American Poetry

American
POETRY

EDITED BY

GAY WILSON ALLEN

NEW YORK UNIVERSITY

WALTER B. RIDEOUT

THE UNIVERSITY OF WISCONSIN

JAMES K. ROBINSON

UNIVERSITY OF CINCINNATI

Harper & Row, Publishers · New York

Acknowledgments for the use of copyright material will be found on pages v-xi which are hereby made part of this copyright page.

Library of Congress Catalog Card Number: 65-19490

C-1

ACKNOWLEDGMENTS

Grateful acknowledgment is made to the publishers and poets who granted permission to reprint the following works.

Conrad Aiken: Eight poems from *Collected Poems* by Conrad Aiken. Copyright 1953 by Conrad Aiken. Reprinted by permission of Oxford University Press, Inc.

Wendell Berry: *November 26, 1963.* Copyright 1963 by Wendell Berry. Reprinted by permission of George Braziller, Inc. "A Man Walking and Singing," "Canticle," "May Song," "Ascent," and "The Guest." © 1964 by Wendell Berry. Reprinted from his volume *The Broken Ground* by permission of Harcourt, Brace & World, Inc.

John Berryman: "Winter Landscape," "Cloud and Flame," and "The Dispossessed" from *The Dispossessed* by John Berryman. Reprinted by permission of John Berryman. "Three Around the Old Gentleman" (Songs 37, 38, and 39). Reprinted from *77 Dream Songs* by John Berryman, by permission of Farrar, Straus & Giroux, Inc. Copyright © 1963 by John Berryman.

Hart Crane: Fifteen poems from *The Collected Poems of Hart Crane*. By permission of Liveright, Publishers, N.Y. Copyright © R, 1961, by Liveright Publishing Corp.

Stephen Crane: "Three Poems" from *The Collected Poems of Stephen Crane*. Reprinted by permission of Alfred A. Knopf, Inc.

Robert Creeley: Five poems. Reprinted with the permission of Charles Scribner's Sons from *For Love* by Robert Creeley. Copyright © 1959, 1962 Robert Creeley.

e. e. cummings: "O sweet spontaneous." Copyright, 1923, 1951, by E. E. Cummings. "a man who had fallen among thieves" and "'next to of course god america i." Copyright, 1926, by Horace Liveright, copyright, 1954, by E. E. Cummings. "somewhere i have never travelled,gladly beyond." Copyright, 1931, 1959, by E. E. Cummings. "anyone lived in a pretty how town" and "my father moved through dooms of love." Copyright, 1940, by E. E. Cummings. "pity this busy monster,manunkind" and "what if a much of a which of a wind." Copyright, 1944, by E. E. Cummings. Reprinted from his volume *Poems 1923–1954* by permission of Harcourt, Brace & World, Inc. "now does our world descend" and "enter no(silence is the blood whose flesh." © 1963 by Marion Morehouse Cummings. Reprinted from *73 Poems* by E. E. Cummings by permission of Harcourt, Brace & World, Inc.

James Dickey: "Between Two Prisoners." Copyright © 1960 by James Dickey. "The Scratch." Copyright © 1960 by James Dickey. "The Heaven of Animals." Copyright © 1961 by James Dickey. Reprinted from *Drowning with Others*, by James Dickey, by permission of Wesleyan University Press.

"The Dusk of Horses" and "The Beholders." Copyright © 1962 by James Dickey. Reprinted from *Helmets,* by James Dickey, by permission of Wesleyan University Press.

Emily Dickinson: Eighty-five poems. Reprinted by permission of the publishers and the Trustees of Amherst College from Thomas H. Johnson, Editor, *The Poems of Emily Dickinson,* Cambridge, Mass.: The Belknap Press of Harvard University Press, Copyright, 1951, 1955, by The President and Fellows of Harvard College. "813 This quiet Dust was Gentlemen and Ladies," "985 The Missing All, prevented Me," "1243 Safe Despair it is that raves," "1333 A little Madness in the Spring," "1670 In Winter in my Room," "1672 Lightly stepped a yellow star," and "1695 There is a solitude of space." Copyright 1914, 1942 by Martha Dickinson Bianchi. "341 After great pain, a formal feeling comes," "376 Of course—I prayed," "448 This was a Poet—It is That," "657 I dwell in Possibility," "721 Behind Me—dips Eternity," "754 My Life had stood—a Loaded Gun," and "1082 Revolution is the Pod." Copyright 1929, © 1957 by Mary L. Hampson. "378 I saw no Way—The Heavens were stitched," and "474 They put Us far apart." Copyright 1935, © 1963 by Martha Dickinson Bianchi. From *The Complete Poems of Emily Dickinson* edited by Thomas H. Johnson, by permission of Little, Brown and Co. "1072 Title divine—is mine" from *Life and Letters of Emily Dickinson* by Martha Dickinson Bianchi, by permission of Houghton Mifflin Company.

H.D.: Six poems from *H.D. Selected Poems,* Grove Press, Inc., copyright © 1957 by Norman Holmes Pearson.

Alan Dugan: "On an East Wind from the Wars," "Love Song: I and Thou," and "Funeral Oration for a Mouse" from *Poems* by Alan Dugan. Reprinted by permission of Alan Dugan. "Elegy" and "Plague of Dead Sharks" from *Poems 2* by Alan Dugan. Reprinted by permission of Yale University Press.

T. S. Eliot: Six poems from *Collected Poems 1909–1962* by T. S. Eliot, copyright, 1936, by Harcourt, Brace & World, Inc.; © 1963, 1964, by T. S. Eliot. Reprinted by permission of Harcourt, Brace & World, Inc. and Faber & Faber Ltd.

Robert Frost: Twenty poems from *Complete Poems of Robert Frost.* Copyright 1916, 1921, 1923, 1928, 1930, 1934, 1939, 1947 by Holt, Rinehart and Winston, Inc. Copyright 1936, 1942 by Robert Frost. Copyright renewed 1944, 1951, © 1956, 1958, 1962 by Robert Frost. Copyright renewed © 1964 by Leslie Frost Ballantine. Reprinted by permission of Holt, Rinehart and Winston, Inc.

Randall Jarrell: "90 North" from *Blood for a Stranger* by Randall Jarrell, copyright, 1942, by Harcourt, Brace & World, Inc. and reprinted with their permission. "Second Air Force" and note thereto and "The Death of the Ball Turret Gunner" and note thereto from *Little Friend, Little Friend,* by Randall Jarrell. Copyright 1945 by Randall Jarrell. Reprinted by permission of Randall Jarrell. "A Camp in the Prussian Forest" from *Losses* by Randall Jarrell, copyright, 1948, by Harcourt, Brace & World, Inc. and reprinted with their permission. "The Orient Express" from *The Seven-League Crutches* by Randall Jarrell, copyright, 1951, by Harcourt, Brace & World, Inc. and reprinted with their permission. "The Woman at the Washington Zoo" from *The Woman at the Washington Zoo* by Randall Jarrell. Copyright © 1960 by Randall Jarrell. Reprinted by permission of Atheneum Publishers.

Robinson Jeffers: "Night," "Birds," and "Apology for Bad Dreams." Copyright 1925 and renewed 1953 by Robinson Jeffers. Reprinted from *The Selected Poetry of Robinson Jeffers*, by permission of Random House, Inc. "Promise of Peace." Copyright 1925 and renewed 1953 by Robinson Jeffers. Reprinted from *Roan Stallion, Tamar and Other Poems*, by Robinson Jeffers, by permission of Random House, Inc. "Hurt Hawks." Copyright 1928 and renewed 1956 by Robinson Jeffers. Reprinted from *The Selected Poetry of Robinson Jeffers*, by permission of Random House, Inc. "The Eye." Copyright 1948 by Robinson Jeffers. Reprinted from *The Double Axe and Other Poems*, by Robinson Jeffers, by permission of Random House, Inc. "Ocean," Copyright 1954 by Robinson Jeffers. Reprinted from *Hungerfield and Other Poems*, by Robinson Jeffers, by permission of Random House, Inc. "Let Them Alone," "But I Am Growing Old and Indolent," and "My Burial Place." © Copyright 1963 by Garth Jeffers and Donnan Jeffers. Reprinted from *The Beginning and the End and Other Poems*, by Robinson Jeffers, by permission of Random House, Inc.

Sidney Lanier: Ten poems from Charles R. Anderson (general editor). *Centennial Edition of the Works and Letters of Sidney Lanier, 1842–1942.* Published by The Johns Hopkins Press, 1945.

Denise Levertov: "Pleasures" and "The Goddess" from *With Eyes at the Back of Our Heads* by Denise Levertov. © 1958, 1959 by Denise Levertov Goodman. Reprinted by permission of New Directions, Publishers. "Come into Animal Presence" and "The Well" from *The Jacob's Ladder*. © 1958, 1959, 1960, 1961 by Denise Levertov Goodman. Reprinted by permission of New Directions, Publishers. "The Novel" from *The Very Thing That Happens* by Russell Edson. © 1964 by Russell Edson. Reprinted by permission of New Directions, Publishers.

Robert Lowell: "In Memory of Arthur Winslow," "Christmas Eve Under Hooker's Statue," "The Drunken Fisherman," "Children of Light," "The Exile's Return," "Colloquy in Black Rock," "The Quaker Graveyard in Nantucket," "As a Plane Tree by the Water," "Mr. Edwards and the Spider," "After the Surprising Conversions," and "Where the Rainbow Ends" from *Lord Weary's Castle*, copyright 1944, 1946, by Robert Lowell. Reprinted by permission of Harcourt, Brace & World, Inc. "Falling Asleep over the Aeneid." Copyright, 1948, by Robert Lowell. Reprinted from his volume *The Mills of the Kavanaughs* by permission of Harcourt, Brace & World, Inc. "Words for Hart Crane" and "Skunk Hour." Reprinted from *Life Studies* by Robert Lowell, by permission of Farrar, Straus & Giroux, Inc. Copyright © 1956, 1959 by Robert Lowell. "The Public Garden." Reprinted from *For the Union Dead* by Robert Lowell, by permission of Farrar, Straus & Company, Inc. Copyright © 1962 by Robert Lowell.

Archibald MacLeish: "Ars Poetica" and "The End of the World" from *Streets in the Moon*, by Archibald MacLeish. Reprinted by permission of Houghton Mifflin Company. "You, Andrew Marvell," "Immortal Autumn," and "'Not Marble nor the Gilded Monuments'" from *New Found Land*, by Archibald MacLeish. Reprinted by permission of Houghton Mifflin Company. "Pole Star" from *Public Speech* by Archibald MacLeish. Copyright 1936, copyright renewed © 1964 by Archibald MacLeish. Reprinted by permission of Holt, Rinehart and Winston, Inc. "Theory of Poetry" from *Songs of Eve*, by Archibald MacLeish. Reprinted by permission of Houghton Mifflin Company.

W. S. Merwin: "Dictum: For a Masque of Deluge" from *A Mask for Janus* by W. S. Merwin. Reprinted by permission of Yale University Press. "When I Came from Colchis" from *The Dancing Bears* by W. S. Merwin. Reprinted by permission of Yale University Press. "The Annunciation." Published in 1956 by Alfred A. Knopf, Inc. Reprinted from *Green with Beasts* by W. S. Merwin, by permission of the publisher. "John Otto." Copyright © 1958 by W. S. Merwin. Reprinted by permission of Harold Ober Associates Incorporated. "In the Night Fields" from *The Moving Target* by W. S. Merwin. Copyright © 1961, © 1963 by W. S. Merwin. Reprinted by permission of Atheneum Publishers.

William Vaughn Moody: "Thammuz." Reprinted by permission of Frederick J. Fawcett.

Marianne Moore: "Poetry" and "No Swan So Fine." Copyright 1935 by Marianne Moore. Renewed 1963 by Marianne Moore and T. S. Eliot. "The Pangolin" and "What Are Years?" Copyright 1941 by Marianne Moore. "The Mind Is an Enchanting Thing" and "In Distrust of Merits." Copyright 1944 by Marianne Moore. "The Steeple-Jack" and "Armour's Undermining Modesty." Copyright 1951 by Marianne Moore. Reprinted with permission of The Macmillan Company from *Collected Poems* by Marianne Moore. "Tom Fool at Jamaica" from *Like a Bulwark* by Marianne Moore. Copyright © 1953 by Marianne Moore. Reprinted by permission of The Viking Press, Inc. "Melchior Vulpius" from *O To Be a Dragon* by Marianne Moore. Copyright © 1958 by Marianne Moore. Reprinted by permission of The Viking Press, Inc.

Ezra Pound: "Portrait d'une Femme," "The Seafarer," "A Virginal," "The Return," "Lament of the Frontier Guard," "Liu Ch'e," and "Hugh Selwyn Mauberley" from *Personæ* by Ezra Pound. Copyright 1926, 1954 by Ezra Pound. Reprinted by permission of New Directions, Publishers. "Canto I" and "Canto II" from *The Cantos* by Ezra Pound. Copyright 1934, 1948 by Ezra Pound. Reprinted by permission of New Directions, Publishers.

John Crowe Ransom: "Winter Remembered," "Bells for John Whiteside's Daughter," and "Captain Carpenter." Copyright, 1924 by Alfred A. Knopf, Inc. Renewed, 1952. "Vision by Sweetwater," "Piazza Piece," "Antique Harvesters," and "The Equilibrists." Copyright, 1927 by Alfred A. Knopf, Inc. Renewed, 1955 by John Crowe Ransom. "Painted Head," "Master's

of Sunday" and "Nostalgia." Copyright 1941 by Karl Shapiro. Copyright 1942 by Karl Jay Shapiro. "V-Letter" and "Elegy for a Dead Soldier." Copyright 1943 by Karl Shapiro. Copyright 1944 by Karl Shapiro. "The Sickness of Adam." Copyright 1951 by Karl Shapiro. Reprinted from *Poems 1940–1953*, by Karl Shapiro, by permission of Random House, Inc.

W. D. Snodgrass: "Returned to Frisco, 1946." Copyright, 1957 by W. D. Snodgrass. "April Inventory." Copyright, 1957 by W. D. Snodgrass. "The Campus on the Hill." Copyright 1958 by W. D. Snodgrass. "Heart's Needle: 5" ("Winter again and it is snowing"). Copyright, 1959 by W. D. Snodgrass. Reprinted from *Heart's Needle* by W. D. Snodgrass by permission of Alfred A. Knopf, Inc. "A Flat One" from *Quarterly Review of Literature*, Vol. X, No. 3, April, 1960. Published by Quarterly Review of Literature, Bard College, Annandale-on-Hudson, New York. Reprinted by permission of W. D. Snodgrass.

Wallace Stevens: "Domination of Black," "The Snow Man," "Le Monocle de Mon Oncle," "A High-Toned Old Christian Woman," "The Emperor of Ice-Cream," "Sunday Morning," "Anecdote of the Jar," "To the One of Fictive Music," "Peter Quince at the Clavier," "Thirteen Ways of Looking at a Blackbird," and "Sea Surface Full of Clouds." Copyright, 1923, 1951 by Wallace Stevens. "The Idea of Order at Key West," "Anglais Mort à Florence," and "A Postcard from the Volcano." Copyright, 1936 by Wallace Stevens. "Study of Two Pears," "The Glass of Water," "The Sense of the Sleight-of-Hand Man," "Mrs. Alfred Uruguay," and "Asides on the Oboe." Copyright, 1942 by Wallace Stevens. "The Motive for Metaphor," "Credences of Summer," and "As You Leave the Room." Copyright, 1947 by Wallace Stevens. "To an Old Philosopher in Rome." Copyright, 1952 by Wallace Stevens. "The World as Meditation." Copyright, 1952 by Wallace Stevens. "The Rock." Copyright, 1954 by Wallace Stevens. All reprinted from *The Collected Poems of Wallace Stevens* by permission of Alfred A. Knopf, Inc.

Allen Tate: Ten poems. Reprinted with the permission of Charles Scribner's Sons from *Poems* by Allen Tate. Copyright 1936, 1945, 1952 Allen Tate. Copyright 1937 Charles Scribner's Sons.

Edward Taylor: "Prologue," "Meditation 1," "The Reflexion," "Meditation 8," "Meditation 38," "The Glory of and Grace in the Church Set Out," "The Joy of Church Fellowship Rightly Attended," "Huswifery," "Upon Wedlock and Death of Children," and "The Ebb and Flow" from Thomas H. Johnson, "Edward Taylor: A Puritan 'Sacred Poet,'" *New England Quarterly*, X (June, 1937), 290–322. Reprinted by permission of *New England Quarterly*. "Meditation 40" from Thomas H. Johnson, "Some Edward Taylor Gleanings," *New England Quarterly*, XVI (June, 1943), 280–296. Reprinted by permission of *New England Quarterly*. "Meditation 6," "Meditation 20," "Meditation 29," "The Preface," "An Address to the Soul Occasioned by a Rain," and "Upon a Spider Catching a Fly." Reprinted from *The Poetical Works of Edward Taylor* edited by Thomas Johnson by permission of Princeton University Press. "Meditation 68A, Second Series" from *The*

Poems of Edward Taylor edited by Donald Stanford. Reprinted by permission of Yale University Press.

Henry David Thoreau: Eleven poems from Carl Bode (ed.). *Collected Poems of Henry Thoreau.* Published by The Johns Hopkins Press, Baltimore, Maryland, 1964.

Richard Wilbur: "First Snow in Alsace" and "Bell Speech" from *The Beautiful Changes and Other Poems,* copyright, 1947, by Richard Wilbur. Reprinted by permission of Harcourt, Brace & World, Inc. "Still, Citizen Sparrow" and "The Death of a Toad" from *Ceremony and Other Poems,* copyright, 1948, 1949, 1950, by Richard Wilbur. Reprinted by permission of Harcourt, Brace & World, Inc. "Lamarck Elaborated" from *Things of This World,* © 1956, by Richard Wilbur. Reprinted by permission of Harcourt, Brace & World, Inc. "Pangloss's Song: A Comic-Opera Lyric." © 1957 by Richard Wilbur. Reprinted from his volume *Advice to a Prophet and Other Poems* by permission of Harcourt, Brace & World, Inc.

William Carlos Williams: "Tract," "The Widow's Lament in Springtime," "Queen-Ann's-Lace," "Spring and All," "To Elsie," "Rain," "The Yachts," and "These" from *Collected Earlier Poems of William Carlos Williams.* Copyright 1938, 1951 by William Carlos Williams. Reprinted by permission of New Directions, Publishers. "Burning the Christmas Greens," "The Injury" and "The Semblables" from *Collected Later Poems of William Carlos Williams.* Copyright 1944, 1948, 1950, 1963 by William Carlos Williams. Reprinted by permission of New Directions, Publishers. "Preface to *Paterson:* Book One" from *Paterson* by William Carlos Williams. Copyright © 1946 by William Carlos Williams. Reprinted by permission of New Directions, Publishers.

The following poems appeared originally in *The New Yorker:* "The Lovers" and "Music" by Conrad Aiken; "Now Does Our World Descend" by E. E. Cummings; "The Heaven of Animals," "The Dusk of Horses," and "The Beholders" by James Dickey; "John Otto" by W. S. Merwin; "Tom Fool at Jamaica" by Marianne Moore; and "V-Letter" by Karl Shapiro.

Contents

Philip Freneau
(1752–1832)

☀

Joel Barlow
(1754–1812)

☀

William Cullen Bryant
(1794–1878)

William Cullen Bryant
(*Continued*)

☀

Ralph Waldo Emerson
(1803–1882)

Ralph Waldo Emerson

(*Continued*)

❂

Henry Wadsworth Longfellow

(1807–1882)

Henry Wadsworth Longfellow

(*Continued*)

❂

John Greenleaf Whittier

(1807–1892)

❂

Edgar Allan Poe

(1809–1849)

Edgar Allan Poe
(Continued)

Oliver Wendell Holmes
(1809–1894)

Oliver Wendell Holmes
(Continued)

Jones Very
(1813–1880)

Walt Whitman
(*Continued*)

From "Calamus"

From "Drum-Taps"

Walt Whitman
(*Continued*)

❖

Herman Melville
(1819–1891)

Frederick Goddard Tuckerman

(1821–1873)

❂

Henry Timrod

(1828–1867)

❂

Emily Dickinson

(1830–1886)

Emily Dickinson

(*Continued*)

Emily Dickinson
(Continued)

Emily Dickinson
(Continued)

Emily Dickinson
(*Continued*)

Emily Dickinson
(*Continued*)

Emily Dickinson

(*Continued*)

❖

Sidney Lanier

(1842–1881)

William Vaughn Moody

(1869–1910)

❖

Edwin Arlington Robinson

(1869–1935)

❖

Stephen Crane

(1871–1900)

From *The Black Riders*

Stephen Crane

(*Continued*)

From *War Is Kind*

Robert Frost

(1874–1963)

Carl Sandburg

(b. 1878)

Carl Sandburg
(*Continued*)

❖

Wallace Stevens
(1879–1955)

Wallace Stevens
(*Continued*)

❖

William Carlos Williams
(1883–1963)

❖

Ezra Pound
(b. 1885)

Ezra Pound

(*Continued*)

❖

H.D.

(1886–1961)

❖

Robinson Jeffers

(1887–1962)

❖

Marianne Moore

(b. 1887)

Marianne Moore

(*Continued*)

❖

John Crowe Ransom

(b. 1888)

❖

T. S. Eliot

(1888–1965)

Conrad Aiken
(b. 1889)

❊

Archibald MacLeish
(b. 1892)

❊

e. e. cummings
(1894–1962)

e. e. cummings
(Continued)

❊

Hart Crane
(1899–1932)

❊

Allen Tate
(b. 1899)

Allen Tate
(*Continued*)

❖

Theodore Roethke
(1908–1963)

❖

Karl Shapiro
(b. 1913)

Randall Jarrell
(b. 1914)

❖

John Berryman
(b. 1914)

❖

Robert Lowell
(b. 1917)

Robert Lowell
(*Continued*)

❖

Richard Wilbur
(b. 1921)

❖

James Dickey
(b. 1923)

❖

Alan Dugan
(b. 1923)

Alan Dugan
(*Continued*)

❖

Denise Levertov
(b. 1923)

❖

W. D. Snodgrass
(b. 1926)

❖

Robert Creeley
(b. 1926)

W. S. Merwin
(b. 1927)

Wendell Berry
(*Continued*)

❂

Wendell Berry
(b. 1934)

❂

Preface

In preparing this volume we have aimed to provide the student and the general reader with a carefully selected anthology covering the entire sweep of American poetic achievement from the Puritan age to the present day. Believing that poets should be studied in depth, we have omitted the great mass of versifiers in order to give ample space to the leading American figures; yet we have balanced depth with breadth in order to include some who, if not of the very first creative order, are nevertheless of distinct literary significance. The important criterion for the selection of the poems themselves has been literary excellence.

On these basic principles we have compiled a work that is sufficiently flexible to meet the needs of a variety of classroom situations. This volume most obviously provides a textbook for courses surveying American poetry or, because of our heavy concentration on nineteenth- and twentieth-century poets, for courses limited to the poetic production of either of these centuries. Especially is the anthology designed as the central volume for survey courses in American literature, to be supplemented by any combination of the abundantly available paperback texts of novels, stories, and nonfictional prose.

Of the fifty poets included twenty wrote before 1900, thirty after that date. The earlier poets whom we consider most important, as indicated by the large number of poems selected from each, are Edward Taylor, William Cullen Bryant, Ralph Waldo Emerson, Henry Wadsworth Longfellow, Edgar Allan Poe, Jones Very, Herman Melville, Walt Whitman, Frederick Goddard Tuckerman, Emily Dickinson, and Stephen Crane. For poets of secondary stature—such figures as Philip Freneau, James Russell Lowell, and Sidney Lanier—we have given lesser though still substantial representation. We believe that our choice of poets and poems is not simply indicative of our individual judgments but reflects current scholarly and critical trends and reassessments as well. For example, though Longfellow's nine-teenth-century reputation as a household giant collapsed in the first decades of the present century, he is here represented by a sizable number of poems, mostly those sonnets and lyrics in which, it is now recognized, his technical skill was fused with a valid emotional impulse. Walt Whitman has long since been assigned a high position in the development of American poetry and is here given an appropriately impressive amount of space; but the large number of poems reprinted from the works of Tuckerman, Very, and Stephen Crane, of Emerson, Melville, and Emily Dickinson accords with the present wide interest in the poetic accomplishment of those writers.

Among the poets of the twentieth century we have given most consideration to Edwin Arlington Robinson, Robert Frost, Wallace Stevens, Ezra Pound, T. S. Eliot, Hart Crane, and Rob-ert Lowell, although such artists as Carl Sandburg, William Carlos Williams, Robinson Jeffers, Marianne Moore, John Crowe Ransom, e. e. cummings, Allen Tate, and Theodore Roethke are also well represented. Besides including generous selections from the work of all those who are by consensus the substantial poets of the present century, we have added a number of poets who are now in the process of establishing critical repu-tations. Our choices among possibilities were necessarily arbi-trary. Other new poets may be as good as those we have chosen; none, we think, are better or show greater promise.

Both poets and their poems are presented in chronological sequence. The poets appear according to date of birth, while the poems of each are given in order of their first printing in an original collection by the poet, the date assigned in brackets following the poem's title being the date of that collection. As teachers and scholars we have been concerned to present a com-plete and accurate text for each poem, using either standard editions or the most recent text that has passed under the poet's hand.

In order to make this volume of maximum usefulness, we have

provided not only the brief biographical sketch that appears at the beginning of each poet's selections, but also a sizable body of notes, located in a single section at the back of the book and arranged for quick reference according to the alphabetical order of the poets' last names. These notes list for each author his major writings, standard editions of his work (if any), biographical and critical studies, and full explanatory notes on individual poems. In addition we have assembled for each poem, where such is available, a convenient list of analyses and detailed discussions. These lists are designed to help the student or general reader confront the poem more fully and to avoid imposing on him any one critical approach or attitude. Like the poet in Melville's poem, any reader of poetry, whether he be general or special, professional or amateur, must himself directly "wrestle with the angel—Art."

We gratefully record the names of a number of persons who have generously assisted us in various ways in the preparation of this book: Edwin Barber, Frank Brunotts, William S. Clark II, James Dickey, James Doolittle, John J. Enck, John J. Espey, Edgar M. Glenn, Daniel Havens, Ian Loram, Richard M. Ludwig, Archimede Marni, Robert D. Mayo, Kathleen Morrison, Betty Payne, Robert O. Payne, Rollin Posey, Aileen Reinstatler, Jean Rideout, Christopher Robinson, Pamela Robinson, Donald E. Stanford, Hugh B. Staples, G. Thomas Tanselle, Carl Trahman, James M. Vail, Lazlo Velics, Dallas Wiebe.

Although *American Poetry* has been a joint undertaking, each editor has had special responsibility in preparing the texts and notes for particular poets, as follows:

Gay Wilson Allen: Philip Freneau, John Greenleaf Whittier, Jones Very, Walt Whitman, Frederick Goddard Tuckerman, Henry Timrod, Stephen Crane, Edwin Arlington Robinson, Carl Sandburg, William Carlos Williams, H[ilda]. D[oolittle]., Robinson Jeffers, Conrad Aiken, Karl Shapiro, Denise Levertov, Robert Creeley, Wendell Berry.

Walter B. Rideout: Anne Bradstreet, Edward Taylor, Ralph Waldo Emerson, Henry David Thoreau, Herman Melville, Emily Dickinson, William Vaughn Moody, Ezra Pound, T. S. Eliot, e. e. cummings, Hart Crane, Theodore Roethke, Randall Jarrell, Robert Lowell, James Dickey, Alan Dugan.

James K. Robinson: Joel Barlow, William Cullen Bryant, Henry Wadsworth Longfellow, Oliver Wendell Holmes, Edgar Allan Poe, James Russell Lowell, Sidney Lanier, Robert Frost, Wallace Stevens, Marianne Moore, John Crowe Ransom, Archibald MacLeish, Allen Tate, John Berryman, Richard Wilbur, W. D. Snodgrass, W. S. Merwin.

GAY WILSON ALLEN

WALTER B. RIDEOUT

JAMES K. ROBINSON

American Poetry

Anne Bradstreet

c. 1612–1672

Anne Bradstreet was born in Northampton, England, the daughter of Thomas Dudley, steward of the Earl of Lincoln. She was probably educated by tutors. In 1628 she married Simon Bradstreet, a Puritan and a graduate of Cambridge. In 1630 the Dudleys and the Bradstreets joined the first settlers of the Massachusetts Bay Colony, in which both Thomas Dudley and Simon Bradstreet were leaders for years. Simon and Anne set up a permanent home at North Andover, Massachusetts, on the Merrimack River. While bearing eight children and managing a large household, she found time to write her "Quaternions" (long, learned, pedestrian poems in groups of four) and a number of lyrics on religion and domestic affairs. After her first book of poems was published in London in 1650, she prepared a revised edition, which did not appear until after her death on September 16, 1672.

THE PROLOGUE   [1650]

To sing of wars, of captains, and of kings,
Of cities founded, commonwealths begun,
For my mean pen are too superior things:
Or how they all, or each, their dates have run;
Let poets and historians set these forth,
My obscure lines shall not so dim their worth.

But when my wondering eyes and envious heart
Great Bartas' sugared lines do but read o'er,
Fool I do grudge the Muses did not part
'Twixt him and me that overfluent store;—   10

A Bartas can do what a Bartas will,
But simple I according to my skill.

From school-boys' tongues no rhetoric we expect,
Nor yet a sweet consort from broken strings,
Nor perfect beauty where's a main defect:
My foolish, broken, blemished Muse so sings;
And this to mend, alas, no art is able,
'Cause nature made it so, irreparable.

Nor can I, like that fluent, sweet-tongued Greek
Who lisped at first, in future times speak plain;   20
By art he gladly found what he did seek—
A full requital of his striving pain.
Art can do much, but this maxim's most sure:
A weak or wounded brain admits no cure.

I am obnoxious to each carping tongue
Who says my hand a needle better fits.
A poet's pen all scorn I should thus wrong;
For such despite they cast on female wits,
If what I do prove well, it won't advance—
They'll say it's stolen, or else it was by chance.   30

But sure the antique Greeks were far more mild,
Else of our sex why feignéd they those Nine,
And Poesy made Calliope's own child?
So 'mongst the rest they placed the Arts Divine.
But this weak knot they will full soon untie—
The Greeks did naught but play the fools and lie.

Let Greeks be Greeks, and women what they are.
Men have precedency, and still excel.
It is but vain unjustly to wage war:
Men can do best, and women know it well.   40
Preëminence in all and each is yours—
Yet grant some small acknowledgment of ours.

And oh, ye high flown quills that soar the skies,
And ever with your prey still catch your praise,

If e'er you deign these lowly lines your eyes,
Give thyme or parsley wreath; I ask no bays.
This mean and unrefinéd ore of mine
Will make your glistering gold but more to shine.

CONTEMPLATIONS   [1678]

Some time now past in the autumnal tide,
   When Phoebus wanted but one hour to bed,
The trees all richly clad, yet void of pride,
   Were gilded o'er by his rich golden head;
Their leaves and fruits seemed painted, but were true
Of green, of red, of yellow, mixéd hue.
Rapt were my senses at this delectable view.

I wist not what to wish, yet sure, thought I,
   If so much excellence abide below
How excellent is He that dwells on high,   10
   Whose power and beauty by his works we know!
Sure He is goodness, wisdom, glory, light,
That hath this under world so richly dight.
More heaven than earth was here, no winter and no night.

Then on a stately oak I cast mine eye,
   Whose ruffling top the clouds seemed to aspire.
How long since thou wast in thine infancy?
   Thy strength and stature more thy years admire.
Hath hundred winters passed since thou wast born,
Or thousand since thou break'st thy shell of horn?   20
If so, all these as naught eternity doth scorn.

Then higher on the glistering sun I gazed,
   Whose beams were shaded by the leafy tree;
The more I looked the more I grew amazed,
   And softly said, What glory's like to thee?
Soul of this world, this universe's eye,
No wonder some made thee a deity.
Had I not better known, alas, the same had I.

Thou as a bridegroom from thy chamber rushes,
   And as a strong man joys to run a race;   30
The morn doth usher thee with smiles and blushes,
   The earth reflects her glances in thy face.
Birds, insects, animals, with vegetive,
Thy heart from death and dulness doth revive,
And in the darksome womb of fruitful nature dive.

Thy swift annual and diurnal course,
   Thy daily straight and yearly oblique path,
Thy pleasing fervor, and thy scorching force
   All mortals here the feeling knowledge hath.
Thy presence makes it day, thy absence night.   40
Quaternal seasons causéd by thy might.
Hail, creature full of sweetness, beauty, and delight!

Art thou so full of glory that no eye
   Hath strength thy shining rays once to behold?
And is thy splendid throne erect so high
   As to approach it can no earthly mould?
How full of glory then must thy Creator be
Who gave this bright light luster unto thee?
Admired, adored, forever be that Majesty.

Silent, alone, where none or saw or heard,   50
   In pathless paths I led my wandering feet;
My humble eyes to lofty skies I reared,
   To sing some song my amazéd muse thought meet.
My great Creator I would magnify
That nature had thus decked liberally.
But ah, and ah again, my imbecility!

I heard the merry grasshopper then sing,
   The black-clad cricket bear a second part;
They kept one tune and played on the same string,
   Seeming to glory in their little art.   60
Shall creatures abject thus their voices raise,
And in their kind resound their maker's praise,
Whilst I as mute can warble forth no higher lays?

When present times look back to ages past,
 And men in being fancy those are dead,
It makes things gone perpetually to last,
 And calls back months and years that long since fled;
It makes a man more aged in conceit
Than was Methuselah or his grandsire great
While of their persons and their acts his mind doth treat.   70

Sometimes in Eden fair he seems to be,
 Sees glorious Adam there made lord of all,
Fancies the apple dangle on the tree
 That turned his sovereign to a naked thrall,
Who like a miscreant was driven from that place
To get his bread with pain and sweat of face—
A penalty imposed on his backsliding race.

Here sits our grandam in retired place,
 And in her lap her bloody Cain new born;
The weeping imp oft looks her in the face,   80
 Bewails his unknown hap and fate forlorn.
His mother sighs to think of paradise,
And how she lost her bliss to be more wise,
Believing him that was and is father of lies.

Here Cain and Abel come to sacrifice;
 Fruits of the earth and fatlings each doth bring.
On Abel's gift the fire descends from skies,
 But no such sign on false Cain's offering.
With sullen hateful looks he goes his ways,
Hath thousand thoughts to end his brother's days,   90
Upon whose blood his future good he hopes to raise.

There Abel keeps his sheep, no ill he thinks;
 His brother comes, then acts his fratricide;
The virgin earth of blood her first draught drinks,
 But since that time she often hath been cloyed.
The wretch with ghastly face and dreadful mind
Thinks each he sees will serve him in his kind,
Though none on earth but kindred near then could
  he find.

Who fancies not his looks now at the bar,
    His face like death, his heart with horror fraught,   100
Nor malefactor ever felt like war
    When deep despair with wish of life hath sought.
Branded with guilt, and crushed with treble woes,
A vagabond to land of Nod he goes,
A city builds, that walls might him secure from foes.

Who thinks not oft upon the fathers' ages,
    Their long descent, how nephews' sons they saw,
The starry observations of those sages,
    And how their precepts to their sons were law;
How Adam sighed to see his progeny   110
Clothed all in his black sinful livery,
Who neither guilt nor yet the punishment could fly?

Our life compare we with their length of days,
    Who to the tenth of theirs doth now arrive?
And though thus short, we shorten many ways,
    Living so little while we are alive—
In eating, drinking, sleeping, vain delight;
So unawares comes on perpetual night,
And puts all pleasures vain unto eternal flight.

When I behold the heavens as in their prime,   120
    And then the earth, though old, still clad in green,
The stones and trees insensible of time,
    Nor age nor wrinkle on their front are seen;
If winter come, and greenness then doth fade,
A spring returns, and they're more youthful made.
But man grows old, lies down, remains where once
    he's laid.

By birth more noble than those creatures all,
    Yet seems by nature and by custom cursed—
No sooner born but grief and care make fall
    That state obliterate he had at first;   130
Nor youth, nor strength, nor wisdom spring again,
Nor habitations long their names retain,
But in oblivion to the final day remain.

Shall I then praise the heavens, the trees, the earth,
   Because their beauty and their strength last longer?
Shall I wish there or never to had birth,
   Because they're bigger and their bodies stronger?
Nay, they shall darken, perish, fade, and die,
And when unmade so ever shall they lie;
But man was made for endless immortality.   140

Under the cooling shadow of a stately elm
   Close sat I by a goodly river's side
Where gliding streams the rocks did overwhelm;
   A lonely place, with pleasures dignified.
I once that loved the shady woods so well
Now thought the rivers did the trees excel,
And if the sun would ever shine there would I dwell.

While on the stealing stream I fixed mine eye
   Which to the longed-for ocean held its course,
I marked nor crooks nor rubs that there did lie   150
   Could hinder aught, but still augment its force.
O happy flood, quoth I, that holds thy race
Till thou arrive at thy beloved place,
Nor is it rocks or shoals that can obstruct thy pace.

Nor is it enough that thou alone mayst slide,
   But hundred brooks in thy clear waves do meet;
So hand in hand along with thee they glide
   To Thetis' house, where all embrace and greet.
Thou emblem true of what I count the best,
Oh, could I lead my rivulets to rest!   160
So may we press to that vast mansion ever blest!

Ye fish which in this liquid region abide,
   That for each season have your habitation,
Now salt, now fresh, where you think best to glide,
   To unknown coasts to give a visitation,
In lakes and ponds you leave your numerous fry;
So nature taught, and yet you know not why,
You watery folk that know not your felicity.

Look how the wantons frisk to taste the air,
    Then to the colder bottom straight they dive;   170
Eftsoon to Neptune's glassy hall repair
    To see what trade the great ones there do drive;
Who forage o'er the spacious sea-green field,
And take the trembling prey before it yield;
Whose armor is their scales, their spreading fins their
    shield.

While musing thus with contemplation fed,
    And thousand fancies buzzing in my brain,
The sweet-tongued philomel perched o'er my head,
    And chanted forth a most melodious strain,
Which rapt me so with wonder and delight   180
I judged my hearing better than my sight,
And wished me wings with her a while to take my flight.

O merry bird, said I, that fears no snares,
    That neither toils nor hoards up in thy barn,
Feels no sad thoughts, nor cruciating cares
    To gain more good or shun what might thee harm,
Thy clothes ne'er wear, thy meat is everywhere,
Thy bed a bough, thy drink the water clear,
Reminds not what is past, nor what's to come dost fear!

The dawning morn with songs thou dost prevent,   190
    Settest hundred notes unto thy feathered crew;
So each one tunes his pretty instrument,
    And, warbling out the old, begins anew.
And thus they pass their youth in summer season,
Then follow thee into a better region
Where winter's never felt by that sweet airy legion.

Man, at the best a creature frail and vain,
    In knowledge ignorant, in strength but weak,
Subject to sorrows, losses, sickness, pain,
    Each storm his state, his mind, his body break,   200
From some of these he never finds cessation,
But day or night, within, without, vexation,
Troubles from foes, from friends, from dearest, nearest
    relation.

And yet this sinful creature, frail and vain,
　　This lump of wretchedness, of sin and sorrow,
This weather-beaten vessel racked with pain,
　　Joys not in hope of an eternal morrow;
Nor all his losses, crosses, and vexation,
In weight, in frequency, and long duration,
Can make him deeply groan for that divine translation.　　210

The mariner that on smooth waves doth glide
　　Sings merrily, and steers his bark with ease,
As if he had command of wind and tide,
　　And now become great master of the seas;
But suddenly a storm spoils all the sport,
And makes him long for a more quiet port,
Which 'gainst all adverse winds may serve for fort.

So he that faileth in this world of pleasure,
　　Feeding on sweets, that never bit of the sour,
That's full of friends, of honor, and of treasure,　　220
　　Fond fool, he takes this earth e'en for heaven's bower.
But sad affliction comes, and makes him see
Here's neither honor, wealth, nor safety;
Only above is found all with security.

O time, the fatal wreck of mortal things,
That draws oblivion's curtains over kings!
Their sumptuous monuments men know them not,
Their names without a record are forgot,
Their parts, their ports, their pomps, all laid in the dust,
Nor wit, nor gold, nor buildings 'scape time's rust.　　230
But he whose name is graved in the white stone
Shall last and shine when all of these are gone.

THE FLESH AND THE SPIRIT　　[1678]

In secret place where once I stood,
Close by the banks of lacrym flood,
I heard two sisters reason on

Things that are past and things to come.
One Flesh was called, who had her eye
On worldly wealth and vanity;
The other Spirit, who did rear
Her thoughts unto a higher sphere.
"Sister," quoth Flesh, "what livest thou on—
Nothing but meditatiön?   10
Doth contemplation feed thee, so
Regardlessly to let earth go?
Can speculation satisfy
Notion without reality?
Dost dream of things beyond the moon,
And dost thou hope to dwell there soon?
Hast treasures there laid up in store
That all in the world thou countest poor?
Art fancy sick, or turned a sot,
To catch at shadows which are not?   20
Come, come, I'll show unto thy sense
Industry hath its recompense.
What canst desire but thou mayst see
True substance in variety?
Dost honor like? Acquire the same,
As some to their immortal fame,
And trophies to thy name erect
Which wearing time shall ne'er deject.
For riches dost thou long full sore?
Behold enough of precious store;   30
Earth hath more silver, pearls, and gold
Than eyes can see or hands can hold.
Affectest thou pleasure? Take thy fill;
Earth hath enough of what you will.
Then let not go what thou mayst find
For things unknown, only in mind."
    Spirit. "Be still, thou unregenerate part;
Disturb no more my settled heart,
For I have vowed, and so will do,
Thee as a foe still to pursue,   40
And combat with thee will and must
Until I see thee laid in the dust.
Sisters we are, yea, twins we be,

Yet deadly feud 'twixt thee and me;
For from one father are we not.
Thou by old Adam wast begot,
But my arise is from above,
Whence my dear Father I do love.
Thou speakest me fair, but hatest me sore;
Thy flattering shows I'll trust no more.   50
How oft thy slave hast thou me made
When I believed what thou hast said,
And never had more cause of woe
Than when I did what thou bad'st do.
I'll stop mine ears at these thy charms,
And count them for my deadly harms.
Thy sinful pleasures I do hate,
Thy riches are to me no bait,
Thine honors do nor will I love,
For my ambition lies above.   60
My greatest honor it shall be
When I am victor over thee,
And triumph shall, with laurel head,
When thou my captive shalt be led.
How I do live thou needst not scoff,
For I have meat thou knowest not of:
The hidden manna I do eat,
The word of life it is my meat.
My thoughts do yield me more content
Than can thy hours in pleasure spent.   70
Nor are they shadows which I catch,
Nor fancies vain at which I snatch,
But reach at things that are so high
Beyond thy dull capacity.
Eternal substance I do see,
With which enrichéd I would be;
Mine eye doth pierce the heavens, and see
What is invisible to thee.
My garments are not silk or gold,
Nor such like trash which earth doth hold,   80
But royal robes I shall have on,
More glorious than the glistering sun.
My crown not diamonds, pearls, and gold,

But such as angels' heads enfold.
The city where I hope to dwell
There's none on earth can parallel:
The stately walls, both high and strong,
Are made of precious jasper stone;
The gates of pearl both rich and clear,
And angels are for porters there;   90
The streets thereof transparent gold,
Such as no eye did e'er behold;
A crystal river there doth run,
Which doth proceed from the Lamb's throne;
Of life there are the waters sure,
Which shall remain for ever pure;
Of sun or moon they have no need,
For glory doth from God proceed—
No candle there, nor yet torch-light,
For there shall be no darksome night.   100
From sickness and infirmity
For evermore they shall be free,
Nor withering age shall e'er come there,
But beauty shall be bright and clear.
This city pure is not for thee,
For things unclean there shall not be.
If I of Heaven may have my fill,
Take thou the world, and all that will."

THE AUTHOR TO HER BOOK   [1678]

Thou ill-formed offspring of my feeble brain,
Who after birth didst by my side remain
Till snatched from thence by friends less wise than true
Who thee abroad exposed to public view,
Made thee, in rags, halting, to the press to trudge,
Where errors were not lessened, all may judge,
At thy return my blushing was not small
My rambling brat—in print—should mother call.
I cast thee by as one unfit for light,
Thy visage was so irksome in my sight;   10

Yet being mine own, at length affection would
Thy blemishes amend, if so I could.
I washed thy face, but more defects I saw,
And rubbing off a spot still made a flaw.
I stretched thy joints to make thee even feet,
Yet still thou runnest more hobbling than is meet.
In better dress to trim thee was my mind,
But naught save homespun cloth in the house I find.
In this array 'mongst vulgars mayst thou roam,
In critics' hands beware thou dost not come,   20
And take thy way where yet thou art not known.
If for thy father asked, say thou hadst none;
And for thy mother, she, alas, is poor,
Which caused her thus to send thee out of door.

TO MY DEAR AND LOVING HUSBAND   [1678]

If ever two were one, then surely we;
If ever man were loved by wife, then thee;
If ever wife was happy in a man,
Compare with me, ye women, if you can.
I prize thy love more than whole mines of gold,
Or all the riches that the East doth hold.
My love is such that rivers cannot quench,
Nor aught but love from thee give recompense.
Thy love is such I can no way repay;
The heavens reward thee manifold, I pray.   10
Then while we live in love let's so persevere
That when we live no more we may live ever.

IN MEMORY OF MY DEAR GRANDCHILD ELIZABETH BRADSTREET, WHO DECEASED AUGUST, 1665, BEING A YEAR AND A HALF OLD   [1678]

Farewell, dear babe, my heart's too much content!
   Farewell, sweet babe, the pleasure of mine eye!

Farewell, fair flower that for a space was lent,
  Then taken away unto eternity!
Blest babe, why should I once bewail thy fate,
Or sigh the days so soon were terminate,
Since thou art settled in an everlasting state?

By nature trees do rot when they are grown,
  And plums and apples throughly ripe do fall,
And corn and grass are in their season mown,   10
  And time brings down what is both strong and tall.
But plants new set to be eradicate,
And buds new blown to have so short a date,
Is by His hand alone that guides nature and fate.

SOME VERSES UPON THE BURNING OF OUR HOUSE, JULY 10TH, 1666   [1867]

In silent night, when rest I took,
For sorrow near I did not look.
I wakened was with thundering noise
And piteous shrieks of dreadful voice.
That fearful sound of "Fire!" and "Fire!"
Let no man know, is my desire.

I, starting up, the light did spy,
And to my God my heart did cry
To strengthen me in my distress,
And not to leave me succorless;   10
Then coming out, beheld apace
The flame consume my dwelling-place.

And when I could no longer look
I blest his name that gave and took,
That laid my goods now in the dust;
Yea, so it was, and so 'twas just—
It was his own; it was not mine.
Far be it that I should repine.

He might of all justly bereft,
But yet sufficient for us left.   20
When by the ruins oft I passed
My sorrowing eyes aside did cast,
And here and there the places spy
Where oft I sat, and long did lie.

Here stood that trunk, and there that chest;
There lay that store I counted best;
My pleasant things in ashes lie,
And them behold no more shall I.
Under thy roof no guest shall sit,
Nor at thy table eat a bit;   30

No pleasant tale shall e'er be told,
Nor things recounted done of old;
No candle e'er shall shine in thee,
Nor bridegroom's voice e'er heard shall be.
In silence ever shalt thou lie.
Adieu, adieu; all's vanity.

Then straight I 'gan my heart to chide:
And did thy wealth on earth abide?
Didst fix thy hope on mouldering dust,
The arm of flesh didst make thy trust?   40
Raise up thy thoughts above the sky,
That dunghill mists away may fly.

Thou hast an house on high erect;
Framed by that mighty Architect,
With glory richly furnished,
Stands permanent though this be fled.
It's purchaséd, and paid for, too,
By Him who hath enough to do—

A prize so vast as is unknown,
Yet, by his gift, is made thine own.   50
There's wealth enough; I need no more.
Farewell, my pelf; farewell, my store;
The world no longer let me love.
My hope and treasure lie above.

Edward Taylor

c. 1642–1729

Edward Taylor was probably born in 1642 in Sketchley, Leicestershire, England, the son of a yeoman farmer. Trained for the "Dissenting," or Puritan, ministry, he may have attended Cambridge University; but in 1668 he left England for the Massachusetts Bay Colony, where he spent three years at Harvard College. In late fall of 1671 he was invited to preach at the frontier community of Westfield, Massachusetts, and he remained that town's minister and physician for over fifty years. Throughout this period he retained his scholarly interests in the classical languages and history. In 1682 he began writing the poems that make up his Preparatory Meditations, *the last being composed in 1725. Shortly thereafter he became an invalid. He died on June 24, 1729, and was buried at Westfield.*

PROLOGUE   [1939]

Lord, Can a Crumb of Earth the Earth outweigh:
    Outmatch all mountains, nay the Chrystall Sky?
Imbosom in't designs that shall Display
    And trace into the Boundless Deity?
    Yea, hand a Pen whose moysture doth guild ore
    Eternall Glory with a glorious glore.

If it its Pen had of an Angels Quill,
    And sharpend on a Pretious Stone ground tite,
And dipt in Liquid Gold, and mov'de by skill
    In Christall leaves should golden Letters write,   10
    It would but blot and blur: yea, jag and jar,
    Unless thou mak'st the Pen and Scribener.

I am this Crumb of Dust which is design'd
   To make my Pen unto thy Praise alone,
And my dull Phancy I would gladly grinde
    Unto an Edge on Zions Pretious Stone:
    And Write in Liquid Gold upon thy Name
    My Letters till thy glory forth doth flame.

Let not th'attempts breake down my Dust I pray,
   Nor laugh thou them to scorn, but pardon give.   20
Inspire this Crumb of Dust till it display
    Thy Glory through't: and then thy dust shall live.
    Its failings then thou'lt overlook I trust,
    They being Slips slipt from thy Crumb of Dust.

Thy Crumb of Dust breaths two words from its breast;
   That thou wilt guide its pen to write aright
To Prove thou art, and that thou art the best,
    And shew thy Properties to shine most bright.
    And then thy Works will shine as flowers on Stems,
    Or as in Jewellary Shops, do jems.   30

From *Preparatory Meditations*

MEDITATION I   [1939]

What Love is this of thine, that Cannot bee
   In thine Infinity, O Lord, Confinde,
Unless it in thy very Person see
    Infinity and Finity Conjoyn'd?
    What! hath thy Godhead, as not satisfi'de,
    Marri'de our Manhood, making it its Bride?

Oh, Matchless Love! Filling Heaven to the brim!
   O'rerunning it: all running o're beside
This World! Nay, Overflowing Hell, wherein
    For thine Elect, there rose a mighty Tide!   10

That there our Veans might through thy Person bleed,
To quench those flames, that else would on us feed.

Oh! that thy love might overflow my Heart!
    To fire the same with Love: for Love I would.
But oh! my streight'ned Breast! my Lifeless Sparke!
    My Fireless Flame! What Chilly Love, and Cold?
    In measure small! In Manner Chilly! See!
    Lord, blow the Coal: Thy Love Enflame in mee.

THE REFLEXION   [1939]

CANTICLES 2: 1.   I am the rose of Sharon.

Lord, art thou at the Table Head above
    Meat, Med'cine, Sweetness, sparkling Beautys, to
Enamour Souls with Flaming Flakes of Love,
    And not my Trencher, nor my Cup o'reflow?
    Ben't I a bidden guest? Oh! sweat mine Eye:
    O'reflow with Teares: Oh! draw thy fountains dry.

Shall I not smell thy sweet, oh! Sharons Rose?
    Shall not mine Eye salute thy Beauty? Why?
Shall thy sweet leaves their Beautious sweets upclose?
    As halfe ashamde my sight should on them ly?   10
    Woe's me! For this my sighs shall be in grain,
    Offer'd on Sorrows Altar for the same.

Had not my Soule's, thy Conduit, Pipes stopt bin
    With mud, what Ravishment would'st thou Convay?
Let Graces Golden Spade dig till the Spring
    Of tears arise, and cleare this filth away.
    Lord, let thy Spirit raise my sighings till
    These Pipes my soule do with thy sweetness fill.

Earth once was Paradise of Heaven below,
    Till inkefac'd sin had it with poyson stockt;   20

And Chast this Paradise away into
   Heav'ns upmost Loft, and it in Glory Lockt.
   But thou, sweet Lord, hast with thy golden Key
   Unlock[t] the Doore, and made a golden day.

Once at thy Feast, I saw thee Pearle-like stand
   'Tween Heaven and Earth, where Heavens Bright glory
     all
In streams fell on thee, as a floodgate and,
   Like Sun Beams through thee on the World to Fall.
   Oh! Sugar sweet then! My Deare sweet Lord, I see
   Saints Heaven-lost Happiness restor'd by thee.   30

Shall Heaven and Earth's bright Glory all up lie,
   Like Sun Beams bundled in the sun in thee?
Dost thou sit Rose at Table Head, where I
   Do sit, and Carv'st no morsell sweet for mee?
   So much before, so little now! Sprindge, Lord,
   Thy Rosie Leaves, and me their Glee afford.

Shall not thy Rose my Garden fresh perfume?
   Shall not thy Beauty my dull Heart assaile?
Shall not thy golden gleams run through this gloom?
   Shall my black Velvet Mask thy fair Face Vaile?   40
   Pass o're my Faults: shine forth, bright sun; arise!
   Enthrone thy Rosy-selfe within mine Eyes.

MEDITATION 6   [1939]

CANTICLES 2: 1.   I am ... the lily of the valleys.

Am I thy gold? Or Purse, Lord, for thy Wealth;
   Whether in mine or mint refinde for thee?
Ime counted so, but count me o're thyselfe,
   Lest gold washt face, and brass in Heart I bee.
   I Feare my Touchstone touches when I try
   Mee, and my Counted Gold too overly.

Am I new minted by thy Stamp indeed?
   Mine Eyes are dim; I cannot clearly see.
Be thou my Spectacles that I may read
   Thine Image and Inscription stampt on mee.   10
   If thy bright Image do upon me stand,
   I am a Golden Angell in thy hand.

Lord, make my Soule thy Plate: thine Image bright
   Within the Circle of the same enfoile.
And on its brims in golden Letters write
   Thy Superscription in an Holy style.
   Then I shall be thy Money, thou my Hord:
   Let me thy Angell bee, bee thou my Lord.

MEDITATION 8   [1939]

     JOHN 6: 51.   I am the living bread.

I ken[n]ing through Astronomy Divine
   The Worlds bright Battlement, wherein I spy
A Golden Path my Pensill cannot line
   From that bright Throne unto my Threshold ly.
   And while my puzzled thoughts about it pore,
   I find the Bread of Life in't at my doore.

When that this Bird of Paradise put in
   This Wicker Cage (my Corps) to tweedle praise
Had peckt the Fruite forbid: and so did fling
   Away its Food, and lost its golden dayes,   10
   It fell into Celestiall Famine sore,
   And never could attain a morsell more.

Alas! alas! Poore Bird, what wilt thou doe?
   This Creatures field no food for Souls e're gave:
And if thou knock at Angells dores, they show
   An Empty Barrell: they no soul bread have.

Alas! Poore Bird, the Worlds White Loafe is done,
And cannot yield thee here the smallest Crumb.

In this sad state, Gods Tender Bowells run
Out streams of Grace: And he to end all strife,   20
The Purest Wheate in Heaven, his deare-dear Son
Grinds, and kneads up into this Bread of Life:
Which Bread of Life from Heaven down came and
stands
Disht in thy Table up by Angells Hands.

Did God mould up this Bread in Heaven, and bake,
Which from his Table came, and to thine goeth?
Doth he bespeake thee thus: This Soule Bread take;
Come, Eate thy fill of this, thy Gods White Loafe?
Its Food too fine for Angells; yet come, take
And Eate thy fill! Its Heavens Sugar Cake.   30

What Grace is this knead in this Loafe? This thing
Souls are but petty things it to admire.
Yee Angells, help: This fill would to the brim
Heav'ns whelm'd-down Chrystall meele Bowle, yea and
higher.
This Bread of Life dropt in thy mouth doth Cry:
Eate, Eate me, Soul, and thou shalt never dy.

MEDITATION 20   [1939]

PHILIPPIANS 2: 9.   Wherefore God also hath highly exalted him.

View, all ye eyes above, this sight which flings
Seraphick Phancies in Chill Raptures high:
A Turffe of Clay, and yet bright Glories King:
From dust to Glory Angell-like to fly.
A Mortall Clod immortaliz'de, behold,
Flyes through the skies swifter than Angells could.

Upon the Wings he of the Winde rode in
   His Bright Sedan, through all the Silver Skies,
And made the Azure Cloud, his Charriot, bring
   Him to the Mountain of Celestiall joyes.   10
   The Prince o'th'Aire durst not an Arrow spend,
   While through his Realm his Charriot did ascend.

He did not in a Fiery Charriot's shine,
   And Whirlewinde, like Elias upward goe.
But th'golden Ladders Jasper rounds did climbe
   Unto the Heavens high from Earth below.
   Each step had on a Golden Stepping Stone
   Of Deity unto his very Throne.

Methinks I see Heavens sparkling Courtiers fly,
   In flakes of Glory down him to attend;   20
And heare Heart Cramping notes of Melody
   Surround his Charriot as it did ascend:
   Mixing their Musick, making e'ry string
   More to inravish, as they this tune sing.

God is Gone up with a triumphant shout:
   The Lord with sounding Trumpets melodies:
Sing Praise, sing Praise, sing Praise, sing Praises out,
   Unto our King sing praise seraphick-wise!
   Lift up your Heads, ye lasting Doore, they sing,
   And let the King of Glory Enter in.   30

Art thou ascended up on high, my Lord,
   And must I be without thee here below?
Art thou the sweetest joy the Heavens afford?
   Oh! that I with thee was! what shall I do?
   Should I pluck Feathers from an Angells Wing,
   They could not waft me up to thee my King.

Lend mee thy Wings, my Lord, I'st fly apace,
   My Soules Arms stud with thy strong Quills, true Faith;
My Quills then Feather with thy Saving Grace,
   My Wings will take the Winde thy Word displai'th.   40
   Then I shall fly up to thy glorious Throne
   With my strong Wings whose Feathers are thine own.

MEDITATION 29   [1939]

> JOHN 20: 17. I ascend unto my Father, and your
> Father; and to my God, and your God.

My shattred Phancy stole away from mee,
  (Wits run a Wooling over Edens Parke)
And in Gods Garden saw a golden Tree,
  Whose Heart was All Divine, and gold its barke:
  Whose glorious limbs and fruitfull branches strong
  With Saints and Angells bright are richly hung.

Thou! thou! my Deare-Deare Lord, art this rich Tree:
  The Tree of Life within Gods Paradise.
I am a Withred Twig, dri'de, fit to bee
  A Chat Cast in thy fire, writh off by Vice.   10
  Yet if thy Milkwhite Gracious Hand will take mee,
  And grafft mee in this golden stock, thou'lt make mee.

Thou'lt make me then its Fruite and Branch to spring.
  And though a nipping Eastwinde blow, and all
Hells Nymps with spite their Dog's sticks thereat ding
  To Dash the Grafft off, and its fruit to fall,
  Yet I shall stand thy Grafft, and Fruits that are
  Fruits of the Tree of Life thy Grafft shall beare.

I being grafft in thee, there up do stand
  In us Relations all that mutuall are.   20
I am thy Patient Pupill, Servant, and
  Thy Sister, Mother, Doove, Spouse, Son, and Heire:
  Thou art my Priest, Physician, Prophet, King,
  Lord, Brother, Bridegroom, Father, Ev'rything.

I being grafft in thee am graffted here
  Into thy Family and kindred Claim
To all in Heaven: God, Saints, and Angells there.
  I thy Relations my Relations name.
  Thy Father's mine, thy God my God, and I
  With Saints and Angells draw Affinity.   30

My Lord, what is it that thou dost bestow?
    The Praise on this account fills up and throngs
Eternity brimfull, doth overflow
    The Heavens vast with rich Angelick Songs.
    How should I blush? how Tremble at this thing,
    Not having yet my gamut, learn'd to sing.

But, Lord, as burnish't Sun Beams forth out fly,
    Let Angell-Shine forth in my Life out flame,
That I may grace thy gracefull Family,
    And not to thy Relations be a shame.   40
    Make mee thy Grafft, be thou my Golden Stock:
    Thy Glory then I'le make my fruits and Crop.

MEDITATION 38   [1939]

> 1 JOHN 2: 1.   And if any man sin, we have an
> advocate with the Father.

Oh! What a thing is Man? Lord, Who am I?
    That thou shouldst give him Law (Oh! golden Line)
To regulate his Thoughts, Words, Life thereby:
    And judge him wilt thereby too in thy time.
    A Court of Justice thou in heaven holdst,
    To try his Case while he's here housd on mould.

How do thy Angells lay before thine eye
    My Deeds both White and Black I dayly doe?
How doth thy Court thou Pannellst there them try?
    But flesh complains. What right for this? let's know!   10
    For right or wrong, I can't appeare unto't.
    And shall a sentence Pass on such a suite?

Soft; blemish not this golden Bench, or place.
    Here is no Bribe, nor Colourings to hide,
Nor Pettifogger to befog the Case;
    But Justice hath her Glory here well tri'de:
    Her spotless Law all spotted Cases tends;
    Without Respect or Disrespect them ends.

God's Judge himselfe, and Christ Atturny is;
   The Holy Ghost Regesterer is founde.   20
Angells the sergeants are, all Creatures kiss
   The booke, and doe as Evidence abounde.
     All Cases pass according to pure Law,
     And in the sentence is no Fret nor flaw.

What saith, my soule? Here all thy Deeds are tri'de.
   Is Christ thy Advocate to pleade thy Cause?
Art thou his Client? Such shall never slide.
     He never lost his Case: he pleads such Laws
     As Carry do the same, nor doth refuse
     The Vilest sinners Case that doth him Choose.   30

This is his Honour, not Dishonour: nay,
   No Habeas-Corpus 'gainst his Clients came;
For all their Fines his Purse doth make down pay.
     He Non-Suites Satan's suite or Casts the same.
     He'l plead thy Case, and not accept a Fee.
     He'l plead Sub Forma Pauperis for thee.

My Case is bad. Lord, be my Advocate.
   My sin is red: I'me under Gods Arrest.
Thou hast the Hit of Pleading; plead my state.
     Although it's bad, thy Plea will make it best.   40
     If thou wilt plead my Case before the King,
     I'le Waggon Loads of Love and Glory bring.

MEDITATION 40   [1960]

     1 JOHN 2: 2. And he is the propitiation for our sins; and
    not for our's only, but also for the sins of the whole world.

Still I complain; I am complaining still.
   Oh woe is me! Was ever Heart like mine?
A Sty of Filth, a Trough of Washing-Swill,
   A Dunghill Pit, a Puddle of mere Slime,
   A Nest of Vipers, Hive of Hornets-stings,
   A Bag of Poyson, Civit-Box of Sins.

Was ever Heart like mine? So bad? black? vile?
　　Is any Divell blacker? Or can Hell
Produce its match? It is the very soile
　　Where Satan reads his charms and sets his spell;　　　　10
　　His Bowling Ally where he sheeres his fleece
　　At Nine Pins, Nine Holes, Morrice, Fox and Geese.

His Palace Garden where his courtiers walke;
　　His Jewells cabbinet. Here his caball
Do sham it and truss up their Privie talk
　　In Fardells of Consults and bundles all.
　　His shambles and his Butchers stall's herein.
　　It is the Fuddling Schoole of every sin.

Was ever Heart like mine? Pride, Passion fell,
　　Ath'ism, Blasphemy pot, pipe it, dance,　　　　　　　20
Play Barlybreaks, and at last couple in Hell:
　　At Cudgells, Kit-Cat, Cards and Dice here prance:
　　At Noddy, Ruff-and-Trump, Jink, Post and Pare,
　　Put, One-and-thirty, and such other ware.

Grace shuffled is away; Patience oft sticks
　　Too soon, or draws itselfe out, and's out put.
Faith's over-trump, and oft doth lose her tricks.
　　Repentance's chalkt up Noddy, and out shut.
　　They Post and Pare off Grace thus, and its shine.
　　Alas! alas! was ever Heart like mine?　　　　　　　30

Sometimes methinks the serpents head I mall:
　　Now all is still: my spirits do recreute.
But ere my Harpe can tune sweet praise, they fall
　　On me afresh and tare me at my Root.
　　They bite like Badgers now: nay worse, although
　　I tooke them toothless sculls, rot long agoe.

My Reason now's more than my sense, I feele
　　I have more sight than sense: Which seems to bee
A Rod of sunbeams t'whip mee for my steele.
　　My Spirits spiritless and dull in mee　　　　　　　40
　　For my dead prayerless Prayers: the Spirits winde
　　Scarce blows my mill about. I little grinde.

Was ever Heart like mine? My Lord, declare
   I know not what to do: What shall I doe?
I wonder, split I don't upon Despare.
    Its grace's wonder that I wrack not so.
    I faintly shun't, although I see this case
    Would say my sin is greater than thy grace.

Hope's Day-peep down hence through this chinck, Christs
    name,
   Propitiation is for sins. Lord, take   50
It so for mine. Thus quench thy burning flame
    In that clear stream that from his side forth brake.
    I can no comfort take while thus I see
    Hells cursed Imps thus jetting strut in mee.

Lord, take thy sword: these Anakims destroy;
   Then soake my soule in Zions Bucking-tub
With Holy Soap, and Nitre, and rich Lye.
    From all Defilement me cleanse, wash, and rub.
    Then wrince, and wring mee out till th'water fall
    As pure as in the Well: not foule at all.   60

And let thy Sun shine on my Head out cleare.
   And bathe my Heart within its radient beams:
Thy Christ make my Propitiation Deare:
    Thy Praise shall from my Heart breake forth in streams.
    This reeching Vertue of Christs blood will quench
    Thy Wrath, slay Sin, and in thy Love mee bench.

MEDITATION 68A   [1960]

Second Series

      MALACHI 4: 2.   The Sun of Righteousness, etc.

Methinks I spy Almighty holding in
   His hand the Crystall Sky and Sun in't bright:
As Candle and bright Lanthorn lightening,
    The World with this bright lanthorns flaming light

Endungeoning all Darkness underground,
Making all Sunshine Day Heavenward abound.

The Spirituall World, this world doth, Lord out vie:
  Its Skie this Crystall Lanthorn doth orematch.
Its Sun, thou Art, that in'ts bright Canopy
  Outshines that Candle, Darkness doth dispatch.   10
  Thy Crystall Globe of Glorious Sunshine furld
  Light, Life and heate in't Sundayeth the World.

The World without the Sun,'s as dungeon, darke.
  The Sun without its Light would Dungeon spring.
The Moon and Stars are but as Chilly Sparks
  Of Dying fire. The Sun Cheeres ery thing.
  But oh thy Light, Lightsom, delightsom falls
  Upon the Soul above all Cordialls.

All Light delights. Yet Dozde wood light is cold.
  Some light hath heate yet Darkness doth it bound   20
As Lamp and Glowworm light. The Stars do hold
  A twinkling lifeless Light. The Sun is found
  A Ball of Light, of Life, Warmth to natures race.
  But thou'rt that Sun, that shines out Saving Grace.

Doz'de wood-light is but glimmer, with no Smoke.
  And Candle Light's a smoaky lifeless thing.
The light lodgd in the glowworm's peticoate
  Is but a Shew. Star light's nights twinkling.
  Moonlight is nightish, Sun makes day: these all
  Without our Visive Organs lightless fall.   30

But thou, my Lord no Dozed Wood Shine art.
  No Smoky Candle Light rose from thy Wick.
Thy Light ne'er linde the glowworms velvet part.
  Thy Shine makes Stars, Moons, Sunlight darkness thick.
  Thou art the Sun of Heavens bright light rose in
  The Heavenly Orbs. And Heavens blesst glories spring.

Were all the trees on earth fir'de Torches made,
  And all her Grass Wax Candles set on flame

This Light could not make day, this lightsom trade
   Would be a darksom Smoke when Sun shines plaine.   40
   But thy Shine, Lord, darkens this Sunshine bright,
   And makes the Seing Organ, and its Light.

Within the Horizontall Hemisphere
   Of this Blesst Sun, Lord, let mee Mansion have.
Make Day, thou Shining Sun, unto mee cleare
   Thy Sorry Servant earnestly doth crave.
   Let not the Moon ere intervene or fix
   Between me and this Sun to make Ecclipse.

O! bright, bright Day. Lord let this Sun Shine flow.
   Drive hence my Sin and Darkness greate profound   50
And up them Coffin in Earths Shade below
   In darkness gross, on th'other side the ground.
   Neer let the Soyle spew fogs to foile the Light
   Of this Sweet Aire pregnant with Sunbeams bright.

How shall my Soule (Such thoughts Enravish mee)
   Under the Canopy of this bright Day
Imparadisde, Lightend and Livend bee
   Bathd in this Sun Shine 'mong bright Angells play
   And with them strive in sweetest tunes expresst
   Which can thy glorious praises sing out best.   60

From *Gods Determinations Touching His Elect*

THE PREFACE   [1939]

   Infinity, when all things it beheld,
In Nothing, and of Nothing all did build,
Upon what Base was fixt the Lath, wherein
He turn'd this Globe, and riggalld it so trim?
Who blew the Bellows of his Furnace Vast?

Or held the Mould wherein the world was Cast?
Who laid its Corner Stone? Or whose Command?
Where stand the Pillars upon which it stands?
Who Lac'de and Fillitted the earth so fine,
With Rivers like green Ribbons Smaragdine?   10
Who made the Sea's its Selvedge, and it locks
Like a Quilt Ball within a Silver Box?
Who Spread its Canopy? Or Curtains Spun?
Who in this Bowling Alley bowld the Sun?
Who made it always when it rises set:
To go at once both down, and up to get?
Who th' Curtain rods made for this Tapistry?
Who hung the twinckling Lanthorns in the Sky?
Who? who did this? or who is he? Why, know
It's Onely Might Almighty this did doe.   20
His hand hath made this noble worke which Stands
His Glorious Handywork not made by hands.
Who spake all things from nothing; and with ease
Can speake all things to nothing, if he please.
Whose Little finger at his pleasure Can
Out mete ten thousand worlds with halfe a Span:
Whose Might Almighty can by half a looks
Root up the rocks and rock the hills by th' roots.
Can take this mighty World up in his hande,
And shake it like a Squitchen or a Wand.   30
Whose single Frown will make the Heavens shake
Like as an aspen leafe the Winde makes quake.
Oh! what a might is this! Whose single frown
Doth shake the world as it would shake it down?
Which All from Nothing fet, from Nothing, All:
Hath All on Nothing set, lets Nothing fall.
Gave All to nothing Man indeed, whereby
Through nothing man all might him Glorify.
In Nothing is imbosst the brightest Gem
More pretious than all pretiousness in them.   40
But Nothing man did throw down all by sin:
And darkened that lightsom Gem in him,
    That now his Brightest Diamond is grown
    Darker by far than any Coalpit Stone.

THE GLORY OF AND GRACE IN THE
CHURCH SET OUT   [1939]

Come now behold
Within this Knot what Flowers do grow:
Spanglde like gold:
Whence Wreaths of all Perfumes do flow.
Most Curious Colours of all sorts you shall
With all Sweet Spirits s[c]ent. Yet thats not all.

Oh! Look, and finde
These Choicest Flowers most richly sweet
Are Disciplinde
With Artificiall Angells meet.   10
An heap of Pearls is precious: but they shall
When set by Art Excell. Yet that's not all.

Christ's Spirit showers
Down in his Word and Sacraments
Upon these Flowers,
The Clouds of Grace Divine Contents.
Such things of Wealthy Blessings on them fall
As make them sweetly thrive. Yet that's not all.

Yet still behold!
All flourish not at once. We see   20
While some Unfold
Their blushing Leaves, some buds there bee:
Here's Faith, Hope, Charity in flower, which call
On yonders in the Bud. Yet that's not all.

But as they stand
Like Beauties reeching in perfume
A Divine Hand
Doth hand them up to Glories room:
Where Each in sweet'ned Songs all Praises shall
Sing all ore heaven for aye. And that's but all.   30

THE JOY OF CHURCH FELLOWSHIP RIGHTLY
ATTENDED   [1939]

In Heaven soaring up, I dropt an Eare
   On Earth: and oh! sweet Melody!
And listening, found it was the Saints who were
   Encoacht for Heaven that sang for Joy.
    For in Christs Coach they sweetly sing,
    As they to Glory ride therein.

Oh! joyous hearts! Enfir'de with holy Flame!
   Is speech thus tasseled with praise?
Will not your inward fire of Joy contain,
   That it in open flames doth blaze?   10
    For in Christ[s] Coach Saints sweetly sing,
    As they to Glory ride therein.

And if a string do slip by Chance, they soon
   Do screw it up again: whereby
They set it in a more melodious Tune
   And a Diviner Harmony.
    For in Christs Coach they sweetly sing,
    As they to Glory ride therein.

In all their Acts, publick and private, nay,
   And secret too, they praise impart.   20
But in their Acts Divine, and Worship, they
   With Hymns do offer up their Heart.
    Thus in Christs Coach they sweetly sing,
    As they to Glory ride therein.

Some few not in; and some whose Time and Place
   Block up this Coaches way, do goe
As Travellers afoot: and so do trace
   The Road that gives them right thereto;
    While in this Coach these sweetly sing,
    As they to Glory ride therein.   30

Miscellaneous Poems

AN ADDRESS TO THE SOUL OCCASIONED BY A
RAIN   [1939]

Ye Flippering Soule,
  Why dost between the Nippers dwell?
Not stay, nor goe. Not yea, nor yet Controle.
  Doth this doe well?
    Rise journy'ng when the skies fall weeping Showers,
    Not o're nor under th' Clouds and Cloudy Powers.

Not yea, nor noe:
  On tiptoes thus? Why sit on thorns?
Resolve the matter: Stay thyselfe or goe:
  Ben't both wayes born.   10
    Wager thyselfe against thy surplic'de see,
    And win thy Coate, or let thy Coate win thee.

Is this th' Effect
  To leaven thus my Spirits all?
To make my heart a Crabtree Cask direct?
  A Verjuc'te Hall?
    As Bottle Ale, whose Spirits prison'd must
    When jogg'd, the bung with Violence doth burst?

Shall I be made
  A sparkling Wildfire Shop,   20
Where my dull Spirits at the Fireball trade
  Do frisk and hop?
    And while the Hammer doth the Anvill pay,
    The fire ball matter sparkles e'ry way.

One sorry fret,
  An anvill Sparke, rose higher,
And in thy Temple falling, almost set
  The house on fire.
    Such fireballs drop[p]ing in the Temple Flame
    Burns up the building: Lord, forbid the same.   30

UPON A SPIDER CATCHING A FLY   [1939]

Thou sorrow, venom Elfe:
  Is this thy play,
To spin a web out of thyselfe
  To Catch a Fly?
    For why?

I saw a pettish wasp
  Fall foule therein:
Whom yet thy whorle pins did no[t hasp]
  Lest he should fling
    His sting.   10

But as afraid, remote
  Didst stand hereat,
And with thy little fingers stroke
  And gently tap
    His back.

Thus gently him didst treate
  Lest he should pet,
And in a froppish, aspish heate
  Should greatly fret
    Thy net.   20

Whereas the silly Fly,
  Caught by its leg,
Thou by the throate took'st hastily,
  And 'hinde the head
    Bite Dead.

This goes to pot, that not
  Nature doth call.
Strive not above what strength hath got,
  Lest in the brawle
    Thou fall.   30

This Frey seems thus to us:
  Hells Spider gets
His intrails spun to whip Cords thus,
  And wove to nets,
    And sets.

To tangle Adams race
  In's stratagems
To their Destructions, Spoil'd, made base
  By venom things,
    Damn'd Sins.   40

But mighty, Gracious Lord,
  Communicate
Thy Grace to breake the Cord; afford
  Us Glorys Gate
    And State.

We'l Nightingaile sing like,
  When pearcht on high
In Glories Cage, thy glory, bright:
  [Yea,] thankfully,
    For joy.   50

HUSWIFERY [1939]

Make me, O Lord, thy Spin[n]ing Wheele compleat;
  Thy Holy Worde my Distaff make for mee.
Make mine Affections thy Swift Flyers neate,
  And make my Soule thy holy Spoole to bee.
  My Conversation make to be thy Reele,
  And reele the yarn thereon spun of thy Wheele.

Make me thy Loome then, knit therein this Twine:
  And make thy Holy Spirit, Lord, winde quills:
Then weave the Web thyselfe, The yarn is fine.
  Thine Ordinances make my Fulling Mills.   10

Then dy the same in Heavenly Colours Choice,
    All pinkt with Varnish't Flowers of Paradise.

Then cloath therewith mine Understanding, Will,
    Affections, Judgment, Conscience, Memory;
My Words and Actions, that their shine may fill
    My wayes with glory and thee glorify.
    Then mine apparell shall display before yee
    That I am Cloathd in Holy robes for glory.

UPON WEDLOCK AND DEATH OF
CHILDREN   [1939]

A Curious Knot God made in Paradise,
    And drew it out inamled neatly Fresh.
It was the True-Love Knot, more sweet than spice,
    And set with all the flowres of Graces dress.
    Its Weddens Knot, that ne're can be unti'de:
    No Alexanders Sword can it divide.

The slips here planted, gay and glorious grow:
    Unless an Hellish breath do sindge their Plumes.
Here Primrose, Cowslips, Roses, Lilies blow,
    With Violets and Pinkes that voide perfumes: 10
    Whose beautious leaves are lac'd with Hony Dew,
    And Chanting birds Chirp out Sweet Musick true.

When in this Knot I planted was, my Stock
    Soon knotted, and a manly flower out brake.
And after it my branch again did knot:
    Brought out another Flowre: its sweet breath'd mate.
    One knot gave tother and tothers place;
    Thence Checkling Smiles fought in each others face.

But oh! a glorious hand from glory came,
    Guarded with Angells, soon did Crop this flowre,   20
Which almost tore the root up of the same,

At that unlookt for, Dolesome, darksome houre.
In Pray're to Christ perfum'de it did ascend,
And Angells bright did it to heaven tend.

But pausing on't this Sweet perfum'd my thought,
    Christ would in Glory have a Flowre, Choice, Prime.
And having Choice, chose this my branch forth brought.
    Lord, take! I thanke thee, thou takst ought of mine;
    It is my pledg in glory; part of mee
    Is now in it, Lord, glorifi'de with thee.   30

But praying o're my branch, my branch did sprout,
    And bore another manly flower, and gay,
And after that another, sweet brake out,
    The which the former hand soon got away.
    But oh! the torture, Vomit, screechings, groans:
    And six weeks fever would pierce hearts like stones.

Griefe o're doth flow: and nature fault would finde
    Were not thy Will my Spell, Charm, Joy, and Gem:
That as I said, I say, take, Lord, they're thine:
    I piecemeale pass to Glory bright in them.   40
    I joy, may I sweet Flowers for Glory breed,
    Whether thou getst them green, or lets them seed.

THE EBB AND FLOW   [1939]

When first thou on me, Lord, wrough'st thy Sweet Print,
    My heart was made thy tinder box.
    My 'ffections were thy tinder in't:
        Where fell thy Sparkes by drops.
Those holy Sparks of Heavenly fire that came
Did ever catch and often out would flame.

But now my Heart is made thy Censar trim,
    Full of thy golden Altars fire,
    To offer up Sweet Incense in

Unto thyselfe intire: 10
I finde my tinder scarce thy sparks can feel
That drop out from thy Holy flint and Steel.

Hence doubts out bud for feare thy fire in mee
   'S a mocking Ignis Fatuus,
    Or lest thine Altars fire out bee,
      It's hid in ashes thus.
Yet when the bellows of thy Spirit blow
Away mine ashes, then thy fire doth glow.

Philip Freneau

1752–1832

Philip Morin Freneau was born in New York City, January 2, 1752, of a French Huguenot father and a Scotch mother, but his youth and much of his later life were spent in New Jersey. At the College of New Jersey (now Princeton University) he collaborated with James Madison and Henry Hugh Brackenridge on Satires Against the Tories *and with Brackenridge on* The Rising Glory of America. *During the American Revolution he was captured by the British while returning from the Caribbean. After his release he wrote fierce satires on the heinous practices of British prison ships and other abuses. During Jefferson's administration he was a strongly partisan editor and journalist, who suffered from Hamilton's enmity. In politics he was a Jeffersonian "democrat," and in theology a Deist. His satires, odes, and attempted epics were in the neoclassic tradition of eighteenth-century English poetry, but some of his lyrics anticipated the romantic movement, which his poetic career overlapped. After commanding a trading vessel engaged in Caribbean shipping, he retired to a farm in Monmouth, New Jersey, where he died in poverty after exposure during a snowstorm.*

THE POWER OF FANCY   [1786]

Wakeful, vagrant, restless thing,
Ever wandering on the wing,
Who thy wondrous source can find,
Fancy, regent of the mind;
A spark from Jove's resplendent throne,
But thy nature all unknown.

This spark of bright, celestial flame,
From Jove's seraphic altar came,
And hence alone in man we trace,
Resemblance to the immortal race.   10

Ah! what is all this mighty whole,
These suns and stars that round us roll!
What are they all, where'er they shine,
But Fancies of the Power Divine!
What is this globe, these lands, and seas,
And heat, and cold, and flowers, and trees,
And life, and death, and beast, and man,
And time—that with the sun began—
But thoughts on reason's scale combin'd,
Ideas of the Almighty mind!   20

On the surface of the brain
Night after night she walks unseen,
Noble fabrics doth she raise
In the woods or on the seas,
On some high, steep, pointed rock,
Where the billows loudly knock
And the dreary tempests sweep
Clouds along the uncivil deep.

Lo! she walks upon the moon,
Listens to the chimy tune   30
Of the bright, harmonious spheres,
And the song of angels hears;
Sees this earth a distant star,
Pendant, floating in the air;
Leads me to some lonely dome,
Where Religion loves to come,
Where the bride of Jesus dwells,
And the deep ton'd organ swells
In notes with lofty anthems join'd,
Notes that half distract the mind.   40

Now like lightning she descends
To the prison of the fiends,
Hears the rattling of their chains,
Feels their never ceasing pains—
But, O never may she tell
Half the frightfulness of hell.

Now she views Arcadian rocks,
Where the shepherds guard their flocks,
And, while yet her wings she spreads,
Sees chrystal streams and coral beds,　　　　50
Wanders to some desert deep,
Or some dark, enchanted steep.
By the full moonlight doth shew
Forests of a dusky blue,
Where, upon some mossy bed,
Innocence reclines her head.

　　Swift, she stretches o'er the seas
To the far off Hebrides,
Canvas on the lofty mast
Could not travel half so fast—　　　　60
Swifter than the eagle's flight
Or instantaneous rays of light!
Lo! contemplative she stands
On Norwegia's rocky lands—
Fickle Goddess, set me down
Where the rugged winters frown
Upon Orca's howling steep,
Nodding o'er the northern deep,
Where the winds tumultuous roar,
Vext that Ossian sings no more.　　　　70
Fancy, to that land repair,
Sweetest Ossian slumbers there;
Waft me far to southern isles
Where the soften'd winter smiles,
To Bermuda's orange shades,
Or Demarara's lovely glades;
Bear me o'er the sounding cape,
Painting death in every shape,
Where daring Anson spread the sail
Shatter'd by the stormy gale—　　　　80
Lo! she leads me wide and far,
Sense can never follow her—
Shape thy course o'er land and sea,
Help me to keep pace with thee,
Lead me to yon' chalky cliff,
Over rock and over reef,

Into Britain's fertile land,
Stretching far her proud command.
Look back and view, thro' many a year,
Cæsar, Julius Cæsar, there.   90
　　Now to Tempe's verdant wood,
Over the mid-ocean flood
Lo! the islands of the sea—
Sappho, Lesbos mourns for thee:
Greece, arouse thy humbled head,
Where are all thy mighty dead,
Who states to endless ruin hurl'd
And carried vengeance through the world?
Troy, thy vanish'd pomp resume,
Or, weeping at thy Hector's tomb,   100
Yet those faded scenes renew,
Whose memory is to Homer due.
Fancy, lead me wandering still
Up to Ida's cloud-topt hill;
Not a laurel there doth grow
But in vision thou shalt show,—
Every sprig on Virgil's tomb
Shall in livelier colours bloom,
And every triumph Rome has seen
Flourish on the years between.   110
　　Now she bears me far away
In the east to meet the day,
Leads me over Ganges' streams,
Mother of the morning beams—
O'er the ocean hath she ran,
Places me on Tinian;
Farther, farther in the east,
Till it almost meets the west,
Let us wandering both be lost
On Taitis sea-beat coast,   120
Bear me from that distant strand,
Over ocean, over land,
To California's golden shore—
Fancy, stop, and rove no more.
　　Now, tho' late, returning home,
Lead me to Belinda's tomb;

Let me glide as well as you
Through the shroud and coffin too,
And behold, a moment, there,
All that once was good and fair—   130
Who doth here so soundly sleep?
Shall we break this prison deep?—
Thunders cannot wake the maid,
Lightnings cannot pierce the shade,
And tho' wintry tempests roar,
Tempests shall disturb no more.
   Yet must those eyes in darkness stay,
That once were rivals to the day?—
Like heaven's bright lamp beneath the main
They are but set to rise again.   140
   Fancy, thou the muses' pride,
In thy painted realms reside
Endless images of things,
Fluttering each on golden wings,
Ideal objects, such a store,
The universe could hold no more:
Fancy, to thy power I owe
Half my happiness below;
By thee Elysian groves were made,
Thine were the notes that Orpheus play'd;   150
By thee was Pluto charm'd so well
While rapture seiz'd the sons of hell—
Come, O come—perceiv'd by none,
You and I will walk alone.

DEATH   [1786]

(from "The House of Night")

Dark was the sky, and not one friendly star
Shone from the zenith or horizon clear,
Mist sate upon the woods, and darkness rode
In her black chariot, with a wild career.

And from the woods the late resounding note
Issued of the loquacious Whip-poor-will,
Hoarse, howling dogs, and nightly roving wolves
Clamour'd from far off cliffs invisible.

Rude, from the wide extended Chesapeke
I heard the winds the dashing waves assail,   10
And saw from far, by picturing fancy form'd,
The black ship travelling through the noisy gale.

*   *   *

O'er a dark field I held my dubious way
Where Jack-a-lanthorn walk'd his lonely round,
Beneath my feet substantial darkness lay,
And screams were heard from the distemper'd ground.

Nor look'd I back, till to a far-off wood
Trembling with fear, my weary feet had sped—
Dark was the night, but at the inchanted dome
I saw the infernal windows flaming red.   20

And from within the howls of Death I heard,
Cursing the dismal night that gave him birth,
Damning his ancient sire, and mother sin,
Who at the gates of hell, accurséd, brought him forth.

(For fancy gave to my enraptur'd soul
An eagle's eye, with keenest glance to see,
And bade those distant sounds distinctly roll,
Which, waking, never had affected me.)

*   *   *

"Though humbled now, dishearten'd and distrest,
Yet, when admitted to the peaceful ground,   30
With heroes, kings and conquerors I shall rest,
Shall sleep as safely, and perhaps as sound."

Dim burnt the lamp, and now the phantom Death
Gave his last groans in horror and despair—

"All hell demands me hence,"—he said, and threw
The red lamp hissing through the midnight air.

THE VANITY OF EXISTENCE   [1786]

To Thyrsis

In youth, gay scenes attract our eyes,
    And not suspecting their decay
Life's flowery fields before us rise,
    Regardless of its winter day.

But vain pursuits and joys as vain,
    Convince us life is but a dream.
Death is to wake, to rise again
    To that true life you best esteem.

So nightly on some shallow tide,
    Oft have I seen a splendid show;   10
Reflected stars on either side,
    And glittering moons were seen below.

But when the tide had ebbed away,
    The scene fantastic with it fled,
A bank of mud around me lay,
    And sea-weed on the river's bed.

TO THE MEMORY OF THE BRAVE
AMERICANS   [1786]

Under General Greene, in South Carolina,
who fell in the action of September 8, 1781

At Eutaw Springs the valiant died;
    Their limbs with dust are covered o'er—

Weep on, ye springs, your tearful tide;
    How many heroes are no more!

If in this wreck or ruin, they
    Can yet be thought to claim a tear,
O smite your gentle breast, and say
    The friends of freedom slumber here!

Thou, who shalt trace this bloody plain,
    If goodness rules thy generous breast,   10
Sigh for the wasted rural reign;
    Sigh for the shepherds, sunk to rest!

Stranger, their humble graves adorn;
    You too may fall, and ask a tear;
'Tis not the beauty of the morn
    That proves the evening shall be clear.—

They saw their injured country's woe;
    The flaming town, the wasted field;
Then rushed to meet the insulting foe;
    They took the spear—but left the shield.   20

Led by thy conquering genius, Greene,
    The Britons they compelled to fly;
None distant viewed the fatal plain,
    None grieved, in such a cause to die—

But, like the Parthian, famed of old,
    Who, flying, still their arrows threw,
These routed Britons, full as bold,
    Retreated, and retreating slew.

Now rest in peace, our patriot band;
    Though far from nature's limits thrown,   30
We trust they find a happier land,
    A brighter sunshine of their own.

THE HURRICANE [1786]

Happy the man who, safe on shore,
   Now trims, at home, his evening fire;
Unmov'd, he hears the tempests roar,
   That on the tufted groves expire:
Alas! on us they doubly fall,
Our feeble barque must bear them all.

Now to their haunts the birds retreat,
   The squirrel seeks his hollow tree,
Wolves in their shaded caverns meet,
   All, all are blest but wretched we— 10
Foredoomed a stranger to repose,
No rest the unsettled ocean knows.

While o'er the dark abyss we roam,
   Perhaps, with last departing gleam,
We saw the sun descend in gloom,
   No more to see his morning beam;
But buried low, by far too deep,
On coral beds, unpitied, sleep!

But what a strange, uncoasted strand
   Is that, where fate permits no day— 20
No charts have we to mark that land,
   No compass to direct that way—
What Pilot shall explore that realm,
What new Columbus take the helm!

While death and darkness both surround,
   And tempests rage with lawless power,
Of friendship's voice I hear no sound,
   No comfort in this dreadful hour—
What friendship can in tempests be,
What comfort on this raging sea? 30

The barque, accustomed to obey,
  No more the trembling pilots guide:
Alone she gropes her trackless way,
  While mountains burst on either side—
Thus, skill and science both must fall;
And ruin is the lot of all.

THE WILD HONEY SUCKLE   [1788]

Fair flower, that dost so comely grow,
Hid in this silent, dull retreat,
Untouched thy honied blossoms blow,
Unseen thy little branches greet:
  No roving foot shall crush thee here,
  No busy hand provoke a tear.

By Nature's self in white arrayed,
She bade thee shun the vulgar eye,
And planted here the guardian shade,
And sent soft waters murmuring by;   10
  Thus quietly thy summer goes,
  Thy days declining to repose.

Smit with those charms, that must decay,
I grieve to see your future doom;
They died—nor were those flowers more gay,
The flowers that did in Eden bloom;
  Unpitying frosts, and Autumn's power
  Shall leave no vestige of this flower.

From morning suns and evening dews
At first thy little being came: 20
If nothing once, you nothing lose,
For when you die you are the same;
  The space between, is but an hour,
  The frail duration of a flower.

THE INDIAN BURYING GROUND   [1788]

In spite of all the learned have said,
    I still my opinion keep;
The posture, that we give the dead,
    Points out the soul's eternal sleep.

Not so the ancients of these lands—
    The Indian, when from life released,
Again is seated with his friends,
    And shares again the joyous feast.

His imaged birds, and painted bowl,
    And venison, for a journey dressed,   10
Bespeak the nature of the soul,
    Activity, that knows no rest.

His bow, for action ready bent,
    And arrows, with a head of stone,
Can only mean that life is spent,
    And not the old ideas gone.

Thou, stranger, that shalt come this way,
    No fraud upon the dead commit—
Observe the swelling turf, and say
    They do not lie, but here they sit.   20

Here still a lofty rock remains,
    On which the curious eye may trace
(Now wasted, half, by wearing rains)
    The fancies of a ruder race.

Here still an aged elm aspires,
    Beneath whose far-projecting shade
(And which the shepherd still admires)
    The children of the forest played!

There oft a restless Indian queen
    (Pale Shebah, with her braided hair)   30

And many a barbarous form is seen
  To chide the man that lingers there.

By midnight moons, o'er moistening dews;
  In habit for the chase arrayed,
The hunter still the deer pursues,
  The hunter and the deer, a shade!

And long shall timorous fancy see
  The painted chief, and pointed spear,
And Reason's self shall bow the knee
  To shadows and delusions here.   40

TO SIR TOBY   [1795]

A Sugar Planter in the interior parts of Jamaica,
near the City of San Jago de la Vega,
(Spanish Town) 1784

> The motions of his spirit are black as night,
> And his affections dark as Erebus.—SHAKESPEARE

If there exists a hell—the case is clear—
Sir Toby's slaves enjoy that portion here:
Here are no blazing brimstone lakes, 'tis true;
But kindled Rum too often burns as blue,
In which some fiend, whom nature must detest,
Steeps Toby's brand and marks poor Cudjoe's breast.
Here whips on whips excite perpetual fears,
And mingled howlings vibrate on my ears:
Here nature's plagues abound, to fret and teaze,
Snakes, scorpions, despots, lizards, centipedes—   10
No art, no care escapes the busy lash;
All have their dues—and all are paid in cash—
The eternal driver keeps a steady eye
On a black herd, who would his vengeance fly,
But chained, imprisoned, on a burning soil,
For the mean avarice of a tyrant, toil!

The lengthy cart-whip guards this monster's reign—
And cracks, like pistols, from the fields of cane.

   Ye powers! who formed these wretched tribes, relate,
What had they done, to merit such a fate!   20
Why were they brought from Eboe's sultry waste,
To see that plenty which they must not taste—
Food, which they cannot buy, and dare not steal;
Yams and potatoes—many a scanty meal!—

   One, with a gibbet wakes his negro's fears,
One to the windmill nails him by the ears;
One keeps his slave in darkened dens, unfed,
One puts the wretch in pickle ere he's dead:
This, from a tree suspends him by the thumbs,
That, from his table grudges even the crumbs!   30

   O'er yond' rough hills a tribe of females go,
Each with her gourd, her infant, and her hoe;
Scorched by a sun that has no mercy here,
Driven by a devil, whom men call overseer—
In chains, twelve wretches to their labours haste;
Twice twelve I saw, with iron collars graced!—

   Are such the fruits that spring from vast domains?
Is wealth, thus got, Sir Toby, worth your pains!—
Who would your wealth on terms, like these, possess,
Where all we see is pregnant with distress—   40
Angola's natives scourged by ruffian hands,
And toil's hard product shipp'd to foreign lands.

   Talk not of blossoms and your endless spring;
What joy, what smile, can scenes of misery bring?—
Though Nature, here, has every blessing spread,
Poor is the labourer—and how meanly fed!—

   Here Stygian paintings light and shade renew,
Pictures of hell, that Virgil's pencil drew:
Here, surly Charons make their annual trip,
And ghosts arrive in every Guinea ship,   50
To find what beasts these western isles afford,
Plutonian scourges, and despotic lords:—

   Here, they, of stuff determined to be free,
Must climb the rude cliffs of the Liguanee;
Beyond the clouds, in skulking haste repair,
And hardly safe from brother traitors there.

ODE   [1795]

God save the Rights of Man!
Give us a heart to scan
Blessings so dear:
Let them be spread around
Wherever man is found,
And with the welcome sound
Ravish his ear.

Let us with France agree,
And bid the world be free,
While tyrants fall!   10
Let the rude savage host
Of their vast numbers boast—
Freedom's almighty trust
Laughs at them all!

Though hosts of slaves conspire
To quench fair Gallia's fire,
Still shall they fail:
Though traitors round her rise,
Leagu'd with her enemies,
To war each patriot flies,   20
And will prevail.

No more is valor's flame
Devoted to a name,
Taught to adore—
Soldiers of Liberty
Disdain to bow the knee,
But teach Equality
To every shore.

The world at last will join
To aid thy grand design,   30
Dear Liberty!
To Russia's frozen lands

The generous flame expands:
On Afric's burning sands
Shall man be free!

In this our western world
Be Freedom's flag unfurl'd
Through all its shores!
May no destructive blast
Our heaven of joy o'ercast,   40
May Freedom's fabric last
While time endures.

If e'er her cause require!—
Should tyrants e'er aspire
To aim their stroke,
May no proud despot daunt—
Should he his standard plant,
Freedom will never want
Her hearts of oak!

AMANDA'S COMPLAINT   [1809]

In shades we live, in shades we die,
Cool zephyrs breathe for our repose;
In shallow streams we love to play,
But, cruel you, that praise deny
Which you might give, and nothing lose,
And then pursue your destined way.

Ungrateful man! when anchoring here,
On shore you came to beg relief;
I shewed you where the fig trees grow,
And wandering with you, free from fear,   10
To hear the story of your grief
I pointed where the cisterns are,
And would have shewn, if streams did flow!

The Men that spurned your ragged crew,
So long exposed to Neptune's rage—

I told them what your sufferings were:
Told them that landsmen never knew
The trade that hastens frozen age,
The life that brings the brow of care.

A lamb, the loveliest of the flock,   20
To your disheartened crew I gave,
Life to sustain on yonder deep—
Sighing, I cast one sorrowing look
When on the margin of the main
You slew the loveliest of my sheep.

Along your native northern shores,
From cape to cape, where'er you stray,
Of all the nymphs that catch the eye,
They scarce can be excelled by our's—
Not in more fragrant shades they play;—   30
The summer suns come not so nigh.

Confess your fault, mistaken swain,
And own, at least, our equal charms—
Have you no flowers of ruddy hue,
That please your fancy on the plain?—
Would you not guard those flowers from harm,
If Nature's self each picture drew!

Vain are your sighs—in vain your tears,
Your barque must still at anchor lay,
And you remain a slave to care;   40
A thousand doubts, a thousand fears,
'Till what you said, you shall unsay,
Bermudian damsels are not fair!

ON A HONEY BEE   [1809]

Drinking from a glass of wine and drowned
therein (by Hezekiah Salem)

Thou, born to sip the lake or spring,
    Or quaff the waters of the stream,

Why hither come, on vagrant wing?—
    Does Bacchus tempting seem—
        Did he, for you, this glass prepare?—
        Will I admit you to a share?

Did storms harass or foes perplex,
    Did wasps or king-birds bring dismay—
Did wars distress, or labours vex,
    Or did you miss your way?—   10
        A better seat you could not take
        Than on the margin of this lake.

Welcome!—I hail you to my glass:
    All welcome, here, you find;
Here, let the cloud of trouble pass,
    Here, be all care resigned.—
        This fluid never fails to please,
        And drown the griefs of men or bees.

What forced you here we cannot know,
    And you will scarcely tell—   20
But cheery we would have you go
    And bid a glad farewell:
        On lighter wings we bid you fly,
        Your dart will now all foes defy.

Yet take not, oh! too deep a drink,
    And in this ocean die;
Here bigger bees than you might sink,
    Even bees full six feet high.
        Like Pharaoh, then, you would be said
        To perish in a sea of red.   30

Do as you please, your will is mine;
    Enjoy it without fear—
And your grave will be this glass of wine,
    Your epitaph—a tear;
        Go, take your seat on Charon's boat,
        We'll tell the hive, you died afloat.

ON THE UNIVERSALITY AND OTHER ATTRIBUTES
OF THE GOD OF NATURE   [1815]

All that we see, about, abroad,
What is it all, but nature's God?
In meaner works discovered here
No less than in the starry sphere.

In seas, on earth, this God is seen;
All that exist, upon him lean;
He lives in all, and never strayed
A moment from the works he made:

His system fixed on general laws
Bespeaks a wise creating cause;   10
Impartially he rules mankind
And all that on this globe we find.

Unchanged in all that seems to change,
Unbounded space is his great range;
To one vast purpose always true,
No time, with him, is old or new.

In all the attributes divine
Unlimited perfectings shine;
In these enwrapt, in these complete,
All virtues in that centre meet.   20

This power doth all powers transcend,
To all intelligence a friend,
Exists, the greatest and the best
Throughout all the worlds, to make them blest.

All that he did he first approved,
He all things into being loved;
O'er all he made he still presides,
For them in life, or death provides.

Joel Barlow

1754–1812

*Born March 24, 1754, at Redding, Connecticut, Joel Barlow graduated
from Yale College in 1778, studied law, and served as an unordained
chaplain until the end of the American Revolution. In Paris during the
French Revolution, Barlow sympathized with the revolutionary side. From
1795 to 1797 he served as American consul in Algiers. Having made a
fortune speculating in securities, he lived comfortably near Washington,
D.C., for several years. Though best represented by such occasional verse as*
The Hasty-Pudding (1796), *Barlow was most serious about writing an
American epic, first published as* The Vision of Columbus (1787),
and in its final form as The Columbiad (1807). *In 1811 he went to
France as ambassador and the following year went to Poland in a futile
attempt to get Napoleon's signature to an important treaty. He caught
cold and died of pneumonia in Zarnowiec, Department of Krakow,
southern Poland, December 26, 1812.*

THE HASTY-PUDDING   [1796]

Omne tulit punctum qui miscuit utile dulci.
(He makes a good breakfast who mixes pudding with molasses.)

CANTO I

Ye Alps audacious, thro' the heav'ns that rise,
To cramp the day and hide me from the skies;
Ye Gallic flags, that o'er their heights unfurl'd,
Bear death to kings, and freedom to the world,
I sing not you. A softer theme I chuse,
A virgin theme, unconscious of the Muse,

But fruitful, rich, well suited to inspire
The purest frenzy of poetic fire.
   Despise it not, ye Bards to terror steel'd,
Who hurl your thunders round the epic field;   10
Nor ye who strain your midnight throats to sing
Joys that the vineyard and the still-house bring;
Or on some distant fair your notes employ,
And speak of raptures that you ne'er enjoy.
I sing the sweets I know, the charms I feel,
My morning incense, and my evening meal,
The sweets of Hasty-Pudding. Come, dear bowl,
Glide o'er my palate, and inspire my soul.
The milk beside thee, smoking from the kine,
Its substance mingled, married in with thine,   20
Shall cool and temper thy superior heat,
And save the pains of blowing while I eat.
   Oh! could the smooth, the emblematic song
Flow like thy genial juices o'er my tongue,
Could those mild morsels in my numbers chime,
And, as they roll in substance, roll in rhyme,
No more thy awkward unpoetic name
Should shun the Muse, or prejudice thy fame;
But rising grateful to th' accustom'd ear,
All Bards should catch it, and all realms revere.   30
   Assist me first with pious toil to trace
Thro' wrecks of time thy lineage and thy race;
Declare what lovely squaw, in dayes of yore,
(Ere great Columbus sought thy native shore)
First gave thee to the world; her works of fame
Have liv'd indeed, but liv'd without a name.
Some tawny Ceres, goddess of her days
First learn'd with stones to crack the well dry'd maize,
Thro' the rough sieve to shake the golden show'r,
In boiling water stir the yellow flour: 40
The yellow flour, bestrew'd and stir'd with haste,
Swells in the flood and thickens to a paste,
Then puffs and wallops, rises to the brim,
Drinks the dry knobs that on the surface swim;
The knobs at last the busy ladle breaks,
And the whole mass its true consistence takes.

Could but her sacred name unknown so long,
Rise, like her labors, to the son of song,
To her, to them, I'd consecrate my lays,
And blow her pudding with the breath of praise.   50
If 'twas Oella, whom I sang before,
I here ascribe her one great virtue more.
Not thro' the rich Peruvian realms alone
The fame of Sol's sweet daughter should be known,
But o'er the world's wide clime should live secure,
Far as his rays extend, as long as they endure.

Dear Hasty-Pudding, what unpromis'd joy
Expands my heart, to meet thee in Savoy!
Doom'd o'er the world thro' devious paths to roam,
Each clime my country, and each house my home,   60
My soul is sooth'd, my cares have found an end,
I greet my long-lost, unforgotten friend.

For Thee thro' Paris, that corrupted town,
How long in vain I wandered up and down,
Where shameless Bacchus, with his drenching hoard,
Cold from his cave usurps the morning board.
London is lost in smoke and steep'd in tea;
No Yankey there can lisp the name of thee;
The uncouth word, a libel on the town,
Would call a proclamation from the crown.   70
For climes oblique, that fear the sun's full rays,
Chill'd in their fogs, exclude the generous maize;
A grain whose rich luxuriant growth requires
Short gentle showers, and bright etherial fires.

But here, tho' distant from our native shore,
With mutual glee we meet and laugh once more.
The same! I know thee by that yellow face,
That strong complexion of true Indian race.
Which time can never change, nor soil impair,
Nor Alpine snows, nor Turkey's morbid air;   80
For endless years, thro' every mild domain,
Where grows the maize, there thou art sure to reign.

But man, more fickle, the bold licence claims,
In different realms to give thee different names.
Thee the soft nations round the warm Levant
Polanta call, the French of course *Polante*.

Ev'n in thy native regions, how I blush
To hear the Pennsylvanians call thee *Mush!*
On Hudson's banks, while men of Belgic spawn
Insult and eat thee by the name *Suppawn.*   90
Thy name is *Hasty-Pudding!* thus our sires
Were wont to greet thee fuming from their fires,
And while they argu'd in thy just defence
With logic clear, they thus explain'd the sense:—
"In *haste* the boiling cauldron, o'er the blaze,
"Receives and cooks the ready-powder'd maize;
"In *haste* 'tis served, and then in equal *haste*,
"With cooling milk, we make the sweet repast.
"No carving to be done, no knife to grate
"The tender ear, and wound the stony plate;   100
"But the smooth spoon, just fitted to the lip,
"And taught with art the yielding mass to dip,
"By frequent journeys to the bowl well stor'd,
"Performs the hasty honors of the board."
Such is thy name, significant and clear,
A name, a sound to every Yankey dear,
But most to me, whose heart and palate chaste
Preserve my pure hereditary taste.
    There are who strive to stamp with disrepute
The luscious food, because it feeds the brute;   110
In tropes of high-strain'd wit, while gaudy prigs
Compare thy nursling man to pamper'd pigs;
With sovereign scorn I treat the vulgar jest,
Nor fear to share thy bounties with the beast.
What though the generous cow gives me to quaff
The milk nutritious; am I then a calf?
Or can the genius of the noisy swine,
Though nurs'd on pudding, thence lay claim to mine?
Sure the sweet song, I fashion to thy praise,
Runs more melodious than the notes they raise.   120
    My song resounding in its grateful glee,
No merit claims; I praise myself in thee.
My father lov'd thee thro' his length of days;
For thee his fields were shaded o'er with maize;
From thee what health, what vigor he possesst,
Ten sturdy freemen from his loins attest;

Thy constellation rul'd my natal morn,
And all my bones were made of Indian corn.
Delicious grain! whatever form it take,
To roast or boil, to smother or to bake,   130
In every dish 'tis welcome still to me,
But most, my *Hasty-Pudding*, most in thee.

    Let the green Succatash with thee contend,
Let beans and corn their sweetest juices blend,
Let butter drench them in its yellow tide,
And a long slice of bacon grace their side;
Not all the plate, how fam'd soe'er it be,
Can please my palate like a bowl of thee.

    Some talk of Hoe-Cake, fair Virginia's pride,
Rich Johnny-Cake this mouth has often tri'd;   140
Both please me well, their virtues much the same;
Alike their fabric, as allied their fame,
Except in dear New-England, where the last
Receive a dash of pumpkin in the paste,
To give it sweetness and improve the taste.
But place them all before me, smoking hot,
The big, round dumplin rolling from the pot;
The pudding of the bag, whose quivering breast,
With suet lin'd, leads on the Yankey feast;
The Charlotte brown, within whose crusty sides   150
A belly soft the pulpy apple hides;
The yellow bread, whose face like amber glows,
And all of Indian that the bake-pan knows—
You tempt me not, my fav'rite greets my eyes,
To that lov'd bowl my spoon by instinct flies.

CANTO II

    To mix the food by vicious rules of art,
To kill the stomach and to sink the heart,
To make mankind to social virtue sour,
Cram o'er each dish, and be what they devour;
For this the kitchen Muse first fram'd her book,   160
Commanding sweat to stream from every cook;
Children no more their antic gambols tri'd,
And friends to physic wonder'd why they died.

Not so the Yankey—his abundant feast,
With simples furnish'd, and with plainness drest,
A numerous offspring gathers round the board,
And cheers alike the servant and the lord;
Whose well-bought hunger prompts the joyous taste,
And health attends them from the short repast.

While the full pail rewards the milk-maid's toil,   170
The mother sees the morning cauldron boil;
To stir the pudding next demands their care,
To spread the table and the bowls prepare;
To feed the children, as their portions cool,
And comb their heads, and send them off to school.

Yet may the simplest dish some rules impart,
For nature scorns not all the aids of art.
Ev'n Hasty-Pudding, purest of all food,
May still be bad, indifferent, or good,
As sage experience the short process guides,   180
Or want of skill, or want of care presides.
Whoe'er would form it on the surest plan,
To rear the child and long sustain the man;
To shield the morals while it mends the size,
And all the powers of every food supplies,
Attend the lessons that the Muse shall bring,
Suspend your spoons, and listen while I sing.

But since, O man! thy life and health demand
Not food alone, but labour from thy hand,
First in the field, beneath the sun's strong rays,   190
Ask of thy mother earth the needful maize;
She loves the race that courts her yielding soil,
And gives her bounties to the sons of toil.

When now the ox, obedient to thy call,
Repays the loan that fill'd the winter stall,
Pursue his traces o'er the furrow'd plain,
And plant in measur'd hills the golden grain.
But when the tender germe begins to shoot,
And the green spire declares the sprouting root,
Then guard your nursling from each greedy foe,   200
Th' insidious worm, the all-devouring crow.
A little ashes, sprinkled round the spire,
Soon steep'd in rain, will bid the worm retire;

The feather'd robber with his hungry maw
Swift flies the field before your man of straw,
A frightful image, such as school-boys bring
When met to burn the Pope, or hang the King.

Thrice in each season, through each variant row
Wield the strong plow-share and the faithful hoe;
The faithful hoe; a double task that takes,   210
To till the summer corn, and roast the winter cakes.

Slow springs the blade, while check'd by chilling rains,
Ere yet the sun the seat of Cancer gains;
But when his fiercest fires emblaze the land,
Then start the juices, then the roots expand;
Then, like a column of Corinthian mould,
The stalk struts upward, and the leaves unfold;
The busy branches all the ridges fill,
Entwine their arms, and kiss from hill to hill.
Here cease to vex them, all your cares are done;   220
Leave the last labors to the parent sun;
Beneath his genial smiles, the well-drest field,
When autumn calls, a plenteous crop shall yield.

Now the strong foliage bears the standards high,
And shoots the tall top-gallants to the sky;
The suckling ears their silky fringes bend,
And pregnant grown, their swelling coats distend;
The loaded stalk, while still the burthen grows,
O'erhangs the space that runs between the rows;
High as a hop-field waves the silent grove,   230
A safe retreat for little thefts of love,
When the pledg'd roasting-ears invite the maid,
To meet her swain beneath the new-form'd shade;
His generous hand unloads the cumbrous hill,
And the green spoils her ready basket fill;
Small compensation for the two-fold bliss,
The promis'd wedding and the present kiss.

Slight depredations these; but now the moon
Calls from his hollow tree the sly raccoon;
And while by night he bears his prize away,   240
The bolder squirrel labors thro' the day.
Both thieves alike, but provident of time,
A virtue rare, that almost hides their crime.

Then let them steal the little stores they can,
And fill their gran'ries from the toils of man;
We've one advantage where they take no part,—
With all their wiles they ne'er have found the art
To boil the Hasty-Pudding; here we shine
Superior far to tenants of the pine;
This envy'd boon to man shall still belong,   250
Unshar'd by them in substance or in song.

   At last the closing season browns the plain,
And ripe October gathers in the grain;
Deep loaded carts the spacious corn-house fill,
The sack distended marches to the mill;
The lab'ring mill beneath the burthen groans,
And show'rs the future pudding from the stones;
Till the glad house-wife greets the powder'd gold,
And the new crop exterminates the old.

CANTO III

   The days grow short; but tho' the falling sun   260
To the glad swain proclaims his day's work done,
Night's pleasing shades his various tasks prolong,
And yield new subjects to my various song.
For now, the corn-house fill'd, the harvest home,
Th' invited neighbors to the *Husking* come;
A frolic scene, where work, and mirth, and play,
Unite their charms, to chace the hours away.

   Where the huge heap lies center'd in the hall,
The lamp suspended from the cheerful wall,
Brown corn-fed nymphs, and strong hard-handed beaux,   270
Alternate rang'd, extend in circling rows,
Assume their seats, the solid mass attack;
The dry husks rustle, and the corn-cobs crack;
The song, the laugh, alternate notes resound,
And the sweet cider trips in silence round.

   The laws of Husking every wight can tell;
And sure no laws he ever keeps so well:
For each red ear a general kiss he gains,
With each smut ear he smuts the luckless swains;
But when to some sweet maid a prize is cast,   280
Red as her lips, and taper as her waist,

She walks the round, and culls one favor'd beau,
Who leaps, the luscious tribute to bestow.
Various the sport, as are the wits and brains
Of well-pleas'd lasses and contending swains;
Till the vast mound of corn is swept away,
And he that gets the last ear, wins the day.

Meanwhile the house-wife urges all her care,
The well-earn'd feast to hasten and prepare.
The sifted meal already waits her hand.   290
The milk is strain'd, the bowls in order stand,
The fire flames high; and, as a pool (that takes
The headlong stream that o'er the mill-dam breaks)
Foams, roars, and rages, with incessant toils,
So the vext cauldron rages, roars and boils.

First with clean salt she seasons well the food,
Then strews the flour, and thickens all the flood.
Long o'er the simmering fire she lets its stand;
To stir it well demands a stronger hand;
The husband takes his turn and round and round   300
The ladle flies; at last the toil is crown'd;
When to the board the thronging huskers pour,
And take their seats as at the corn before.

I leave them to their feast. There still belong
More copious matters to my faithful song.
For rules there are, tho' ne'er unfolded yet,
Nice rules and wise, how pudding should be ate.

Some with molasses grace the luscious treat,
And mix, like Bards, the useful with the sweet.
A wholesome dish, and well deserving praise,   310
A great resource in those bleak wintry days,
When the chill'd earth lies buried deep in snow,
And raging Boreas dries the shivering cow.

Blest cow! thy praise shall still my notes employ,
Great source of health, the only source of joy;
Mother of Egypt's God,—but sure, for me,
Were I to leave my God, I'd worship thee.
How oft thy teats these pious hands have prest!
How oft thy bounties proved my only feast!
How oft I've fed thee with my fav'rite grain!   320
And roar'd, like thee, to find thy children slain!

Ye swains who know her various worth to prize,
Ah! house her well from Winter's angry skies.
Potatoes, pumpkins, should her sadness cheer,
Corn from your crib, and mashes from your beer;
When spring returns she'll well acquit the loan,
And nurse at once your infants and her own.

Milk then with pudding I should always chuse;
To this in future I confine my Muse,
Till she in haste some farther hints unfold,   330
Well for the young, nor useless to the old.
First in your bowl the milk abundant take,
Then drop with care along the silver lake
Your flakes of pudding; these at first will hide
Their little bulk beneath the swelling tide;
But when their growing mass no more can sink,
When the soft island looms above the brink,
Then check your hand; you've got the portion's due,
So taught our sires, and what they taught is true.

There is a choice in spoons. Tho' small appear   340
The nice distinction, yet to me 'tis clear.
The deep-bowl'd Gallic spoon, contriv'd to scoop
In ample draughts the thin diluted soup,
Performs not well in these substantial things,
Whose mass adhesive to the metal clings;
Where the strong labial muscles must embrace,
The gentle curve, and sweep the hollow space.
With ease to enter and discharge the freight,
A bowl less concave but still more dilate,
Becomes the pudding best. The shape, the size,   350
A secret rests unknown to vulgar eyes.
Experienc'd feeders can alone impart
A rule so much above the lore of art.
These tuneful lips, that thousand spoons have tried,
With just precision could the point decide.
Tho' not in song; the muse but poorly shines
In cones, and cubes, and geometric lines,
Yet the true form, as near as she can tell,
Is that small section of a goose-egg shell,
Which in two equal portions shall divide   360
The distance from the centre to the side.

Fear not to slaver; 'tis no deadly sin.
Like the free Frenchman, from your joyous chin
Suspend the ready napkin; or, like me,
Poise with one hand your bowl upon your knee;
Just in the zenith your wise head project,
Your full spoon, rising in a line direct,
Bold as a bucket, heeds no drops that fall,
The wide-mouth'd bowl will surely catch them all!

From *The Columbiad*

[ONE CENTRED SYSTEM] [1807]

Eager he look'd. Another train of years
Had roll'd unseen, and brighten'd still their spheres;
Earth more resplendent in the floods of day
Assumed new smiles, and flush'd around him lay.
Green swell the mountains, calm the oceans roll,
Fresh beams of beauty kindle round the pole;
Thro all the range where shores and seas extend,
In tenfold pomp the works of peace ascend.
Robed in the bloom of spring's eternal year,
And ripe with fruits the same glad fields appear;   10
O'er hills and vales perennial gardens run,
Cities unwall'd stand sparkling to the sun;
The streams all freighted from the bounteous plain
Swell with the load and labor to the main,
Whose stormless waves command a steadier gale
And prop the pinions of a bolder sail:
Sway'd with the floating weight each ocean toils,
And joyous nature's full perfection smiles.
Fill'd with unfolding fate, the vision'd age
Now leads its actors on a broader stage;   20
When clothed majestic in the robes of state,
Moved by one voice, in general congress meet
The legates of all empires. Twas the place
Where wretched men first firm'd their wandering pace;

Ere yet beguiled, the dark delirious hordes
Began to fight for altars and for lords;
Nile washes still the soil, and feels once more
The works of wisdom press his peopled shore.

    In this mid site, this monumental clime,
Rear'd by all realms to brave the wrecks of time   30
A spacious dome swells up, commodious great,
The last resort, the unchanging scene of state.
On rocks of adamant the walls ascend,
Tall columns heave and sky-like arches bend;
Bright o'er the golden roofs the glittering spires
Far in the concave meet the solar fires;
Four blazing fronts, with gates unfolding high,
Look with immortal splendor round the sky:
Hither the delegated sires ascend,
And all the cares of every clime attend.   40

    As that blest band, the guardian guides of heaven,
To whom the care of stars and suns is given,
(When one great circuit shall have proved their spheres,
And time well taught them how to wind their years)
Shall meet in general council; call'd to state
The laws and labors that their charge await;
To learn, to teach, to settle how to hold
Their course more glorious, as their lights unfold:
From all the bounds of space (the mandate known)
They wing their passage to the eternal throne;   50
Each thro his far dim sky illumes the road,
And sails and centres tow'rd the mount of God;
There, in mid universe, their seats to rear,
Exchange their counsels and their works compare:
So, from all tracts of earth, this gathering throng
In ships and chariots shape their course along,
Reach with unwonted speed the place assign'd
To hear and give the counsels of mankind.

    South of the sacred mansion, first resort
The assembled sires, and pass the spacious court.   60
Here in his porch earth's figured Genius stands,
Truth's mighty mirror poizing in his hands;
Graved on the pedestal and chased in gold,
Man's noblest arts their symbol forms unfold,
His tillage and his trade; with all the store

Of wondrous fabrics and of useful lore:
Labors that fashion to his sovereign sway
Earth's total powers, her soil and air and sea;
Force them to yield their fruits at his known call,
And bear his mandates round the rolling ball.   70
Beneath the footstool all destructive things,
The mask of priesthood and the mace of kings,
Lie trampled in the dust; for here at last
Fraud, folly, error all their emblems cast.
Each envoy here unloads his wearied hand
Of some old idol from his native land;
One flings a pagod on the mingled heap,
One lays a crescent, one a cross to sleep;
Swords, sceptres, mitres, crowns and globes and stars,
Codes of false fame and stimulants to wars   80
Sink in the settling mass; since guile began,
These are the agents of the woes of man.
   Now the full concourse, where the arches bend,
Pour thro by thousands and their seats ascend.
Far as the centred eye can range around,
Or the deep trumpet's solemn voice resound,
Long rows of reverend sires sublime extend,
And cares of worlds on every brow suspend.
High in the front, for soundest wisdom known,
A sire elect in peerless grandeur shone;   90
He open'd calm the universal cause,
To give each realm its limit and its laws,
Bid the last breath of tired contention cease,
And bind all regions in the leagues of peace;
Till one confederate, condependent sway
Spread with the sun and bound the walks of day,
One centred system, one all-ruling soul
Live thro the parts and regulate the whole.
   Here then, said Hesper, with a blissful smile,
Behold the fruits of thy long years of toil.   100
To yon bright borders of Atlantic day
Thy swelling pinions led the trackless way,
And taught mankind such useful deeds to dare,
To trace new seas and happy nations rear;
Till by fraternal hands their sails unfurl'd
Have waved at last in union o'er the world.

William Cullen Bryant

1794–1878

William Cullen Bryant was born November 3, 1794, at Cummington, Massachusetts. He spent a year at Williams College, then studied law and was admitted to the bar in Massachusetts. In 1825 he moved to New York, first to edit the New York Review, *a year later to become assistant editor of the* New York Evening Post, *and in 1829 to begin a half century as that newspaper's great liberal editor. Though most of his best poetry had been written by the time he was forty, in later life he wrote poetry, literary criticism, travel letters, and tales in addition to many distinguished editorials. He died June 12, 1878, in Roslyn, Long Island, New York.*

THANATOPSIS   [1821]

To him who in the love of Nature holds
Communion with her visible forms, she speaks
A various language; for his gayer hours
She has a voice of gladness, and a smile
And eloquence of beauty, and she glides
Into his darker musings, with a mild
And healing sympathy, that steals away
Their sharpness, ere he is aware. When thoughts
Of the last bitter hour come like a blight
Over thy spirit, and sad images   10
Of the stern agony, and shroud, and pall,
And breathless darkness, and the narrow house,
Make thee to shudder, and grow sick at heart;—
Go forth, under the open sky, and list

To Nature's teachings, while from all around—
Earth and her waters, and the depths of air—
Comes a still voice—Yet a few days, and thee
The all-beholding sun shall see no more
In all his course; nor yet in the cold ground,
Where thy pale form was laid, with many tears,   20
Nor in the embrace of ocean, shall exist
Thy image. Earth, that nourished thee, shall claim
Thy growth, to be resolved to earth again,
And, lost each human trace, surrendering up
Thine individual being, shalt thou go
To mix for ever with the elements,
To be a brother to the insensible rock
And to the sluggish clod, which the rude swain
Turns with his share, and treads upon. The oak
Shall send his roots abroad, and pierce thy mould.   30

    Yet not to thine eternal resting-place
Shalt thou retire alone, nor couldst thou wish
Couch more magnificent. Thou shalt lie down
With patriarchs of the infant world—with kings,
The powerful of the earth—the wise, the good,
Fair forms, and hoary seers of ages past,
All in one mighty sepulchre. The hills
Rock-ribbed and ancient as the sun—the vales
Stretching in pensive quietness between;
The venerable woods—rivers that move   40
In majesty, and the complaining brooks
That make the meadows green; and, poured round all,
Old Ocean's gray and melancholy waste,—
Are but the solemn decorations all
Of the great tomb of man. The golden sun,
The planets, all the infinite host of heaven,
Are shining on the sad abodes of death,
Through the still lapse of ages. All that tread
The globe are but a handful to the tribes
That slumber in its bosom.—Take the wings   50
Of morning, pierce the Barcan wilderness,
Or lose thyself in the continuous woods
Where rolls the Oregon, and hears no sound,

Save his own dashings—yet the dead are there:
And millions in those solitudes, since first
The flight of years began, have laid them down
In their last sleep—the dead reign there alone,
So shalt thou rest, and what if thou withdraw
In silence from the living, and no friend
Take note of thy departure? All that breathe   60
Will share thy destiny. The gay will laugh
When thou art gone, the solemn brood of care
Plod on, and each one as before will chase
His favorite phantom; yet all these shall leave
Their mirth and their employments, and shall come,
And make their bed with thee. As the long train
Of ages glide away, the sons of men,
The youth in life's green spring, and he who goes
In the full strength of years, matron and maid,
The speechless babe, and the gray-headed man—   70
Shall one by one be gathered to thy side,
By those, who in their turn shall follow them.

So live, that when thy summons comes to join
The innumerable caravan, which moves
To that mysterious realm, where each shall take
His chamber in the silent halls of death,
Thou go not, like the quarry-slave at night,
Scourged to his dungeon, but, sustained and soothed
By an unfaltering trust, approach thy grave,
Like one who wraps the drapery of his couch   80
About him, and lies down to pleasant dreams.

THE YELLOW VIOLET   [1821]

When beechen buds begin to swell,
    And woods the blue-bird's warble know,
The yellow violet's modest bell
    Peeps from the last year's leaves below.

Ere russet fields their green resume,
    Sweet flower, I love, in forest bare,

To meet thee, when thy faint perfume
    Alone is in the virgin air.

Of all her train, the hands of Spring
    First plant thee in the watery mould,   10
And I have seen thee blossoming
    Beside the snow-bank's edges cold.

Thy parent sun, who bade thee view
    Pale skies, and chilling moisture sip,
Has bathed thee in his own bright hue,
    And streaked with jet thy glowing lip.

Yet slight thy form, and low thy seat,
    And earthward bent thy gentle eye,
Unapt the passing view to meet,
    When loftier flowers are flaunting nigh.   20

Oft, in the sunless April day,
    Thy early smile has stayed my walk;
But midst the gorgeous blooms of May,
    I passed thee on thy humble stalk.

So they, who climb to wealth, forget
    The friends in darker fortunes tried.
I copied them—but I regret
    That I should ape the ways of pride.

And when again the genial hour
    Awakes the painted tribes of light,   30
I'll not o'erlook the modest flower
    That made the woods of April bright.

INSCRIPTION FOR THE ENTRANCE TO A
WOOD   [1821]

    Stranger, if thou hast learned a truth which needs
No school of long experience, that the world

Is full of guilt and misery, and hast seen
Enough of all its sorrows, crimes, and cares,
To tire thee of it, enter this wild wood
And view the haunts of Nature. The calm shade
Shall bring a kindred calm, and the sweet breeze
That makes the green leaves dance, shall waft a balm
To thy sick heart. Thou wilt find nothing here
Of all that pained thee in the haunts of men,   10
And made thee loathe thy life. The primal curse
Fell, it is true, upon the unsinning earth,
But not in vengeance. God hath yoked to guilt
Her pale tormentor, misery. Hence, these shades
Are still the abodes of gladness; the thick roof
Of green and stirring branches is alive
And musical with birds, that sing and sport
In wantonness of spirit; while below
The squirrel, with raised paws and form erect,
Chirps merrily. Throngs of insects in the shade   20
Try their thin wings and dance in the warm beam
That waked them into life. Even the green trees
Partake the deep contentment; as they bend
To the soft winds, the sun from the blue sky
Looks in and sheds a blessing on the scene.
Scarce less the cleft-born wild-flower seems to enjoy
Existence, than the wingèd plunderer
That sucks its sweets. The mossy rocks themselves,
And the old and ponderous trunks of prostrate trees
That lead from knoll to knoll a causey rude   30
Or bridge the sunken brook, and their dark roots,
With all their earth upon them, twisting high,
Breathe fixed tranquillity. The rivulet
Sends forth glad sounds, and tripping o'er its bed
Of pebbly sands, or leaping down the rocks,
Seems, with continuous laughter, to rejoice
In its own being. Softly tread the marge,
Lest from her midway perch thou scare the wren
That dips her bill in water. The cool wind,
That stirs the stream in play, shall come to thee,   40
Like one that loves thee nor will let thee pass
Ungreeted, and shall give its light embrace.

TO A WATERFOWL [1821]

Whither, midst falling dew,
While glow the heavens with the last steps of day,
Far, through their rosy depths, dost thou pursue
    Thy solitary way?

Vainly the fowler's eye
Might mark thy distant flight to do thee wrong,
As, darkly seen against the crimson sky,
    Thy figure floats along.

Seek'st thou the plashy brink
Of weedy lake, or marge of river wide,   10
Or where the rocking billows rise and sink
    On the chafed ocean-side?

There is a Power whose care
Teaches thy way along that pathless coast—
The desert and illimitable air—
    Lone wandering, but not lost.

All day thy wings have fanned,
At that far height, the cold, thin atmosphere,
Yet stoop not, weary, to the welcome land,
    Though the dark night is near.   20

And soon that toil shall end;
Soon shalt thou find a summer home, and rest,
And scream among thy fellows; reeds shall bend,
    Soon, o'er thy sheltered nest.

Thou'rt gone, the abyss of heaven
Hath swallowed up thy form; yet, on my heart
Deeply has sunk the lesson thou hast given,
    And shall not soon depart.

He who, from zone to zone,
Guides through the boundless sky thy certain flight,   30

In the long way that I must tread alone,
    Will lead my steps aright.

GREEN RIVER   [1821]

    When breezes are soft and skies are fair,
I steal an hour from study and care,
And hie me away to the woodland scene,
Where wanders the stream with waters of green,
As if the bright fringe of herbs on its brink
Had given their stain to the waves they drink;
And they, whose meadows it murmurs through,
Have named the stream from its own fair hue.

    Yet pure its waters—its shallows are bright
With colored pebbles and sparkles of light,   10
And clear the depths where its eddies play,
And dimples deepen and whirl away,
And the plane-tree's speckled arms o'ershoot
The swifter current that mines its root,
Through whose shifting leaves, as you walk the hill,
The quivering glimmer of sun and rill
With a sudden flash on the eye is thrown,
Like the ray that streams from the diamond-stone.
Oh, loveliest there the spring days come,
With blossoms, and birds, and wild-bees' hum;   20
The flowers of summer are fairest there,
And freshest the breath of the summer air;
And sweetest the golden autumn day
In silence and sunshine glides away.

    Yet, fair as thou art, thou shunnest to glide,
Beautiful stream! by the village side;
But windest away from haunts of men,
To quiet valley and shaded glen;
And forest, and meadow, and slope of hill,
Around thee, are lonely, lovely, and still,   30
Lonely—save when, by thy rippling tides,
From thicket to thicket the angler glides;

Or the simpler comes, with basket and book,
For herbs of power on thy banks to look;
Or haply, some idle dreamer, like me,
To wander, and muse, and gaze on thee,
Still—save the chirp of birds that feed
On the river cherry and seedy reed,
And thy own wild music gushing out
With mellow murmur of fairy shout,   40
From dawn to the blush of another day,
Like traveller singing along his way.

    That fairy music I never hear,
Nor gaze on those waters so green and clear,
And mark them winding away from sight,
Darkened with shade or flashing with light,
While o'er them the vine to its thicket clings,
And the zephyr stoops to freshen his wings,
But I wish that fate had left me free
To wander these quiet haunts with thee,   50
Till the eating cares of earth should depart,
And the peace of the scene pass into my heart;
And I envy thy stream, as it glides along
Through its beautiful banks in a trance of song.

    Though forced to drudge for the dregs of men,
And scrawl strange words with the barbarous pen,
And mingle among the jostling crowd,
Where the sons of strife are subtle and loud—
I often come to this quiet place,
To breathe the airs that ruffle thy face,   60
And gaze upon thee in silent dream,
For in thy lonely and lovely stream
An image of that calm life appears
That won my heart in my greener years.

A WINTER PIECE   [1832]

    The time has been that these wild solitudes,
Yet beautiful as wild, were trod by me

Oftener than now; and when the ills of life
Had chafed my spirit—when the unsteady pulse
Beat with strange flutterings— I would wander forth
And seek the woods. The sunshine on my path
Was to me as a friend. The swelling hills,
The quiet dells retiring far between,
With gentle invitation to explore
Their windings, were a calm society   10
That talked with me and soothed me. Then the chant
Of birds, and chime of brooks, and soft caress
Of the fresh sylvan air, made me forget
The thoughts that broke my peace, and I began
To gather simples by the fountain's brink,
And lose myself in day-dreams. While I stood
In Nature's loneliness, I was with one
With whom I early grew familiar, one
Who never had a frown for me, whose voice
Never rebuked me for the hours I stole   20
From cares I loved not, but of which the world
Deems highest, to converse with her. When shrieked
The bleak November winds, and smote the woods,
And the brown fields were herbless, and the shades,
That met above the merry rivulet,
Were spoiled, I sought, I loved them still; they seemed
Like old companions in adversity.
Still there was beauty in my walks; the brook
Bordered with sparkling frost-work, was as gay
As with its fringe of summer flowers. Afar,   30
The village with its spires, the path of streams
And dim receding valleys, hid before
By interposing trees, lay visible
Through the bare grove, and my familiar haunts
Seemed new to me. Nor was I slow to come
Among them, when the clouds, from their still skirts,
Had shaken down on earth the feathery snow,
And all was white. The pure keen air abroad,
Albeit it breathed no scent of herb, nor heard
Love-call of bird nor merry hum of bee,   40
Was not the air of death. Bright mosses crept
Over the spotted trunks, and the close buds,

That lay along the boughs, instinct with life,
Patient, and waiting the soft breath of Spring,
Feared not the piercing spirit of the North.
The snow-bird twittered on the beechen bough,
And 'neath the hemlock, whose thick branches bent
Beneath its bright cold burden, and kept dry
A circle, on the earth, of withered leaves,
The partridge found a shelter. Through the snow   50
The rabbit sprang away. The lighter track
Of fox, and the raccoon's broad path, were there,
Crossing each other. From his hollow tree
The squirrel was abroad, gathering the nuts
Just fallen, that asked the winter cold and sway
Of winter blast, to shake them from their hold.

But Winter has yet brighter scenes—he boasts
Splendors beyond what gorgeous Summer knows;
Or Autumn with his many fruits, and woods
All flushed with many hues. Come when the rains   60
Have glazed the snow and clothed the trees with ice,
While the slant sun of February pours
Into the bowers a flood of light. Approach!
The incrusted surface shall upbear thy steps,
And the broad arching portals of the grove
Welcome thy entering. Look! the massy trunks
Are cased in the pure crystal; each light spray,
Nodding and tinkling in the breath of heaven,
Is studded with its trembling water-drops,
That glimmer with an amethystine light.   70
But round the parent-stem the long low boughs
Bend, in a glittering ring, and arbors hide
The glassy floor. Oh! you might deem the spot
The spacious cavern of some virgin mine,
Deep in the womb of earth—where the gems grow,
And diamonds put forth radiant rods and bud
With amethyst and topaz—and the place
Lit up, most royally, with the pure beam
That dwells in them. Or haply the vast hall
Of fairy palace, that outlasts the night,   80
And fades not in the glory of the sun;—

Where crystal columns send forth slender shafts
And crossing arches; and fantastic aisles
Wind from the sight in brightness, and are lost
Among the crowded pillars. Raise thine eye;
Thou seest no cavern roof, no palace vault;
There the blue sky and the white drifting cloud
Look in. Again the wildered fancy dreams
Of spouting fountains, frozen as they rose,
And fixed, with all their branching jets, in air,   90
And all their sluices sealed. All, all is light;
Light without shade. But all shall pass away
With the next sun. From numberless vast trunks
Loosened, the crashing ice shall make a sound
Like the far roar of rivers, and the eve
Shall close o'er the brown woods as it was wont.

  And it is pleasant, when the noisy streams
Are just set free, and milder suns melt off
The plashy snow, save only the firm drift
In the deep glen or the close shade of pines—   100
'Tis pleasant to behold the wreaths of smoke
Roll up among the maples of the hill,
Where the shrill sound of youthful voices wakes
The shriller echo, as the clear pure lymph,
That from the wounded trees, in twinkling drops,
Falls, mid the golden brightness of the morn,
Is gathered in with brimming pails, and oft,
Wielded by sturdy hands, the stroke of axe
Makes the woods ring. Along the quiet air,
Come and float calmly off the soft light clouds,   110
Such as you see in summer, and the winds
Scarce stir the branches. Lodged in sunny cleft,
Where the cold breezes come not, blooms alone
The little wind-flower, whose just opened eye
Is blue as the spring heaven it gazes at—
Startling the loiterer in the naked groves
With unexpected beauty, for the time
Of blossoms and green leaves is yet afar.
And ere it comes, the encountering winds shall oft
Muster their wrath again, and rapid clouds   120

Shade heaven, and bounding on the frozen earth
Shall fall their volleyed stores, rounded like hail
And white like snow, and the loud North again
Shall buffet the vexed forest in his rage.

SUMMER WIND   [1832]

　　It is a sultry day; the sun has drunk
The dew that lay upon the morning grass;
There is no rustling in the lofty elm
That canopies my dwelling, and its shade
Scarce cools me. All is silent, save the faint
And interrupted murmur of the bee,
Settling on the sick flowers, and then again
Instantly on the wing. The plants around
Feel the too potent fervors: the tall maize
Rolls up its long green leaves; the clover droops   10
Its tender foliage, and declines its blooms.
But far in the fierce sunshine tower the hills,
With all their growth of woods, silent and stern,
As if the scorching heat and dazzling light
Were but an element they loved. Bright clouds,
Motionless pillars of the brazen heaven—
Their bases on the mountains—their white tops
Shining in the far ether—fire the air
With a reflected radiance, and make turn
The gazer's eye away. For me, I lie   20
Languidly in the shade, where the thick turf,
Yet virgin from the kisses of the sun,
Retains some freshness, and I woo the wind
That still delays his coming. Why so slow,
Gentle and voluble spirit of the air?
Oh, come and breathe upon the fainting earth
Coolness and life. Is it that in his caves
He hears me? See, on yonder woody ridge,
The pine is bending his proud top, and now
Among the nearer groves, chestnut and oak   30

Are tossing their green boughs about. He comes;
Lo, where the grassy meadow runs in waves!
The deep distressful silence of the scene
Breaks up with mingling of unnumbered sounds
And universal motion. He is come,
Shaking a shower of blossoms from the shrubs,
And bearing on their fragrance; and he brings
Music of birds, and rustling of young boughs,
And sound of swaying branches, and the voice
Of distant waterfalls. All the green herbs   40
Are stirring in his breath; a thousand flowers,
By the road-side and the borders of the brook,
Nod gayly to each other; glossy leaves
Are twinkling in the sun, as if the dew
Were on them yet, and silver waters break
Into small waves and sparkle as he comes.

A FOREST HYMN   [1832]

   The groves were God's first temples. Ere man learned
To hew the shaft, and lay the architrave,
And spread the roof above them—ere he framed
The lofty vault, to gather and roll back
The sound of anthems; in the darkling wood,
Amid the cool and silence, he knelt down,
And offered to the Mightiest solemn thanks
And supplication. For his simple heart
Might not resist the sacred influences
Which, from the stilly twilight of the place,   10
And from the gray old trunks that high in heaven
Mingled their mossy boughs, and from the sound
Of the invisible breath that swayed at once
All their green tops, stole over him, and bowed
His spirit with the thought of boundless power
And inaccessible majesty. Ah, why
Should we, in the world's riper years, neglect
God's ancient sanctuaries, and adore

Only among the crowd, and under roofs
That our frail hands have raised? Let me, at least,　　20
Here, in the shadow of this aged wood,
Offer one hymn—thrice happy, if it find
Acceptance in His ear.

　　　　　　Father, thy hand
Hath reared these venerable columns, thou
Didst weave this verdant roof. Thou didst look down
Upon the naked earth, and, forthwith, rose
All these fair ranks of trees. They, in thy sun,
Budded, and shook their green leaves in thy breeze,
And shot toward heaven. The century-living crow
Whose birth was in their tops, grew old and died　　30
Among their branches, till, at last, they stood,
As now they stand, massy, and tall, and dark,
Fit shrine for humble worshipper to hold
Communion with his Maker. These dim vaults,
These winding aisles, of human pomp or pride
Report not. No fantastic carvings show
The boast of our vain race to change the form
Of thy fair works. But thou art here—thou fill'st
The solitude. Thou art in the soft winds
That run along the summit of these trees　　40
In music; thou art in the cooler breath
That from the inmost darkness of the place
Comes, scarcely felt; the barky trunks, the ground,
The fresh moist ground, are all instinct with thee.
Here is continual worship;—Nature, here,
In the tranquillity that thou dost love,
Enjoys thy presence. Noiselessly, around,
From perch to perch, the solitary bird
Passes; and yon clear spring, that, midst its herbs,
Wells softly forth and wandering steeps the roots　　50
Of half the mighty forest, tells no tale
Of all the good it does. Thou hast not left
Thyself without a witness, in the shades,
Of thy perfections. Grandeur, strength, and grace
Are here to speak of thee. This mighty oak—
By whose immovable stem I stand and seem

Almost annihilated—not a prince,
In all that proud old world beyond the deep,
E'er wore his crown as loftily as he
Wears the green coronal of leaves with which   60
Thy hand has graced him. Nestled at his root
Is beauty, such as blooms not in the glare
Of the broad sun. That delicate forest flower,
With scented breath and look so like a smile,
Seems, as it issues from the shapeless mould,
An emanation of the indwelling Life,
A visible token of the upholding Love,
That are the soul of this great universe.

My heart is awed within me when I think
Of the great miracle that still goes on,   70
In silence, round me—the perpetual work
Of thy creation, finished, yet renewed
Forever. Written on thy works I read
The lesson of thy own eternity.
Lo! all grow old and die—but see again,
How on the faltering footsteps of decay
Youth presses—ever gay and beautiful youth
In all its beautiful forms. These lofty trees
Wave not less proudly that their ancestors
Moulder beneath them. Oh, there is not lost   80
One of earth's charms: upon her bosom yet,
After the flight of untold centuries,
The freshness of her far beginning lies
And yet shall lie. Life mocks the idle hate
Of his arch-enemy Death—yea, seats himself
Upon the tyrant's throne—the sepulchre,
And of the triumphs of his ghastly foe
Makes his own nourishment. For he came forth
From thine own bosom, and shall have no end.

There have been holy men who hid themselves   90
Deep in the woody wilderness, and gave
Their lives to thought and prayer, till they outlived
The generation born with them, nor seemed
Less aged than the hoary trees and rocks

Around them;—and there have been holy men
Who deemed it were not well to pass life thus.
But let me often to these solitudes
Retire, and in thy presence reassure
My feeble virtue. Here its enemies,
The passions, at thy plainer footsteps shrink   100
And tremble and are still. O God! when thou
Dost scare the world with tempests, set on fire
The heavens with falling thunderbolts, or fill,
With all the waters of the firmament,
The swift dark whirlwind that uproots the woods
And drowns the villages; when, at thy call,
Uprises the great deep and throws himself
Upon the continent, and overwhelms
Its cities—who forgets not, at the sight
Of these tremendous tokens of thy power,   110
His pride, and lays his strifes and follies by?
Oh, from these sterner aspects of thy face
Spare me and mine, nor let us need the wrath
Of the mad unchained elements to teach
Who rules them. Be it ours to meditate,
In these calm shades, thy milder majesty,
And to the beautiful order of thy works
Learn to conform the order of our lives.

"OH FAIREST OF THE RURAL MAIDS"
[1832]

Oh fairest of the rural maids!
Thy birth was in the forest shades;
Green boughs, and glimpses of the sky,
Were all that met thine infant eye.

Thy sports, thy wanderings, when a child,
Were ever in the sylvan wild;
And all the beauty of the place
Is in thy heart and on thy face.

The twilight of the trees and rocks
Is in the light shade of thy locks;   10
Thy step is as the wind, that weaves
Its playful way among the leaves.

Thine eyes are springs, in whose serene
And silent waters heaven is seen;
Their lashes are the herbs that look
On their young figures in the brook.

The forest depths, by foot unpressed,
Are not more sinless than thy breast;
The holy peace, that fills the air
Of those calm solitudes, is there.   20

THE EVENING WIND   [1832]

Spirit that breathest through my lattice, thou
   That cool'st the twilight of the sultry day,
Gratefully flows thy freshness round my brow;
   Thou hast been out upon the deep at play,
Riding all day the wild blue waves till now,
   Roughening their crests, and scattering high their spray,
And swelling the white sail. I welcome thee
To the scorched land, thou wanderer of the sea!

Nor I alone; a thousand bosoms round
   Inhale thee in the fulness of delight;   10
And languid forms rise up, and pulses bound
   Livelier, at coming of the wind of night;
And, languishing to hear thy grateful sound,
   Lies the vast inland stretched beyond the sight.
Go forth into the gathering shade; go forth,
God's blessing breathed upon the fainting earth!

Go, rock the little wood-bird in his nest,
   Curl the still waters, bright with stars, and rouse

The wide old wood from his majestic rest,
   Summoning from the innumerable boughs   20
The strange, deep harmonies that haunt his breast:
   Pleasant shall be thy way where meekly bows
The shutting flower, and darkling waters pass,
And where the o'ershadowing branches sweep the grass.

The faint old man shall lean his silver head
   To feel thee; thou shalt kiss the child asleep,
And dry the moistened curls that overspread
   His temples, while his breathing grows more deep;
And they who stand about the sick man's bed,
   Shall joy to listen to thy distant sweep,   30
And softly part his curtains to allow
Thy visit, grateful to his burning brow.

Go—but the circle of eternal change,
   Which is the life of Nature, shall restore,
With sounds and scents from all thy mighty range,
   Thee to thy birthplace of the deep once more;
Sweet odors in the sea-air, sweet and strange,
   Shall tell the home-sick mariner of the shore;
And, listening to thy murmur, he shall deem
He hears the rustling leaf and running stream.   40

TO COLE, THE PAINTER, DEPARTING FOR EUROPE [1832]

Thine eyes shall see the light of distant skies;
   Yet, COLE! thy heart shall bear to Europe's strand
   A living image of our own bright land,
Such as upon thy glorious canvas lies;
Lone lakes—savannas where the bison roves—
   Rocks rich with summer garlands—solemn streams—
   Skies, where the desert eagle wheels and screams—
Spring bloom and autumn blaze of boundless groves.
Fair scenes shall greet thee where thou goest—fair,

But different—everywhere the trace of men,   10
   Paths, homes, graves, ruins, from the lowest glen
To where life shrinks from the fierce Alpine air.
   Gaze on them, till the tears shall dim thy sight,
   But keep that earlier, wilder image bright.

TO THE FRINGED GENTIAN   [1832]

Thou blossom bright with autumn dew,
And colored with the heaven's own blue,
That openest when the quiet light
Succeeds the keen and frosty night.

Thou comest not when violets lean
O'er wandering brooks and springs unseen,
Or columbines, in purple dressed,
Nod o'er the ground-bird's hidden nest.

Thou waitest late and com'st alone,
When woods are bare and birds are flown,   10
And frosts and shortening days portend
The aged year is near his end.

Then doth thy sweet and quiet eye
Look through its fringes to the sky,
Blue—blue—as if that sky let fall
A flower from its cerulean wall.

I would that thus, when I shall see
The hour of death draw near to me,
Hope, blossoming within my heart,
May look to heaven as I depart.   20

THE PRAIRIES   [1834]

These are the gardens of the Desert, these
The unshorn fields, boundless and beautiful,

For which the speech of England has no name—
The Prairies. I behold them for the first,
And my heart swells, while the dilated sight
Takes in the encircling vastness. Lo! they stretch,
In airy undulations, far away,
As if the occean, in his gentlest swell,
Stood still, with all his rounded billows fixed,
And motionless forever.—Motionless?—   10
No—they are all unchained again. The clouds
Sweep over with their shadows, and, beneath,
The surface rolls and fluctuates to the eye;
Dark hollows seem to glide along and chase
The sunny ridges. Breezes of the South!
Who toss the golden and the flame-like flowers,
And pass the prairie-hawk that, poised on high,
Flaps his broad wings, yet moves not—ye have played
Among the palms of Mexico and vines
Of Texas, and have crisped the limpid brooks   20
That from the fountains of Sonora glide
Into the calm Pacific—have ye fanned
A nobler or a lovelier scene than this?
Man hath no power in all this glorious work:
The hand that built the firmament hath heaved
And smoothed these verdant swells, and sown their slopes
With herbage, planted them with island groves,
And hedged them round with forests. Fitting floor
For this magnificent temple of the sky—
With flowers whose glory and whose multitude   30
Rival the constellations! The great heavens
Seem to stoop down upon the scene in love,—
A nearer vault, and of a tenderer blue,
Than that which bends above our eastern hills.

As o'er the verdant waste I guide my steed,
Among the high rank grass that sweeps his sides
The hollow beating of his footstep seems
A sacrilegious sound. I think of those
Upon whose rest he tramples. Are they here—
The dead of other days?—and did the dust   40
Of these fair solitudes once stir with life

And burn with passion? Let the mighty mounds
That overlook the rivers, or that rise
In the dim forest crowded with old oaks,
Answer. A race, that long has passed away,
Built them;—a disciplined and populous race
Heaped, with long toil, the earth, while yet the Greek
Was hewing the Pentelicus to forms
Of symmetry, and rearing on its rock
The glittering Parthenon. These ample fields   50
Nourished their harvests, here their herds were fed,
When haply by their stalls the bison lowed,
And bowed his manèd shoulder to the yoke.
All day this desert murmured with their toils,
Till twilight blushed, and lovers walked, and wooed
In a forgotten language, and old tunes,
From instruments of unremembered form,
Gave the soft winds a voice. The red man came—
The roaming hunter tribes, warlike and fierce,
And the mound-builders vanished from the earth.   60
The solitude of centuries untold
Has settled where they dwelt. The prairie-wolf
Hunts in their meadows, and his fresh-dug den
Yawns by my path. The gopher mines the ground
Where stood their swarming cities. All is gone;
All—save the piles of earth that hold their bones,
The platforms where they worshipped unknown gods,
The barriers which they builded from the soil
To keep the foe at bay—till o'er the walls
The wild beleaguerers broke, and, one by one,   70
The strongholds of the plain were forced, and heaped
With corpses. The brown vultures of the wood
Flocked to those vast uncovered sepulchres,
And sat unscared and silent at their feast.
Haply some solitary fugitive,
Lurking in marsh and forest, till the sense
Of desolation and of fear became
Bitterer than death, yielded himself to die.
Man's better nature triumphed then. Kind words
Welcomed and soothed him; the rude conquerors   80
Seated the captive with their chiefs; he chose

A bride among their maidens, and at length
Seemed to forget—yet ne'er forgot—the wife
Of his first love, and her sweet little ones,
Butchered, amid their shrieks, with all his race.

Thus change the forms of being. Thus arise
Races of living things, glorious in strength,
And perish, as the quickening breath of God
Fills them, or is withdrawn. The red man, too,
Has left the blooming wilds he ranged so long,   90
And, nearer to the Rocky Mountains, sought
A wilder hunting-ground. The beaver builds
No longer by these streams, but far away,
On waters whose blue surface ne'er gave back
The white man's face—among Missouri's springs,
And pools whose issues swell the Oregon—
He rears his little Venice. In these plains
The bison feeds no more. Twice twenty leagues
Beyond remotest smoke of hunter's camp,
Roams the majestic brute, in herds that shake   100
The earth with thundering steps—yet here I meet
His ancient footprints stamped beside the pool.

Still this great solitude is quick with life.
Myriads of insects, gaudy as the flowers
They flutter over, gentle quadrupeds,
And birds, that scarce have learned the fear of man,
Are here, and sliding reptiles of the ground,
Startlingly beautiful. The graceful deer
Bounds to the wood at my approach. The bee,
A more adventurous colonist than man,   110
With whom he came across the eastern deep,
Fills the savannas with his murmurings,
And hides his sweets, as in the golden age,
Within the hollow oak. I listen long
To his domestic hum, and think I hear
The sound of that advancing multitude
Which soon shall fill these deserts. From the ground
Comes up the laugh of children, the soft voice
Of maidens, and the sweet and solemn hymn

Of Sabbath worshippers. The low of herds   120
Blends with the rustling of the heavy grain
Over the dark brown furrows. All at once
A fresher wind sweeps by, and breaks my dream,
And I am in the wilderness alone.

EARTH   [1836]

A midnight black with clouds is in the sky;
I seem to feel, upon my limbs, the weight
Of its vast brooding shadow. All in vain
Turns the tired eye in search of form; no star
Pierces the pitchy veil; no ruddy blaze,
From dwellings lighted by the cheerful hearth,
Tinges the flowering summits of the grass.
No sound of life is heard, no village hum,
Nor measured tramp of footstep in the path,
Nor rush of wind, while, on the breast of Earth,   10
I lie and listen to her mighty voice:
A voice of many tones—sent up from streams
That wander through the gloom, from woods unseen
Swayed by the sweeping of the tides of air,
From rocky chasms where darkness dwells all day,
And hollows of the great invisible hills,
And sands that edge the ocean, stretching far
Into the night—a melancholy sound!

O Earth! dost thou too sorrow for the past
Like man thy offspring? Do I hear thee mourn   20
Thy childhood's unreturning hours, thy springs
Gone with their genial airs and melodies,
The gentle generations of thy flowers,
And thy majestic groves of olden time,
Perished with all their dwellers? Dost thou wail
For that fair age of which the poets tell,
Ere yet the winds grew keen with frost, or fire
Fell with the rains or spouted from the hills,
To blast thy greenness, while the virgin night

Was guiltless and salubrious as the day?   30
Or haply dost thou grieve for those that die—
For living things that trod thy paths awhile,
The love of thee and heaven—and now they sleep
Mixed with the shapeless dust on which thy herds
Trample and graze? I too must grieve with thee,
O'er loved ones lost. Their graves are far away
Upon thy mountains; yet, while I recline
Alone, in darkness, on thy naked soil,
The mighty nourisher and burial-place
Of man, I feel that I embrace their dust.   40

Ha! how the murmur deepens! I perceive
And tremble at its dreadful import. Earth
Uplifts a general cry for guilt and wrong,
And heaven is listening. The forgotten graves
Of the heart-broken utter forth their plaint.
The dust of her who loved and was betrayed,
And him who died neglected in his age;
The sepulchres of those who for mankind
Labored, and earned the recompense of scorn;
Ashes of martyrs for the truth, and bones   50
Of those who, in the strife for liberty,
Were beaten down, their corses given to dogs,
Their names to infamy, all find a voice.
The nook in which the captive, overtoiled,
Lay down to rest at last, and that which holds
Childhood's sweet blossoms, crushed by cruel hands,
Send up a plaintive sound. From battle-fields,
Where heroes madly drave and dashed their hosts
Against each other, rises up a noise,
As if the armèd multitudes of dead   60
Stirred in their heavy slumber. Mournful tones
Come from the green abysses of the sea—
A story of the crimes the guilty sought
To hide beneath its waves. The glens, the groves,
Paths in the thicket, pools of running brook,
And banks and depths of lake, and streets and lanes
Of cities, now that living sounds are hushed,
Murmur of guilty force and treachery.

Here, where I rest, the vales of Italy
Are round me, populous from early time,   70
And field of the tremendous warfare waged
'Twixt good and evil. Who, alas! shall dare
Interpret to man's ear the mingled voice
That comes from her old dungeons yawning now
To the black air, her amphitheatres,
Where the dew gathers on the mouldering·stones,
And fanes of banished gods, and open tombs,
And roofless palaces, and streets and hearths
Of cities dug from their volcanic graves?
I hear a sound of many languages,   80
The utterance of nations now no more,
Driven out by mightier, as the days of heaven
Chase one another from the sky. The blood
Of freemen shed by freemen, till strange lords
Came in their hour of weakness, and made fast
The yoke that yet is worn, cries out to heaven.

What then shall cleanse thy bosom, gentle Earth,
From all its painful memories of guilt?
The whelming flood, or the renewing fire,
Or the slow change of time?—that so, at last,   90
The horrid tale of perjury and strife,
Murder and spoil, which men call history,
May seem a fable, like the inventions told
By poets of the gods of Greece. O thou,
Who sittest far beyond the Atlantic deep,
Among the sources of thy glorious streams,
My native Land of Groves! a newer page
In the great record of the world is thine;
Shall it be fairer? Fear, and friendly Hope,
And Envy, watch the issue, while the lines,   100
By which thou shalt be judged, are written down.

THE ANTIQUITY OF FREEDOM   [1842]

Here are old trees, tall oaks, and gnarléd pines,
That stream with gray-green mosses; here the ground

Was never trenched by spade, and flowers spring up
Unsown, and die ungathered. It is sweet
To linger here, among the flitting birds
And leaping squirrels, wandering brooks, and winds
That shake the leaves, and scatter, as they pass,
A fragrance from the cedars, thickly set
With pale-blue berries. In these peaceful shades—
Peaceful, unpruned, immeasurably old—   10
My thoughts go up the long dim path of years,
Back to the earliest days of liberty.

   O Freedom! thou art not, as poets dream,
A fair young girl, with light and delicate limbs,
And wavy tresses gushing from the cap
With which the Roman master crowned his slave
When he took off the gyves. A bearded man,
Armed to the teeth, art thou; one mailéd hand
Grasps the broad shield, and one the sword; thy brow,
Glorious in beauty though it be, is scarred   20
With tokens of old wars; thy massive limbs
Are strong with struggling. Power at thee has launched
His bolts, and with his lightnings smitten thee;
They could not quench the life thou hast from heaven;
Merciless Power has dug thy dungeon deep,
And his swart armorers, by a thousand fires,
Have forged thy chain; yet, while he deems thee bound,
The links are shivered, and the prison-walls
Fall outward; terribly thou springest forth,
As springs the flame above a burning pile,   30
And shoutest to the nations, who return
Thy shoutings, while the pale oppressor flies.

   Thy birthright was not given by human hands:
Thou wert twin-born with man. In pleasant fields,
While yet our race was few, thou sat'st with him,
To tend the quiet flock and watch the stars,
And teach the reed to utter simple airs.
Thou by his side, amid the tangled wood,
Didst war upon the panther and the wolf,
His only foes; and thou with him didst draw   40
The earliest furrow on the mountain-side,

Soft with the deluge. Tyranny himself,
Thy enemy, although of reverend look,
Hoary with many years, and far obeyed,
Is later born than thou; and as he meets
The grave defiance of thine elder eye,
The usurper trembles in his fastnesses.

Thou shalt wax stronger with the lapse of years,
But he shall fade into a feebler age—
Feebler, yet subtler. He shall weave his snares,   50
And spring them on thy careless steps, and clap
His withered hands, and from their ambush call
His hordes to fall upon thee. He shall send
Quaint maskers, wearing fair and gallant forms
To catch thy gaze, and uttering graceful words
To charm thy ear; while his sly imps, by stealth,
Twine round thee threads of steel, light thread on thread,
That grow to fetters; or bind down thy arms
With chains concealed in chaplets. Oh! not yet
Mayst thou unbrace thy corslet, nor lay by   60
Thy sword; nor yet, O Freedom! close thy lids
In slumber; for thine enemy never sleeps,
And thou must watch and combat till the day
Of the new earth and heaven. But wouldst thou rest
Awhile from tumult and the frauds of men,
These old and friendly solitudes invite
Thy visit. They, while yet the forest-trees
Were young upon the unviolated earth,
And yet the moss-stains on the rock were new,
Beheld thy glorious childhood, and rejoiced.   70

"OH MOTHER OF A MIGHTY RACE"
[1854]

Oh mother of a mighty race,
Yet lovely in thy youthful grace!
The elder dames, thy haughty peers,

Admire and hate thy blooming years.
> With words of shame
And taunts of scorn they join thy name.

For on thy cheeks the glow is spread
That tints thy morning hills with red;
Thy step—the wild-deer's rustling feet
Within thy woods are not more fleet; 10
> Thy hopeful eye
Is bright as thine own sunny sky.

Ay, let them rail—those haughty ones,
While safe thou dwellest with thy sons.
They do not know how loved thou art,
How many a fond and fearless heart
> Would rise to throw
Its life between thee and the foe.

They know not, in their hate and pride,
What virtues with thy children bide; 20
How true, how good, thy graceful maids
Make bright, like flowers, the valley-shades;
> What generous men
Spring, like thine oaks, by hill and glen;—

What cordial welcomes greet the guest
By thy lone rivers of the West;
How faith is kept, and truth revered,
And man is loved, and God is feared,
> In woodland homes,
And where the ocean border foams. 30

There's freedom at thy gates and rest
For Earth's down-trodden and opprest,
A shelter for the hunted head,
For the starved laborer toil and bread.
> Power, at thy bounds,
Stops and calls back his baffled hounds.

Oh, fair young mother! on thy brow
Shall sit a nobler grace than now.

Deep in the brightness of the skies
The thronging years in glory rise,   40
      And, as they fleet,
Drop strength and riches at thy feet.

Thine eye, with every coming hour,
Shall brighten, and thy form shall tower;
And when thy sisters, elder born,
Would brand thy name with words of scorn,
      Before thine eye,
Upon their lips the taunt shall die.

THE POET   [1864]

Thou, who wouldst wear the name
   Of poet mid thy brethren of mankind,
And clothe in words of flame
   Thoughts that shall live within the general mind!
Deem not the framing of a deathless lay
The pastime of a drowsy summer day.

But gather all thy powers,
   And wreak them on the verse that thou dost weave,
And in thy lonely hours,
   At silent morning or at wakeful eve,   10
While the warm current tingles through thy veins,
Set forth the burning words in fluent strains.

No smooth array of phrase,
   Artfully sought and ordered though it be,
Which the cold rhymer lays
   Upon his page with languid industry,
Can wake the listless pulse to livelier speed,
Or fill with sudden tears the eyes that read.

The secret wouldst thou know
   To touch the heart or fire the blood at will?   20

Let thine own eyes o'erflow;
  Let thy lips quiver with the passionate thrill;
Seize the great thought, ere yet its power be past,
And bind, in words, the fleet emotion fast.

Then, should thy verse appear
  Halting and harsh, and all unaptly wrought,
Touch the crude line with fear,
  Save in the moment of impassioned thought;
Then summon back the original glow, and mend
The strain with rapture that with fire was penned.   30

Yet let no empty gust
  Of passion find an utterance in thy lay,
A blast that whirls the dust
  Along the howling street and dies away;
But feelings of calm power and mighty sweep,
Like currents journeying through the windless deep.

Seek'st thou, in living lays,
  To limn the beauty of the earth and sky?
Before thine inner gaze
  Let all that beauty in clear vision lie;   40
Look on it with exceeding love, and write
The words inspired by wonder and delight.

Of tempests wouldst thou sing,
  Or tell of battles—make thyself a part
Of the great tumult; cling
  To the tossed wreck with terror in thy heart;
Scale, with the assaulting host, the rampart's height,
And strike and struggle in the thickest fight.

So shalt thou frame a lay
  That haply may endure from age to age,   50
And they who read shall say:
  "What witchery hangs upon this poet's page!
What art is his the written spells to find
That sway from mood to mood the willing mind!"

THE DEATH OF LINCOLN   [1871]

Oh, slow to smite and swift to spare,
   Gentle and merciful and just!
Who, in the fear of God, didst bear
   The sword of power, a nation's trust!

In sorrow by thy bier we stand,
   Amid the awe that hushes all,
And speak the anguish of a land
   That shook with horror at thy fall.

Thy task is done; the bond are free:
   We bear thee to an honored grave,   10
Whose proudest monument shall be
   The broken fetters of the slave.

Pure was thy life: its bloody close
   Hath placed thee with the sons of light,
Among the noble host of those
   Who perished in the cause of Right.

Ralph Waldo Emerson

1803–1882

Emerson was born on May 25, 1803, in Boston; his father, a Unitarian minister, died eight years later. The impoverished family moved to Concord, Massachusetts, in 1814. Emerson worked his way through Harvard, receiving his degree in 1821. After four years of teaching, he studied at the Divinity School in Cambridge, was licensed to preach in 1826, was a minister from 1829 to 1832 at the Second (Unitarian) Church in Boston, but then resigned his pulpit on doctrinal grounds. He spent most of 1833 traveling in Europe on the first of three trips abroad. In the next year he settled in Concord, but until the last years of his life he made frequent lecture trips to various parts of the United States. His first book, Nature *(1836), was followed in the next two decades by the bulk of his more important works—several books of essays, lectures, and poems. He was a founding member of the Transcendental Club and from 1842 to 1844 was sole editor of the Transcendentalist magazine,* The Dial. *Beginning in 1871 he began to fail in health and memory. He died at Concord, April 27, 1882.*

THE SPHINX   [1847]

The Sphinx is drowsy,
  Her wings are furled:
Her ear is heavy,
  She broods on the world.
"Who'll tell me my secret,
  The ages have kept?—
I awaited the seer
  While they slumbered and slept:—

"The fate of the man-child,
  The meaning of man;   10
Known fruit of the unknown;
  Dædalian plan;
Out of sleeping a waking,
  Out of waking a sleep;
Life death overtaking;
  Deep underneath deep?

"Erect as a sunbeam,
  Upspringeth the palm;
The elephant browses,
  Undaunted and calm;   20
In beautiful motion
  The thrush plies his wings;
Kind leaves of his covert,
  Your silence he sings.

"The waves, unashamèd,
  In difference sweet,
Play glad with the breezes,
  Old playfellows meet;
The journeying atoms,
  Primordial wholes,   30
Firmly draw, firmly drive,
  By their animate poles.

"Sea, earth, air, sound, silence,
  Plant, quadruped, bird,
By one music enchanted,
  One deity stirred,—
Each the other adorning,
  Accompany still;
Night veileth the morning,
  The vapor the hill.   40

"The babe by its mother
  Lies bathèd in joy;
Glide its hours uncounted,—
  The sun is its toy;

Shines the peace of all being,
  Without cloud, in its eyes;
And the sum of the world
  In soft miniature lies.

"But man crouches and blushes,
  Absconds and conceals;   50
He creepeth and peepeth,
  He palters and steals;
Infirm, melancholy,
  Jealous glancing around,
An oaf, an accomplice,
  He poisons the ground.

"Out spoke the great mother,
  Beholding his fear;—
At the sound of her accents
  Cold shuddered the sphere:—   60
'Who has drugged my boy's cup?
  Who has mixed my boy's bread?
Who, with sadness and madness,
  Has turned my child's head?'"

I heard a poet answer
  Aloud and cheerfully,
"Say on, sweet Sphinx! thy dirges
  Are pleasant songs to me.
Deep love lieth under
  These pictures of time;   70
They fade in the light of
  Their meaning sublime.

"The fiend that man harries
  Is love of the Best;
Yawns the pit of the Dragon,
  Lit by rays from the Blest.
The Lethe of Nature
  Can't trance him again,
Whose soul sees the perfect,
  Which his eyes seek in vain.   80

"To vision profounder,
  Man's spirit must dive;
His aye-rolling orb
  At no goal will arrive;
The heavens that now draw him
  With sweetness untold,
Once found,—for new heavens
  He spurneth the old.

"Pride ruined the angels,
  Their shame them restores;   90
Lurks the joy that is sweetest
  In stings of remorse.
Have I a lover
  Who is noble and free?—
I would he were nobler
  Than to love me.

"Eterne alternation
  Now follows, now flies;
And under pain, pleasure,—
  Under pleasure, pain lies.   100
Love works at the centre,
  Heart-heaving alway;
Forth speed the strong pulses
  To the borders of day.

"Dull Sphinx, Jove keep thy five wits;
  Thy sight is growing blear;
Rue, myrrh and cummin for the Sphinx,
  Her muddy eyes to clear!"
The old Sphinx bit her thick lip,—
  Said, "Who taught thee me to name?   110
I am thy spirit, yoke-fellow;
  Of thine eye I am eyebeam.

"Thou art the unanswered question;
  Couldst see thy proper eye,
Alway it asketh, asketh;
  And each answer is a lie.
So take thy quest through nature,

It through thousand natures ply;
Ask on, thou clothed eternity;
　　Time is the false reply."   120

Uprose the merry Sphinx,
　　And crouched no more in stone;
She melted into purple cloud,
　　She silvered in the moon;
She spired into a yellow flame;
　　She flowered in blossoms red;
She flowed into a foaming wave:
　　She stood Monadnoc's head.

Thorough a thousand voices
　　Spoke the universal dame;   130
"Who telleth one of my meanings
　　Is master of all I am."

EACH AND ALL   [1847]

Little thinks, in the field, yon red-cloaked clown
Of thee from the hill-top looking down;
The heifer that lows in the upland farm,
Far-heard, lows not thine ear to charm;
The sexton, tolling his bell at noon,
Deems not that great Napoleon
Stops his horse, and lists with delight,
Whilst his files sweep round yon Alpine height;
Nor knowest thou what argument
Thy life to thy neighbor's creed has lent.   10
All are needed by each one;
Nothing is fair or good alone.
I thought the sparrow's note from heaven,
Singing at dawn on the alder bough;
I brought him home, in his nest, at even;
He sings the song, but it cheers not now,
For I did not bring home the river and sky;—
He sang to my ear,—they sang to my eye.

The delicate shells lay on the shore;
The bubbles of the latest wave   20
Fresh pearls to their enamel gave,
And the bellowing of the savage sea
Greeted their safe escape to me.
I wiped away the weeds and foam,
I fetched my sea-born treasures home;
But the poor, unsightly, noisome things
Had left their beauty on the shore
With the sun and the sand and the wild uproar.
The lover watched his graceful maid,
As 'mid the virgin train she strayed,   30
Nor knew her beauty's best attire
Was woven still by the snow-white choir.
At last she came to his hermitage,
Like the bird from the woodlands to the cage;—
The gay enchantment was undone,
A gentle wife, but fairy none.
Then I said, "I covet truth;
Beauty is unripe childhood's cheat;
I leave it behind with the games of youth:"—
As I spoke, beneath my feet   40
The ground-pine curled its pretty wreath,
Running over the club-moss burrs;
I inhaled the violet's breath;
Around me stood the oaks and firs;
Pine-cones and acorns lay on the ground;
Over me soared the eternal sky,
Full of light and of deity;
Again I saw, again I heard,
The rolling river, the morning bird;—
Beauty through my senses stole;   50
I yielded myself to the perfect whole.

THE PROBLEM   [1847]

I like a church; I like a cowl;
I love a prophet of the soul;

And on my heart monastic aisles
Fall like sweet strains, or pensive smiles;
Yet not for all his faith can see
Would I that cowlèd churchman be.

Why should the vest on him allure,
Which I could not on me endure?

Not from a vain or shallow thought
His awful Jove young Phidias brought;   10
Never from lips of cunning fell
The thrilling Delphic oracle;
Out from the heart of nature rolled
The burdens of the Bible old;
The litanies of nations came,
Like the volcano's tongue of flame,
Up from the burning core below,—
The canticles of love and woe:
The hand that rounded Peter's dome
And groined the aisles of Christian Rome   20
Wrought in a sad sincerity;
Himself from God he could not free;
He builded better than he knew;—
The conscious stone to beauty grew.

Know'st thou what wove yon woodbird's nest
Of leaves, and feathers from her breast?
Or how the fish outbuilt her shell,
Painting with morn each annual cell?
Or how the sacred pine-tree adds
To her old leaves new myriads?   30
Such and so grew these holy piles,
Whilst love and terror laid the tiles.
Earth proudly wears the Parthenon,
As the best gem upon her zone,
And Morning opes with haste her lids
To gaze upon the Pyramids;
O'er England's abbeys bends the sky,
As on its friends, with kindred eye;
For out of Thought's interior sphere

These wonders rose to upper air;   40
And Nature gladly gave them place,
Adopted them into her race,
And granted them an equal date
With Andes and with Ararat.

These temples grew as grows the grass;
Art might obey, but not surpass.
The passive Master lent his hand
To the vast soul that o'er him planned;
And the same power that reared the shrine
Bestrode the tribes that knelt within.   50
Ever the fiery Pentecost
Girds with one flame the countless host,
Trances the heart through chanting choirs,
And through the priest the mind inspires.
The word unto the prophet spoken
Was writ on tables yet unbroken;
The word by seers or sibyls told,
In groves of oak, or fanes of gold,
Still floats upon the morning wind,
Still whispers to the willing mind.   60
One accent of the Holy Ghost
The heedless world hath never lost.
I know what say the fathers wise,—
The Book itself before me lies,
Old *Chrysostom*, best Augustine,
And he who blent both in his line,
The younger *Golden Lips* or mines,
Taylor, the Shakspeare of divines.
His words are music in my ear,
I see his cowlèd portrait dear;   70
And yet, for all his faith could see,
I would not the good bishop be.

URIEL   [1847]

It fell in the ancient periods
    Which the brooding soul surveys,

Or ever the wild Time coined itself
  Into calendar months and days.

This was the lapse of Uriel,
Which in Paradise befell.
Once, among the Pleiads walking,
Seyd overheard the young gods talking;
And the treason, too long pent,
To his ears was evident.   10
The young deities discussed
Laws of form, and metre just,
Orb, quintessence, and sunbeams,
What subsisteth, and what seems.
One, with low tones that decide,
And doubt and reverend use defied,
With a look that solved the sphere,
And stirred the devils everywhere,
Gave his sentiment divine
Against the being of a line.   20
"Line in nature is not found;
Unit and universe are round;
In vain produced, all rays return;
Evil will bless, and ice will burn."
As Uriel spoke with piercing eye,
A shudder ran around the sky;
The stern old war-gods shook their heads,
The seraphs frowned from myrtle-beds;
Seemed to the holy festival
The rash word boded ill to all;   30
The balance-beam of Fate was bent;
The bounds of good and ill were rent;
Strong Hades could not keep his own,
But all slid to confusion.

A sad self-knowledge, withering, fell
On the beauty of Uriel;
In heaven once eminent, the god
Withdrew, that hour, into his cloud;
Whether doomed to long gyration
In the sea of generation,   40
Or by knowledge grown too bright

To hit the nerve of feebler sight.
Straightway, a forgetting wind
Stole over the celestial kind,
And their lips the secret kept,
If in ashes the fire-seed slept.
But now and then, truth-speaking things
Shamed the angels' veiling wings;
And, shrilling from the solar course,
Or from fruit of chemic force,   50
Procession of a soul in matter,
Or the speeding change of water,
Or out of the good of evil born,
Came Uriel's voice of cherub scorn,
And a blush tinged the upper sky,
And the gods shook, they knew not why.

ALPHONSO OF CASTILE   [1847]

I, Alphonso, live and learn,
Seeing Nature go astern.
Things deteriorate in kind;
Lemons run to leaves and rind;
Meagre crop of figs and limes;
Shorter days and harder times.
Flowering April cools and dies
In the insufficient skies.
Imps, at high midsummer, blot
Half the sun's disk with a spot;   10
'T will not now avail to tan
Orange cheek or skin of man.
Roses bleach, the goats are dry,
Lisbon quakes, the people cry.
Yon pale, scrawny fisher fools,
Gaunt as bitterns in the pools,
Are no brothers of my blood;—
They discredit Adamhood.
Eyes of gods! ye must have seen,

O'er your ramparts as ye lean,   20
The general debility;
Of genius the sterility;
Mighty projects countermanded;
Rash ambition, brokenhanded;
Puny man and scentless rose
Tormenting Pan to double the dose.
Rebuild or ruin: either fill
Of vital force the wasted rill,
Or tumble all again in heap
To weltering Chaos and to sleep.   30

Say, Seigniors, are the old Niles dry,
Which fed the veins of earth and sky,
That mortals miss the loyal heats,
Which drove them erst to social feats;
Now, to a savage selfness grown,
Think nature barely serves for one;
With science poorly mask their hurt;
And vex the gods with question pert,
Immensely curious whether you
Still are rulers, or Mildew?   40

Masters, I'm in pain with you;
Masters, I'll be plain with you;
In my palace of Castile,
I, a king, for kings can feel.
There my thoughts the matter roll,
And solve and oft resolve the whole.
And, for I'm styled Alphonse the Wise,
Ye shall not fail for sound advice.
Before ye want a drop of rain,
Hear the sentiment of Spain.   50

You have tried famine: no more try it;
Ply us now with a full diet;
Teach your pupils now with plenty,
For one sun supply us twenty.
I have thought it thoroughly over,—
State of hermit, state of lover;

We must have society,
We cannot spare variety.
Hear you, then, celestial fellows!
Fits not to be overzealous;   60
Steads not to work on the clean jump,
Nor wine nor brains perpetual pump.
Men and gods are too extense;
Could you slacken and condense?
Your rank overgrowths reduce
Till your kinds abound with juice?
Earth, crowded, cries, "Too many men!"
My counsel is, kill nine in ten,
And bestow the shares of all
On the remnant decimal.   70
Add their nine lives to this cat;
Stuff their nine brains in one hat;
Make his frame and forces square
With the labors he must dare;
Thatch his flesh, and even his years
With the marble which he rears.
There, growing slowly old at ease
No faster than his planted trees,
He may, by warrant of his age,
In schemes of broader scope engage.   80
So shall ye have a man of the sphere
Fit to grace the solar year.

MITHRIDATES   [1847]

I cannot spare water or wine,
    Tobacco-leaf, or poppy, or rose;
From the earth-poles to the Line,
    All between that works or grows,
Every thing is kin of mine.

Give me agates for my meat;
Give me cantharids to eat;

From air and ocean bring me foods,
From all zones and altitudes;—

From all natures, sharp and slimy,   10
    Salt and basalt, wild and tame:
Tree and lichen, ape, sea-lion,
    Bird, and reptile, be my game.

Ivy for my fillet band;
Blinding dog-wood in my hand;
Hemlock for my sherbet cull me,
And the prussic juice to lull me;
Swing me in the upas boughs,
Vampyre-fanned, when I carouse.

Too long shut in strait and few,   20
Thinly dieted on dew,
I will use the world, and sift it,
To a thousand humors shift it,
As you spin a cherry.
O doleful ghosts, and goblins merry!
O all you virtues, methods, mights,
Means, appliances, delights,
Reputed wrongs and braggart rights,
Smug routine, and things allowed,
Minorities, things under cloud!   30
Hither! take me, use me, fill me,
Vein and artery, though ye kill me!

HAMATREYA   [1847]

Bulkeley, Hunt, Willard, Hosmer, Meriam, Flint,
Possessed the land which rendered to their toil
Hay, corn, roots, hemp, flax, apples, wool and wood.
Each of these landlords walked amidst his farm,
Saying, "'T is mine, my children's and my name's.
How sweet the west wind sounds in my own trees!

How graceful climb those shadows on my hill!
I fancy these pure waters and the flags
Know me, as does my dog: we sympathize;
And, I affirm, my actions smack of the soil."   10

Where are these men? Asleep beneath their grounds:
And strangers, fond as they, their furrows plough.
Earth laughs in flowers, to see her boastful boys
Earth-proud, proud of the earth which is not theirs;
Who steer the plough, but cannot steer their feet
Clear of the grave.
They added ridge to valley, brook to pond,
And sighed for all that bounded their domain;
"This suits me for a pasture; that's my park;
We must have clay, lime, gravel, granite-ledge,   20
And misty lowland, where to go for peat.
The land is well,—lies fairly to the south.
'T is good, when you have crossed the sea and back,
To find the sitfast acres where you left them."
Ah! the hot owner sees not Death, who adds
Him to his land, a lump of mould the more.
Hear what the Earth says:—

                        EARTH-SONG

            "Mine and yours;
            Mine, not yours.
            Earth endures;   30
            Stars abide—
            Shine down in the old sea;
            Old are the shores;
            But where are old men?
            I who have seen much,
            Such have I never seen.

            "The lawyer's deed
            Ran sure,
            In tail,
            To them, and to their heirs   40
            Who shall succeed,

Without fail,
Forevermore.

"Here is the land,
Shaggy with wood,
With its old valley,
Mound and flood.
But the heritors?—
Fled like the flood's foam.
The lawyer, and the laws,   50
And the kingdom,
Clean swept herefrom.

"They called me theirs,
Who so controlled me;
Yet every one
Wished to stay, and is gone,
How am I theirs,
If they cannot hold me,
But I hold them?"

When I heard the Earth-song   60
I was no longer brave;
My avarice cooled
Like lust in the chill of the grave.

THE RHODORA   [1847]

On Being Asked, Whence Is the Flower?

In May, when sea-winds pierced our solitudes,
I found the fresh Rhodora in the woods,
Spreading its leafless blooms in a damp nook,
To please the desert and the sluggish brook.
The purple petals, fallen in the pool,
Made the black water with their beauty gay;
Here might the red-bird come his plumes to cool,

And court the flower that cheapens his array.
Rhodora! if the sages ask thee why
This charm is wasted on the earth and sky,   10
Tell them, dear, that if eyes were made for seeing,
Then Beauty is its own excuse for being:
Why thou wert there, O rival of the rose!
I never thought to ask, I never knew:
But, in my simple ignorance, suppose
The self-same Power that brought me there brought you.

THE SNOW-STORM   [1847]

Announced by all the trumpets of the sky,
Arrives the snow, and, driving o'er the fields,
Seems nowhere to alight: the whited air
Hides hills and woods, the river, and the heaven,
And veils the farm-house at the garden's end.
The sled and traveller stopped, the courier's feet
Delayed, all friends shut out, the housemates sit
Around the radiant fireplace, enclosed
In a tumultuous privacy of storm.

   Come see the north wind's masonry.   10
Out of an unseen quarry evermore
Furnished with tile, the fierce artificer
Curves his white bastions with projected roof
Round every windward stake, or tree, or door.
Speeding, the myriad-handed, his wild work
So fanciful, so savage, nought cares he
For number or proportion. Mockingly,
On coop or kennel he hangs Parian wreaths;
A swan-like form invests the hidden thorn;
Fills up the farmer's lane from wall to wall,   20
Maugre the farmer's sighs; and at the gate
A tapering turret overtops the work.
And when his hours are numbered, and the world
Is all his own, retiring, as he were not,

Leaves, when the sun appears, astonished Art
To mimic in slow structures, stone by stone,
Built in an age, the mad wind's night-work,
The frolic architecture of the snow.

ODE   [1847]

Inscribed to W. H. Channing

Though loath to grieve
The evil time's sole patriot,
I cannot leave
My honied thought
For the priest's cant,
Or statesman's rant.

If I refuse
My study for their politique,
Which at the best is trick,
The angry Muse   10
Puts confusion in my brain.

But who is he that prates
Of the culture of mankind,
Of better arts and life?
Go, blindworm, go,
Behold the famous States
Harrying Mexico
With rifle and with knife!

Or who, with accent bolder,
Dare praise the freedom-loving mountaineer?   20
I found by thee, O rushing Contoocook!
And in thy valleys, Agiochook!
The jackals of the negro-holder.

The God who made New Hampshire
Taunted the lofty land

With little men;—
Small bat and wren
House in the oak:—
If earth-fire cleave
The upheaved land, and bury the folk,   30
The southern crocodile would grieve.
Virtue palters; Right is hence;
Freedom praised, but hid;
Funeral eloquence
Rattles the coffin-lid.

What boots thy zeal,
O glowing friend,
That would indignant rend
The northland from the south?
Wherefore? to what good end?   40
Boston Bay and Bunker Hill
Would serve things still;—
Things are of the snake.

The horseman serves the horse,
The neatherd serves the neat,
The merchant serves the purse,
The eater serves his meat;
'T is the day of the chattel,
Web to weave, and corn to grind;
Things are in the saddle,   50
And ride mankind.

There are two laws discrete,
Not reconciled,—
Law for man, and law for thing;
The last builds town and fleet,
But it runs wild,
And doth the man unking.

'T is fit the forest fall,
The steep be graded,
The mountain tunnelled,   60

The sand shaded,
The orchard planted,
The glebe tilled,
The prairie granted,
The steamer built.

Let man serve law for man;
Live for friendship, live for love,
For truth's and harmony's behoof;
The state may follow how it can,
As Olympus follows Jove.   70

   Yet do not I implore
The wrinkled shopman to my sounding woods,
Nor bid the unwilling senator
Ask votes of thrushes in the solitudes.
Every one to his chosen work;—
Foolish hands may mix and mar;
Wise and sure the issues are.
Round they roll till dark is light,
Sex to sex, and even to odd;—
The over-god   80
Who marries Right to Might,
Who peoples, unpeoples,—
He who exterminates
Races by stronger races,
Black by white faces,—
Knows to bring honey
Out of the lion;
Grafts gentlest scion
On pirate and Turk.

The Cossack eats Poland,   90
Like stolen fruit;
Her last noble is ruined,
Her last poet mute:
Straight, into double band
The victors divide;
Half for freedom strike and stand;—
The astonished Muse finds thousands at her side.

ODE TO BEAUTY   [1847]

Who gave thee, O Beauty,
The keys of this breast,—
Too credulous lover
Of blest and unblest?
Say, when in lapsed ages
Thee knew I of old?
Or what was the service
For which I was sold?
When first my eyes saw thee,
I found me thy thrall,   10
By magical drawings,
Sweet tyrant of all!
I drank at thy fountain
False waters of thirst;
Thou intimate stranger,
Thou latest and first!
Thy dangerous glances
Make women of men;
New-born, we are melting
Into nature again.   20

Lavish, lavish promiser,
Nigh persuading gods to err!
Guest of million painted forms,
Which in turn thy glory warms!
The frailest leaf, the mossy bark,
The acorn's cup, the raindrop's arc,
The swinging spider's silver line,
The ruby of the drop of wine,
The shining pebble of the pond,
Thou inscribest with a bond,   30
In thy momentary play,
Would bankrupt nature to repay.

Ah, what avails it
To hide or to shun

Whom the Infinite One
Hath granted his throne?
The heaven high over
Is the deep's lover;
The sun and sea,
Informed by thee,   40
Before me run
And draw me on,
Yet fly me still,
As Fate refuses
To me the heart Fate for me chooses.
Is it that my opulent soul
Was mingled from the generous whole;
Sea-valleys and the deep of skies
Furnished several supplies;
And the sands whereof I'm made   50
Draw me to them, self-betrayed?
I turn the proud portfolio
Which holds the grand designs
Of Salvator, of Guercino,
And Piranesi's lines.
I hear the lofty pæans
Of the masters of the shell,
Who heard the starry music
And recount the numbers well;
Olympian bards who sung   60
Divine Ideas below,
Which always find us young
And always keep us so.
Oft, in streets or humblest places,
I detect far-wandered graces,
Which, from Eden wide astray,
In lowly homes have lost their way.

Thee gliding through the sea of form,
Like the lightning through the storm,
Somewhat not to be possessed,   70
Somewhat not to be caressed,
No feet so fleet could ever find,
No perfect form could ever bind.

Thou eternal fugitive,
Hovering over all that live,
Quick and skilful to inspire
Sweet, extravagant desire,
Starry space and lily-bell
Filling with thy roseate smell,
Wilt not give the lips to taste   80
Of the nectar which thou hast.

All that's good and great with thee
Works in close conspiracy;
Thou hast bribed the dark and lonely
To report thy features only,
And the cold and purple morning
Itself with thoughts of thee adorning;
The leafy dell, the city mart,
Equal trophies of thine art;
E'en the flowing azure air   90
Thou hast touched for my despair;
And, if I languish into dreams,
Again I meet the ardent beams.
Queen of things! I dare not die
In Being's deeps past ear and eye;
Lest there I find the same deceiver
And be the sport of Fate forever.
Dread Power, but dear! if God thou be,
Unmake me quite, or give thyself to me!

GIVE ALL TO LOVE   [1847]

Give all to love;
Obey thy heart;
Friends, kindred, days,
Estate, good-fame,
Plans, credit and the Muse,—
Nothing refuse.

'T is a brave master;
Let it have scope:
Follow it utterly,
Hope beyond hope: 10
High and more high
It dives into noon,
With wing unspent,
Untold intent;
But it is a god,
Knows its own path
And the outlets of the sky.

It was never for the mean;
It requireth courage stout.
Souls above doubt, 20
Valor unbending,
It will reward,—
They shall return
More than they were,
And ever ascending.

Leave all for love;
Yet, hear me, yet,
One word more thy heart behoved,
One pulse more of firm endeavor,—
Keep thee to-day, 30
To-morrow, forever,
Free as an Arab
Of thy beloved.

Cling with life to the maid;
But when the surprise,
First vague shadow of surmise
Flits across her bosom young,
Of a joy apart from thee,
Free be she, fancy-free;
Nor thou detain her vesture's hem, 40
Nor the palest rose she flung
From her summer diadem.

Though thou loved her as thyself,
As a self of purer clay,
Though her parting dims the day,
Stealing grace from all alive;
Heartily know,
When half-gods go,
The gods arrive.

THE APOLOGY   [1847]

Think me not unkind and rude
    That I walk alone in grove and glen;
I go to the god of the wood
    To fetch his word to men.

Tax not my sloth that I
    Fold my arms beside the brook;
Each cloud that floated in the sky
    Writes a letter in my book.

Chide me not, laborious band,
    For the idle flowers I brought;   10
Every aster in my hand
    Goes home loaded with a thought.

There was never mystery
    But 't is figured in the flowers;
Was never secret history
    But birds tell it in the bowers.

One harvest from thy field
    Homeward brought the oxen strong;
A second crop thine acres yield,
    Which I gather in a song.   20

MERLIN   [1847]

I

Thy trivial harp will never please
Or fill my craving ear;
Its chords should ring as blows the breeze,
Free, peremptory, clear.
No jingling serenader's art,
Nor tinkle of piano strings,
Can make the wild blood start
In its mystic springs.
The kingly bard
Must smite the chords rudely and hard,   10
As with hammer or with mace;
That they may render back
Artful thunder, which conveys
Secrets of the solar track,
Sparks of the supersolar blaze.
Merlin's blows are strokes of fate,
Chiming with the forest tone,
When boughs buffet boughs in the wood;
Chiming with the gasp and moan
Of the ice-imprisoned flood;   20
With the pulse of manly hearts;
With the voice of orators;
With the din of city arts;
With the cannonade of wars;
With the marches of the brave;
And prayers of might from martyrs' cave.

Great is the art,
Great be the manners, of the bard.
He shall not his brain encumber
With the coil of rhythm and number;   30
But, leaving rule and pale forethought,
He shall aye climb
For his rhyme.

"Pass in, pass in," the angels say,
"In to the upper doors,
Nor count compartments of the floors,
But mount to paradise
By the stairway of surprise."

Blameless master of the games,
King of sport that never shames,   40
He shall daily joy dispense
Hid in song's sweet influence.
Forms more cheerly live and go,
What time the subtle mind
Sings aloud the tune whereto
Their pulses beat,
And march their feet,
And their members are combined.

By Sybarites beguiled,
He shall no task decline;   50
Merlin's mighty line
Extremes of nature reconciled,—
Bereaved a tyrant of his will,
And made the lion mild.
Songs can the tempest still,
Scattered on the stormy air,
Mould the year to fair increase,
And bring in poetic peace.

He shall not seek to weave,
In weak, unhappy times,   60
Efficacious rhymes;
Wait his returning strength.
Bird that from the nadir's floor
To the zenith's top can soar,—
The soaring orbit of the muse exceeds that journey's
     length.
Nor profane affect to hit
Or compass that, by meddling wit,
Which only the propitious mind
Publishes when 't is inclined.

There are open hours 70
When the God's will sallies free,
And the dull idiot might see
The flowing fortunes of a thousand years;—
Sudden, at unawares,
Self-moved, fly-to the doors,
Nor sword of angels could reveal
What they conceal.

II

The rhyme of the poet
Modulates the king's affairs;
Balance-loving Nature 80
Made all things in pairs.
To every foot its antipode;
Each color with its counter glowed;
To every tone beat answering tones,
Higher or graver;
Flavor gladly blends with flavor;
Leaf answers leaf upon the bough;
And match the paired cotyledons.
Hands to hands, and feet to feet,
In one body grooms and brides; 90
Eldest rite, two married sides
In every mortal meet.
Light's far furnace shines,
Smelting balls and bars,
Forging double stars,
Glittering twins and trines.
The animals are sick with love,
Lovesick with rhyme;
Each with all propitious Time
Into chorus wove. 100

Like the dancers' ordered band,
Thoughts come also hand in hand;
In equal couples mated,
Or else alternated;
Adding by their mutual gage,
One to other, health and age.

Solitary fancies go
Short-lived wandering to and fro,
Most like to bachelors,
Or an ungiven maid,   110
Not ancestors,
With no posterity to make the lie afraid,
Or keep truth undecayed.
Perfect-paired as eagle's wings,
Justice is the rhyme of things;
Trade and counting use
The self-same tuneful muse;
And Nemesis,
Who with even matches odd,
Who athwart space redresses   120
The partial wrong,
Fills the just period,
And finishes the song.

Subtle rhymes, with ruin rife,
Murmur in the house of life,
Sung by the Sisters as they spin;
In perfect time and measure they
Build and unbuild our echoing clay.
As the two twilights of the day
Fold us music-drunken in.   130

BACCHUS   [1847]

Bring me wine, but wine which never grew
In the belly of the grape,
Or grew on vine whose tap-roots, reaching through
Under the Andes to the Cape,
Suffer no savor of the earth to scape.

Let its grapes the morn salute
From a nocturnal root,
Which feels the acrid juice

Of Styx and Erebus;
And turns the woe of Night,   10
By its own craft, to a more rich delight.

We buy ashes for bread;
We buy diluted wine;
Give me of the true,—
Whose ample leaves and tendrils curled
Among the silver hills of heaven
Draw everlasting dew;
Wine of wine,
Blood of the world,
Form of forms, and mould of statures,   20
That I intoxicated,
And by the draught assimilated,
May float at pleasure through all natures;
The bird-language rightly spell,
And that which roses say so well.

Wine that is shed
Like the torrents of the sun
Up the horizon walls,
Or like the Atlantic streams, which run
When the South Sea calls.   30

Water and bread,
Food which needs no transmuting,
Rainbow-flowering, wisdom-fruiting,
Wine which is already man,
Food which teach and reason can.

Wine which Music is,—
Music and wine are one,—
That I, drinking this,
Shall hear far Chaos talk with me;
Kings unborn shall walk with me;   40
And the poor grass shall plot and plan
What it will do when it is man.
Quickened so, will I unlock
Every crypt of every rock.

I thank the joyful juice
For all I know;—
Winds of remembering
Of the ancient being blow,
And seeming-solid walls of use
Open and flow.   50

Pour, Bacchus! the remembering wine;
Retrieve the loss of me and mine!
Vine for vine be antidote,
And the grape requite the lote!
Haste to cure the old despair,—
Reason in Nature's lotus drenched,
The memory of ages quenched;
Give them again to shine;
Let wine repair what this undid;
And where the infection slid,   60
A dazzling memory revive;
Refresh the faded tints,
Recut the aged prints,
And write my old adventures with the pen
Which on the first day drew,
Upon the tablets blue,
The dancing Pleiads and eternal men.

BLIGHT   [1847]

            Give me truths;
For I am weary of the surfaces,
And die of inanition. If I knew
Only the herbs and simples of the wood,
Rue, cinquefoil, gill, vervain and agrimony,
Blue-vetch and trillium, hawkweed, sassafras,
Milkweeds and murky brakes, quaint pipes and sundew,
And rare and virtuous roots, which in these woods
Draw untold juices from the common earth,
Untold, unknown, and I could surely spell   10

Their fragrance, and their chemistry apply
By sweet affinities to human flesh,
Driving the foe and stablishing the friend,—
O, that were much, and I could be a part
Of the round day, related to the sun
And planted world, and full executor
Of their imperfect functions.
But these young scholars, who invade our hills,
Bold as the engineer who fells the wood,
And travelling often in the cut he makes,   20
Love not the flower they pluck, and know it not,
And all their botany is Latin names.
The old men studied magic in the flowers,
And human fortunes in astronomy,
And an omnipotence in chemistry,
Preferring things to names, for these were men,
Were unitarians of the united world,
And, wheresoever their clear eye-beams fell,
They caught the footsteps of the SAME. Our eyes
Are armed, but we are strangers to the stars,   30
And strangers to the mystic beast and bird,
And strangers to the plant and to the mine.
The injured elements say, "Not in us;"
And night and day, ocean and continent,
Fire, plant and mineral say, "Not in us;"
And haughtily return us stare for stare.
For we invade them impiously for gain;
We devastate them unreligiously,
And coldly ask their pottage, not their love.
Therefore they shove us from them, yield to us   40
Only what to our griping toil is due;
But the sweet affluence of love and song,
The rich results of the divine consents
Of man and earth, of world beloved and lover,
The nectar and ambrosia, are withheld;
And in the midst of spoils and slaves, we thieves
And pirates of the universe, shut out
Daily to a more thin and outward rind,
Turn pale and starve. Therefore, to our sick eyes,
The stunted trees look sick, the summer short,   50

Clouds shade the sun, which will not tan our hay,
And nothing thrives to reach its natural term;
And life, shorn of its venerable length,
Even at its greatest space is a defeat,
And dies in anger that it was a dupe;
And, in its highest noon and wantonness,
Is early frugal, like a beggar's child;
Even in the hot pursuit of the best aims
And prizes of ambition, checks its hand,
Like Alpine cataracts frozen as they leaped,   60
Chilled with a miserly comparison
Of the toy's purchase with the length of life.

MUSKETAQUID   [1847]

Because I was content with these poor fields,
Low, open meads, slender and sluggish streams,
And found a home in haunts which others scorned,
The partial wood-gods overpaid my love,
And granted me the freedom of their state,
And in their secret senate have prevailed
With the dear, dangerous lords that rule our life,
Made moon and planets parties to their bond,
And through my rock-like, solitary wont
Shot million rays of thought and tenderness.   10
For me, in showers, in sweeping showers, the Spring
Visits the valley;—break away the clouds,—
I bathe in the morn's soft and silvered air,
And loiter willing by yon loitering stream.
Sparrows far off, and nearer, April's bird,
Blue-coated,—flying before from tree to tree,
Courageous sing a delicate overture
To lead the tardy concert of the year.
Onward and nearer rides the sun of May;
And wide around, the marriage of the plants   20
Is sweetly solemnized. Then flows amain
The surge of summer's beauty; dell and crag,

Hollow and lake, hillside and pine arcade,
Are touched with genius. Yonder ragged cliff
Has thousand faces in a thousand hours.

Beneath low hills, in the broad interval
Through which at will our Indian rivulet
Winds mindful still of sannup and of squaw,
Whose pipe and arrow oft the plough unburies,
Here in pine houses built of new-fallen trees,   30
Supplanters of the tribe, the farmers dwell.
Traveller, to thee, perchance, a tedious road,
Or, it may be, a picture; to these men,
The landscape is an armory of powers,
Which, one by one, they know to draw and use.
They harness beast, bird, insect, to their work;
They prove the virtues of each bed of rock,
And, like the chemist 'mid his loaded jars,
Draw from each stratum its adapted use
To drug their crops or weapon their arts withal.   40
They turn the frost upon their chemic heap,
They set the wind to winnow pulse and grain,
They thank the spring-flood for its fertile slime,
And, on cheap summit-levels of the snow,
Slide with the sledge to inaccessible woods
O'er meadows bottomless. So, year by year,
They fight the elements with elements
(That one would say, meadow and forest walked,
Transmuted in these men to rule their like),
And by the order in the field disclose   50
The order regnant in the yeoman's brain.

What these strong masters wrote at large in miles,
I followed in small copy in my acre;
For there's no rood has not a star above it;
The cordial quality of pear or plum
Ascends as gladly in a single tree
As in broad orchards resonant with bees;
And every atom poises for itself,
And for the whole. The gentle deities
Showed me the lore of colors and of sounds,   60

The innumerable tenements of beauty,
The miracle of generative force,
Far-reaching concords of astronomy
Felt in the plants and in the punctual birds;
Better, the linked purpose of the whole,
And, chiefest prize, found I true liberty
In the glad home plain-dealing Nature gave.
The polite found me impolite; the great
Would mortify me, but in vain; for still
I am a willow of the wilderness,   70
Loving the wind that bent me. All my hurts
My garden spade can heal. A woodland walk,
A quest of river-grapes, a mocking thrush,
A wild-rose, or rock-loving columbine,
Salve my worst wounds.
For thus the wood-gods murmured in my ear:
"Dost love our manners? Canst thou silent lie?
Canst thou, thy pride forgot, like Nature pass
Into the winter night's extinguished mood?
Canst thou shine now, then darkle,   80
And being latent, feel thyself no less?
As, when the all-worshipped moon attracts the eye,
The river, hill, stems, foliage are obscure,
Yet envies none, none are unenviable."

THRENODY   [1847]

The South-wind brings
Life, sunshine and desire,
And on every mount and meadow
Breathes aromatic fire;
But over the dead he has no power,
The lost, the lost, he cannot restore;
And, looking over the hills, I mourn
The darling who shall not return.

I see my empty house,
I see my trees repair their boughs;   10

And he, the wondrous child,
Whose silver warble wild
Outvalued every pulsing sound
Within the air's cerulean round,—
The hyacinthine boy, for whom
Morn well might break and April bloom,
The gracious boy, who did adorn
The world whereinto he was born,
And by his countenance repay
The favor of the loving Day,—   20
Has disappeared from the Day's eye;
Far and wide she cannot find him;
My hopes pursue, they cannot bind him.
Returned this day, the South-wind searches,
And finds young pines and budding birches;
But finds not the budding man;
Nature, who lost, cannot remake him;
Fate let him fall, Fate can't retake him;
Nature, Fate, men, him seek in vain.

And whither now, my truant wise and sweet,   30
O, whither tend thy feet?
I had the right, few days ago,
Thy steps to watch, thy place to know:
How have I forfeited the right?
Hast thou forgot me in a new delight?
I hearken for thy household cheer,
O eloquent child!
Whose voice, an equal messenger,
Conveyed thy meaning mild.
What though the pains and joys   40
Whereof it spoke were toys
Fitting his age and ken,
Yet fairest dames and bearded men,
Who heard the sweet request,
So gentle, wise and grave,
Bended with joy to his behest
And let the world's affairs go by,
A while to share his cordial game,
Or mend his wicker wagon-frame,

Still plotting how their hungry ear   50
That winsome voice again might hear;
For his lips could well pronounce
Words that were persuasions.

Gentlest guardians marked serene
His early hope, his liberal mien;
Took counsel from his guiding eyes
To make this wisdom earthly wise.
Ah, vainly do these eyes recall
The school-march, each day's festival,
When every morn my bosom glowed   60
To watch the convoy on the road;
The babe in willow wagon closed,
With rolling eyes and face composed;
With children forward and behind,
Like Cupids studiously inclined;
And he the chieftain paced beside,
The centre of the troop allied,
With sunny face of sweet repose,
To guard the babe from fancied foes.
The little captain innocent   70
Took the eye with him as he went;
Each village senior paused to scan
And speak the lovely caravan.
From the window I look out
To mark thy beautiful parade,
Stately marching in cap and coat
To some tune by fairies played;—
A music heard by thee alone
To works as noble led thee on.

Now Love and Pride, alas! in vain,   80
Up and down their glances strain.
The painted sled stands where it stood;
The kennel by the corded wood;
His gathered sticks to stanch the wall
Of the snow-tower, when snow should fall;
The ominous hole he dug in the sand,
And childhood's castles built or planned;

His daily haunts I well discern,—
The poultry-yard, the shed, the barn,—
And every inch of garden ground   90
Paced by the blessed feet around,
From the roadside to the brook
Whereinto he loved to look.
Step the meek fowls where erst they ranged;
The wintry garden lies unchanged;
The brook into the stream runs on;
But the deep-eyed boy is gone.

On that shaded day,
Dark with more clouds than tempests are,
When thou didst yield thy innocent breath   100
In birdlike heavings unto death,
Night came, and Nature had not thee;
I said, "We are mates in misery."
The morrow dawned with needless glow;
Each snowbird chirped, each fowl must crow;
Each tramper started; but the feet
Of the most beautiful and sweet
Of human youth had left the hill
And garden,—they were bound and still.
There's not a sparrow or a wren,   110
There's not a blade of autumn grain,
Which the four seasons do not tend
And tides of life and increase lend;
And every chick of every bird,
And weed and rock-moss is preferred.
O ostrich-like forgetfulness!
O loss of larger in the less!
Was there no star that could be sent,
No watcher in the firmament,
No angel from the countless host   120
That loiters round the crystal coast,
Could stoop to heal that only child,
Nature's sweet marvel undefiled,
And keep the blossom of the earth,
Which all her harvests were not worth?
Not mine,—I never called thee mine,

But Nature's heir,—if I repine,
And seeing rashly torn and moved
Not what I made, but what I loved,
Grow early old with grief that thou   130
Must to the wastes of Nature go,—
'T is because a general hope
Was quenched, and all must doubt and grope.
For flattering planets seemed to say
This child should ills of ages stay,
By wondrous tongue, and guided pen,
Bring the flown Muses back to men.
Perchance not he but Nature ailed,
The world and not the infant failed.
It was not ripe yet to sustain   140
A genius of so fine a strain,
Who gazed upon the sun and moon
As if he came unto his own,
And, pregnant with his grander thought,
Brought the old order into doubt.
His beauty once their beauty tried;
They could not feed him, and he died,
And wandered backward as in scorn,
To wait an æon to be born.
Ill day which made this beauty waste,   150
Plight broken, this high face defaced!
Some went and came about the dead;
And some in books of solace read;
Some to their friends the tidings say;
Some went to write, some went to pray;
One tarried here, there hurried one;
But their heart abode with none.
Covetous death bereaved us all,
To aggrandize one funeral.
The eager fate which carried thee   160
Took the largest part of me:
For this losing is true dying;
This is lordly man's down-lying,
This his slow but sure reclining,
Star by star his world resigning.

O child of paradise,
Boy who made dear his father's home,
In whose deep eyes
Men read the welfare of the times to come,
I am too much bereft.   170
The world dishonored thou hast left.
O truth's and nature's costly lie!
O trusted broken prophecy!
O richest fortune sourly crossed!
Born for the future, to the future lost!

The deep Heart answered, "Weepest thou?
Worthier cause for passion wild
If I had not taken the child.
And deemest thou as those who pore,
With aged eyes, short way before,—   180
Think'st Beauty vanished from the coast
Of matter, and thy darling lost?
Taught he not thee—the man of eld,
Whose eyes within his eyes beheld
Heaven's numerous hierarchy span
The mystic gulf from God to man?
To be alone wilt thou begin
When worlds of lovers hem thee in?
To-morrow, when the masks shall fall
That dizen Nature's carnival,   190
The pure shall see by their own will,
Which overflowing Love shall fill,
'T is not within the force of fate
The fate-conjoined to separate.
But thou, my votary, weepest thou?
I gave thee sight—where is it now?
I taught thy heart beyond the reach
Of ritual, bible, or of speech;
Wrote in thy mind's transparent table,
As far as the incommunicable;   200
Taught thee each private sign to raise
Lit by the supersolar blaze.
Past utterance, and past belief,

And past the blasphemy of grief,
The mysteries of Nature's heart;
And though no Muse can these impart,
Throb thine with Nature's throbbing breast,
And all is clear from east to west.

"I came to thee as to a friend;
Dearest, to thee I did not send   210
Tutors, but a joyful eye,
Innocence that matched the sky,
Lovely locks, a form of wonder,
Laughter rich as woodland thunder,
That thou might'st entertain apart
The richest flowering of all art:
And, as the great all-loving Day
Through smallest chambers takes its way,
That thou might'st break thy daily bread
With prophet, savior and head;   220
That thou might'st cherish for thine own
The riches of sweet Mary's Son,
Boy-Rabbi, Israel's paragon.
And thoughtest thou such guest
Would in thy hall take up his rest?
Would rushing life forget her laws,
Fate's glowing revolution pause?
High omens ask diviner guess;
Not to be conned to tediousness
And know my higher gifts unbind   230
The zone that girds the incarnate mind.
When the scanty shores are full
With Thought's perilous, whirling pool;
When frail Nature can no more,
Then the Spirit strikes the hour:
My servant Death, with solving rite,
Pours finite into infinite.
Wilt thou freeze love's tidal flow,
Whose streams through Nature circling go?
Nail the wild star to its track   240
On the half-climbed zodiac?
Light is light which radiates,

Blood is blood which circulates,
Life is life which generates,
And many-seeming life is one,—
Wilt thou transfix and make it none?
Its onward force too starkly pent
In figure, bone and lineament?
Wilt thou, uncalled, interrogate,
Talker! the unreplying Fate?   250
Nor see the genius of the whole
Ascendant in the private soul,
Beckon it when to go and come,
Self-announced its hour of doom?
Fair the soul's recess and shrine,
Magic-built to last a season;
Masterpiece of love benign,
Fairer that expansive reason
Whose omen 't is, and sign.
Wilt thou not ope thy heart to know   260
What rainbows teach, and sunsets show?
Verdict which accumulates
From lengthening scroll of human fates,
Voice of earth to earth returned,
Prayers of saints that inly burned,—
Saying, *What is excellent,*
As God lives, is permanent;
Hearts are dust, hearts' loves remain;
Heart's love will meet thee again.
Revere the Maker; fetch thine eye   270
Up to his style, and manners of the sky.
Not of adamant and gold
Built he heaven stark and cold;
No, but a nest of bending reeds,
Flowering grass and scented weeds;
Or like a traveller's fleeing tent,
Or bow above the tempest bent;
Built of tears and sacred flames,
And virtue reaching to its aims;
Built of furtherance and pursuing,   280
Not of spent deeds, but of doing.
Silent rushes the swift Lord

Through ruined systems still restored,
Broadsowing, bleak and void to bless,
Plants with worlds the wilderness;
Waters with tears of ancient sorrow
Apples of Eden ripe to-morrow.
House and tenant go to ground,
Lost in God, in Godhead found."

CONCORD HYMN   [1847]

Sung at the Completion of the Battle Monument,
July 4, 1837

By the rude bridge that arched the flood,
    Their flag to April's breeze unfurled,
Here once the embattled farmers stood
    And fired the shot heard round the world.

The foe long since in silence slept;
    Alike the conqueror silent sleeps;
And Time the ruined bridge has swept
    Down the dark stream which seaward creeps.

On this green bank, by this soft stream,
    We set to-day a votive stone;   10
That memory may their deed redeem,
    When, like our sires, our sons are gone.

Spirit, that made those heroes dare
    To die, and leave their children free,
Bid Time and Nature gently spare
    The shaft we raise to them and thee.

BRAHMA   [1867]

If the red slayer think he slays,
    Or if the slain think he is slain,

They know not well the subtle ways
    I keep, and pass, and turn again.

Far or forgot to me is near;
    Shadow and sunlight are the same;
The vanished gods to me appear;
    And one to me are shame and fame.

They reckon ill who leave me out;
    When me they fly, I am the wings;   10
I am the doubter and the doubt,
    And I the hymn the Brahmin sings.

The strong gods pine for my abode,
    And pine in vain the sacred Seven;
But thou, meek lover of the good!
    Find me, and turn thy back on heaven.

DAYS   [1867]

Daughters of Time, the hypocritic Days,
Muffled and dumb like barefoot dervishes,
And marching single in an endless file,
Bring diadems and fagots in their hands.
To each they offer gifts after his will,
Bread, kingdoms, stars, and sky that holds them all.
I, in my pleached garden, watched the pomp,
Forgot my morning wishes, hastily
Took a few herbs and apples, and the Day
Turned and departed silent. I, too late,   10
Under her solemn fillet saw the scorn.

TWO RIVERS   [1867]

Thy summer voice, Musketaquit,
Repeats the music of the rain;

But sweeter rivers pulsing flit
Through thee, as thou through Concord Plain.

Thou in thy narrow banks art pent:
The stream I love unbounded goes
Through flood and sea and firmament;
Through light, through life, it forward flows.

I see the inundation sweet,
I hear the spending of the stream   10
Through years, through men, through Nature fleet,
Through love and thought, through power and dream.

Musketaquit, a goblin strong,
Of shard and flint makes jewels gay;
They lose their grief who hear his song,
And where he winds is the day of day.

So forth and brighter fares my stream,—
Who drink it shall not thirst again;
No darkness stains its equal gleam,
And ages drop in it like rain.   20

WALDEINSAMKEIT   [1867]

I do not count the hours I spend
In wandering by the sea;
The forest is my loyal friend,
Like God it useth me.

In plains that room for shadows make
Of skirting hills to lie,
Bound in by streams which give and take
Their colors from the sky;

Or on the mountain-crest sublime,
Or down the oaken glade,   10

O what have I to do with time?
For this the day was made.

Cities of mortals woe-begone
Fantastic care derides,
But in the serious landscape lone
Stern benefit abides.

Sheen will tarnish, honey cloy,
And merry is only a mask of sad,
But, sober on a fund of joy,
The woods at heart are glad.   20

There the great Planter plants
Of fruitful worlds the grain,
And with a million spells enchants
The souls that walk in pain.

Still on the seeds of all he made
The rose of beauty burns;
Through times that wear and forms that fade,
Immortal youth returns.

The black ducks mounting from the lake,
The pigeon in the pines,   30
The bittern's boom, a desert make
Which no false art refines.

Down in yon watery nook,
Where bearded mists divide,
The gray old gods whom Chaos knew,
The sires of Nature, hide.

Aloft, in secret veins of air,
Blows the sweet breath of song,
O, few to scale those uplands dare,
Though they to all belong!   40

See thou bring not to field or stone
The fancies found in books;

Leave authors' eyes, and fetch your own,
To brave the landscape's looks.

Oblivion here thy wisdom is,
Thy thrift, the sleep of cares;
For a proud idleness like this
Crowns all thy mean affairs.

TERMINUS   [1867]

It is time to be old,
To take in sail:—
The god of bounds,
Who sets to seas a shore,
Came to me in his fatal rounds,
And said: "No more!
No farther shoot
Thy broad ambitious branches, and thy root.
Fancy departs: no more invent;
Contract thy firmament   10
To compass of a tent.
There's not enough for this and that,
Make thy option which of two;
Economize the failing river,
Not the less revere the Giver,
Leave the many and hold the few.
Timely wise accept the terms,
Soften the fall with wary foot;
A little while
Still plan and smile,   20
And,—fault of novel germs,—
Mature the unfallen fruit.
Curse, if thou wilt, thy sires,
Bad husbands of their fires,
Who, when they gave thee breath,
Failed to bequeath
The needful sinew stark as once,

The Baresark marrow to thy bones,
But left a legacy of ebbing veins,
Inconstant heat and nerveless reins,—   30
Amid the Muses, left thee deaf and dumb,
Amid the gladiators, halt and numb."

   As the bird trims her to the gale,
I trim myself to the storm of time,
I man the rudder, reef the sail,
Obey the voice at eve obeyed at prime:
"Lowly faithful, banish fear,
Right onward drive unharmed;
The port, well worth the cruise, is near,
And every wave is charmed."   40

COMPENSATION   [1867]

The wings of Time are black and white,
Pied with morning and with night.
Mountain tall and ocean deep
Trembling balance duly keep.
In changing moon and tidal wave
Glows the feud of Want and Have.
Gauge of more and less through space,
Electric star or pencil plays,
The lonely Earth amid the balls
That hurry through the eternal halls,   10
A makeweight flying to the void,
Supplemental asteroid,
Or compensatory spark,
Shoots across the neutral Dark.

Man's the elm, and Wealth the vine;
Stanch and strong the tendrils twine:
Though the frail ringlets thee deceive,
None from its stock that vine can reave.
Fear not, then, thou child infirm,

There's no god dare wrong a worm;   20
Laurel crowns cleave to deserts,
And power to him who power exerts.
Hast not thy share? On winged feet,
Lo! it rushes thee to meet;
And all that Nature made thy own,
Floating in air or pent in stone,
Will rive the hills and swim the sea,
And, like thy shadow, follow thee.

Henry Wadsworth Longfellow

1807–1882

Born February 27, 1807, in Portland, Maine, Longfellow went through the Portland Academy and graduated from Bowdoin College. He spent three years in Europe, then taught modern languages for a half-dozen years at Bowdoin and for nearly twenty years at Harvard. In 1854 he resigned his professorship to devote himself wholly to poetry and other literary projects. He died March 24, 1882, in Cambridge, Massachusetts.

HYMN TO THE NIGHT   [1839]

'Ασπασίη, τρίλλιστος

I heard the trailing garments of the Night
  Sweep through her marble halls!
I saw her sable skirts all fringed with light
  From the celestial walls!

I felt her presence, by its spell of might,
  Stoop o'er me from above;
The calm, majestic presence of the Night,
  As of the one I love.

I heard the sounds of sorrow and delight,
  The manifold, soft chimes,   10

That fill the haunted chambers of the Night,
   Like some old poet's rhymes.

From the cool cisterns of the midnight air
   My spirit drank repose;
The fountain of perpetual peace flows there,—
   From those deep cisterns flows.

O holy Night! from thee I learn to bear
   What man has borne before!
Thou layest thy finger on the lips of Care,
   And they complain no more.   20

Peace! Peace! Orestes-like I breathe this prayer!
   Descend with broad-winged flight,
The welcome, the thrice-prayed for, the most fair,
   The best-beloved Night!

THE SKELETON IN ARMOR   [1842]

"Speak! speak! thou fearful guest!
Who, with thy hollow breast
Still in rude armor drest,
   Comest to daunt me!
Wrapt not in Eastern balms,
But with thy fleshless palms
Stretched, as if asking alms,
   Why dost thou haunt me?"

Then, from those cavernous eyes
Pale flashes seemed to rise,
As when the Northern skies
   Gleam in December;   10
And, like the water's flow
Under December's snow,
Came a dull voice of woe
   From the heart's chamber.

"I was a Viking old!
My deeds, though manifold,
No Skald in song has told,
    No Saga taught thee!   20
Take heed, that in thy verse
Thou dost the tale rehearse,
Else dread a dead man's curse;
    For this I sought thee.

"Far in the Northern Land,
By the wild Baltic's strand,
I, with my childish hand,
    Tamed the gerfalcon;
And, with my skates fast-bound,
Skimmed the half-frozen Sound,   30
That the poor whimpering hound
    Trembled to walk on.

"Oft to his frozen lair
Tracked I the grisly bear,
While from my path the hare
    Fled like a shadow;
Oft through the forest dark
Followed the were-wolf's bark,
Until the soaring lark
    Sang from the meadow.   40

"But when I older grew,
Joining a corsair's crew,
O'er the dark sea I flew
    With the marauders.
Wild was the life we led;
Many the souls that sped,
Many the hearts that bled,
    By our stern orders.

"Many a wassail-bout
Wore the long Winter out;   50
Often our midnight shout
    Set the cocks crowing,

As we the Berserk's tale
Measured in cups of ale,
Draining the oaken pail,
  Filled to o'erflowing.

"Once as I told in glee
Tales of the stormy sea,
Soft eyes did gaze on me,
  Burning yet tender;   60
And as the white stars shine
On the dark Norway pine,
On that dark heart of mine
  Fell their soft splendor.

"I wooed the blue-eyed maid,
Yielding, yet half afraid,
And in the forest's shade
  Our vows were plighted.
Under its loosened vest
Fluttered her little breast,   70
Like birds within their nest
  By the hawk frighted.

"Bright in her father's hall
Shields gleamed upon the wall,
Loud sang the minstrels all,
  Chanting his glory;
When of old Hildebrand
I asked his daughter's hand,
Mute did the minstrels stand
  To hear my story.   80

"While the brown ale he quaffed,
Loud then the champion laughed,
And as the wind-gusts waft
  The sea-foam brightly,
So the loud laugh of scorn,
Out of those lips unshorn,
From the deep drinking-horn
  Blew the foam lightly.

"She was a Prince's child,
I but a Viking wild,   90
And though she blushed and smiled,
    I was discarded!
Should not the dove so white
Follow the sea-mew's flight,
Why did they leave that night
    Her nest unguarded?

"Scarce had I put to sea,
Bearing the maid with me,
Fairest of all was she
    Among the Norsemen!   100
When on the white sea-strand,
Waving his armed hand,
Saw we old Hildebrand,
    With twenty horsemen.

"Then launched they to the blast,
Bent like a reed each mast,
Yet we were gaining fast,
    When the wind failed us;
And with a sudden flaw
Came round the gusty Skaw,   110
So that our foe we saw
    Laugh as he hailed us.

"And as to catch the gale
Round veered the flapping sail,
'Death!' was the helmsman's hail,
    'Death without quarter!'
Mid-ships with iron keel
Struck we her ribs of steel;
Down her black hulk did reel
    Through the black water!   120

"As with his wings aslant,
Sails the fierce cormorant,
Seeking some rocky haunt,
    With his prey laden,—

So toward the open main,
Beating to sea again,
Through the wild hurricane,
    Bore I the maiden.

"Three weeks we westward bore,
And when the storm was o'er,   130
Cloud-like we saw the shore
    Stretching to leeward;
There for my lady's bower
Built I the lofty tower,
Which, to this very hour,
    Stands looking seaward.

"There lived we many years;
Time dried the maiden's tears;
She had forgot her fears,
    She was a mother;   140
Death closed her mild blue eyes,
Under that tower she lies;
Ne'er shall the sun arise
    On such another!

"Still grew my bosom then,
Still as a stagnant fen!
Hateful to me were men,
    The sunlight hateful!
In the vast forest here,
Clad in my warlike gear,   150
Fell I upon my spear,
    Oh, death was grateful!

"Thus, seamed with many scars,
Bursting these prison bars,
Up to its native stars
    My soul ascended!
There from the flowing bowl
Deep drinks the warrior's soul,
Skoal! to the Northland! *skoal!*"
    Thus the tale ended.   160

THE ARSENAL AT SPRINGFIELD [1846]

This is the Arsenal. From floor to ceiling,
  Like a huge organ, rise the burnished arms;
But from their silent pipes no anthem pealing
  Startles the villages with strange alarms.

Ah! what a sound will rise, how wild and dreary,
  When the death-angel touches those swift keys!
What loud lament and dismal Miserere
  Will mingle with their awful symphonies!

I hear even now the infinite fierce chorus,
  The cries of agony, the endless groan,   10
Which, through the ages that have gone before us,
  In long reverberations reach our own.

On helm and harness rings the Saxon hammer,
  Through Cimbric forest roars the Norseman's song,
And loud, amid the universal clamor,
  O'er distant deserts sounds the Tartar gong.

I hear the Florentine, who from his palace
  Wheels out his battle-bell with dreadful din,
And Aztec priests upon their teocallis
  Beat the wild war-drums made of serpent's skin;   20

The tumult of each sacked and burning village;
  The shout that every prayer for mercy drowns;
The soldiers' revels in the midst of pillage;
  The wail of famine in beleaguered towns;

The bursting shell, the gateway wrenched asunder,
  The rattling musketry, the clashing blade;
And ever and anon, in tones of thunder
  The diapason of the cannonade.

Is it, O man, with such discordant noises,
  With such accursed instruments as these,   30

Thou drownest Nature's sweet and kindly voices,
    And jarrest the celestial harmonies?

Were half the power, that fills the world with terror,
    Were half the wealth bestowed on camps and courts,
Given to redeem the human mind from error,
    There were no need of arsenals or forts:

The warrior's name would be a name abhorred!
    And every nation, that should lift again
Its hand against a brother, on its forehead
    Would wear forevermore the curse of Cain!   40

Down the dark future, through long generations,
    The echoing sounds grow fainter and then cease;
And like a bell, with solemn, sweet vibrations,
    I hear once more the voice of Christ say, "Peace!"

Peace! and no longer from its brazen portals
    The blast of War's great organ shakes the skies!
But beautiful as songs of the immortals,
    The holy melodies of love arise.

SEAWEED   [1846]

When descends on the Atlantic
        The gigantic
Storm-wind of the equinox,
Landward in his wrath he scourges
        The toiling surges,
Laden with seaweed from the rocks:

From Bermuda's reefs; from edges
        Of sunken ledges,
In some far-off, bright Azore;
From Bahama, and the dashing,   10
        Silver-flashing
Surges of San Salvador;

From the tumbling surf, that buries
    The Orkneyan skerries,
Answering the hoarse Hebrides;
And from wrecks of ships, and drifting
    Spars, uplifting
On the desolate, rainy seas;—

Ever drifting, drifting, drifting
    On the shifting   20
Currents of the restless main;
Till in sheltered coves, and reaches
    Of sandy beaches,
All have found repose again.

So when storms of wild emotion
    Strike the ocean
Of the poet's soul, erelong
From each cave and rocky fastness,
    In its vastness,
Floats some fragment of a song: 30

From the far-off isles enchanted,
    Heaven has planted
With the golden fruit of Truth;
From the flashing surf, whose vision
    Gleams Elysian
In the tropic clime of Youth;

From the strong Will, and the Endeavor
    That forever
Wrestle with the tides of Fate;
From the wreck of Hopes far-scattered,   40
    Tempest-shattered,
Floating waste and desolate;—

Ever drifting, drifting, drifting
    On the shifting
Currents of the restless heart;
Till at length in books recorded,
    They, like hoarded
Household words, no more depart.

THE FIRE OF DRIFT-WOOD   [1850]

Devereux Farm, Near Marblehead

We sat within the farm-house old,
   Whose windows, looking o'er the bay,
Gave to the sea-breeze damp and cold
   An easy entrance, night and day.

Not far away we saw the port,
   The strange, old-fashioned, silent town,
The lighthouse, the dismantled fort,
   The wooden houses, quaint and brown.

We sat and talked until the night,
   Descending, filled the little room;   10
Our faces faded from the sight,
   Our voices only broke the gloom.

We spake of many a vanished scene,
   Of what we once had thought and said,
Of what had been, and might have been,
   And who was changed, and who was dead;

And all that fills the hearts of friends,
   When first they feel, with secret pain,
Their lives thenceforth have separate ends,
   And never can be one again;   20

The first slight swerving of the heart,
   That words are powerless to express,
And leave it still unsaid in part,
   Or say it in too great excess.

The very tones in which we spake
   Had something strange, I could but mark;
The leaves of memory seemed to make
   A mournful rustling in the dark.

Oft died the words upon our lips,
    As suddenly, from out the fire   30
Built of the wreck of stranded ships,
    The flames would leap and then expire.

And, as their splendor flashed and failed,
    We thought of wrecks upon the main,
Of ships dismasted, that were hailed
    And sent no answer back again.

The windows, rattling in their frames,
    The ocean, roaring up the beach,
The gusty blast, the bickering flames,
    All mingled vaguely in our speech;   40

Until they made themselves a part
    Of fancies floating through the brain,
The long-lost ventures of the heart,
    That send no answers back again.

O flames that glowed! O hearts that yearned!
    They were indeed too much akin,
The drift-wood fire without that burned,
    The thoughts that burned and glowed within.

IN THE CHURCHYARD AT CAMBRIDGE
[1858]

In the village churchyard she lies,
Dust is in her beautiful eyes,
    No more she breathes, nor feels, nor stirs;
At her feet and at her head
Lies a slave to attend the dead,
    But their dust is white as hers.

Was she, a lady of high degree,
So much in love with the vanity
    And foolish pomp of this world of ours?

Or was it Christian charity,   10
And lowliness and humility,
  The richest and rarest of all dowers?

Who shall tell us? No one speaks;
No color shoots into those cheeks,
  Either of anger or of pride,
At the rude question we have asked;
Nor will the mystery be unmasked
  By those who are sleeping at her side.

Hereafter?—And do you think to look
On the terrible pages of that Book   20
  To find her failings, faults, and errors?
Ah, you will then have other cares,
In your own shortcomings and despairs,
  In your own secret sins and terrors!

THE JEWISH CEMETERY AT NEWPORT   [1858]

How strange it seems! These Hebrews in their graves,
  Close by the street of this fair seaport town,
Silent beside the never-silent waves,
  At rest in all this moving up and down!

The trees are white with dust, that o'er their sleep
  Wave their broad curtains in the south-wind's breath,
While underneath these leafy tents they keep
  The long, mysterious Exodus of Death.

And these sepulchral stones, so old and brown,
  That pave with level flags their burial-place,   10
Seem like the tablets of the Law, thrown down
  And broken by Moses at the mountain's base.

The very names recorded here are strange,
  Of foreign accent, and of different climes;

Alvares and Rivera interchange
  With Abraham and Jacob of old times.

"Blessed be God, for he created Death!"
  The mourners said, "and Death is rest and peace;"
Then added, in the certainty of faith,
  "And giveth Life that nevermore shall cease."   20

Closed are the portals of their Synagogue,
  No Psalms of David now the silence break,
No Rabbi reads the ancient Decalogue
  In the grand dialect the Prophets spake.

Gone are the living, but the dead remain,
  And not neglected; for a hand unseen,
Scattering its bounty, like a summer rain,
  Still keeps their graves and their remembrance green.

How came they here? What burst of Christian hate,
  What persecution, merciless and blind,   30
Drove o'er the sea—that desert desolate—
  These Ishmaels and Hagars of mankind?

They lived in narrow streets and lanes obscure,
  Ghetto and Judenstrass, in mirk and mire;
Taught in the school of patience to endure
  The life of anguish and the death of fire.

All their lives long, with the unleavened bread
  And bitter herbs of exile and its fears,
The wasting famine of the heart they fed,
  And slaked its thirst with marah of their tears.   40

Anathema maranatha! was the cry
  That rang from town to town, from street to street:
At every gate the accursed Mordecai
  Was mocked and jeered, and spurned by Christian feet.

Pride and humiliation hand in hand
  Walked with them through the world where'er they
     went;

Trampled and beaten were they as the sand,
  And yet unshaken as the continent.

For in the background figures vague and vast
  Of patriarchs and of prophets rose sublime,   50
And all the great traditions of the Past
  They saw reflected in the coming time.

And thus forever with reverted look
  The mystic volume of the world they read,
Spelling it backward, like a Hebrew book,
  Till life became a Legend of the Dead.

But ah! what once has been shall be no more!
  The groaning earth in travail and in pain
Brings forth its races, but does not restore,
  And the dead nations never rise again.   60

THE ROPEWALK   [1858]

In that building, long and low,
With its windows all a-row,
  Like the port-holes of a hulk,
Human spiders spin and spin,
Backward down their threads so thin
  Dropping, each a hempen bulk.

At the end, an open door;
Squares of sunshine on the floor
  Light the long and dusky lane;
And the whirring of a wheel,   10
Dull and drowsy, makes me feel
  All its spokes are in my brain.

As the spinners to the end
Downward go and reascend,

Gleam the long threads in the sun;
While within this brain of mine
Cobwebs brighter and more fine
  By the busy wheel are spun.

Two fair maidens in a swing,
Like white doves upon the wing,   20
  First before my vision pass;
Laughing, as their gentle hands
Closely clasp the twisted strands,
  At their shadow on the grass.

Then a booth of mountebanks,
With its smell of tan and planks,
  And a girl poised high in air
On a cord, in spangled dress,
With a faded loveliness,
  And a weary look of care.   30

Then a homestead among farms,
And a woman with bare arms
  Drawing water from a well;
As the bucket mounts apace,
With it mounts her own fair face,
  As at some magician's spell.

Then an old man in a tower,
Ringing loud the noontide hour,
  While the rope coils round and round
Like a serpent at his feet,
And again, in swift retreat,   40
  Nearly lifts him from the ground.

Then within a prison-yard,
Faces fixed, and stern, and hard,
  Laughter and indecent mirth;
Ah! it is the gallows-tree!
Breath of Christian charity,
  Blow, and sweep it from the earth!

Then a school-boy, with his kite
Gleaming in a sky of light,   50
  And an eager, upward look;
Steeds pursued through lane and field;
Fowlers with their snares concealed;
  And an angler by a brook.

Ships rejoicing in the breeze,
Wrecks that float o'er unknown seas,
  Anchors dragged through faithless sand;
Sea-fog drifting overhead,
And, with lessening line and lead,
  Sailors feeling for the land.   60

All these scenes do I behold,
These, and many left untold,
  In that building long and low;
While the wheel goes round and round,
With a drowsy, dreamy sound.
  And the spinners backward go.

MY LOST YOUTH   [1858]

Often I think of the beautiful town
  That is seated by the sea;
Often in thought go up and down
The pleasant streets of that dear old town,
  And my youth comes back to me.
    And a verse of a Lapland song
    Is haunting my memory still:
  "A boy's will is the wind's will,
And the thoughts of youth are long, long thoughts."

I can see the shadowy lines of its trees,   10
  And catch, in sudden gleams,
The sheen of the far-surrounding seas,

And islands that were the Hesperides
   Of all my boyish dreams.
      And the burden of that old song,
      It murmurs and whispers still:
   "A boy's will is the wind's will,
And the thoughts of youth are long, long thoughts."

I remember the black wharves and the slips,
   And the sea-tides tossing free;   20
And Spanish sailors with bearded lips,
And the beauty and mystery of the ships,
   And the magic of the sea.
      And the voice of that wayward song
      Is singing and saying still:
   "A boy's will is the wind's will,
And the thoughts of youth are long, long thoughts."

I remember the bulwarks by the shore,
   And the fort upon the hill;
The sunrise gun, with its hollow roar,   30
The drum-beat repeated o'er and o'er,
   And the bugle wild and shrill.
      And the music of that old song
      Throbs in my memory still:
   "A boy's will is the wind's will,
And the thoughts of youth are long, long thoughts."

I remember the sea-fight far away,
   How it thundered o'er the tide!
And the dead captains, as they lay
In their graves, o'erlooking the tranquil bay   40
   Where they in battle died.
      And the sound of that mournful song
      Goes through me with a thrill:
   "A boy's will is the wind's will,
And the thoughts of youth are long, long thoughts."

I can see the breezy dome of groves,
   The shadows of Deering's Woods;
And the friendships old and the early loves

Come back with a Sabbath sound, as of doves
 In quiet neighborhoods.   50
  And the verse of that sweet old song,
  It flutters and murmurs still:
 "A boy's will is the wind's will,
And the thoughts of youth are long, long thoughts."

I remember the gleams and glooms that dart
 Across the school-boy's brain;
The song and the silence in the heart,
That in part are prophecies, and in part
 Are longings wild and vain.
  And the voice of that fitful song   60
  Sings on, and is never still:
 "A boy's will is the wind's will,
And the thoughts of youth are long, long thoughts."

There are things of which I may not speak;
 There are dreams that cannot die;
There are thoughts that make the strong heart weak,
And bring a pallor into the cheek,
 And a mist before the eye.
  And the words of that fatal song
  Come over me like a chill: 70
 "A boy's will is the wind's will,
And the thoughts of youth are long, long thoughts."

Strange to me now are the forms I meet
 When I visit the dear old town;
But the native air is pure and sweet,
And the trees that o'ershadow each well-known street,
 As they balance up and down,
  Are singing the beautiful song,
  Are sighing and whispering still:
 "A boy's will is the wind's will,   80
And the thoughts of youth are long, long thoughts."

And Deering's Woods are fresh and fair,
 And with joy that is almost pain
My heart goes back to wander there,

And among the dreams of the days that were,
   I find my lost youth again.
     And the strange and beautiful song,
     The groves are repeating it still:
  "A boy's will is the wind's will,
And the thoughts of youth are long, long thoughts."   90

SNOW-FLAKES   [1863]

Out of the bosom of the Air,
   Out of the cloud-folds of her garments shaken,
Over the woodlands brown and bare,
   Over the harvest-fields forsaken,
     Silent, and soft, and slow
     Descends the snow.

Even as our cloudy fancies take
   Suddenly shape in some divine expression,
Even as the troubled heart doth make
   In the white countenance confession,   10
     The troubled sky reveals
     The grief it feels.

This is the poem of the air,
   Slowly in silent syllables recorded;
This is the secret of despair,
   Long in its cloudy bosom hoarded,
     Now whispered and revealed
     To wood and field.

KILLED AT THE FORD   [1867]

He is dead, the beautiful youth,
The heart of honor, the tongue of truth,

He, the life and light of us all,
Whose voice was blithe as a bugle-call,
Whom all eyes followed with one consent,
The cheer of whose laugh, and whose pleasant word,
Hushed all murmurs of discontent.

Only last night, as we rode along,
Down the dark of the mountain gap,
To visit the picket-guard at the ford,   10
Little dreaming of any mishap,
He was humming the words of some old song:
"Two red roses he had on his cap
And another he bore at the point of his sword."

Sudden and swift a whistling ball
Came out of a wood, and the voice was still;
Something I heard in the darkness fall,
And for a moment my blood grew chill;
I spake in a whisper, as he who speaks
In a room where some one is lying dead;   20
But he made no answer to what I said.

We lifted him up to his saddle again,
And through the mire and the mist and the rain
Carried him back to the silent camp,
And laid him as if asleep on his bed;
And I saw by the light of the surgeon's lamp
Two white roses upon his cheeks,
And one, just over his heart, blood-red!

And I saw in a vision how far and fleet
That fatal bullet went speeding forth,   30
Till it reached a town in the distant North,
Till it reached a house in a sunny street,
Till it reached a heart that ceased to beat
Without a murmur, without a cry;
And a bell was tolled, in that far-off town,
For one who had passed from cross to crown,
And the neighbors wondered that she should die.

DIVINA COMMEDIA   [1867]

I

Oft have I seen at some cathedral door
   A laborer, pausing in the dust and heat,
   Lay down his burden, and with reverent feet
   Enter, and cross himself, and on the floor
Kneel to repeat his paternoster o'er;
   Far off the noises of the world retreat;
   The loud vociferations of the street
   Become an undistinguishable roar.
So, as I enter here from day to day,
   And leave my burden at this minster gate,   10
   Kneeling in prayer, and not ashamed to pray,
The tumult of the time disconsolate
   To inarticulate murmurs dies away,
   While the eternal ages watch and wait.

II

How strange the sculptures that adorn these towers!
   This crowd of statues, in whose folded sleeves
   Birds build their nests; while canopied with leaves
   Parvis and portal bloom like trellised bowers,
And the vast minster seems a cross of flowers!
   But fiends and dragons on the gargoyled eaves   20
   Watch the dead Christ between the living thieves,
   And, underneath, the traitor Judas lowers!
Ah! from what agonies of heart and brain,
   What exultations trampling on despair,
   What tenderness, what tears, what hate of wrong,
What passionate outcry of a soul in pain,
   Uprose this poem of the earth and air,
   This mediæval miracle of song!

III

I enter, and I see thee in the gloom
   Of the long aisles, O poet saturnine!   30
   And strive to make my steps keep pace with thine.

The air is filled with some unknown perfume;
The congregation of the dead make room
    For thee to pass; the votive tapers shine;
    Like rooks that haunt Ravenna's groves of pine
    The hovering echoes fly from tomb to tomb.
From the confessionals I hear arise
    Rehearsals of forgotten tragedies,
    And lamentations from the crypts below;
And then a voice celestial that begins   40
    With the pathetic words, "Although your sins
    As scarlet be," and ends with "as the snow."

IV

With snow-white veil and garments as of flame,
    She stands before thee, who so long ago
    Filled thy young heart with passion and the woe
    From which thy song and all its splendors came;
And while with stern rebuke she speaks thy name,
    The ice about thy heart melts as the snow
    On mountain heights, and in swift overflow
    Comes gushing from thy lips in sobs of shame.   50
Thou makest full confession; and a gleam,
    As of the dawn on some dark forest cast,
    Seems on thy lifted forehead to increase;
Lethe and Eunoe—the remembered dream
    And the forgotten sorrow—bring at last
    That perfect pardon which is perfect peace.

V

I lift mine eyes, and all the windows blaze
    With forms of Saints and holy men who died,
    Here martyred and hereafter glorified;
    And the great Rose upon its leaves displays   60
Christ's Triumph, and the angelic roundelays,
    With splendor upon splendor multiplied;
    And Beatrice again at Dante's side
    No more rebukes, but smiles her words of praise.
And then the organ sounds, and unseen choirs
    Sing the old Latin hymns of peace and love
    And benedictions of the Holy Ghost;

And the melodious bells among the spires
 O'er all the house-tops and through heaven above
 Proclaim the elevation of the Host!   70

VI

O star of morning and of liberty!
 O bringer of the light, whose splendor shines
 Above the darkness of the Apennines,
 Forerunner of the day that is to be!
The voices of the city and the sea,
 The voices of the mountains and the pines,
 Repeat thy song, till the familiar lines
 Are footpaths for the thought of Italy!
Thy flame is blown abroad from all the heights,
 Through all the nations, and a sound is heard, 80
 As of a mighty wind, and men devout,
Strangers of Rome, and the new proselytes,
 In their own language hear thy wondrous word,
 And many are amazed and many doubt.

THE CHALLENGE [1873]

I have a vague remembrance
 Of a story, that is told
In some ancient Spanish legend
 Or chronicle of old.

It was when brave King Sanchez
 Was before Zamora slain,
And his great besieging army
 Lay encamped upon the plain.

Don Diego de Ordoñez
 Sallied forth in front of all,   10
And shouted loud his challenge
 To the warders on the wall.

All the people of Zamora,
  Both the born and the unborn,
As traitors did he challenge
  With taunting words of scorn.

The living, in their houses,
  And in their graves, the dead!
And the waters of their rivers,
  And their wine, and oil, and bread!   20

There is a greater army,
  That besets us round with strife,
A starving, numberless army,
  At all the gates of life.

The poverty-stricken millions
  Who challenge our wine and bread,
And impeach us all as traitors,
  Both the living and the dead.

And whenever I sit at the banquet,
  Where the feast and song are high,   30
Amid the mirth and the music
  I can hear that fearful cry.

And hollow and haggard faces
  Look into the lighted hall,
And wasted hands are extended
  To catch the crumbs that fall.

For within there is light and plenty,
  And odors fill the air;
But without there is cold and darkness,
  And hunger and despair.   40

And there in the camp of famine
  In wind and cold and rain,
Christ, the great Lord of the army,
  Lies dead upon the plain!

AFTERMATH   [1873]

When the summer fields are mown,
When the birds are fledged and flown,
   And the dry leaves strew the path;
With the falling of the snow,
With the cawing of the crow,
Once again the fields we mow
   And gather in the aftermath.

Not the sweet, new grass with flowers
Is this harvesting of ours;
   Not the upland clover bloom;   10
But the rowen mixed with weeds,
Tangled tufts from marsh and meads,
Where the poppy drops its seeds
   In the silence and the gloom.

THE SICILIAN'S TALE   [1873]

The Monk of Casal-Maggiore

Once on a time, some centuries ago,
   In the hot sunshine two Franciscan friars
Wended their weary way, with footsteps slow,
   Back to their convent, whose white walls and spires
Gleamed on the hillside like a patch of snow;
   Covered with dust they were, and torn by briers,
And bore like sumpter-mules upon their backs
The badge of poverty, their beggar's sacks.

The first was Brother Anthony, a spare
   And silent man, with pallid cheeks and thin,   10
Much given to vigils, penance, fasting, prayer,
   Solemn and gray, and worn with discipline,

As if his body but white ashes were,
   Heaped on the living coals that glowed within;
A simple monk, like many of his day,
Whose instinct was to listen and obey.

A different man was Brother Timothy,
   Of larger mould and of a coarser paste;
A rubicund and stalwart monk was he,
   Broad in the shoulders, broader in the waist,   20
Who often filled the dull refectory
   With noise by which the convent was disgraced,
But to the mass-book gave but little heed,
By reason he had never learned to read.

Now, as they passed the outskirts of a wood,
   They saw, with mingled pleasure and surprise,
Fast tethered to a tree an ass, that stood
   Lazily winking his large, limpid eyes.
The farmer Gilbert, of that neighborhood,
   His owner was, who, looking for supplies   30
Of fagots, deeper in the wood had strayed,
Leaving his beast to ponder in the shade.

As soon as Brother Timothy espied
   The patient animal, he said: "Good-lack!
Thus for our needs doth Providence provide;
   We'll lay our wallets on the creature's back."
This being done, he leisurely untied
   From head and neck the halter of the jack,
And put it round his own, and to the tree
Stood tethered fast as if the ass were he.   40

And, bursting forth into a merry laugh,
   He cried to Brother Anthony: "Away!
And drive the ass before you with your staff;
   And when you reach the convent you may say
You left me at a farm, half tired and half
   Ill with a fever, for a night and day,
And that the farmer lent this ass to bear
Our wallets, that are heavy with good fare."

Now Brother Anthony, who knew the pranks
  Of Brother Timothy, would not persuade   50
Or reason with him on his quirks and cranks,
  But, being obedient, silently obeyed;
And, smiting with his staff the ass's flanks,
  Drove him before him over hill and glade,
Safe with his provend to the convent gate,
Leaving poor Brother Timothy to his fate.

Then Gilbert, laden with fagots for his fire,
  Forth issued from the wood, and stood aghast
To see the ponderous body of the friar
  Standing where he had left his donkey last.   60
Trembling he stood, and dared not venture nigher,
  But stared, and gaped, and crossed himself full fast;
For, being credulous and of little wit,
He thought it was some demon from the pit.

While speechless and bewildered thus he gazed,
  And dropped his load of fagots on the ground,
Quoth Brother Timothy: "Be not amazed
  That where you left a donkey should be found
A poor Franciscan friar, half-starved and crazed,
  Standing demure and with a halter bound;   70
But set me free, and hear the piteous story
Of Brother Timothy of Casal-Maggiore.

"I am a sinful man, although you see
  I wear the consecrated cowl and cape;
You never owned an ass, but you owned me,
  Changed and transformed from my own natural shape
All for the deadly sin of gluttony,
  From which I could not otherwise escape,
Than by this penance, dieting on grass,
And being worked and beaten as an ass.   80

"Think of the ignominy I endured;
  Think of the miserable life I led,
The toil and blows to which I was inured,
  My wretched lodging in a windy shed,

My scanty fare so grudgingly procured,
  The damp and musty straw that formed my bed!
But, having done this penance for my sins,
My life as man and monk again begins."

The simple Gilbert, hearing words like these,
  Was conscience-stricken, and fell down apace   90
Before the friar upon his bended knees,
  And with a suppliant voice implored his grace;
And the good monk, now very much at ease,
  Granted him pardon with a smiling face,
Nor could refuse to be that night his guest,
It being late, and he in need of rest.

Upon a hillside, where the olive thrives,
  With figures painted on its whitewashed walls,
The cottage stood; and near the humming hives
  Made murmurs as of far-off waterfalls;   100
A place where those who love secluded lives
  Might live content, and, free from noise and brawls,
Like Claudian's Old Man of Verona here
Measure by fruits the slow-revolving year.

And, coming to this cottage of content,
  They found his children, and the buxom wench
His wife, Dame Cicely, and his father, bent
  With years and labor, seated on a bench,
Repeating over some obscure event
  In the old wars of Milanese and French;   110
All welcomed the Franciscan, with a sense
Of sacred awe and humble reverence.

When Gilbert told them what had come to pass,
  How beyond question, cavil, or surmise,
Good Brother Timothy had been their ass,
  You should have seen the wonder in their eyes;
You should have heard them cry "Alas! alas!"
  Have heard their lamentations and their sighs!
For all believed the story, and began
To see a saint in this afflicted man.   120

Forthwith there was prepared a grand repast,
    To satisfy the craving of the friar
After so rigid and prolonged a fast;
    The bustling housewife stirred the kitchen fire;
Then her two barn-yard fowls, her best and last,
    Were put to death, at her express desire,
And served up with a salad in a bowl,
And flasks of country wine to crown the whole.

It would not be believed should I repeat
    How hungry Brother Timothy appeared;   130
It was a pleasure but to see him eat,
    His white teeth flashing through his russet beard,
His face aglow and flushed with wine and meat,
    His roguish eyes that rolled and laughed and leered!
Lord! how he drank the blood-red country wine
As if the village vintage were divine!

And all the while he talked without surcease,
    And told his merry tales with jovial glee
That never flagged, but rather did increase,
    And laughed aloud as if insane were he,   140
And wagged his red beard, matted like a fleece,
    And cast such glances at Dame Cicely
That Gilbert now grew angry with his guest,
And thus in words his rising wrath expressed.

"Good father," said he, "easily we see
    How needful in some persons, and how right,
Mortification of the flesh may be.
    The indulgence you have given it tonight,
After long penance, clearly proves to me
    Your strength against temptation is but slight,   150
And shows the dreadful peril you are in
Of a relapse into your deadly sin.

"To-morrow morning, with the rising sun,
    Go back unto your convent, nor refrain
From fasting and from scourging, for you run
    Great danger to become an ass again,

Since monkish flesh and asinine are one;
   Therefore be wise, nor longer here remain,
Unless you wish the scourge should be applied
By other hands, that will not spare your hide."   160

When this the monk had heard, his color fled
   And then returned, like lightning in the air,
Till he was all one blush from foot to head,
   And even the bald spot in his russet hair
Turned from its usual pallor to bright red!
   The old man was asleep upon his chair.
Then all retired, and sank into the deep
And helpless imbecility of sleep.

They slept until the dawn of day drew near,
   Till the cock should have crowed, but did not crow,   170
For they had slain the shining chanticleer
   And eaten him for supper, as you know.
The monk was up betimes and of good cheer,
   And, having breakfasted, made haste to go,
As if he heard the distant matin bell,
And had but little time to say farewell.

Fresh was the morning as the breath of kine;
   Odors of herbs commingled with the sweet
Balsamic exhalations of the pine;
   A haze was in the air presaging heat;   180
Uprose the sun above the Apennine,
   And all the misty valleys at its feet
Were full of the delirious song of birds,
Voices of men, and bells, and low of herds.

All this to Brother Timothy was naught;
   He did not care for scenery, nor here
His busy fancy found the thing it sought;
   But when he saw the convent walls appear,
And smoke from kitchen chimneys upwards caught
   And whirled aloft into the atmosphere,   190
He quickened his slow footsteps, like a beast
That scents the stable a league off at least.

And as he entered through the convent gate
   He saw there in the court the ass, who stood
Twirling his ears about, and seemed to wait,
   Just as he found him waiting in the wood;
And told the Prior that, to alleviate
   The daily labors of the brotherhood,
The owner, being a man of means and thrift,
Bestowed him on the convent as a gift.   200

And thereupon the Prior for many days
   Revolved this serious matter in his mind,
And turned it over many different ways,
   Hoping that some safe issue he might find;
But stood in fear of what the world would say,
   If he accepted presents of this kind.
Employing beast of burden for the packs
That lazy monks should carry on their backs.

Then, to avoid all scandal of the sort,
   And stop the mouth of cavil, he decreed   210
That he would cut the tedious matter short,
   And sell the ass with all convenient speed,
Thus saving the expense of his support,
   And hoarding something for a time of need.
So he despatched him to the neighboring Fair,
And freed himself from cumber and from care.

It happened now by chance, as some might say,
   Others perhaps would call it destiny,
Gilbert was at the Fair; and heard a bray,
   And nearer came, and saw that it was he,   220
And whispered in his ear, "Ah, lackaday!
   Good father, the rebellious flesh, I see,
Has changed you back into an ass again,
And all my admonitions were in vain."

The ass, who felt this breathing in his ear,
   Did not turn round to look, but shook his head,
As if he were not pleased these words to hear,
   And contradicted all that had been said.

And this made Gilbert cry in voice more clear,
   "I know you well; your hair is russet-red;   230
Do not deny it; for you are the same
Franciscan friar, and Timothy by name."

The ass, though now the secret had come out,
   Was obstinate, and shook his head again;
Until a crowd was gathered round about
   To hear this dialogue between the twain;
And raised their voices in a noisy shout
   When Gilbert tried to make the matter plain,
And flouted him and mocked him all day long
With laughter and with jibes and scraps of song.   240

"If this be Brother Timothy," they cried,
   "Buy him, and feed him on the tenderest grass;
Thou canst not do too much for one so tried
   As to be twice transformed into an ass."
So simple Gilbert bought him, and untied
   His halter, and o'er mountain and morass
He led him homeward, talking as he went
Of good behavior and a mind content.

The children saw them coming, and advanced,
   Shouting with joy, and hung about his neck,—   250
Not Gilbert's, but the ass's,—round him danced,
   And wove green garlands wherewithal to deck
His sacred person; for again it chanced
   Their childish feelings, without rein or check,
Could not discriminate in any way
A donkey from a friar of Orders Gray.

"O Brother Timothy," the children said,
   "You have come back to us just as before;
We were afraid, and thought that you were dead,
   And we should never see you any more."   260
And then they kissed the white star on his head,
   That like a birth-mark or a badge he wore,

And patted him upon the neck and face,
And said a thousand things with childish grace.

Thenceforward and forever he was known
   As Brother Timothy, and led alway
A life of luxury, till he had grown
   Ungrateful, being stuffed with corn and hay,
And very vicious. Then in angry tone,
   Rousing himself, poor Gilbert said one day,   270
"When simple kindness is misunderstood
A little flagellation may do good."

His many vices need not here be told;
   Among them was a habit that he had
Of flinging up his heels at young and old,
   Breaking his halter, running off like mad
O'er pasture-lands and meadow, wood and wold,
   And other misdemeanors quite as bad;
But worst of all was breaking from his shed
At night, and ravaging the cabbage-bed.   280

So Brother Timothy went back once more
   To his old life of labor and distress;
Was beaten worse than he had been before;
   And now, instead of comfort and caress,
Came labors manifold and trials sore;
   And as his toils increased his food grew less,
Until at last the great consoler, Death,
Ended his many sufferings with his breath.

Great was the lamentation when he died;
   And mainly that he died impenitent;   290
Dame Cicely bewailed, the children cried,
   The old man still remembered the event
In the French war, and Gilbert magnified
   His many virtues, as he came and went,
And said: "Heaven pardon Brother Timothy,
And keep us from the sin of gluttony."

CHAUCER   [1875]

An old man in a lodge within a park;
   The chamber walls depicted all around
   With portraitures of huntsman, hawk, and hound,
   And the hurt deer. He listeneth to the lark,
Whose song comes with the sunshine through the dark
   Of painted glass in leaden lattice bound;
   He listeneth and he laugheth at the sound,
   Then writeth in a book like any clerk.
He is the poet of the dawn, who wrote
   The Canterbury Tales, and his old age   10
   Made beautiful with song; and as I read
I hear the crowing cock, I hear the note
   Of lark and linnet, and from every page
   Rise odors of ploughed field or flowery mead.

MILTON   [1875]

I pace the sounding sea-beach and behold
   How the voluminous billows roll and run,
   Upheaving and subsiding, while the sun
   Shines through their sheeted emerald far unrolled,
And the ninth wave, slow gathering fold by fold
   All its loose-flowing garments into one,
   Plunges upon the shore, and floods the dun
   Pale reach of sands, and changes them to gold.
So in majestic cadence rise and fall
   The mighty undulations of thy song,   10
   O sightless bard, England's Mæonides!
And ever and anon, high over all
   Uplifted, a ninth wave superb and strong,
   Floods all the soul with its melodious seas.

KEATS   [1875]

The young Endymion sleeps Endymion's sleep;
   The shepherd-boy whose tale was left half told!
   The solemn grove uplifts its shield of gold
   To the red rising moon, and loud and deep
The nightingale is singing from the steep;
   It is midsummer, but the air is cold;
   Can it be death? Alas, beside the fold
A shepherd's pipe lies shattered near his sheep.
Lo! in the moonlight gleams a marble white,
   On which I read: "Here lieth one whose name   10
   Was writ in water." And was this the meed
Of his sweet singing? Rather let me write:
   "The smoking flax before it burst to flame
   Was quenched by death, and broken the bruised reed."

THE SOUND OF THE SEA   [1875]

The sea awoke at midnight from its sleep,
   And round the pebbly beaches far and wide
   I heard the first wave of the rising tide
   Rush onward with uninterrupted sweep;
A voice out of the silence of the deep,
   A sound mysteriously multiplied
   As of a cataract from the mountain's side,
   Or roar of winds upon a wooded steep.
So comes to us at times, from the unknown
   The inaccessible solitudes of being,   10
   The rushing of the sea-tides of the soul;
And inspirations, that we deem our own,
   Are some divine foreshadowing and foreseeing
   Of things beyond our reason or control.

THE HARVEST MOON   [1875]

It is the Harvest Moon! On gilded vanes
   And roofs of villages, on woodland crests
   And their aerial neighborhoods of nests
   Deserted, on the curtained window-panes
Of rooms where children sleep, on country lanes
   And harvest-fields, its mystic splendor rests!
   Gone are the birds that were our summer guests;
   With the last sheaves return the laboring wains!
All things are symbols: the external shows
   Of Nature have their image in the mind,   10
   As flowers and fruits and falling of the leaves;
The song-birds leave us at the summer's close,
   Only the empty nests are left behind,
   And pipings of the quail among the sheaves.

NATURE   [1878]

As a fond mother, when the day is o'er,
   Leads by the hand her little child to bed,
   Half willing, half reluctant to be led,
   And leave his broken playthings on the floor,
Still gazing at them through the open door,
   Nor wholly reassured and comforted
   By promises of others in their stead,
   Which, though more splendid, may not please him more;
So Nature deals with us, and takes away
   Our playthings one by one, and by the hand   10
   Leads us to rest so gently, that we go
Scarce knowing if we wish to go or stay,
   Being too full of sleep to understand
   How far the unknown transcends the what we know.

THE CHAMBER OVER THE GATE   [1880]

Is it so far from thee
Thou canst no longer see,
In the Chamber over the Gate,
That old man desolate,
Weeping and wailing sore
For his son, who is no more?
    O Absalom, my son!

Is it so long ago
That cry of human woe
From the walled city came,   10
Calling on his dear name,
That it has died away
In the distance of to-day?
    O Absalom, my son!

There is no far or near,
There is neither there nor here,
There is neither soon nor late,
In that Chamber over the Gate,
Nor any long ago
To that cry of human woe,   20
    O Absalom, my son!

From the ages that are past
The voice sounds like a blast,
Over seas that wreck and drown,
Over tumult of traffic and town;
And from ages yet to be
Come the echoes back to me,
    O Absalom, my son!

Somewhere at every hour
The watchman on the tower   30
Looks forth, and sees the fleet
Approach of the hurrying feet

Of messengers, that bear
The tidings of despair.
  O Absalom, my son!

He goes forth from the door,
Who shall return no more.
With him our joy departs;
The light goes out in our hearts;
In the Chamber over the Gate   40
We sit disconsolate.
  O Absalom, my son!

That 't is a common grief
Bringeth but slight relief;
Ours is the bitterest loss,
Ours is the heaviest cross;
And forever the cry will be
"Would God I had died for thee,
  O Absalom, my son!"

THE TIDE RISES, THE TIDE FALLS   [1880]

The tide rises, the tide falls,
The twilight darkens, the curlew calls;
Along the sea-sands damp and brown
The traveller hastens toward the town,
    And the tide rises, the tide falls.

Darkness settles on roofs and walls,
But the sea, the sea in the darkness calls;
The little waves, with their soft, white hands,
Efface the footprints in the sands,
    And the tide rises, the tide falls.   10

The morning breaks; the steeds in their stalls
Stamp and neigh, as the hostler calls;
The day returns, but nevermore
Returns the traveller to the shore,
    And the tide rises, the tide falls.

JUGURTHA   [1880]

How cold are thy baths, Apollo!
  Cried the African monarch, the splendid,
As down to his death in the hollow
  Dark dungeons of Rome he descended,
  Uncrowned, unthroned, unattended;
How cold are thy baths, Apollo!

How cold are thy baths, Apollo!
  Cried the Poet, unknown, unbefriended,
As the vision, that lured him to follow,
  With the mist and the darkness blended,   10
  And the dream of his life was ended;
How cold are thy baths, Apollo!

THE CROSS OF SNOW   [1886]

In the long, sleepless watches of the night,
  A gentle face—the face of one long dead—
  Looks at me from the wall, where round its head
  The night-lamp casts a halo of pale light.
Here in this room she died; and soul more white
  Never through martyrdom of fire was led
  To its repose; nor can in books be read
  The legend of a life more benedight.
There is a mountain in the distant West
  That, sun-defying, in its deep ravines   10
  Displays a cross of snow upon its side.
Such is the cross I wear upon my breast
  These eighteen years, through all the changing scenes
  And seasons, changeless since the day she died.

John Greenleaf Whittier

1807–1892

John Greenleaf Whittier was born December 17, 1807, near Haver-hill, Massachusetts, where the Whittiers had settled in 1647. The poet's father, John, was a poor farmer and a Quaker. His mother, Abigail Hussey, encouraged him to write poetry, aided by the Abolitionist William Lloyd Garrison, who was impressed by the boy's precocity. After publishing many poems in small newspapers, Whittier became a major propagandist for the Abolitionist movement. But as war drew near, he turned to personal reminiscence, as in Snow-Bound, *universally acknowledged as his masterpiece. Mainly self-educated, color-blind, tone-deaf, and handicapped by poor health, Whittier nevertheless became one of the most influential and respected American poets of his time. Though his reputation has declined, he will be remembered for his homely poems of rural New England in the nineteenth century. But the regionalism of his subject matter should not blind the student to Whittier's affinities with poets of the past, especially Milton, Spenser, the metaphysical poets of the seventeenth century, Burns, and other British poets.*

MEMORIES   [1843]

A beautiful and happy girl,
   With step as light as summer air,
Eyes glad with smiles, and brow of pearl,
Shadowed by many a careless curl
   Of unconfined and flowing hair;
A seeming child in everything,
   Save thoughtful brow and ripening charms,

As Nature wears the smile of Spring
  When sinking into Summer's arms.

A mind rejoicing in the light 10
  Which melted through its graceful bower,
Leaf after leaf, dew-moist and bright,
And stainless in its holy white,
  Unfolding like a morning flower:
A heart, which, like a fine-toned lute,
  With every breath of feeling woke,
And, even when the tongue was mute,
  From eye and lip in music spoke.

How thrills once more the lengthening chain
  Of memory, at the thought of thee! 20
Old hopes which long in dust have lain.
Old dreams, come thronging back again,
  And boyhood lives again in me;
I feel its glow upon my cheek,
  Its fulness of the heart is mine,
As when I leaned to hear thee speak,
  Or raised my doubtful eye to thine.

I hear again thy low replies,
  I feel thy arm within my own,
And timidly again uprise 30
The fringèd lids of hazel eyes,
  With soft brown tresses overblown.
Ah! memories of sweet summer eves,
  Of moonlit wave and willowy way,
Of stars and flowers, and dewy leaves,
  And smiles and tones more dear than they!

Ere this, thy quiet eye hath smiled
  My picture of thy youth to see,
When, half a woman, half a child,
Thy very artlessness beguiled, 40
  And folly's self seemed wise in thee;
I too can smile, when o'er that hour
  The lights of memory backward stream,

Yet feel the while that manhood's power
   Is vainer than my boyhood's dream.

Years have passed on, and left their trace,
   Of graver care and deeper thought;
And unto me the calm, cold face
Of manhood, and to thee the grace
   Of woman's pensive beauty brought.   50
More wide, perchance, for blame than praise.
   The school-boy's humble name has flown;
Thine, in the green and quiet ways
   Of unobtrusive goodness known.

And wider yet in thought and deed
   Diverge our pathways, one in youth;
Thine the Genevan's sternest creed,
While answers to my spirit's need
   The Derby dalesman's simple truth.
For thee, the priestly rite and prayer,   60
   And holy day, and solemn psalm;
For me, the silent reverence where
   My brethren gather, slow and calm.

Yet hath thy spirit left on me
   An impress Time has worn not out,
And something of myself in thee,
A shadow from the past, I see,
   Lingering, even yet, thy way about;
Not wholly can the heart unlearn
   That lesson of its better hours,   70
Not yet has Time's dull footstep worn
   To common dust that path of flowers.

Thus, while at times before our eyes
   The shadows melt, and fall apart,
And, smiling through them, round us lies
The warm light of our morning skies,—
   The Indian Summer of the heart!
In secret sympathies of mind,
   In founts of feeling which retain

Their pure, fresh flow, we yet may find   80
   Our early dreams not wholly vain!

PROEM   [1849]

   I love the old melodious lays
Which softly melt the ages through,
    The songs of Spenser's golden days,
    Arcadian Sidney's silvery phrase,
Sprinkling our noon of time with freshest morning dew.

   Yet, vainly in my quiet hours
To breathe their marvellous notes I try;
    I feel them, as the leaves and flowers
    In silence feel the dewy showers,
And drink with glad, still lips the blessing of the sky.   10

   The rigor of a frozen clime,
The harshness of an untaught ear,
    The jarring words of one whose rhyme
    Beat often Labor's hurried time,
Or Duty's rugged march through storm and strife,
     are here.

   Of mystic beauty, dreamy grace,
No rounded art the lack supplies;
    Unskilled the subtle lines to trace,
    Or softer shades of Nature's face,
I view her common forms with unanointed eyes.   20

   Nor mine the seer-like power to show
The secrets of the heart and mind;
    To drop the plummet-line below
    Our common world of joy and woe.
A more intense despair or brighter hope to find.

   Yet here at least an earnest sense
Of human right and weal is shown;

A hate of tyranny intense,
    And hearty in its vehemence,
As if my brother's pain and sorrow were my own.   30

    O Freedom! if to me belong
Nor mighty Milton's gift divine,
    Nor Marvell's wit and graceful song,
    Still with a love as deep and strong
As theirs, I lay, like them, my best gifts on thy shrine!

ICHABOD   [1850]

So fallen! so lost! the light withdrawn
    Which once he wore!
The glory from his gray hairs gone
    Forevermore!

Revile him not, the Tempter hath
    A snare for all;
And pitying tears, not scorn and wrath,
    Befit his fall!

Oh, dumb be passion's stormy rage,
    When he who might   10
Have lighted up and led his age,
    Falls back in night.

Scorn! would the angels laugh, to mark
    A bright soul driven,
Fiend-goaded, down the endless dark,
    From hope and heaven!

Let not the land once proud of him
    Insult him now,
Nor brand with deeper shame his dim,
    Dishonored brow.   20

But let its humbled sons, instead,
    From sea to lake,
A long lament, as for the dead,
    In sadness make.

Of all we loved and honored, naught
    Save power remains;
A fallen angel's pride of thought,
    Still strong in chains.

All else is gone; from those great eyes
    The soul has fled: 30
When faith is lost, when honor dies,
    The man is dead!

Then, pay the reverence of old days
    To his dead fame;
Walk backward, with averted gaze,
    And hide the shame!

SKIPPER IRESON'S RIDE   [1860]

Of all the rides since the birth of time,
Told in story or sung in rhyme,—
On Apuleius's Golden Ass,
Or one-eyed Calender's horse of brass,
Witch astride of a human back,
Islam's prophet on Al-Borák,—
The strangest ride that ever was sped
Was Ireson's, out from Marblehead!
    Old Floyd Ireson, for his hard heart,
      Tarred and feathered and carried in a cart   10
        By the women of Marblehead!

Body of turkey, head of owl,
Wings a-droop like a rained-on fowl,
Feathered and ruffled in every part,

Skipper Ireson stood in the cart.
Scores of women, old and young,
Strong of muscle, and glib of tongue,
Pushed and pulled up the rocky lane,
Shouting and singing the shrill refrain:
   "Here's Flud Oirson, fur his horrd horrt,   20
    Torr'd an' futherr'd an' corr'd in a corrt
      By the women o' Morble'ead!"

Wrinkled scolds with hands on hips,
Girls in bloom of cheek and lips,
Wild-eyed, free-limbed, such as chase
Bacchus round some antique vase,
Brief of skirt, with ankles bare,
Loose of kerchief and loose of hair,
With conch-shells blowing and fish-horns' twang,
Over and over the Mænads sang: 30
   "Here's Flud Oirson, fur his horrd horrt,
    Torr'd an' futherr'd an' corr'd in a corrt
      By the women o' Morble'ead!"

Small pity for him!—He sailed away
From a leaking ship in Chaleur Bay,—
Sailed away from a sinking wreck,
With his own town's-people on her deck!
"Lay by! lay by!" they called to him.
Back he answered, "Sink or swim!
Brag of your catch of fish again!"   40
And off he sailed through the fog and rain!
   Old Floyd Ireson, for his hard heart,
    Tarred and feathered and carried in a cart
      By the women of Marblehead!

Fathoms deep in dark Chaleur
That wreck shall lie forevermore.
Mother and sister, wife and maid,
Looked from the rocks of Marblehead
Over the moaning and rainy sea,—
Looked for the coming that might not be!   50
What did the winds and the sea-birds say

Of the cruel captain who sailed away?—
   Old Floyd Ireson, for his hard heart,
   Tarred and feathered and carried in a cart
     By the women of Marblehead!

Through the street, on either side,
Up flew windows, doors swung wide;
Sharp-tongued spinsters, old wives gray,
Treble lent the fish-horn's bray.
Sea-worn grandsires, cripple-bound,   60
Hulks of old sailors run aground,
Shook head, and fist, and hat, and cane,
And cracked with curses the hoarse refrain:
   "Here's Flud Oirson, fur his horrd horrt,
   Torr'd an' futherr'd an' corr'd in a corrt
     By the women o' Morble'ead!"

Sweetly along the Salem road
Bloom of orchard and lilac showed.
Little the wicked skipper knew
Of the fields so green and the sky so blue.   70
Riding there in his sorry trim,
Like an Indian idol glum and grim,
Scarcely he seemed the sound to hear
Of voices shouting, far and near:
   "Here's Flud Oirson, fur his horrd horrt,
   Torr'd an' futherr'd an' corr'd in a corrt
     By the women o' Morble'ead!"

"Hear me, neighbors!" at last he cried,—
"What to me is this noisy ride?
What is the shame that clothes the skin   80
To the nameless horror that lives within?
Waking or sleeping, I see a wreck,
And hear a cry from a reeling deck!
Hate me and curse me,—I only dread
The hand of God and the face of the dead!"
   Said old Floyd Ireson, for his hard heart,
   Tarred and feathered and carried in a cart
     By the women of Marblehead!

Then the wife of the skipper lost at sea
Said, "God has touched him! why should we!"   90
Said an old wife mourning her only son,
"Cut the rogue's tether and let him run!"
So with soft relentings and rude excuse,
Half scorn, half pity, they cut him loose,
And gave him a cloak to hide him in,
And left him alone with his shame and sin.
   Poor Floyd Ireson, for his hard heart,
    Tarred and feathered and carried in a cart
     By the women of Marblehead!

THE OLD BURYING-GROUND   [1860]

Our vales are sweet with fern and rose,
   Our hills are maple-crowned;
But not from them our fathers chose
   The village burying-ground.

The dreariest spot in all the land
   To Death they set apart;
With scanty grace from Nature's hand,
   And none from that of art.

A winding wall of mossy stone,
   Frost-flung and broken, lines   10
A lonesome acre thinly grown
   With grass and wandering vines.

Without the wall a birch-tree shows
   Its drooped and tasselled head;
Within, a stag-horn sumach grows,
   Fern-leafed, with spikes of red.

There, sheep that graze the neighboring plain
   Like white ghosts come and go,
The farm-horse drags his fetlock chain,
   The cow-bell tinkles slow.   20

Low moans the river from its bed,
　　The distant pines reply;
Like mourners shrinking from the dead,
　　They stand apart and sigh.

Unshaded smites the summer sun,
　　Unchecked the winter blast;
The school-girl learns the place to shun,
　　With glances backward cast.

For thus our fathers testified,
　　That he might read who ran,   30
The emptiness of human pride,
　　The nothingness of man.

They dared not plant the grave with flowers,
　　Nor dress the funeral sod,
Where, with a love as deep as ours,
　　They left their dead with God.

The hard and thorny path they kept
　　From beauty turned aside;
Nor missed they over those who slept
　　The grace to life denied.   40

Yet still the wilding flowers would blow,
　　The golden leaves would fall,
The seasons come, the seasons go,
　　And God be good to all.

Above the graves the blackberry hung
　　In bloom and green its wreath,
And harebells swung as if they rung
　　The chimes of peace beneath.

The beauty Nature loves to share,
　　The gifts she hath for all,   50
The common light, the common air,
　　O'ercrept the graveyard's wall.

It knew the glow of eventide,
  The sunrise and the noon,
And glorified and sanctified
  It slept beneath the moon.

With flowers or snow-flakes for its sod,
  Around the seasons ran,
And evermore the love of God
  Rebuked the fear of man.   60

We dwell with fears on either hand
  Within a daily strife,
And spectral problems waiting stand
  Before the gates of life.

The doubts we vainly seek to solve,
  The truths we know, are one;
The known and nameless stars revolve
  Around the Central Sun.

And if we reap as we have sown,
  And take the dole we deal,   70
The law of pain is love alone,
  The wounding is to heal.

Unharmed from change to change we glide,
  We fall as in our dreams;
The far-off terror at our side
  A smiling angel seems.

Secure on God's all-tender heart
  Alike rest great and small;
Why fear to lose our little part,
  When He is pledged for all?   80

O fearful heart and troubled brain!
  Take hope and strength from this,—
That Nature never hints in vain,
  Nor prophesies amiss.

Her wild birds sing the same sweet stave,
   Her lights and airs are given
Alike to playground and the grave;
   And over both is Heaven.

TELLING THE BEES   [1860]

Here is the place; right over the hill
   Runs the path I took;
You can see the gap in the old wall still,
   And the stepping-stones in the shallow brook.

There is the house, with the gate red-barred,
   And the poplars tall;
And the barn's brown length, and the cattle-yard,
   And the white horns tossing above the wall.

There are the beehives ranged in the sun;
   And down by the brink   10
Of the brook are her poor flowers, weed-o'errun,
   Pansy and daffodil, rose and pink.

A year has gone, as the tortoise goes,
   Heavy and slow;
And the same rose blows, and the same sun glows,
   And the same brook sings of a year ago.

There's the same sweet clover-smell in the breeze;
   And the June sun warm
Tangles his wings of fire in the trees,
   Setting, as then, over Fernside farm.   20

I mind me how with a lover's care
   From my Sunday coat
I brushed off the burrs, and smoothed my hair.
   And cooled at the brookside my brow and throat.

Since we parted, a month had passed,—
    To love, a year;
Down through the beeches I looked at last
    On the little red gate and the well-sweep near.

I can see it all now,—the slantwise rain
    Of light through the leaves,   30
The sundown's blaze on her window-pane,
    The bloom of her roses under the eaves.

Just the same as a month before,—
    The house and the trees,
The barn's brown gable, the vine by the door,—
    Nothing changed but the hives of bees.

Before them, under the garden wall,
    Forward and back,
Went drearily singing the chore-girl small,
    Draping each hive with a shred of black.   40

Trembling, I listened: the summer sun
    Had the chill of snow;
For I knew she was telling the bees of one
    Gone on the journey we all must go!

Then I said to myself, "My Mary weeps
    For the dead to-day:
Haply her blind old grandsire sleeps
    The fret and the pain of his age away."

But her dog whined low; on the doorway sill,
    With his cane to his chin,   50
The old man sat; and the chore-girl still
    Sung to the bees stealing out and in.

And the song she was singing ever since
    In my ear sounds on:—
"Stay at home, pretty bees, fly not hence!
    Mistress Mary is dead and gone!"

MY PLAYMATE   [1860]

The pines were dark on Ramoth hill,
  Their song was soft and low;
The blossoms in the sweet May wind
  Were falling like the snow.

The blossoms drifted at our feet,
  The orchard birds sang clear;
The sweetest and the saddest day
  It seemed of all the year.

For, more to me than birds or flowers,
  My playmate left her home,   10
And took with her the laughing spring,
  The music and the bloom.

She kissed the lips of kith and kin,
  She laid her hand in mine:
What more could ask the bashful boy
  Who fed her father's kine?

She left us in the bloom of May:
  The constant years told o'er
Their seasons with as sweet May morns,
  But she came back no more.   20

I walk, with noiseless feet, the round
  Of uneventful years;
Still o'er and o'er I sow the spring
  And reap the autumn ears.

She lives where all the golden year
  Her summer roses blow;
The dusky children of the sun
  Before her come and go.

There haply with her jewelled hands
  She smooths her silken gown,—   30

No more the homespun lap wherein
   I shook the walnuts down.

The wild grapes wait us by the brook,
   The brown nuts on the hill,
And still the May-day flowers make sweet
   The woods of Follymill.

The lilies blossom in the pond,
   The bird builds in the tree,
The dark pines sing on Ramoth hill
   The slow song of the sea.   40

I wonder if she thinks of them,
   And how the old time seems,—
If ever the pines of Ramoth wood
   Are sounding in her dreams.

I see her face, I hear her voice;
   Does she remember mine?
And what to her is now the boy
   Who fed her father's kine?

What cares she that the orioles build
   For other eyes than ours,—   50
That other hands with nuts are filled,
   And other laps with flowers?

O playmate in the golden time!
   Our mossy seat is green,
Its fringing violets blossom yet,
   The old trees o'er it lean.

The winds so sweet with birch and fern
   A sweeter memory blow;
And there in spring the veeries sing
   The song of long ago.   60

And still the pines of Ramoth wood
   Are moaning like the sea,—

The moaning of the sea of change
　　Between myself and thee!

BARBARA FRIETCHIE　　[1864]

Up from the meadows rich with corn,
Clear in the cool September morn,

The clustered spires of Frederick stand
Green-walled by the hills of Maryland.

Round about them orchards sweep,
Apple and peach tree fruited deep,

Fair as the garden of the Lord
To the eyes of the famished rebel horde,

On that pleasant morn of the early fall
When Lee marched over the mountain wall;　　　　10

Over the mountains winding down,
Horse and foot, into Frederick town.

Forty flags with their silver stars,
Forty flags with their crimson bars,

Flapped in the morning wind: the sun
Of noon looked down, and saw not one.

Up rose old Barbara Frietchie then,
Bowed with her fourscore years and ten;

Bravest of all in Frederick town,
She took up the flag the men hauled down;　　　　20

In her attic window the staff she set,
To show that one heart was loyal yet.

Up the street came the rebel tread,
Stonewall Jackson riding ahead.

Under his slouched hat left and right
He glanced; the old flag met his sight.

"Halt"—the dust-brown ranks stood fast.
"Fire!"—out blazed the rifle-blast.

It shivered the window, pane and sash;
It rent the banner with seam and gash.   30

Quick, as it fell, from the broken staff
Dame Barbara snatched the silken scarf.

She leaned far out on the window-sill,
And shook it forth with a royal will.

"Shoot, if you must, this old gray head,
But spare your country's flag," she said.

A shade of sadness, a blush of shame,
Over the face of the leader came;

The nobler nature within him stirred
To life at that woman's deed and word;   40

"Who touches a hair of yon gray head
Dies like a dog! March on!" he said.

All day long through Frederick street
Sounded the tread of marching feet:

All day long that free flag tost
Over the heads of the rebel host.

Ever its torn folds rose and fell
On the loyal winds that loved it well;

And through the hill-gaps sunset light
Shone over it with a warm good-night.   50

Barbara Frietchie's work is o'er,
And the Rebel rides on his raids no more.

Honor to her! and let a tear
Fall, for her sake, on Stonewall's bier.

Over Barbara Frietchie's grave,
Flag of Freedom and Union, wave!

Peace and order and beauty draw
Round thy symbol of light and law;

And ever the stars above look down
On thy stars below in Frederick town!   60

SNOW-BOUND   [1866]

A Winter Idyl

> To the Memory of the Household It Describes
> This Poem Is Dedicated by the Author

The sun that brief December day
Rose cheerless over hills of gray,
And, darkly circled, gave at noon
A sadder light than waning moon.
Slow tracing down the thickening sky
Its mute and ominous prophecy,
A portent seeming less than threat,
It sank from sight before it set.
A chill no coat, however stout,
Of homespun stuff could quite shut out,   10
A hard, dull bitterness of cold,
That checked, mid-vein, the circling race
Of life-blood in the sharpened face,
The coming of the snow-storm told.
The wind blew east; we heard the roar
Of Ocean on his wintry shore,

And felt the strong pulse throbbing there
Beat with low rhythm our inland air.

Meanwhile we did our nightly chores,—
Brought in the wood from out of doors,   20
Littered the stalls, and from the mows
Raked down the herd's-grass for the cows:
Heard the horse whinnying for his corn;
And, sharply clashing horn on horn,
Impatient down the stanchion rows
The cattle shake their walnut bows;
While, peering from his early perch
Upon the scaffold's pole of birch,
The cock his crested helmet bent
And down his querulous challenge sent.   30

Unwarmed by any sunset light
The gray day darkened into night,
A night made hoary with the swarm
And whirl-dance of the blinding storm,
As zigzag, wavering to and fro,
Crossed and recrossed the wingëd snow:
And ere the early bedtime came
The white drift piled the window-frame,
And through the glass the clothes-line posts
Looked in like tall and sheeted ghosts.   40

So all night long the storm roared on:
The morning broke without a sun;
In tiny spherule traced with lines
Of Nature's geometric signs,
In starry flake, and pellicle,
All day the hoary meteor fell;
And, when the second morning shone,
We looked upon a world unknown,
On nothing we could call our own.
Around the glistening wonder bent   50
The blue walls of the firmament,
No cloud above, no earth below,—
A universe of sky and snow!

The old familiar sights of ours
Took marvellous shapes; strange domes and towers
Rose up where sty or corn-crib stood,
Or garden-wall, or belt of wood;
A smooth white mound the brush-pile showed,
A fenceless drift what once was road;
The bridle-post an old man sat 60
With loose-flung coat and high cocked hat;
The well-curb had a Chinese roof;
And even the long sweep, high aloof,
In its slant splendor, seemed to tell
Of Pisa's leaning miracle.

A prompt, decisive man, no breath
Our father wasted: "Boys, a path!"
Well pleased, (for when did farmer boy
Count such a summons less than joy?)
Our buskins on our feet we drew; 70
With mittened hands, and caps drawn low,
To guard our necks and ears from snow,
We cut the solid whiteness through.
And, where the drift was deepest, made
A tunnel walled and overlaid
With dazzling crystal: we had read
Of rare Aladdin's wondrous cave,
And to our own his name we gave,
With many a wish the luck were ours
To test his lamp's supernal powers. 80
We reached the barn with merry din,
And roused the prisoned brutes within.
The old horse thrust his long head out,
And grave with wonder gazed about;
The cock his lusty greeting said,
And forth his speckled harem led;
The oxen lashed their tails, and hooked,
And mild reproach of hunger looked;
The hornëd patriarch of the sheep,
Like Egypt's Amun roused from sleep, 90
Shook his sage head with gesture mute,
And emphasized with stamp of foot.

All day the gusty north-wind bore
The loosening drift its breath before;
Low circling round its southern zone,
The sun through dazzling snow-mist shone.
No church-bell lent its Christian tone
To the savage air, no social smoke
Curled over woods of snow-hung oak.
A solitude made more intense   100
By dreary-voicëd elements,
The shrieking of the mindless wind,
The moaning tree-boughs swaying blind,
And on the glass the unmeaning beat
Of ghostly finger-tips of sleet.
Beyond the circle of our hearth
No welcome sound of toil or mirth
Unbound the spell, and testified
Of human life and thought outside.
We minded that the sharpest ear   110
The buried brooklet could not hear,
The music of whose liquid lip
Had been to us companionship,
And, in our lonely life, had grown
To have an almost human tone.

As night drew on, and, from the crest
Of wooded knolls that ridged the west,
The sun, a snow-blown traveller, sank
From sight beneath the smothering bank,
We piled, with care, our nightly stack   120
Of wood against the chimney-back,—
The oaken log, green, huge, and thick,
And on its top the stout back-stick;
The knotty forestick laid apart,
And filled between with curious art
The ragged brush; then hovering near,
We watched the first red blaze appear,
Heard the sharp crackle, caught the gleam
On whitewashed wall and sagging beam,
Until the old, rude-furnished room   130
Burst, flower-like, into rosy bloom;

While radiant with a mimic flame
Outside the sparkling drift became,
And through the bare-boughed lilac-tree
Our own warm hearth seemed blazing free.
The crane and pendent trammels showed,
The Turks' heads on the andirons glowed;
While childish fancy, prompt to tell
The meaning of the miracle.,
Whispered the old rhyme: "*Under the tree,*   140
When fire outdoors burns merrily,
There the witches are making tea."

The moon above the eastern wood
Shone at its full; the hill-range stood
Transfigured in the silver flood,
Its blown snows flashing cold and keen,
Dead white, save where some sharp ravine
Took shadow, or the sombre green
Of hemlocks turned to pitchy black
Against the whiteness at their back   150
For such a world and such a night
Most fitting that unwarming light,
Which only seemed where'er it fell
To make the coldness visible.

Shut in from all the world without,
We sat the clean-winged hearth about,
Content to let the north-wind roar
In baffled rage at pane and door,
While the red logs before us beat
The frost-line back with tropic heat;   160
And ever, when a louder blast
Shook beam and rafter as it passed,
The merrier up its roaring draught
The great throat of the chimney laughed;
The house-dog on his paws outspread
Laid to the fire his drowsy head,
The cat's dark silhouette on the wall
A couchant tiger's seemed to fall;
And, for the winter fireside meet,

Between the andirons' straddling feet,   170
The mug of cider simmered slow,
The apples sputtered in a row,
And, close at hand, the basket stood
With nuts from brown October's wood.

What matter how the night behaved?
What matter how the north-wind raved?
Blow high, blow low, not all its snow
Could quench our hearth-fire's ruddy glow.
O Time and Change!—with hair as gray
As was my sire's that winter day,   180
How strange it seems, with so much gone
Of life and love, to still live on!
Ah, brother! only I and thou
Are left of all that circle now,—
The dear home faces whereupon
That fitfull firelight paled and shone.
Henceforward, listen as we will,
The voices of that hearth are still;
Look where we may, the wide earth o'er,
Those lighted faces smile no more.   190
We tread the paths their feet have worn,
    We sit beneath their orchard trees,
    We hear, like them, the hum of bees
And rustle of the bladed corn;
We turn the pages that they read,
    Their written words we linger o'er,
But in the sun they cast no shade,
No voice is heard, no sign is made,
    No step is on the conscious floor!
Yet Love will dream, and Faith will trust,   200
(Since He who knows our need is just,)
That somehow, somewhere, meet we must.
Alas for him who never sees
The stars shine through his cypress-trees!
Who, hopeless, lays his dead away,
Nor looks to see the breaking day
Across the mournful marbles play!
Who hath not learned, in hours of faith,

The truth to flesh and sense unknown,
That Life is ever lord of Death,   210
    And Love can never lose its own!

We sped the time with stories old,
Wrought puzzles out, and riddles told,
Or stammered from our school-book lore
"The Chief of Gambia's golden shore."
How often since, when all the land
Was clay in Slavery's shaping hand,
As if a far-blown trumpet stirred
The languorous sin-sick air, I heard:
"Does not the voice of reason cry,   220
    Claim the first right which Nature gave,
From the red scourge of bondage fly,
    Nor deign to live a burdened slave!"
Our father rode again his ride
On Memphremagog's wooded side;
Sat down again to moose and samp
In trapper's hut and Indian camp;
Lived o'er the old idyllic ease
Beneath St. François' hemlock-trees;
Again for him the moonlight shone   230
On Norman cap and bodiced zone;
Again he heard the violin play
Which led the village dance away,
And mingled in its merry whirl
The grandam and the laughing girl.
Or, nearer home, our steps he led
Where Salisbury's level marshes spread
    Mile-wide as flies the laden bee;
Where merry mowers, hale and strong,
Swept, scythe on scythe, their swaths along   240
    The low green prairies of the sea.
We shared the fishing off Boar's Head,
    And round the rocky Isles of Shoals
    The hake-broil on the drift-wood coals;
The chowder on the sand-beach made,
Dipped by the hungry, steaming hot,
With spoons of clam-shell from the pot.

We heard the tales of witchcraft old,
And dream and sign and marvel told
To sleepy listeners as they lay   250
Stretched idly on the salted hay,
Adrift along the winding shores,
When favoring breezes deigned to blow
The square sail of the gundelow
And idle lay the useless oars.

Our mother, while she turned her wheel
Or run the new-knit stocking-heel,
Told how the Indian hordes came down
At midnight on Cocheco town,
And how her own great-uncle bore   260
His cruel scalp-mark to fourscore.
Recalling, in her fitting phrase,
    So rich and picturesque and free,
    (The common unrhymed poetry
Of simple life and country ways,)
The story of her early days,—
She made us welcome to her home;
Old hearths grew wide to give us room;
We stole with her a frightened look
At the gray wizard's conjuring-book,   270
The fame whereof went far and wide
Through all the simple country side;
We heard the hawks at twilight play,
The boat-horn on Piscataqua,
The loon's weird laughter far away;
We fished her little trout-brook, knew
What flowers in wood and meadow grew,
What sunny hillsides autumn-brown
She climbed to shake the ripe nuts down,
Saw where in sheltered cove and bay   280
The ducks' black squadron anchored lay,
And heard the wild-geese calling loud
Beneath the gray November cloud.

Then, haply, with a look more grave,
And soberer tone, some tale she gave

From painful Sewel's ancient tome,
Beloved in every Quaker home,
Of faith fire-winged by martyrdom,
Or Chalkley's Journal, old and quaint,—
Gentlest of skippers, rare sea-saint!—   290
Who, when the dreary calms prevailed,
And water-butt and bread-cask failed,
And cruel, hungry eyes pursued
His portly presence mad for food,
With dark hints muttered under breath
Of casting lots for life or death,
Offered, if Heaven withheld supplies,
To be himself the sacrifice.
Then, suddenly, as if to save
The good man from his living grave,   300
A ripple on the water grew,
A school of porpoise flashed in view.
"Take, eat," he said, "and be content;
These fishes in my stead are sent
By Him who gave the tangled ram
To spare the child of Abraham."

Our uncle, innocent of books,
Was rich in lore of fields and brooks,
The ancient teachers never dumb
Of Nature's unhoused lyceum.   310
In moons and tides and weather wise,
He read the clouds as prophecies,
And foul or fair could well divine,
By many an occult hint and sign,
Holding the cunning-warded keys
To all the woodcraft mysteries;
Himself to Nature's heart so near
That all her voices in his ear
Of beast or bird had meanings clear,
Like Apollonius of old,   320
Who knew the tales the sparrows told,
Or Hermes, who interpreted
What the sage cranes of Nilus said;
A simple, guileless, childlike man,

Content to live where life began;
Strong only on his native grounds,
The little world of sights and sounds
Whose girdle was the parish bounds,
Whereof his fondly partial pride
The common features magnified,   330
As Surrey hills to mountains grew
In White of Selborne's loving view,—
He told how teal and loon he shot,
And how the eagle's eggs he got,
The feats on pond and river done,
The prodigies of rod and gun;
Till, warming with the tales he told,
Forgotten was the outside cold,
The bitter wind unheeded blew,
From ripening corn the pigeons flew,   340
The partridge drummed i' the wood, **the mink**
Went fishing down the river-brink.
In fields with bean or clover gay,
The woodchuck, like a hermit gray,
    Peered from the doorway of his cell;
The muskrat plied the mason's trade,
And tier by tier his mud-walls laid;
And from the shagbark overhead
    The grizzled squirrel dropped his shell.

Next, the dear aunt, whose smile of cheer   350
And voice in dreams I see and hear,—
The sweetest woman ever Fate
Perverse denied a household mate,
Who, lonely, homeless, not the less
Found peace in love's unselfishness,
And welcome wheresoe'er she went,
A calm and gracious element,
Whose presence seemed the sweet income
And womanly atmosphere of home,—
Called up her girlhood memories,   360
The huskings and the apple-bees,
The sleigh-rides and the summer sails,
Weaving through all the poor details

And homespun warp of circumstance
A golden woof-thread of romance.
For well she kept her genial mood
And simple faith of maidenhood;
Before her still a cloud-land lay,
The mirage loomed across her way;
The morning dew, that dries so soon   370
With others, glistened at her noon;
Through years of toil and soil and care,
From glossy tress to thin gray hair,
All unprofaned she held apart
The virgin fancies of the heart.
Be shame to him of woman born
Who hath for such but thought of scorn.

There, too, our elder sister plied
Her evening task the stand beside;
A full, rich nature, free to trust,   380
Truthful and almost sternly just,
Impulsive, earnest, prompt to act,
And make her generous thought a fact,
Keeping with many a light disguise
The secret of self-sacrifice.
O heart sore-tried! thou hast the best
That Heaven itself could give thee,—rest,
Rest from all bitter thoughts and things!
    How many a poor one's blessing went
    With thee beneath the low green tent   390
Whose curtain never outward swings!

As one who held herself a part
Of all she saw, and let her heart
    Against the household bosom lean,
Upon the motley-braided mat
Our youngest and our dearest sat,
Lifting her large, sweet, asking eyes,
    Now bathed in the unfading green
And holy peace of Paradise.
Oh, looking from some heavenly hill,   400

Or from the shade of saintly palms,
Or silver reach of river calms,
Do those large eyes behold me still?
With me one little year ago:—
The chill weight of the winter snow
For months upon her grave has lain;
And now, when summer south-winds blow
And brier and harebell bloom again,
I tread the pleasant paths we trod,
I see the violet-sprinkled sod   410
Whereon she leaned, too frail and weak
The hillside flowers she loved to seek,
Yet following me where'er I went
With dark eyes full of love's content.
The birds are glad; the brier-rose fills
The air with sweetness; all the hills
Stretch green to June's unclouded sky;
But still I wait with ear and eye
For something gone which should be nigh,
A loss in all familiar things,   420
In flower that blooms, and bird that sings.
And yet, dear heart! remembering thee,
Am I not richer than of old?
Safe in thy immortality,
What change can reach the wealth I hold?
What chance can mar the pearl and gold
Thy love hath left in trust with me?
And while in life's late afternoon,
Where cool and long the shadows grow,
I walk to meet the night that soon   430
Shall shape and shadow overflow,
I cannot feel that thou art far,
Since near at need the angels are;
And when the sunset gates unbar,
Shall I not see thee waiting stand,
And, white against the evening star,
The welcome of thy beckoning hand?

Brisk wielder of the birch and rule,
The master of the district school

Held at the fire his favored place,   440
Its warm glow lit a laughing face
Fresh-hued and fair, where scarce appeared
The uncertain prophecy of beard.
He teased the mitten-blinded cat,
Played cross-pins on my uncle's hat,
Sang songs, and told us what befalls
In classic Dartmouth's college halls.
Born the wild Northern hills among,
From whence his yeoman father wrung
By patient toil subsistence scant,   450
Not competence and yet not want,
He early gained the power to pay
His cheerful, self-reliant way;
Could doff at ease his scholar's gown
To peddle wares from town to town;
Or through the long vacation's reach
In lonely lowland districts teach,
Where all the droll experience found
At stranger hearths in boarding round,
The moonlit skater's keen delight,   460
The sleigh-drive through the frosty night,
The rustic party, with its rough
Accompaniment of blind-man's-buff,
And whirling-plate, and forfeits paid,
His winter task a pastime made.
Happy the snow-locked homes wherein
He tuned his merry violin,
Or played the athlete in the barn,
Or held the good dame's winding-yarn,
Or mirth-provoking versions told   470
Of classic legends rare and old,
Wherein the scenes of Greece and Rome
Had all the commonplace of home,
And little seemed at best the odds
'Twixt Yankee pedlers and old gods;
Where Pindus-born Arachthus took
The guise of any grist-mill brook,
And dread Olympus at his will
Became a huckleberry hill.

A careless boy that night he seemed;   480
    But at his desk he had the look
And air of one who wisely schemed,
    And hostage from the future took
    In trainëd thought and lore of book.
Large-brained, clear-eyed, of such as he
Shall Freedom's young apostles be,
Who, following in War's bloody trail,
Shall every lingering wrong assail;
All chains from limb and spirit strike,
Uplift the black and white alike;   490
Scatter before their swift advance
The darkness and the ignorance,
The pride, the lust, the squalid sloth,
Which nurtured Treason's monstrous growth,
Made murder pastime, and the hell
Of prison-torture possible;
The cruel lie of caste refute,
Old forms remould, and substitute
For Slavery's lash the freeman's will,
For blind routine, wise-handed skill;   500
A school-house plant on every hill,
Stretching in radiate nerve-lines thence
The quick wires of intelligence;
Till North and South together brought
Shall own the same electric thought,
In peace a common flag salute,
And, side by side in labor's free
And unresentful rivalry,
Harvest the fields wherein they fought.

Another guest that winter night   510
Flashed back from lustrous eyes the light.
Unmarked by time, and yet not young,
The honeyed music of her tongue
And words of meekness scarcely told
A nature passionate and bold,
Strong, self-concentred, spurning guide,
Its milder features dwarfed beside
Her unbent will's majestic pride.

She sat among us, at the best,
A not unfeared, half-welcome guest,   520
Rebuking with her cultured phrase
Our homeliness of words and ways.
A certain pard-like, treacherous grace
Swayed the lithe limbs and drooped the lash,
Lent the white teeth their dazzling flash;
And under low brows, black with night,
Rayed out at times a dangerous light;
The sharp heat-lightnings of her face
Presaging ill to him whom Fate
Condemned to share her love or hate.   530
A woman tropical, intense
In thought and act, in soul and sense,
She blended in a like degree
The vixen and the devotee.
Revealing with each freak or feint
   The temper of Petruchio's Kate,
The raptures of Siena's saint.
Her tapering hand and rounded wrist
Had facile power to form a fist;
The warm, dark languish of her eyes   540
Was never safe from wrath's surprise.
Brows saintly calm and lips devout
Knew every change of scowl and pout;
And the sweet voice had notes more high
And shrill for social battle-cry.

Since then what old cathedral town
Has missed her pilgrim staff and gown,
What convent-gate has held its lock
Against the challenge of her knock!
Through Smyrna's plague-hushed thoroughfares,   550
Up sea-set Malta's rocky stairs,
Gray olive slopes of hills that hem
Thy tombs and shrines, Jerusalem,
Or startling on her desert throne
The crazy Queen of Lebanon
With claims fantastic as her own,
Her tireless feet have held their way;

And still, unrestful, bowed, and gray,
She watches under Eastern skies,
   With hope each day renewed and fresh,   560
   The Lord's quick coming in the flesh
Whereof she dreams and prophesies!

Where'er her troubled path may be,
   The Lord's sweet pity with her go!
The outward wayward life we see,
   The hidden springs we may not know.
Nor is it given us to discern
   What threads the fatal sisters spun,
   Through what ancestral years has run
The sorrow with the woman born,   570
What forged her cruel chain of moods,
What set her feet in solitudes,
   And held the love within her mute,
What mingled madness in the blood,
   A life-long discord and annoy,
   Water of tears with oil of joy,
And hid within the folded bud
   Perversities of flower and fruit.
It is not ours to separate
The tangled skein of will and fate,   580
To show what metes and bounds should stand
Upon the soul's debatable land,
And between choice and Providence
Divide the circle of events;
But He who knows our frame is just,
Merciful and compassionate,
And full of sweet assurances
And hope for all the language is,
That He remembereth we are dust!

At last the great logs, crumbling low,   590
Sent out a dull and duller glow,
The bull's-eye watch that hung in view,
Ticking its weary circuit through,
Pointed with mutely warning sign
Its black hand to the hour of nine.

That sign the pleasant circle broke:
My uncle ceased his pipe to smoke,
Knocked from its bowl the refuse gray,
And laid it tenderly away;
Then roused himself to safely cover 600
The dull red brands with ashes over.
And while, with care, our mother laid
The work aside, her steps she stayed
One moment, seeking to express
Her grateful sense of happiness
For food and shelter, warmth and health,
And love's contentment more than wealth,
With simple wishes (not the weak,
Vain prayers which no fulfilment seek,
But such as warm the generous heart, 610
O'er-prompt to do with Heaven its part)
That none might lack, that bitter night,
For bread and clothing, warmth and light.

Within our beds awhile we heard
The wind that round the gables roared,
With now and then a ruder shock,
Which made our very bedsteads rock.
We heard the loosened clapboards tost,
The board-nails snapping in the frost;
And on us, through the unplastered wall, 620
Felt the light sifted snow-flakes fall.
But sleep stole on, as sleep will do
When hearts are light and life is new;
Faint and more faint the murmurs grew,
Till in the summer-land of dreams
They softened to the sound of streams,
Low stir of leaves, and dip of oars,
And lapsing waves on quiet shores.

Next morn we wakened with the shout
Of merry voices high and clear; 630
And saw the teamsters drawing near
To break the drifted highways out.

Down the long hillside treading slow
We saw the half-buried oxen go,
Shaking the snow from heads uptost,
Their straining nostrils white with frost.
Before our door the straggling train
Drew up, an added team to gain.
The elders threshed their hands a-cold,
   Passed, with the cider-mug, their jokes   640
   From lip to lip; the younger folks
Down the loose snow-banks, wrestling, rolled,
Then toiled again the cavalcade
   O'er windy hill, through clogged ravine,
   And woodland paths that wound between
Low drooping pine-boughs winter-weighed.
From every barn a team afoot,
At every house a new recruit,
Where, drawn by Nature's subtlest law,
Haply the watchful young men saw   650
Sweet doorway pictures of the curls
And curious eyes of merry girls,
Lifting their hands in mock defence
Against the snow-ball's compliments,
And reading in each missive tost
The charm with Eden never lost.

We heard once more the sleigh-bell's sound;
   And, following where the teamsters led,
The wise old Doctor went his round,
Just pausing at our door to say,   660
In the brief autocratic way
Of one who, prompt at Duty's call,
Was free to urge her claim on all,
   That some poor neighbor sick abed
At night our mother's aid would need.
For, one in generous thought and deed,
   What mattered in the sufferer's sight
   The Quaker matron's inward light,
The Doctor's mail of Calvin's creed?
All hearts confess the saints elect   670
   Who, twain in faith, in love agree,

And melt not in an acid sect
   The Christian pearl of charity!

So days went on: a week had passed
Since the great world was heard from last.
The Almanac we studied o'er,
Read and reread our little store
Of books and pamphlets, scarce a score;
One harmless novel, mostly hid
From younger eyes, a book forbid,   680
And poetry, (or good or bad,
A single book was all we had,)
Where Ellwood's meek, drab-skirted Muse,
   A stranger to the heathen Nine,
   Sang, with a somewhat nasal whine,
The wars of David and the Jews.
At last the floundering carrier bore
The village paper to our door.
Lo! broadening outward as we read,
To warmer zones the horizon spread;   690
In panoramic length unrolled
We saw the marvels that it told.
Before us passed the painted Creeks,
   And daft McGregor on his raids
   In Costa Rica's everglades.
And up Taygetos winding slow
Rode Ypsilanti's Mainote Greeks,
A Turk's head at each saddle-bow!
Welcome to us its week-old news,
Its corner for the rustic Muse,   700
   Its monthly gauge of snow and rain,
Its record, mingling in a breath
The wedding bell and dirge of death;
Jest, anecdote, and love-lorn tale,
The latest culprit sent to jail;
Its hue and cry of stolen and lost,
Its vendue sales and goods at cost,
   And traffic calling loud for gain.
We felt the stir of hall and street,
The pulse of life that round us beat;   710

The chill embargo of the snow
Was melted in the genial glow;
Wide swung again our ice-locked door,
And all the world was ours once more!

Clasp, Angel of the backward look
    And folded wings of ashen gray
    And voice of echoes far away,
The brazen covers of thy book;
The weird palimpsest old and vast,
Wherein thou hid'st the spectral past;   720
Where, closely mingling, pale and glow
The characters of joy and woe;
The monographs of outlived years,
Or smile-illumed or dim with tears,
    Green hills of life that slope to death,
And haunts of home, whose vistaed trees
Shade off to mournful cypresses
    With the white amaranths underneath.
Even while I look, I can but heed
    The restless sands' incessant fall,   730
Importunate hours that hours succeed,
Each clamorous with its own sharp need,
    And duty keeping pace with all.
Shut down and clasp the heavy lids;
I hear again the voice that bids
The dreamer leave his dream midway
For larger hopes and graver fears:
Life greatens in these later years,
The century's aloe flowers to-day!

Yet, haply, in some lull of life,   740
Some Truce of God which breaks its strife,
The worldling's eyes shall gather dew,
    Dreaming in throngful city ways
Of winter joys his boyhood knew;
And dear and early friends—the few
Who yet remain—shall pause to view
    These Flemish pictures of old days;
Sit with me by the homestead hearth,

And stretch the hands of memory forth
  To warm them at the wood-fire's blaze!   750
And thanks untraced to lips unknown
Shall greet me like the odors blown
From unseen meadows newly mown,
Or lilies floating in some pond,
Wood-fringed, the wayside gaze beyond;
The traveller owns the grateful sense
Of sweetness near, he knows not whence,
And, pausing, takes with forehead bare
The benediction of the air.

LAUS DEO!   [1867]

   It is done!
  Clang of bell and roar of gun
Send the tidings up and down.
   How the belfries rock and reel!
   How the great guns, peal on peal,
Fling the joy from town to town!

   Ring, O bells!
  Every stroke exulting tells
Of the burial hour of crime.
   Loud and long, that all may hear,   10
   Ring for every listening ear
Of Eternity and Time!

   Let us kneel:
  God's own voice is in that peal,
And this spot is holy ground.
   Lord, forgive us! What are we,
   That our eyes this glory see,
That our ears have heard the sound!

   For the Lord
  On the whirlwind is abroad;   20

In the earthquake He has spoken;
  He has smitten with His thunder
  The iron walls asunder,
And the gates of brass are broken!

    Loud and long
  Lift the old exulting song;
Sing with Miriam by the sea,
  He has cast the mighty down;
  Horse and rider sink and drown;
"He hath triumphed gloriously!"   30

    Did we dare,
  In our agony of prayer,
Ask for more than He has done?
  When was ever His right hand
  Over any time or land
Stretched as now beneath the sun?

    How they pale,
  Ancient myth and song and tale,
In this wonder of our days,
  When the cruel rod of war   40
  Blossoms white with righteous law,
And the wrath of man is praise!

    Blotted out!
  All within and all about
Shall a fresher life begin;
  Freer breathe the universe
  As it rolls its heavy curse
On the dead and buried sin!

    It is done!
  In the circuit of the sun   50
Shall the sound thereof go forth.
  It shall bid the sad rejoice,
  It shall give the dumb a voice,
It shall belt with joy the earth!

Ring and swing,
Bells of joy! On morning's wing
Send the song of praise abroad!
With a sound of broken chains
Tell the nations that He reigns,
Who alone is Lord and God!   60

PRELUDE   [1869]

(from "Among the Hills")

Along the roadside, like the flowers of gold
That tawny Incas for their gardens wrought,
Heavy with sunshine droops the goldenrod,
And the red pennons of the cardinal-flowers
Hang motionless upon their upright staves.
The sky is hot and hazy, and the wind,
Wing-weary with its long flight from the south,
Unfelt; yet, closely scanned, yon maple leaf
With faintest motion, as one stirs in dreams,
Confesses it. The locust by the wall   10
Stabs the noon-silence with his sharp alarm.
A single hay-cart down the dusty road
Creaks slowly, with its driver fast asleep
On the load's top. Against the neighboring hill,
Huddled along the stone wall's shady side,
The sheep show white, as if a snowdrift still
Defied the dog-star. Through the open door
A drowsy smell of flowers—gray heliotrope,
And white sweet clover, and shy mignonette—
Comes faintly in, and silent chorus lends   20
To the pervading symphony of peace.

No time is this for hands long over-worn
To task their strength: and (unto Him be praise
Who giveth quietness!) the stress and strain
Of years that did the work of centuries

Have ceased, and we can draw our breath once more
Freely and full. So, as yon harvesters
Make glad their nooning underneath the elms
With tale and riddle and old snatch of song,
I lay aside grave themes, and idly turn   30
The leaves of memory's sketch-book, dreaming o'er
Old summer pictures of the quiet hills,
And human life, as quiet, at their feet.

And yet not idly all. A farmer's son,
Proud of field-lore and harvest craft, and feeling
All their fine possibilities, how rich
And restful even poverty and toil
Become when beauty, harmony, and love
Sit at their humble hearth as angels sat
At evening in the patriarch's tent, when man   40
Makes labor noble, and his farmer's frock
The symbol of a Christian chivalry
Tender and just and generous to her
Who clothes with grace all duty; still, I know
Too well the picture has another side,—
How wearily the grind of toil goes on
Where love is wanting, how the eye and ear
And heart are starved amidst the plenitude
Of nature, and how hard and colorless
Is life without an atmosphere. I look   50
Across the lapse of half a century,
And call to mind old homesteads, where no flower
Told that the spring had come, but evil weeds,
Nightshade and rough-leaved burdock in the place
Of the sweet doorway greeting of the rose
And honeysuckle, where the house walls seemed
Blistering in sun, without a tree or vine
To cast the tremulous shadow of its leaves
Across the curtainless windows, from whose panes
Fluttered the signal rags of shiftlessness.   60
Within, the cluttered kitchen floor, unwashed
(Broom-clean I think they called it); the best room
Stifling with cellar-damp, shut from the air
In hot midsummer, bookless, pictureless

Save the inevitable sampler hung
Over the fireplace, or a mourning piece,
A green-haired woman, peony-cheeked, beneath
Impossible willows; the wide-throated hearth
Bristling with faded pine-boughs half concealing
The piled-up rubbish at the chimney's back;   70
And, in sad keeping with all things about them,
Shrill, querulous women, sour and sullen men,
Untidy, loveless, old before their time,
With scarce a human interest save their own
Monotonous round of small economies,
Or the poor scandal of the neighborhood;
Blind to the beauty everywhere revealed,
Treading the May-flowers with regardless feet;
For them the song-sparrow and the bobolink
Sang not, nor winds made music in the leaves;   80
For them in vain October's holocaust
Burned, gold and crimson, over all the hills,
The sacramental mystery of the woods.
Church-goers, fearful of the unseen Powers,
But grumbling over pulpit-tax and pew-rent,
Saving, as shrewd economists, their souls
And winter pork with the least possible outlay
Of salt and sanctity; in daily life
Showing as little actual comprehension
Of Christian charity and love and duty,   90
As if the Sermon on the Mount had been
Outdated like a last year's almanac:
Rich in broad woodlands and in half-tilled fields,
And yet so pinched and bare and comfortless,
The veriest straggler limping on his rounds,
The sun and air his sole inheritance,
Laughed at a poverty that paid its taxes,
And hugged his rags in self-complacency!

Not such should be the homesteads of a land
Where whoso wisely wills and acts may dwell   100
As king and lawgiver, in broad-acred state,
With beauty, art, taste, culture, books, to make
His hour of leisure richer than a life

Of fourscore to the barons of old time,
Our yeoman should be equal to his home
Set in the fair, green valleys, purple walled,
A man to match his mountains, not to creep
Dwarfed and abased below them. I would fain
In this light way (of which I needs must own
With the knife-grinder of whom Canning sings,   110
"Story, God bless you! I have none to tell you!")
Invite the eye to see and heart to feel
The beauty and the joy within their reach,—
Home, and home loves, and the beatitudes
Of nature free to all. Haply in years
That wait to take the places of our own,
Heard where some breezy balcony looks down
On happy homes, or where the lake in the moon
Sleeps dreaming of the mountains, fair as Ruth,
In the old Hebrew pastoral, at the feet   120
Of Boaz, even this simple lay of mine
May seem the burden of a prophecy,
Finding its late fulfilment in a change
Slow as the oak's growth, lifting manhood up
Through broader culture, finer manners, love,
And reverence, to the level of the hills.

O Golden Age, whose light is of the dawn,
And not of sunset, forward, not behind,
Flood the new heavens and earth, and with thee bring
All the old virtues, whatsoever things   130
Are pure and honest and of good repute,
But add thereto whatever bard has sung
Or seer has told of when in trance and dream
They saw the Happy Isles of prophecy!
Let Justice hold her scale, and Truth divide
Between the right and wrong; but give the heart
The freedom of its fair inheritance;
Let the poor prisoner, cramped and starved so long,
At Nature's table feast his ear and eye
With joy and wonder; let all harmonies   140
Of sound, form, color, motion, wait upon
The princely guest, whether in soft attire

Of leisure clad, or the coarse frock of toil,
And, lending life to the dead form of faith,
Give human nature reverence for the sake
Of One who bore it, making it divine
With the ineffable tenderness of God;
Let common need, the brotherhood of prayer,
The heirship of an unknown destiny,
The unsolved mystery round about us, make   150
A man more precious than the gold of Ophir.
Sacred, inviolate, unto whom all things
Should minister, as outward types and signs
Of the eternal beauty which fulfils
The one great purpose of creation, Love,
The sole necessity of Earth and Heaven!

AT LAST   [1883]

When on my day of life the night is falling,
    And, in the winds from unsunned spaces blown,
I hear far voices out of darkness calling
    My feet to paths unknown,

Thou who hast made my home of life so pleasant,
    Leave not its tenant when its walls decay;
O Love Divine, O Helper ever present,
    Be Thou my strength and stay!

Be near me when all else is from me drifting:
    Earth, sky, home's pictures, days of shade and shine,   10
And kindly faces to my own uplifting
    The love which answers mine.

I have but Thee, my Father! let Thy spirit
    Be with me then to comfort and uphold;
No gate of pearl, no branch of palm I merit,
    Nor street of shining gold.

Suffice it if—my good and ill unreckoned,
  And both forgiven through Thy abounding grace—
I find myself by hands familiar beckoned
  Unto my fitting place.   20

Some humble door among Thy many mansions,
  Some sheltering shade where sin and striving cease,
And flows forever through heaven's green expansions
  The river of Thy peace.

There, from the music round about me stealing,
  I fain would learn the new and holy song,
And find at last, beneath Thy trees of healing,
  The life for which I long.

Edgar Allan Poe

1809–1849

Born January 19, 1809, in Boston to strolling actors, Edgar Allan Poe lost both parents before he reached the age of three. Taken into the home of a Richmond, Virginia, merchant, John Allan (whose surname he adopted as his middle name), Poe lived in England (1815–1820), studied briefly at the University of Virginia, served in the United States Army, and was admitted to and dismissed from West Point (1831). His literary career as poet, short story writer, critic, literary theorist, editor, and journalist took him to New York, Richmond, Philadelphia, and Baltimore. During most of his life he was plagued by ill health, alcoholism, and poverty. He died of undetermined causes in Baltimore, October 7, 1849.

TAMERLANE   [1827]

Kind solace in a dying hour!
    Such, father, is not (now) my theme—
I will not madly deem that power
        Of Earth may shrive me of the sin
        Unearthly pride hath revell'd in—
    I have no time to dote or dream:
You call it hope—that fire of fire!
It is but agony of desire:
If I *can* hope—oh, God! I can—
    Its fount is holier—more divine—   10
I would not call thee fool, old man,
    But such is not a gift of thine.

Know thou the secret of a spirit
  Bow'd from its wild pride into shame.
O yearning heart! I did inherit
  Thy withering portion with the fame,
The searing glory which hath shone
Amid the jewels of my throne,
Halo of Hell! and with a pain
Not Hell shall make me fear again—   20
O craving heart, for the lost flowers
And sunshine of my summer hours!
The undying voice of that dead time,
With its interminable chime,
Rings, in the spirit of a spell,
Upon thy emptiness—a knell.

I have not always been as now:
The fever'd diadem on my brow
  I claim'd and won usurpingly—
Hath not the same fierce heirdom given   30
  Rome to the Cæsar—this to me?
  The heritage of a kingly mind,
And a proud spirit which hath striven
    Triumphantly with human kind.

On mountain soil I first drew life:
  The mists of the Taglay have shed
  Nightly their dews upon my head,
And, I believe, the winged strife
And tumult of the headlong air
Have nestled in my very hair.   40

So late from Heaven—that dew—it fell
  ('Mid dreams of an unholy night)
Upon me with the touch of Hell,
  While the red flashing of the light
From clouds that hung, like banners, o'er,
  Appeared to my half-closing eye
  The pageantry of monarchy,
And the deep trumpet-thunder's roar
  Came hurriedly upon me, telling

    Of human battle, where my voice,   50
  My own voice, silly child! was swelling
    (O! how my spirit would rejoice,
And leap within me at the cry)
The battle-cry of Victory!

The rain came down upon my head
  Unshelter'd—and the heavy wind
    Rendered me mad and deaf and blind.
It was but man, I thought, who shed
Laurels upon me: and the rush,
  The torrent of the chilly air   60
Gurgled within my ear the crush
  Of empires—with the captive's prayer—
The hum of suitors—and the tone
Of flattery 'round a sovereign's throne.

My passions, from that hapless hour,
  Usurp'd a tyranny which men
Have deem'd, since I have reach'd to power,
    My innate nature—be it so:
  But, father, there liv'd one who, then,
Then—in my boyhood—when their fire   70
    Burn'd with a still intenser glow
(For passion must, with youth, expire)
  E'en *then* who knew this iron heart
  In woman's weakness had a part.

I have no words—alas!—to tell
The loveliness of loving well!
Nor would I now attempt to trace
The more than beauty of a face
Whose lineaments, upon my mind,
Are—shadows on th' unstable wind: 80
Thus I remember having dwelt
  Some page of early lore upon,
With loitering eye, till I have felt
The letters—with their meaning —melt
  To fantasies—with none.

O, she was worthy of all love!
   Love—as in infancy was mine—
'Twas such as angel minds above
   Might envy; her young heart the shrine
On which my every hope and thought   90
   Were incense—then a goodly gift,
     For they were childish and upright—
Pure—as her young example taught:
   Why did I leave it, and, adrift,
     Trust to the fire within, for light?

We grew in age—and love—together—
   Roaming the forest and the wild;
My breast her shield in wintry weather—
   And, when the friendly sunshine smil'd,
And she would mark the opening skies,   100
I saw no Heaven—but in her eyes.

Young Love's first lesson is—the heart:
   For 'mid that sunshine and those smiles,
When, from our little cares apart,
   And laughing at her girlish wiles,
I'd throw me on her throbbing breast,
   And pour my spirit out in tears—
There was no need to speak the rest—
   No need to quiet any fears
Of her—who ask'd no reason why,   110
But turn'd on me her quiet eye!

Yet *more* than worthy of the love
My spirit struggled with, and strove,
When, on the mountain peak, alone,
Ambition lent it a new tone—
I had no being—but in thee:
   The world, and all it did contain
In the earth—the air—the sea—
   Its joy—its little lot of pain
That was new pleasure—the ideal,   120
   Dim, vanities of dreams by night—
And dimmer nothings which were real—

(Shadows—and a more shadowy light!)
Parted upon their misty wings,
    And, so, confusedly, became
      Thine image and—a name—a name!
Two separate—yet most intimate things.

I was ambitious—have you known
    The passion, father? You have not:
A cottager, I mark'd a throne   130
Of half the world as all my own,
    And murmur'd at such lowly lot—
But, just like any other dream,
    Upon the vapor of the dew
My own had past, did not the beam
    Of beauty which did while it thro'
The minute—the hour—the day—oppress
My mind with double loveliness.

We walk'd together on the crown
Of a high mountain which look'd down   140
Afar from its proud natural towers
    Of rock and forest, on the hills—
The dwindled hills! begirt with bowers
    And shouting with a thousand rills.

I spoke to her of power and pride,
    But mystically—in such guise
That she might deem it nought beside
    The moment's converse; in her eyes
I read, perhaps too carelessly,
    A mingled feeling with my own—   150
The flush on her bright cheek, to me
    Seem'd to become a queenly throne
Too well that I should let it be
    Light in the wilderness alone.

I wrapp'd myself in grandeur then
    And donn'd a visionary crown—
      Yet it was not that Fantasy
      Had thrown her mantle over me—

But that, among the rabble—men,
   Lion ambition is chain'd down—   160
And crouches to a keeper's hand—
Not so in deserts where the grand—
The wild—the terrible conspire
With their own breath to fan his fire.

Look 'round thee now on Samarcand!—
   Is she not queen of Earth? her pride
Above all cities? in her hand
   Their destinies? in all beside
Of glory which the world hath known
Stands she not nobly and alone?   170
Falling—her veriest stepping-stone
Shall form the pedestal of a throne—
And who her sovereign? Timour—he
   Whom the astonished people saw
Striding o'er empires haughtily
   A diadem'd outlaw!

O, human love! thou spirit given,
On Earth, of all we hope in Heaven!
Which fall'st into the soil like rain
Upon the Siroc-wither'd plain,   180
And, failing in thy power to bless,
But leav'st the heart a wilderness!
Idea! which bindest life around
With music of so strange a sound
And beauty of so wild a birth—
Farewell! for I have won the Earth.

When Hope, the eagle that tower'd, could see
   No cliff beyond him in the sky,
His pinions were bent droopingly—
   And homeward turn'd his soften'd eye.   190
'Twas sunset: when the sun will part
There comes a sullenness of heart
To him who still would look upon
The glory of the summer sun.
That soul will hate the ev'ning mist

So often lovely, and will list
To the sound of the coming darkness (known
To those whose spirits harken) as one
Who, in a dream of night, *would* fly
But *cannot* from a danger nigh.   200

What tho' the moon—the white moon—
Shed all the splendor of her noon,
Her smile is chilly—and *her* beam,
In that time of dreariness, will seem
(So like you gather in your breath)
A portrait taken after death.
And boyhood is a summer sun
Whose waning is the dreariest one.
For all we live to know is known,
And all we seek to keep hath flown.   210
Let life, then, as the day-flower, fall
With the noon-day beauty—which is all.

I reach'd my home—my home no more—
    For all had flown who made it so.
I pass'd from out its mossy door,
    And, tho' my tread was soft and low,
A voice came from the threshold stone
Of one whom I had earlier known—
    O, I defy thee, Hell, to show
    On beds of fire that burn below,   220
    An humbler heart—a deeper wo.

Father, I firmly do believe—
    I *know*—for Death who comes for me
        From regions of the blest afar,
Where there is nothing to deceive,
        Hath left his iron gate ajar,
    And rays of truth you cannot see
    Are flashing thro' Eternity—
I do believe that Eblis hath
A snare in every human path—   230
Else how, when in the holy grove
I wandered of the idol, Love,

Who daily scents his snowy wings
With incense of burnt offerings
From the most unpolluted things,
Whose pleasant bowers are yet so riven
Above with trellis'd rays from Heaven
No mote may shun—no tiniest fly—
The light'ning of his eagle eye—
How was it that Ambition crept,   240
 Unseen, amid the revels there,
Till growing bold, he laughed and leapt
 In the tangles of Love's very hair?

EVENING STAR   [1827]

'T was noontide of summer,
 And mid-time of night;
And stars, in their orbits,
 Shone pale, thro' the light
Of the brighter, cold moon,
 'Mid planets her slaves,
Herself in the Heavens,
 Her beam on the waves.
 I gaz'd a while
 On her cold smile;   10
Too cold—too cold for me.
 There pass'd, as a shroud,
 A fleecy cloud,
And I turn'd away to thee,
 Proud Evening Star,
 In thy glory afar,
And dearer thy beam shall be;
 For joy to my heart
 Is the proud part
Thou bearest in Heav'n at night,   20
 And more I admire
 Thy distant fire
Than that colder, lowly light.

A DREAM WITHIN A DREAM   [1827]

Take this kiss upon the brow!
And, in parting from you now,
Thus much let me avow—
You are not wrong, who deem
That my days have been a dream;
Yet if Hope has flown away
In a night, or in a day,
In a vision, or in none,
Is it therefore the less *gone*?
All that we see or seem   10
Is but a dream within a dream.

I stand amid the roar
Of a surf-tormented shore,
And I hold within my hand
Grains of the golden sand—
How few! yet how they creep
Through my fingers to the deep,
While I weep—while I weep!
O God! can I not grasp
Them with a tighter clasp?   20
O God! can I not save
One from the pitiless wave?
Is *all* that we see or seem
But a dream within a dream?

SONNET—TO SCIENCE   [1829]

Science! true daughter of Old Time thou art!
    Who alterest all things with thy peering eyes.
Why preyest thou thus upon the poet's heart,
    Vulture, whose wings are dull realities?

How should he love thee? or how deem thee wise,
 Who wouldst not leave him in his wandering
To seek for treasure in the jewelled skies,
 Albeit he soared with an undaunted wing?
Hast thou not dragged Diana from her car?
 And driven the Hamadryad from the wood   10
To seek a shelter in some happier star?
 Hast thou not torn the Naiad from her flood,
The Elfin from the green grass, and from me
The summer dream beneath the tamarind tree?

AL AARAAF [1829]

PART I

O! Nothing earthly save the ray
(Thrown back from flowers) of Beauty's eye,
As in those gardens where the day
Springs from the gems of Circassy—
O! nothing earthly save the thrill
Of melody in woodland rill—
Or (music of the passion-hearted)
Joy's voice so peacefully departed
That, like the murmur in the shell,
Its echo dwelleth and will dwell—   10
Oh, nothing of the dross of ours—
Yet all the beauty—all the flowers
That list our Love, and deck our bowers—
Adorn yon world afar, afar—
The wandering star.

 'T was a sweet time for Nesace—for there
Her world lay lolling on the golden air,
Near four bright suns—a temporary rest—
An oasis in desert of the blest.
Away—away—'mid seas of rays that roll   20
Empyrean splendor o'er th' unchained soul—
The soul that scarce (the billows are so dense)

Can struggle to its destin'd eminence—
To distant spheres, from time to time, she rode,
And late to ours, the favor'd one of God—
But, now, the ruler of an anchor'd realm,
She throws aside the sceptre—leaves the helm,
And, amid incense and high spiritual hymns,
Laves in quadruple light her angel limbs.

Now happiest, loveliest in yon lovely Earth,   30
Whence sprang the "Idea of Beauty" into birth
(Falling in wreaths thro' many a startled star,
Like woman's hair 'mid pearls, until, afar,
It lit on hills Achaian, and there dwelt),
She look'd into Infinity—and knelt.
Rich clouds, for canopies, about her curled—
Fit emblems of the model of her world—
Seen but in beauty—not impeding sight
Of other beauty glittering thro' the light—
A wreath that twined each starry form around,   40
And all the opal'd air in color bound.

All hurriedly she knelt upon a bed
Of flowers: of lilies such as rear'd the head
On the fair Capo Deucato, and sprang
So eagerly around about to hang
Upon the flying footsteps of —deep pride—
Of her who lov'd a mortal—and so died.
The Sephalica, budding with young bees,
Uprear'd its purple stem around her knees:
And gemmy flower, of Trebizond misnam'd—   50
Inmate of highest stars, where erst it sham'd
All other loveliness: its honied dew
(The fabled nectar that the heathen knew)
Deliriously sweet, was dropp'd from Heaven,
And fell on gardens of the unforgiven
In Trebizond—and on a sunny flower
So like its own above, that, to this hour,
It still remaineth, torturing the bee
With madness, and unwonted reverie:
In Heaven, and all its environs, the leaf   60

And blossom of the fairy plant, in grief
Disconsolate linger—grief that hangs her head,
Repenting follies that full long have fled,
Heaving her white breast to the balmy air,
Like guilty beauty, chasten'd, and more fair:
Nyctanthes, too, as sacred as the light
She fears to perfume, perfuming the night:
And Clytia pondering between many a sun,
While pettish tears adown her petals run:
And that aspiring flower that sprang on Earth—   70
And died, ere scarce exalted into birth,
Bursting its odorous heart in spirit to wing
Its way to Heaven, from garden of a king:
And Valisnerian lotus thither flown
From struggling with the waters of the Rhone:
And thy most lovely purple perfume, Zante!
Isola d'oro!—Fior di Levante!
And the Nelumbo bud that floats for ever
With Indian Cupid down the holy river—
Fair flowers, and fairy! to whose care is given   80
To bear the Goddess' song, in odors, up to Heaven:

   "Spirit! that dwellest where,
    In the deep sky,
   The terrible and fair,
    In beauty vie!
  Beyond the line of blue—
    The boundary of the star
  Which turneth at the view
    Of thy barrier and thy bar—
  Of the barrier overgone   90
    By the comets who were cast
  From their pride, and from their throne
    To be drudges till the last—
  To be carriers of fire
    (The red fire of their heart)
  With speed that may not tire
    And with pain that shall not part—
  Who livest—*that* we know—
    In Eternity—we feel—

But the shadow of whose brow   100
    What spirit shall reveal?
Tho' the beings whom thy Nesace,
    Thy messenger, hath known,
Have dream'd for thy Infinity
    A model of their own—
Thy will is done, oh, God!
    The star hath ridden high
Thro' many a tempest, but she rode
    Beneath thy burning eye;
And here, in thought, to thee—   110
    In thought that can alone
Ascend thy empire and so be
    A partner of thy throne—
By winged Fantasy,
    My embassy is given,
Till secrecy shall knowledge be
    In the environs of Heaven."

She ceas'd—and buried then her burning cheek
Abash'd, amid the lilies there, to seek
A shelter from the fervour of His eye;   121
For the stars trembled at the Deity.
She stirr'd not—breath'd not—for a voice was there
How solemnly pervading the calm air!
A sound of silence on the startled ear
Which dreamy poets name "the music of the sphere."
Ours is a world of words: Quiet we call
"Silence"—which is the merest word of all.
All Nature speaks, and ev'n ideal things
Flap shadowy sounds from visionary wings—
But ah! not so when, thus, in realms on high   130
The eternal voice of God is passing by,
And the red winds are withering in the sky!

"What tho' in worlds which sightless cycles run,
Link'd to a little system and one sun—
Where all my love is folly, and the crowd
Still think my terrors but the thunder cloud,
The storm, the earthquake, and the ocean-wrath

(Ah! will they cross me in my angrier path?)
What tho' in worlds which own a single sun
The sands of Time grow dimmer as they run,   140
Yet thine is my resplendency, so given
To bear my secrets thro' the upper Heaven.
Leave tenantless thy crystal home, and fly,
With all thy train, athwart the moony sky—
Apart—like fire-flies in Sicilian night,
And wing to other worlds another light!
Divulge the secrets of thy embassy
To the proud orbs that twinkle—and so be
To ev'ry heart a barrier and a ban
Lest the stars totter in the guilt of man!"   150

   Up rose the maiden in the yellow night,
The single-mooned eve!—on Earth we plight
Our faith to one love—and one moon adore—
The birth-place of young Beauty had no more.
As sprang that yellow star from downy hours
Up rose the maiden from her shrine of flowers,
And bent o'er sheeny mountain and dim plain
Her way—but left not yet her Therasæan reign.

PART II

High on a mountain of enamell'd head—
Such as the drowsy shepherd on his bed   160
Of giant pasturage lying at his ease,
Raising his heavy eyelid, starts and sees
With many a mutter'd "hope to be forgiven,"
What time the moon is quadrated in Heaven—
Of rosy head, that towering far away
Into the sunlit ether, caught the ray
Of sunken suns at eve—at noon of night,
While the moon danc'd with the fair stranger light—
Uprear'd upon such height arose a pile
Of gorgeous columns on th' unburthen'd air,   170
Flashing from Parian marble that twin smile
Far down upon the wave that sparkled there,
And nursled the young mountain in its lair.

Of molten stars their pavement, such as fall
Thro' the ebon air, besilvering the pall
Of their own dissolution, while they die—
Adorning then the dwellings of the sky.
A dome, by linked light from Heaven let down,
Sat gently on these columns as a crown—
A window of one circular diamond, there,   180
Look'd out above into the purple air,
And rays from God shot down that meteor chain
And hallow'd all the beauty twice again,
Save when, between th' Empyrean and that ring,
Some eager spirit flapp'd his dusky wing.
But on the pillars Seraph eyes have seen
The dimness of this world: that greyish green
That Nature loves the best for Beauty's grave
Lurk'd in each cornice, round each architrave—
And every sculptur'd cherub thereabout   190
That from his marble dwelling peeréd out,
Seem'd earthly in the shadow of his niche—
Achaian statues in a world so rich!
Friezes from Tadmor and Persepolis—
From Balbec, and the stilly, clear abyss
Of beautiful Gomorrah! O, the wave
Is now upon thee—but too late to save!

  Sound loves to revel in a summer night:
Witness the murmur of the grey twilight
That stole upon the ear, in Eyraco,   200
Of many a wild star gazer long ago—
That stealeth ever on the ear of him
Who, musing, gazeth on the distance dim,
And sees the darkness coming as a cloud—
Is not its form—its voice—most palpable and loud?

But what is this?—it cometh—and it brings
A music with it—'tis the rush of wings—
A pause—and then a sweeping, falling strain,
And Nesace is in her halls again.
From the wild energy of wanton haste   210
  Her cheeks were flushing, and her lips apart;

And zone that clung around her gentle waist
  Had burst beneath the heaving of her heart.
Within the centre of that hall to breathe
She paus'd and panted, Zanthe! all beneath,
The fairy light that kiss'd her golden hair
And long'd to rest, yet could but sparkle there!

  Young flowers were whispering in melody
To happy flowers that night—and tree to tree;
Fountains were gushing music as they fell   220
In many a star-lit grove, or moon-lit dell;
Yet silence came upon material things—
Fair flowers, bright waterfalls and angel wings—
And sound alone, that from the spirit sprang,
Bore burthen to the charm the maiden sang:

      "'Neath blue-bell or streamer—
        Or tufted wild spray
    That keeps from the dreamer
        The moonbeam away—
    Bright beings! that ponder,   230
        With half closing eyes,
  On the stars which your wonder
        Hath drawn from the skies,
  Till they glance thro' the shade, and
        Come down to your brow
  Like—eyes of the maiden
        Who calls on you now—
  Arise! from your dreaming
        In violet bowers,
  To duty beseeming   240
        These star-litten hours—
  And shake from your tresses,
        Encumber'd with dew,
  The breath of those kisses
        That cumber them too
  (O, how, without you, Love!
        Could angels be blest?)—
  Those kisses of true love
        That lull'd ye to rest!

Up!—shake from your wing   250
    Each hindering thing:
The dew of the night—
    It would weigh down your flight;
And true love caresses—
    O! leave them apart:
They are light on the tresses,
    But lead on the heart.

"Ligeia! Ligeia!
    My beautiful one!
Whose harshest idea   260
    Will to melody run,
O! is it thy will
    On the breezes to toss?
Or, capriciously still,
    Like the lone Albatross,
Incumbent on night
    (As she on the air)
To keep watch with delight
    On the harmony there?

"Ligeia! wherever   270
    Thy image may be,
No magic shall sever
    Thy music from thee.
Thou hast bound many eyes
    In a dreamy sleep—
But the strains shall arise
    Which *thy* vigilance keep:
The sound of the rain
    Which leaps down to the flower,
And dances again   280
    In the rhythm of the shower—
The murmur that springs
    From the growing of grass
Are the music of things—
    But are modell'd, alas!—
Away, then, my dearest,
    O! hie thee away

To springs that lie clearest
    Beneath the moon-ray—
To lone lake that smiles,   290
    In its dream of deep rest,
At the many star-isles
    That enjewel its breast—
Where wild flowers, creeping,
    Have mingled their shade,
On its margin is sleeping
    Full many a maid—
Some have left the cool glade, and
    Have slept with the bee—
Arouse them, my maiden,   300
    On moorland and lea—
Go! breathe on their slumber,
    All softly in ear,
The musical number
    They slumber'd to hear—
For what can awaken
    An angel so soon,
Whose sleep hath been taken
    Beneath the cold moon,
As the spell which no slumber   310
    Of witchery may test,
The rhythmical number
    Which lull'd him to rest?"

Spirits in wing, and angels' to the view,
A thousand seraphs burst th' Empyrean thro',
Young dreams still hovering on their drowsy flight—
Seraphs in all but "Knowledge," the keen light
That fell, refracted, thro' thy bounds, afar
O Death! from eye of God upon that star:
Sweet was that error—sweeter still that death—   320
Sweet was that error—ev'n with *us* the breath
Of Science dims the mirror of our joy—
To them 't were the Simoom, and would destroy—
For what (to them) availeth it to know
That Truth is Falsehood—or that Bliss is Woe?
Sweet was their death—with them to die was rife

With the last ecstasy of satiate life—
Beyond that death no immortality—
But sleep that pondereth and is not "to be"—
And there—oh! may my weary spirit dwell—   330
Apart from Heaven's Eternity—and yet how far from
    Hell!

    What guilty spirit, in what shrubbery dim,
Heard not the stirring summons of that hymn?
But two: they fell: for Heaven no grace imparts
To those who hear not for their beating hearts.
A maiden-angel and her seraph-lover—
O! where (and ye may seek the wide skies over)
Was Love, the blind, near sober Duty known?
Unguided Love hath fallen—'mid "tears of perfect moan."

    He was a goodly spirit—he who fell: 340
A wanderer by moss-y-mantled well—
A gazer on the lights that shine above—
A dreamer in the moonbeam by his love:
What wonder? for each star is eye-like there,
And looks so sweetly down on Beauty's hair;
And they, and ev'ry mossy spring were holy
To his love-haunted heart and melancholy.
The night had found (to him a night of wo)
Upon a mountain crag, young Angelo—
Beetling it bends athwart the solemn sky,   350
And scowls on starry worlds that down beneath it lie.
Here sate he with his love—his dark eye bent
With eagle gaze along the firmament:
Now turn'd it upon her—but ever then
It trembled to the orb of EARTH again.

    "Ianthe, dearest, see! how dim that ray!
How lovely 'tis to look so far away!
She seem'd not thus upon that autumn eve
I left her gorgeous halls—nor mourn'd to leave,
That eve—that eve—I should remember well—   360
The sun-ray dropp'd, in Lemnos, with a spell
On th' Arabesque carving of a gilded hall

Wherein I sate, and on the draperied wall—
And on my eyelids—O the heavy light!
How drowsily it weigh'd them into night!
On flowers, before, and mist, and love they ran
With Persian Saadi in his Gulistan:
But O that light—I slumber'd—Death, the while,
Stole o'er my senses in that lovely isle
So softly that no single silken hair   370
Awoke that slept—or knew that he was there.

    "The last spot of Earth's orb I trod upon
Was a proud temple call'd the Parthenon.
More beauty clung around her column'd wall
Than ev'n thy glowing bosom beats withal,
And when old Time my wing did disenthral—
Thence sprang I—as the eagle from his tower,
And years I left behind me in an hour.
What time upon her airy bounds I hung,
One half the garden of her globe was flung,   380
Unrolling as a chart unto my view—
Tenantless cities of the desert too!
Ianthe, beauty crowded on me then,
And half I wish'd to be again of men."

    "My Angelo! and why of them to be?
A brighter dwelling-place is here for thee,
And greener fields than in yon world above,
And woman's loveliness—and passionate love."

    "But, list, Ianthe! when the air so soft
Fail'd, as my pennon'd spirit leapt aloft,   390
Perhaps my brain grew dizzy—but the world
I left so late was into chaos hurl'd—
Sprang from her station, on the winds apart,
And roll'd, a flame, the fiery Heaven athwart.
Methought, my sweet one, then I ceased to soar,
And fell—not swiftly as I rose before,
But with a downward, tremulous motion thro'
Light, brazen rays, this golden star unto!
Nor long the measure of my falling hours,

For nearest of all stars was thine to ours—   400
Dread star! that came, amid a night of mirth,
A red Dædalion on the timid Earth."

    "We came—and to thy Earth—but not to us
Be given our lady's bidding to discuss:
We came, my love; around, above, below,
Gay fire-fly of the night we come and go,
Nor ask a reason save the angel-nod
She grants to us, as granted by her God—
But, Angelo, than thine grey Time unfurl'd
Never his fairy wing o'er fairier world!   410
Dim was its little disk, and angel eyes
Alone could see the phantom in the skies,
When first Al Aaraaf knew her course to be
Headlong thitherward o'er the starry sea—
But when its glory swell'd upon the sky,
As glowing Beauty's bust beneath man's eye,
We paus'd before the heritage of men,
And thy star trembled—as doth Beauty then!"

    Thus, in discourse, the lovers whiled away
The night that waned and waned and brought no day.   420
They fell: for Heaven to them no hope imparts
Who hear not for the beating of their hearts.

ROMANCE   [1829]

Romance, who loves to nod and sing,
With drowsy head and folded wing,
Among the green leaves as they shake
Far down within some shadowy lake,
To me a painted paroquet
Hath been—a most familiar bird—
Taught me my alphabet to say,
To lisp my very earliest word,

While in the wild wood I did lie,
A child—with a most knowing eye.   10

Of late, eternal Condor years
So shake the very Heaven on high
With tumult as they thunder by,
I have no time for idle cares
Through gazing on the unquiet sky.
And when an hour with calmer wings
Its down upon my spirit flings—
That little time with lyre and rhyme
To while away—forbidden things!
My heart would feel to be a crime   20
Unless it trembled with the strings.

TO HELEN   [1831]

Helen, thy beauty is to me
   Like those Nicéan barks of yore,
That gently, o'er a perfumed sea,
   The weary, way-worn wanderer bore
   To his own native shore.

On desperate seas long wont to roam,
   Thy hyacinth hair, thy classic face,
Thy Naiad airs have brought me home
   To the glory that was Greece,
And the grandeur that was Rome.   10

Lo! in yon brilliant window-niche
   How statue-like I see thee stand,
   The agate lamp within thy hand!
Ah, Psyche, from the regions which
   Are Holy Land!

ISRAFEL   [1831]

> *And the angel Israfel, whose*
> *heart-strings are a lute, and*
> *who has the sweetest voice*
> *of all God's creatures.*—KORAN

In Heaven a spirit doth dwell
  "Whose heart-strings are a lute";
None sing so wildly well
As the angel Israfel,
And the giddy stars (so legends tell),
Ceasing their hymns, attend the spell
  Of his voice, all mute.

Tottering above
  In her highest noon,
  The enamoured moon   10
Blushes with love,
  While, to listen, the red levin
  (With the rapid Pleiads, even,
  Which were seven,)
  Pauses in Heaven.

And they say (the starry choir
  And the other listening things)
That Israfeli's fire
  Is owing to that lyre
  By which he sits and sings—   20
The trembling living wire
  Of those unusual strings

But the skies that angel trod,
  Where deep thoughts are a duty—
Where Love's a grown-up God—
  Where the Houri glances are
Imbued with all the beauty
  Which we worship in a star.

Therefore, thou art not wrong,
  Israfeli, who despisest 30
An unimpassioned song;
To thee the laurels belong,
  Best bard, because the wisest!
Merrily live, and long!

The ecstasies above
  With thy burning measures suit—
Thy grief, thy joy, thy hate, thy love,
  With the fervour of thy lute—
  Well may the stars be mute!

Yes, Heaven is thine; but this 40
  Is a world of sweets and sours;
  Our flowers are merely—flowers,
And the shadow of thy perfect bliss
  Is the sunshine of ours.

If I could dwell
Where Israfel
  Hath dwelt, and he where I,
He might not sing so wildly well
  A mortal melody,
While a bolder note than this might swell 50
  From my lyre within the sky.

THE CITY IN THE SEA   [1831]

Lo! Death has reared himself a throne
In a strange city lying alone
Far down within the dim West,
Where the good and the bad and the worst and the best
Have gone to their eternal rest.
There shrines and palaces and towers
(Time-eaten towers that tremble not!)
Resemble nothing that is ours.

Around, by lifting winds forgot,
Resignedly beneath the sky   10
The melancholy waters lie.

No rays from the holy heaven come down
On the long night-time of that town;
But light from out the lurid sea
Streams up the turrets silently—
Gleams up the pinnacles far and free—
Up domes—up spires—up kingly halls—
Up fanes—up Babylon-like walls—
Up shadowy long-forgotten bowers
Of sculptured ivy and stone flowers—   20
Up many and many a marvellous shrine
Whose wreathéd friezes intertwine
The viol, the violet, and the vine.

Resignedly beneath the sky
The melancholy waters lie.
So blend the turrets and shadows there
That all seem pendulous in air,
While from a proud tower in the town
Death looks gigantically down.

There open fanes and gaping graves   30
Yawn level with the luminous waves;
But not the riches there that lie
In each idol's diamond eye—
Not the gaily-jewelled dead
Tempt the waters from their bed;
For no ripples curl, alas!
Along that wilderness of glass—
No swellings tell that winds may be
Upon some far-off happier sea—
No heavings hint that winds have been   40
On seas less hideously serene.

But lo, a stir is in the air!
The wave—there is a movement there!
As if the towers had thrust aside,

In slightly sinking, the dull tide—
As if their tops had feebly given
A void within the filmy Heaven.
The waves have now a redder glow—
The hours are breathing faint and low—
And when, amid no earthly moans,   50
Down, down that town shall settle hence,
Hell, rising from a thousand thrones,
Shall do it reverence.

THE SLEEPER   [1831]

At midnight, in the month of June,
I stand beneath the mystic moon.
An opiate vapor, dewy, dim
Exhales from out her golden rim,
And, softly dripping, drop by drop,
Upon the quiet mountain top,
Steals drowsily and musically
Into the universal valley.
The rosemary nods upon the grave;
The lily lolls upon the wave;   10
Wrapping the fog about its breast,
The ruin moulders into rest;
Looking like Lethe, see! the lake
A conscious slumber seems to take,
And would not, for the world, awake.
All Beauty sleeps!—and lo! where lies
Irene, with her Destinies!

Oh, lady bright! can it be right—
This window open to the night?
The wanton airs, from the tree-top,   20
Laughingly through the lattice drop—
The bodiless airs, a wizard rout,
Flit through thy chamber in and out,

And wave the curtain canopy
So fitfully—so fearfully—
Above the closed and fringéd lid
'Neath which thy slumb'ring soul lies hid,
That, o'er the floor and down the wall,
Like ghosts the shadows rise and fall!
Oh, lady dear, hast thou no fear?   30
Why and what art thou dreaming here?
Sure thou art come o'er far-off seas,
A wonder to these garden trees!
Strange is thy pallor! strange thy dress!
Strange, above all, thy length of tress,
And this all solemn silentness!

The lady sleeps! Oh, may her sleep,
Which is enduring, so be deep!
Heaven have her in its sacred keep!
This chamber changed for one more holy,   40
This bed for one more melancholy,
I pray to God that she may lie
Forever with unopened eye,
While the pale sheeted ghosts go by!

My love, she sleeps! Oh, may her sleep,
As it is lasting, so be deep!
Soft may the worms about her creep!
Far in the forest, dim and old,
For her may some tall vault unfold—
Some vault that oft hath flung its black   50
And wingéd pannels fluttering back,
Triumphant, o'er the crested palls
Of her grand family funerals—

Some sepulchre, remote, alone,
Against whose portal she hath thrown,
In childhood, many an idle stone—
Some tomb from out whose sounding door
She ne'er shall force an echo more,
Thrilling to think, poor child of sin!
It was the dead who groaned within.   60

LENORE   [1831]

Ah, broken is the golden bowl!—the spirit flown forever!
Let the bell toll!—a saintly soul floats on the Stygian
    river:—
And, Guy de Vere, hast *thou* no tear?—weep now or never
    more!
See! on yon drear and rigid bier low lies thy love, Lenore!
Come, let the burial rite be read—the funeral song be
    sung!—
An anthem for the queenliest dead that ever died so
    young—
A dirge for her the doubly dead in that she died so young.

"Wretches! ye loved her for her wealth, and ye hated her
    for her pride;
And, when she fell in feeble health, ye blessed her—that
    she died:—
How *shall* the ritual, then, be read—the requiem how be
    sung   10
By you—by yours, the evil eye,—by yours, the slanderous
    tongue
That did to death the innocence that died, and died so
    young?"

Peccavimus; yet rave not thus! but let a Sabbath song
Go up to God so solemnly the dead may feel no wrong!
The sweet Lenore hath gone before, with Hope that flew
    beside,
Leaving thee wild for the dear child that should have been
    thy bride—
For her, the fair and debonair, that now so lowly lies,
The life upon her yellow hair, but not within her eyes—
The life still there upon her hair, the death upon her eyes.

"Avaunt!—avaunt! to friends from fiends the indignant
    ghost is riven—   20
From Hell unto a high estate within the utmost Heaven—

From moan and groan to a golden throne beside the King of
    Heaven:—
Let *no* bell toll, then, lest her soul, amid its hallowed mirth,
Should catch the note as it doth float up from the damnéd
    Earth!
And I—tonight my heart is light:—no dirge will I upraise,
But waft the angel on her flight with a Pæan of old days!"

THE VALLEY OF UNREST   [1831]

Once it smiled a silent dell
Where the people did not dwell;
They had gone unto the wars,
Trusting to the mild-eyed stars,
Nightly, from their azure towers,
To keep watch above the flowers,
In the midst of which all day
The red sun-light lazily lay.
Now each visitor shall confess
The sad valley's restlessness.   10
Nothing there is motionless—
Nothing save the airs that brood
Over the magic solitude.
Ah, by no wind are stirred those trees
That palpitate like the chill seas
Around the misty Hebrides!
Ah, by no wind those clouds are driven
That rustle through the unquiet Heaven
Uneasily, from morn till even,
Over the violets there that lie   20
In myriad types of the human eye—
Over the lilies there that wave
And weep above a nameless grave!
They wave:—from out their fragrant tops
Eternal dews come down in drops.
They weep:—from off their delicate stems
Perennial tears descend in gems.

THE COLISEUM   [1845]

Type of the antique Rome! Rich reliquary
Of lofty contemplation left to Time
By buried centuries of pomp and power!
At length—at length—after so many days
Of weary pilgrimage and burning thirst
(Thirst for the springs of lore that in thee lie),
I kneel, an altered and an humble man,
Amid thy shadows, and so drink within
My very soul thy grandeur, gloom, and glory!

Vastness! and Age! and Memories of Eld!   10
Silence! and Desolation! and dim Night!
I feel ye now—I feel ye in your strength—
O spells more sure than e'er Judæan king
Taught in the gardens of Gethsemane!
O charms more potent than the rapt Chaldee
Ever drew down from out the quiet stars!

Here, where a hero fell, a column falls!
Here, where the mimic eagle glared in gold,
A midnight vigil holds the swarthy bat!
Here, where the dames of Rome their gilded hair   20
Waved to the wind, now wave the reed and thistle!
Here, where on golden throne the monarch lolled,
Glides, spectre-like, unto his marble home,
Lit by the wan light of the hornéd moon,
The swift and silent lizard of the stones!

But stay! these walls—these ivy-clad arcades—
These mouldering plinths—these dead and blackened
      shafts—
These vague entablatures—this crumbling frieze—
These shattered cornices—this wreck—this ruin—
These stones—alas! these gray stones—are they all—   30
All of the famed and the colossal left
By the corrosive Hours to Fate and me?

"Not all"—the Echoes answer me—"not all!
Prophetic sounds and loud, arise forever
From us, and from all Ruin, unto the wise,
As melody from Memnon to the Sun.
We rule the hearts of mightiest men—we rule
With a despotic sway all giant minds.
We are not impotent—we pallid stones.
Not all our power is gone—not all our fame—   40
Not all the magic of our high renown—
Not all the wonder that encircles us—
Not all the mysteries that in us lie—
Not all the memories that hang upon
And cling around about us as a garment,
Clothing us in a robe of more than glory."

TO ONE IN PARADISE   [1845]

Thou wast that all to me, love,
    For which my soul did pine—
A green isle in the sea, love,
    A fountain and a shrine,
All wreathed with fairy fruits and flowers,
    And all the flowers were mine.

Ah, dream too bright to last!
    Ah, starry Hope! that didst arise
But to be overcast!
    A voice from out the Future cries,   10
"On! on!"—but o'er the Past
    (Dim gulf!) my spirit hovering lies
Mute, motionless, aghast!

For, alas! alas! with me
    The light of Life is o'er!
No more—no more—no more—
    (Such language holds the solemn sea
To the sands upon the shore)

Shall bloom the thunder-blasted tree,
Or the stricken eagle soar!

And all my days are trances,
    And all my nightly dreams
Are where thy grey eye glances,
    And where thy footstep gleams—
In what ethereal dances,
    By what eternal streams.

THE HAUNTED PALACE   [1845]

In the greenest of our valleys,
    By good angels tenanted,
Once a fair and stately palace—
    Radiant palace—reared its head.
In the monarch Thought's dominion—
    It stood there!
Never seraph spread a pinion
    Over fabric half so fair!

Banners yellow, glorious, golden,
    On its roof did float and flow,   10
(This—all this—was in the olden
    Time long ago,)
And every gentle air that dallied,
    In that sweet day,
Along the ramparts plumed and pallid,
    A wingéd odor went away.

Wanderers in that happy valley,
    Through two luminous windows, saw
Spirits moving musically
    To a lute's well-tunéd law,   20
Round about a throne where, sitting,
    Porphyrogene!
In state his glory well befitting,
    The ruler of the realm was seen.

And all with pearl and ruby glowing
   Was the fair palace door,
Through which came flowing, flowing, flowing,
   And sparkling evermore,
A troop of Echoes, whose sweet duty
   Was but to sing,   30
In voices of surpassing beauty,
   The wit and wisdom of their king.

But evil things, in robes of sorrow,
   Assailed the monarch's high estate.
(Ah, let us mourn!—for never morrow
   Shall dawn upon him, desolate!)
And round about his home the glory
   That blushed and bloomed,
Is but a dim-remembered story
   Of the old time entombed.   40

And travellers, now, within that valley,
   Through the red-litten windows see
Vast forms that move fantastically
   To a discordant melody,
While, like a ghastly rapid river,
   Through the pale door
A hideous throng rush out forever,
   And laugh—but smile no more.

SONNET—SILENCE   [1845]

There are some qualities—some incorporate things,
   That have a double life, which thus is made
A type of that twin entity which springs
   From matter and light, evinced in solid and shade.
There is a two-fold *Silence*—sea and shore—
   Body and soul. One dwells in lonely places,
   Newly with grass o'ergrown; some solemn graces,
Some human memories and tearful lore,

Render him terrorless: his name's "No More."
He is the corporate Silence: dread him not!   10
    No power hath he of evil in himself;
But should some urgent fate (untimely lot!)
    Bring thee to meet his shadow (nameless elf,
That haunteth the lone regions where hath trod
No foot of man), commend thyself to God!

THE CONQUEROR WORM   [1845]

Lo! 't is a gala night
    Within the lonesome latter years!
An angel throng, bewinged, bedight
    In veils, and drowned in tears,
Sit in a theatre, to see
    A play of hopes and fears,
While the orchestra breathes fitfully
    The music of the spheres.

Mimes, in the form of God on high,
    Mutter and mumble low,   10
And hither and thither fly—
    Mere puppets they, who come and go
At bidding of vast formless things
    That shift the scenery to and fro,
Flapping from out their Condor wings
    Invisible Wo!

That motley drama—oh, be sure
    It shall not be forgot!
With its Phantom chased for evermore
    By a crowd that seize it not,   20
Through a circle that ever returneth in
    To the self-same spot,
And much of Madness, and more of Sin,
    And Horror the soul of the plot.

But see, amid the mimic rout,
   A crawling shape intrude!
A blood-red thing that writhes from out
   The scenic solitude!
It writhes!—it writhes!—with mortal pangs
   The mimes become its food,   30
And seraphs sob at vermin fangs
   In human gore imbued.

Out—out are the lights—out all!
   And, over each quivering form,
The curtain, a funeral pall,
   Comes down with the rush of a storm,
While the angels, all pallid and wan,
   Uprising, unveiling, affirm
That the play is the tragedy, "Man,"
   And its hero, the Conqueror Worm.   40

DREAM-LAND   [1845]

   By a route obscure and lonely,
   Haunted by ill angels only,
   Where an Eidolon, named NIGHT,
   On a black throne reigns upright,
   I have reached these lands but newly
   From an ultimate dim Thule—
From a wild weird clime that lieth, sublime,
      Out of SPACE—out of TIME.

   Bottomless vales and boundless floods,
   And chasms, and caves, and Titan woods,   10
   With forms that no man can discover
   For the tears that drip all over;
   Mountains toppling evermore
   Into seas without a shore;
   Seas that restlessly aspire,
   Surging, unto skies of fire;

Lakes that endlessly outspread
Their lone waters, lone and dead,—
Their still waters, still and chilly
With the snows of the lolling lily.   20

By the lakes that thus outspread
Their lone waters, lone and dead,—
Their sad waters, sad and chilly
With the snows of the lolling lily,—
By the mountains—near the river
Murmuring lowly, murmuring ever,—
By the grey woods,—by the swamp
Where the toad and the newt encamp,—
By the dismal tarns and pools
   Where dwell the Ghouls,—   30
By each spot the most unholy—
In each nook most melancholy,—
There the traveller meets, aghast,
Sheeted Memories of the Past—
Shrouded forms that start and sigh
As they pass the wanderer by—
White-robed forms of friends long given,
In agony, to the Earth—and Heaven.

For the heart whose woes are legion
'T is a peaceful, soothing region—   40
For the spirit that walks in shadow
'T is—oh, 't is an Eldorado!
But the traveller, travelling through it,
May not—dare not openly view it;
Never its mysteries are exposed
To the weak human eye unclosed;
So wills its King, who hath forbid
The uplifting of the fringéd lid;
And thus the sad Soul that here passes
Beholds it but through darkened glasses.   50

By a route obscure and lonely,
Haunted by ill angels only,
Where an Eidolon, named Night,

On a black throne reigns upright,
I have wandered home but newly
From this ultimate dim Thule.

THE RAVEN   [1845]

Once upon a midnight dreary, while I pondered, weak and
    weary,
Over many a quaint and curious volume of forgotten
    lore—
While I nodded, nearly napping, suddenly there came a
    tapping,
As of some one gently rapping, rapping at my chamber
    door.
"'T is some visitor," I muttered, "tapping at my chamber
    door—
                    Only this and nothing more."

Ah, distinctly I remember it was in the bleak December;
And each separate dying ember wrought its ghost upon the
    floor.
Eagerly I wished the morrow;—vainly I had sought to
    borrow
From my books surcease of sorrow—sorrow for the lost
    Lenore—   10
For the rare and radiant maiden whom the angels name
    Lenore—
                    Nameless *here* for evermore.

And the silken, sad, uncertain rustling of each purple curtain
Thrilled me—filled me with fantastic terrors never felt
    before;
So that now, to still the beating of my heart, I stood repeating,
"'T is some visitor entreating entrance at my chamber
    door—
Some late visitor entreating entrance at my chamber
    door;—
                    This it is and nothing more."

Presently my soul grew stronger; hesitating then no
    longer,
"Sir," said I, "or Madam, truly your forgiveness I
    implore;   20
But the fact is I was napping, and so gently you came
    rapping,
And so faintly you came tapping, tapping at my chamber
    door,
That I scarce was sure I heard you"—here I opened wide
    the door;—
                    Darkness there and nothing more.

Deep into that darkness peering, long I stood there
    wondering, fearing,
Doubting, dreaming dreams no mortal ever dared to dream
    before;
But the silence was unbroken, and the stillness gave no
    token,
And the only word there spoken was the whispered word,
    "Lenore?"
This I whispered, and an echo murmured back the word,
    "Lenore!"
                    Merely this and nothing more.   30

Back into the chamber turning, all my soul within me
    burning,
Soon again I heard a tapping somewhat louder than
    before.
"Surely," said I, "Surely that is something at my window
    lattice;
Let me see, then, what thereat is, and this mystery
    explore—
Let my heart be still a moment and this mystery ex-
    plore;—
                  'T is the wind and nothing more!"

Open here I flung the shutter, when, with many a flirt and
    flutter,
In there stepped a stately Raven of the saintly days of
    yore;

Not the least obeisance made he; not a minute stopped or
    stayed he;
But, with mien of lord or lady, perched above my chamber
    door—   40
Perched upon a bust of Pallas just above my chamber
    door—
                    Perched, and sat, and nothing more.

Then this ebony bird beguiling my sad fancy into smiling,
By the grave and stern decorum of the countenance it
    wore,
"Though thy crest be shorn and shaven, thou," I said,
    "art sure no craven,
Ghastly grim and ancient Raven wandering from
    the Nightly shore—
Tell me what thy lordly name is on the Night's Plutonian
    shore!"
                    Quoth the Raven, "Nevermore."

Much I marvelled this ungainly fowl to hear discourse so
    plainly,
Though its answer little meaning—little relevancy bore;   50
For we cannot help agreeing that no living human being
Ever yet was blessed with seeing bird above his chamber
    door—
Bird or beast upon the sculptured bust above his chamber
    door,
                    With such name as "Nevermore."

But the Raven, sitting lonely on the placid bust, spoke
    only
That one word, as if his soul in that one word he did
    outpour.
Nothing farther then he uttered—not a feather then he
    fluttered—
Till I scarcely more than muttered, "Other friends have
    flown before—
On the morrow *he* will leave me, as my Hopes have flown
    before."
                    Then the bird said, "Nevermore." 60

Startled at the stillness broken by reply so aptly spoken,
"Doubtless," said I, "what it utters is its only stock and
    store
Caught from some unhappy master whom unmerciful
    Disaster
Followed fast and followed faster till his songs one burden
    bore—
Till the dirges of his Hope that melancholy burden
    bore
                    Of 'Never—nevermore.'"

But the Raven still beguiling my sad fancy into smiling,
Straight I wheeled a cushioned seat in front of bird and bust
    and door;
Then, upon the velvet sinking, I betook myself to linking
Fancy unto fancy, thinking what this ominous bird of
    yore—   70
What this grim, ungainly, ghastly, gaunt, and ominous bird
    of yore
                    Meant in croaking "Nevermore."

This I sat engaged in guessing, but no syllable expressing
To the fowl whose fiery eyes now burned into my bosom's
    core;
This and more I sat divining, with my head at ease
    reclining
On the cushion's velvet lining that the lamp-light gloated
    o'er,
But whose velvet-violet lining with the lamp-light gloating
    o'er,
                    She shall press, ah, nevermore!

Then, methought, the air grew denser, perfumed from an
    unseen censer
Swung by seraphim whose foot-falls tinkled on the tufted
    floor.   80
"Wretch," I cried, "thy God hath lent thee—by these angels
    he hath sent thee
Respite—respite and nepenthe from thy memories of
    Lenore;

Quaff, oh, quaff this kind nepenthe and forget this lost
    Lenore!"
                        Quoth the Raven, "Nevermore."

"Prophet!" said I, "thing of evil!—prophet still, if bird or
    devil!—
Whether Tempter sent, or whether tempest tossed thee here
    ashore,
Desolate yet all undaunted, on this desert land enchanted—
On this home by Horror haunted—tell me truly, I
    implore—
Is there—*is* there balm in Gilead?—tell me—tell me, I
    implore!"
                        Quoth the Raven, "Nevermore."   90

"Prophet!" said, I, "thing of evil!—prophet still, if bird or
    devil!
By that Heaven that bends above us—by that God we both
    adore—
Tell this soul with sorrow laden if, within the distant Aidenn,
It shall clasp a sainted maiden whom the angels name
    Lenore—
Clasp a rare and radiant maiden whom the angels name
    Lenore."
                        Quoth the Raven, "Nevermore."

"Be that word our sign of parting, bird or fiend!" I
    shrieked, upstarting—
"Get thee back into the tempest and the Night's Plutonian
    shore!
Leave no black plume as a token of that lie thy soul hath
    spoken!
Leave my loneliness unbroken!—quit the bust above my
    door!   100
Take thy beak from out my heart, and take thy form from
    off my door!"
                        Quoth the Raven, "Nevermore."

And the Raven, never flitting, still is sitting, *still* is sitting
On the pallid bust of Pallas just above my chamber door;

And his eyes have all the seeming of a demon's that is
    dreaming,
And the lamp-light o'er him streaming throws his shadow
    on the floor;
And my soul from out that shadow that lies floating on the
    floor
                 Shall be lifted—nevermore!

ULALUME—A BALLAD   [1850]

The skies they were ashen and sober;
    The leaves they were crispéd and sere—
    The leaves they were withering and sere:
It was night, in the lonesome October
    Of my most immemorial year:
It was hard by the dim lake of Auber,
    In the misty mid region of Weir—
It was down by the dank tarn of Auber,
    In the ghoul-haunted woodland of Weir.

Here once, through an alley Titanic,   10
    Of cypress, I roamed with my Soul—
    Of cypress, with Psyche, my Soul.
These were days when my heart was volcanic
    As the scoriac rivers that roll—
    As the lavas that restlessly roll
Their sulphurous currents down Yaanek
    In the ultimate climes of the Pole—
That groan as they roll down Mount Yaanek
    In the realms of the Boreal Pole.

Our talk had been serious and sober,   20
    But our thoughts they were palsied and sere—
    Our memories were treacherous and sere—
For we knew not the month was October,
    And we marked not the night of the year
    (Ah, night of all nights in the year!)—
We noted not the dim lake of Auber

(Though once we had journeyed down here)—
We remembered not the dank tarn of Auber.
    Nor the ghoul-haunted woodland of Weir.

And now, as the night was senescent   30
    And star-dials pointed to morn—
    As the star-dials hinted of morn—
At the end of our path a liquescent
    And nebulous lustre was born,
Out of which a miraculous crescent
    Arose with a duplicate horn—
Astarte's bediamonded crescent
    Distinct with its duplicate horn.

And I said: "She is warmer than Dian;
    She rolls through an ether of sighs—   40
    She revels in a region of sighs.
She has seen that the tears are not dry on
    These cheeks, where the worm never dies,
And has come past the stars of the Lion,
    To point us the path to the skies—
    To the Lethean peace of the skies—
Come up, in despite of the Lion,
    To shine on us with her bright eyes—
Come up through the lair of the Lion,
    With love in her luminous eyes."   50

But Psyche, uplifting her finger,
    Said: "Sadly this star I mistrust—
    Her pallor I strangely mistrust:
Ah, hasten!—ah, let us not linger!
    Ah, fly!—let us fly!—for we must."
In terror she spoke, letting sink her
    Wings until they trailed in the dust—
In agony sobbed, letting sink her
    Plumes till they trailed in the dust—
    Till they sorrowfully trailed in the dust.   60

I replied: "This is nothing but dreaming:
    Let us on by this tremulous light!

Let us bathe in this crystalline light!
Its Sibyllic splendor is beaming
    With Hope and in Beauty to-night:—
    See!—it flickers up the sky through the night!
Ah, we safely may trust to its gleaming,
    And be sure it will lead us aright—
We surely may trust to a gleaming,
    That cannot but guide us aright,   70
    Since it flickers up to Heaven through the night."

Thus I pacified Psyche and kissed her,
    And tempted her out of her gloom—
    And conquered her scruples and gloom;
And we passed to the end of the vista,
    But were stopped by the door of a tomb—
    By the door of a legended tomb;
And I said—"What is written, sweet sister,
    On the door of this legended tomb?"
    She replied: "Ulalume—Ulalume!—   80
    'Tis the vault of thy lost Ulalume!"

Then my heart it grew ashen and sober
    As the leaves that were crispéd and sere—
    As the leaves that were withering and sere;
And I cried: "It was surely October
    On *this* very night of last year
    That I journeyed—I journeyed down here!—
    That I brought a dread burden down here—
    On this night of all nights in the year,
    Ah, what demon has tempted me here?   90
Well I know, now, this dim lake of Auber—
    This misty mid region of Weir—
Well I know, now, this dank tarn of Auber,
    This ghoul-haunted woodland of Weir."

Said we, then—the two, then: "Ah, can it
    Have been that the woodlandish ghouls—
    The pitiful, the merciful ghouls—
To bar up our way and to ban it

From the secret that lies in these wolds—
From the thing that lies hidden in these wolds—   100
Have drawn up the spectre of a planet
From the limbo of lunary souls—
This sinfully scintillant planet
From the Hell of the planetary souls?"

ELDORADO   [1850]

Gaily bedight,
A gallant knight,
In sunshine and in shadow,
Had journeyed long,
Singing a song,
In search of Eldorado.

But he grew old—
This knight so bold—
And o'er his heart a shadow
Fell as he found   10
No spot of ground
That looked like Eldorado.

And, as his strength
Failed him at length,
He met a pilgrim shadow—
"Shadow," said he,
"Where can it be—
This land of Eldorado?"

"Over the Mountains
Of the Moon,
Down the Valley of the Shadow,   20
Ride, boldly ride,"
The shade replied,—
"If you seek for Eldorado!"

FOR ANNIE   [1850]

Thank Heaven! the crisis,
    The danger, is past,
And the lingering illness
    Is over at last—
And the fever called "Living"
    Is conquered at last.

Sadly, I know
    I am shorn of my strength,
And no muscle I move
    As I lie at full length—   10
But no matter!—I feel
    I am better at length.

And I rest so composedly,
    Now, in my bed,
That any beholder
    Might fancy me dead—
Might start at beholding me,
    Thinking me dead.

The moaning and groaning,
    The sighing and sobbing,   20
Are quieted now,
    With that horrible throbbing
At heart:—ah, that horrible,
    Horrible throbbing!

The sickness—the nausea—
    The pitiless pain—
Have ceased, with the fever
    That maddened my brain—
With the fever called "Living"
    That burned in my brain.   30

And oh! of all tortures
 That torture the worst
Has abated—the terrible
 Torture of thirst
For the naphthaline river
 Of Passion accurst:—
I have drank of a water
 That quenches all thirst:—

Of a water that flows,
 With a lullaby sound,   40
From a spring but a very few
 Feet under ground—
From a cavern not very far
 Down under ground.

And ah! let it never
 Be foolishly said
That my room it is gloomy
 And narrow my bed;
For man never slept
 In a different bed—   50
And, to *sleep*, you must slumber
 In just such a bed.

My tantalized spirit
 Here blandly reposes,
Forgetting, or never
 Regretting, its roses—
Its old agitations
 Of myrtles and roses:

For now, while so quietly
 Lying, it fancies   60
A holier odor
 About it, of pansies—
A rosemary odor,
 Commingled with pansies—
With rue and the beautiful
 Puritan pansies.

And so it lies happily,
  Bathing in many
A dream of the truth
  And the beauty of Annie—   70
Drowned in a bath
  Of the tresses of Annie.

She tenderly kissed me,
  She fondly caressed,
And then I fell gently
  To sleep on her breast—
Deeply to sleep
  From the heaven of her breast.

When the light was extinguished,
  She covered me warm,   80
And she prayed to the angels
  To keep me from harm—
To the queen of the angels
  To shield me from harm.

And I lie so composedly,
  Now, in my bed,
(Knowing her love),
  That you fancy me dead—
And I rest so contentedly,
  Now, in my bed   90
(With her love at my breast),
  That you fancy me dead—
That you shudder to look at me,
  Thinking me dead:—

But my heart it is brighter
  Than all of the many
Stars in the sky,
  For it sparkles with Annie—
It glows with the light
  Of the love of my Annie—   100
With the thought of the light
  Of the eyes of my Annie.

TO MY MOTHER   [1850]

Because I feel that, in the Heavens above,
　　The angels, whispering to one another,
Can find, among their burning terms of love,
　　None so devotional as that of "Mother,"
Therefore by that dear name I long have called you—
　　You who are more than mother unto me,
And fill my heart of hearts, where Death installed you
　　In setting my Virginia's spirit free.
My mother—my own mother, who died early,
　　Was but the mother of myself; but you   10
Are mother to the one I loved so dearly,
　　And thus are dearer than the mother I knew
By that infinity with which my wife
　　Was dearer to my soul than its soul-life.

ANNABEL LEE   [1850]

It was many and many a year ago,
　　　In a kingdom by the sea,
That a maiden there lived whom you may know
　　　By the name of Annabel Lee;
And this maiden she lived with no other thought
　　　Than to love and be loved by me.

She was a child and *I* was a child,
　　　In this kingdom by the sea,
But we loved with a love that was more than love—
　　　I and my Annabel Lee—   10
With a love that the wingéd seraphs of Heaven
　　　Coveted her and me.

And this was the reason that, long ago,
　　　In this kingdom by the sea,

A wind blew out of a cloud by night
    Chilling my Annabel Lee;
So that her highborn kinsmen came
    And bore her away from me,
To shut her up in a sepulchre
    In this kingdom by the sea.   20

The angels, not half so happy in Heaven,
    Went envying her and me:—
Yes!—that was the reason (as all men know,
    In this kingdom by the sea)
That the wind came out of the cloud, chilling
    And killing my Annabel Lee.

But our love it was stronger by far than the love
    Of those who were older than we—
    Of many far wiser than we—
And neither the angels in Heaven above   30
    Nor the demons down under the sea,
Can ever dissever my soul from the soul
    Of the beautiful Annabel Lee:—

For the moon never beams, without bringing me dreams
    Of the beautiful Annabel Lee;
And the stars never rise but I see the bright eyes
    Of the beautiful Annabel Lee:
And so, all the night-tide, I lie down by the side
Of my darling, my darling, my life and my bride,
    In the sepulchre there by the sea—   40
    In her tomb by the side of the sea.

Oliver Wendell Holmes

1809–1894

Born August 29, 1809, at Cambridge, Massachusetts, Oliver Wendell Holmes was educated at Phillips Academy and Harvard. He studied law briefly, then medicine in Europe and at Harvard. For nearly thirty-five years he taught anatomy and physiology at the Harvard Medical School. Concurrently a man of letters, he wrote poetry and fiction, delivered lectures on English poetry, and delighted readers of the Atlantic Monthly *with the* Autocrat *papers. He died in Boston, October 7, 1894.*

THE BALLAD OF THE OYSTERMAN   [1836]

It was a tall young oysterman lived by the river-side,
His shop was just upon the bank, his boat was on the tide;
The daughter of a fisherman, that was so straight and slim,
Lived over on the other bank, right opposite to him.

It was the pensive oysterman that saw a lovely maid,
Upon a moonlight evening, a-sitting in the shade;
He saw her wave her handkerchief, as much as if to say,
"I'm wide awake, young oysterman, and all the folks
  away."

Then up arose the oysterman, and to himself said he,
"I guess I'll leave the skiff at home, for fear that folks
  should see;
I read it in the story-book, that, for to kiss his dear,
Leander swam the Hellespont,—and I will swim this here."

And he has leaped into the waves, and crossed the shining
    stream,
And he has clambered up the bank, all in the moonlight
    gleam;
O there were kisses sweet as dew, and words as soft as
    rain,—
But they have heard her father's step, and in he leaps again!

Out spoke the ancient fisherman,—"O what was that, my
    daughter?"
"'T was nothing but a pebble, sir, I threw into the water."
"And what is that, pray tell me, love, that paddles off so
    fast?"
"It's nothing but a porpoise, sir, that's been a-swimming
    past."   20

Out spoke the ancient fisherman,—"Now bring me my
    harpoon!
I'll get into my fishing-boat, and fix the fellow soon."
Down fell that pretty innocent, as falls a snow-white lamb,
Her hair drooped round her pallid cheeks, like seaweed on
    a clam.

Alas for those two loving ones! she waked not from her
    swound,
And he was taken with the cramp, and in the waves was
    drowned;
But Fate has metamorphosed them, in pity of their woe,
And now they keep an oyster-shop for mermaids down
    below.

OLD IRONSIDES   [1836]

Ay, tear her tattered ensign down!
    Long has it waved on high,
And many an eye has danced to see
    That banner in the sky;

Beneath it rung the battle shout,
   And burst the cannon's roar;—
The meteor of the ocean air
   Shall sweep the clouds no more.

Her deck, once red with heroes' blood,
   Where knelt the vanquished foe,   10
When winds were hurrying o'er the flood,
   And waves were white below,
No more shall feel the victor's tread,
   Or know the conquered knee;—
The harpies of the shore shall pluck
   The eagle of the sea!

Oh, better that her shattered hulk
   Should sink beneath the wave;
Her thunders shook the mighty deep,
   And there should be her grave;   20
Nail to the mast her holy flag,
   Set every threadbare sail,
And give her to the god of storms,
   The lightning and the gale!

THE LAST LEAF   [1836]

I saw him once before,
As he passed by the door,
   And again
The pavement stones resound,
As he totters o'er the ground
   With his cane.

They say that in his prime,
Ere the pruning-knife of Time
   Cut him down,
Not a better man was found   10
By the Crier on his round
   Through the town.

But now he walks the streets,
And he looks at all he meets
    Sad and wan,
And he shakes his feeble head,
That it seems as if he said,
    "They are gone."

The mossy marbles rest
On the lips that he has prest   20
    In their bloom,
And the names he loved to hear
Have been carved for many a year
    On the tomb.

My grandmamma has said—
Poor old lady, she is dead
    Long ago—
That he had a Roman nose,
And his cheek was like a rose
    In the snow;   30

But now his nose is thin,
And it rests upon his chin
    Like a staff,
And a crook is in his back,
And a melancholy crack
    In his laugh.

I know it is a sin
For me to sit and grin
    At him here;
But the old three-cornered hat,   40
And the breeches, and all that,
    Are so queer!

And if I should live to be
The last leaf upon the tree
    In the spring,
Let them smile, as I do now,
At the old forsaken bough
    Where I cling.

THE CHAMBERED NAUTILUS   [1858]

This is the ship of pearl, which, poets feign,
   Sails the unshadowed main,—
   The venturous bark that flings
On the sweet summer wind its purpled wings
In gulfs enchanted, where the Siren sings,
   And coral reefs lie bare,
Where the cold sea-maids rise to sun their streaming hair.

Its webs of living gauze no more unfurl;
   Wrecked is the ship of pearl!
   And every chambered cell,   10
Where its dim dreaming life was wont to dwell,
As the frail tenant shaped his growing shell,
   Before thee lies revealed,—
Its irised ceiling rent, its sunless crypt unsealed!

Year after year beheld the silent toil
   That spread his lustrous coil;
   Still, as the spiral grew,
He left the past year's dwelling for the new,
Stole with soft step its shining archway through,
   Built up its idle door,   20
Stretched in his last-found home, and knew the old no
     more.

Thanks for the heavenly message brought by thee,
   Child of the wandering sea,
   Cast from her lap, forlorn!
From thy dead lips a clearer note is born
Than ever Triton blew from wreathèd horn!
   While on mine ear it rings,
Through the deep caves of thought I hear a voice that
     sings:—

Build thee more stately mansions, O my soul,
   As the swift seasons roll!   30
   Leave thy low-vaulted past!

Let each new temple, nobler than the last,
Shut thee from heaven with a dome more vast,
    Till thou at length art free,
Leaving thine outgrown shell by life's unresting sea!

THE LIVING TEMPLE   [1858]

Not in the world of light alone,
Where God has built his blazing throne,
Nor yet alone in earth below,
With belted seas that come and go,
And endless isles of sunlit green,
Is all thy Maker's glory seen:
Look in upon thy wondrous frame,—
Eternal wisdom still the same!

The smooth soft air with pulse-like waves
Flows murmuring through its hidden caves,   10
Whose streams of brightening purple rush,
Fired with a new and livelier blush,
While all their burden of decay
The ebbing current steals away,
And red with Nature's flame they start
From the warm fountains of the heart.

No rest that throbbing slave may ask,
Forever quivering o'er his task,
While far and wide a crimson jet
Leaps forth to fill the woven net   20
Which in unnumbered crossing tides
The flood of burning life divides,
Then, kindling each decaying part,
Creeps back to find the throbbing heart.

But warmed with that unchanging flame
Behold the outward moving frame,
Its living marbles jointed strong
With glistening band and silvery thong,

And linked to reason's guiding reins
By myriad rings in trembling chains,   30
Each graven with the threaded zone
Which claims it as the master's own.

See how yon beam of seeming white
Is braided out of seven-hued light,
Yet in those lucid globes no ray
By any chance shall break astray.
Hark how the rolling surge of sound,
Arches and spirals circling round,
Wakes the hushed spirit through thine ear
With music it is heaven to hear.   40

Then mark the cloven sphere that holds
All thought in its mysterious folds;
That feels sensation's faintest thrill,
And flashes forth the sovereign will;
Think on the stormy world that dwells
Locked in its dim and clustering cells!
The lightning gleams of power it sheds
Along its hollow glassy threads!

O Father! grant thy love divine
To make these mystic temples thine!   50
When wasting age and wearying strife
Have sapped the leaning walls of life,
When darkness gathers over all,
And the last tottering pillars fall,
Take the poor dust thy mercy warms,
And mould it into heavenly forms!

THE DEACON'S MASTERPIECE   [1858]

or, The Wonderful "One-Hoss Shay"

> A Logical Story

Have you heard of the wonderful one-hoss shay,
That was built in such a logical way

It ran a hundred years to a day,
And then, of a sudden, it—ah, but stay,
I'll tell you what happened without delay,
Scaring the parson into fits,
Frightening people out of their wits,—
Have you ever heard of that, I say?

Seventeen hundred and fifty-five.
Georgius Secundus was then alive,—   10
Snuffy old drone from the German hive.
That was the year when Lisbon-town
Saw the earth open and gulp her down,
And Braddock's army was done so brown,
Left without a scalp to its crown.
It was on the terrible Earthquake-day
That the Deacon finished the one-hoss shay.

Now in building of chaises, I tell you what,
There is always *somewhere* a weakest spot,—
In hub, tire, felloe, in spring or thill,   20
In panel, or crossbar, or floor, or sill,
In screw, bolt, thoroughbrace,—lurking still,
Find it somewhere you must and will,—
Above or below, or within or without,—
And that's the reason, beyond a doubt,
That a chaise *breaks down*, but doesn't *wear out*.

But the Deacon swore (as Deacons do,
With an "I dew vum," or an "I tell *yeou*")
He would build one shay to beat the taown
'N' the keounty 'n' all the kentry raoun';   30
It should be so built that it *couldn'* break daown:
"Fur," said the Deacon, "'t's mighty plain
Thut the weakes' places mus' stan' the strain;
'N' the way t' fix it, uz I maintain,
                    Is only jest
T' make that place uz strong uz the rest."

So the Deacon inquired of the village folk
Where he could find the strongest oak,
That couldn't be split nor bent nor broke,—

That was for spokes and floor and sills;   40
He sent for lancewood to make the thills;
The crossbars were ash, from the straightest trees,
The panels of white-wood, that cuts like cheese,
But lasts like iron for things like these;
The hubs of logs from the "Settler's ellum,"—
Last of its timber,—they couldn't sell 'em,
Never an axe had seen their chips,
And the wedges flew from between their lips,
Their blunt ends frizzled like celery-tips;
Step and prop-iron, bolt and screw,   50
Spring, tire, axle, and linchpin too,
Steel of the finest, bright and blue;
Thoroughbrace bison-skin, thick and wide;
Boot, top, dasher, from tough old hide
Found in the pit when the tanner died.
That was the way he "put her through."
"There!" said the Deacon, "naow she'll dew!"

Do! I tell you, I rather guess
She was a wonder, and nothing less!
Colts grew horses, beards turned gray,   60
Deacon and deaconess dropped away,
Children and grandchildren—where were they?
But there stood the stout old one-hoss shay
As fresh as on Lisbon-earthquake-day!

EIGHTEEN HUNDRED;—it came and found
The Deacon's masterpiece strong and sound.
Eighteen hundred increased by ten;—
"Hahnsum kerridge" they called it then.
Eighteen hundred and twenty came;—
Running as usual; much the same.   70
Thirty and forty at last arrive,
And then come fifty, and FIFTY-FIVE.

Little of all we value here
Wakes on the morn of its hundredth year
Without both feeling and looking queer.
In fact, there's nothing that keeps its youth,

So far as I know, but a tree and truth.
(This is a moral that runs at large;
Take it.—You're welcome.—No extra charge.)

FIRST OF NOVEMBER,—the Earthquake-day,—   80
There are traces of age in the one-hoss shay,
A general flavor of mild decay,
But nothing local, as one may say.
There couldn't be,— for the Deacon's art
Had made it so like in every part
That there wasn't a chance for one to start.
For the wheels were just as strong as the thills,
And the floor was just as strong as the sills,
And the panels just as strong as the floor,
And the whipple-tree neither less nor more,   90
And the back-crossbar as strong as the fore,
And spring and axle and hub *encore*.
And yet, *as a whole*, it is past a doubt
In another hour it will be *worn out!*

First of November, 'Fifty-five!
This morning the parson takes a drive.
Now, small boys, get out of the way!
Here comes the wonderful one-hoss shay,
Drawn by a rat-tailed, ewe-necked bay.
"Huddup!" said the parson.—Off went they.   100
The parson was working his Sunday's text,—
Had got to *fifthly*, and stopped perplexed
At what the—Moses—was coming next.
All at once the horse stood still,
Close by the meet'n'-house on the hill.
First a shiver, and then a thrill,
Then something decidedly like a spill,—
And the parson was sitting upon a rock,
At half past nine by the meet'n'-house clock,—
Just the hour of the Earthquake shock!   110
What do you think the parson found,
When he got up and stared around?
The poor old chaise in a heap or mound,
As if it had been to the mill and ground!

You see, of course, if you're not a dunce,
How it went to pieces all at once,—
All at once, and nothing first,—
Just as bubbles do when they burst.

End of the wonderful one-hoss shay.
Logic is logic. That's all I say. 120

CONTENTMENT [1858]

"Man wants but little here below"

Little I ask; my wants are few;
    I only wish a hut of stone,
(A *very plain* brown stone will do,)
    That I may call my own;—
And close at hand is such a one,
In yonder street that fronts the sun.

Plain food is quite enough for me;
    Three courses are as good as ten;—
If Nature can subsist on three,
    Thank Heaven for three. Amen! 10
I always thought cold victual nice;—
My *choice* would be vanilla-ice.

I care not much for gold or land;—
    Give me a mortgage here and there,—
Some good bank-stock, some note of hand,
    Or trifling railroad share,—
I only ask that Fortune send
A *little* more than I shall spend.

Honors are silly toys, I know,
    And titles are but empty names; 20
I would, *perhaps*, be Plenipo,—
    But only near St. James;

I'm very sure I should not care
To fill our Gubernator's chair.

Jewels are baubles; 't is a sin
    To care for such unfruitful things;—
One good-sized diamond in a pin,—
    Some, *not so large*, in rings,—
A ruby, and a pearl, or so,
Will do for me;—I laugh at show.   30

My dame should dress in cheap attire;
    (Good, heavy silks are never dear;)—
I own perhaps I *might* desire
    Some shawls of true Cashmere,—
Some marrowy crapes of China silk,
Like wrinkled skins on scalded milk.

I would not have the horse I drive
    So fast that folks must stop and stare;
An easy gait—two forty-five—
    Suits me; I do not care;—   40
Perhaps, for just a *single spurt*,
Some seconds less would do no hurt.

Of pictures, I should like to own
    Titians and Raphaels three or four,—
I love so much their style and tone,
    One Turner, and no more,
(A landscape,—foreground golden dirt,—
The sunshine painted with a squirt.)

Of books but few,—some fifty score
    For daily use, and bound for wear;   50
The rest upon an upper floor;—
    Some *little* luxury *there*
Of red morocco's gilded gleam
And vellum rich as country cream.

Busts, cameos, gems,—such things as these,
    Which others often show for pride,

I value for their power to please,
   And selfish churls deride;—
One Stradivarius, I confess,
Two Meerschaums, I would fain possess.   60

Wealth's wasteful tricks I will not learn,
   Nor ape the glittering upstart fool;—
Shall not carved tables serve my turn,
   But *all* must be of buhl?
Give grasping pomp its double share,—
I ask but *one* recumbent chair.

Thus humble let me live and die,
   Nor long for Midas' golden touch;
If Heaven more generous gifts deny,
   I shall not miss them *much*,—   70
Too grateful for the blessing lent
Of simple tastes and mind content!

THE TWO STREAMS   [1860]

   Behold the rocky wall
   That down its sloping sides
Pours the swift rain-drops, blending, as they fall,
   In rushing river-tides!

   Yon stream, whose sources run
   Turned by a pebble's edge,
Is Athabasca, rolling toward the sun
   Through the cleft mountain-ledge.

   The slender rill had strayed,
   But for the slanting stone,   10
To evening's ocean, with the tangled braid
   Of foam-flecked Oregon.

   So from the heights of Will
   Life's parting stream descends,

And, as a moment turns its slender rill,
  Each widening torrent bends,—

  From the same cradle's side,
  From the same mother's knee,—
One to long darkness and the frozen tide,
  One to the Peaceful Sea!   20

MANHOOD   [1872]

(from "Wind-Clouds and Star-Drifts")

I claim the right of knowing whom I serve,
Else is my service idle; He that asks
My homage asks it from a reasoning soul.
To crawl is not to worship; we have learned
A drill of eyelids, bended neck and knee,
Hanging our prayers on hinges, till we ape
The flexures of the many-jointed worm.
Asia has taught her Allahs and salaams
To the world's children,—we have grown to men!
We who have rolled the sphere beneath our feet   10
To find a virgin forest, as we lay
The beams of our rude temple, first of all
Must frame its doorway high enough for man
To pass unstooping; knowing as we do
That He who shaped us last of living forms
Has long enough been served by creeping things,
Reptiles that left their footprints in the sand
Of old sea margins that have turned to stone,
And men who learned their ritual; we demand
To know Him first, then trust Him and then love   20
When we have found Him worthy of our love,
Tried by our own poor hearts and not before;
He must be truer than the truest friend,
He must be tenderer than a woman's love,
A father better than the best of sires;

Kinder than she who bore us, though we sin
Oftener than did the brother we are told
We—poor ill-tempered mortals—must forgive,
Though seven times sinning threescore times and ten.

This is the new world's gospel: Be ye men!   30
Try well the legends of the children's time;
Ye are the chosen people, God has led
Your steps across the desert of the deep
As now across the desert of the shore;
Mountains are cleft before you as the sea
Before the wandering tribe of Israel's sons;
Still onward rolls the thunderous caravan,
Its coming printed on the western sky,
A cloud by day, by night a pillared flame;
Your prophets are a hundred unto one   40
Of them of old who cried, ''Thus saith the Lord;''
They told of cities that should fall in heaps,
But yours of mightier cities that shall rise
Where yet the lonely fishers spread their nets,
Where hides the fox and hoots the midnight owl;
The tree of knowledge in your garden grows
Not single, but at every humble door;
Its branches lend you their immortal food,
That fills you with the sense of what ye are,
No servants of an altar hewed and carved   50
From senseless stone by craft of human hands,
Rabbi, or dervish, brahmin, bishop, bonze,
But masters of the charm with which they work
To keep your hands from that forbidden tree!

Ye that have tasted that divinest fruit,
Look on this world of yours with opened eyes!
Ye are as gods! Nay, makers of your gods,—
Each day ye break an image in your shrine
And plant a fairer image where it stood:
Where is the Moloch of your fathers' creed,   60
Whose fires of torment burned for span-long babes?
Fit object for a tender mother's love!
Why not? It was a bargain duly made

For these same infants through the surety's act
Intrusted with their all for earth and heaven,
By Him who chose their guardian, knowing well
His fitness for the task,—this, even this,
Was the true doctrine only yesterday
As thoughts are reckoned,—and to-day you hear
In words that sound as if from human tongues   70
Those monstrous, uncouth horrors of the past
That blot the blue of heaven and shame the earth
As would the saurians of the age of slime,
Awaking from their stony sepulchres
And wallowing hateful in the eye of day!

DOROTHY Q.   [1875]

A Family Portrait

Grandmother's mother: her age, I guess,
Thirteen summers, or something less;
Girlish bust, but womanly air;
Smooth, square forehead with uprolled hair;
Lips that lover has never kissed;
Taper fingers and slender wrist;
Hanging sleeves of stiff brocade;
So they painted the little maid.

On her hand a parrot green
Sits unmoving and broods serene.   10
Hold up the canvas full in view,—
Look! there's a rent the light shines through,
Dark with a century's fringe of dust,—
That was a Red-Coat's rapier-thrust!
Such is the tale the lady old,
Dorothy's daughter's daughter, told.

Who the painter was none may tell,—
One whose best was not over well;

Hard and dry, it must be confessed,
Flat as a rose that has long been pressed;   20
Yet in her cheek the hues are bright,
Dainty colors of red and white,
And in her slender shape are seen
Hint and promise of stately mien.

Look not on her with eyes of scorn,—
Dorothy Q. was a lady born!
Ay! since the galloping Normans came,
England's annals have known her name;
And still to the three-hilled rebel town
Dear is that ancient name's renown,   30
For many a civic wreath they won,
The youthful sire and the gray-haired son.

O Damsel Dorothy! Dorothy Q.!
Strange is the gift that I owe to you;
Such a gift as never a king
Save to daughter or son might bring,—
All my tenure of heart and hand,
All my title to house and land;
Mother and sister and child and wife
And joy and sorrow and death and life!   40

What if a hundred years ago
Those close-shut lips had answered No,
When forth the tremulous question came
That cost the maiden her Norman name,
And under the folds that look so still
The bodice swelled with the bosom's thrill?
Should I be I, or would it be
One tenth another, to nine tenths me?

Soft is the breath of a maiden's YES:
Not the light gossamer stirs with less;   50
But never a cable that holds so fast
Through all the battles of wave and blast,
And never an echo of speech or song
That lives in the babbling air so long!

There were tones in the voice that whispered then
You may hear to-day in a hundred men.

O lady and lover, how faint and far
Your images hover,—and here we are,
Solid and stirring in flesh and bone,—
Edward's and Dorothy's—all their own,—   60
A goodly record for Time to show
Of a syllable spoken so long ago!—
Shall I bless you, Dorothy, or forgive
For the tender whisper that bade me live?

It shall be a blessing, my little maid!
I will heal the stab of the Red-Coat's blade,
And freshen the gold of the tarnished frame,
And gild with a rhyme your household name;
So you shall smile on us brave and bright
As first you greeted the morning's light,   70
And live untroubled by woes and fears
Through a second youth of a hundred years.

TWO SONNETS: HARVARD   [1880]

"Christo et Ecclesiæ"   1700

To God's anointed and his chosen flock:
    So ran the phrase the black-robed conclave chose
    To guard the sacred cloisters that arose
Like David's altar on Moriah's rock.
Unshaken still those ancient arches mock
    The ram's-horn summons of the windy foes
    Who stand like Joshua's army while it blows
And wait to see them toppling with the shock.
Christ and the Church. *Their* church, whose narrow door
    Shut out the many, who if over bold   10
    Like hunted wolves were driven from the fold,
Bruised with the flails these godly zealots bore,

Mindful that Israel's altar stood of old
Where echoed once Araunah's threshing-floor.

1643   "Veritas"   1878

TRUTH: So the frontlet's older legend ran,
 On the brief record's opening page displayed;
 Not yet those clear-eyed scholars were afraid
Lest the fair fruit that wrought the woe of man
By far Euphrates—where our sire began
 His search for truth, and, seeking, was betrayed— 20
 Might work new treason in their forest shade,
Doubling the curse that brought life's shortened span.
Nurse of the future, daughter of the past,
 That stern phylactery best becomes thee now:
 Lift to the morning star thy marble brow!
Cast thy brave truth on every warring blast!
 Stretch thy white hand to that forbidden bough,
And let thine earliest symbol be thy last!

THE PEAU DE CHAGRIN OF STATE
STREET   [1891]

How beauteous is the bond
In the manifold array
Of its promises to pay,
While the eight per cent it gives
And the rate at which one lives
  Correspond!

But at last the bough is bare
Where the coupons one by one
Through their ripening days have run,
And the bond, a beggar now,   10
Seeks investment anyhow,
  Anywhere!

Jones Very

1813–1880

Jones Very was born in Salem, Massachusetts, on August 28, 1813, the son of a sea captain, with whom he sailed as a child. Graduated from Harvard College in 1836, he entered the Divinity School and was a tutor in Greek in Harvard College. In 1838 he withdrew from Harvard at the request of the trustees after experiencing a religious frenzy. He spent a month in the McLean Asylum in Somerville, but was declared sane and released. From this time on he believed that his will was completely submissive to God's will. For the remainder of his life he lived quietly in his parental home with his family in Salem, served as a lay preacher in the Unitarian Church, and wrote poetry. His subject was his own mystical experiences, which resembled the quietism of the Quakers more than the orthodox Unitarianism he professed. He was admired by Emerson and some of the other American Transcendentalists, but was neglected until rediscovered in the twentieth century by Yvor Winters and other critics.

TO THE CANARY BIRD   [1839]

I cannot hear thy voice with others' ears,
Who make of thy lost liberty a gain;
And in a tale of blighted hopes and fears
Feel not that every note is born with pain.
Alas! that with thy music's gentle swell
Past days of joy should through thy memory throng,
And each to thee their words of sorrow tell,
While ravished sense forgets thee in thy song.
The heart that on the past and future feeds,
And pours in human words its thoughts divine,   10

Though at each birth the spirit inly bleeds,
Its song may charm the listening ear like thine,
And men with gilded cage and praise will try
To make the bard, like thee, forget his native sky.

THY BEAUTY FADES   [1839]

Thy beauty fades and with it too my love,
For 'twas the self-same stalk that bore its flower;
Soft fell the rain, and breaking from above
The sun looked out upon our nuptial hour;
And I had thought forever by thy side
With bursting buds of hope in youth to dwell,
But one by one Time strewed thy petals wide,
And every hope's wan look a grief can tell:
For I had thoughtless lived beneath his sway,
Who like a tyrant dealeth with us all,   10
Crowning each rose, though rooted on decay,
With charms that shall the spirit's love enthral,
And for a season turn the soul's pure eyes
From virtue's changeless bloom that time and death defies.

THE NEW BIRTH   [1839]

'Tis a new life;—thoughts move not as they did
With slow uncertain steps across my mind,
In thronging haste fast pressing on they bid
The portals open to the viewless wind
That comes not save when in the dust is laid
The crown of pride that gilds each mortal brow,
And from before man's vision melting fade
The heavens and earth;—their walls are falling now.—
Fast crowding on, each thought asks utterance strong;
Storm-lifted waves swift rushing to the shore;   10

On from the sea they send their shouts along,
Back through the cave-worn rocks their thunders roar;
And I a child of God by Christ made free
Start from death's slumbers to Eternity.

NATURE   [1839]

The bubbling brook doth leap when I come by,
Because my feet find measure with its call,
The birds know when the friend they love is nigh,
For I am known to them both great and small;
The flower that on the lovely hill-side grows
Expects me there when Spring their bloom has given;
And many a tree and bush my wanderings knows,
And e'en the clouds and silent stars of heaven;
For he who with his Maker walks aright,
Shall be their lord as Adam was before;   10
His ear shall catch each sound with new delight,
Each object wear the dress which then it wore;
And he, as when erect in soul he stood,
Hear from his Father's lips that all is good.

LIFE   [1839]

It is not life upon Thy gifts to live,
But, to grow fixed with deeper roots in Thee;
And when the sun and shower their bounties give,
To send out thick-leaved limbs; a fruitful tree,
Whose green head meets the eye for many a mile,
Whose moss-grown arms their rigid branches rear,
And full-faced fruits their blushing welcome smile
As to its goodly shade our feet draw near;
Who tastes its gifts shall never hunger more,
For 'tis the Father spreads the pure repast,   10

Who, while we eat, renews the ready store,
Which at his bounteous board must ever last;
For none the bridegroom's supper shall attend,
Who will not hear and make his word their friend.

THE GARDEN   [1839]

I saw the spot where our first parents dwelt;
And yet it wore to me no face of change,
For while amid its fields and groves I felt
As if I had not sinned, nor thought it strange;
My eye seemed but a part of every sight,
My ear heard music in each sound that rose,
Each sense forever found a new delight,
Such as the spirit's vision only knows;
Each act some new and ever-varying joy
Did by my father's love for me prepare;   10
To dress the spot my ever fresh employ,
And in the glorious whole with Him to share;
No more without the flaming gate to stray,
No more for sin's dark stain the debt of death to pay.

THE COLUMBINE   [1839]

Still, still my eye will gaze long fixed on thee,
Till I forget that I am called a man,
And at thy side fast-rooted seem to be,
And the breeze comes my cheek with thine to fan.
Upon this craggy hill our life shall pass,
A life of summer days and summer joys,
Nodding our honey-bells mid pliant grass
In which the bee half hid his time employs;
And here we'll drink with thirsty pores the rain,
And turn dew-sprinkled to the rising sun,   10

And look when in the flaming west again
His orb across the heaven its path has run;
Here left in darkness on the rocky steep,
My weary eyes shall close like folding flowers in sleep.

THE DEAD   [1839]

I see them,—crowd on crowd they walk the earth,
Dry leafless trees no autumn wind laid bare;
And in their nakedness find cause for mirth,
And all unclad would winter's rudeness dare;
No sap doth through their clattering branches flow,
Whence springing leaves and blossoms bright appear;
Their hearts the living God have ceased to know
Who gives the spring time to th' expectant year;
They mimic life, as if from him to steal
His glow of health to paint the livid cheek;   10
They borrow words for thoughts they cannot feel,
That with a seeming heart their tongue may speak;
And in their show of life more dead they live
Than those that to the earth with many tears they give.

THE SLAVE   [1839]

I saw him forging link by link his chain,
Yet while he felt its strength he thought him free,
And sighed for those borne o'er the barren main
To bondage that to his would freedom be;
Yet on he walked with eyes far-gazing still
On wrongs that from his own dark bosom flowed,
And while he thought to do his master's will
He but the more his disobedience showed;
I heard a wild rose by the stony wall,
Whose fragrance reached me in the passing gale,   10

A lesson give—it gave alike to all—
And I repeat the moral of its tale,
"That from the spot where deep its dark roots grew
Bloomed forth the fragrant rose that all delight to view."

LOVE   [1839]

I asked of Time to tell me where was Love;
He pointed to her footsteps on the snow,
Where first the angel lighted from above,
And bid me note the way and onward go;
Through populous streets of cities spreading wide,
By lonely cottage rising on the moor,
Where bursts from sundered cliff the struggling tide,
To where it hails the sea with answering roar,
She led me on; o'er mountains' frozen head,
Where mile on mile still stretches on the plain,   10
Then homeward whither first my feet she led,
I traced her path along the snow again,
But there the sun had melted from the earth
The prints where first she trod, a child of mortal birth.

THY BROTHER'S BLOOD   [1839]

I have no Brother,—they who meet me now
Offer a hand with their own wills defiled,
And, while they wear a smooth unwrinkled brow,
Know not that Truth can never be beguiled;
Go wash the hand that still betrays thy guilt;—
Before the spirit's gaze what stain can hide?
Abel's red blood upon the earth is spilt,
And by thy tongue it cannot be denied;
I hear not with the ear,—the heart doth tell
Its secret deeds to me untold before;   10

Go, all its hidden plunder quickly sell,
Then shalt thou cleanse thee from thy brother's gore,
Then will I take thy gift;—that bloody stain
Shall not be seen upon thy hand again.

THE HAND AND FOOT   [1886]

The hand and foot that stir not, they shall find
Sooner than all the rightful place to go;
Now in their motion free as roving wind,
Though first no snail more limited and slow;
I mark them full of labor all the day,
Each active motion made in perfect rest;
They cannot from their path mistaken stray,
Though 't is not theirs, yet in it they are blest;
The bird has not their hidden track found out,
Nor cunning fox, though full of art he be;   10
It is the way unseen, the certain route,
Where ever bound, yet thou art ever free;
The path of Him, whose perfect law of love
Bids spheres and atoms in just order move.

PSYCHE   [1886]

I saw a worm, with many a fold;
    It spun itself a silken tomb;
And there in winter time enrolled,
    It heeded not the cold or gloom.

Within a small, snug nook it lay,
    Nor snow nor sleet could reach it there,
Nor wind was felt in gusty day,
    Nor biting cold of frosty air.

Spring comes with bursting buds and grass,
    Around him stirs a warmer breeze;   10

The chirping insects by him pass,
    His hiding place not yet he leaves.

But summer came; its fervid breath
    Was felt within the sleeper's cell;
And, waking from his sleep of death,
    I saw him crawl from out his shell.

Slow and with pain he first moved on,
    And of the dust he seemed to be;
A day passed by; the worm was gone,
    It soared on golden pinions free!   20

THE BARBERRY-BUSH   [1886]

The bush that has most briers and bitter fruit
Waits till the frost has turned its green leaves red,
Its sweetened berries will thy palate suit,
And thou mayst find e'en there a homely bread;
Upon the hills of Salem scattered wide,
Their yellow blossoms gain the eye in Spring;
And straggling e'en upon the turnpike's side,
Their ripened branches to your hand they bring;
I've plucked them oft in boyhood's early hour,
That then I gave such name, and thought it true;   10
But now I know that other fruit as sour,
Grows on what now thou callest *Me* and *You*;
Yet wilt thou wait the autumn that I see,
Will sweeter taste than these red berries be.

MAN IN HARMONY WITH NATURE   [1886]

The flowers I pass have eyes that look at me,
The birds have ears that hear my spirit's voice,
And I am glad the leaping brook to see,
Because it does at my light step rejoice.

Come, brothers, all who tread the grassy hill,
Or wander thoughtless o'er the blooming fields,
Come, learn the sweet obedience of the will;
Then every sight and sound new pleasure yields.
Nature shall seem another house of thine,
When He who formed thee bids it live and play;   10
And in thy rambles e'en the creeping vine
Shall keep with thee a jocund holiday,
And every plant, and bird, and insect, be
Thine own companions born for harmony.

ON THE COMPLETION OF THE PACIFIC
TELEGRAPH   [1886]

Swift to the western bounds of this wide land,
Swifter than light, the Electric Message flies;
The continent is in a moment spanned,
And furthest West to furthest East replies.
While War asunder drives the nearest States,
And doth to them all intercourse deny;
Science new bonds of Union still creates,
And the most distant brings forever nigh!
I hail this omen for our Country's cause;
For it the stars do in their courses fight!   10
In vain men strive against the eternal laws
Of Peace, and Liberty, and social Right,
Rebel against the light, and hope to stay
The dawn on earth of Freedom's perfect day.

THE BROKEN BOWL   [1886]

The fountain flows, but where the bowl
    To catch from heaven the living stream
That ever shall refresh the soul,
    And make life's ills a passing dream?

'T is broken at the cistern, broke;
   Its waters spilled upon the ground;
The words of old the preacher spoke,
   I too their truth like him have found.

Prepare, prepare new vessels still,
   Though broken fragments round thee lie;   10
Thou must from hence thy pitcher fill,
   And often drink, or thou wilt die.

Behold the Rock, that smitten gave
   To Israel, on the burning sand,
Life in its cool, refreshing wave;
   'T will flow when smitten by thy hand.

Ho all that thirst! come, drink ye all!
   The fountain pours its waters free.
Come, heed the Saviour's earnest call;
   Come, every one who thirsts, to me.   20

THE APRIL SNOW   [1886]

It will not stay! The robe so pearly white,
Which fell in folds on Nature's bosom bare
And sparkled in the winter moonbeam's light,
A vesture such as sainted spirits wear,—
It will not stay! Look! from the open plain
It melts beneath the glance of April's sun;
Nor can the rock's cool shade the snow detain;
It feeds the brooks which down the hill-side run.
Why should it linger? Many-tinted flowers
And the green grass its place will quickly fill,   10
And, with new life from sun and kindly showers,
With beauty deck the meadow and the hill,
Till we regret to see the earth resume
This snowy mantle for her robe of bloom.

SOUL-SICKNESS   [1886]

How many of the body's health complain,
When they some deeper malady conceal;
Some unrest of the soul, some secret pain,
Which thus its presence doth to them reveal.
Vain would we seek, by the physician's aid,
A name for this soul-sickness e'er to find;
A remedy for health and strength decayed,
Whose cause and cure are wholly of the mind.
To higher nature is the soul allied,
And restless seeks its being's Source to know;   10
Finding nor health nor strength in aught beside;
How often vainly sought in things below,
Whether in sunny clime, or sacred stream,
Or plant of wondrous powers of which we dream!

THE CLOUDED MORNING   [1886]

The morning comes, and thickening clouds prevail,
   Hanging like curtains all the horizon round,
Or overhead in heavy stillness sail;
   So still is day, it seems like night profound;
Scarce by the city's din the air is stirred,
   And dull and deadened comes its every sound;
The cock's shrill, piercing voice subdued is heard,
   By the thick fold of muffling vapors drowned.
Dissolved in mists the hills and trees appear,
   Their outlines lost and blended with the sky;   10
And well-known objects, that to all are near,
   No longer seem familiar to the eye,
But with fantastic forms they mock the sight,
As when we grope amid the gloom of night.

ABDOLONYMUS THE SIDONIAN   [1886]

The clash of arms which shook the Persian state
Did not disturb the peasant at his toil;
In his small garden-plot more truly great
Than he who stretched his sceptre o'er its soil,
He wanted naught but what his hands supplied,
Content with fruits, the bounty of his field;
There would he, in old age, in peace have died,
But worth and greatness could not be concealed!
O'erlooked were many who would Sidon rule,
Ambitious princes, seeking kingly sway;   10
Who, trained in arms, had learned from War's proud
        school,
By fire and sword to win to thrones their way.
The crown and purple robe to him were sent,
Who peaceful lived with poverty content.

THE FUGITIVE SLAVES   [1886]

Ye sorrowing people! who from bondage fly,
And cruel laws that men against you make,—
Think not that none there are who hear your cry
And for yourselves and children thought will take.
Though now bowed down with sorrow and with fear,
Lift up your heads! for you are not alone;
Some Christian hearts are left your flight to cheer,
Some human hearts not wholly turned to stone;
God to His angels shall give strictest charge,
And in their hands they'll bear you safe from harm,   10
Where in a freer land you'll roam at large,
Nor dread pursuit, nor start at each alarm;
Till in His time you shall return again,
No more to feel man's wrath or dread his chain.

ON VISITING THE GRAVES OF HAWTHORNE
AND THOREAU   [1886]

Beneath these shades, beside yon winding stream,
Lies Hawthorne's manly form, the mortal part!
The soul, that loved to meditate and dream,
Might linger here unwilling to depart,
But that a higher life has called away
To fairer scenes, to nobler work and thought.
Why should the spirit then on earth delay,
That has a glimpse of such bright regions caught!
And near another, Nature's child, doth rest,—
Thoreau, who loved each woodland path to tread;   10
So gently sleeping on his mother's breast!
Living, though numbered with the numerous dead.
We mourn! But hope will whisper in the heart,
We meet again! and meet no more to part.

THE NEW MAN   [1886]

The hands must touch and handle many things,
The eyes long waste their glances all in vain;
The feet course still in idle, mazy rings,
Ere man himself, the lost, shall back regain
The hand that ever moves, the eyes that see,
While day holds out his shining lamp on high,
And, strait as flies the honey-seeking bee,
Direct the feet to unseen flowers they spy;
These, when they come, the man revealed from heaven,
Shall labor all the day in quiet rest,   10
And find at eve the covert duly given,
Where with the bird they find sweet sleep and rest,
That shall their wasted strength to health restore,
And bid them seek with morn the hills and fields once more.

THE NEW WORLD   [1886]

The night that has no star lit up by God,
The day that round men shines who still are blind,
The earth their grave-turned feet for ages trod,
And sea swept over by His mighty wind,—
All these have passed away; the melting dream
That flitted o'er the sleepers' half-shut eye,
When touched by morning's golden-darting beam;
And he beholds around the earth and sky
What ever real stands; the rolling spheres,
And heaving billows of the boundless main,   10
That show, though time is past, no trace of years,
And earth restored he sees as his again,
The earth that fades not, and the heavens that stand,
Their strong foundations laid by God's right hand!

Henry David Thoreau

1817–1862

Thoreau was born July 12, 1817, at Concord, Massachusetts. He graduated from Harvard College in 1837 and in the same year became associated with Emerson and began making regular entries in his journals, which reveal his intense interest in nature, in human individualism, and in the transcendental unity of the two. After graduation he tried lecturing and schoolteaching, and he contributed frequently to the Transcendentalist magazine, The Dial *(1840–1844); but he also helped his father make pencils, did odd jobs about Concord, and worked occasionally as a surveyor. Most of his poetry was composed within a few years after his graduation, and by the middle 1840's he had come to regard himself as primarily a writer of prose. With his brother John he took a two-week trip on the Concord and Merrimack Rivers in 1839, and from July 4, 1845, to September 6, 1847, he lived by himself at Walden Pond near Concord; the two experiences formed the bases for the two books he published during his lifetime. An opponent of the Mexican War, author of the still-influential essay "Civil Disobedience" (1849), he spoke out in the 1850's against slavery. Although, as he said, he "travelled a good deal in Concord," he also went on lecture trips and on several excursions to Cape Cod, the Maine woods, and Canada. Already declining in health, he went to Minnesota in 1861. He died in Concord of tuberculosis, May 6, 1862.*

WITHIN THE CIRCUIT OF THIS PLODDING LIFE [1895]

Within the circuit of this plodding life
There enter moments of an azure hue,

Untarnished fair as is the violet
Or anemone, when the spring strews them
By some meandering rivulet, which make
The best philosophy untrue that aims
But to console man for his grievances.
I have remembered when the winter came,
High in my chamber in the frosty nights,
When in the still light of the cheerful moon,   10
On every twig and rail and jutting spout,
The icy spears were adding to their length
Against the arrows of the coming sun,
How in the shimmering noon of summer past
Some unrecorded beam slanted across
The upland pastures where the Johnswort grew;
Or heard, amid the verdure of my mind,
The bee's long smothered hum, on the blue flag
Loitering amidst the mead; or busy rill,
Which now through all its course stands still and dumb   20
Its own memorial,—purling at its play
Along the slopes, and through the meadows next,
Until its youthful sound was hushed at last
In the staid current of the lowland stream;
Or seen the furrows shine but late upturned,
And where the fieldfare followed in the rear,
When all the fields around lay bound and hoar
Beneath a thick integument of snow.
So by God's cheap economy made rich
To go upon my winter's task again.   30

GREAT GOD, I ASK THEE FOR NO MEANER
PELF   [1895]

Great God, I ask thee for no meaner pelf
Than that I may not disappoint myself,
That in my action I may soar as high,
As I can now discern with this clear eye.

And next in value, which thy kindness lends,
That I may greatly disappoint my friends,
Howe'er they think or hope that it may be,
They may not dream how thou'st distinguished me.

That my weak hand may equal my firm faith,
And my life practice more than my tongue saith;   10
That my low conduct may not show,
Nor my relenting lines,
That I thy purpose did not know,
Or overrated thy designs.

LIGHT-WINGED SMOKE, ICARIAN BIRD [1895]

Light-winged Smoke, Icarian bird,
Melting thy pinions in thy upward flight,
Lark without song, and messenger of dawn,
Circling above the hamlets as thy nest;
Or else, departing dream, and shadowy form
Of midnight vision, gathering up thy skirts;
By night star-veiling, and by day
Darkening the light and blotting out the sun;
Go thou my incense upward from this hearth,
And ask the gods to pardon this clear flame.   10

THOUGH ALL THE FATES SHOULD PROVE UNKIND [1895]

Though all the fates should prove unkind,
Leave not your native land behind.
The ship, becalmed, at length stands still;
The steed must rest beneath the hill;
But swiftly still our fortunes pace
To find us out in every place.

The vessel, though her masts be firm,
Beneath her copper bears a worm;
Around the cape, across the line,
Till fields of ice her course confine;   10
It matters not how smooth the breeze,
How shallow or how deep the seas,
Whether she bears Manilla twine,
Or in her hold Madeira wine,
Or China teas, or Spanish hides,
In port or quarantine she rides;
Far from New England's blustering shore,
New England's worm her hulk shall bore,
And sink her in the Indian seas,
Twine, wine, and hides, and China teas.   20

WOOF OF THE SUN, ETHEREAL GAUZE   [1895]

Woof of the sun, ethereal gauze,
Woven of Nature's richest stuffs,
Visible heat, air-water, and dry sea,
Last conquest of the eye;
Toil of the day displayed, sun-dust,
Aerial surf upon the shores of earth,
Ethereal estuary, frith of light,
Breakers of air, billows of heat,
Fine summer spray on inland seas;
Bird of the sun, transparent-winged   10
Owlet of noon, soft-pinioned,
From heath or stubble rising without song;
Establish thy serenity o'er the fields.

LATELY, ALAS, I KNEW A GENTLE BOY   [1895]

Lately, alas, I knew a gentle boy,
    Whose features all were cast in Virtue's mould,

As one she had designed for Beauty's toy,
    But after manned him for her own strong-hold.

On every side he open was as day,
    That you might see no lack of strength within,
For walls and ports do only serve alway
    For a pretence to feebleness and sin.

Say not that Cæsar was victorious,
    With toil and strife who stormed the House of Fame,   10
In other sense this youth was glorious,
    Himself a kingdom wheresoe'er he came.

No strength went out to get him victory,
    When all was income of its own accord;
For where he went none other was to see,
    But all were parcel of their noble lord.

He forayed like the subtile haze of summer,
    That stilly shows fresh landscapes to our eyes,
And revolutions works without a murmur,
    Or rustling of a leaf beneath the skies.   20

So was I taken unawares by this,
    I quite forgot my homage to confess;
Yet now am forced to know, though hard it is,
    I might have loved him had I loved him less.

Each moment as we nearer drew to each,
    A stern respect withheld us farther yet,
So that we seemed beyond each other's reach,
    And less acquainted than when first we met.

We two were one while we did sympathize,
    So could we not the simplest bargain drive;   30
And what avails it now that we are wise,
    If absence doth this doubleness contrive?

Eternity may not the chance repeat,
    But I must tread my single way alone,

In sad remembrance that we once did meet,
 And know that bliss irrevocably gone.

The spheres henceforth my elegy shall sing,
 For elegy has other subject none;
Each strain of music in my ears shall ring
 Knell of departure from that other one.   40

Make haste and celebrate my tragedy;
 With fitting strain resound ye woods and fields;
Sorrow is dearer in such case to me
 Than all the joys other occasion yields.

   ————

Is't then too late the damage to repair?
 Distance, forsooth, from my weak grasp hath reft
The empty husk, and clutched the useless tare,
 But in my hands the wheat and kernel left.

If I but love that virtue which he is,
 Though it be scented in the morning air,   50
Still shall we be truest acquaintances,
 Nor mortals know a sympathy more rare.

THE INWARD MORNING   [1895]

Packed in my mind lie all the clothes
 Which outward nature wears,
And in its fashion's hourly change
 It all things else repairs.

In vain I look for change abroad,
 And can no difference find,
Till some new ray of peace uncalled
 Illumes my inmost mind.

What is it gilds the trees and clouds,
 And paints the heavens so gay,   10

But yonder fast-abiding light
  With its unchanging ray?

Lo, when the sun streams through the wood,
  Upon a winter's morn,
Where'er his silent beams intrude
  The murky night is gone.

How could the patient pine have known
  The morning breeze would come,
Or humble flowers anticipate
  The insect's noonday hum,—   20

Till the new light with morning cheer
  From far streamed through the aisles,
And nimbly told the forest trees
  For many stretching miles?

I've heard within my inmost soul
  Such cheerful morning news,
In the horizon of my mind
  Have seen such orient hues,

As in the twilight of the dawn,
  When the first birds awake,   30
Are heard within some silent wood,
  Where they the small twigs break,

Or in the eastern skies are seen,
  Before the sun appears,
The harbingers of summer heats
  Which from afar he bears.

MY BOOKS I'D FAIN CAST OFF, I CANNOT READ [1895]

My books I'd fain cast off, I cannot read,
'Twixt every page my thoughts go stray at large

Down in the meadow, where is richer feed,
And will not mind to hit their proper targe.

Plutarch was good, and so was Homer too,
Our Shakespeare's life were rich to live again,
What Plutarch read, that was not good nor true,
Nor Shakespeare's books, unless his books were men.

Here while I lie beneath this walnut bough,
What care I for the Greeks or for Troy town,   10
If juster battles are enacted now
Between the ants upon this hummock's crown?

Bid Homer wait till I the issue learn,
If red or black the gods will favor most,
Or yonder Ajax will the phalanx turn,
Struggling to heave some rock against the host.

Tell Shakespeare to attend some leisure hour,
For now I've business with this drop of dew,
And see you not, the clouds prepare a shower,—
I'll meet him shortly when the sky is blue.   20

This bed of herd's-grass and wild oats was spread
Last year with nicer skill than monarchs use,
A clover tuft is pillow for my head,
And violets quite overtop my shoes.

And now the cordial clouds have shut all in,
And gently swells the wind to say all's well,
The scattered drops are falling fast and thin,
Some in the pool, some in the flower-bell.

I am well drenched upon my bed of oats;
But see that globe come rolling down its stem,   30
Now like a lonely planet there it floats,
And now it sinks into my garment's hem.

Drip drip the trees for all the country round,
And richness rare distils from every bough,

The wind alone it is makes every sound,
Shaking down crystals on the leaves below.

For shame the sun will never show himself,
Who could not with his beams e'er melt me so,
My dripping locks,—they would become an elf,
Who in a beaded coat does gayly go.   40

I AM A PARCEL OF VAIN STRIVINGS TIED   [1895]

I am a parcel of vain strivings tied
      By a chance bond together,
   Dangling this way and that, their links
      Were made so loose and wide,
            Methinks,
         For milder weather.

A bunch of violets without their roots,
      And sorrel intermixed,
   Encircled by a wisp of straw
      Once coiled about their shoots,   10
            The law
         By which I'm fixed.

A nosegay which Time clutched from out
      Those fair Elysian fields,
   With weeds and broken stems, in haste,
      Doth make the rabble rout
            That waste
         The day he yields.

And here I bloom for a short hour unseen,
      Drinking my juices up,   20
   With no root in the land
      To keep my branches green,
            But stand
         In a bare cup.

Some tender buds were left upon my stem
    In mimicry of life,
  But ah! the children will not know,
    Till time has withered them,
       The woe
      With which they're rife.   30

But now I see I was not plucked for naught,
    And after in life's vase
Of glass set while I might survive,
    But by a kind hand brought
       Alive
      To a strange place.

That stock thus thinned will soon redeem its hours,
    And by another year,
  Such as God knows, with freer air,
    More fruits and fairer flowers   40
       Will bear,
      While I droop here.

INSPIRATION   [1895]

Whate'er we leave to God, God does,
    And blesses us;
The work we choose should be our own,
    God lets alone.

If with light head erect I sing,
    Though all the muses lend their force,
From my poor love of anything,
    The verse is weak and shallow as its source.

But if with bended neck I grope,
    Listening behind me for my wit,   10
With faith superior to hope,
    More anxious to keep back than forward it,

Making my soul accomplice there
    Unto the flame my heart hath lit,
Then will the verse forever wear,—
    Time cannot bend the line which God hath writ.

Always the general show of things
    Floats in review before my mind,
And such true love and reverence brings,
    That sometimes I forget that I am blind.   20

But now there comes unsought, unseen,
    Some clear, divine electuary,
And I who had but sensual been,
    Grow sensible, and as God is, am wary.

I hearing get who had but ears,
    And sight, who had but eyes before,
I moments live who lived but years,
    And truth discern who knew but learning's lore.

I hear beyond the range of sound,
    I see beyond the range of sight,   30
New earths and skies and seas around,
    And in my day the sun doth pale his light.

A clear and ancient harmony
    Pierces my soul through all its din,
As through its utmost melody,—
    Farther behind than they—farther within.

More swift its bolt than lightning is,
    Its voice than thunder is more loud,
It doth expand my privacies
    To all, and leave me single in the crowd.   40

It speaks with such authority,
    With so serene and lofty tone,
That idle Time runs gadding by,
    And leaves me with Eternity alone.

Then chiefly is my natal hour,
  And only then my prime of life,
Of manhood's strength it is the flower,
  'Tis peace's end and war's beginning strife.

'T hath come in summer's broadest noon,
  By a grey wall or some chance place,   50
Unseasoned time, insulted June,
  And vexed the day with its presuming face.

Such fragrance round my couch it makes,
  More rich than are Arabian drugs,
That my soul scents its life and wakes
  The body up beneath its perfumed rugs.

Such is the Muse—the heavenly maid,
  The star that guides our mortal course,
Which shows where life's true kernel's laid,
  Its wheat's fine flower, and its undying force.   60

She with one breath attunes the spheres,
  And also my poor human heart,
With one impulse propels the years
  Around, and gives my throbbing pulse its start.

I will not doubt forever more,
  Nor falter from a steadfast faith,
For though the system be turned o'er,
  God takes not back the word which once he saith.

I will then trust the love untold
  Which not my worth nor want has bought,   70
Which wooed me young and woos me old,
  And to this evening hath me brought.

My memory I'll educate
  To know the one historic truth,
Remembering to the latest date
  The only true and sole immortal youth.

Be but thy inspiration given,
   No matter through what danger sought,
I'll fathom hell or climb to heaven,
   And yet esteem that cheap which love has bought.   80

Fame cannot tempt the bard
   Who's famous with his God,
Nor laurel him reward
   Who hath his Maker's nod.

THE FALL OF THE LEAF   [1895]

Thank God who seasons thus the year,
   And sometimes kindly slants his rays;
For in his winter he's most near
   And plainest seen upon the shortest days.

Who gently tempers now his heats,
   And then his harsher cold, lest we
Should surfeit on the summer's sweets,
   Or pine upon the winter's crudity.

A sober mind will walk alone,
   Apart from nature, if need be,   10
And only its own seasons own;
   For nature leaving its humanity.

Sometimes a late autumnal thought
   Has crossed my mind in green July,
And to its early freshness brought
   Late ripened fruits, and an autumnal sky.

. . . .

The evening of the year draws on,
   The fields a later aspect wear;

Since Summer's garishness is gone,
    Some grains of night tincture the noontide air.   20

Behold! the shadows of the trees
    Now circle wider 'bout their stem,
Like sentries that by slow degrees
    Perform their rounds, gently protecting them.

And as the year doth decline,
    The sun allows a scantier light;
Behind each needle of the pine
    There lurks a small auxiliar to the night.

I hear the cricket's slumbrous lay
    Around, beneath me, and on high;   30
It rocks the night, it soothes the day,
    And everywhere is Nature's lullaby.

But most he chirps beneath the sod,
    When he has made his winter bed;
His creak grown fainter but more broad,
    A film of autumn o'er the summer spread.

Small birds, in fleets migrating by,
    Now beat across some meadow's bay,
And as they tack and veer on high,
    With faint and hurried click beguile the way.   40

Far in the woods, these golden days,
    Some leaf obeys its Maker's call;
And through their hollow aisles it plays
    With delicate touch the prelude of the Fall.

Gently withdrawing from its stem,
    It lightly lays itself along
Where the same hand hath pillowed them,
    Resigned to sleep upon the old year's throng.

The loneliest birch is brown and sere,
    The furthest pool is strewn with leaves,   50

Which float upon their watery bier,
    Where is no eye that sees, no heart that grieves.

The jay screams through the chestnut wood;
    The crisped and yellow leaves around
Are hue and texture of my mood—
    And these rough burrs my heirlooms on the ground.

The threadbare trees, so poor and thin—
    They are no wealthier than I;
But with as brave a core within
    They rear their boughs to the October sky.   60

Poor knights they are which bravely wait
    The charge of Winter's cavalry,
Keeping a simple Roman state,
    Discumbered of their Persian luxury.

James Russell Lowell

*James Russell Lowell was born February 22, 1819, at "Elmwood,"
Cambridge, Massachusetts, the son of a Unitarian clergyman. He was
educated at Harvard and the Harvard Law School. He briefly practiced
law, then turned to journalism and literature. In 1855 he succeeded
Longfellow as professor of modern languages at Harvard, two years
later became the first editor of the* Atlantic Monthly *and, with
Charles Eliot Norton, edited the* North American Review. *A
prominent Republican, Lowell became Minister to Spain in 1877 and,
from 1880 to 1885, was Ambassador to Great Britain. He died
August 12, 1891, at his birthplace.*

TO THE DANDELION   [1848]

   Dear common flower, that grow'st beside the way,
Fringing the dusty road with harmless gold,
      First pledge of blithesome May,
Which children pluck, and, full of pride uphold,
   High-hearted buccaneers, o'erjoyed that they
An Eldorado in the grass have found,
      Which not the rich earth's ample round
  May match in wealth, thou art more dear to me
Than all the prouder summer-blooms may be.

   Gold such as thine ne'er drew the Spanish prow   10
Through the primeval hush of Indian seas,
      Nor wrinkled the lean brow
Of age, to rob the lover's heart of ease;

'T is the Spring's largess, which she scatters now
To rich and poor alike, with lavish hand,
    Though most hearts never understand
  To take it at God's value, but pass by
The offered wealth with unrewarded eye.

Thou art my tropics and mine Italy;
To look at thee unlocks a warmer clime;   20
    The eyes thou givest me
Are in the heart, and heed not space or time:
  Not in mid June the golden-cuirassed bee
Feels a more summer-like warm ravishment
    In the white lily's breezy tent,
  His fragrant Sybaris, than I, when first
From the dark green thy yellow circles burst.

Then think I of deep shadows on the grass,
Of meadows where in sun the cattle graze,
    Where, as the breezes pass,   30
The gleaming rushes lean a thousand ways,
  Of leaves that slumber in a cloudy mass,
Or whiten in the wind, of waters blue
    That from the distance sparkle through
  Some woodland gap, and of a sky above,
Where one white cloud like a stray lamb doth move.

My childhood's earliest thoughts are linked with thee;
The sight of thee calls back the robin's song,
    Who, from the dark old tree
Beside the door, sang clearly all day long;   40
  And I, secure in childish piety,
Listened as if I heard an angel sing
    With news from heaven, which he could bring
  Fresh every day to my untainted ears
When birds and flowers and I were happy peers.

How like a prodigal doth nature seem,
When thou, for all thy gold, so common art!
    Thou teachest me to deem
More sacredly of every human heart,

Since each reflects in joy its scanty gleam   50
Of heaven, and could some wondrous secret show,
　　　Did we but pay the love we owe,
　　And with a child's undoubting wisdom look
　　On all these living pages of God's book.

From *A Fable for Critics*

[EMERSON]　　[1848]

"There comes Emerson first, whose rich words, every
　　one,
Are like gold nails in temples to hang trophies on,
Whose prose is grand verse, while his verse, the Lord
　　knows,
Is some of it pr— No, 't is not even prose;
I'm speaking of metres; some poems have welled
From those rare depths of soul that have ne'er been
　　excelled;
They 're not epics, but that does n't matter a pin,
In creating, the only hard thing 's to begin;
A grass-blade 's no easier to make than an oak;
If you 've once found the way, you 've achieved the
　　grand stroke;   10
In the worst of his poems are mines of rich matter,
But thrown in a heap with a crash and a clatter;
Now it is not one thing nor another alone
Makes a poem, but rather the general tone,
The something pervading, uniting the whole,
The before unconceived, unconceivable soul,
So that just in removing this trifle or that, you
Take away, as it were, a chief limb of the statue;
Roots, wood, bark, and leaves singly perfect may be,
But, clapt hodge-podge together, they don't make a tree.   20

"But, to come back to Emerson (whom, by the way,
I believe we left waiting),—his is, we may say,

A Greek head on right Yankee shoulders, whose range
Has Olympus for one pole, for t' other the Exchange;
He seems, to my thinking (although I 'm afraid
The comparison must, long ere this, have been made),
A Plotinus-Montaigne, where the Egyptian's gold mist
And the Gascon's shrewd wit cheek-by-jowl coexist;
All admire, and yet scarcely six converts he 's got
To I don't (nor they either) exactly know what;   30
For though he builds glorious temples, 't is odd
He leaves never a doorway to get in a god.
'T is refreshing to old-fashioned people like me
To meet such a primitive Pagan as he,
In whose mind all creation is duly respected
As parts of himself—just a little projected;
And who 's willing to worship the stars and the sun,
A convert to—nothing but Emerson.
So perfect a balance there is in his head,
That he talks of things sometimes as if they were dead;   40
Life, nature, love, God, and affairs of that sort,
He looks at as merely ideas; in short,
As if they were fossils stuck round in a cabinet,
Of such vast extent that our earth 's a mere dab in it;
Composed just as he is inclined to conjecture her,
Namely, one part pure earth, ninety-nine parts pure
    lecturer;
You are filled with delight at his clear demonstration,
Each figure, word, gesture, just fits the occasion,
With the quiet precision of science he 'll sort 'em,
But you can't help suspecting the whole a *post mortem*.   50

    "There are persons, mole-blind to the soul's make and
        style,
Who insist on a likeness 'twixt him and Carlyle;
To compare him with Plato would be vastly fairer,
Carlyle 's the more burly, but E. is the rarer;
He sees fewer objects, but clearlier, truelier,
If C. 's as original, E. 's more peculiar;
That he 's more of a man you might say of the one,
Of the other he 's more of an Emerson;
C. 's the Titan, as shaggy of mind as of limb,—

E. the clear-eyed Olympian, rapid and slim;   60
The one 's two thirds Norseman, the other half Greek,
Where the one 's most abounding, the other 's to seek;
C.'s generals require to be seen in the mass,—
E.'s specialties gain if enlarged by the glass;
C. gives nature and God his own fits of the blues,
And rims common-sense things with mystical hues,—
E. sits in a mystery calm and intense,
And looks coolly around him with sharp common-sense;
C. shows you how every-day matters unite
With the dim transdiurnal recesses of night,—   70
While E., in a plain, preternatural way,
Makes mysteries matters of mere every day;
C. draws all his characters quite *à la* Fuseli,—
Not sketching their bundles of muscles and thews illy,
He paints with a brush so untamed and profuse,
They seem nothing but bundles of muscles and thews;
E. is rather like Flaxman, lines strait and severe,
And a colorless outline, but full, round, and clear;—
To the men he thinks worthy he frankly accords
The design of a white marble statue in words.   80
C. labors to get at the centre, and then
Take a reckoning from there of his actions and men;
E. calmly assumes the said centre as granted,
And, given himself, has whatever is wanted."

·   ·   ·   ·   ·

[BRYANT]   [1848]

"There is Bryant, as quiet, as cool, and as dignified,
As a smooth, silent iceberg, that never is ignified,
Save when by reflection 't is kindled o' nights
With a semblance of flame by the chill Northern Lights.
He may rank (Griswold says so) first bard of your nation
(There's no doubt that he stands in supreme iceolation),
Your topmost Parnassus he may set his heel on,

But no warm applauses come, peal following peal on,—
He 's too smooth and too polished to hang any zeal on:
Unqualified merits, I 'll grant, if you choose, he has 'em,   10
But he lacks the one merit of kindling enthusiasm;
If he stir you at all, it is just, on my soul,
Like being stirred up with the very North Pole.

"He is very nice reading in summer, but *inter
Nos*, we don't want *extra* freezing in winter;
Take him up in the depth of July, my advice is,
When you feel an Egyptian devotion to ices.
But, deduct all you can, there 's enough that 's right good
     in him,
He has a true soul for field, river, and wood in him;
And his heart, in the midst of brick walls, or where'er it is,   20
Glows, softens, and thrills with the tenderest charities—
To you mortals that delve in this trade-ridden planet?
No, to old Berkshire's hills, with their limestone and granite.
If you 're one who *in loco* (add *foco* here) *desipis*,
You will get of his outermost heart (as I guess) a piece;
But you 'd get deeper down if you came as a precipice,
And would break the last seal of its inwardest fountain,
If you only could palm yourself off for a mountain.
Mr. Quivis, or somebody quite as discerning,
Some scholar who 's hourly expecting his learning,   30
Calls B. the American Wordsworth; but Wordsworth
May be rated at more than your whole tuneful herd 's
     worth.
No, don't be absurd, he 's an excellent Bryant;
But, my friends, you 'll endanger the life of your client,
By attempting to stretch him up into a giant:
If you choose to compare him, I think there are two per-
-sons fit for a parallel—Thompson and Cowper;[1]
I don't mean exactly,—there 's something of each,
There 's T.'s love of nature, C.'s penchant to preach;
Just mix up their minds so that C.'s spice of craziness   40

[1] To demonstrate quickly and easily how per-
     -versely absurd 't is to sound this name *Cowper*,
     As people in general call him named *super*,
     I remark that he rhymes it himself with horse-trooper.

Shall balance and neutralize T.'s turn for laziness,
And it gives you a brain cool, quite frictionless, quiet,
Whose internal police nips the buds of all riot,—
A brain like a permanent strait-jacket put on
The heart that strives vainly to burst off a button,—
A brain which, without being slow or mechanic,
Does more than a larger less drilled, more volcanic;
He 's a Cowper condensed, with no craziness bitten,
And the advantage that Wordsworth before him had
    written.

   "But, my dear little bardlings, don't prick up your ears   50
Nor suppose I would rank you and Bryant as peers;
If I call him an iceberg, I don't mean to say
There is nothing in that which is grand in its way;
He is almost the one of your poets that knows
How much grace, strength, and dignity lie in Repose;
If he sometimes fall short, he is too wise to mar
His thought's modest fulness by going too far;
'T would be well if your authors should all make a trial
Of what virtue there is in severe self-denial,
And measure their writings by Hesiod's staff,   60
Which teaches that all has less value than half."

[WHITTIER]   [1848]

   "There is Whittier, whose swelling and vehement heart
Strains the strait-breasted drab of the Quaker apart,
And reveals the live Man, still supreme and erect,
Underneath the bemummying wrappers of sect;
There was ne'er a man born who had more of the swing
Of the true lyric bard and all that kind of thing;
And his failures arise (though he seem not to know it)
From the very same cause that has made him a poet,—
A fervor of mind which knows no separation
'Twixt simple excitement and pure inspiration,   10
As my Pythoness erst sometimes erred from not knowing
If 't were I or mere wind through her tripod was blowing;

Let his mind once get head in its favorite direction
And the torrent of verse bursts the dams of reflection,
While, borne with the rush of the metre along,
The poet may chance to go right or go wrong,
Content with the whirl and delirium of song;
Then his grammar 's not always correct, nor his rhymes,
And he 's prone to repeat his own lyrics sometimes,
Not his best, though, for those are struck off at white-heats   20
When the heart in his breast like a trip-hammer beats,
And can ne'er be repeated again any more
Than they could have been carefully plotted before:
Like old what 's-his-name there at the battle of Hastings
(Who, however, gave more than mere rhythmical bastings),
Our Quaker leads off metaphorical fights
For reform and whatever they call human rights,
Both singing and striking in front of the war,
And hitting his foes with the mallet of Thor;
Anne haec, one exclaims, on beholding his knocks,   30
Vestis filii tui, O leather-clad Fox?
Can that be thy son, in the battle's mid din,
Preaching brotherly love and then driving it in
To the brain of the tough old Goliath of sin,
With the smoothest of pebbles from Castaly's spring
Impressed on his hard moral sense with a sling?

"All honor and praise to the right-hearted bard
Who was true to The Voice when such service was hard,
Who himself was so free he dared sing for the slave
When to look but a protest in silence was brave;   40
All honor and praise to the women and men
Who spoke out for the dumb and the down-trodden
        then!"

[HAWTHORNE]   [1848]

"There is Hawthorne, with genius so shrinking and rare
That you hardly at first see the strength that is there;

A frame so robust, with a nature so sweet,
So earnest, so graceful, so lithe and so fleet,
Is worth a descent from Olympus to meet;
'T is as if a rough oak that for ages had stood,
With his gnarled bony branches like ribs of the wood,
Should bloom, after cycles of struggle and scathe,
With a single anemone trembly and rathe;
His strength is so tender, his wildness so meek,   10
That a suitable parallel sets one to seek,—
He 's a John Bunyan Fouqué, a Puritan Tieck;
When Nature was shaping him, clay was not granted
For making so full-sized a man as she wanted,
So, to fill out her model, a little she spared
From some finer-grained stuff for a woman prepared,
And she could not have hit a more excellent plan
For making him fully and perfectly man."

[COOPER]   [1848]

   "Here 's Cooper, who 's written six volumes to show
He 's as good as a lord: well, let 's grant that he 's so;
If a person prefer that description of praise,
Why, a coronet 's certainly cheaper than bays;
But he need take no pains to convince us he 's not
(As his enemies say) the American Scott.
Choose any twelve men, and let C. read aloud
That one of his novels of which he 's most proud,
And I 'd lay any bet that, without ever quitting
Their box, they 'd be all, to a man, for acquitting.   10
He has drawn you one character, though, that is new,
One wildflower he's plucked that is wet with the dew
Of this fresh Western world, and, the thing not to mince,
He has done naught but copy it ill ever since;
His Indians, with proper respect be it said,
Are just Natty Bumppo, daubed over with red,
And his very Long Toms are the same useful Nat,
Rigged up in duck pants and a sou'wester hat

(Though once in a Coffin, a good chance was found
To have slipped the old fellow away underground).   20
All his other men-figures are clothes upon sticks,
The *dernière chemise* of a man in a fix
(As a captain besieged, when his garrison 's small,
Sets up caps upon poles to be seen o'er the wall);
And the women he draws from one model don't vary,
All sappy as maples and flat as a prairie.
When a character 's wanted, he goes to the task
As a cooper would do in composing a cask;
He picks out the staves, of their qualities heedful,
Just hoops them together as tight as is needful,   30
And, if the best fortune should crown the attempt, he
Has made at the most something wooden and empty.

  "Don't suppose I would underrate Cooper's abilities;
If I thought you 'd do that, I should feel very ill at ease;
The men who have given to *one* character life
And objective existence are not very rife;
You may number them all, both prose-writers and singers,
Without overrunning the bounds of your fingers,
And Natty won't go to oblivion quicker
Than Adams the parson or Primrose the vicar.   40

  "There is one thing in Cooper I like, too, and that is
That on manners he lectures his countrymen gratis;
Not precisely so either, because, for a rarity,
He is paid for his tickets in unpopularity.
Now he may overcharge his American pictures,
But you 'll grant there 's a good deal of truth in his
        strictures;
And I honor the man who is willing to sink
Half his present repute for the freedom to think,
And, when he has thought, be his cause strong or weak,
Will risk t' other half for the freedom to speak,   50
Caring naught for what vengeance the mob has in store.
Let the mob be the upper ten thousand or lower."

                .   .   .   .   .

[POE AND LONGFELLOW]   [1848]

"There comes Poe, with his raven, like Barnaby Rudge,
Three fifths of him genius and two fifths sheer fudge,
Who talks like a book of iambs and pentameters,
In a way to make people of common sense damn metres,
Who has written some things quite the best of their kind,
But the heart somehow seems all squeezed out by the mind,
Who— But hey-day! What 's this? Messieurs Mathews and
    Poe,
You must n't fling mud-balls at Longfellow so,
Does it make a man worse that his character 's such
As to make his friends love him (as you think) too much?   10
Why, there is not a bard at this moment alive
More willing than he that his fellows should thrive;
While you are abusing him thus, even now
He would help either one of you out of a slough;
You may say that he 's smooth and all that till you 're
    hoarse,
But remember that elegance also is force;
After polishing granite as much as you will,
The heart keeps its tough old persistency still;
Deduct all you can, *that* still keeps you at bay;
Why, he 'll live till men weary of Collins and Gray.   20
I 'm not over-fond of Greek metres in English,
To me rhyme 's a gain, so it be not too jinglish,
And your modern hexameter verses are no more
Like Greek ones than sleek Mr. Pope is like Homer;
As the roar of the sea to the coo of a pigeon is,
So, compared to your moderns, sounds old Melesigenes;
I may be too partial, the reason, perhaps, o't is
That I've heard the old blind man recite his own
    rhapsodies,
And my ear with that music impregnate may be,
Like the poor exiled shell with the soul of the sea,   30
Or as one can't bear Strauss when his nature is cloven
To its deeps within deeps by the stroke of Beethoven;

But, set that aside, and 't is truth that I speak,
Had Theocritus written in English, not Greek,
I believe that his exquisite sense would scarce change a line
In that rare, tender, virgin-like pastoral Evangeline.
That 's not ancient nor modern, its place is apart
Where time has no sway, in the realm of pure Art,
'T is a shrine of retreat from Earth's hubbub and strife
As quiet and chaste as the author's own life."   40

[LOWELL]   [1848]

"There is Lowell, who's striving Parnassus to climb
With a whole bale of *isms* tied together with rhyme,
He might get on alone, spite of brambles and boulders,
But he can't with that bundle he has on his shoulders,
The top of the hill he will ne'er come nigh reaching
Till he learns the distinction 'twixt singing and preaching;
His lyre has some chords that would ring pretty well,
But he'd rather by half make a drum of the shell,
And rattle away till he's old as Methusalem,
At the head of a march to the last new Jerusalem."   10

ODE RECITED AT THE HARVARD COMMEMORATION   [1865]

I

Weak-winged is song,
Nor aims at that clear-ethered height
Whither the brave deed climbs for light:
      We seem to do them wrong,
Bringing our robin's-leaf to deck their hearse
Who in warm life-blood wrote their nobler verse,
Our trivial song to honor those who come
With ears attuned to strenuous trump and drum,

And shaped in squadron-strophes their desire,
Live battle-odes whose lines were steel and fire: 10
 Yet sometimes feathered words are strong,
A gracious memory to buoy up and save
From Lethe's dreamless ooze, the common grave
 Of the unventurous throng.

II

To-day our Reverend Mother welcomes back
 Her wisest Scholars, those who understood
The deeper teaching of her mystic tome,
 And offered their fresh lives to make it good:
  No lore of Greece or Rome,
No science peddling with the names of things, 20
Or reading stars to find inglorious fates,
  Can lift our life with wings
Far from Death's idle gulf that for the many waits,
  And lengthen out our dates
With that clear fame whose memory sings
In manly hearts to come, and nerves them and dilates:
Nor such thy teaching, Mother of us all!
  Not such the trumpet-call
  Of thy diviner mood,
  That could thy sons entice 30
From happy homes and toils, the fruitful nest
Of those half-virtues which the world calls best,
  Into War's tumult rude;
  But rather far that stern device
The sponsors chose that round thy cradle stood
  In the dim, unventured wood,
  The VERITAS that lurks beneath
  The letter's unprolific sheath,
 Life of whate'er makes life worth living,
Seed-grain of high emprise, immortal food, 40
 One heavenly thing whereof earth hath the giving.

III

Many loved Truth, and lavished life's best oil
 Amid the dust of books to find her,

Content at last, for guerdon of their toil,
  With the cast mantle she hath left behind her.
    Many in sad faith sought for her,
    Many with crossed hands sighed for her;
    But these, our brothers, fought for her;
    At life's dear peril wrought for her,
    So loved her that they died for her,   50
    Tasting the raptured fleetness
    Of her divine completeness:
    Their higher instinct knew
Those love her best who to themselves are true,
And what they dare to dream of, dare to do;
    They followed her and found her
    Where all may hope to find,
Not in the ashes of the burnt-out mind,
But beautiful, with danger's sweetness round her.
    Where faith made whole with deed   60
    Breathes its awakening breath
    Into the lifeless creed,
    They saw her plumed and mailed,
    With sweet, stern face unveiled,
And all-repaying eyes, look proud on them in death.

IV

Our slender life runs rippling by, and glides
  Into the silent hollow of the past;
    What is there that abides
  To make the next age better for the last?
    Is earth too poor to give us   70
  Something to live for here that shall outlive us?
    Some more substantial boon
Than such as flows and ebbs with Fortune's fickle moon?
    The little that we see
    From doubt is never free;
    The little that we do
    Is but half-nobly true;
    With our laborious hiving
What men call treasure, and the gods call dross,
  Life seems a jest of Fate's contriving,   80
  Only secure in every one's conniving,

A long account of nothings paid with loss,
Where we poor puppets, jerked by unseen wires,
    After our little hour of strut and rave,
With all our pasteboard passions and desires,
Loves, hates, ambitions, and immortal fires,
    Are tossed pell-mell together in the grave.
    But stay! no age was e'er degenerate,
    Unless men held it at too cheap a rate,
    For in our likeness still we shape our fate.   90
            Ah, there is something here
    Unfathomed by the cynic's sneer,
    Something that gives our feeble light
    A high immunity from Night,
    Something that leaps life's narrow bars
To claim its birthright with the hosts of heaven;
    A seed of sunshine that can leaven
    Our earthly dulness with the beams of stars,
            And glorify our clay
With light from fountains elder than the Day;   100
    A conscience more divine than we,
    A gladness fed with secret tears,
    A vexing, forward-reaching sense
    Of some more noble permanence;
            A light across the sea,
    Which haunts the soul and will not let it be,
Still beaconing from the heights of undegenerate years.

                    V

            Whither leads the path
            To ampler fates that leads?
            Not down through flowery meads,   110
            To reap an aftermath
        Of youth's vainglorious weeds,
        But up the steep, amid the wrath
    And shock of deadly-hostile creeds,
        Where the world's best hope and stay
By battle's flashes gropes a desperate way,
And every turf the fierce foot clings to bleeds.
        Peace hath her not ignoble wreath,
        Ere yet the sharp, decisive word

Light the black lips of cannon, and the sword   120
    Dreams in its easeful sheath;
But some day the live coal behind the thought,
    Whether from Baäl's stone obscene,
    Or from the shrine serene
    Of God's pure altar brought,
Bursts up in flame; the war of tongue and pen
Learns with what deadly purpose it was fraught,
And, helpless in the fiery passion caught,
Shakes all the pillared state with shock of men:
Some day the soft Ideal that we wooed   130
Confronts us fiercely, foe-beset, pursued,
And cries reproachful: "Was it, then, my praise,
And not myself was loved? Prove now thy truth;
I claim of thee the promise of thy youth;
Give me thy life, or cower in empty phrase,
The victim of thy genius, not its mate!"
  Life may be given in many ways,
  And loyalty to Truth be sealed
As bravely in the closet as the field,
    So bountiful is Fate;   140
    But then to stand beside her,
    When craven churls deride her,
To front a lie in arms and not to yield,
    This shows, methinks, God's plan
    And measure of a stalwart man,
    Limbed like the old heroic breeds,
    Who stands self-poised on manhood's solid earth,
    Not forced to frame excuses for his birth,
Fed from within with all the strength he needs.

            VI

Such was he, our Martyr-Chief,   150
    Whom late the Nation he had led,
    With ashes on her head,
Wept with the passion of an angry grief:
Forgive me, if from present things I turn
To speak what in my heart will beat and burn,
And hang my wreath on his world-honored urn.
    Nature, they say, doth dote,

And cannot make a man
Save on some worn-out plan,
Repeating us by rote: 160
For him her Old-World moulds aside she threw,
And, choosing sweet clay from the breast
Of the unexhausted West,
With stuff untainted shaped a hero new,
Wise, steadfast in the strength of God, and true.
How beautiful to see
Once more a shepherd of mankind indeed,
Who loved his charge, but never loved to lead;
One whose meek flock the people joyed to be,
Not lured by any cheat of birth,   170
But by his clear-grained human worth,
And brave old wisdom of sincerity!
They knew that outward grace is dust;
They could not choose but trust
In that sure-footed mind's unfaltering skill,
And supple-tempered will
That bent like perfect steel to spring again and thrust.
His was no lonely mountain-peak of mind,
Thrusting to thin air o'er our cloudy bars,
A sea-mark now, now lost in vapors blind;   180
Broad prairie rather, genial, level-lined,
Fruitful and friendly for all human kind,
Yet also nigh to heaven and loved of loftiest stars.
Nothing of Europe here,
Or, then, of Europe fronting mornward still,
Ere any names of Serf and Peer
Could Nature's equal scheme deface
And thwart her genial will;
Here was a type of the true elder race,
And one of Plutarch's men talked with us face to face.   190
I praise him not; it were too late;
And some innative weakness there must be
In him who condescends to victory
Such as the Present gives, and cannot wait,
Safe in himself as in a fate.
So always firmly he:
He knew to bide his time,

And can his fame abide,
Still patient in his simple faith sublime,
          Till the wise years decide.   200
     Great captains, with their guns and drums,
          Disturb our judgment for the hour,
               But at last silence comes;
     These all are gone, and, standing like a tower,
     Our children shall behold his fame,
          The kindly-earnest, brave, foreseeing man,
Sagacious, patient, dreading praise, not blame,
     New birth of our new soil, the first American.

                         VII

Long as man's hope insatiate can discern
     Or only guess some more inspiring goal   210
     Outside of Self, enduring as the pole,
Along whose course the flying axles burn
Of spirits bravely-pitched, earth's manlier brood;
     Long as below we cannot find
The meed that stills the inexorable mind;
So long this faith to some ideal Good,
Under whatever mortal names it masks,
Freedom, Law, Country, this ethereal mood
That thanks the Fates for their severer tasks,
     Feeling its challenged pulses leap,   220
     While others skulk in subterfuges cheap,
And, set in Danger's van, has all the boon it asks,
     Shall win man's praise and woman's love,
     Shall be a wisdom that we set above
All other skills and gifts to culture dear,
     A virtue round whose forehead we inwreathe
     Laurels that with a living passion breathe
When other crowns grow, while we twine them, sear.
     What brings us thronging these high rites to pay,
And seal these hours the noblest of our year,   230
     Save that our brothers found this better way?

                         VIII

We sit here in the Promised Land
That flows with Freedom's honey and milk;
But 't was they won it, sword in hand,

Making the nettle danger soft for us as silk.
   We welcome back our bravest and our best;—
   Ah me! not all! some come not with the rest,
Who went forth brave and bright as any here!
I strive to mix some gladness with my strain,
         But the sad strings complain,   240
         And will not please the ear:
I sweep them for a pæan, but they wane
         Again and yet again
Into a dirge, and die away, in pain.
In these brave ranks I only see the gaps,
Thinking of dear ones whom the dumb turf wraps,
Dark to the triumph which they died to gain:
   Fitlier may others greet the living,
   For me the past is unforgiving;
      I with uncovered head   250
      Salute the sacred dead,
Who went, and who return not.—Say not so!
'T is not the grapes of Canaan that repay,
But the high faith that failed not by the way;
Virtue treads paths that end not in the grave;
No ban of endless night exiles the brave;
      And to the saner mind
We rather seem the dead that stayed behind.
Blow, trumpets, all your exultations blow!
For never shall their aureoled presence lack: 260
I see them muster in a gleaming row,
With ever-youthful brows that nobler show;
We find in our dull road their shining track;
      In every nobler mood
We feel the orient of their spirit glow,
Part of our life's unalterable good,
Of all our saintlier aspiration;
      They come transfigured back,
Secure from change in their high-hearted ways,
Beautiful evermore, and with the rays   270
Of morn on their white Shields of Expectation!

         IX

   But is there hope to save
Even this ethereal essence from the grave?

What ever 'scaped Oblivion's subtle wrong
Save a few clarion names, or golden threads of song?
      Before my musing eye
    The mighty ones of old sweep by,
   Disvoicëd now and insubstantial things,
   As noisy once as we; poor ghosts of kings,
Shadows of empire wholly gone to dust,   280
   And many races, nameless long ago,
  To darkness driven by that imperious gust
Of ever-rushing Time that here doth blow:
   O visionary world, condition strange,
  Where naught abiding is but only Change,
Where the deep-bolted stars themselves still shift and
     range!
  Shall we to more continuance make pretence?
Renown builds tombs; a life-estate is Wit;
     And, bit by bit,
The cunning years steal all from us but woe;   290
  Leaves are we, whose decays no harvest sow.
     But, when we vanish hence,
  Shall they lie forceless in the dark below,
  Save to make green their little length of sods,
  Or deepen pansies for a year or two,
  Who now to us are shining-sweet as gods?
  Was dying all they had the skill to do?
  That were not fruitless: but the Soul resents
  Such short-lived service, as if blind events
  Ruled without her, or earth could so endure;   300
  She claims a more divine investiture
  Of longer tenure than Fame's airy rents;
  Whate'er she touches doth her nature share;
  Her inspiration haunts the ennobled air,
     Gives eyes to mountains blind,
  Ears to the deaf earth, voices to the wind,
  And her clear trump sings succor everywhere
  By lonely bivouacs to the wakeful mind;
  For soul inherits all that soul could dare:
     Yea, Manhood hath a wider span   310
  And larger privilege of life than man.
  The single deed, the private sacrifice,

So radiant now through proudly-hidden tears,
Is covered up erelong from mortal eyes
With thoughtless drift of the deciduous years;
But that high privilege that makes all men peers,
That leap of heart whereby a people rise
        Up to a noble anger's height,
And, flamed on by the Fates, not shrink, but grow more
    bright,
    That swift validity in noble veins,   320
    Of choosing danger and disdaining shame,
        Of being set on flame
By the pure fire that flies all contact base
But wraps its chosen with angelic might,
    These are imperishable gains,
Sure as the sun, medicinal as light,
    These hold great futures in their lusty reins
And certify to earth a new imperial race.

           x

    Who now shall sneer?
    Who dare again to say we trace   330
    Our lines to a plebeian race?
      Roundhead and Cavalier!
Dumb are those names erewhile in battle loud;
Dream-footed as the shadow of a cloud,
    They flit across the ear:
That is best blood that hath most iron in 't.
To edge resolve with, pouring without stint
    For what makes manhood dear.
    Tell us not of Plantagenets,
Hapsburgs, and Guelfs, whose thin bloods crawl   340
Down from some victor in a border-brawl!
    How poor their outworn coronets,
Matched with one leaf of that plain civic wreath
Our brave for honor's blazon shall bequeath,
    Through whose desert a rescued Nation sets
Her heel on treason, and the trumpet hears
Shout victory, tingling Europe's sullen ears
    With vain resentments and more vain regrets!

XI

Not in anger, not in pride,
Pure from passion's mixture rude   350
Ever to base earth allied,
But with far-heard gratitude,
Still with heart and voice renewed,
To heroes living and dear martyrs dead,
The strain should close that consecrates our brave.
Lift the heart and lift the head!
Lofty be its mood and grave,
Not without a martial ring,
Not without a prouder tread
And a peal of exultation: 360
Little right has he to sing
Through whose heart in such an hour
Beats no march of conscious power,
Sweeps no tumult of elation!
'T is no Man we celebrate,
By his country's victories great,
A hero half, and half the whim of Fate,
But the pith and marrow of a Nation
Drawing force from all her men,
Highest, humblest, weakest, all,   370
For her time of need, and then
Pulsing it again through them,
Till the basest can no longer cower,
Feeling his soul spring up divinely tall,
Touched but in passing by her mantle-hem.
Come back, then, noble pride, for 't is her dower!
How could poet ever tower,
If his passions, hopes, and fears,
If his triumphs and his tears,
Kept not measure with his people?   380
Boom, cannon, boom to all the winds and waves!
Clash out, glad bells, from every rocking steeple!
Banners, adance with triumph, bend your staves!
And from every mountain-peak
Let beacon-fire to answering beacon speak,
Katahdin tell Monadnock, Whiteface he,

And so leap on in light from sea to sea,
    Till the glad news be sent
    Across a kindling continent,
Making earth feel more firm and air breathe braver: 390
"Be proud! for she is saved, and all have helped to save
    her!
    She that lifts up the manhood of the poor,
    She of the open soul and open door,
    With room about her hearth for all mankind!
    The fire is dreadful in her eyes no more;
    From her bold front the helm she doth unbind,
    Sends all her handmaid armies back to spin,
    And bids her navies, that so lately hurled
    Their crashing battle, hold their thunders in,
    Swimming like birds of calm along the unharmful
      shore.   400
    No challenge sends she to the elder world,
    That looked askance and hated; a light scorn
    Plays o'er her mouth, as round her mighty knees
    She calls her children back, and waits the morn
Of nobler day, enthroned between her subject seas."

XII

Bow down, dear Land, for thou hast found release!
   Thy God, in these distempered days,
   Hath taught thee the sure wisdom of His ways,
And through thine enemies hath wrought thy peace!
    Bow down in prayer and praise!   410
No poorest in thy borders but may now
Lift to the juster skies a man's enfranchised brow.
O Beautiful! my Country! ours once more!
Smoothing thy gold of war-dishevelled hair
O'er such sweet brows as never other wore,
    And letting thy set lips,
    Freed from wrath's pale eclipse,
The rosy edges of their smile lay bare,
What words divine of lover or of poet
Could tell our love and make thee know it,   420
Among the Nations bright beyond compare?
    What were our lives without thee?

What all our lives to save thee?
We reck not what we gave thee;
We will not dare to doubt thee,
But ask whatever else, and we will dare!

SUNTHIN' IN THE PASTORAL LINE   [1867]

Once git a smell o' musk into a draw,
An' it clings hold like precerdents in law:
Your gra'ma'am put it there,—when, goodness knows,—
To jes' this-worldify her Sunday-clo'es;
But the old chist wun't sarve her gran'son's wife,
(For, 'thout new funnitoor, wut good in life?)
An' so ole clawfoot, from the precinks dread
O' the spare chamber, slinks into the shed,
Where, dim with dust, it fust or last subsides
To holdin' seeds an' fifty things besides;   10
But better days stick fast in heart an' husk,
An' all you keep in 't gits a scent o' musk.

Jes' so with poets: wut they 've airly read
Gits kind o' worked into their heart an' head,
So 's 't they can't seem to write but jest on sheers
With furrin countries or played-out ideers,
Nor hev a feelin', ef it doos n't smack
O' wut some critter chose to feel 'way back:
This makes 'em talk o' daisies, larks, an' things,
Ez though we 'd nothin' here that blows an' sings,—   20
(Why, I 'd give more for one live bobolink
Than a square mile o' larks in printer's ink,)—
This makes 'em think our fust o' May is May,
Which 't ain't, for all the almanicks can say.

O little city-gals, don't never go it
Blind on the word o' noospaper or poet!
They 're apt to puff, an' May-day seldom looks
Up in the country ez it doos in books;

They 're no more like than hornets'-nests an' hives,
Or printed sarmons be to holy lives.   30
I, with my trouses perched on cowhide boots,
Tuggin' my foundered feet out by the roots,
Hev seen ye come to fling on April's hearse
Your muslin nosegays from the milliner's,
Puzzlin' to find dry ground your queen to choose,
An' dance your throats sore in morocker shoes:
I 've seen ye an' felt proud, thet, come wut would,
Our Pilgrim stock wuz pethed with hardihood.
Pleasure doos make us Yankees kind o' winch,
Ez though 't wuz sunthin' paid for by the inch;   40
But yit we du contrive to worry thru,
Ef Dooty tells us thet the thing 's to du,
An' kerry a hollerday, ef we set out,
Ez stiddily ez though 't wuz a redoubt.

I, country-born an' bred, know where to find
Some blooms thet make the season suit the mind,
An' seem to metch the doubtin' bluebird's notes,—
Half-vent'rin' liverworts in furry coats,
Bloodroots, whose rolled-up leaves ef you oncurl,
Each on 'em 's cradle to a baby-pearl,—   50
But these are jes' Spring's pickets; sure ez sin,
The rebble frosts 'll try to drive 'em in;
For half our May 's so awfully like May n't,
't would rile a Shaker or an evrige saint;
Though I own up I like our back'ard springs
Thet kind o' haggle with their greens an' things,
An' when you 'most give up, 'uthout more words
Toss the fields full o' blossoms, leaves, an' birds:
Thet 's Northun natur', slow an' apt to doubt,
But when it *doos* git stirred, ther' 's no gin-out!   60

Fust come the blackbirds clatt'rin' in tall trees,
An' settlin' things in windy Congresses,—
Queer politicians, though, for I 'll be skinned
Ef all on 'em don't head aginst the wind.
'fore long the trees begin to show belief,—
The maple crimsons to a coral-reef,

Then saffern swarms swing off from all the willers
So plump they look like yaller caterpillars,
Then gray hossches'nuts leetle hands unfold
Softer 'n a baby's be at three days old: 70
Thet 's robin-redbreast's almanick; he knows
Thet arter this ther' 's only blossom-snows;
So, choosin' out a handy crotch an' spouse,
He goes to plast'rin' his adobë house.

Then seems to come a hitch,—things lag behind,
Till some fine mornin' Spring makes up her mind,
An' ez, when snow-swelled rivers cresh their dams
Heaped-up with ice thet dovetails in an' jams,
A leak comes spirtin' thru some pin-hole cleft,
Grows stronger, fercer, tears out right an' left,   80
Then all the waters bow themselves an' come,
Suddin, in one gret slope o' shedderin' foam,
Jes' so our Spring gits everythin' in tune
An' gives one leap from Aperl into June:
Then all comes crowdin' in; afore you think,
Young oak-leaves mist the side-hill woods with pink;
The catbird in the laylock-bush is loud;
The orchards turn to heaps o' rosy cloud;
Red-cedars blossom tu, though few folks know it,
An' look all dipt in sunshine like a poet;   90
The lime-trees pile their solid stacks o' shade
An' drows'ly simmer with the bees' sweet trade;
In ellum-shrouds the flashin' hangbird clings
An' for the summer vy'ge his hammock slings;
All down the loose-walled lanes in archin' bowers
The barb'ry droops its strings o' golden flowers,
Whose shrinkin' hearts the school-gals love to try
With pins,—they'll worry yourn so, boys, bimeby!
But I don't love your cat'logue style,—do you?—
Ez ef to sell off Natur' by vendoo;   100
One word with blood in 't 's twice ez good ez two:
'nuff sed, June's bridesman, poet o' the year,
Gladness on wings, the bobolink, is here;
Half-hid in tip-top apple blooms he swings,
Or climbs aginst the breeze with quiverin' wings,

Or, givin' way to 't in a mock despair,
Runs down, a brook o' laughter, thru the air.

I ollus feel the sap start in my veins
In Spring, with curus heats an' prickly pains,
Thet drive me, when I git a chance, to walk 110
Off by myself to hev a privit talk
With a queer critter thet can't seem to 'gree
Along o' me like most folks,—Mister Me.
Ther' 's times when I 'm unsoshle ez a stone,
An' sort o' suffercate to be alone,—
I 'm crowded jes' to think thet folks are nigh,
An' can't bear nothin' closer than the sky;
Now the wind 's full ez shifty in the mind
Ez wut it is ou'-doors, ef I ain't blind,
An' sometimes, in the fairest sou'west weather, 120
My innard vane pints east for weeks together,
My natur' gits all goose-flesh, an' my sins
Come drizzlin' on my conscience sharp ez pins:
Wal, et sech times I jes' slip out o' sight
An' take it out in a fair stan'-up fight
With the one cuss I can't lay on the shelf,
The crook'dest stick in all the heap,—Myself.

'T wuz so las' Sabbath arter meetin'-time:
Findin' my feelin's would n't noways rhyme
With nobody's, but off the hendle flew 130
An' took things from an east-wind pint o' view,
I started off to lose me in the hills
Where the pines be, up back o' 'Siah's Mills:
Pines, ef you 're blue, are the best friends I know,
They mope an' sigh an' sheer your feelin's so,—
They hesh the ground beneath so, tu, I swan,
You half-forgit you 've gut a body on.
Ther' 's a small school'us' there where four roads meet,
The door-steps hollered out by little feet,
An' side-posts carved with names whose owners grew 140
To gret men, some on 'em, an' deacons, tu;
't ain't used no longer, coz the town hez gut
A high-school, where they teach the Lord knows wut:

Three-story larnin' 's pop'lar now; I guess
We thriv' ez wal on jes' two stories less,
For it strikes me ther' 's sech a thing ez sinnin'
By overloadin' children's underpinnin':
Wal, here it wuz I larned my A B C,
An' it's a kind o' favorite spot with me.

We 're curus critters: Now ain't jes' the minute   150
Thet ever fits us easy while we 're in it;
Long ez 't wuz futur', 't would be perfect bliss,—
Soon ez it 's past, *thet* time 's wuth ten o' this;
An' yit there ain't a man thet need be told
Thet Now 's the only bird lays eggs o' gold.
A knee-high lad, I used to plot an' plan
An' think 't wuz life's cap-sheaf to be a man;
Now, gittin' gray, there 's nothin' I enjoy
Like dreamin' back along into a boy:
So the ole school'us' is a place I choose   160
Afore all others, ef I want to muse;
I set down where I used to set, an' git
My boyhood back, an' better things with it,—
Faith, Hope, an' sunthin', ef it is n't Cherrity,
It 's want o' guile, an' thet 's ez gret a rerrity,—
While Fancy's cushin', free to Prince and Clown,
Makes the hard bench ez soft ez milk-weed-down.

Now, 'fore I knowed, thet Sabbath arternoon
When I sot out to tramp myself in tune,
I found me in the school'us' on my seat,   170
Drummin' the march to No-wheres with my feet.
Thinkin' o' nothin', I 've heerd ole folks say
Is a hard kind o' dooty in its way:
It 's thinkin' everythin' you ever knew,
Or ever hearn, to make your feelin's blue.
I sot there tryin' thet on for a spell:
I thought o' the Rebellion, then o' Hell,
Which some folks tell ye now is jest a metterfor
(A the'ry, p'raps, it wun't *feel* none the better for);
I thought o' Reconstruction, wut we 'd win   180
Patchin' our patent self-blow-up agin:

I thought ef this 'ere milkin' o' the wits,
So much a month, warn't givin' Natur' fits,—
Ef folks warn't druv, findin' their own milk fail,
To work the cow thet hez an iron tail,
An' ef idees 'thout ripenin' in the pan
Would send up cream to humor ary man:
From this to thet I let my worryin' creep,
Till finally I must ha' fell aleep.

Our lives in sleep are some like streams thet glide   190
'twixt flesh an' sperrit boundin' on each side,
Where both shores' shadders kind o' mix an' mingle
In sunthin' thet ain't jes' like either single;
An' when you cast off moorin's from To-day,
An' down towards To-morrer drift away,
The imiges thet tengle on the stream
Make a new upside-down'ard world o' dream:
Sometimes they seem like sunrise-streaks an' warnin's
O' wut 'll be in Heaven on Sabbath-mornin's,
An', mixed right in ez ef jest out o' spite,   200
Sunthin' thet says your supper ain't gone right.
I 'm gret on dreams, an' often when I wake,
I 've lived so much it makes my mem'ry ache,
An' can't skurce take a cat-nap in my cheer
'thout hevin' 'em, some good, some bad, all queer.

Now I wuz settin' where I 'd ben, it seemed,
An' ain't sure yit whether I r'ally dreamed,
Nor, ef I did, how long I might ha' slep',
When I hearn some un stompin' up the step,
An' lookin' round, ef two an' two make four,   210
I see a Pilgrim Father in the door.
He wore a steeple-hat, tall boots, an' spurs
With rowels to 'em big ez ches'nut-burrs,
An' his gret sword behind him sloped away
Long 'z a man's speech thet dunno wut to say.—
"Ef your name 's Biglow, an' your given-name
Hosee," sez he, "it 's arter you I came;
I 'm your gret-gran'ther multiplied by three."—
"My *wut*?" sez I.—"Your gret-gret-gret," sez he:

"You would n't ha' never ben here but for me.   220
Two hundred an' three year ago this May
The ship I come in sailed up Boston Bay;
I 'd been a cunnle in our Civil War,—
But wut on airth hev *you* gut up one for?
Coz we du things in England, 't ain't for you
To git a notion you can du 'em tu:
I 'm told you write in public prints: ef true,
It 's nateral you should know a thing or two."—
"Thet air 's an argymunt I can't endorse,—
't would prove, coz you wear spurs, you kep' a horse: 230
For brains," sez I, "wutever you may think,
Ain't boun' to cash the drafts o' pen-an'-ink,—
Though mos' folks write ez ef they hoped jes' quickenin'
The churn would argoo skim-milk into thickenin';
But skim-milk ain't a thing to change its view
O' wut it 's meant for more 'n a smoky flue.
But du pray tell me, 'fore we furder go,
How in all Natur' did you come to know
'bout our affairs," sez I, "in Kingdom-Come?"—
"Wal, I worked round at sperrit-rappin' some,   240
An' danced the tables till their legs wuz gone,
In hopes o' larnin' wut wuz goin' on,"
Sez he, "but mejums lie so like all-split
Thet I concluded it wuz best to quit.
But, come now, ef you wun't confess to knowin',
You 've some conjectures how the thing 's a-goin'."—
"Gran'ther," sez I, "a vane warn't never known
Nor asked to hev a jedgment of its own;
An' yit, ef 't ain't gut rusty in the jints,
It 's safe to trust its say on certin pints: 250
It knows the wind's opinions to a T,
An' the wind settles wut the weather 'll be."
"I never thought a scion of our stock
Could grow the wood to make a weather-cock;
When I wuz younger 'n you, skurce more 'n a shaver,
No airthly wind," sez he, "could make me waver!"
(Ez he said this, he clinched his jaw an' forehead,
Hitchin' his belt to bring his sword-hilt forrard.)—
"Jes so it wuz with me," sez I, "I swow,

When *I* wuz younger 'n wut you see me now,—   260
Nothin' from Adam's fall to Huldy's bonnet,
Thet I warn't full cocked with my jedgment on it;
But now I 'm gittin' on in life, I find
It 's a sight harder to make up my mind,—
Nor I don't often try tu, when events
Will du it for me free of all expense.
The moral question 's ollus plain enough,—
It 's jes' the human-natur' side thet 's tough;
Wut 's best to think may n't puzzle me nor you,—
The pinch comes in decidin' wut to *du*;   270
Ef you *read* History, all runs smooth ez grease,
Cos there the men ain't nothin' more 'n idees,—
But come to *make* it, ez we must to-day,
Th' idees hev arms an' legs an' stop the way:
It 's easy fixin' things in facts an' figgers,—
They can't resist, nor warn't brought up with niggers;
But come to try your the'ry on,—why, then
Your facts an' figgers change to ign'ant men
Actin' ez ugly—"—"Smite 'em hip an' thigh!"
Sez gran'ther, "and let every man-child die!   280
Oh for three weeks o' Crommle an' the Lord!
Up, Isr'el, to your tents an' grind the sword!"—
"Thet kind o' thing worked wal in old Judee,
But you forgit how long it 's ben A. D.;
You think thet 's ellerkence,—I call it shoddy,
A thing," sez I, "wun't cover soul nor body;
I like the plain all-wool o' common-sense,
Thet warms ye now, an' will a twelve-month hence.
You took to follerin' where the Prophets beckoned,
An', fust you knowed on, back come Charles the Second;   290
Now wut I want 's to hev all *we* gain stick,
An' not to start Millennium too quick;
We hain't to punish only, but to keep,
An' the cure 's gut to go a cent'ry deep."
"Wal, milk-an'-water ain't the best o' glue,"
Sez he, "an' so you 'll find afore you 're thru;
Ef reshness venters sunthin', shilly-shally
Loses ez often wut 's ten times the vally.
Thet exe of ourn, when Charles's neck gut split,

Opened a gap thet ain't bridged over yit: 300
Slav'ry 's your Charles, the Lord hez gin the exe"—
"Our Charles," sez I, "hez gut eight million necks.
The hardest question ain't the black man's right,
The trouble is to 'mancipate the white;
One 's chained in body an' can be sot free,
But t' other 's chained in soul to an idee:
It 's a long job, but we shall worry thru it;
Ef bagnets fail, the spellin'-book must du it."
"Hosee," sez he, "I think you 're goin' to fail:
The rettlesnake ain't dangerous in the tail;   310
This 'ere rebellion 's nothin but the rettle,—
You 'll stomp on thet an' think you 've won the bettle;
It 's Slavery thet 's the fangs an' thinkin' head,
An' ef you want selvation, cresh it dead,—
An' cresh it suddin, or you 'll larn by waitin'
Thet Chance wun't stop to listen to debatin'!"—
"God's truth!" sez I,—"an' ef I held the club,
An' knowed jes' where to strike,—but there's the rub!"—
"Strike soon," sez he, "or you 'll be deadly ailin',—
Folks thet 's afeared to fail are sure o' failin';   320
God hates your sneakin' creturs thet believe
He 'll settle things they run away an' leave!"
He brought his foot down fercely, ez he spoke,
An' give me sech a startle thet I woke.

THE WASHERS OF THE SHROUD   [1868]

Along a river-side, I know not where,
I walked one night in mystery of dream;
A chill creeps curdling yet beneath my hair,
To think what chanced me by the pallid gleam
Of a moon-wraith that waned through haunted air.

Pale fireflies pulsed within the meadow-mist
Their halos, wavering thistledowns of light;

The loon, that seemed to mock some goblin tryst,
Laughed; and the echoes, huddling in affright,
Like Odin's hounds, fled baying down the night.   10

Then all was silent, till there smote my ear
A movement in the stream that checked my breath:
Was it the slow plash of a wading deer?
But something said, "This water is of Death!
The Sisters wash a shroud,—ill thing to hear!"

I, looking then, beheld the ancient Three
Known to the Greek's and to the Northman's creed,
That sit in shadow of the mystic Tree,
Still crooning, as they weave their endless brede,
One song: "Time was, Time is, and Time shall be."   20

No wrinkled crones were they, as I had deemed,
But fair as yesterday, to-day, to-morrow,
To mourner, lover, poet, ever seemed;
Something too high for joy, too deep for sorrow,
Thrilled in their tones, and from their faces gleamed.

"Still men and nations reap as they have strawn,"
So sang they, working at their task the while;
"The fatal raiment must be cleansed ere dawn:
For Austria? Italy? the Sea-Queen's isle?
O'er what quenched grandeur must our shroud be **drawn**?   30

"Or is it for a younger, fairer corse,
That gathered States like children round his knees,
That tamed the wave to be his posting-horse,
Feller of forests, linker of the seas,
Bridge-builder, hammerer, youngest son of Thor's?

"What make we, murmur'st thou? and what are we?
When empires must be wound, we bring the shroud,
The time-old web of the implacable Three:
Is it too coarse for him, the young and proud?
Earth's mightiest deigned to wear it,—why not he?"   40

"Is there no hope?" I moaned, "so strong, so fair!
Our Fowler whose proud bird would brook erewhile
No rival's swoop in all our western air!
Gather the ravens, then, in funeral file
For him, life's morn yet golden in his hair?

"Leave me not hopeless, ye unpitying dames!
I see, half seeing. Tell me, ye who scanned
The stars, Earth's elders, still must noblest aims
Be traced upon oblivious ocean-sands?
Must Hesper join the wailing ghosts of names?"   50

"When grass-blades stiffen with red battle-dew,
Ye deem we choose the victor and the slain:
Say, choose we them that shall be leal and true
To the heart's longing, the high faith of brain?
Yet there the victory lies, if ye but knew.

"Three roots bear up Dominion: Knowledge, Will,—
These twain are strong, but stronger yet the third,—
Obedience,—'t is the great tap-root that still,
Knit round the rock of Duty, is not stirred,
Though Heaven-loosed tempests spend their utmost skill.   60

"Is the doom sealed for Hesper? 'T is not we
Denounce it, but the Law before all time:
The brave makes danger opportunity;
The waverer, paltering with the chance sublime,
Dwarfs it to peril: which shall Hesper be?

"Hath he let vultures climb his eagle's seat
To make Jove's volts purveyors of their maw?
Hath he the Many's plaudits found more sweet
Than Wisdom? held Opinion's wind for Law?
Then let him hearken for the doomster's feet!   70

"Rough are the steps, slow-hewn in flintiest rock,
States climb to power by; slippery those with gold
Down which they stumble to eternal mock:
No chafferer's hand shall long the sceptre hold,
Who, given a Fate to shape, would sell the block.

"We sing old Sagas, songs of weal and woe,
Mystic because too cheaply understood;
Dark sayings are not ours; men hear and know,
See Evil weak, see strength alone in Good,
Yet hope to stem God's fire with walls of tow.   80

"Time Was unlocks the riddle of Time Is,
That offers choice of glory or of gloom;
The solver makes Time Shall Be surely his.
But hasten, Sisters! for even now the tomb
Grates its slow hinge and calls from the abyss."

"But not for him," I cried, "not yet for him,
Whose large horizon, westering, star by star
Wins from the void to where on Ocean's rim
The sunset shuts the world with golden bar,
Not yet his thews shall fail, his eye grow dim!   90

"His shall be larger manhood, saved for those
That walk unblenching through the trial-fires;
Not suffering, but faint heart, is worst of woes,
And he no base-born son of craven sires,
Whose eye need blench confronted with his foes.

"Tears may be ours, but proud, for those who win
Death's royal purple in the foeman's lines;
Peace, too, brings tears; and mid the battle-din,
The wiser ear some text of God divines,
For the sheathed blade may rust with darker sin.   100

"God, give us peace! not such as lulls to sleep,
But sword on thigh, and brow with purpose knit!
And let our Ship of State to harbor sweep,
Her ports all up, her battle-lanterns lit,
And her leashed thunders gathering for their leap!"

So cried I with clenched hands and passionate pain,
Thinking of dear ones by Potomac's side;
Again the loon laughed mocking, and again
The echoes bayed far down the night and died,
While waking I recalled my wandering brain.   110

AUSPEX   [1888]

My heart, I cannot still it,
Nest that had song-birds in it;
And when the last shall go,
The dreary days, to fill it,
Instead of lark or linnet,
Shall whirl dead leaves and snow.

Had they been swallows only,
Without the passion stronger
That skyward longs and sings,—
Woe's me, I shall be lonely   10
When I can feel no longer
The impatience of their wings!

A moment, sweet delusion,
Like birds the brown leaves hover;
But it will not be long
Before their wild confusion
Fall wavering down to cover
The poet and his song.

THE RECALL   [1888]

Come back before the birds are flown,
Before the leaves desert the tree,
And, through the lonely alleys blown,
Whisper their vain regrets to me
Who drive before a blast more rude,
The plaything of my gusty mood,
In vain pursuing and pursued!

Nay, come although the boughs be bare,
Though snowflakes fledge the summer's nest,

And in some far Ausonian air 10
The thrush, your minstrel, warm his breast.
Come, sunshine's treasurer, and bring
To doubting flowers their faith in spring,
To birds and me the need to sing!

ON RECEIVING A COPY OF MR. AUSTIN DOBSON'S "OLD WORLD IDYLLS" [1888]

I

At length arrived, your book I take
To read in for the author's sake;
Too gray for new sensations grown,
Can charm to Art or Nature known
This torpor from my senses shake?

Hush! my parched ears what runnels slake?
Is a thrush gurgling from the brake?
Has Spring, on all the breezes blown,
At length arrived?

Long may you live such songs to make, 10
And I to listen while you wake,
With skill of late disused, each tone
Of the *Lesboum barbiton*,
At mastery, through long finger-ache,
At length arrived.

II

As I read on, what changes steal
O'er me and through, from head to heel?
A rapier thrusts coat-skirt aside,
My rough Tweeds bloom to silken pride,—
Who was it laughed? Your hand, Dick Steele! 20

Down vistas long of clipt *charmille*
Watteau as Pierrot leads the reel;

Tabor and pipe the dancers guide
As I read on.

While in and out the verses wheel
The wind-caught robes trim feet reveal,
Lithe ankles that to music glide,
But chastely and by chance descried;
Art? Nature? Which do I most feel
As I read on?   30

VERSES   [1895]

Intended to Go with a Posset Dish to My
Dear Little Goddaughter, 1882

In good old times, which means, you know,
The time men wasted long ago,
And we must blame our brains or mood
If that we squander seems less good,
In those blest days when wish was act
And fancy dreamed itself to fact,
Godfathers used to fill with guineas
The cups they gave their pickaninnies,
Performing functions at the chrism
Not mentioned in the Catechism.   10
No millioner, poor I fill up
With wishes my more modest cup,
Though had I Amalthea's horn
It should be hers the newly born.
Nay, shudder not! I should bestow it
So brimming full she couldn't blow it.
Wishes are n't horses: true, but still
There are worse roadsters than goodwill.
And so I wish my darling health,
And just to round my couplet, wealth,   20
With faith enough to bridge the chasm
'Twixt Genesis and Protoplasm,

And bear her o'er life's current vext
From this world to a better next,
Where the full glow of God puts out
Poor reason's farthing candle, Doubt.
I 've wished her healthy, wealthy, wise,
What more can godfather devise?
But since there's room for countless wishes
In these old-fashioned posset dishes, 30
I 'll wish her from my plenteous store
Of these commodities two more,
Her father's wit, veined through and through
With tenderness that Watts (but whew!
Celia's aflame, I mean no stricture
On his Sir Josh-surpassing picture)—
I wish her next, and 't is the soul
Of all I've dropt into the bowl,
Her mother's beauty—nay, but two
So fair at once would never do. 40
Then let her but the half possess,
Troy was besieged ten years for less.
Now if there's any truth in Darwin,
And we from what was, all we are win,
I simply wish the child to be
A sample of Heredity,
Enjoying to the full extent
Life's best, the Unearned Increment
Which Fate her Godfather to flout
Gave *him* in legacies of gout. 50
Thus, then, the cup is duly filled;
Walk steady, dear, lest all be spilled.

Walt Whitman

1819–1892

Walter Whitman was born on May 31, 1819, on Long Island. He was the son of a struggling carpenter-farmer, after whom he was named. In 1823 the Whitman family moved to Brooklyn, where Walt attended public school, learned printing, became a journalist and editor, and finally a house builder, until he printed the first Leaves of Grass *in 1855 at his own expense. Though he became an editor again for two years and wrote frequently for newspapers throughout his life, after 1855 his main occupation was writing poems for successive editions of* Leaves of Grass, *most of which he published himself. The twelve untitled poems of the 1855 edition became the nucleus of his evolving book, ending only with the " deathbed edition" of 1891–1892, the tenth. Emerson was the only famous American author to recognize the merits of the first edition, and at his death in 1892 Whitman was still more admired in Europe than in his own country. In the twentieth century, however, Whitman attained recognition as one of the two or three greatest poets in American literature. His prose is also of some importance and reveals the realistic background of his poetry. During the Civil War he volunteered his services in military hospitals and wrote detailed accounts of his experiences with the sick and wounded. These, with his vivid accounts of other Civil War scenes, were collected in the autobiographical prose work,* Specimen Days *(1882–1883). After the war Whitman was employed as a government clerk until stricken by paralysis in 1873, after which he lived in Camden, N.J., until his death. His tomb in Harleigh Cemetery has become an international shrine, as has also his birthplace near Huntington, Long Island, and his modest home on Mickle Street in Camden.*

SONG OF MYSELF   [1855]

[1]

I celebrate myself,
And what I assume you shall assume,
For every atom belonging to me as good belongs to you.

I loafe and invite my soul,
I lean and loafe at my ease....observing a spear of
    summer grass.

[2]

Houses and rooms are full of perfumes....the shelves are
    crowded with perfumes,
I breathe the fragrance myself, and know it and like it,
The distillation would intoxicate me also, but I shall not
    let it.

The atmosphere is not a perfume....it has no taste of the
    distillation....it is odorless,
It is for my mouth forever....I am in love with it,   10
I will go to the bank by the wood and become undisguised
    and naked,
I am mad for it to be in contact with me.

The smoke of my own breath,
Echoes, ripples, and buzzed whispers....loveroot,
    silkthread, crotch and vine,
My respiration and inspiration....the beating of my
    heart....the passing of blood and air through my
    lungs,
The sniff of green leaves and dry leaves, and of the shore
    and darkcolored sea-rocks, and of hay in the barn,
The sound of the belched words of my voice....words
    loosed to the eddies of the wind,
A few light kisses....a few embraces....a reaching
    around of arms,
The play of shine and shade on the trees as the supple
    boughs wag,

The delight alone or in the rush of the streets, or along the
    fields and hillsides,   20
The feeling of health....the full-noon trill....the song
    of me rising from bed and meeting the sun.

Have you reckoned a thousand acres much? Have you
    reckoned the earth much?
Have you practiced so long to learn to read?
Have you felt so proud to get at the meaning of poems?

Stop this day and night with me and you shall possess the
    origin of all poems,
You shall possess the good of the earth and sun....there
    are millions of suns left,
You shall no longer take things at second or third hand
    ....nor look through the eyes of the dead....nor feed
    on the spectres in books,
You shall not look through my eyes either, nor take things
    from me,
You shall listen to all sides and filter them from yourself.

[3]

I have heard what the talkers were talking....the talk of
    the beginning and the end,   30
But I do not talk of the beginning or the end.

There was never any more inception than there is now,
Nor any more youth or age than there is now;
And will never be any more perfection than there is now,
Nor any more heaven or hell than there is now.

Urge and urge and urge,
Always the procreant urge of the world.

Out of the dimness opposite equals advance....Always
    substance and increase,
Always a knit of identity....always distinction....always a
    breed of life.

To elaborate is no avail....Learned and unlearned feel
    that it is so.   40

Sure as the most certain sure....plumb in the uprights,
  well entretied, braced in the beams,
Stout as a horse, affectionate, haughty, electrical,
I and this mystery here we stand.

Clear and sweet is my soul....and clear and sweet is all
  that is not my soul.

Lack one lacks both....and the unseen is proved by the
  seen,
Till that becomes unseen and receives proof in its turn.

Showing the best and dividing it from the worst, age vexes
  age,
Knowing the perfect fitness and equanimity of things,
  while they discuss I am silent, and go bathe and
  admire myself.

Welcome is every organ and attribute of me, and of any
  man hearty and clean,
Not an inch nor a particle of an inch is vile, and none shall
  be less familiar than the rest.   50

I am satisfied....I see, dance, laugh, sing;
As God comes a loving bedfellow and sleeps at my side all
  night and close on the peep of the day,
And leaves for me baskets covered with white towels
  bulging the house with their plenty,
Shall I postpone my acceptation and realization and
  scream at my eyes,
That they turn from gazing after and down the road,
And forthwith cipher and show me to a cent,
Exactly the contents of one, and exactly the contents of
  two, and which is ahead?

[4]

Trippers and askers surround me,
People I meet....the effect upon me of my early life....of
  the ward and city I live in....of the nation,
The latest news....discoveries, inventions, societies....
  authors old and new,   60

My dinner, dress, associates, looks, business, compliments,
    dues,
The real or fancied indifference of some man or woman I
    love,
The sickness of one of my folks—or of myself....or
    ill-doing....or loss or lack of money....or
    depressions or exaltations,
They come to me days and nights and go from me again,
But they are not the Me myself.

Apart from the pulling and hauling stands what I am,
Stands amused, complacent, compassionating, idle, unitary,
Looks down, is erect, bends an arm on an impalpable
    certain rest,
Looks with its sidecurved head curious what will come
    next,
Both in and out of the game, and watching and wondering
    at it.   70

Backward I see in my own days where I sweated through
    fog with linguists and contenders,
I have no mockings or arguments....I witness and wait.

                              [5]
I believe in you my soul....the other I am must not abase
    itself to you,
And you must not be abased to the other.

Loafe with me on the grass....loose the stop from your
    throat,
Not words, not music or rhyme I want....not custom or
    lecture, not even the best,
Only the lull I like, the hum of your valved voice.

I mind how we lay in June, such a transparent summer
    morning;
You settled your head athwart my hips and gently turned
    over upon me,
And parted the shirt from my bosom-bone, and plunged
    your tongue to my barestript heart,   80

And reached till you felt my beard, and reached till you
    held my feet.

Swiftly arose and spread around me the peace and joy and
    knowledge that pass all the art and argument of the
    earth;
And I know that the hand of God is the elderhand of my
    own,
And I know that the spirit of God is the eldest brother of
    my own,
And that all the men ever born are also my brothers....
    and the women my sisters and lovers,
And that a kelson of the creation is love;
And limitless are leaves stiff or drooping in the fields,
And brown ants in the little wells beneath them,
And mossy scabs of the wormfence, and heaped stones, and
    elder and mullen and pokeweed.

[6]

A child said, What is the grass? fetching it to me with full
    hands;   90
How could I answer the child?....I do not know what it
    is any more than he.

I guess it must be the flag of my disposition, out of hopeful
    green stuff woven.

Or I guess it is the handkerchief of the Lord,
A scented gift and remembrancer designedly dropped,
Bearing the owner's name someway in the corners, that we
    may see and remark, and say Whose?

Or I guess the grass is itself a child....the produced babe
    of the vegetation.

Or I guess it is a uniform hieroglyphic,
And it means, Sprouting alike in broad zones and narrow
    zones,
Growing among black folks as among white,
Kanuck, Tuckahoe, Congressman, Cuff, I give them the
    same, I receive them the same.   100

And now it seems to me the beautiful uncut hair of graves.

Tenderly will I use you curling grass,
It may be you transpire from the breasts of young men,
It may be if I had known them I would have loved them;
It may be you are from old people and from women, and
        from offspring taken soon out of their mothers' laps,
And here you are the mothers' laps.

This grass is very dark to be from the white heads of old
        mothers,
Darker than the colorless beards of old men,
Dark to come from under the faint red roofs of mouths.

O I perceive after all so many uttering tongues!   110
And I perceive they do not come from the roofs of mouths
        for nothing.

I wish I could translate the hints about the dead young
        men and women,
And the hints about old men and mothers, and the
        offspring taken soon out of their laps.

What do you think has become of the young and old men?
And what do you think has become of the women and
        children?

They are alive and well somewhere;
The smallest sprout shows there is really no death,
And if ever there was it led forward life, and does not wait
        at the end to arrest it,
And ceased the moment life appeared.

All goes onward and outward. . . .and nothing collapses,   120
And to die is different from what any one supposed, and
        luckier.

[7]

Has any one supposed it lucky to be born?
I hasten to inform him or her it is just as lucky to die, and
        I know it.

I pass death with the dying, and birth with the new-washed
    babe....and am not contained between my hat and
    boots,
And peruse manifold objects, no two alike, and every one
    good,
The earth good, and the stars good, and their adjuncts all
    good.

I am not an earth nor an adjunct of an earth,
I am the mate and companion of people, all just as
    immortal and fathomless as myself;
They do not know how immortal, but I know.

Every kind for itself and its own....for me mine male and
    female,   130
For me all that have been boys and that love women,
For me the man that is proud and feels how it stings to be
    slighted,
For me the sweetheart and the old maid....for me
    mothers and the mothers of mothers,
For me lips that have smiled, eyes that have shed tears,
For me children and the begetters of children.

Who need be afraid of the merge?
Undrape....you are not guilty to me, nor stale nor
    discarded,
I see through the broadcloth and gingham whether or no,
And am around, tenacious, acquisitive, tireless....and can
    never be shaken away.

[8]

The little one sleeps in its cradle,   140
I lift the gauze and look a long time, and silently brush
    away flies with my hand.

The youngster and the redfaced girl turn aside up the
    bushy hill,
I peeringly view them from the top.

The suicide sprawls on the bloody floor of the bedroom,

It is so....I witnessed the corpse....there the pistol had
    fallen.

The blab of the pave....the tires of carts and sluff of
    bootsoles and talk of the promenaders,
The heavy omnibus, the driver with his interrogating
    thumb, the clank of the shod horses on the granite
    floor,
The carnival of sleighs, the clinking and shouted jokes and
    pelts of snowballs;
The hurrahs for popular favorites....the fury of roused
    mobs,
The flap of the curtained litter—the sick man inside, borne
    to the hospital,   150
The meeting of enemies, the sudden oath, the blows and
    fall,
The excited crowd—the policeman with his star quickly
    working his passage to the centre of the crowd;
The impassive stones that receive and return so many
    echoes,
The souls moving along....are they invisible while the
    least atom of the stones is visible?
What groans of overfed or half-starved who fall on the
    flags sunstruck or in fits,
What exclamations of women taken suddenly, who hurry
    home and give birth to babes,
What living and buried speech is always vibrating here....
    what howls restrained by decorum,
Arrests of criminals, slights, adulterous offers made,
    acceptances, rejections with convex lips,
I mind them or the resonance of them....I come again
    and again.

[9]

The big doors of the country-barn stand open and ready,   160
The dried grass of the harvest-time loads the slow-drawn
    wagon,
The clear light plays on the brown gray and green inter-
    tinged,
The armfuls are packed to the sagging mow:

I am there....I help....I came stretched atop of the load,
I felt its soft jolts....one leg reclined on the other,
I jump from the crossbeams, and seize the clover and
    timothy,
And roll head over heels, and tangle my hair full of wisps.

[10]

Alone far in the wilds and mountains I hunt,
Wandering amazed at my own lightness and glee,
In the late afternoon choosing a safe spot to pass the night, 170
Kindling a fire and broiling the freshkilled game,
Soundly falling asleep on the gathered leaves, my dog and
    gun by my side.

The Yankee clipper is under her three skysails....she cuts
    the sparkle and scud,
My eyes settle the land....I bend at her prow or shout
    joyously from the deck.

The boatmen and clamdiggers arose early and stopped for
    me,
I tucked my trowser-ends in my boots and went and had a
    good time,
You should have been with us that day round the
    chowder-kettle.

I saw the marriage of the trapper in the open air in the
    far-west....the bride was a red girl,
Her father and his friends sat near by crosslegged and
    dumbly smoking....they had moccasins to their feet
    and large thick blankets hanging from their shoulders;
On a bank lounged the trapper....he was dressed mostly
    in skins....his luxuriant beard and curls protected his
    neck,   180
One hand rested on his rifle....the other hand held firmly
    the wrist of the red girl,
She had long eyelashes....her head was bare....her
    coarse straight locks descended upon her voluptuous
    limbs and reached to her feet.

The runaway slave came to my house and stopped outside,
I heard his motions crackling the twigs of the woodpile,
Through the swung half-door of the kitchen I saw him
    limpsey and weak,
And went where he sat on a log, and led him in and
    assured him,
And brought water and filled a tub for his sweated body
    and bruised feet,
And gave him a room that entered from my own, and gave
    him some coarse clean clothes,
And remember perfectly well his revolving eyes and his
    awkwardness,
And remember putting plasters on the galls of his neck and
    ankles;   190
He staid with me a week before he was recuperated and
    passed north,
I had him sit next me at table.... my firelock leaned in the
    corner.

[11]

Twenty-eight young men bathe by the shore,
Twenty-eight young men, and all so friendly,
Twenty-eight years of womanly life, and all so lonesome.

She owns the fine house by the rise of the bank,
She hides handsome and richly drest aft the blinds of the
    window.

Which of the young men does she like the best?
Ah the homeliest of them is beautiful to her.

Where are you off to, lady? for I see you,   200
You splash in the water there, yet stay stock still in your
    room.

Dancing and laughing along the beach came the twenty-
    ninth bather,
The rest did not see her, but she saw them and loved them.

The beards of the young men glistened with wet, it ran
    from their long hair,
Little streams passed all over their bodies.

An unseen hand also passed over their bodies,
It descended tremblingly from their temples and ribs.

The young men float on their backs, their white bellies
    swell to the sun....they do not ask who seizes fast to
    them,
They do not know who puffs and declines with pendant
    and bending arch,
They do not think whom they souse with spray.   210

[12]

The butcher-boy puts off his killing-clothes, or sharpens
    his knife at the stall in the market,
I loiter enjoying his repartee and his shuffle and
    breakdown.

Blacksmiths with grimed and hairy chests environ the
    anvil,
Each has his main-sledge....they are all out....there is a
    great heat in the fire.

From the cinder-strewed threshold I follow their move-
    ments,
The lithe sheer of their waists plays even with their
    massive arms,
Overhand the hammers roll—overhand so slow—overhand
    so sure,
They do not hasten, each man hits in his place.

[13]

The negro holds firmly the reins of his four horses....the
    block swags underneath on its tied-over chain,
The negro that drives the huge dray of the stoneyard....
    steady and tall he stands poised on one leg on the
    stringpiece,   220
His blue shirt exposes his ample neck and breast and
    loosens over his hipband,
His glance is calm and commanding....he tosses the
    slouch of his hat away from his forehead,
The sun falls on his crispy hair and moustache....falls on
    the black of his polish'd and perfect limbs.

I behold the picturesque giant and love him....and I do
    not stop there,
I go with the team also.

In me the caresser of life wherever moving....backward
    as well as forward slueing,
To niches aside and junior bending.

Oxen that rattle the yoke or halt in the shade, what is that
    you express in your eyes?
It seems to me more than all the print I have read in my
    life.

My tread scares the wood-drake and wood-duck on my
    distant and daylong ramble,   230
They rise together, they slowly circle around.
....I believe in those winged purposes,
And acknowledge the red yellow and white playing within
    me,
And consider the green and violet and the tufted crown
    intentional;
And do not call the tortoise unworthy because she is not
    something else,
And the mocking bird in the swamp never studied the
    gamut, yet trills pretty well to me,
And the look of the bay mare shames silliness out of me.

[14]

The wild gander leads his flock through the cool night,
Ya-honk! he says, and sounds it down to me like an
    invitation;
The pert may suppose it meaningless, but I listen closer,   240
I find its purpose and place up there toward the November
    sky.

The sharphoofed moose of the north, the cat on the
    housesill, the chickadee, the prairie-dog,
The litter of the grunting sow as they tug at her teats,
The brood of the turkeyhen, and she with her halfspread
    wings,
I see in them and myself the same old law.

The press of my foot to the earth springs a hundred
    affections,
They scorn the best I can do to relate them.

I am enamoured of growing outdoors,
Of men that live among cattle or taste of the ocean or
    woods,
Of the builders and steerers of ships, of the wielders of
    axes and mauls, of the drivers of horses,   250
I can eat and sleep with them week in and week out.

What is commonest and cheapest and nearest and easiest is
    Me,
Me going in for my chances, spending for vast returns,
Adorning myself to bestow myself on the first that will
    take me,
Not asking the sky to come down to my goodwill,
Scattering it freely forever.

[15]

The pure contralto sings in the organloft,
The carpenter dresses his plank. . . . the tongue of his
    foreplane whistles its wild ascending lisp,
The married and unmarried children ride home to their
    thanksgiving dinner,
The pilot seizes the king-pin, he heaves down with a
    strong arm,   260
The mate stands braced in the whaleboat, lance and
    harpoon are ready,
The duck-shooter walks by silent and cautious stretches,
The deacons are ordained with crossed hands at the altar,
The spinning-girl retreats and advances to the hum of the
    big wheel,
The farmer stops by the bars of a Sunday and looks at the
    oats and rye,
The lunatic is carried at last to the asylum a confirmed
    case,
He will never sleep any more as he did in the cot in his
    mother's bedroom;
The jour printer with gray head and gaunt jaws works at
    his case,

He turns his quid of tobacco, his eyes get blurred with the
    manuscript;
The malformed limbs are tied to the anatomist's table,   270
What is removed drops horribly in a pail;
The quadroon girl is sold at the stand....the drunkard
    nods by the barroom stove,
The machinist rolls up his sleeves....the policeman travels
    his beat....the gatekeeper marks who pass,
The young fellow drives the express-wagon....I love him
    though I do not know him;
The half-breed straps on his light boots to compete in the
    race,
The western turkey-shooting draws old and young....
    some lean on their rifles, some sit on logs,
Out from the crowd steps the marksman and takes his
    position and levels his piece;
The groups of newly-come immigrants cover the wharf or
    levee,
The woollypates hoe in the sugarfield, the overseer views
    them from his saddle;
The bugle calls in the ballroom, the gentlemen run for
    their partners, the dancers bow to each other;   280
The youth lies awake in the cedar-roofed garret and harks
    to the musical rain,
The Wolverine sets traps on the creek that helps fill the
    Huron,
The reformer ascends the platform, he spouts with his
    mouth and nose,
The company returns from its excursion, the darkey brings
    up the rear and bears the well-riddled target,
The squaw wrapt in her yellow-hemmed cloth is offering
    moccasins and beadbags for sale,
The connoisseur peers along the exhibition-gallery with
    halfshut eyes bent sideways,
The deckhands make fast the steamboat, the plank is
    thrown for the shoregoing passengers,
The young sister holds out the skein, the elder sister winds
    it off in a ball and stops now and then for the knots,
The one-year wife is recovering and happy, a week ago she
    bore her first child,

The cleanhaired Yankee girl works with her sewing-
  machine or in the factory or mill,   290
The nine months' gone is in the parturition chamber, her
  faintness and pains are advancing;
The pavingman leans on his twohanded rammer—the
  reporter's lead flies swiftly over the notebook—the
  signpainter is lettering with red and gold,
The canal-boy trots on the towpath—the bookkeeper
  counts at his desk—the shoemaker waxes his thread,
The conductor beats time for the band and all the
  performers follow him,
The child is baptised—the convert is making the first
  professions,
The regatta is spread on the bay. . . . how the white sails
  sparkle!
The drover watches his drove, he sings out to them that
  would stray,
The pedlar sweats with his pack on his back—the
  purchaser higgles about the odd cent,
The camera and plate are prepared, the lady must sit for
  her daguerreotype,
The bride unrumples her white dress, the minutehand of
  the clock moves slowly,   300
The opium eater reclines with rigid head and just-opened
  lips,
The prostitute draggles her shawl, her bonnet bobs on her
  tipsy and pimpled neck,
The crowd laugh at her blackguard oaths, the men jeer
  and wink to each other,
(Miserable! I do not laugh at your oaths nor jeer you,)
The President holds a cabinet council, he is surrounded by
  the great secretaries,
On the piazza walk five friendly matrons with twined
  arms;
The crew of the fish-smack pack repeated layers of halibut
  in the hold,
The Missourian crosses the plains toting his wares and his
  cattle,
The fare-collector goes through the train—he gives notice
  by the jingling of loose change,

The floormen are laying the floor—the tinners are tinning
the roof—the masons are calling for mortar,   310
In single file each shouldering his hod pass onward the
laborers;
Seasons pursuing each other the indescribable crowd is
gathered....it is the Fourth of July....what salutes
of cannon and small arms!
Seasons pursuing each other the plougher ploughs and the
mower mows and the wintergrain falls in the ground;
Off on the lakes the pikefisher watches and waits by the
hole in the frozen surface,
The stumps stand thick round the clearing, the squatter
strikes deep with his axe,
The flatboatmen make fast toward dusk near the cotton-
wood or pekantrees,
The coon-seekers go now through the regions of the Red
river, or through those drained by the Tennessee, or
through those of the Arkansas,
The torches shine in the dark that hangs on the
Chattahoochee or Altamahaw;
Patriarchs sit at supper with sons and grandsons and great
grandsons around them,
In walls of adobe, in canvas tents, rest hunters and
trappers after their day's sport.   320
The city sleeps and the country sleeps,
The living sleep for their time....the dead sleep for their
time,
The old husband sleeps by his wife and the young husband
sleeps by his wife;
And these one and all tend inward to me, and I tend
outward to them,
And such as it is to be of these more or less I am.

[16]

I am of old and young, of the foolish as much as the
wise,
Regardless of others, ever regardful of others,
Maternal as well as paternal, a child as well as a man,
Stuffed with the stuff that is coarse, and stuffed with the
stuff that is fine,

One of the great nation, the nation of many nations—the
    smallest the same and the largest the same,   330
A southerner soon as a northerner, a planter nonchalant
    and hospitable,
A Yankee bound my own way....ready for trade....my
    joints the limberest joints on earth and the sternest
    joints on earth,
A Kentuckian walking the vale of the Elkhorn in my
    deerskin leggings,
A boatman over the lakes or bays or along coasts....a
    Hoosier, a Badger, a Buckeye,
A Louisianian or Georgian, a poke-easy from sandhills and
    pines,
At home on Canadian snowshoes or up in the bush, or
    with fishermen off Newfoundland,
At home in the fleet of iceboats, sailing with the rest and
    tacking,
At home on the hills of Vermont or in the woods of
    Maine or the Texan ranch,
Comrade of Californians....comrade of free north-
    westerners, loving their big proportions,
Comrade of raftsmen and coalmen—comrade of all who
    shake hands and welcome to drink and meat;   340
A learner with the simplest, a teacher of the thoughtfulest,
A novice beginning experient of myriads of seasons,
Of every hue and trade and rank, of every caste and
    religion,
Not merely of the New World but of Africa Europe or
    Asia....a wandering savage,
A farmer, mechanic, or artist....a gentleman, sailor, lover
    or quaker,
A prisoner, fancy-man, rowdy, lawyer, physician or priest.

I resist anything better than my own diversity,
And breathe the air and leave plenty after me,
And am not stuck up, and am in my place.

The moth and the fisheggs are in their place,   350
The suns I see and the suns I cannot see are in their place,
The palpable is in its place and the impalpable is in its place.

[17]

These are the thoughts of all men in all ages and lands,
     they are not original with me,
If they are not yours as much as mine they are nothing or
     next to nothing,
If they do not enclose everything they are next to nothing,
If they are not the riddle and the untying of the riddle they
     are nothing,
If they are not just as close as they are distant they are
     nothing.

This is the grass that grows wherever the land is and the
     water is,
This is the common air that bathes the globe.

This is the breath of laws and songs and behaviour,   360
This is the tasteless water of souls....this is the true
     sustenance,
It is for the illiterate....it is for the judges of the supreme
     court....it is for the federal capitol and the state
     capitols,
It is for the admirable communes of literary men and
     composers and singers and lecturers and engineers and
     savans,
It is for the endless races of working people and farmers
     and seamen.

[18]

This is the trill of a thousand clear cornets and scream of
     the octave flute and strike of triangles.

I play not a march for victors only....I play great marches
     for conquered and slain persons.

Have you heard that it was good to gain the day?
I also say it is good to fall....battles are lost in the same
     spirit in which they are won.

I sound triumphal drums for the dead....I fling through
     my embouchures the loudest and gayest music to them,

Vivas to those who have failed, and to those whose
     war-vessels sank in the sea, and those themselves who
     sank in the sea,   370
And to all generals that lost engagements, and all over-
     come heroes, and the numberless unknown heroes
     equal to the greatest heroes known.

[19]

This is the meal pleasantly set....this is the meat and
     drink for natural hunger,
It is for the wicked just the same as the righteous....I
     make appointments with all,
I will not have a single person slighted or left away,
The keptwoman and sponger and thief are hereby invited
     ....the heavy-lipped slave is invited....the
     venerealee is invited,
There shall be no difference between them and the rest.

This is the press of a bashful hand....this is the float and
     odor of hair,
This is the touch of my lips to yours....this is the
     murmur of yearning,
This is the far-off depth and height reflecting my own face,
This is the thoughtful merge of myself and the outlet again.   380

Do you guess I have some intricate purpose?
Well I have....for the April rain has, and the mica on the
     side of a rock has.

Do you take it I would astonish?
Does the daylight astonish? or the early redstart twittering
     through the woods?
Do I astonish more than they?

This hour I tell things in confidence,
I might not tell everybody but I will tell you.

[20]

Who goes there! hankering, gross, mystical, nude?
How is it I extract strength from the beef I eat?

What is a man anyhow? What am I? and what are you?   390
All I mark as my own you shall offset it with your own,
Else it were time lost listening to me.

I do not snivel that snivel the world over,
That months are vacuums and the ground but wallow and
      filth,
That life is a suck and a sell, and nothing remains at the
      end but threadbare crape and tears.

Whimpering and truckling fold with powders for invalids
    ....conformity goes to the fourth-removed,
I cock my hat as I please indoors or out.

Shall I pray? Shall I venerate and be ceremonious?
I have pried through the strata and analyzed to a hair,
And counselled with doctors and calculated close and
      found no sweeter fat than sticks to my own bones.   400

In all people I see myself, none more and not one a
      barleycorn less,
And the good or bad I say of myself I say of them.

And I know I am solid and sound,
To me the converging objects of the universe perpetually
      flow,
All are written to me, and I must get what the writing
      means.

And I know I am deathless,
I know this orbit of mine cannot be swept by a carpenter's
      compass,
I know I shall not pass like a child's carlacue cut with a
      burnt stick at night.

I know I am august,
I do not trouble my spirit to vindicate itself or be under-
      stood,   410
I see that the elementary laws never apologize,
I reckon I behave no prouder than the level I plant my
      house by after all.

I exist as I am, that is enough,
If no other in the world be aware I sit content,
And if each and all be aware I sit content.

One world is aware, and by far the largest to me, and that
    is myself,
And whether I come to my own today or in ten thousand
    or ten million years,
I can cheerfully take it now, or with equal cheerfulness I
    can wait.

My foothold is tenoned and mortised in granite,
I laugh at what you call dissolution,   420
And I know the amplitude of time.

[21]

I am the poet of the body,
And I am the poet of the soul.

The pleasures of heaven are with me, and the pains of hell
    are with me,
The first I graft and increase upon myself. . . . the latter I
    translate into a new tongue.

I am the poet of the woman the same as the man,
And I say it is as great to be a woman as to be a man,
And I say there is nothing greater than the mother of men.

I chant a new chant of dilation or pride,
We have had ducking and deprecating about enough,   430
I show that size is only development.

Have you outstript the rest? Are you the President?
It is a trifle. . . . they will more than arrive there every one,
    and still pass on.

I am he that walks with the tender and growing night;
I call to the earth and sea half-held by the night.

Press close barebosomed night! Press close magnetic
    nourishing night!

Night of south winds! Night of the large few stars!
Still nodding night! Mad naked summer night!

Smile O voluptuous coolbreathed earth!
Earth of the slumbering and liquid trees!   440
Earth of departed sunset! Earth of the mountains misty-
    topt!
Earth of the vitreous pour of the full moon just tinged
    with blue!
Earth of shine and dark mottling the tide of the river!
Earth of the limpid gray of clouds brighter and clearer for
    my sake!
Far-swooping elbowed earth! Rich apple-blossomed earth!
Smile, for your lover comes!

Prodigal! you have given me love!....therefore I to you
    give love!
O unspeakable passionate love!

Thruster holding me tight and that I hold tight!
We hurt each other as the bridegroom and the bride hurt
    each other.   450

[22]

You sea! I resign myself to you also.....I guess what you
    mean,
I behold from the beach your crooked inviting fingers,
I believe you refuse to go back without feeling of me;
We must have a turn together....I undress....hurry me
    out of sight of the land,
Cushion me soft....rock me in billowy drowse,
Dash me with amorous wet....I can repay you.

Sea of stretched ground-swells!
Sea breathing broad and convulsive breaths!
Sea of the brine of life! Sea of unshovelled and
    always-ready graves!
Howler and scooper of storms! Capricious and dainty sea!   460
I am integral with you....I too am of one phase and of
    all phases.

Partaker of influx and efflux.....extoller of hate and
    conciliation,
Extoller of amies and those that sleep in each others' arms.

I am he attesting sympathy;
Shall I make my list of things in the house and skip the
    house that supports them?

I am the poet of commonsense and of the demonstrable
    and of immortality;
And am not the poet of goodness only....I do not decline
    to be the poet of wickedness also.

Washes and razors for foofoos....for me freckles and a
    bristling beard.

What blurt is it about virtue and about vice?
Evil propels me, and reform of evil propels me....I stand
    indifferent,   470
My gait is no faultfinder's or rejecter's gait,
I moisten the roots of all that has grown.

Did you fear some scrofula out of the unflagging
    pregnancy?
Did you guess the celestial laws are yet to be worked over
    and rectified?

I step up to say that what we do is right and what we
    affirm is right....and some is only the ore of right,
Witnesses of us....one side a balance and the antipodal
    side a balance,
Soft doctrine as steady help as stable doctrine,
Thoughts and deeds of the present our rouse and early
    start.

This minute that comes to me over the past decillions,
There is no better than it and now.   480

What behaved well in the past or behaves well today is not
    such a wonder,

The wonder is always and always how there can be a mean
    man or an infidel.

[23]

Endless unfolding of words of ages!
And mine a word of the modern....a word en masse.

A word of the faith that never balks,
One time as good as another time....here or
    henceforward it is all the same to me.

A word of reality....materialism first and last imbueing.

Hurrah for positive science! Long live exact
    demonstration!
Fetch stonecrop and mix it with cedar and branches of lilac;
This is the lexicographer or chemist....this made a
    grammar of the old cartouches,   490
These mariners put the ship through dangerous unknown
    seas,
This is the geologist, and this works with the scalpel, and
    this is a mathematician.

Gentlemen I receive you, and attach and clasp hands with
    you,
The facts are useful and real....they are not my dwelling
    ....I enter by them to an area of the dwelling.

I am less the reminder of property or qualities, and more
    the reminder of life,
And go on the square for my own sake and for other's sake,
And make short account of neuters and geldings, and
    favor men and women fully equipped,
And beat the gong of revolt, and stop with fugitives and
    them that plot and conspire.

[24]

Walt Whitman, an American, one of the roughs, a kosmos,
Disorderly fleshy and sensual....eating drinking and
    breeding,   500

No sentimentalist....no stander above men and women or
    apart from them....no more modest than immodest.

Unscrew the locks from the doors!
Unscrew the doors themselves from their jambs!

Whoever degrades another degrades me....and whatever is
    done or said returns at last to me,
And whatever I do or say I also return.

Through me the afflatus surging and surging....through
    me the current and index.

I speak the password primeval....I give the sign of
    democracy;
By God! I will accept nothing which all cannot have their
    counterpart of on the same terms.

Through me many long dumb voices,
Voice of the interminable generations of slaves,   510
Voices of prostitutes and of deformed persons,
Voices of the diseased and despairing, and of thieves and
    dwarfs,
Voices of cycles of preparation and accretion,
And of the threads that connect the stars—and of wombs,
    and of the fatherstuff,
And of the rights of them the others are down upon,
Of the trivial and flat and foolish and despised,
Of fog in the air and beetles rolling balls of dung.

Through me forbidden voices,
Voices of sexes and lusts....voices veiled, and I remove
    the veil,
Voices indecent by me clarified and transfigured.   520

I do not press my finger across my mouth,
I keep as delicate around the bowels as around the head
    and heart,
Copulation is no more rank to me than death is.

I believe in the flesh and the appetites,

Seeing hearing and feeling are miracles, and each part and
    tag of me is a miracle.

Divine am I inside and out, and I make holy whatever I
    touch or am touched from;
The scent of these arm-pits is aroma finer than prayer,
This head is more than churches or bibles or creeds.

If I worship any particular thing it shall be some of the
    spread of my body;
Translucent mould of me it shall be you,   530
Shaded ledges and rests, firm masculine coulter, it shall be
    you,
Whatever goes to the tilth of me it shall be you,
You my rich blood, your milky stream pale strippings of
    my life;
Breast that presses against other breasts it shall be you,
My brain it shall be your occult convolutions,
Root of washed sweet-flag, timorous pond-snipe, nest of
    guarded duplicate eggs, it shall be you,
Mixed tussled hay of head and beard and brawn it shall be
    you,
Trickling sap of maple, fibre of manly wheat, it shall be
    you;
Sun so generous it shall be you,
Vapors lighting and shading my face it shall be you,   540
You sweaty brooks and dews it shall be you,
Winds whose soft-tickling genitals rub against me it shall
    be you,
Broad muscular fields, branches of liveoak, loving lounger
    in my winding paths, it shall be you,
Hands I have taken, face I have kissed, mortal I have ever
    touched, it shall be you.

I dote on myself....there is that lot of me, and all so
    luscious,
Each moment and whatever happens thrills me with joy.

I cannot tell how my ankles bend....nor whence the
    cause of my faintest wish,

Nor the cause of the friendship I emit....nor the cause of
    the friendship I take again.

To walk up my stoop is unaccountable....I pause to
    consider if it really be,
That I eat and drink is spectacle enough for the great
    authors and schools,   550
A morning-glory at my window satisfies me more than the
    metaphysics of books.

To behold the daybreak!
The little light fades the immense and diaphanous shadows,
The air tastes good to my palate.

Hefts of the moving world at innocent gambols, silently
    rising, freshly exuding,
Scooting obliquely high and low.

Something I cannot see puts upward libidinous prongs,
Seas of bright juice suffuse heaven.

The earth by the sky staid with....the daily close of their
    junction,
The heaved challenge from the east that moment over my
    head,   560
The mocking taunt, See then whether you shall be
    master!

[25]
Dazzling and tremendous how quick the sunrise would kill
    me,
If I could not now and always send sunrise out of me.

We also ascend dazzling and tremendous as the sun,
We found our own my soul in the calm and cool of the
    daybreak.

My voice goes after what my eyes cannot reach,
With the twirl of my tongue I encompass worlds and
    volumes of worlds.

Speech is the twin of my vision....it is unequal to
    measure itself.
It provokes me forever,
It says sarcastically, Walt, you understand enough....why
    don't you let it out then?   570

Come now I will not be tantalized....you conceive too
    much of articulation.

Do you not know how the buds beneath are folded?
Waiting in gloom protected by frost,
The dirt receding before my prophetical screams,
I underlying causes to balance them at last,
My knowledge my live parts....it keeping tally with the
    meaning of things,
Happiness....which whoever hears me let him or her set
    out in search of this day.

My final merit I refuse you....I refuse putting from me
    the best I am.

Encompass worlds but never try to encompass me,
I crowd your noisiest talk by looking toward you.   580

Writing and talk do not prove me,
I carry the plenum of proof and every thing else in my
    face,
With the hush of my lips I confound the topmost skeptic.

[26]

I think I will do nothing for a long time but listen,
And accrue what I hear into myself....and let sounds
    contribute toward me.

I hear the bravuras of birds....the bustle of growing
    wheat....gossip of flames....clack of sticks cooking
    my meals.

I hear the sound of the human voice....a sound I love,

I hear all sounds as they are tuned to their uses....sounds
     of the city and sounds out of the city....sounds of
     the day and night;
Talkative young ones to those that like them....the
     recitative of fish-pedlars and fruit-pedlars....the loud
     laugh of workpeople at their meals,
The angry base of disjointed friendship....the faint tones
     of the sick,   590
The judge with hands tight to the desk, his shaky lips
     pronouncing a death-sentence,
The heave'e'yo of stevedores unlading ships by the
     wharves....the refrain of the anchor-lifters;
The ring of alarm-bells....the cry of fire....the whirr
     of swift-streaking engines and hose-carts with pre-
     monitory tinkles and colored lights,
The steam-whistle....the solid roll of the train of
     approaching cars;
The slow-march played at night at the head of the
     association,
They go to guard some corpse....the flag-tops are draped
     with black muslin.

I hear the violincello or man's heart complaint,
And hear the keyed cornet or else the echo of sunset.

I hear the chorus....it is a grand-opera....this indeed is
     music!

A tenor large and fresh as the creation fills me,   600
The orbic flex of his mouth is pouring and filling me full.

I hear the trained soprano....she convulses me like the
     climax of my love-grip;
The orchestra whirls me wider than Uranus flies,
It wrenches unnamable ardors from my breast,
It throbs me to gulps of the farthest down horror,
It sails me....I dab with bare feet....they are licked by
     the indolent waves,
I am exposed....cut by bitter and poisoned hail,

Steeped amid honeyed morphine....my windpipe
    squeezed in the fakes of death,
Let up again to feel the puzzle of puzzles,
And that we call Being.   610

[27]

To be in any form, what is that?
If nothing lay more developed the quahaug and its callous
    shell were enough.

Mine is no callous shell,
I have instant conductors all over me whether I pass or
    stop,
They seize every object and lead it harmlessly through me.

I merely stir, press, feel with my fingers, and am happy,
To touch my person to some one else's is about as much
    as I can stand.

[28]

Is this then a touch?....quivering me to a new identity,
Flames and ether making a rush for my veins,
Treacherous tip of me reaching and crowding to help
    them,   620
My flesh and blood playing out lightning, to strike what is
    hardly different from myself,
On all sides prurient provokers stiffening my limbs,
Straining the udder of my heart for its withheld drip,
Behaving licentious toward me, taking no denial,
Depriving me of my best as for a purpose,
Unbuttoning my clothes and holding me by the bare waist,
Deluding my confusion with the calm of the sunlight and
    pasture fields,
Immodestly sliding the fellow-senses away,
They bribed to swap off with touch, and go and graze at
    the edges of me,
No consideration, no regard for my draining strength or
    my anger,   630
Fetching the rest of the herd around to enjoy them awhile,
Then all uniting to stand on a headland and worry me.

The sentries desert every other part of me,
They have left me helpless to a red marauder,
They all come to the headland to witness and assist against
    me.

I am given up by traitors;
I talk wildly....I have lost my wits....I and nobody else
    am the greatest traitor,
I went myself first to the headland....my own hands
    carried me there.

You villain touch! what are you doing?....my breath is
    tight in its throat;
Unclench your floodgates! you are too much for me.   640

[29]

Blind loving wrestling touch! Sheathed hooded sharp-
    toothed touch!
Did it make you ache so leaving me?

Parting tracked by arriving....perpetual payment of the
    perpetual loan,
Rich showering rain, and recompense richer afterward.

Sprouts take and accumulate....stand by the curb prolific
    and vital,
Landscapes projected masculine full-sized and golden.

[30]

All truths wait in all things,
They neither hasten their own delivery nor resist it,
They do not need the obstetric forceps of the surgeon,
The insignificant is as big to me as any,   650
What is less or more than a touch?

Logic and sermons never convince,
The damp of the night drives deeper into my soul.

Only what proves itself to every man and woman is so,
Only what nobody denies is so.

A minute and a drop of me settle my brain;
I believe the soggy clods shall become lovers and lamps,
And a compend of compends is the meat of a man or
    woman,
And a summit and flower there is the feeling they have for
    each other,
And they are to branch boundlessly out of that lesson until
    it becomes omnific,   660
And until every one shall delight us, and we them.

[31]

I believe a leaf of grass is no less than the journeywork of
    the stars,
And the pismire is equally perfect, and a grain of sand, and
    the egg of the wren,
And the tree-toad is a chef-d'œuvre for the highest,
And the running blackberry would adorn the parlors of
    heaven,
And the narrowest hinge in my hand puts to scorn all
    machinery,
And the cow crunching with depressed head surpasses any
    statue,
And a mouse is miracle enough to stagger sextillions of
    infidels,
And I could come every afternoon of my life to look at the
    farmer's girl boiling her iron tea-kettle and baking
    shortcake.

I find I incorporate gneiss and coal and long-threaded
    moss and fruits and grains and esculent roots,   670
And am stucco'd with quadrupeds and birds all over,
And have distanced what is behind me for good reasons,
And call any thing close again when I desire it.

In vain the speeding or shyness,
In vain the plutonic rocks send their old heat against my
    approach,
In vain the mastodon retreats beneath its own powdered
    bones,
In vain objects stand leagues off and assume manifold shapes,

In vain the ocean settling in hollows and the great
    monsters lying low,
In vain the buzzard houses herself with the sky,
In vain the snake slides through the creepers and logs,   680
In vain the elk takes to the inner passes of the woods,
In vain the razorbilled auk sails far north to Labrador,
I follow quickly....I ascend to the nest in the fissure of
    the cliff.

[32]

I think I could turn and live awhile with the animals....
    they are so placid and self-contained,
I stand and look at them sometimes half the day long.

They do not sweat and whine about their condition,
They do not lie awake in the dark and weep for their sins,
They do not make me sick discussing their duty to God,
Not one is dissatisfied....not one is demented with the
    mania of owning things,
Not one kneels to another nor to his kind that lived
    thousands of years ago,   690
Not one is respectable or industrious over the whole earth.

So they show their relations to me and I accept them;
They bring me tokens of myself....they evince them
    plainly in their possession.

I do not know where they got those tokens,
I must have passed that way untold times ago and
    negligently dropt them,
Myself moving forward then and now and forever,
Gathering and showing more always and with velocity,
Infinite and omnigenous and the like of these among them;
Not too exclusive toward the reachers of my
    remembrancers,
Picking out here one that shall be my amie,   700
Choosing to go with him on brotherly terms.

A gigantic beauty of a stallion, fresh and responsive to my
    caresses,

Head high in the forehead and wide between the ears,
Limbs glossy and supple, tail dusting the ground,
Eyes well apart and full of sparkling wickedness....ears
    finely cut and flexibly moving.

His nostrils dilate....my heels embrace him....his well
    built limbs tremble with pleasure....we speed around
    and return.

I but use you a moment and then I resign you stallion....
    and do not need your paces, and outgallop them,
And myself as I stand or sit pass faster than you.

[33]

Swift wind! Space! My Soul! Now I know it is true what
    I guessed at;
What I guessed when I loafed on the grass,   710
What I guessed while I lay alone in my bed....and again
    as I walked the beach under the paling stars of the
    morning.

My ties and ballasts leave me....I travel....I sail....my
    elbows rest in the sea-gaps,
I skirt the sierras....my palms cover continents,
I am afoot with my vision.

By the city's quadrangular houses....in log-huts, or
    camping with lumbermen,
Along the ruts of the turnpike....along the dry gulch and
    rivulet bed,
Hoeing my onion-patch, and rows of carrots and parsnips
    ....crossing savannas....trailing in forests,
Prospecting....gold-digging....girdling the trees of a
    new purchase,
Scorched ankle-deep by the hot sand....hauling my boat
    down the shallow river;
Where the panther walks to and fro on a limb overhead
    ....where the buck turns furiously at the hunter,   720
Where the rattlesnake suns his flabby length on a rock....
    where the otter is feeding on fish,

Where the alligator in his tough pimples sleeps by the
    bayou,
Where the black bear is searching for roots or honey....
    where the beaver pats the mud with his paddle-tail;
Over the growing sugar....over the cottonplant....over
    the rice in its low moist field;
Over the sharp-peaked farmhouse with its scalloped scum
    and slender shoots from the gutters;
Over the western persimmon....over the longleaved corn
    and the delicate blue-flowered flax;
Over the white and brown buckwheat, a hummer and a
    buzzer there with the rest,
Over the dusky green of the rye as it ripples and shades
    in the breeze;
Scaling mountains....pulling myself cautiously up....
    ....holding on by low scragged limbs,
Walking the path worn in the grass and beat through the
    leaves of the brush;   730
Where the quail is whistling betwixt the woods and the
    wheatlot,
Where the bat flies in the July eve....where the great
    goldbug drops through the dark;
Where the flails keep time on the barn floor,
Where the brook puts out of the roots of the old tree and
    flows to the meadow,
Where cattle stand and shake away flies with the tremulous
    shuddering of their hides,
Where the cheese-cloth hangs in the kitchen, and andirons
    straddle the hearth-slab, and cobwebs fall in festoons
    from the rafters;
Where triphammers crash....where the press is whirling
    its cylinders;
Wherever the human heart beats with terrible throes out
    of its ribs;
Where the pear-shaped balloon is floating aloft....
    floating in it myself and looking composedly down;
Where the life-car is drawn on the slipnoose....where the
    heat hatches pale-green eggs in the dented sand,   740
Where the she-whale swims with her calves and never for-
    sakes them,

Where the steamship trails hindways its long pennant of
    smoke,
Where the ground-shark's fin cuts like a black chip out of
    the water,
Where the half-burned brig is riding on unknown currents,
Where shells grow to her slimy deck, and the dead are
    corrupting below;
Where the striped and starred flag is borne at the head of
    the regiments;
Approaching Manhattan, up by the long-stretching island,
Under Niagara, the cataract falling like a veil over my
    countenance;
Upon a door-step....upon the horse-block of hard wood
    outside,
Upon the race-course, or enjoying pic-nics or jigs or a
    good game of base-ball,   750
At he-festivals with blackguard jibes and ironical license
    and bull-dances and drinking and laughter,
At the cider-mill, tasting the sweet of the brown sqush....
    sucking the juice through a straw,
At apple-peelings, wanting kisses for all the red fruit I find,
At musters and beach-parties and friendly bees and
    huskings and house-raisings;
Where the mockingbird sounds his delicious gurgles, and
    cackles and screams and weeps,
Where the hay-rick stands in the barnyard, and the dry-
    stalks are scattered, and the brood cow waits in the
    hovel,
Where the bull advances to do his masculine work, and the
    stud to the mare, and the cock is treading the hen,
Where the heifers browse, and the geese nip their food
    with short jerks;
Where the sundown shadows lengthen over the limitless
    and lonesome prairie,
Where the herds of buffalo make a crawling spread of the
    square miles far and near;   760
Where the hummingbird shimmers....where the neck of
    the longlived swan is curving and winding;
Where the laughing-gull scoots by the slappy shore and
    laughs her near-human laugh;

Where beehives range on a gray bench in the garden
half-hid by the high weeds;
Where the band-necked partridges roost in a ring on the
ground with their heads out;
Where burial coaches enter the arched gates of a cemetery;
Where winter wolves bark amid wastes of snow and
icicled trees;
Where the yellow-crowned heron comes to the edge of the
marsh at night and feeds upon small crabs;
Where the splash of swimmers and divers cools the warm
noon;
Where the katydid works her chromatic reed on the
walnut-tree over the well;
Through patches of citrons and cucumbers with silver-
wired leaves,   770
Through the salt-lick or orange glade....or under conical
firs;
Through the gymnasium....through the curtained
saloon....through the office or public hall;
Pleased with the native and pleased with the foreign....
pleased with the new and old,
Pleased with women, the homely as well as the handsome,
Pleased with the quakeress as she puts off her bonnet and
talks melodiously,
Pleased with the primitive tunes of the choir of the
whitewashed church,
Pleased with the earnest words of the sweating Methodist
preacher, or any preacher....looking seriously at the
camp-meeting;
Looking in at the shop-windows in Broadway the whole
forenoon....pressing the flesh of my nose to the
thick plate-glass,
Wandering the same afternoon with my face turned up to
the clouds;
My right and left arms round the sides of two friends and
I in the middle;   780
Coming home with the bearded and dark-cheeked
bush-boy....riding behind him at the drape of the day;
Far from the settlements studying the print of animals'
feet, or the moccasin print;

By the cot in the hospital reaching lemonade to a feverish
    patient,
By the coffined corpse when all is still, examining with a
    candle;
Voyaging to every port to dicker and adventure;
Hurrying with the modern crowd, as eager and fickle as any,
Hot toward one I hate, ready in my madness to knife him;
Solitary at midnight in my back yard, my thoughts gone
    from me a long while,
Walking the old hills of Judea with the beautiful gentle
    god by my side;
Speeding through space....speeding through heaven and
    the stars,   790
Speeding amid the seven satellites and the broad ring and
    the diameter of eighty thousand miles,
Speeding with tailed meteors....throwing fire-balls like
    the rest,
Carrying the crescent child that carries its own full mother
    in its belly:
Storming enjoying planning loving cautioning,
Backing and filling, appearing and disappearing,
I tread day and night such roads.

I visit the orchards of God and look at the spheric product,
And look at quintillions ripened, and look at quintillions
    green.

I fly the flight of the fluid and swallowing soul,
My course runs below the soundings of plummets.   800

I help myself to material and immaterial,
No guard can shut me off, no law can prevent me.

I anchor my ship for a little while only,
My messengers continually cruise away or bring their
    returns to me.

I go hunting polar furs and the seal....leaping chasms
    with a pike-pointed staff....clinging to topples of
    brittle and blue.

I ascend to the foretruck....I take my place late at night
    in the crow's nest....we sail through the arctic sea
    ....it is plenty light enough,
Through the clear atmosphere I stretch around on the
    wonderful beauty,
The enormous masses of ice pass me and I pass them....
    the scenery is plain in all directions,
The white-topped mountains point up in the distance....
    I fling out my fancies toward them;
We are about approaching some great battlefield in which
    we are soon to be engaged,   810
We pass the colossal outposts of the encampment....we
    pass with still feet and caution;
Or we are entering by the suburbs some vast and ruined
    city....the blocks and fallen architecture more than
    all the living cities of the globe.

I am a free companion....I bivouac by invading
    watchfires.

I turn the bridegroom out of bed and stay with the bride
    myself,
And tighten her all night to my thighs and lips.

My voice is the wife's voice, the screech by the rail of the
    stairs,
They fetch my man's body up dripping and drowned.

I understand the large hearts of heroes,
The courage of present times and all times;
How the skipper saw the crowded and rudderless wreck of
    the steamship, and death chasing it up and down the
    storm,   820
How he knuckled tight and gave not back one inch, and
    was faithful of days and faithful of nights,
And chalked in large letters on a board, Be of good cheer,
    We will not desert you;
How he saved the drifting company at last,
How the lank loose-gowned women looked when boated
    from the side of their prepared graves,

How the silent old-faced infants, and the lifted sick, and
    the sharp-lipped unshaved men;
All this I swallow and it tastes good....I like it well, and
    it becomes mine,
I am the man....I suffered....I was there.

The disdain and calmness of martyrs,
The mother condemned for a witch and burnt with dry
    wood, and her children gazing on;
The hounded slave that flags in the race and leans by the
    fence, blowing and covered with sweat,   830
The twinges that sting like needles his legs and neck,
The murderous buckshot and the bullets,
All these I feel or am.

I am the hounded slave....I wince at the bite of the dogs,
Hell and despair are upon me....crack and again crack the
    marksmen,
I clutch the rails of the fence....my gore dribs thinned
    with the ooze of my skin,
I fall on the weeds and stones,
The riders spur their unwilling horses and haul close,
They taunt my dizzy ears....they beat me violently over
    the head with their whip-stocks.

Agonies are one of my changes of garments;   840
I do not ask the wounded person how he feels....I
    myself become the wounded person,
My hurt turns livid upon me as I lean on a cane and
    observe.

I am the mashed fireman with breastbone broken....
    tumbling walls buried me in their debris,
Heat and smoke I inspired....I heard the yelling shouts of
    my comrades,
I heard the distant click of their picks and shovels;
They have cleared the beams away....they tenderly lift
    me forth.

I lie in the night air in my red shirt....the pervading hush
    is for my sake,

Painless after all I lie, exhausted but not so unhappy,
White and beautiful are the faces around me....the heads
    are bared of their fire-caps,
The kneeling crowd fades with the light of the torches   850

Distant and dead resuscitate,
They show as the dial or move as the hands of me....and
    I am the clock myself.

I am an old artillerist, and tell of some fort's bombardment
    ....and am there again.

Again the reveille of drummers....again the attacking
    cannon and mortars and howitzers,
Again the attacked send their cannon responsive.

I take part....I see and hear the whole,
The cries and curses and roar....the plaudits for well
    aimed shots,
The ambulanza slowly passing and trailing its red drip,
Workmen searching after damages and to make
    indispensable repairs,
The fall of grenades through the rent roof....the fan-
    shaped explosion,   860
The whizz of limbs heads stone wood and iron high in the
    air.

Again gurgles the mouth of my dying general....he
    furiously waves with his hand,
He gasps through the clot....Mind not me....mind....
    the entrenchments.

[34]

I tell not the fall of Alamo....not one escaped to tell the
    fall of Alamo,
The hundred and fifty are dumb yet at Alamo.

Hear now the tale of a jetblack sunrise,
Hear of the murder in cold blood of four hundred and
    twelve young men.

Retreating they had formed in a hollow square with their
    baggage for breastworks,
Nine hundred lives out of the surrounding enemy's nine
    times their number was the price they took in advance,
Their colonel was wounded and their ammunition gone,   870
They treated for an honorable capitulation, received
    writing and seal, gave up their arms, and marched
    back prisoners of war.

They were the glory of the race of rangers,
Matchless with a horse, a rifle, a song, a supper or a
    courtship,
Large, turbulent, brave, handsome, generous, proud and
    affectionate,
Bearded, sunburnt, dressed in the free costume of hunters,
Not a single one over thirty years of age.

The second Sunday morning they were brought out in
    squads and massacred. . . . it was beautiful early summer,
The work commenced about five o'clock and was over by
    eight.

None obeyed the command to kneel,
Some made a mad and helpless rush. . . . some stood stark
    and straight,   880
A few fell at once, shot in the temple or heart. . . . the
    living and dead lay together,
The maimed and mangled dug in the dirt. . . . the new-
    comers saw them there;
Some half-killed attempted to crawl away,
These were dispatched with bayonets or battered with the
    blunts of muskets;
A youth not seventeen years old seized his assassin till two
    more came to release him,
The three were all torn, and covered with the boy's blood.

At eleven o'clock began the burning of the bodies;
And that is the tale of the murder of the four hundred and
    twelve young men,
And that was a jetblack sunrise.

[35]

Did you read in the seabooks of the oldfashioned frigate-
     fight?   890
Did you learn who won by the light of the moon and stars?

Our foe was no skulk in his ship, I tell you,
His was the English pluck, and there is no tougher or
     truer, and never was, and never will be;
Along the lowered eve he came, horribly raking us.

We closed with him. . . . the yards entangled. . . . the
     cannon touched,
My captain lashed fast with his own hands.

We had received some eighteen-pound shots under the
     water,
On our lower-gun-deck two large pieces had burst at the
     first fire, killing all around and blowing up overhead.

Ten o'clock at night, and the full moon shining and the
     leaks on the gain, and five feet of water reported,
The master-at-arms loosing the prisoners confined in the
     after-hold to give them a chance for themselves.   900

The transit to and from the magazine was now stopped by
     the sentinels,
They saw so many strange faces they did not know whom
     to trust.

Our frigate was afire. . . . the other asked if we demanded
     quarters? if our colors were struck and the fighting
     done?

I laughed content when I heard the voice of my little
     captain,
We have not struck, he composedly cried, We have just
     begun our part of the fighting.

Only three guns were in use,
One was directed by the captain himself against the
     enemy's mainmast,

Two well-served with grape and canister silenced his
    musketry and cleared his decks.

The tops alone seconded the fire of this little battery,
    especially the maintop,
They all held out bravely during the whole of the action.   910

Not a moment's cease,
The leaks gained fast on the pumps....the fire eat toward
    the powder-magazine,
One of the pumps was shot away....it was generally
    thought we were sinking.

Serene stood the little captain,
He was not hurried....his voice was neither high nor low,
His eyes gave more light to us than our battle-lanterns.

Toward twelve at night, there in the beams of the moon
    they surrendered to us.

[36]

Stretched and still lay the midnight,
Two great hulls motionless on the breast of the darkness,
Our vessel riddled and slowly sinking....preparations to
    pass to the one we had conquered,   920
The captain on the quarter deck coldly giving his orders
    through a countenance white as a sheet,
Near by the corpse of the child that served in the cabin,
The dead face of an old salt with long white hair and
    carefully curled whiskers,
The flames spite of all that could be done flickering aloft
    and below,
The husky voices of the two or three officers yet fit for
    duty,
Formless stacks of bodies and bodies by themselves....
    dabs of flesh upon the masts and spars,
The cut of cordage and dangle of rigging....the slight
    shock of the soothe of waves,
Black and impassive guns, and litter of powder-parcels,
    and the strong scent,

Delicate sniffs of the seabreeze....smells of sedgy grass
    and fields by the shore....death-messages given in
    charge to survivors,
The hiss of the surgeon's knife and the gnawing teeth of
    his saw,   930
The wheeze, the cluck, the swash of falling blood....the
    short wild scream, the long dull tapering groan,
These so....these irretrievable.

[37]

O Christ! My fit is mastering me!
What the rebel said gaily adjusting his throat to the rope-
    noose,
What the savage at the stump, his eye-sockets empty, his
    mouth spirting whoops and defiance,
What stills the traveler come to the vault at Mount
    Vernon,
What sobers the Brooklyn boy as he looks down the shores
    of the Wallabout and remembers the prison ships,
What burnt the gums of the redcoat at Saratoga when he
    surrendered his brigades,
These become mine and me every one, and they are but
    little,
I become as much more as I like.   940

I become any presence or truth of humanity here,
And see myself in prison shaped like another man,
And feel the dull unintermitted pain.

For me the keepers of convicts shoulder their carbines and
    keep watch,
It is I let out in the morning and barred at night. .

Not a mutineer walks handcuffed to the jail, but I am
    handcuffed to him and walk by his side,
I am less the jolly one there, and more the silent one with
    sweat on my twitching lips.

Not a youngster is taken for larceny, but I go too and am
    tried and sentenced.

Not a cholera patient lies at the last gasp, but I also lie at
    the last gasp,
My face is ash-colored, my sinews gnarl....away from me
    people retreat.   950

Askers embody themselves in me, and I am embodied in
    them,
I project my hat and sit shamefaced and beg.

I rise extatic through all, and sweep with the true
    gravitation,
The whirling and whirling is elemental within me.

[38]

Somehow I have been stunned. Stand back!
Give me a little time beyond my cuffed head and slumbers
    and dreams and gaping,
I discover myself on a verge of the usual mistake.

That I could forget the mockers and insults!
That I could forget the trickling tears and the blows of the
    bludgeons and hammers!
That I could look with a separate look on my own
    crucifixion and bloody crowning!   960

I remember....I resume the overstaid fraction,
The grave of rock multiplies what has been confided to
    it....or to any graves,
The corpses rise....the gashes heal....the fastenings roll
    away.

I troop forth replenished with supreme power, one of an
    average unending procession,
We walk the roads of Ohio and Massachusetts and Virginia
    and Wisconsin and New York and New Orleans and
    Texas and Montreal and San Francisco and Charleston
    and Savannah and Mexico,
Inland and by the seacoast and boundary lines....and we
    pass the boundary lines.

Our swift ordinances are on their way over the whole
    earth,
The blossoms we wear in our hats are the growth of two
    thousand years.

Eleves I salute you,
I see the approach of your numberless gangs....I see you
    understand yourselves and me,
And know that they who have eyes are divine, and the   970
    blind and lame are equally divine,
And that my steps drag behind yours yet go before them,
And are aware how I am with you no more than I am with
    everybody.

[39]

The friendly and flowing savage....Who is he?
Is he waiting for civilization or past it and mastering it?

Is he some southwesterner raised outdoors? Is he
    Canadian?
Is he from the Mississippi country? or from Iowa, Oregon
    or California? or from the mountains? or prairie life or
    bush-life? or from the sea?

Wherever he goes men and women accept and desire him,
They desire he should like them and touch them and
    speak to them and stay with them.

Behaviour lawless as snow-flakes....words simple as
    grass....uncombed head and laughter and naivete;   980
Slowstepping feet and the common features, and the
    common modes and emanations,
They descend in new forms from the tips of his fingers,
They are wafted with the odor of his body or breath....
    they fly out of the glance of his eyes.

[40]

Flaunt of the sunshine I need not your bask....lie over,
You light surfaces only....I force the surfaces and the
    depths also.

Earth! you seem to look for something at my hands,
Say old topknot! what do you want?

Man or woman! I might tell how I like you, but cannot,
And might tell what it is in me and what it is in you, but
    cannot,
And might tell the pinings I have....the pulse of my
    nights and days.   990

Behold I do not give lectures or a little charity,
What I give I give out of myself.

You there, impotent, loose in the knees, open your
    scarfed chops till I blow grit within you,
Spread your palms and lift the flaps of your pockets,
I am not to be denied....I compel....I have stores
    plenty and to spare,
And any thing I have I bestow.

I do not ask who you are....that is not important to
    me,
You can do nothing and be nothing but what I will
    infold you.

To a drudge of the cottonfields or emptier of privies I
    lean....on his right cheek I put the family kiss,
And in my soul I swear I never will deny him.   1000

On women fit for conception I start bigger and nimbler
    babes,
This day I am jetting the stuff of far more arrogant
    republics.

To any one dying....thither I speed and twist the knob
    of the door,
Turn the bedclothes toward the foot of the bed,
Let the physician and the priest go home.

I seize the descending man....I raise him with resistless
    will.

O despairer, here is my neck,
By God! you shall not go down! Hang your whole
     weight upon me.

I dilate you with tremendous breath.... I buoy you up;
Every room of the house do I fill with an armed force
     ....lovers of me, bafflers of graves: 1010
Sleep! I and they keep guard all night;
Not doubt, not decease shall dare to lay finger upon you,
I have embraced you, and henceforth possess you to
     myself,
And when you rise in the morning you will find what I
     tell you is so.

[41]

I am he bringing help for the sick as they pant on their
     backs,
And for strong upright men I bring yet more needed help.

I heard what was said of the universe,
Heard it and heard of several thousand years;
It is middling well as far as it goes.... but is that all?

Magnifying and applying come I,   1020
Outbidding at the start the old cautious hucksters,
The most they offer for mankind and eternity less than a
     spirt of my own seminal wet,
Taking myself the exact dimensions of Jehovah and
     laying them away,
Lithographing Kronos and Zeus his son, and Hercules his
     grandson,
Buying drafts of Osiris and Isis and Belus and Brahma
     and Adonai,
In my portfolio placing Manito loose, and Allah on a leaf,
     and the crucifix engraved,
With Odin, and the hideous-faced Mexitli, and all idols
     and images,
Honestly taking them all for what they are worth, and not
     a cent more,
Admitting they were alive and did the work of their day,

Admitting they bore mites as for unfledged birds who
    have now to rise and fly and sing for themselves,   1030
Accepting the rough deific sketches to fill out better in
    myself.... bestowing them freely on each man and
    woman I see,
Discovering as much or more in a framer framing a house,
Putting higher claims for him there with his rolled-up
    sleeves, driving the mallet and chisel;
Not objecting to special revelations.... considering a
    curl of smoke or a hair on the back of my hand as
    curious as any revelation;
Those ahold of fire-engines and hook-and-ladder ropes
    more to me than the gods of the antique wars,
Minding their voices peal through the crash of
    destruction,
Their brawny limbs passing safe over charred laths....
    their white foreheads whole and unhurt out of the
    flames;
By the mechanic's wife with her babe at her nipple
    interceding for every person born;
Three scythes at harvest whizzing in a row from three
    lusty angels with shirts bagged out at their waists;
The snag-toothed hostler with red hair redeeming sins
    past and to come,   1040
Selling all he possesses and traveling on foot to fee
    lawyers for his brother and sit by him while he is
    tried for forgery:
What was strewn in the amplest strewing the square rod
    about me, and not filling the square rod then;
The bull and the bug never worshipped half enough,
Dung and dirt more admirable than was dreamed,
The supernatural of no account.... myself waiting my
    time to be one of the supremes,
The day getting ready for me when I shall do as much
    good as the best, and be as prodigious,
Guessing when I am it will not tickle me much to receive
    puffs out of pulpit or print;
By my life-lumps! becoming already a creator!
Putting myself here and now to the ambushed womb of
    the shadows!

[42]

....A call in the midst of the crowd,   1050
My own voice, orotund sweeping and final.

Come my children,
Come my boys and girls, and my women and household
    and intimates,
Now the performer launches his nerve....he has passed
    his prelude on the reeds within.

Easily written loosefingered chords! I feel the thrum of
    their climax and close.

My head [r]evolves on my neck,
Music rolls, but not from the organ....folks are around
    me, but they are no household of mine.

Ever the hard and unsunk ground,
Ever the eaters and drinkers....ever the upward and
    downward sun....ever the air and the ceaseless
    tides,
Ever myself and my neighbors, refreshing and wicked
    and real,   1060
Ever the old inexplicable query....ever that thorned
    thumb—that breath of itches and thirsts,
Ever the vexer's hoot! till we find where the sly one
    hides and bring him forth;
Ever love....ever the sobbing liquid of life,
Ever the bandage under the chin....ever the trestles of
    death.

Here and there with dimes on the eyes walking,
To feed the greed of the belly the brains liberally
    spooning,
Tickets buying or taking or selling, but in to the feast
    never once going;
Many sweating and ploughing and thrashing, and then the
    chaff for payment receiving,
A few idly owning, and they the wheat continually
    claiming.

This is the city....and I am one of the citizens;   1070
Whatever interests the rest interests me....politics,
        churches, newspapers, schools,
Benevolent societies, improvements, banks, tariffs,
        steamships, factories, markets,
Stocks and stores and real estate and personal estate.

They who piddle and patter here in collars and tailed
        coats....I am aware who they are....and that they
        are not worms or fleas,
I acknowledge the duplicates of myself under all the
        scrape-lipped and pipe-legged concealments.

The weakest and shallowest is deathless with me,
What I do and say the same waits for them,
Every thought that flounders in me the same flounders in
        them.

I know perfectly well my own egotism,
And know my omnivorous words, and cannot say any
        less,   1080
And would fetch you whoever you are flush with myself.

My words are words of a questioning, and to indicate
        reality;
This printed and bound book....but the printer and the
        printing-office boy?
The marriage estate and settlement....but the body and
        mind of the bridegroom? also those of the bride?
The panorama of the sea....but the sea itself?
The well-taken photographs....but your wife or friend
        close and solid in your arms?
The fleet of ships of the line and all the modern
        improvements....but the craft and pluck of the
        admiral?
The dishes and fare and furniture....but the host and
        hostess, and the look out of their eyes?
The sky up there....yet here or next door or across the
        way?
The saints and sages in history....but you yourself?   1090

Sermons and creeds and theology. . . . but the human
    brain, and what is called reason, and what is called
    love, and what is called life?

[43]

I do not despise you priests;
My faith is the greatest of faiths and the least of faiths,
Enclosing all worship ancient and modern, and all
    between ancient and modern,
Believing I shall come again upon the earth after five
    thousand years,
Waiting responses from oracles. . . . honoring the gods
    . . . . saluting the sun,
Making a fetish of the first rock or stump. . . . powowing
    with sticks in the circle of obis,
Helping the lama or brahmin as he trims the lamps of the
    idols,
Dancing yet through the streets in a phallic procession
    . . . . rapt and austere in the woods, a gymnosophist,
Drinking mead from the skull-cup. . . . to shasta and
    vedas admirant. . . . minding the koran,   1100
Walking the teokallis, spotted with gore from the stone
    and knife—beating the serpent-skin drum;
Accepting the gospels, accepting him that was crucified,
    knowing assuredly that he is divine,
To the mass kneeling—to the puritan's prayer rising—
    sitting patiently in a pew,
Ranting and frothing in my insane crisis—waiting dead-
    like till my spirit arouses me;
Looking forth on pavement and land, and outside of
    pavement and land,
Belonging to the winders of the circuit of circuits.

One of that centripetal and centrifugal gang,
I turn and talk like a man leaving charges before a
    journey.

Down-hearted doubters, dull and excluded,
Frivolous sullen moping angry affected disheartened
    atheistical,   1110

I know every one of you, and know the unspoken
    interrogatories,
By experience I know them.

How the flukes splash!
How they contort rapid as lightning, with spasms and
    spouts of blood!

Be at peace bloody flukes of doubters and sullen mopers,
I take my place among you as much as among any;
The past is the push of you and me and all precisely the
    same,
And the day and night are for you and me and all,
And what is yet untried and afterward is for you and me
    and all.

I do not know what is untried and afterward,   1120
But I know it is sure and alive and sufficient.

Each who passes is considered, and each who stops is
    considered, and not a single one can it fail.

It cannot fail the young man who died and was buried,
Nor the young woman who died and was put by his
    side,
Nor the little child that peeped in at the door and then
    drew back and was never seen again,
Nor the old man who has lived without purpose, and
    feels it with bitterness worse than gall,
Nor him in the poorhouse tubercled by rum and the bad
    disorder,
Nor the numberless slaughtered and wrecked....nor the
    brutish koboo, called the ordure of humanity,
Nor the sacs merely floating with open mouths for food
    to slip in,
Nor any thing in the earth, or down in the oldest graves
    of the earth,   1130
Nor any thing in the myriads of spheres, nor one of the
    myriads of myriads that inhabit them,
Nor the present, nor the least wisp that is known.

[44]

It is time to explain myself....let us stand up.

What is known I strip away....I launch all men and
    women forward with me into the unknown.

The clock indicates the moment....but what does
    eternity indicate?

Eternity lies in bottomless reservoirs....its buckets are
    rising forever and ever,
They pour and they pour and they exhale away.

We have thus far exhausted trillions of winters and
    summers;
There are trillions ahead, and trillions ahead of them.

Births have brought us richness and variety,   1140
And other births will bring us richness and variety.

I do not call one greater and one smaller,
That which fills its period and place is equal to any.

Were mankind murderous or jealous upon you my brother
    or my sister?
I am sorry for you....they are not murderous or jealous
    upon me;
All has been gentle with me....I keep no account with
    lamentation;
What have I to do with lamentation?

I am an acme of things accomplished, and I an encloser
    of things to be.

My feet strike an apex of the apices of the stairs,
On every step bunches of ages, and larger bunches
    between the steps,   1150
All below duly traveled—and still I mount and mount.

Rise after rise bow the phantoms behind me,

Afar down I see the huge first Nothing, the vapor from
    the nostrils of death,
I know I was even there....I waited unseen and always,
And slept while God carried me through the lethargic
    mist,
And took my time....and took no hurt from the fœtid
    carbon.

Long I was hugged close....long and long.

Immense have been the preparations for me,
Faithful and friendly the arms that have helped me.

Cycles ferried my cradle, rowing and rowing like cheerful
    boatmen;   1160
For room to me stars kept aside in their own rings,
They sent influences to look after what was to hold me.

Before I was born out of my mother generations guided
    me,
My embryo has never been torpid....nothing could
    overlay it;
For it the nebula cohered to an orb....the long slow
    strata piled to rest it on....vast vegetables gave it
    sustenance,
Monstrous sauroids transported it in their mouths and
    deposited it with care.

All forces have been steadily employed to complete and
    delight me,
Now I stand on this spot with my soul.

[45]

Span of youth! Ever-pushed elasticity! Manhood balanced
    and florid and full!

My lovers suffocate me!   1170
Crowding my lips, and thick in the pores of my skin,
Jostling me through streets and public halls....coming
    naked to me at night,

Crying by day Ahoy from the rocks of the river....
    swinging and chirping over my head,
Calling my name from flowerbeds or vines or tangled
    underbrush,
Or while I swim in the bath....or drink from the pump
    at the corner....or the curtain is down at the opera
    ....or I glimpse at a woman's face in the railroad car;
Lighting on every moment of my life,
Bussing my body with soft and balsamic busses,
Noiselessly passing handfuls out of their hearts and giving
    them to be mine.

Old age superbly rising! Ineffable grace of dying days!

Every condition promulges not only itself....it
    promulges what grows after and out of itself,   1180
And the dark hush promulges as much as any.

I open my scuttle at night and see the far-sprinkled
    systems,
And all I see, multiplied as high as I can cipher, edge but
    the rim of the farther systems.

Wider and wider they spread, expanding and always
    expanding,
Outward and outward and forever outward.

My sun has his sun, and round him obediently wheels,
He joins with his partners a group of superior circuit,
And greater sets follow, making specks of the greatest
    inside them.

There is no stoppage, and never can be stoppage;
If I and you and the worlds and all beneath or upon their
    surfaces, and all the palpable life, were this moment
    reduced back to a pallid float, it would not avail in
    the long run,   1190
We should surely bring up again where we now stand,
And as surely go as much farther, and then farther and
    farther.

A few quadrillions of eras, a few octillions of cubic
    leagues, do not hazard the span, or make it
    impatient,
They are but parts....any thing is but a part.

See ever so far....there is limitless space outside of that,
Count ever so much....there is limitless time around
    that.

Our rendezvous is fitly appointed....God will be there
    and wait till we come.

[46]

I know I have the best of time and space—and that I was
    never measured, and never will be measured.

I tramp a perpetual journey,
My signs are a rain-proof coat and good shoes and a staff
    cut from the woods;   1200
No friend of mine takes his ease in my chair,
I have no chair, nor church nor philosophy;
I lead no man to a dinner-table or library or exchange,
But each man and each woman of you I lead upon a
    knoll,
My left hand hooks you round the waist,
My right hand points to landscapes of continents, and a
    plain public road.

Not I, not any one else can travel that road for you,
You must travel it for yourself.

It is not far....it is within reach,
Perhaps you have been on it since you were born, and
    did not know,   1210
Perhaps it is every where on water and on land.

Shoulder your duds, and I will mine, and let us hasten
    forth;
Wonderful cities and free nations we shall fetch as we
    go.

If you tire, give me both burdens, and rest the chuff of
    your hand on my hip,
And in due time you shall repay the same service to me;
For after we start we never lie by again.

This day before dawn I ascended a hill and looked at the
    crowded heaven,
And I said to my spirit, When we become the enfolders
    of those orbs and the pleasure and knowledge of every
    thing in them, shall we be filled and satisfied then?
And my spirit said No, we level that lift to pass and
    continue beyond.

You are also asking me questions, and I hear you;   1220
I answer that I cannot answer....you must find out for
    yourself.

Sit awhile wayfarer,
Here are biscuits to eat and here is milk to drink,
But as soon as you sleep and renew yourself in sweet
    clothes I will certainly kiss you with my goodbye kiss
    and open the gate for your egress hence.

Long enough have you dreamed contemptible dreams,
Now I wash the gum from your eyes,
You must habit yourself to the dazzle of the light and of
    every moment of your life.

Long have you timidly waded, holding a plank by the
    shore,
Now I will you to be a bold swimmer,
To jump off in the midst of the sea, and rise again and nod
    to me and shout, and laughingly dash with your hair.   1230

[47]

I am the teacher of athletes,
He that by me spreads a wider breast than my own proves
    the width of my own,
He most honors my style who learns under it to destroy
    the teacher.

The boy I love, the same becomes a man not through
    derived power but in his own right,
Wicked, rather than virtuous out of conformity or fear,
Fond of his sweetheart, relishing well his steak,
Unrequited love or a slight cutting him worse than a
    wound cuts,
First rate to ride, to fight, to hit the bull's eye, to sail a
    skiff, to sing a song or play on the banjo,
Preferring scars and faces pitted with smallpox over all
    latherers and those that keep out of the sun.

I teach straying from me, yet who can stray from me?   1240
I follow you whoever you are from the present hour;
My words itch at your ears till you understand them.

I do not say these things for a dollar, or to fill up the time
    while I wait for a boat;
It is you talking just as much as myself. . . . I act as the
    tongue of you,
It was tied in your mouth. . . . in mine it begins to be
    loosened.

I swear I will never mention love or death inside a house,
And I swear I never will translate myself at all, only to
    him or her who privately stays with me in the open
    air.

If you would understand me go to the heights or water-
    shore,
The nearest gnat is an explanation and a drop or the
    motion of waves a key,
The maul the oar and the handsaw second my words.   1250

No shuttered room or school can commune with me,
But roughs and little children better than they.

The young mechanic is closest to me. . . . he knows me
    pretty well,
The woodman that takes his axe and jug with him shall
    take me with him all day,

The farmboy ploughing in the field feels good at the
    sound of my voice,
In vessels that sail my words must sail. . . . I go with
    fishermen and seamen, and love them,
My face rubs to the hunter's face when he lies down
    alone in his blanket,
The driver thinking of me does not mind the jolt of his
    wagon,
The young mother and old mother shall comprehend me,
The girl and the wife rest the needle a moment and
    forget where they are,   1260
They and all would resume what I have told them.

[48]

I have said that the soul is not more than the body,
And I have said that the body is not more than the soul,
And nothing, not God, is greater to one than one's-self is,
And whoever walks a furlong without sympathy walks
    to his own funeral, dressed in his shroud,
And I or you pocketless of a dime may purchase the pick
    of the earth,
And to glance with an eye or show a bean in its pod
    confounds the learning of all times,
And there is no trade or employment but the young man
    following it may become a hero,
And there is no object so soft but it makes a hub for the
    wheeled universe,
And any man or woman shall stand cool and supercilious
    before a million universes.   1270

And I call to mankind, Be not curious about God,
For I who am curious about each am not curious about
    God,
No array of terms can say how much I am at peace about
    God and about death.

I hear and behold God in every object, yet I understand
    God not in the least,
Nor do I understand who there can be more wonderful
    than myself.

Why should I wish to see God better than this day?
I see something of God each hour of the twenty-four,
      and each moment then,
In the faces of men and women I see God, and in my
      own face in the glass;
I find letters from God dropped in the street, and every
      one is signed by God's name,
And I leave them where they are, for I know that others
      will punctually come forever and ever.   1280

[49]

And as to you death, and you bitter hug of mortality....
      it is idle to try to alarm me.

To his work without flinching the accoucheur comes,
I see the elderhand pressing receiving supporting,
I recline by the sills of the exquisite flexible doors....and
      mark the outlet, and mark the relief and escape.

And as to you corpse I think you are good manure, but
      that does not offend me,
I smell the white roses sweetscented and growing,
I reach to the leafy lips....I reach to the polished breasts
      of melons.

And as to you life, I reckon you are the leavings of many
      deaths,
No doubt I have died myself ten thousand times before.

I hear you whispering there O stars of heaven,   1290
O suns....O grass of graves....O perpetual transfers
      and promotions....if you do not say anything how
      can I say anything?

Of the turbid pool that lies in the autumn forest,
Of the moon that descends the steeps of the soughing
      twilight,
Toss, sparkles of day and dusk....toss on the black
      stems that decay in the muck,
Toss to the moaning gibberish of the dry limbs.

I ascend from the moon. . . . I ascend from the night,
And perceive of the ghastly glitter the sunbeams
    reflected,
And debouch to the steady and central from the offspring
    great or small.

[50]

There is that in me. . . . I do not know what is is. . . . but I
    know it is in me.

Wrenched and sweaty. . . . calm and cool then my body
    becomes;   1300
I sleep. . . . I sleep long.

I do not know it. . . . it is without name. . . . it is a word
    unsaid,
It is not in any dictionary or utterance or symbol.

Something it swings on more than the earth I swing
    on,
To it the creation is the friend whose embracing awakes
    me.

Perhaps I might tell more. . . . Outlines! I plead for my
    brothers and sisters.

Do you see O my brothers and sisters?
It is not chaos or death. . . . it is form and union and
    plan. . . . it is eternal life. . . . it is happiness.

[51]

The past and present wilt. . . . I have filled them and
    emptied them,
And proceed to fill my next fold of the future.   1310

Listener up there! Here you. . . . what have you to confide
    to me?
Look in my face while I snuff the sidle of evening,
Talk honestly, for no one else hears you, and I stay only
    a minute longer.

Do I contradict myself?
Very well then....I contradict myself;
I am large....I contain multitudes.

I concentrate toward them that are nigh....I wait on the
        door-slab.

Who has done his day's work and will soonest be through
        with his supper?
Who wishes to walk with me?

Will you speak before I am gone? Will you prove already
        too late?   1320

[52]

The spotted hawk swoops by and accuses me....he
        complains of my gab and my loitering.

I too am not a bit tamed....I too am untranslatable,
I sound my barbaric yawp over the roofs of the world.

The last scud of day holds back for me,
It flings my likeness after the rest and true as any on the
        shadowed wilds,
It coaxes me to the vapor and the dusk.

I depart as air....I shake my white locks at the runaway
        sun,
I effuse my flesh in eddies and drift it in lacy jags.

I bequeath myself to the dirt to grow from the grass I love,
If you want me again look for me under your bootsoles.   1330

You will hardly know who I am or what I mean,
But I shall be good health to you nevertheless,
And filter and fibre your blood.

Failing to fetch me at first keep encouraged,
Missing me one place search another,
I stop some where waiting for you.

FROM "TO THINK OF TIME" [1855]

[1]

To think of time....to think through the retrospection,
To think of today..and the ages continued henceforward.

Have you guessed you yourself would not continue?
    Have you dreaded those earth-beetles?
Have you feared the future would be nothing to you?

Is today nothing? Is the beginningless past nothing?
If the future is nothing they are just as surely nothing.

To think that the sun rose in the east....that men and
    women were flexible and real and alive....that every
    thing was real and alive;
To think that you and I did not see feel think nor bear
    our part,
To think that we are now here and bear our part.

[2]

Not a day passes..not a minute or second without an
    accouchement;   10
Not a day passes..not a minute or second without a
    corpse.

When the dull nights are over, and the dull days also,
When the soreness of lying so much in bed is over,
When the physician, after long putting off, gives the silent
    and terrible look for an answer,
When the children come hurried and weeping, and the
    brothers and sisters have been sent for,
When medicines stand unused on the shelf, and the
    camphor-smell has pervaded the rooms,
When the faithful hand of the living does not desert the
    hand of the dying,
When the twitching lips press lightly on the forehead of
    the dying,

When the breath ceases and the pulse of the heart ceases,
Then the corpse-limbs stretch on the bed, and the living
    look upon them,   20
They are palpable as the living are palpable.

The living look upon the corpse with their eyesight,
But without eyesight lingers a different living and looks
    curiously on the corpse.

[3]

To think that the rivers will come to flow, and the snow
    fall, and fruits ripen. .and act upon others as upon us
    now. . . .yet not act upon us;
To think of all these wonders of city and country. .and
    others taking great interest in them. .and we taking
    small interest in them.

To think how eager we are in building our houses,
To think others shall be just as eager. .and we quite
    indifferent.

I see one building the house that serves him a few years
    . . . .or seventy or eighty years at most;
I see one building the house that serves him longer than
    that.

Slowmoving and black lines creep over the whole earth
    . . . .they never cease. . . .they are the burial lines,   30
He that was President was buried, and he that is now
    President shall surely be buried.

[4]

Cold dash of waves at the ferrywharf,
Posh and ice in the river. . . .half-frozen mud in the
    streets,
A gray discouraged sky overhead. . . .the short last
    daylight of December,
A hearse and stages. . . .other vehicles give place,

The funeral of an old stagedriver....the cortege mostly
     drivers.

Rapid the trot to the cemetery,
Duly rattles the deathbell....the gate is passed....the
     grave is halted at....the living alight....the hearse
     uncloses,
The coffin is lowered and settled....the whip is laid on
     the coffin,
The earth is swiftly shovelled in....a minute..no one
     moves or speaks....it is done,
He is decently put away....is there anything more?   40

He was a goodfellow,
Freemouthed, quicktempered, not badlooking, able to take
     his own part,
Witty, sensitive to a slight, ready with life or death for a
     friend,
Fond of women,..played some..eat hearty and drank
     hearty,
Had known what it was to be flush..grew lowspirited
     toward the last..sickened..was helped by a
     contribution,
Died aged forty-one years..and that was his funeral.

Thumb extended or finger uplifted,
Apron, cape, gloves, strap....wetweather clothes....
     whip carefully chosen....boss, spotter, starter, and
     hostler,
Somebody loafing on you, or you loafing on somebody
     ....headway....man before and man behind,   50
Good day's work or bad day's work....pet stock or
     mean stock....first out or last out....turning in at
     night,
To think that these are so much and so nigh to other
     drivers..and he there takes no interest in them.

.   .   .   .   .

CROSSING BROOKLYN FERRY   [1856]

1

Flood-tide below me! I see you face to face!
Clouds of the west—sun there half an hour high—I see you
    also face to face.

Crowds of men and women attired in the usual costumes,
    how curious you are to me!
On the ferry-boats the hundreds and hundreds that cross,
    returning home, are more curious to me than you
    suppose,
And you that shall cross from shore to shore years hence
    are more to me, and more in my meditations, than you
    might suppose.

2

The impalpable sustenance of me from all things at all hours
    of the day,
The simple, compact, well-join'd scheme, myself
    disintegrated, every one disintegrated yet part of the
    scheme,
The similitudes of the past and those of the future,
The glories strung like beads on my smallest sights and
    hearings, on the walk in the street and the passage over
    the river,
The current rushing so swiftly and swimming with me far
    away,   10
The others that are to follow me, the ties between me and
    them,
The certainty of others, the life, love, sight, hearing of
    others.

Others will enter the gates of the ferry and cross from
    shore to shore,
Others will watch the run of the flood-tide,
Others will see the shipping of Manhattan north and west,
    and the heights of Brooklyn to the south and east,

Others will see the islands large and small;
Fifty years hence, others will see them as they cross, the
    sun half an hour high,
A hundred years hence, or ever so many hundred years
    hence, others will see them,
Will enjoy the sunset, the pouring-in of the flood-tide, the
    falling-back to the sea of the ebb-tide.

3

It avails not, time nor place—distance avails not,   20
I am with you, you men and women of a generation, or
    ever so many generations hence,
Just as you feel when you look on the river and sky, so I
    felt,
Just as any of you is one of a living crowd, I was one of a
    crowd,
Just as you are refresh'd by the gladness of the river and
    the bright flow, I was refresh'd,
Just as you stand and lean on the rail, yet hurry with the
    swift current, I stood yet was hurried,
Just as you look on the numberless masts of ships and the
    thick-stemm'd pipes of steamboats, I look'd.

I too many and many a time cross'd the river of old,
Watched the Twelfth-month sea-gulls, saw them high in
    the air floating with motionless wings, oscillating their
    bodies,
Saw how the glistening yellow lit up parts of their bodies
    and left the rest in strong shadow,
Saw the slow-wheeling circles and the gradual edging
    toward the south,   30
Saw the reflection of the summer sky in the water,
Had my eyes dazzled by the shimmering track of beams,
Look'd at the fine centrifugal spokes of light round the
    shape of my head in the sunlit water,
Look'd on the haze on the hills southward and south-
    westward,
Look'd on the vapor as it flew in fleeces tinged with
    violet,
Look'd toward the lower bay to notice the vessels arriving,

Saw their approach, saw aboard those that were near me,
Saw the white sails of schooners and sloops, saw the ships
    at anchor,
The sailors at work in the rigging or out astride the spars,
The round masts, the swinging motion of the hulls, the
    slender serpentine pennants,   40
The large and small steamers in motion, the pilots in their
    pilot-houses,
The white wake left by the passage, the quick tremulous
    whirl of the wheels,
The flags of all nations, the falling of them at sunset,
The scallop-edged waves in the twilight, the ladled cups,
    the frolicsome crests and glistening,
The stretch afar growing dimmer and dimmer, the gray
    walls of the granite storehouses by the docks,
On the river the shadowy group, the big steam-tug closely
    flank'd on each side by the barges, the hay-boat, the
    belated lighter,
On the neighboring shore the fires from the foundry
    chimneys burning high and glaringly into the night,
Casting their flicker of black contrasted with wild red and
    yellow light over the tops of houses, and down into
    the clefts of streets.

4

These and all else were to me the same as they are to you,
I loved well those cities, loved well the stately and rapid
    river,   50
The men and women I saw were all near to me,
Others the same—others who look back on me because I
    look'd forward to them,
(The time will come, though I stop here to-day and
    to-night.)

5

What is it then between us?
What is the count of the scores or hundreds of years
    between us?

Whatever it is, it avails not—distance avails not, and place
    avails not,

I too lived, Brooklyn of ample hills was mine,
I too walk'd the streets of Manhattan island, and bathed
    in the waters around it,
I too felt the curious abrupt questionings stir within me,
In the day among crowds of people sometimes they came
    upon me,   60
In my walks home late at night or as I lay in my bed they
    came upon me,
I too had been struck from the float forever held in
    solution,
I too had receiv'd identity by my body,
That I was I knew was of my body, and what I should be I
    knew I should be of my body.

6

It is not upon you alone the dark patches fall,
The dark threw its patches down upon me also,
The best I had done seem'd to me blank and suspicious,
My great thoughts as I supposed them, were they not in
    reality meagre?
Nor is it you alone who know what it is to be evil,
I am he who knew what it was to be evil,   70
I too knitted the old knot of contrariety,
Blabb'd, blush'd, resented, lied, stole, grudg'd,
Had guile, anger, lust, hot wishes I dared not speak,
Was wayward, vain, greedy, shallow, sly, cowardly,
    malignant,
The wolf, the snake, the hog, not wanting in me,
The cheating look, the frivolous word, the adulterous wish,
    not wanting,
Refusals, hates, postponements, meanness, laziness, none of
    these wanting,
Was one with the rest, the days and haps of the rest,
Was call'd by my nighest name by clear loud voices of
    young men as they saw me approaching or passing,
Felt their arms on my neck as I stood, or the negligent
    leaning of their flesh against me as I sat,   80
Saw many I loved in the street or ferry-boat or public
    assembly, yet never told them a word,
Lived the same life with the rest, the same old laughing,
    gnawing, sleeping,

Play'd the part that still looks back on the actor or actress,
The same old role, the role that is what we make it, as
        great as we like,
Or as small as we like, or both great and small.

                                    7

Closer yet I approach you,
What thought you have of me now, I had as much of you
        —I laid in my stores in advance,
I consider'd long and seriously of you before you were born.

Who was to know what should come home to me?
Who knows but I am enjoying this?   90
Who knows, for all the distance, but I am as good as
        looking at you now, for all you cannot see me?

                                    8

Ah, what can ever be more stately and admirable to me
        than mast-hemm'd Manhattan?
River and sunset and scallop-edg'd waves of flood-tide?
The sea-gulls oscillating their bodies, the hay-boat in the
        twilight, and the belated lighter?
What gods can exceed these that clasp me by the hand, and
        with voices I love call me promptly and loudly by my
        nighest name as I approach?

What is more subtle than this which ties me to the woman
        or man that looks in my face?
Which fuses me into you now, and pours my meaning into
        you?

We understand then do we not?
What I promis'd without mentioning it, have you not
        accepted?
What the study could not teach—what the preaching could
        not accomplish is accomplish'd, is it not?   100

                                    9

Flow on, river! flow with the flood-tide, and ebb with the
        ebb-tide!

Frolic on, crested and scallop-edg'd waves!

Gorgeous clouds of the sunset! drench with your splendor
    me, or the men and women generations after me!

Cross from shore to shore, countless crowds of passengers!

Stand up, tall masts of Mannahatta! stand up, beautiful hills
    of Brooklyn!

Throb, baffled and curious brain! throw out questions and
    answers!

Suspend here and everywhere, eternal float of solution!

Gaze, loving and thirsting eyes, in the house or street or
    public assembly!

Sound out, voices of young men! loudly and musically call
    me by my nighest name!

Live, old life! play the part that looks back on the actor or
    actress!   110

Play the old role, the role that is great or small according
    as one makes it!

Consider, you who peruse me, whether I may not in
    unknown ways be looking upon you;

Be firm, rail over the river, to support those who lean
    idly, yet haste with the hasting current;

Fly on, sea-birds! fly sideways, or wheel in large circles
    high in the air;

Receive the summer sky, you water, and faithfully hold it
    till all downcast eyes have time to take it from you!

Diverge, fine spokes of light, from the shape of my head,
    or any one's head, in the sunlit water!

Come on, ships from the lower bay! pass up or down,
    white-sail'd schooners, sloops, lighters!

Flaunt away, flags of all nations! be duly lower'd at sunset!

Burn high your fires, foundry chimneys! cast black shadows
    at nightfall! cast red and yellow light over the tops of
    the houses!

Appearances, now or henceforth, indicate what you are,   120

You necessary film, continue to envelop the soul,

About my body for me, and your body for you, be hung
    our divinest aromas,

Thrive, cities—bring your freight, bring your shows, ample
    and sufficient rivers,

Expand, being than which none else is perhaps more spiritual,

Keep your places, objects than which none else is more
    lasting.

You have waited, you always wait, you dumb, beautiful
    ministers,
We receive you with free sense at last, and are insatiate
    henceforward,
Not you any more shall be able to foil us, or withhold
    yourselves from us,
We use you, and do not cast you aside—we plant you
    permanently within us,
We fathom you not—we love you—there is perfection in
    you also,   130
You furnish your parts toward eternity,
Great or small, you furnish your parts toward the soul.

OUT OF THE CRADLE ENDLESSLY
ROCKING   [1860]

Out of the cradle endlessly rocking,
Out of the mocking-bird's throat, the musical shuttle,
Out of the Ninth-month midnight,
Over the sterile sands and the fields beyond, where the
    child leaving his bed wander'd alone, bareheaded,
    barefoot,
Down from the shower'd halo,
Up from the mystic play of shadows twining and twisting
    as if they were alive,
Out from the patches of briers and blackberries,
From the memories of the bird that chanted to me,
From your memories sad brother, from the fitful risings
    and fallings I heard,
From under that yellow half-moon late-risen and swollen
    as if with tears,   10
From those beginning notes of yearning and love there in
    the mist,
From the thousand responses of my heart never to cease,

From the myriad thence-arous'd words,
From the word stronger and more delicious than any,
From such as now they start the scene revisiting,
As a flock, twittering, rising, or overhead passing,
Borne hither, ere all eludes me, hurriedly,
A man, yet by these tears a little boy again,
Throwing myself on the sand, confronting the waves,
I, chanter of pains and joys, uniter of here and hereafter,   20
Taking all hints to use them, but swiftly leaping beyond
        them,
A reminiscence sing.

Once Paumanok,
When the lilac-scent was in the air and Fifth-month grass
        was growing,
Up this seashore in some briers,
Two feather'd guests from Alabama, two together,
And their nest, and four light-green eggs spotted with
        brown,
And every day the he-bird to and fro near at hand,
And every day the she-bird crouch'd on her nest, silent,
        with bright eyes,
And every day I, a curious boy, never too close, never
        disturbing them,   30
Cautiously peering, absorbing, translating.

Shine! shine! shine!
Pour down your warmth, great sun!
While we bask, we two together.

Two together!
Winds blow south, or winds blow north,
Day come white, or night come black,
Home, or rivers and mountains from home,
Singing all time, minding no time,
While we two keep together.   40

Till of a sudden,
May-be kill'd, unknown to her mate,
One forenoon the she-bird crouch'd not on the nest,

Nor return'd that afternoon, nor the next,
Nor ever appear'd again.

And thenceforward all summer in the sound of the sea,
And at night under the full of the moon in calmer weather,
Over the hoarse surging of the sea,
Or flitting from brier to brier by day,
I saw, I heard at intervals the remaining one, the he-bird,   50
The solitary guest from Alabama.

Blow! blow! blow!
Blow up sea-winds along Paumanok's shore;
I wait and I wait till you blow my mate to me.

Yes, when the stars glisten'd,
All night long on the prong of a moss-scallop'd stake,
Down almost amid the slapping waves,
Sat the lone singer wonderful causing tears.

He call'd on his mate,
He pour'd forth the meanings which I of all men know.   60

Yes my brother I know,
The rest might not, but I have treasur'd every note,
For more than once dimly down to the beach gliding,
Silent, avoiding the moonbeams, blending myself with the
        shadows,
Recalling now the obscure shapes, the echoes, the sounds
        and sights after their sorts,
The white arms out in the breakers tirelessly tossing,
I, with bare feet, a child, the wind wafting my hair,
Listen'd long and long.

Listen'd to keep, to sing, now translating the notes,
Following you my brother.   70

Soothe! soothe! soothe!
Close on its wave soothes the wave behind,
And again another behind embracing and lapping, every one close,
But my love soothes not me, not me.

Low hangs the moon, it rose late,
It is lagging—O I think it is heavy with love, with love.

O madly the sea pushes upon the land,
With love, with love.

O night! do I not see my love fluttering out among the breakers?
What is that little black thing I see there in the white?   80

Loud! loud! loud!
Loud I call to you, my love!
High and clear I shoot my voice over the waves,
Surely you must know who is here, is here,
You must know who I am, my love.

Low-hanging moon!
What is that dusky spot in your brown yellow?
O it is the shape, the shape of my mate!
O moon do not keep her from me any longer.

Land! land! O land!   90
Whichever way I turn, O I think you could give me my mate back
*   again if you only would,*
For I am almost sure I see her dimly whichever way I look.

O rising stars!
Perhaps the one I want so much will rise, will rise with some of
*   you.*

O throat! O trembling throat!
Sound clearer through the atmosphere!
Pierce the woods, the earth,
Somewhere listening to catch you must be the one I want.

Shake out carols!
Solitary here, the night's carols!   100
Carols of lonesome love! death's carols!
Carols under that lagging, yellow, waning moon!
O under the moon where she droops almost down into the sea!
O reckless despairing carols.

But soft! sink low!
Soft! let me just murmur,
And do you wait a moment you husky-nois'd sea,
For somewhere I believe I heard my mate responding to me,
So faint, I must be still, be still to listen,
But not altogether still, for then she might not come immediately
      to me.   110

Hither my love!
Here I am! here!
With this just-sustain'd note I announce myself to you,
This gentle call is for you my love, for you.

Do not be decoy'd elsewhere,
That is the whistle of the wind, it is not my voice,
That is the fluttering, the fluttering of the spray,
Those are the shadows of leaves.

O darkness! O in vain!
O I am very sick and sorrowful.   120

O brown halo in the sky near the moon, drooping upon the sea!
O troubled reflection in the sea!
O throat! O throbbing heart!
And I singing uselessly, uselessly all the night.

O past! O happy life! O songs of joy!
In the air, in the woods, over fields,
Loved! loved! loved! loved! loved!
But my mate no more, no more with me!
We two together no more.

The aria sinking,   130
All else continuing, the stars shining,
The winds blowing, the notes of the bird continuous
    echoing,
With angry moans the fierce old mother incessantly
    moaning,
On the sands of Paumanok's shore gray and rustling,
The yellow half-moon enlarged, sagging down, drooping,
    the face of the sea almost touching,

The boy ecstatic, with his bare feet the waves, with his hair
    the atmosphere dallying,
The love in the heart long pent, now loose, now at last
    tumultuously bursting,
The aria's meaning, the ears, the soul, swiftly depositing,
The strange tears down the cheeks coursing,
The colloquy there, the trio, each uttering,   140
The undertone, the savage old mother incessantly crying,
To the boy's soul's questions sullenly timing, some
    drown'd secret hissing,
To the outsetting bard.

Demon or bird! (said the boy's soul,)
Is it indeed toward your mate you sing? or is it really to
    me?
For I, that was a child, my tongue's use sleeping, now I
    have heard you,
Now in a moment I know what I am for, I awake,
And already a thousand singers, a thousand songs, clearer,
    louder and more sorrowful than yours,
A thousand warbling echoes have started to life within me,
    never to die.

O you singer solitary, singing by yourself, projecting me,   150
O solitary me listening, never more shall I cease
    perpetuating you,
Never more shall I escape, never more the reverberations,
Never more the cries of unsatisfied love be absent from
    me,
Never again leave me to be the peaceful child I was before
    what there in the night,
By the sea under the yellow and sagging moon,
The messenger there arous'd, the fire, the sweet hell
    within,
The unknown want, the destiny of me.

O give me the clew! (it lurks in the night here somewhere,)
O if I am to have so much, let me have more!

A word then, (for I will conquer it,)   160
The word final, superior to all,

Subtle, sent up—what is it?—I listen;
Are you whispering it, and have been all the time, you sea
    waves?
Is that it from your liquid rims and wet sands?

Whereto answering, the sea,
Delaying not, hurrying not,
Whisper'd me through the night, and very plainly before
    daybreak,
Lisp'd to me the low and delicious word death,
And again death, death, death, death,
Hissing melodious, neither like the bird nor like my
    arous'd child's heart,   170
But edging near as privately for me rustling at my feet,
Creeping thence steadily up to my ears and laving me
    softly all over,
Death, death, death, death, death.

Which I do not forget,
But fuse the song of my dusky demon and brother,
That he sang to me in the moonlight on Paumanok's
    gray beach,
With the thousand responsive songs at random,
My own songs awaked from that hour,
And with them the key, the word up from the waves,
The word of the sweetest song and all songs,   180
That strong and delicious word which, creeping to my
    feet,
(Or like some old crone rocking the cradle, swathed in
    sweet garments, bending aside,)
The sea whisper'd me.

From "Children of Adam"   [1860]

TO THE GARDEN THE WORLD

To the garden the world anew ascending,
Potent mates, daughters, sons, preluding,

The love, the life of their bodies, meaning and being,
Curious here behold my resurrection after slumber,
The revolving cycles in their wide sweep having brought
      me again,
Amorous, mature, all beautiful to me, all wondrous,
My limbs and the quivering fire that ever plays through
      them, for reasons, most wondrous,
Existing I peer and penetrate still,
Content with the present, content with the past,
By my side or back of me Eve following,   10
Or in front, and I following her just the same.

FROM PENT-UP ACHING RIVERS

From pent-up aching rivers,
From that of myself without which I were nothing,
From what I am determin'd to make illustrious, even if I
      stand sole among men,
From my own voice resonant, singing the phallus,
Singing the song of procreation,
Singing the need of superb children and therein superb
      grown people,
Singing the muscular urge and the blending,
Singing the bedfellow's song, (O resistless yearning!
O for any and each the body correlative attracting!
O for you whoever you are your correlative body! O it,
      more than all else, you delighting!)   10
From the hungry gnaw that eats me night and day,
From native moments, from bashful pains, singing them,
Seeking something yet unfound though I have diligently
      sought it many a long year,
Singing the true song of the soul fitful at random,
Renascent with grossest Nature or among animals,
Of that, of them and what goes with them my poems
      informing,
Of the smell of apples and lemons, of the pairing of birds,
Of the wet of woods, of the lapping of waves,

Of the mad pushes of waves upon the land, I them
    chanting,
The overture lightly sounding, the strain anticipating,   20
The welcome nearness, the sight of the perfect body,
The swimmer swimming naked in the bath, or motionless
    on his back lying and floating,
The female form approaching, I pensive, love-flesh
    tremulous aching,
The divine list for myself or you or for any one making,
The face, the limbs, the index from head to foot, and
    what it arouses,
The mystic deliria, the madness amorous, the utter
    abandonment,
(Hark close and still what I now whisper to you,
I love you, O you entirely possess me,
O that you and I escape from the rest and go utterly off,
    free and lawless,
Two hawks in the air, two fishes swimming in the sea not
    more lawless than we;)   30
The furious storm through me careering, I passionately
    trembling,
The oath of the inseparableness of two together, of the
    woman that loves me and whom I love more than my
    life, that oath swearing,
(O I willingly stake all for you,
O let me be lost if it must be so!
O you and I! what is it to us what the rest do or think?
What is all else to us? only that we enjoy each other and
    exhaust each other if it must be so;)
From the master, the pilot I yield the vessel to,
The general commanding me, commanding all, from him
    permission taking,
From time the programme hastening, (I have loiter'd too
    long as it is,)
From sex, from the warp and from the woof,   40
From privacy, from frequent repinings alone,
From plenty of persons near and yet the right person not
    near,
From the soft sliding of hands over me and thrusting of
    fingers through my hair and beard,

From the long sustain'd kiss upon the mouth or bosom,
From the close pressure that makes me or any man drunk,
    fainting with excess,
From what the divine husband knows, from the work of
    fatherhood,
From exultation, victory and relief from the bedfellow's
    embrace in the night,
From the act-poems of eyes, hands, hips and bosoms,
From the cling of the trembling arm,
From the bending curve and the clinch,   50
From side by side the pliant coverlet off-throwing,
From the one so unwilling to have me leave, and me just
    as unwilling to leave,
(Yet a moment O tender waiter, and I return,)
From the hour of shining stars and dropping dews,
From the night a moment I emerging flitting out,
Celebrate you act divine and you children prepared for,
And you stalwart loins.

AGES AND AGES RETURNING AT INTERVALS

Ages and ages returning at intervals,
Undestroy'd, wandering immortal,
Lusty, phallic, with the potent original loins, perfectly sweet,
I, chanter of Adamic songs,
Through the new garden the West, the great cities calling,
Deliriate, thus prelude what is generated, offering these,
    offering myself,
Bathing myself, bathing my songs in Sex,
Offspring of my loins.

AS ADAM EARLY IN THE MORNING

As Adam early in the morning,
Walking forth from the bower refresh'd with sleep,
Behold me where I pass, hear my voice, approach,

Touch me, touch the palm of your hand to my body as I pass,
Be not afraid of my body.

From "Calamus" [1860]

IN PATHS UNTRODDEN

In paths untrodden,
In the growth by margins of pond-waters,
Escaped from the life that exhibits itself,
From all the standards hitherto publish'd, from the
    pleasures, profits, conformities,
Which too long I was offering to feed my soul,
Clear to me now standards not yet publish'd, clear to me
    that my soul,
That the soul of the man I speak for rejoices in comrades,
Here by myself away from the clank of the world,
Tallying and talk'd to here by tongues aromatic,
No longer abash'd, (for in this secluded spot I can respond
    as I would not dare elsewhere,)   10
Strong upon me the life that does not exhibit itself, yet
    contains all the rest,
Resolv'd to sing no songs to-day but those of manly
    attachment,
Projecting them along that substantial life,
Bequeathing hence types of athletic love,
Afternoon this delicious Ninth-month in my forty-first year,
I proceed for all who are or have been young men,
To tell the secret of my nights and days,
To celebrate the need of comrades.

SCENTED HERBAGE OF MY BREAST

Scented herbage of my breast,
Leaves from you I glean, I write, to be perused best
    afterwards,

Tomb-leaves, body-leaves growing up above me above
    death,
Perennial roots, tall leaves, O the winter shall not freeze
    you delicate leaves,
Every year shall you bloom again, out from where you
    retired you shall emerge again;
O I do not know whether many passing by will discover
    you or inhale your faint odor, but I believe a few will;
O slender leaves! O blossoms of my blood! I permit you
    to tell in your own way of the heart that is under you,
O I do not know what you mean there underneath
    yourselves, you are not happiness,
You are often more bitter than I can bear, you burn and
    sting me,
Yet you are beautiful to me you faint-tinged roots, you
    make me think of death,   10
Death is beautiful from you, (what indeed is finally
    beautiful except death and love?)
O I think it is not for life I am chanting here my chant of
    lovers, I think it must be for death,
For how calm, how solemn it grows to ascend to the
    atmosphere of lovers,
Death or life I am then indifferent, my soul declines to
    prefer,
(I am not sure but the high soul of lovers welcomes death
    most),
Indeed O death, I think now these leaves mean precisely
    the same as you mean,
Grow up taller sweet leaves that I may see! grow up out of
    my breast!
Spring away from the conceal'd heart there!
Do not fold yourself so in your pink-tinged roots timid
    leaves!
Do not remain down there so ashamed, herbage of my
    breast!   20
Come I am determin'd to unbare this broad breast of mine,
    I have long enough stifled and choked;
Emblematic and capricious blades I leave you, now you
    serve me not,
I will say what I have to say by itself,

I will sound myself and comrades only, I will never again
    utter a call only their call,
I will raise with it immortal reverberations through the
    States,
I will give an example to lovers to take permanent shape
    and will through the States,
Through me shall the words be said to make death
    exhilarating.
Give me your tone therefore O death, that I may accord
    with it,
Give me yourself, for I see that you belong to me now
    above all, and are folded inseparably together, you love
    and death are,
Nor will I allow you to balk me any more with what I was
    calling life,   30
For now it is convey'd to me that you are the purports
    essential,
That you hide in these shifting forms of life, for reasons,
    and that they are mainly for you,
That you beyond them come forth to remain, the real
    reality,
That behind the mask of materials you patiently wait, no
    matter how long,
That you will one day perhaps take control of all,
That you will perhaps dissipate this entire show of
    appearance,
That may-be you are what it is all for, but it does not last
    so very long,
But you will last very long.

I SAW IN LOUISIANA A LIVE-OAK GROWING

I saw in Louisiana a live-oak growing,
All alone stood it and the moss hung down from the
    branches,
Without any companion it grew there uttering joyous leaves
    of dark green,

And its look, rude, unbending, lusty, made me think of
    myself,
But I wonder'd how it could utter joyous leaves standing
    alone there without its friend near, for I knew I could
    not,
And I broke off a twig with a certain number of leaves
    upon it, and twined around it a little moss,
And brought it away, and I have placed it in sight in my
    room,
It is not needed to remind me as of my own dear
    friends,
(For I believe lately I think of little else than of them,)
Yet it remains to me a curious token, it makes me think of
    manly love;   10
For all that, and though the live-oak glistens there in
    Louisiana solitary in a wide flat space,
Uttering joyous leaves all its life without a friend a lover
    near,
I know very well I could not.

WHEN I HEARD AT THE CLOSE OF THE DAY

When I heard at the close of the day how my name had
    been receiv'd with plaudits in the capitol, still it was not
    a happy night for me that follow'd,
And else when I carous'd, or when my plans were
    accomplish'd, still I was not happy,
But the day when I rose at dawn from the bed of perfect
    health, refresh'd, singing, inhaling the ripe breath of
    autumn,
When I saw the full moon in the west grow pale and
    disappear in the morning light,
When I wander'd alone over the beach, and undressing
    bathed, laughing with the cool waters, and saw the
    sun rise,
And when I thought how my dear friend my lover was on
    his way coming, O then I was happy,

O then each breath tasted sweeter, and all that day my food
    nourish'd me more, and the beautiful day pass'd well,
And the next came with equal joy, and with the next at
    evening came my friend,
And that night while all was still I heard the waters roll
    slowly continually up the shores,
I heard the hissing rustle of the liquid and sands as directed
    to me whispering to congratulate me,   10
For the one I love most lay sleeping by me under the same
    cover in the cool night,
In the stillness in the autumn moonbeams his face was
    inclined toward me,
And his arm lay lightly around my breast—and that night I
    was happy.

HERE THE FRAILEST LEAVES OF ME

Here the frailest leaves of me and yet my strongest lasting,
Here I shade and hide my thoughts, I myself do not expose
    them,
And yet they expose me more than all my other poems.

I DREAM'D IN A DREAM

I dream'd in a dream I saw a city invincible to the attacks
    of the whole of the rest of the earth,
I dream'd that was the new city of Friends,
Nothing was greater there than the quality of robust love,
    it led the rest,
It was seen every hour in the actions of the men of that
    city,
And in all their looks and words.

From "Drum-Taps" [1865]

BEAT! BEAT! DRUMS!

Beat! beat! drums—blow! bugles, blow!
Through the windows—through doors—burst like a
    ruthless force,
Into the solemn church, and scatter the congregation,
Into the school where the scholar is studying;
Leave not the bridegroom quiet—no happiness must he
    have now with his bride,
Nor the peaceful farmer any peace, ploughing his field or
    gathering his grain,
So fierce you whirr and pound you drums—so shrill you
    bugles blow.

Beat! beat! drums—blow! bugles! blow!
Over the traffic of cities—over the rumble of wheels in the
    streets;
Are beds prepared for sleepers at night in the houses? no
    sleepers must sleep in those beds,   10
No bargainers' bargains by day—no brokers or speculators
    —would they continue?
Would the talkers be talking? would the singer attempt to
    sing?
Would the lawyer rise in the court to state his case before
    the judge?
Then rattle quicker, heavier drums—you bugles wilder
    blow.

Beat! beat! drums!—blow! bugles! blow!
Make no parley—stop for no expostulation,
Mind not the timid—mind not the weeper or prayer,
Mind not the old man beseeching the young man,
Let not the child's voice be heard, nor the mother's
    entreaties,

Make even the trestles to shake the dead where they lie
    awaiting the hearses,   20
So strong you thump O terrible drums—so loud you
    bugles blow.

CAVALRY CROSSING A FORD

A line in long array where they wind betwixt green islands,
They take a serpentine course, their arms flash in the sun—
    hark to the musical clank,
Behold the silvery river, in it the splashing horses loitering
    stop to drink,
Behold the brown-faced men, each group, each person a
    picture, the negligent rest on the saddles,
Some emerge on the opposite bank, others are just
    entering the ford—while,
Scarlet and blue and snowy white,
The guidon flags flutter gayly in the wind.

BIVOUAC ON A MOUNTAIN SIDE

I see before me now a traveling army halting,
Below a fertile valley spread, with barns and the orchards
    of summer,
Behind, the terraced sides of a mountain, abrupt, in places
    rising high,
Broken, with rocks, with clinging cedars, with tall shapes
    dingily seen,
The numerous camp-fires scatter'd near and far, some
    away up on the mountain,
The shadowy forms of men and horses, looming,
    large-sized, flickering,
And over all the sky—the sky! far, far out of reach,
    studded, breaking out, the eternal stars.

BY THE BIVOUAC'S FITFUL FLAME

By the bivouac's fitful flame,
A procession winding around me, solemn and sweet and
      slow—but first I note,
The tents of the sleeping army, the fields' and woods' dim
      outline,
The darkness lit by spots of kindled fire, the silence,
Like a phantom far or near an occasional figure moving,
The shrubs and trees, (as I lift my eyes they seem to be
      stealthily watching me,)
While wind in procession thoughts, O tender and
      wondrous thoughts,
Of life and death, of home and the past and loved, and of
      those that are far away;
A solemn and slow procession there as I sit on the ground,
By the bivouac's fitful flame.   10

THE WOUND-DRESSER

1

An old man bending I come among new faces,
Years looking backward resuming in answer to children,
Come tell us old man, as from young men and maidens
      that love me,
(Arous'd and angry, I'd thought to beat the alarum, and
      urge relentless war,
But soon my fingers fail'd me, my face droop'd and I
      resign'd myself,
To sit by the wounded and soothe them, or silently watch
      the dead;)
Years hence of these scenes, of these furious passions,
      these chances,
Of unsurpass'd heroes, (was one side so brave? the other
      was equally brave;)

Now be witness again, paint the mightiest armies of earth,
Of those armies so rapid so wondrous what saw you to
    tell us?   10
What stays with you latest and deepest? of curious panics,
Of hard-fought engagements or sieges tremendous what
    deepest remains?

2

O maidens and young men I love and that love me,
What you ask of my days those the strangest and sudden
    your talking recalls,
Soldier alert I arrive after a long march cover'd with sweat
    and dust,
In the nick of time I come, plunge in the fight, loudly
    shout in the rush of successful charge,
Enter the captur'd works—yet lo, like a swift-running
    river they fade,
Pass and are gone they fade—I dwell not on soldiers' perils
    or soldiers' joys,
(Both I remember well—many the hardships, few the
    joys, yet I was content.)

But in silence, in dreams' projections,   20
While the world of gain and appearance and mirth goes on,
So soon what is over forgotten, and waves wash the
    imprints off the sand,
With hinged knees returning I enter the doors, (while for
    you up there,
Whoever you are, follow without noise and be of strong
    heart.)

Bearing the bandages, water and sponge,
Straight and swift to my wounded I go,
Where they lie on the ground after the battle brought in,
Where their priceless blood reddens the grass the ground,
Or to the rows of the hospital tent, or under the roof'd
    hospital,
To the long rows of cots up and down each side I return,   30
To each and all one after another I draw near, not one do
    I miss,

An attendant follows holding a tray, he carries a refuse
     pail,
Soon to be fill'd with clotted rags and blood, emptied, and
     fill'd again.

I onward go, I stop,
With hinged knees and steady hand to dress wounds,
I am firm with each, the pangs are sharp yet unavoidable,
One turns to me his appealing eyes—poor boy! I never
     knew you,
Yet I think I could not refuse this moment to die for you,
     if that would save you.

3

On, on I go, (open doors of time! open hospital doors!)
The crush'd head I dress, (poor crazed hand tear not the
     bandage away,)   40
The neck of the cavalry-man with the bullet through and
     through I examine,
Hard the breathing rattles, quite glazed already the eye, yet
     life struggles hard,
(Come sweet death! be persuaded O beautiful death!
In mercy come quickly.)

From the stump of the arm, the amputated hand,
I undo the clotted lint, remove the slough, wash off the
     matter and blood,
Back on his pillow the soldier bends with curv'd neck and
     side falling head,
His eyes are closed, his face is pale, he dares not look on
     the bloody stump,
And has not yet look'd on it.

I dress a wound in the side, deep, deep,   50
But a day or two more, for see the frame all wasted and
     sinking,
And the yellow-blue countenance see.

I dress the perforated shoulder, the foot with the bullet-
     wound,

Cleanse the one with a gnawing and putrid gangrene, so
    sickening, so offensive,
While the attendant stands behind aside me holding the
    tray and pail.

I am faithful, I do not give out,
The fractur'd thigh, the knee, the wound in the abdomen,
These and more I dress with impassive hand, (yet deep in
    my breast a fire, a burning flame.)

4

Thus in silence in dreams' projections,
Returning, resuming, I thread my way through the
    hospitals,   60
The hurt and wounded I pacify with soothing hand,
I sit by the restless all the dark night, some are so young,
Some suffer so much, I recall the experience sweet and sad,
(Many a soldier's loving arms about this neck have cross'd
    and rested,
Many a soldier's kiss dwells on these bearded lips.)

A SIGHT IN CAMP IN THE DAYBREAK
GRAY AND DIM

A sight in camp in the daybreak gray and dim,
As from my tent I emerge so early sleepless,
As slow I walk in the cool fresh air the path near by the
    hospital tent,
Three forms I see on stretchers lying, brought out there
    untended lying,
Over each the blanket spread, ample brownish woolen
    blanket,
Gray and heavy blanket, folding, covering all.

Curious I halt and silent stand,
Then with light fingers I from the face of the nearest the
    first just lift the blanket;

Who are you elderly man so gaunt and grim, with
    well-gray'd hair, and flesh all sunken about the eyes?
Who are you my dear comrade?   10

Then to the second I step—and who are you my child and
    darling?
Who are you sweet boy with cheeks yet blooming?

Then to the third—a face nor child nor old, very calm, as
    of beautiful yellow-white ivory;
Young man I think I know you—I think this face is the
    face of the Christ himself,
Dead and divine and brother of all, and here again he
    lies.

TO THE LEAVEN'D SOIL THEY TROD

To the leaven'd soil they trod calling I sing for the last,
(Forth from my tent emerging for good, loosing, untying
    the tent-ropes,)
In the freshness the forenoon air, in the far-stretching
    circuits and vistas again to peace restored,
To the fiery fields emanative and the endless vistas beyond,
    to the South and the North,
To the leaven'd soil of the general Western world to attest
    my songs,
To the Alleghanian hills and the tireless Mississippi,
To the rocks I calling sing, and all the trees in the woods,
To the plains of the poems of heroes, to the prairies
    spreading wide,
To the far-off sea and the unseen winds, and the sane
    impalpable air;
And responding they answer all, (but not in words,)   10
The average earth, the witness of war and peace,
    acknowledges mutely,
The prairie draws me close, as the father to bosom broad
    the son,

The Northern ice and rain that began me nourish me to
    the end,
But the hot sun of the South is to fully ripen my songs.

O CAPTAIN! MY CAPTAIN!   [1865]

O Captain! my Captain! our fearful trip is done,
The ship has weather'd every rack, the prize we sought is
            won,
The port is near, the bells I hear, the people all exulting,
While follow eyes the steady keel, the vessel grim and
            daring;
    But O heart! heart! heart!
      O the bleeding drops of red,
        Where on the deck my Captain lies,
          Fallen cold and dead.

O Captain! my Captain! rise up and hear the bells;
Rise up—for you the flag is flung—for you the bugle trills,   10
For you bouquets and ribbon'd wreaths—for you the
          shores a-crowding,
For you they call, the swaying mass, their eager faces
          turning;
    Here Captain! dear father!
      The arm beneath your head!
        It is some dream that on the deck,
         You've fallen cold and dead.

My Captain does not answer, his lips are pale and still,
My father does not feel my arm, he has no pulse nor will,
The ship is anchor'd safe and sound, its voyage closed and
          done,
From fearful trip the victor ship comes in with object won;   20
      Exult O shores, and ring O bells!
     But I with mournful tread,
       Walk the deck my Captain lies,
        Fallen cold and dead.

WHEN LILACS LAST IN THE DOORYARD
BLOOM'D   [1865]

1

When lilacs last in the dooryard bloom'd,
And the great star early droop'd in the western sky in the
    night,
I mourn'd, and yet shall mourn with ever-returning spring.

Ever-returning spring, trinity sure to me you bring,
Lilac blooming perennial and drooping star in the west,
And thought of him I love.

2

O powerful western fallen star!
O shades of night—O moody, tearful night!
O great star disappear'd—O the black murk that hides the
    star!
O cruel hands that hold me powerless—O helpless soul of
    me!   10
O harsh surrounding cloud that will not free my soul.

3

In the dooryard fronting an old farm-house near the
    white-wash'd palings,
Stands the lilac-bush tall-growing with heart-shaped leaves
    of rich green,
With many a pointed blossom rising delicate, with the
    perfume strong I love,
With every leaf a miracle—and from this bush in the
    dooryard,
With delicate-color'd blossoms and heart-shaped leaves of
    rich green,
A sprig with its flower I break.

4

In the swamp in secluded recesses,
A shy and hidden bird is warbling a song.

Solitary the thrush,   20
The hermit withdrawn to himself, avoiding the
    settlements,
Sings by himself a song.

Song of the bleeding throat,
Death's outlet song of life, (for well dear brother I know,
If thou wast not granted to sing thou would'st surely
    die.)

5

Over the breast of the spring, the land, amid cities,
Amid lanes and through old woods, where lately the
    violets peep'd from the ground, spotting the gray
    debris,
Amid the grass in the fields each side of the lanes, passing
    the endless grass,
Passing the yellow-spear'd wheat, every grain from its
    shroud in the dark-brown fields uprisen,
Passing the apple-tree blows of white and pink in the
    orchards,   30
Carrying a corpse to where it shall rest in the grave,
Night and day journeys a coffin.

6

Coffin that passes through lanes and streets,
Through day and night with the great cloud darkening the
    land,
With the pomp of the inloop'd flags with the cities draped
    in black,
With the show of the States themselves as of crape-veil'd
    women standing,
With processions long and winding and the flambeaus of
    the night,
With the countless torches lit, with the silent sea of faces
    and the unbared heads,
With the waiting depot, the arriving coffin, and the sombre
    faces,
With dirges through the night, with the thousand voices
    rising strong and solemn,   40

With all the mournful voices of the dirges pour'd around
    the coffin,
The dim-lit churches and the shuddering organs—where
    amid these you journey,
With the tolling tolling bells' perpetual clang,
Here, coffin that slowly passes,
I give you my sprig of lilac.

7

(Nor for you, for one alone,
Blossoms and branches green to coffins all I bring,
For fresh as the morning, thus would I chant a song for
    you O sane and sacred death.

All over bouquets of roses,
O death, I cover you over with roses and early lilies,   50
But mostly and now the lilac that blooms the first,
Copious I break, I break the sprigs from the bushes,
With loaded arms I come, pouring for you,
For you and the coffins all of you O death.)

8

O western orb sailing the heaven,
Now I know what you must have meant as a month since
    I walk'd,
As I walk'd in silence the transparent shadowy night,
As I saw you had something to tell as you bent to me
    night after night,
As you droop'd from the sky low down as if to my side,
    (while the other stars all look'd on,)
As we wander'd together the solemn night, (for something
    I know not what kept me from sleep,)   60
As the night advanced, and I saw on the rim of the west
    how full you were of woe,
As I stood on the rising ground in the breeze in the cool
    transparent night,
As I watch'd where you pass'd and was lost in the nether-
    ward black of the night,
As my soul in its trouble dissatisfied sank, as where you
    sad orb,
Concluded, dropt in the night, and was gone.

9

Sing on there in the swamp,
O singer bashful and tender, I hear your notes, I hear your
    call,
I hear, I come presently, I understand you,
But a moment I linger, for the lustrous star has detain'd
    me,
The star my departing comrade holds and detains me.   70

10

O how shall I warble myself for the dead one there I
    loved?
And how shall I deck my song for the large sweet soul
    that has gone?
And what shall my perfume be for the grave of him I
    love?

Sea-winds blown from east and west,
Blown from the Eastern sea and blown from the Western
    sea, till there on the prairies meeting,
These and with these and the breath of my chant,
I'll perfume the grave of him I love.

11

O what shall I hang on the chamber walls?
And what shall the pictures be that I hang on the
    walls,
To adorn the burial-house of him I love?   80

Pictures of growing spring and farms and homes,
With the Fourth-month eve at sundown, and the gray
    smoke lucid and bright,
With floods of the yellow gold of the gorgeous, indolent,
    sinking sun, burning, expanding the air,
With the fresh sweet herbage under foot, and the pale
    green leaves of the trees prolific,
In the distance the flowing glaze, the breast of the river,
    with a wind-dapple here and there,
With ranging hills on the banks, with many a line against
    the sky, and shadows,

And the city at hand with dwellings so dense, and stacks
    of chimneys,
And all the scenes of life and the workshops, and the
    workmen homeward returning.

12

Lo, body and soul—this land,
My own Manhattan with spires, and the sparkling and
    hurrying tides, and the ships,   90
The varied and ample land, the South and the North in the
    light, Ohio's shores and flashing Missouri,
And ever the far-spreading prairies cover'd with grass and
    corn.

Lo, the most excellent sun so calm and haughty,
The violet and purple morn with just-felt breezes,
The gentle soft-born measureless light,
The miracle spreading bathing all, the fulfill'd noon,
The coming eve delicious, the welcome night and the stars,
Over my cities shining all, enveloping man and land.

13

Sing on, sing on you gray-brown bird,
Sing from the swamps, the recesses, pour your chant from
    the bushes,   100
Limitless out of the dusk, out of the cedars and pines.

Sing on dearest brother, warble your reedy song,
Loud human song, with voice of uttermost woe.

O liquid and free and tender!
O wild and loose to my soul—O wondrous singer!
You only I hear—yet the star holds me, (but will soon
    depart,)
Yet the lilac with mastering odor holds me.

14

Now while I sat in the day and look'd forth,
In the close of the day with its light and the fields of
    spring, and the farmers preparing their crops,

In the large unconscious scenery of my land with its lakes
    and forests,   110
In the heavenly aerial beauty, (after the perturb'd winds
    and the storms,)
Under the arching heavens of the afternoon swift passing,
    and the voices of children and women,
The many-moving sea-tides, and I saw the ships how they
    sail'd,
And the summer approaching with richness, and the fields
    all busy with labor,
And the infinite separate houses, how they all went on,
    each with its meals and minutia of daily usages,
And the streets how their throbbings throbb'd, and the
    cities pent—lo, then and there,
Falling upon them all and among them all, enveloping me
    with the rest,
Appear'd the cloud, appear'd the long black trail,
And I knew death, its thought, and the sacred knowledge
    of death.

Then with the knowledge of death as walking one side of
    me,   120
And the thought of death close-walking the other side of
    me,
And I in the middle as with companions, and as holding
    the hands of companions,
I fled forth to the hiding receiving night that talks not,
Down to the shores of the water, the path by the swamp in
    the dimness,
To the solemn shadowy cedars and ghostly pines so still.

And the singer so shy to the rest receiv'd me,
The gray-brown bird I know receiv'd us comrades three,
And he sang the carol of death, and a verse for him I love.

From deep secluded recesses,
From the fragrant cedars and the ghostly pines so still,   130
Came the carol of the bird.

And the charm of the carol rapt me,

As I held as if by their hands my comrades in the night,
And the voice of my spirit tallied the song of the bird.

Come lovely and soothing death,
Undulate round the world, serenely arriving, arriving,
In the day, in the night, to all, to each,
Sooner or later delicate death.

Prais'd be the fathomless universe,
For life and joy, and for objects and knowledge curious,   140
And for love, sweet love—but praise! praise! praise!
For the sure-enwinding arms of cool-enfolding death.

Dark mother always gliding near with soft feet,
Have none chanted for thee a chant of fullest welcome?
Then I chant it for thee, I glorify thee above all,
I bring thee a song that when thou must indeed come, come
        unfalteringly.

Approach strong deliveress,
When it is so, when thou hast taken them I joyously sing the
        dead,
Lost in the loving floating ocean of thee,
Laved in the flood of thy bliss O death.   150

From me to thee glad serenades,
Dances for thee I propose saluting thee, adornments and feastings
        for thee,
And the sights of the open landscape and the high-spread sky
        are fitting,
And life and the fields, and the huge and thoughtful night.

The night in silence under many a star,
The ocean shore and the husky whispering wave whose voice I know,
And the soul turning to thee O vast and well-veil'd death,
And the body gratefully nestling close to thee.

Over the tree-tops I float thee a song,
Over the rising and sinking waves, over the myriad fields and the
        prairies wide,   160

Over the dense-pack'd cities all and the teeming wharves and ways,
I float this carol with joy, with joy to thee O death.

15

To the tally of my soul,
Loud and strong kept up the gray-brown bird,
With pure deliberate notes spreading filling the night.

Loud in the pines and cedars dim,
Clear in the freshness moist and the swamp-perfume,
And I with my comrades there in the night.

While my sight that was bound in my eyes unclosed,
As to long panoramas of visions.   170

And I saw askant the armies,
I saw as in noiseless dreams hundreds of battle-flags,
Borne through the smoke of the battles and pierc'd with
        missiles I saw them,
And carried hither and yon through the smoke, and torn
        and bloody,
And at last but a few shreds left on the staffs, (and all in
        silence,)
And the staffs all splinter'd and broken.

I saw battle-corpses, myriads of them,
And the white skeletons of young men, I saw them,
I saw the debris and debris of all the slain soldiers of the war,
But I saw they were not as was thought,   180
They themselves were fully at rest, they suffer'd not,
The living remain'd and suffer'd, the mother suffer'd,
And the wife and the child and the musing comrade
        suffer'd,
And the armies that remain'd suffer'd.

16

Passing the visions, passing the night,
Passing, unloosing the hold of my comrades' hands,
Passing the song of the hermit bird and the tallying song
        of my soul,

Victorious song, death's outlet song, yet varying ever-
    altering song,
As low and wailing, yet clear the notes, rising and falling,
    flooding the night,
Sadly sinking and fainting, as warning and warning, and
    yet again bursting with joy,   190
Covering the earth and filling the spread of the heaven,
As that powerful psalm in the night I heard from recesses,
Passing, I leave thee lilac with heart-shaped leaves,
I leave thee there in the dooryard, blooming, returning
    with spring.

I cease from my song for thee,
From my gaze on thee in the west, fronting the west,
    communing with thee,
O comrade lustrous with silver face in the night.

Yet each to keep and all, retrievements out of the night,
The song, the wondrous chant of the gray-brown bird,
And the tallying chant, the echo arous'd in my soul,   200
With the lustrous and drooping star with the countenance
    full of woe,
With the holders holding my hand nearing the call of the
    bird,
Comrades mine and I in the midst, and their memory ever
    to keep, for the dead I loved so well,
For the sweetest, wisest soul of all my days and lands—and
    this for his dear sake,
Lilac and star and bird twined with the chant of my soul,
There in the fragrant pines and the cedars dusk and dim.

SPARKLES FROM THE WHEEL   [1871]

Where the city's ceaseless crowd moves on the livelong
    day,
Withdrawn I join a group of children watching, I pause
    aside with them.

By the curb toward the edge of the flagging,
A knife-grinder works at his wheel sharpening a great
      knife,
Bending over he carefully holds it to the stone, by foot and
      knee,
With measur'd tread he turns rapidly, as he presses with
      light but firm hand,
Forth issue then in copious golden jets,
Sparkles from the wheel.

The scene and all its belongings, how they seize and affect
      me,
The sad sharp-chinn'd old man with worn clothes and
      broad shoulder-band of leather,   10
Myself effusing and fluid, a phantom curiously floating
      now here absorb'd and arrested,
The group, (an unminded point set in a vast surrounding,)
The attentive, quiet children, the loud, proud, restive base
      of the streets,
The low hoarse purr of the whirling stone, the light-
      press'd blade,
Diffusing, dropping, sideways-darting, in tiny showers of
      gold,
Sparkles from the wheel.

A NOISELESS PATIENT SPIDER   [1871]

A noiseless patient spider,
I mark'd where on a little promontory it stood isolated,
Mark'd how to explore the vacant vast surrounding,
It launch'd forth filament, filament, filament, out of itself,
Ever unreeling them, ever tirelessly speeding them.

And you O my soul where you stand,
Surrounded, detached, in measureless oceans of space,
Ceaselessly musing, venturing, throwing, seeking the
      spheres to connect them,

Till the bridge you will need be form'd, till the ductile
    anchor hold,
Till the gossamer thread you fling catch somewhere, O my
    soul.   10

TO A LOCOMOTIVE IN WINTER   [1876]

Thee for my recitative,
Thee in the driving storm even as now, the snow, the
    winter-day declining,
Thee in thy panoply, thy measur'd dual throbbing and thy
    beat convulsive,
Thy black cylindric body, golden brass and silvery steel,
Thy ponderous side-bars, parallel and connecting rods,
    gyrating, shuttling at thy sides,
Thy metrical, now swelling pant and roar, now tapering in
    the distance,
Thy great protruding head-light fix'd in front,
Thy long, pale, floating vapor-pennants, tinged with
    delicate purple,
The dense and murky clouds out-belching from thy
    smoke-stack,
Thy knitted frame, thy springs and valves, the tremulous
    twinkle of thy wheels,   10
Thy train of cars, behind, obedient, merrily following,
Through gale or calm, now swift, now slack, yet steadily
    careering;
Type of the modern—emblem of motion and power—pulse
    of the continent,
For once come serve the Muse and merge in verse, even as
    here I see thee,
With storm and buffeting gusts of wind and falling snow,
By day thy warning ringing bell to sound its notes,
By night thy silent signal lamps to swing.

Fierce-throated beauty!
Roll through my chant with all thy lawless music, thy
    swinging lamps at night,

Thy madly-whistled laughter, echoing, rumbling like an
    earthquake, rousing all,   20
Law of thyself complete, thine own track firmly holding,
(No sweetness debonair of tearful harp or glib piano thine,)
Thy trills of shrieks by rocks and hills return'd,
Launch'd o'er the prairies wide, across the lakes,
To the free skies unpent and glad and strong.

GOOD-BYE MY FANCY!   [1891]

Good-bye my Fancy!
Farewell dear mate, dear love!
I'm going away, I know not where,
Or to what fortune, or whether I may ever see you again,
So Good-bye my Fancy.

Now for my last—let me look back a moment;
The slower fainter ticking of the clock is in me,
Exit, nightfall, and soon the heart-thud stopping.

Long have we lived, joy'd, caress'd together;
Delightful!—now separation—Good-bye my Fancy.   10

Yet let me not be too hasty,
Long indeed have we lived, slept, filter'd, become really
    blended into one;
Then if we die together, (yes, we'll remain one,)
If we go anywhere we'll go together to meet what happens,
May-be we'll be better off and blither, and learn something,
May-be it is yourself now really ushering me to the true
    songs, (who knows?)
May-be it is you the mortal knob really undoing, turning—
    so now finally,
Good-bye—and hail! my Fancy.

Herman Melville

1819–1891

Herman Melville was born August 1, 1819, in New York City, the son of a merchant who died bankrupt when Herman was twelve. After employment as a clerk, as a cabin boy on a sea voyage, and as a school teacher, Melville shipped in January, 1841, on the Acushnet, *a whaler bound for the Pacific. After deserting ship in the Marquesas Islands the next year, he made his way to Tahiti and Honolulu, served as ordinary seaman on the frigate* United States, *and was discharged in October, 1844, in Boston. He began writing books based on his travels and immediately won popular success as a romancer. In 1850 he settled at Pittsfield, Massachusetts, where he became friends with Nathaniel Hawthorne and wrote* Moby-Dick *and several other fictional works. Late in the 1850's, his fame as a novelist having declined, he began composing verse. A visit to the Holy Land in January, 1857, subsequently inspired his long poem* Clarel. *He moved back to New York in 1863 and from 1866 to 1885 was a customs inspector. He died in New York on September 28, 1891.*

THE PORTENT   [1866]

(1859)

Hanging from the beam,
   Slowly swaying (such the law),
Gaunt the shadow on your green,
   Shenandoah!
The cut is on the crown
(Lo, John Brown),
And the stabs shall heal no more.

Hidden in the cap
   Is the anguish none can draw;
So your future veils its face,   10
   Shenandoah!
But the streaming beard is shown
(Weird John Brown),
The meteor of the war.

MISGIVINGS   [1866]

(1860)

When ocean-clouds over inland hills
   Sweep storming in late autumn brown,
And horror the sodden valley fills,
   And the spire falls crashing in the town,
I muse upon my country's ills—
The tempest bursting from the waste of Time
On the world's fairest hope linked with man's foulest crime.

Nature's dark side is heeded now—
   (Ah! optimist-cheer disheartened flown)—
A child may read the moody brow   10
   Of yon black mountain lone.
With shouts the torrents down the gorges go,
   And storms are formed behind the storm we feel:
The hemlock shakes in the rafter, the oak in the driving keel.

THE CONFLICT OF CONVICTIONS   [1866]

(1860-1)

On starry heights
   A bugle wails the long recall;

Derision stirs the deep abyss,
   Heaven's ominous silence over all.
Return, return, O eager Hope,
   And face man's latter fall.
Events, they make the dreamers quail;
Satan's old age is strong and hale,
A disciplined captain, gray in skill,
And Raphael a white enthusiast still;   10
Dashed aims, at which Christ's martyrs pale,
Shall Mammon's slaves fulfill?

> *(Dismantle the fort,*
> *Cut down the fleet—*
> *Battle no more shall be!*
> *While the fields for fight in æons to come*
> *Congeal beneath the sea.)*

The terrors of truth and dart of death
   To faith alike are vain;
Though comets, gone a thousand years,   20
      Return again,
Patient she stands—she can no more—
And waits, nor heeds she waxes hoar.

> *(At a stony gate,*
> *A statue of stone,*
> *Weed overgrown—*
> *Long 'twill wait!)*

But God His former mind retains,
   Confirms his old decree;
The generations are inured to pains,   30
   And strong Necessity
Surges, and heaps Time's strand with wrecks.
   The People spread like a weedy grass,
   The thing they will they bring to pass,
And prosper to the apoplex.
The rout it herds around the heart,
   The ghost is yielded in the gloom;
Kings wag their heads—Now save thyself
   Who wouldst rebuild the world in bloom.

(Tide-mark   40
And top of the ages' strife,
Verge where they called the world to come,
The last advance of life—
Ha ha, the rust on the Iron Dome!)

Nay, but revere the hid event;
  In the cloud a sword is girded on,
I mark a twinkling in the tent
  Of Michael the warrior one.
Senior wisdom suits not now,
The light is on the youthful brow.   50

(Ay, in caves the miner see:
His forehead bears a blinking light;
Darkness so he feebly braves—
A meagre wight!)

But He who rules is old—is old;
Ah! faith is warm, but heaven with age is cold.

(Ho ho, ho ho,
The cloistered doubt
Of olden times
Is blurted out!)   60

The Ancient of Days forever is young,
  Forever the scheme of Nature thrives;
I know a wind in purpose strong—
  It spins *against* the way it drives.
What if the gulfs their slimed foundations bare?
So deep must the stones be hurled
Whereon the throes of ages rear
The final empire and the happier world.

(The poor old Past,
The Future's slave,   70
She dredged through pain and crime
To bring about the blissful Prime,
Then—perished. There's a grave!)

Power unanointed may come—
Dominion (unsought by the free)
   And the Iron Dome,
Stronger for stress and strain,
Fling her huge shadow athwart the main;
But the Founders' dream shall flee.
Age after age shall be   80
As age after age has been,
(From man's changeless heart their way they win);
And death be busy with all who strive—
Death, with silent negative.

       YEA AND NAY—
       EACH HATH HIS SAY;
       BUT GOD HE KEEPS THE MIDDLE WAY.
       NONE WAS BY
       WHEN HE SPREAD THE SKY;
       WISDOM IS VAIN, AND PROPHESY.   90

THE MARCH INTO VIRGINIA   [1866]

Ending in the First Manassas (July, 1861)

Did all the lets and bars appear
   To every just or larger end,
Whence should come the trust and cheer?
   Youth must its ignorant impulse lend—
Age finds place in the rear.
   All wars are boyish, and are fought by boys,
The champions and enthusiasts of the state:
   Turbid ardors and vain joys
      Not barrenly abate—
Stimulants to the power mature,   10
   Preparatives of fate.

Who here forecasteth the event?
What heart but spurns at precedent

And warnings of the wise,
Contemned foreclosures of surprise?
The banners play, the bugles call,
The air is blue and prodigal.
　No berrying party, pleasure-wooed,
No picnic party in the May,
Ever went less loth than they   20
　Into that leafy neighborhood.
In Bacchic glee they file toward Fate,
Moloch's uninitiate;
Expectancy, and glad surmise
Of battle's unknown mysteries.
All they feel is this: 'tis glory,
A rapture sharp, though transitory,
Yet lasting in belaureled story.
So they gayly go to fight,
Chatting left and laughing right.   30

But some who this blithe mood present,
　As on in lightsome files they fare,
Shall die experienced ere three days are spent—
　Perish, enlightened by the vollied glare;
Or shame survive, and, like to adamant,
　The throe of Second Manassas share.

A UTILITARIAN VIEW OF THE
MONITOR'S FIGHT　[1866]

Plain be the phrase, yet apt the verse,
　More ponderous than nimble;
For since grimed War here laid aside
His Orient pomp, 'twould ill befit
　　Overmuch to ply
　The rhyme's barbaric cymbal.

Hail to victory without the gaud
　Of glory; zeal that needs no fans

Of banners; plain mechanic power
Plied cogently in War now placed—   10
     Where War belongs—
  Among the trades and artisans.

Yet this was battle, and intense—
  Beyond the strife of fleets heroic;
Deadlier, closer, calm 'mid storm;
No passion; all went on by crank,
     Pivot, and screw,
  And calculations of caloric.

Needless to dwell; the story's known.
  The ringing of those plates on plates   20
Still ringeth round the world—
The clangor of that blacksmiths' fray.
     The anvil-din
  Resounds this message from the Fates:

War shall yet be, and to the end;
  But war-paint shows the streaks of weather;
War yet shall be, but warriors
Are now but operatives; War's made
     Less grand than Peace,
  And a singe runs through lace and feather.   30

SHILOH   [1866]

A Requiem (April, 1862)

Skimming lightly, wheeling still,
  The swallows fly low
Over the field in clouded days,
  The forest-field of Shiloh—
Over the field where April rain
Solaced the parched ones stretched in pain
Through the pause of night

That followed the Sunday fight
    Around the church of Shiloh—
The church so lone, the log-built one,   10
That echoed to many a parting groan
        And natural prayer
    Of dying foemen mingled there—
Foemen at morn, but friends at eve—
    Fame or country least their care:
(What like a bullet can undeceive!)
    But now they lie low,
While over them the swallows skim,
    And all is hushed at Shiloh.

MALVERN HILL   [1866]

(July, 1862)

Ye elms that wave on Malvern Hill
    In prime of morn and May,
Recall ye how McClellan's men
        Here stood at bay?
While deep within yon forest dim
    Our rigid comrades lay—
Some with the cartridge in their mouth,
Others with fixed arms lifted South—
        Invoking so
The cypress glades? Ah wilds of woe!   10

The spires of Richmond, late beheld
    Through rifts in musket-haze,
Were closed from view in clouds of dust
        On leaf-walled ways,
Where streamed our wagons in caravan;
    And the Seven Nights and Days
Of march and fast, retreat and fight,
Pinched our grimed faces to ghastly plight—
        Does the elm wood
Recall the haggard beards of blood?   20

The battle-smoked flag, with stars eclipsed,
  We followed (it never fell!)—
In silence husbanded our strength—
    Received their yell;
Till on this slope we patient turned
  With cannon ordered well;
Reverse we proved was not defeat;
But ah, the sod what thousands meet!—
    Does Malvern Wood
Bethink itself, and muse and brood?   30

> *We elms of Malvern Hill*
>   *Remember every thing;*
> *But sap the twig will fill:*
> *Wag the world how it will,*
>   *Leaves must be green in Spring.*

THE HOUSE-TOP   [1866]

A Night Piece (July, 1863)

No sleep. The sultriness pervades the air
And binds the brain—a dense oppression, such
As tawny tigers feel in matted shades,
Vexing their blood and making apt for ravage.
Beneath the stars the roofy desert spreads
Vacant as Libya. All is hushed near by.
Yet fitfully from far breaks a mixed surf
Of muffled sound, the Atheist roar of riot.
Yonder, where parching Sirius set in drought,
Balefully glares red Arson—there—and there.   10
The Town is taken by its rats—ship-rats
And rats of the wharves. All civil charms
And priestly spells which late held hearts in awe—
Fear-bound, subjected to a better sway
Than sway of self; these like a dream dissolve,
And man rebounds whole æons back in nature.
Hail to the low dull rumble, dull and dead,

And ponderous drag that shakes the wall.
Wise Draco comes, deep in the midnight roll
Of black artillery; he comes, though late;   20
In code corroborating Calvin's creed
And cynic tyrannies of honest kings;
He comes, nor parlies; and the Town, redeemed,
Gives thanks devout; nor, being thankful, heeds
The grimy slur on the Republic's faith implied,
Which holds that Man is naturally good,
And—more—is Nature's Roman, never to be scourged.

A DIRGE FOR MC PHERSON   [1866]

Killed in Front of Atlanta (July, 1864)

Arms reversed and banners craped—
     Muffled drums;
Snowy horses sable-draped—
     McPherson comes.

          But, tell us, shall we know him more,
          Lost-Mountain and lone Kenesaw?

Brave the sword upon the pall—
     A gleam in gloom;
So a bright name lighteth all
     McPherson's doom.   10

Bear him through the chapel-door—
     Let priest in stole
Pace before the warrior
     Who led. Bell—toll!

Lay him down within the nave,
     The Lesson read—
Man is noble, man is brave,
     But man's—a weed.

Take him up again and wend
    Graveward, nor weep: 20
There's a trumpet that shall rend
    This Soldier's sleep.

Pass the ropes the coffin round,
    And let descend;
Prayer and volley—let it sound
    McPherson's end.

        True fame is his, for life is o'er—
        Sarpedon of the mighty war.

ON THE GRAVE OF A YOUNG CAVALRY OFFICER KILLED IN THE VALLEY OF VIRGINIA   [1866]

Beauty and youth, with manners sweet, and friends—
    Gold, yet a mind not unenriched had he
Whom here low violets veil from eyes.
    But all these gifts transcended be:
His happier fortune in this mound you see.

COMMEMORATIVE OF A NAVAL VICTORY
[1866]

Sailors there are of gentlest breed,
    Yet strong, like every goodly thing;
The discipline of arms refines,
    And the wave gives tempering.
    The damasked blade its beam can fling;
It lends the last grave grace:
The hawk, the hound, and sworded nobleman
    In Titian's picture for a king,
Are of hunter or warrior race.

In social halls a favored guest   10
    In years that follow victory won,
How sweet to feel your festal fame
    In woman's glance instinctive thrown:
    Repose is yours—your deed is known,
It musks the amber wine;
It lives, and sheds a light from storied days
    Rich as October sunsets brown,
Which make the barren place to shine.

But seldom the laurel wreath is seen
    Unmixed with pensive pansies dark;   20
There's a light and a shadow on every man
    Who at last attains his lifted mark—
    Nursing through night the ethereal spark.
Elate he never can be;
He feels that spirits which glad had hailed his worth,
    Sleep in oblivion.—The shark
Glides white through the phosphorus sea.

EPILOGUE   [1876]

(from *Clarel*)

If Luther's day expand to Darwin's year,
Shall that exclude the hope—foreclose the fear?

    Unmoved by all the claims our times avow,
The ancient Sphinx still keeps the porch of shade;
And comes Despair, whom not her calm may cow,
And coldly on that adamantine brow
Scrawls undeterred his bitter pasquinade.
But Faith (who from the scrawl indignant turns)
With blood warm oozing from her wounded trust,
Inscribes even on her shards of broken urns   10
The sign o' the cross—*the spirit above the dust!*

Yea, ape and angel, strife and old debate—
The harps of heaven and dreary gongs of hell;
Science the feud can only aggravate—
No umpire she betwixt the chimes and knell:
The running battle of the star and clod
Shall run forever—if there be no God.

Degrees we know, unknown in days before;
The light is greater, hence the shadow more;
And tantalized and apprehensive Man   20
Appealing—Wherefore ripen us to pain?
Seems there the spokesman of dumb Nature's train.
But through such strange illusions have they passed
Who in life's pilgrimage have baffled striven—
Even death may prove unreal at the last,
And stoics be astounded into heaven.

Then keep thy heart, though yet but ill-resigned—
Clarel, thy heart, the issues there but mind;
That like the crocus budding through the snow—
That like a swimmer rising from the deep—   30
That like a burning secret which doth go
Even from the bosom that would hoard and keep;
Emerge thou mayst from the last whelming sea,
And prove that death but routs life into victory.

THE ÆOLIAN HARP   [1888]

At the Surf Inn

List the harp in window wailing
    Stirred by fitful gales from sea:
Shrieking up in mad crescendo—
    Dying down in plaintive key!

Listen: less a strain ideal
    Than Ariel's rendering of the Real.
What that Real is, let hint
    A picture stamped in memory's mint.

Braced well up, with beams aslant,
Betwixt the continents sails the *Phocion*,   10
To Baltimore bound from Alicant.
Blue breezy skies white fleeces fleck
Over the chill blue white-capped ocean:
From yard-arm comes—"Wreck ho, a wreck!"

Dismasted and adrift,
Long time a thing forsaken;
Overwashed by every wave
Like the slumbering kraken;
Heedless if the billow roar,
Oblivious of the lull,   20
Leagues and leagues from shoal or shore,
It swims—a levelled hull:
Bulwarks gone—a shaven wreck,
Nameless, and a grass-green deck.
A lumberman: perchance, in hold
Prostrate pines with hemlocks rolled.

It has drifted, waterlogged,
Till by trailing weeds beclogged:
   Drifted, drifted, day by day,
   Pilotless on pathless way.   30
It has drifted till each plank
Is oozy as the oyster-bank:
   Drifted, drifted, night by night,
   Craft that never shows a light;
Nor ever, to prevent worse knell,
Tolls in fog the warning bell.

From collision never shrinking,
Drive what may through darksome smother;
Saturate, but never sinking,
Fatal only to the *other*!   40
   Deadlier than the sunken reef
Since still the snare it shifteth,
   Torpid in dumb ambuscade
Waylayingly it drifteth.

O, the sailors—O, the sails!
O, the lost crews never heard of!
Well the harp of Ariel wails
Thoughts that tongue can tell no word of!

THE MALDIVE SHARK   [1888]

About the Shark, phlegmatical one,
Pale sot of the Maldive sea,
The sleek little pilot-fish, azure and slim,
How alert in attendance be.
From his saw-pit of mouth, from his charnel of maw
They have nothing of harm to dread,
But liquidly glide on his ghastly flank
Or before his Gorgonian head;
Or lurk in the port of serrated teeth
In white triple tiers of glittering gates,   10
And there find a haven when peril's abroad,
An asylum in jaws of the Fates!
They are friends; and friendly they guide him to prey,
Yet never partake of the treat—
Eyes and brains to the dotard lethargic and dull,
Pale ravener of horrible meat.

THE BERG   [1888]

(A Dream)

I saw a ship of martial build
(Her standards set, her brave apparel on)
Directed as by madness mere
Against a stolid iceberg steer,
Nor budge it, though the infatuate ship went down.
The impact made huge ice-cubes fall
Sullen, in tons that crashed the deck;

But that one avalanche was all—
No other movement save the foundering wreck.

Along the spurs of ridges pale,   10
Not any slenderest shaft and frail,
A prism over glass-green gorges lone,
Toppled; nor lace of traceries fine,
Nor pendant drops in grot or mine
Were jarred, when the stunned ship went down.
Nor sole the gulls in cloud that wheeled
Circling one snow-flanked peak afar,
But nearer fowl the floes that skimmed
And crystal beaches, felt no jar.
No thrill transmitted stirred the lock   20
Of jack-straw needle-ice at base;
Towers undermined by waves—the block
Atilt impending—kept their place.
Seals, dozing sleek on sliddery ledges
Slipt never, when by loftier edges
Through very inertia overthrown,
The impetuous ship in bafflement went down.

Hard Berg (methought), so cold, so vast,
With mortal damps self-overcast;
Exhaling still thy dankish breath—   30
Adrift dissolving, bound for death;
Though lumpish thou, a lumbering one—
A lumbering lubbard loitering slow,
Impingers rue thee and go down,
Sounding thy precipice below,
Nor stir the slimy slug that sprawls
Along thy dead indifference of walls.

PEBBLES   [1888]

I

Though the Clerk of the Weather insist,
   And lay down the weather-law,
Pintado and gannet they wist

That the winds blow whither they list
  In tempest or flaw.

II

Old are the creeds, but stale the schools,
  Revamped as the mode may veer,
But Orm from the schools to the beaches strays,
And, finding a Conch hoar with time, he delays
  And reverent lifts it to ear.   10
That Voice, pitched in far monotone,
  Shall it swerve? shall it deviate ever?
The Seas have inspired it, and Truth—
  Truth, varying from sameness never.

III

In hollows of the liquid hills
  Where the long Blue Ridges run,
The flattery of no echo thrills,
  For echo the seas have none;
Nor aught that gives man back man's strain—
The hope of his heart, the dream in his brain.   20

IV

On ocean where the embattled fleets repair,
Man, suffering inflictor, sails on sufferance there.

V

Implacable I, the old implacable Sea:
  Implacable most when most I smile serene—
Pleased, not appeased, by myriad wrecks in me.

VI

Curled in the comb of yon billow Andean,
  Is it the Dragon's heaven-challenging crest?
Elemental mad ramping of ravening waters—
  Yet Christ on the Mount, and the dove in her nest!

VII

Healed of my hurt, I laud the inhuman Sea—   30
Yea, bless the Angels Four that there convene;

For healed I am even by their pitiless breath
Distilled in wholesome dew named rosmarine.

AFTER THE PLEASURE PARTY   [1891]

Lines Traced Under an Image of Amor Threatening

Fear me, virgin whosoever
Taking pride from love exempt,
Fear me, slighted. Never, never
Brave me, nor my fury tempt:
Downy wings, but wroth they beat
Tempest even in reason's seat.

Behind the house the upland falls
With many an odorous tree—
White marbles gleaming through green halls,
Terrace by terrace, down and down,   10
And meets the starlit Mediterranean Sea.

  'Tis Paradise. In such an hour
Some pangs that rend might take release.
Nor less perturbed who keeps this bower
Of balm, nor finds balsamic peace?
From whom the passionate words in vent
After long revery's discontent?

  Tired of the homeless deep,
Look how their flight yon hurrying billows urge,
Hitherward but to reap   20
Passive repulse from the iron-bound verge!
Insensate, can they never know
'Tis mad to wreck the impulsion so?

  An art of memory is, they tell:
But to forget! forget the glade
Wherein Fate sprung Love's ambuscade,
To flout pale years of cloistral life

And flush me in this sensuous strife.
'Tis Vesta struck with Sappho's smart.
No fable her delirious leap: 30
With more of cause in desperate heart,
Myself could take it—but to sleep!

   Now first I feel, what all may ween,
That soon or late, if faded e'en,
One's sex asserts itself. Desire,
The dear desire through love to sway,
Is like the Geysers that aspire—
Through cold obstruction win their fervid way.
But baffled here—to take disdain,
To feel rule's instinct, yet not reign;   40
To dote, to come to this drear shame—
Hence the winged blaze that sweeps my soul
Like prairie fires that spurn control,
Where withering weeds incense the flame.

   And kept I long heaven's watch for this,
Contemning love, for this, even this?
O terrace chill in Northern air,
O reaching ranging tube I placed
Against yon skies, and fable chased
Till, fool, I hailed for sister there   50
Starred Cassiopea in Golden Chair.
In dream I throned me, nor I saw
In cell the idiot crowned with straw.

   And yet, ah yet scarce ill I reigned,
Through self-illusion self-sustained,
When now—enlightened, undeceived—
What gain I barrenly bereaved!
Than this can be yet lower decline—
Envy and spleen, can these be mine?

   The peasant girl demure that trod   60
Beside our wheels that climbed the way,
And bore along a blossoming rod
That looked the sceptre of May-Day—

On her—to fire this petty hell,
His softened glance how moistly fell!
The cheat! on briars her buds were strung;
And wiles peeped forth from mien how meek.
The innocent bare-foot! young, so young!
To girls, strong man's a novice weak.
To tell such beads! And more remain,   70
Sad rosary of belittling pain.

When after lunch and sallies gay,
Like the Decameron folk we lay
In sylvan groups; and I—let be!
O, dreams he, can he dream that one
Because not roseate feels no sun?
The plain lone bramble thrills with Spring
As much as vines that grapes shall bring.

Me now fair studies charm no more.
Shall great thoughts writ, or high themes sung   80
Damask wan cheeks—unlock his arm
About some radiant ninny flung?
How glad with all my starry lore,
I'd buy the veriest wanton's rose
Would but my bee therein repose.

Could I remake me! or set free
This sexless bound in sex, then plunge
Deeper than Sappho, in a lunge
Piercing Pan's paramount mystery!
For, Nature, in no shallow surge   90
Against thee either sex may urge,
Why hast thou made us but in halves—
Co-relatives? This makes us slaves.
If these co-relatives never meet
Self-hood itself seems incomplete.
And such the dicing of blind fate
Few matching halves here meet and mate.
What Cosmic jest or Anarch blunder
The human integral clove asunder

And shied the fractions through life's gate?   100

   Ye stars that long your votary knew
Rapt in her vigil, see me here!
Whither is gone the spell ye threw
When rose before me Cassiopea?
Usurped on by love's stronger reign—
But lo, your very selves do wane:
Light breaks—truth breaks! Silvered no more,
But chilled by dawn that brings the gale
Shivers yon bramble above the vale,
And disillusion opens all the shore.   110

   One knows not if Urania yet
The pleasure-party may forget;
Or whether she lived down the strain
Of turbulent heart and rebel brain;
For Amor so resents a slight,
And her's had been such haught disdain,
He long may wreak his boyish spite,
And boy-like, little reck the pain.

   One knows not, no. But late in Rome
(For queens discrowned a congruous home)   120
Entering Albani's porch she stood
Fixed by an antique pagan stone
Colossal carved. No anchorite seer,
Not Thomas a Kempis, monk austere,
Religious more are in their tone;
Yet far, how far from Christian heart
That form august of heathen Art.
Swayed by its influence, long she stood,
Till surged emotion seething down,
She rallied and this mood she won: 130

   Languid in frame for me,
To-day by Mary's convent shrine,
Touched by her picture's moving plea
In that poor nerveless hour of mine,

I mused—A wanderer still must grieve.
Half I resolved to kneel and believe,
Believe and submit, the veil take on.
But thee, armed Virgin! less benign,
Thee now I invoke, thou mightier one.
Helmeted woman—if such term   140
Befit thee, far from strife
Of that which makes the sexual feud
And clogs the aspirant life—
O self-reliant, strong and free,
Thou in whom power and peace unite,
Transcender! raise me up to thee,
Raise me and arm me!

               Fond appeal.
For never passion peace shall bring,
Nor Art inanimate for long   150
Inspire. Nothing may help or heal
While Amor incensed remembers wrong.
Vindictive, not himself he'll spare;
For scope to give his vengeance play
Himself he'll blaspheme and betray.

   Then for Urania, virgins everywhere,
O pray! Example take too, and have care.

THE RAVAGED VILLA   [1891]

In shards the sylvan vases lie,
   Their links of dance undone,
And brambles wither by thy brim,
   Choked fountain of the sun!
The spider in the laurel spins,
   The weed exiles the flower:
And, flung to kiln, Apollo's bust
   Makes lime for Mammon's tower.

MONODY   [1891]

To have known him, to have loved him
    After loneness long;
And then to be estranged in life,
    And neither in the wrong;
And now for death to set his seal—
    Ease me, a little ease, my song!

By wintry hills his hermit-mound
    The sheeted snow-drifts drape,
And houseless there the snow-bird flits
    Beneath the fir-trees' crape: 10
Glazed now with ice the cloistral vine
    That hid the shyest grape.

ART   [1891]

In placid hours well-pleased we dream
Of many a brave unbodied scheme.
But form to lend, pulsed life create,
What unlike things must meet and mate:
A flame to melt—a wind to freeze;
Sad patience—joyous energies;
Humility—yet pride and scorn;
Instinct and study; love and hate;
Audacity—reverence. These must mate,
And fuse with Jacob's mystic heart,   10
To wrestle with the angel—Art.

Frederick Goddard Tuckerman

1821–1873

Frederick Goddard Tuckerman, son of a wealthy businessman, was born in Boston on February 4, 1821. At the age of sixteen he entered Harvard, where Jones Very was his tutor, but withdrew at the end of the year. Later he completed the requirements for the LL.B. degree in the Law School and was admitted to the Bar, though he never practiced. In 1847 he married Miss Hannah Lucinda Jones and made his home in Greenfield, Massachusetts, devoting his time to domestic life and his hobbies, astronomy, botany, and poetry. The death of his wife in 1857 was the great sorrow of his life and was the subject of many of his sonnets. In 1860 he privately printed a volume of his poems, which was reissued in 1864 by Ticknor and Fields. It won high praise from Tennyson, whom he had visited in England, from Emerson and other American poets, but was largely forgotten until Witter Bynner edited a selection in 1931. The Cricket, published in 1950 from notebook manuscripts, was praised by Yvor Winters and other critics. Many poems remained in manuscript until N. Scott Momaday edited them in The Complete Poems of Frederick Goddard Tuckerman, *1965.*

THE QUESTION   [1860]

How shall I array my love?
How should I arrange my fair?
Leave her standing white and silent
In the richness of her hair?
Motion silent, beauty bare,

In the glory of her hair?
Or, for place and drapery,
Ravage land, and sack the sea?

Or from darkest summer sky,
When the white belts, riding high,   10
Cut the clear like ribs of pearl,
On the eastern upland's curl,
In the time of dusk and dew
Tear away a breadth of blue?

Touched from twilight's rosy bars,
With each twinkling tuft of stars,
And, shaking out the glints of gold,
Catch her softly from the cold?—
Catch, and lift her to the cloud,
Where to crown her, passing proud,   20
Gliding, glistening woods of June,
Reach the rain-ring from the moon?

Or—to fold her warmer-wise—
Let me try, in garb and guise
Gathered from this mortal globe;
Roll her beauty in a robe
Of the Persian lilac stain,
Purple, dim with filigrane;
Belted-in with rarer red
Than India's leaf ere figurèd,   30
Put a crown upon her head—
Then to lead her, high and cold,
Where, from a step of silver rolled
A crimson floweth on the floor;
Like a river riding o'er
Pearl, and priceless marbles bright,—
Onyx, myrrhine, marcasite,
And the jasper green!—nor these alone!
But the famed Phengites stone,—
And leading upward to the throne.   40
Prop and pillar, roof and rise,
All ashake with drops and dyes,

And the diamond's precious eyes;
And she, as if a sudden storm
Had fallen upon her face and form;
Diamonds like raindrops rare,
Pearls like hailstones in her hair;
In the lamplight's ruddy stream,
Jewels crossed with jewels gleam
On jewels, jewel-circled there;   50
While, round her wrists and ankles bare,
Gems of jewels glimpse and gaze,—
Hyacinth, rose-stone, idocrase.

Or she stealeth, soft arrayed
Like a white Hæmonian maid
Winding under cypress shade;
Cedar shade, and paths of green,
With the porch and pillar, white between;
Amaranth eyes do mine behold,
Hair like the pale marigold: 60
Dreamily she seems to me
Hero, or Herodice!
With a sidelong motion sweet,
Thro' flowers she draws her feet;
This way now the ripples come,—
Shower myrtles, myrrh, and gum,
With heliochryse and ámomum!

Ah, not so, New England's flower!
Separate must her beauty be
From stars of old mythology,—   70
Priestesses, or Crysophoræ,
Nor fairy garb, nor kingly dower,
May fit her in her radiant hour;
Free and bold her steps must flow,
All men see her come and go;
At her feet the planet lies,
Day and night are in her eyes,
Over her the star-flag strewn:
Lo! she standeth there alone,
Pride, in her dark glances, king!   80

Love, her cheek rose-colouring;
In a garden all her own,
Lo! she standeth, crownèd on
With rare roses, round her drawn
Texture like the webs of dawn
On the rose-beds lingering,
While my heart to her I bring;
Heart and garden all her own—
What, in truth, cares such a one,
Though my arm could round her throw   90
Gleam of gods or crowns bestow?
Or though the old gods could confer
All godlike gifts and grace on her?
The young Medusa's locks divine,
Pelops' shoulder eburnine,
Lips that drew the Ismenean bees,
Tears of the Heliades,
Dropped into shimmering shells that be
About the indraught of the sea.

The river-riches of the sphere,   100
All that the dark sea-bottoms bear,
The wide earth's green convexity,
The inexhaustible blue sky,
Hold not a prize, so proud, so high,
That it could grace her, gay or grand,
By garden-gale and rose-breath fanned;
Or as tonight I saw her stand,
Lovely in the meadow-land,
With a clover in her hand.

REFRIGERIUM   [1860]

Let them lie,—their day is over;
   Only night and stillness be:
Let the slow rain come and bring
   Brake and star-grass, speedwell, harebell,

All the fulness of the spring;
　　What reck I of friend and lover?
Foe by foe laid lovingly?

What are mounds of green earth, either?
　　What, to me, unfriendly bones
Death hath pacified and won　　　　　　　　　　　　　　　10
　　To a reconcilèd patience,
Though their very graves have run
　　In the blending earth together,
And the spider links the stones?

To the hills I wander, crying,—
　　Where we stood in days of old,
Stood and saw the sunset die,
　　Watched through tears the passing purple,—
"Oh, my darling, misery
　　Has been mine; but thou wert lying　　　　　　　20
In a slumber sweet and cold."

Sonnets: Part I　[1860]

XXII

The morning comes; not slow, with reddening gold,
But wildly driven, with windy shower, and sway
As though the wind would blow the dark away!
Voices of wail, of misery multifold,
Wake with the light, and its harsh glare obey;
And yet I walk betimes this day of spring,
Still my own private portion reckoning,
Not to compute, though every tear be told.
Oh, might I on the gale my sorrow fling!
But sweep, sweep on, wild blast! Who bids thee stay?　　10
Across the stormy headlands shriek and sing;
And, earlier than the daytime, bring the day

To pouring eyes, half-quenched with watery sight,
And breaking hearts that hate the morning light!

XXIV

Perhaps a dream; yet surely truth has beamed
Oft from the gate of dreams upon the brain;
As on yon mountain, black with thunder-rain,
Today through cloudy clefts the glory streamed.
Why do men doubt, and balance, and disdain,
Where she, the gentler spirit, seeks to skim
Light from the vague,—though thick the shadows swim;
Still counting what she may not all explain,—
Not to be lost, or lightly disesteemed,—
Though cloudy of shape it seem, and meaning dim?   10
Did Manoah's wife doubt ere she showed to him
The angel standing in the golden grain?
Had Deborah fear? Or was that vision vain
That Actia, Arlotte, and Mandané dreamed?

XXV

By this low fire I often sit to woo
Memory to bring the days forever done;
And call the mountains, where our love begun,
And the dear happy woodlands dipped in dew;
And pore upon the landscape, like a book
But cannot find her: or there rise to me
Gardens and groves in light and shadow outspread:
Or, on a headland far away, I see
Men marching slow in orderly review;
And bayonets flash, as, wheeling from the sun,   10
Rank after rank give fire: or, sad, I look
On miles of moonlit brine, with many a bed
Of wave-weed heaving,—there the wet sands shine,
And just awash, the low reef lifts its line.

XXVI

For Nature daily through her grand design
Breathes contradiction where she seems most clear:

For I have held of her the gift to hear;
And felt, indeed, endowed of sense divine,
When I have found, by guarded insight fine,
Cold April flowers in the green end of June;
And thought myself possessed of Nature's ear,
When, by the lonely mill-brook, unto mine,
Seated on slab, or trunk asunder sawn,
The night-hawk blew his horn at sunny noon;　　　　10
And in the rainy midnight I have heard
The ground-sparrow's long twitter from the pine,
And the cat-bird's silver song—the wakeful bird
That to the lighted window sings for dawn.

Sonnets: Part II [1860]

VII

His heart was in his garden; but his brain
Wandered at will among the fiery stars:
Bards, heroes, prophets, Homers, Hamilcars,
With many angels, stood, his eye to gain;
The devils, too, were his familiars.
And yet the cunning florist held his eyes
Close to the ground,—a tulip-bulb his prize,—
And talked of tan and bone-dust, cutworms, grubs,
As though all Nature held no higher strain;
Or, if he spoke of Art, he made the theme　　　　10
Flow through box-borders, turf, and flower-tubs;
Or, like a garden-engine's, steered the stream,—
Now spouted rainbows to the silent skies;
Now kept it flat, and raked the walks and shrubs.

VIII

Companions were we in the grove and glen!
Through belts of summer wandered hour on hour,
Ransacking sward and swamp to deck his bower,—

River, and reservoir of mountain rain;
Nor sought for hard-named herb, or plant of power,
But Whippoorwill-shoe and quaint Sidesaddle-flower.
And still he talked, asserting, thought is free
And wisest souls by their own action shine:
"For beauty," he said, "is where'er we look,
Growing alike in waste and guarded ground, 10
And, like the May-flower, gathered equally
On desolate hills, where scantily the pine
Drops his dry wisps about the barren rock,
And in the angles of the fences found."

IX

But unto him came swift calamity,
In the sweet spring-time, when his beds were green;
And my heart waited, trustfully serene,
For the new blossom on my household-tree.
But flowers, and gods, and quaint Philosophy,
Are poor, in truth, to fill the empty place;
Nor any joy, nor season's jollity,
Can aught, indeed, avail to grace our grief.
Can spring return to him a brother's face,
Or bring my darling back to me—to me? 10
Undimmed the May went on with bird and bower;
The summer filled and faded like a flower:
But rainy Autumn and the red-turned leaf
Found us at tears and wept for company.

X

Thy baby, too, the child that was to be,
Thro' happier days,—a brightening sun above,—
Held to thy heart with more forgetful love,—
So proud a portion of thyself to me:
We talked it o'er,—the bliss that was to bless;
The birth, the baby robes, the christening,
And all our hearts were carried in this thing.

Cold, cold she lies where houseless tempests blow;
The baby's face is here, almost a woe;
And I, so seared in soul, so sapped and shrunk,   10
Gaze hopeless,—careless, in my changed estate
To fall at once, or in the wilderness
Stand like a charred and fire-hardened trunk,
To break the axe's edge of time and Fate!

XI

Still pressing through these weeping solitudes,
Perchance I snatch a beam of comfort bright,—
And pause, to fix the gleam, or lose it quite,
That darkens as I move, or but intrudes,
To baffle and forelay: as sometimes here,
When late at night the wearied engineer
Driving his engine up through Whately woods
Sees on the track a glimmering lantern-light,
And checks his crashing speed,—with hasty hand
Reversing and retarding. But, again!   10
Look where it burns, a furlong on before!—
The witchlight of the reedy-river-shore,
The pilot of the forest and the fen,
Not to be left, but with the waste woodland.

XII

How most unworthy, echoing in mine ears,
The verse sounds on!—Life, Love, Experience, Art,
Fused into grief; and like a grief-filled heart,
Where all emotion tends and turns to tears,
Broken by its own strength of passion and need;
Unworthy, though the bitter waters start
In these dim eyes, reviewing thought and word;
The high desire, the faint accomplished deed;
Unuttered love and loss,—and feverish
Beatings against a gate forever barred.   10
Yet over and again I range and read
The blotted page, re-turning leaf and leaf;
And half-believe the words are what I wish,
And pore upon my verse, and court my grief,—

XIII

Even as a lover, dreaming, unaware,
Calls o'er his mistress' features hour by hour,
Nor thinks of simple dress, and humble dower;
But pictures to himself her graces rare,—
Dark eyes, dark lashes, and harmonious hair
Caught lightly up with amaryllis flower,
Hæmanthus, eardrop, or auricula:
And deems within wide Nature's bound and law
All to beseem her beauty but designed—
Of pure or proud; nor counts himself too bold   10
To fit her forehead with the perfect gold;
Or round her girlish temples belt and bind
Some lamp of jewels, lovelier than the whole,—
Green diamond, or gem of girasol!

XIV

The breeze is sharp, the sky is hard and blue,—
Blue with white tails of cloud. On such a day,
Upon a neck of sand o'erblown with spray,
We stood in silence the great sea to view;
And marked the bathers at their shuddering play
Run in and out with the succeeding wave,
While from our footsteps broke the trembling turf.
Again I hear the drenching of the wave;
The rocks rise dark, with wall and weedy cave;
Her voice is in mine ears, her answer yet: 10
Again I see, above the froth and fret,
The blue loft standing like eternity!
And white feet flying from the surging surf
And simmering suds of the sea!

XV

Gertrude and Gulielma, sister-twins,
Dwelt in the valley, at the farm-house old;
Nor grief had touched their locks of dark and gold,
Nor dimmed the fragrant whiteness of their skins:
Both beautiful, and one in height and mould;

Yet one had loveliness which the spirit wins
To other worlds,—eyes, forehead, smile and all,
More softly serious than the twilight's fall.
The other—can I e'er forget the day,
When, stealing from a laughing group away,   10
To muse with absent eye, and motion slow,
Her beauty fell upon me like a blow?—
Gertrude! with red flowerlip, and silk black hair!
Yet Gulielma was by far more fair!

XVI

Under the mountain, as when I first knew
Its low black roof, and chimney creeper-twined,
The red house stands; and yet my footsteps find
Vague in the walks, waste balm and feverfew.
But they are gone; no soft-eyed sisters trip
Across the porch or lintels; where, behind,
The mother sat,—sat knitting with pursed lip.
The house stands vacant in its green recess,
Absent of beauty as a broken heart;
The wild rain enters; and the sunset wind   10
Sighs in the chambers of their loveliness,
Or shakes the pane; and in the silent noons,
The glass falls from the window, part by part,
And ringeth in the grassy stones.

XVII

Roll on, sad world! Not Mercury or Mars
Could swifter speed, or slower, round the sun,
Than in this year of variance thou hast done
For me. Yet pain, fear, heart-break, woes and wars
Have natural limit; from his dread eclipse
The swift sun hastens, and the night debars
The day, but to bring in the day more bright;
The flowers renew their odorous fellowships;
The moon runs round and round; the slow earth dips,
True to her poise, and lifts, the planet-stars   10

Roll and return from circle to ellipse;
The day is dull and soft, the eave-trough drips;
And yet I know the splendour of the light
Will break anon: Lo! where the gray is white!

XXXI

My Anna! When for her my head was bowed,
The circle of the world, sky, mountain, main,
Drew inward to one spot; and now again
Wide Nature narrows to the shell and shroud.
In the late dawn they will not be forgot,
And evenings early-dark, when the low rain
Begins at nightfall, though no tempests rave,
I know the rain is falling on her grave;
The morning views it, and the sunset cloud
Points with a finger to that lonely spot;   10
The crops, that up the valley rolling go,
Ever towards her slumber bow and blow!
I look on the sweeping corn, and the surging rye,
And with every gust of wind my heart goes by!

XXXII

Oh for the face and footstep!—Woods and shores!
That looked upon us in life's happiest flush;
That saw our figures breaking from the brush;
That heard our voices calling through the bowers!
How are ye darkened! Deepest tears upgush
From the heart's heart; and, gathering more and more,
Blindness, and strangling tears,—as now before
Your shades I stand, and find ye still so fair!
And thou, sad mountain-stream! thy stretches steal
Thro' fern and flag, as when we gathered flowers   10
Along thy reeds and shallows cold; or where—
Over the red reef with a rolling roar—
The woods, thro' glimmering gaps of green, reveal,
Sideward, the River turning like a wheel.

XXXIII

One still dark night, I sat alone and wrote:
So still it was, that distant Chanticleer
Seemed to cry out his warning at my ear,—
Save for the brooding echo in his throat.
Sullen I sat; when, like the night-wind's note,
A voice said, "Wherefore doth he weep and fear?
Doth he not know no cry to God is dumb?"
Another spoke: "His heart is dimmed and drowned
With grief." I knew the shape that bended then
To kiss me, when suddenly I once again,   10
Across the watches of the starless gloom,
Heard the cock scream and pause; the morning bell,
Into the gulfs of Night dropped One; the vision fell,—
And left me listening to the sinking sound.

XXXIV

My Anna! though thine earthly steps are done;
Nor in the garden, nor beside the door,
Shall I behold thee standing any more,—
I would not hide my face from light, nor shun
The full completion of this wordly day.
What though beside my feet no other one
May set her own, to walk the forward way?
I will not fear to take the path alone;
Loving, for thy sake, things that cheer and bless,—
Kind words, pure deeds, and gentlest charities.   10
Nor will I cease to hold a hope and aim;
But, prophet-like, of these will make my bread,
And feed my soul at peace; as Esdras fed
On flowers, until the vision and the glory came!

Henry Timrod

1828–1867

*Henry Timrod was born in Charleston, South Carolina, on December 8,
1828, into a family of modest means. His grandfather was an emigrant
German tailor and his father a bookdealer. After a classical education in
a private academy and the University of Georgia, though illness and
poverty prevented him from graduating, he struggled to support himself
by teaching and writing. He started* Russell's Magazine *in order to
give the South a magazine comparable to the* Atlantic Monthly *in
New England, but the South was not ready for such a venture. In 1860
his only volume of poems was published in Boston. During the early
months of the Civil War he served in the Confederate Army, until discharged because of illness. He married and tried to support his family
by journalism, but the devastation of the war made this impossible, and
he died of malnutrition and tuberculosis. Many poets, in the North as
well as the South, felt that his death was a tragic loss of unfulfilled
talent.*

CHARLESTON   [1873]

Calm as that second summer which precedes
    The first fall of the snow,
In the broad sunlight of heroic deeds,
    The City bides the foe.

As yet, behind their ramparts stern and proud,
    Her bolted thunders sleep—
Dark Sumter, like a battlemented cloud,
    Looms o'er the solemn deep.

No Calpe frowns from lofty cliff or scar
   To guard the holy strand;   10
But Moultrie holds in leash her dogs of war
   Above the level sand.

And down the dunes a thousand guns lie couched,
   Unseen, beside the flood—
Like tigers in some Orient jungle crouched
   That wait and watch for blood.

Meanwhile, through streets still echoing with trade,
   Walk grave and thoughtful men,
Whose hands may one day wield the patriot's blade
   As lightly as the pen.   20

And maidens, with such eyes as would grow dim
   Over a bleeding hound,
Seem each one to have caught the strength of him
   Whose sword she sadly bound.

Thus girt without and garrisoned at home,
   Day patient following day,
Old Charleston looks from roof, and spire, and dome,
   Across her tranquil bay.

Ships, through a hundred foes, from Saxon lands
   And spicy Indian ports   30
Bring Saxon steel and iron to her hands,
   And Summer to her courts.

But still, along yon dim Atlantic line,
   The only hostile smoke
Creeps like a harmless mist above the brine,
   From some frail, floating oak.

Shall the Spring dawn, and she still clad in smiles,
   And with an unscathed brow,
Rest in the strong arms of her palm-crowned isles,
   As fair and free as now?   40

We know not; in the temple of the Fates
   God has inscribed her doom;
And, all untroubled in her faith, she waits
   The triumph or the tomb.

SPRING   [1873]

Spring, with that nameless pathos in the air
Which dwells with all things fair,
Spring, with her golden suns and silver rain,
Is with us once again.

Out in the lonely woods the jasmine burns
Its fragrant lamps, and turns
Into a royal court with green festoons
The banks of dark lagoons.

In the deep heart of every forest tree
The blood is all aglee,   10
And there's a look about the leafless bowers
As if they dreamed of flowers.

Yet still on every side we trace the hand
Of Winter in the land,
Save where the maple reddens on the lawn,
Flushed by the season's dawn;

Or where, like those strange semblances we find
That age to childhood bind,
The elm puts on, as if in Nature's scorn,
The brown of Autumn corn.   20

As yet the turf is dark, although you know
That, not a span below,
A thousand germs are groping through the gloom,
And soon will burst their tomb.

Already, here and there, on frailest stems
Appear some azure gems,
Small as might deck, upon a gala day,
The forehead of a fay.

In gardens you may note amid the dearth
The crocus breaking earth;   30
And near the snowdrop's tender white and green,
The violet in its screen.

But many gleams and shadows need must pass
Along the budding grass,
And weeks go by, before the enamored South
Shall kiss the rose's mouth.

Still there's a sense of blossoms yet unborn
In the sweet airs of morn;
One almost looks to see the very street
Grow purple at his feet.   40

At times a fragrant breeze comes floating by,
And brings, you know not why,
A feeling as when eager crowds await
Before a palace gate

Some wondrous pageant; and you scarce would start,
If from a beech's heart,
A blue-eyed Dryad, stepping forth, should say,
"Behold me! I am May!"

Ah! who would couple thoughts of war and crime
With such a blessëd time!   50
Who in the west wind's aromatic breath
Could hear the call of Death!

Yet not more surely shall the Spring awake
The voice of wood and brake,
Than she shall rouse, for all her tranquil charms,
A million men to arms.

There shall be deeper hues upon her plains
Than all her sunlit rains,
And every gladdening influence around,
Can summon from the ground.   60

Oh! standing on this desecrated mould,
Methinks that I behold,
Lifting her bloody daisies up to God,
Spring kneeling on the sod,

And calling, with the voice of all her rills,
Upon the ancient hills
To fall and crush the tyrants and the slaves
Who turn her meads to graves.

THE UNKNOWN DEAD   [1873]

The rain is plashing on my sill,
But all the winds of Heaven are still;
And so it falls with that dull sound
Which thrills us in the church-yard ground,
When the first spadeful drops like lead
Upon the coffin of the dead.
Beyond my streaming window-pane,
I cannot see the neighboring vane,
Yet from its old familiar tower
The bell comes, muffled, through the shower.   10
What strange and unsuspected link
Of feeling touched, has made me think—
While with a vacant soul and eye
I watch that gray and stony sky—
Of nameless graves on battle-plains
Washed by a single winter's rains,
Where, some beneath Virginian hills,
And some by green Atlantic rills,
Some by the waters of the West,
A myriad unknown heroes rest.   20

Ah! not the chiefs, who, dying, see
Their flags in front of victory,
Or, at their life-blood's noble cost
Pay for a battle nobly lost,
Claim from their monumental beds
The bitterest tears a nation sheds.
Beneath yon lonely mound—the spot
By all save some fond few forgot—
Lie the true martyrs of the fight
Which strikes for freedom and for right.   30
Of them, their patriot zeal and pride,
The lofty faith that with them died,
No grateful page shall farther tell
Than that so many bravely fell;
And we can only dimly guess
What worlds of all this world's distress,
What utter woe, despair, and dearth,
Their fate has brought to many a hearth.
Just such a sky as this should weep
Above them, always, where they sleep;   40
Yet, haply, at this very hour,
Their graves are like a lover's bower;
And Nature's self, with eyes unwet,
Oblivious of the crimson debt
To which she owes her April grace,
Laughs gayly o'er their burial-place.

ODE   [1873]

Sung on the Occasion of Decorating the Graves
of the Confederate Dead, at Magnolia Cemetery,
Charleston, S.C., 1867

                              I

Sleep sweetly in your humble graves,
    Sleep, martyrs of a fallen cause;
Though yet no marble column craves
    The pilgrim here to pause.

II

In seeds of laurel in the earth
   The blossom of your fame is blown,
And somewhere, waiting for its birth,
   The shaft is in the stone!

III

Meanwhile, behalf the tardy years
   Which keep in trust your storied tombs,   10
Behold! your sisters bring their tears,
   And these memorial blooms.

IV

Small tributes! but your shades will smile
   More proudly on these wreaths to-day,
Than when some cannon-moulded pile
   Shall overlook this bay.

V

Stoop, angels, hither from the skies!
   There is no holier spot of ground
Than where defeated valor lies,
   By mourning beauty crowned!   20

Emily Dickinson

1830–1886

Emily Dickinson was born December 10, 1830, in Amherst, Massachusetts. Her father, Edward Dickinson, was a lawyer, Congressman, and treasurer of Amherst College. In 1847 she entered South Hadley Female Seminary, now Mount Holyoke College, but returned in less than a year to Amherst, where she lived the rest of her life. On a brief visit to Philadelphia in 1854 she met Charles Wadsworth, a Presbyterian minister, and apparently fell in love with him; but he does not seem to have returned her love. She had already begun writing poetry in the 1850's; and in 1862, the year that Wadsworth accepted a call to a church in San Francisco, she began her few years of greatest productivity and sought critical assistance from Thomas Wentworth Higginson, who became her first editor. Though she had numerous friends, she became increasingly bound to her home and garden in her last years. Only seven of her poems were published during her lifetime; her first volume appeared posthumously in 1890. She died May 15, 1886.

49   [1890]

I never lost as much but twice,
And that was in the sod.
Twice have I stood a beggar
Before the door of God!

Angels—twice descending
Reimbursed my store—
Burglar! Banker—Father!
I am poor once more!

67 [1890]

Success is counted sweetest
By those who ne'er succeed.
To comprehend a nectar
Requires sorest need.

Not one of all the purple Host
Who took the Flag today
Can tell the definition
So clear of Victory

As he defeated—dying—
On whose forbidden ear   10
The distant strains of triumph
Burst agonized and clear!

76 [1890]

Exultation is the going
Of an inland soul to sea,
Past the houses—past the headlands—
Into deep Eternity—

Bred as we, among the mountains,
Can the sailor understand
The divine intoxication
Of the first league out from land?

80 [1896]

Our lives are Swiss—
So still—so Cool—

Till some odd afternoon
The Alps neglect their Curtains
And we look farther on!

Italy stands the other side!
While like a guard between—
The solemn Alps—
The siren Alps
Forever intervene!   10

1 2 6   [1890]

To fight aloud, is very brave—
But *gallanter*, I know
Who charge within the bosom
The Cavalry of Wo—

Who win, and nations do not see—
Who fall—and none observe—
Whose dying eyes, no Country
Regards with patriot love—

We trust, in plumed procession
For such, the Angels go—   10
Rank after Rank, with even feet—
And Uniforms of Snow.

1 2 8   [1891]

Bring me the sunset in a cup,
Reckon the morning's flagon's up
And say how many Dew,
Tell me how far the morning leaps—

Tell me what time the weaver sleeps
Who spun the breadths of blue!

Write me how many notes there be
In the new Robin's extasy
Among astonished boughs—
How many trips the Tortoise makes— 10
How many cups the Bee partakes,
The Debauchee of Dews!

Also, who laid the Rainbow's piers,
Also, who leads the docile spheres
By withes of supple blue?
Whose fingers string the stalactite—
Who counts the wampum of the night
To see that none is due?

Who built this little Alban House
And shut the windows down so close 20
My spirit cannot see?
Who'll let me out some gala day
With implements to fly away,
Passing Pomposity?

130   [1890]

These are the days when Birds come back—
A very few—a Bird or two—
To take a backward look.

These are the days when skies resume
The old—old sophistries of June—
A blue and gold mistake.

Oh fraud that cannot cheat the Bee—
Almost thy plausibility
Induces my belief.

Till ranks of seeds their witness bear—   10
And softly thro' the altered air
Hurries a timid leaf.

Oh Sacrament of summer days,
Oh Last Communion in the Haze—
Permit a child to join.

Thy sacred emblems to partake—
Thy consecrated bread to take
And thine immortal wine!

160   [1891]

Just lost, when I was saved!
Just felt the world go by!
Just girt me for the onset with Eternity,
When breath blew back,
And on the other side
I heard recede the disappointed tide!

Therefore, as One returned, I feel,
Odd secrets of the line to tell!
Some Sailor, skirting foreign shores—
Some pale Reporter, from the awful doors   10
Before the Seal!

Next time, to stay!
Next time, the things to see
By Ear unheard,
Unscrutinized by Eye—

Next time, to tarry,
While the Ages steal—
Slow tramp the Centuries,
And the Cycles wheel!

165   [1890]

A *Wounded* Deer—leaps highest—
I've heard the Hunter tell—
'Tis but the Extasy of *death*—
And then the Brake is still!

The *Smitten* Rock that gushes!
The *trampled* Steel that springs!
A Cheek is always redder
Just where the Hectic stings!

Mirth is the Mail of Anguish—
In which it Cautious Arm,   10
Lest anybody spy the blood
And "you're hurt" exclaim!

187   [1890]

How many times these low feet staggered—
Only the soldered mouth can tell—
Try—can you stir the awful rivet—
Try—can you lift the hasps of steel!

Stroke the cool forehead—hot so often—
Lift—if you care—the listless hair—
Handle the adamantine fingers
Never a thimble—more—shall wear—

Buzz the dull flies—on the chamber window—
Brave—shines the sun through the freckled pane—   10
Fearless—the cobweb swings from the ceiling—
Indolent Housewife—in Daisies—lain!

2 I 4   [1890]

I taste a liquor never brewed—
From Tankards scooped in Pearl—
Not all the Vats upon the Rhine*
Yield such an Alcohol!

Inebriate of Air—am I—
And Debauchee of Dew—
Reeling—thro endless summer days—
From inns of Molten Blue—

When "Landlords" turn the drunken Bee
Out of the Foxglove's door—   10
When Butterflies—renounce their "drams"—
I shall but drink the more!

Till Seraphs swing their snowy Hats—
And Saints—to windows run—
To see the little Tippler
Leaning against the—Sun—*

2 I 6   [1890]

Safe in their Alabaster Chambers—
Untouched by Morning
And untouched by Noon—
Sleep the meek members of the Resurrection—
Rafter of satin,
And Roof of stone.

Light laughs the breeze
In her Castle above them—
Babbles the Bee in a stolid Ear,

* See notes to ll. 3 and 16 on p. 1095.

Pipe the Sweet Birds in ignorant cadence—   10
Ah, what sagacity perished here!

version of 1859

Safe in their Alabaster Chambers—
Untouched by Morning—
And untouched by Noon—
Lie the meek members of the Resurrection—
Rafter of Satin—and Roof of Stone!

Grand go the Years—in the Crescent—above them—
Worlds scoop their Arcs—
And Firmaments—row—
Diadems—drop—and Doges—surrender—
Soundless as dots—on a Disc of Snow—   10

version of 1861

241   [1890]

I like a look of Agony,
Because I know it's true—
Men do not sham Convulsion,
Nor simulate, a Throe—

The Eyes glaze once—and that is Death—
Impossible to feign
The Beads upon the Forehead
By homely Anguish strung.

249   [1891]

Wild Nights—Wild Nights!
Were I with thee
Wild Nights should be
Our luxury!

Futile—the Winds—
To a Heart in port—
Done with the Compass—
Done with the Chart!

Rowing in Eden—
Ah, the Sea!   10
Might I but moor—Tonight—
In Thee!

2 5 8   [1890]

There's a certain Slant of light,
Winter Afternoons—
That oppresses, like the Heft
Of Cathedral Tunes—

Heavenly Hurt, it gives us—
We can find no scar,
But internal difference,
Where the Meanings, are—

None may teach it—Any—
'Tis the Seal Despair—   10
An imperial affliction
Sent us of the Air—

When it comes, the Landscape listens—
Shadows—hold their breath—
When it goes, 'tis like the Distance
On the look of Death—

2 8 0   [1896]

I felt a Funeral, in my Brain,
And Mourners to and fro

Kept treading—treading—till it seemed
That Sense was breaking through—

And when they all were seated,
A Service, like a Drum—
Kept beating—beating—till I thought
My Mind was going numb—

And then I heard them lift a Box
And creak across my Soul   10
With those same Boots of Lead, again,
Then Space—began to toll,

As all the Heavens were a Bell,
And Being, but an Ear,
And I, and Silence, some strange Race
Wrecked, solitary, here—

And then a Plank in Reason, broke,
And I dropped down, and down—
And hit a World, at every plunge,
And Finished knowing—then—   20

287   [1896]

A Clock stopped—
Not the Mantel's—
Geneva's farthest skill
Cant put the puppet bowing—
That just now dangled still—

An awe came on the Trinket!
The Figures hunched, with pain—
Then quivered out of Decimals—
Into Degreeless Noon—

It will not stir for Doctor's—   10
This Pendulum of snow—
The Shopman importunes it—
While cool—concernless No—

Nods from the Gilded pointers—
Nods from the Seconds slim—
Decades of Arrogance between
The Dial life—
And Him—

290   [1896]

Of Bronze—and Blaze—
The North—Tonight—
So adequate—it forms—
So preconcerted with itself
So distant—to alarms—
An Unconcern so sovreign
To Universe, or me—
Infects my simple spirit
With Taints of Majesty—
Till I take vaster attitudes—   10
And strut upon my stem—
Disdaining Men, and Oxygen,
For Arrogance of them—

My Splendors, are Menagerie—
But their Competeless Show
Will entertain the Centuries
When I, am long ago,
An Island in dishonored Grass—
Whom none but Beetles—know.*

303   [1890]

The Soul selects her own Society—
Then—shuts the Door—
To her divine Majority—
Present no more—

* See note to l. 19 on p. 1096.

Unmoved—she notes the Chariots—pausing—
At her low Gate—
Unmoved—an Emperor be kneeling
Upon her Mat—

I've known her—from an ample nation—
Choose One—   10
Then—close the Valves of her attention—
Like Stone—

3 1 8   [1890]

I'll tell you how the Sun rose—
A Ribbon at a time—
The Steeples swam in Amethyst—
The news, like Squirrels, ran—
The Hills untied their Bonnets—
The Bobolinks—begun—
Then I said softly to myself—
"That must have been the Sun"!
But how he set—I know not—
There seemed a purple stile   10
That little Yellow boys and girls
Were climbing all the while—
Till when they reached the other side,
A Dominie in Gray—
Put gently up the evening Bars—
And led the flock away—

3 2 2   [1890]

There came a Day at Summer's full,
Entirely for me—
I thought that such were for the Saints,
Where Resurrections—be—

The Sun, as common, went abroad,
The flowers, accustomed, blew,
As if no soul the solstice passed
That maketh all things new—

The time was scarce profaned, by speech—
The symbol of a word   10
Was needless, as at Sacrament,
The Wardrobe—of our Lord—

Each was to each The Sealed Church,
Permitted to commune this—time—
Lest we too awkward show
At Supper of the Lamb.

The Hours slid fast—as Hours will,
Clutched tight, by greedy hands—
So faces on two Decks, look back,
Bound to opposing lands—   20

And so when all the time had leaked,
Without external sound
Each bound the Other's Crucifix—
We gave no other Bond—

Sufficient troth, that we shall rise—
Deposed—at length, the Grave—
To that new Marriage,
Justified—through Calvaries of Love—

328   [1891]

A Bird came down the Walk—
He did not know I saw—
He bit an Angleworm in halves
And ate the fellow, raw,

And then he drank a Dew
From a convenient Grass—
And then hopped sidewise to the Wall
To let a Beetle pass—

He glanced with rapid eyes
That hurried all around—   10
They looked like frightened Beads, I thought—
He stirred his Velvet Head

Like one in danger, Cautious,
I offered him a Crumb
And he unrolled his feathers
And rowed him softer home—

Than Oars divide the Ocean,
Too silver for a seam—
Or Butterflies, off Banks of Noon
Leap, plashless as they swim.   20

341   [1929]

After great pain, a formal feeling comes—
The Nerves sit ceremonious, like Tombs—
The stiff Heart questions was it He, that bore,
And Yesterday, or Centuries before?

The Feet, mechanical, go round—
Of Ground, or Air, or Ought—
A Wooden way
Regardless grown,
A Quartz contentment, like a stone—

This is the Hour of Lead—   10
Remembered, if outlived,
As Freezing persons, recollect the Snow—
First—Chill—then Stupor—then the letting go—

348   [1891]

I dreaded that first Robin, so,
But He is mastered, now,
I'm some accustomed to Him grown,
He hurts a little, though—

I thought if I could only live
Till that first Shout got by—
Not all Pianos in the Woods
Had power to mangle me—

I dared not meet the Daffodils—
For fear their Yellow Gown   10
Would pierce me with a fashion
So foreign to my own—

I wished the Grass would hurry—
So—when 'twas time to see—
He'd be too tall, the tallest one
Could stretch—to look at me—

I could not bear the Bees should come,
I wished they'd stay away
In those dim countries where they go,
What word had they, for me?   20

They're here, though; not a creature failed—
No Blossom stayed away
In gentle deference to me—
The Queen of Calvary—

Each one salutes me, as he goes,
And I, my childish Plumes,
Lift, in bereaved acknowledgement
Of their unthinking Drums—

376   [1929]

Of Course—I prayed—
And did God Care?
He cared as much as on the Air
A Bird—had stamped her foot—
And cried "Give Me"—
My Reason—Life—
I had not had—but for Yourself—
'Twere better Charity
To leave me in the Atom's Tomb—
Merry, and Nought, and gay, and numb—   10
Than this smart Misery.

378   [1935]

I saw no Way—The Heavens were stitched—
I felt the Columns close—
The Earth reversed her Hemispheres—
I touched the Universe—

And back it slid—and I alone—
A Speck upon a Ball—
Went out upon Circumference—
Beyond the Dip of Bell—

401   [1896]

What Soft—Cherubic Creatures—
These Gentlewomen are—
One would as soon assault a Plush—
Or violate a Star—

Such Dimity Convictions—
A Horror so refined
Of freckled Human Nature—
Of Deity—ashamed—

It's such a common—Glory—
A Fisherman's—Degree—   10
Redemption—Brittle Lady—
Be so—ashamed of Thee—

435   [1890]

Much Madness is divinest Sense—
To a discerning Eye—
Much Sense—the starkest Madness—
'Tis the Majority
In this, as All, prevail—
Assent—and you are sane—
Demur—you're straightway dangerous—
And handled with a Chain—

441   [1890]

This is my letter to the World
That never wrote to Me—
The simple News that Nature told—
With tender Majesty

Her Message is committed
To Hands I cannot see—
For love of Her—Sweet—countrymen—
Judge tenderly—of Me

448   [1929]

This was a Poet—It is That
Distills amazing sense
From ordinary Meanings—
And Attar so immense

From the familiar species
That perished by the Door—
We wonder it was not Ourselves
Arrested it—before—

Of Pictures, the Discloser—
The Poet—it is He—   10
Entitles Us—by Contrast—
To ceaseless Poverty—

Of Portion—so unconscious—
The Robbing—could not harm—
Himself—to Him—a Fortune—
Exterior—to Time—

449   [1890]

I died for Beauty—but was scarce
Adjusted in the Tomb
When One who died for Truth, was lain
In an adjoining Room—

He questioned softly "Why I failed"?
"For Beauty", I replied—
"And I—for Truth—Themself are One—
We Bretheren, are", He said—

And so, as Kinsmen, met a Night—
We talked between the Rooms—   10
Until the Moss had reached our lips—
And covered up—our names—

465   [1896]

I heard a Fly buzz—when I died—
The Stillness in the Room
Was like the Stillness in the Air—
Between the Heaves of Storm—

The Eyes around—had wrung them dry—
And Breaths were gathering firm
For that last Onset—when the King
Be witnessed—in the Room—

I willed my Keepsakes—Signed away
What portion of me be   10
Assignable—and then it was
There interposed a Fly—

With Blue—uncertain stumbling Buzz—
Between the light—and me—
And then the Windows failed—and then
I could not see to see—

474   [1935]

They put Us far apart—
As separate as Sea
And Her unsown Peninsula—
We signified "These see"—

They took away our Eyes—
They thwarted Us with Guns—
"I see Thee" each responded straight
Through Telegraphic Signs—

With Dungeons—They devised—
But through their thickest skill—   10
And their opaquest Adamant—
Our Souls saw—just as well—

They summoned Us to die—
With sweet alacrity
We stood upon our stapled feet—
Condemned—but just—to see—

Permission to recant—
Permission to forget—
We turned our backs upon the Sun
For perjury of that—   20

Not Either—noticed Death—
Of Paradise—aware—
Each other's Face—was all the Disc
Each other's setting—saw—

502   [1891]

At least—to pray—is left—is left—
Oh Jesus—in the Air—
I know not which thy chamber is—
I'm knocking—everywhere—

Thou settest Earthquake in the South—
And Maelstrom, in the Sea—
Say, Jesus Christ of Nazareth—
Hast thou no Arm for Me?

5 I I   [1890]

If you were coming in the Fall,
I'd brush the Summer by
With half a smile, and half a spurn,
As Housewives do, a Fly.

If I could see you in a year,
I'd wind the months in balls—
And put them each in separate Drawers,
For fear the numbers fuse—

If only Centuries, delayed,
I'd count them on my Hand,   10
Subtracting, till my fingers dropped
Into Van Dieman's Land.

If certain, when this life was out—
That your's and mine, should be—
I'd toss it yonder, like a Rind,
And take Eternity—

But, now, uncertain of the length
Of this, that is between,
It goads me, like the Goblin Bee—
That will not state—it's sting.   20

5 2 6   [1891]

To hear an Oriole sing
May be a common thing—
Or only a divine.

It is not of the Bird
Who sings the same, unheard,
As unto Crowd—

The Fashion of the Ear
Attireth that it hear
In Dun, or fair—

So whether it be Rune,   10
Or whether it be none
Is of within.

The "Tune is in the Tree—"
The Skeptic—showeth me—
"No Sir! In Thee!"

536   [1890]

The Heart asks Pleasure—first—
And then—Excuse from Pain—
And then—those little Anodynes
That deaden suffering—

And then—to go to sleep—
And then—if it should be
The will of it's Inquisitor
The privilege to die—

556   [1890]

The Brain, within it's Groove
Runs evenly—and true—
But let a Splinter swerve—
'Twere easier for You—

To put a Current back—
When Floods have slit the Hills—
And scooped a Turnpike for Themselves—
And trodden out the Mills—

5 8 5   [1891]

I like to see it lap the Miles—
And lick the Valleys up—
And stop to feed itself at Tanks—
And then—prodigious step

Around a Pile of Mountains—
And supercilious peer
In Shanties—by the sides of Roads—
And then a Quarry pare

To fit it's Ribs—*
And crawl between   10
Complaining all the while
In horrid—hooting stanza—
Then chase itself down Hill—

And neigh like Boanerges—
Then—punctual as—a Star*
Stop—docile and omnipotent
At it's own stable door—

6 2 0   [1890]

It makes no difference abroad—
The Seasons—fit—the same—
The Mornings blossom into Noons—
And split their Pods of Flame—

Wild flowers—kindle in the Woods—
The Brooks slam—all the Day—
No Black bird bates his Banjo—
For passing Calvary—

* See notes to ll. 9 and 15 on p. 1098.

Auto da Fe—and Judgment—
Are nothing to the Bee—   10
His separation from His Rose—
To Him—sums Misery—

640   [1890]

I cannot live with You—
It would be Life—
And Life is over there—
Behind the Shelf

The Sexton keeps the Key to—
Putting up
Our Life—His Porcelain—
Like a Cup—

Discarded of the Housewife—
Quaint—or Broke—   10
A newer Sevres pleases—
Old Ones crack—

I could not die—with You—
For One must wait
To shut the Other's Gaze down—
You—could not—

And I—Could I stand by
And see You—freeze—
Without my Right of Frost—
Death's privilege?   20

Nor could I rise—with You—
Because Your Face
Would put out Jesus'—
That New Grace

Glow plain—and foreign
On my homesick Eye—
Except that You than He
Shone closer by—

They'd judge Us—How—
For You—served Heaven—You know,   30
Or sought to—
I could not—

Because You saturated Sight—
And I had no more Eyes
For sordid excellence
As Paradise

And were You lost, I would be—
Though My Name
Rang loudest
On the Heavenly fame—   40

And were You—saved—
And I—condemned to be
Where You were not—
That self—were Hell to Me—

So We must meet apart—
You there—I—here—
With just the Door ajar
That Oceans are—and Prayer—
And that White Sustenance—
Despair—   50

650   [1890]

Pain—has an Element of Blank—
It cannot recollect
When it begun—or if there were
A time when it was not—

It has no Future—but itself—
It's Infinite contain
It's Past—enlightened to perceive
New Periods—of Pain.

657   [1929]

I dwell in Possibility—
A fairer House than Prose—
More numerous of Windows—
Superior—for Doors—

Of Chambers as the Cedars—
Impregnable of Eye—
And for an Everlasting Roof
The Gambrels of the Sky—

Of Visiters—the fairest—
For Occupation—This—   10
The spreading wide my narrow Hands
To gather Paradise—

664   [1891]

Of all the Souls that stand create—
I have elected—One—
When Sense from Spirit—files away—
And Subterfuge—is done—
When that which is—and that which was—
Apart—intrinsic—stand—
And this brief Tragedy of Flesh—
Is shifted—like a Sand—
When Figures show their royal Front—
And Mists—are carved away,   10
Behold the Atom—I preferred—
To all the lists of Clay!

675   [1891]

Essential Oils—are wrung—
The Attar from the Rose
Be not expressed by Suns—alone—
It is the gift of Screws—

The General Rose—decay—
But this—in Lady's Drawer
Make Summer—When the Lady lie
In Ceaseless Rosemary—

712   [1890]

Because I could not stop for Death—
He kindly stopped for me—
The Carriage held but just Ourselves—
And Immortality.

We slowly drove—He knew no haste
And I had put away
My labor and my leisure too,
For His Civility—

We passed the School, where Children strove
At Recess—in the Ring—   10
We passed the Fields of Gazing Grain—
We passed the Setting Sun—

Or rather—He passed Us—
The Dews drew quivering and chill—
For only Gossamer, my Gown—
My Tippet—only Tulle—

We paused before a House that seemed
A Swelling of the Ground—

The Roof was scarcely visible—
The Cornice—in the Ground—   20

Since then—'tis Centuries—and yet
Feels shorter than the Day
I first surmised the Horses Heads
Were toward Eternity—

7 2 1   [1929]

Behind Me—dips Eternity—
Before Me—Immortality—
Myself—the Term between—
Death but the Drift of Eastern Gray,
Dissolving into Dawn away,
Before the West begin—

'Tis Kingdoms—afterward—they say—
In perfect—pauseless Monarchy—
Whose Prince—is Son of None—
Himself—His Dateless Dynasty—   10
Himself—Himself diversify—
In Duplicate divine—

'Tis Miracle before Me—then—
'Tis Miracle behind—between—
A Crescent in the Sea—
With Midnight to the North of Her—
And Midnight to the South of Her—
And Maelstrom—in the Sky—

7 4 2   [1945]

Four Trees—upon a solitary Acre—
Without Design

Or Order, or Apparent Action—
Maintain—

The Sun—upon a Morning meets them—
The Wind—
No nearer Neighbor—have they—
But God—

The Acre gives them—Place—
They—Him—Attention of Passer by—   10
Of Shadow, or of Squirrel, haply—
Or Boy—

What Deed is Their's unto the General Nature—
What Plan
They severally—retard—or further—
Unknown—

754   [1929]

My life had stood—a Loaded Gun—
In Corners—till a Day
The Owner passed—identified—
And carried Me away—

And now We roam in Sovreign Woods—
And now We hunt the Doe—
And every time I speak for Him—
The Mountains straight reply—

And do I smile, such cordial light
Upon the Valley glow—   10
It is as a Vesuvian face
Had let it's pleasure through—

And when at Night—Our good Day done—
I guard My Master's Head—

'Tis better than the Eider-Duck's
Deep Pillow—to have shared—

To foe of His—I'm deadly foe—
None stir the second time—
On whom I lay a Yellow Eye—
Or an emphatic Thumb—   20

Though I than He—may longer live
He longer must—than I—
For I have but the power to kill,
Without—the power to die—

764   [1890]

Presentiment—is that long Shadow—on the Lawn—
Indicative that Suns go down—

The Notice to the startled Grass
That Darkness—is about to pass—

813   [1914]

This quiet Dust was Gentlemen and Ladies
And Lads and Girls—
Was laughter and ability and Sighing
And Frocks and Curls.

This Passive Place a Summer's nimble mansion
Where Bloom and Bees
Exist an Oriental Circuit
Then cease, like these—

822   [1945]

This Consciousness that is aware
Of Neighbors and the Sun
Will be the one aware of Death
And that itself alone

Is traversing the interval
Experience between
And most profound experiment
Appointed unto Men—

How adequate unto itself
It's properties shall be   10
Itself unto itself and none
Shall make discovery.

Adventure most unto itself
The Soul condemned to be—
Attended by a single Hound
It's own identity.

829   [1891]

Ample make this Bed—
Make this Bed with Awe—
In it wait till Judgment break
Excellent and Fair.

Be it's Mattress straight—
Be it's Pillow round—
Let no Sunrise' yellow noise
Interrupt this Ground—

861   [1896]

Split the Lark—and you'll find the Music—
Bulb after Bulb, in Silver rolled—
Scantily dealt to the Summer Morning
Saved for your Ear when Lutes be old.

Loose the Flood—you shall find it patent—
Gush after Gush, reserved for you—
Scarlet Experiment! Sceptic Thomas!
Now, do you doubt that your Bird was true?

870   [1945]

Finding is the first Act
The second, loss,
Third, Expedition for
The "Golden Fleece"

Fourth, no Discovery—
Fifth, no Crew—
Finally, no Golden Fleece—
Jason—sham—too.

875   [1896]

I stepped from Plank to Plank
A slow and cautious way
The Stars about my Head I felt
About my Feet the Sea.

I knew not but the next
Would be my final inch—
This gave me that precarious Gait
Some call Experience.

888   [1945]

When I have seen the Sun emerge
From His amazing House—
And leave a Day at every Door
A Deed, in every place—

Without the incident of Fame
Or accident of Noise—
The Earth has seemed to me a Drum,
Pursued of little Boys

946   [1896]

It is an honorable Thought
And makes One lift One's Hat
As One met sudden Gentlefolk
Upon a daily Street

That We've immortal Place
Though Pyramids decay
And Kingdoms, like the Orchard
Flit Russetly away

949   [1945]

Under the Light, yet under,
Under the Grass and the Dirt,

Under the Beetle's Cellar
Under the Clover's Root,

Further than Arm could stretch
Were it Giant long,
Further than Sunshine could
Were the Day Year long,

Over the Light, yet over,
Over the Arc of the Bird—   10
Over the Comet's chimney—
Over the Cubit's Head,

Further than Guess can gallop
Further than Riddle ride—
Oh for a Disc to the Distance
Between Ourselves and the Dead!

9 8 5   [1914]

The Missing All, prevented Me
From missing minor Things.
If nothing larger than a World's
Departure from a Hinge
Or Sun's extinction, be observed
'Twas not so large that I
Could lift my Forehead from my work
For Curiosity.

9 8 6   [1891]

A narrow Fellow in the Grass
Occasionally rides—
You may have met Him—did you not
His notice sudden is—

The Grass divides as with a Comb—
A spotted shaft is seen—
And then it closes at your feet
And opens further on—

He likes a Boggy Acre
A Floor too cool for Corn—   10
Yet when a Boy, and Barefoot—
I more than once at Noon
Have passed, I thought, a Whip lash
Unbraiding in the Sun
When stooping to secure it
It wrinkled, and was gone—

Several of Nature's People
I know, and they know me—
I feel for them a transport
Of cordiality—   20

But never met this Fellow
Attended, or alone
Without a tighter breathing
And Zero at the Bone—

997   [1945]

Crumbling is not an instant's Act
A fundamental pause
Delapidation's processes
Are organized Decays.

'Tis first a Cobweb on the Soul
A Cuticle of Dust
A Borer in the Axis
An Elemental Rust—

Ruin is formal—Devils work
Consecutive and slow—   10

Fail in an instant, no man did
Slipping—is Crashe's law.

1 0 5 2   [1890]

I never saw a Moor—
I never saw the Sea—
Yet know I how the Heather looks
And what a Billow be.

I never spoke with God
Nor visited in Heaven—
Yet certain am I of the spot
As if the Checks were given—

1 0 6 8   [1891]

Further in Summer than the Birds
Pathetic from the Grass
A minor Nation celebrates
It's unobtrusive Mass.

No Ordinance be seen
So gradual the Grace
A pensive Custom it becomes
Enlarging Loneliness.

Antiquest felt at Noon
When August burning low   10
Arise this spectral Canticle
Repose to typify

Remit as yet no Grace
No Furrow on the Glow

Yet a Druidic Difference
Enhances Nature now

1072   [1924]

Title divine—is mine!
The Wife—without the Sign!
Acute Degree—conferred on me—
Empress of Calvary!
Royal—all but the Crown!
Betrothed—without the swoon
God sends us Women—
When you—hold—Garnet to Garnet—
Gold—to Gold—
Born—Bridalled—Shrouded—   10
In a Day—
Tri Victory—*
"My Husband"—women say—
Stroking the Melody—
Is *this*—the way?

1078   [1890]

The Bustle in a House
The Morning after Death
Is solemnest of industries
Enacted upon Earth—

The Sweeping up the Heart
And putting Love away
We shall not want to use again
Until Eternity.

* See note to l. 12 on p. 1099.

1082   [1929]

Revolution is the Pod
Systems rattle from
When the Winds of Will are stirred
Excellent is Bloom

But except it's Russet Base
Every Summer be
The Entomber of itself,
So of Liberty—

Left inactive on the Stalk
All it's Purple fled   10
Revolution shakes it for
Test if it be dead.

1084   [1891]

At Half past Three, a single Bird
Unto a silent Sky
Propounded but a single term
Of cautious melody.

At Half past Four, Experiment
Had subjugated test
And lo, Her silver Principle
Supplanted all the rest.

At Half past Seven, Element
Nor Implement, be seen—   10
And Place was where the Presence was
Circumference between.

1129   [1945]

Tell all the Truth but tell it slant—
Success in Circuit lies
Too bright for our infirm Delight
The Truth's superb surprise
As Lightning to the Children eased
With explanation kind
The Truth must dazzle gradually
Or every man be blind—

1176   [1896]

We never know how high we are
Till we are asked to rise
And then if we are true to plan
Our statures touch the skies—

The Heroism we recite
Would be a normal thing
Did not ourselves the Cubits warp
For fear to be a King—

1207   [1891]

He preached upon "Breadth" till it argued him narrow—
The Broad are too broad to define
And of "Truth" until it proclaimed him a Liar—
The Truth never flaunted a Sign—

Simplicity fled from his counterfeit presence
As Gold the Pyrites would shun—
What confusion would cover the innocent Jesus
To meet so enabled a Man!

1243   [1914]

Safe Despair it is that raves—
Agony is frugal.
Puts itself severe away
For it's own perusal.

Garrisoned no Soul can be
In the Front of Trouble—
Love is one, not aggregate—
Nor is Dying double—

1304   [1896]

Not with a Club, the Heart is broken
Nor with a Stone—
A Whip so small you could not see it
I've known

To lash the Magic Creature
Till it fell,
Yet that Whip's Name
Too noble then to tell.

Magnanimous as Bird
By Boy descried—   10
Singing unto the Stone
Of which it died—

Shame need not crouch
In such an Earth as Our's—
Shame—stand erect—
The Universe is your's.

1333   [1914]

A little Madness in the Spring
Is wholesome even for the King,
But God be with the Clown—
Who ponders this tremendous scene—
This whole Experiment of Green—
As if it were his own!

1393   [1891]

Lay this Laurel on the One
Too intrinsic for Renown—
Laurel—vail your deathless tree—
Him you chasten, that is He!

1463   [1891]

A Route of Evanescence
With a revolving Wheel—
A Resonance of Emerald—
A Rush of Cochineal—
And every Blossom on the Bush
Adjusts it's tumbled Head—
The mail from Tunis, probably,
An easy Morning's Ride—

1540   [1891]

As imperceptibly as Grief
The Summer lapsed away—

Too imperceptible at last
To seem like Perfidy—
A Quietness distilled
As Twilight long begun,
Or Nature spending with herself
Sequestered Afternoon—
The Dusk drew earlier in—
The Morning foreign shone—   10
A courteous, yet harrowing Grace,
As Guest, that would be gone—
And thus, without a Wing
Or service of a Keel
Our Summer made her light escape
Into the Beautiful.

1587   [1890]

He ate and drank the precious Words—
His Spirit grew robust—
He knew no more that he was poor,
Nor that his frame was Dust—

He danced along the dingy Days
And this Bequest of Wings
Was but a Book—What Liberty
A loosened spirit brings—

1612   [1945]

The Auctioneer of Parting
His "Going, going, gone"
Shouts even from the Crucifix,
And brings his Hammer down—
He only sells the Wilderness,
The prices of Despair

Range from a single human Heart
To Two—not any more—

1624   [1890]

Apparently with no surprise
To any happy Flower
The Frost beheads it at it's play—
In accidental power—
The blonde Assassin passes on—
The Sun proceeds unmoved
To measure off another Day
For an Approving God.

1670   [1914]

In Winter in my Room
I came upon a Worm
Pink lank and warm
But as he was a worm
And worms presume
Not quite with him at home
Secured him by a string
To something neighboring
And went along.

A Trifle afterward
A thing occurred
I'd not believe it if I heard
But state with creeping blood
A snake with mottles rare
Surveyed my chamber floor
In feature as the worm before

10

But ringed with power
The very string with which
I tied him—too
When he was mean and new   20
That string was there—

I shrank—"How fair you are"!
Propitiation's claw—
"Afraid he hissed
Of me"?
"No cordiality"—
He fathomed me—
Then to a Rhythm *Slim*
Secreted in his Form
As Patterns swim   30
Projected him.

That time I flew
Both eyes his way
Lest he pursue
Nor ever ceased to run
Till in a distant Town
Towns on from mine
I set me down
This was a dream—

1672   [1914]

Lightly stepped a yellow star
To it's lofty place
Loosed the Moon her silver hat
From her lustral Face
All of Evening softly lit
As an Astral Hall
Father I observed to Heaven
You are punctual—

1695   [1914]

There is a solitude of space
A solitude of sea
A solitude of death, but these
Society shall be
Compared with that profounder site
That polar privacy
A soul admitted to itself—
Finite Infinity.

1712   [1945]

A Pit—but Heaven over it—
And Heaven beside, and Heaven abroad;
And yet a Pit—
With Heaven over it.

To stir would be to slip—
To look would be to drop—
To dream—to sap the Prop
That holds my chances up.
Ah! Pit! With Heaven over it!

The depth is all my thought—   10
I dare not ask my feet—
'Twould start us where we sit
So straight you'd scarce suspect
It was a Pit—with fathoms under it
Its Circuit just the same
Seed—summer—tomb—
Whose Doom to whom

1732 [1896]

My life closed twice before its close;
It yet remains to see
If Immortality unveil
A third event to me,

So huge, so hopeless to conceive
As these that twice befel.
Parting is all we know of heaven,
And all we need of hell.

Sidney Lanier

1842–1881

Born February 3, 1842, at Macon, Georgia, Sidney Lanier graduated from Oglethorpe University in 1860. A year later, he joined the Confederate Army, participated in the Seven Days' Battle, and spent the winter of 1864-1865 as a prisoner of war. On the verge of tuberculosis much of his life, he was successively a teacher, law clerk, flautist in the Peabody Orchestra, Baltimore, and a lecturer in English at Johns Hopkins University. All this time he was writing poetry. In August, 1881, he went to the mountains at Lynn, North Carolina, and died there September 7.

THAR'S MORE IN THE MAN THAN THAR IS IN THE LAND   [1877]

I knowed a man, which he lived in Jones,
Which Jones is a county of red hills and stones,
And he lived pretty much by gittin' of loans,
And his mules was nuthin' but skin and bones,
And his hogs was flat as his corn-bread pones,
And he had 'bout a thousand acres o' land.

This man—which his name it was also Jones—
He swore that he'd leave them old red hills and stones,
Fur he couldn't make nuthin' but yallerish cotton,
And little o' *that*, and his fences was rotten,
And what little corn he had, *hit* was boughten,
And dinged ef a livin' was in the land.

10

And the longer he swore the madder he got,
And he riz and he walked to the stable lot,
And he hollered to Tom to come thar and hitch,
Fur to emigrate somewhar whar land was rich,
And to quit rasin' cock-burrs, thistles and sich,
And a wastin' ther time on the cussed land.

So him and Tom they hitched up the mules,
Pertestin' that folks was mighty big fools   20
That 'ud stay in Georgy ther lifetime out,
Jest scratchin' a livin' when all of 'em mought
Git places in Texas whar cotton would sprout
By the time you could plant it in the land.

And he driv by a house whar a man named Brown
Was a livin', not fur from the edge o' town,
And he bantered Brown fur to buy his place,
And said that bein' as money was skace,
And bein' as sheriffs was hard to face,
Two dollars an acre would git the land.   30

They closed at a dollar and fifty cents,
And Jones he bought him a waggin and tents,
And loaded his corn, and his wimmin, and truck,
And moved to Texas, which it tuck
His entire pile, with the best of luck,
To git thar and git him a little land.

But Brown moved out on the old Jones farm,
And he rolled up his breeches and bared his arm,
And he picked all the rocks from off'n the groun',
And he rooted it up and he plowed it down,   40
Then he sowed his corn and his wheat in the land.

Five years glid by, and Brown, one day
(Which he'd got so fat that he wouldn't weigh),
Was a settin' down, sorter lazily,
To the bulliest dinner you ever see,
When one o' the children jumped on his knee
And says, "Yan's Jones, which you bought his land."

And thar was Jones, standin' out at the fence,
And he hadn't no waggin, nor mules, nor tents,
Fur he had left Texas afoot and cum   50
To Georgy to see if he couldn't git sum
Employment, and he was a lookin' as hum-
Ble as ef he had never owned any land.

But Brown he axed him in, and he sot
Him down to his vittles smokin' hot,
And when he had filled hisself and the floor
Brown looked at him sharp and riz and swore
That, "whether men's land was rich or poor
Thar was more in the *man* than thar was in the *land*."

CORN   [1877]

To-day the woods are trembling through and through
With shimmering forms, that flash before my view,
Then melt in green as dawn-stars melt in blue.
    The leaves that wave against my cheek caress
        Like women's hands; the embracing boughs express
            A subtlety of mighty tenderness;
The copse-depths into little noises start,
That sound anon like beatings of a heart,
Anon like talk 'twixt lips not far apart.
    The beech dreams balm, as a dreamer hums a song;   10
        Through that vague wafture, expirations strong
        Throb from young hickories breathing deep and long
With stress and urgence bold of prisoned spring
                And ecstasy of burgeoning.
    Now, since the dew-plashed road of morn is dry,
        Forth venture odors of more quality
        And heavenlier giving. Like Jove's locks awry,
                Long muscadines
Rich-wreathe the spacious foreheads of great pines,
And breathe ambrosial passion from their vines.   20
    I pray with mosses, ferns and flowers shy
        That hide like gentle nuns from human eye

To lift adoring perfumes to the sky.
I hear faint bridal-sighs of brown and green
Dying to silent hints of kisses keen
As far lights fringe into a pleasant sheen.
　I start at fragmentary whispers, blown
　From undertalks of leafy souls unknown,
　Vague purports sweet, of inarticulate tone.

Dreaming of gods, men, nuns and brides, between　　　30
Old companies of oaks that inward lean
To join their radiant amplitudes of green
　I slowly move, with ranging looks that pass
　Up from the matted miracles of grass
Into yon veined complex of space
Where sky and leafage interlace
　So close, the heaven of blue is seen
　Inwoven with a heaven of green.

I wander to the zigzag-cornered fence
Where sassafras, intrenched in brambles dense,　　　40
Contests with stolid vehemence
　The march of culture, setting limb and thorn
　As pikes against the army of the corn.

There, while I pause, my fieldward-faring eyes
Take harvests, where the stately corn-ranks rise,
　　　　　Of inward dignities
And large benignities and insights wise,
　　　　　Graces and modest majesties.
Thus, without theft, I reap another's field;
Thus, without tilth, I house a wondrous yield,　　　50
And heap my heart with quintuple crops concealed.

Look, out of line one tall corn-captain stands
Advanced beyond the foremost of his bands,
　And waves his blades upon the very edge
　And hottest thicket of the battling hedge.
Thou lustrous stalk, that ne'er mayst walk nor talk,
　Still shalt thou type the poet-soul sublime
　That leads the vanward of his timid time
　And sings up cowards with commanding rhyme—

Soul calm, like thee, yet fain, like thee, to grow   60
By double increment, above, below;
   Soul homely, as thou art, yet rich in grace like thee,
   Teaching the yeomen selfless chivalry
   That moves in gentle curves of courtesy;
Soul filled like thy long veins with sweetness tense,
        By every godlike sense
Transmuted from the four wild elements.
        Drawn to high plans,
   Thou lift'st more stature than a mortal man's,
Yet ever piercest downward in the mould   70
        And keepest hold
   Upon the reverend and steadfast earth
        That gave thee birth;
   Yea, standest smiling in thy future grave,
        Serene and brave,
   With unremitting breath
   Inhaling life from death,
Thine epitaph writ fair in fruitage eloquent,
        Thyself thy monument.

    As poets should,   80
Thou hast built up thy hardihood
With universal food,
   Drawn in select proportion fair
   From honest mould and vagabond air;
From darkness of the dreadful night,
        And joyful light;
   From antique ashes, whose departed flame
   In thee has finer life and longer fame;
From wounds and balms,
From storms and calms,   90
From potsherds and dry bones
     And ruin-stones.

Into thy vigorous substance thou hast wrought
Whate'er the hand of Circumstance hath brought;
   Yea, into cool solacing green hast spun
   White radiance hot from out the sun.
So thou dost mutually leaven

Strength of earth with grace of heaven;
   So thou dost marry new and old
   Into a one of higher mould;   100
   So thou dost reconcile the hot and cold,
     The dark and bright,
And many a heart-perplexing opposite,
          And so,
   Akin by blood to high and low,
Fitly thou playest out thy poet's part,
Richly expending thy much-bruisèd heart
   In equal care to nourish lord in hall
     Or beast in stall:
   Thou took'st from all that thou might'st give to all.   110

O steadfast dweller on the selfsame spot
Where thou wast born, that still repinest not—
Type of the home-fond heart, the happy lot!—
   Deeply thy mild content rebukes the land
   Whose flimsy homes, built on the shifting sand
Of trade, for ever rise and fall
With alternation whimsical,
   Enduring scarce a day,
   Then swept away
By swift engulfments of incalculable tides   120
Whereon capricious Commerce rides.

Look, thou substantial spirit of content!
Across this little vale, thy continent,
   To where, beyond the mouldering mill,
   Yon old deserted Georgian hill
Bares to the sun his piteous aged crest
     And seamy breast,
   By restless-hearted children left to lie
   Untended there beneath the heedless sky,
   As barbarous folk expose their old to die.   130

Upon that generous-rounding side,
     With gullies scarified
   Where keen Neglect his lash hath plied,
Dwelt one I knew of old, who played at toil,

And gave to coquette Cotton soul and soil.
  Scorning the slow reward of patient grain,
  He sowed his heart with hopes of swifter gain,
  Then sat him down and waited for the rain.
He sailed in borrowed ships of usury—
A foolish Jason on a treacherous sea,   140
Seeking the Fleece and finding misery.
  Lulled by smooth-rippling loans, in idle trance
  He lay, content that unthrift Circumstance
  Should plough for him the stony field of Chance.
Yea, gathering crops whose worth no man might tell,
He staked his life on games of Buy-and-Sell,
And turned each field into a gambler's hell.
  Aye, as each year began,
  My farmer to the neighboring city ran;
Passed with a mournful anxious face   150
Into the banker's inner place;
Parleyed, excused, pleaded for longer grace;
  Railed at the drought, the worm, the rust, the grass;
  Protested ne'er again 'twould come to pass;
  With many an *oh* and *if* and *but alas*
Parried or swallowed searching questions rude,
And kissed the dust to soften Dives's mood.
At last, small loans by pledges great renewed,
  He issues smiling from the fatal door,
  And buys with lavish hand his yearly store   160
  Till his small borrowings will yield no more.
Aye, as each year declined,
With bitter heart and ever-brooding mind
He mourned his fate unkind.
  In dust, in rain, with might and main,
  He nursed his cotton, cursed his grain,
  Fretted for news that made him fret again,
Snatched at each telegram of Future Sale,
And thrilled with Bulls' or Bears' alternate wail—
In hope or fear alike for ever pale.   170
  And thus from year to year, through hope and fear,
  With many a curse and many a secret tear,
  Striving in vain his cloud of debt to clear,
          At last

He woke to find his foolish dreaming past,
   And all his best-of-life the easy prey
    Of squandering scamps and quacks that lined his way
           With vile array,
From rascal statesman down to petty knave;
Himself, at best, for all his bragging brave,   180
A gamester's catspaw and a banker's slave.
   Then, worn and gray, and sick with deep unrest,
  He fled away into the oblivious West,
          Unmourned, unblest.

Old hill! old hill! thou gashed and hairy Lear
Whom the divine Cordelia of the year,
E'en pitying Spring, will vainly strive to cheer—
   King, that no subject man nor beast may own,
   Discrowned, undaughtered and alone—
Yet shall the great God turn thy fate,   190
And bring thee back into thy monarch state
         And majesty immaculate.
Lo, through hot waverings of the August morn,
   Thou givest from thy vasty sides forlorn
   Visions of golden treasuries of corn—
Ripe largesse lingering for some bolder heart
That manfully shall take thy part,
         And tend thee,
         And defend thee,
With antique sinew and with modern art.   200

THE SYMPHONY   [1877]

"O Trade! O Trade! would thou wert dead!
The Time needs heart—'tis tired of head:
We're all for love," the violins said.
"Of what avail the rigorous tale
Of bill for coin and box for bale?
Grant thee, O Trade! thine uttermost hope:
Level red gold with blue sky-slope,

And base it deep as devils grope:
When all's done, what hast thou won
Of the only sweet that's under the sun?   10
Ay, canst thou buy a single sigh
Of true love's least, least ecstasy?"
Then, with a bridegroom's heart-beats trembling,
All the mightier strings assembling
Ranged them on the violins' side
As when the bridegroom leads the bride,
And, heart in voice, together cried:
"Yea, what avail the endless tale
Of gain by cunning and plus by sale?
Look up the land, look down the land—   20
The poor, the poor, the poor, they stand
Wedged by the pressing of Trade's hand
Against an inward-opening door
That pressure tightens evermore:
They sigh a monstrous foul-air sigh
For the outside leagues of liberty,
Where Art, sweet lark, translates the sky
Into a heavenly melody.
'Each day, all day' (these poor folks say),
'In the same old year-long, drear-long way,   30
We weave in the mills and heave in the kilns,
We sieve mine-meshes under the hills,
And thieve much gold from the Devil's bank tills,
To relieve, O God, what manner of ills?—
The beasts, they hunger, and eat, and die;
And so do we, and the world's a sty;
Hush, fellow-swine: why nuzzle and cry?
Swinehood hath no remedy
Say many men, and hasten by,
Clamping the nose and blinking the eye.   40
But who said once, in the lordly tone,
Man shall not live by bread alone
But all that cometh from the Throne?
  Hath God said so?
  But Trade saith *No:*
And the kilns and the curt-tongued mills say *Go:*
There's plenty that can, if you can't: we know.

Move out, if you think you're underpaid.
The poor are prolific; we're not afraid;
　Trade is trade.'"　　　　　　　　　　　　　　　50
Thereat this passionate protesting
　Meekly changed, and softened till
It sank to sad requesting
　And suggesting sadder still:
"And oh, if men might some time see
How piteous-false the poor decree
That trade no more than trade must be!
Does business mean, *Die, you—live, I?*
Then 'Trade is trade' but sings a lie:
'Tis only war grown miserly.　　　　　　　　60
If business is battle, name it so:
War-crimes less will shame it so,
And widows less will blame it so.
Alas: for the poor to have some part
In yon sweet living lands of Art,
Makes problem not for head, but heart.
Vainly might Plato's brain revolve it:
Plainly the heart of a child could solve it."

And then, as when from words that seem but rude
We pass to silent pain that sits abrood　　　　70
Back in our heart's great dark and solitude,
So sank the strings to gentle throbbing
Of long chords change-marked with sobbing—
Motherly sobbing, not distinctlier heard
Than half wing-openings of the sleeping bird,
Some dream of danger to her young hath stirred.

Then stirring and demurring ceased, and lo!
Every least ripple of the string's song-flow
Died to a level with each level bow
And made a great chord tranquil-surfaced so,　　80
As a brook beneath his curving bank doth go
To linger in the sacred dark and green
Where many boughs the still pool overlean
And many leaves make shadow with their sheen.
　But presently

A velvet flute-note fell down pleasantly
Upon the bosom of that harmony,
And sailed and sailed incessantly,
As if a petal from a wild-rose blown
Had fluttered down upon that pool of tone   90
And boatwise dropped o' the convex side
And floated down the glassy tide
And clarified and glorified
The solemn spaces where the shadows bide.
From the warm concave of that fluted note
Somewhat, half song, half odor, forth did float,
As if a rose might somehow be a throat:
"When Nature from her far-off glen
Flutes her soft messages to men,
The flute can say them o'er again;   100
Yea, Nature, singing sweet and lone,
Breathes through life's strident polyphone
The flute-voice in the world of tone.
    Sweet friends,
    Man's love ascends
To finer and diviner ends
Than man's mere thought e'er comprehends.
    For I, e'en I,
    As here I lie,
A petal on a harmony,   110
Demand of Science whence and why
Man's tender pain, man's inward cry,
When he doth gaze on earth and sky?
I am not overbold:
    I hold
Full powers from Nature manifold.
I speak for each no-tonguèd tree
That, spring by spring, doth nobler be,
And dumbly and most wistfully
His mighty prayerful arms outspreads   120
Above men's oft-unheeding heads,
And his big blessing downward sheds.
I speak for all-shaped blooms and leaves,
Lichens on stones and moss on eaves,
Grasses and grains in ranks and sheaves;

Broad-fronded ferns and keen-leaved canes,
And briery mazes bounding lanes,
And marsh-plants, thirsty-cupped for rains,
And milky stems and sugary veins;
For every long-armed woman-vine   130
That round a piteous tree doth twine;
For passionate odors, and divine
Pistils, and petals crystalline;
All purities of shady springs,
All shynesses of film-winged things
That fly from tree-trunks and bark-rings;
All modesties of mountain-fawns
That leap to covert from wild lawns,
And tremble if the day but dawns;
All sparklings of small beady eyes   140
Of birds, and sidelong glances wise
Wherewith the jay hints tragedies;
All piquancies of prickly burs,
And smoothnesses of downs and furs
Of eiders and of minevers;
All limpid honeys that do lie
At stamen-bases, nor deny
The humming-birds' fine roguery,
Bee-thighs, nor any butterfly;
All gracious curves of slender wings,   150
Bark-mottlings, fibre-spiralings,
Fern-wavings and leaf-flickerings;
Each dial-marked leaf and flower-bell
Wherewith in every lonesome dell
Time to himself his hours doth tell;
All tree-sounds, rustlings of pine-cones,
Wind-sighings, doves' melodious moans,
And night's unearthly under-tones;
All placid lakes and waveless deeps,
All cool reposing mountain-steeps,   160
Vale-calms and tranquil lotos-sleeps;—
Yea, all fair forms, and sounds, and lights,
And warmths, and mysteries, and mights,
Of Nature's utmost depths and heights,
—These doth my timid tongue present,

Their mouthpiece and leal instrument
And servant, all love-eloquent.
I heard, when '*All for love*' the violins cried:
So, Nature calls through all her system wide,
Give me thy love, O man, so long denied.   170
Much time is run, and man hath changed his ways,
Since Nature, in the antique fable-days,
Was hid from man's true love by proxy fays,
False fauns and rascal gods that stole her praise.
The nymphs, cold creatures of man's colder brain,
Chilled Nature's streams till man's warm heart was fain
Never to lave its love in them again.
Later, a sweet Voice *Love thy neighbor* said;
Then first the bounds of neighborhood outspread
Beyond all confines of old ethnic dread.   180
Vainly the Jew might wag his covenant head:
'*All men are neighbors,*' so the sweet Voice said.
So, when man's arms had circled all man's race,
The liberal compass of his warm embrace
Stretched bigger yet in the dark bounds of space;
With hands a-grope he felt smooth Nature's grace,
Drew her to breast and kissed her sweetheart face:
Yea man found neighbors in great hills and trees
And streams and clouds and suns and birds and bees,
And throbbed with neighbor-loves in loving these.   190
But oh, the poor! the poor! the poor!
That stand by the inward-opening door
Trade's hand doth tighten ever more,
And sigh their monstrous foul-air sigh
For the outside hills of liberty,
Where Nature spreads her wild blue sky
For Art to make into melody!
Thou Trade! thou king of the modern days!
     Change thy ways,
     Change thy ways;   200
Let the sweaty laborers file
     A little while,
     A little while,
Where Art and Nature sing and smile.
Trade! is thy heart all dead, all dead?

And hast thou nothing but a head?
I'm all for heart," the flute-voice said,
And into sudden silence fled,
Like as a blush that while 'tis red
Dies to a still, still white instead.   210

  Thereto a thrilling calm succeeds,
Till presently the silence breeds
A little breeze among the reeds
That seems to blow by sea-marsh weeds:
Then from the gentle stir and fret
Sings out the melting clarionet,
Like as a lady sings while yet
Her eyes with salty tears are wet.
"O Trade! O Trade!" the Lady said,
"I too will wish thee utterly dead   220
If all thy heart is in thy head.
For O my God! and O my God!
What shameful ways have women trod
At beckoning of Trade's golden rod!
Alas when sighs are traders' lies,
And heart's-ease eyes and violet eyes
  Are merchandise!
O purchased lips that kiss with pain!
O cheeks coin-spotted with smirch and stain!
O trafficked hearts that break in twain!   230
—And yet what wonder at my sisters' crime?
So hath Trade withered up Love's sinewy prime,
Men love not women as in olden time.
Ah, not in these cold merchantable days
Deem men their life an opal gray, where plays
The one red Sweet of gracious ladies'-praise.
Now, comes a suitor with sharp prying eye—
Says, *Here, you Lady, if you'll sell, I'll buy:*
Come, heart for heart—a trade? What! weeping? why?
Shame on such wooers' dapper mercery!   240
I would my lover kneeling at my feet
In humble manliness should cry, *O sweet!*
I know not if thy heart my heart will greet:
I ask not if thy love my love can meet:

Whate'er thy worshipful soft tongue shall say,
I'll kiss thine answer, be it yea or nay:
I do but know I love thee, and I pray
To be thy knight until my dying day.
Woe him that cunning trades in hearts contrives!
Base love good women to base loving drives.   250
If men loved larger, larger were our lives;
And wooed they nobler, won they nobler wives."

There thrust the bold straightforward horn
To battle for that lady lorn,
With heartsome voice of mellow scorn,
Like any knight in knighthood's morn.
    "Now comfort thee," said he,
        "Fair Lady.
For God shall right thy grievous wrong.
And man shall sing thee a true-love song,   260
Voiced in act his whole life long,
    Yea, all thy sweet life long,
        Fair Lady.
Where's he that craftily hath said,
The day of chivalry is dead?
I'll prove that lie upon his head,
    Or I will die instead,
        Fair Lady.
Is Honor gone into his grave?
Hath Faith become a caitiff knave,   270
And Selfhood turned into a slave
    To work in Mammon's Cave,
        Fair Lady?
Will Truth's long blade ne'er gleam again?
Hath Giant Trade in dungeons slain
All great contempts of mean-got gain
    And hates of inward stain,
        Fair Lady?
For aye shall name and fame be sold,
And place be hugged for the sake of gold,   280
And smirch-robed Justice feebly scold
    At Crime all money-bold,
        Fair Lady?

Shall self-wrapt husbands aye forget
Kiss-pardons for the daily fret
Wherewith sweet wifely eyes are wet—
 Blind to lips kiss-wise set—
  Fair Lady?
Shall lovers higgle, heart for heart,
Till wooing grows a trading mart   290
Where much for little, and all for part,
 Make love a cheapening art,
  Fair Lady?
Shall woman scorch for a single sin
That her betrayer can revel in,
And she be burnt, and he but grin
 When that the flames begin,
  Fair Lady?
Shall ne'er prevail the woman's plea,
We maids would far, far whiter be   300
If that our eyes might sometimes see
 Men maids in purity,
  Fair Lady?
Shall Trade aye salve his conscience-aches
With jibes at Chivalry's old mistakes—
The wars that o'erhot knighthood makes
 For Christ's and ladies' sakes,
  Fair Lady?
Now by each knight that e'er hath prayed
To fight like a man and love like a maid,   310
Since Pembroke's life, as Pembroke's blade,
 I' the scabbard, death, was laid,
  Fair Lady,
I dare avouch my faith is bright
That God doth right and God hath might,
Nor time hath changed His hair to white,
 Nor His dear love to spite,
  Fair Lady.
I doubt no doubts: I strive, and shrive my clay,
And fight my fight in the patient modern way 320
For true love and for thee—ah me! and pray
 To be thy knight until my dying day,
  Fair Lady."

Made end that knightly horn, and spurred away
Into the thick of the melodious fray.

And then the hautboy played and smiled,
And sang like any large-eyed child,
Cool-hearted and all undefiled.
  "Huge Trade!" he said,
"Would thou wouldst lift me on thy head,   330
And run where'er my finger led!
Once said a Man—and wise was He—
Never shalt thou the heavens see,
Save as a little child thou be."
Then o'er sea-lashings of commingling tunes
The ancient wise bassoons,
    Like weird
    Gray-beard
Old harpers sitting on the high-sea-dunes,
    Chanted runes: 340
"Bright-waved gain, gray waved loss,
The sea of all doth lash and toss,
One wave forward and one across:
But now 'twas trough, now 'tis crest,
And worst doth foam and flash to best,
    And curst to blest.

"Life! Life! thou sea-fugue, writ from east to west,
    Love, Love alone can pore
    On thy dissolving score
    Of harsh half-phrasings,   350
        Blotted ere writ,
    And double erasings
        Of chords most fit.
Yea, Love, sole music-master blest,
May read thy weltering palimpsest.
To follow Time's dying melodies through,
And never to lose the old in the new,
And ever to solve the discords true—
    Love alone can do.
And ever Love hears the poor-folks' crying,   360
And ever Love hears the women's sighing,

And ever sweet knighthood's death-defying,
And ever wise childhood's deep implying,
But never a trader's glozing and lying.

"And yet shall Love himself be heard,
Though long deferred, though long deferred:
O'er the modern waste a dove hath whirred:
Music is Love in search of a word."

THE WAVING OF THE CORN   [1884]

  Ploughman, whose gnarly hand yet kindly wheeled
Thy plough to ring this solitary tree
  With clover, whose round plat, reserved a-field,
In cool green radius twice my length may be—
  Scanting the corn thy furrows else might yield,
To pleasure August, bees, fair thoughts, and me,
    That here come oft together—daily I,
    Stretched prone in summer's mortal ecstasy,
Do stir with thanks to thee, as stirs this morn
      With waving of the corn.   10

  Unseen, the farmer's boy from round the hill
Whistles a snatch that seeks his soul unsought,
  And fills some time with tune, howbeit shrill;
The cricket tells straight on his simple thought—
  Nay, 'tis the cricket's way of being still;
The peddler bee drones in, and gossips naught;
    Far down the wood, a one-desiring dove
    Times me the beating of the heart of love:
And these be all the sounds that mix, each morn,
      With waving of the corn.   20

  From here to where the louder passions dwell,
Green leagues of hilly separation roll:
  Trade ends where yon far clover ridges swell.
Ye terrible Towns, ne'er claim the trembling soul

That, craftless all to buy or hoard or sell,
From out your deadly complex quarrel stole
    To company with large amiable trees,
        Suck honey summer with unjealous bees,
And take Time's strokes as softly as this morn
            Takes waving of the corn.   30

EVENING SONG   [1884]

Look off, dear Love, across the sallow sands,
    And mark yon meeting of the sun and sea;
How long they kiss, in sight of all the lands!
            Ah, longer, longer, we.

Now in the sea's red vintage melts the sun,
    As Egypt's pearl dissolved in rosy wine,
And Cleopatra Night drinks all. 'Tis done!
            Love, lay thine hand in mine.

Come forth, sweet stars, and comfort Heaven's heart:
    Glimmer, ye waves, round else unlighted sands;   10
O Night, divorce our sun and sky apart—
            Never our lips, our hands.

SONG OF THE CHATTAHOOCHEE   [1884]

    Out of the hills of Habersham,
        Down the valleys of Hall,
I hurry amain to reach the plain,
Run the rapid and leap the fall,
Split at the rock and together again,
Accept my bed, or narrow or wide,
And flee from folly on every side
With a lover's pain to attain the plain

Far from the hills of Habersham,
Far from the valleys of Hall.   10

All down the hills of Habersham,
   All through the valleys of Hall,
The rushes cried *Abide, abide*,
The willful waterweeds held me thrall,
The laving laurel turned my tide,
The ferns and the fondling grass said *Stay*,
The dewberry dipped for to work delay,
And the little reeds sighed *Abide, abide*,
   Here in the hills of Habersham,
   Here in the valleys of Hall.   20

High o'er the hills of Habersham,
   Veiling the valleys of Hall,
The hickory told me manifold
Fair tales of shade, the poplar tall
Wrought me her shadowy self to hold,
The chestnut, the oak, the walnut, the pine,
Overleaning, with flickering meaning and sign,
Said, *Pass not, so cold, these manifold*
   Deep shades of the hills of Habersham,
   These glades in the valleys of Hall.   30

And oft in the hills of Habersham,
   And oft in the valleys of Hall,
The white quartz shone, and the smooth brook-stone
Did bar me of passage with friendly brawl,
And many a luminous jewel lone
—Crystals clear or a-cloud with mist,
Ruby, garnet and amethyst—
Made lures with the lights of streaming stone
   In the clefts of the hills of Habersham,
   In the beds of the valleys of Hall.   40

But oh, not the hills of Habersham,
   And oh, not the valleys of Hall
Avail: I am fain for to water the plain.
Downward the voices of Duty call—

Downward, to toil and be mixed with the main,
The dry fields burn, and the mills are to turn,
And a myriad flowers mortally yearn,
And the lordly main from beyond the plain
　　Call o'er the hills of Habersham,
　　Calls through the valleys of Hall.   50

THE HARLEQUIN OF DREAMS   [1884]

Swift through some trap mine eyes have never found,
　　Dim-panelled in the painted scene of sleep,
　　Thou, giant Harlequin of Dreams, dost leap
Upon my spirit's stage. Then sight and sound,
Then space and time, then language, mete and bound,
　　And all familiar forms that firmly keep
　　Man's reason in the road, change faces, peep
Betwixt the legs, and mock the daily round.
Yet thou canst more than mock: sometimes my tears
　　At midnight break through bounden lids—a sign   10
　　　　Thou hast a heart; and oft thy little leaven
Of dream-taught wisdom works me bettered years.
　　In one night witch, saint, trickster, fool divine,
　　I think thou'rt Jester at the Court of Heaven!

THE REVENGE OF HAMISH   [1884]

It was three slim does and a ten-tined buck in the bracken lay;
　　And all of a sudden the sinister smell of a man,
　　Awaft on a wind-shaft, wavered and ran
Down the hill-side and sifted along through the bracken and
　　　　passed that way.

Then Nan got a-tremble at nostril; she was the daintiest
　　doe;

In the print of her velvet flank on the velvet fern
  She reared, and rounded her ears in turn.
Then the buck leapt up, and his head as a king's to a
    crown did go

Full high in the breeze, and he stood as if Death had the form
    of a deer;
  And the two slim does full lazily stretching arose,   10
  For their day-dream slowlier came to a close,
Till they woke and were still, breath-bound with waiting
    and wonder and fear.

Then Alan the huntsman sprang over the hillock, the hounds
    shot by,
  The does and the ten-tined buck made a marvellous
    bound,
  The hounds swept after with never a sound,
But Alan loud winded his horn, in sign that the quarry was
    nigh.

For at dawn of that day proud Maclean of Lochbuy to the
    hunt had waxed wild,
  And he cursed at old Alan till Alan fared off with the
    hounds
  For to drive him the deer to the lower glen-grounds:
"I will kill a red deer," quoth Maclean, "in the sight of the
    wife and the child."   20

So gayly he paced with the wife and the child to his chosen
    stand;
  But he hurried tall Hamish the henchman ahead: "Go
    turn,"—
  Cried Maclean—"if the deer seek to cross to the burn,
Do thou turn them to me: nor fail, lest thy back be red as
    thy hand."

Now hard-fortuned Hamish, half blown of his breath with
    the height of the hill,
  Was white in the face when the ten-tined buck and the does
  Drew leaping to burn-ward; huskily rose

His shouts, and his nether lip twitched, and his legs were
    o'erweak for his will.

So the deer darted lightly by Hamish and bounded away to
    the burn.
    But Maclean never bating his watch tarried waiting below   30
    Still Hamish hung heavy with fear for to go
All the space of an hour; then he went, and his face was
    greenish and stern,

And his eye sat back in the socket, and shrunken the
    eyeballs shone,
    As withdrawn from a vision of deeds it were shame to see.
    "Now, now, grim henchman, what is't with thee?"
Brake Maclean, and his wrath rose red as a beacon the wind
    hath upblown.

"Three does and a ten-tined buck made out," spoke
    Hamish, full mild,
    "And I ran for to turn, but my breath it was blown, and
    they passed;
    I was weak, for ye called ere I broke me my fast."
Cried Maclean: "Now a ten-tined buck in the sight of the
    wife and the child
                                        40

I had killed if the gluttonous kern had not wrought me a
    snail's own wrong!"
    Then he sounded, and down came kinsmen and clansmen
    all:
    "Ten blows, for ten tine, on his back let fall,
And reckon no stroke if the blood follow not at the bite of
    thong!"

So Hamish made bare, and took him his strokes; at the
    last he smiled.
    "Now I'll to the burn," quoth Maclean, "for it still may
    be,
    If a slimmer-paunched henchman will hurry with me,
I shall kill me the ten-tined buck for a gift to the wife and
    the child!"

Then the clansmen departed, by this path and that; and over
    the hill
    Sped Maclean with an outward wrath for an inward shame; 50
    And that place of the lashing full quiet became;
And the wife and the child stood sad; and bloody-backed
    Hamish sat still.

But look! red Hamish has risen; quick about and about turns
    he.
    "There is none betwixt me and the crag-top!" he screams
      under breath.
    Then, livid as Lazarus lately from death,
He snatches the child from the mother, and clambers the
    crag toward the sea.

Now the mother drops breath; she is dumb, and her heart
    goes dead for a space,
    Till the motherhood, mistress of death, shrieks, shrieks
      through the glen,
    And that place of the lashing is live with men,
And Maclean, and the gillie that told him, dash up in a
    desperate race.   60

Not a breath's time for asking; an eye-glance reveals all the
    tale untold.
    They follow mad Hamish afar up the crag toward the sea,
    And the lady cries: "Clansmen, run for a fee!—
Yon castle and lands to the two first hands that shall hook
    him and hold

Fast Hamish back from the brink!"—and ever she flies up
    the steep,
    And the clansmen pant, and they sweat, and they jostle
      and strain.
    But, mother, 'tis vain; but, father, 'tis vain;
Stern Hamish stands bold on the brink, and dangles the
    child o'er the deep.

Now a faintness falls on the men that run, and they all
    stand still.

And the wife prays Hamish as if he were God, on her
    knees,   70
  Crying: "Hamish! O Hamish! but please, but please
For to spare him!" and Hamish still dangles the child,
    with a wavering will.

On a sudden he turns; with a sea-hawk scream, and a
    gibe, and a song,
  Cries: "So; I will spare ye the child if, in sight of ye all,
Ten blows on Maclean's bare back shall fall,
And ye reckon no stroke if the blood follow not at the
    bite of the thong!"

Then Maclean he set hardly his tooth to his lip that his
    tooth was red,
  Breathed short for a space, said: "Nay, but it never
    shall be!
  Let me hurl off the damnable hound in the sea!"
But the wife: "Can Hamish go fish us the child from the
    sea, if dead?   80

Say yea!—Let them lash *me*, Hamish?"—"Nay!"—
    "Husband, the lashing will heal;
  But, oh, who will heal me the bonny sweet bairn in his
    grave?
  Could ye cure me my heart with the death of a knave?
Quick! Love! I will bare thee—so—kneel!" Then Maclean
    'gan slowly to kneel

With never a word, till presently downward he jerked to
    the earth.
  Then the henchman—he that smote Hamish—would
    tremble and lag;
  "Strike, hard!" quoth Hamish, full stern, from the
    crag;
Then he struck him, and "One!" sang Hamish, and
    danced with the child in his mirth.

And no man spake beside Hamish; he counted each stroke
    with a song.

When the last stroke fell, then he moved him a pace
    down the height,   90
  And he held forth the child in the heartaching sight
Of the mother, and looked all pitiful grave, as repenting
    a wrong.

And there as the motherly arms stretched out with the
    thanksgiving prayer—
  And there as the mother crept up with a fearful swift
    pace,
    Till her finger nigh felt of the bairnie's face—
In a flash fierce Hamish turned round and lifted the child
    in the air,

And sprang with the child in his arms from the horrible
    height in the sea,
  Shrill screeching, "Revenge!" in the wind-rush; and
    pallid Maclean,
    Age-feeble with anger and impotent pain,
Crawled up on the crag, and lay flat, and locked hold of
    dead roots of a tree—   100

And gazed hungrily o'er, and the blood from his back drip-
    dripped in the brine,
  And a sea-hawk flung down a skeleton fish as he flew,
  And the mother stared white on the waste of blue,
And the wind drove a cloud to seaward, and the sun
    began to shine.

THE MARSHES OF GLYNN   [1884]

Glooms of the live-oaks, beautiful-braided and woven
With intricate shades of the vines that myriad-cloven
  Clamber the forks of the multiform boughs,—
    Emerald twilights,—
    Virginal shy lights,
Wrought of the leaves to allure to the whisper of vows,

When lovers pace timidly down through the green colon-
    nades
 Of the dim sweet woods, of the dear dark woods,
  Of the heavenly woods and glades,
That run to the radiant marginal sand-beach within   10
 The wide sea-marshes of Glynn;—

Beautiful glooms, soft dusks in the noon-day fire,—
Wildwood privacies, closets of lone desire,
Chamber from chamber parted with wavering arras of
    leaves,—
Cells for the passionate pleasure of prayer to the soul that
    grieves,
 Pure with a sense of the passing of saints through the
    wood,
 Cool for the dutiful weighing of ill with good;—

O braided dusks of the oak and woven shades of the vine.
While the riotous noon-day sun of the June-day long did
    shine,
Ye held me fast in your heart and I held you fast in mine; 20
 But now when the noon is no more, and riot is rest,
 And the sun is a-wait at the ponderous gate of the West,
  And the slant yellow beam down the wood-aisle doth
    seem
  Like a lane into heaven that leads from a dream,—
Ay, now, when my soul all day hath drunken the soul of the oak,
And my heart is at ease from men, and the wearisome
    sound of the stroke
 Of the scythe of time and the trowel of trade is low,
 And belief overmasters doubt, and I know that I know,
 And my spirit is grown to a lordly great compass within,
 That the length and the breadth and the sweep of the
    marshes of Glynn   30
 Will work me no fear like the fear they have wrought me
    of yore
  When length was fatigue, and when breadth was but
    bitterness sore,
  And when terror and shrinking and dreary unnamable
    pain

Drew over me out of the merciless miles of the plain,—
   Oh, now, unafraid, I am fain to face
     The vast sweet visage of space.
  To the edge of the wood I am drawn, I am drawn,
Where the gray beach glimmering runs, as a belt of the
         dawn,
     For a mete and a mark
     To the forest-dark:—   40
      So:
   Affable live-oak, leaning low,—
Thus—with your favor—soft, with a reverent hand,
(Not lightly touching your person, Lord of the land!)
Bending your beauty aside, with a step I stand
     On the firm-packed sand,
     Free
  By a world of marsh that borders a world of sea.
Sinuous southward and sinuous northward the shimmering
         band
Of the sand-beach fastens the fringe of the marsh to the
         folds of the land.   50
Inward and outward to northward and southward the
         beach-lines linger and curl
As a silver-wrought garment that clings to and follows
         the firm sweet limbs of a girl.
Vanishing, swerving, evermore curving again into sight,
Softly the sand-beach wavers away to a dim gray looping
         of light.
And what if behind me to westward the wall of the woods
         stands high?
The world lies east: how ample, the marsh and the sea
         and the sky!
A league and a league of marsh-grass, waist-high, broad in
         the blade,
Green, and all of a height, and unflecked with a light or a
         shade,
     Stretch leisurely off, in a pleasant plain,
     To the terminal blue of the main.   60

  Oh, what is abroad in the marsh and the terminal sea?
  Somehow my soul seems suddenly free

From the weighing of fate and the sad discussion of sin,
By the length and the breadth and the sweep of the
                    marshes of Glynn.
Ye marshes, how candid and simple and nothing-withhold-
                    ing and free
Ye publish yourselves to the sky and offer yourselves to
                    the sea!
Tolerant plains, that suffer the sea and the rains and the
                    sun,
Ye spread and span like the catholic man who hath
                    mightily won
   God out of knowledge and good out of infinite pain
   And sight out of blindness and purity out of a stain.   70

   As the marsh-hen secretly builds on the watery sod,
   Behold I will build me a nest on the greatness of God:
   I will fly in the greatness of God as the marsh-hen flies
   In the freedom that fills all the space 'twixt the marsh and
                    the skies:
   By so many roots as the marsh-grass sends in the sod
   I will heartily lay me a-hold on the greatness of God:
   Oh, like to the greatness of God is the greatness within
   The range of the marshes, the liberal marshes of Glynn.

And the sea lends large, as the marsh: lo, out of his plenty
                    the sea
   Pours fast: full soon the time of the flood-tide must be: 80
      Look how the grace of the sea doth go
   About and about through the intricate channels that flow
            Here and there,
            Everywhere,
Till his waters have flooded the uttermost creeks and the
                    low-lying lanes,
      And the marsh is meshed with a million veins,
   That like as with rosy and silvery essences flow
      In the rose-and-silver evening glow.
            Farewell, my lord Sun!
   The creeks overflow: a thousand rivulets run   90
   'Twixt the roots of the sod; the blades of the marsh-grass
                    stir;

Passeth a hurrying sound of wings that westward whirr;
Passeth, and all is still; and the currents cease to run;
     And the sea and the marsh are one.
     How still the plains of the waters be!
     The tide is in his ecstasy.
     The tide is at his highest height:
        And it is night.

  And now from the Vast of the Lord will the waters of
        sleep
    Roll in on the souls of men,   100
   But who will reveal to our waking ken
   The forms that swim and the shapes that creep
     Under the waters of sleep?
And I would I could know what swimmeth below when
        the tide comes in
On the length and the breadth of the marvellous marshes
        of Glynn.

A BALLAD OF TREES AND THE MASTER   [1884]

Into the woods my Master went,
  Clean forspent, forspent.
Into the woods my Master came,
  Forspent with love and shame.
But the olives they were not blind to Him,
The little gray leaves were kind to Him:
The thorn-tree had a mind to Him
  When into the woods He came.

Out of the woods my Master went,
  And He was well content.   10
Out of the woods my Master came,
  Content with death and shame.
When Death and Shame would woo Him last,
From under the trees they drew Him last:
'Twas on a tree they slew Him—last
  When out of the woods He came.

William Vaughn Moody

1869–1910

William Vaughn Moody was born July 8, 1869, at Spencer, Indiana, and brought up in New Albany on the Ohio River. He was educated at Harvard, spending his senior year in Europe as a tutor and receiving his B.A. in 1893. The next year he took his master's degree at Harvard and began teaching English there. From 1895 to 1902 he was an instructor and assistant professor of English at the University of Chicago. A conscientious and brilliant lecturer, his first interest was not his teaching or his scholarly work but his writing of poetry and plays, and the income from his and Robert Morss Lovett's A History of English Literature *(1902) enabled him to devote full time to it. His prose play* The Great Divide, *which opened in New York in October, 1906, was a two-year popular success. At the time of his death he was working on the last of a trilogy of poetic dramas. He died at Colorado Springs, Colorado, on October 17, 1910.*

GLOUCESTER MOORS   [1901]

A mile behind is Gloucester town
Where the fishing fleets put in,
A mile ahead the land dips down
And the woods and farms begin.
Here, where the moors stretch free
In the high blue afternoon,
Are the marching sun and talking sea,
And the racing winds that wheel and flee
On the flying heels of June.

Jill-o'er-the-ground is purple blue,   10
Blue is the quaker-maid,
The wild geranium holds its dew
Long in the boulder's shade.
Wax-red hangs the cup
From the huckleberry boughs,
In barberry bells the grey moths sup,
Or where the choke-cherry lifts high up
Sweet bowls for their carouse.

Over the shelf of the sandy cove
Beach-peas blossom late.   20
By copse and cliff the swallows rove
Each calling to his mate.
Seaward the sea-gulls go,
And the land-birds all are here;
That green-gold flash was a vireo,
And yonder flame where the marsh-flags grow
Was a scarlet tanager.

This earth is not the steadfast place
We landsmen build upon;
From deep to deep she varies pace,   30
And while she comes is gone.
Beneath my feet I feel
Her smooth bulk heave and dip;
With velvet plunge and soft upreel
She swings and steadies to her keel
Like a gallant, gallant ship.

These summer clouds she sets for sail,
The sun is her masthead light,
She tows the moon like a pinnace frail
Where her phosphor wake churns bright.   40
Now hid, now looming clear,
On the face of the dangerous blue
The star fleets tack and wheel and veer,
But on, but on does the old earth steer
As if her port she knew.

God, dear God! Does she know her port,
Though she goes so far about?
Or blind astray, does she make her sport
To brazen and chance it out?
I watched when her captains passed: 50
She were better captainless.
Men in the cabin, before the mast,
But some were reckless and some aghast,
And some sat gorged at mess.

By her battened hatch I leaned and caught
Sounds from the noisome hold,—
Cursing and sighing of souls distraught
And cries too sad to be told.
Then I strove to go down and see;
But they said, "Thou art not of us!"   60
I turned to those on the deck with me
And cried, "Give help!" But they said, "Let be:
Our ship sails faster thus."

Jill-o'er-the-ground is purple blue,
Blue is the quaker-maid,
The alder-clump where the brook comes through
Breeds cresses in its shade.
To be out of the moiling street
With its swelter and its sin!
Who has given to me this sweet,   70
And given my brother dust to eat?
And when will his wage come in?

Scattering wide or blown in ranks,
Yellow and white and brown,
Boats and boats from the fishing banks
Come home to Gloucester town.
There is cash to purse and spend,
There are wives to be embraced,
Hearts to borrow and hearts to lend,
And hearts to take and keep to the end,—   80
O little sails, make haste!

But thou, vast outbound ship of souls,
What harbor town for thee?
What shapes, when thy arriving tolls,
Shall crowd the banks to see?
Shall all the happy shipmates then
Stand singing brotherly?
Or shall a haggard ruthless few
Warp her over and bring her to,
While the many broken souls of men   90
Fester down in the slaver's pen,
And nothing to say or do?

AN ODE IN TIME OF HESITATION   [1901]

(After seeing at Boston the statue of Robert Gould Shaw, killed
while storming Fort Wagner, July 18, 1863, at the head of the first
enlisted Negro regiment, the Fifty-fourth Massachusetts.)

I

Before the solemn bronze Saint Gaudens made
To thrill the heedless passer's heart with awe,
And set here in the city's talk and trade
To the good memory of Robert Shaw,
This bright March morn I stand,
And hear the distant spring come up the land;
Knowing that what I hear is not unheard
Of this boy soldier and his Negro band,
For all their gaze is fixed so stern ahead,
For all the fatal rhythm of their tread.   10
The land they died to save from death and shame
Trembles and waits, hearing the spring's great
        name,
And by her pangs these resolute ghosts are stirred.

II

Through street and mall the tides of people go
Heedless; the trees upon the Common show

No hint of green; but to my listening heart
The still earth doth impart
Assurance of her jubilant emprise,
And it is clear to my long-searching eyes
That love at last has might upon the skies.   20
The ice is runneled on the little pond;
A telltale patter drips from off the trees;
The air is touched with southland spiceries,
As if but yesterday it tossed the frond
Of pendant mosses where the live-oaks grow
Beyond Virginia and the Carolines,
Or had its will among the fruits and vines
Of aromatic isles asleep beyond
Florida and the Gulf of Mexico.

III

Soon shall the Cape Ann children shout in glee,   30
Spying the arbutus, spring's dear recluse;
Hill lads at dawn shall hearken the wild goose
Go honking northward over Tennessee;
West from Oswego to Sault Sainte-Marie,
And on to where the Pictured Rocks are hung,
And yonder where, gigantic, wilful, young,
Chicago sitteth at the northwest gates,
With restless violent hands and casual tongue
Moulding her mighty fates,
The Lakes shall robe them in ethereal sheen;   40
And like a larger sea, the vital green
Of springing wheat shall vastly be outflung
Over Dakota and the prairie states.
By desert people immemorial
On Arizonan mesas shall be done
Dim rites unto the thunder and the sun;
Nor shall the primal gods lack sacrifice
More splendid, when the white Sierras call
Unto the Rockies straightway to arise
And dance before the unveiled ark of the year,   50
Sounding their windy cedars as for shawms,
Unrolling rivers clear
For flutter of broad phylacteries;

While Shasta signals to Alaskan seas
That watch old sluggish glaciers downward creep
To fling their icebergs thundering from the steep,
And Mariposa through the purple calms
Gazes at far Hawaii crowned with palms
Where East and West are met,—
A rich seal on the ocean's bosom set   60
To say that East and West are twain,
With different loss and gain:
The Lord hath sundered them; let them be sundered yet.

IV

Alas! what sounds are these that come
Sullenly over the Pacific seas,—
Sounds of ignoble battle, striking dumb
The season's half-awakened ecstasies?
Must I be humble, then,
Now when my heart hath need of pride?
Wild love falls on me from these sculptured men;   70
By loving much the land for which they died
I would be justified.
My spirit was away on pinions wide
To soothe in praise of her its passionate mood
And ease it of its ache of gratitude.
Too sorely heavy is the debt they lay
On me and the companions of my day.
I would remember now
My country's goodliness, make sweet her name.
Alas! what shade art thou   80
Of sorrow or of blame
Liftest the lyric leafage from her brow,
And pointest a slow finger at her shame?

V

Lies! lies! It cannot be! The wars we wage
Are noble, and our battles still are won
By justice for us, ere we lift the gage.
We have not sold our loftiest heritage.
The proud republic hath not stooped to cheat
And scramble in the market-place of war;

Her forehead weareth yet its solemn star.   90
Here is her witness: this, her perfect son,
This delicate and proud New England soul
Who leads despisèd men, with just-unshackled feet,
Up the large ways where death and glory meet,
To show all peoples that our shame is done,
That once more we are clean and spirit-whole.

VI

Crouched in the sea fog on the moaning sand
All night he lay, speaking some simple word
From hour to hour to the slow minds that heard,
Holding each poor life gently in his hand   100
And breathing on the base rejected clay
Till each dark face shone mystical and grand
Against the breaking day;
And lo, the shard the potter cast away
Was grown a fiery chalice crystal-fine
Fulfilled of the divine
Great wine of battle wrath by God's ring-finger stirred.
Then upward, where the shadowy bastion loomed
Huge on the mountain in the wet sea light,
Whence now, and now, infernal flowerage bloomed,   110
Bloomed, burst, and scattered down its deadly seed,—
They swept, and died like freemen on the height,
Like freemen, and like men of noble breed;
And when the battle fell away at night
By hasty and contemptuous hands were thrust
Obscurely in a common grave with him
The fair-haired keeper of their love and trust.
Now limb doth mingle with dissolvèd limb
In nature's busy old democracy
To flush the mountain laurel when she blows   120
Sweet by the southern sea,
And heart with crumbled heart climbs in the rose:—
The untaught hearts with the high heart that knew
This mountain fortress for no earthly hold
Of temporal quarrel, but the bastion old
Of spiritual wrong,
Built by an unjust nation sheer and strong,

Expugnable but by a nation's rue
And bowing down before that equal shrine
By all men held divine,   130
Whereof his band and he were the most holy sign.

VII

O bitter, bitter shade!
Wilt thou not put the scorn
And instant tragic question from thine eye?
Do thy dark brows yet crave
That swift and angry stave—
Unmeet for this desirous morn—
That I have striven, striven to evade?
Gazing on him, must I not deem they err
Whose careless lips in street and shop aver   140
As common tidings, deeds to make his cheek
Flush from the bronze, and his dead throat to speak?
Surely some elder singer would arise,
Whose harp hath leave to threaten and to mourn
Above this people when they go astray.
Is Whitman, the strong spirit, overworn?
Has Whittier put his yearning wrath away?
I will not and I dare not yet believe!
Though furtively the sunlight seems to grieve,
And the spring-laden breeze   150
Out of the gladdening west is sinister
With sounds of nameless battle overseas;
Though when we turn and question in suspense
If these things be indeed after these ways,
And what things are to follow after these,
Our fluent men of place and consequence
Fumble and fill their mouths with hollow phrase,
Or for the end-all of deep arguments
Intone their dull commercial liturgies—
I dare not yet believe! My ears are shut!   160
I will not hear the thin satiric praise
And muffled laughter of our enemies,
Bidding us never sheathe our valiant sword
Till we have changed our birthright for a gourd
Of wild pulse stolen from a barbarian's hut;

Showing how wise it is to cast away
The symbols of our spiritual sway,
That so our hands with better ease
May wield the driver's whip and grasp the jailer's keys.

VIII

Was it for this our fathers kept the law?   170
This crown shall crown their struggle and their ruth?
Are we the eagle nation Milton saw
Mewing its mighty youth,
Soon to possess the mountain winds of truth,
And be a swift familiar of the sun
Where aye before God's face his trumpets run?
Or have we but the talons and the maw,
And for the abject likeness of our heart
Shall some less lordly bird be set apart?—
Some gross-billed wader where the swamps are fat?   180
Some gorger in the sun? Some prowler with the bat?

IX

Ah no!
We have not fallen so.
We are our fathers' sons: let those who lead us know!
'T was only yesterday sick Cuba's cry
Came up the tropic wind, "Now help us, for we die!"
Then Alabama heard,
And rising, pale, to Maine and Idaho
Shouted a burning word.
Proud state with proud impassioned state conferred,   190
And at the lifting of a hand sprang forth,
East, west, and south, and north,
Beautiful armies. Oh, by the sweet blood and young
Shed on the awful hill slope at San Juan,
By the unforgotten names of eager boys
Who might have tasted girls' love and been stung
With the old mystic joys
And starry griefs, now the spring nights come on,
But that the heart of youth is generous,—
We charge you, ye who lead us,   200
Breathe on their chivalry no hint of stain!

Turn not their new-world victories to gain!
One least leaf plucked for chaffer from the bays
Of their dear praise,
One jot of their pure conquest put to hire,
The implacable republic will require;
With clamor, in the glare and gaze of noon,
Or subtly, coming as a thief at night,
But surely, very surely, slow or soon
That insult deep we deeply will requite.   210
Tempt not our weakness, our cupidity!
For save we let the island men go free,
Those baffled and dislaureled ghosts
Will curse us from the lamentable coasts
Where walk the frustrate dead.
The cup of trembling shall be drainèd quite,
Eaten the sour bread of astonishment,
With ashes of the hearth shall be made white
Our hair, and wailing shall be in the tent;
Then on your guiltier head   220
Shall our intolerable self-disdain
Wreak suddenly its anger and its pain;
For manifest in that disastrous light
We shall discern the right
And do it, tardily.—O ye who lead,
Take heed!
Blindness we may forgive, but baseness we will smite.

ON A SOLDIER FALLEN IN THE PHILIPPINES [1901]

Streets of the roaring town,
Hush for him, hush, be still!
He comes, who was stricken down
Doing the word of our will.
Hush! Let him have his state,
Give him his soldier's crown.
The grists of trade can wait
Their grinding at the mill,

But he cannot wait for his honor, now the trumpet has
   been blown;
Wreathe pride now for his granite brow, lay love on his
   breast of stone.   10

  Toll! Let the great bells toll
  Till the clashing air is dim.
  Did we wrong this parted soul?
  We will make up it to him.
  Toll! Let him never guess
  What work we set him to.
  Laurel, laurel, yes;
  He did what we bade him do.
Praise, and never a whispered hint but the fight he fought
   was good;
Never a word that the blood on his sword was his
   country's own heart's-blood.   20

  A flag for the soldier's bier
  Who dies that his land may live;
  O, banners, banners here,
  That he doubt not nor misgive!
  That he heed not from the tomb
  The evil days draw near
  When the nation, robed in gloom,
  With its faithless past shall strive.
Let him never dream that his bullet's scream went wide of
   its island mark,
Home to the heart of his darling land where she stumbled
   and sinned in the dark.   30

THE MENAGERIE [1901]

Thank God my brain is not inclined to cut
Such capers every day! I'm just about
Mellow, but then—There goes the tent-flap shut.
Rain's in the wind. I thought so: every snout
Was twitching when the keeper turned me out.

That screaming parrot makes my blood run cold.
Gabriel's trump! the big bull elephant
Squeals "Rain!" to the parched herd. The monkeys scold,
And jabber that it's rain water they want.
(It makes me sick to see a monkey pant.)   10

I'll foot it home, to try and make believe
I'm sober. After this I stick to beer,
And drop the circus when the sane folks leave.
A man's a fool to look at things too near:
They look back, and begin to cut up queer.

Beasts do, at any rate; especially
Wild devils caged. They have the coolest way
Of being something else than what you see:
You pass a sleek young zebra nosing hay,
A nylghau looking bored and distingué,—   20

And think you've seen a donkey and a bird.
Not on your life! Just glance back, if you dare.
The zebra chews, the nylghau hasn't stirred;
But something's happened, Heaven knows what or where
To freeze your scalp and pompadour your hair.

I'm not precisely an æolian lute
Hung in the wandering winds of sentiment,
But drown me if the ugliest, meanest brute
Grunting and fretting in that sultry tent
Didn't just floor me with embarrassment!   30

'T was like a thunder-clap from out the clear,—
One minute they were circus beasts, some grand,
Some ugly, some amusing, and some queer:
Rival attractions to the hobo band,
The flying jenny, and the peanut stand.

Next minute they were old hearth-mates of mine!
Lost people, eyeing me with such a stare!
Patient, satiric, devilish, divine;
A gaze of hopeless envy, squalid care,
Hatred, and thwarted love, and dim despair.   40

Within my blood my ancient kindred spoke,—
Grotesque and monstrous voices, heard afar
Down ocean caves when behemoth awoke,
Or through fern forests roared the plesiosaur
Locked with the giant-bat in ghastly war.

And suddenly, as in a flash of light,
I saw great Nature working out her plan;
Through all her shapes from mastodon to mite
Forever groping, testing, passing on
To find at last the shape and soul of Man.   50

Till in the fullness of accomplished time,
Comes brother Forepaugh, upon business bent,
Tracks her through frozen and through torrid clime,
And shows us, neatly labeled in a tent,
The stages of her huge experiment;

Blabbing aloud her shy and reticent hours;
Dragging to light her blinking, slothful moods;
Publishing fretful seasons when her powers
Worked wild and sullen in her solitudes,
Or when her mordant laughter shook the woods.   60

Here, round about me, were her vagrant births;
Sick dreams she had, fierce projects she essayed;
Her qualms, her fiery prides, her crazy mirths;
The troublings of her spirit as she strayed,
Cringed, gloated, mocked, was lordly, was afraid,

On that long road she went to seek mankind;
Here were the darkling coverts that she beat
To find the Hider she was sent to find;
Here the distracted footprints of her feet
Whereby her soul's Desire she came to greet.   70

But why should they, her botch-work, turn about
And stare disdain at me, her finished job?
Why was the place one vast suspended shout
Of laughter? Why did all the daylight throb
With soundless guffaw and dumb-stricken sob?

Helpless I stood among those awful cages;
The beasts were walking loose, and I was bagged!
I, I, last product of the toiling ages,
Goal of heroic feet that never lagged,—
A little man in trousers, slightly jagged.   80

Deliver me from such another jury!
The Judgment-day will be a picnic to 't.
Their satire was more dreadful than their fury,
And worst of all was just a kind of brute
Disgust, and giving up, and sinking mute.

Survival of the fittest, adaptation,
And all their other evolution terms,
Seem to omit one small consideration,
To wit, that tumblebugs and angleworms
Have souls: there's soul in everything that squirms.   90

And souls are restless, plagued, impatient things,
All dream and unaccountable desire;
Crawling, but pestered with the thought of wings;
Spreading through every inch of earth's old mire
Mystical hanker after something higher.

Wishes *are* horses, as I understand.
I guess a wistful polyp that has strokes
Of feeling faint to gallivant on land
Will come to be a scandal to his folks;
Legs he will sprout, in spite of threats and jokes.   100

And at the core of every life that crawls
Or runs or flies or swims or vegetates—
Churning the mammoth's heart-blood, in the galls
Of shark and tiger planting gorgeous hates,
Lighting the love of eagles for their mates;

Yes, in the dim brain of the jellied fish
That is and is not living—moved and stirred
From the beginning a mysterious wish,
A vision, a command, a fatal Word:
The name of Man was uttered, and they heard.   110

Upward along the æons of old war
They sought him: wing and shank-bone, claw and bill
Were fashioned and rejected; wide and far
They roamed the twilight jungles of their will;
But still they sought him, and desired him still.

Man they desired, but mind you, Perfect Man,
The radiant and the loving, yet to be!
I hardly wonder, when they came to scan
The upshot of their strenuosity,
They gazed with mixed emotions upon *me*.   120

Well, my advice to you is, Face the creatures,
Or spot them sideways with your weather eye,
Just to keep tab on their expansive features;
It isn't pleasant when you're stepping high
To catch a giraffe smiling on the sly.

If nature made you graceful, don't get gay
Back-to before the hippopotamus;
If meek and godly, find some place to play
Besides right where three mad hyenas fuss:
You may hear language that we won't discuss.   130

If you're a sweet thing in a flower-bed hat,
Or her best fellow with your tie tucked in,
Don't squander love's bright springtime girding at
An old chimpanzee with an Irish chin:
There may be hidden meaning in his grin.

THE BRACELET OF GRASS   [1901]

The opal heart of afternoon
Was clouding on to throbs of storm,
Ashen within the ardent west
The lips of thunder muttered harm,
And as a bubble like to break

Hung heaven's trembling amethyst,
When with the sedge-grass by the lake
I braceleted her wrist.

And when the ribbon grass was tied,
Sad with the happiness we planned,   10
Palm linked in palm we stood awhile
And watched the raindrops dot the sand;
Until the anger of the breeze
Chid all the lake's bright breathing down,
And ravished all the radiancies
From her deep eyes of brown.

We gazed from shelter on the storm,
And through our hearts swept ghostly pain
To see the shards of day sweep past,
Broken, and none might mend again.   20
Broken, that none shall ever mend;
Loosened, that none shall ever tie.
O the wind and the wind, will it never end?
O the sweeping past of the ruined sky!

FADED PICTURES   [1901]

Only two patient eyes to stare
Out of the canvas. All the rest—
The warm green gown, the small hands pressed
Light in the lap, the braided hair

That must have made the sweet low brow
So earnest, centuries ago,
When some one saw it change and glow—
All faded! Just the eyes burn now.

I dare say people pass and pass
Before the blistered little frame,   10
And dingy work without a name
Stuck in behind its square of glass.

But I, well, I left Raphael
Just to come drink these eyes of hers,
To think away the stains and blurs
And make all new again and well.

Only, for tears my head will bow,
Because there on my heart's last wall,
Scarce one tint left to tell it all,
A picture keeps its eyes, somehow.   20

THAMMUZ   [1912]

Daughters, daughters, do ye grieve?
Crimson dark the freshes flow!
Were ye violent at eve?
Crimson stains where the rushes grow!
What is this that I must know?

Mourners by the dark red waters,
Met ye Thammuz at his play?
Was your mood upon you, daughters?
Had ye drunken? O how grey
Looks your hair in the rising day!   10

Mourners, mourn not overmuch
That ye slew your lovely one.
Such ye are; and be ye such!
Lift your heads; the waters run
Ruby bright in the climbing sun.

Raven hair and hair of gold,
Look who bendeth over you!
This is not the shepherd old;
This is Thammuz, whom ye slew,
Radiant Thammuz, risen anew!   20

Edwin Arlington Robinson

1869–1935

Edwin Arlington Robinson was born December 22, 1869, in Head Tide, Maine, but grew up in Gardiner, Maine, the "Tilbury Town" of his poems. He studied at Harvard as a special student from 1891 to 1893, then tried various means of supporting himself in Boston and New York. Through the assistance of President Theodore Roosevelt he became a clerk in the New York Customs House from 1905 to 1910, when he resigned to devote his entire time to writing. He was helped by Mrs. Edward MacDowell, the wife of the composer, who turned her home, Hillcrest, at Peterborough, New Hampshire, into a colony for composers, writers, and artists after her husband's death in 1908. From 1911 on Robinson spent his summers at the MacDowell colony and produced his most successful writing there. He was awarded the Pulitzer Prize three times and became a famous poet, though he never courted popularity. He died on April 6, 1935, in New York City.

GEORGE CRABBE   [1896]

Give him the darkest inch your shelf allows,
Hide him in lonely garrets, if you will,—
But his hard, human pulse is throbbing still
With the sure strength that fearless truth endows.
In spite of all fine science disavows,
Of his plain excellence and stubborn skill
There yet remains what fashion cannot kill,
Though years have thinned the laurel from his brows.

Whether or not we read him, we can feel
From time to time the vigor of his name   10
Against us like a finger for the shame
And emptiness of what our souls reveal
In books that are as altars where we kneel
To consecrate the flicker, not the flame.

LUKE HAVERGAL   [1896]

Go to the western gate, Luke Havergal,
There where the vines cling crimson on the wall,
And in the twilight wait for what will come.
The leaves will whisper there of her, and some,
Like flying words, will strike you as they fall;
But go, and if you listen she will call.
Go to the western gate, Luke Havergal—
Luke Havergal.

No, there is not a dawn in eastern skies
To rift the fiery night that's in your eyes;   10
But there, where western glooms are gathering,
The dark will end the dark, if anything:
God slays Himself with every leaf that flies,
And hell is more than half of paradise.
No, there is not a dawn in eastern skies—
In eastern skies.

Out of a grave I come to tell you this,
Out of a grave I come to quench the kiss
That flames upon your forehead with a glow
That blinds you to the way that you must go.   20
Yes, there is yet one way to where she is,
Bitter, but one that faith may never miss.
Out of a grave I come to tell you this—
To tell you this.

There is the western gate, Luke Havergal,
There are the crimson leaves upon the wall.

Go, for the winds are tearing them away,—
Nor think to riddle the dead words they say,
Nor any more to feel them as they fall;
But go, and if you trust her she will call.   30
There is the western gate, Luke Havergal—
Luke Havergal.

CREDO   [1896]

I cannot find my way: there is no star
In all the shrouded heavens anywhere;
And there is not a whisper in the air
Of any living voice but one so far
That I can hear it only as a bar
Of lost, imperial music, played when fair
And angel fingers wove, and unaware,
Dead leaves to garlands where no roses are.

No, there is not a glimmer, nor a call,
For one that welcomes, welcomes when he fears,   10
The black and awful chaos of the night;
For through it all—above, beyond it all—
I know the far-sent message of the years,
I feel the coming glory of the Light.

CLIFF KLINGENHAGEN   [1897]

Cliff Klingenhagen had me in to dine
With him one day; and after soup and meat,
And all the other things there were to eat,
Cliff took two glasses and filled one with wine
And one with wormwood. Then, without a sign
For me to choose at all, he took the draught
Of bitterness himself, and lightly quaffed
It off, and said the other one was mine.

And when I asked him what the deuce he meant
By doing that, he only looked at me   10
And smiled, and said it was a way of his.
And though I know the fellow, I have spent
Long time a-wondering when I shall be
As happy as Cliff Klingenhagen is.

HOW ANNANDALE WENT OUT   [1910]

"They called it Annandale—and I was there
To flourish, to find words, and to attend:
Liar, physician, hypocrite, and friend,
I watched him; and the sight was not so fair
As one or two that I have seen elsewhere:
An apparatus not for me to mend—
A wreck, with hell between him and the end,
Remained of Annandale; and I was there.

"I knew the ruin as I knew the man;
So put the two together, if you can,   10
Remembering the worst you know of me.
Now view yourself as I was, on the spot—
With a slight kind of engine. Do you see?
Like this . . . You wouldn't hang me? I thought not."

MINIVER CHEEVY   [1910]

Miniver Cheevy, child of scorn,
    Grew lean while he assailed the seasons;
He wept that he was ever born,
    And he had reasons.

Miniver loved the days of old
    When swords were bright and steeds were prancing;

The vision of a warrior bold
   Would set him dancing.

Miniver sighed for what was not,
   And dreamed, and rested from his labors;   10
He dreamed of Thebes and Camelot,
   And Priam's neighbors.

Miniver mourned the ripe renown
   That made so many a name so fragrant;
He mourned Romance, now on the town,
   And Art, a vagrant.

Miniver loved the Medici,
   Albeit he had never seen one;
He would have sinned incessantly
   Could he have been one.   20

Miniver cursed the commonplace
   And eyed a khaki suit with loathing;
He missed the mediæval grace
   Of iron clothing.

Miniver scorned the gold he sought,
   But sore annoyed was he without it;
Miniver thought, and thought, and thought,
   And thought about it.

Miniver Cheevy, born too late,
   Scratched his head and kept on thinking;   30
Miniver coughed, and called it fate,
   And kept on drinking.

FOR A DEAD LADY   [1910]

No more with overflowing light
Shall fill the eyes that now are faded,
Nor shall another's fringe with night

Their woman-hidden world as they did.
No more shall quiver down the days
The flowing wonder of her ways,
Whereof no language may requite
The shifting and the many-shaded.

The grace, divine, definitive,
Clings only as a faint forestalling;   10
The laugh that love could not forgive
Is hushed, and answers to no calling;
The forehead and the little ears
Have gone where Saturn keeps the years;
The breast where roses could not live
Has done with rising and with falling.

The beauty, shattered by the laws
That have creation in their keeping,
No longer trembles at applause,
Or over children that are sleeping;   20
And we who delve in beauty's lore
Know all that we have known before
Of what inexorable cause
Makes Time so vicious in his reaping.

THE GIFT OF GOD   [1916]

Blessed with a joy that only she
Of all alive shall ever know,
She wears a proud humility
For what it was that willed it so,—
That her degree should be so great
Among the favored of the Lord
That she may scarcely bear the weight
Of her bewildering reward.

As one apart, immune, alone,
Or featured for the shining ones,   10

And like to none that she has known
Of other women's other sons,—
The firm fruition of her need,
He shines anointed; and he blurs
Her vision, till it seems indeed
A sacrilege to call him hers.

She fears a little for so much
Of what is best, and hardly dares
To think of him as one to touch
With aches, indignities, and cares;   20
She sees him rather at the goal,
Still shining; and her dream foretells
The proper shining of a soul
Where nothing ordinary dwells.

Perchance a canvass of the town
Would find him far from flags and shouts,
And leave him only the renown
Of many smiles and many doubts;
Perchance the crude and common tongue
Would havoc strangely with his worth;   30
But she, with innocence unwrung,
Would read his name around the earth.

And others, knowing how this youth
Would shine, if love could make him great,
When caught and tortured for the truth
Would only writhe and hesitate;
While she, arranging for his days
What centuries could not fulfill,
Transmutes him with her faith and praise,
And has him shining where she will.   40

She crowns him with her gratefulness,
And says again that life is good;
And should the gift of God be less
In him than in her motherhood,
His fame, though vague, will not be small,
As upward through her dream he fares,

Half clouded with a crimson fall
Of roses thrown on marble stairs.

HILLCREST   [1916]

To Mrs. Edward MacDowell

No sound of any storm that shakes
Old island walls with older seas
Comes here where now September makes
An island in a sea of trees.

Between the sunlight and the shade
A man may learn till he forgets
The roaring of a world remade,
And all his ruins and regrets;

And if he still remembers here
Poor fights he may have won or lost,—   10
If he be ridden with the fear
Of what some other fight may cost,—

If, eager to confuse too soon,
What he has known with what may be,
He reads a planet out of tune
For cause of his jarred harmony,—

If here he venture to unroll
His index of adagios,
And he be given to console
Humanity with what he knows,—   20

He may by contemplation learn
A little more than what he knew,
And even see great oaks return
To acorns out of which they grew.

He may, if he but listen well,
Through twilight and the silence here,

Be told what there are none may tell
To vanity's impatient ear;

And he may never dare again
Say what awaits him, or be sure   30
What sunlit labyrinth of pain
He may not enter and endure.

Who knows to-day from yesterday
May learn to count no thing too strange;
Love builds of what Time takes away,
Till Death itself is less than Change.

Who sees enough in his duress
May go as far as dreams have gone;
Who sees a little may do less
Than many who are blind have done;   40

Who sees unchastened here the soul
Triumphant has no other sight
Than has a child who sees the whole
World radiant with his own delight.

Far journeys and hard wandering
Await him in whose crude surmise
Peace, like a mask, hides everything
That is and has been from his eyes;

And all his wisdom is unfound,
Or like a web that error weaves   50
On airy looms that have a sound
No louder now than falling leaves.

EROS TURANNOS   [1916]

She fears him, and will always ask
   What fated her to choose him;
She meets in his engaging mask
   All reasons to refuse him;

But what she meets and what she fears
Are less than are the downward years,
Drawn slowly to the foamless weirs
    Of age, were she to lose him.

Between a blurred sagacity
    That once had power to sound him,   10
And Love, that will not let him be
    The Judas that she found him,
Her pride assuages her almost,
As if it were alone the cost.—
He sees that he will not be lost,
    And waits and looks around him.

A sense of ocean and old trees
    Envelops and allures him;
Tradition, touching all he sees,
    Beguiles and reassures him;   20
And all her doubts of what he says
Are dimmed with what she knows of days—
Till even prejudice delays
    And fades, and she secures him.

The falling leaf inaugurates
    The reign of her confusion;
The pounding wave reverberates
    The dirge of her illusion;
And home, where passion lived and died,
Becomes a place where she can hide,   30
While all the town and harbor side
    Vibrate with her seclusion.

We tell you, tapping on our brows,
    The story as it should be,—
As if the story of a house
    Were told, or ever could be;
We'll have no kindly veil between
Her visions and those we have seen,—
As if we guessed what hers have been,
    Or what they are or would be.   40

Meanwhile we do no harm; for they
    That with a god have striven,
Not hearing much of what we say,
    Take what the god has given;
Though like waves breaking it may be,
Or like a changed familiar tree,
Or like a stairway to the sea
    Where down the blind are driven.

BEWICK FINZER   [1916]

Time was when his half million drew
    The breath of six per cent;
But soon the worm of what-was-not
    Fed hard on his content:
And something crumbled in his brain
    When his half million went.

Time passed, and filled along with his
    The place of many more;
Time came, and hardly one of us
    Had credence to restore,   10
From what appeared one day, the man
    Whom we had known before.

The broken voice, the withered neck,
    The coat worn out with care,
The cleanliness of indigence,
    The brilliance of despair,
The fond imponderable dreams
    Of affluence,—all were there.

Poor Finzer, with his dreams and schemes,
    Fares hard now in the race,   20
With heart and eye that have a task
    When he looks in the face
Of one who might so easily
    Have been in Finzer's place.

He comes unfailing for the loan
   We give and then forget;
He comes, and probably for years
   Will he be coming yet,—
Familiar as an old mistake,
   And futile as regret.   30

THE MAN AGAINST THE SKY   [1916]

Between me and the sunset, like a dome
Against the glory of a world on fire,
Now burned a sudden hill,
Bleak, round, and high, by flame-lit height made higher,
With nothing on it for the flame to kill
Save one who moved and was alone up there
To loom before the chaos and the glare
As if he were the last god going home
Unto his last desire.

Dark, marvelous, and inscrutable he moved on   10
Till down the fiery distance he was gone,
Like one of those eternal, remote things
That range across a man's imaginings
When a sure music fills him and he knows
What he may say thereafter to few men,—
The touch of ages having wrought
An echo and a glimpse of what he thought
A phantom or a legend until then;
For whether lighted over ways that save,
Or lured from all repose,   20
If he go on too far to find a grave,
Mostly alone he goes.

Even he, who stood where I had found him,
On high with fire all round him,
Who moved along the molten west,
And over the round hill's crest
That seemed half ready with him to go down,

Flame-bitten and flame-cleft,
As if there were to be no last thing left
Of a nameless unimaginable town,—   30
Even he who climbed and vanished may have taken
Down to the perils of a depth not known,
From death defended though by men forsaken,
The bread that every man must eat alone;
He may have walked while others hardly dared
Look on to see him stand where many fell;
And upward out of that, as out of hell,
He may have sung and striven
To mount where more of him shall yet be given,
Bereft of all retreat,   40
To sevenfold heat,—
As on a day when three in Dura shared
The furnace, and were spared
For glory by that king of Babylon
Who made himself so great that God, who heard,
Covered him with long feathers, like a bird.

Again, he may have gone down easily,
By comfortable altitudes, and found,
As always, underneath him solid ground
Whereon to be sufficient and to stand   50
Possessed already of the promised land,
Far stretched and fair to see:
A good sight, verily,
And one to make the eyes of her who bore him
Shine glad with hidden tears.
Why question of his ease of who before him,
In one place or another where they left
Their names as far behind them as their bones,
And yet by dint of slaughter toil and theft,
And shrewdly sharpened stones,   60
Carved hard the way for his ascendency
Through deserts of lost years?
Why trouble him now who sees and hears
No more than what his innocence requires,
And therefore to no other height aspires
Than one at which he neither quails nor tires?

He may do more by seeing what he sees
Than others eager for iniquities;
He may, by seeing all things for the best,
Incite futurity to do the rest.   70

Or with an even likelihood,
He may have met with atrabilious eyes
The fires of time on equal terms and passed
Indifferently down, until at last
His only kind of grandeur would have been,
Apparently, in being seen.
He may have had for evil or for good
No argument; he may have had no care
For what without himself went anywhere
To failure or to glory, and least of all   80
For such a stale, flamboyant miracle;
He may have been the prophet of an art
Immovable to old idolatries;
He may have been a player without a part,
Annoyed that even the sun should have the skies
For such a flaming way to advertise;
He may have been a painter sick at heart
With Nature's toiling for a new surprise;
He may have been a cynic, who now, for all
Of anything divine that his effete   90
Negation may have tasted,
Saw truth in his own image, rather small,
Forebore to fever the ephemeral,
Found any barren height a good retreat
From any swarming street,
And in the sun saw power superbly wasted:
And when the primitive old-fashioned stars
Came out again to shine on joys and wars
More primitive, and all arrayed for doom,
He may have proved a world a sorry thing   100
In his imagining,
And life a lighted highway to the tomb.

Or, mounting with infirm unsearching tread,
His hopes to chaos led,

He may have stumbled up there from the past,
And with an aching strangeness viewed the last
Abysmal conflagration of his dreams,—
A flame where nothing seems
To burn but flame itself, by nothing fed;
And while it all went out,   110
Not even the faint anodyne of doubt
May then have eased a painful going down
From pictured heights of power and lost renown,
Revealed at length to his outlived endeavor
Remote and unapproachable forever;
And at his heart there may have gnawed
Sick memories of a dead faith foiled and flawed
And long dishonored by the living death
Assigned alike by chance
To brutes and hierophants;   120
And anguish fallen on those he loved around him
May once have dealt the last blow to confound him,
And so have left him as death leaves a child,
Who sees it all too near;
And he who knows no young way to forget
May struggle to the tomb unreconciled.
Whatever suns may rise or set
There may be nothing kinder for him here
Than shafts and agonies;
And under these   130
He may cry out and stay on horribly;
Or, seeing in death too small a thing to fear,
He may go forward like a stoic Roman
Where pangs and terrors in his pathway lie,—
Or, seizing the swift logic of a woman,
Curse God and die.

Or maybe there, like many another one
Who might have stood aloft and looked ahead,
Black-drawn against wild red,
He may have built, unawed by fiery gules   140
That in him no commotion stirred,
A living reason out of molecules
Why molecules occurred,

And one for smiling when he might have sighed
Had he seen far enough,
And in the same inevitable stuff
Discovered an odd reason too for pride
In being what he must have been by laws
Infrangible and for no kind of cause.
Deterred by no confusion or surprise   150
He may have seen with his mechanic eyes
A world without a meaning, and had room,
Alone amid magnificence and doom,
To build himself an airy monument
That should, or fail him in his vague intent,
Outlast an accidental universe—
To call it nothing worse—
Or, by the burrowing guile
Of Time disintegrated and effaced,
Like once-remembered mighty trees go down   160
To ruin, of which by man may now be traced
No part sufficient even to be rotten,
And in the book of things that are forgotten
Is entered as a thing not quite worth while.
He may have been so great
That satraps would have shivered at his frown,
And all he prized alive may rule a state
No larger than a grave that holds a clown;
He may have been a master of his fate,
And of his atoms,—ready as another   170
In his emergence to exonerate
His father and his mother;
He may have been a captain of a host,
Self-eloquent and ripe for prodigies,
Doomed here to swell by dangerous degrees,
And then give up the ghost.
Nahum's great grasshoppers were such as these,
Sun-scattered and soon lost.

Whatever the dark road he may have taken,
This man who stood on high   180
And faced alone the sky,

Whatever drove or lured or guided him—
A vision answering a faith unshaken,
An easy trust assumed of easy trials,
A sick negation born of weak denials,
A crazed abhorrence of an old condition,
A blind attendance on a brief ambition,—
Whatever stayed him or derided him,
His way was even as ours;
And we, with all our wounds and all our powers,   190
Must each await alone at his own height
Another darkness or another light;
And there, of our poor self dominion reft,
If inference and reason shun
Hell, Heaven, and Oblivion,
May thwarted will (perforce precarious,
But for our conservation better thus)
Have no misgiving left
Of doing yet what here we leave undone?
Or if unto the last of these we cleave,   200
Believing or protesting we believe
In such an idle and ephemeral
Florescence of the diabolical,—
If, robbed of two fond old enormities,
Our being had no onward auguries,
What then were this great love of ours to say
For launching other lives to voyage again
A little farther into time and pain,
A little faster in a futile chase
For a kingdom and a power and a Race   210
That would have still in sight
A manifest end of ashes and eternal night?
Is this the music of the toys we shake
So loud,—as if there might be no mistake
Somewhere in our indomitable will?
Are we no greater than the noise we make
Along one blind atomic pilgrimage
Whereon by crass chance billeted we go
Because our brains and bones and cartilage
Will have it so?   220

If this we say, then let us all be still
About our share in it, and live and die
More quietly thereby.

Where was he going, this man against the sky?
You know not, nor do I.
But this we know, if we know anything:
That we may laugh and fight and sing
And of our transience here make offering
To an orient Word that will not be erased,
Or, save in incommunicable gleams   230
Too permanent for dreams,
Be found or known.
No tonic and ambitious irritant
Of increase or of want
Has made an otherwise insensate waste
Of ages overthrown
A ruthless, veiled, implacable foretaste
Of other ages that are still to be
Depleted and rewarded variously
Because a few, by fate's economy,   240
Shall seem to move the world the way it goes;
No soft evangel of equality,
Safe cradled in a communal repose
That huddles into death and may at last
Be covered well with equatorial snows—
And all for what, the devil only knows—
Will aggregate an inkling to confirm
The credit of a sage or of a worm,
Or tell us why one man in five
Should have a care to stay alive   250
While in his heart he feels no violence
Laid on his humor and intelligence
When infant Science makes a pleasant face
And waves again that hollow toy, the Race;
No planetary trap where souls are wrought
For nothing but the sake of being caught
And sent again to nothing will attune
Itself to any key of any reason
Why man should hunger through another season

To find out why 'twere better late than soon   260
To go away and let the sun and moon
And all the silly stars illuminate
A place for creeping things,
And those that root and trumpet and have wings,
And herd and ruminate,
Or dive and flash and poise in rivers and seas,
Or by their loyal tails in lofty trees
Hang screeching lewd victorious derision
Of man's immortal vision.

Shall we, because Eternity records   270
Too vast an answer for the time-born words
We spell, whereof so many are dead that once
In our capricious lexicons
Were so alive and final, hear no more
The Word itself, the living word
That none alive has ever heard
Or ever spelt,
And few have ever felt
Without the fears and old surrenderings
And terrors that began   280
When Death let fall a feather from his wings
And humbled the first man?
Because the weight of our humility,
Wherefrom we gain
A little wisdom and much pain,
Falls here too sore and there too tedious,
Are we in anguish or complacency,
Not looking far enough ahead
To see by what mad couriers we are led
Along the roads of the ridiculous,   290
To pity ourselves and laugh at faith
And while we curse life bear it?
And if we see the soul's dead end in death,
Are we to fear it?
What folly is here that has not yet a name
Unless we say outright that we are liars?
What have we seen beyond our sunset fires
That lights again the way by which we came?

Why pay we such a price, and one we give
So clamoringly, for each racked empty day   300
That leads one more last human hope away,
As quiet fiends would lead past our crazed eyes
Our children to an unseen sacrifice?
If after all that we have lived and thought,
All comes to Nought,—
If there be nothing after Now,
And we be nothing anyhow,
And we know that,—why live?
'Twere sure but weaklings' vain distress
To suffer dungeons where so many doors   310
Will open on the cold eternal shores
That look sheer down
To the dark tideless floods of Nothingness
Where all who know may drown.

DEMOS   [1920]

All you that are enamored of my name
      And least intent on what most I require,
      Beware; for my design and your desire,
Deplorably, are not as yet the same.
Beware, I say, the failure and the shame
      Of losing that for which you now aspire
      So blindly, and of hazarding entire
The gift that I was bringing when I came.

Give as I will, I cannot give you sight
      Whereby to see that with you there are some   10
      To lead you, and be led. But they are dumb
Before the wrangling and the shrill delight
      Of your deliverance that has not come,
And shall not, if I fail you—as I might.

II

So little have you seen of what awaits
      Your fevered glimpse of a democracy

Confused and foiled with an equality
Not equal to the envy it creates,
That you see not how near you are the gates
    Of an old king who listens fearfully   **20**
    To you that are outside and are to be
The noisy lords of imminent estates.

Rather be then your prayer that you shall have
    Your kingdom undishonored. Having all,
    See not the great among you for the small,
But hear their silence; for the few shall save
    The many, or the many are to fall—
Still to be wrangling in a noisy grave.

THE DARK HILLS   [1920]

Dark hills at evening in the west,
Where sunset hovers like a sound
Of golden horns that sang to rest
Old bones of warriors under ground,
Far now from all the bannered ways
Where flash the legions of the sun,
You fade—as if the last of days
Were fading, and all wars were done.

MR. FLOOD'S PARTY   [1921]

Old Eben Flood, climbing alone one night
Over the hill between the town below
And the forsaken upland hermitage
That held as much as he should ever know
On earth again of home, paused warily.
The road was his with not a native near;
And Eben, having leisure, said aloud,
For no man else in Tilbury Town to hear:

"Well, Mr. Flood, we have the harvest moon
Again, and we may not have many more;   10
The bird is on the wing, the poet says,
And you and I have said it here before.
Drink to the bird." He raised up to the light
The jug that he had gone so far to fill,
And answered huskily: "Well, Mr. Flood,
Since you propose it, I believe I will."

Alone, as if enduring to the end
A valiant armor of scarred hopes outworn,
He stood there in the middle of the road
Like Roland's ghost winding a silent horn.   20
Below him, in the town among the trees,
Where friends of other days had honored him,
A phantom salutation of the dead
Rang thinly till old Eben's eyes were dim.

Then, as a mother lays her sleeping child
Down tenderly, fearing it may awake,
He set the jug down slowly at his feet
With trembling care, knowing that most things break;
And only when assured that on firm earth
It stood, as the uncertain lives of men   30
Assuredly did not, he paced away,
And with his hand extended paused again:

"Well, Mr. Flood, we have not met like this
In a long time; and many a change has come
To both of us, I fear, since last it was
We had a drop together. Welcome home!"
Convivially returning with himself,
Again he raised the jug up to the light;
And with an acquiescent quaver said:
"Well, Mr. Flood, if you insist, I might.   40

"Only a very little, Mr. Flood—
For auld lang syne. No more, sir; that will do."
So, for the time, apparently it did,
And Eben evidently thought so too;

For soon amid the silver loneliness
Of night he lifted up his voice and sang,
Secure, with only two moons listening,
Until the whole harmonious landscape rang—

"For auld lang syne." The weary throat gave out,
The last word wavered, and the song was done.   50
He raised again the jug regretfully
And shook his head, and was again alone.
There was not much that was ahead of him,
And there was nothing in the town below—
Where strangers would have shut the many doors
That many friends had opened long ago.

THE SHEAVES   [1925]

Where long the shadows of the wind had rolled,
Green wheat was yielding to the change assigned;
And as by some vast magic undivined
The world was turning slowly into gold.
Like nothing that was ever bought or sold
It waited there, the body and the mind;
And with a mighty meaning of a kind
That tells the more the more it is not told.

So in a land where all days are not fair,
Fair days went on till on another day   10
A thousand golden sheaves were lying there,
Shining and still, but not for long to stay—
As if a thousand girls with golden hair
Might rise from where they slept and go away.

KARMA   [1925]

Christmas was in the air and all was well
With him, but for a few confusing flaws

In divers of God's images. Because
A friend of his would neither buy nor sell,
Was he to answer for the axe that fell?
He pondered; and the reason for it was,
Partly, a slowly freezing Santa Claus
Upon the corner, with his beard and bell.

Acknowledging an improvident surprise,
He magnified a fancy that he wished   10
The friend whom he had wrecked were here again.
Not sure of that, he found a compromise;
And from the fulness of his heart he fished
A dime for Jesus who had died for men.

Stephen Crane

1871–1900

Stephen Crane was born in Newark, New Jersey, on November 1,
1871, the fourteenth child of the Reverend Jonathan Crane. Both his
father and his mother, Mary Helen Peck, were militant leaders in the
Methodist Church. One of Crane's dominant characteristics was his
rebellion against his parents' religion, and much of his poetry ruminates
on religious and theological questions. He began writing poetry soon after
completing The Red Badge of Courage *(1895). His technique is said*
to have derived from Whitman and Emily Dickinson, but it more closely
resembles contemporary French vers libre, *though there is no evidence*
that Crane had read it. The only extended study of Crane's poetry is by
Daniel G. Hoffman, but John Berryman has also explored the psy-
chology of his symbolism. The poems had few readers until they were
republished in 1930. Since then Stephen Crane's reputation as a poet
has slowly gained favor.

From *The Black Riders* [1895]

I

Black riders came from the sea.
There was clang and clang of spear and shield,
And clash and clash of hoof and heel,
Wild shouts and the wave of hair
In the rush upon the wind:
Thus the ride of Sin.

III

In the desert
I saw a creature, naked, bestial,
Who, squatting upon the ground,
Held his heart in his hands,
And ate of it.
I said, "Is it good, friend?"
"It is bitter—bitter," he answered;
"But I like it
Because it is bitter,
And because it is my heart."   10

VI

God fashioned the ship of the world carefully.
With the infinite skill of an All-Master
Made He the hull and the sails,
Held He the rudder
Ready for adjustment.
Erect stood He, scanning His work proudly.
Then—at fateful time—a wrong called,
And God turned, heeding.
Lo, the ship, at this opportunity, slipped slyly,
Making cunning noiseless travel down the ways.   10
So that, for ever rudderless, it went upon the seas
Going ridiculous voyages,
Making quaint progress,
Turning as with serious purpose
Before stupid winds.
And there were many in the sky
Who laughed at this thing.

VIII

I looked here;
I looked there;
Nowhere could I see my love.
And—this time—
She was in my heart.
Truly, then, I have no complaint,
For though she be fair and fairer,
She is none so fair as she
In my heart.

IX

I stood upon a high place,
And saw, below, many devils
Running, leaping,
And carousing in sin.
One looked up, grinning,
And said, "Comrade! Brother!"

X

Should the wide world roll away,
Leaving black terror,
Limitless night,
Nor God, nor man, nor place to stand
Would be to me essential,
If thou and thy white arms were there,
And the fall to doom a long way.

XII

"And the sins of the fathers shall be visited upon the heads of
the children, even unto the third and fourth generation of them
that hate me."

Well, then, I hate Thee, unrighteous picture;
Wicked image, I hate Thee;
So, strike with Thy vengeance
The heads of those little men
Who come blindly.
It will be a brave thing.

XIV

There was crimson clash of war.
Lands turned black and bare;
Women wept;
Babes ran, wondering.
There came one who understood not these things.
He said, "Why is this?"
Whereupon a million strove to answer him.
There was such intricate clamour of tongues,
That still the reason was not.

XVIII

In heaven,
Some little blades of grass
Stood before God.
"What did you do?"
Then all save one of the little blades
Began eagerly to relate

The merits of their lives.
This one stayed a small way behind,
Ashamed.
Presently, God said,   10
"And what did you do?"
The little blade answered, "O my lord,
Memory is bitter to me,
For, if I did good deeds,
I know not of them."
Then God, in all His splendor,
Arose from His throne.
"Oh, best little blade of grass!" He said.

XIX

A god in wrath
Was beating a man;
He cuffed him loudly
With thunderous blows
That rang and rolled over the earth.
All people came running.
The man screamed and struggled,
And bit madly at the feet of the god.
The people cried,
"Ah, what a wicked man!"   10
And—
"Ah, what a redoubtable god!"

XXI

There was, before me,
Mile upon mile
Of snow, ice, burning sand.
And yet I could look beyond all this,

To a place of infinite beauty;
And I could see the loveliness of her
Who walked in the shade of the trees.
When I gazed,
All was lost
But this place of beauty and her.
When I gazed,
And in my gazing, desired,
Then came again
Mile upon mile,
Of snow, ice, burning sand.

XXIII

Places among the stars,
Soft gardens near the sun,
Keep your distant beauty;
Shed no beams upon my weak heart.
Since she is here
In a place of blackness,
Not your golden days
Nor your silver nights
Can call me to you.
Since she is here   10
In a place of blackness,
Here I stay and wait.

XXIV

I saw a man pursuing the horizon;
Round and round they sped.
I was disturbed at this;
I accosted the man.
"It is futile," I said,
"You can never—"

"You lie," he cried,
And ran on.

XXVIII

"Truth," said a traveller,
"Is a rock, a mighty fortress;
Often have I been to it,
Even to its highest tower,
From whence the world looks black."

"Truth," said a traveller,
"Is a breath, a wind,
A shadow, a phantom;
Long have I pursued it,
But never have I touched   10
The hem of its garment."

And I believed the second traveller;
For truth was to me
A breath, a wind,
A shadow, a phantom,
And never had I touched
The hem of its garment.

XXIX

Behold, from the land of the farther suns
I returned.
And I was in a reptile-swarming place,
Peopled, otherwise, with grimaces,
Shrouded above in black impenetrableness.
I shrank, loathing,
Sick with it.
And I said to Him,

"What is this?"
He made answer slowly,   10
"Spirit, this is a world;
This was your home."

XXXIV

I stood upon a highway,
And, behold, there came
Many strange peddlers.
To me each one made gestures,
Holding forth little images, saying,
"This is my pattern of God.
Now this is the God I prefer."

But I said, "Hence!
Leave me with mine own,
And take you yours away;   10
I can't buy of your patterns of God,
The little gods you may rightly prefer."

XXXIX

The livid lightnings flashed in the clouds;
The leaden thunders crashed.
A worshipper raised his arm.
"Hearken! hearken! The voice of God!"

"Not so," said a man.
"The voice of God whispers in the heart
So softly
That the soul pauses,
Making no noise,
And strives for these melodies,   10
Distant, sighing, like faintest breath,
And all the being is still to hear."

XLI

Love walked alone.
The rocks cut her tender feet,
And the brambles tore her fair limbs.
There came a companion to her,
But, alas, he was no help,
For his name was heart's pain.

XLVI

Many red devils ran from my heart
And out upon the page.
They were so tiny
The pen could mash them.
And many struggled in the ink.
It was strange
To write in this red muck
Of things from my heart.

XLIX

I stood musing in a black world,
Not knowing where to direct my feet.
And I saw the quick stream of men
Pouring ceaselessly,
Filled with eager faces,
A torrent of desire.
I called to them,
"Where do you go? What do you see?"
A thousand voices called to me.
A thousand fingers pointed.   10
"Look! Look! There!"

I know not of it.
But, lo! in the far sky shone a radiance
Ineffable, divine,—
A vision painted upon a pall;
And sometimes it was,
And sometimes it was not.
I hesitated.
Then from the stream
Came roaring voices,   20
Impatient:
"Look! Look! There!"

So again I saw,
And leaped, unhesitant,
And struggled and fumed
With outspread clutching fingers.
The hard hills tore my flesh;
The ways bit my feet.
At last I looked again.
No radiance in the far sky,   30
Ineffable, divine;
No vision painted upon a pall;
And always my eyes ached for the light.
Then I cried in despair,
"I see nothing! Oh, where do I go?"
The torrent turned again its faces:
"Look! Look! There!"

And at the blindness of my spirit
They screamed,
"Fool! Fool! Fool!"   40

LI

A man went before a strange God—
The God of many men, sadly wise.
And the Deity thundered loudly,

Fat with rage, and puffing,
"Kneel, mortal, and cringe
And grovel and do homage
To My Particularly Sublime Majesty."

The man fled.

Then the man went to another God,—
The God of his inner thoughts.   10
And this one looked at him
With soft eyes
Lit with infinite comprehension,
And said, "My poor child!"

LIV

"It was wrong to do this," said the angel.
"You should live like a flower,
Holding malice like a puppy,
Waging war like a lambkin."

"Not so," quoth the man
Who had no fear of spirits;
"It is only wrong for angels
Who can live like the flowers,
Holding malice like the puppies,
Waging war like the lambkins."   10

LX

Upon the road of my life,
Passed me many fair creatures,
Clothed all in white, and radiant.
To one, finally, I made speech:

"Who art thou?"
But she, like the others,
Kept cowled her face,
And answered in haste, anxiously,
"I am Good Deed, forsooth;
You have often seen me."   10
"Not uncowled," I made reply.
And with rash and strong hand,
Though she resisted,
I drew away the veil
And gazed at the features of vanity.
She, shamefaced, went on;
And after I had mused a time,
I said of myself,
                    "Fool!"

LXVI

If I should cast off this tattered coat,
And go free into the mighty sky;
If I should find nothing there
But a vast blue,
Echoless, ignorant—
What then?

LXVII

God lay dead in heaven;
Angels sang the hymn of the end;
Purple winds went moaning,
Their wings drip-dripping
With blood
That fell upon the earth.
It, groaning thing,

Turned black and sank.
Then from the far caverns
Of dead sins   10
Came monsters, livid with desire.
They fought,
Wrangled over the world,
A morsel.
But of all sadness this was sad—
A woman's arms tried to shield
The head of a sleeping man
From the jaws of the final beast.

THE BLUE BATTALIONS   [1898]

When a people reach the top of a hill,
Then does God lean toward them,
Shortens tongues and lengthens arms.
A vision of their dead comes to the weak.
The moon shall not be too old
Before the new battalions rise,
                    Blue battalions.
The moon shall not be too old
When the children of change shall fall
Before the new battalions,   10
                    The blue battalions.

Mistakes and virtues will be trampled deep.
A church and a thief shall fall together.
A sword will come at the bidding of the eyeless,
The God-led, turning only to beckon,
    Swinging a creed like a censer
    At the head of the new battalions,
                    Blue battalions.
    March the tools of nature's impulse,
    Men born of wrong, men born of right,   20
    Men of the new battalions,
                    The blue battalions.

The clang of swords is Thy wisdom,
The wounded make gestures like Thy Son's;
The feet of mad horses is one part—
Ay, another is the hand of a mother on the brow of a
        youth.
    Then, swift as they charge through a shadow,
    The men of the new battalions,
                        Blue battalions—
God lead them high, God lead them far,   30
God lead them far, God lead them high,
These new battalions.
                    The blue battalions.

From *War Is Kind* [1899]

[1]

Do not weep, maiden, for war is kind.
Because your lover threw wild hands toward the sky
And the affrighted steed ran on alone,
Do not weep.
War is kind.

        Hoarse, booming drums of the regiment,
        Little souls who thirst for fight,
        These men were born to drill and die.
        The unexplained glory flies above them,
        Great is the battle-god, great, and his kingdom—   10
        A field where a thousand corpses lie.

Do not weep, babe, for war is kind.
Because your father tumbled in the yellow trenches,
Raged at his breast, gulped and died,
Do not weep.
War is kind.

Swift blazing flag of the regiment,
Eagle with crest of red and gold,
These men were born to drill and die.
Point for them the virtue of slaughter,   20
Make plain to them the excellence of killing
And a field where a thousand corpses lie.

Mother whose heart hung humble as a button
On the bright splendid shroud of your son,
Do not weep.
War is kind.

[VI]

I explain the silvered passing of a ship at night,
The sweep of each sad lost wave,
The dwindling boom of the steel thing's striving,
The little cry of a man to a man,
A shadow falling across the greyer night,
And the sinking of the small star;
Then the waste, the far waste of waters,
And the soft lashing of black waves
For long and in loneliness.

Remember, thou, O ship of love,   10
Thou leavest a far waste of waters,
And the soft lashing of black waves
For long and in loneliness.

[VII]

"I have heard the sunset song of the birches,
A white melody in the silence,
I have seen a quarrel of the pines.

At nightfall
The little grasses have rushed by me
With the wind men.
These things have I lived," quoth the maniac,
"Possessing only eyes and ears.
But you—
You don green spectacles before you look at roses."   10

[XI]

On the desert
A silence from the moon's deepest valley.
Fire rays fall athwart the robes
Of hooded men, squat and dumb.
Before them, a woman
Moves to the blowing of shrill whistles
And distant thunder of drums,
While mystic things, sinuous, dull with terrible color,
Sleepily fondle her body
Or move at her will, swishing stealthily over the sand.   10
The snakes whisper softly;
The whispering, whispering snakes,
Dreaming and swaying and staring,
But always whispering, softly whispering.
The wind streams from the lone reaches
Of Arabia, solemn with night,
And the wild fire makes shimmer of blood
Over the robes of the hooded men
Squat and dumb.
Bands of moving bronze, emerald, yellow,   20
Circle the throat and the arms of her,
And over the sands serpents move warily
Slow, menacing and submissive,
Swinging to the whistles and drums,
The whispering, whispering snakes,
Dreaming and swaying and staring,
But always whispering, softly whispering.

The dignity of the accursèd;
The glory of slavery, despair, death,
Is in the dance of the whispering snakes.   30

[XII]

A newspaper is a collection of half-injustices
Which, bawled by boys from mile to mile,
Spreads its curious opinion
To a million merciful and sneering men,
While families cuddle the joys of the fireside
When spurred by tale of dire lone agony.
A newspaper is a court
Where every one is kindly and unfairly tried
By a squalor of honest men.
A newspaper is a market   10
Where wisdom sells its freedom
And melons are crowned by the crowd.
A newspaper is a game
Where his error scores the player victory
While another's skill wins death.
A newspaper is a symbol;
It is feckless life's chronicle,
A collection of loud tales
Concentrating eternal stupidities,
That in remote ages lived unhaltered,   20
Roaming through a fenceless world.

[XVIII]

In the night
Grey heavy clouds muffled the valleys,
And the peaks looked toward God alone.
    "O Master that movest the wind with a finger,
    Humble, idle, futile peaks are we.

Grant that we may run swiftly across the world
To huddle in worship at Thy feet."

In the morning
A noise of men at work came the clear blue miles,
And the little black cities were apparent.   10
  "O Master that knowest the meaning of raindrops,
  Humble, idle, futile peaks are we.
  Give voice to us, we pray, O Lord,
  That we may sing Thy goodness to the sun."

In the evening
The far valleys were sprinkled with tiny lights.
  "O Master,
  Thou that knowest the value of kings and birds,
  Thou hast made us humble, idle, futile peaks.
  Thou only needest eternal patience;   20
  We bow to Thy wisdom, O Lord—
  Humble, idle, futile peaks."

In the night
Grey clouds muffled the valleys,
And the peaks looked toward God alone.

[XIX]

The chatter of a death-demon from a tree-top.

Blood—blood and torn grass—
Had marked the rise of his agony—
This lone hunter.
The grey-green woods impassive
Had watched the threshing of his limbs.

A canoe with flashing paddle,
A girl with soft searching eyes,
A call: "John!"

.   .   .   .

Come, arise, hunter!   10
Can you not hear?

The chatter of a death-demon from a tree-top.

[XXI]

A man said to the universe:
"Sir, I exist!"
"However," replied the universe,
"The fact has not created in me
A sense of obligation."

[XXIII]

There was a land where lived no violets.
A traveller at once demanded: "Why?"
The people told him:
"Once the violets of this place spoke thus:
'Until some woman freely gives her lover
To another woman
We will fight in bloody scuffle.'"
Sadly the people added:
"There are no violets here."

THREE POEMS   [1930]

I

A man adrift on a slim spar
A horizon smaller than the rim of a bottle
Tented waves rearing lashy dark points
The near whine of froth in circles.
                    God is cold.

The incessant raise and swing of the sea
And growl after growl of crest
The sinkings, green, seething, endless
The upheaval half-completed.
                    God is cold.   10

The seas are in the hollow of The Hand;
Oceans may be turned to a spray
Raining down through the stars
Because of a gesture of pity toward a babe.
Oceans may become grey ashes,
Die with a long moan and a roar
Amid the tumult of the fishes
And the cries of the ships,
Because The Hand beckons the mice.
A horizon smaller than a doomed assassin's cap,   20
Inky, surging tumults
A reeling, drunken sky and no sky
A pale hand sliding from a polished spar.
                    God is cold.

The puff of a coat imprisoning air:
A face kissing the water-death
A weary slow sway of a lost hand
And the sea, the moving sea, the sea.
                    God is cold.

II

Chant you loud of punishments,
Of the twisting of the heart's poor strings
Of the crash of the lightning's fierce revenge.

Then sing I of the supple-souled men
And the strong, strong gods
That shall meet in times hereafter
And the amaze of the gods
At the strength of the men.
—The strong, strong gods—
—And the supple-souled men—   10

III

A naked woman and a dead dwarf;
Poor dwarf!
Reigning with foolish kings
And dying mid bells and wine
Ending with a desperate comic palaver
While before thee and after thee
Endures the eternal clown—
—The eternal clown—
A naked woman.

Robert Frost

1874–1963

Robert Frost was born March 26, 1874, in San Francisco of New England parentage. When Frost was eleven his father died and his mother took him back to her parents' home in Lawrence, Massachusetts, where she taught school. Frost studied at Harvard for two years, then tried teaching, newspaper work, shoemaking, and farming. From 1912 to 1915 he lived in England, where he first won recognition as a poet. Back in the United States, he taught at several colleges, for twenty years at Amherst. He received the Pulitzer Prize for Poetry four times and numerous other awards and honors. He died in Boston on January 29, 1963.

THE TUFT OF FLOWERS   [1913]

I went to turn the grass once after one
Who mowed it in the dew before the sun.

The dew was gone that made his blade so keen
Before I came to view the leveled scene.

I looked for him behind an isle of trees;
I listened for his whetstone on the breeze.

But he had gone his way, the grass all mown,
And I must be, as he had been,—alone,

"As all must be," I said within my heart,
"Whether they work together or apart."

But as I said it, swift there passed me by
On noiseless wing a bewildered butterfly,

Seeking with memories grown dim o'er night
Some resting flower of yesterday's delight.

And once I marked his flight go round and round,
As where some flower lay withering on the ground.

And then he flew as far as eye could see,
And then on tremulous wing came back to me.

I thought of questions that have no reply,
And would have turned to toss the grass to dry;   20

But he turned first, and led my eye to look
At a tall tuft of flowers beside a brook,

A leaping tongue of bloom the scythe had spared
Beside a reedy brook the scythe had bared.

The mower in the dew had loved them thus,
By leaving them to flourish, not for us,

Nor yet to draw one thought of ours to him,
But from sheer morning gladness at the brim.

The butterfly and I had lit upon,
Nevertheless, a message from the dawn,   30

That made me hear the wakening birds around,
And hear his long scythe whispering to the ground,

And feel a spirit kindred to my own;
So that henceforth I worked no more alone;

But glad with him, I worked as with his aid,
And weary, sought at noon with him the shade;

And dreaming, as it were, held brotherly speech
With one whose thought I had not hoped to reach.

"Men work together," I told him from the heart,
"Whether they work together or apart." 40

MENDING WALL [1914]

Something there is that doesn't love a wall,
That sends the frozen-ground-swell under it,
And spills the upper boulders in the sun;
And makes gaps even two can pass abreast.
The work of hunters is another thing:
I have come after them and made repair
Where they have left not one stone on a stone,
But they would have the rabbit out of hiding,
To please the yelping dogs. The gaps I mean,
No one has seen them made or heard them made, 10
But at spring mending-time we find them there.
I let my neighbor know beyond the hill;
And on a day we meet to walk the line
And set the wall between us once again.
We keep the wall between us as we go.
To each the boulders that have fallen to each.
And some are loaves and some so nearly balls
We have to use a spell to make them balance:
"Stay where you are until our backs are turned!"
We wear our fingers rough with handling them. 20
Oh, just another kind of outdoor game,
One on a side. It comes to little more:
There where it is we do not need the wall:
He is all pine and I am apple orchard.
My apple trees will never get across
And eat the cones under his pines, I tell him.
He only says, "Good fences make good neighbors."
Spring is the mischief in me, and I wonder
If I could put a notion in his head:
"*Why* do they make good neighbors? Isn't it 30
Where there are cows? But here there are no cows.
Before I built a wall I'd ask to know

What I was walling in or walling out,
And to whom I was like to give offense.
Something there is that doesn't love a wall,
That wants it down." I could say "Elves" to him,
But it's not elves exactly, and I'd rather
He said it for himself. I see him there
Bringing a stone grasped firmly by the top
In each hand, like an old-stone savage armed.   40
He moves in darkness as it seems to me,
Not of woods only and the shade of trees.
He will not go behind his father's saying,
And he likes having thought of it so well
He says again, "Good fences make good neighbors."

HOME BURIAL   [1914]

He saw her from the bottom of the stairs
Before she saw him. She was starting down,
Looking back over her shoulder at some fear.
She took a doubtful step and then undid it
To raise herself and look again. He spoke
Advancing toward her: "What is it you see
From up there always—for I want to know."
She turned and sank upon her skirts at that,
And her face changed from terrified to dull.
He said to gain time: "What is it you see,"   10
Mounting until she cowered under him.
"I will find out now—you must tell me, dear."
She, in her place, refused him any help
With the least stiffening of her neck and silence.
She let him look, sure that he wouldn't see,
Blind creature; and awhile he didn't see.
But at last he murmured, "Oh," and again, "Oh."

"What is it—what?" she said.

                    "Just that I see."

"You don't," she challenged. "Tell me what it is."

"The wonder is I didn't see at once.   20
I never noticed it from here before.
I must be wonted to it—that's the reason.
The little graveyard where my people are!
So small the window frames the whole of it.
Not so much larger than a bedroom, is it?
There are three stones of slate and one of marble,
Broad-shouldered little slabs there in the sunlight
On the sidehill. We haven't to mind *those*.
But I understand: it is not the stones,
But the child's mound—"

           "Don't, don't, don't, don't," she cried.

She withdrew shrinking from beneath his arm   31
That rested on the bannister, and slid downstairs;
And turned on him with such a daunting look,
He said twice over before he knew himself:
"Can't a man speak of his own child he's lost?"

"Not you! Oh, where's my hat? Oh, I don't need it!
I must get out of here. I must get air.
I don't know rightly whether any man can."

"Amy! Don't go to someone else this time.
Listen to me. I won't come down the stairs."   40
He sat and fixed his chin between his fists.
"There's something I should like to ask you, dear."

"You don't know how to ask it."

           "Help me, then."

Her fingers moved the latch for all reply.

"My words are nearly always an offense.
I don't know how to speak of anything

So as to please you. But I'might be taught
I should suppose. I can't say I see how.
A man must partly give up being a man
With women-folk. We could have some arrangement   50
By which I'd bind myself to keep hands off
Anything special you're a-mind to name.
Though I don't like such things 'twixt those that love.
Two that don't love can't live together without them.
But two that do can't live together with them."
She moved the latch a little. "Don't—don't go.
Don't carry it to someone else this time.
Tell me about it if it's something human.
Let me into your grief. I'm not so much
Unlike other folks as your standing there   60
Apart would make me out. Give me my chance.
I do think, though, you overdo it a little.
What was it brought you up to think it the thing
To take your mother-loss of a first child
So inconsolably—in the face of love.
You'd think his memory might be satisfied—"

"There you go sneering now!"

                        "I'm not, I'm not!
You make me angry. I'll come down to you.
God, what a woman! And it's come to this,
A man can't speak of his own child that's dead."   70

"You can't because you don't know how to speak.
If you had any feelings, you that dug
With your own hand—how could you?—his little grave;
I saw you from that very window there,
Making the gravel leap and leap in air,
Leap up, like that, like that, and land so lightly
And roll back down the mound beside the hole.
I thought, Who is that man? I didn't know you.
And I crept down the stairs and up the stairs
To look again, and still your spade kept lifting.   80
Then you came in. I heard your rumbling voice

Out in the kitchen, and I don't know why,
But I went near to see with my own eyes.
You could sit there with the stains on your shoes
Of the fresh earth from your own baby's grave
And talk about your everyday concerns.
You had stood the spade up against the wall
Outside there in the entry, for I saw it."

"I shall laugh the worst laugh I ever laughed.
I'm cursed. God, if I don't believe I'm cursed."   90

"I can repeat the very words you were saying.
'Three foggy mornings and one rainy day
Will rot the best birch fence a man can build.'
Think of it, talk like that at such a time!
What had how long it takes a birch to rot
To do with what was in the darkened parlor.
You *couldn't* care! The nearest friends can go
With anyone to death, comes so far short
They might as well not try to go at all.
No, from the time when one is sick to death,   100
One is alone, and he dies more alone.
Friends make pretense of following to the grave,
But before one is in it, their minds are turned
And making the best of their way back to life
And living people, and things they understand.
But the world's evil. I won't have grief so
If I can change it. Oh, I won't, I won't!"

"There, you have said it all and you feel better.
You won't go now. You're crying. Close the door.
The heart's gone out of it: why keep it up.   110
Amy! There's someone coming down the road!"

"*You*—oh, you think the talk is all. I must go—
Somewhere out of this house. How can I make you—"

"If—you—do!" She was opening the door wider.
"Where do you mean to go? First tell me that.
I'll follow and bring you back by force. I *will!*—"

AFTER APPLE-PICKING [1914]

My long two-pointed ladder's sticking through a tree
Toward heaven still,
And there's a barrel that I didn't fill
Beside it, and there may be two or three
Apples I didn't pick upon some bough.
But I am done with apple-picking now.
Essence of winter sleep is on the night,
The scent of apples: I am drowsing off.
I cannot rub the strangeness from my sight
I got from looking through a pane of glass 10
I skimmed this morning from the drinking trough
And held against the world of hoary grass.
It melted, and I let if fall and break.
But I was well
Upon my way to sleep before it fell,
And I could tell
What form my dreaming was about to take.
Magnified apples appear and disappear,
Stem end and blossom end,
And every fleck of russet showing clear. 20
My instep arch not only keeps the ache,
It keeps the pressure of a ladder-round.
I feel the ladder sway as the boughs bend.
And I keep hearing from the cellar bin
The rumbling sound
Of load on load of apples coming in.
For I have had too much
Of apple-picking: I am overtired
Of the great harvest I myself desired.
There were ten thousand thousand fruit to touch, 30
Cherish in hand, lift down, and not let fall.
For all
That struck the earth,
No matter if not bruised or spiked with stubble,
Went surely to the cider-apple heap
As of no worth.

One can see what will trouble
This sleep of mine, whatever sleep it is.
Were he not gone,
The woodchuck could say whether it's like his   40
Long sleep, as I describe its coming on,
Or just some human sleep.

THE ROAD NOT TAKEN   [1916]

Two roads diverged in a yellow wood,
And sorry I could not travel both
And be one traveler, long I stood
And looked down one as far as I could
To where it bent in the undergrowth;

Then took the other, as just as fair,
And having perhaps the better claim,
Because it was grassy and wanted wear;
Though as for that the passing there
Had worn them really about the same,   10

And both that morning equally lay
In leaves no step had trodden black.
Oh, I kept the first for another day!
Yet knowing how way leads on to way,
I doubted if I should ever come back.

I shall be telling this with a sigh
Somewhere ages and ages hence:
Two roads diverged in a wood, and I—
I took the one less traveled by,
And that has made all the difference.   20

THE OVEN BIRD   [1916]

There is a singer everyone has heard,
Loud, a mid-summer and a mid-wood bird,

Who makes the solid tree trunks sound again.
He says that leaves are old and that for flowers
Mid-summer is to spring as one to ten.
He says the early petal-fall is past
When pear and cherry bloom went down in showers
On sunny days a moment overcast;
And comes that other fall we name the fall.
He says the highway dust is over all.   10
The bird would cease and be as other birds
But that he knows in singing not to sing.
The question that he frames in all but words
Is what to make of a diminished thing.

THE WITCH OF COÖS   [1923]

(from "Two Witches")

I stayed the night for shelter at a farm
Behind the mountain, with a mother and son,
Two old-believers. They did all the talking.

MOTHER. Folks think a witch who has familiar spirits
She could call up to pass a winter evening,
But won't, should be burned at the stake or something.
Summoning spirits isn't "Button, button,
Who's got the button," I would have them know.

SON. Mother can make a common table rear
And kick with two legs like an army mule.   10

MOTHER. And when I've done it, what good have I done?
Rather than tip a table for you, let me
Tell you what Ralle the Sioux Control once told me.
He said the dead had souls, but when I asked him
How could that be—I thought the dead were souls,
He broke my trance. Don't that make you suspicious
That there's something the dead are keeping back?
Yes, there's something the dead are keeping back.

SON. You wouldn't want to tell him what we have
Up attic, mother?   20

MOTHER. Bones—a skeleton.

SON. But the headboard of mother's bed is pushed
Against the attic door: the door is' nailed.
It's harmless. Mother hears it in the night
Halting perplexed behind the barrier
Of door and headboard. Where it wants to get
Is back into the cellar where it came from.

MOTHER. We'll never let them, will we, son! We'll never!

SON. It left the cellar forty years ago
And carried itself like a pile of dishes   30
Up one flight from the cellar to the kitchen,
Another from the kitchen to the bedroom,
Another from the bedroom to the attic,
Right past both father and mother, and neither stopped it.
Father had gone upstairs; mother was downstairs.
I was a baby: I don't know where I was.

MOTHER. The only fault my husband found with me—
I went to sleep before I went to bed,
Especially in winter when the bed
Might just as well be ice and the clothes snow.   40
The night the bones came up the cellar-stairs
Toffile had gone to bed alone and left me,
But left an open door to cool the room off
So as to sort of turn me out of it.
I was just coming to myself enough
To wonder where the cold was coming from,
When I heard Toffile upstairs in the bedroom
And thought I heard him downstairs in the cellar.
The board we had laid down to walk dry-shod on
When there was water in the cellar in spring   50
Struck the hard cellar bottom. And then someone
Began the stairs, two footsteps for each step,
The way a man with one leg and a crutch,

Or a little child, comes up. It wasn't Toffile:
It wasn't anyone who could be there.
The bulkhead double-doors were double-locked
And swollen tight and buried under snow.
The cellar windows were banked up with sawdust
And swollen tight and buried under snow.
It was the bones. I knew them—and good reason.			60
My first impulse was to get to the knob
And hold the door. But the bones didn't try
The door; they halted helpless on the landing,
Waiting for things to happen in their favor.
The faintest restless rustling ran all through them.
I never could have done the thing I did
If the wish hadn't been too strong in me
To see how they were mounted for this walk.
I had a vision of them put together
Not like a man, but like a chandelier.				70
So suddenly I flung the door wide on him.
A moment he stood balancing with emotion,
And all but lost himself. (A tongue of fire
Flashed out and licked along his upper teeth.
Smoke rolled inside the sockets of his eyes.)
Then he came at me with one hand outstretched,
The way he did in life once; but this time
I struck the hand off brittle on the floor,
And fell back from him on the floor myself.
The finger-pieces slid in all directions.				80
(Where did I see one of those pieces lately?
Hand me my button-box—it must be there.)
I sat up on the floor and shouted, "Toffile,
It's coming up to you." It had its choice
Of the door to the cellar or the hall.
It took the hall door for the novelty,
And set off briskly for so slow a thing,
Still going every which way in the joints, though,
So that it looked like lightning or a scribble,
From the slap I had just now given its hand.			90
I listened till it almost climbed the stairs
From the hall to the only finished bedroom,
Before I got up to do anything;

Then ran and shouted, "Shut the bedroom door,
Toffile, for my sake!" "Company?" he said,
"Don't make me get up; I'm too warm in bed."
So lying forward weakly on the handrail
I pushed myself upstairs, and in the light
(The kitchen had been dark) I had to own
I could see nothing. "Toffile, I don't see it.   100
It's with us in the room though. It's the bones."
"What bones?" "The cellar bones—out of the grave."
That made him throw his bare legs out of bed
And sit up by me and take hold of me.
I wanted to put out the light and see
If I could see it, or else mow the room,
With our arms at the level of our knees,
And bring the chalk-pile down. "I'll tell you what—
It's looking for another door to try.
The uncommonly deep snow has made him think   110
Of his old song, *The Wild Colonial Boy*,
He always used to sing along the tote road.
He's after an open door to get outdoors.
Let's trap him with an open door up attic."
Toffile agreed to that, and sure enough,
Almost the moment he was given an opening,
The steps began to climb the attic stairs.
I heard them. Toffile didn't seem to hear them.
"Quick!" I slammed to the door and held the knob.
"Toffile, get nails." I made him nail the door shut   120
And push the headboard of the bed against it.
Then we asked was there anything
Up attic that we'd never want again.
The attic was less to us than the cellar.
If the bones liked the attic, let them have it.
Let them stay in the attic. When they sometimes
Come down the stairs at night and stand perplexed
Behind the door and headboard of the bed,
Brushing their chalky skull with chalky fingers,
With sounds like the dry rattling of a shutter,   130
That's what I sit up in the dark to say—
To no one any more since Toffile died.
Let them stay in the attic since they went there.

I promised Toffile to be cruel to them
For helping them be cruel once to him.

SON. We think they had a grave down in the cellar.

MOTHER. We know they had a grave down in the cellar.

SON. We never could find out whose bones they were.

MOTHER. Yes, we could too, son. Tell the truth for once.
They were a man's his father killed for me.   140
I mean a man he killed instead of me.
The least I could do was to help dig their grave.
We were about it one night in the cellar.
Son knows the story: but 'twas not for him
To tell the truth, suppose the time had come.
Son looks surprised to see me end a lie
We'd kept all these years between ourselves
So as to have it ready for outsiders.
But tonight I don't care enough to lie—
I don't remember why I ever cared.   150
Toffile, if he were here, I don't believe
Could tell you why he ever cared himself. . . .

She hadn't found the finger-bone she wanted
Among the buttons poured out in her lap.
I verified the name next morning: Toffile.
The rural letter box said Toffile Lajway.

STOPPING BY WOODS ON A SNOWY
EVENING   [1923]

Whose woods these are I think I know.
His house is in the village though;
He will not see me stopping here
To watch his woods fill up with snow.

My little horse must think it queer
To stop without a farmhouse near
Between the woods and frozen lake
The darkest evening of the year.

He gives his harness bells a shake
To ask if there is some mistake.   10
The only other sound's the sweep
Of easy wind and downy flake.

The woods are lovely, dark and deep,
But I have promises to keep,
And miles to go before I sleep,
And miles to go before I sleep.

FOR ONCE, THEN, SOMETHING   [1923]

Others taunt me with having knelt at well-curbs
Always wrong to the light, so never seeing
Deeper down in the well than where the water
Gives me back in a shining surface picture
Me myself in the summer heaven godlike
Looking out of a wreath of fern and cloud puffs.
Once, when trying with chin against a well-curb,
I discerned, as I thought, beyond the picture,
Through the picture, a something white, uncertain,
Something more of the depths—and then I lost it.   10
Water came to rebuke the too clear water.
One drop fell from a fern, and lo, a ripple
Shook whatever it was lay there at bottom,
Blurred it, blotted it out. What was that whiteness?
Truth? A pebble of quartz? For once, then, something.

THE ONSET   [1923]

Always the same, when on a fated night
At last the gathered snow lets down as white

As may be in dark woods, and with a song
It shall not make again all winter long
Of hissing on the yet uncovered ground,
I almost stumble looking up and round,
As one who overtaken by the end
Gives up his errand, and lets death descend
Upon him where he is, with nothing done
To evil, no important triumph won,   10
More than if life had never been begun.

Yet all the precedent is on my side;
I know that winter death has never tried
The earth but it has failed: the snow may heap
In long storms an undrifted four feet deep
As measured against maple, birch, and oak,
It cannot check the peeper's silver croak;
And I shall see the snow all go down hill
In water of a slender April rill
That flashes tail through last year's withered brake   20
And dead weeds, like a disappearing snake,
Nothing will be left white but here a birch,
And there a clump of houses with a church.

TO EARTHWARD   [1923]

Love at the lips was touch
As sweet as I could bear;
And once that seemed too much;
I lived on air

That crossed me from sweet things
The flow of—was it musk
From hidden grapevine springs
Down hill at dusk?

I had the swirl and ache
From sprays of honeysuckle   10

That when they're gathered shake
Dew on the knuckle.

I craved strong sweets, but those
Seemed strong when I was young;
The petal of the rose
It was that stung.

Now no joy but lacks salt
That is not dashed with pain
And weariness and fault;
I crave the stain   20

Of tears, the aftermark
Of almost too much love,
The sweet of bitter bark
And burning clove.

When stiff and sore and scarred
I take away my hand
From leaning on it hard
In grass and sand,

The hurt is not enough:
I long for weight and strength   30
To feel the earth as rough
To all my length.

TWO LOOK AT TWO   [1923]

Love and forgetting might have carried them
A little further up the mountain side
With night so near, but not much further up.
They must have halted soon in any case
With thoughts of the path back, how rough it was
With rock and washout, and unsafe in darkness;
When they were halted by a tumbled wall
With barbed-wire binding. They stood facing this,
Spending what onward impulse they still had

In one last look the way they must not go,   10
On up the failing path, where, if a stone
Or earthslide moved at night, it moved itself;
No footstep moved it. "This is all," they sighed,
"Good-night to woods." But not so; there was more.
A doe from round a spruce stood looking at them
Across the wall, as near the wall as they.
She saw them in their field, they her in hers.
The difficulty of seeing what stood still,
Like some up-ended boulder split in two,
Was in her clouded eyes: they saw no fear there.   20
She seemed to think that two thus they were safe.
Then, as if they were something that, though strange,
She could not trouble her mind with too long,
She sighed and passed unscared along the wall.
"*This*, then, is all. What more is there to ask?"
But no, not yet. A snort to bid them wait.
A buck from round the spruce stood looking at them
Across the wall as near the wall as they.
This was an antlered buck of lusty nostril,
Not the same doe come back into her place.   30
He viewed them quizzically with jerks of head,
As if to ask, "Why don't you make some motion?
Or give some sign of life? Because you can't.
I doubt if you're as living as you look."
Thus till he had them almost feeling dared
To stretch a proffering hand—and a spell-breaking.
Then he too passed unscared along the wall.
Two had seen two, whichever side you spoke from.
"This *must* be all." It was all. Still they stood,
A great wave from it going over them,   40
As if the earth in one unlooked-for-favor
Had made them certain earth returned their love.

ACQUAINTED WITH THE NIGHT   [1928]

I have been one acquainted with the night.
I have walked out in rain—and back in rain.
I have outwalked the furthest city light.

I have looked down the saddest city lane.
I have passed by the watchman on his beat
And dropped my eyes, unwilling to explain.

I have stood still and stopped the sound of feet
When far away an interrupted cry
Came over houses from another street,

But not to call me back or say good-by;   10
And further still at an unearthly height,
One luminary clock against the sky

Proclaimed the time was neither wrong nor right.
I have been one acquainted with the night.

WEST-RUNNING BROOK   [1928]

"Fred, where is north?"

                    "North? North is there, my love.
The brook runs west."

                    "West-running Brook then call it."
(West-running Brook men call it to this day.)
"What does it think it's doing running west
When all the other country brooks flow east
To reach the ocean? It must be the brook
Can trust itself to go by contraries
The way I can with you—and you with me—
Because we're—we're—I don't know what we are.
What are we?"

               "Young or new?"

                    "We must be something.   10
We've said we two. Let's change that to we three.
As you and I are married to each other,
We'll both be married to the brook. We'll build

Our bridge across it, and the bridge shall be
Our arm thrown over it asleep beside it.
Look, look, it's waving to us with a wave
To let us know it hears me."

                     "Why, my dear,
That wave's been standing off this jut of shore—"
(The black stream, catching on a sunken rock,
Flung backward on itself in one white wave,   20
And the white water rode the black forever,
Not gaining but not losing, like a bird
White feathers from the struggle of whose breast
Flecked the dark stream and flecked the darker pool
Below the point, and were at last driven wrinkled
In a white scarf against the far shore alders.)
"That wave's been standing off this jut of shore
Ever since rivers, I was going to say,
Were made in heaven. It wasn't waved to us."

"It wasn't, yet it was. If not to you   30
It was to me—in an annunciation."

"Oh, if you take it off to lady-land,
As't were the country of the Amazons
We men must see you to the confines of
And leave you there, ourselves forbid to enter,—
It is your brook! I have no more to say."

"Yes, you have, too. Go on. You thought of something."

"Speaking of contraries, see how the brook
In that white wave runs counter to itself.
It is from that in water we were from   40
Long, long before we were from any creature.
Here we, in our impatience of the steps,
Get back to the beginning of beginnings,
The stream of everything that runs away.
Some say existence like a Pirouot
And Pirouette, forever in one place,
Stands still and dances, but it runs away,

It seriously, sadly, runs away
To fill the abyss' void with emptiness.
It flows beside us in this water brook,   50
But it flows over us. It flows between us
To separate us for a panic moment.
It flows between us, over us, and *with* us.
And it is time, strength, tone, light, life, and love—
And even substance lapsing unsubstantial;
The universal cataract of death
That spends to nothingness—and unresisted,
Save by some strange resistance in itself,
Not just a swerving, but a throwing back,
As if regret were in it and were sacred.   60
It has this throwing backward on itself.
So that the fall of most of it is always
Raising a little, sending up a little.
Our life runs down in sending up the clock.
The brook runs down in sending up our life.
The sun runs down in sending up the brook.
And there is something sending up the sun.
It is this backward motion toward the source,
Against the stream, that most we see ourselves in,
The tribute of the current to the source.   70
It is from this in nature we are from.
It is most us."

            "Today will be the day
You said so."

            "No, today will be the day
You said the brook was called West-running Brook."

"Today will be the day of what we both said."

TWO TRAMPS IN MUD TIME   [1936]

Out of the mud two strangers came
And caught me splitting wood in the yard.

And one of them put me off my aim
By hailing cheerily "Hit them hard!"
I knew pretty well why he dropped behind
And let the other go on a way.
I knew pretty well what he had in mind:
He wanted to take my job for pay.

Good blocks of oak it was I split,
As large around as the chopping block;   10
And every piece I squarely hit
Fell splinterless as a cloven rock.
The blows that a life of self-control
Spares to strike for the common good
That day, giving a loose to my soul,
I spent on the unimportant wood.

The sun was warm but the wind was chill.
You know how it is with an April day
When the sun is out and the wind is still,
You're one month on in the middle of May.   20
But if you so much as dare to speak,
A cloud comes over the sunlit arch,
A wind comes off a frozen peak,
And you're two months back in the middle of March.

A bluebird comes tenderly up to alight
And turns to the wind to unruffle a plume
His song so pitched as not to excite
A single flower as yet to bloom.
It is snowing a flake: and he half knew
Winter was only playing possum.   30
Except in color he isn't blue,
But he wouldn't advise a thing to blossom.

The water for which we may have to look
In summertime with a witching-wand,
In every wheelrut's now a brook,
In every print of a hoof a pond.
Be glad of water, but don't forget

The lurking frost in the earth beneath
That will steal forth after the sun is set
And show on the water its crystal teeth.   40

The time when most I loved my task
These two must make me love it more
By coming with what they came to ask.
You'd think I never had felt before
The weight of an ax-head poised aloft,
The grip on earth of outspread feet.
The life of muscles rocking soft
And smooth and moist in vernal heat.

Out of the woods two hulking tramps
(From sleeping God knows where last night,   50
But not long since in the lumber camps).
They thought all chopping was theirs of right.
Men of the woods and lumberjacks,
They judged me by their appropriate tool.
Except as a fellow handled an ax,
They had no way of knowing a fool.

Nothing on either side was said.
They knew they had but to stay their stay
And all their logic would fill my head:
As that I had no right to play   60
With what was another man's work for gain.
My right might be love but theirs was need.
And where the two exist in twain
Theirs was the better right—agreed.

But yield who will to their separation,
My object in life is to unite
My avocation and my vocation
As my two eyes make one in sight.
Only where love and need are one,
And the work is play for mortal stakes,   70
Is the deed ever really done
For Heaven and the future's sakes.

DESERT PLACES   [1936]

Snow falling and night falling fast, oh, fast
In a field I looked into going past,
And the ground almost covered smooth in snow,
But a few weeds and stubble showing last.

The woods around it have it—it is theirs.
All animals are smothered in their lairs.
I am too absent-spirited to count;
The loneliness includes me unawares.

And lonely as it is that loneliness
Will be more lonely ere it will be less—   10
A blanker whiteness of benighted snow
With no expression, nothing to express.

They cannot scare me with their empty spaces
Between stars—on stars where no human race is.
I have it in me so much nearer home
To scare myself with my own desert places.

NEITHER OUT FAR NOR IN DEEP   [1936]

The people along the sand
All turn and look one way.
They turn their back on the land.
They look at the sea all day.

As long as it takes to pass
A ship keeps raising its hull;
The wetter ground like glass
Reflects a standing gull.

The land may vary more;
But wherever the truth may be—   10
The water comes ashore,
And the people look at the sea.

They cannot look out far.
They cannot look in deep.
But when was that ever a bar
To any watch they keep?

DESIGN   [1936]

I found a dimpled spider, fat and white,
On a white heal-all, holding up a moth
Like a white piece of rigid satin cloth—
Assorted characters of death and blight
Mixed ready to begin the morning right,
Like the ingredients of a witches' broth—
A snow-drop spider, a flower like a froth,
And dead wings carried like a paper kite.

What had that flower to do with being white,
The wayside blue and innocent heal-all?   10
What brought the kindred spider to that height,
Then steered the white moth thither in the night?
What but design of darkness to appall?—
If design govern in a thing so small.

THE GIFT OUTRIGHT   [1942]

The land was ours before we were the land's.
She was our land more than a hundred years
Before we were her people. She was ours
In Massachusetts, in Virginia,

But we were England's, still colonials,
Possessing what we still were unpossessed by,
Possessed by what we now no more possessed.
Something we were withholding made us weak
Until we found out that it was ourselves
We were withholding from our land of living,   10
And forthwith found salvation in surrender.
Such as we were we gave ourselves outright
(The deed of gift was many deeds of war)
To the land vaguely realizing westward,
But still unstoried, artless, unenhanced,
Such as she was, such as she would become.

DIRECTIVE   [1947]

Back out of all this now too much for us,
Back in a time made simple by the loss
Of detail, burned, dissolved, and broken off
Like graveyard marble sculpture in the weather,
There is a house that is no more a house
Upon a farm that is no more a farm
And in a town that is no more a town.
The road there, if you'll let a guide direct you
Who only has at heart your getting lost,
May seem as if it should have been a quarry—   10
Great monolithic knees the former town
Long since gave up pretence of keeping covered.
And there's a story in a book about it:
Besides the wear of iron wagon wheels
The ledges show lines ruled southeast northwest,
The chisel work of an enormous Glacier
That braced his feet against the Arctic Pole.
You must not mind a certain coolness from him
Still said to haunt this side of Panther Mountain.
Nor need you mind the serial ordeal   20
Of being watched from forty cellar holes
As if by eye pairs out of forty firkins.

As for the woods' excitement over you
That sends light rustle rushes to their leaves,
Charge that to upstart inexperience.
Where were they all not twenty years ago?
They think too much of having shaded out
A few old pecker-fretted apple trees.
Make yourself up a cheering song of how
Someone's road home from work this once was,   30
Who may be just ahead of you on foot
Or creaking with a buggy load of grain.
The height of the adventure is the height
Of country where two village cultures faded
Into each other. Both of them are lost.
And if you're lost enough to find yourself
By now, pull in your ladder road behind you
And put a sign up CLOSED to all but me.
Then make yourself at home. The only field
Now left's no bigger than a harness gall.   40
First there's the children's house of make believe,
Some shattered dishes underneath a pine,
The playthings in the playhouse of the children.
Weep for what little things could make them glad.
Then for the house that is no more a house,
But only a belilaced cellar hole,
Now slowly closing like a dent in dough.
This was no playhouse but a house in earnest.
Your destination and your destiny's
A brook that was the water of the house,   50
Cold as a spring as yet so near its source,
Too lofty and original to rage.
(We know the valley streams that when aroused
Will leave their tatters hung on barb and thorn.)
I have kept hidden in the instep arch
Of an old cedar at the waterside
A broken drinking goblet like the Grail
Under a spell so the wrong ones can't find it,
So can't get saved, as Saint Mark says they mustn't.
(I stole the goblet from the children's playhouse.)   60
Here are your waters and your watering place.
Drink and be whole again beyond confusion.

Carl Sandburg

b. 1878

Carl Sandburg was born in Galesburg, Illinois, January 6, 1878, the son of poor Swedish immigrants. At thirteen he quit school, worked at many jobs during his teens, wandered through the West, served eight months in the Army during the Spanish-American War, then atten-ded Lombard College, where he began to write poetry. In 1907 and 1908 he worked as a district organizer for the Social-Democratic Party in Wisconsin, then moved to Chicago, where he worked on a newspaper and contributed poems to Harriet Monroe's newly founded Poetry: A Magazine of Verse, *which helped to usher in a new epoch in American poetry. It was Sandburg's monumental biography of Lincoln, however, that won a Pulitzer Prize in 1939. He had already become well known as a collector and singer of folk ballads. The legend of Sandburg as the poet of Chicago, "Hog Butcher for the World," has obscured his growth away from regionalism and folksy democracy, as his elegy for Franklin D. Roosevelt shows. Embedded in his voluminous* Complete Poems *are a few lyrics which deserve to be remembered as lasting contributions to American poetry.*

CHICAGO   [1916]

Hog Butcher for the World,
Tool Maker, Stacker of Wheat,
Player with Railroads and the Nation's Freight Handler;
Stormy, husky, brawling,
City of the Big Shoulders:

They tell me you are wicked and I believe them, for I have
    seen your painted women under the gas lamps luring
    the farm boys.
And they tell me you are crooked and I answer: Yes, it is
    true I have seen the gunman kill and go free to kill
    again.
And they tell me you are brutal and my reply is: On the
    faces of women and children I have seen the marks of
    wanton hunger.
And having answered so I turn once more to those who
    sneer at this my city, and I give them back the sneer
    and say to them:
Come and show me another city with lifted head singing
    so proud to be alive and coarse and strong and
    cunning.   10
Flinging magnetic curses amid the toil of piling job on job,
    here is a tall bold slugger set vivid against the little
    soft cities;
Fierce as a dog with tongue lapping for action, cunning as
    a savage pitted against the wilderness,
          Bareheaded,
          Shoveling,
          Wrecking,
          Planning,
          Building, breaking, rebuilding,
Under the smoke, dust all over his mouth, laughing with
    white teeth,
Under the terrible burden of destiny laughing as a young
    man laughs,
Laughing even as an ignorant fighter laughs who has never
    lost a battle,   20
Bragging and laughing that under his wrist is the pulse,
    and under his ribs the heart of the people,
                         Laughing!
Laughing the stormy, husky, brawling laughter of Youth,
    half-naked, sweating, proud to be Hog Butcher,
        Tool Maker, Stacker of Wheat, Player with Railroads
    and Freight Handler to the Nation.

SKETCH   [1916]

The shadows of the ships
Rock on the crest
In the low blue lustre
Of the tardy and the soft inrolling tide.

A long brown bar at the dip of the sky
Puts an arm of sand in the span of salt.

The lucid and endless wrinkles
Draw in, lapse and withdraw.
Wavelets crumble and white spent bubbles
Wash on the floor of the beach.   10

    Rocking on the crest
    In the low blue lustre
    Are the shadows of the ships.

FOG   [1916]

The fog comes
on little cat feet.

It sits looking
over harbor and city
on silent haunches
and then moves on.

POOL   [1916]

Out of the fire
Came a man sunken

To less than cinders,
A tea-cup of ashes or so.
And I,
The gold in the house,
Writhed into a stiff pool.

PRAYERS OF STEEL   [1918]

Lay me on an anvil, O God.
Beat me and hammer me into a crowbar.
Let me pry loose old walls.
Let me lift and loosen old foundations.

Lay me on an anvil, O God.
Beat me and hammer me into a steel spike.
Drive me into the girders that hold a skyscraper together.
Take red-hot rivets and fasten me into the central girders.
Let me be the great nail holding a skyscraper through blue
    nights into white stars. ·   10

WILDERNESS   [1918]

There is a wolf in me . . . fangs pointed for tearing gashes . . . a
    red tongue for raw meat . . . and the hot lapping of blood—I
    keep this wolf because the wilderness gave it to me and the
    wilderness will not let it go.

There is a fox in me . . . a silver-gray fox . . . I sniff and guess . . .
    I pick things out of the wind and air . . . I nose in the dark
    night and take sleepers and eat them and hide the feathers
    . . . I circle and loop and double-cross.

There is a hog in me . . . a snout and a belly . . . a machinery for
    eating and grunting . . . a machinery for sleeping satisfied in
    the sun—I got this too from the wilderness and the wilder-
    ness will not let it go.

There is a fish in me ... I know I came from salt-blue water-
    gates ... I scurried with shoals of herring ... I blew
    waterspouts with porpoises ... before land was ... before
    the water went down ... before Noah ... before the first
    chapter of Genesis.

There is a baboon in me ... clambering-clawed ... dog-faced ...
    yawping a galoot's hunger ... hairy under the armpits ...
    here are the hawk-eyed hankering men ... here are the
    blonde and blue-eyed women ... here they hide curled
    asleep waiting ... ready to snarl and kill ... ready to sing
    and give milk ... waiting—I keep the baboon because the
    wilderness says so.

There is an eagle in me and a mocking bird ... and the eagle
    flies among the Rocky Mountains of my dreams and fights
    among the Sierra crags of what I want ... and the mocking
    bird warbles in the early forenoon before the dew is gone,
    warbles in the underbrush of my Chattanoogas of hope,
    gushes over the blue Ozark foothills of my wishes—And I
    got the eagle and the mockingbird from the wilderness.

O, I got a zoo, I got a menagerie, inside my ribs, under my bony
    head, under my red-valve heart—and I got something else:
    it is a man-child heart, a woman-child heart: it is a father and
    mother and lover: it came from God-Knows-Where: it is
    going to God-Knows-Where—For I am the keeper of the
    zoo: I say yes and no: I sing and kill and work: I am a pal of
    the world: I came from the wilderness.

HANDFULS   [1918]

Blossoms of babies
Blinking their stories
Come soft
On the dusk and the babble;
Little red gamblers,
Handfuls that slept in the dust.

Summers of rain,
Winters of drift,
Tell off the years;
And they go back   10
Who came soft—
Back to the sod,
To silence and dust;
Gray gamblers,
Handfuls again.

COOL TOMBS   [1918]

When Abraham Lincoln was shoveled into the tombs, he forgot
the copperheads and the assassin . . . in the dust, in the cool
tombs.

When Ulysses Grant lost all thought of con men and Wall Street,
cash and collateral turned ashes . . . in the dust, in the cool
tombs.

Pocahontas' body, lovely as a poplar, sweet as a red haw in
November or a pawpaw in May, did she wonder? does she
remember? . . . in the dust, in the cool tombs?

Take any streetful of people buying clothes and groceries,
cheering a hero or throwing confetti and blowing tin horns
. . . tell me if the lovers are losers . . . tell me if any get more
than the lovers . . . in the dust . . . in the cool tombs.

FOUR PRELUDES ON PLAYTHINGS OF THE
WIND   [1920]

"The past is a bucket of ashes."

I

The woman named Tomorrow
sits with a hairpin in her teeth

and takes her time
and does her hair the way she wants it
and fastens at last the last braid and coil
and puts the hairpin where it belongs
and turns and drawls: Well, what of it?
My grandmother, Yesterday, is gone.
What of it? Let the dead be dead.

2

The doors were cedar   10
and the panels strips of gold
and the girls were golden girls
and the panels read and the girls chanted:
     We are the greatest city,
     the greatest nation:
     nothing like us ever was.

The doors are twisted on broken hinges.
Sheets of rain swish through on the wind
     where the golden girls ran and the panels read:
     We are the greatest city,   20
     the greatest nation,
     nothing like us ever was.

3

It has happened before.
Strong men put up a city and got
     a nation together,
And paid singers to sing and women
     to warble: We are the greatest city,
       the greatest nation,
       nothing like us ever was.

And while the singers sang   30
and the strong men listened
and paid the singers well
and felt good about it all,
     there were rats and lizards who listened
     . . . and the only listeners left now
     . . . are . . . the rats . . . and the lizards.

And there are black crows
crying "Caw, caw,"
bringing mud and sticks
building a nest
over the words carved   40
on the doors where the panels were cedar
and the strips on the panels were gold
and the golden girls came singing:
     We are the greatest city,
     the greatest nation:
     nothing like us ever was.

The only singers now are crows crying "Caw, caw,"
And the sheets of rain whine in the wind and doorways.
And the only listeners now are . . . the rats . . . and the lizards.

4

The feet of the rats   50
scribble on the doorsills;
the hieroglyphs of the rat footprints
chatter the pedigrees of the rats
and babble of the blood
and gabble of the breed
of the grandfathers and the great-grandfathers
of the rats.

And the wind shifts
and the dust on a doorsill shifts
and even the writing of the rat footprints   60
tells us nothing, nothing at all
about the greatest city, the greatest nation
where the strong men listened
and the women warbled: Nothing like us ever was.

WHEN DEATH CAME APRIL TWELVE 1945   [1950]

Can a bell ring in the heart
telling the time, telling a moment,
telling off a stillness come,

in the afternoon a stillness come
and now never come morning?

Now never again come morning,
say the tolling bells repeating it,
now on the earth in blossom days,
in earthy days and potato planting,
now to the stillness of the earth,   10
to the music of dust to dust
and the drop of ashes to ashes
he returns and it is the time,
the afternoon time and never come morning,
the voice never again, the face never again.

A bell rings in the heart telling it
and the bell rings again and again
remembering what the first bell told,
the going away, the great heart still—
and they will go on remembering   20
and they is you and you and me and me.

And there will be roses and spring blooms
flung on the moving oblong box, emblems endless
flung from nearby, from faraway earth corners,
from frontline tanks nearing Berlin
          unseen flowers of regard to The Commander,
from battle stations over the South Pacific
          silent tokens saluting The Commander.

And the whitening bones of men at sea bottoms
or huddled and mouldering men at Aachen,   30
          they may be murmuring,
          "Now he is one of us,"
          one answering muffled drums
in the realm and sphere of the shadow battalions.

Can a bell ring proud in the heart
          over a voice yet lingering,
          over a face past any forgetting,
          over a shadow alive and speaking,
over echoes and lights come keener, come deeper?

Can a bell ring in the heart   40
in time with the tall headlines,
the high fidelity transmitters,
the somber consoles rolling sorrow,
the choirs in ancient laments—chanting:
            "Dreamer, sleep deep,
            Toiler, sleep long,
            Fighter, be rested now,
            Commander, sweet good night."

Wallace Stevens

1879–1955

*Wallace Stevens was born October 2, 1879, in Reading, Pennsylvania.
He attended Harvard from 1897 to 1900 and then studied law at the
New York Law School. After he was admitted to the Bar in 1904, he
engaged in general practice in New York. From 1916 on he was employed
by the Hartford Accident and Indemnity Company of Hartford,
Connecticut. In 1934 he became a vice-president of the company and
continued throughout the rest of his life the two occupations of insurance
executive and poet. Little known to the general public for most of his
career, he received a number of awards in his last years, including the
Bollingen Prize (1949) and the Pulitzer Prize (1955). He died on
August 2, 1955, in Hartford.*

DOMINATION OF BLACK   [1923]

At night, by the fire,
The colors of the bushes
And of the fallen leaves,
Repeating themselves,
Turned in the room,
Like the leaves themselves
Turning in the wind.
Yes: but the color of the heavy hemlocks
Came striding.
And I remembered the cry of the peacocks.   10

The colors of their tails
Were like the leaves themselves
Turning in the wind,

In the twilight wind.
They swept over the room,
Just as they flew from the boughs of the hemlocks
Down to the ground.
I heard them cry—the peacocks.
Was it a cry against the twilight
Or against the leaves themselves   20
Turning in the wind,
Turning as the flames
Turned in the fire,
Turning as the tails of the peacocks
Turned in the loud fire,
Loud as the hemlocks
Full of the cry of the peacocks?
Or was it a cry against the hemlocks?

Out of the window
I saw how the planets gathered   30
Like the leaves themselves
Turning in the wind.
I saw how the night came,
Came striding like the color of the heavy hemlocks
I felt afraid.
And I remembered the cry of the peacocks.

THE SNOW MAN   [1923]

One must have a mind of winter
To regard the frost and the boughs
Of the pine-trees crusted with snow;

And have been cold a long time
To behold the junipers shagged with ice,
The spruces rough in the distant glitter

Of the January sun; and not to think
Of any misery in the sound of the wind,
In the sound of a few leaves,

Which is the sound of the land   10
Full of the same wind
That is blowing in the same bare place

For the listener, who listens in the snow,
And, nothing himself, beholds
Nothing that is not there and the nothing that is.

LE MONOCLE DE MON ONCLE   [1923]

"Mother of heaven, regina of the clouds,
O sceptre of the sun, crown of the moon,
There is not nothing, no, no, never nothing,
Like the clashed edges of two words that kill."
And so I mocked her in magnificent measure.
Or was it that I mocked myself alone?
I wish that I might be a thinking stone.
The sea of spuming thought foists up again
The radiant bubble that she was. And then
A deep up-pouring from some saltier well   10
Within me, bursts its watery syllable.

II

A red bird flies across the golden floor.
It is a red bird that seeks out his choir
Among the choirs of wind and wet and wing.
A torrent will fall from him when he finds.
Shall I uncrumple this much-crumpled thing?
I am a man of fortune greeting heirs;
For it has come that thus I greet the spring.
These choirs of welcome choir for me farewell.
No spring can follow past meridian.   20
Yet you persist with anecdotal bliss
To make believe a starry *connnaissance*.

III

Is it for nothing, then, that old Chinese
Sat tittivating by their mountain pools

Or in the Yangtse studied out their beards?
I shall not play the flat historic scale.
You know how Utamaro's beauties sought
The end of love in their all-speaking braids.
You know the mountainous coiffures of Bath.
Alas! Have all the barbers lived in vain   30
That not one curl in nature has survived?
Why, without pity on these studious ghosts,
Do you come dripping in your hair from sleep?

IV

This luscious and impeccable fruit of life
Falls, it appears, of its own weight to earth.
When you were Eve, its acrid juice was sweet,
Untasted, in its heavenly, orchard air.
An apple serves as well as any skull
To be the book in which to read a round,
And is as excellent, in that it is composed   40
Of what, like skulls, comes rotting back to ground.
But it excels in this, that as the fruit
Of love, it is a book too mad to read
Before one merely reads to pass the time.

V

In the high west there burns a furious star.
It is for fiery boys that star was set
And for sweet-smelling virgins close to them.
The measure of the intensity of love
Is measure, also, of the verve of earth.
For me, the firefly's quick, electric stroke   50
Ticks tediously the time of one more year.
And you? Remember how the crickets came
Out of their mother grass, like little kin,
In the pale nights, when your first imagery
Found inklings of your bond to all that dust.

VI

If men at forty will be painting lakes
The ephemeral blues must merge for them in one,
The basic slate, the universal hue.

There is a substance in us that prevails.
But in our amours amorists discern   60
Such fluctuations that their scrivening
Is breathless to attend each quirky turn.
When amorists grow bald, then amours shrink
Into the compass and curriculum
Of introspective exiles, lecturing.
It is a theme for Hyacinth alone.

VII

The mules that angels ride come slowly down
The blazing passes, from beyond the sun.
Descensions of their tinkling bells arrive.
These muleteers are dainty of their way.   70
Meantime, centurions guffaw and beat
Their shrilling tankards on the table-boards.
This parable, in sense, amounts to this:
The honey of heaven may or may not come,
But that of earth both comes and goes at once.
Suppose these couriers brought amid their train
A damsel heightened by eternal bloom.

VIII

Like a dull scholar, I behold, in love,
An ancient aspect touching a new mind.
It comes, it blooms, it bears its fruit and dies.   80
This trivial trope reveals a way of truth.
Our bloom is gone. We are the fruit thereof.
Two golden gourds distended on our vines,
Into the autumn weather, splashed with frost,
Distorted by hale fatness, turned grotesque.
We hang like warty squashes, streaked and rayed,
The laughing sky will see the two of us
Washed into rinds by rotting winter rains.

IX

In verses wild with motion, full of din,
Loudened by cries, by clashes, quick and sure   90
As the deadly thought of men accomplishing
Their curious fates in war, come, celebrate

The faith of forty, ward of Cupido.
Most venerable heart, the lustiest conceit
Is not too lusty for your broadening.
I quiz all sounds, all thoughts, all everything
For the music and manner of the paladins
To make oblation fit. Where shall I find
Bravura adequate to this great hymn?

X

The fops of fancy in their poems leave   100
Memorabilia of the mystic spouts,
Spontaneously watering their gritty soils.
I am a yeoman, as such fellows go.
I know no magic trees, no balmy boughs,
No silver-ruddy, gold-vermilion fruits.
But, after all, I know a tree that bears
A semblance to the thing I have in mind.
It stands gigantic, with a certain tip
To which all birds come sometime in their time.
But when they go that tip still tips the tree.   110

XI

If sex were all, then every trembling hand
Could make us squeak, like dolls, the wished-for words.
But note the unconscionable treachery of fate,
That makes us weep, laugh, grunt and groan, and shout
Doleful heroics, pinching gestures forth
From madness or delight, without regard
To that first, foremost law. Anguishing hour!
Last night, we sat beside a pool of pink,
Clippered with lilies scudding the bright chromes,
Keen to the point of starlight, while a frog   120
Boomed from his very belly odious chords.

XII

A blue pigeon it is, that circles the blue sky,
On sidelong wing, around and round and round.
A white pigeon it is, that flutters to the ground,
Grown tired of flight. Like a dark rabbi, I
Observed, when young, the nature of mankind,
In lordly study. Every day, I found

Man proved a gobbet in my mincing world.
Like a rose rabbi, later, I pursued,
And still pursue, the origin and course   130
Of love, but until now I never knew
That fluttering things have so distinct a shade.

A HIGH-TONED OLD CHRISTIAN WOMAN   [1923]

Poetry is the supreme fiction, madame.
Take the moral law and make a nave of it
And from the nave build haunted heaven. Thus,
The conscience is converted into palms,
Like windy citherns hankering for hymns.
We agree in principle. That's clear. But take
The opposing law and make a peristyle,
And from the peristyle project a masque
Beyond the planets. Thus, our bawdiness,
Unpurged by epitaph, indulged at last,   10
Is equally converted into palms,
Squiggling like saxophones. And palm for palm,
Madame, we are where we began. Allow,
Therefore, that in the planetary scene
Your disaffected flagellants, well-stuffed,
Smacking their muzzy bellies in parade,
Proud of such novelties of the sublime,
Such tink and tank and tunk-a-tunk-tunk,
May, merely may, madame, whip from themselves
A jovial hullabaloo among the spheres.   20
This will make widows wince. But fictive things
Wink as they will. Wink most when widows wince.

THE EMPEROR OF ICE-CREAM   [1923]

Call the roller of big cigars,
The muscular one, and bid him whip
In kitchen cups concupiscent curds.

Let the wenches dawdle in such dress
As they are used to wear, and let the boys
Bring flowers in last month's newspapers.
Let be be finale of seem.
The only emperor is the emperor of ice-cream.

Take from the dresser of deal,
Lacking the three glass knobs, that sheet   10
On which she embroidered fantails once
And spread it so as to cover her face.
If her horny feet protrude, they come
To show how cold she is, and dumb.
Let the lamp affix its beam.
The only emperor is the emperor of ice-cream.

SUNDAY MORNING   [1923]

                          I

Complacencies of the peignoir, and late
Coffee and oranges in a sunny chair,
And the green freedom of a cockatoo
Upon a rug mingle to dissipate
The holy hush of ancient sacrifice.
She dreams a little, and she feels the dark
Encroachment of that old catastrophe,
As a calm darkens among water-lights.
The pungent oranges and bright, green wings
Seem things in some procession of the dead,   10
Winding across wide water, without sound.
The day is like wide water, without sound,
Stilled for the passing of her dreaming feet
Over the seas, to silent Palestine,
Dominion of the blood and sepulchre.

                          II

Why should she give her bounty to the dead?
What is divinity if it can come

Only in silent shadows and in dreams?
Shall she not find in comforts of the sun,
In pungent fruit and bright, green wings, or else   20
In any balm or beauty of the earth,
Things to be cherished like the thought of heaven?
Divinity must live within herself:
Passions of rain, or moods in falling snow;
Grievings in loneliness, or unsubdued
Elations when the forest blooms; gusty
Emotions on wet roads on autumn nights;
All pleasures and all pains, remembering
The bough of summer and the winter branch.
These are the measures destined for her soul.   30

III

Jove in the clouds had his inhuman birth.
No mother suckled him, no sweet land gave
Large-mannered motions to his mythy mind.
He moved among us, as a muttering king,
Magnificent, would move among his hinds,
Until our blood, commingling, virginal,
With heaven, brought such requital to desire
The very hinds discerned it, in a star.
Shall our blood fail? Or shall it come to be
The blood of paradise? And shall the earth   40
Seem all of paradise that we shall know?
The sky will be much friendlier then than now,
A part of labor and a part of pain,
And next in glory to enduring love,
Not this dividing and indifferent blue.

IV

She says, "I am content when wakened birds,
Before they fly, test the reality
Of misty fields, by their sweet questionings;
But when the birds are gone, and their warm fields
Return no more, where, then, is paradise?"   50
There is not any haunt of prophecy,
Nor any old chimera of the grave,
Neither the golden underground, nor isle

Melodious, where spirits gat them home,
Nor visionary south, nor cloudy palm
Remote on heaven's hill, that has endured
As April's green endures; or will endure
Like her remembrance of awakened birds,
Or her desire for June and evening, tipped
By the consummation of the swallow's wings.   60

V

She says, "But in contentment I still feel
The need of some imperishable bliss."
Death is the mother of beauty; hence from her,
Alone, shall come fulfilment to our dreams
And our desires. Although she strews the leaves
Of sure obliteration on our paths,
The path sick sorrow took, the many paths
Where triumph rang its brassy phrase, or love
Whispered a little out of tenderness,
She makes the willow shiver in the sun   70
For maidens who were wont to sit and gaze
Upon the grass, relinquished to their feet.
She causes boys to pile new plums and pears
On disregarded plate. The maidens taste
And stray impassioned in the littering leaves.

VI

Is there no change of death in paradise?
Does ripe fruit never fall? Or do the boughs
Hang always heavy in that perfect sky,
Unchanging, yet so like our perishing earth,
With rivers like our own that seek for seas   80
They never find, the same receding shores
That never touch with inarticulate pang?
Why set the pear upon those river-banks
Or spice the shores with odors of the plum?
Alas, that they should wear our colors there,
The silken weavings of our afternoons,
And pick the strings of our insipid lutes!
Death is the mother of beauty, mystical,
Within whose burning bosom we devise
Our earthly mothers waiting, sleeplessly.   90

VII

Supple and turbulent, a ring of men
Shall chant in orgy on a summer morn
Their boisterous devotion to the sun,
Not as a god, but as a god might be,
Naked among them, like a savage source.
Their chant shall be a chant of paradise,
Out of their blood, returning to the sky;
And in their chant shall enter, voice by voice,
The windy lake wherein their lord delights,
The trees, like serafin, and echoing hills,   100
That choir among themselves long afterward.
They shall know well the heavenly fellowship
Of men that perish and of summer morn.
And whence they came and whither they shall go
The dew upon their feet shall manifest.

VIII

She hears, upon that water without sound,
A voice that cries, "The tomb in Palestine
Is not the porch of spirits lingering.
It is the grave of Jesus, where he lay."
We live in an old chaos of the sun,   110
Or old dependency of day and night,
Or island solitude, unsponsored, free,
Of that wide water, inescapable.
Deer walk upon our mountains, and the quail
Whistle about us their spontaneous cries;
Sweet berries ripen in the wilderness;
And, in the isolation of the sky,
At evening, casual flocks of pigeons make
Ambiguous undulations as they sink,
Downward to darkness, on extended wings.   120

ANECDOTE OF THE JAR   [1923]

I placed a jar in Tennessee,
And round it was, upon a hill.

It made the slovenly wilderness
Surround that hill.

The wilderness rose up to it,
And sprawled around, no longer wild.
The jar was round upon the ground
And tall and of a port in air.

It took dominion everywhere.
The jar was gray and bare.   10
It did not give of bird or bush,
Like nothing else in Tennessee.

TO THE ONE OF FICTIVE MUSIC   [1923]

Sister and mother and diviner love,
And of the sisterhood of the living dead
Most near, most clear, and of the clearest bloom,
And of the fragrant mothers the most dear
And queen, and of diviner love the day
And flame and summer and sweet fire, no thread
Of cloudy silver sprinkles in your gown
Its venom of renown, and on your head
No crown is simpler than the simple hair.

Now, of the music summoned by the birth   10
That separates us from the wind and sea,
Yet leaves us in them, until earth becomes,
By being so much of the things we are,
Gross effigy and simulacrum, none
Gives motion to perfection more serene
Than yours, out of our imperfections wrought,
Most rare, or ever of more kindred air
In the laborious weaving that you wear.

For so retentive of themselves are men
That music is intensest which proclaims   20

The near, the clear, and vaunts the clearest bloom,
And of all vigils musing the obscure,
That apprehends the most which sees and names,
As in your name, an image that is sure,
Among the arrant spices of the sun,
O bough and bush and scented vine, in whom
We give ourselves our likest issuance.

Yet not too like, yet not so like to be
Too near, too clear, saving a little to endow
Our feigning with the strange unlike, whence springs   30
The difference that heavenly pity brings.
For this, musician, in your girdle fixed
Bear other perfumes. On your pale head wear
A band entwining, set with fatal stones.
Unreal, give back to us what once you gave:
The imagination that we spurned and crave.

PETER QUINCE AT THE CLAVIER   [1923]

I

Just as my fingers on these keys
Make music, so the selfsame sounds
On my spirit make a music, too.

Music is feeling, then, not sound;
And thus it is that what I feel,
Here in this room, desiring you,

Thinking of your blue-shadowed silk,
Is music. It is like the strain
Waked in the elders by Susanna.

Of a green evening, clear and warm,   10
She bathed in her still garden, while
The red-eyed elders watching, felt

The basses of their beings throb
In witching chords, and their thin blood
Pulse pizzicati of Hosanna.

II

In the green water, clear and warm,
Susanna lay.
She searched
The touch of springs,
And found   20
Concealed imaginings.
She sighed,
For so much melody.

Upon the bank, she stood
In the cool
Of spent emotions.
She felt, among the leaves,
The dew
Of old devotions.

She walked upon the grass,   30
Still quavering.
The winds were like her maids,
On timid feet,
Fetching her woven scarves,
Yet wavering.

A breath upon her hand
Muted the night.
She turned—
A cymbal crashed,
And roaring horns.   40

III

Soon, with a noise like tambourines,
Came her attendant Byzantines.

They wondered why Susanna cried
Against the elders by her side;

And as they whispered, the refrain
Was like a willow swept by rain.

Anon, their lamps' uplifted flame
Revealed Susanna and her shame.

And then, the simpering Byzantines
Fled, with a noise like tambourines.   50

IV

Beauty is momentary in the mind—
The fitful tracing of a portal;
But in the flesh it is immortal.
The body dies; the body's beauty lives.
So evenings die, in their green going,
A wave, interminably flowing.
So gardens die, their meek breath scenting
The cowl of winter, done repenting.
So maidens die, to the auroral
Celebration of a maiden's choral.   60
Susanna's music touched the bawdy strings
Of those white elders; but, escaping,
Left only Death's ironic scraping.
Now, in its immortality, it plays
On the clear viol of her memory,
And makes a constant sacrament of praise.

THIRTEEN WAYS OF LOOKING AT A BLACKBIRD   [1923]

I

Among twenty snowy mountains,
The only moving thing
Was the eye of the blackbird.

II

I was of three minds,
Like a tree
In which there are three blackbirds.

III

The blackbird whirled in the autumn winds.
It was a small part of the pantomime.

IV

A man and a woman
Are one.   10
A man and a woman and a blackbird
Are one.

V

I do not know which to prefer,
The beauty of inflections
Or the beauty of innuendoes,
The blackbird whistling
Or just after.

VI

Icicles filled the long window
With barbaric glass.
The shadow of the blackbird   20
Crossed it, to and fro.
The mood
Traced in the shadow
An indecipherable cause.

VII

O thin men of Haddam,
Why do you imagine golden birds?
Do you not see how the blackbird
Walks around the feet
Of the women about you?

VIII

I know noble accents   30
And lucid, inescapable rhythms;
But I know, too,
That the blackbird is involved
In what I know.

IX

When the blackbird flew out of sight,
It marked the edge
Of one of many circles.

X

At the sight of blackbirds
Flying in a green light,
Even the bawds of euphony   40
Would cry out sharply.

XI

He rode over Connecticut
In a glass coach.
Once, a fear pierced him,
In that he mistook
The shadow of his equipage
For blackbirds.

XII

The river is moving.
The blackbird must be flying.

XIII

It was evening all afternoon.   50
It was snowing
And it was going to snow.
The blackbird sat
In the cedar-limbs.

SEA SURFACE FULL OF CLOUDS   [1931]

I

In that November off Tehuantepec,
The slopping of the sea grew still one night
And in the morning summer hued the deck

And made one think of rosy chocolate
And gilt umbrellas. Paradisal green
Gave suavity to the perplexed machine

Of ocean, which like limpid water lay.
Who, then, in that ambrosial latitude
Out of the light evolved the moving blooms,

Who, then, evolved the sea-blooms from the clouds   10
Diffusing balm in that Pacific calm?
C'était mon enfant, mon bijou, mon âme.

The sea-clouds whitened far below the calm
And moved, as blooms move, in the swimming green
And in its watery radiance, while the hue

Of heaven in an antique reflection rolled
Round those flotillas. And sometimes the sea
Poured brilliant iris on the glistening blue.

II

In that November off Tehuantepec
The slopping of the sea grew still one night.   20
At breakfast jelly yellow streaked the deck

And made one think of chop-house chocolate
And sham umbrellas. And a sham-like green
Capped summer-seeming on the tense machine

Of ocean, which in sinister flatness lay.
Who, then, beheld the rising of the clouds
That strode submerged in that malevolent sheen,

Who saw the mortal massives of the blooms
Of water moving on the water-floor?
C'était mon frère du ciel, ma vie, mon or.   30

The gongs rang loudly as the windy booms
Hoo-hooed it in the darkened ocean-blooms.

The gongs grew still. And then blue heaven spread

Its crystalline pendentives on the sea
And the macabre of the water-glooms
In an enormous undulation fled.

III

In that November off Tehuantepec,
The slopping of the sea grew still one night
And a pale silver patterned on the deck

And made one think of porcelain chocolate   40
And pied umbrellas. An uncertain green,
Piano-polished, held the tranced machine

Of ocean, as a prelude holds and holds.
Who, seeing silver petals of white blooms
Unfolding in the water, feeling sure

Of the milk within the saltiest spurge, heard, then,
The sea unfolding in the sunken clouds?
Oh! C'était mon extase et mon amour.

So deeply sunken were they that the shrouds,
The shrouding shadows, made the petals black   50
Until the rolling heaven made them blue,

A blue beyond the rainy hyacinth,
And smiting the crevasses of the leaves
Deluged the ocean with a sapphire blue.

IV

In that November off Tehuantepec
The night-long slopping of the sea grew still.
A mallow morning dozed upon the deck

And made one think of musky chocolate
And frail umbrellas. A too-fluent green
Suggested malice in the dry machine   60

Of ocean, pondering dank stratagem.
Who then beheld the figures of the clouds
Like blooms secluded in the thick marine?

Like blooms? Like damasks that were shaken off
From the loosed girdles in the spangling must.
C'était ma foi, la nonchalance divine.

The nakedness would rise and suddenly turn
Salt masks of beard and mouths of bellowing,
Would—But more suddenly the heaven rolled

Its bluest sea-clouds in the thinking green,   70
And the nakedness became the broadest blooms,
Mile-mallows that a mallow sun cajoled.

V

In that November off Tehuantepec
Night stilled the slopping of the sea. The day
Came, bowing and voluble, upon the deck,

Good clown. . . . One thought of Chinese chocolate
And large umbrellas. And a motley green
Followed the drift of the obese machine

Of ocean, perfected in indolence.
What pistache one, ingenious and droll,   80
Beheld the sovereign clouds as jugglery

And the sea as turquoise-turbaned Sambo, neat
At tossing saucers—cloudy-conjuring sea?
C'était mon esprit bâtard, l'ignominie.

The sovereign clouds came clustering. The conch
Of loyal conjuration trumped. The wind
Of green blooms turning crisped the motley hue

To clearing opalescence. Then the sea
And heaven rolled as one and from the two
Came fresh transfigurings of freshest blue.   90

THE IDEA OF ORDER AT KEY WEST   [1935]

She sang beyond the genius of the sea.
The water never formed to mind or voice,
Like a body wholly body, fluttering
Its empty sleeves; and yet its mimic motion
Made constant cry, caused constantly a cry,
That was not ours although we understood,
Inhuman, of the veritable ocean.

The sea was not a mask. No more was she.
The song and water were not medleyed sound
Even if what she sang was what she heard,   10
Since what she sang was uttered word by word.
It may be that in all her phrases stirred
The grinding water and the gasping wind;
But it was she and not the sea we heard.

For she was the maker of the song she sang.
The ever-hooded, tragic-gestured sea
Was merely a place by which she walked to sing.
Whose spirit is this? we said, because we knew
It was the spirit that we sought and knew
That we should ask this often as she sang.   20

If it was only the dark voice of the sea
That rose, or even colored by many waves;
If it was only the outer voice of sky
And cloud, of the sunken coral water-walled,
However clear, it would have been deep air,
The heaving speech of air, a summer sound
Repeated in a summer without end
And sound alone. But it was more than that,
More even than her voice, and ours, among
The meaningless plungings of water and the wind,   30
Theatrical distances, bronze shadows heaped
On high horizons, mountainous atmospheres
Of sky and sea.

                    It was her voice that made
The sky acutest at its vanishing.
She measured to the hour its solitude.
She was the single artificer of the world
In which she sang. And when she sang, the sea,
Whatever self it had, became the self
That was her song, for she was the maker. Then we,
As we beheld her striding there alone,   40
Knew that there never was a world for her
Except the one she sang and, singing, made.

Ramon Fernandez, tell me, if you know,
Why, when the singing ended and we turned
Toward the town, tell why the glassy lights,
The lights in the fishing boats at anchor there,
As the night descended, tilting in the air,
Mastered the night and portioned out the sea,
Fixing emblazoned zones and fiery poles,
Arranging, deepening, enchanting night.   50

Oh! Blessed rage for order, pale Ramon,
The maker's rage to order words of the sea,
Words of the fragrant portals, dimly-starred,
And of ourselves and of our origins,
In ghostlier demarcations, keener sounds.

ANGLAIS MORT A FLORENCE   [1935]

A little less returned for him each spring.
Music began to fail him. Brahms, although
His dark familiar, often walked apart.

His spirit grew uncertain of delight,
Certain of its uncertainty, in which
That dark companion left him unconsoled

For a self returning mostly memory.
Only last year he said that the naked moon
Was not the moon he used to see, to feel

(In the pale coherences of moon and mood   10
When he was young), naked and alien,
More leanly shining from a lankier sky.

Its ruddy pallor had grown cadaverous.
He used his reason, exercised his will,
Turning in time to Brahms as alternate

In speech. He was that music and himself.
They were particles of order, a single majesty:
But he remembered the time when he stood alone.

He stood at last by God's help and the police;
But he remembered the time when he stood alone.   20
He yielded himself to that single majesty;

But he remembered the time when he stood alone,
When to be and delight to be seemed to be one,
Before the colors deepened and grew small.

A POSTCARD FROM THE VOLCANO   [1936]

Children picking up our bones
Will never know that these were once
As quick as foxes on the hill;

And that in autumn, when the grapes
Made sharp air sharper by their smell
These had a being, breathing frost;

And least will guess that with our bones
We left much more, left what still is
The look of things, left what we felt

At what we saw. The spring clouds blow   10
Above the shuttered mansion-house,
Beyond our gate and the windy sky

Cries out a literate despair.
We knew for long the mansion's look
And what we said of it became

A part of what it is ... Children,
Still weaving budded aureoles,
Will speak our speech and never know,

Will say of the mansion that it seems
As if he that lived there left behind   20
A spirit storming in blank walls,

A dirty house in a gutted world,
A tatter of shadows peaked to white,
Smeared with the gold of the opulent sun.

STUDY OF TWO PEARS   [1942]

I

Opusculum paedagogum.
The pears are not viols,
Nudes or bottles.
They resemble nothing else.

II

They are yellow forms
Composed of curves
Bulging toward the base.
They are touched red.

III

They are not flat surfaces
Having curved outlines.
They are round   10
Tapering toward the top.

IV

In the way they are modelled
There are bits of blue.
A hard dry leaf hangs
From the stem.

V

The yellow glistens.
It glistens with various yellows,
Citrons, oranges and greens
Flowering over the skin.   20

VI

The shadows of the pears
Are blobs on the green cloth.
The pears are not seen
As the observer wills.

THE GLASS OF WATER   [1942]

That the glass would melt in heat,
That the water would freeze in cold,
Shows that this object is merely a state,
One of many, between two poles. So,
In the metaphysical, there are these poles.

Here in the centre stands the glass. Light
Is the lion that comes down to drink. There
And in that state, the glass is a pool.
Ruddy are his eyes and ruddy are his claws
When light comes down to wet his frothy jaws   10

And in the water winding weeds move round.
And there and in another state—the refractions,
The *metaphysica*, the plastic parts of poems
Crash in the mind—But, fat Jocundus, worrying
About what stands here in the centre, not the glass,

But in the centre of our lives, this time, this day,
It is a state, this spring among the politicians
Playing cards. In a village of the indigenes,
One would have still to discover. Among the dogs
        and dung,
One would continue to contend with one's ideas.   20

THE SENSE OF THE SLEIGHT-OF-HAND
MAN   [1942]

One's grand flights, one's Sunday baths,
One's tootings at the weddings of the soul
Occur as they occur. So bluish clouds
Occurred above the empty house and the leaves
Of the rhododendrons rattled their gold,
As if someone lived there. Such floods of white
Came bursting from the clouds. So the wind
Threw its contorted strength around the sky.

Could you have said the bluejay suddenly
Would swoop to earth? It is a wheel, the rays   10
Around the sun. The wheel survives the myths.
The fire eye in the clouds survives the gods.
To think of a dove with an eye of grenadine
And pines that are cornets, so it occurs,
And a little island full of geese and stars:
It may be that the ignorant man, alone,
Has any chance to mate his life with life
That is the sensual, pearly spouse, the life
That is fluent in even the wintriest bronze.

MRS. ALFRED URUGUAY   [1942]

So what said the others and the sun went down
And, in the brown blues of evening, the lady said,
In the donkey's ear, "I fear that elegance
Must struggle like the rest." She climbed until
The moonlight in her lap, mewing her velvet,

And her dress were one and she said, "I have said no
To everything, in order to get at myself.
I have wiped away moonlight like mud. Your innocent ear
And I, if I rode naked, are what remain."

The moonlight crumbled to degenerate forms,   10
While she approached the real, upon her mountain,
With lofty darkness. The donkey was there to ride,
To hold by the ear, even though it wished for a bell,
Wished faithfully for a falsifying bell.
Neither the moonlight could change it. And for her,
To be, regardless of velvet, could never be more
Than to be, she could never differently be,
Her no and no made yes impossible.

Who was it passed her there on a horse all will,
What figure of capable imagination?   20
Whose horse clattered on the road on which she rose,
As it descended, blind to her velvet and
The moonlight? Was it a rider intent on the sun,
A youth, a lover with phosphorescent hair,
Dressed poorly, arrogant of his streaming forces,
Lost in an integration of the martyrs' bones,
Rushing from what was real; and capable?

The villages slept as the capable man went down,
Time swished on the village clocks and dreams were alive,
The enormous gongs gave edges to their sounds,   30
As the rider, no chevalere and poorly dressed,
Impatient of the bells and midnight forms,
Rode over the picket rocks, rode down the road,
And, capable, created in his mind,
Eventual victor, out of the martyrs' bones,
The ultimate elegance: the imagined land.

ASIDES ON THE OBOE   [1942]

The prologues are over. It is a question, now,
Of final belief. So, say that final belief
Must be in a fiction. It is time to choose.

I

That obsolete fiction of the wide river in
An empty land; the gods that Boucher killed;
And the metal heroes that time granulates—
The philosophers' man alone still walks in dew,
Still by the sea-side mutters milky lines
Concerning an immaculate imagery.
If you say on the hautboy man is not enough,   10
Can never stand as god, is ever wrong
In the end, however naked, tall, there is still
The impossible possible philosophers' man,
The man who has had the time to think enough,
The central man, the human globe, responsive
As a mirror with a voice, the man of glass,
Who in a million diamonds sums us up.

II

He is the transparence of the place in which
He is and in his poems we find peace.
He sets this peddler's pie and cries in summer,   20
The glass man, cold and numbered, dewily cries,
"Thou art not August unless I make thee so."
Clandestine steps upon imagined stairs
Climb through the night, because his cuckoos call.

III

One year, death and war prevented the jasmine scent
And the jasmine islands were bloody martyrdoms.
How was it then with the central man? Did we
Find peace? We found the sum of men. We found,
If we found the central evil, the central good.
We buried the fallen without jasmine crowns.   30
There was nothing he did not suffer, no; nor we.

It was not as if the jasmine ever returned.
But we and the diamond globe at last were one.
We had always been partly one. It was as we came
To see him, that we were wholly one, as we heard
Him chanting for those buried in their blood,
In the jasmine haunted forests, that we knew
The glass man, without external reference.

THE MOTIVE FOR METAPHOR [1947]

You like it under the trees in autumn,
Because everything is half dead.
The wind moves like a cripple among the leaves
And repeats words without meaning.

In the same way, you were happy in spring,
With the half colors of quarter-things,
The slightly brighter sky, the melting clouds,
The single bird, the obscure moon—

The obscure moon lighting an obscure world
Of things that would never be quite expressed,   10
Where you yourself were never quite yourself
And did not want nor have to be,

Desiring the exhilarations of changes:
The motive for metaphor, shrinking from
The weight of primary noon,
The A B C of being,

The ruddy temper, the hammer
Of red and blue, the hard sound—
Steel against intimation—the sharp flash,
The vital, arrogant, fatal, dominant X.   20

CREDENCES OF SUMMER [1947]

I

Now in midsummer come and all fools slaughtered
And spring's infuriations over and a long way
To the first autumnal inhalations, young broods
Are in the grass, the roses are heavy with a weight
Of fragrance and the mind lays by its trouble.

Now the mind lays by its trouble and considers.
The fidgets of remembrance come to this.
This is the last day of a certain year
Beyond which there is nothing left of time.
It comes to this and the imagination's life.   10

There is nothing more inscribed nor thought nor felt
And this must comfort the heart's core against
Its false disasters—these fathers standing round,
These mothers touching, speaking, being near,
These lovers waiting in the soft dry grass.

II

Postpone the anatomy of summer, as
The physical pine, the metaphysical pine.
Let's see the very thing and nothing else.
Let's see it with the hottest fire of sight.
Burn everything not part of it to ash.   20

Trace the gold sun about the whitened sky
Without evasion by a single metaphor.
Look at it in its essential barrenness
And say this, this is the centre that I seek.
Fix it in an eternal foliage

And fill the foliage with arrested peace,
Joy of such permanence, right ignorance
Of change still possible. Exile desire
For what is not. This is the barrenness
Of the fertile thing that can attain no more.   30

III

It is the natural tower of all the world,
The point of survey, green's green apogee,
But a tower more precious than the view beyond,
A point of survey squatting like a throne,
Axis of everything, green's apogee

And happiest folk-land, mostly marriage-hymns.
It is the mountain on which the tower stands,

It is the final mountain. Here the sun,
Sleepless, inhales his proper air, and rests.
This is the refuge that the end creates.   40

It is the old man standing on the tower,
Who reads no book. His ruddy ancientness
Absorbs the ruddy summer and is appeased,
By an understanding that fulfils his age,
By a feeling capable of nothing more.

IV

One of the limits of reality
Presents itself in Oley when the hay,
Baked through long days, is piled in mows. It is
A land too ripe for enigmas, too serene.
There the distant fails the clairvoyant eye   50

And the secondary senses of the ear
Swarm, not with secondary sounds, but choirs,
Not evocations but last choirs, last sounds
With nothing else compounded, carried full,
Pure rhetoric of a language without words.

Things stop in that direction and since they stop
The direction stops and we accept what is
As good. The utmost must be good and is
And is our fortune and honey hived in the trees
And mingling of colors at a festival.   60

V

One day enriches a year. One woman makes
The rest look down. One man becomes a race,
Lofty like him, like him perpetual.
Or do the other days enrich the one?
And is the queen humble as she seems to be,

The charitable majesty of her whole kin?
The bristling soldier, weather-foxed, who looms
In the sunshine is a filial form and one
Of the land's children, easily born, its flesh,
Not fustian. The more than casual blue   70

Contains the year and other years and hymns
And people, without souvenir. The day
Enriches the year, not as embellishment.
Stripped of remembrance, it displays its strength—
The youth, the vital son, the heroic power.

VI

The rock cannot be broken. It is the truth.
It rises from land and sea and covers them.
It is a mountain half way green and then,
The other immeasurable half, such rock
As placid air becomes. But it is not   80

A hermit's truth nor symbol in hermitage.
It is the visible rock, the audible,
The brilliant mercy of a sure repose,
On this present ground, the vividest repose,
Things certain sustaining us in certainty.

It is the rock of summer, the extreme,
A mountain luminous half way in bloom
And then half way in the extremest light
Of sapphires flashing from the central sky,
As if twelve princes sat before a king.   90

VII

Far in the woods they sang their unreal songs,
Secure. It was difficult to sing in face
Of the object. The singers had to avert themselves
Or else avert the object. Deep in the woods
They sang of summer in the common fields.

They sang desiring an object that was near,
In face of which desire no longer moved,
Nor made of itself that which it could not find . . .
Three times the concentred self takes hold, three times
The thrice concentred self, having possessed   100

The object, grips it in savage scrutiny,
Once to make captive, once to subjugate

Or yield to subjugation, once to proclaim
The meaning of the capture, this hard prize,
Fully made, fully apparent, fully found.

VIII

The trumpet of morning blows in the clouds and through
The sky. It is the visible announced,
It is the more than visible, the more
Than sharp, illustrious scene. The trumpet cries
This is the successor of the invisible.   110

This is its substitute in stratagems
Of the spirit. This, in sight and memory,
Must take its place, as what is possible
Replaces what is not. The resounding cry
Is like ten thousand tumblers tumbling down

To share the day. The trumpet supposes that
A mind exists, aware of division, aware
Of its cry as clarion, its diction's way
As that of a personage in a multitude:
Man's mind grown venerable in the unreal.   120

IX

Fly low, cock bright, and stop on a bean pole. Let
Your brown breast redden, while you wait for warmth.
With one eye watch the willow, motionless.
The gardener's cat is dead, the gardener gone
And last year's garden grows salacious weeds.

A complex of emotions falls apart,
In an abandoned spot. Soft, civil bird,
The decay that you regard: of the arranged
And of the spirit of the arranged, *douceurs*,
Tristesses, the fund of life and death, suave bush   130

And polished beast, this complex falls apart.
And on your bean pole, it may be, you detect
Another complex of other emotions, not
So soft, so civil, and you make a sound,
Which is not part of the listener's own sense.

X

The personae of summer play the characters
Of an inhuman author, who meditates
With the gold bugs, in blue meadows, late at night.
He does not hear his characters talk. He sees
Them mottled, in the moodiest costumes,   140

Of blue and yellow, sky and sun, belted
And knotted, sashed and seamed, half pales of red,
Half pales of green, appropriate habit for
The huge decorum, the manner of the time,
Part of the mottled mood of summer's whole,

In which the characters speak because they want
To speak, the fat, the roseate characters,
Free, for a moment, from malice and sudden cry,
Complete in a completed scene, speaking
Their parts as in a youthful happiness.   150

TO AN OLD PHILOSOPHER IN ROME   [1954]

On the threshold of heaven, the figures in the street
Become the figures of heaven, the majestic movement
Of men growing small in the distances of space,
Singing, with smaller and still smaller sound,
Unintelligible absolution and an end—

The threshold, Rome, and that more merciful Rome
Beyond, the two alike in the make of the mind.
It is as if in a human dignity
Two parallels become one, a perspective, of which
Men are part both in the inch and in the mile.   10

How easily the blown banners change to wings . . .
Things dark on the horizons of perception,

Become accompaniments of fortune, but
Of the fortune of the spirit, beyond the eye,
Not of its sphere, and yet not far beyond,

The human end in the spirit's greatest reach,
The extreme of the known in the presence of the extreme
Of the unknown. The newsboys' muttering
Becomes another murmuring; the smell
Of medicine, a fragrantness not to be spoiled . . .   20

The bed, the books, the chair, the moving nuns,
The candle as it evades the sight, these are
The sources of happiness in the shape of Rome,
A shape within the ancient circles of shapes,
And these beneath the shadow of a shape

In a confusion on bed and books, a portent
On the chair, a moving transparence on the nuns,
A light on the candle tearing against the wick
To join a hovering excellence, to escape
From fire and be part only of that of which   30

Fire is the symbol: the celestial possible.
Speak to your pillow as if it was yourself.
Be orator but with an accurate tongue
And without eloquence, O, half-asleep,
Of the pity that is the memorial of this room,

So that we feel, in this illumined large,
The veritable small, so that each of us
Beholds himself in you, and hears his voice
In yours, master and commiserable man,
Intent on your particles of nether-do,   40

Your dozing in the depths of wakefulness,
In the warmth of your bed, at the edge of your chair, alive
Yet living in two worlds, impenitent
As to one, and, as to one, most penitent,
Impatient for the grandeur that you need

In so much misery; and yet finding it
Only in misery, the afflatus of ruin,
Profound poetry of the poor and of the dead,
As in the last drop of the deepest blood,
As it falls from the heart and lies there to be seen,   50

Even as the blood of an empire, it might be,
For a citizen of heaven though still of Rome.
It is poverty's speech that seeks us out the most.
It is older than the oldest speech of Rome.
This is the tragic accent of the scene.

And you—it is you that speak it, without speech,
The loftiest syllables among loftiest things,
The one invulnerable man among
Crude captains, the naked majesty, if you like,
Of bird-nest arches and of rain-stained-vaults.   60

The sounds drift in. The buildings are remembered.
The life of the city never lets go, nor do you
Ever want it to. It is part of the life in your room.
Its domes are the architecture of your bed.
The bells keep on repeating solemn names

In choruses and choirs of choruses,
Unwilling that mercy should be a mystery
Of silence, that any solitude of sense
Should give you more than their peculiar chords
And reverberations clinging to whisper still.   70

It is a kind of total grandeur at the end,
With every visible thing enlarged and yet
No more than a bed, a chair and moving nuns,
The immensest theatre, the pillared porch,
The book and candle in your ambered room,

Total grandeur of a total edifice,
Chosen by an inquisitor of structures
For himself. He stops upon this threshold,

As if the design of all his words takes form
And frame from thinking and is realized.   80

THE ROCK   [1954]

I

Seventy Years Later

It is an illusion that we were ever alive,
Lived in the houses of mothers, arranged ourselves
By our own motions in a freedom of air.

Regard the freedom of seventy years ago.
It is no longer air. The houses still stand,
Though they are rigid in rigid emptiness.

Even our shadows, their shadows, no longer remain.
The lives these lived in the mind are at an end.
They never were . . . The sounds of the guitar

Were not and are not. Absurd. The words spoken   10
Were not and are not. It is not to be believed.
The meeting at noon at the edge of the field seems like

An invention, an embrace between one desperate clod
And another in a fantastic consciousness,
In a queer assertion of humanity:

A theorem proposed between the two—
Two figures in a nature of the sun,
In the sun's design of its own happiness,

As if nothingness contained a métier,
A vital assumption, an impermanence   20
In its permanent cold, an illusion so desired

That the green leaves came and covered the high rock,
That the lilacs came and bloomed, like a blindness cleaned,
Exclaiming bright sight, as it was satisfied,

In a birth of sight. The blooming and the musk
Were being alive, an incessant being alive,
A particular of being, that gross universe.

II
The Poem as Icon

It is not enough to cover the rock with leaves.
We must be cured of it by a cure of the ground
Or a cure of ourselves, that is equal to a cure   30

Of the ground, a cure beyond forgetfulness.
And yet the leaves, if they broke into bud,
If they broke into bloom, if they bore fruit,

And if we ate the incipient colorings
Of their fresh culls might be a cure of the ground.
The fiction of the leaves is the icon

Of the poem, the figuration of blessedness,
And the icon is the man. The pearled chaplet of spring,
The magnum wreath of summer, time's autumn snood,

Its copy of the sun, these cover the rock.   40
These leaves are the poem, the icon and the man.
These are a cure of the ground and of ourselves,

In the predicate that there is nothing else.
They bud and bloom and bear their fruit without change.
They are more than leaves that cover the barren rock

They bud the whitest eye, the pallidest sprout,
New senses in the engenderings of sense,
The desire to be at the end of distances,

The body quickened and the mind in root.
They bloom as a man loves, as he lives in love.   50
They bear their fruit so that the year is known,

As if its understanding was brown skin,

The honey in its pulp, the final found,
The plenty of the year and of the world.

In this plenty, the poem makes meanings of the rock,
Of such mixed motion and such imagery
That its barrenness becomes a thousand things

And so exists no more. This is the cure
Of leaves and of the ground and of ourselves.
His words are both the icon and the man. 60

III
Forms of the Rock in a Night-Hymn

The rock is the gray particular of man's life,
The stone from which he rises, up—and—ho,
The step to the bleaker depths of his descents . . .

The rock is the stern particular of the air,
The mirror of the planets, one by one,
But through man's eye, their silent rhapsodist,

Turquoise the rock, at odious evening bright
With redness that sticks fast to evil dreams;
The difficult rightness of half-risen day.

The rock is the habitation of the whole, 70
Its strength and measure, that which is near, point A
In a perspective that begins again

At B: the origin of the mango's rind.
It is the rock where tranquil must adduce
Its tranquil self, the main of things, the mind,

The starting point of the human and the end,
That in which space itself is contained, the gate
To the enclosure, day, the things illumined

By day, night and that which night illumines,
Night and its midnight-minting fragrances, 80
Night's hymn of the rock, as in a vivid sleep.

THE WORLD AS MEDITATION   [1954]

> *J'ai passé trop de temps à travailler mon violon, à voyager. Mais l'exercice essentiel du compositeur—la méditation—rien ne l'a jamais suspendu en moi ... Je vis un rêve permanent, qui ne s'arrête ni nuit ni jour.*
> —GEORGES ENESCO

Is it Ulysses that approaches from the east,
The interminable adventurer? The trees are mended.
That winter is washed away. Someone is moving

On the horizon and lifting himself up above it.
A form of fire approaches the cretonnes of Penelope,
Whose mere savage presence awakens the world in which
    she dwells.

She has composed, so long, a self with which to welcome him,
Companion to his self for her, which she imagined,
Two in a deep-founded sheltering, friend and dear friend.

The trees had been mended, as an essential exercise   10
In an inhuman meditation, larger than her own.
No winds like dogs watched over her at night.

She wanted nothing he could not bring her by coming alone.
She wanted no fetchings. His arms would be her necklace
And her belt, the final fortune of their desire.

But was it Ulysses? Or was it only the warmth of the sun
On her pillow? The thought kept beating in her like her
    heart.
The two kept beating together. It was only day.

It was Ulysses and it was not. Yet they had met,
Friend and dear friend and a planet's encouragement.   20
The barbarous strength within her would never fail.

She would talk a little to herself as she combed her hair.
Repeating his name with its patient syllables,
Never forgetting him that kept coming constantly so near.

AS YOU LEAVE THE ROOM   [1957]

You speak. You say: Today's character is not
A skeleton out of its cabinet. Nor am I.

That poem about the pineapple, the one
About the mind as never satisfied,

The one about the credible hero, the one
About summer, are not what skeletons think about.

I wonder, have I lived a skeleton's life,
As a disbeliever in reality,

A countryman of all the bones in the world?
Now, here, the snow I had forgotten becomes   10

Part of a major reality, part of
An appreciation of a reality

And thus an elevation, as if I left
With something I could touch, touch every way.

And yet nothing has been changed except what is
Unreal, as if nothing had been changed at all.

William Carlos Williams

1883–1963

*William Carlos Williams was born September 17, 1883, in Rutherford,
New Jersey. He attended schools in this country, France, and Switzerland,
and took the M.D. degree in 1906 at the University of Pennsylvania,
where he knew Ezra Pound and Hilda Doolittle. After interning for
two years in New York hospitals, he studied pediatrics at Leipzig for
a year, then returned to Rutherford, where he practiced pediatrics and
wrote poetry until a few years before his death. In 1926 he received the
Dial Award and in 1931 the Guarantors Prize given by Poetry.
Williams believed that American speech has its own characteristic
rhythms, which he attempted to reproduce in his poems. He also published
several volumes of novels, short stories, essays, and dramas.*

TRACT [1917]

I will teach you my townspeople
how to perform a funeral
for you have it over a troop
of artists—
unless one should scour the world—
you have the ground sense necessary.

See! the hearse leads.
I begin with a design for a hearse.
For Christ's sake not black—
nor white either—and not polished!   10
Let it be weathered—like a farm wagon—
with gilt wheels (this could be

applied fresh at small expense)
or no wheels at all:
a rough dray to drag over the ground.

Knock the glass out!
My God—glass, my townspeople!
For what purpose? Is it for the dead
to look out or for us to see
how well he is housed or to see   20
the flowers or the lack of them—
or what?
To keep the rain and snow from him?
He will have a heavier rain soon:
pebbles and dirt and what not.
Let there be no glass—
and no upholstery, phew!
and no little brass rollers
and small easy wheels on the bottom—
my townspeople what are you thinking of?   30

A rough plain hearse then
with gilt wheels and no top at all.
On this the coffin lies
by its own weight.

                    No wreaths please—
especially no hot house flowers.
Some common memento is better,
something he prized and is known by:
his old clothes—a few books perhaps—
God knows what! You realize
how we are about these things   40
my townspeople—
something will be found—anything
even flowers if he had come to that.
So much for the hearse.

For heaven's sake though see to the driver!
Take off the silk hat! In fact
that's no place at all for him—

up there unceremoniously
dragging our friend out to his own dignity!
Bring him down—bring him down!   50
Low and inconspicuous! I'd not have him ride
on the wagon at all—damn him—
the undertaker's understrapper!
Let him hold the reins
and walk at the side
and inconspicuously too!

Then briefly as to yourselves:
Walk behind—as they do in France,
seventh class, or if you ride
Hell take curtains! Go with some show   60
of inconvenience; sit openly—
to the weather as to grief.
Or do you think you can shut grief in?
What—from us? We who have perhaps
nothing to lose? Share with us
share with us—it will be money
in your pockets.

                    Go now
I think you are ready.

THE WIDOW'S LAMENT IN SPRINGTIME
[1921]

Sorrow is my own yard
where the new grass
flames as it has flamed
often before but not
with the cold fire
that closes round me this year.
Thirtyfive years
I lived with my husband.
The plumtree is white today
with masses of flowers.   10

Masses of flowers
load the cherry branches
and color some bushes
yellow and some red
but the grief in my heart
is stronger than they
for though they were my joy
formerly, today I notice them
and turned away forgetting.
Today my son told me   20
that in the meadows,
at the edge of the heavy woods
in the distance, he saw
trees of white flowers.
I feel that I would like
to go there
and fall into those flowers
and sink into the marsh near them.

QUEEN-ANN'S-LACE   [1921]

Her body is not so white as
anemone petals nor so smooth—nor
so remote a thing. It is a field
of the wild carrot taking
the field by force; the grass
does not raise above it.
Here is no question of whiteness,
white as can be, with a purple mole
at the center of each flower.
Each flower is a hand's span   10
of her whiteness. Wherever
his hand has lain there is
a tiny purple blemish. Each part
is a blossom under his touch
to which the fibres of her being
stem one by one, each to its end,

until the whole field is a
white desire, empty, a single stem,
a cluster, flower by flower,
a pious wish to whiteness gone over—   20
or nothing.

SPRING AND ALL   [1923]

By the road to the contagious hospital
under the surge of the blue
mottled clouds driven from the
northeast—a cold wind. Beyond, the
waste of broad, muddy fields
brown with dried weeds, standing and fallen

patches of standing water
the scattering of tall trees

All along the road the reddish
purplish, forked, upstanding, twiggy   10
stuff of bushes and small trees
with dead, brown leaves under them
leafless vines—

Lifeless in appearance, sluggish
dazed spring approaches—

They enter the new world naked,
cold, uncertain of all
save that they enter. All about them
the cold, familiar wind—

Now the grass, tomorrow   20
the stiff curl of wildcarrot leaf
One by one objects are defined—
It quickens: clarity, outline of leaf

But now the stark dignity of
entrance—Still, the profound change
has come upon them: rooted, they
grip down and begin to awaken

TO ELSIE   [1923]

The pure products of America
go crazy—
mountain folk from Kentucky

or the ribbed north end of
Jersey
with its isolate lakes and

valleys, its deaf-mutes, thieves
old names
and promiscuity between

devil-may-care men who have taken   10
to railroading
out of sheer lust of adventure—

and young slatterns, bathed
in filth
from Monday to Saturday

to be tricked out that night
with gauds
from imaginations which have no

peasant traditions to give them
character   20
but flutter and flaunt

sheer rags—succumbing without
emotion
save numbed terror

under some hedge of choke-cherry
or viburnum—
which they cannot express—

Unless it be that marriage
perhaps
with a dash of Indian blood   30

will throw up a girl so desolate
so hemmed round
with disease or murder

that she'll be rescued by an
agent—
reared by the state and

sent out at fifteen to work in
some hard-pressed
house in the suburbs—

some doctor's family, some Elsie—   40
voluptuous water
expressing with broken

brain the truth about us—
her great
ungainly hips and flopping breasts

addressed to cheap
jewelry
and rich young men with fine eyes

as if the earth under our feet
were   50
an excrement of some sky

and we degraded prisoners
destined
to hunger until we eat filth

while the imagination strains
after deer
going by fields of goldenrod in

the stifling heat of September
Somehow
it seems to destroy us   60

It is only in isolate flecks that
something
is given off

No one
to witness
and adjust, no one to drive the car

RAIN   [1934]

As the rain falls
so does
        your love

bathe every
            open
object of the world—

In houses
the priceless dry
                rooms
of illicit love   10
where we live
hear the wash of the
                    rain—

There
      paintings

and fine
        metalware
woven stuffs—
all the whorishness
of our   20
        delight
sees
from its window

the spring wash
of your love
                the falling
rain—

The trees
are become
beasts fresh-risen   30
from the sea—
water

trickles
from the crevices of
their hides—

So my life is spent
                        to keep out love
with which
she rains upon

                the world   40

of spring

        drips

so spreads

        the words

far apart to let in

                         her love

And running in between

the drops

                    the rain

is a kind physician   50

                              the rain
of her thoughts over
the ocean
                    every

where

            walking with
invisible swift feet
over

            the helpless
                         waves—   60

Unworldly love
that has no hope
                    of the world

                              and that
cannot change the world
to its delight—

            The rain
falls upon the earth
and grass and flowers

come   70
            perfectly

into form from its
                         liquid

clearness

      But love is
unworldly

       and nothing
comes of it but love

following
and falling endlessly   80
from
     her thoughts

THE YACHTS   [1935]

contend in a sea which the land partly encloses
shielding them from the too-heavy blows
of an ungoverned ocean which when it chooses

tortures the biggest hulls, the best man knows
to pit against its beatings, and sinks them pitilessly.
Mothlike in mists, scintillant in the minute

brilliance of cloudless days, with broad bellying sails
they glide to the wind tossing green water
from their sharp prows while over them the crew crawls

ant-like, solicitously grooming them, releasing,   10
making fast as they turn, lean far over and having
caught the wind again, side by side, head for the mark.

In a well guarded arena of open water surrounded by
lesser and greater craft which, sycophant, lumbering
and flittering follow them, they appear youthful, rare

as the light of a happy eye, live with the grace
of all that in the mind is feckless, free and
naturally to be desired. Now the sea which holds them

is moody, lapping their glossy sides, as if feeling
for some slightest flaw but fails completely.   20
Today no race. Then the wind comes again. The yachts

move, jockeying for a start, the signal is set and they
are off. Now the waves strike at them but they are too
well made, they slip through, though they take in canvas.

Arms with hands grasping seek to clutch at the prows.
Bodies thrown recklessly in the way are cut aside.
It is a sea of faces about them in agony, in despair

until the horror of the race dawns staggering the mind,
the whole sea become an entanglement of watery bodies
lost to the world bearing what they cannot hold. Broken,   30

beaten, desolate, reaching from the dead to be taken up
they cry out, failing, failing! their cries rising
in waves still as the skillful yachts pass over.

THESE   [1938]

are the desolate, dark weeks
when nature in its barrenness
equals the stupidity of man.

The year plunges into night
and the heart plunges
lower than night

to an empty, windswept place
without sun, stars or moon
but a peculiar light as of thought

that spins a dark fire—   10
whirling upon itself until,
in the cold, it kindles

to make a man aware of nothing
that he knows, not loneliness
itself—Not a ghost but

would be embraced—emptiness,
despair—(They
whine and whistle) among

the flashes and booms of war;
houses of whose rooms   20
the cold is greater than can be thought,

the people gone that we loved,
the beds lying empty, the couches
damp, the chairs unused—

Hide it away somewhere
out of the mind, let it get roots
and grow, unrelated to jealous

ears and eyes—for itself.
In this mine they come to dig—all.
Is this the counterfoil to sweetest   30

music? The source of poetry that
seeing the clock stopped, says,
The clock has stopped

that ticked yesterday so well?
and hears the sound of lakewater
splashing—that is now stone.

PREFACE TO *PATERSON*: BOOK ONE   [1946]

> Rigor of beauty is the quest. But how will you find beauty when it
> is locked in the mind past all remonstrance?

To make a start,
out of particulars

and make them general, rolling
up the sum, by defective means—
Sniffing the trees,
just another dog
among a lot of dogs. What
else is there? And to do?
The rest have run out—
after the rabbits.   10
Only the lame stands—on
three legs. Scratch front and back.
Deceive and eat. Dig
a musty bone

For the beginning is assuredly
the end—since we know nothing, pure
and simple, beyond
our own complexities.

                    Yet there is
no return: rolling up out of chaos,   20
a nine months' wonder, the city
the man, an identity—it can't be
otherwise—an
interpenetration, both ways. Rolling
up! obverse, reverse;
the drunk the sober; the illustrious
the gross; one. In ignorance
a certain knowledge and knowledge,
undispersed, its own undoing.

                    (The multiple seed,   30
packed tight with detail, soured,
is lost in the flux and the mind,
distracted, floats off in the same
scum)

Rolling up, rolling up heavy with
numbers.

                    It is the ignorant sun
rising in the slot of
hollow suns risen, so that never in this
world will a man live well in his body   40
save dying—and not know himself
dying; yet that is
the design. Renews himself
thereby, in addition and subtraction,
walking up and down.

          and the craft,
subverted by thought, rolling up, let
him beware lest he turn to no more than
the writing of stale poems . . .
Minds like beds always made up,   50
               (more stony than a shore)
unwilling or unable.

                    Rolling in, top up,
under, thrust and recoil, a great clatter:
lifted as air, boated, multicolored, a
wash of seas—
from mathematics to particulars—

               divided as the dew,
floating mists, to be rained down and
regathered into a river that flows   60
and encircles:

          shells and animalcules
generally and so to man,

               to Paterson.

THE SEMBLABLES   [1946]

The red brick monastery in
the suburbs over against the dust-

hung acreage of the unfinished
and all but subterranean

munitions plant: those high
brick walls behind which at Easter
the little orphans and bastards
in white gowns sing their Latin

responses to the hoary ritual
while frankincense and myrrh   10
round out the dark chapel making
an enclosed sphere of it

of which they are the worm:
that cell outside the city beside
the polluted stream and dump
heap, uncomplaining, and the field

of upended stones with a photo
under glass fastened here and there
to one of them near the deeply
carved name to distinguish it: 20

that trinity of slate gables
the unembellished windows piling
up, the chapel with its round
window between the dormitories

peaked by the bronze belfry
peaked in turn by the cross,
verdegris—faces all silent
that miracle that has burst sexless

from between the carrot rows.
Leafless white birches, their   30
empty tendrils swaying in
the all but no breeze guard

behind the spiked monastery fence
the sacred statuary. But ranks

of brilliant car-tops row on row
give back in all his glory the

late November sun and hushed
attend, before that tumbled
ground, those sightless walls
and shovelled entrances where no   40

one but a lonesome cop swinging
his club gives sign, that agony
within where the wrapt machines
are praying . . .

BURNING THE CHRISTMAS GREENS   [1950]

Their time past, pulled down
cracked and flung to the fire
—go up in a roar

All recognition lost, burnt clean
clean in the flame, the green
dispersed, a living red,
flame red, red as blood wakes
on the ash—

and ebbs to a steady burning
the rekindled bed become   10
a landscape of flame

At the winter's midnight
we went to the trees, the coarse
holly, the balsam and
the hemlock for their green

At the thick of the dark
the moment of the cold's

deepest plunge we brought branches
cut from the green trees

to fill our need, and over   20
doorways, about paper Christmas
bells covered with tin foil
and fastened by red ribbons

we stuck the green prongs
in the windows hung
woven wreaths and above pictures
the living green. On the

mantle we built a green forest
and among those hemlock
sprays put a herd of small   30
white deer as if they

were walking there. All this!
and it seemed gentle and good
to us. Their time past,
relief! The room bare. We

stuffed the dead grate
with them upon the half burnt out
log's smoldering eye, opening
red and closing under them

and we stood there looking down.   40
Green is a solace
a promise of peace, a fort
against the cold (though we

did not say so) a challenge
above the snow's
hard shell. Green (we might
have said) that, where

small birds hide and dodge
and lift their plaintive

rallying cries, blocks for them   50
and knocks down

the unseeing bullets of
the storm. Green spruce boughs
pulled down by a weight of
snow—Transformed!

Violence leaped and appeared.
Recreant! roared to life
as the flame rose through and
our eyes recoiled from it.

In the jagged flames green   60
to red, instant and alive. Green!
those sure abutments . . . Gone!
lost to mind

and quick in the contracting
tunnel of the grate
appeared a world! Black
mountains, black and red—as

yet uncolored—and ash white,
an infant landscape of shimmering
ash and flame and we, in   70
that instant, lost,

breathless to be witnesses,
as if we stood
ourselves refreshed among
the shining fauna of that fire.

THE INJURY   [1951]

From this hospital bed
I can hear an engine

breathing—somewhere
   in the night:

—Soft coal, soft coal,
   soft coal!

And I know it is men
   breathing
shoveling, resting—

—Go about it   10
the slow way, if you can
find any way—
               Christ!
who's a bastard?
        —quit
and quit shoveling.

A man breathing
   and it quiets and
the puff of steady
work begins   20
          slowly: Chug.
Chug. Chug. Chug. . . .
        fading off.
Enough coal at least
   for this small job

   Soft! Soft!
—enough for one small
engine, enough for that.

A man shoveling
working and not lying here   30
   in this
hospital bed—powerless
—with the white-throat
   calling in the
poplars before dawn, his
faint flute-call,

triple tongued, piercing
the shingled curtain
of the new leaves;
  drowned out by   40
  car wheels
singing now on the rails,
taking the curve,
  slowly,
    a long wail,
high pitched:
  rounding
    the curve—
—the slow way because
(if you can find any way) that is   50
the only way left now
      for you.

Ezra Pound

b. 1885

Ezra Pound was born October 30, 1885, in Hailey, Idaho, but grew up in Pennsylvania. He was educated at the University of Pennsylvania and at Hamilton College, from which he graduated in 1905. After taking a master's degree at Pennsylvania and, briefly, teaching French and Spanish at Wabash College, Indiana, he left in 1908 for Europe, soon settling in London. A leading figure in the new poetry movements, such as Imagism, he helped found and edit Blast *(1914–1915) and from 1917 to 1919 was London editor of* The Little Review. *He left London for Paris in 1920, and from 1924 on lived in Italy. During these years he published, in addition to his poetry, books on art, literature, and economics. In 1941 he began to broadcast propaganda from Rome, attacking the American war effort. Brought back a prisoner to the United States in 1945 on the charge of treason, he was declared insane and placed in St. Elizabeth's Hospital, Washington, D.C., before he could be tried. When his* Pisan Cantos *received the Bollingen Award in 1949, he became the subject of national controversy. In 1958 his indictment for treason was dismissed, and he returned to Italy, where he now lives.*

PORTRAIT D'UNE FEMME   [1912]

Your mind and you are our Sargasso Sea,
London has swept about you this score years
And bright ships left you this or that in fee:
Ideas, old gossip, oddments of all things,
Strange spars of knowledge and dimmed wares of price.
Great minds have sought you—lacking someone else.

You have been second always. Tragical?
No. You preferred it to the usual thing:
One dull man, dulling and uxorious,
One average mind—with one thought less, each year. 10
Oh, you are patient, I have seen you sit
Hours, where something might have floated up.
And now you pay one. Yes, you richly pay.
You are a person of some interest, one comes to you
And takes strange gain away:
Trophies fished up; some curious suggestion;
Fact that leads nowhere; and a tale or two,
Pregnant with mandrakes, or with something else
That might prove useful and yet never proves,
That never fits a corner or shows use, 20
Or finds its hour upon the loom of days:
The tarnished, gaudy, wonderful old work;
Idols and ambergris and rare inlays,
These are your riches, your great store; and yet
For all this sea-hoard of deciduous things,
Strange woods half sodden, and new brighter stuff:
In the slow float of differing light and deep,
No! there is nothing! In the whole and all,
Nothing that's quite your own.
     Yet this is you. 30

THE SEAFARER [1912]

From the Anglo-Saxon

May I for my own self song's truth reckon,
Journey's jargon, how I in harsh days
Hardship endured oft.
Bitter breast-cares have I abided,
Known on my keel many a care's hold,
And dire sea-surge, and there I oft spent
Narrow nightwatch nigh the ship's head
While she tossed close to cliffs. Coldly afflicted,

My feet were by frost benumbed.
Chill its chains are; chafing sighs   10
Hew my heart round and hunger begot
Mere-weary mood. Lest man know not
That he on dry land loveliest liveth,
List how I, care-wretched, on ice-cold sea,
Weathered the winter, wretched outcast
Deprived of my kinsmen;
Hung with hard ice-flakes, where hail-scur flew,
There I heard naught save the harsh sea
And ice-cold wave, at whiles the swan cries,
Did for my games the gannet's clamour,   20
Sea-fowls' loudness was for me laughter,
The mews' singing all my mead-drink.
Storms, on the stone-cliffs beaten, fell on the stern
In icy feathers; full oft the eagle screamed
With spray on his pinion.
                              Not any protector
May make merry man faring needy.
This he little believes, who aye in winsome life
Abides 'mid burghers some heavy business,
Wealthy and wine-flushed, how I weary oft   30
Must bide above brine.
Neareth nightshade, snoweth from north,
Frost froze the land, hail fell on earth then,
Corn of the coldest. Nathless there knocketh now
The heart's thought that I on high streams
The salt-wavy tumult traverse alone.
Moaneth alway my mind's lust
That I fare forth, that I afar hence
Seek out a foreign fastness.
For this there's no mood-lofty man over earth's midst,   40
Not though he be given his good, but will have in his
        youth greed;
Nor his deed to the daring, nor his king to the faithful
But shall have his sorrow for sea-fare
Whatever his lord will.
He hath not heart for harping, nor in ring-having
Nor winsomeness to wife, nor world's delight
Nor any whit else save the wave's slash,

Yet longing comes upon him to fare forth on the water.
Bosque taketh blossom, cometh beauty of berries,
Fields to fairness, land fares brisker,   50
All this admonisheth man eager of mood,
The heart turns to travel so that he then thinks
On flood-ways to be far departing.
Cuckoo calleth with gloomy crying,
He singeth summerward, bodeth sorrow,
The bitter heart's blood. Burgher knows not—
He the prosperous man—what some perform
Where wandering them widest draweth.
So that but now my heart burst from my breastlock,
My mood 'mid the mere-flood,   60
Over the whale's acre, would wander wide.
On earth's shelter cometh oft to me,
Eager and ready, the crying lone-flyer,
Whets for the whale-path the heart irresistibly,
O'er tracks of ocean; seeing that anyhow
My lord deems to me this dead life
On loan and on land, I believe not
That any earth-weal eternal standeth
Save there be somewhat calamitous
That, ere a man's tide go, turn it to twain.   70
Disease or oldness or sword-hate
Beats out the breath from doom-gripped body.
And for this, every earl whatever, for those speaking
          after—
Laud of the living, boasteth some last word,
That he will work ere he pass onward,
Frame on the fair earth 'gainst foes his malice,
Daring ado, . . .
So that all men shall honour him after
And his laud beyond them remain 'mid the English,
Aye, for ever, a lasting life's-blast,   80
Delight 'mid the doughty.
                              Days little durable,
And all arrogance of earthen riches,
There come now no kings nor Cæsars
Nor gold-giving lords like those gone.
Howe'er in mirth most magnified,

Whoe'er lived in life most lordliest,
Drear all this excellence, delights undurable!
Waneth the watch, but the world holdeth.
Tomb hideth trouble. The blade is layed low.   90
Earthly glory ageth and seareth.
No man at all going the earth's gait,
But age fares against him, his face paleth,
Grey-haired he groaneth, knows gone companions,
Lordly men, are to earth o'ergiven,
Nor may he then the flesh-cover, whose life ceaseth,
Nor eat the sweet nor feel the sorry,
Nor stir hand nor think in mid heart,
And though he strew the grave with gold,
His born brothers, their buried bodies   100
Be an unlikely treasure hoard.

A VIRGINAL   [1912]

No, no! Go from me. I have left her lately.
I will not spoil my sheath with lesser brightness,
For my surrounding air hath a new lightness;
Slight are her arms, yet they have bound me straitly
And left me cloaked as with a gauze of æther;
As with sweet leaves; as with subtle clearness.
Oh, I have picked up magic in her nearness
To sheathe me half in half the things that sheathe her.
No, no! Go from me. I have still the flavour,
Soft as spring wind that's come from birchen bowers.   10
Green come the shoots, aye April in the branches,
As winter's wound with her sleight hand she staunches,
Hath of the trees a likeness of the savour:
As white their bark, so white this lady's hours.

THE RETURN   [1912]

See, they return; ah, see the tentative
        Movements, and the slow feet,

The trouble in the pace and the uncertain
Wavering!

See, they return, one, and by one,
With fear, as half-awakened;
As if the snow should hesitate
And murmur in the wind,
            and half turn back;
These were the "Wing'd-with-Awe,"   10
            Inviolable.

Gods of the wingèd shoe!
With them the silver hounds,
            sniffing the trace of air!

Haie! Haie!
      These were the swift to harry;
These were the keen-scented;
These were the souls of blood.

Slow on the leash,
            pallid the leash-men!   20

LAMENT OF THE FRONTIER GUARD   [1915]

By the North Gate, the wind blows full of sand,
Lonely from the beginning of time until now!
Trees fall, the grass goes yellow with autumn.
I climb the towers and towers
            to watch out the barbarous land:
Desolate castle, the sky, the wide desert.
There is no wall left to this village.
Bones white with a thousand frosts,
High heaps, covered with trees and grass;
Who brought this to pass?   10
Who has brought the flaming imperial anger?
Who has brought the army with drums and with kettle-
      drums?

Barbarous kings.
A gracious spring, turned to blood-ravenous autumn,
A turmoil of wars-men, spread over the middle kingdom,
Three hundred and sixty thousand,
And sorrow, sorrow like rain.
Sorrow to go, and sorrow, sorrow returning.
Desolate, desolate fields,
And no children of warfare upon them,   20
        No longer the men for offence and defence.
Ah, how shall you know the dreary sorrow at the North
        Gate,
With Rihoku's name forgotten,
And we guardsmen fed to the tigers.

By Rihaku

LIU CH'E   [1916]

The rustling of the silk is discontinued,
Dust drifts over the court-yard,
There is no sound of foot-fall, and the leaves
Scurry into heaps and lie still,
And she the rejoicer of the heart is beneath them:

A wet leaf that clings to the threshold.

HUGH SELWYN MAUBERLEY   [1920]

(LIFE AND CONTACTS)

"VOCAT ÆSTUS IN UMBRAM"
            Nemesianus, Ec. IV.

I

E. P. ODE POUR L'ELECTION DE SON SEPULCHRE

For three years, out of key with his time,
He strove to resuscitate the dead art

Of poetry; to maintain "the sublime"
In the old sense. Wrong from the start—

No, hardly, but seeing he had been born
In a half savage country, out of date;
Bent resolutely on wringing lilies from the acorn;
Capaneus; trout for factitious bait;

Ἴδμεν γάρ τοι πάνθ', ὅσ' ἐνὶ Τροίῃ
Caught in the unstopped ear;   10
Giving the rocks small lee-way
The chopped seas held him, therefore, that year.

His true Penelope was Flaubert,
He fished by obstinate isles;
Observed the elegance of Circe's hair
Rather than the mottoes on sun-dials.

Unaffected by "the march of events,"
He passed from men's memory in *l'an trentiesme*
De son eage; the case presents
No adjunct to the Muses' diadem.   20

II

The age demanded an image
Of its accelerated grimace,
Something for the modern stage,
Not, at any rate, an Attic grace;

Not, not certainly, the obscure reveries
Of the inward gaze;
Better mendacities
Than the classics in paraphrase!

The "age demanded" chiefly a mould in plaster,
Made with no loss of time,   30
A prose kinema, not, not assuredly, alabaster
Of the "sculpture" of rhyme.

III

The tea-rose tea-gown, etc.
Supplants the mousseline of Cos,
The pianola "replaces"
Sappho's barbitos.

Christ follows Dionysus,
Phallic and ambrosial
Made way for macerations;
Caliban casts out Ariel.   40

All things are a flowing,
Sage Heracleitus says;
But a tawdry cheapness
Shall outlast our days.

Even the Christian beauty
Defects—after Samothrace;
We see τὸ καλὸν
Decreed in the market place.

Faun's flesh is not to us,
Nor the saint's vision.   50
We have the press for wafer;
Franchise for circumcision.

All men, in law, are equals.
Free of Pisistratus,
We choose a knave or an eunuch
To rule over us.

O bright Apollo,
τίν' ἄνδρα, τίν' ἥρωα, τίνα θεὸν,
What god, man, or hero
Shall I place a tin wreath upon!   60

IV

These fought in any case,
and some believing,
            pro domo, in any case . . .

Some quick to arm,
some for adventure,
some from fear of weakness,
some from fear of censure,
some for love of slaughter, in imagination,
learning later . . .
some in fear, learning love of slaughter;   70

Died some, pro patria,
                non "dulce" non "et decor" . . .
walked eye-deep in hell
believing in old men's lies, then unbelieving
came home, home to a lie,
home to many deceits,
home to old lies and new infamy;
usury age-old and age-thick
and liars in public places.

Daring as never before, wastage as never before.   80
Young blood and high blood,
fair cheeks, and fine bodies;

fortitude as never before

frankness as never before,
disillusions as never told in the old days,
hysterias, trench confessions,
laughter out of dead bellies.

                                v

There died a myriad,
And of the best, among them,
For an old bitch gone in the teeth,   90
For a botched civilization,

Charm, smiling at the good mouth,
Quick eyes gone under earth's lid,

For two gross of broken statues,
For a few thousand battered books.

YEUX GLAUQUES

Gladstone was still respected,
When John Ruskin produced
"King's Treasuries"; Swinburne
And Rossetti still abused.

Fœtid Buchanan lifted up his voice   100
When that faun's head of hers
Became a pastime for
Painters and adulterers.

The Burne-Jones cartons
Have preserved her eyes;
Still, at the Tate, they teach
Cophetua to rhapsodize;

Thin like brook-water,
With a vacant gaze.
The English Rubaiyat was still-born   110
In those days.

The thin, clear gaze, the same
Still darts out faun-like from the half-ruin'd face,
Questing and passive. . . .
"Ah, poor Jenny's case" . . .

Bewildered that a world
Shows no surprise
At her last maquero's
Adulteries.

"SIENA MI FE'; DISFECEMI MAREMMA"

Among the pickled fœtuses and bottled bones,   120
Engaged in perfecting the catalogue,
I found the last scion of the
Senatorial families of Strasbourg, Monsieur Verog.

For two hours he talked of Gallifet;
Of Dowson; of the Rhymers' Club;
Told me how Johnson (Lionel) died
By falling from a high stool in a pub . . .

But showed no trace of alcohol
At the autopsy, privately performed—
Tissue preserved—the pure mind   130
Arose toward Newman as the whiskey warmed.

Dowson found harlots cheaper than hotels;
Headlam for uplift; Image impartially imbued
With raptures for Bacchus, Terpsichore and the Church.
So spoke the author of "The Dorian Mood,"

M. Verog, out of step with the decade,
Detached from his contemporaries,
Neglected by the young,
Because of these reveries.

BRENNBAUM

The sky-like limpid eyes,   140
The circular infant's face,
The stiffness from spats to collar
Never relaxing into grace;

The heavy memories of Horeb, Sinai and the forty years,
Showed only when the daylight fell
Level across the face
Of Brennbaum "The Impeccable."

MR. NIXON

In the cream gilded cabin of his steam yacht
Mr. Nixon advised me kindly, to advance with fewer
Dangers of delay. "Consider   150
      "Carefully the reviewer.

"I was as poor as you are;
"When I began I got, of course,
"Advance on royalties, fifty at first," said Mr. Nixon,
"Follow me, and take a column,
"Even if you have to work free.

"Butter reviewers. From fifty to three hundred
"I rose in eighteen months;

"The hardest nut I had to crack
"Was Dr. Dundas.   160

"I never mentioned a man but with the view
"Of selling my own works.
"The tip's a good one, as for literature
"It gives no man a sinecure.

"And no one knows, at sight, a masterpiece.
"And give up verse, my boy,
"There's nothing in it."

.   .   .   .

Likewise a friend of Bloughram's once advised me:
Don't kick against the pricks,
Accept opinion. The "Nineties" tried your game   170
And died, there's nothing in it.

X

Beneath the sagging roof
The stylist has taken shelter,
Unpaid, uncelebrated,
At last from the world's welter

Nature receives him;
With a placid and uneducated mistress
He exercises his talents
And the soil meets his distress.

The haven from sophistications and contentions   180
Leaks through its thatch;
He offers succulent cooking;
The door has a creaking latch.

XI

"Conservatrix of Milésien"
Habits of mind and feeling,
Possibly. But in Ealing
With the most bank-clerkly of Englishmen?

No, "Milésian" is an exaggeration.
No instinct has survived in her

Older than those her grandmother   190
Told her would fit her station.

XII

"Daphne with her thighs in bark
Stretches toward me her leafy hands,"—
Subjectively. In the stuffed-satin drawing-room
I await The Lady Valentine's commands,

Knowing my coat has never been
Of precisely the fashion
To stimulate, in her,
A durable passion;

Doubtful, somewhat, of the value   200
Of well-gowned approbation
Of literary effort,
But never of The Lady Valentine's vocation:

Poetry, her border of ideas,
The edge, uncertain, but a means of blending
With other strata
Where the lower and higher have ending;

A hook to catch the Lady Jane's attention,
A modulation toward the theatre,
Also, in the case of revolution,   210
A possible friend and comforter.

.   .   .   .

Conduct, on the other hand, the soul
"Which the highest cultures have nourished"
To Fleet St. where
Dr. Johnson flourished;

Beside this thoroughfare
The sale of half-hose has
Long since superseded the cultivation
Of Pierian roses.

ENVOI (1919)

Go, dumb-born book, 220
Tell her that sang me once that song of Lawes:
Hadst thou but song
As thou hast subjects known,
Then were there cause in thee that should condone
Even my faults that heavy upon me lie,
And build her glories their longevity.

Tell her that sheds
Such treasure in the air,
Recking naught else but that her graces give
Life to the moment, 230
I would bid them live
As roses might, in magic amber laid,
Red overwrought with orange and all made
One substance and one colour
Braving time.

Tell her that goes
With song upon her lips
But sings not out the song, nor knows
The maker of it, some other mouth,
May be as fair as hers, 240
Might, in new ages, gain her worshippers,
When our two dusts with Waller's shall be laid,
Siftings on siftings in oblivion,
Till change hath broken down
All things save Beauty alone.

MAUBERLEY

1920

"Vacuos exercet aera morsus."

I

Turned from the "eau-forte
Par Jaquemart"
To the strait head
Of Messalina:

"His true Penelope   250
Was Flaubert,"
And his tool
The engraver's.

Firmness,
Not the full smile,
His art, but an art
In profile;

Colourless
Pier Francesca,
Pisanello lacking the skill   260
To forge Achaia.

II

"*Qu'est ce qu'ils savent de l'amour, et qu'est ce qu'ils peuvent
comprendre?*
*S'ils ne comprennent pas la poésie, s'ils ne sentent pas la
musique, qu'est ce qu'ils peuvent comprendre de cette passion en
comparaison avec laquelle la rose est grossière et le parfum des
violettes un tonnerre?*"   CAID ALI

For three years, diabolus in the scale,
He drank ambrosia,
All passes, ANANGKE prevails,
Came end, at last, to that Arcadia.

He had moved amid her phantasmagoria,
Amid her galaxies,
NUKTIS 'AGALMA

.   .   .   .

Drifted ... drifted precipitate,
Asking time to be rid of ...   270
Of his bewilderment; to designate
His new found orchid. ...

To be certain ... certain ...
(Amid ærial flowers) ... time for arrangements—
Drifted on
To the final estrangement;

Unable in the supervening blankness
To sift TO AGATHON from the chaff
Until he found his sieve . . .
Ultimately, his seismograph: 280

—Given that is his "fundamental passion,"
This urge to convey the relation
Of eye-lid and cheek-bone
By verbal manifestations;

To present the series
Of curious heads in medallion—

He had passed, inconscient, full gaze,
The wide-banded irides
And botticellian sprays implied
In their diastasis;   290

Which anæthesis, noted a year late,
And weighed, revealed his great affect,
(Orchid), mandate
Of Eros, a retrospect.

                    .   .   .

Mouths biting empty air,
The still stone dogs,
Caught in metamorphosis, were
Left him as epilogues.

"THE AGE DEMANDED"
VIDE POEM II. Page 766
For this agility chance found
Him of all men, unfit   300
As the red-beaked steeds of
The Cytheræan for a chain bit.

The glow of porcelain
Brought no reforming sense
To his perception
Of the social inconsequence.

Thus, if her colour
Came against his gaze,
Tempered as if
It were through a perfect glaze   310

He made no immediate application
Of this to relation of the state
To the individual, the month was more temperate
Because this beauty had been.

> The coral isle, the lion-coloured sand
> Burst in upon the porcelain revery:
> Impetuous troubling
> Of his imagery.

Mildness, amid the neo-Nietzschean clatter,
His sense of graduations,   320
Quite out of place amid
Resistance to current exacerbations,

Invitation, mere invitation to perceptivity
Gradually led him to the isolation
Which these presents place
Under a more tolerant, perhaps, examination.

By constant elimination
The manifest universe
Yielded an armour
Against utter consternation,   330

A Minoan undulation,
Seen, we admit, amid ambrosial circumstances
Strengthened him against
The discouraging doctrine of chances,

And his desire for survival,
Faint in the most strenuous moods,
Became an Olympian *apathein*
In the presence of selected perceptions.

A pale gold, in the aforesaid pattern,
The unexpected palms   340
Destroying, certainly, the artist's urge,
Left him delighted with the imaginary
Audition of the phantasmal sea-surge,

Incapable of the least utterance or composition,
Emendation, conservation of the "better tradition,"
Refinement of medium, elimination of superfluities,
August attraction or concentration.

Nothing, in brief, but maudlin confession,
Irresponse to human aggression,
Amid the precipitation, down-float   350
Of insubstantial manna,
Lifting the faint susurrus
Of his subjective hosannah.

Ultimate affronts to
Human redundancies;

Non-esteem of self-styled "his betters"
Leading, as he well knew,
To his final
Exclusion from the world of letters.

IV

Scattered Moluccas   360
Not knowing, day to day,
The first day's end, in the next noon;
The placid water
Unbroken by the Simoon;

Thick foliage
Placid beneath warm suns,
Tawn fore-shores
Washed in the cobalt of oblivions;

Or through dawn-mist
The grey and rose   370

Of the juridical
Flamingoes;

A consciousness disjunct,
Being but this overblotted
Series
Of intermittences;

Coracle of Pacific voyages,
The unforecasted beach;
Then on an oar
Read this: 380

"I was
And I no more exist;
Here drifted
An hedonist."

MEDALLION

Luini in porcelain!
The grand piano
Utters a profane
Protest with her clear soprano.

The sleek head emerges
From the gold-yellow frock
As Anadyomene in the opening   390
Pages of Reinach.

Honey-red, closing the face-oval,
A basket-work of braids which seem as if they were
Spun in King Minos' hall
From metal, or intractable amber;

The face-oval beneath the glaze,
Bright in its suave bounding-line, as,
Beneath half-watt rays,
The eyes turn topaz.   400

CANTO I   [1925]

And then went down to the ship,
Set keel to breakers, forth on the godly sea, and
We set up mast and sail on that swart ship,
Bore sheep aboard her, and our bodies also
Heavy with weeping, and winds from sternward
Bore us out onward with bellying canvas,
Circe's this craft, the trim-coifed goddess.
Then sat we amidships, wind jamming the tiller,
Thus with stretched sail, we went over sea till day's end.
Sun to his slumber, shadows o'er all the ocean,   10
Came we then to the bounds of deepest water,
To the Kimmerian lands, and peopled cities
Covered with close-webbed mist, unpierced ever
With glitter of sun-rays
Nor with stars stretched, nor looking back from heaven
Swartest night stretched over wretched men there.
The ocean flowing backward, came we then to the place
Aforesaid by Circe.
Here did they rites, Perimedes and Eurylochus,
And drawing sword from my hip   20
I dug the ell-square pitkin;
Poured we libations unto each the dead,
First mead and then sweet wine, water mixed with white
        flour.
Then prayed I many a prayer to the sickly death's-heads;
As set in Ithaca, sterile bulls of the best
For sacrifice, heaping the pyre with goods,
A sheep to Tiresias only, black and a bell-sheep.
Dark blood flowed in the fosse,
Souls out of Erebus, cadaverous dead, of brides
Of youths and of the old who had borne much;   30
Souls stained with recent tears, girls tender,
Men many, mauled with bronze lance heads,
Battle spoil, bearing yet dreory arms,
These many crowded about me; with shouting,

Fallor upon me, cried to my men for more beasts;
Slaughtered the herds, sheep slain of bronze;
Poured ointment, cried to the gods,
To Pluto the strong, and praised Proserpine;
Unsheathed the narrow sword,
I sat to keep off the impetuous impotent dead,   40
Till I should hear Tiresias.
But first Elpenor came, our friend Elpenor,
Unburied, cast on the wide earth,
Limbs that we left in the house of Circe,
Unwept, unwrapped in sepulchre, since toils urged other.
Pitiful spirit. And I cried in hurried speech:
"Elpenor, how art thou come to this dark coast?
"Cam'st thou afoot, outstripping seamen?"
          And he in heavy speech:
"Ill fate and abundant wine. I slept in Circe's ingle.   50
"Going down the long ladder unguarded,
"I fell against the buttress,
"Shattered the nape-nerve, the soul sought Avernus.
"But thou, O King, I bid remember me, unwept, unburied,
"Heap up mine arms, be tomb by sea-bord, and inscribed:
"*A man of no fortune, and with a name to come.*
"And set my oar up, that I swung mid fellows."

And Anticlea came, whom I beat off, and then Tiresias
     Theban,
Holding his golden wand, knew me, and spoke first:
"A second time? why? man of ill star,   60
"Facing the sunless dead and this joyless region?
"Stand from the fosse, leave me my bloody bever
"For soothsay."
          And I stepped back,
And he strong with the blood, said then: "Odysseus
"Shalt return through spiteful Neptune, over dark seas,
"Lose all companions." And then Anticlea came.
Lie quiet Divus. I mean, that is Andreas Divus,
In officina Wecheli, 1538, out of Homer.
And he sailed, by Sirens and thence outward and away   70
And unto Circe.
          Venerandam,

In the Cretan's phrase, with the golden crown, Aphrodite,
Cypri munimenta sortita est, mirthful, oricalchi, with
    golden
Girdles and breast bands, thou with dark eyelids
Bearing the golden bough of Argicida. So that:

CANTO II   [1925]

Hang it all, Robert Browning,
            there can be but the one "Sordello."
But Sordello, and my Sordello?
Lo Sordels si fo di Mantovana.
So-shu churned in the sea.
Seal sports in the spray-whited circles of cliff-wash,
Sleek head, daughter of Lir,
            eyes of Picasso
Under black fur-hood, lithe daughter of Ocean;
And the wave runs in the beach-groove;   10
"Eleanor, ἐλέναυς and ἑλέπτολις!"
            And poor old Homer blind, blind, as a bat,
Ear, ear for the sea-surge, murmur of old men's voices:
"Let her go back to the ships,
Back among Grecian faces, lest evil come on our own,
Evil and further evil, and a curse cursed on our children,
Moves, yes she moves like a goddess
And has the face of a god
            and the voice of Schoeney's daughters,
And doom goes with her in walking,   20
Let her go back to the ships,
            back among Grecian voices."
And by the beach-run, Tyro,
            Twisted arms of the sea-god,
Lithe sinews of water, gripping her, cross-hold,
And the blue-gray glass of the wave tents them,
Glare azure of water, cold-welter, close cover.
Quiet sun-tawny sand-stretch,
The gulls broad out their wings,
            nipping between the splay feathers;   30

Snipe come for their bath,
              bend out their wing-joints,
Spread wet wings to the sun-film,
And by Scios,
              to left of the Naxos passage,
Naviform rock overgrown,
              algæ cling to its edge,
There is a wine-red glow in the shallows,
              a tin flash in the sun-dazzle.

The ship landed in Scios,   40
              men wanting spring-water,
And by the rock-pool a young boy loggy with vine-must,
              "To Naxos? Yes, we'll take you to Naxos,
Cum' along lad." "Not that way!"
"Aye, that way is Naxos."
              And I said: "It's a straight ship."
And an ex-convict out of Italy
              knocked me into the fore-stays,
(He was wanted for manslaughter in Tuscany)
              And the whole twenty against me,   50
Mad for a little slave money.
              And they took her out of Scios
And off her course . . .
              And the boy came to, again, with the racket,
And looked out over the bows,
              and to eastward, and to the Naxos passage.
God-sleight then, god-sleight:
              Ship stock fast in sea-swirl,
Ivy upon the oars, King Pentheus,
              grapes with no seed but sea-foam,   60
Ivy in scupper-hole.
Aye, I, Accetes, stood there,
              and the god stood by me,
Water cutting under the keel,
Sea-break from stern forrards,
              wake running off from the bow,
And where was gunwale, there now was vine-trunk,
And tenthril where cordage had been,
              grape-leaves on the rowlocks,

Heavy vine on the oarshafts,   70
And, out of nothing, a breathing,
          hot breath on my ankles,
Beasts like shadows in glass,
          a furred tail upon nothingness.
Lynx-purr, and heathery smell of beasts,
          where tar smell had been,
Sniff and pad-foot of beasts,
          eye-glitter out of black air.
The sky overshot, dry, with no tempest,
Sniff and pad-foot of beasts,   80
          fur brushing my knee-skin,
Rustle of airy sheaths,
          dry forms in the *æther*.
And the ship like a keel in ship-yard,
          slung like an ox in smith's sling,
Ribs stuck fast in the ways,
          grape-cluster over pin-rack,
          void air taking pelt.
Lifeless air become sinewed,
          feline leisure of panthers,   90
Leopards sniffing the grape shoots by scupper-hole,
Crouched panthers by fore-hatch,
And the sea blue-deep about us,
          green-ruddy in shadows,
And Lyæus: "From now, Accœtes, my altars,
Fearing no bondage,
          fearing no cat of the wood,
Safe with my lynxes,
          feeding grapes to my leopards,
Olibanum is my incense,   100
          the vines grow in my homage."

The back-swell now smooth in the rudder-chains,
Black snout of a porpoise
          where Lycabs had been,
Fish-scales on the oarsmen.
          And I worship.
I have seen what I have seen.
          When they brought the boy I said:

"He has a god in him,
           though I do not know which god."   110
And they kicked me into the fore-stays.
I have seen what I have seen:
           Medon's face like the face of a dory,
Arms shrunk into fins. And you, Pentheus,
Had as well listen to Tiresias, and to Cadmus,
           or your luck will go out of you.
Fish-scales over groin muscles,
           lynx-purr amid sea . . .
And of a later year,
           pale in the wine-red algæ,   120
If you will lean over the rock,
           the coral face under wave-tinge,
Rose-paleness under water-shift,
           Ileuthyeria, fair Dafne of sea-bords,
The swimmer's arms turned to branches,
Who will say in what year,
           fleeing what band of tritons,
The smooth brows, seen, and half seen,
           now ivory stillness.

And So-shu churned in the sea, So-shu also,   130
           using the long moon for a churn-stick . . .
Lithe turning of water,
           sinews of Poseidon,
Black azure and hyaline,
           glass wave over Tyro,
Close cover, unstillness,
           bright welter of wave-cords,
Then quiet water,
           quiet in the buff sands,
Sea-fowl stretching wing-joints,   140
           splashing in rock-hollows and sand-hollows
In the wave-runs by the half-dune;
Glass-glint of wave in the tide-rips against sunlight,
           pallor of Hesperus,
Grey peak of the wave,
           wave, colour of grape's pulp,

Olive grey in the near,
          far, smoke grey of the rock-slide,
Salmon-pink wings of the fish-hawk
          cast grey shadows in water,   150
The tower like a one-eyed great goose
          cranes up out of the olive-grove,

And we have heard the fauns chiding Proteus
          in the smell of hay under the olive-trees,
And the frogs singing against the fauns
          in the half-light.
And . . .

H.D.

1886–1961

H[ilda]. D[oolittle]. *was born in Bethlehem, Pennsylvania, on September 10, 1886, the daughter of Charles L. Doolittle, a professor of astronomy at Lehigh University, later director of the Flower Observatory in Philadelphia. While a student at Bryn Mawr she became a friend of Ezra Pound and William Carlos Williams, then students at the University of Pennsylvania. In 1911 she went to Europe and Pound claimed her for his Imagist movement, having her sign her poems "H.D. Imagist." She married Richard Aldington, but later separated from him after the birth of a daughter and a nervous breakdown. The novelist Winifred Bryher helped her regain health and visited Greece with her. She was treated by Freud, who was interested in her dreams, visions, and vicarious experiences of ancient Greece. The "classical world" in H.D.'s poems is neither the historical Greece of the Golden Age nor the sentimental Greece of Victorian poetry, but an imaginative world of her own creation, of unearthly beauty and Puritan austerity. Hilda Doolittle died in Zurich on September 17, 1961.*

ADONIS   [1916]

1.

Each of us like you
has died once,
each of us like you
has passed through drift of wood-leaves,
cracked and bent
and tortured and unbent
in the winter-frost,
then burnt into gold points,

lighted afresh,
crisp amber, scales of gold-leaf,   10
gold turned and re-welded
in the sun-heat;

each of us like you
has died once,
each of us has crossed an old wood-path
and found the winter-leaves
so golden in the sun-fire
that even the live wood-flowers
were dark.

2.

Not the gold on the temple-front   20
where you stand
is as gold as this,
not the gold that fastens your sandal,
nor the gold reft
through your chiselled locks,
is as gold as this last year's leaf,
not all the gold hammered and wrought
and beaten
on your lover's face,
brow and bare breast   30
is as golden as this:

each of us like you
has died once,
each of us like you
stands apart, like you
fit to be worshipped.

HEAT   [1916]

O wind, rend open the heat,
cut apart the heat,
rend it to tatters.

Fruit cannot drop
through this thick air—
fruit cannot fall into heat
that presses up and blunts
the points of pears
and rounds the grapes.

Cut the heat—   10
plough through it,
turning it on either side
of your path.

PEAR TREE   [1916]

Silver dust,
lifted from the earth,
higher than my arms reach,
you have mounted,
O, silver,
higher than my arms reach,
you front us with great mass;

no flower ever opened
so staunch a white leaf,
no flower ever parted silver   10
from such rare silver;

O, white pear,
your flower-tufts
thick on the branch
bring summer and ripe fruits
in their purple hearts.

OREAD   [1916]

Whirl up, sea—
whirl your pointed pines,

splash your great pines
on our rocks,
hurl your green over us,
cover us with your pools of fir.

FROM CITRON-BOWER   [1916]

From citron-bower be her bed,
cut from branch of tree a-flower,
fashioned for her maidenhead.

From Lydian apples, sweet of hue,
cut the width of board and lathe,
carve the feet from myrtle-wood.

Let the palings of her bed
be quince and box-wood overlaid
with the scented bark of yew.

That all the wood in blossoming,   10
may calm her heart and cool her blood,
for losing of her maidenhood.

ERIGE COR TUUM AD ME IN CAELUM   [1957]

(September 1940)

                    1.
Lift up your eyes on high,
under the sky—
indeed?
watch planets swerve and lend
lustre to partner-planet,
as they serve
magnetic stress, and turn

subservient to your hands,
your will that guides
majestic cycle of obedient tides?   10

lift up our eyes to you?
no, God, we stare and stare,
upon a nearer thing
that greets us here,
Death, violent and near.

2.

The alchemy and mystery is this,
no cross to kiss,
but a cross pointing on a compass-face,
east, west, south, north;

the secret of the ages is revealed,   20
the book un-sealed,
the fisherman entangled in his nets
felled where he waded
for the evening catch,
the house-door
swinging on the broken latch,
the woman with her basket on the quay,
shading her eyes to see,
if the last boat
really is the last,   30
the house-dog lost,
the little hen escaped,
the precious hay-rick scattered,
and the empty cage,
the book of life is open,
turn and read:

the linnet picking at the wasted seed,
is holy ghost,
the weed,
broken by iron axle,   40
is the flower
magicians bartered for.

Robinson Jeffers

1887–1962

John Robinson Jeffers was born on January 10, 1887, in Pittsburgh, where his father taught Old Testament in Western Theological Seminary. He was a precocious child, began reading Greek at the age of five, traveled extensively with his parents in Europe, and studied at boarding schools in Geneva, Lausanne, Zurich, and Leipzig. In 1903 the Jeffers family moved to California and Robinson entered Occidental College, from which he graduated in 1905. He then attended in quick succession the University of California at Los Angeles, the University of Zurich, the College of Physicians at the University of California, and the School of Forestry at the University of Washington. A small inheritance gave him independence in 1912, and he began his long career as poet. He married Una Call Kuster, and they settled at Carmel, California, where Jeffers built his famous stone tower and wrote his powerful, violent tragedies. He won literary recognition with Tamar and Other Poems *in 1924, and his* Medea *was a sensation on Broadway, with Judith Anderson playing Medea, in 1947. A few of his poems continue to have an audience, even though critical attention since the 1930's has diminished.*

NIGHT   [1925]

The ebb slips from the rock, the sunken
Tide-rocks lift streaming shoulders
Out of the slack, the slow west
Sombering its torch; a ship's light
Shows faintly, far out,
Over the weight of the prone ocean
On the low cloud.

Over the dark mountain, over the dark pinewood,
Down the long dark valley along the shrunken river,
Returns the splendor without rays, the shining of shadow,   10
Peace-bringer, the matrix of all shining and quieter of
          shining.
Where the shore widens on the bay she opens dark wings
And the ocean accepts her glory. O soul worshipful of her
You like the ocean have grave depths where she dwells
          always,
And the film of waves above that takes the sun takes also
Her, with more love. The sun-lovers have a blond favorite,
A father of lights and noises, wars, weeping and laughter,
Hot labor, lust and delight and the other blemishes.
          Quietness
Flows from her deeper fountain; and he will die; and she is
          immortal.

Far off from here the slender   20
Flocks of the mountain forest
Move among stems like towers
Of the old redwoods to the stream,
No twig crackling; dip shy
Wild muzzles into the mountain water
Among the dark ferns.

O passionately at peace you being secure will pardon
The blasphemies of glowworms, the lamp in my tower,
          the fretfulness
Of cities, the cressets of the planets, the pride of the stars.
This August night in a rift of cloud Antares reddens,   30
The great one, the ancient torch, a lord among lost
          children,
The earth's orbit doubled would not girdle his greatness,
          one fire
Globed, out of grasp of the mind enormous; but to you O
          Night
What? Not a spark? What flicker of a spark in the faint far
          glimmer
Of a lost fire dying in the desert, dim coals of a sand-pit the
          Bedouins

Wandered from at dawn . . . Ah singing prayer to what gulfs
    tempted
Suddenly are you more lost? To us the near-hand mountain
Be a measure of height, the tide-worn cliff at the sea-gate a
    measure of continuance.

The tide, moving the night's
Vastness with lonely voices,   40
Turns, the deep dark-shining
Pacific leans on the land,
Feeling his cold strength
To the outmost margins: you Night will resume
The stars in your time.

O passionately at peace when will that tide draw
    shoreward?
Truly the spouting fountains of light, Antares, Arcturus,
Tire of their flow, they sing one song but they think
    silence.
The striding winter giant Orion shines, and dreams
    darkness.
And life, the flicker of men and moths and the wolf on
    the hill,   50
Though furious for continuance, passionately feeding,
    passionately
Remaking itself upon its mates, remembers deep inward
The calm mother, the quietness of the womb and the egg,
The primal and the latter silences: dear Night it is
    memory
Prophesies, prophecy that remembers, the charm of the
    dark.
And I and my people, we are willing to love the four-score
    years
Heartily; but as a sailor loves the sea, when the helm is for
    harbor.

Have men's minds changed,
Or the rock hidden in the deep of the waters of the soul
Broken the surface? A few centuries   60
Gone by, was none dared not to people

The darkness beyond the stars with harps and habitations.
But now, dear is the truth. Life is grown sweeter and lonelier,
And death is no evil.

BIRDS   [1925]

The fierce musical cries of a couple of sparrowhawks hunt-
    ing on the headland,
Hovering and darting, their heads northwestward,
Prick like silver arrows shot through a curtain the noise of
    the ocean
Trampling its granite; their red backs gleam
Under my window around the stone corners; nothing grace-
    fuller, nothing
Nimbler in the wind. Westward the wave-gleaners,
The old gray sea-going gulls are gathered together, the
    northwest wind wakening
Their wings to the wild spirals of the wind-dance.
Fresh as the air, salt as the foam, play birds in the bright
    wind, fly falcons
Forgetting the oak and the pinewood, come gulls   10
From the Carmel sands and the sands at the river-mouth,
    from Lobos and out of the limitless
Power of the mass of the sea, for a poem
Needs multitude, multitudes of thoughts, all fierce, all flesh-
    eaters, musically clamorous
Bright hawks that hover and dart headlong, and ungainly
Gray hungers fledged with desire of transgression, salt
    slimed beaks, from the sharp
Rock-shores of the world and the secret waters.

APOLOGY FOR BAD DREAMS   [1927]

I

In the purple light, heavy with redwood, the slopes drop
    seaward,

Headlong convexities of forest, drawn in together to the
    steep ravine. Below, on the sea-cliff,
A lonely clearing; a little field of corn by the streamside; a
    roof under spared trees. Then the ocean
Like a great stone someone has cut to a sharp edge and
    polished to shining. Beyond it, the fountain
And furnace of incredible light flowing up from the sunk
    sun. In the little clearing a woman
Is punishing a horse; she had tied the halter to a sapling at
    the edge of the wood, but when the great whip
Clung to the flanks the creature kicked so hard she feared
    he would snap the halter; she called from the house
The young man her son; who fetched a chain tie-rope, they
    working together
Noosed the small rusty links round the horse's tongue
And tied him by the swollen tongue to the tree.   10
Seen from this height they are shrunk to insect size,
Out of all human relation. You cannot distinguish
The blood dripping from where the chain is fastened,
The beast shuddering; but the thrust neck and the legs
Far apart. You can see the whip fall on the flanks . . .
The gesture of the arm. You cannot see the face of the
    woman.
The enormous light beats up out of the west across the
    cloud-bars of the trade-wind. The ocean
Darkens, the high clouds brighten, the hills darken together.
    Unbridled and unbelievable beauty
Covers the evening world . . . not covers, grows apparent
    out of it, as Venus down there grows out
From the lit sky. What said the prophet? "I create good: and
    I create evil: I am the Lord."   20

II

This coast crying out for tragedy like all beautiful places,
(The quiet ones ask for quieter suffering: but here the granite
    cliff the gaunt cypresses crown
Demands what victim? The dykes of red lava and black
    what Titan? The hills like pointed flames
Beyond Soberanes, the terrible peaks of the bare hills under
    the sun, what immolation?)

This coast crying out for tragedy like all beautiful places:
    and like the passionate spirit of humanity
Pain for its bread: God's, many victims', the painful deaths,
    the horrible transfigurations: I said in my heart,
"Better invent than suffer: imagine victims
Lest your own flesh be chosen the agonist, or you
Martyr some creature to the beauty of the place." And
    I said,
"Burn sacrifices once a year to magic   30
Horror away from the house, this little house here
You have built over the ocean with your own hands
Beside the standing boulders: for what are we,
The beast that walks upright, with speaking lips
And little hair, to think we should always be fed,
Sheltered, intact, and self-controlled? We sooner more liable
Than the other animals. Pain and terror, the insanities of
    desire; not accidents but essential,
And crowd up from the core." I imagined victims for
    those wolves, I made them phantoms to follow,
They have hunted the phantoms and missed the house. It is
    not good to forget over what gulfs the spirit
Of the beauty of humanity, the petal of a lost flower blown
    seaward by the night-wind, floats to its quietness.   40

III

Boulders blunted like an old bear's teeth break up from the
    headland; below them
All the soil is thick with shells, the tide-rock feasts of a dead
    people.
Here the granite flanks are scarred with ancient fire, the
    ghosts of the tribe
Crouch in the nights beside the ghost of a fire, they try to
    remember the sunlight,
Light has died out of their skies. These have paid something
    for the future
Luck of the country, while we living keep old griefs in
    memory: though God's
Envy is not a likely fountain of ruin, to forget evils calls
    down

Sudden reminders from the cloud; remembered deaths be our
    redeemers;

Imagined victims our salvation: white as the half moon at
    midnight

Someone flamelike passed me, saying, "I am Tamar
    Cauldwell, I have my desire,"   50

Then the voice of the sea returned, when she had gone by,
    the stars to their towers.

... Beautiful country burn again, Point Pinos down to the
    Sur Rivers

Burn as before with bitter wonders, land and ocean and the
    Carmel water.

IV

He brays humanity in a mortar to bring the savor

From the bruised root: a man having bad dreams, who invents
    victims, is only the ape of that God.

He washes it out with tears and many waters, calcines it with
    fire in the red crucible,

Deforms it, makes it horrible to itself: the spirit flies out and
    stands naked, he sees the spirit,

He takes it in the naked ecstasy; it breaks in his hand, the
    atom is broken, the power that massed it

Cries to the power that moves the stars, "I have come home
    to myself, behold me.

I bruised myself in the flint mortar and burnt me   60

In the red shell, I tortured myself, I flew forth,

Stood naked of myself and broke me in fragments,

And here am I moving the stars that are me."

I have seen these ways of God: I know of no reason ·

For fire and change and torture and the old returnings.

He being sufficient might be still. I think they admit no
    reason; they are the ways of my love.

Unmeasured power, incredible passion, enormous craft: no
    thought apparent but burns darkly

Smothered with its own smoke in the human brain-vault:
    no thought outside: a certain measure in phenomena:

The fountains of the boiling stars, the flowers on the foreland,
    the ever-returning roses of dawn.

HURT HAWKS   [1928]

I

The broken pillar of the wing jags from the clotted shoulder,
The wing trails like a banner in defeat,
No more to use the sky forever but live with famine
And pain a few days: cat nor coyote
Will shorten the week of waiting for death, there is game
    without talons.
He stands under the oak-bush and waits
The lame feet of salvation; at night he remembers freedom
And flies in a dream, the dawns ruin it.
He is strong and pain is worse to the strong, incapacity is
    worse.
The curs of the day come and torment him   10
At distance, no one but death the redeemer will humble
    that head,
The intrepid readiness, the terrible eyes.
The wild God of the world is sometimes merciful to those
That ask mercy, not often to the arrogant.
You do not know him, you communal people, or you have
    forgotten him;
Intemperate and savage, the hawk remembers him;
Beautiful and wild, the hawks, and men that are dying,
    remember him.

II

I'd sooner, except the penalties, kill a man than a hawk; but
    the great redtail
Had nothing left but unable misery
From the bone too shattered for mending, the wing that
    trailed under his talons when he moved.   20
We had fed him six weeks, I gave him freedom,
He wandered over the foreland hill and returned in the
    evening, asking for death,
Not like a beggar, still eyed with the old
Implacable arrogance. I gave him the lead gift in the twilight.
    What fell was relaxed,

Owl-downy, soft feminine feathers; but what
Soared: the fierce rush: the night-herons by the flooded river
    cried fear at its rising
Before it was quite unsheathed from reality.

PROMISE OF PEACE   [1935]

The heads of strong old age are beautiful
Beyond all grace of youth. They have strange quiet,
Integrity, health, soundness, to the full
They've dealt with life and been atempered by it.
A young man must not sleep, his years are war
Civil and foreign but the former's worse;
But the old can breathe in safety now they are
Forgetting what youth meant, the being perverse,
Running the fool's gauntlet and getting cut
By the whips of the five senses. As for me,   10
If I should wish to live long it were but
To trade those fevers for tranquillity,
Thinking though that's entire and sweet in the grave
How shall the dead taste the deep treasure they have?

THE EYE   [1948]

The Atlantic is a stormy moat; and the Mediterranean,
The blue pool in the old garden,
More than five thousand years has drunk sacrifice
Of ships and blood, and shines in the sun; but here the
    Pacific—
Our ships, planes, wars are perfectly irrelevant.
Neither our present blood-feud with the brave dwarfs
Nor any future world-quarrel of westering
And eastering man, the bloody migrations, greed of
    power, clash of faiths—

Is a speck of dust on the great scale-pan.
Here from this mountain shore, headland beyond stormy
     headland plunging like dolphins through the blue sea-
     smoke   10
Into pale sea—look west at the hill of water: it is half the
     planet: this dome, this half-globe, this bulging
Eyeball of water, arched over to Asia,
Australia and white Antarctica: those are the eyelids that
     never close; this is the staring unsleeping
Eye of the earth; and what it watches is not our wars.

OCEAN   [1954]

The gray whales are going south: I see their fountains
Rise from black sea: great dark bulks of hot blood
Plowing the deep cold sea to their trysting-place
Off Mexican California, where water is warm, and love
Finds massive joy: from the flukes to the blowhole the
     whole giant
Flames like a star. In February storm the ocean
Is black and rainbowed; the high spouts of white spray
Rise and fall over in the wind. There is no April in the
     ocean;
How do these creatures know that spring is at hand?
     They remember their ancestors
That crawled on earth: the little fellows like otters, who
     took to sea   10
And have grown great. Go out to the ocean, little ones,
You will grow great or die.

                                   And there the small trout
Flicker in the streams that tumble from the coast mountain,
Little quick flames of life: but from time to time
One of them goes mad, wanting room and freedom; he
     slips between the rock jaws
And takes to sea, where from time immemorial
The long sharks wait. If he lives he becomes a steelhead,

A rainbow trout grown beyond nature in the ocean. Go
    out to the great ocean,
Grow great or die.

            O ambitious children,
It would be wiser no doubt to rest in the brook   20
And remain little. But if the devil drives
I hope you will scull far out to the wide ocean and find
    your fortune, and beware of teeth.

It is not important. There are deeps you will never reach
    and peaks you will never explore,
Where the great squids and kraken lie in the gates, in the
    awful twilight
The whip-armed hungers; and mile under mile below,
Deep under deep, on the deep floor, in the darkness
Under the weight of the world: like lighted galleons the
    ghost-fish,
With phosphorescent portholes along their flanks,
Sail over and eat each other: the condition of life,
To eat each other: but in the slime below   30
Prodigious worms as great and as slow as glaciers burrow
    in the sediment,
Mindless and blind, huge tubes of muddy flesh
Sucking not meat but carrion, drippings and offal
From the upper sea. They move a yard in a year,
Where there are no years, no sun, no seasons, darkness
    and slime;
They spend nothing on action, all on gross flesh.

                O ambitious ones,
Will you grow great, or die? It hardly matters; the words are
    comparative;
Greatness is but less little; and death's changed life.

MY BURIAL PLACE   [1963]

I have told you in another poem, whether you've read it or
    not,

About a beautiful place the hard-wounded
Deer go to die in; their bones lie mixed in their little
        graveyard
Under leaves by a flashing cliff-brook, and if
They have ghosts they like it, the bones and mixed antlers
        are well content.
Now comes for me the time to engage
My burial place: put me in a beautiful place far off from men,
No cemetery, no necropolis,
And for God's sake no columbarium, nor yet no funeral.

But if the human animal were precious   10
As the quick deer or that hunter in the night the lonely puma
I should be pleased to lie in one grave with 'em.

LET THEM ALONE   [1963]

If God has been good enough to give you a poet
Then listen to him. But for God's sake let him alone until
        he is dead; no prizes, no ceremony,
They kill the man. A poet is one who listens
To Nature and his own heart; and if the noise of the world
        grows up around him, and if he is tough enough,
He can shake off his enemies but not his friends.
That is what withered Wordsworth and muffled Tennyson,
        and would have killed Keats; that is what makes
Hemingway play the fool and Faulkner forget his art.

BUT I AM GROWING OLD AND INDOLENT   [1963]

I have been warned. It is more than thirty years since I
        wrote—
Thinking of the narrative poems I made, which always
Ended in blood and pain, though beautiful enough—my
        pain, my blood,

They were my creatures—I understood, and wrote to
        myself:
"Make sacrifices once a year to magic
Horror away from the house"—for that hangs imminent
Over all men and all houses—"This little house here
You have built over the ocean with your own hands
Beside the standing sea-boulders . . . " So I listened
To my Demon warning me that evil would come   10
If my work ceased, if I did not make sacrifice
Of storied and imagined lives, Tamar and Cawdor
And Thurso's wife—"imagined victims be our
        redeemers"—
At that time I was sure of my fates and felt
My poems guarding the house, well-made watchdogs
Ready to bite.
                But time sucks out the juice,
A man grows old and indolent.

Marianne Moore

b. 1887

Born November 15, 1887, in St. Louis, Missouri, Marianne Moore spent much of her girlhood in Carlisle, Pennsylvania. After graduating from Bryn Mawr in 1909, she taught at the government Indian school at Carlisle from 1911 to 1915, worked as an assistant in a branch of the New York Public Library, and from 1925 to 1929 was acting editor of The Dial. *In 1924 her book* Observations *won the* Dial *Award, and in 1952 her* Collected Poems *received the Pulitzer Prize and other awards.*

POETRY   [1921]

I, too, dislike it: there are things that are important beyond
       all this fiddle.
  Reading it, however, with a perfect contempt for it, one
       discovers in
  it after all, a place for the genuine.
    Hands that can grasp, eyes
    that can dilate, hair that can rise
      if it must, these things are important not because a

high-sounding interpretation can be put upon them but be-
      cause they are   10
  useful. When they become so derivative as to become
      unintelligible,
  the same thing may be said for all of us, that we
    do not admire what
    we cannot understand: the bat
      holding on upside down or in quest of something to

eat, elephants pushing, a wild horse taking a roll, a tireless
            wolf under
    a tree, the immovable critic twitching his skin like a horse
            that feels a flea, the base-   20
    ball fan, the statistician—
        nor is it valid
            to discriminate against "business documents and

school-books"; all these phenomena are important. One
            must make a distinction
    however: when dragged into prominence by half poets,
            the result is not poetry,
    nor till the poets among us can be
        "literalists of
        the imagination"—above   30
            insolence and triviality and can present

for inspection, "imaginary gardens with real toads in them,"
            shall we have
    it. In the meantime, if you demand on the one hand,
    the raw material of poetry in
        all its rawness and
        that which is on the other hand
            genuine, you are interested in poetry.

THE STEEPLE-JACK   [1935]

Dürer would have seen a reason for living
        in a town like this, with eight stranded whales
    to look at; with the sweet sea air coming into your house
    on a fine day, from water etched
            with waves as formal as the scales
    on a fish

One by one in two's and three's, the seagulls keep
        flying back and forth over the town clock,
    or sailing around the lighthouse without moving their
            wings—

rising steadily with a slight   10
        quiver of the body—or flock
mewing where

a sea the purple of the peacock's neck is
        paled to greenish azure as Dürer changed
the pine green of the Tyrol to peacock blue and guinea
gray. You can see a twenty-five-
        pound lobster; and fish-nets arranged
to dry. The

whirlwind fife-and-drum of the storm bends the salt
        marsh grass, disturbs stars in the sky and the   20
star on the steeple; it is a privilege to see so
much confusion. Disguised by what
        might seem the opposite, the sea-
side flowers and

trees are favored by the fog so that you have
        the tropics at first hand: the trumpet-vine,
fox-glove, giant snap-dragon, a salpiglossis that has
spots and stripes; morning-glories, gourds,
        or moon-vines trained on fishing-twine
at the back   30

door; cat-tails, flags, blueberries and spiderwort,
        stripped grass, lichens, sunflowers, asters, daisies—
yellow and crab-claw ragged sailors with green bracts—
        toad-plant,
petunias, ferns; pink lilies, blue
        ones, tigers; poppies; black sweet-peas.
The climate

is not right for the banyan, frangipani, or
        jack-fruit trees; or an exotic serpent
life. Ring lizard and snake-skin for the foot, if you see fit;
but here they've cats, not cobras, to   40
        keep down the rats. The diffident
little newt

with white pin-dots on black horizontal spaced
    out bands lives here; yet there is nothing that
ambition can buy or take away. The college student
named Ambrose sits on the hillside
    with his not-native books and hat
and sees boats

at sea progress white and rigid as if in
    a groove. Liking an elegance of which   50
the source is not bravado, he knows by heart the antique
sugar-bowl shaped summer-house of
    interlacing slats, and the pitch
of the church

spire, not true, from which a man in scarlet lets
    down a rope as a spider spins a thread;
he might be part of a novel, but on the sidewalk a
sign says C. J. Poole, Steeple Jack,
    in black and white; and one in red
and white says   60

Danger. The church portico has four fluted
    columns, each a single piece of stone, made
modester by white-wash. This would be a fit haven for
waifs, children, animals, prisoners,
    and presidents who have repaid
sin-driven

senators by not thinking about them. The
    place has a school-house, a post-office in a
store, fish-houses, hen-houses, a three-masted
        schooner on
the stocks. The hero, the student,   70
    the steeple-jack, each in his way,
is at home.

It could not be dangerous to be living
    in a town like this, of simple people,
who have a steeple-jack placing danger-signs by the church

while he is gilding the solid-
    pointed star, which on a steeple
stands for hope.

NO SWAN SO FINE   [1935]

"No water so still as the
   dead fountains of Versailles." No swan,
with swart blind look askance
and gondoliering legs, so fine
   as the chintz china one with fawn-
brown eyes and toothed gold
collar on to show whose bird it was.

Lodged in the Louis Fifteenth
   candelabrum-tree of cockscomb-
tinted buttons, dahlias,   10
sea-urchins, and everlastings,
   it perches on the branching foam
of polished sculptured
flowers—at ease and tall. The king is dead.

THE PANGOLIN   [1936]

Another armored animal—scale
    lapping scale with spruce-cone regularity until they
form the uninterrupted central
    tail-row! This near artichoke with heads and legs and
              grit-equipped giz-
   zard the night miniature artist engineer is
        Leonardo—da Vinci's replica—
           impressive animal and toiler of whom we seldom
              hear.

Armor seems extra. But for him,   10
    the closing ear-ridge—
        or bare ear lacking even this small
        eminence and similarly safe

contracting nose and eye apertures
    impenetrably closable, are not. A true ant-eater,
not cockroach-eater, who endures
    exhausting solitary trips through unfamiliar ground at
        night,
    returning before sunrise; stepping in the moonlight,
        on the moonlight peculiarly, that the outside   20
            edges of his hands may bear the weight and save
            the claws
        for digging. Serpentined about
           the tree, he draws
            away from danger unpugnaciously,
            with no sound but a harmless hiss. Keeping

the fragile grace of the Thomas-
    of-Leighton Buzzard Westminster Abbey wrought-
        iron vine, he
rolls himself into a ball that has   30
    power to defy all effort to unroll it; strongly intailed,
        neat
head for core, on neck not breaking off, with curled-in
        feet.
        Nevertheless he has sting-proof scales; and nest
           of rocks closed with earth from inside, which he
            can thus darken.
        Sun and moon and day and night and man and beast
           each with a splendor
            which man in all his vileness cannot   40
            set aside; each with an excellence!

"Fearful yet to be feared," the armored
    ant-eater met by the driver-ant does not turn back, but
engulfs what he can, the flattened sword-
    edged leafpoints on the tail and artichoke set leg- and
        body-plates

quivering violently when it retaliates
and swarms on him. Compact like the furled
fringed frill
on the hat-brim of Gargallo's hollow iron head   50
of a
matador, he will drop and will
then walk away
unhurt, although if unintruded on,
he cautiously works down the tree, helped

by his tail. The giant-pangolin-
tail, graceful tool, as prop or hand or broom or axe,
tipped like
the elephant's trunk with special skin,
is not lost on this ant- and stone-swallowing uninjurable   60
artichoke which simpletons thought a living fable
whom the stones had nourished, whereas ants had
done
so. Pangolins are not aggressive animals; between
dusk and day they have the measured
tread of the machine—
the slow frictionless creep of a thing
made graceful by adversities, con-

versities. To explain grace requires
a curious hand. If that which is at all were not forever,   70
why would those who graced the spires
with animals and gathered there to rest, on cold luxurious
low stone seats—a monk and monk and monk—between
the thus
ingenious roof-supports, have slaved to confuse
grace with a kindly manner, time in which to pay
a debt,
the cure for sins, a graceful use
of what are yet
approved stone mullions branching out across   80
the perpendiculars? A sailboat

was the first machine. Pangolins, made
for moving quietly also, are models of exactness,
on four legs; or hind feet plantigrade,

with certain postures of a man. Beneath sun and moon,
        man slaving
to make his life more sweet, leaves half the flowers
        worth having,
    needing to choose wisely how to use the strength;
        a paper-maker like the wasp; a tractor of food-   90
            stuffs,
    like the ant; spidering a length
        of web from bluffs
            above a stream; in fighting, mechanicked
            like the pangolin; capsizing in

disheartenment. Bedizened or stark
    naked, man, the self, the being we call human, writing-
master to this world, griffons a dark
    "Like does not like like that is obnoxious"; and writes
            error with four   100
r's. Among animals, one has a sense of humor.
        Humor saves a few steps, it saves years. Un-
            ignorant
        modest and unemotional, and all emotion,
        he has everlasting vigor,
            power to grow,
                although there are few creatures who can make
                    one
                breathe faster and make one erecter.

Not afraid of anything is he,
        and then goes cowering forth, tread paced to meet an   110
            obstacle
at every step. Consistent with the
    formula—warm blood, no gills, two pairs of hands and
            a few hairs—that
is a mammal; there he sits in his own habitat,
        serge-clad, strong-shod. The prey of fear, he, always
            curtailed, extinguished, thwarted by the dusk,
                work partly done,
        says to the alternating blaze,
            "Again the sun!   120
                anew each day; and new and new and new,
                that comes into and steadies my soul."

WHAT ARE YEARS? [1941]

What is our innocence,
what is our guilt? All are
    naked, none is safe. And whence
is courage: the unanswered question,
the resolute doubt,—
dumbly calling, deafly listening—that
in misfortune, even death,
        encourages others
        and in its defeat, stirs

    the soul to be strong? He   10
sees deep and is glad, who
    accedes to mortality
and in his imprisonment rises
upon himself as
the sea in a chasm, struggling to be
free and unable to be,
        in its surrendering
        finds its continuing.

    So he who strongly feels,
behaves. The very bird,   20
    grown taller as he sings, steels
his form straight up. Though he is captive,
his mighty singing
says, satisfaction is a lowly
thing, how pure a thing is joy.
        This is mortality,
        this is eternity.

THE MIND IS AN ENCHANTING THING [1944]

is an enchanted thing
    like the glaze on a

katydid-wing
  subdivided by sun
  till the nettings are legion.
Like Gieseking playing Scarlatti;

like the apteryx-awl
  as a beak, or the
kiwi's rain-shawl   10
   of haired feathers, the mind
   feeling its way as though blind,
walks along with its eyes on the ground.

It has memory's ear
  that can hear without
having to hear.
   Like the gyroscope's fall,
   truly unequivocal
because trued by regnant certainty,

it is a power of   20
  strong enchantment. It
is like the dove-
   neck animated by
   sun; it is memory's eye;
it's conscientious inconsistency.

It tears off the veil; tears
  the temptation, the
mist the heart wears,
   from its eyes—if the heart
   has a face; it takes apart   30
dejection. It's fire in the dove-neck's

iridescence; in the
  inconsistencies
of Scarlatti.
   Unconfusion submits
   its confusion to proof; it's
not a Herod's oath that cannot change.

IN DISTRUST OF MERITS   [1944]

Strengthened to live, strengthened to die for
      medals and positioned victories?
They're fighting, fighting, fighting the blind
      man who thinks he sees—
who cannot see that the enslaver is
enslaved; the hater, harmed. O shining O
            firm star, O tumultuous
                  ocean lashed till small things go
                  as they will, the mountainous
                        wave makes us who look, know   10

depth. Lost at sea before they fought! O
      star of David, star of Bethlehem,
O black imperial lion
      of the Lord—emblem
of a risen world—be joined at last, be
joined. There is hate's crown beneath which all is
            death; there's love's without which none
                  is king; the blessed deeds bless
                  the halo. As contagion
                        of sickness makes sickness,   20

contagion of trust can make trust. They're
      fighting in deserts and caves, one by
one, in battalions and squadrons;
      they're fighting that I
may yet recover from the disease, My
Self; some have it lightly; some will die. "Man
            wolf to man"; yes. We devour
                  ourselves. The enemy could not
                  have made a greater breach in our
                        defenses. One pilot-   30

ing a blind man can escape him, but
      Job disheartened by false comfort knew,
that nothing can be so defeating

as a blind man who
can see. O alive who are dead, who are
proud not to see, O small dust of the earth
      that walks so arrogantly,
         trust begets power and faith is
      an affectionate thing. We
       vow, we make this promise   40

to the fighting—it's a promise—"We'll
    never hate black, white, red, yellow, Jew,
Gentile, Untouchable." We are
   not competent to
make our vows. With set jaw they are fighting,
fighting, fighting—some we love whom we know,
      some we love but know not—that
         hearts may feel and not be numb.
      It cures me; or am I what
       I can't believe in? Some   50

in snow, some on crags, some in quicksands,
    little by little, much by much, they
are fighting fighting fighting that where
   there was death there may
be life. "When a man is prey to anger,
he is moved by outside things; when he holds
      his ground in patience patience
         patience, that is action or
      beauty," the soldier's defense
       and hardest armor for   60

the fight. The world's an orphans' home. Shall
    we never have peace without sorrow?
without pleas of the dying for
   help that won't come? O
quiet form upon the dust, I cannot
look and yet I must. If these great patient
      dyings—all these agonies
         and woundbearings and bloodshed—
      can teach us how to live, these
       dyings were not wasted.   70

Hate-hardened heart, O heart of iron,
    iron is iron till it is rust.
There never was a war that was
    not inward; I must
fight till I have conquered in myself what
causes war, but I would not believe it.
        I inwardly did nothing.
          O Iscariotlike crime!
        Beauty is everlasting
          and dust is for a time.   80

ARMOUR'S UNDERMINING MODESTY   [1951]

    At first I thought a pest
    Must have alighted on my wrist.
    It was a moth almost an owl,
    Its wings were furred so well,
with backgammon-board wedges interlacing
on the wing—

    like cloth of gold in a pattern
    of scales with a hair-seal Persian
    sheen. Once, self-determination
    made an axe of a stone   10
and hacked things out with hairy paws. The consequence—
        our mis-set
alphabet.

    Arise, for it is day.
    Even gifted scholars lose their way
    through faulty etymology.
    No wonder we hate poetry,
and stars and harps and the new moon. If tributes cannot
be implicit,

    give me diatribes and the fragrance of iodine,   20
    the cork oak acorn grown in Spain;

the pale-ale-eyed impersonal look
which the sales-placard gives the bock beer buck.
What is more precise than precision? Illusion.
Knights we've known,

like those familiar
now unfamiliar knights who sought the Grail, were
ducs in old Roman fashion
without the addition
of wreaths and silver rods, and armour gilded   30
or inlaid.

They did not let self bar
their usefulness to others who were
different. Though Mars is excessive
in being preventive,
heroes need not write an ordinall of attributes to enumer-
          ate
what they hate.

I should, I confess,
like to have a talk with one of them about excess,   40
and armour's undermining modesty
instead of innocent depravity.
A mirror-of-steel uninsistence should countenance
continence,

objectified and not by chance,
there in its frame of circumstance
of innocence and altitude
in an unhackneyed solitude.
There is the tarnish; and there, the imperishable wish

TOM FOOL AT JAMAICA   [1956]

Look at Jonah embarking from Joppa, deterred by
the whale; hard going for a statesman whom nothing could
          detain,

although one who would not rather die than repent.
    Be infallible at your peril, for your system will fail,
and select as a model the schoolboy in Spain
    who at the age of six, portrayed a mule and jockey
        who had pulled up for a snail.

"There is submerged magnificence, as Victor Hugo
said." *Sentir avec ardeur*; that's it; magnetized by feeling.
    Tom Fool "makes an effort and makes it oftener   10
        than the rest"—out on April first, a day of some
            significance
in the ambiguous sense—the smiling
    Master Atkinson's choice, with that mark of a champion,
        the extra
        spurt when needed. Yes, yes. "Chance

is a regrettable impurity"; like Tom Fool's
left white hind foot—an unconformity; though judging by
    results, a kind of cottontail to give him confidence.
        Up in the cupola comparing speeds, Signor Capossela
            keeps his head.
"It's tough," he said; "but I get 'em; and why shouldn't I?
I'm relaxed, I'm confident, and I don't bet." Sensational.
        He does not   20
        bet on his animated

valentines—his pink and black-striped, sashed or dotted
    silks.
Tom Fool is "a handy horse," with a chiseled foot. You've
        the beat
    of a dancer to a measure or harmonious rush
        of a porpoise at the prow where the racers all win easily—
like centaurs' legs in tune, as when kettledrums compete;
    nose rigid and suede nostrils spread, a light left hand on
        the rein, till
        well—this is a rhapsody.

Of course, speaking of champions, there was Fats Waller
with the feather touch, giraffe eyes, and that hand
        alighting in   30

Ain't Misbehavin'! Ozzie Smith and Eubie Blake
   ennoble the atmosphere; you recall the Lippizan
      school;
the time Ted Atkinson charged by on Tiger Skin—
   no pursuers in sight—cat-loping along. And you may
      have seen a monkey
   on a greyhound. "But Tom Fool . . .

MELCHIOR VULPIUS   [1959]

c. 1560–1615

a contrapuntalist—
               composer of chorales
   and wedding-hymns to Latin words
   but best of all an anthem:
      "God be praised for conquering faith
      which feareth neither pain nor death."

We have to trust this art—
                  this mastery which none
   can understand. Yet someone has
   acquired it and is able to   10
      direct it. Mouse-skin-bellows'-breath
      expanding into rapture saith

"Hallelujah." Almost
            utmost absolutist
   and fugue-ist, Amen; slowly building
   from miniature thunder,
      crescendos antidoting death—
      love's signature cementing faith.

John Crowe Ransom

b. 1888

John Crowe Ransom was born April 30, 1888, in Pulaski, Tennessee, the son of a clergyman. After graduating from Vanderbilt in 1909, he spent three years at Oxford as a Rhodes Scholar. Most of the time between 1914 and 1937 he taught English at Vanderbilt; he also served in the field artillery during World War I and held a Guggenheim Fellowship in England in 1931–1932. He was a founder and editor of The Fugitive *in Nashville from 1922 to 1925, and he founded* The Kenyon Review *in 1938, the year after he had become Professor of English at Kenyon College. Since retirement from teaching in 1958 he has been visiting professor at several universities. For his* Selected Poems *(1963) he won the National Book Award for Poetry.*

WINTER REMEMBERED   [1924]

Two evils, monstrous either one apart,
Possessed me, and were long and loath at going:
A cry of Absence, Absence, in the heart,
And in the wood the furious winter blowing.

Think not, when fire was bright upon my bricks,
And past the tight boards hardly a wind could enter,
I glowed like them, the simple burning sticks,
Far from my cause, my proper heat and center.

Better to walk forth in the frozen air
And wash my wound in the snows; that would be healing;   10
Because my heart would throb less painful there,
Being caked with cold, and past the smart of feeling.

And where I walked, the murderous winter blast
Would have this body bowed, these eyeballs streaming,
And though I think this heart's blood froze not fast
It ran too small to spare one drop for dreaming.

Dear love, these fingers that had known your touch,
And tied our separate forces first together,
Were ten poor idiot fingers not worth much,
Ten frozen parsnips hanging in the weather.   20

BELLS FOR JOHN WHITESIDE'S
DAUGHTER   [1924]

There was such speed in her little body,
And such lightness in her footfall,
It is no wonder her brown study
Astonishes us all.

Her wars were bruited in our high window.
We looked among orchard trees and beyond
Where she took arms against her shadow,
Or harried unto the pond

The lazy geese, like a snow cloud
Dripping their snow on the green grass,   10
Tricking and stopping, sleepy and proud,
Who cried in goose, Alas,

For the tireless heart within the little
Lady with rod that made them rise
From their noon apple-dreams and scuttle
Goose-fashion under the skies!

But now go the bells, and we are ready,
In one house we are sternly stopped
To say we are vexed at her brown study,
Lying so primly propped.   20

CAPTAIN CARPENTER   [1924]

Captain Carpenter rose up in his prime
Put on his pistols and went riding out
But had got wellnigh nowhere at that time
Till he fell in with ladies in a rout.

It was a pretty lady and all her train
That played with him so sweetly but before
An hour she'd taken a sword with all her main
And twined him of his nose for evermore.

Captain Carpenter mounted up one day
And rode straightway into a stranger rogue   10
That looked unchristian but be that as may
The Captain did not wait upon prologue.

But drew upon him out of his great heart
The other swung against him with a club
And cracked his two legs at the shinny part
And let him roll and stick like any tub.

Captain Carpenter rode many a time
From male and female took he sundry harms
He met the wife of Satan crying "I'm
The she-wolf bids you shall bear no more arms."   20

Their strokes and counters whistled in the wind
I wish he had delivered half his blows
But where she should have made off like a hind
The bitch bit off his arms at the elbows.

And Captain Carpenter parted with his ears
To a black devil that used him in this wise
O Jesus ere his threescore and ten years
Another had plucked out his sweet blue eyes.

Captain Carpenter got up on his roan
And sallied from the gate in hell's despite   30

I heard him asking in the grimmest tone
If any enemy yet there was to fight?

"To any adversary it is fame
If he risk to be wounded by my tongue
Or burnt in two beneath my red heart's flame
Such are the perils he is cast among.

"But if he can he has a pretty choice
From an anatomy with little to lose
Whether he cut my tongue and take my voice
Or whether it be my round red heart he choose."   40

It was the neatest knave that ever was seen
Stepping in perfume from his lady's bower
Who at this word put in his merry mien
And fell on Captain Carpenter like a tower.

I would not knock old fellows in the dust
But there lay Captain Carpenter on his back
His weapons were the old heart in his bust
And a blade shook between rotten teeth alack.

The rogue in scarlet and grey soon knew his mind
He wished to get his trophy and depart   50
With gentle apology and touch refined
He pierced him and produced the Captain's heart.

God's mercy rest on Captain Carpenter now
I thought him Sirs an honest gentleman
Citizen husband soldier and scholar enow
Let jangling kites eat of him if they can.

But God's deep curses follow after those
That shore him of his goodly nose and ears
His legs and strong arms at the two elbows
And eyes that had not watered seventy years.   60

The curse of hell upon the sleek upstart
That got the Captain finally on his back

And took the red red vitals of his heart
And made the kites to whet their beaks clack clack.

VISION BY SWEETWATER   [1927]

Go and ask Robin to bring the girls over
To Sweetwater, said my Aunt; and that was why
It was like a dream of ladies sweeping by
The willows, clouds, deep meadowgrass, and the river.

Robin's sisters and my Aunt's lily daughter
Laughed and talked, and tinkled light as wrens
If there were a little colony all hens
To go walking by the steep turn of Sweetwater.

Let them alone, dear Aunt, just for one minute
Till I go fishing in the dark of my mind: 10
Where have I seen before, against the wind,
These bright virgins, robed and bare of bonnet,

Flowing with music of their strange quick tongue
And adventuring with delicate paces by the stream,—
Myself a child, old suddenly at the scream
From one of the white throats which it hid among?

PIAZZA PIECE   [1927]

—I am a gentleman in a dustcoat trying
To make you hear. Your ears are soft and small
And listen to an old man not at all,
They want the young men's whispering and sighing.
But see the roses on your trellis dying
And hear the spectral singing of the moon;
For I must have my lovely lady soon,
I am a gentleman in a dustcoat trying.

—I am a lady young in beauty waiting
Until my truelove comes, and then we kiss. 10
But what grey man among the vines is this
Whose words are dry and faint as in a dream?
Back from my trellis, Sir, before I scream!
I am a lady young in beauty waiting.

ANTIQUE HARVESTERS   [1927]

> (Scene: Of the Mississippi the bank sinister,
> and of the Ohio the bank sinister.)

Tawny are the leaves turned but they still hold,
And it is harvest; what shall this land produce?
A meager hill of kernels, a runnel of juice;
Declension looks from our land, it is old.
Therefore let us assemble, dry, grey, spare,
And mild as yellow air.

"I hear the croak of a raven's funeral wing."
The young men would be joying in the song
Of passionate birds; their memories are not long.
What is it thus rehearsed in sable? "Nothing." 10
Trust not but the old endure, and shall be older
Than the scornful beholder.

We pluck the spindling ears and gather the corn.
One spot has special yield? "On this spot stood
Heroes and drenched it with their only blood."
And talk meets talk, as echoes from the horn
Of the hunter—echoes are the old men's arts,
Ample are the chambers of their hearts.

Here come the hunters, keepers of a rite;
The horn, the hounds, the lank mares coursing by 20
Straddled with archetypes of chivalry;
And the fox, lovely ritualist, in flight
Offering his unearthly ghost to quarry;
And the fields, themselves to harry.

Resume, harvesters. The treasure is full bronze
Which you will garner for the Lady, and the moon
Could tinge it no yellower than does this noon;
But the grey will quench it shortly—the fields, men, stones.
Pluck fast, dreamers; prove as you amble slowly
Not less than men, not wholly.   30

Bare the arm, dainty youths, bend the knees
Under bronze burdens. And by an autumn tone
As by a grey, as by a green, you will have known
Your famous Lady's image; for so have these;
And if one say that easily will your hands
More prosper in other lands,

Angry as wasp-music be your cry then:
"Forsake the Proud Lady, of the heart of fire,
The look of snow, to the praise of a dwindled choir,
Song of degenerate specters that were men?   40
The sons of the fathers shall keep her, worthy of
What these have done in love."

True, it is said of our Lady, she ageth.
But see, if you peep shrewdly, she hath not stooped;
Take no thought of her servitors that have drooped,
For we are nothing; and if one talk of death—
Why, the ribs of the earth subsist frail as a breath
If but God wearieth.

THE EQUILIBRISTS   [1927]

Full of her long white arms and milky skin
He had a thousand times remembered sin.
Alone in the press of people traveled he,
Minding her jacinth, and myrrh, and ivory.

Mouth he remembered: the quaint orifice
From which came heat that flamed upon the kiss,

Till cold words came down spiral from the head.
Grey doves from the officious tower illsped.

Body: it was a white field ready for love,
On her body's field, with the gaunt tower above,   10
The lilies grew, beseeching him to take,
If he would pluck and wear them, bruise and break.

Eyes talking: Never mind the cruel words,
Embrace my flowers, but not embrace the swords.
But what they said, the doves came straightway flying
And unsaid: Honor, Honor, they came crying.

Importunate her doves. Too pure, too wise,
Clambering on his shoulder, saying, Arise,
Leave me now, and never let us meet,
Eternal distance now command thy feet.   20

Predicament indeed, which thus discovers
Honor among thieves, Honor between lovers.
O such a little word is Honor, they feel!
But the grey word is between them cold as steel.

At length I saw these lovers fully were come
Into their torture of equilibrium;
Dreadfully had forsworn each other, and yet
They were bound each to each, and they did not forget.

And rigid as two painful stars, and twirled
About the clustered night their prison world,   30
They burned with fierce love always to come near,
But Honor beat them back and kept them clear.

Ah, the strict lovers, they are ruined now!
I cried in anger. But with puddled brow
Devising for those gibbeted and brave
Came I descanting: Man, what would you have?

For spin your period out, and draw your breath,
A kinder saeculum begins with Death.

Would you ascend to Heaven and bodiless dwell?
Or take your bodies honorless to Hell?   40

In Heaven you have heard no marriage is,
No white flesh tinder to your lecheries,
Your male and female tissue sweetly shaped
Sublimed away, and furious blood escaped.

Great lovers lie in Hell, the stubborn ones
Infatuate of the flesh upon the bones;
Stuprate, they rend each other when they kiss,
The pieces kiss again, no end to this.

But still I watched them spinning, orbited nice.
Their flames were not more radiant than their ice.   50
I dug in the quiet earth and wrought the tomb
And made these lines to memorize their doom:—

> #### EPITAPH
> *Equilibrists lie here; stranger, tread light;*
> *Close, but untouching in each other's sight;*
> *Mouldered the lips and ashy the tall skull,*
> *Let them lie perilous and beautiful.*

PAINTED HEAD   [1945]

By dark severance the apparition head
Smiles from the air a capital on no
Column or a Platonic perhaps head
On a canvas sky depending from nothing;

Stirs up an old illusion of grandeur
By tickling the instinct of heads to be
Absolute and to try decapitation
And to play truant from the body bush;

But too happy and beautiful for those sorts
Of head (homekeeping heads are happiest)   10

Discovers maybe thirty unwidowed years
Of not dishonoring the faithful stem;

Is nameless and has authored for the evil
Historian headhunters neither book
Nor state and is therefore distinct from tart
Heads with crowns and guilty gallery heads;

Wherefore the extravagant device of art
Unhousing by abstraction this once head
Was capital irony by a loving hand
That knew the no treason of a head like this;   20

Makes repentance in an unlovely head
For having vinegarly traduced the flesh
Till, the hurt flesh recusing, the hard egg
Is shrunken to its own deathlike surface;

And an image thus. The body bears the head
(So hardly one they terribly are two)
Feeds and obeys and unto please what end?
Not to the glory of tyrant head but to

The being of body. Beauty is of body.
The flesh contouring shallowly on a head   30
Is a rock-garden needing body's love
And best bodiness to colorify

The big blue birds sitting and sea-shell flats
And caves and on the iron acropolis
To spread the hyacinthine hair and rear
The olive garden for the nightingales.

MASTER'S IN THE GARDEN AGAIN   [1963]

(To the memory of Thomas Hardy)

i

Evening comes early, and soon discovers
Exchange between these conjugate lovers.

"Conrad! dear man, surprise! aren't you bold
To be sitting so late in your sodden garden?"

"Woman! intrusion! does this promise well?
I'm nursing my knees, they are not very cold.
Have you known the fall of the year when it fell?
Indeed it's a garden, but if you will pardon,
The health of a garden is reason's burden."

"Conrad! your feet are dripping in muck,   10
The neuralgia will settle in your own neck,
And whose health is it that catches an asthma?
Come in from foul weather for pity's sake!"

"No," says the thinker. "Concede. I am here,
Keeping guard of my garden and minding miasma.
You're lonely, my loony? Your house is up there.
Go and wait. If you won't, I'll go jump in the lake."

                              ii
And the master's back has not uncurved
Nor the autumn's blow for an instant swerved.

Autumn days in our section   20
Are the most used-up thing on earth
(Or in the waters under the earth)
Having no more color nor predilection
Than cornstalks too wet for the fire
And black leaves pitched onto the byre.

The show is of death. There is no defection.

                              iii
He will play out his mood before he takes food.

By the bob of the Power the dark skies lower,
By the bite of Its frost the children were lost
Who hurt no one where they shone in the sun,   30
But the valiant heart knows a better part
Than to do with an "O did It lay them low,
But we're a poor sinner just going to dinner."

See the tell-tale art of the champion heart.

Here's temple and brow, which frown like the law.
If the arm lies low, yet the rage looks high.
The accusing eye? that's a fierce round O.
The offense was raw, says the fix in the jaw.
We'll raise a rare row! we'll heave a brave blow!

A pantomime blow, if it damns him to do,   40
A yell mumming too. But it's gay garden now,
Play sweeter than pray, that the darkened be gay.

PRELUDE TO AN EVENING   [1963]

Do not enforce the tired wolf
Dragging his infected wound homeward
To sit tonight with the warm children
Saying the pretty Kings of France.

You are my scholar. Then languish, expire
With each day's terror and next week's doom
Till we're twice espoused, in love and ruin,
And grave but smiling though the heavens fall.

The images of the invaded mind
Were monstrous only in the dreams   10
Of your most brief enchanted headful.
Suppose a miracle of confusion:—

That dreamed and undreamt become each other
And mix the night and day of your soul.
For it never mattered your twice crying
From mouth unbeautied against the pillow

To avert the gun of the same old soldier,
If quickly cry, cock-crow or bell
Breaking the improbable black spell
Annihilated the poor phantom.   20

And now? To confirm our strange supposal,
Apparitions wait upon sunny mornings;
You in your peignoir commend the heaped oranges
Gold on the platter for cheeky children

But freeze at the turbulence under the floor
Where unclean spirits yawn and thrash;
The day-long clock will strike your fears;
The heels detonating the stair's cavern.

Freshening the water in the blue bowls
For the buckberries with not all your love   30
You listen for a low lost wind to awaken
The warning sibilance of pines.

Finally evening. Hear me denouncing
Our equal and conniving Furies;
You making Noes but they lack conviction;
Smoothing the heads of the hungry children.

I would have us magnificent at my coming;
Two souls tight-clasped; and a swamp of horrors.
O you shall be handsome and brave at fearing.
Now my step quickens; and meets a huge No!   40

Whose No was it? like the hoarse policeman's,
Clopping onstage in the Name of the Law.
That was Me; forbidding tricks at homecoming;
At the moment of coming to its white threshold.

I went to the nations of disorder
To be freed of the memory of good and evil;
There even your image was disfigured;
Then the boulevards rocked; they said, Go back.

I am here; and to balk my ruffian I bite
The tongue devising all that treason;   50
Then creep in my wounds to the sovereign flare
Of the room where you shine on the good children.

T. S. Eliot

1888–1965

Thomas Stearns Eliot was born September 26, 1888, in St. Louis, Missouri, of a family originally long in New England. At first more interested in philosophy and theology than in literature, he graduated from Harvard in 1910, spent a year in Paris at the Sorbonne, and returned for three years of graduate study at Harvard in philosophy and Indic philology. He left the United States in 1914 and did not return until 1932, when he made the first of several visits to this country. From 1914 to 1915 he studied at Oxford and subsequently worked for Lloyd's Bank in London for a number of years. He was assistant editor of The Egoist *from 1917 to 1919 and editor of the influential* Criterion *from 1922 until it ceased publication in 1939. For a number of years he was a director of Faber and Faber, the London publishing house. In 1927 he became a British subject and soon attracted attention as a spokesman for the Anglo-Catholic branch of the Church of England. He was almost as well known for his essays as for his poetry, and from the middle 1930's he showed an increasing interest in writing verse dramas. In 1948 he became one of the few American writers to receive the Nobel Prize for Literature. He died in London on January 4, 1965.*

THE LOVE SONG OF J. ALFRED PRUFROCK   [1917]

> *S'io credessi che mia risposta fosse*
> *a persona che mai tornasse al mondo,*
> *questa fiamma staria senza più scosse.*
> *Ma per ciò che giammai di questo fondo*
> *non tornò vivo alcun, s'i'odo il vero,*
> *senza tema d'infamia ti rispondo.*

Let us go then, you and I,
When the evening is spread out against the sky

Like a patient etherised upon a table;
Let us go, through certain half-deserted streets,
The muttering retreats
Of restless nights in one-night cheap hotels
And sawdust restaurants with oyster-shells:
Streets that follow like a tedious argument
Of insidious intent
To lead you to an overwhelming question ...   10
Oh, do not ask, "What is it?"
Let us go and make our visit.

In the room the women come and go
Talking of Michelangelo.

The yellow fog that rubs its back upon the window-panes,
The yellow smoke that rubs its muzzle on the window-
        panes,
Licked its tongue into the corners of the evening,
Lingered upon the pools that stand in drains,
Let fall upon its back the soot that falls from chimneys,
Slipped by the terrace, made a sudden leap,   20
And seeing that it was a soft October night,
Curled once about the house, and fell asleep.

And indeed there will be time
For the yellow smoke that slides along the street
Rubbing its back upon the window-panes;
There will be time, there will be time
To prepare a face to meet the faces that you meet;
There will be time to murder and create,
And time for all the works and days of hands
That lift and drop a question on your plate;   30
Time for you and time for me,
And time yet for a hundred indecisions,
And for a hundred visions and revisions,
Before the taking of a toast and tea.

In the room the women come and go
Talking of Michelangelo.

And indeed there will be time
To wonder, "Do I dare?" and, "Do I dare?"
Time to turn back and descend the stair,
With a bald spot in the middle of my hair—   40
(They will say: "How his hair is growing thin!")
My morning coat, my collar mounting firmly to the chin,
My necktie rich and modest, but asserted by a simple pin—
(They will say: "But how his arms and legs are thin!")
Do I dare
Disturb the universe?
In a minute there is time
For decisions and revisions which a minute will reverse.

For I have known them all already, known them all—
Have known the evenings, mornings, afternoons,   50
I have measured out my life with coffee spoons;
I know the voices dying with a dying fall
Beneath the music from a farther room.
　　So how should I presume?

And I have known the eyes already, known them all—
The eyes that fix you in a formulated phrase,
And when I am formulated, sprawling on a pin,
When I am pinned and wriggling on the wall,
Then how should I begin
To spit out all the butt-ends of my days and ways?   60
　　And how should I presume?

And I have known the arms already, known them all—
Arms that are braceleted and white and bare
(But in the lamplight, downed with light brown hair!)
Is it perfume from a dress
That makes me so digress?
Arms that lie along a table, or wrap about a shawl.
　　And should I then presume?
　　And how should I begin?

· · · · ·

Shall I say, I have gone at dusk through narrow streets   70

And watched the smoke that rises from the pipes
Of lonely men in shirt-sleeves, leaning out of windows? ...

I should have been a pair of ragged claws
Scuttling across the floors of silent seas.

.   .   .   .   .

And the afternoon, the evening, sleeps so peacefully!
Smoothed by long fingers,
Asleep ... tired ... or it malingers,
Stretched on the floor, here beside you and me.
Should I, after tea and cakes and ices,
Have the strength to force the moment to its crisis?   80
But though I have wept and fasted, wept and prayed,
Though I have seen my head (grown slightly bald) brought
        in upon a platter,
I am no prophet—and here's no great matter;
I have seen the moment of my greatness flicker,
And I have seen the eternal Footman hold my coat, and
        snicker,
And in short, I was afraid.

And would it have been worth it, after all,
After the cups, the marmalade, the tea,
Among the porcelain, among some talk of you and me,
Would it have been worth while,   90
To have bitten off the matter with a smile,
To have squeezed the universe into a ball
To roll it towards some overwhelming question,
To say: "I am Lazarus, come from the dead,
Come back to tell you all, I shall tell you all"—
If one, settling a pillow by her head,
        Should say: "That is not what I meant at all.
        That is not it, at all."

And would it have been worth it, after all,
Would it have been worth while,   100
After the sunsets and the dooryards and the sprinkled
        streets,

After the novels, after the teacups, after the skirts that trail
    along the floor—
And this, and so much more?—
It is impossible to say just what I mean!
But as if a magic lantern threw the nerves in patterns on a
    screen:
Would it have been worth while
If one, settling a pillow or throwing off a shawl,
And turning toward the window, should say:
    "That is not it at all,
    That is not what I meant, at all."   110

        .   .   .   .   .

No! I am not Prince Hamlet, nor was meant to be;
Am an attendant lord, one that will do
To swell a progress, start a scene or two,
Advise the prince; no doubt, an easy tool,
Deferential, glad to be of use,
Politic, cautious, and meticulous;
Full of high sentence, but a bit obtuse;
At times, indeed, almost ridiculous—
Almost, at times, the Fool.

I grow old ... I grow old ...   120
I shall wear the bottoms of my trousers rolled.

Shall I part my hair behind? Do I dare to eat a peach?
I shall wear white flannel trousers, and walk upon the
    beach.
I have heard the mermaids singing, each to each.

I do not think that they will sing to me.

I have seen them riding seaward on the waves
Combing the white hair of the waves blown back
When the wind blows the water white and black.

We have lingered in the chambers of the sea
By sea-girls wreathed with seaweed red and brown   130
Till human voices wake us, and we drown.

SWEENEY AMONG THE NIGHTINGALES   [1919]

ὤμοι, πέπληγμαι καιρίαν πληγὴν ἔσω.

Apeneck Sweeney spreads his knees
Letting his arms hang down to laugh,
The zebra stripes along his jaw
Swelling to maculate giraffe.

The circles of the stormy moon
Slide westward toward the River Plate,
Death and the Raven drift above
And Sweeney guards the hornèd gate.

Gloomy Orion and the Dog
Are veiled; and hushed the shrunken seas;   10
The person in the Spanish cape
Tries to sit on Sweeney's knees

Slips and pulls the table cloth
Overturns a coffee-cup,
Reorganized upon the floor
She yawns and draws a stocking up;

The silent man in mocha brown
Sprawls at the window-sill and gapes;
The waiter brings in oranges
Bananas figs and hothouse grapes;   20

The silent vertebrate in brown
Contracts and concentrates, withdraws;
Rachel *née* Rabinovitch
Tears at the grapes with murderous paws;

She and the lady in the cape
Are suspect, thought to be in league;
Therefore the man with heavy eyes
Declines the gambit, shows fatigue,

Leaves the room and reappears
Outside the window, leaning in,   30
Branches of wistaria
Circumscribe a golden grin;

The host with someone indistinct
Converses at the door apart,
The nightingales are singing near
The Convent of the Sacred Heart,

And sang within the bloody wood
When Agamemnon cried aloud,
And let their liquid siftings fall
To stain the stiff dishonoured shroud.   40

GERONTION [1920]

*Thou hast nor youth nor age
But as it were an after dinner sleep
Dreaming of both.*

Here I am, an old man in a dry month,
Being read to by a boy, waiting for rain.
I was neither at the hot gates
Nor fought in the warm rain
Nor knee deep in the salt marsh, heaving a cutlass,
Bitten by flies, fought.
My house is a decayed house,
And the Jew squats on the window sill, the owner,
Spawned in some estaminet of Antwerp,
Blistered in Brussels, patched and peeled in London.   10
The goat coughs at night in the field overhead;
Rocks, moss, stonecrop, iron, merds.
The woman keeps the kitchen, makes tea,
Sneezes at evening, poking the peevish gutter.
                              I an old man,
A dull head among windy spaces.

Signs are taken for wonders. "We would see a sign!"
The word within a word, unable to speak a word,
Swaddled with darkness. In the juvescence of the year
Came Christ the tiger   20

In depraved May, dogwood and chestnut, flowering judas,
To be eaten, to be divided, to be drunk
Among whispers; by Mr. Silvero
With caressing hands, at Limoges
Who walked all night in the next room;

By Hakagawa, bowing among the Titians;
By Madame de Tornquist, in the dark room
Shifting the candles; Fräulein von Kulp
Who turned in the hall, one hand on the door.
        Vacant shuttles   30
Weave the wind. I have no ghosts,
An old man in a draughty house
Under a windy knob.

After such knowledge, what forgiveness? Think now
History has many cunning passages, contrived corridors
And issues, deceives with whispering ambitions,
Guides us by vanities. Think now
She gives when our attention is distracted
And what she gives, gives with such supple confusions
That the giving famishes the craving. Gives too late   40
What's not believed in, or is still believed,
In memory only, reconsidered passion. Gives too soon
Into weak hands, what's thought can be dispensed with
Till the refusal propagates a fear. Think
Neither fear nor courage saves us. Unnatural vices
Are fathered by our heroism. Virtues
Are forced upon us by our impudent crimes.
These tears are shaken from the wrath-bearing tree.

The tiger springs in the new year. Us he devours. Think at
        last
We have not reached conclusion, when I   50
Stiffen in a rented house. Think at last

I have not made this show purposelessly
And it is not by any concitation
Of the backward devils.
I would meet you upon this honestly.
I that was near your heart was removed therefrom
To lose beauty in terror, terror in inquisition.
I have lost my passion: why should I need to keep it
Since what is kept must be adulterated?
I have lost my sight, smell, hearing, taste and touch: 60
How should I use them for your closer contact?

These with a thousand small deliberations
Protract the profit of their chilled delirium,
Excite the membrane, when the sense has cooled,
With pungent sauces, multiply variety
In a wilderness of mirrors. What will the spider do,
Suspend its operations, will the weevil
Delay? De Bailhache, Fresca, Mrs. Cammel, whirled
Beyond the circuit of the shuddering Bear
In fractured atoms. Gull against the wind, in the windy straits   70
Of Belle Isle, or running on the Horn.
White feathers in the snow, the Gulf claims,
And an old man driven by the Trades
To a sleepy corner.
                              Tenants of the house,
Thoughts of a dry brain in a dry season.

THE WASTE LAND   [1922]

> "*Nam Sibyllam quidem Cumis ego ipse oculis meis vidi in ampulla pen-
> dere, et cum illi pueri dicerent: Σίβυλλα τί θέλεις; respondebat illa:
> ἀποθανεῖν θέλω.*"
>
>   For Ezra Pound
>   *il miglior fabbro.*

I. THE BURIAL OF THE DEAD

April is the cruellest month, breeding
Lilacs out of the dead land, mixing
Memory and desire, stirring

Dull roots with spring rain.
Winter kept us warm, covering
Earth in forgetful snow, feeding
A little life with dried tubers.
Summer surprised us, coming over the Starnbergersee
With a shower of rain; we stopped in the colonnade,
And went on in sunlight, into the Hofgarten,   10
And drank coffee, and talked for an hour.
Bin gar keine Russin, stamm' aus Litauen, echt deutsch.
And when we were children, staying at the arch-duke's,
My cousin's, he took me out on a sled,
And I was frightened. He said, Marie,
Marie, hold on tight. And down we went.
In the mountains, there you feel free.
I read, much of the night, and go south in the winter.

What are the roots that clutch, what branches grow
Out of this stony rubbish? Son of man,   20
You cannot say, or guess, for you know only
A heap of broken images, where the sun beats,
And the dead tree gives no shelter, the cricket no relief,
And the dry stone no sound of water. Only
There is shadow under this red rock,
(Come in under the shadow of this red rock),
And I will show you something different from either
Your shadow at morning striding behind you
Or your shadow at evening rising to meet you;
I will show you fear in a handful of dust.   30
              Frisch weht der Wind
              Der Heimat zu
              Mein Irisch Kind,
              Wo weilest du?
"You gave me hyacinths first a year ago;
"They called me the hyacinth girl."
—Yet when we came back, late, from the hyacinth garden,
Your arms full, and your hair wet, I could not
Speak, and my eyes failed, I was neither
Living nor dead, and I knew nothing,   40
Looking into the heart of light, the silence.
Oed' und leer das Meer.

Madame Sosostris, famous clairvoyante,
Had a bad cold, nevertheless
Is known to be the wisest woman in Europe,
With a wicked pack of cards. Here, said she,
Is your card, the drowned Phoenician Sailor,
(Those are pearls that were his eyes. Look!)
Here is Belladonna, the Lady of the Rocks,
The lady of situations.   50
Here is the man with three staves, and here the Wheel,
And here is the one-eyed merchant, and this card,
Which is blank, is something he carries on his back,
Which I am forbidden to see. I do not find
The Hanged Man. Fear death by water.
I see crowds of people, walking round in a ring.
Thank you. If you see dear Mrs. Equitone,
Tell her I bring the horoscope myself:
One must be so careful these days.

Unreal City,   60
Under the brown fog of a winter dawn,
A crowd flowed over London Bridge, so many,
I had not thought death had undone so many.
Sighs, short and infrequent, were exhaled,
And each man fixed his eyes before his feet.
Flowed up the hill and down King William Street,
To where Saint Mary Woolnoth kept the hours
With a dead sound on the final stroke of nine.
There I saw one I knew, and stopped him, crying:
        "Stetson!
"You who were with me in the ships at Mylae!   70
"That corpse you planted last year in your garden,
"Has it begun to sprout? Will it bloom this year?
"Or has the sudden frost disturbed its bed?
"O keep the Dog far hence, that's friend to men,
"Or with his nails he'll dig it up again!
"You! hypocrite lecteur!—mon semblable,—mon frère!"

II. A GAME OF CHESS

The Chair she sat in, like a burnished throne,
Glowed on the marble, where the glass

Held up by standards wrought with fruited vines
From which a golden Cupidon peeped out   80
(Another hid his eyes behind his wing)
Doubled the flames of sevenbranched candelabra
Reflecting light upon the table as
The glitter of her jewels rose to meet it,
From satin cases poured in rich profusion.
In vials of ivory and coloured glass
Unstoppered, lurked her strange synthetic perfumes,
Unguent, powdered, or liquid—troubled, confused
And drowned the sense in odours; stirred by the air
That freshened from the window, these ascended   90
In fattening the prolonged candle-flames,
Flung their smoke into the laquearia,
Stirring the pattern on the coffered ceiling.
Huge sea-wood fed with copper
Burned green and orange, framed by the coloured stone,
In which sad light a carvèd dolphin swam.
Above the antique mantel was displayed
As though a window gave upon the sylvan scene
The change of Philomel, by the barbarous king
So rudely forced; yet there the nightingale   100
Filled all the desert with inviolable voice
And still she cried, and still the world pursues,
"Jug Jug" to dirty ears.
And other withered stumps of time
Were told upon the walls; staring forms
Leaned out, leaning, hushing the room enclosed.
Footsteps shuffled on the stair.
Under the firelight, under the brush, her hair
Spread out in fiery points
Glowed into words, then would be savagely still.   110

"My nerves are bad to-night. Yes, bad. Stay with me.
"Speak to me. Why do you never speak. Speak.
  "What are you thinking of? What thinking? What?
"I never know what you are thinking. Think."

I think we are in rats' alley
Where the dead men lost their bones.

"What is that noise?"
                          The wind under the door.
"What is that noise now? What is the wind doing?"
                          Nothing again nothing.   120
                                        "Do
"You know nothing? Do you see nothing? Do you
     remember
"Nothing?"

     I remember
Those are pearls that were his eyes.
"Are you alive, or not? Is there nothing in your head?"
                                                         But

O O O O that Shakespeherian Rag—
It's so elegant
So intelligent   130
"What shall I do now? What shall I do?"
"I shall rush out as I am, and walk the street
"With my hair down, so. What shall we do tomorrow?
"What shall we ever do?"
                          The hot water at ten.
And if it rains, a closed car at four.
And we shall play a game of chess,
Pressing lidless eyes and waiting for a knock upon the door.

When Lil's husband got demobbed, I said—
I didn't mince my words, I said to her myself,   140
HURRY UP PLEASE ITS TIME
Now Albert's coming back, make yourself a bit smart.
He'll want to know what you done with that money he
     gave you
To get yourself some teeth. He did, I was there.
You have them all out, Lil, and get a nice set,
He said, I swear, I can't bear to look at you.
And no more can't I, I said, and think of poor Albert,
He's been in the army four years, he wants a good time,
And if you don't give it him, there's others will, I said.
Oh is there, she said. Something o' that, I said.   150
Then I'll know who to thank, she said, and give me a
     straight look.

Hurry up please its time
If you don't like it you can get on with it, I said.
Others can pick and choose if you can't.
But if Albert makes off, it won't be for lack of telling.
You ought to be ashamed, I said, to look so antique.
(And her only thirty-one.)
I can't help it, she said, pulling a long face,
It's them pills I took, to bring it off, she said.
(She's had five already, and nearly died of young George.)   160
The chemist said it would be all right, but I've never been
    the same.
You *are* a proper fool, I said.
Well, if Albert won't leave you alone, there it is, I said,
What you get married for if you don't want children?
Hurry up please its time
Well, that Sunday Albert was home, they had a hot
    gammon,
And they asked me in to dinner, to get the beauty of it
    hot—
Hurry up please its time
Hurry up please its time
Goonight Bill. Goonight Lou. Goonight May. Goonight.   170
Ta ta. Goonight. Goonight.
Good night, ladies, good night, sweet ladies, good night,
    good night.

III. THE FIRE SERMON

The river's tent is broken; the last fingers of leaf
Clutch and sink into the wet bank. The wind
Crosses the brown land, unheard. The nymphs are
    departed.
Sweet Thames, run softly, till I end my song.
The river bears no empty bottles, sandwich papers,
Silk handkerchiefs, cardboard boxes, cigarette ends
Or other testimony of summer nights. The nymphs are
    departed.
And their friends, the loitering heirs of City directors;   180
Departed, have left no addresses.
By the waters of Leman I sat down and wept . . .
Sweet Thames, run softly till I end my song,
Sweet Thames, run softly, for I speak not loud or long.

But at my back in a cold blast I hear
The rattle of the bones, and chuckle spread from ear to ear.

A rat crept softly through the vegetation
Dragging its slimy belly on the bank
While I was fishing in the dull canal
On a winter evening round behind the gashouse   190
Musing upon the king my brother's wreck
And on the king my father's death before him.
White bodies naked on the low damp ground
And bones cast in a little low dry garret,
Rattled by the rat's foot only, year to year.
But at my back from time to time I hear·
The sound of horns and motors, which shall bring
Sweeney to Mrs. Porter in the spring.
O the moon shone bright on Mrs. Porter
And on her daughter   200
They wash their feet in soda water
Et O ces voix d'enfants, chantant dans la coupole!

Twit twit twit
Jug jug jug jug jug jug
So rudely forc'd.
Tereu

Unreal City
Under the brown fog of a winter noon
Mr. Eugenides, the Smyrna merchant
Unshaven, with a pocket full of currants   210
C.i.f. London: documents at sight,
Asked me in demotic French
To luncheon at the Cannon Street Hotel
Followed by a weekend at the Metropole.

At the violet hour, when the eyes and back
Turn upward from the desk, when the human engine waits
Like a taxi throbbing waiting,
I Tiresias, though blind, throbbing between two lives,
Old man with wrinkled female breasts, can see
At the violet hour, the evening hour that strives   220
Homeward, and brings the sailor home from sea,

The typist home at teatime, clears her breakfast, lights
Her stove, and lays out food in tins.
Out of the window perilously spread
Her drying combinations touched by the sun's last rays,
On the divan are piled (at night her bed)
Stockings, slippers, camisoles, and stays.
I Tiresias, old man with wrinkled dugs
Perceived the scene, and foretold the rest—
I too awaited the expected guest.   230
He, the young man carbuncular, arrives,
A small house agent's clerk, with one bold stare,
One of the low on whom assurance sits
As a silk hat on a Bradford millionaire.
The time is now propitious, as he guesses,
The meal is ended, she is bored and tired,
Endeavours to engage her in caresses
Which still are unreproved, if undesired.
Flushed and decided, he assaults at once;
Exploring hands encounter no defence;   240
His vanity requires no response,
And makes a welcome of indifference.
(And I Tiresias have foresuffered all
Enacted on this same divan or bed;
I who have sat by Thebes below the wall
And walked among the lowest of the dead.)
Bestows one final patronising kiss,
And gropes his way, finding the stairs unlit . . .

She turns and looks a moment in the glass,
Hardly aware of her departed lover;   250
Her brain allows one half-formed thought to pass:
"Well now that's done: and I'm glad it's over."
When lovely woman stoops to folly and
Paces about her room again, alone,
She smoothes her hair with automatic hand,
And puts a record on the gramophone.

"This music crept by me upon the waters"
And along the Strand, up Queen Victoria Street.
O City city, I can sometimes hear
Beside a public bar in Lower Thames Street,   260

The pleasant whining of a mandoline
And a clatter and a chatter from within
Where fishmen lounge at noon: where the walls
Of Magnus Martyr hold
Inexplicable splendour of Ionian white and gold.

      The river sweats
      Oil and tar
      The barges drift
      With the turning tide
      Red sails   270
      Wide
      To leeward, swing on the heavy spar.
      The barges wash
      Drifting logs
      Down Greenwich reach
      Past the Isle of Dogs.
            Weialala leia
            Wallala leialala

      Elizabeth and Leicester
      Beating oars   280
      The stern was formed
      A gilded shell
      Red and gold
      The brisk swell
      Rippled both shores
      Southwest wind
      Carried down stream
      The peal of bells
      White towers
            Weialala leia   290
            Wallala leialala

"Trams and dusty trees.
Highbury bore me. Richmond and Kew
Undid me. By Richmond I raised my knees
Supine on the floor of a narrow canoe."

"My feet are at Moorgate, and my heart
Under my feet. After the event

He wept. He promised 'a new start.'
I made no comment. What should I resent?"

"On Margate Sands.   300
I can connect
Nothing with nothing.
The broken fingernails of dirty hands.
My people humble people who expect
Nothing."
                    la la

To Carthage then I came

Burning burning burning burning
O Lord Thou pluckest me out
O Lord Thou pluckest   310

burning

IV. DEATH BY WATER

Phlebas the Phoenician, a fortnight dead,
Forgot the cry of gulls, and the deep sea swell
And the profit and loss.
                              A current under sea
Picked his bones in whispers. As he rose and fell
He passed the stages of his age and youth
Entering the whirlpool.
                              Gentile or Jew
O you who turn the wheel and look to windward,   320
Consider Phlebas, who was once handsome and tall as you.

V. WHAT THE THUNDER SAID

After the torchlight red on sweaty faces
After the frosty silence in the gardens
After the agony in stony places
The shouting and the crying
Prison and palace and reverberation
Of thunder of spring over distant mountains
He who was living is now dead

We who were living are now dying
With a little patience   330

Here is no water but only rock
Rock and no water and the sandy road
The road winding above among the mountains
Which are mountains of rock without water
If there were water we should stop and drink
Amongst the rock one cannot stop or think
Sweat is dry and feet are in the sand
If there were only water amongst the rock
Dead mountain mouth of carious teeth that cannot spit
Here one can neither stand nor lie nor sit   340
There is not even silence in the mountains
But dry sterile thunder without rain
There is not even solitude in the mountains
But red sullen faces sneer and snarl
From doors of mudcracked houses
                    If there were water
    And no rock
    If there were rock
    And also water
    And water   350
    A spring
    A pool among the rock
    If there were the sound of water only
    Not the cicada
    And dry grass singing
    But sound of water over a rock
    Where the hermit-thrush sings in the pine trees
    Drip drop drip drop drop drop drop
    But there is no water

Who is the third who walks always beside you?   360
When I count, there are only you and I together
But when I look ahead up the white road
There is always another one walking beside you
Gliding wrapt in a brown mantle, hooded
I do not know whether a man or a woman
—But who is that on the other side of you?

What is that sound high in the air
Murmur of maternal lamentation
Who are those hooded hordes swarming
Over endless plains, stumbling in cracked earth   370
Ringed by the flat horizon only
What is the city over the mountains
Cracks and reforms and bursts in the violet air
Falling towers
Jerusalem Athens Alexandria
Vienna London
Unreal

A woman drew her long black hair out tight
And fiddled whisper music on those strings
And bats with baby faces in the violet light   380
Whistled, and beat their wings
And crawled head downward down a blackened wall
And upside down in air were towers
Tolling reminiscent bells, that kept the hours
And voices singing out of empty cisterns and exhausted
        wells

In this decayed hole among the mountains
In the faint moonlight, the grass is singing
Over the tumbled graves, about the chapel
There is the empty chapel, only the wind's home.
It has no windows, and the door swings,   390
Dry bones can harm no one.
Only a cock stood on the rooftree
Co co rico co co rico
In a flash of lightning. Then a damp gust
Bringing rain

Ganga was sunken, and the limp leaves
Waited for rain, while the black clouds
Gathered far distant, over Himavant.
The jungle crouched, humped in silence.
Then spoke the thunder   400
DA
Datta: what have we given?
My friend, blood shaking my heart

The awful daring of a moment's surrender
Which an age of prudence can never retract
By this, and this only, we have existed
Which is not to be found in our obituaries
Or in memories draped by the beneficent spider
Or under seals broken by the lean solicitor
In our empty rooms   410
DA
Dayadhvam: I have heard the key
Turn in the door once and turn once only
We think of the key, each in his prison
Thinking of the key, each confirms a prison
Only at nightfall, aethereal rumours
Revive for a moment a broken Coriolanus
DA
Damyata: The boat responded
Gaily, to the hand expert with sail and oar   420
The sea was calm, your heart would have responded
Gaily, when invited, beating obedient
To controlling hands

                I sat upon the shore
Fishing, with the arid plain behind me
Shall I at least set my lands in order?
London Bridge is falling down falling down falling down
Poi s'ascose nel foco che gli affina
Quando fiam uti chelidon—O swallow swallow
Le Prince d'Aquitaine à la tour abolie   430
These fragments I have shored against my ruins
Why then Ile fit you. Hieronymo's mad againe.
Datta. Dayadhvam. Damyata.
       Shantih   shantih   shantih

THE HOLLOW MEN   [1925]

      Mistah Kurtz—he dead.
           A penny for the Old Guy

        I

We are the hollow men
We are the stuffed men

Leaning together
Headpiece filled with straw. Alas!
Our dried voices, when
We whisper together
Are quiet and meaningless
As wind in dry grass
Or rats' feet over broken glass
In our dry cellar   10

Shape without form, shade without colour,
Paralysed force, gesture without motion;

Those who have crossed
With direct eyes, to death's other Kingdom
Remember us—if at all—not as lost
Violent souls, but only
As the hollow men
The stuffed men.

                        II

Eyes I dare not meet in dreams
In death's dream kingdom   20
These do not appear:
There, the eyes are
Sunlight on a broken column
There, is a tree swinging
And voices are
In the wind's singing
More distant and more solemn
Than a fading star.

Let me be no nearer
In death's dream kingdom   30
Let me also wear
Such deliberate disguises
Rat's coat, crowskin, crossed staves
In a field
Behaving as the wind behaves
No nearer—

Not that final meeting
In the twilight kingdom

III

This is the dead land
This is cactus land   40
Here the stone images
Are raised, here they receive
The supplication of a dead man's hand
Under the twinkle of a fading star.

Is it like this
In death's other kingdom
Waking alone
At the hour when we are
Trembling with tenderness
Lips that would kiss   50
Form prayers to broken stone.

IV

The eyes are not here
There are no eyes here
In this valley of dying stars
In this hollow valley
This broken jaw of our lost kingdoms

In this last of meeting places
We grope together
And avoid speech
Gathered on this beach of the tumid river   60

Sightless, unless
The eyes reappear
As the perpetual star
Multifoliate rose
Of death's twilight kingdom
The hope only
Of empty men.

V

Here we go round the prickly pear
Prickly pear prickly pear
Here we go round the prickly pear   70
At five o'clock in the morning.

Between the idea
And the reality
Between the motion
And the act
Falls the Shadow
      For Thine is the Kingdom

Between the conception
And the creation
Between the emotion   80
And the response
Falls the Shadow
        Life is very long

Between the desire
And the spasm
Between the potency
And the existence
Between the essence
And the descent
Falls the Shadow   90
      For Thine is the Kingdom

For Thine is
Life is
For Thine is the

This is the way the world ends
This is the way the world ends
This is the way the world ends
Not with a bang but a whimper.

ASH-WEDNESDAY   [1930]

I

Because I do not hope to turn again
Because I do not hope

Because I do not hope to turn
Desiring this man's gift and that man's scope
I no longer strive to strive towards such things
(Why should the agèd eagle stretch its wings?)
Why should I mourn
The vanished power of the usual reign?

Because I do not hope to know again
The infirm glory of the positive hour   10
Because I do not think
Because I know I shall not know
The one veritable transitory power
Because I cannot drink
There, where trees flower, and springs flow, for there is
      nothing again

Because I know that time is always time
And place is always and only place
And what is actual is actual only for one time
And only for one place
I rejoice that things are as they are and   20
I renounce the blessèd face
And renounce the voice
Because I cannot hope to turn again
Consequently I rejoice, having to construct something
Upon which to rejoice

And pray to God to have mercy upon us
And I pray that I may forget
These matters that with myself I too much discuss
Too much explain
Because I do not hope to turn again   30
Let these words answer
For what is done, not to be done again
May the judgement not be too heavy upon us

Because these wings are no longer wings to fly
But merely vans to beat the air
The air which is now thoroughly small and dry
Smaller and dryer than the will

Teach us to care and not to care
Teach us to sit still.

Pray for us sinners now and at the hour of our death   40
Pray for us now and at the hour of our death.

II

Lady, three white leopards sat under a juniper-tree
In the cool of the day, having fed to satiety
On my legs my heart my liver and that which had been
          contained
In the hollow round of my skull. And God said
Shall these bones live? shall these
Bones lives? And that which had been contained
In the bones (which were already dry) said chirping:
Because of the goodness of this Lady
And because of her loveliness, and because   50
She honours the Virgin in meditation,
We shine with brightness. And I who am here dissembled
Proffer my deeds to oblivion, and my love
To the posterity of the desert and the fruit of the gourd.
It is this which recovers
My guts the strings of my eyes and the indigestible portions
Which the leopards reject. The Lady is withdrawn
In a white gown, to contemplation, in a white gown.
Let the whiteness of bones atone to forgetfulness.
There is no life in them. As I am forgotten   60
And would be forgotten, so I would forget
Thus devoted, concentrated in purpose. And God said
Prophesy to the wind, to the wind only for only
The wind will listen. And the bones sang chirping
With the burden of the grasshopper, saying

Lady of silences
Calm and distressed
Torn and most whole
Rose of memory
Rose of forgetfulness   70
Exhausted and life-giving
Worried reposeful

The single Rose
Is now the Garden
Where all loves end
Terminate torment
Of love unsatisfied
The greater torment
Of love satisfied
End of the endless   80
Journey to no end
Conclusion of all that
Is inconclusible
Speech without word and
Word of no speech
Grace to the Mother
For the Garden
Where all love ends.

Under a juniper-tree the bones sang, scattered and shining
We are glad to be scattered, we did little good to each other,   90
Under a tree in the cool of the day, with the blessing of
        sand,
Forgetting themselves and each other, united
In the quiet of the desert. This is the land which ye
Shall divide by lot. And neither division nor unity
Matters. This is the land. We have our inheritance.

                                    III

At the first turning of the second stair
I turned and saw below
The same shape twisted on the banister
Under the vapour in the fetid air
Struggling with the devil of the stairs who wears   100
The deceitful face of hope and of despair.

At the second turning of the second stair
I left them twisting, turning below;
There were no more faces and the stair was dark,
Damp, jaggèd, like an old man's mouth drivelling, beyond
        repair,
Or the toothed gullet of an agèd shark.

At the first turning of the third stair
Was a slotted window bellied like the fig's fruit
And beyond the hawthorn blossom and a pasture scene
The broadbacked figure drest in blue and green   110
Enchanted the maytime with an antique flute.
Blown hair is sweet, brown hair over the mouth blown,
Lilac and brown hair;
Distraction, music of the flute, stops and steps of the mind
          over the third stair,
Fading, fading; strength beyond hope and despair
Climbing the third stair.

Lord, I am not worthy
Lord, I am not worthy

          but speak the word only.

IV

Who walked between the violet and the violet   120
Who walked between
The various ranks of varied green
Going in white and blue, in Mary's colour,
Talking of trivial things
In ignorance and in knowledge of eternal dolour
Who moved among the others as they walked,
Who then made strong the fountains and made fresh the
          springs

Made cool the dry rock and made firm the sand
In blue of larkspur, blue of Mary's colour,
Sovegna vos   130

Here are the years that walk between, bearing
Away the fiddles and the flutes, restoring
One who moves in the time between sleep and waking,
          wearing

White light folded, sheathed about her, folded.
The new years walk, restoring
Through a bright cloud of tears, the years, restoring

With a new verse the ancient rhyme. Redeem
The time. Redeem
The unread vision in the higher dream
While jewelled unicorns draw by the gilded hearse.   140

The silent sister veiled in white and blue
Between the yews, behind the garden god,
Whose flute is breathless, bent her head and signed but
    spoke no word

But the fountain sprang up and the bird sang down
Redeem the time, redeem the dream
The token of the word unheard, unspoken

Till the wind shake a thousand whispers from the yew

And after this our exile

V

If the lost word is lost, if the spent word is spent
If the unheard, unspoken   150
Word is unspoken, unheard;
Still is the unspoken word, the Word unheard,
The Word without a word, the Word within
The world and for the world;
And the light shone in darkness and
Against the Word the unstilled world still whirled
About the centre of the silent Word.

    O my people, what have I done unto thee.

Where shall the word be found, where will the word
Resound? Not here, there is not enough silence   160
Not on the sea or on the islands, not
On the mainland, in the desert or the rain land,
For those who walk in darkness
Both in the day time and in the night time
The right time and the right place are not here
No place of grace for those who avoid the face
No time to rejoice for those who walk among noise and
    deny the voice

Will the veiled sister pray for
Those who walk in darkness, who chose thee and oppose
        thee,
Those who are torn on the horn between season and
        season, time and time, between   170
Hour and hour, word and word, power and power, those
        who wait
In darkness? Will the veiled sister pray
For children at the gate
Who will not go away and cannot pray:
Pray for those who chose and oppose

            O my people, what have I done unto thee.

Will the veiled sister between the slender
Yew trees pray for those who offend her
And are terrified and cannot surrender
And affirm before the world and deny between the rocks   180
In the last desert between the last blue rocks
The desert in the garden the garden in the desert
Of drouth, spitting from the mouth the withered apple-
        seed.

            O my people.

                                VI

Although I do not hope to turn again
Although I do not hope
Although I do not hope to turn

Wavering between the profit and the loss
In this brief transit where the dreams cross
The dreamcrossed twilight between birth and dying   190
(Bless me father) though I do not wish to wish these things
From the wide window towards the granite shore
The white sails still fly seaward, seaward flying
Unbroken wings

And the lost heart stiffens and rejoices
In the lost lilac and the lost sea voices

And the weak spirit quickens to rebel
For the bent golden-rod and the lost sea smell
Quickens to recover
The cry of quail and the whirling plover   200
And the blind eye creates
The empty forms between the ivory gates
And smell renews the salt savour of the sandy earth

This is the time of tension between dying and birth
The place of solitude where three dreams cross
Between blue rocks
But when the voices shaken from the yew-tree drift away
Let the other yew be shaken and reply.

Blessèd sister, holy mother, spirit of the fountain, spirit of
        the garden,
Suffer us not to mock ourselves with falsehood   210
Teach us to care and not to care
Teach us to sit still
Even among these rocks,
Our peace in His will
And even among these rocks
Sister, mother
And spirit of the river, spirit of the sea,
Suffer me not to be separated

And let my cry come unto Thee.

Conrad Aiken

b. 1889

Conrad Potter Aiken was born in Savannah, Georgia, August 5, 1889, but while still a small child was sent to New Bedford, Massachusetts, to live with relatives when his father, a distinguished physician, killed his mother and committed suicide. He wrote his first poem at the age of nine, and at thirteen began memorizing Poe's lyrics, his first literary influence. He graduated a year after the Harvard class of 1910, which included T. S. Eliot, Van Wyck Brooks, and Walter Lippman. He was probably influenced by French Symbolism, as Eliot was, and certainly by the psychology and philosophy of William James, Freud, and Bergson. Music profoundly affected his capacity for verbal melody. Since 1914 he has published prodigiously: poetry, fiction, criticism, and an autobiography called Ushant *(1952). His* Selected Poems *(1929) won a Pulitzer Prize, and from 1950 to 1952 he was Consultant in Poetry to the Library of Congress.*

THE ROAD   [1925]

Three then came forward out of darkness, one
An old man bearded, his old eyes red with weeping,
A peasant, with hard hands. 'Come now,' he said,
'And see the road, for which our people die.
Twelve miles of road we've made, a little only,
Westward winding. Of human blood and stone
We build; and in a thousand years will come
Beyond the hills to sea.'

               I went with them,
Taking a lantern, which upon their faces

Showed years and grief; and in a time we came   10
To the wild road which wound among wild hills
Westward; and so along this road we stooped,
Silent, thinking of all the dead men, there
Compounded with sad clay. Slowly we moved:
For they were old and weak, had given all
Their life, to build this twelve poor miles of road,
Muddy, under the rain. And in my hand
Turning the lantern, here or there, I saw
Deep holes of water where the raindrop splashed,
And rainfilled footprints in the grass, and heaps   20
Of broken stone, and rusted spades and picks,
And helves of axes. And the old man spoke,
Holding my wrist: 'Three hundred years it took
To build these miles of road: three hundred years;
And human lives unnumbered. But the day
Will come when it is done.' Then spoke another,
One not so old, but old, whose face was wrinkled:
'And when it comes, our people will all sing
For joy, passing from east to west, or west
To east, returning, with the light behind them;   30
All meeting in the road and singing there.'
And the third said: 'The road will be their life;
A heritage of blood. Grief will be in it,
And beauty out of grief. And I can see
How all the women's faces will be bright.
In that time, laughing, they will remember us.
Blow out your lantern now, for day is coming.'
My lantern blown out, in a little while
We climbed in long light up a hill, where climbed
The dwindling road, and ended in a field.   40
Peasants were working in the field, bowed down
With unrewarded work, and grief, and years
Of pain. And as we passed them, one man fell
Into a furrow that was bright with water
And gave a cry that was half cry half song—
'The road . . . the road . . . the road . . . ' And all then fell
Upon their knees and sang.

                              We four passed on
Over the hill, to westward. Then I felt

How tears ran down my face, tears without number;
And knew that all my life henceforth was weeping,   50
Weeping, thinking of human grief, and human
Endeavour fruitless in a world of pain.
And when I held my hands up they were old;
I knew my face would not be young again.

SEA HOLLY   [1925]

Begotten by the meeting of rock with rock,
The mating of rock and rock, rocks gnashing together;
Created so, and yet forgetful, walks
The seaward path, puts up her left hand, shades
Blue eyes, the eyes of rock, to see better
In slanting light the ancient sheep (which kneels
Biting the grass) the while her other hand,
Hooking the wicker handle, turns the basket
Of eggs. The sea is high to-day. The eggs
Are cheaper. The sea is blown from the southwest,   10
Confused, taking up sand and mud in waves,
The waves break, sluggish, in brown foam, the wind
Disperses (on the sheep and hawthorn) spray,—
And on her cheeks, the cheeks engendered of rock,
And eyes, the colour of rock. The left hand
Falls from the eyes, and undecided slides
Over the left breast on which muslin lightly
Rests, touching the nipple, and then down
The hollow side, virgin as rock, and bitterly
Caresses the blue hip.

                    It was for this,   20
This obtuse taking of the seaward path,
This stupid hearing of larks, this hooking
Of wicker, this absent observation of sheep
Kneeling in harsh sea-grass, the cool hand shading
The spray-stung eyes—it was for this the rock
Smote itself. The sea is higher to-day,

And eggs are cheaper. The eyes of rock take in
The seaward path that winds toward the sea,
The thistle-prodder, old woman under a bonnet,
Forking the thistles, her back against the sea,   30
Pausing, with hard hands on the handle, peering
With rock eyes from her bonnet.

                            It was for this,
This rock-lipped facing of brown waves, half sand
And half water, this tentative hand that slides
Over the breast of rock, and into the hollow
Soft side of muslin rock, and then fiercely
Almost as rock against the hip of rock—
It was for this in midnight the rocks met,
And dithered together, cracking and smoking.

                            It was for this   40
Barren beauty, barrenness of rock that aches
On the seaward path, seeing the fruitful sea,
Hearing the lark of rock that sings, smelling
The rock-flower of hawthorn, sweetness of rock—
It was for this, stone pain in the stony heart,
The rock loved and laboured; and all is lost.

ELDER TREE   [1925]

'The sensual will have its moment? The brain
Sleep? . . . You can prophesy? . . . '

                    —Thus laughed the woman,
Tall, thin, and bitter as an elder tree,
Lifting her white face like a crown of bloom.
And so I swore by darkness, trees, and blood,
And rivers underground, and felt my brain,
(Thus challenged by her brain) fall steeply down
Like a dead leaf upon the rushing flood.

'Yes, I can prophesy,' I laughed in answer;
And lost my life in hers, which brighter shone,   10
Radiant and derisive. 'Never yet,'
She darkly smiled, 'has voice of man flown in
To break my chords of being. You but waste
The evening, with its bank of clouds, where stars
Plunge down to swim . . . Look, how the lights now come
Like perforations in that wall of trees—
Where through the Ultimate winks!'

              And she was still,
Clasping long hands around her lifted knee.
These touched I twice, with teasing finger-tip,
Three times and four, then wearied. But the darkness   20
And that profounder sound where rushed the river,
Nocturnal, under all, and moving all,—
Took both of us, annulled the brain, devoured
The elder tree, with white faint face of bloom,
And me, who sat beneath it.

              Then my blood
Was filled with elder blossom cold and white,
My arms embraced the tree of singing wood,
My hands took leaves and broke them. We were lost,
Thus mingled, in the world. No speech we had.
Till suddenly (as at the end of death,   30
The darkness being silent) we stood up
Once more; the woman hushed, an elder tree,
And I a voice. And then she smiled, and said—
'Ah, it is true! The sensual has its moment.
The trickster brain—thank God—can be deposed . . . '

Then I, 'Look now! how all the trees rush back
From the dark stream! and every blade of grass
New-washed in starlight!'

            'Starlight?' . . . She laughed, rustling,—
Rustling, nodding her elder-blossom face,—
'Not starlight, no! The trees, the grass, the brain,   40
Come back again from blood; and they are strong.'

THE ROOM   [1925]

Through that window—all else being extinct
Except itself and me—I saw the struggle
Of darkness against darkness. Within the room
It turned and turned, dived downward. Then I saw
How order might—if chaos wished—become:
And saw the darkness crush upon itself,
Contracting powerfully; it was as if
It killed itself: slowly: and with much pain.
Pain. The scene was pain, and nothing but pain.
What else, when chaos draws all forces inward   10
To shape a single leaf? . . .

                    For the leaf came,
Alone and shining in the empty room;
After a while the twig shot downward from it;
And from the twig a bough; and then the trunk,
Massive and coarse; and last the one black root.
The black root cracked the walls. Boughs burst the
          window:
The great tree took possession.

                         Tree of trees!
Remember (when time comes) how chaos died
To shape the shining leaf. Then turn, have courage,
Wrap arms and roots together, be convulsed   20
With grief, and bring back chaos out of shape.
I will be watching then as I watch now.
I will praise darkness now, but then the leaf.

DOCTORS' ROW   [1942]

Snow falls on the cars in Doctors' Row and hoods the
          headlights;
snow piles on the brownstone steps, the basement deadlights;

fills up the letters and names and brass degrees
on the bright brass plates, and the bright brass holes for keys.

Snow hides, as if on purpose, the rows of bells
which open the doors to separate cells and hells:
to the waiting-rooms, where the famous prepare for headlines,
and humbler citizens for their humbler deadlines.

And in and out, and out and in, they go,
the lamentable devotees of Doctors' Row;   10
silent and circumspect—indeed, liturgical;
their cries and prayers prescribed, their penance surgical.

No one complains—no one presumes to shriek—
the walls are very thick, and the voices weak.
Or the cries are whisked away in noiseless cabs,
while nurse, in the alley, empties a pail of swabs.

Miserable street!—through which your sweetheart hurries,
lowers her chin, as the snow-cloud stings and flurries;
thinks of the flower-stall, by the church, where you
wait like a clock, for two, for half-past two;   20

thinks of the roses banked on the steps in snow.
of god in heaven, and the world above, below;
widens her vision beyond the storm, her sight
the infinite rings of an immense delight;

all to be lived and loved—O glorious All!
Eastward or westward, Plato's turning wall;
the sky's blue streets swept clean of silent birds
for an audience of gods, and superwords.

NORTH INFINITY STREET   [1942]

The alarm clocks tick in a thousand furnished rooms,
tick and are wound for a thousand separate dooms;

all down both sides of North Infinity Street
you hear that contrapuntal pawnshop beat.

Hall bedrooms, attic rooms, where the gas-ring sings,
rooms in the basement where the loud doorbell rings;
carpeted or bare, by the rail at the head of the stair,
the curtains drawn, a mirror, a bed, and a chair,

in midnight darkness, when the last footfall creaks,
in northeast rain, when the broken window leaks,   10
at dawn, to the sound of dishes, the kitchen steam,
at dusk, when the muted radio croons a dream,

there, amid combs and the waiting shoes and socks,
and the bathrobes hung in closets, tick the clocks:
on the chest of drawers, on the table beside the bed,
facing the pillow, facing the recumbent head:

yes, from here to forever, from here to never,
one long sidereal curve of ticking fever,
all down both sides of North Infinity Street
you hear that contrapuntal pawnshop beat.   20

THE LOVERS   [1942]

In this glass palace are flowers in golden baskets.
In that grim brownstone castle are silver caskets.
The caskets watch and wait, and the baskets wait,
for a certain day and hour, and a certain gate.

Wonderfully glow the colors in this bright palace.
Superb the *flora*, in pyx and vase and chalice.
The glass is steamed with a stifling tuberose breath;
and lilies too, of the valley of the shadow of death.

The caskets are satin-lined, with silver handles;
and the janitor sings 'they'll soon be lighting candles.'   10

He sweeps the sidewalk, and as he sweeps he sings,
in praise of a hearse with completely noiseless springs.

Hush—the conspiracy works, it has crossed the street:
some day, and it's not far off, the lovers will meet:
casket and basket will soon set forth together
on a joyful journey, no matter how bleak the weather:

in a beautiful beetle-black hearse with noiseless tread,
basket and casket together will hie to bed;
and start on a pullman journey to a certain gate,
punctually, at a certain hour, on a certain date.   20

MUSIC   [1942]

The calyx of the oboe breaks,
silver and soft the flower it makes.
And next, beyond, the flute-notes seen
now are white and now are green.

What are these sounds, what daft device,
mocking at flame, mimicking ice?
Musicians, will you never rest
from strange translation of the breast?

The heart, from which all horrors come,
grows like a vine, its gourd a drum;   10
the living pattern sprawls and climbs
eager to bear all worlds and times:

trilling leaf and tinkling grass
glide into darkness clear as glass;
then the musicians cease to play
and the world is waved away.

Archibald MacLeish

b. 1892

Archibald MacLeish was born May 7, 1892, in Glencoe, Illinois. He graduated from Yale in 1915 and received a degree from the Harvard Law School in 1919 after service as an officer of field artillery in World War I. For three years he practiced law in Boston and in 1923 went to France for five years. During the 1930's he was on the staff of Fortune, *from 1939 to 1944 he was Librarian of Congress, and in 1944–1945 he was Assistant Secretary of State. In 1949 he became professor of English at Harvard, a post from which he retired in 1962. MacLeish has won three Pulitzer Prizes: for* Conquistador *in 1933, for* Collected Poems *in 1953, and for the verse play* J.B. *in 1959.*

ARS POETICA   [1926]

A poem should be palpable and mute
As a globed fruit,

Dumb
As old medallions to the thumb,

Silent as the sleeve-worn stone
Of casement ledges where the moss has grown—

A poem should be wordless
As the flight of birds.

                    *

A poem should be motionless in time
As the moon climbs,   10

Leaving, as the moon releases
Twig by twig the night-entangled trees,

Leaving, as the moon behind the winter leaves,
Memory by memory the mind—

A poem should be motionless in time
As the moon climbs.

*

A poem should be equal to:
Not true.

For all the history of grief
An empty doorway and a maple leaf.   20

For love
The leaning grasses and two lights above the sea—

A poem should not mean
But be.

THE END OF THE WORLD   [1926]

Quite unexpectedly as Vasserot
The armless ambidextrian was lighting
A match between his great and second toe
And Ralph the lion was engaged in biting
The neck of Madame Sossman while the drum
Pointed, and Teeny was about to cough
In waltz-time swinging Jocko by the thumb—
Quite unexpectedly the top blew off:

And there, there overhead, there, there, hung over
Those thousands of white faces, those dazed eyes,   10
There in the starless dark the poise, the hover,
There with vast wings across the canceled skies,

There in the sudden blackness the black pall
Of nothing, nothing, nothing—nothing at all.

YOU, ANDREW MARVELL   [1930]

And here face down beneath the sun
And here upon earth's noonward height
To feel the always coming on
The always rising of the night:

To feel creep up the curving east
The earthy chill of dusk and slow
Upon those under lands the vast
And ever climbing shadow grow

And strange at Ecbatan the trees
Take leaf by leaf the evening strange   10
The flooding dark about their knees
The mountains over Persia change

And now at Kermanshah the gate
Dark empty and the withered grass
And through the twilight now the late
Few travelers in the westward pass

And Baghdad darken and the bridge
Across the silent river gone
And through Arabia the edge
Of evening widen and steal on   20

And deepen on Palmyra's street
The wheel rut in the ruined stone
And Lebanon fade out and Crete
High through the clouds and overblown

And over Sicily the air
Still flashing with the landward gulls

And loom and slowly disappear
The sails above the shadowy hulls

And Spain go under and the shore
Of Africa the gilded sand   30
And evening vanish and no more
The low pale light across that land

Nor now the long light on the sea:

And here face downward in the sun
To feel how swift how secretly
The shadow of the night comes on . . .

IMMORTAL AUTUMN   [1930]

I speak this poem now with grave and level voice
In praise of autumn, of the far-horn-winding fall.

I praise the flower-barren fields, the clouds, the tall
Unanswering branches where the wind makes sullen noise.

I praise the fall: it is the human season.
                                        Now
No more the foreign sun does meddle at our earth,
Enforce the green and bring the fallow land to birth,
Nor winter yet weigh all with silence the pine bough,

But now in autumn with the black and outcast crows
Share we the spacious world: the whispering year is gone: 10
There is more room to live now: the once secret dawn
Comes late by daylight and the dark unguarded goes.

Between the mutinous brave burning of the leaves
And winter's covering of our hearts with his deep snow
We are alone: there are no evening birds: we know
The naked moon: the tame stars circle at our eaves.

It is the human season. On this sterile air
Do words outcarry breath: the sound goes on and on.
I hear a dead man's cry from autumn long since gone.

I cry to you beyond upon this bitter air.   20

"NOT MARBLE NOR THE GILDED MONUMENTS" [1930]

For Adele

The praisers of women in their proud and beautiful poems,
Naming the grave mouth and the hair and the eyes,
Boasted those they loved should be forever remembered:
These were lies.

The words sound but the face in the Istrian sun is
        forgotten.
The poet speaks but to her dead ears no more.
The sleek throat is gone—and the breast that was
        troubled to listen:
Shadow from door.

Therefore I will not praise your knees nor your fine
        walking
Telling you men shall remember your name as long   10
As lips move or breath is spent or the iron of English
Rings from a tongue.

I shall say you were young, and your arms straight, and
        your mouth scarlet:
I shall say you will die and none will remember you:
Your arms change, and none remember the swish of your
        garments,
Nor the click of your shoe.

Not with my hand's strength, not with difficult labor
Springing the obstinate words to the bones of your breast

And the stubborn line to your young stride and the breath
    to your breathing
And the beat to your haste   20
Shall I prevail on the hearts of unborn men to remember.

(What is a dead girl but a shadowy ghost
Or a dead man's voice but a distant and vain affirmation
Like dream words most)

Therefore I will not speak of the undying glory of women.
I will say you were young and straight and your skin fair
And you stood in the door and the sun was a shadow of
    leaves on your shoulders
And a leaf on your hair—

I will not speak of the famous beauty of dead women:
I will say the shape of a leaf lay once on your hair.   30
Till the world ends and the eyes are out and the mouths
    broken
Look! It is there!

POLE STAR   [1936]

Where the wheel of light is turned,
Where the axle of the night is
Turned, is motionless, where holds
And has held ancient sureness always:

Where of faring men the eyes
At oar bench at the rising bow
Have seen—torn shrouds between—the Wain
And that star's changelessness, not changing:

There upon that intent star,
Trust of wandering men, of truth   10
The most reminding witness, we
Fix our eyes also, waylost, the wanderers:

We too turn now to that star:
We too in whose trustless hearts
All truth alters and the lights
Of earth are out now turn to that star:

Liberty of man and mind
That once was mind's necessity
And made the West blaze up has burned
To bloody embers and the lamp's out: 20

Hope that was a noble flame
Has fanned to violence and feeds
On cities and the flesh of men
And chokes where unclean smoke defiles it:

Even the small spark of pride
That taught the tyrant once is dark
Where gunfire rules the starving street
And justice cheats the dead of honor:

Liberty and pride and hope—
Every guide-mark of the mind   30
That led our blindness once has vanished.
This star will not. Love's star will not.

Love that has beheld the face
A man has with a man's eyes in it
Bloody from the slugger's blows
Or heard the cold child cry for hunger—

Love that listens where the good,
The virtuous, the men of faith,
Proclaim the paradise on earth
And murder starve and burn to make it—   40

Love that cannot either sleep
Or keep rich music in the ear
Or lose itself for the wild beat
The anger in the blood makes raging—

Love that hardens into hate,
Love like hatred and as bright,
Love is that one waking light
That leads now when all others darken.

THEORY OF POETRY   [1954]

Know the world by heart
Or never know it!
Let the pedant stand apart—
Nothing he can name will show it:
Also him of intellectual art.
None know it
Till they know the world by heart.

Take heart then, poet!

e. e. cummings

1894–1962

Edward Estlin Cummings was born October 14, 1894, in Cambridge, Massachusetts. His father was then teaching at Harvard and later became minister of the Old South Church in Boston. Cummings took his A.B. from Harvard in 1915 and his M.A. in 1916. During World War I he was in the Norton-Harjes Volunteer Ambulance Unit until, through a military censor's error, he was placed for three months in a French detention camp. After the war he studied painting in Paris. Later he moved back to New York, where he continued to paint and to write poetry throughout his life, though he experimented in other literary forms as well. In 1950 the Academy of American Poets awarded him a Fellowship for "great achievement." He died at North Conway, New Hampshire, on September 3, 1962.

O SWEET SPONTANEOUS   [1923]

O sweet spontaneous
earth how often have
the
doting

          fingers of
prurient philosophers pinched
and
poked

thee
, has the naughty thumb

of science prodded
thy

    beauty   . how
often have religions taken
thee upon their scraggy knees
squeezing and

buffeting thee that thou mightest conceive
gods
    (but
true   20

to the incomparable
couch of death thy
rhythmic
lover

    thou answerest

them only with

        spring)

A MAN WHO HAD FALLEN AMONG THIEVES
[1926]

a man who had fallen among thieves
lay by the roadside on his back
dressed in fifteenthrate ideas
wearing a round jeer for a hat

fate per a somewhat more than less
emancipated evening
had in return for consciousness
endowed him with a changeless grin

whereon a dozen staunch and leal
citizens did graze at pause   10
then fired by hypercivic zeal
sought newer pastures or because

swaddled with a frozen brook
of pinkest vomit out of eyes
which noticed nobody he looked
as if he did not care to rise

one hand did nothing on the vest
its wideflung friend clenched weakly dirt
while the mute trouserfly confessed
a button solemnly inert.   20

Brushing from whom the stiffened puke
i put him all into my arms
and staggered banged with terror through
a million billion trillion stars

"NEXT TO OF COURSE GOD AMERICA I
[1926]

"next to of course god america i
love you land of the pilgrims' and so forth oh
say can you see by the dawn's early my
country 'tis of centuries come and go
and are no more what of it we should worry
in every language even deafanddumb
thy sons acclaim your glorious name by gorry
by jingo by gee by gosh by gum
why talk of beauty what could be more beaut-
iful than these heroic happy dead   10
who rushed like lions to the roaring slaughter
they did not stop to think they died instead
then shall the voices of liberty be mute?"

He spoke. And drank rapidly a glass of water

SOMEWHERE I HAVE NEVER TRAVELLED, GLADLY BEYOND [1931]

somewhere i have never travelled,gladly beyond
any experience,your eyes have their silence:
in your most frail gesture are things which enclose me,
or which i cannot touch because they are too near

your slightest look easily will unclose me
though i have closed myself as fingers,
you open always petal by petal myself as Spring opens
(touching skilfully,mysteriously)her first rose

or if your wish be to close me,i and
my life will shut very beautifully,suddenly,   10
as when the heart of this flower imagines
the snow carefully everywhere descending;

nothing which we are to perceive in this world equals
the power of your intense fragility:whose texture
compels me with the colour of its countries,
rendering death and forever with each breathing

(i do not know what it is about you that closes
and opens;only something in me understands
the voice of your eyes is deeper than all roses)
nobody,not even the rain,has such small hands   20

ANYONE LIVED IN A PRETTY HOW TOWN
[1940]

anyone lived in a pretty how town
(with up so floating many bells down)
spring summer autumn winter
he sang his didn't he danced his did.

Women and men(both little and small)
cared for anyone not at all
they sowed their isn't they reaped their same
sun moon stars rain

children guessed(but only a few
and down they forgot as up they grew   10
autumn winter spring summer)
that noone loved him more by more

when by now and tree by leaf
she laughed his joy she cried his grief
bird by snow and stir by still
anyone's any was all to her

someones married their everyones
laughed their cryings and did their dance
(sleep wake hope and then)they
said their nevers they slept their dream   20

stars rain sun moon
(and only the snow can begin to explain
how children are apt to forget to remember
with up so floating many bells down)

one day anyone died i guess
(and noone stooped to kiss his face)
busy folk buried them side by side
little by little and was by was

all by all and deep by deep
and more by more they dream their sleep   30
noone and anyone earth by april
wish by spirit and if by yes.

Women and men(both dong and ding)
summer autumn winter spring
reaped their sowing and went their came
sun moon stars rain

MY FATHER MOVED THROUGH DOOMS OF
LOVE   [1940]

my father moved through dooms of love
through sames of am through haves of give,
singing each morning out of each night
my father moved through depths of height

this motionless forgetful where
turned at his glance to shining here;
that if(so timid air is firm)
under his eyes would stir and squirm

newly as from unburied which
floats the first who,his april touch   10
drove sleeping selves to swarm their fates
woke dreamers to their ghostly roots

and should some why completely weep
my father's fingers brought her sleep:
vainly no smallest voice might cry
for he could feel the mountains grow.

Lifting the valleys of the sea
my father moved through griefs of joy;
praising a forehead called the moon
singing desire into begin   20

joy was his song and joy so pure
a heart of star by him could steer
and pure so now and now so yes
the wrists of twilight would rejoice

keen as midsummer's keen beyond
conceiving mind of sun will stand,
so strictly(over utmost him
so hugely)stood my father's dream

his flesh was flesh his blood was blood:
no hungry man but wished him food;   30
no cripple wouldn't creep one mile
uphill to only see him smile.

Scorning the pomp of must and shall
my father moved through dooms of feel;
his anger was as right as rain
his pity was as green as grain

septembering arms of year extend
less humbly wealth to foe and friend
than he to foolish and to wise
offered immeasurable is   40

proudly and(by octobering flame
beckoned)as earth will downward climb,
so naked for immortal work
his shoulders marched against the dark

his sorrow was as true as bread:
no liar looked him in the head;
if every friend became his foe
he'd laugh and build a world with snow.

My father moved through theys of we,
singing each new leaf out of each tree   50
(and every child was sure that spring
danced when she heard my father sing)

then let men kill which cannot share,
let blood and flesh be mud and mire,
scheming imagine,passion willed,
freedom a drug that's bought and sold

giving to steal and cruel kind,
a heart to fear,to doubt a mind,
to differ a disease of same,
conform the pinnacle of am   60

though dull were all we taste as bright,
bitter all utterly things sweet,
maggoty minus and dumb death
all we inherit,all bequeath

and nothing quite so least as truth
—i say though hate were why men breathe—
because my father lived his soul
love is the whole and more than all

PITY THIS BUSY MONSTER,MANUNKIND   [1944]

pity this busy monster,manunkind,

not. Progress is a comfortable disease:
your victim(death and life safely beyond)

plays with the bigness of his littleness
—electrons deify one razorblade
into a mountainrange;lenses extend

unwish through curving wherewhen till unwish
returns on its unself.
                        A world of made
is not a world of born—pity poor flesh

and trees,poor stars and stones,but never this   10
fine specimen of hypermagical

ultraomnipotence. We doctors know

a hopeless case if—listen:there's a hell
of a good universe next door;let's go

WHAT IF A MUCH OF A WHICH OF A WIND   [1944]

what if a much of a which of a wind
gives the truth to summer's lie;

bloodies with dizzying leaves the sun
and yanks immortal stars awry?
Blow king to beggar and queen to seem
(blow friend to fiend:blow space to time)
—when skies are hanged and oceans drowned,
the single secret will still be man

what if a keen of a lean wind flays
screaming hills with sleet and snow: 10
strangles valleys by ropes of thing
and stifles forests in white ago?
Blow hope to terror;blow seeing to blind
(blow pity to envy and soul to mind)
—whose hearts are mountains,roots are trees,
it's they shall cry hello to the spring

what if a dawn of a doom of a dream
bites this universe in two,
peels forever out of his grave
and sprinkles nowhere with me and you?   20
Blow soon to never and never to twice
(blow life to isn't:blow death to was)
—all nothing's only our hugest home;
the most who die,the more we live

NOW DOES OUR WORLD DESCEND   [1963]

now does our world descend
the path to nothingness
(cruel now cancels kind;
friends turn to enemies)
therefore lament,my dream
and don a doer's doom

create is now contrive;
imagined,merely know
(freedom:what makes a slave)
therefore,my life,lie down   10

and more by most endure
all that you never were

hide,poor dishonoured mind
who thought yourself so wise;
and much could understand
concerning no and yes:
if they've become the same
it's time you unbecame

where climbing was and bright
is darkness and to fall   20
(now wrong's the only right
since brave are cowards all)
therefore despair,my heart
and die into the dirt

but from this endless end
of briefer each our bliss—
where seeing eyes go blind
(where lips forget to kiss)
where everything's nothing
—arise,my soul;and sing   30

ENTER NO(SILENCE IS THE BLOOD WHOSE
FLESH   [1963]

enter no(silence is the blood whose flesh
is singing)silence:but unsinging. In
spectral such hugest how hush,one

dead leaf stirring makes a crash

—far away(as far as alive)lies
april;and i breathe-move-and-seem some
perpetually roaming whylessness—

autumn has gone:will winter never come?

o come,terrible anonymity;enfold
phantom me with the murdering minus of cold   10
—open this ghost with millionary knives of wind—
scatter his nothing all over what angry skies and

gently
        (very whiteness:absolute peace,
never imaginable mystery)
                            descend

Hart Crane

1899–1932

Harold Hart Crane was born July 21, 1899, in Garrettsville, Ohio, the son of a prosperous manufacturer. He grew up in Cleveland, but in 1916 went to New York and proceeded through a series of jobs both there and in several Midwestern cities to support himself while writing poetry. With financial help from Otto Kahn from 1925 on, he worked for several years at The Bridge, *his most important achievement. After a year in Mexico on a Guggenheim Fellowship, he committed suicide on April 26, 1932, by jumping into the Gulf of Mexico from the ship that was returning him to the United States.*

BLACK TAMBOURINE   [1926]

The interests of a black man in a cellar
Mark tardy judgment on the world's closed door.
Gnats toss in the shadow of a bottle,
And a roach spans a crevice in the floor.

Æsop, driven to pondering, found
Heaven with the tortoise and the hare;
Fox brush and sow ear top his grave
And mingling incantations on the air.

The black man, forlorn in the cellar,
Wanders in some mid-kingdom, dark, that lies,   10
Between his tambourine, stuck on the wall,
And, in Africa, a carcass quick with flies.

PRAISE FOR AN URN   [1926]

In Memoriam: Ernest Nelson

It was a kind and northern face
That mingled in such exile guise
The everlasting eyes of Pierrot
And, of Gargantua, the laughter.

His thoughts, delivered to me
From the white coverlet and pillow,
I see now, were inheritances—
Delicate riders of the storm.

The slant moon on the slanting hill
Once moved us toward presentiments   10
Of what the dead keep, living still,
And such assessments of the soul

As, perched in the crematory lobby,
The insistent clock commented on,
Touching as well upon our praise
Of glories proper to the time.

Still, having in mind gold hair,
I cannot see that broken brow
And miss the dry sound of bees
Stretching across a lucid space.   20

Scatter these well-meant idioms
Into the smoky spring that fills
The suburbs, where they will be lost.
They are no trophies of the sun.

CHAPLINESQUE   [1926]

We make our meek adjustments,
Contented with such random consolations

As the wind deposits
In slithered and too ample pockets.

For we can still love the world, who find
A famished kitten on the step, and know
Recesses for it from the fury of the street,
Or warm torn elbow coverts.

We will sidestep, and to the final smirk
Dally the doom of that inevitable thumb   10
That slowly chafes its puckered index toward us,
Facing the dull squint with what innocence
And what surprise!

And yet these fine collapses are not lies
More than the pirouettes of any pliant cane;
Our obsequies are, in a way, no enterprise.
We can evade you, and all else but the heart:
What blame to us if the heart live on.

The game enforces smirks; but we have seen
The moon in lonely alleys make   20
A grail of laughter of an empty ash can,
And through all sound of gaiety and quest
Have heard a kitten in the wilderness.

REPOSE OF RIVERS   [1926]

The willows carried a slow sound,
A sarabande the wind mowed on the mead.
I could never remember
That seething, steady leveling of the marshes
Till age had brought me to the sea.

Flags, weeds. And remembrance of steep alcoves
Where cypresses shared the noon's
Tyranny; they drew me into hades almost.

And mammoth turtles climbing sulphur dreams
Yielded, while sun-silt rippled them   10
Asunder . . .

How much I would have bartered! the black gorge
And all the singular nestings in the hills
Where beavers learn stitch and tooth.
The pond I entered once and quickly fled—
I remember now its singing willow rim.

And finally, in that memory all things nurse;
After the city that I finally passed
With scalding unguents spread and smoking darts
The monsoon cut across the delta   20
At gulf gates . . . There, beyond the dykes

I heard wind flaking sapphire, like this summer,
And willows could not hold more steady sound.

THE WINE MENAGERIE   [1926]

Invariably when wine redeems the sight,
Narrowing the mustard scansions of the eyes,
A leopard ranging always in the brow
Asserts a vision in the slumbering gaze.

Then glozening decanters that reflect the street
Wear me in crescents on their bellies. Slow
Applause flows into liquid cynosures:
—I am conscripted to their shadows' glow.

Against the imitation onyx wainscoting
(Painted emulsion of snow, eggs, yarn, coal, manure)   10
Regard the forceps of the smile that takes her.
Percussive sweat is spreading to his hair. Mallets,
Her eyes, unmake an instant of the world . . .

What is it in this heap the serpent pries—
Whose skin, facsimile of time, unskeins
Octagon, sapphire transepts round the eyes;
—From whom some whispered carillon assures
Speed to the arrow into feathered skies?

Sharp to the window-pane guile drags a face,
And as the alcove of her jealousy recedes   20
An urchin who has left the snow
Nudges a cannister across the bar
While August meadows somewhere clasp his brow.

Each chamber, transept, coins some squint,
Remorseless line, minting their separate wills—
Poor streaked bodies wreathing up and out,
Unwitting the stigma that each turn repeals:
Between black tusks the roses shine!

New thresholds, new anatomies! Wine talons
Build freedom up about me and distill   30
This competence—to travel in a tear
Sparkling alone, within another's will.

Until my blood dreams a receptive smile
Wherein new purities are snared; where chimes
Before some flame of gaunt repose a shell
Tolled once, perhaps, by every tongue in hell.
—Anguished, the wit that cries out of me:

"Alas,—these frozen billows of your skill!
Invent new dominoes of love and bile . . .
Ruddy, the tooth implicit of the world   40
Has followed you. Though in the end you know
And count some dim inheritance of sand,
How much yet meets the treason of the snow.

"Rise from the dates and crumbs. And walk away,
Stepping over Holofernes' shins—
Beyond the wall, whose severed head floats by
With Baptist John's. Their whispering begins.

"—And fold your exile on your back again;
Petrushka's valentine pivots on its pin."

FOR THE MARRIAGE OF FAUSTUS AND
HELEN   [1926]

> "And so we may arrive by Talmud skill
> And profane Greek to raise the building up
> Of Helen's house against the Ismaelite,
> King of Thogarma, and his habergeons
> Brimstony, blue and fiery; and the force
> Of King Abaddon, and the beast of Cittim;
> Which Rabbi David Kimchi, Onkelos,
> And Aben Ezra do interpret Rome."—THE ALCHEMIST

I

The mind has shown itself at times
Too much the baked and labeled dough
Divided by accepted multitudes.
Across the stacked partitions of the day—
Across the memoranda, baseball scores,
The stenographic smiles and stock quotations
Smutty wings flash out equivocations.

The mind is brushed by sparrow wings;
Numbers, rebuffed by asphalt, crowd
The margins of the day, accent the curbs,   10
Convoying divers dawns on every corner
To druggist, barber and tobacconist,
Until the graduate opacities of evening
Take them away as suddenly to somewhere
Virginal perhaps, less fragmentary, cool.

> *There is the world dimensional for
> those untwisted by the love of things
> irreconcilable . . .*

And yet, suppose some evening I forgot
The fare and transfer, yet got by that way   20
Without recall,—lost yet poised in traffic.
Then I might find your eyes across an aisle,

Still flickering with those prefigurations—
Prodigal, yet uncontested now,
Half-riant before the jerky window frame.

There is some way, I think, to touch
Those hands of yours that count the nights
Stippled with pink and green advertisements.
And now, before its arteries turn dark,
I would have you meet this bartered blood.   30
Imminent in his dream, none better knows
The white wafer cheek of love, or offers words
Lightly as moonlight on the eaves meets snow.

Reflective conversion of all things
At your deep blush, when ecstasies thread
The limbs and belly, when rainbows spread
Impinging on the throat and sides . . .
Inevitable, the body of the world
Weeps in inventive dust for the hiatus
That winks above it, bluet in your breasts.   40

The earth may glide diaphanous to death;
But if I lift my arms it is to bend
To you who turned away once, Helen, knowing
The press of troubled hands, too alternate
With steel and soil to hold you endlessly.
I meet you, therefore, in that eventual flame
You found in final chains, no captive then—
Beyond their million brittle, bloodshot eyes;
White, through white cities passed on to assume
That world which comes to each of us alone.   50

Accept a lone eye riveted to your plane,
Bent axle of devotion along companion ways
That beat, continuous, to hourless days—
One inconspicuous, glowing orb of praise.

II

Brazen hypnotics glitter here;
Glee shifts from foot to foot,

Magnetic to their tremolo.
This crashing opéra bouffe,
Blest excursion! this ricochet
From roof to roof—   60
Know, Olympians, we are breathless
While nigger cupids scour the stars!

A thousand light shrugs balance us
Through snarling hails of melody.
White shadows slip across the floor
Splayed like cards from a loose hand;
Rhythmic ellipses lead into canters
Until somewhere a rooster banters.

Greet naïvely—yet intrepidly
New soothings, new amazements   70
That cornets introduce at every turn—
And you may fall downstairs with me
With perfect grace and equanimity.
Or, plaintively scud past shores
Where, by strange harmonic laws
All relatives, serene and cool,
Sit rocked in patent armchairs.

O, I have known metallic paradises
Where cuckoos clucked to finches
Above the deft catastrophes of drums.   80
While titters hailed the groans of death
Beneath gyrating awnings I have seen
The incunabula of the divine grotesque.
This music has a reassuring way.

The siren of the springs of guilty song—
Let us take her on the incandescent wax
Striated with nuances, nervosities
That we are heir to: she is still so young,
We cannot frown upon her as she smiles,
Dipping here in this cultivated storm   90
Among slim skaters of the gardened skies.

III

Capped arbiter of beauty in this street
That narrows darkly into motor dawn,—
You, here beside me, delicate ambassador
Of intricate slain numbers that arise
In whispers, naked of steel;

                              religious gunman!
Who faithfully, yourself, will fall too soon,
And in other ways than as the wind settles
On the sixteen thrifty bridges of the city: 100
Let us unbind our throats of fear and pity.

                       We even,
Who drove speediest destruction
In corymbulous formations of mechanics,—
Who hurried the hill breezes, spouting malice
Plangent over meadows, and looked down
On rifts of torn and empty houses
Like old women with teeth unjubilant
That waited faintly, briefly and in vain:

We know, eternal gunman, our flesh remembers   110
The tensile boughs, the nimble blue plateaus,
The mounted, yielding cities of the air!
That saddled sky that shook down vertical
Repeated play of fire—no hypogeum
Of wave or rock was good against one hour.

We did not ask for that, but have survived,
And will persist to speak again before
All stubble streets that have not curved
To memory, or known the ominous lifted arm
That lowers down the arc of Helen's brow   120
To saturate with blessing and dismay.

A goose, tobacco and cologne—
Three-winged and gold-shod prophecies of heaven,
The lavish heart shall always have to leaven
And spread with bells and voices, and atone
The abating shadows of our conscript dust.

Anchises' navel, dripping of the sea,—
The hands Erasmus dipped in gleaming tides,
Gathered the voltage of blown blood and vine;
Delve upward for the new and scattered wine,   130
O brother-thief of time, that we recall.
Laugh out the meager penance of their days
Who dare not share with us the breath released,
The substance drilled and spent beyond repair
For golden, or the shadow of gold hair.

Distinctly praise the years, whose volatile
Blamed bleeding hands extend and thresh the height
The imagination spans beyond despair,
Outpacing bargain, vocable and prayer.

AT MELVILLE'S TOMB   [1926]

Often beneath the wave, wide from this ledge
The dice of drowned men's bones he saw bequeath
An embassy. Their numbers as he watched,
Beat on the dusty shore and were obscured.

And wrecks passed without sound of bells,
The calyx of death's bounty giving back
A scattered chapter, livid hieroglyph,
The portent wound in corridors of shells.

Then in the circuit calm of one vast coil,
Its lashings charmed and malice reconciled,   10
Frosted eyes there were that lifted altars;
And silent answers crept across the stars.

Compass, quadrant and sextant contrive
No farther tides . . . High in the azure steeps
Monody shall not wake the mariner.
This fabulous shadow only the sea keeps.

VOYAGES   [1926]

I

Above the fresh ruffles of the surf
Bright striped urchins flay each other with sand.
They have contrived a conquest for shell shucks,
And their fingers crumble fragments of baked weed
Gaily digging and scattering.

And in answer to their treble interjections
The sun beats lightning on the waves,
The waves fold thunder on the sand;
And could they hear me I would tell them:

O brilliant kids, frisk with your dog,   10
Fondle your shells and sticks, bleached
By time and the elements; but there is a line
You must not cross nor ever trust beyond it
Spry cordage of your bodies to caresses
Too lichen-faithful from too wide a breast.
The bottom of the sea is cruel.

II

And yet this great wink of eternity,
Of rimless floods, unfettered leewardings,
Samite sheeted and processioned where
Her undinal vast belly moonward bends,   20
Laughing the wrapt inflections of our love;

Take this Sea, whose diapason knells
On scrolls of silver snowy sentences,
The sceptred terror of whose sessions rends
As her demeanors motion well or ill,
All but the pieties of lovers' hands.

And onward, as bells off San Salvador
Salute the crocus lustres of the stars,
In these poinsettia meadows of her tides,—

Adagios of islands, O my Prodigal, 30
Complete the dark confessions her veins spell.

Mark how her turning shoulders wind the hours,
And hasten while her penniless rich palms
Pass superscription of bent foam and wave,—
Hasten, while they are true,—sleep, death, desire,
Close round one instant in one floating flower.

Bind us in time, O Seasons clear, and awe.
O minstrel galleons of Carib fire,
Bequeath us to no earthly shore until
Is answered in the vortex of our grave 40
The seal's wide spindrift gaze toward paradise.

III

Infinite consanguinity it bears—
This tendered theme of you that light
Retrieves from sea plains where the sky
Resigns a breast that every wave enthrones;
While ribboned water lanes I wind
Are laved and scattered with no stroke
Wide from your side, whereto this hour
The sea lifts, also, reliquary hands.

And so, admitted through black swollen gates 50
That must arrest all distance otherwise,—
Past whirling pillars and lithe pediments,
Light wrestling there incessantly with light,
Star kissing star through wave on wave unto
Your body rocking!
　　　　　　　and where death, if shed,
Presumes no carnage, but this single change,—
Upon the steep floor flung from dawn to dawn
The silken skilled transmemberment of song;

Permit me voyage, love, into your hands . . . 60

IV

Whose counted smile of hours and days, suppose
I know as spectrum of the sea and pledge

Vastly now parting gulf on gulf of wings
Whose circles bridge, I know, (from palms to the severe
Chilled albatross's white immutability)
No stream of greater love advancing now
Than, singing, this mortality alone
Through clay aflow immortally to you.

All fragrance irrefragibly, and claim
Madly meeting logically in this hour   70
And region that is ours to wreathe again,
Portending eyes and lips and making told
The chancel port and portion of our June—

Shall they not stem and close in our own steps
Bright staves of flowers and quills to-day as I
Must first be lost in fatal tides to tell?
In signature of the incarnate word
The harbor shoulders to resign in mingling
Mutual blood, transpiring as foreknown
And widening noon within your breast for gathering   80
All bright insinuations that my years have caught
For islands where must lead inviolably
Blue latitudes and levels of your eyes,—

In this expectant, still exclaim receive
The secret oar and petals of all love.

                                    v

Meticulous, past midnight in clear rime,
Infrangible and lonely, smooth as though cast
Together in one merciless white blade—
The bay estuaries fleck the hard sky limits.

—As if too brittle or too clear to touch!   90
The cables of our sleep so swiftly filed,
Already hang, shred ends from remembered stars.
One frozen trackless smile . . . What words
Can strangle this deaf moonlight? For we

Are overtaken. Now no cry, no sword
Can fasten or deflect this tidal wedge,

Slow tyranny of moonlight, moonlight loved
And changed . . . "There's

Nothing like this in the world," you say,
Knowing I cannot touch your hand and look   100
Too, into that godless cleft of sky
Where nothing turns but dead sands flashing.

"—And never to quite understand!" No,
In all the argosy of your bright hair I dreamed
Nothing so flagless as this piracy.

                          But now
Draw in your head, alone and too tall here.
Your eyes already in the slant of drifting foam;
Your breath sealed by the ghosts I do not know:
Draw in your head and sleep the long way home.   110

VI

Where icy and bright dungeons lift
Of swimmers their lost morning eyes,
And ocean rivers, churning, shift
Green borders under stranger skies,

Steadily as a shell secretes
Its beating leagues of monotone,
Or as many waters trough the sun's
Red kelson past the cape's wet stone;

O rivers mingling toward the sky
And harbor of the phœnix' breast—   120
My eyes pressed black against the prow,
—Thy derelict and blinded guest

Waiting, afire, what name, unspoke,
I cannot claim: let thy waves rear
More savage than the death of kings,
Some splintered garland for the seer.

Beyond siroccos harvesting
The solstice thunders, crept away,

Like a cliff swinging or a sail
Flung into April's inmost day—   130

Creation's blithe and petalled word
To the lounged goddess when she rose
Conceding dialogue with eyes
That smile unsearchable repose—

Still fervid covenant, Belle Isle,
—Unfolded floating dais before
Which rainbows twine continual hair—
Belle Isle, white echo of the oar!

The imaged Word, it is, that holds
Hushed willows anchored in its glow.   140
It is the unbetrayable reply
Whose accent no farewell can know.

TO BROOKLYN BRIDGE   [1930]

(Proem to *The Bridge*)

How many dawns, chill from his rippling rest
The seagull's wings shall dip and pivot him,
Shedding white rings of tumult, building high
Over the chained bay waters Liberty—

Then, with inviolate curve, forsake our eyes
As apparitional as sails that cross
Some page of figures to be filed away;
—Till elevators drop us from our day . . .

I think of cinemas, panoramic sleights
With multitudes bent toward some flashing scene   10
Never disclosed, but hastened to again,
Foretold to other eyes on the same screen;

And Thee, across the harbor, silver-paced
As though the sun took step of thee, yet left
Some motion ever unspent in thy stride,—
Implicitly thy freedom staying thee!

Out of some subway scuttle, cell or loft
A bedlamite speeds to thy parapets,
Tilting there momently, shrill shirt ballooning,
A jest falls from the speechless caravan.   20

Down Wall, from girder into street noon leaks,
A rip-tooth of the sky's acetylene;
All afternoon the cloud-flown derricks turn . . .
Thy cables breathe the North Atlantic still.

And obscure as that heaven of the Jews,
Thy guerdon . . . Accolade thou dost bestow
Of anonymity time cannot raise:
Vibrant reprieve and pardon thou dost show.

O harp and altar, of the fury fused,
(How could mere toil align thy choiring strings!)   30
Terrific threshold of the prophet's pledge,
Prayer of pariah, and the lover's cry,—

Again the traffic lights that skim thy swift
Unfractioned idiom, immaculate sigh of stars,
Beading thy path—condense eternity:
And we have seen night lifted in thine arms.

Under thy shadow by the piers I waited;
Only in darkness is thy shadow clear.
The City's fiery parcels all undone,
Already snow submerges an iron year . . .   40

O Sleepless as the river under thee,
Vaulting the sea, the prairies' dreaming sod,
Unto us lowliest sometime sweep, descend
And of the curveship lend a myth to God.

THE RIVER   [1930]

(from *The Bridge*)

Stick your patent name on a signboard
brother—all over—going west—young man   . . . and past
Tintex—Japalac—Certain-teed Overalls ads   the din and
                                                slogans of
and lands sakes! under the new playbill ripped the year—
in the guaranteed corner—see Bert Williams what?
Minstrels when you steal a chicken just
save me the wing for if it isn't
Erie it ain't for miles around a
Mazda—and the telegraphic night coming on Thomas

a Ediford—and whistling down the tracks   10
a headlight rushing with the sound—can you
imagine—while an EXPRESS makes time like
SCIENCE—COMMERCE and the HOLYGHOST
RADIO ROARS IN EVERY HOME WE HAVE THE NORTHPOLE
WALLSTREET AND VIRGINBIRTH WITHOUT STONES OR
WIRES OR EVEN RUNNing brooks connecting ears
and no more sermons windows flashing roar
Breathtaking—as you like it . . . eh?

                    So the 20th Century—so
whizzed the Limited—roared by and left   20
three men, still hungry on the tracks, ploddingly
watching the tail lights wizen and converge, slipping gimleted and neatly out of sight.

                    *

The last bear, shot drinking in the Dakotas
Loped under wires that span the mountain stream.
Keen instruments, strung to a vast precision
Bind town to town and dream to ticking dream.   to those
But some men take their liquor slow—and count   whose
                                                 addresses are
—Though they'll confess no rosary nor clue—   never near

The river's minute by the far brook's year.   30
Under a world of whistles, wires and steam
Caboose-like they go ruminating through
Ohio, Indiana—blind baggage—
To Cheyenne tagging . . . Maybe Kalamazoo.

Time's rendings, time's blendings they construe
As final reckonings of fire and snow;
Strange bird-wit, like the elemental gist
Of unwalled winds they offer, singing low
My Old Kentucky Home and *Casey Jones*,
Some Sunny Day. I heard a road-gang chanting so.   40
And afterwards, who had a colt's eyes—one said,
"Jesus! Oh I remember watermelon days!" And sped
High in a cloud of merriment, recalled
"—And when my Aunt Sally Simpson smiled," he
        drawled—
"It was almost Louisiana, long ago."

"There's no place like Booneville though, Buddy,"
One said, excising a last burr from his vest,
"—For early trouting." Then peering in the can,
"—But I kept on the tracks." Possessed, resigned,
He trod the fire down pensively and grinned,   50
Spreading dry shingles of a beard. . . .

                              Behind
My father's cannery works I used to see
Rail-squatters ranged in nomad raillery,
The ancient men—wifeless or runaway
Hobo-trekkers that forever search
An empire wilderness of freight and rails.
Each seemed a child, like me, on a loose perch,
Holding to childhood like some termless play.
John, Jake or Charley, hopping the slow freight   60
—Memphis to Tallahassee—riding the rods,
Blind fists of nothing, humpty-dumpty clods.

Yet they touch something like a key perhaps.
From pole to pole across the hills, the states

—They know a body under the wide rain;
Youngsters with eyes like fjords, old reprobates
With racetrack jargon,—dotting immensity
They lurk across her, knowing her yonder breast
Snow-silvered, sumac-stained or smoky blue—
Is past the valley-sleepers, south or west.
—As I have trod the rumorous midnights, too,

but who have touched her, knowing her without name

70

And past the circuit of the lamp's thin flame
(O Nights that brought me to her body bare!)
Have dreamed beyond the print that bound her name.
Trains sounding the long blizzards out—I heard
Wail into distances I knew were hers.
Papooses crying on the wind's long mane
Screamed redskin dynasties that fled the brain,
—Dead echoes! But I knew her body there,
Time like a serpent down her shoulder, dark,
And space, an eaglet's wing, laid on her hair.

80

Under the Ozarks, domed by Iron Mountain,
The old gods of the rain lie wrapped in pools
Where eyeless fish curvet a sunken fountain
And re-descend with corn from querulous crows.
Such pilferings make up their timeless eatage,
Propitiate them for their timber torn
By iron, iron—always the iron dealt cleavage!
They doze now, below axe and powder horn.

nor the myths of her fathers . . .

And Pullman breakfasters glide glistening steel
From tunnel into field—iron strides the dew—
Straddles the hill, a dance of wheel on wheel.
You have a half-hour's wait at Siskiyou,
Or stay the night and take the next train through.
Southward, near Cairo passing, you can see
The Ohio merging,—borne down Tennessee;
And if it's summer and the sun's in dusk
Maybe the breeze will lift the River's musk
—As though the waters breathed that you might know
Memphis Johnny, Steamboat Bill, Missouri Joe.
Oh, lean from the window, if the train slows down,

90

100

As though you touched hands with some ancient clown,
—A little while gaze absently below
And hum *Deep River* with them while they go.

Yes, turn again and sniff once more—look see,
O Sheriff, Brakeman and Authority—
Hitch up your pants and crunch another quid,
For you, too, feed the River timelessly.
And few evade full measure of their fate;
Always they smile out eerily what they seem.   110
I could believe he joked at heaven's gate—
Dan Midland—jolted from the cold brake-beam.

Down, down—born pioneers in time's despite,
Grimed tributaries to an ancient flow—
They win no frontier by their wayward plight,
But drift in stillness, as from Jordan's brow.

You will not hear it as the sea; even stone
Is not more hushed by gravity . . . But slow,
As loth to take more tribute—sliding prone
Like one whose eyes were buried long ago   120

The River, spreading, flows—and spends your dream.
What are you, lost within this tideless spell?
You are your father's father, and the stream—
A liquid theme that floating niggers swell.

Damp tonnage and alluvial march of days—
Nights turbid, vascular with silted shale
And roots surrendered down of moraine clays:
The Mississippi drinks the farthest dale.

O quarrying passion, undertowed sunlight!
The basalt surface drags a jungle grace   130
Ochreous and lynx-barred in lengthening might;
Patience! and you shall reach the biding place!

Over De Soto's bones the freighted floors
Throb past the City storied of three thrones.

Down two more turns the Mississippi pours
(Anon tall ironsides up from salt lagoons)

And flows within itself, heaps itself free.
All fades but one thin skyline 'round . . . Ahead
No embrace opens but the stinging sea;
The River lifts itself from its long bed,   140

Poised wholly on its dream, a mustard glow
Tortured with history, its one will—flow!
—The Passion spreads in wide tongues, choked and slow,
Meeting the Gulf, hosannas silently below.

THE TUNNEL   [1930]

(from *The Bridge*)

> To Find the Western path
> Right thro' the Gates of Wrath.—BLAKE

Performances, assortments, résumés—
Up Times Square to Columbus Circle lights
Channel the congresses, nightly sessions,
Refractions of the thousand theatres, faces—
Mysterious kitchens. . . . You shall search them all.
Some day by heart you'll learn each famous sight
And watch the curtain lift in hell's despite;
You'll find the garden in the third act dead,
Finger your knees—and wish yourself in bed
With tabloid crime-sheets perched in easy sight.   10

> Then let you reach your hat
> and go.
> As usual, let you—also
> walking down—exclaim
> to twelve upward leaving
> a subscription praise
> for what time slays.

Or can't you quite make up your mind to ride;
A walk is better underneath the L a brisk
Ten blocks or so before? But you find yourself   20
Preparing penguin flexions of the arms,—
As usual you will meet the scuttle yawn:
The subway yawns the quickest promise home.

Be minimum, then, to swim the hiving swarms
Out of the Square, the Circle burning bright—
Avoid the glass doors gyring at your right,
Where boxed alone a second, eyes take fright
—Quite unprepared rush naked back to light:
And down beside the turnstile press the coin
Into the slot. The gongs already rattle.   30

      And so
      of cities you bespeak
      subways, rivered under streets
      and rivers. . . . In the car
      the overtone of motion
      underground, the monotone
      of motion is the sound
      of other faces, also underground—

"Let's have a pencil Jimmy—living now
at Floral Park   40
Flatbush—on the Fourth of July—
like a pigeon's muddy dream—potatoes
to dig in the field—travlin the town—too—
night after night—the Culver line—the
girls all shaping up—it used to be—"

Our tongues recant like beaten weather vanes.
This answer lives like verdigris, like hair
Beyond extinction, surcease of the bone;
And repetition freezes—"What

"what do you want? getting weak on the links?   50
fandaddle daddy don't ask for change—IS THIS
FOURTEENTH? it's half past six she said—if

you don't like my gate why did you
swing on it, why *didja*
swing on it
anyhow—"

    And somehow anyhow swing—

The phonographs of hades in the brain
Are tunnels that re-wind themselves, and love
A burnt match skating in a urinal—   60
Somewhere above Fourteenth TAKE THE EXPRESS
To brush some new presentiment of pain—

"But I want service in this office SERVICE
I said—after
the show she cried a little afterwards but—"

Whose head is swinging from the swollen strap?
Whose body smokes along the bitten rails,
Bursts from a smoldering bundle far behind
In back forks of the chasms of the brain,—
Puffs from a riven stump far out behind   70
In interborough fissures of the mind . . .?

And why do I often meet your visage here,
Your eyes like agate lanterns—on and on
Below the toothpaste and the dandruff ads?
—And did their riding eyes right through your side,
And did their eyes like unwashed platters ride?
And Death, aloft,—gigantically down
Probing through you—toward me, O evermore!
And when they dragged your retching flesh,
Your trembling hands that night through Baltimore—   80
That last night on the ballot rounds, did you
Shaking, did you deny the ticket, Poe?

For Gravesend Manor change at Chambers Street.
The platform hurries along to a dead stop.

The intent escalator lifts a serenade
Stilly

Of shoes, umbrellas, each eye attending its shoe, then
Bolting outright somewhere above where streets
Burst suddenly in rain. . . . The gongs recur:
Elbows and levers, guard and hissing door.   90
Thunder is galvothermic here below. . . . The car
Wheels off. The train rounds, bending to a scream,
Taking the final level for the dive
Under the river—
And somewhat emptier than before,
Demented, for a hitching second, humps; then
Lets go. . . . Toward corners of the floor
Newspapers wing, revolve and wing.
Blank windows gargle signals through the roar.

And does the Dæmon take you home, also,   100
Wop washerwoman, with the bandaged hair?
After the corridors are swept, the cuspidors—
The gaunt sky-barracks cleanly now, and bare,
O Genoese, do you bring mother eyes and hands
Back home to children and to golden hair?

Dæmon, demurring and eventful yawn!
Whose hideous laughter is a bellows mirth
—Or the muffled slaughter of a day in birth—
O cruelly to inoculate the brinking dawn
With antennæ toward worlds that glow and sink;—   110
To spoon us out more liquid than the dim
Locution of the eldest star, and pack
The conscience navelled in the plunging wind,
Umbilical to call—and straightway die!

O caught like pennies beneath soot and steam,
Kiss of our agony thou gatherest;
Condensed, thou takest all—shrill ganglia
Impassioned with some song we fail to keep.
And yet, like Lazarus, to feel the slope,
The sod and billow breaking,—lifting ground,   120
—A sound of waters bending astride the sky
Unceasing with some Word that will not die . . . !

*

A tugboat, wheezing wreaths of steam,
Lunged past, with one galvanic blare stove up the River.
I counted the echoes assembling, one after one,
Searching, thumbing the midnight on the piers.
Lights, coasting, left the oily tympanum of waters;
The blackness somewhere gouged glass on a sky.
And this thy harbor, O my City, I have driven under,
Tossed from the coil of ticking towers.... Tomorrow,   130
And to be.... Here by the River that is East—
Here at the waters' edge the hands drop memory;
Shadowless in that abyss they unaccounting lie.
How far away the star has pooled the sea—
Or shall the hands be drawn away, to die?

Kiss of our agony Thou gatherest,
                    O Hand of Fire
                                gatherest—

O CARIB ISLE!   [1933]

The tarantula rattling at the lily's foot
Across the feet of the dead, laid in white sand
Near the coral beach—nor zigzag fiddler crabs
Side-stilting from the path (that shift, subvert
And anagrammatize your name)—No, nothing here
Below the palsy that one eucalyptus lifts
In wrinkled shadows—mourns.

                            And yet suppose
I count these nacreous frames of tropic death,
Brutal necklaces of shells around each grave   10
Squared off so carefully. Then

To the white sand I may speak a name, fertile
Albeit in a stranger tongue. Tree names, flower names
Deliberate, gainsay death's brittle crypt. Meanwhile
The wind that knots itself in one great death—
Coils and withdraws. So syllables want breath.

But where is the Captain of the doubloon isle
Without a turnstile? Who but catchword crabs
Patrols the dry groins of the underbrush?
What man, or What   20
Is Commissioner of the mildew throughout the ambushed
    senses?
His Carib mathematics web the eyes' baked lenses!

Under the poinciana, of a noon or afternoon
Let fiery blossoms clot the light, render my ghost
Sieved upward, white and black along the air
Until it meets the blue's comedian host.

Let not the pilgrim see himself again
For slow evisceration bound like those huge terrapin
Each daybreak on the wharf, their brine-caked eyes;
—Spiked, overturned; such thunder in their strain!   30

Slagged on the hurricane—I, cast within its flow,
Congeal by afternoons here, satin and vacant.
You have given me the shell, Satan,—carbonic amulet
Sere of the sun exploded in the sea.

ROYAL PALM   [1933]

For Grace Hart Crane

Green rustlings, more than regal charities
Drift coolly from that tower of whispered light.
Amid the noontide's blazed asperities
I watched the sun's most gracious anchorite

Climb up as by communings, year on year
Uneaten of the earth or aught earth holds,
And the grey trunk, that's elephantine, rear
Its frondings sighing in ætherial folds.

Forever fruitless, and beyond that yield
Of sweat the jungle presses with hot love   10

And tendril till our deathward breath is sealed—
It grazes the horizons, launched above

Mortality—ascending emerald-bright,
A fountain at salute, a crown in view—
Unshackled, casual of its azured height
As though it soared suchwise through heaven too.

THE HURRICANE   [1933]

Lo, Lord, Thou ridest!
Lord, Lord, Thy swifting heart

Naught stayeth, naught now bideth
But's smithereened apart!

Ay! Scripture flee'th stone!
Milk-bright, Thy chisel wind

Rescindeth flesh from bone
To quivering whittlings thinned—

Swept—whistling straw! Battered,
Lord, e'en boulders now out-leap   10

Rock sockets, levin-lathered!
Nor, Lord, may worm out-deep

Thy drum's gambade, its plunge abscond!
Lord God, while summits crashing

Whip sea-kelp screaming on blond
Sky-seethe, high heaven dashing—

Thou ridest to the door, Lord!
Thou bidest wall nor floor, Lord!

THE BROKEN TOWER   [1933]

The bell-rope that gathers God at dawn
Dispatches me as though I dropped down the knell
Of a spent day—to wander the cathedral lawn
From pit to crucifix, feet chill on steps from hell.

Have you not heard, have you not seen that corps
Of shadows in the tower, whose shoulders sway
Antiphonal carillons launched before
The stars are caught and hived in the sun's ray?

The bells, I say, the bells break down their tower;
And swing I know not where. Their tongues engrave   10
Membrane through marrow, my long-scattered score
Of broken intervals. . . . And I, their sexton slave!

Oval encyclicals in canyons heaping
The impasse high with choir. Banked voices slain!
Pagodas, campaniles with reveilles outleaping—
O terraced echoes prostrate on the plain! . . .

And so it was I entered the broken world
To trace the visionary company of love, its voice
An instant in the wind (I know not whither hurled)
But not for long to hold each desperate choice.   20

My word I poured. But was it cognate, scored
Of that tribunal monarch of the air
Whose thigh embronzes earth, strikes crystal Word
In wounds pledged once to hope—cleft to despair?

The steep encroachments of my blood left me
No answer (could blood hold such a lofty tower
As flings the question true?)—or is it she
Whose sweet mortality stirs latent power?—

And through whose pulse I hear, counting the strokes
My veins recall and add, revived and sure   30

The angelus of wars my chest evokes:
What I hold healed, original now, and pure . . .

And builds, within, a tower that is not stone
(Not stone can jacket heaven)—but slip
Of pebbles—visible wings of silence sown
In azure circles, widening as they dip

The matrix of the heart, lift down the eye
That shrines the quiet lake and swells a tower . . .
The commodious, tall decorum of that sky
Unseals her earth, and lifts love in its shower.   40

Allen Tate

b. 1899

Born November 19, 1899, in Winchester, Kentucky, Allen Tate was educated at Vanderbilt University and was a founder and editor (1922–1925), of the Nashville literary magazine The Fugitive. *During the next twenty-five years he wrote poetry, fiction, and criticism in New York and France, taught at several universities, held the Chair of Poetry at the Library of Congress (1943–1944), and edited the* Sewanee Review *(1944–1946). Since 1951 he has been professor of English at the University of Minnesota.*

MR. POPE   [1928]

When Alexander Pope strolled in the city
Strict was the glint of pearl and gold sedans.
Ladies leaned out more out of fear than pity
For Pope's tight back was rather a goat's than man's.

Often one thinks the urn should have more bones
Than skeletons provide for speedy dust,
The urn gets hollow, cobwebs brittle as stones
Weave to the funeral shell a frivolous rust.

And he who dribbled couplets like a snake
Coiled to a lithe precision in the sun   10
Is missing. The jar is empty; you may break
It only to find that Mr. Pope is gone.

What requisitions of a verity
Prompted the wit and rage between his teeth

One cannot say. Around a crooked tree
A moral climbs whose name should be a wreath.

THE SUBWAY   [1928]

Dark accurate plunger down the successive knell
Of arch on arch, where ogives burst a red
Reverberance of hail upon the dead
Thunder like an exploding crucible!
Harshly articulate, musical steel shell
Of angry worship, hurled religiously
Upon your business of humility
Into the iron forestries of hell:

Till broken in the shift of quieter
Dense altitudes tangential of your steel,   10
I am become geometries, and glut
Expansions like a blind astronomer
Dazed, while the worldless heavens bulge and reel
In the cold revery of an idiot.

ODE TO THE CONFEDERATE DEAD   [1928]

Row after row with strict impunity
The headstones yield their names to the element,
The wind whirrs without recollection;
In the riven troughs the splayed leaves
Pile up, of nature the casual sacrament
To the seasonal eternity of death;
Then driven by the fierce scrutiny
Of heaven to their election in the vast breath,
They sough the rumour of mortality.

Autumn is desolation in the plot   10
Of a thousand acres where these memories grow

From the inexhaustible bodies that are not
Dead, but feed the grass row after rich row.
Think of the autumns that have come and gone!—
Ambitious November with the humors of the year,
With a particular zeal for every slab,
Staining the uncomfortable angels that rot
On the slabs, a wing chipped here, an arm there:
The brute curiosity of an angel's stare
Turns you, like them, to stone,   20
Transforms the heaving air
Till plunged to a heavier world below
You shift your sea-space blindly
Heaving, turning like the blind crab.

   Dazed by the wind, only the wind
   The leaves flying, plunge

You know who have waited by the wall
The twilight certainty of an animal,
Those midnight restitutions of the blood
You know—the immitigable pines, the smoky frieze   30
Of the sky, the sudden call: you know the rage,
The cold pool left by the mounting flood,
Of muted Zeno and Parmenides.
You who have waited for the angry resolution
Of those desires that should be yours tomorrow,
You know the unimportant shrift of death
And praise the vision
And praise the arrogant circumstance
Of those who fall
Rank upon rank, hurried beyond decision—   40
Here by the sagging gate, stopped by the wall.

   Seeing, seeing only the leaves
   Flying, plunge and expire

Turn your eyes to the immoderate past,
Turn to the inscrutable infantry rising
Demons out of the earth—they will not last.
Stonewall, Stonewall, and the sunken fields of hemp,

Shiloh, Antietam, Malvern Hill, Bull Run.
Lost in that orient of the thick-and-fast
You will curse the setting sun.   50

   Cursing only the leaves crying
   Like an old man in a storm

You hear the shout, the crazy hemlocks point
With troubled fingers to the silence which
Smothers you, a mummy, in time.

                    The hound bitch
Toothless and dying, in a musty cellar
Hears the wind only.

              Now that the salt of their blood
Stiffens the saltier oblivion of the sea,
Seals the malignant purity of the flood,
What shall we who count our days and bow   60
Our heads with a commemorial woe
In the ribboned coats of grim felicity,
What shall we say of the bones, unclean,
Whose verdurous anonymity will grow?
The ragged arms, the ragged heads and eyes
Lost in these acres of the insane green?
The gray lean spiders come, they come and go;
In a tangle of willows without light
The singular screech-owl's tight
Invisible lyric seeds the mind   70
With the furious murmur of their chivalry.

   We shall say only the leaves
   Flying, plunge and expire

We shall say only the leaves whispering
In the improbable mist of nightfall
That flies on multiple wing;
Night is the beginning and the end
And in between the ends of distraction
Waits mute speculation, the patient curse

That stones the eyes, or like the jaguar leaps   80
For his own image in a jungle pool, his victim.
What shall we say who have knowledge
Carried to the heart? Shall we take the act
To the grave? Shall we, more hopeful, set up the grave
In the house? The ravenous grave?

                                        Leave now
The shut gate and the decomposing wall:
The gentle serpent, green in the mulberry bush,
Riots with his tongue through the hush—
Sentinel of the grave who counts us all!

THE CROSS   [1932]

There is a place that some men know,
I cannot see the whole of it
Nor how I came there. Long ago
Flame burst out of a secret pit
Crushing the world with such a light
The day-sky fell to moonless black,
The kingly sun to hateful night
For those, once seeing, turning back:
For love so hates mortality
Which is the providence of life   10
She will not let it blesséd be
But curses it with mortal strife,
Until beside the blinding rood
Within that world-destroying pit
—Like young wolves that have tasted blood,
Of death, men taste no more of it.
So blind, in so severe a place
(All life before in the black grave)
The last alternatives they face
Of life, without the life to save,   20
Being from all salvation weaned—
A stag charged both at heel and head:

Who would come back is turned a fiend
Instructed by the fiery dead.

SONNETS AT CHRISTMAS (1934)   [1936]

I

This is the day His hour of life draws near,
Let me get ready from head to foot for it
Most handily with eyes to pick the year
For small feed to reward a feathered wit.
Some men would see it an epiphany
At ease, at food and drink, others at chase
Yet I, stung lassitude, with ecstasy
Unspent argue the season's difficult case
So: Man, dull critter of enormous head,
What would he look at in the coiling sky?   10
But I must kneel again unto the Dead
While Christmas bells of paper white and red,
Figured with boys and girls spilt from a sled,
Ring out the silence I am nourished by.

II

Ah, Christ, I love you rings to the wild sky
And I must think a little of the past:
When I was ten I told a stinking lie
That got a black boy whipped; but now at last
The going years, caught in an accurate glow,
Reverse like balls englished upon green baize—   20
Let them return, let the round trumpets blow
The ancient crackle of the Christ's deep gaze.
Deafened and blind, with senses yet unfound,
Am I, untutored to the after-wit
Of knowledge, knowing a nightmare has no sound;
Therefore with idle hands and head I sit
In late December before the fire's daze
Punished by crimes of which I would be quit.

THE MEDITERRANEAN   [1936]

Quem das finem, rex magne, dolorum?

Where we went in the boat was a long bay
A slingshot wide, walled in by towering stone—
Peaked margin of antiquity's delay,
And we went there out of time's monotone:

Where we went in the black hull no light moved
But a gull white-winged along the feckless wave,
The breeze, unseen but fierce as a body loved,
That boat drove onward like a willing slave:

Where we went in the small ship the seaweed
Parted and gave to us the murmuring shore,   10
And we made feast and in our secret need
Devoured the very plates Aeneas bore:

Where derelict you see through the low twilight
The green coast that you, thunder-tossed, would win,
Drop sail, and hastening to drink all night
Eat dish and bowl to take that sweet land in!

Where we feasted and caroused on the sandless
Pebbles, affecting our day of piracy,
What prophecy of eaten plates could landless
Wanderers fulfil by the ancient sea?   20

We for that time might taste the famous age
Eternal here yet hidden from our eyes
When lust of power undid its stuffless rage;
They, in a wineskin, bore earth's paradise.

Let us lie down once more by the breathing side
Of Ocean, where our live forefathers sleep
As if the Known Sea still were a month wide—
Atlantis howls but is no longer steep!

What country shall we conquer, what fair land
Unman our conquest and locate our blood?   30
We've cracked the hemispheres with careless hand!
Now, from the Gates of Hercules we flood

Westward, westward till the barbarous brine
Whelms us to the tired land where tasseling corn,
Fat beans, grapes sweeter than muscadine
Rot on the vine: in that land were we born.

AENEAS AT WASHINGTON   [1936]

I myself saw furious with blood
Neoptolemus, at his side the black Atridae,
Hecuba and the hundred daughters, Priam
Cut down, his filth drenching the holy fires.
In that extremity I bore me well,
A true gentleman, valorous in arms,
Disinterested and honourable. Then fled:
That was a time when civilization
Run by the few fell to the many, and
Crashed to the shout of men, the clang of arms: 10
Cold victualing I seized, I hoisted up
The old man my father upon my back,
In the smoke made by sea for a new world
Saving little—a mind imperishable
If time is, a love of past things tenuous
As the hesitation of receding love.

(To the reduction of uncitied littorals
We brought chiefly the vigor of prophecy,
Our hunger breeding calculation
And fixed triumphs)
                                    I saw the thirsty dove   20
In the glowing fields of Troy, hemp ripening
And tawny corn, the thickening Blue Grass
All lying rich forever in the green sun.

I see all things apart, the towers that men
Contrive I too contrived long, long ago.
Now I demand little. The singular passion
Abides its object and consumes desire
In the circling shadow of its appetite.
There was a time when the young eyes were slow,
Their flame steady beyond the firstling fire,   30
I stood in the rain, far from home at nightfall
By the Potomac, the great Dome lit the water,
The city my blood had built I knew no more
While the screech-owl whistled his new delight
Consecutively dark.

              Stuck in the wet mire
Four thousand leagues from the ninth buried city
I thought of Troy, what we had built her for.

PASTORAL   [1936]

The enquiring fields, courtesies
And tribulations of the air—
Be still and give them peace:

The girl in the gold hair
With her young man in clover
In shadow of the day's glare

And there they were by the river
Where a leaf's light interval
Ringed the deep hurrying mirror;

Yet naught there to befall   10
Such meditations as beguile
Courage when love grows tall

For tall he was in green style
Of a willow shaking the pool.
"Let time be quiet as a mile,"

He said, "time is love's fool."
Yet time he would appease:
"Time, be easy and cool."

The enquiring courtesies
Of first dusk then debated   20
To cloud their agonies:

She, her head back, waited
Barbarous the stalking tide;
He, nor balked nor sated

But plunged into the wide
Area of mental ire,
Lay at her wandering side.

SEASONS OF THE SOUL   [1944]

To the memory of John Peale Bishop, 1892–1944

> *Allor porsi la mano un poco avante,*
> *e colsi un ramicel da un gran pruno;*
> *e il tronco suo gridò: Perchè mi schiante?*

I. SUMMER

Summer, this is our flesh,
The body you let mature;
If now while the body is fresh
You take it, shall we give
The heart, lest heart endure
The mind's tattering
Blow of greedy claws?
Shall mind itself still live
If like a hunting king
It falls to the lion's jaws?   10

Under the summer's blast
The soul cannot endure
Unless by sleight or fast

It seize or deny its day
To make the eye secure.
Brothers-in-arms, remember
The hot wind dries and draws
With circular delay
The flesh, ash from the ember,
Into the summer's jaws.   20

It was a gentle sun
When, at the June solstice
Green France was overrun
With caterpillar feet.
No head knows where its rest is
Or may lie down with reason
When war's usurping claws
Shall take the heart escheat—
Green field in burning season
To stain the weevil's jaws.   30

The southern summer dies
Evenly in the fall:
We raise our tired eyes
Into a sky of glass,
Blue, empty, and tall
Without tail or head
Where burn the equal laws
For Balaam and his ass
Above the invalid dead,
Who cannot lift their jaws.   40

When was it that the summer
(Daylong a liquid light)
And a child, the new-comer,
Bathed in the same green spray,
Could neither guess the night?
The summer had no reason;
Then, like a primal cause
It had its timeless day
Before it kept the season
Of time's engaging jaws.   50

Two men of our summer world
Descended winding hell
And when their shadows curled
They fearfully confounded
The vast concluding shell:
Stopping, they saw in the narrow
Light a centaur pause
And gaze, then his astounded
Beard, with a notched arrow,
Part back upon his jaws.   60

II. AUTUMN

It had an autumn smell
And that was how I knew
That I was down a well:
I was no longer young;
My lips were numb and blue,
The air was like fine sand
In a butcher's stall
Or pumice to the tongue:
And when I raised my hand
I stood in the empty hall.   70

The round ceiling was high
And the gray light like shale
Thin, crumbling, and dry:
No rug on the bare floor
Nor any carved detail
To which the eye could glide;
I counted along the wall
Door after closed door
Through which a shade might slide
To the cold and empty hall.   80

I will leave this house, I said,
There is the autumn weather—
Here, nor living nor dead;
The lights burn in the town
Where men fear together.
Then on the bare floor,
But tiptoe lest I fall,

I walked years down
Towards the front door
At the end of the empty hall.   90

The door was false—no key
Or lock, and I was caught
In the house; yet I could see
I had been born to it
For miles of running brought
Me back where I began.
I saw now in the wall
A door open a slit
And a fat grizzled man
Come out into the hall: 100

As in a moonlit street
Men meeting are too shy
To check their hurried feet
But raise their eyes and squint
As through a needle's eye
Into the faceless gloom,—
My father in a gray shawl
Gave me an unseeing glint
And entered another room!
I stood in the empty hall   110

And watched them come and go
From one room to another,
Old men, old women—slow,
Familiar; girls, boys;
I saw my downcast mother
Clad in her street-clothes,
Her blue eyes long and small,
Who had no look or voice
For him whose vision froze
Him in the empty hall.   120

III. WINTER

Goddess sea-born and bright,
Return into the sea
Where eddying twilight

Gathers upon your people—
Cold goddess, hear our plea!
Leave the burnt earth, Venus,
For the drying God above,
Hanged in his windy steeple,
No longer bears for us
The living wound of love.   130

All the sea-gods are dead.
You, Venus, come home
To your salt maidenhead,
The tossed anonymous sea
Under shuddering foam—
Shade for lovers, where
A shark swift as your dove
Shall pace our company
All night to nudge and tear
The livid wound of love.   140

And now the winter sea:
Within her hollow rind
What sleek facility
Of sea-conceited scop
To plumb the nether mind!
Eternal winters blow
Shivering flakes, and shove
Bodies that wheel and drop—
Cold soot upon the snow
Their livid wound of love.   150

Beyond the undertow
The gray sea-foliage
Transpires a phosphor glow
Into the circular miles:
In the centre of his cage
The pacing animal
Surveys the jungle cove
And slicks his slithering wiles
To turn the venereal awl
In the livid wound of love.   160

Beyond the undertow
The rigid madrepore
Resists the winter's flow—
Headless, unageing oak
That gives the leaf no more.
Wilfully as I stood
Within the thickest grove
I seized a branch, which broke;
I heard the speaking blood
(From the livid wound of love)   170

Drip down upon my toe:
"We are the men who died
Of self-inflicted woe,
Lovers whose strategem
Led to their suicide."
I touched my sanguine hair
And felt it drip above
Their brother who, like them,
Was maimed and did not bear
The living wound of love.   180

IV. SPRING

Irritable spring, infuse
Into the burning breast
Your combustible juice
That as a liquid soul
Shall be the body's guest
Who lights, but cannot stay
To comfort this unease
Which, like a dying coal,
Hastens the cooler day
Of the mother of silences.   190

Back in my native prime
I saw the orient corn
All space but no time,
Reaching for the sun
Of the land where I was born:
It was a pleasant land

Where even death could please
Us with an ancient pun—
All dying for the hand
Of the mother of silences.   200

In time of bloody war
Who will know the time?
Is it a new spring star
Within the timing chill,
Talking, or just a mime,
That rises in the blood—
Thin Jack-and-Jilling seas
Without the human will?
Its light is at the flood,
Mother of silences!   210

It burns us each alone
Whose burning arrogance
Burns up the rolling stone,
This earth—Platonic cave
Of vertiginous chance!
Come, tired Sisyphus,
Cover the cave's egress
Where light reveals the slave,
Who rests when sleeps with us
The mother of silences.   220

Come, old woman, save
Your sons who have gone down
Into the burning cave:
Come, mother, and lean
At the window with your son
And gaze through its light frame
These fifteen centuries
Upon the shirking scene
Where men, blind, go lame:
Then, mother of silences,   230

Speak, that we may hear;
Listen, while we confess

That we conceal our fear;
Regard us, while the eye
Discerns by sight or guess
Whether, as sheep foregather
Upon their crooked knees,
We have begun to die;
Whether your kindness, mother,
Is mother of silences.   240

THE SWIMMERS   [1961]

SCENE: Montgomery County, Kentucky, July 1911

Kentucky water, clear springs: a boy fleeing
    To water under the dry Kentucky sun,
    His four little friends in tandem with him, seeing

Long shadows of grapevine wriggle and run
    Over the green swirl; mullein under the ear
    Soft as Nausicaä's palm; sullen fun

Savage as childhood's thin harmonious tear:
    O fountain, bosom source undying-dead
    Replenish me the spring of love and fear

And give me back the eye that looked and fled   10
    When a thrush idling in the tulip tree
    Unwound the cold dream of the copperhead.

—Along the creek the road was winding; we
    Felt the quicksilver sky. I see again
    The shrill companions of that odyssey:

Bill Eaton, Charlie Watson, "Nigger" Layne
    The doctor's son, Harry Duèsler who played
    The flute; and Tate, with water on the brain.

Dog-days: the dusty leaves where rain delayed
   Hung low on poison-oak and scuppernong,   20
   And we were following the active shade

Of water, that bells and bickers all night long.
   "No more'n a mile," Layne said. All five stood still.
   Listening, I heard what seemed at first a song;

Peering, I heard the hooves come down the hill.
   The posse passed, twelve horse; the leader's face
   Was worn as limestone on an ancient sill.

Then, as sleepwalkers shift from a hard place
   In bed, and rising to keep a formal pledge
   Descend a ladder into empty space,   30

We scuttled down the bank below a ledge
   And marched stiff-legged in our common fright
   Along a hog-track by the riffle's edge:

Into a world where sound shaded the sight
   Dropped the dull hooves again; the horsemen came
   Again, all but the leader. It was night

Momently and I feared: eleven same
   Jesus-Christers unmembered and unmade,
   Whose Corpse had died again in dirty shame.

The bank then levelling in a speckled glade,   40
   We stopped to breathe above the swimming-hole;
   I gazed at its reticulated shade

Recoiling in blue fear, and felt it roll
   Over my ears and eyes and lift my hair
   Like seaweed tossing on a sunk atoll.

I rose again. Borne on the copper air
   A distant voice green as a funeral wreath
   Against a grave: "That dead nigger there."

The melancholy sheriff slouched beneath
  A giant sycamore; shaking his head   50
  He plucked a sassafras twig and picked his teeth:

"We come too late." He spoke to the tired dead
  Whose ragged shirt soaked up the viscous flow
  Of blood in which It lay discomfited.

A butting horse-fly gave one ear a blow
  And glanced off, as the sheriff kicked the rope
  Loose from the neck and hooked it with his toe

Away from the blood.—I looked back down the slope:
  The friends were gone that I had hoped to greet.—
  A single horseman came at a slow lope   60

And pulled up at the hanged man's horny feet;
  The sheriff noosed the feet, the other end
  The stranger tied to his pommel in a neat

Slip-knot. I saw the Negro's body bend
  And straighten, as a fish-line cast transverse
  Yields to the current that it must subtend.

The sheriff's Goddamn was a murmured curse
  Not for the dead but for the blinding dust
  That boxed the cortège in a cloudy hearse

And dragged it towards our town. I knew I must   70
  Not stay till twilight in that silent road;
  Sliding my bare feet into the warm crust,

I hopped the stonecrop like a panting toad
  Mouth open, following the heaving cloud
  That floated to the court-house square its load

Of limber corpse that took the sun for shroud.
  There were three figures in the dying sun
  Whose light were company where three was crowd.

My breath crackled the dead air like a shotgun
    As, sheriff and the stranger disappearing,   80
    The faceless head lay still. I could not run

Or walk, but stood. Alone in the public clearing
    This private thing was owned by all the town,
    Though never claimed by us within my hearing.

Theodore Roethke

1908–1963

Theodore Roethke was born May 25, 1908, in Saginaw, Michigan, and grew up, as he says, "in and around a beautiful green-house owned by my father and uncle." He graduated from the University of Michigan in 1929 and received his M.A. there in 1936. He taught English at Lafayette College, Pennsylvania State University, and Bennington College, and from 1947 onward was associate professor and professor of English and poet in residence at the University of Washington. He held a Guggenheim Fellowship in 1945, was a Fulbright lecturer in Italy in 1955, and in 1953 received the Pulitzer and other prizes for The Waking. *He was a member of the National Institute of Arts and Letters. He died on August 1, 1963, on Bainbridge Island, across Puget Sound from Seattle.*

OPEN HOUSE   [1941]

My secrets cry aloud.
I have no need for tongue.
My heart keeps open house,
My doors are widely swung.
An epic of the eyes
My love, with no disguise.

My truths are all foreknown,
This anguish self-revealed.
I'm naked to the bone,
With nakedness my shield.
Myself is what I wear:
I keep the spirit spare.

10

The anger will endure,
The deed will speak the truth
In language strict and pure.
I stop the lying mouth:
Rage warps my clearest cry
To witless agony.

CUTTINGS, *later*   [1948]

This urge, wrestle, resurrection of dry sticks,
Cut stems struggling to put down feet,
What saint strained so much,
Rose on such lopped limbs to a new life?

I can hear, underground, that sucking and sobbing,
In my veins, in my bones I feel it,—
The small waters seeping upward,
The tight grains parting at last.
When sprouts break out,
Slippery as fish,   10
I quail, lean to beginnings, sheath-wet.

DOLOR   [1948]

I have known the inexorable sadness of pencils,
Neat in their boxes, dolor of pad and paper-weight,
All the misery of manila folders and mucilage,
Desolation in immaculate public places,
Lonely reception room, lavatory, switchboard,
The unalterable pathos of basin and pitcher,
Ritual of multigraph, paper-clip, comma,
Endless duplication of lives and objects.
And I have seen dust from the walls of institutions,
Finer than flour, alive, more dangerous than silica,   10
Sift, almost invisible, through long afternoons of tedium,

Dropping a fine film on nails and delicate eyebrows,
Glazing the pale hair, the duplicate gray standard faces.

THE LOST SON   [1948]

I   THE FLIGHT

At Woodlawn I heard the dead cry:
I was lulled by the slamming of iron,
A slow drip over stones,
Toads brooding in wells.
All the leaves stuck out their tongues;
I shook the softening chalk of my bones,
Saying,
Snail, snail, glister me forward,
Bird, soft-sigh me home.
Worm, be with me.   10
This is my hard time.

Fished in an old wound,
The soft pond of repose;
Nothing nibbled my line,
Not even the minnows came.

Sat in an empty house
Watching shadows crawl,
Scratching.
There was one fly.

Voice, come out of the silence.   20
Say something.
Appear in the form of a spider
Or a moth beating the curtain.

Tell me:
Which is the way I take;
Out of what door do I go,
Where and to whom?

Dark hollows said, lee to the wind,
The moon said, back of an eel,
The salt said, look by the sea,   30
Your tears are not enough praise,
You will find no comfort here,
In the kingdom of bang and blab.

Running lightly over spongy ground,
Past the pasture of flat stones,
The three elms,
The sheep strewn on a field,
Over a rickety bridge
Toward the quick-water, wrinkling and rippling.

Hunting along the river,   40
Down among the rubbish, the bug-riddled foliage,
By the muddy pond-edge, by the bog-holes,
By the shrunken lake, hunting, in the heat of summer.

The shape of a rat?
    It's bigger than that.
    It's less than a leg
    And more than a nose,
    Just under the water
    It usually goes.

Is it soft like a mouse?   50
Can it wrinkle its nose?
Could it come in the house
On the tips of its toes?

    Take the skin of a cat
    And the back of an eel,
    Then roll them in grease,—
    That's the way it would feel.

    It's sleek as an otter
    With wide webby toes
    Just under the water   60
    It usually goes.

2   THE PIT

Where do the roots go?
  Look down under the leaves.
Who put the moss there?
  These stones have been here too long.
Who stunned the dirt into noise?
  Ask the mole, he knows.
I feel the slime of a wet nest.
  Beware Mother Mildew.
Nibble again, fish nerves.   70

3   THE GIBBER

At the wood's mouth,
By the cave's door,
I listened to something
I had heard before.

Dogs of the groin
Barked and howled,
The sun was against me,
The moon would not have me.

The weeds whined,
The snakes cried,   80
The cows and briars
Said to me: Die.

What a small song. What slow clouds. What dark water.
Hath the rain a father? All the caves are ice. Only the
      snow's here.
I'm cold. I'm cold all over. Rub me in father and mother.
Fear was my father, Father Fear.
His look drained the stones.

      What gliding shape
      Beckoning through halls,
      Stood poised on the stair,   90
      Fell dreamily down?

      From the mouths of jugs
      Perched on many shelves,

I saw substance flowing
That cold morning.

Like a slither of eels
That watery cheek
As my own tongue kissed
My lips awake.

Is this the storm's heart? The ground is unstilling itself.   100
My veins are running nowhere. Do the bones cast out
    their fire?
Is the seed leaving the old bed? These buds are live as
    birds.
Where, where are the tears of the world?
Let the kisses resound, flat like a butcher's palm;
Let the gestures freeze; our doom is already decided.
All the windows are burning! What's left of my life?
I want the old rage, the lash of primordial milk!
Good-bye, good-bye, old stones, the time-order is going,
I have married my hands to perpetual agitation,
I run, I run to the whistle of money.   110

Money money money
Water water water

How cool the grass is.
Has the bird left?
The stalk still sways.
Has the worm a shadow?
What do the clouds say?

These sweeps of light undo me.
Look, look, the ditch is running white!
I've more veins than a tree!   120
Kiss me, ashes, I'm falling through a dark swirl.

4   THE RETURN

The way to the boiler was dark,
Dark all the way,

Over slippery cinders
Through the long greenhouse.

The roses kept breathing in the dark.
They had many mouths to breathe with.
My knees made little winds underneath
Where the weeds slept.

There was always a single light   130
Swinging by the fire-pit,
Where the fireman pulled out roses,
The big roses, the big bloody clinkers.

Once I stayed all night.
The light in the morning came slowly over the white
Snow.
There were many kinds of cool
Air.
Then came steam.

Pipe-knock.   140

Scurry of warm over small plants.
Ordnung! Ordnung!
Papa is coming!

A fine haze moved off the leaves;
Frost melted on far panes;
The rose, the chrysanthemum turned toward the light.
Even the hushed forms, the bent yellowy weeds
Moved in a slow up-sway.

            5   (IT WAS BEGINNING WINTER.)
It was beginning winter,
An in-between time,   150
The landscape still partly brown:
The bones of weeds kept swinging in the wind,
Above the blue snow.

It was beginning winter.
The light moved slowly over the frozen field,

Over the dry seed-crowns,
The beautiful surviving bones
Swinging in the wind.

Light traveled over the field;
Stayed.   160
The weeds stopped swinging.
The mind moved, not alone,
Through the clear air, in the silence.

   Was it light?
   Was it light within?
   Was it light within light?
   Stillness becoming alive,
   Yet still?

   A lively understandable spirit
   Once entertained you.   170
   It will come again.
   Be still.
   Wait.

ELEGY FOR JANE   [1953]

My Student, Thrown by a Horse

I remember the neckcurls, limp and damp as tendrils;
And her quick look, a sidelong pickerel smile;
And how, once startled into talk, the light syllables
      leaped for her,
And she balanced in the delight of her thought,
A wren, happy, tail into the wind,
Her song trembling the twigs and small branches.
The shade sang with her;
The leaves, their whispers turned to kissing;
And the mold sang in the bleached valleys under the rose.

Oh, when she was sad, she cast herself down into such a
      pure depth,   10

Even a father could not find her:
Scraping her cheek against straw;
Stirring the clearest water.

My sparrow, you are not here,
Waiting like a fern, making a spiny shadow.
The sides of wet stones cannot console me,
Nor the moss, wound with the last light.

If only I could nudge you from this sleep,
My maimed darling, my skittery pigeon.
Over this damp grave I speak the words of my love: 20
I, with no rights in this matter,
Neither father nor lover.

FOUR FOR SIR JOHN DAVIES   [1953]

I

THE DANCE

Is that dance slowing in the mind of man
That made him think the universe could hum?
The great wheel turns its axle when it can;
I need a place to sing, and dancing-room,
And I have made a promise to my ears
I'll sing and whistle romping with the bears.

For they are all my friends: I saw one slide
Down a steep hillside on a cake of ice,—
Or was that in a book? I think with pride:
A caged bear rarely does the same thing twice   10
In the same way: O watch his body sway!—
This animal remembering to be gay.

I tried to fling my shadow at the moon,
The while my blood leaped with a wordless song.
Though dancing needs a master, I had none
To teach my toes to listen to my tongue.

But what I learned there, dancing all alone,
Was not the joyless motion of a stone.

I take this cadence from a man named Yeats;
I take it, and I give it back again: 20
For other tunes and other wanton beats
Have tossed my heart and fiddled through my brain.
Yes, I was dancing-mad, and how
That came to be the bears and Yeats would know.

2

THE PARTNER

Between such animal and human heat
I find myself perplexed. What is desire?—
The impulse to make someone else complete?
That woman would set sodden straw on fire.
Was I the servant of a sovereign wish,
Or ladle rattling in an empty dish?   30

We played a measure with commingled feet:
The lively dead had taught us to be fond.
Who can embrace the body of his fate?
Light altered light along the living ground.
She kissed me close, and then did something else.
My marrow beat as wildly as my pulse.

I'd say it to my horse: we live beyond
Our outer skin. Who's whistling up my sleeve?
I see a heron prancing in his pond;
I know a dance the elephants believe.   40
The living all assemble! What's the cue?—
Do what the clumsy partner wants to do!

Things loll and loiter. Who condones the lost?
This joy outleaps the dog. Who cares? Who cares?
I gave her kisses back, and woke a ghost.
O what lewd music crept into our ears!
The body and the soul know how to play
In that dark world where gods have lost their way.

3
THE WRAITH

Incomprehensible gaiety and dread
Attended what we did. Behind, before,   50
Lay all the lonely pastures of the dead;
The spirit and the flesh cried out for more.
We two, together, on a darkening day
Took arms against our own obscurity.

Did each become the other in that play?
She laughed me out, and then she laughed me in;
In the deep middle of ourselves we lay;
When glory failed, we danced upon a pin.
The valley rocked beneath the granite hill;
Our souls looked forth, and the great day stood still.   60

There was a body, and it cast a spell,—
God pity those but wanton to the knees,—
The flesh can make the spirit visible;
We woke to find the moonlight on our toes.
In the rich weather of a dappled wood
We played with dark and light as children should.

What shape leaped forward at the sensual cry?—
Sea-beast or bird flung toward the ravaged shore?
Did space shake off an angel with a sigh?
We rose to meet the moon, and saw no more.   70
It was and was not she, a shape alone,
Impaled on light, and whirling slowly down.

4
THE VIGIL

Dante attained the purgatorial hill,
Trembled at hidden virtue without flaw,
Shook with a mighty power beyond his will,—
Did Beatrice deny what Dante saw?
All lovers live by longing, and endure:
Summon a vision and declare it pure.

Though everything's astonishment at last,
Who leaps to heaven at a single bound?   80
The links were soft between us; still, we kissed;
We undid chaos to a curious sound:
The waves broke easy, cried to me in white;
Her look was morning in the dying light.

The visible obscures. But who knows when?
Things have their thoughts: they are the shards of me;
I thought that once, and thought comes round again;
Rapt, we leaned forth with what we could not see.
We danced to shining; mocked before the black
And shapeless night that made no answer back.   90

The world is for the living. Who are they?
We dared the dark to reach the white and warm.
She was the wind when wind was in my way;
Alive at noon, I perished in her form.
Who rise from flesh to spirit know the fall:
The word outleaps the world, and light is all.

THE WAKING   [1953]

I wake to sleep, and take my waking slow.
I feel my fate in what I cannot fear.
I learn by going where I have to go.

We think by feeling. What is there to know?
I hear my being dance from ear to ear.
I wake to sleep, and take my waking slow.

Of those so close beside me, which are you?
God bless the Ground! I shall walk softly there,
And learn by going where I have to go.

Light takes the Tree; but who can tell us how?   10
The lowly worm climbs up a winding stair;
I wake to sleep, and take my waking slow.

Great Nature has another thing to do
To you and me; so take the lively air,
And, lovely, learn by going where to go.

This shaking keeps me steady. I should know.
What falls away is always. And is near.
I wake to sleep, and take my waking slow.
I learn by going where I have to go.

WORDS FOR THE WIND   [1958]

I

Love, love, a lily's my care,
She's sweeter than a tree.
Loving, I use the air
Most lovingly: I breathe;
Mad in the wind I wear
Myself as I should be,
All's even with the odd,
My brother the vine is glad.

Are flower and seed the same?
What do the great dead say?   10
Sweet Phoebe, she's my theme:
She sways whenever I sway.
"O love me while I am,
You green thing in my way!"
I cried, and the birds came down
And made my song their own.

Motion can keep me still:
She kissed me out of thought
As a lovely substance will;
She wandered; I did not: 20
I stayed, and light fell
Across her pulsing throat;
I stared, and a garden stone
Slowly became the moon.

The shallow stream runs slack;
The wind creaks slowly by;
Out of a nestling's beak
Comes a tremulous cry
I cannot answer back;
A shape from deep in the eye—   30
That woman I saw in a stone—
Keeps pace when I walk alone.

2

The sun declares the earth;
The stones leap in the stream;
On a wide plain, beyond
The far stretch of a dream,
A field breaks like the sea;
The wind's white with her name,
And I walk with the wind.

The dove's my will today.   40
She sways, half in the sun:
Rose, easy on a stem,
One with the sighing vine,
One to be merry with,
And pleased to meet the moon.
She likes wherever I am.

Passion's enough to give
Shape to a random joy:
I cry delight: I know
The root, the core of a cry.   50
Swan-heart, arbutus-calm,
She moves when time is shy:
Love has a thing to do.

A fair thing grows more fair;
The green, the springing green
Makes an intenser day
Under the rising moon;
I smile, no mineral man;
I bear, but not alone,
The burden of this joy.   60

3

Under a southern wind,
The birds and fishes move
North, in a single stream;
The sharp stars swing around;
I get a step beyond
The wind, and there I am,
I'm odd and full of love.

Wisdom, where is it found?—
Those who embrace, believe.
Whatever was, still is,   70
Says a song tied to a tree.
Below, on the ferny ground,
In rivery air, at ease,
I walk with my true love.

What time's my heart? I care.
I cherish what I have
Had of the temporal:
I am no longer young
But the winds and waters are;
What falls away will fall;   80
All things bring me to love.

4

The breath of a long root,
The shy perimeter
Of the unfolding rose,
The green, the altered leaf,
The oyster's weeping foot,
And the incipient star—
Are part of what she is.
She wakes the ends of life.

Being myself, I sing   90
The soul's immediate joy.
Light, light, where's my repose?
A wind wreathes round a tree.
A thing is done: a thing
Body and spirit know

When I do what she does:
Creaturely creature, she!—

I kiss her moving mouth,
Her swart hilarious skin;
She breaks my breath in half;   100
She frolicks like a beast;
And I dance round and round,
A fond and foolish man,
And see and suffer myself
In another being, at last.

THE SONG   [1958]

1

I met a ragged man;
He looked beyond me when
I tried to meet his eyes.
What have I done to you?
I cried, and backed away.
Dust in a corner stirred,
And the walls stretched wide.

2

I went running down a road,
In a country of bleak stone,
And shocks of ragged corn;   10
When I stayed for breath, I lay
With the saxifrage and fern
At the edge of a raw field.
I stared at a fissure of ground
Ringed round with crumbled clay:
The old house of a crab;
Stared, and began to sing.

3

I sang to whatever had been
Down in that watery hole:

I wooed with a low tune;   20
You could say I was mad.
And a wind woke in my hair,
And the sweat poured from my face,
When I heard, or thought I heard,
Another join my song
With the small voice of a child,
Close, and yet far away.

Mouth upon mouth, we sang,
My lips pressed upon stone.

FIRST MEDITATION   [1958]

(from "Meditations of an Old Woman")

                         I

On love's worst ugly day,
The weeds hiss at the edge of the field,
The small winds make their chilly indictments.
Elsewhere, in houses, even pails can be sad;
While stones loosen on the obscure hillside,
And a tree tilts from its roots,
Toppling down an embankment.

The spirit moves, but not always upward,
While animals eat to the north,
And the shale slides an inch in the talus,   10
The bleak wind eats at the weak plateau,
And the sun brings joy to some.
But the rind, often, hates the life within.

How can I rest in the days of my slowness?
I've become a strange piece of flesh,
Nervous and cold, bird-furtive, whiskery,
With a cheek soft as a hound's ear.
What's left is light as a seed;
I need an old crone's knowing.

2

Often I think of myself as riding—   20
Alone, on a bus through western country.
I sit above the back wheels, where the jolts are hardest,
And we bounce and sway along toward the midnight,
The lights tilting up, skyward, as we come over a little rise,
Then down, as we roll like a boat from a wave-crest.
All journeys, I think, are the same:
The movement is forward, after a few wavers,
And for a while we are all alone,
Busy, obvious with ourselves,
The drunken soldier, the old lady with her peppermints;   30
And we ride, we ride, taking the curves
Somewhat closer, the trucks coming
Down from behind the last ranges,
Their black shapes breaking past;
And the air claps between us,
Blasting the frosted windows,
And I seem to go backward,
Backward in time:

> Two song sparrows, one within a greenhouse,
> Shuttling its throat while perched on a wind-vent,   40
> And another, outside, in the bright day,
> With a wind from the west and the trees all in motion.
> One sang, then the other,
> The songs tumbling over and under the glass,
> And the men beneath them wheeling in dirt to the
>   cement benches,
> The laden wheelbarrows creaking and swaying,
> And the up-spring of the plank when a foot left the
>   runway.

Journey within a journey:
The ticket mislaid or lost, the gate
Inaccessible, the boat always pulling out   50
From the rickety wooden dock,
The children waving;
Or two horses plunging in snow, their lines tangled,
A great wooden sleigh careening behind them,

Swerving up a steep embankment.
For a moment they stand above me,
Their black skins shuddering:
Then they lurch forward,
Lunging down a hillside.

3

As when silt drifts and sifts down through muddy pond-
    water,   60
Settling in small beads around weeds and sunken branches,
And one crab, tentative, hunches himself before moving
    along the bottom,
Grotesque, awkward, his extended eyes looking at nothing
    in particular,
Only a few bubbles loosening from the ill-matched
    tentacles,
The tail and smaller legs slipping and sliding slowly
    backward—
So the spirit tries for another life,
Another way and place in which to continue;
Or a salmon, tired, moving up a shallow stream,
Nudges into a back-eddy, a sandy inlet,
Bumping against sticks and bottom-stones, then swinging   70
Around, back into the tiny maincurrent, the rush of
    brownish-white water,
Still swimming forward—
So, I suppose, the spirit journeys.

4

I have gone into the waste lonely places
Behind the eye; the lost acres at the edge of smoky cities.
What's beyond never crumbles like an embankment,
Explodes like a rose, or thrusts wings over the Caribbean.
There are no pursuing forms, faces on walls:
Only the motes of dust in the immaculate hallways,
The darkness of falling hair, the warnings from lint and
    spiders,   80
The vines graying to a fine powder.
There is no riven tree, or lamb dropped by an eagle.

There are still times, morning and evening:
The cerulean, high in the elm,
Thin and insistent as a cicada,
And the far phoebe, singing,
The long plaintive notes floating down,
Drifting through leaves, oak and maple,
Or the whippoorwill, along the smoky ridges,
A single bird calling and calling;   90
A fume reminds me, drifting across wet gravel;
A cold wind comes over stones;
A flame, intense, visible,
Plays over the dry pods,
Runs fitfully along the stubble,
Moves over the field,
Without burning.
    In such times, lacking a god,
    I am still happy.

Karl Shapiro

b. 1913

Karl Shapiro was born November 10, 1913, in Baltimore, Maryland. He attended the University of Virginia, Johns Hopkins University, and studied library science for a year at the Enoch Pratt Free Library in Baltimore. From 1941 to 1945 he served in the United States Army. While in Australia, New Guinea, and other South Pacific areas, he sent poems to his fiancée in New York, who arranged for their publication. V-Letter and Other Poems *won several prizes, including the Pulitzer. In 1946–1947 he was Consultant in Poetry to the Library of Congress, and from 1947 to 1950 lecturer at Johns Hopkins University. He then edited* Poetry *for five years and joined the English Department at the University of Nebraska, where he also edited* Prairie Schooner. *Recently he has been conducting a critical war against Eliot and Pound and championing Whitman, D. H. Lawrence, and Henry Miller.*

THE DOME OF SUNDAY   [1942]

With focus sharp as Flemish-painted face
In film of varnish brightly fixed
And through a polished hand-lens deeply seen,
Sunday at noon through hyaline thin air
Sees down the street,
And in the camera of my eye depicts
Row-houses and row-lives:
Glass after glass, door after door the same,
Face after face the same, the same,
The brutal visibility the same;   10

As if one life emerging from one house
Would pause, a single image caught between
Two facing mirrors where vision multiplies
Beyond perspective,
A silent clatter in the high-speed eye
Spinning out photo-circulars of sight.

I see slip to the curb the long machines
Out of whose warm and windowed rooms pirouette
Shellacked with silk and light
The hard legs of our women.   20
Our women are one woman, dressed in black.
The carmine printed mouth
And cheeks as soft as muslin-glass belong
Outright to one dark dressy man,
Merely a swagger at her curvy side.
This is their visit to themselves:
All day from porch to porch they weave
A nonsense pattern through the even glare,
Stealing in surfaces
Cold vulgar glances at themselves.   30

And high up in the heated room all day
I wait behind the plate glass pane for one,
Hot as a voyeur for a glimpse of one,
The vision to blot out this woman's sheen;
All day my sight records expensively
Row-houses and row-lives.

But nothing happens; no diagonal
With melting shadow falls across the curb:
Neither the blinded negress lurching through fatigue,
Nor exiles bleeding from their pores,   40
Nor that bright bomb slipped lightly from its rack
To splinter every silvered glass and crystal prism,
Witch-bowl and perfume bottle
And billion candle-power dressing-bulb,
No direct hit to smash the shatter-proof
And lodge at last the quivering needle

Clean in the eye of one who stands transfixed
In fascination of her brightness.

THE POTOMAC [1942]

The thin Potomac scarcely moves
But to divide Virginia from today;
    Rider, whichever is your way
You go due south and neither South improves;
Not this, of fractured columns and queer rents
    And rags that charm the nationalist,
Not that, the axle of the continents,
Nor the thin sky that flows unprejudiced
This side and that, cleansing the poisoned breath.

For Thomas died a Georgian death   10
And now the legion bones of Arlington
    Laid out in marble alphabets
Stare on the great tombs of the capitol
    Where heroes calcified and cool
    Ponder the soldier named Unknown
Whose lips are guarded with live bayonets.

Yet he shall speak though sentries walk
And columns with their cold Corinthian stalk
    Shed gold-dust pollen on Brazil
    To turn the world to Roman chalk;   20
Yet he shall speak, yet he shall speak
    Whose sulphur lit the flood-lit Dome,
    Whose hands were never in the kill,
Whose will was furrows of Virginia loam.

But not like London blown apart by boys
Who learned the books of love in English schools,
His name shall strike the fluted columns down;
These shall lie buried deep as fifty Troys,
The money fade like leaves from green to brown,
And embassies dissolve to molecules.   30

NOSTALGIA   [1942]

My soul stands at the window of my room,
    And I ten thousand miles away;
My days are filled with Ocean's sound of doom,
    Salt and cloud and the bitter spray.
Let the wind blow, for many a man shall die.

My selfish youth, my books with gilded edge,
    Knowledge and all gaze down the street;
The potted plants upon the window ledge
    Gaze down with selfish lives and sweet.
Let the wind blow, for many a man shall die.   10

My night is now her day, my day her night,
    So I lie down, and so I rise;
The sun burns close, the star is losing height,
    The clock is hunted down the skies.
Let the wind blow, for many a man shall die.

Truly a pin can make the memory bleed,
    A word explode the inward mind
And turn the skulls and flowers never freed
    Into the air, no longer blind.
Let the wind blow, for many a man shall die.   20

Laughter and grief join hands. Always the heart
    Clumps in the breast with heavy stride;
The face grown lined and wrinkled like a chart,
    The eyes bloodshot with tears and tide.
Let the wind blow, for many a man shall die.

ELEGY FOR A DEAD SOLDIER   [1944]

I

A white sheet on the tail-gate of a truck
Becomes an altar; two small candlesticks

Sputter at each side of the crucifix
Laid round with flowers brighter than the blood,
Red as the red of our apocalypse,
Hibiscus that a marching man will pluck
To stick into his rifle or his hat,
And great blue morning-glories pale as lips
That shall no longer taste or kiss or swear.
The wind begins a low magnificat,   10
The chaplain chats, the palmtrees swirl their hair,
The columns come together through the mud.

II

We too are ashes as we watch and hear
The psalm, the sorrow, and the simple praise
Of one whose promised thoughts of other days
Were such as ours, but now wholly destroyed,
The service record of his youth wiped out,
His dream dispersed by shot, must disappear.
What can we feel but wonder at a loss
That seems to point at nothing but the doubt   20
Which flirts our sense of luck into the ditch?
Reader of Paul who prays beside this fosse,
Shall we believe our eyes or legends rich
With glory and rebirth beyond the void?

III

For this comrade is dead, dead in the war,
A young man out of millions yet to live,
One cut away from all that war can give,
Freedom of self and peace to wander free.
Who mourns in all this sober multitude
Who did not feel the bite of it before   30
The bullet found its aim? This worthy flesh,
This boy laid in a coffin and reviewed—
Who has not wrapped himself in this same flag,
Heard the light fall of dirt, his wound still fresh,
Felt his eyes closed, and heard the distant brag
Of the last volley of humanity?

IV

By chance I saw him die, stretched on the ground,
A tattooed arm lifted to take the blood

Of someone else sealed in a tin. I stood
During the last delirium that stays   40
The intelligence a tiny moment more,
And then the strangulation, the last sound.
The end was sudden, like a foolish play,
A stupid fool slamming a foolish door,
The absurd catastrophe, half-prearranged,
And all the decisive things still left to say.
So we disbanded, angrier and unchanged,
Sick with the utter silence of dispraise.

V

We ask for no statistics of the killed,
For nothing political impinges on   50
This single casualty, or all those gone,
Missing or healing, sinking or dispersed,
Hundreds of thousands counted, millions lost.
More than an accident and less than willed
Is every fall, and this one like the rest.
However others calculate the cost,
To us the final aggregate is *one*,
One with a name, one transferred to the blest;
And though another stoops and takes the gun,
We cannot add the second to the first.   60

VI

I would not speak for him who could not speak
Unless my fear were true: he was not wronged,
He knew to which decision he belonged
But let it choose itself. Ripe in instinct,
Neither the victim nor the volunteer,
He followed, and the leaders could not seek
Beyond the followers. Much of this he knew;
The journey was a detour that would steer
Into the Lincoln Highway of a land
Remorselessly improved, excited, new,   70
And that was what he wanted. He had planned
To earn and drive. He and the world had winked.

VII

No history deceived him, for he knew
Little of times and armies not his own;

He never felt that peace was but a loan,
Had never questioned the idea of gain.
Beyond the headlines once or twice he saw
The gathering of a power by the few
But could not tell their names; he cast his vote,
Distrusting all the elected but not the law.   80
He laughted at socialism; *on mourrait*
Pour les industriels? He shed his coat
And not for brotherhood, but for his pay.
To him the red flag marked the sewer main.

VIII

Above all else he loathed the homily,
The slogan and the ad. He paid his bill
But not for Congressmen at Bunker Hill.
Ideals were few and those there were not made
For conversation. He belonged to church
But never spoke of God. The Christmas tree,   90
The Easter egg, baptism, he observed,
Never denied the preacher on his perch,
And would not sign Resolved That or Whereas.
Softness he had and hours and nights reserved
For thinking, dressing, dancing to the jazz.
His laugh was real, his manners were home made.

IX

Of all men poverty pursued him least;
He was ashamed of all the down and out,
Spurned the panhandler like an uneasy doubt,
And saw the unemployed as a vague mass   100
Incapable of hunger or revolt.
He hated other races, south or east,
And shoved them to the margin of his mind.
He could recall the justice of the Colt,
Take interest in a gang-war like a game.
His ancestry was somewhere far behind
And left him only his peculiar name.
Doors opened, and he recognized no class.

X

His children would have known a heritage,
Just or unjust, the richest in the world,   110

The quantum of all art and science curled
In the horn of plenty, bursting from the horn,
A people bathed in honey, Paris come,
Vienna transferred with the highest wage,
A World's Fair spread to Phoenix, Jacksonville,
Earth's capitol, the new Byzantium,
Kingdom of man—who knows? Hollow or firm,
No man can ever prophesy until
Out of our death some undiscovered germ,
Whole toleration or pure peace is born.   120

XI

The time to mourn is short that best becomes
The military dead. We lift and fold the flag,
Lay bare the coffin with its written tag,
And march away. Behind, four others wait
To lift the box, the heaviest of loads.
The anesthetic afternoon benumbs,
Sickens our senses, forces back our talk.
We know that others on tomorrow's roads
Will fall, ourselves perhaps, the man beside,
Over the world the threatened, all who walk: 130
And could we mark the grave of him who died
We would write this beneath his name and date:

EPITAPH

Underneath this wooden cross there lies
A Christian killed in battle. You who read,
Remember that this stranger died in pain;
And passing here, if you can lift your eyes
Upon a peace kept by a human creed,
Know that one soldier has not died in vain.

V-LETTER   [1944]

I love you first because your face is fair,
    Because your eyes Jewish and blue,

Set sweetly with the touch of foreignness
Above the cheekbones, stare rather than dream.
Often your countenance recalls a boy
      Blue-eyed and small, whose silent mischief
Tortured his parents and compelled my hate
      To wish his ugly death.
Because of this reminder, my soul's trouble,
And for your face, so often beautiful,   10
      I love you, wish you life.

I love you first because you wait, because
      For your own sake, I cannot write
Beyond these words. I love you for these words
That sting and creep like insects and leave filth.
I love you for the poverty you cry
      And I bend down with tears of steel
That melt your hand like wax, not for this war
      The droplets shattering
Those candle-glowing fingers of my joy,   20
But for your name of agony, my love,
      That cakes my mouth with salt.

And all your imperfections and perfections
      And àll your magnitude of grace
And all this love explained and unexplained
Is just a breath. I see you woman-size
And this looms larger and more goddess-like
      Than silver goddesses on screens.
I see you in the ugliness of light,
      Yet you are beautiful,   30
And in the dark of absence your full length
Is such as meets my body to the full
      Though I am starved and huge.

You turn me from these days as from a scene
      Out of an open window far
Where lies the foreign city and the war.
You are my home and in your spacious love
I dream to march as under flaring flags
      Until the door is gently shut.

Give me the tearless lesson of your pride,   40
       Teach me to live and die
As one deserving anonymity,
The mere devotion of a house to keep
       A woman and a man.

Give me the free and poor inheritance
       Of our own kind, not furniture
Of education, nor the prophet's pose,
The general cause of words, the hero's stance,
The ambitions incommensurable with flesh,
       But the drab makings of a room   50
Where sometimes in the afternoon of thought
       The brief and blinding flash
May light the enormous chambers of your will
And show the gracious Parthenon that time
       Is ever measured by.

As groceries in a pantry gleam and smile
       Because they are important weights
Bought with the metal minutes of your pay,
So do these hours stand in solid rows,
The dowry for a use in common life.   60
       I love you first because your years
Lead to my matter-of-fact and simple death
       Or to our open marriage,
And I pray nothing for my safety back,
Not even luck, because our love is whole
       Whether I live or fail.

THE SICKNESS OF ADAM   [1953]

(from "Adam and Eve")

In the beginning, at every step, he turned
As if by instinct to the East to praise
The nature of things. Now every path was learned
He lost the lifted, almost flower-like gaze

Of a temple dancer. He began to walk
Slowly, like one accustomed to be alone.
He found himself lost in the field of talk;
Thinking became a garden of its own.

In it were new things: words he had never said,
Beasts he had never seen and knew were not   10
In the true garden, terrors, and tears shed
Under a tree by him, for some new thought.

And the first anger. Once he flung a staff
At softly coupling sheep and struck the ram.
It broke away. And God heard Adam laugh
And for his laughter made the creature lame.

And wanderlust. He stood upon the Wall
To search the unfinished countries lying wide
And waste, where not a living thing could crawl,
And yet he would descend, as if to hide.   20

His thought drew down the guardian at the gate,
To whom man said, "What danger am I in?"
And the angel, hurt in spirit, seemed to hate
The wingless thing that worried after sin,

For it said nothing but marvelously unfurled
Its wings and arched them shimmering overhead,
Which must have been the signal from the world
That the first season of our life was dead.

Adam fell down with labor in his bones,
And God approached him in the cool of day   30
And said, "This sickness in your skeleton
Is longing. I will remove it from your clay."

He said also, "I made you strike the sheep."
It began to rain and God sat down beside
The sinking man. When he was fast asleep
He wet his right hand deep in Adam's side

And drew the graceful rib out of his breast.
Far off, the latent streams began to flow
And birds flew out of Paradise to nest
On earth. Sadly the angel watched them go.   40

Randall Jarrell

b. 1914

Randall Jarrell was born May 6, 1914, in Nashville, Tennessee. He studied psychology and English at Vanderbilt University, where he had two years of graduate work. After teaching at Kenyon College (1937–1939) and the University of Texas (1939–1942), he enlisted in the Army Air Corps. In 1946–1947 he taught at Sarah Lawrence College and was literary editor of The Nation. *Since 1947 he has been associate professor and professor of English at the Woman's College of the University of North Carolina, and in addition has taught at Princeton, Indiana University, the University of Illinois, the University of Cincinnati, and the Salzburg (Austria) Seminar in American Civilization. He has been Consultant in Poetry at the Library of Congress for two years, received a National Book Award in 1960, and is a member of the National Institute of Arts and Letters.*

90 NORTH [1942]

At home, in my flannel gown, like a bear to its floe,
I clambered to bed; up the globe's impossible sides
I sailed all night—till at last, with my black beard,
My furs and my dogs, I stood at the northern pole.

There in the childish night my companions lay frozen,
The stiff furs knocked at my starveling throat,
And I gave my great sigh: the flakes came huddling,
Were they really my end? In the darkness I turned to my
    rest.

—Here, the flag snaps in the glare and silence
Of the unbroken ice. I stand here,   10
The dogs bark, my beard is black, and I stare
At the North Pole . . .
                        And now what? Why, go back.

Turn as I please, my step is to the south.
The world—my world spins on this final point
Of cold and wretchedness: all lines, all winds
End in this whirlpool I at last discover.

And it is meaningless. In the child's bed
After the night's voyage, in that warm world
Where people work and suffer for the end
That crowns the pain—in that Cloud-Cuckoo-Land   20

I reached my North and it had meaning.
Here at the actual pole of my existence,
Where all that I have done is meaningless,
Where I die or live by accident alone—

Where, living or dying, I am still alone;
Here where North, the night, the berg of death
Crowd me out of the ignorant darkness,
I see at last that all the knowledge

I wrung from the darkness—that the darkness flung me—
Is worthless as ignorance: nothing comes from nothing,   30
The darkness from the darkness. Pain comes from the
    darkness
And we call it wisdom. It is pain.

SECOND AIR FORCE   [1945]

Far off, above the plain the summer dries,
The great loops of the hangars sway like hills.
Buses and weariness and loss, the nodding soldiers

Are wire, the bare frame building, and a pass
To what was hers; her head hides his square patch
And she thinks heavily: My son is grown.
She sees a world: sand roads, tar-paper barracks,
The bubbling asphalt of the runways, sage,
The dunes rising to the interminable ranges,
The dim flights moving over clouds like clouds.   10
The armorers in their patched faded green,
Sweat-stiffened, banded with brass cartridges,
Walk to the line; their Fortresses, all tail,
Stand wrong and flimsy on their skinny legs,
And the crews climb to them clumsily as bears.
The head withdraws into its hatch (a boy's),
The engines rise to their blind laboring roar,
And the green, made beasts run home to air.
Now in each aspect death is pure.
(At twilight they wink over men like stars   20
And hour by hour, through the night, some see
The great lights floating in—from Mars, from Mars.)
How emptily the watchers see them gone.

They go, there is silence; the woman and her son
Stand in the forest of the shadows, and the light
Washes them like water. In the long-sunken city
Of evening, the sunlight stills like sleep
The faint wonder of the drowned; in the evening,
In the last dreaming light, so fresh, so old,
The soldiers pass like beasts, unquestioning,   30
And the watcher for an instant understands
What there is then no need to understand;
But she wakes from her knowledge, and her stare,
A shadow now, moves emptily among
The shadows learning in their shadowy fields
The empty missions.
                              Remembering,
She hears the bomber calling, *Little Friend!*
To the fighter hanging in the hostile sky,
And sees the ragged flame eat, rib by rib,
Along the metal of the wing into her heart: 40
The lives stream out, blossom, and float steadily

To the flames of the earth, the flames
That burn like stars above the lands of men.

She saves from the twilight that takes everything
A squadron shipping, in its last parade—
Its dogs run by it, barking at the band—
A gunner walking to his barracks, half-asleep,
Starting at something, stumbling (above, invisible,
The crews in the steady winter of the sky
Tremble in their wired fur); and feels for them   50
The love of life for life. The hopeful cells
Heavy with someone else's death, cold carriers
Of someone else's victory, grope past their lives
Into her own bewilderment: The years meant *this*?

But for them the bombers answer everything.

THE DEATH OF THE BALL TURRET GUNNER   [1945]

From my mother's sleep I fell into the State,
And I hunched in its belly till my wet fur froze.
Six miles from earth, loosed from its dream of life,
I woke to black flak and the nightmare fighters.
When I died they washed me out of the turret with a hose.

A CAMP IN THE PRUSSIAN FOREST   [1948]

I walk beside the prisoners to the road.
Load on puffed load,
Their corpses, stacked like sodden wood,
Lie barred or galled with blood

By the charred warehouse. No one comes today
In the old way
To knock the fillings from their teeth;
The dark, coned, common wreath

Is plaited for their grave—a kind of grief.
The living leaf   10
Clings to the planted profitable
Pine if it is able;

The boughs sigh, mile on green, calm, breathing mile,
From this dead file
The planners ruled for them. . . . One year
They sent a million here:

Here men were drunk like water, burnt like wood.
The fat of good
And evil, the breast's star of hope
Were rendered into soap.   20

I paint the star I sawed from yellow pine—
And plant the sign
In soil that does not yet refuse
Its usual Jews

Their first asylum. But the white, dwarfed star—
This dead white star—
Hides nothing, pays for nothing; smoke
Fouls it, a yellow joke,

The needles of the wreath are chalked with ash,
A filmy trash   30
Litters the black woods with the death
Of men; and one last breath

Curls from the monstrous chimney. . . . I laugh aloud
Again and again;
The star laughs from its rotting shroud
Of flesh. O star of men!

THE ORIENT EXPRESS   [1951]

One looks from the train
Almost as one looked as a child. In the sunlight
What I see still seems to me plain,
I am safe; but at evening
As the lands darken, a questioning
Precariousness comes over everything.

Once after a day of rain
I lay longing to be cold; and after a while
I was cold again, and hunched shivering
Under the quilt's many colors, gray   10
With the dull ending of the winter day.
Outside me there were a few shapes
Of chairs and tables, things from a primer;
Outside the window
There were the chairs and tables of the world. . . .
I saw that the world
That had seemed to me the plain
Gray mask of all that was strange
Behind it—of all that *was*—was all.

But it is beyond belief.   20
One thinks, "Behind everything
An unforced joy, an unwilling
Sadness (a willing sadness, a forced joy)
Moves changelessly"; one looks from the train
And there is something, the same thing
Behind everything: all these little villages,
A passing woman, a field of grain,
The man who says good-bye to his wife—
A path through a wood full of lives, and the train
Passing, after all unchangeable   30
And not now ever to stop, like a heart—

It is like any other work of art.
It is and never can be changed.
Behind everything there is always
The unknown unwanted life.

THE WOMAN AT THE WASHINGTON
ZOO   [1960]

The saris go by me from the embassies.

Cloth from the moon. Cloth from another planet.
They look back at the leopard like the leopard.

And I. . . .
        this print of mine, that has kept its color
Alive through so many cleanings; this dull null
Navy I wear to work, and wear from work, and so
To my bed, so to my grave, with no
Complaints, no comment: neither from my chief,
The Deputy Chief Assistant, nor his chief—
Only I complain. . . . this serviceable   10
Body that no sunlight dyes, no hand suffuses
But, dome-shadowed, withering among columns,
Wavy beneath fountains—small, far-off, shining
In the eyes of animals, these beings trapped
As I am trapped but not, themselves, the trap,
Aging, but without knowledge of their age,
Kept safe here, knowing not of death, for death—
Oh, bars of my own body, open, open!

The world goes by my cage and never sees me.
And there come not to me, as come to these,   20
The wild beasts, sparrows pecking the llamas' grain,
Pigeons settling on the bears' bread, buzzards
Tearing the meat the flies have clouded. . . .
                  Vulture,
When you come for the white rat that the foxes left,
Take off the red helmet of your head, the black
Wings that have shadowed me, and step to me as man:
The wild brother at whose feet the white wolves fawn,
To whose hand of power the great lioness
Stalks, purring. . . .
          You know what I was,
You see what I am: change me, change me!   30

John Berryman

b. 1914

Born October 25, 1914, in McAlester, Oklahoma, John Berryman
attended school in South Kent, Connecticut, and took B.A. degrees at
Columbia College in 1936 and Clare College, Cambridge, in 1938. He
has held Rockefeller, Guggenheim and Partisan Review fellowships
and has taught at Wayne University, Harvard, Princeton, the University
of California, and Brown. Since 1955 he has been at the University of
Minnesota, where he is now professor of humanities. Throughout his
teaching career Berryman has been a writer of short stories, literary
criticism, and poetry. In 1965 he won the Pulitzer Prize for Poetry.

WINTER LANDSCAPE   [1948]

The three men coming down the winter hill
In brown, with tall poles and a pack of hounds
At heel, through the arrangement of the trees,
Past the five figures at the burning straw,
Returning cold and silent to their town,

Returning to the drifted snow, the rink
Lively with children, to the older men,
The long companions they can never reach,
The blue light, men with ladders, by the church
The sledge and shadow in the twilit street,   10

Are not aware that in the sandy time
To come, the evil waste of history
Outstretched, they will be seen upon the brow

Of that same hill: when all their company
Will have been irrecoverably lost,

These men, this particular three in brown
Witnessed by birds will keep the scene and say
By their configuration with the trees,
The small bridge, the red houses and the fire,
What place, what time, what morning occasion   20

Sent them into the wood, a pack of hounds
At heel and the tall poles upon their shoulders,
Thence to return as now we see them and
Ankle-deep in snow down the winter hill
Descend, while three birds watch and the fourth flies.

CLOUD AND FLAME   [1948]

The summer cloud in summer blue
Capricious from the wind will run,
Laughing into the tender sun,
Knowing the work that it must do.
When One says liberty is vain
The cloud will come to summer rain.

After his college failure, Swift
Eight hours a day against his age
Began to document his rage
Towards the decades of strife and shift.   10
From claims that pride or party made
He kept in an exacting shade.

Cornford in a retreat was lost;
A stray shot like an aimless joke
His learning, spirit, at one stroke
Dispersed, his generation's cost.
The harvest value of his head
Is less than cloud, is less than bread.

The One recalls the many burn,
Prepared or unprepared: one flame   20
Within a shade can strike its name,
Another sees the cloud return.
And Thirkill saw the Christ's head shake
At Hastings, by the Bloody Lake.

THE DISPOSSESSED   [1948]

'and something that . . that is theirs—no longer ours'
stammered to me the Italian page. A wood
seeded & towered suddenly. I understood.—

The Leading Man's especially, and the Juvenile Lead's,
and the Leading Lady's thigh that switches & warms,
and their grimaces, and their flying arms:

our arms, our story. Every seat was sold.
A crone met in a clearing sprouts a beard
and has a tirade. Not a word we heard.

Movement of stone within a woman's heart,   10
abrupt & dominant. They gesture how
fings really are. Rarely a child sings now.

My harpsichord weird as a koto drums
adagio for twilight, for the storm-worn dove
no more de-iced, and the spidery business of love.

The Juvenile Lead's the Leader's arm, one arm
running the whole bole, branches, roots, (O watch)
and the faceless fellow waving from her crotch,

Stalin-unanimous! who procured a vote
and care not use it, who have kept an eye   20
and care not use it, percussive vote, clear eye.

That which a captain and a weaponeer
one day and one more day did, we did, *ach*
we did not, *They* did . . cam slid, the great lock

lodged, and no soul of us all was near was near,—
an evil sky (where the umbrella bloomed)
twirled its mustaches, hissed, the ingenue fumed,

poor virgin, and no hero rides. The race
is done. Drifts through, between the cold black trunks,
the peachblow glory of the perishing sun   30

in empty houses where old things take place.

THREE AROUND THE OLD GENTLEMAN   [1964]

37

His malice was a pimple down his good
big face, with its sly eyes. I must be sorry
Mr Frost has left:
I like it so less I don't understood—
he couldn't hear or see well—all we sift—
but this is a *bad* story.

He had fine stories and was another man
in private; difficult, always. Courteous,
on the whole, in private.
He apologize to Henry, off & on,   10
for two blue slanders; which was good of him.
I don't know how he made it.

Quickly, off stage with all but kindness, now.
I can't say what I have in mind. Bless Frost,
any odd god around.
Gentle his shift, I decussate & command,
stoic deity. For a while here we possessed
an unusual man.

38

The Russian grin bellows his condolence
tó the family: ah but it's Kay,
& Ted, & Chis & Anne,

Henry thinks of: who eased his fearful way
from here, in here, to there. This wants thought.
I won't make it out.

Maybe the source of noble such may come
clearer to dazzled Henry. It may come.
I'd say it will come with pain,
in mystery. I'd rather leave it alone.   10
I do leave it alone.
And down with the listener.

Now he has become, abrupt, an industry.
Professional-Friends-Of-Robert-Frost all over
gap wide their mouths
while the quirky medium of so many truths
is quiet. Let's be quiet. Let us listen:
—What for, Mr Bones?
                    —while he begins to have it out with Horace.

39

Goodbye, sir, & fare well. You're in the clear.
'Nobody' (Mark says   you said) 'is ever found out.'
I figure you were right,
having as Henry got away with murder
for long. Some jarred clock tell me it's late,
not for you who went straight

but for the lorn. Our roof is lefted off
lately: the shooter, and the bourbon man,
and then you got tired.
I'm afraid that's it. I figure you with love,   10
lifey, deathy, but I have a little sense
the rest of us are fired

or fired: be with us: we will blow our best,
our sad wild riffs come easy in that case,
thinking you over,
knowing you resting, who was reborn to rest,
your gorgeous sentence done. Nothing's the same,
sir,—taking cover.

Robert Lowell

b. 1917

Robert Trail Spence Lowell, Jr., was born March 1, 1917, in Boston, the son of a naval officer and a member of the family that includes James Russell Lowell and Amy Lowell. He attended Harvard for two years and then transferred to Kenyon College, where he majored in classics and graduated in 1940. In the same year he entered the Roman Catholic Church. During World War II he was a conscientious objector and served a jail sentence. In 1947 he was appointed Consultant in Poetry at the Library of Congress for a year, was awarded a Guggenheim Fellowship, and received the Pulitzer Prize for Poetry. His volume Life Studies *received a National Book Award in 1959. He has taught at the State University of Iowa, Kenyon, Boston University, and Harvard. He now lives in New York City.*

IN MEMORY OF ARTHUR WINSLOW   [1944]

I
DEATH FROM CANCER

This Easter, Arthur Winslow, less than dead,
Your people set you up in Phillips' House
To settle off your wrestling with the crab—
The claws drop flesh upon your yachting blouse
Until longshoreman Charon come and stab
Through your adjusted bed
And crush the crab. On Boston Basin, shells
Hit water by the Union Boat Club wharf:
You ponder why the coxes' squeakings dwarf
The *resurrexit dominus* of all the bells.   10

Grandfather Winslow, look, the swanboats coast
That island in the Public Gardens, where
The bread-stuffed ducks are brooding, where with tub
And strainer the mid-Sunday Irish scare
The sun-struck shallows for the dusky chub
This Easter, and the ghost
Of risen Jesus walks the waves to run
Arthur upon a trumpeting black swan
Beyond Charles River to the Acheron
Where the wide waters and their voyager are one.   20

II

DUNBARTON

The stones are yellow and the grass is gray
Past Concord by the rotten lake and hill
Where crutch and trumpet meet the limousine
And half-forgotten Starks and Winslows fill
The granite plot and the dwarf pines are green
From watching for the day
When the great year of the little yeomen come
Bringing its landed Promise and the faith
That made the Pilgrim Makers take a lathe
And point their wooden steeples lest the Word be dumb.   30

O fearful witnesses, your day is done:
The minister from Boston waves your shades,
Like children, out of sight and out of mind.
The first selectman of Dunbarton spreads
Wreaths of New Hampshire pine cones on the lined
Casket where the cold sun
Is melting. But, at last, the end is reached;
We start our cars. The preacher's mouthings still
Deafen my poor relations on the hill:
Their sunken landmarks echo what our fathers preached.   40

III

FIVE YEARS LATER

This Easter, Arthur Winslow, five years gone
I came to mourn you, not to praise the craft
That netted you a million dollars, late

Hosing out gold in Colorado's waste,
Then lost it all in Boston real estate.
Now from the train, at dawn
Leaving Columbus in Ohio, shell
On shell of our stark culture strikes the sun
To fill my head with all our fathers won
When Cotton Mather wrestled with the fiends from hell.   50

You must have hankered for our family's craft:
The block-house Edward made, the Governor,
At Marshfield, and the slight coin-silver spoons
The Sheriff beat to shame the gaunt Revere,
And General Stark's coarse bas-relief in bronze
Set on your granite shaft
In rough Dunbarton; for what else could bring
You, Arthur, to the veined and alien West
But devil's notions that your gold as least
Could give back life to men who whipped or backed the
    King?   60

IV

A PRAYER FOR MY GRANDFATHER TO OUR LADY

Mother, for these three hundred years or more
Neither our clippers nor our slavers reached
The haven of your peace in this Bay State:
Neither my father nor his father. Beached
On these dry flats of fishy real estate,
O Mother, I implore
Your scorched, blue thunderbreasts of love to pour
Buckets of blessings on my burning head
Until I rise like Lazarus from the dead:
Lavabis nos et super nivem delabor   70

"On Copley Square, I saw you hold the door
To Trinity, the costly Church, and saw
The painted Paradise of harps and lutes
Sink like Atlantis in the Devil's jaw
And knock the Devil's teeth out by the roots;
But when I strike for shore
I find no painted idols to adore:

Hell is burned out, heaven's harp-strings are slack.
Mother, run to the chalice, and bring back
Blood on your finger-tips for Lazarus who was poor."   80

CHRISTMAS EVE UNDER HOOKER'S
STATUE [1944]

Tonight a blackout. Twenty years ago
I hung my stocking on the tree, and hell's
Serpent entwined the apple in the toe
To sting the child with knowledge. Hooker's heels
Kicking at nothing in the shifting snow,
A cannon and a cairn of cannon balls
Rusting before the blackened Statehouse, know
How the long horn of plenty broke like glass
In Hooker's gauntlets. Once I came from Mass;

Now storm-clouds shelter Christmas, once again   10
Mars meets his fruitless star with open arms,
His heavy sabre flashes with the rime,
The war-god's bronzed and empty forehead forms
Anonymous machinery from raw men;
The cannon on the Common cannot stun
The blundering butcher as he rides on Time—
The barrel clinks with holly. I am cold:
I ask for bread, my father gives me mould;

His stocking is full of stones, Santa in red
Is crowned with wizened berries. Man of war,   20
Where is the summer's garden? In its bed
The ancient speckled serpent will appear,
And black-eyed susan with her frizzled head.
When Chancellorsville mowed down the volunteer,
"All wars are boyish," Herman Melville said;
But we are old, our fields are running wild:
Till Christ again turn wanderer and child.

THE DRUNKEN FISHERMAN   [1944]

Wallowing in this bloody sty,
I cast for fish that pleased my eye
(Truly Jehovah's bow suspends
No pots of gold to weight its ends);
Only the blood-mouthed rainbow trout
Rose to my bait. They flopped about
My canvas creel until the moth
Corrupted its unstable cloth.

A calendar to tell the day;
A handkerchief to wave away   10
The gnats; a couch unstuffed with storm
Pouching a bottle in one arm;
A whiskey bottle full of worms;
And bedroom slacks: are these fit terms
To mete the worm whose molten rage
Boils in the belly of old age?

Once fishing was a rabbit's foot—
O wind blow cold, O wind blow hot,
Let suns stay in or suns step out:
Life danced a jig on the sperm-whale's spout—   20
The fisher's fluent and obscene
Catches kept his conscience clean.
Children, the raging memory drools
Over the glory of past pools.

Now the hot river, ebbing, hauls
Its bloody waters into holes;
A grain of sand inside my shoe
Mimics the moon that might undo
Man and Creation too; remorse,
Stinking, has puddled up its source;   30
Here tantrums thrash to a whale's rage.
This is the pot-hole of old age.

Is there no way to cast my hook
Out of this dynamited brook?
The Fisher's sons must cast about
When shallow waters peter out.
I will catch Christ with a greased worm,
And when the Prince of Darkness stalks
My bloodstream to its Stygian term . . .
On water the Man-Fisher walks.   40

CHILDREN OF LIGHT   [1944]

Our fathers wrung their bread from stocks and stones
And fenced their gardens with the Redman's bones;
Embarking from the Nether Land of Holland,
Pilgrims unhouseled by Geneva's night,
They planted here the Serpent's seeds of light;
And here the pivoting searchlights probe to shock
The riotous glass houses built on rock,
And candles gutter by an empty altar,
And light is where the landless blood of Cain
Is burning, burning the unburied grain.   10

THE EXILE'S RETURN   [1946]

There mounts in squalls a sort of rusty mire,
Not ice, not snow, to leaguer the Hôtel
De Ville, where braced pig-iron dragons grip
The blizzard to their rigor mortis. A bell
Grumbles when the reverberations strip
The thatching from its spire,
The search-guns click and spit and split up timber
And nick the slate roofs on the Holstenwall
Where torn-up tilestones crown the victor. Fall
And winter, spring and summer, guns unlimber   10
And lumber down the narrow gabled street

Past your gray, sorry and ancestral house
Where the dynamited walnut tree
Shadows a squat, old, wind-torn gate and cows
The Yankee commandant. You will not see
Strutting children or meet
The peg-leg and reproachful chancellor
With a forget-me-not in his button-hole
When the unseasoned liberators roll
Into the Market Square, ground arms before   20
The Rathaus; but already lily-stands
Burgeon the risen Rhineland, and a rough
Cathedral lifts its eye. Pleasant enough,
Voi ch'entrate, and your life is in your hands.

COLLOQUY IN BLACK ROCK   [1946]

Here the jack-hammer jabs into the ocean;
My heart, you race and stagger and demand
More blood-gangs for your nigger-brass percussions,
Till I, the stunned machine of your devotion,
Clanging upon this cymbal of a hand,
Am rattled screw and footloose. All discussions

End in low water, slump, and dumps and death.
My heart, beat faster, faster. In Black Mud
Hungarian machinists give their blood
For the martyr Stephen, who was stoned to death.   10

Black Mud, a name to conjure with: O mud
For watermelons gutted to the crust,
Mud for the mole-tide harbor, mud for mouse,
Mud for the armored Diesel fishing tubs that thud
A year and a day to wind and tidal rust,
The heart-skip and the quake that shakes my house

To Jericho, a clay and trumpet death.
My heart, beat faster, faster. In Black Mud

Stephen the martyr was broken down to blood:
Our ransom is the rubble of his death.   20

Christ walks on the black water. In Black Mud
Darts the Kingfisher. On Corpus Christi, heart,
Over the drum-beat of St. Stephen's choir
I hear him, *Stupor Mundi*, and the mud
Flies from his hunching wings and beak—my heart,
The blue kingfisher dives on you in fire.

THE QUAKER GRAVEYARD IN NANTUCKET   [1946]

(For Warren Winslow, Dead at Sea)

> *Let man have dominion over the fishes of the sea and the fowls of the air
> and the beasts and the whole earth, and every creeping creature that moveth
> upon the earth.*

I

A brackish reach of shoal off Madaket,—
The sea was still breaking violently and night
Had steamed into our North Atlantic Fleet,
When the drowned sailor clutched the drag-net. Light
Flashed from his matted head and marble feet,
He grappled at the net
With the coiled, hurdling muscles of his thighs:
The corpse was bloodless, a botch of reds and whites,
Its open, staring eyes
Were lustreless dead-lights   10
Or cabin-windows on a stranded hulk
Heavy with sand. We weight the body, close
Its eyes and heave it seaward whence it came,
Where the heel-headed dogfish barks its nose
On Ahab's void and forehead; and the name
Is blocked in yellow chalk.
Sailors, who pitch this portent at the sea
Where dreadnoughts shall confess
Its heel-bent deity,

When you are powerless   20
To sand-bag this Atlantic bulwark, faced
By the earth-shaker, green, unwearied, chaste
In his steel scales: ask for no Orphean lute
To pluck life back. The guns of the steeled fleet
Recoil and then repeat
The hoarse salute.

II

Whenever winds are moving and their breath
Heaves at the roped-in bulwarks of this pier,
The terns and sea-gulls tremble at your death
In these home waters. Sailor, can you hear   30
The Pequod's sea wings, beating landward, fall
Headlong and break on our Atlantic wall
Off 'Sconset, where the yawing S-boats splash
The bellbuoy, with ballooning spinnakers,
As the entangled, screeching mainsheet clears
The blocks: off Madaket, where lubbers lash
The heavy surf and throw their long lead squids
For blue-fish? Sea-gulls blink their heavy lids
Seaward. The winds' wings beat upon the stones,
Cousin, and scream for you and the claws rush   40
At the sea's throat and wring it in the slush
Of this old Quaker graveyard where the bones
Cry out in the long night for the hurt beast
Bobbing by Ahab's whaleboats in the East.

III

All you recovered from Poseidon died
With you, my cousin, and the harrowed brine
Is fruitless on the blue beard of the god,
Stretching beyond us to the castles in Spain,
Nantucket's westward haven. To Cape Cod
Guns, cradled on the tide,   50
Blast the eelgrass about a waterclock
Of bilge and backwash, roil the salt and sand
Lashing earth's scaffold, rock
Our warships in the hand
Of the great God, where time's contrition blues

Whatever it was these Quaker sailors lost
In the mad scramble of their lives. They died
When time was open-eyed,
Wooden and childish; only bones abide
There, in the nowhere, where their boats were tossed   60
Sky-high, where mariners had fabled news
Of IS, the whited monster. What it cost
Them is their secret. In the sperm-whale's slick
I see the Quakers drown and hear their cry:
"If God himself had not been on our side,
If God himself had not been on our side,
When the Atlantic rose against us, why,
Then it had swallowed us up quick."

IV

This is the end of the whaleroad and the whale
Who spewed Nantucket bones on the thrashed swell   70
And stirred the troubled waters to whirlpools
To send the Pequod packing off to hell:
This is the end of them, three-quarters fools,
Snatching at straws to sail
Seaward and seaward on the turntail whale,
Spouting out blood and water as it rolls,
Sick as a dog to these Atlantic shoals:
Clamavimus, O depths. Let the sea-gulls wail

For water, for the deep where the high tide
Mutters to its hurt self, mutters and ebbs.   80
Waves wallow in their wash, go out and out,
Leave only the death-rattle of the crabs,
The beach increasing, its enormous snout
Sucking the ocean's side.
This is the end of running on the waves;
We are poured out like water. Who will dance
The mast-lashed master of Leviathans
Up from this field of Quakers in their unstoned graves?

V

When the whale's viscera go and the roll
Of its corruption overruns this world   90

Beyond tree-swept Nantucket and Wood's Hole
And Martha's Vineyard, Sailor, will your sword
Whistle and fall and sink into the fat?
In the great ash-pit of Jehoshaphat
The bones cry for the blood of the white whale,
The fat flukes arch and whack about its ears,
The death-lance churns into the sanctuary, tears
The gun-blue swingle, heaving like a flail,
And hacks the coiling life out: it works and drags
And rips the sperm-whale's midriff into rags,   100
Gobbets of blubber spill to wind and weather,
Sailor, and gulls go round the stoven timbers
Where the morning stars sing out together
And thunder shakes the white surf and dismembers
The red flag hammered in the mast-head. Hide,
Our steel, Jonas Messias, in Thy side.

VI

OUR LADY OF WALSINGHAM

There once the penitents took off their shoes
And then walked barefoot the remaining mile;
And the small trees, a stream and hedgerows file
Slowly along the munching English lane,   110
Like cows to the old shrine, until you lose
Track of your dragging pain.
The stream flows down under the druid tree,
Shiloah's whirlpools gurgle and make glad
The castle of God. Sailor, you were glad
And whistled Sion by that stream. But see:

Our Lady, too small for her canopy,
Sits near the altar. There's no comeliness
At all or charm in that expressionless
Face with its heavy eyelids. As before,   120
This face, for centuries a memory,
Non est species, neque decor,
Expressionless, expresses God: it goes
Past castled Sion. She knows what God knows,
Not Calvary's Cross nor crib at Bethlehem
Now, and the world shall come to Walsingham.

VII

The empty winds are creaking and the oak
Splatters and splatters on the cenotaph,
The boughs are trembling and a gaff
Bobs on the untimely stroke   130
Of the greased wash exploding on a shoal-bell
In the old mouth of the Atlantic. It's well;
Atlantic, you are fouled with the blue sailors,
Sea-monsters, upward angel, downward fish:
Unmarried and corroding, spare of flesh
Mart once of supercilious, wing'd clippers,
Atlantic, where your bell-trap guts its spoil
You could cut the brackish winds with a knife
Here in Nantucket, and cast up the time
When the Lord God formed man from the sea's slime   140
And breathed into his face the breath of life,
And blue-lung'd combers lumbered to the kill.
The Lord survives the rainbow of His will.

AS A PLANE TREE BY THE WATER   [1946]

Darkness has called to darkness, and disgrace
Elbows about our windows in this planned
Babel of Boston where our money talks
And multiplies the darkness of a land
Of preparation where the Virgin walks
And roses spiral her enamelled face
Or fall to splinters on unwatered streets.
Our Lady of Babylon, go by, go by,
I was once the apple of your eye;
Flies, flies are on the plane tree, on the streets.   10

The flies, the flies, the flies of Babylon
Buzz in my ear-drums while the devil's long
Dirge of the people detonates the hour
For floating cities where his golden tongue
Enchants the masons of the Babel Tower

To raise tomorrow's city to the sun
That never sets upon these hell-fire streets
Of Boston, where the sunlight is a sword
Striking at the withholder of the Lord:
Flies, flies are on the plane tree, on the streets.   20

Flies strike the miraculous waters of the iced
Atlantic and the eyes of Bernadette
Who saw Our Lady standing in the cave
At Massabielle, saw her so squarely that
Her vision put out reason's eyes. The grave
Is open-mouthed and swallowed up in Christ.
O walls of Jericho! And all the streets
To our Atlantic wall are singing: "Sing,
Sing for the resurrection of the King."
Flies, flies are on the plane tree, on the streets.   30

MR. EDWARDS AND THE SPIDER   [1946]

I saw the spiders marching through the air,
  Swimming from tree to tree that mildewed day
    In latter August when the hay
    Came creaking to the barn. But where
      The wind is westerly,
  Where gnarled November makes the spiders fly
  Into the apparitions of the sky,
    They purpose nothing but their ease and die
Urgently beating east to sunrise and the sea;

  What are we in the hands of the great God?   10
  It was in vain you set up thorn and briar
    In battle array against the fire
    And treason crackling in your blood;
      For the wild thorns grow tame
  And will do nothing to oppose the flame;
  Your lacerations tell the losing game
    You play against a sickness past your cure.
How will the hands be strong? How will the heart endure?

A very little thing, a little worm,
Or hourglass-blazoned spider, it is said,   20
    Can kill a tiger. Will the dead
    Hold up his mirror and affirm
      To the four winds the smell
And flash of his authority? It's well
If God who holds you to the pit of hell,
Much as one holds a spider, will destroy,
Baffle and dissipate your soul. As a small boy

On Windsor Marsh, I saw the spider die
When thrown into the bowels of fierce fire:
    There's no long struggle, no desire   30
    To get up on its feet and fly—
      It stretches out its feet
And dies. This is the sinner's last retreat;
Yes, and no strength exerted on the heat
Then sinews the abolished will, when sick
And full of burning, it will whistle on a brick.

But who can plumb the sinking of that soul?
Josiah Hawley, picture yourself cast
    Into a brick-kiln where the blast
    Fans your quick vitals to a coal—   40
      If measured by a glass,
How long would it seem burning! Let there pass
A minute, ten, ten trillion; but the blaze
Is infinite eternal: this is death,
To die and know it. This is the Black Widow, death.

AFTER THE SURPRISING CONVERSIONS   [1946]

September twenty-second, Sir: today
I answer. In the latter part of May,
Hard on our Lord's Ascension, it began
To be more sensible. A gentleman

Of more than common understanding, strict
In morals, pious in behavior, kicked
Against our goad. A man of some renown,
An useful, honored person in the town,
He came of melancholy parents; prone
To secret spells, for years they kept alone—   10
His uncle, I believe, was killed of it:
Good people, but of too much or little wit.
I preached one Sabbath on a text from Kings;
He showed concernment for his soul. Some things
In his experience were hopeful. He
Would sit and watch the wind knocking a tree
And praise this countryside our Lord has made.
Once when a poor man's heifer died, he laid
A shilling on the doorsill; though a thirst
For loving shook him like a snake, he durst   20
Not entertain much hope of his estate
In heaven. Once we saw him sitting late
Behind his attic window by a light
That guttered on his Bible; through that night
He meditated terror, and he seemed
Beyond advice or reason, for he dreamed
That he was called to trumpet Judgment Day
To Concord. In the latter part of May
He cut his throat. And though the coroner
Judged him delirious, soon a noisome stir   30
Palsied our village. At Jehovah's nod
Satan seemed more let loose amongst us: God
Abandoned us to Satan, and he pressed
Us hard, until we thought we could not rest
Till we had done with life. Content was gone.
All the good work was quashed. We were undone.
The breath of God had carried out a planned
And sensible withdrawal from this land;
The multitude, once unconcerned with doubt,
Once neither callous, curious nor devout,   40
Jumped at broad noon, as though some peddler groaned
At it in its familiar twang: "My friend,
Cut your own throat. Cut your own throat. Now! Now!"
September twenty-second, Sir, the bough

Cracks with the unpicked apples, and at dawn
The small-mouth bass breaks water, gorged with spawn.

WHERE THE RAINBOW ENDS   [1946]

I saw the sky descending, black and white,
Not blue, on Boston where the winters wore
The skulls to jack-o'-lanterns on the slates,
And Hunger's skin-and-bone retrievers tore
The chickadee and shrike. The thorn tree waits
Its victim and tonight
The worms will eat the deadwood to the foot
Of Ararat: the scythers, Time and Death,
Helmed locusts, move upon the tree of breath;
The wild ingrafted olive and the root   10

Are withered, and a winter drifts to where
The Pepperpot, ironic rainbow, spans
Charles River and its scales of scorched-earth miles
I saw my city in the Scales, the pans
Of judgment rising and descending. Piles
Of dead leaves char the air—
And I am a red arrow on this graph
Of Revelations. Every dove is sold
The Chapel's sharp-shinned eagle shifts its hold
On serpent-Time, the rainbow's epitaph.   20

In Boston serpents whistle at the cold.
The victim climbs the altar steps and sings:
"Hosannah to the lion, lamb, and beast
Who fans the furnace face of IS with wings:
I breathe the ether of my marriage feast."
At the high altar, gold
And a fair cloth. I kneel and the wings beat
My cheek. What can the dove of Jesus give
You now but wisdom, exile? Stand and live,
The dove has brought an olive branch to eat.   30

FALLING ASLEEP OVER THE AENEID   [1950]

> (An old man in Concord forgets to go to morning service. He
> falls asleep, while reading Vergil, and dreams that he is Aeneas
> at the funeral of Pallas, an Italian prince.)

The sun is blue and scarlet on my page,
And *yuck-a, yuck-a, yuck-a, yuck-a,* rage
The yellowhammers mating. Yellow fire
Blankets the captives dancing on their pyre,
And the scorched lictor screams and drops his rod.
Trojans are singing to their drunken God,
Ares. Their helmets catch on fire. Their files
Clank by the body of my comrade—miles
Of filings! Now the scythe-wheeled chariot rolls
Before their lances long as vaulting poles,   10
And I stand up and heil the thousand men,
Who carry Pallas to the bird-priest. Then
The bird-priest groans, and as his birds foretold,
I greet the body, lip to lip. I hold
The sword that Dido used. It tries to speak,
A bird with Dido's sworded breast. Its beak
Clangs and ejaculates the Punic word
I hear the bird-priest chirping like a bird.
I groan a little. "Who am I, and why?"
It asks, a boy's face, though its arrow-eye   20
Is working from its socket. "Brother, try,
O Child of Aphrodite, try to die:
To die is life." His harlots hang his bed
With feathers of his long-tailed birds. His head
Is yawning like a person. The plumes blow;
The beard and eyebrows ruffle. Face of snow,
You are the flower that country girls have caught,
A wild bee-pillaged honey-suckle brought
To the returning bridegroom—the design
Has not yet left it, and the petals shine;   30
The earth, its mother, has, at last, no help:
It is itself. The broken-winded yelp
Of my Phoenician hounds, that fills the brush

With snapping twigs and flying, cannot flush
The ghost of Pallas. But I take his pall,
Stiff with its gold and purple, and recall
How Dido hugged it to her, while she toiled,
Laughing—her golden threads, a serpent coiled
In cypress. Now I lay it like a sheet;
It clinks and settles down upon his feet,   40
The careless yellow hair that seemed to burn
Beforehand. Left foot, right foot—as they turn,
More pyres are rising: armored horses, bronze,
And gagged Italians, who must file by ones
Across the bitter river, when my thumb
Tightens into their wind-pipes. The beaks drum;
Their headman's cow-horned death's-head bites its tongue,
And stiffens, as it eyes the hero slung
Inside his feathered hammock on the crossed
Staves of the eagles that we winged. Our cost   50
Is nothing to the lovers, whoring Mars
And Venus, father's lover. Now his car's
Plumage is ready, and my marshals fetch
His squire, Acoetes, white with age, to hitch
Aethon, the hero's charger, and its ears
Prick, and it steps and steps, and stately tears
Lather its teeth; and then the harlots bring
The hero's charms and baton—but the King,
Vain-glorious Turnus, carried off the rest.
"I was myself, but Ares thought it best   60
The way it happened." At the end of time,
He sets his spear, as my descendants climb
The knees of Father Time, his beard of scalps,
His scythe, the arc of steel that crowns the Alps.
The elephants of Carthage hold those snows,
Turms of Numidian horse unsling their bows,
The flaming turkey-feathered arrows swarm
Beyond the Alps "Pallas," I raise my arm
And shout, "Brother, eternal health. Farewell
Forever," Church is over, and its bell   70
Frightens the yellowhammers, as I wake
And watch the whitecaps wrinkle up the lake.
Mother's great-aunt, who died when I was eight,
Stands by our parlor sabre. "Boy, it's late.

Vergil must keep the Sabbath." Eighty years!
It all comes back. My Uncle Charles appears.
Blue-capped and bird-like. Phillips Brooks and Grant
Are frowning at his coffin, and my aunt,
Hearing his colored volunteers parade
Through Concord, laughs, and tells her English maid   80
To clip his yellow nostril hairs, and fold
His colors on him . . . It is I, I hold
His sword to keep from falling, for the dust
On the stuffed birds is breathless, for the bust
Of young Augustus weighs on Vergil's shelf:
It scowls into my glasses at itself.

WORDS FOR HART CRANE   [1959]

"When the Pulitzers showered on some dope
or screw who flushed our dry mouths out with soap,
few people would consider why I took
to stalking sailors, and scattered Uncle Sam's
phoney gold-plated laurels to the birds.
Because I knew my Whitman like a book,
stranger in America, tell my country: I,
Catullus redivivus, once the rage
of the Village and Paris, used to play my role
of homosexual, wolfing the stray lambs   10
who hungered by the Place de la Concorde.
My profit was a pocket with a hole.
Who asks for me, the Shelley of my age,
must lay his heart out for my bed and board."

SKUNK HOUR   [1959]

(For Elizabeth Bishop)

Nautilus Island's hermit
heiress still lives through winter in her Spartan cottage;

her sheep still graze above the sea.
Her son's a bishop. Her farmer
is first selectman in our village;
she's in her dotage.

Thirsting for
the hierarchic privacy
of Queen Victoria's century,
she buys up all   10
the eyesores facing her shore,
and lets them fall.

The season's ill—
we've lost our summer millionaire,
who seemed to leap from an L. L. Bean
catalogue. His nine-knot yawl
was auctioned off to lobstermen.
A red fox stain covers Blue Hill.

And now our fairy
decorator brightens his shop for fall;   20
his fishnet's filled with orange cork,
orange, his cobbler's bench and awl;
there is no money in his work,
he'd rather marry.

One dark night,
my Tudor Ford climbed the hill's skull;
I watched for love-cars. Lights turned down,
they lay together, hull to hull,
where the graveyard shelves on the town....
My mind's not right.   30

A car radio bleats,
"Love, O careless Love...." I hear
my ill-spirit sob in each blood cell,
as if my hand were at its throat....
I myself am hell;
nobody's here—

only skunks, that search
in the moonlight for a bite to eat.
They march on their soles up Main Street:
white stripes, moonstruck eyes' red fire   40
under the chalk-dry and spar spire
of the Trinitarian Church.

I stand on top
of our back steps and breathe the rich air—
a mother skunk with her column of kittens swills the
      garbage pail.
She jabs her wedge-head in a cup
of sour cream, drops her ostrich tail,
and will not scare.

THE PUBLIC GARDEN   [1964]

Burnished, burned-out, still burning as the year
you lead me to our stamping ground.
The city and its cruising cars surround
the Public Garden. All's alive—
the children crowding home from school at five,
punting a football in the bricky air,
the sailors and their pick-ups under trees
with Latin labels. And the jaded flock
of swanboats paddles to its dock.
The park is drying.   10
Dead leaves thicken to a ball
inside the basin of a fountain, where
the heads of four stone lions stare
and suck on empty fawcets. Night
deepens. From the arched bridge, we see
the shedding park-bound mallards, how they keep
circling and diving in the lanternlight,
searching for something hidden in the muck.
And now the moon, earth's friend, that cared so much
for us, and cared so little, comes again—   20

always a stranger! As we walk,
it lies like chalk
over the waters. Everything's aground.
Remember summer? Bubbles filled
the fountain, and we splashed. We drowned
in Eden, while Jehovah's grass-green lyre
was rustling all about us in the leaves
that gurgled by us, turning upside down ...
The fountain's failing waters flash around
the garden. Nothing catches fire.   30

Richard Wilbur

b. 1921

Born March 1, 1921, in New York City, Richard Wilbur graduated from Amherst College, served in the United States Army in Europe in World War II, was a member of the Society of Fellows and took an M.A. at Harvard, and taught at Harvard and at Wellesley. He has won a number of fellowships, prizes, and awards for his poetry, most notably the Pulitzer Prize in 1957. He is now professor of English at Wesleyan University in Connecticut.

FIRST SNOW IN ALSACE   [1947]

The snow came down last night like moths
Burned on the moon; it fell till dawn,
Covered the town with simple cloths.

Absolute snow lies rumpled on
What shellbursts scattered and deranged,
Entangled railings, crevassed lawn.

As if it did not know they'd changed,
Snow smoothly clasps the roofs of homes
Fear-gutted, trustless and estranged.

The ration stacks are milky domes;   10
Across the ammunition pile
The snow has climbed in sparkling combs.

You think: beyond the town a mile
Or two, this snowfall fills the eyes
Of soldiers dead a little while.

Persons and persons in disguise,
Walking the new air white and fine,
Trade glances quick with shared surprise.

At children's windows, heaped, benign,
As always, winter shines the most,   20
And frost makes marvelous designs.

The night guard coming from his post,
Ten first-snows back in thought, walks slow
And warms him with a boyish boast:

He was the first to see the snow.

BELL SPEECH   [1947]

The selfsame toothless voice for death or bridal:
It has been long since men would give the time
To tell each someone's-change with a special chime,
And a toll for every year the dead walked through.
And mostly now, above this urgent idle
Town, the bells mark time, as they can do.

This bavardage of early and of late
Is what is wanted, and yet the bells beseech
By some excess that's in their stricken speech
Less meanly to be heard. Were this not so,   10
Why should Great Paul shake every window plate
To warn me that my pocket watch is slow?

Whether or not attended, bells will chant
With a clear dumb sound, and wide of any word
Expound our hours, clear as the waves are heard
Crashing at Mount Desert, from far at sea,
And dumbly joining, as the night's descent
Makes deltas into dark of every tree.

Great Paul, great pail of sound, still dip and draw
Dark speech from the deep and quiet steeple well,   20
Bring dark for doctrine, do but dim and quell
All voice in yours, while earth will give you breath.
Still gather to a language without flaw
Our loves, and all the hours of our death.

STILL, CITIZEN SPARROW   [1950]

Still, citizen sparrow, this vulture which you call
Unnatural, let him but lumber again to air
Over the rotten office, let him bear
The carrion ballast up, and at the tall

Tip of the sky lie cruising. Then you'll see
That no more beautiful bird is in heaven's height,
No wider more placid wings, no watchfuller flight;
He shoulders nature there, the frightfully free,

The naked-headed one. Pardon him, you
Who dart in the orchard aisles, for it is he   10
Devours death, mocks mutability,
Has heart to make an end, keeps nature new.

Thinking of Noah, childheart, try to forget
How for so many bedlam hours his saw
Soured the song of birds with its wheezy gnaw,
And the slam of his hammer all the day beset

The people's ears. Forget that he could bear
To see the towns like coral under the keel,
And the fields so dismal deep. Try rather to feel
How high and weary it was, on the waters where   20

He rocked his only world, and everyone's.
Forgive the hero, you who would have died

Gladly with all you knew; he rode that tide
To Ararat; all men are Noah's sons.

THE DEATH OF A TOAD   [1950]

A toad the power mower caught,
Chewed and clipped of a leg, with a hobbling hop has got
    To the garden verge, and sanctuaried him
    Under the cineraria leaves, in the shade
        Of the ashen heartshaped leaves, in a dim,
            Low, and a final glade.

The rare original heartsblood goes,
Spends on the earthen hide, in the folds and wizenings, flows
    In the gutters of the banked and staring eyes. He lies
    As still as if he would return to stone,   10
        And soundlessly attending, dies
            Toward some deep monotone,

Toward misted and ebullient seas
And cooling shores, toward lost Amphibia's emperies.
    Day dwindles, drowning, and at length is gone
    In the wide and antique eyes, which still appear
        To watch, across the castrate lawn,
            The haggard daylight steer.

LAMARCK ELABORATED   [1956]

"The environment creates the organ."

The Greeks were wrong who said our eyes have rays;
Not from these sockets or these sparkling poles
Comes the illumination of our days.
It was the sun that bored these two blue holes.

It was the song of doves begot the ear
And not the ear that first conceived of sound:
That organ bloomed in vibrant atmosphere,
As music conjured Ilium from the ground.

The yielding water, the repugnant stone,
The poisoned berry and the flaring rose   10
Attired in sense the tactless finger-bone
And set the taste-buds and inspired the nose.

Out of our vivid ambiance came unsought
All sense but that most formidably dim.
The shell of balance rolls in seas of thought.
It was the mind that taught the head to swim.

Newtonian numbers set to cosmic lyres
Whelmed us in whirling worlds we could not know,
And by the imagined floods of our desires
The voice of Sirens gave us vertigo.   20

PANGLOSS'S SONG: A COMIC-OPERA
LYRIC   [1961]

I

Dear boy, you will not hear me speak
   With sorrow or with rancor
Of what has paled my rosy cheek
   And blasted it with canker;
'Twas Love, great Love, that did the deed
   Through Nature's gentle laws,
And how should ill effects proceed
   From so divine a cause?

Sweet honey comes from bees that sting,
   As you are well aware;   10
To one adept in reasoning,
Whatever pains disease may bring

Are but the tangy seasoning
   To Love's delicious fare.

II

Columbus and his men, they say,
   Conveyed the virus hither
Whereby my features rot away
   And vital powers wither;
Yet had they not traversed the seas
   And come infected back,   20
Why, think of all the luxuries
   That modern life would lack!

All bitter things conduce to sweet,
   As this example shows;
Without the little spirochete
We'd have no chocolate to eat,
Nor would tobacco's fragrance greet
   The European nose.

III

Each nation guards its native land
   With cannon and with sentry,   30
Inspectors look for contraband
   At every port of entry,
Yet nothing can prevent the spread
   Of Love's divine disease:
It rounds the world from bed to bed
   As pretty as you please.

Men worship Venus everywhere,
   As plainly may be seen;
The decorations which I bear
Are nobler than the Croix de Guerre,   40
And gained in service of our fair
   And universal Queen.

James Dickey

b. 1923

James Dickey was born February 2, 1923, in Atlanta, Georgia, and educated at Clemson College and Vanderbilt University. During both World War II and the Korean War he served in the Air Force. After holding a Sewanee Review *fellowship in poetry in 1954–1955, he worked for nearly six years in advertising, leaving business in 1961 to hold a Guggenheim Fellowship. He has taught at Rice Institute and the University of Florida and at Reed College, where he was poet in residence. He is now writer in residence at San Fernando Valley State College.*

THE HEAVEN OF ANIMALS   [1962]

Here they are. The soft eyes open.
If they have lived in a wood
It is a wood.
If they have lived on plains
It is grass rolling
Under their feet forever.

Having no souls, they have come,
Anyway, beyond their knowing.
Their instincts wholly bloom
And they rise.   10
The soft eyes open.

To match them, the landscape flowers,
Outdoing, desperately
Outdoing what is required:

The richest wood,
The deepest field.

For some of these,
It could not be the place
It is, without blood.
These hunt, as they have done,   20
But with claws and teeth grown perfect,

More deadly than they can believe.
They stalk more silently,
And crouch on the limbs of trees,
And their descent
Upon the bright backs of their prey

May take years
In a sovereign floating of joy.
And those that are hunted
Know this as their life,   30
Their reward: to walk

Under such trees in full knowledge
Of what is in glory above them,
And to feel no fear,
But acceptance, compliance.
Fulfilling themselves without pain

At the cycle's center,
They tremble, they walk
Under the tree,
They fall, they are torn,   40
They rise, they walk again.

BETWEEN TWO PRISONERS   [1962]

I would not wish to sit
In my shape bound together with wire,

Wedged into a child's sprained desk
In the schoolhouse under the palm tree.
Only those who did could have done it.

One bled from a cut on his temple,
And sat with his yellow head bowed,
His wound for him painfully thinking.
A belief in words grew upon them
That the unbound, who walk, cannot know.   10

The guard at the window leaned close
In a movement he took from the palm tree,
To hear, in a foreign tongue,
All things which cannot be said.
In the splintering clapboard room

They rested the sides of their faces
On the tops of the desks as they talked.
Because of the presence of children
In the deep signs carved in the desk tops,
Signs on the empty blackboard   20

Began, like a rain, to appear.
In the luminous chalks of all colors,
Green face, yellow breast, white sails
Whose wing feathers made the wall burn
Like a waterfall seen in a fever,

An angel came boldly to light
From his hands casting green, ragged bolts.
Each having the shape of a palm leaf.
Also traced upon darkness in chalk
Was the guard at the rear window leaning   30

Through the red, vital strokes of his tears.
Behind him, men lying with swords
As with women, heard themselves sing,
And woke, then, terribly knowing
That they were a death squad, singing

In its sleep, in the middle of a war.
A wind sprang out of the tree.
The guard awoke by the window,
And found he had talked to himself
All night, in two voices, of Heaven.   40

He stood in the sunlit playground
Where the quiet boys knelt together
In their bloodletting trusses of wire,
And saw their mussed, severed heads
Make the ground jump up like a dog.

I watched the small guard be hanged
A year later, to the day,
In a closed horse stall in Manila.
No one knows what language he spoke
As his face changed into all colors,   50

And gave off his red, promised tears,
Or if he learned blindly to read
A child's deep, hacked hieroglyphics
Which can call up an angel from nothing,
Or what was said for an instant, there,

In the tied, scribbled dark, between him
And a figure drawn hugely in chalk,
Speaking words that can never be spoken
Except in a foreign tongue,
In the end, at the end of a war.   60

THE SCRATCH   [1962]

Once hid in a fiery twist
Of brier, it binds my wrist.
In this marked place, on a stone,
I watchfully sit down
To lift it wisely, and see

Blood come, as at a play,
Which shall fall outside my life.
It knows neither stone nor leaf,
Nor how it has come from my heart
To find its true color in light.   10
The glaze of my death is upon it
In the shadowy sun, and yet
A merciful rust shall set in
To kill, not me, but my pain.
My arm opened up by a thorn,
I feel the no-soul of the rock;
I hear, through the trees, the cock
Shout out his long-necked cry.
My patience comes over the wood,
And, caught in the silence of blood,   20
The wind in the leaves stands still
And delivers its green to my will.
I raise my other-armed sleeve,
And wipe, in a kind of love,
The wellspring of love from its bed,
And, glancing about for the dead,
Look distantly off at my blood
As it forms upon air, as if
It were the first blood of my life,
And the last thing of earth that I owned.   30
I conjure up sons, all crowned,
Who this drop shall not inherit,
And women who shall not share it,
Who might have borne me that son
To sit on a moss-backed stone
And master the kingdom of silence
Forever: as I do, once.
I feel more alive thereby
Than when the same blood in my eye
Of sleep, brought my real son,   40
Or my wife, that heavenly one.
I have had no vision but this
Of blood unable to pass
Between father and son,
Yet wedding the brain and the stone,

The cock's cutting cry and the thorn,
And binding me, whole, in a wood,
To a prince of impossible blood.
The rock shall inherit my soul.
The gem at my wrist is dull,   50
And may or may never fall.
Which will be, I do not know.
I shall dream of a crown till I do.

THE DUSK OF HORSES   [1964]

Right under their noses, the green
Of the field is paling away
Because of something fallen from the sky.

They see this, and put down
Their long heads deeper in grass
That only just escapes reflecting them

As the dream of a millpond would.
The color green flees over the grass
Like an insect, following the red sun over

The next hill. The grass is white.   10
There is no cloud so dark and white at once;
There is no pool at dawn that deepens

Their faces and thirsts as this does.
Now they are feeding on solid
Cloud, and, one by one,

With nails as silent as stars among the wood
Hewed down years ago and now rotten,
The stalls are put up around them.

Now if they lean, they come
On wood on any side. Not touching it, they sleep.   20
No beast ever lived who understood

What happened among the sun's fields,
Or cared why the color of grass
Fled over the hill while he stumbled,

Led by the halter to sleep
On his four taxed, worthy legs.
Each thinks he awakens where

The sun is black on the rooftop,
That the green is dancing in the next pasture,
And that the way to sleep   30

In a cloud, or in a risen lake,
Is to walk as though he were still
In the drained field standing, head down,

To pretend to sleep when led,
And thus to go under the ancient white
Of the meadow, as green goes

And whiteness comes up through his face
Holding stars and rotten rafters,
Quiet, fragrant, and relieved.

THE BEHOLDERS   [1964]

Far away under us, they are mowing on the green steps
Of the valley, taking long, unending swings
Among the ripe wheat.
It is something about them growing,
Growing smaller, that makes us look up and see
That what has come over them is a storm.

It is a blue-black storm the shape of this valley,
And includes, perhaps, in its darkness,
Three men in the air
Taking long, limber swings, cutting water.   10

Swaths start to fall and, on earth,
The men come closer together as they mow.

Now in the last stand of wheat they bend.
From above, we watch over them like gods,
Our chins on our hands,
Our great eyes staring, our throats dry
And aching to cry down on their heads
Some curse or blessing,

Some word we have never known, but we feel
That when the right time arrives, and more stillness,   20
Lightning will leap
From our mouths in reasonless justice
As they arc their scythes more slowly, taking care
Not to look up.

As darkness increases there comes
A dancing into each of their swings,
A dancing like men in a cloud.
We two are coming together
Also, along the wall.
No lightning yet falls from us   30

Where their long hooks catch on the last of the sun
And the color of the wheat passes upward,
Drawn off like standing water
Into the cloud, turning green;
The field becomes whiter and darker,
And fire in us gathers and gathers

Not to call down death to touch brightly
The only metal for miles
In the hands of judged, innocent men,
But for our use only, who in the first sheaves of rain   40
Sit thunderstruck, having now the power to speak
With deadly intent of love.

Alan Dugan

b. 1923

Alan Dugan was born February 12, 1923, in Brooklyn, New York. His college education, which began at Queens College (Flushing, New York), was interrupted by service with the Air Force during World War II. He then attended Olivet College and Mexico City College, where he received his B.A. in 1950. After graduation he first worked in advertising and publishing and then became a plastics model-maker in a medical supply house in New York. He makes his home in Manhattan, although he has also lived in Italy and France. For his first book of poems he received the Yale Series of Younger Poets Award, a National Book Award, a Pulitzer Prize, and the Prix de Rome of the American Academy of Arts and Letters.

ON AN EAST WIND FROM THE WARS   [1961]

The wind came in for several thousand miles all night
and changed the close lie of your hair this morning. It
has brought well-travelled sea-birds who forget
their passage, singing. Old songs from the old
battle- and burial-grounds seem new in new lands.
They have to do with spring as new in seeming as
the old air idling in your hair in fact. So new,
so ignorant of any weather not your own,
you like it, breathing in a wind that swept
the battlefields of their worst smells, and took the dead   10
unburied to the potter's field of air. For miles
they sweetened on the sea-spray, the foul washed off,
and what is left is spring to you, love, sweet,

the salt blown past your shoulder luckily. No
wonder your laugh rings like a chisel as it cuts
your children's new names in the tombstone of thin air.

LOVE SONG: I AND THOU   [1961]

Nothing is plumb, level or square:
    the studs are bowed, the joists
are shaky by nature, no piece fits
    any other piece without a gap
or pinch, and bent nails
    dance all over the surfacing
like maggots. By Christ
    I am no carpenter. I built
the roof for myself, the walls
    for myself, the floors   10
for myself, and got
    hung up in it myself. I
danced with a purple thumb
    at this house-warming, drunk
with my prime whiskey: rage.
    Oh I spat rage's nails
into the frame-up of my work:
    it held. It settled plumb,
level, solid, square and true
    for that great moment. Then   20
it screamed and went on through,
    skewing as wrong the other way.
God damned it. This is hell,
    but I planned it, I sawed it,
I nailed it, and I
    will live in it until it kills me.
I can nail my left palm
    to the left-hand cross-piece but
I can't do everything myself.
    I need a hand to nail the right,   30
a help, a love, a you, a wife.

FUNERAL ORATION FOR A MOUSE   [1961]

This, Lord, was an anxious brother and
a living diagram of fear: full of health himself,
he brought diseases like a gift
to give his hosts. Masked in a cat's moustache
but sounding like a bird, he was a ghost
of lesser noises and a kitchen pest
for whom some ladies stand on chairs. So,
Lord, accept our felt though minor guilt
for an ignoble foe and ancient sin:
          the murder of a guest   10
who shared our board: just once he ate
too slowly, dying in our trap
from necessary hunger and a broken back.

Humors of love aside, the mousetrap was our own
opinion of the mouse, but for the mouse
it was the tree of knowledge with
its consequential fruit, the true cross
and the gate of hell. Even to approach
it makes him like or better than
its maker: his courage as a spoiler never once   20
impressed us, but to go out cautiously at night,
into the dining room;—what bravery, what
hunger! Younger by far, in dying he
was older than us all: his mobile tail and nose
spasmed in the pinch of our annoyance. Why,
then, at that snapping sound, did we, victorious,
begin to laugh without delight?

Our stomachs, deep in an analysis
of their own stolen baits
(and asking, "Lord, Host, to whom are we the pests?"),   30
contracted and demanded a retreat
from our machine and its effect of death,
as if the mouse's fingers, skinnier
than hairpins and as breakable as cheese,

could grasp our grasping lives, and in
their drowning movement pull us under too,
into the common death beyond the mousetrap.

ELEGY   [1963]

I know but will not tell
you, Aunt Irene, why there
are soap-suds in the whiskey:
Uncle Robert had to have
a drink while shaving. May
there be no bloodshed in your house
this morning of my father's death
and no unkept appearance
in the living, since he has
to wear the rouge and lipstick   10
of your ceremony, mother,
for the first and last time:
father, hello and goodbye.

PLAGUE OF DEAD SHARKS   [1963]

Who knows whether the sea heals or corrodes?
The wading, wintered pack-beasts of the feet
slough off, in spring, the dead rind of the shoes'
leather detention, the big toes' yellow horn
shines with a natural polish, and the whole
person seems to profit. The opposite appears
when dead sharks wash up along the beach
for no known reason. What is more built
for winning than the swept-back teeth,
water-finished fins, and pure bad eyes   10
these old, efficient forms of appetite
are dressed in? Yet it looks as if the sea

digested what it wished of them with viral ease
and threw up what was left to stink and dry.
If this shows how the sea approaches life
in its propensity to feed as animal entire,
then sharks are comforts, feet are terrified,
but they vacation in the mystery and why not?
Who knows whether the sea heals or corrodes?:
what the sun burns up of it, the moon puts back.   20

Denise Levertov

b. 1923

Denise Levertov was born on October 24, 1923, at Ilford, Essex, England. Her mother was Welsh and her father a Russian Jew who had been converted to Christianity while a student at Königsberg and became an Anglican priest. She was educated at home, which was visited frequently by Jewish booksellers, German theologians, Russian priests in exile, Viennese opera singers, and Zionists. She and her American husband, Mitchell Goodman, came to New York in 1948, and the poetic career which she had begun auspiciously in England flourished in this country. William Carlos Williams had an early influence on her style and subject matter, but as Kenneth Rexroth has written, she "has evolved a style of her own, clear, sparse, immediate and vibrant with a special sensibility and completely feminine insight."

PLEASURES   [1960]

I like to find
what's not found
at once, but lies

within something of another nature,
in repose, distinct.
Gull feathers of glass, hidden

in white pulp: the bones of squid
which I pull out and lay
blade by blade on the draining board—

tapered as if for swiftness, to pierce   10
the heart, but fragile, substance
belying design.   Or a fruit, *mamey*,

cased in rough brown peel, the flesh
rose-amber, and the seed:
the seed a stone of wood, carved and

polished, walnut-colored, formed
like a brazilnut, but large,
large enough to fill
the hungry palm of a hand.

I like the juicy stem of grass that grows   20
within the coarser leaf folded round,
and the butteryellow glow
in the narrow flute from which the morning-glory
opens blue and cool on a hot morning.

THE GODDESS   [1960]

She in whose lipservice
I passed my time,
whose name I knew, but not her face,
came upon me where I lay in Lie Castle!

Flung me across the room, and
room after room (hitting the walls, re-
bounding—to the last
sticky wall—wrenching away from it
pulled hair out!)
till I lay   10
outside the outer walls!

There in cold air
lying still where her hand had thrown me,
I tasted the mud that splattered my lips:

the seeds of a forest were in it,
asleep and growing! I tasted
her power!

The silence was answering my silence,
a forest was pushing itself
out of sleep between my submerged fingers.   20

I bit on a seed and it spoke on my tongue
of day that shone already among stars
in the water-mirror of low ground,
and a wind rising ruffled the lights:
she passed near me returning from the encounter,
she who plucked me from the close rooms,

without whom nothing
flowers, fruits, sleeps in season,
without whom nothing
speaks in its own tongue, but returns   30
lie for lie!

COME INTO ANIMAL PRESENCE   [1961]

Come into animal presence.
No man is so guileless as
the serpent. The lonely white
rabbit on the roof is a star
twitching its ears at the rain.
The llama intricately
folding its hind legs to be seated
not disdains but mildly
disregards human approval.
What joy when the insouciant   10
armadillo glances at us and doesn't
quicken his trotting
across the track into the palm brush.

What is this joy? That no animal
falters, but knows what it must do?
That the snake has no blemish,
that the rabbit inspects his strange surroundings
in white star-silence? The llama
rests in dignity, the armadillo
has some intention to pursue in the palm-forest.   20
Those who were sacred have remained so,
holiness does not dissolve, it is a presence
of bronze, only the sight that saw it
faltered and turned from it.
And old joy returns in holy presence.

THE WELL   [1961]

The Muse
   in her dark habit,
trim-waisted,
   wades into deep water.

The spring where she
   will fill her pitcher to the brim
wells out
   below the lake's surface, among
papyrus, where a stream
   enters the lake and is crossed   10
by the bridge on which I stand.

She stoops
   to gently dip and deep enough.
Her face resembles
   the face of the young actress who played
Miss Annie Sullivan, she who
   spelled the word 'water' into the palm
of Helen Keller, opening
   the doors of the world.

In the baroque park,   20
   transformed as I neared the water
   to Valentines, a place of origin,
I stand on a bridge of one span
and see this calm act, this gathering up
   of life, of spring water

and the Muse gliding then
   in her barge without sails, without
oars or motor, across
   the dark lake, and I know

no interpretation of these mysteries   30
   although I know she is the Muse
and that the humble
   tributary of Roding is
one with Alpheus, the god who as a river
flowed through the salt sea to his love's well

so that my heart leaps
   in wonder.
Cold, fresh, deep, I feel the word 'water'
   spelled in my left palm.

THE NOVEL   [1964]

A wind is blowing. The book being written
shifts, halts, pages
yellow and white drawing apart
and inching together in
new tries. A single white half-sheet
skims out under the door.

And cramped in their not yet
halfwritten leaves, a man and a woman
grimace in pain. Their cat
yawning its animal secret,   10

stirs in the monstrous limbo of erasure.
They live (when they live) in fear

of blinding, of burning, of choking under a
mushroom cloud in the year of the roach.
And they want (like us) the eternity
of today, they want this fear to be
struck out at once by a thick black
magic marker, everywhere, every page,

the whole sheets of it crushed, crackling,
and tossed in the fire   20
     and when they were fine ashes
     the stove would cool and be cleaned
     and a jar of flowers would be put to stand
     on top of the stove in the spring light.

Meanwhile from page to page they
buy things, acquiring the look of a
full life; they argue, make silence bitter,
play journeys, move house, implant
despair in each other
and then in the nick of time   30

they save one another with tears,
remorse, tenderness—
hooked on those wonder-drugs.
Yet they do have
—don't they—like us—
their days of grace, they

halt, stretch, a vision
breaks in on the cramped grimace,
inscape of transformation.
Something sundered begins to knit.   40
By scene, by sentence, something is rendered
back into life, back to the gods.

W. D. Snodgrass

b. 1926

Born January 5, 1926, in Wilkinsburg, Pennsylvania, W. D. Snod-grass grew up in Beaver Falls, studied music at Geneva College (Pennsylvania), served three years in the United States Navy, then took B.A., M.A., and M.F.A. degrees at the State University of Iowa. He has taught at Cornell and the University of Rochester and has been, since 1959, a member of the English faculty at Wayne State University in Detroit. His first book of poems, Heart's Needle, *won the £1000 award in poetry of the Ingram Merrill Foundation and the Pulitzer Prize for Poetry in 1960.*

RETURNED TO FRISCO, 1946   [1959]

We shouldered like pigs along the rail to try
And catch that first gray outline of the shore
Of our first life. A plane hung in the sky
From which a girl's voice sang: " . . . you're home once
    more."

For that one moment, we were dulled and shaken
By fear. What could still catch us by surprise?
We had known all along we would be taken
By hawkers, known what authoritative lies

Would plan us as our old lives had been planned.
We had stood years and, then, scrambled like rabbits   10
Up hostile beaches; why should we fear this land
Intent on luxuries and its old habits?

A seagull shrieked for garbage. The Bay Bridge,
Busy with noontime traffic, rose ahead.
We would have liberty, the privilege
Of lingering over steak and white, soft bread

Served by women, free to get drunk or fight,
Free, if we chose, to blow in our back pay
On smart girls or trinkets, free to prowl all night
Down streets giddy with lights, to sleep all day,   20

Pay our own way and make our own selections;
Free to choose just what they meant we should;
To turn back finally to our old affections,
The ties that lasted and which must be good.

Off the port side, through haze, we could discern
Alcatraz, lavender with flowers. Barred,
The Golden Gate, fading away astern,
Stood like the closed gate of your own backyard.

THE CAMPUS ON THE HILL   [1959]

Up the reputable walks of old established trees
They stalk, children of the *nouveaux riches;* chimes
Of the tall Clock Tower drench their heads in blessing:
"I don't wanna play at your house;
I don't like you any more."
My house stands opposite, on the other hill,
Among meadows, with the orchard fences down and
    falling;
Deer come almost to the door.
You cannot see it, even in this clearest morning.
White birds hang in the air between   10
Over the garbage landfill and those homes thereto adjacent,
Hovering slowly, turning, settling down
Like the flakes sifting imperceptibly onto the little town
In a waterball of glass.

And yet, this morning, beyond this quiet scene,
The floating birds, the backyards of the poor,
Beyond the shopping plaza, the dead canal, the hillside
    lying tilted in the air,
Tomorrow has broken out today:
Riot in Algeria, in Cyprus, in Alabama;
Aged in wrong, the empires are declining,   20
And China gathers, soundlessly, like evidence.
What shall I say to the young on such a morning?—
Mind is the one salvation?—also grammar?—
No; my little ones lean not toward revolt. They
Are the Whites, the vaguely furiously driven, who resist
Their souls with such passivity
As would make Quakers swear. All day, dear Lord, all
    day
They wear their godhead lightly.
They look out from their hill and say,
To themselves, "We have nowhere to go but down;   30
The great destination is to stay."
Surely the nations will be reasonable;
They look at the world—don't they?—the world's way?
The clock just now has nothing more to say.

APRIL INVENTORY   [1959]

The green catalpa tree has turned
All white; the cherry blooms once more.
In one whole year I haven't learned
A blessed thing they pay you for.
The blossoms snow down in my hair;
The trees and I will soon be bare.

The trees have more than I to spare.
The sleek, expensive girls I teach,
Younger and pinker every year,
Bloom gradually out of reach.   10
The pear tree lets its petals drop
Like dandruff on a tabletop.

The girls have grown so young by now
I have to nudge myself to stare.
This year they smile and mind me how
My teeth are falling with my hair.
In thirty years I may not get
Younger, shrewder, or out of debt.

The tenth time, just a year ago,
I made myself a little list   20
Of all the things I'd ought to know,
Then told my parents, analyst,
And everyone who's trusted me
I'd be substantial, presently.

I haven't read one book about
A book or memorized one plot.
Or found a mind I did not doubt.
I learned one date. And then forgot.
And one by one the solid scholars
Get the degrees, the jobs, the dollars.   30

And smile above their starchy collars.
I taught my classes Whitehead's notions;
One lovely girl, a song of Mahler's.
Lacking a source-book or promotions,
I showed one child the colors of
A luna moth and how to love.

I taught myself to name my name,
To bark back, loosen love and crying;
To ease my woman so she came,
To ease an old man who was dying.   40
I have not learned how often I
Can win, can love, but choose to die.

I have not learned there is a lie
Love shall be blonder, slimmer, younger;
That my equivocating eye
Loves only by my body's hunger;
That I have forces, true to feel,
Or that the lovely world is real.

While scholars speak authority
And wear their ulcers on their sleeves,   50
My eyes in spectacles shall see
These trees procure and spend their leaves.
There is a value underneath
The gold and silver in my teeth.

Though trees turn bare and girls turn wives,
We shall afford our costly seasons;
There is a gentleness survives
That will outspeak and has it reasons.
There is a loveliness exists,
Preserves us, not for specialists.   60

HEART'S NEEDLE: 5   [1959]

Winter again and it is snowing;
Although you are still three,
You are already growing
Strange to me.

You chatter about new playmates, sing
Strange songs; you do not know
Hey ding-a-ding-a-ding
Or where I go

Or when I sang for bedtime, *Fox
Went out on a chilly night*,   10
Before I went for walks
And did not write;

You never mind the squalls and storms
That are renewed long since;
Outside, the thick snow swarms
Into my prints

And swirls out by warehouses, sealed,
Dark cowbarns, huddled, still,

Beyond to the blank field,
The fox's hill   20

Where he backtracks and sees the paw,
Gnawed off, he cannot feel;
Conceded to the jaw
Of toothed, blue steel.

A FLAT ONE   [1960]

Old Fritz, on this rotating bed
For seven wasted months you lay
Unfit to move, shrunken, gray,
No good to yourself or anyone
But to be babied—changed and bathed and fed.
        At long last, that's all done.

Before each meal, twice every night,
We set pads on your bedsores, shut
Your catheter tube off, then brought
The second canvas-and-black-iron   10
Bedframe and clamped you in between them, tight,
        Scared, so we could turn

You over. We washed you, covered you,
Cut up each bite of meat you ate;
We watched your lean jaws masticate
As ravenously your useless food
As thieves at hard labor in their chains chew
        Or insects in the wood.

Such pious sacrifice to give
You all you could demand of pain: 20
Receive this haddock's body, slain
For you, old tyrant; take this blood
Of a tomato, shed that you might live.
        You had that costly food.

You seem to be all finished, so
We'll plug your recalcitrant anus
And tie up your discouraged penis
In a great, snow-white bow of gauze.
We wrap, you, pin you, and cart you down below,
                Below, below, because   30

Your credit has finally run out.
On our steel table, trussed and carved,
You'll find this world's hardworking, starved
Teeth working in your precious skin.
The earth turns, in the end, by turn about
                And opens to take you in.

Seven months gone down the drain; thank God
That's through. Throw out the four-by-fours,
Swagsticks, the thick salve for bedsores,
Throw out the diaper pads and drug   40
Containers, pile the bedclothes in a wad,
                And rinse the cider jug

Half filled with the last urine. Then
Empty out the cotton cans,
Autoclave the bowls and spit pans,
Unhook the pumps and all the red
Tubes—catheter, suction, oxygen;
                Next, wash the empty bed.

—All this Dark Age machinery
On which we had tormented you   50
To life. Last, we collect the few
Belongings: snapshots, some odd bills,
Your mail, and half a pack of Luckies we
                Won't light you after meals.

Old man, these seven months you've lain
Determined—not that you would live—
Just not to die. No one would give
You one chance you could ever wake
From that first night, much less go well again,
                Much less go home and make   60

Your living; how could you hope to find
A place for yourself in all creation?—
Pain was your only occupation.
And pain that should content and will
A man to give it up, nerved you to grind
    Your clenched teeth, breathing, till

Your skin broke down, your calves went flat
And your legs lost all sensation. Still,
You took enough morphine to kill
A strong man. Finally, nitrogen   70
Mustard: you could last two months after that;
    It would kill you then.

Even then you wouldn't quit,
Old soldier, yet you must have known
Inside the animal had grown
Sick of the world, made up its mind
To stop. Your mind ground on its separate
    Way, merciless and blind,

Into these last weeks when the breath
Would only come in fits and starts   80
That puffed out your sections like the parts
Of some enormous, damaged bug.
You waited, not for life, not for your death,
    Just for the deadening drug

That made your life seem bearable.
You still whispered you would not die.
Yet in the nights I heard you cry
Like a whipped child; in fierce old age
You whimpered, tears stood on your gun-metal
    Blue cheeks shaking with rage   90

And terror. So much pain would fill
Your room that when I left I'd pray
That if I came back the next day
I'd find you gone. You stayed for me—
Nailed to your own rapacious, stiff self-will.
    You've shook loose, finally.

They'd say this was a worthwhile job
Unless they tried it. It is mad
To throw our good lives after bad;
    Waste time, drugs, and our minds, while strong   100
Men starve. How many young men did we rob
        To keep you hanging on?

I can't think we did *you* much good.
Well, when you died, none of us wept.
You killed for us, and so we kept
    You, because we need to earn *our* pay.
No. We'd still have to help you try. We would
        Have killed for you today.

Robert Creeley

b. 1926

Robert Creeley was born May 21, 1926, in Massachusetts. He attended Harvard and served in the American Field Service in India and Burma. He has also lived in Guatemala, Majorca, and France. As editor of the Black Mountain Review *he encouraged many talented young poets. His own poems owe something to the late William Carlos Williams, but he has evolved his own idiom and is generally regarded as one of the gifted poets of his generation. He teaches at the University of New Mexico and writes fiction as well as poetry.*

HART CRANE   [1957]

For Slater Brown

I

He had been stuttering, by the edge
of the street, one foot still
on the sidewalk, and the other
in the gutter . . .

like a bird, say, wired to flight, the
wings, pinned to their motion, stuffed.

The words, several, and for each, several
senses.
        "It is very difficult to sum up
briefly . . ."   10
                It always was.

(Slater, let me come home.
The letters have proved insufficient.
The mind cannot hang to them as it could
to the words.

There are ways beyond
what I have here to work with,
what my head cannot push to any kind
of conclusion.

But my own ineptness   20
cannot bring them to hand,
the particulars of those times
we had talked.)

"Men kill themselves because they are
afraid of death, he says . . . "

The push
            beyond and
into
Respect, they said he respected the
ones with the learning, lacking it   30
himself
            (Waldo Frank & his
6 languages)
                    What had seemed
important
While Crane sailed to Mexico I was writing
(so that one betrayed
                        himself)

He slowed
            (without those friends to keep going, to   40
keep up), stopped
                    dead and the head could not
go further
            without those friends
. . . And so it was I entered the broken world
Hart Crane.
                Hart

THE WAY [1959]

My love's manners in bed
are not to be discussed by me,
as mine by her
I would not credit comment upon gracefully.

Yet I ride by the margin of that lake in
the wood, the castle,
and the excitement of strongholds;
and have a small boy's notion of doing good.

Oh well, I will say here,
knowing each man,   10
let you find a good wife too,
and love her as hard as you can.

THE ROSE [1962]

For Bobbie

Up and down
she walks, listless
form, a movement
quietly misled.

Now, speak to her.
"Did you want
to go, then why
don't you."

She went. There were
things she left   10
in the room
as a form of it.

He follows, walking.
Where do they walk now?

Do they talk now
where they are

in that other place
grown monstrous,
quiet quiet air
as breath.   20

And all about a rosy
mark discloses
her nature
to him, vague and unsure.

There roses, here roses,
flowers, a pose of
nature, her
nature has disclosed to him.

Yet breathing, crouched
in the dark,   30
he is there
also, recovers,

to bring her back
to herself, himself.
The room wavers,
wavers.

And as if,
as if a cloud had
broken at last
open   40

and all the rain
from that,
from that had fallen
on them,

on them there is a mark
of her nature, her flowers,

and his room, his nature
to come home to.

THE WIFE   [1962]

I know two women
   and the one
is tangible substance,
   flesh and bone.

The other in my mind
   occurs.
She keeps her strict
   proportion there.

But how should I
   propose to live
with two such creatures
   in my bed—   10

or how shall he
   who has a wife
yield two to one
   and watch the other die.

THE SNOW   [1962]

The broken snow should leave the traces
of yesterday's walks, the paths worn in,
and bring friends to our door
somewhere in the dark winter.

Sometime in April I will get at last
the flowers promised you long ago,—

to think of it
will help us through.

The night is a pleasure to us,
I think sleeping, and what warmth secures   10
me you bring,
giving at last freely of yourself.

Myself was old, was confused, was wanting,—
to sing of an old song,
through the last echo of hurting,
brought now home.

W. S. Merwin

b. 1927

Born September 30, 1927, in New York City, W. S. Merwin grew up in Union City, New Jersey, and Scranton, Pennsylvania, took a B.A. at Princeton, where he studied Romance Languages in the Graduate School. From 1949 until 1951 he was a tutor in France, Portugal, and Majorca, in 1956 served as playwright in residence at the Poet's Theater, Cambridge, Massachusetts. His first volume of poetry was selected for the Yale Series of Younger Poets; his second won him the Kenyon Review *Fellowship for Poetry; his third was selected by the British Poetry Book Society.*

DICTUM: FOR A MASQUE OF DELUGE   [1952]

For Dido

There will be the cough before the silence, then
Expectation; and the hush of portent
Must be welcomed by a diffident music
Lisping and dividing its renewals;
Shadows will lengthen and sway, and, casually
As in a latitude of diversion
Where growth is topiary, and the relaxed horizons
Are accustomed to the trespass of surprise,
One with a mask of Ignorance will appear
Musing on the wind's strange pregnancy.   10

And to him one must enter from the south
In a feigned haste, with disaster on his lips,
And tales of distended seas, continents

Submerged, worlds drowned, and of drownings
Into mirrors; unto this foreboding
Let them add sidelong but increasing mention,
With darkening syllables, of shadows, as though
They stood and traded restlessness beneath
A gathering dark, until their figures seem
But a flutter of speech down an expense of wind.   20

So, with talk, like a blather of rain, begun,
Weather will break and the artful world will rush
Incontinent. There must be a vessel.
There must be rummage and shuffling for salvation
Till on that stage and violence, among
Curtains of tempest and shaking sea,
A covered basket, where a child might lie,
Timbered with osiers and floated on a shadow,
Glides adrift, as improbably sailing
As a lotus flower bearing a bull.   30

Hills are to be forgotten; the patter of speech
Must lilt upon flatness. The beasts will come;
And as they come, let one man, by the ark,
Drunken with desolation, his tongue
Rounding the full statement of the seasons,
Tremble and stare, his eyes seeming to chase
A final clatter of doomed crows, to seek
An affirmation, a mercy, an island,
Or hills crested with towns, and to find only
Cities of cloud already crumbling.   40

And these the beasts: the bull from the lotus flower
With wings at his shoulders; and a goat, winged;
A serpent undulating in the air;
A lion with wings like falling leaves;
These are to wheel on a winged wheel above
The sullen ark, while hare, swine, crocodile,
Camel and mouse come; and the sole man, always,
Lurches on childish limbs above the basket—
To his mere humanity seas shall not attain
With tempest, nor the obscure sky with torches.   50

(Why is it rumored that these beasts come in pairs
When the anatomies of their existence
Are wrought for singularity? They walk
Beside their shadows; their best motions are
Figments on the drapery of the air.
Their propagation is a redoubling
Merely of dark against the wall, a planetary
Leaning in the night unto their shadows
And stiffening to the moment of eclipse;
Shadows will be their lean progeny.)   60

At last the sigh of recession: the land
Wells from the water; the beasts depart; the man
Whose shocked speech must conjure a landscape
As of some country where the dead years keep
A circle of silence, a drying vista of ruin,
Musters himself, rises, and stumbling after
The dwindling beasts, under the all-colored
Paper rainbow, whose arc he sees as promise,
Moves in an amazement of resurrection,
Solitary, impoverished, renewed.   70

A falling frond may seem all trees. If so
We know the tone of falling. We shall find
Dictions for rising, words for departure;
And time will be sufficient before that revel
To teach an order and rehearse the days
Till the days are accomplished: so now the dove
Makes assignations with the olive tree,
Slurs with her voice the gestures of the time:
The day foundering, the dropping sun
Heavy, the wind a low portent of rain.   80

WHEN I CAME FROM COLCHIS   [1954]

When I came from Colchis
Where the spring fields lay green,

A land famed for fine linen,
Bounded northerly
By the glistering Caucasus,
By the Euxine westerly,

Most I spoke of fine linen
But did, in truth, tell something
Of Jason who had come sailing
And poised upon that shore   10
His fabulous excursion.
All turned the incredulous ear.

From Troy, over the water
Returning, I recounted
The tale of wrecked walls, but said
That gray waves lap and surround
That shore as any other.
With a shrewd smile they listened.

Now if, amazed, I come
From the deep bourn of your hand,   20
A stranger up from the sunned
Sea of your eyes, lady,
What fable should I tell them,
That they should believe me?

THE ANNUNCIATION   [1956]

It was not night, not even when the darkness came
That came blacker than any night, and more fearful,
Like a bell beating and I under its darkness dying
To the stun of the sound. Before that
It was not dark nor loud nor any way strange,
Just the empty kitchen, with the smell of the bean-flowers
In their late blossom, coming in at the window,
And the stillness, just that empty hour of the afternoon
                    When it is hard indeed to believe in time.

When the young grass sleeps white in the sun, and the
      tree's shadow   10
Lies so still on the small stone by the doorway
You would think the stone was only a shadow
Rounded, and nothing beneath, and the air
Forgets to move, forgets, and you can hear a humming,
It is like a humming, but it is not a sound
But the edges of the silence whirring
To tell you how deep the silence is. When, even
Though it is spring, and the coldness of winter
And the coldness of morning still under the air,
If you do not think, you can feel already   20
The turned summer, the daze, the dryness,
           The light heavy in the air.

So that time is hard to believe, but it is with you
More than ever, for you can feel the stillness
Rushing more sudden than ever, in the open day
More secret than ever, and farther and harder
To understand, and all so still. And I was thinking
Can it be true, like the stone under the shadow;
Can it be true? And thinking how they tell
That a woman is for a man, and that from a man   30
She learns many things and can make names for them
That, before, she was empty of. And of this man
That will take me as a woman, and he is a good man.
And yet thinking how men and women, even
Together in their understanding, are lost
In that secret, and the names they made. And sometimes
You can stand in that emptiness till you are thinking
Of nothing, and it sounds as though a kind
Of joy began whirring at the edge of that sadness,
Like a sudden peace that was there, but it is not whirring   40
It is so still, but you are drawn out on it
Till you are as empty as the hushed hour,
          And there is no word for it all.

That was the way it was, and in the fragrant light
That came in at the window, I was standing
Still, that way, seeing nothing but the light,

As though I was gliding out on the peaceful light
Like water; and what I was, in myself
I was nothing. And had even forgotten whatever
I should have been doing; only in my two hands   50
I was holding a cup, I remember, the kind
You would measure flour or drink water in,
But wherever I was going with it, and why,
I had stopped and forgotten, because of the secret
Way of the stillness, and myself, and the light,
So that now, the reason why I was holding
That cup in my hands is one of the things I cannot
                    Remember nor understand.

Then the darkness began: it brushed
Just lightly first, like it might be the wing   60
Of a bird, a soft bird, that flutters,
As it comes down. It brushed the hem of the light
And in my eyes, where I was nothing. But grew
Clouding between my eyes and the light
And rushing upon me, the way the shadow
Of a cloud will rush over the sunned fields
In a time of wind; and the black coming down
In its greatness, between my eyes and the light,
Was like wings growing, and the blackness
Of their shadow growing as they came down   70
Whirring and beating, cold and like thunder, until
All the light was gone, and only that noise
And terrible darkness, making everything shake
Like the end of it was come, and there was
No word for it, and I thought Lord, Lord, and thought
How if I had not gone out on the light
And been hidden away on the vanished light
So that myself I was empty and nothing
I would surely have died, because the thing
That the darkness was, and the wings and the shaking   80
That there was no word for it, was a thing that in myself
I could not have borne and lived. And still came
Nearer and darker, beating, and there was
Like a whisper in the feathers there, in the wings'
Great wind, like a whirring of words, but I could not

Say the shape of them, and it came to me
They were like a man, but none has yet come to me,
And I could not say how. Only, in the place
Where, myself, I was nothing, there was suddenly
A great burning under the darkness, a fire   90
Like fighting up into the wings' lash and the beating
Blackness, and flames like the tearing of teeth,
With noise like rocks rending, such that no word
Can call it as it was there, and for fire only,
Without the darkness beating and the wind, had I
Been there, had I not been far on the hiding light
I could not have borne it and lived. And then the
     stillness:
The wings giving way all at once, and the fire quiet
Leaving neither day nor darkness, but only the silence
That closed like a last clap of the thunder   100
And was perfect. And the light lying beyond, like a ring,
And the things in it lying, and everything still
With no moving at all, and no pulse, nor any breath,
And no rushing in that stillness, for time was not there,
Nor the emptiness, the way time falls into emptiness,
But only fullness, like it was forever,
Like it was everything from the beginning and always,
In itself and still, and not even waiting,
Because it was there. And in the silence
And in the fullness it came, it was there   110
Like it had not come but was there, whatever it was
                    That above all I cannot name.

Though in itself it was like a word, and it was
Like no man and no word that ever was known,
Come where I was; and because I was nothing
It could be there. It was a word for
The way the light and the things in the light
Were looking into the darkness, and the darkness
And the things of the darkness were looking into the light
In the fullness, and the way the silence   120
Was hearing, like it was hearing a great song
And the song was hearing the silence forever
And forever and ever. And I knew the name for it;

There in the place where I was nothing in
The fullness, I knew, it, and held it and knew
The way of it, and the word for how it was one,
I held it, and the word for why. Or almost,
Or believed I knew it, believed, like an echo
That when it comes you believe you know
The word, while it rings, but when it is gone   130
You had not learned it, and cannot find it, even
Though the sound still breathes in your ear. Because
Then the light looked away from the darkness
Again, and the song slid into the silence
And was lost again, and the fullness rose, going,
And the sound of its going was the sound of wings
Rushing away in darkness, and the sound
That came after them was the stillness rushing
Again, and time sudden and hard to believe,
And forever was emptiness again, where time fell,   140
And I was standing there in myself, in the light,
With only the shape of the word that is wonder,
                    And that same cup still in my hands.

And I could not say how long it had been
That I had stood there forever, while the end
Looked into the beginning, and they were one
And the word for one. Because the shadow
Had not changed on the stone, and nothing had moved
In all that time, if it was in time at all,
Because nothing had changed. But I did not doubt   150
For the wonder that was in me, quickening,
Like in your ear the shape of a sound
When the sound is gone. And because when
At last I moved my hand, slowly, slowly,
Like it could not believe, to touch myself, to see
If it could be true, if I had truly come back
From the light, and touched myself like something
Hard to believe, I knew I was not the same
And could not say how. Then a long time I stood there
Pondering the way of it in my heart, and how   160
                    The coming of it was a blessing.

Afterwards, though, there was the emptiness
And not as it was before: not drifting
About the place where I stood, like the afternoon
Light and the smell of the bean-flowers, but as though
There was emptiness only, and the great falling
And nothing besides, and it was all inside me
In the place where I had been nothing: the stillness
Rushing, and time not hard to believe then
But undeniable in the pain of its falling,   170
And the darkness where time fell and men and women
Together in their understanding, and the names
That they made and everything from the beginning
Like they were falling inside me, in the emptiness
That I was, and because of me they were falling,
Because I had been nothing. So that I thought then
That that was the change I had known, the only change,
But yet I would not believe that, but I cannot
Say why. And so that I would have prayed
That it be removed from me, the grief of it,   180
The keen that was in me at all their falling
In the emptiness that I was be removed from me,
But then how should I have named it, and what am I
That He should be mindful of? But I prayed,
But for that I did not pray, but yet I
Cannot say why, but in my heart that also
I pondered. And it went when its time was,
Because in the place where we are, the shadow
Moves and there is the stone again, and the day
Going and things to be done, the same   190
As always, the way they have to be; and because
Such emptiness as that was, you could not
Bear it for long and live, or I could not.
So I moved away about something
That all that time I should have been doing, with
That cup in my hands; whatever it was
               I have forgotten again.

And I moved away because you must live
Forward, which is away from whatever

It was that you had, though you think when you have it   200
That it will stay with you forever. Like that word
I thought I had known and held surely and that it
Was with me always. In the evening
Between the shadows the light lifts and slides
Out and out, and the cold that was under the air
Is the darkness you remember, and how it was
There all the time and you had forgotten.
It carries its own fragrance. And there is this man
Will take me as a woman, and he is a good man,
And I will learn what I am, and the new names. Only   210
If I could remember, if I could only remember
The way that word was, and the sound of it. Because
There is that in me still that draws all that I am
Backwards, as weeds are drawn down when the water
Flows away; and if I could only shape
And hear again that word and the way of it—
But you must grow forward, and I know
That I cannot. And yet it is there in me:
As though if I could only remember
The word, if I could make it with my breath   220
It would be with me forever as it was
Then in the beginning, when it was
The end and the beginning, and the way
They were one; and time and the things of falling
Would not fall into emptiness but into
The light, and the word tell the way of their falling
Into the light forever, if I could remember
                    And make the word with my breath.

JOHN OTTO   [1960]

John Otto of Brunswick, ancestor
On my mother's side, Latin scholar,
Settler of the Cumberland Valley,
Schoolmaster, sire of a family,
Why, one day in your white age,

Did you heave up onto your old man's legs
In the house near Blain, in Perry County,
And shut the gate and shuffle away
From the home of eighty years or so
And what cronies were left, and follow   10
The road out of the valley, up the hill,
Over the south mountain, to Carlisle,
The whole way on foot, in the wagon tracks,
To die of fatigue there, at ninety-six?
I can see Carlisle Valley spread below
And you, John, coming over the hill's brow,
Stopping for breath and a long look;
I can hear your breath come sharp and quick,
But why it was that you climbed up there
None of us remembers any more.   20
To see your son and his family?
Was the house too quiet in Perry County?
To ask some question, tell some secret,
Or beg some pardon before too late?
Or was it to look once again
On another valley green in the sun
Almost as in the beginning, to remind
Your eyes of a promise in the land?

IN THE NIGHT FIELDS   [1963]

I heard the sparrows shouting "Eat, eat,"
And then the day dragged its carcass in back of the hill.
Slowly the tracks darkened.

The smoke rose steadily from no fires.
The old hunger, left in the old darkness,
Turned like a hanged knife.
I would have preferred a quiet life.
The bugs of regret began their services
Using my spine as a rosary. I left the maps
For the spiders.   10
Let's go, I said.

                    Light of the heart,
The wheat had started lighting its lanterns,
And in every house in heaven there were lights waving
Hello good-bye. But that's
Another life.
Snug on the crumbling earth
The old bottles lay dreaming of new wine.
I picked up my breast, which had gone out.
By other lights I go looking for yours

Through the standing harvest of my lost arrows.   20
Under the moon the shadow
Practices mowing. Not for me, I say,
Please not for my
Benefit. A man cannot live by bread
Alone.

Wendell Berry

b. 1934

Wendell Berry was born in Henry County, Kentucky, August 5, 1934. He holds A.B. and M.A. degrees from the University of Kentucky. In 1958–1959 he held a Wallace Stegner Fellowship in writing at Stanford University, and a Guggenheim Fellowship in 1961. His first novel, Nathan Coulter, *was published in 1960. An elegy for President Kennedy,* November 26, 1963, *was published in the spring of 1964 by George Braziller with drawings by Ben Shahn. Berry's first book of poems,* The Broken Ground, *was published in the autumn of 1964. After teaching at New York University from 1962 to 1964 he joined the Department of English at the University of Kentucky.*

A MAN WALKING AND SINGING   [1964]

For James Baker Hall

I

It is no longer necessary to sleep
in order to dream of our destruction.

We take form within our death, the figures
emerging like shadows in fire.

Who is it? speaking to me of death's beauty.

I think it is my own black angel, as near me
as my flesh. I am never divided from his darkness.
His face is the black mask of my face. My eyes

live in his black eye-holes. On his black wings
I rise to sing.
                        His mouthing presences attend   10
my singing, masquerading his black ambiguous
absolute:
                Die more lightly than live,
they say. Death is more gay.
                                        There's no argument
against its certainty, at least, they say.

I know they know as surely as I live my death
exists, and has my shape.

                        2

But the man so forcefully walking,
say where he goes,
say what he hears and what he sees
and what he knows   20
to cause him to stride so merrily.

He goes in spring
through the evening street
to buy bread,

green trees leaning
over the sidewalk,
forsythia yellow
beneath the windows,
birds singing
as birds sing   30
only in spring,

and he sings, his footsteps
beating the measure of his song.

In an open window
a man and a woman
leaning together
at the room's center

embrace and kiss
as if they met
in passing,   40
the spring wind
lifting the curtain.

His footsteps carry him
past the window,
deeper into his song.

His singing becomes conglomerate
of all he sees,
leaving the street behind him
runged as a ladder
or the staff of a song.   50

                    3
To his death? Yes.

He walks and sings to his death.

And winter will equal spring.

And for the lovers, even
while they kiss, even though
it is spring, the day ends.

But to the sound of his passing
he sings. It is a kind of triumph
that he grieves—thinking
of the white lilacs in bloom,   60
profuse, fragrant, white
in excess of all seasonal need,

and of the mockingbird's crooked
arrogant notes, hooking him to the sky
as though no flight
or dying could equal him
at his momentary song.

CANTICLE   [1964]

For Robert Hazel

1

What death means is not this—
the spirit, triumphant in the body's fall,
praising its absence, feeding on music.
If life can't justify and explain itself,
death can't justify and explain it.
A creed and a grave never did equal the life
of anything. Yellow flowers sprout in the clefts
of ancient stones at the beginning of April.
The black clothes of the priests are turned
against the frail yellow of sunlight and petal;   10
they wait in their blackness to earn joy
by dying. They trust that nothing holy is free,
and so their lives are paid. Money slots
in the altar rails can make a jukebox of the world,
the mind paying its gnawed coins for the safety of ignorance.

2

Now while blood and heat run in the mind,
yellow flowers gouging out of the cracked stones
bloom into a consuming question
which is its own answer, and is all.
There's nothing here but earth, no matter what it buries.   20

3

The black face of the coal merchant opens with his singing,
and his blackened lungs breathe out his song.
He mentions the daily and several colors of the world.
His song is a part of a singing into which the trees
move, and fill themselves with all their living
and their sounds. Dirt and offal assail the dead
with music, and they vanish out of their bodies.
The coal man laughs in the black of his opened doorway;
in his sooty face his mouth filled with laughter

is like a red tulip blooming out of the dirt;   30
his eyes are clarified, seeing the young leaves
over his doorway drop their shadows at his feet;
his laughter is useful as money and holy as altars.
Now the hyacinths are full born. The rain is on them.
They are like nothing ever imagined or written down.
I choose and sing these shapes and breathings of the ground.
I wear this yellow blossom like an eye.

MAY SONG   [1964]

For whatever is let go
there's a taker.
The living discovers itself

where no preparation
was made for it,
where its only privilege

is to live if it can.
The window flies from the dark
of the subway mouth

into the sunlight   10
stained with the green
of the spring weeds

that crowd the improbable
black earth
of the embankment,

their stout leaves
like the tongues and bodies
of a herd, feeding

on the new heat,
drinking at the seepage   20
of the stones:

the freehold of life,
triumphant
even in the waste

of those who possess it.
But it is itself the possessor,
we know at last,

seeing it send out weeds
to take back
whatever is left: 30

Proprietor, pasturing foliage
on the rubble,
making use

of the useless—a beauty
we have less than not
deserved.

ASCENT   [1964]

I

This mud, my genesis,
slicks and shines
in the rinsed morning.

Under all my sleeps
the river has plodded its furrow
to be wakened to

—intact for all my days
have taken from it, the sum
of its running.

The meshes of the sun   10
leap up, netting the leaves
like schools of fish.

2

Walking on the world
in which the final explosion
is planted, arrived

at another waking, the body
recognizes itself gladly.
The familiar persists,

nothing but the night has gone.
Having made peace again   20
with the loss of time,

I climb the bent road
in the opening of the ledged stone,
in the crease of my mind,

a surface tension of the known
answering the weight
of my feet, bearing me

like a water-strider walking
on the roof of drowning.

3

The wind crossing it, the green field   30
moves in itself, into itself,
like the iris of my green eye.

Along the deep alleys of the grass
the living waken and go
in their commonwealth

toward whatever singing
the morning will carry
on its branches.

Under its shingles and leaves,
flight of bomber and hummingbird,   40
the town survives its nightmares

—colony of white mushrooms
grown up during the night
out of the leaf-fall of its grove.

THE GUEST   [1964]

Washed into the doorway
by the wake of the traffic,
he wears humanity
like a third-hand shirt
—blackened with enough
of Manhattan's dirt to sprout
a tree, or poison one.
His empty hand has led him
where he has come to.
Our differences claim us.   10
He holds out his hand,
in need of all that's mine.

And so we're joined, as deep
as son and father. His life
is offered me to choose.

*Shall I begin servitude
to him? Let this cup pass.
Who am I?* But charity must
suppose, knowing no better,
that this is a man fallen   20
among thieves, or come
to this strait by no fault
—that our difference
is not a judgment,
though I can afford to eat
and am made his judge.

I am, I nearly believe,
the Samaritan who fell

into the ambush of his heart
on the way to another place.   30
My stranger waits, his hand
held out like something to read,
as though its emptiness
is an accomplishment.
I give him a smoke and the price
of a meal, no more

—not sufficient kindness
nor believable sham.
I paid him to remain strange
to my threshold and table,   40
to permit me to forget him—
knowing I won't. He's the guest
of my knowing, though not asked.

NOVEMBER 26, 1963   [1964]

We know the winter earth upon the body of the young Presi-
        dent, and the early dark falling;

we know the veins grown quiet in his temples and wrists,
        and his hands and eyes grown quiet;

we know his name written in the black capitals of his death,
        and the mourners standing in the rain, and the leaves
        falling;

we know his death's horses and drums; the roses, bells,
        candles, crosses; the faces hidden in veils;

we know the children who begin the youth of loss greater
        than they can dream now;

we know the nightlong coming of faces into the candlelight
        before his coffin, and their passing;

we know the mouth of the grave waiting, the bugle and rifles,
    the mourners turning away;

we know the young dead body carried in the earth into the
    first deep night of its absence;

we know our streets and days slowly opening into the time
    he is not alive, filling with our footsteps and voices;

we know ourselves, the bearers of the light of the earth he is
    given to, and of the light of all his lost days;   10

we know the long approach of summers toward the healed
    ground where he will be waiting, no longer the keeper
    of what he was.

NOTES AND
SELECTED BIBLIOGRAPHY

LIST OF ABBREVIATIONS

Am. Lit.	*American Literature*
Am. Quart.	*American Quarterly*
Am. Schol.	*American Scholar*
Am. Sp.	*American Speech*
Atlantic	*Atlantic Monthly*
Coll. Eng.	*College English*
Eng. Jour.	*English Journal*
Hud. Rev.	*Hudson Review*
Jour. Aesth. & Art Crit.	*Journal of Aesthetics and Art Criticism*
Ken. Rev.	*Kenyon Review*
Mod. Lang. Notes	*Modern Language Notes*
Mod. Phil.	*Modern Philology*
New Eng. Quart.	*New England Quarterly*
No. Am. Rev.	*North American Review*
Part. Rev.	*Partisan Review*
Phil. Quart.	*Philological Quarterly*
PMLA	*Publications of the Modern Language Association of America*
Sewanee Rev.	*Sewanee Review*
So. Atl. Quart.	*South Atlantic Quarterly*
So. Rev.	*Southern Review*
Stud. Phil.	*Studies in Philology*
Times Lit. Sup.	*The [London] Times Literary Supplement*
Tulane Stud. Eng.	*Tulane Studies in English*
U. Kans. City Rev.	*University of Kansas City Review*
Va. Quart. Rev.	*Virginia Quarterly Review*
West. Hum. Rev.	*Western Humanities Review*
West. Rev.	*Western Review*
Yale Rev.	*Yale Review*

NOTES

CONRAD AIKEN
b. 1881

Bibliography

Stallman, R. W. "Annotated Checklist on Conrad Aiken: A Critical Study,"
    Wake XI (1952), 114–121.

Major Writings

Earth Triumphant (1914)
Turns and Movies (1916)
The Jig of Forslin (1916)
Nocturnes of Remembered Spring (1917)
The Charnel Rose (1918)
Skepticisms (1919, criticism)
The House of Dust (1920)
Punch: The Immortal Liar (1921)
Priapus and the Pool (1922; enlarged edition, 1925)
The Pilgrimage of Festus (1923)
Blue Voyage (1927, novel)
John Deth and Other Poems (1930)
Preludes for Memnon (1931)
Landscape West of Eden (1934)
Time in the Rock (1936)
And in the Human Heart (1940)
Brownstone Eclogues and Other Poems (1942)
The Kid (1947)
Divine Pilgrim (1949)
Skylight One (1949)
Ushant (1952, autobiography)
Sheepfold Hill (1953)
Collected Poems (1953)
Letter from Li Po and Other Poems (1955)
Collected Short Stories (1960)
Selected Poems (1961)

Criticism

Beach, Joseph Warren. "Conrad Aiken and T. S. Eliot: Echoes and Over-tones," *PMLA*, LXIX (1954), 753–762.

Blackmur, R. P. "Conrad Aiken: The Poet," *Atlantic*, CXCII (December, 1953), 77–82.

Blanchard, Rufus A. "Metamorphosis of a Dream," *Sewanee Rev.*, LXV (1957).

Brown, C. S. "Music and Conrad Aiken," *Georgia Review*, II (1948), 40–51.

Brown, C. S. "The Poetry of Conrad Aiken," *Georgia Review*, VIII (1954), 315–322.

Carlson, Eric W. "The Range of Symbolism in Poetry," *So. Atl. Quart.*, XLVIII (1949), 442–451.

Dahlberg, Edward. "A Long Lotus Sleep," *Poetry*, LXXXI (1953), 313–321.

Deutsch, Babette. *Poetry in Our Time*, pp. 181–182. New York: Columbia University Press, 1956.

Fitzgerald, S. M. "Aiken's Search for Self-Awareness," *Commonweal*, LVII (1952), pp. 77–82.

Gregory, Horace, and Zaturenska, Marya. "The Heritage of the *Yellow Book* and Conrad Aiken," pp. 217–225, in *A History of American Poetry: 1900–1940.* New York: Harcourt, Brace and Co., 1942.

Hoffman, Dan G. "Poetic Symbols from the Public Domain," *Southern Folklore Quarterly*, Vol. XII (1948), pp. 293–297.

Martin, Jay. *Conrad Aiken: A Life of His Art.* Princeton: Princeton University Press, 1962.

Comments on Poems

The text source of both the 1925 poems, first collected in the enlarged *Priapus and the Pool*, and the 1942 poems is *Collected Poems*.

Critical discussions of individual poems have been almost invariably superficial. Aiken's complicated symbolism waits for a competent critic.

Doctors' Row

This poem and the three that follow were published in *Brownstone Eclogues*, a title which suggests some of the ironies of "Doctors' Row," "North Infinity Street," and "The Lovers." Although "eclogue" was originally applied to various kinds of poems, since Theocritus and Virgil it has suggested pastoral poetry, whereas Aiken treats the life in doctors' offices, sordid "Infinity Street" (with the metaphor play on time, debt, and death), and the "marriage" of the undertaker's parlor and the flower shop—the latter a parody-satire on one of the traditional subjects of eclogues, the courtship of shepherd and shepherdess.

26. *Plato's turning wall:* to illustrate his doctrine of the Immortality of the Soul, Plato argued by analogy in *Phaedo* that man does not experience truth itself but only the shadow of truth, as if he were dwelling in a "hollow of the earth" and could see only the shadows of real things cast by a light above and behind him. The moving shadow could create the illusion that the wall itself revolves.

JOEL BARLOW
1754-1812

Bibliography

Howard, Leon. "A Check List: Joel Barlow," pp. 421–424 in *The Connecticut Wits*. Chicago: University of Chicago Press, 1943.

Major Writings

The Vision of Columbus (1787)
The Hasty-Pudding (1796)
The Political Writings of Joel Barlow (1796)
The Columbiad (1807)

Biography

Dos Passos, John. "Citizen Barlow of the Republic of the World," pp. 256–380 in *The Ground We Stand On*. New York: Harcourt, Brace & Co., 1941.

Howard, Leon. *The Connecticut Wits*. Chicago: University of Chicago Press, 1943.

Todd, C. B. *Life and Letters of Joel Barlow, LL.D.* New York: G. P. Putnam's Sons, 1886.

Tyler, M. C. "The Literary Strivings of Mr. Joel Barlow," pp. 129–180 in *Three Men of Letters*. New York: G. P. Putnam's Sons, 1895.

Woodress, James. *A Yankee's Odyssey: The Life of Joel Barlow*. Philadelphia: J. B. Lippincott, 1958.

Zunder, T. A. *The Early Days of Joel Barlow, a Connecticut Wit*. New Haven, Conn.: Yale University Press, 1934.

Criticism

Blau, J. L. "Joel Barlow, Enlightened Religionist," *Journal of the History of Ideas*, X (1949), 430–444.

Boynton, P. H. "Joel Barlow Advises the Privileged Classes," *New Eng. Quart.*, III (1939), 477–499.

Christensen, M. A. "Deism in Joel Barlow's Early Work: Heterodox Passages in *The Vision of Columbus*," *Am. Lit.*, XXVII (1956), 509–520.

Dorfman, Joseph. "Joel Barlow: Trafficker in Trade and Letters," *Political Science Quarterly*, LIX (1944), 83–100.

Erdman, D. V. "William Blake's Debt to Joel Barlow," *Am. Lit.*, XXVI (1954), 94–98.

Howard, Leon. *The Vision of Joel Barlow*. Los Angeles: The Grey Bow Press, 1937.

Pearce, R. H. "Toward an American Epic," *Hud. Rev.*, XII (1959), 362–377.

Tinker, C. B. "Joel Barlow's *Vision of Columbus*," pp. 37–42 in *Essays in Retrospect*. New Haven, Conn.: Yale University Press, 1948.

Comments on Poems

The Hasty-Pudding

This poem, written in the Savoy, France, was inspired by a dish of New England hasty pudding served him at a Chambéry inn. A literal translation of the Latin first line of the epigraph runs, "He has gained all approval who has mixed the useful with the pleasant."

Discussed in Howard, *The Connecticut Wits*, p. 295; Woodress, *A Yankee's Odyssey*, pp. 135–136.

The text is that which appeared in the *New York Weekly Magazine* in January, 1796.

3. *Ye Gallic flags:* French flags. The French took Savoy in 1792 from the Kingdom of Sardinia.

43. *wallops:* (dialectal) bubbles.

51. *Oella:* a supposed ancestress of the Incas who originated spinning. Barlow "sang before" of her in *The Vision of Columbus* (1787).

89. *Belgic spawn:* the Dutch.

90. *Suppawn:* one of the numerous spellings of the eastern American Indian word for boiled corn meal or mush.

207. *burn the Pope:* probably refers to Guy Fawkes Day, November 5, anniversary of the discovery of the English Gunpowder Plot of 1605.

213. *Cancer:* sign of zodiac for summer solstice.

[One Centred System]

These lines are excerpted from Book X, ll. 529–634, of Barlow's epic, *The Columbiad* (1807), the enlarged version of *The Vision of Columbus* (1787). The text is that which appeared in *The Columbiad: A Poem* (London: Richard Phillips, 1809).

Discussed in Howard, *The Connecticut Wits*, pp. 309–326.

1. *he:* Christopher Columbus.

23. *the place:* Egypt, which Barlow saw as the first seat of civilization, is perhaps chosen here because it is also a "mid site," (l. 29) centrally located.

77. *pagod:* pagoda, representing Buddhism, or perhaps Eastern religions generally.

78. *crescent:* emblem of Mohammedanism. *cross:* emblem of Christianity.

99. *Hesper:* The West, that is, America.

WENDELL BERRY
b. 1934

Major Writings

Nathan Coulter (1960, novel)
November 26, 1963 (1964)
The Broken Ground (1964)

JOHN BERRYMAN
b. 1914

Major Writings

Poems (1942)
The Dispossessed (1948)
Stephen Crane (1950)
Homage to Mistress Bradstreet (1956)
His Thought Made Pockets & The Plane Buckt (1958)
77 Dream Songs (1964)

Criticism

Ciardi, John. "The Researched Mistress," *Saturday Review*, 40 (March 23,
   1957), 36–37.
Eberhart, Richard. "Song of the Nerves," *Poetry*, 73 (1948), 43–45.
Elliott, G. P. "Poetry Chronicle," *Hud. Rev.*, XVII (1964), 457–459.
Kunitz, Stanley. "No Middle Flight," *Poetry*, 90 (1957), 244–249.
Lowell, Robert. "The Poetry of John Berryman," *New York Review of Books*,
   II (May 28, 1964), 3–4.
Rich, Adrienne. "Mr. Bones, He Lives," *Nation*, 198 (May 25, 1964), 538, 540.

Comments on Poems

Winter Landscape
   This poem first appeared in an anthology, *Five Young American Poets*. Norfolk, Conn.: New Directions, 1940. The poem takes its images from the painting *Hunters in the Snow*, by the Flemish painter Pieter Breughel the Elder
(*c.* 1525–1569).

Cloud and Flame
   7. *After his college failure, Swift:* Jonathan Swift neglected his studies at
Trinity College, Dublin, and took an undistinguished degree.
   13. *Cornford:* John Cornford (1915–1936), young English poet who was
killed fighting for the Loyalist cause in the Spanish Civil War.
   23. *Thirkill:* Thirkill the Sacrist. Just before leaving for Hastings to meet
the invading army of William of Normandy, King Harold of England visited
the church at Waltham, Essex, which contained the Holy Rood of Montacute
and Waltham. "The holy image, whose head had hitherto stood erect, bowed
itself toward the King who lay prostrated beneath it. One eye alone, that of
the sacrist Thurkill, was privileged to behold the actual working of the divine
wonder. But many there were who had seen the image in former days, and
who bare witness how its head from that day bowed toward the ground, as
if to say 'It is finished,' as if to say that all was over with the hopes and the
career of him who had so devoutly honoured him." E. A. Freeman, *The
History of the Norman Conquest* (New York: Macmillan, 1873), III, 287.

The Dispossessed

Discussed by John Berryman, pp. 135–136 in Paul Engle and Joseph Langland (eds.), *Poet's Choice* (Dial Press, 1962).

1. *"and something that . . . that is theirs—no longer ours"*: a line spoken by The Father, one of the "characters of the comedy in the making," in Luigi Pirandello's play, *Six Characters in Search of an Author*, Act II. The Leading Man, The Juvenile Lead, and The Leading Lady are among "the actors of the company" in the same play.

Three Around the Old Gentleman

The "Three" are songs 37, 38, and 39 of *77 Dream Songs*, a version of what Berryman calls "a poem in progress." The "Old Gentleman" is Robert Frost, who died in Boston January 29, 1963, of a pulmonary embolism.

37

10. *Henry*: the speaker in the poem, Henry Pussycat, a Negro musician.

38

1. *The Russian grin*: Nikita S. Khrushchev (b. 1894), Chairman of the Council of Ministers of the U.S.S.R. (1958–1964) and First Secretary of the Central Committee of the Communist Party (1953–1964).

2. *Kay*: Kathleen (Mrs. Theodore) Morrison, Frost's secretary for many years.

3. *Ted*: Theodore Morrison, writer and professor of English at Harvard. *Chis & Anne*: Chisholm and Anne Gentry of Ripton, Vermont. Anne, the daughter of the Theodore Morrisons, from the time she was two lived near Frost in Cambridge, Massachusetts, and in Ripton. Her husband, Chisholm Ferrell Gentry, is a printer.

18. *Mr. Bones*: another name for the speaker, Henry Pussycat.

39

2. *Mark*: Mark Van Doren, American poet and critic; emeritus professor of English, Columbia University.

8. *the shooter*: Ernest Hemingway, a lifelong hunter, who died July 2, 1961, of a gunshot wound. *the bourbon man*: William Faulkner, who died July 6, 1962, was reputedly enthusiastic about bourbon whiskey.

ANNE BRADSTREET
c. 1612–1672

Bibliography

Hopkins, F. E. (ed.). "Editor's Note," pp. xxxiii–xliv in *The Poems of Mrs. Anne Bradstreet (1612-1672) Together with Her Prose Remains*. New York: The Duodecimos, 1897.

Wegelin, Oscar. "A List of Editions of the Poems of Anne Bradstreet, with Several Additional Books Relating to Her," *American Book Collector*, IV (1933), 15–16.

Major Writings

The Tenth Muse Lately Sprung up in America: Or Severall Poems, Compiled with Great Variety of Wit and Learning, Full of Delight (1650)
Several Poems Compiled with Great Variety of Wit and Learning, Full of Delight (1678)

Standard Editions

Ellis, J. H. (ed.). *The Works of Anne Bradstreet in Prose and Verse.* Charlestown, Mass.: Abram E. Cutter, 1867.

Hopkins, F. E. (ed.). *The Poems of Mrs. Anne Bradstreet (1612–1672) Together with Her Prose Remains.* New York: The Duodecimos, 1897.

Biography

Berryman, John. *Homage to Mistress Bradstreet.* New York: Farrar, Straus and Cudahy, 1956. (Poem.)

Bradstreet, Metta. "Anne Bradstreet: Her Life and Works," *Historical Collections of the Topsfield* [Massachusetts] *Historical Society,* I (1895), 3–7.

Campbell, Helen. *Anne Bradstreet and Her Time.* Boston: D. Lothrop Co., 1891.

Morison, S. E. "Mistress Anne Bradstreet," pp. 320–336 in *Builders of the Bay Colony.* Boston: Houghton Mifflin and Co., 1930.

Richardson, L. N. "Anne Bradstreet," pp. 577–578 in Allen Johnson (ed.), *Dictionary of American Biography,* Vol. II. New York: Charles Scribner's Sons, 1929.

Criticism

Murdock, K. B. " 'A Little Recreation of Poetry,' " pp. 137–172 in *Literature & Theology in Colonial New England.* Cambridge, Mass.: Harvard University Press, 1949.

Pearce, R. H. "Anne Bradstreet," pp. 22–24 in *The Continuity of American Poetry.* Princeton, N.J.: Princeton University Press, 1961.

Tyler, M. C. "Anne Bradstreet," pp. 277–292 in *A History of American Literature During the Colonial Time,* rev. ed., Vol. I. New York: G. P. Putnam's Sons, 1897.

White, E. W. "The Tenth Muse—A Tercentenary Appraisal of Anne Bradstreet," *William and Mary Quarterly,* VIII (1951), 355–377.

Comments on Poems

The texts of the Bradstreet poems are from the F. E. Hopkins edition, *The Poems of Mrs. Anne Bradstreet,* which is dependable although the seventeenth-century spelling and punctuation are modernized. A few minor variations from the Ellis text, which reproduces the 1678 edition, have been listed in the notes.

The Prologue

Prologue to *The Tenth Muse Lately Sprung up in America*.

8. *Bartas:* Guillaume de Salluste du Bartas (1544–1590), her favorite poet, was a French soldier and author of long religious poems. An English translation by Joshua Sylvester was published in 1605.

19. *sweet-tongued Greek:* Demosthenes, the orator.

43. *oh:* the spelling in both Ellis' and Hopkins' texts. The meaning of the line suggests that the correct spelling is "O," the exclamation used in direct address, in which case the comma following it should be deleted.

Contemplations

29–30. *Thou . . . run a race:* see Psalms 19 : 4–5.

68. *conceit:* conception, thought.

69. *Methuselah or his grandsire:* see Genesis 5 : 18–27.

75. *miscreant was:* in the Ellis text, "miscreant's," which is metrically more regular.

136. *there or:* so spelled in both the Ellis and the Hopkins texts; possibly a printer's error for "therefor" (therefore).

158. *Thetis' house:* the ocean. Thetis was a daughter of Nereus, a sea god in Greek mythology.

162. *abide:* in the Ellis text, "'bide," which is metrically more regular.

178. *philomel:* the nightingale, a bird found in England and in poetry but not in the American colonies.

190. *prevent:* anticipate.

206. *racked:* in the Ellis text, "wrackt" (wrecked).

231. *he . . . white stone:* see Revelation 2 : 17. The reference here is to the redemption of the soul.

The Flesh and the Spirit

Samuel Eliot Morison calls this poem "one of the best expressions in English literature of the conflict described by Saint Paul in the eighth chapter of his Epistle to the Romans."

2. *lacrym:* from Latin *lacrimae*, "tears."

67. *hidden manna:* see Revelation 2 : 17.

85–106. *The city . . . shall not be:* these lines are based on the description of the Heavenly City in Revelation 21 : 10–27 and 22 : 1–5.

97. *Of sun or moon:* in the Ellis text, "Nor Sun, nor Moon."

The Author to Her Book

Anne Bradstreet's brother-in-law, the Reverend John Woodbridge, arranged for the publication of the 1650 edition of her poems while he was in London, despite the fact that she had never intended them to be published. This poem was printed in the posthumous second edition (1678), which she had prepared herself.

To My Dear and Loving Husband

One of four poems addressed to her husband included in the 1678 edition along with, as the title page states, "several other Poems found amongst her Papers after her Death."

In Memory of My Dear Grandchild Elizabeth Bradstreet
 Elizabeth was the first child of her eldest son, Samuel.
 Discussed in Murdock, *Literature & Theology*, pp. 151–152.

Some Verses upon the Burning of Our House, July 10th, 1666
 After Mrs. Bradstreet's death this poem was found on a "loose paper" by
her son, Simon, Jr., from whose note the title is taken. It was first printed in
the Ellis edition of 1867. In the burning of the house at North Andover she
lost many papers, books, and other valuable belongings.
 14. *I blest . . . took:* see Job 1 : 21.
 49. *prize*: in the Ellis text, "Prise"; in the Hopkins text, "price."

WILLIAM CULLEN BRYANT
1794–1878

Bibliography

McDowell, Tremaine (ed.). "Selected Bibliography," pp. lxxiii–lxxxii in
 William Cullen Bryant: Representative Selections. New York: American
 Book Company, 1935.

Major Writings

Poems (1821)
Poems (1832)
Poems (1836)
The Fountain and Other Poems (1842)
Poems (1854)
Thirty Poems (1864)
Poems (1871)
Poems (1875, 3 Vols.)

Standard Editions

Godwin, Parke (ed.). *The Poetical Works of William Cullen Bryant*, 2 Vols. New
 York: D. Appleton and Company, 1883.
McDowell, Tremaine (ed.). *William Cullen Bryant: Representative Selections*.
 New York: American Book Company, 1935.
Sturges, H. C. (ed.). *The Poetical Works of William Cullen Bryant*. New York:
 D. Appleton and Company, 1903.

Biography

Godwin, Parke. *A Biography of William Cullen Bryant, with Extracts from His
 Private Correspondence*, 2 Vols. New York: D. Appleton and Company,
 1883.

Nevins, Allan. *The Evening Post: A Century of Journalism.* New York: Boni and Liveright, 1922.

Peckham, H. H. *Gotham Yankee: A Biography of William Cullen Bryant.* New York: Vantage Press, 1950.

Criticism

Allen, Gay Wilson. "William Cullen Bryant," pp. 27–55 in *American Prosody.* New York: American Book Company, 1935.

Arms, George. "Bryant," pp. 9–19 in *The Fields Were Green.* Stanford, Calif.: Stanford University Press, 1953.

Bradley, W. A. *William Cullen Bryant.* New York: The Macmillan Company, 1905.

Glicksberg, C. I. "William Cullen Bryant, a Reinterpretation," *Revue Anglo-Américaine*, XI (1934), 495–504.

Herrick, M. T. "Rhetoric and Poetry in Bryant," *Am. Lit.*, VII (1935), 188–194.

Hudson, W. P. "Archibald Alison and William Cullen Bryant," *Am. Lit.*, XII (1940), 59–68.

McDowell, Tremaine. "Bryant's Practice in Composition and Revision," *PMLA*, LII (1937), 474–502.

McLean, A. F., Jr. *William Cullen Bryant.* New York: Twayne Publishers, 1964.

Monroe, Harriet. "Aere Perennius," *Poetry*, VI (1915), 197–200.

Murray, D. M. "Dr. Peter Bryant: Preceptor in Poetry to William Cullen Bryant," *New Eng. Quart.*, XXXIII (1960) 513–522.

Ringe, D. A. "Kindred Spirits: Bryant and Cole," *Am. Quart.*, VI (1954), 233–244.

Sanford, Charles. "The Concept of the Sublime in Bryant and Cole," *Am. Lit.*, XXVII (1957), 434–448.

Schick, J. S. "William Cullen Bryant and Théophile Gautier," *Modern Language Journal*, XVII (1933), 260–267.

Comments on Poems

Thanatopsis

The first draft was written in 1811. The poem was first published, in an expanded version, in the *North American Review* in 1817 and further expanded for inclusion in *Poems* (1821). The title, from the Greek, means "on death."

Discussed in Arms, *The Fields Were Green*, pp. 14–15; W. C. Bryant II, *New Eng. Quart.*, XXI (1948), 163–184; W. F. Johnson, *No. Am. Rev.* CCXXIV (1927), 556–572; A. I. Ladu, *Am. Lit.*, XI (1939), 80–81; Tremaine McDowell, *Am. Lit.*, I (1929), 14–26; A. F. McLean, Jr., *Am. Lit.*, XXXI (1960), 474–479; C. W. Nichols, *Am. Lit.*, XI (1939) 217–218; Carl Van Doren, *Nation*, CI (1915), 432–433.

51. *Barcan:* American desert, by analogy with name for desert in Libya, North Africa.

53. *Oregon:* Columbia River.

Inscription for the Entrance to a Wood
  Discussed in G. Giovannini and Walter Gierasch, *Explicator*, IV (1946), 40.
  11. *The primal curse:* see Genesis 3 : 17.
  30. *causey:* causeway.

To a Waterfowl
  The genesis of this poem is described in Godwin, *A Biography of William Cullen Bryant*, I, 143–144.
  Discussed in Arms, *The Fields Were Green*, pp. 17–18; W. C. Bryant II, *New Eng. Quart.*, XXX (1957), 181–189; Donald Davie, pp. 130–137 in John Wain (ed.), *Interpretations* (Routledge and Kegan Paul, 1955); McLean, *William Cullen Bryant*, pp. 31–33.

Green River
  Green River flows near Great Barrington, Massachusetts, where the young Bryant practiced law.
  Discussed in Arms, *The Fields Were Green*, p. 13.
  33. *simpler:* gatherer of simples, herbs.

A Forest Hymn
  Discussed in McLean, *William Cullen Bryant*, pp. 58–60.

"Oh Fairest of the Rural Maids"
  Written in 1820 to Frances Fairchild, who in 1821 became Bryant's wife.
  16. *the brook:* perhaps the Seekonk, which flows into Green River near Great Barrington, Massachusetts.

The Evening Wind
  Discussed in Arms, *The Fields Were Green*, p. 18.

To Cole, the Painter, Departing for Europe
  Bryant's close friend, Thomas Cole (1801–1848), a native of England, was founder of the Hudson River School of landscape painters.

The Prairies
  This poem was first published in a minor volume, *Poems* (1834), one of three poems added to those published in *Poems* (1832).
  Inspired by a first sight of the prairies in Illinois, where Bryant visited his two brothers in the summer of 1832.
  Discussed in C. D. Eby, Jr., *Papers of the Bibliographical Society of America*, LVI (1962), 356–357; McLean, *William Cullen Bryant*, pp. 41–44; R. N. Miller, *Am. Lit.*, XXI (1949), 227–232.
  3. *the speech of England: prairie* is a French word.
  21. *Sonora:* state in northwestern Mexico bordering on California and the Gulf of California.
  42. *the mighty mounds:* Bryant follows popular belief in describing burial mounds as the work of "Mound Builders," who were thought to be ancestors of modern American Indians.
  48. *Pentelicus:* marble from the quarries of Pentelikon, in Greece near Athens.

52. *the bison lowed:* Bryant mistakenly assumes that bisons were successfully domesticated by the "Mound Builders."

67. *the platforms:* pyramidal mounds with temples on the top.

72. *brown vultures of the wood:* wolves.

95. *among Missouri's springs:* at the headwaters of the Missouri River in what are now Montana and Wyoming.

96. *Oregon:* Columbia River.

Earth

Written in Pisa, Italy, in 1834.

Discussed in McLean, *William Cullen Bryant*, pp. 44–46.

36. *O'er loved ones lost:* Bryant refers to his father, who died in 1820, and his favorite sister, who died in 1824 and who are buried in the Berkshire Mountains.

52. *corses:* corpses, bodies.

79. *volcanic graves:* such cities as Pompeii and Herculaneum, buried by the eruption of Mt. Vesuvius in A.D. 79.

84. *strange lords:* reference to French, Spanish, and Austrian domination of partitioned Italy.

The Poet

Discussed in Arms, *The Fields Were Green*, pp. 12–13.

The Death of Lincoln

Written for the funeral procession of the dead Lincoln through New York City in April, 1865.

HART CRANE
1899–1932

Bibliography

Rowe, H. D. *Hart Crane: A Bibliography*. Denver: Alan Swallow, 1955.

Major Writings

White Buildings: Poems (1926)
The Bridge: A Poem (1930)
The Collected Poems of Hart Crane (1933, Waldo Frank, ed.)
The Letters of Hart Crane, 1916–1932 (1952, Brom Weber, ed.)

Biography

Horton, Philip. *Hart Crane: The Life of an American Poet*. New York: W. W. Norton Co., 1937. Republished in Compass Books, Viking Press, 1957.
Weber, Brom. *Hart Crane: A Biographical and Critical Study*. New York: The Bodley Press, 1948.

Criticism

Alvarez, A. *Stewards of Excellence: Studies in Modern English and American Poets*, pp. 107–123. New York: Charles Scribner's Sons, 1958.

Blackmur, R. P. *The Double Agent*, pp. 121–140. New York: Arrow Editions, 1935. Reprinted in *Form and Value in Modern Poetry*, pp. 269–285. New York: Anchor, 1957.

Dembo, L. S. "Hart Crane's Early Poetry," *U. Kans. City Rev.*, XXVII (1961), 181–187.

Deutsch, Babette. *Poetry in Our Time*, pp. 312–330. New York: Holt, Rinehart and Winston, 1952.

Hazo, Samuel. *Hart Crane: An Introduction and Interpretation*. New York: Barnes and Noble, 1963.

Herman, Barbara. "The Language of Hart Crane," *Sewanee Rev.*, LVIII (1950), 52–67.

Munson, G. B. *Destinations*, pp. 160–177. New York: J. H. Sears & Co., 1928.

Quinn, Vincent. *Hart Crane*. New York: Twayne Publishers, 1963.

Rosenthal, M. L. *The Modern Poets: A Critical Introduction*, pp. 168–182. New York: Oxford University Press, 1960.

Swallow, Alan. "Hart Crane," *U. Kans. City Rev.*, XVI (1949), 103–118.

Tate, Allen. *On the Limits of Poetry*, pp. 225–237. New York: The Swallow Press and William Morrow & Co., 1948. Reprinted in *The Man of Letters in the Modern World*, pp. 283–294. New York: Meridian Books, 1955.

Winters, Yvor. "The Progress of Hart Crane," *Poetry*, XXXVI (1930), 153–165.

Zabel, M. D. "The Book of Hart Crane," *Poetry*, XLII (1933), 33–39.

Comments on Poems

The texts of Crane's poems are all taken from *The Collected Poems of Hart Crane*.

Black Tambourine

Discussed in Dembo, *U. Kans. City Rev.*, XXVII (1961), 183–184; Hazo, *Hart Crane*, pp. 24–26.

Praise for an Urn

Ernest Nelson was a Norwegian immigrant, a lithographer, who had settled in Cleveland, where he and Crane became acquainted. He died and was cremated in December, 1921.

Discussed in Dembo, *U. Kans. City Rev.*, XXVII (1961), 185–186; Hazo, *Hart Crane*, pp. 28–31; Quinn, *Hart Crane*, pp. 37–38; Swallow, *U. Kans. City Rev.*, XVI (1949), 115; Mark Van Doren, *Introduction to Poetry* (William Sloane Associates, 1950), pp. 102–107.

Chaplinesque

Charles Spencer (Charlie) Chaplin (b. 1889), American movie actor, was particularly famous in the 1920's and 1930's for the wistful humor of his comedy parts. Crane's poem was inspired by his having seen Chaplin and Jackie Coogan in the movie *The Kid* in the fall of 1921.

Discussed in Glauco Cambon, *The Inclusive Flame* (Indiana University Press, 1963), pp. 168–169; Deutsch, *Poetry in Our Time*, pp. 317–318; Hazo, *Hart Crane*, pp. 34–38; R. W. B. Lewis, *Massachusetts Review*, IV (1963), 745–767; Weber, *Hart Crane*, pp. 107–110.

Repose of Rivers
    Discussed in Hazo, *Hart Crane*, pp. 39–40; Rosenthal, *The Modern Poets*, p. 178; J. D. Young, *Xavier University Studies*, II (1963), 121–137.

The Wine Menagerie
    Discussed in Blackmur, *The Double Agent*, pp. 130–134; Glauco Cambon, *The Inclusive Flame* (Indiana University Press, 1963), pp. 173–175; Hazo, *Hart Crane*, pp. 43–46; Quinn, *Hart Crane*, pp. 52–54; Frajam Taylor, *Accent*, VIII 1947), 34–40.

    45. *Holofernes:* invading general of Biblical times killed by Judith in order to save the Jewish city of Bethulia. See the Book of Judith in the Apocrypha.

    47. *Baptist John's:* John the Baptist, for whose head Salome danced. See Matthew 14 : 1–11 and Mark 6 : 14–28.

    49. *Petrushka's valentine:* Petrouchka, a legendary Russian folk figure. Crane may be referring to Igor Stravinsky's ballet *Petrouchka*, completed May, 1911, and first performed in New York on January 24, 1916.

For the Marriage of Faustus and Helen
    The epigraph is from Ben Jonson's play *The Alchemist* (1610), IV, iii.
    Discussed in Joseph Frank, *Sewanee Rev.*, LVII (1949), 155–156; Hazo, *Hart Crane*, pp. 48–55; W. C. Jumper, *Explicator*, XVII (1959), 8; Quinn, *Hart Crane*, pp. 57–70; Weber, *Hart Crane*, pp. 179–187.

    83. *incunabula:* beginnings, first stages.

    104. *corymbulous:* like corymbs, or flower clusters.

    114. *hypogeum:* an underground chamber.

    127. *Anchises' navel:* Anchises was the crippled father of Aeneas in Virgil's *Aeneid*. Crane is probably referring here to the sea voyages of Aeneas and Anchises after the Fall of Troy, as described in Book III of Virgil's epic.

    128. *Erasmus:* Desiderius Erasmus (*c.* 1466–1536), Dutch humanist scholar and writer.

At Melville's Tomb
    This poem, with its echoes from the conclusion to *Moby-Dick*, is one indication of Crane's deep interest in the works of Herman Melville.

    Discussed in J. W. Beach, *West. Rev.*, XX (1956), 191–192; Hazo, *Hart Crane*, pp. 32–34; Harriet Monroe and Hart Crane, *Poetry*, XXIX (1926), 34–41 (exchange of letters reprinted in Appendix B of Weber, *Hart Crane*, pp. 416–422; Crane's letter to Miss Monroe explaining the poem and his technique is reprinted in Appendix II of Horton, *Hart Crane*, pp. 329–334); Quinn, *Hart Crane*, pp. 41–42.

Voyages
    Discussed in J. W. Beach, *West. Rev.*, XX (1956), 183–196; Deutsch, *Poetry in Our Time*, pp. 319–321; Elizabeth Drew, *Directions in Modern Poetry* (W. W.

Norton Co., 1940), pp. 212–217; J. S. Friedman and Ruth Perlmutter, *Explicator*, XIX (1960), 4; Hazo, *Hart Crane*, pp. 55–67; H. C. Morris, *Accent*, XIV (1954), 291–299; W. V. O'Connor, *Sense and Sensibility in Modern Poetry* (University of Chicago Press, 1948), pp. 73–75; Quinn, *Hart Crane*, pp. 105–115; Sidney Richman, *Wisconsin Studies in Contemporary Literature*, III (1962), 65–78; Rosenthal, *The Modern Poets*, pp. 179–182; M. F. Schulz, *Explicator*, XIV (1956), 46; C. C. Walcutt, *Explicator*, IV (1946), 53; James Zigarell, *Explicator*, XIII (1954), 7.

20. *undinal:* Crane combines a reference to the tidal pull of the moon with a reference to Undine, the water nymph or sprite who desired the love of a mortal man. The name Undine is derived from the Latin *unda*, "wave."

132. *lounged goddess:* Aphrodite, the Greek goddess of love, whose name, derived from *aphros*, "foam," links her to the sea.

135. *Belle Isle:* imagined island so named from the French for "Beautiful Island" for its connotative value.

To Brooklyn Bridge

The most thorough discussion of *The Bridge*, of which "To Brooklyn Bridge," "The River," and "The Tunnel" are parts, is L. S. Dembo, *Hart Crane's Sanskrit Charge: A Study of "The Bridge"* (Cornell University Press, 1960). See also J. W. Beach, *Accent*, VII (1947), 245–246; Glauco Cambon, *The Inclusive Flame* (Indiana University Press, 1963), pp. 120–182; S. K. Coffman, Jr., *PMLA*, LXVI (1951), 65–77; Deutsch, *Poetry in Our Time*, pp. 322–327; Paul Friedman, *Psychoanalytic Quarterly*, XXI (1952), 49–80; Brewster Ghiselin, *Part. Rev.*, XVI (1949), 679–686; Hazo, *Hart Crane*, pp. 68–123; F. J. Hoffman, *The Twenties* (Viking Press, 1955), pp. 223–239; Howard Moss, *Poetry*, LXII (1943), 32–45; W. V. O'Connor, *Sense and Sensibility in Modern Poetry* (University of Chicago Press, 1948), pp. 19–25; R. H. Pearce, *The Continuity of American Poetry* (Princeton University Press, 1961), pp. 101–111; Quinn, *Hart Crane*, pp. 71–103; Sister M. B. Quinn, *The Metamorphic Tradition in Modern Poetry* (Rutgers University Press, 1955), pp. 147–167; Rosenthal, *The Modern Poets*, pp. 169–176; Bernice Slote, *Start with the Sun* (by J. E. Miller, Jr., Karl Shapiro, and Bernice Slote; University of Nebraska Press, 1960), pp. 137–165; Swallow, *U. Kans. City Rev.*, XVI (1949), 116–118; Tate, *On the Limits of Poetry*, pp. 228–237; John Unterecker, *Wisconsin Studies in Contemporary Literature*, III (1962), 5–20; Albert Van Nostrand in R. M. Ludwig (ed.), *Aspects of American Poetry* (Ohio State University Press, 1962), pp. 171–202; H. H. Waggoner, *The Heel of Elohim* (University of Oklahoma Press, 1950), pp. 171–192; Weber, *Hart Crane*, pp. 317–378; H. W. Wells, *The American Way of Poetry* (Columbia University Press, 1943), pp. 191–204; Yvor Winters, *In Defense of Reason* (Alan Swallow, 1947), pp. 577–603.

21. *Wall:* Wall Street in New York City.

The River

For discussions see "To Brooklyn Bridge."

5. *Bert Williams:* Negro vaudeville comedian who died in 1922.

9–10. *Thomas a Ediford:* a combined name for Thomas A. Edison and Henry Ford, selected as representative of a machine civilization. The name is a punning reference to Thomas à Becket, the twelfth-century English saint.

82. *Iron Mountain:* a hill of iron ore situated in southeastern Missouri and actually in the St. Francois Mountains rather than the Ozarks.

93. *Siskiyou:* a county and a mountain range, but not a community, in northern California close to the Oregon border.

95. *Cairo:* small city located at the extreme southern tip of Illinois, where the Ohio River flows into the Mississippi.

112. *Dan Midland:* a famous hobo, who was killed in the manner described while "riding the rods."

116. *Jordan's brow:* perhaps a reference to the section of the Palestinian River Jordan where it flows slowly before entering the Dead Sea.

133. *De Soto's bones:* when Hernando de Soto, discoverer of the Mississippi River, died in 1542, his men buried him in the Mississippi near the future site of New Orleans.

134. *the City:* New Orleans, which in its history has been under French, Spanish, and finally American government.

The Tunnel

The epigraph is the first two lines of "Morning" by the English poet William Blake (1757–1827).

For discussions see "To Brooklyn Bridge."

2. *Up Times Square to Columbus Circle:* standing at Times Square at Broadway and Forty-second Street, the poet looks north up Broadway toward Columbus Circle at the southwest corner of Central Park.

19. *the L:* elevated trains; here the Sixth Avenue "El." The "El" was a feature of New York's transportation system until 1955.

52. *Fourteenth:* Fourteenth Street in Manhattan. The poet is taking the subway south under Manhattan Island and will go under the East River across to Brooklyn.

72. *your visage:* the poet addresses Edgar Allan Poe. See l. 82.

73. *agate lanterns:* cf. the "agate lamp" of Poe's "To Helen," l. 13.

77. *And Death . . . down:* an echo of Poe's "The City in the Sea," ll. 28–29.

79–82. *And when . . . Poe:* the events that led up to Poe's death in Baltimore on October 7, 1849, are still not certainly known.

83. *Chambers Street:* near the southern tip of Manhattan at the end of Brooklyn Bridge.

104. *O Genoese:* an echo, as is l. 137 and "Columbus Circle," of a preceding section of *The Bridge*, "Ave Maria," a monologue by Christopher Columbus, who was probably born in Genoa, Italy. Possibly also an echo of "Ah Genoese" in Walt Whitman's "Passage to India," l. 65.

O Carib Isle!

Discussed in Hazo, *Hart Crane*, pp. 128–129; Quinn, *Hart Crane*, pp. 34–35.

Royal Palm

Grace Hart Crane was the poet's mother.

Discussed in Hazo, *Hart Crane*, pp. 126–127.

The Hurricane

Discussed in Hazo, *Hart Crane*, pp. 124–125; Quinn, *Hart Crane*, pp. 34–35.

The Broken Tower

The church in this poem is that of San Sebastián y Santa Prisca in Taxco, Mexico, where Crane lived in the final months of his life.

Discussed in Marius Bewley, *Accent*, XIX (1959), 75–85; Henry Braun, *Boston University Studies in English*, V (1961), 167–177; Hazo, *Hart Crane*, pp. 129–132; Herbert Martey, *U. Kans. City Rev.*, XVIII (1952), 199–205; Quinn, *Hart Crane*, pp. 55–56; Muriel Rukeyser, *The Life of Poetry* (A. A. Wyn, 1949), pp. 32–33.

STEPHEN CRANE
1871–1900

Bibliography

Stolpher, J. R. *Stephen Crane: A List of His Writings and Articles About Him.* Newark, N.J.: Public Library, 1930.

Williams, Ames W., and Starrett, Vincent. *Stephen Crane: A Bibliography.* Glendale, Calif.: John Valentine, 1948.

Major Writings

Maggie: A Girl of the Streets (1893, fiction)
The Black Riders (1895)
The Red Badge of Courage (1895, fiction)
War Is Kind (1899)
Whilomville Stories (1900, fiction)

Standard Edition

Follett, Wilson (ed.). New York: Alfred A. Knopf, 1930.

Biography

Beer, Thomas. *Stephen Crane: A Study in American Letters.* Garden City, N.Y.: Garden City Publishing Co., 1927.

Berryman, John. *Stephen Crane.* New York: William Sloane Associates, 1950.

Criticism

Gregory, Horace, and Zaturenska, Marya. *A History of American Poetry: 1900–1940*, pp. 133–137. New York: Harcourt, Brace and Co., 1946.

Hoffman, D. G. *The Poetry of Stephen Crane.* New York: Columbia University Press, 1957.

Stallman, Robert W. (ed.). *Stephen Crane: An Omnibus.* New York: Alfred A. Knopf, 1952.

Comments on Poems

The Black Riders

The text source of these poems from *The Black Riders* is the 1895 edition published in Boston by Copeland and Day. All poems were printed in capital letters and quotation marks appeared at the beginning of each line. The 1895 text has been faithfully followed except for these two typographical peculiarities. The 1930 edition contains some slight variations.

I

1. *Black riders:* Hoffman in *The Poetry of Stephen Crane*, pp. 81–82, suggests that "*all* the poems are like the black riders that come from the sea (conventionally a symbol of the unconscious) . . ."

III

Hoffman, *The Poetry of Stephen Crane*, pp. 54–55, finds the origin of the imagery of this poem in a chapter called "The Depraved Heart" in an evangelical book entitled *What Must I Do to Be Saved?* owned by the poet's father.

IX

6. "*Comrade! Brother!*": Stallman in *Stephen Crane: An Omnibus*, p. 570, sees the influence of Hawthorne's "Young Goodman Brown" in this poem, but Hoffman in *The Poetry of Stephen Crane*, p. 80, says: "'Comrade! Brother!' reminds us also of Baudelaire's '*Hypocrite lecteur—mon semblable—mon frère*." For T. S. Eliot's use of the phrase see *The Waste Land*, l. 76.

X

6. *white arms:* both Berryman, *Stephen Crane*, p. 302, and Hoffman, *The Poetry of Stephen Crane*, p. 126, regard this as a Freudian symbol, erotic and Oedipal.

XII

Epigraph from Exodus 20 : 5.

XXVIII

2. *rock . . . fortress:* "The Lord is my rock, my fortress," Psalms 18 : 2.

11. *hem of its garment:* ". . . touched the hem of his [Jesus'] garment," Matthew 9 : 20; "And besought him [Jesus] that they might only touch the hem of his garment . . . ," Matthew 14 : 36.

XLI

Hoffman, *The Poetry of Stephen Crane*, p. 195, calls attention to the similarity of imagery in this poem to Olive Schreiner's *Dreams*, which Crane had read; but his sardonic dreams contrast sharply with her sentimental ones.

XLVI

This poem might be called an allegory of Crane's process of writing poems, suggesting the origin of the imagery in the psyche of the poet.

LXVII

15–18. Beer, *Stephen Crane*, p. 122, sees an actual experience reflected in these lines: in the Bowery Crane "had seen a young streetwalker cover the head of a drunken procurer with her body while the fellow's assailants were trying to stamp his face to pieces; Crane ran to bring help and the police arrested the girl for cursing."

The Blue Battalions

This poem was published in *The Philistine* (a short-lived Boston literary magazine) in June, 1898, but for some reason Crane did not include it in *War Is Kind*, published the following year. However, when Amy Lowell edited the two books of poems for *The Works of Stephen Crane* (Alfred A. Knopf, 1926), she placed this poem at the end of the *War Is Kind* group and gave it the number XXVII; in *The Collected Poems of Stephen Crane* (1930) this erroneous place and number are retained, and the error has been perpetuated in many anthologies. Hoffman, *The Poetry of Stephen Crane*, p. 187, thinks that in this poem, and some others, the poet's imagination attempts to move in two directions at the same time: toward "a wry, ironic, seemingly colloquial diction" and toward a "crude sort of allegory."

War Is Kind

XI
4. *hooded men:* apparently nomadic Arabs, watching a dancing houri.

XIX
9–10. No editorial omission; thus in Crane's text.

Three Poems

These unpublished poems were discovered in 1928 among some Crane manuscripts which had been in the posession of Cora Taylor, Crane's common-law wife. They were first published in *The Bookman*, April, 1929, and then reprinted in *The Collected Poems of Stephen Crane* (1930). The dates of composition are unknown, and the order is not significant.

ROBERT CREELEY
b. 1926

Major Writings

Le Fou (1952)
The Immortal Proposition (1953)
The Kind of Act of (1953)
The Gold Diggers (1954)
All That Is Lovely in Men (1955)
If You (1956)
The Whip (1957)
A Form of Women (1959)
For Love: Poems 1950–1960 (1962)

Criticism

For Creeley's theories on poetics see Donald M. Allen (ed.), *The New American Poetry: 1945–1960* (Grove Press, 1960).

The review of *For Love* in the San Francisco *Chronicle* (July 1, 1962, p. 4, by James Shevill) remarked that "most of these poems deal with the tangle and wonder of love." Paul Carroll in the *Nation*, 95 (1962), 77, called them "close-to-the-bone, fiercely personal poems." Dudley Fitts reviewed the volume in the *Saturday Review*, 45 (August 4, 1962), 22, and Kenneth Rexroth in the *New York Times Book Review* (November 4, 1962), p. 38.

Comments on Poems

Hart Crane

Slater Brown: close friend of Hart Crane; one of the expatriates discussed by Malcolm Cowley in *Exile's Return* (Viking Press, 1951). See also Brom Weber, *Hart Crane* (The Bodley Press, 1948), p. 207 *et passim*.

1–10. *stuttering:* Crane stuttered when strongly moved or unable to say what he wished.

11. Crane was briefly happy on Slater Brown's farm at Patterson, New York. Cf. Brom Weber, *Hart Crane*, pp. 246 ff.

31. *Waldo Frank:* journalist, novelist, translator, author of books interpreting Latin America; he befriended Crane personally and with critical support.

35. *Mexico:* in 1931, having received a Guggenheim Fellowship, Crane went to Mexico, hoping to finish *The Bridge* and other poems.

44. *broken world:* allusion to Crane's poem "The Broken Tower," in which the ringing of bells shatters the tower, as the poet's uncontrollable emotions shattered his life while in Mexico and led to his suicide a few months later. See notes on Hart Crane's "The Broken Tower."

E. E. CUMMINGS
1894–1962

Bibliography

Firmage, G. J. *E. E. Cummings: A Bibliography*. Middletown, Conn.: Wesleyan University Press, 1960.

Lauter, Paul. *E. E. Cummings: Index to First Lines and Bibliography of Works by and about the Poet*. Denver: Alan Swallow, 1955.

Major Writings

The Enormous Room (1922, autobiography)
Tulips and Chimneys (1923)
& (1925)
is 5 (1926)

Him (1927, play)
W (*Viva*) (1931)
Eimi (1933, a report on a trip to the U.S.S.R.)
no thanks (1935)
50 POEMS (1940)
1 x 1 (1944)
XAIPE (1950)
i: six nonlectures (1953, autobiography)
Poems, 1923–1954 (1954)
95 Poems (1958)
73 Poems (1963)

Biography

Norman, Charles. *The Magic-Maker: E. E. Cummings*. New York: The Macmillan Co., 1958.

Criticism

Arthos, John. "The Poetry of E. E. Cummings," *Am. Lit.*, XIV (1943), 372–390.

Axelrod, Joseph. "Cummings and Phonetics," *Poetry*, LXV (1944), 88–94.

Baum, S. V. "E. E. Cummings: The Technique of Immediacy," *So. Atl. Quart.*, LIII (1954), 70–88.

Baum, S. V. (ed.). *EΣTI: e e c: E. E. Cummings and the Critics*. East Lansing, Mich.: Michigan State University Press, 1962.

Blackmur, R. P. *Form and Value in Modern Poetry*, pp. 287–312. New York: Anchor, 1957.

Frankenberg, Lloyd. *Pleasure Dome: On Reading Modern Poetry*, pp. 159–194. Boston: Houghton Mifflin and Co., 1949.

Friedman, Norman. *E. E. Cummings: The Art of His Poetry*. Baltimore: The Johns Hopkins Press, 1960.

Friedman, Norman. *E. E. Cummings: The Growth of a Writer*. Carbondale, Ill.: Southern Illinois University Press, 1964.

Harvard Wake, No. 5 (1946). Cummings number.

Marks, B. A. *E. E. Cummings*. New York: Twayne Publishers, 1964.

Sickels, E. M. "The Unworld of E. E. Cummings," *Am. Lit.*, XXVI (1954), 223–238.

Spencer, Theodore. "Technique as Joy," *Perspectives USA*, No. 2 (1953), 23–29.

Von Abele, Rudolph. "'Only to Grow': Change in the Poetry of E. E. Cummings," *PMLA*, LXX (1955), 913–933.

Watson, Barbara. "The Dangers of Security: E. E. Cummings' Revolt Against the Future," *Ken. Rev.*, XVIII (1956), 519–537.

Comments on Poems

The texts of the first eight poems by Cummings are taken from *Poems, 1923–1954*; the last two, from *73 Poems*.

O sweet spontaneous
  Discussed in Marks, *E. E. Cummings*, pp. 69–71.

anyone lived in a pretty how town
  Discussed in H. C. Barrows, Jr., and W. R. Steinhoff, *Explicator*, IX (1950),
1; Arthur Carr, *Explicator*, XI (1952), 6; George Haines, *Sewanee Rev.*, LIX
(1951), 216–217; Marks, *E. E. Cummings*, pp. 38–45; R. C. Walsh, *Explicator*,
XXII (1964), 72.

my father moved through dooms of love
  Discussed in George Haines, *Sewanee Rev.*, LIX (1951), 215–216; Sister
J. M. Lechner, *Renascence*, XII (1960), 183.

pity this busy monster,manunkind
  Discussed in John Britton, *Explicator*, XVIII (1959), 5; J. W. Gargano,
Explicator, XX (1961), 21.

what if a much of a which of a wind
  Discussed in Friedman, *E. E. Cummings: The Art of His Poetry*, pp. 37–39;
Marks, *E. E. Cummings*, pp. 59–60, 118–119; S. E. Whicher, *Explicator*, XII
(1953), 14.

JAMES DICKEY
b. 1923

Major Writings

Into the Stone and Other Poems (1960)
Drowning with Others (1962)
Helmets (1964)
Two Poems of the Air (1964)
The Suspect in Poetry (1964, criticism)

Criticism

"Crunk." "The Work of James Dickey," *The Sixties*, No. 7 (1964), 41–57.
Nemerov, Howard. "Poems of Darkness and a Specialized Light," *Sewanee
  Rev.*, LXXI (1963), 99–104.

EMILY DICKINSON
1830–1886

Bibliography

Emily Dickinson, December 10, 1830–May 15, 1886: A Bibliography. Amherst,
  Mass.: The Jones Library, 1930.
Hampson, A. L. *Emily Dickinson: A Bibliography*. Northampton, Mass.: The
  Hampshire Bookshop, 1930.

Concordance

Rosenbaum, S. P. *A Concordance to the Poems of Emily Dickinson.* Ithaca, N.Y.:
    Cornell University Press, 1965.

Major Writings

Poems by Emily Dickinson (1890, M. L. Todd and T. W. Higginson, eds.)
Poems by Emily Dickinson, Second Series (1891, T. W. Higginson and M. L. Todd,
    eds.)
Poems by Emily Dickinson, Third Series (1896, M. L. Todd, ed.)
The Single Hound: Poems of a Lifetime (1914, M. D. Bianchi, ed.)
The Complete Poems of Emily Dickinson (1924, M. D. Bianchi and A. L. Hampson,
    eds.)
Further Poems of Emily Dickinson (1929, M. D. Bianchi and A. L. Hampson,
    eds.)
The Poems of Emily Dickinson, Centenary Edition (1930, M. D. Bianchi and
    A. L. Hampson, eds.)
Unpublished Poems of Emily Dickinson (1935, M. D. Bianchi and A. L.
    Hampson, eds.)
Poems by Emily Dickinson (1937, M. D. Bianchi and A. L. Hampson, eds.)
Bolts of Melody: New Poems of Emily Dickinson (1945, M. L. Todd and M. T.
    Bingham, eds.)
The Letters of Emily Dickinson (1958, 3 Vols., T. H. Johnson and Theodora
    Ward, eds.)
The Complete Poems of Emily Dickinson (1960, T. H. Johnson, ed.)

Standard Edition

Johnson, T. H. (ed.). *The Poems of Emily Dickinson,* 3 Vols. Cambridge, Mass.:
    The Belknap Press of Harvard University Press, 1955.

Biography

Johnson, T. H. *Emily Dickinson: An Interpretive Biography.* Cambridge, Mass.:
    The Belknap Press of Harvard University Press, 1955.
Leyda, Jay. *The Years and Hours of Emily Dickinson,* 2 Vols. New Haven, Conn.:
    Yale University Press, 1960.
Ward, Theodora. *The Capsule of the Mind: Chapters in the Life of Emily Dickin-
    son.* Cambridge, Mass.: The Belknap Press of Harvard University Press,
    1961.
Whicher, G. F. *This Was a Poet: A Critical Biography of Emily Dickinson.* New
    York: Charles Scribner's Sons, 1939.

Criticism

Adams, R. P. "Pure Poetry: Emily Dickinson," *Tulane Stud. Eng.,* VII (1957),
    133–152.
Anderson, C. R. *Emily Dickinson's Poetry: Stairway of Surprise.* New York:
    Holt, Rinehart and Winston, 1960.

Banzer, Judith. "'Compound Manner': Emily Dickinson and the Meta-physical Poets," *Am. Lit.*, XXXII (1961), 417–433.

Blake, C. R., and Wells, C. F. (eds.). *The Recognition of Emily Dickinson: Selected Criticism Since 1890.* Ann Arbor, Mich.: The University of Michigan Press, 1964.

Carpenter, F. I. "Emily Dickinson and the Rhymes of Dream," *U. Kans. City Rev.*, XX (1953), 113–120.

Chase, Richard. *Emily Dickinson.* New York: William Sloane Associates, 1951.

Griffith, Clark. *The Long Shadow: Emily Dickinson's Tragic Poetry.* Princeton, N.J.: Princeton University Press, 1964.

Howard, William. "Emily Dickinson's Poetic Vocabulary," *PMLA*, LXXII (1957), 225–248.

MacLeish, Archibald; Bogan, Louise; and Wilbur, Richard. *Emily Dickinson: Three Views.* Amherst, Mass.: Amherst College Press, 1960. The Mac-Leish essay is expanded as "The Private World: Poems of Emily Dickinson," pp. 91–114 in *Poetry and Experience.* Boston: Houghton Mifflin and Co., 1961.

Tate, Allen. "Emily Dickinson," pp. 3–25 in *Reactionary Essays on Poetry and Ideas.* New York: Charles Scribner's Sons, 1936.

Thackrey, D. E. "Emily Dickinson's Approach to Poetry," *University of Nebraska Studies*, n. s. No. 13 (1954), 1–82.

Warren, Austin. "Emily Dickinson," *Sewanee Rev.*, LXV (1957), 565–586.

Wells, H. W. *Introduction to Emily Dickinson.* Chicago: Packard and Co., 1947.

Winters, Yvor. "Emily Dickinson and the Limits of Judgment," pp. 149–165 in *Maule's Curse: Seven Studies in the History of American Obscurantism.* Norfolk, Conn.: New Directions, 1938.

Comments on Poems

The texts of Emily Dickinson's poems here printed are taken from the three-volume edition by Thomas H. Johnson, which aimed at giving a "literal rendering" of the manuscripts as a means of overcoming the textual problems faced, and sometimes created, by previous editors. The numbers that appear in the place of titles are those assigned by Johnson to indicate probable chronology of composition of the poems, while the dates in brackets are those of first publication in a collection of Emily Dickinson's poetry. For both variant versions, which are numerous in the manuscripts, and the composition dates of the poems one should go to the volumes of this 1955 edition. In a very few instances an alternative reading given in Johnson's notes and adopted by him in the one-volume *Complete Poems of Emily Dickinson* (1960) has been substituted in this 1955 text. Alternative readings are marked with an asterisk and the 1955 readings given in the Notes.

49 I never lost as much but twice
   Discussed in Johnson, *Emily Dickinson*, p. 89.

67 Success is counted sweetest
   This was the last Dickinson poem to be published during her lifetime. It

appeared, somewhat altered, in *A Masque of Poets* (1878), an anthology of anonymous verse edited by Thomas Niles.

Discussed in D. S. R. Welland, in Carl Bode (ed.), *The Great Experiment in American Literature* (Heinemann, 1961), pp. 62–64; Whicher, *This Was a Poet*, pp. 202–203; Wilbur, *Emily Dickinson: Three Views*, pp. 40–41.

128 Bring me the sunset in a cup
19. *Alban:* white. "Alban house" refers to the speaker's body.

130 These are the days when Birds come back
Discussed in Adams, *Tulane Stud. Eng.*, VII (1957), 145–146; Anderson, *Emily Dickinson's Poetry*, pp. 145–149; George Arms, *Explicator*, II (1944), 29; Johnson, *Emily Dickinson*, pp. 187–188; Marshall Van Deusen, *Explicator*, XII (1954), 40.

160 Just lost, when I was saved
Discussed in Johnson, *Emily Dickinson*, pp. 89–90, 153.
13–15. *the things . . . by Eye:* see 1 Corinthians 2 : 9.

165 A *Wounded* Deer—leaps highest
Discussed in Griffith, *The Long Shadow*, pp. 299–301.

187 How many times these low feet staggered
Discussed in Anderson, *Emily Dickinson's Poetry*, pp. 229–230; Johnson, *Emily Dickinson*, pp. 90–91, 209.

214 I taste a liquor never brewed
Published anonymously under the title "The May-Wine" in the *Springfield Daily Republican*, May 4, 1861, with revisions probably representing editorial regularization of meter and rhyme.
Discussed in Anderson, *Emily Dickinson's Poetry*, pp. 73–75; Chase, *Emily Dickinson*, pp. 228–230; W. W. Douglas, *English "A" Analyst* (Northwestern University), No. 4, pp. 1–3; Johnson, *Emily Dickinson*, pp. 91–92; Genevieve Taggard, *The Life and Mind of Emily Dickinson* (Knopf, 1930), pp. 267–270.
3. *Vats . . . Rhine:* in 1955 edition: "Frankfort Berries."
16. *Leaning . . . Sun:* in 1955 edition: "From Manzanilla come!"

216 Safe in their Alabaster Chambers
The first version of this poem (1859) was published anonymously under the title "The Sleeping" in the *Springfield Daily Republican*, March 1, 1862. Johnson presents evidence (*Poems*, I, pp. 152–155) that the poet did not find even the second version (1861) satisfactory. The two versions were combined into a single poem in *Poems* (1890).
Discussed in Anderson, *Emily Dickinson's Poetry*, pp. 270–275; Chase, *Emily Dickinson*, p. 233; William Howard and Mother Angela Carson, *Explicator*, XVII (1959), 62; Johnson, *Emily Dickinson*, pp. 106–108; John Wheatcroft, *Bucknell Review*, X (1961), 124–127.

241 I like a look of Agony
Discussed in Johnson, *Emily Dickinson*, p. 95.

249 Wild Nights—Wild Nights
Discussed in Anderson, *Emily Dickinson's Poetry*, pp. 169–170.

258 There's a certain Slant of light
Discussed in Adams, *Tulane Stud. Eng.*, VII (1957), 146–149; Anderson, *Emily Dickinson's Poetry*, pp. 215–218; Chase, *Emily Dickinson*, p. 141; Griffith, *The Long Shadow*, pp. 26–29, 173; Johnson, *Emily Dickinson*, pp. 189–190; Laurence Perrine, *Explicator*, XI (1953), 50; Thackrey, *University of Nebraska Studies*, n. s. No. 13 (1954), 76–80; Winters, *Maule's Curse*, pp. 162–164.

280 I felt a Funeral, in my Brain
Discussed in Anderson, *Emily Dickinson's Poetry*, pp. 208–210; Griffith, *The Long Shadow*, pp. 245–255; Johnson, *Emily Dickinson*, p. 212; George Monteiro, *Mod. Lang. Notes*, LXXV (1960), 656–663.

287 A Clock stopped
Discussed in Anderson, *Emily Dickinson's Poetry*, pp. 234–238; D. W. Bolin, *Explicator*, XXII (1963), 27; Johnson, *Emily Dickinson*, pp. 211–212; E. R. Miner, *Explicator*, XIII (1954), 18; Laurence Perrine, *Explicator.* XIV (1955), 4; William Rossky, *Explicator*, XXII (1963), 3.

290 Of Bronze—and Blaze
Discussed in Anderson, *Emily Dickinson's Poetry*, pp. 47–54; David Hiatt, *Explicator*, XXI (1962), 6.
    19. *Beetles*: in 1955 edition: "Daisies."

303 The Soul selects her own Society
Discussed in Anderson, *Emily Dickinson's Poetry*, pp. 170–171; Griffith, *The Long Shadow*, pp. 210–212; H. F. Pommer, *Explicator*, III (1945), 32; Mark Van Doren, *Introduction to Poetry* (William Sloane Associates, 1951), pp. 39–42.

318 I'll tell you how the Sun rose
Discussed in Griffith *The Long Shadow*, pp. 111–112; Johnson, *Emily Dickinson*, pp. 108–109; Wilbur Scott, *Explicator*, VII (1948), 14; S. M. Wilson, *Am. Lit.*, XXXV (1963), 56–57.

322 There came a Day at Summer's full
Discussed in Mother Mary Anthony, *Massachusetts Review*, II (1961), 557–561; Griffith, *The Long Shadow*, pp. 158–161; Caroline Hogue, *Explicator*, XI (1952) 17; William Howard, *Explicator*, XII (1954), 41.
    8. *That . . . new:* perhaps an echo of Revelation 21 : 5.

328 A Bird came down the Walk
Discussed in Anderson, *Emily Dickinson's Poetry*, pp. 117–119; Carpenter, *U. Kans. City Rev.*, XX (1953), 119–120; J. P. Kirby, *Explicator*, II (1944), 61.

341 After great pain, a formal feeling comes
Johnson notes (*Poems*, I, p. 273) but does not follow Emily Dickinson's own reordering of lines that reverses ll. 6 and 7 and produces far more syntactical sense:

> The Feet, mechanical, go round—
> A Wooden way
> Of Ground, or Air, or Ought—
> Regardless grown,
> A Quartz contentment, like a stone—

Discussed in Anderson, *Emily Dickinson's Poetry*, pp. 210–211; Chase, *Emily Dickinson*, p. 232; Elizabeth Drew, *Poetry: A Modern Guide to Its Understanding and Enjoyment* (Norton, 1959), pp. 124–125; Griffith, *The Long Shadow*, pp. 241–245; Johnson, *Emily Dickinson*, pp. 97–98; Francis Manley, *Mod. Lang. Notes*, LXXIII (1958), 260–264.

348 I dreaded that first Robin, so

Johnson dates this poem early 1862 and notes: "On 11 January 1862, the *Daily News* of Philadelphia reported Charles Wadsworth's call to Calvary Church in San Francisco, where he arrived on 28 May." (*Poems*, I, pp. 278–279.)

Discussed in Anderson, *Emily Dickinson's Poetry*, pp. 198–202; R. St. C. Smith, *Explicator*, V (1947), 31.

376 Of Course—I prayed

Discussed in Whicher, *This Was a Poet*, pp. 272–273.

401 What Soft—Cherubic Creatures

Discussed in Anderson, *Emily Dickinson's Poetry*, pp. 12–14; S. M. Wilson, *Am. Lit.*, XXXV (1963), 55–56.

5. *Dimity:* a thin cotton fabric.

449 I died for Beauty—but was scarce

Discussed in Carpenter, *U. Kans. City Rev.*, XX (1953), 116–117; Chase, *Emily Dickinson*, pp. 141, 196–198.

465 I heard a Fly buzz—when I died

Discussed in Anderson, *Emily Dickinson's Poetry*, pp. 231–232; Chase, *Emily Dickinson*, pp. 246–249; John Ciardi, *Explicator*, XIV (1956), 22; Gerhard Friedrich, *Explicator*, XIII (1955), 35; Caroline Hogue, *Explicator*, XX (1961) 26; Johnson, *Emily Dickinson*, pp. 213–214.

502 At least—to pray—is left—is left

Discussed in Griffith, *The Long Shadow*, p. 67 fn.

511 If you were coming in the Fall

1. *you:* possibly Charles Wadsworth.

12. *Van Dieman's Land:* Tasmania. Until 1853 Tasmania was officially named Van Dieman's Land in honor of Antony Van Dieman, who was Governor-General of the Dutch East Indies when the island was discovered, in 1642, by Abel Tasman, the Dutch navigator.

526 To hear an Oriole sing

Discussed in Anderson, *Emily Dickinson's Poetry*, pp. 88–89.

536 The Heart asks Pleasure—first
Discussed in Carpenter, *U. Kans. City Rev.*, XX (1953), 115.

556 The Brain, within it's Groove
Discussed in Griffith, *The Long Shadow*, pp. 195–196.

585 I like to see it lap the Miles
Edward Dickinson had helped establish the Amherst & Belchertown Railway in 1853.

Discussed in Anderson, *Emily Dickinson's Poetry*, pp. 15–16; Chase, *Emily Dickinson*, pp. 227–228; Nathalia Wright, *Mod. Lang. Notes*, LXXII (1957), 101–103.
   9. *Ribs:* in 1955 edition: "sides."
   14. *Boanerges:* "The sons of thunder." See Mark 3 : 17.
   15. *punctual as:* in 1955 edition: "prompter than."

620 It makes no difference abroad
Discussed in Wilbur, *Emily Dickinson: Three Views*, p. 42.

640 I cannot live with You
Discussed in Eunice Glenn, *Sewanee Rev.*, LI (1943), 582–585.
   1. *You:* possibly Charles Wadsworth.
   11. *Sevres:* Sèvres, fine porcelain named after a suburb of Paris where it is made.

657 I dwell in Possibility
Discussed in Johnson, *Emily Dickinson*, p. 142.

664 Of all the Souls that stand create
Discussed in Anderson, *Emily Dickinson's Poetry*, pp. 171–172; Chase, *Emily Dickinson*, pp. 159–160; Johnson, *Emily Dickinson*, p. 101; Whicher, *This Was a Poet*, pp. 284–285.

675 Essential Oils—are wrung
Discussed in Anderson, *Emily Dickinson's Poetry*, pp. 64–68.

712 Because I could not stop for Death
Discussed in Anderson, *Emily Dickinson's Poetry*, pp. 241–249; Chase, *Emily Dickinson*, pp. 161, 249–251; Eunice Glenn, *Sewanee Rev.*, LI (1943), 585–588; Griffith, *The Long Shadow*, pp. 127–135; T. C. Hoepfner, *Am. Lit.*, XXIX (1957), 96; Johnson, *Emily Dickinson*, pp. 222–224; Tate, *Reactionary Essays on Poetry and Ideas*, pp. 13–16; John Wheatcroft, *Bucknell Review*, X (1961), 108–114; Winters, *Maule's Curse*, pp. 154–156.

721 Behind Me—dips Eternity
Discussed in Anderson, *Emily Dickinson's Poetry*, pp. 280–283; Wells, *Introduction to Emily Dickinson*, pp. 149–150.

754 My Life had stood—a Loaded Gun
Discussed in Anderson, *Emily Dickinson's Poetry*, pp. 172–176; Johnson, *Emily Dickinson*, pp. 138–140; Laurence Perrine, *Explicator*, XXI (1962), 21;

The Poetry Workshop, Columbus, Ga., *Explicator*, XV (1957), 51; Whicher, *This Was a Poet*, pp. 278–279.

764 Presentiment—is that long Shadow—on the Lawn
   Discussed in Chase, *Emily Dickinson*, pp. 140–141; Griffith, *The Long Shadow*, pp. 84–92; D. H. Hirsch, *American Notes and Queries*, I (1962–1963), 36–37.

822 This Consciousness that is aware
   Discussed in C. R. Anderson, *Am. Lit.*, XXXI (1959), 307; Johnson, *Emily Dickinson*, pp. 249–251; MacLeish, *Poetry and Experience*, pp. 107–109.

829 Ample make this Bed
   Discussed in Anderson, *Emily Dickinson's Poetry*, p. 271.

861 Split the Lark—and you'll find the Music
   Discussed in Anderson, *Emily Dickinson's Poetry*, pp. 89–90.
   7. *Sceptic Thomas:* the doubting disciple of Jesus. See John 20 : 24–25.

946 It is an honorable Thought
   Discussed in Ralph Marcellino, *Classical Journal*, L (1954), 126.
   5–6. *That . . . decay* Marcellino suggests that these lines are a reminiscence of Horace, *Odes* 3 : 30.

986 A narrow Fellow in the Grass
   First published anonymously under the title "The Snake" in the *Springfield Daily Republican* for February 14, 1866.
   Discussed in Adams, *Tulane Stud. Eng.*, VII (1957), 142–145; Anderson, *Emily Dickinson's Poetry*, pp. 120–121.

997 Crumbling is not an instant's Act
   Discussed in C. R. Anderson, *Am. Lit.*, XXXI (1959), 297–298.

1052 I never saw a Moor
   Discussed in Griffith, *The Long Shadow*, pp. 3–4, 109–110; William Howard, *Explicator*, XXI (1962), 13.
   8. *Checks:* Johnson notes that this word seems to be used "in the accepted colloquial sense of railroad tickets." (*Poems*, II, p. 742.)

1068 Further in Summer than the Birds
   Discussed in Adams, *Tulane Stud. Eng.*, VII (1957), 150–151; Anderson, *Emily Dickinson's Poetry*, pp. 150–156; F. I. Carpenter, *Explicator*, VIII (1950), 33; Carpenter, *U. Kans. City Rev.*, XX (1953), 118; Chase, *Emily Dickinson*, pp. 171–172; R. H. and H. L. Elias, *Explicator*, XI (1952), 5; Griffith, *The Long Shadow*, pp. 84–92; Johnson, *Emily Dickinson*, pp. 185–187; René Rapin, *Explicator*, XII (1954), 24; Marshall Van Deusen, *Explicator*, XIII (1955), 33; Winters, *Maule's Curse*, pp. 159–160.
   3. *minor Nation:* insects.

1072 Title divine—is mine
   Discussed in Anderson, *Emily Dickinson's Poetry*, pp. 182–183; Eunice Glenn, *Sewanee Rev.*, LI (1943), 578–580.
   12. *Tri Victory:* in 1955 edition this line is omitted.

1078 The Bustle in a House
Discussed in R. J. Jordan, *Explicator*, XXI (1963), 49.

1084 At Half past Three, a single Bird
Discussed in MacLeish, *Poetry and Experience*, pp. 94–95; J. C. Ransom, *Perspectives USA*, No. 15 (1956), 11; R. W. Russell, *Explicator*, XVI (1957), 3.

1207 He preached upon "Breadth" till it argued him narrow
6. *Pyrites:* iron sulfide, a yellow mineral also called "fool's gold."

1304 Not with a Club, the Heart is broken
Discussed in Anderson, *Emily Dickinson's Poetry*, p. 193; Mordecai Marcus, *Explicator*, XX (1962), 54.

1333 A little Madness in the Spring
Discussed in Anderson, *Emily Dickinson's Poetry*, p. 81.

1393 Lay this Laurel on the One
For the circumstances surrounding the composition of this elegy on the poet's father, see Johnson, *Poems*, III, pp. 960–962.
Discussed in MacLeish, *Poetry and Experience*, p. 99.

1463 A Route of Evanescence
In a letter to Higginson, Emily Dickinson entitled this poem "A Humming-Bird."
Discussed in Adams, *Tulane Stud. Eng.*, VII (1957), 138–143; Anderson, *Emily Dickinson's Poetry*, pp. 113–117; Frank Davidson, *New Eng. Quart.*, XVIII (1945), 407–408; Rebecca Patterson, *Educational Leader*, XXII (July, 1958), 12–19; Grover Smith, *Explicator*, VII (1949), 54; Whicher, *This Was a Poet*, p. 262.
7. *The mail from Tunis:* Frank Davidson links this with Shakespeare's *The Tempest*, II, i, ll. 246–248.

1540 As imperceptibly as Grief
Discussed in Adams, *Tulane Stud. Eng.*, VII (1957), 149–150; Anderson, *Emily Dickinson's Poetry*, pp. 149–150; Carpenter, *U. Kans. City Rev.*, XX (1953), 118–119; Winters, *Maule's Curse*, pp. 161–163.

1587 He ate and drank the precious Words
Discussed in Anderson, *Emily Dickinson's Poetry*, pp. 44–45.

1612 The Auctioneer of Parting
Discussed in Anderson, *Emily Dickinson's Poetry*, pp. 196–198.

1624 Apparently with no surprise
Discussed in Anderson, *Emily Dickinson's Poetry*, pp. 158–159.

1670 In Winter in my Room
Discussed in Griffith, *The Long Shadow*, pp. 177–183, 284–288.

1672 Lightly stepped a yellow star
Discussed in Anderson, *Emily Dickinson's Poetry*, pp. 27–29; Whicher, *This Was a Poet*, p. 184.

H.D.
1886–1961

Major Writings

Sea Garden (1916)
Hymen (1921)
Heliodora and Other Poems (1924)
Collected Poems (1925, 1940)
Hippolytus Temporizes (1927)
Red Roses for Bronze (1931)
The Walls Do Not Fall (1944)
The Flowering of the Rod (1946)
Selected Poems (1957)
Helen in Egypt (1961)

Criticism

Blackmur, R. P. "The Lesser Satisfactions," *Poetry*, XLI (1932), 94–100.
Doggett, F. H. "H.D., a Study in Sensitivity," *Sewanee Rev.*, XXXVII (1929), 1–9.
Hughes, Glenn. *Imagism and the Imagists*, pp. 124 ff. Stanford, Calif.: Stanford University Press, 1931.
Swann, T. B. *The Classical World of H.D.* Lincoln, Neb.: University of Nebraska Press, 1962.
Watts, Harold. "H.D. and the Age of Myth," *Sewanee Rev.*, LVI (1948), 287–303.

Comments on Poems

The text source of these poems is *Sea Garden* (1916), except for "Erige Cor Tuum ad Me in Caelum," which is from *Selected Poems* (1957).

Adonis
As Swann points out (*The Classical World of H.D.*, p. 94), this poem is not about "Adonis, the prince beloved by Aphrodite," but the Oriental "hero-god whose cult flourished throughout the Mediterranean world and whose death and rebirth symboblized the decay of winter and the bloom of spring." He is one of H.D.'s chaste Olympian heroes who stands for both purification and rebirth.

Oread
"The sea here is equated with an immense oread, a nymph of the mountains, whose violence is purification," Swann, *The Classical World of H.D.*, pp. 24–25. This poem became famous as a showpiece of Imagism. H.D.'s husband, Richard Aldington, wrote Japanese haiku, which this poem

resembles, but probably, as Swann suggests (p. 25), the strongest influence was the short poems of the *Greek Anthology*, a collection first compiled in the first century B.C., later supplemented.

From Citron-Bower

The trees mentioned in the poem are noted for their flowers, fruit, and pleasant odors. They are both decorative and symbolically healing.

Erige Cor Tuum ad Me in Caelum

The Latin title: "Lift up your heart to me (God) on high." Although not a direct quotation, the words echo several passages in the Bible, such as "To Thee I lift up my soul," Psalms 25: 1.

September 1940: the Nazi bombing of Great Britain began July 10, 1940, and became intense the following autumn. One of the worst days was September 7, 1940. At the outbreak of World War II H.D. returned to England and experienced the terror and hardships of the bombings.

ALAN DUGAN
b. 1923

Major Writings

Poems (1961)
Poems 2 (1963)

Criticism

Lyttle, David. "The Poems of Alan Dugan," *Approach*, No. 46 (1963), 17–19.

T. S. ELIOT
1888–1965

Bibliography

Gallup, D. C. *T. S. Eliot: A Bibliography Including Contributions to Periodicals and Foreign Translations.* New York: Harcourt, Brace and Co., 1953.

Major Writings

Prufrock and Other Observations (1917)
Poems (1919)
Ara Vos Prec (1920)
The Waste Land (1922)
Poems, 1909–1925 (1925)

Ash-Wednesday (1930)
Selected Essays (1932; enlarged edition, 1950)
Murder in the Cathedral (1935, verse drama)
The Family Reunion: A Play (1939, verse drama)
Four Quartets (1943)
The Cocktail Party: A Comedy (1950, verse drama)
The Complete Poems and Plays (1952)
The Confidential Clerk: A Play (1954, verse drama)
On Poetry and Poets (1957, essays)
The Elder Statesman: A Play (1959, verse drama)
Collected Plays (1962)
Collected Poems, 1909–1962 (1963)

Criticism

Drew, Elizabeth. *T. S. Eliot: The Design of His Poetry*. New York: Charles Scribner's Sons, 1949.

Frye, Northrop. *T. S. Eliot*. New York: Grove Press, 1963.

Gardner, Helen. *The Art of T. S. Eliot*. New York: E. P. Dutton, 1950.

Kenner, Hugh. *The Invisible Poet: T. S. Eliot*. New York: Ivan Obolensky, 1959.

Lucy, Sean. *T. S. Eliot and the Idea of Tradition*. London: Cohen & West, 1960.

March, Richard, and Tambimuttu, M. J. *T. S. Eliot: A Symposium*. Chicago: Henry Regnery, 1949.

Matthiessen, F. O. *The Achievement of T. S. Eliot: An Essay on the Nature of Poetry*, 3rd ed. New York: Oxford University Press, 1958.

Maxwell, D. E. S. *The Poetry of T. S. Eliot*. New York: Hillary House, 1959.

Rajan, B. (ed.). *T. S. Eliot: A Study of His Writings by Several Hands*. London: Dennis Dobson, 1947.

Smidt, Kristian. *Poetry and Belief in the Work of T. S. Eliot,* rev. ed. New York: Humanities Press, 1961.

Smith, Grover. *T. S. Eliot's Poetry and Plays: A Study in Sources and Meaning*. Chicago: University of Chicago Press, 1956.

Unger, Leonard (ed.). *T. S. Eliot: A Selected Critique*. New York: Holt, Rinehart and Winston, 1948.

Williamson, George. *A Reader's Guide to T. S. Eliot: A Poem-by-Poem Analysis*. New York: The Noonday Press, 1953. Reprinted as a paperback, The Noonday Press, 1957.

Comments on Poems

The texts of the Eliot poems are from *Collected Poems, 1909–1962* and contain some dozen minor differences from the texts in *The Complete Poems and Plays*. An authoritative text of Eliot's poetry is in the process of being established.

Because the critical literature on Eliot is so vast, no listing of discussions will be made for the individual poems. The books by Drew, Matthiessen,

Smith, and Williamson cited under Criticism are particularly valuable for detailed analyses of the poems included in this anthology.

The Love Song of J. Alfred Prufrock

The epigraph is from Dante's *Inferno,* XXVII, 61–66, the words of Guido da Montefeltro to the poet: "If I thought my answer were to one who ever could return to the world, this flame should shake no more; but since none ever did return alive from this depth, if what I hear be true, without fear of infamy I answer thee."

82–83. *Though I . . . no prophet:* see Matthew 14 : 3–11. The "prophet" is John the Baptist.

94. *Lazarus:* see John 11 : 1–44 for the raising of Lazarus from the dead by Christ.

113. *swell a progress:* increase the number in the prince's retinue on a journey.

121. *I shall . . . rolled:* with the bottoms turned up into cuffs in the manner of the young dandies of the 1900's. At that time trousers were customarily worn without cuffs.

Sweeney Among the Nightingales

The epigraph is from Aeschylus' *Agamemnon,* l. 1343: "Ay me! I am smitten deep with a mortal blow."

6. *River Plate:* British for Rio de la Plata, the estuary on which is situated the city of Buenos Aires, Argentina.

7. *Raven:* the constellation Corvus. In folklore and literature ravens have often been associated with death and disaster.

8. *hornèd gate:* see Virgil's *Aeneid,* book vi, ll. 893–896, where Aeneas, in Hades, is told that there are two gates of Sleep—the gate of horn, through which true dreams pass, and the gate of ivory, through which the false pass. This part of the *Aeneid* is taken from the *Odyssey,* xix, ll. 562–567, where Penelope describes the two gates of Dreams. In Eliot's poem "the hornèd gate" is also perhaps the gate of death.

9. *Orion and the Dog:* the constellations Orion and Canis Major, though "Dog" may refer to Sirius, the Dog Star, in Canis Major.

35. *nightingales:* Smith points out that these are brought into the poem from Sophocles' *Oedipus at Colonus,* where they sing in the grove of the Furies, the "bloody wood" of l. 37.

38. *Agamemnon:* leader of the Greeks at the siege of Troy, who upon his return home is killed by Aegisthus, his wife's lover. Dying, Agamemnon speaks the words here used in the epigraph.

Gerontion

The title, coined from the Greek *geron,* means "little old man."

The epigraph is from the Duke's speech to Claudio in Shakespeare's *Measure for Measure,* Act III, scene 1, ll. 32–34.

12. *merds:* dung.

17. *"We . . . sign":* see Matthew 12 : 38–39.

18–19. *The word . . . darkness:* see John 1 : 1 and Luke 2 : 12.

23. *Mr. Silvero:* like those which follow, the name of an acquaintance re-called by the old man "speaking" the poem.

24. *Limoges:* city in central France noted for its fine porcelain.

41. *is still:* previous editions of Eliot's poem read "if still."

48. *wrath-bearing tree:* see Genesis 2 : 16–17; 3.

53. *concitation:* excitation or stirring up.

55. *you:* Christ.

68. *De Bailhache . . . Cammel:* other remembered acquaintances.

69. *Bear:* either of the constellations also known as the Dippers.

The Waste Land

The epigraph, in Latin and Greek, is from Chapter 48 of the *Satyricon* by Petronius: "For I myself saw with my own eyes the Sibyl of Cumae hanging in a cage; and when the boys cried to her: 'Sibyl, what do you want?'; she would reply: 'I want to die.'"

The Italian dedication, "the better craftsman," is from Dante's *Purgatorio,* XXVI, 117, where the reference is to Arnaut Daniel, the twelfth-century Provençal poet. Pound helped Eliot compress the original version of *The Waste Land* from some eight hundred lines into the present length.

The notes that Eliot appended to his poem follow, interspersed with additional editorial comment. After the introductory statement by Eliot himself, each of his notes has been designated by inserting his name in brackets immediately after the line number and by placing the note itself in quotation marks.

Notes on "The Waste Land"

Not only the title, but the plan and a good deal of the incidental symbolism of the poem were suggested by Miss Jessie L. Weston's book on the Grail legend: *From Ritual to Romance* (Cambridge). Indeed, so deeply am I indebted, Miss Weston's book will elucidate the difficulties of the poem much better than my notes can do; and I recommend it (apart from the great interest of the book itself) to any who think such elucidation of the poem worth the trouble. To another work of anthropology I am indebted in general, one which has influenced our generation profoundly; I mean *The Golden Bough;* I have used especially the two volumes *Adonis, Attis, Osiris.* Anyone who is acquainted with these works will immediately recognize in the poem certain references to vegetation ceremonies.

I. The Burial of the Dead

8. *Starnbergersee:* a resort lake near Munich in Germany.

10. *Hofgarten:* a public park in Munich with a zoo and outdoor cafés.

12. *Bin . . . deutsch:* (German) "I am not Russian, I come from Lithuania, pure German."

20. [Eliot] "Cf. Ezekiel II, i."

23. [Eliot] "Cf. Ecclesiastes XII, v."

25. *There is . . . rock:* cf. Isaiah 32 : 1–2.

31–34. [Eliot] "V. Tristan und Isolde, I, verses 5–8." The translation from the German is: "Fresh blows the wind / to the homeland; / my Irish child, / where are you waiting?"

37. *hyacinth garden:* in Greek mythology, when Hyacinth, a Spartan boy, was accidentally killed, the hyacinth flower grew from his blood. Hyacinth's death and rebirth were celebrated in Sparta in early summer and were related to vegetation cults. The fertility ritual theme of the poem is here connected with a scene involving romantic love.

42. [Eliot] "Id. III, verse 24." The translation of this verse from the German is: "Desolate and empty is the sea."

46. [Eliot] "I am not familiar with the exact constitution of the Tarot pack of cards, from which I have obviously departed to suit my own convenience. The Hanged Man, a member of the traditional pack, fits my purpose in two ways: because he is associated in my mind with the Hanged God of Frazer, and because I associate him with the hooded figure in the passage of the disciples to Emmaus in Part V. The Phoenician Sailor and the Merchant appear later; also the 'crowds of people,' and Death by Water is executed in Part IV. The Man with Three Staves (an authentic member of the Tarot pack) I associate, quite arbitrarily, with the Fisher King himself." Originally the Tarot pack of cards was used by Eastern magicians, but it is now employed by fortunetellers like the fictitious Madame Sosostris (accent on the second syllable). The pack is still used in central Europe in playing the popular game of tarok (in French, *tarot*).

48. *Those . . . eyes:* from Shakespeare's *The Tempest*, Act I, scene 2, line 398, Ariel's song.

60. [Eliot] "Cf. Baudelaire:

'Fourmillante cité, cité pleine de rêves,
'Où le spectre en plein jour raccroche le passant.'"

These are the opening lines of "Les Sept Vieillards" ("The Seven Old Men"), Poem 90 in Charles Baudelaire's *Les Fleurs du Mal* (*Flowers of Evil*). The translation from the French is: "Swarming city, city full of dreams, / where the ghost in broad daylight accosts the passerby."

63. [Eliot] "Cf. Inferno III, 55–57:

'si lunga tratta
di gente, ch'io non avrei mai creduto
che morte tanta n' avesse disfatta.'"

(Italian) "so long a train of people, I should never have believed Death had undone so many."

64. [Eliot] "Cf. Inferno IV, 25–27:

'Quivi, secondo che per ascoltare,
'non avea pianto, ma' che di sospiri,
'che l'aura eterna facevan tremare.'"

(Italian) "Here was no plaint, that could be heard, except of sighs, which caused the eternal air to tremble."

67. *Saint Mary Woolnoth:* an Anglican church built in the eighteenth century at the corner of King William and Lombard streets.

68. [Eliot] "A phenomenon which I have often noticed."

70. *Mylae:* a naval battle (260 B.C.) in the Punic Wars in which the Romans defeated the Carthaginians.

74. [Eliot] "Cf. the Dirge in Webster's *White Devil.*" See John Webster's *The White Devil,* Act V, scene 4, lines 97–98.

76. [Eliot] "V. Baudelaire, Preface to *Fleurs du Mal.*" The translation of this line from the French is: "'hypocritical reader!—my likeness,—my brother!'"

II. A Game of Chess

77. [Eliot] "Cf. *Antony and Cleopatra*, II, ii, l. 190."

92. [Eliot] "Laquearia. V. *Aeneid*, I, 726:

> dependent lychni laquearibus aureis incensi, et noctem
> flammis funalia vincunt."·

(Latin) "lighted lamps hang from the golden laquearia (fretted ceiling), and flaming torches drive out the night."

98. [Eliot] "Sylvan scene. V. Milton, *Paradise Lost*, IV, 140."

99. [Eliot] "V. Ovid, *Metamorphoses*, VI, Philomela." King Tereus of Thrace, according to this passage in Ovid's poem, rapes Philomela, sister of his wife, Procne, and then cuts off her tongue. In revenge the sisters kill Tereus' son and feed him to Tereus. When Tereus pursues them, the gods change him into a hoopoe, Philomela into a nightingale, and Procne into a swallow.

100. [Eliot] "Cf. Part III, l. 204."

103. "*Jug Jug*": see note to lines 204 and 206.

115. [Eliot] "Cf. Part III, l. 195."

118. [Eliot] "Cf. Webster: 'Is the wind in that door still?'" See John Webster, *The Devil's Law Case*, Act III, scene 2, line 162.

126. [Eliot] "Cf. Part I, l. 37, 48."

128. *that Shakespeherian Rag:* B. R. McElderry, Jr., has pointed out that "That Shakespearian Rag" was a popular ragtime piece in 1912. The first two lines of the chorus are: "That Shakespearian rag— / Most intelligent, very elegant. . . ."

138. [Eliot] "Cf. the game of chess in Middleton's *Women beware Women.*" See Act II, scene 2 of this play by Thomas Middleton.

139. *demobbed:* (British slang) demobilized from the army.

141. *Hurry . . . time:* call of the London pubkeeper at closing time.

161. *chemist:* (British) "druggist."

166. *gammon:* (usually British) ham, side of bacon.

171. *Ta ta:* (British slang) "good-by."

172. *Good . . . night:* cf. Shakespeare's *Hamlet*, Act IV, scene 5, ll. 72–74.

III. The Fire Sermon

176. [Eliot] "V. Spenser, *Prothalamion.*"

182. *Leman:* name for Lake Geneva in Switzerland. The line is a paraphrase of Psalm 137 : 1.

185. *But . . . hear:* see note to line 196.

192. [Eliot] "Cf. *The Tempest*, I, ii." The reference is to lines 389–390 in this scene of *The Tempest*.

196. [Eliot] "Cf. Marvell, *To His Coy Mistress.*" The reference is to lines

21–22 of the poem by Andrew Marvell. Cf. MacLeish's use of this passage in "You, Andrew Marvell" (p. 875).

197. [Eliot] "Cf. Day, *Parliament of Bees:*

> 'When of the sudden, listening, you shall hear,
> 'A noise of horns and hunting, which shall bring
> 'Actaeon to Diana in the spring,
> 'Where all shall see her naked skin . . .'"

John Day (1574–*c.* 1640) was an English dramatist, whose *The Parliament of Bees* (1607) is a group of eclogues.

199. [Eliot] "I do not know the origin of the ballad from which these lines are taken: it was reported to me from Sydney, Australia."

202. [Eliot] "V. Verlaine, *Parsifal.*" The translation of this verse from the French is: 'And O those children's voices, singing in the cupola!'

204 and 206. *Jug . . . Tereu:* the words used by the Elizabethans to represent the song of the nightingale. Cf. Trico's song in Act V, scene 1 of *Campaspe* by John Lyly (1554?–1606), English novelist and dramatist.

210. [Eliot] "The currants were quoted at a price 'carriage and insurance free to London'; and the Bill of Lading etc. were to be handed to the buyer upon payment of the sight draft."

213. *Cannon Street Hotel:* hotel in London on Cannon Street, a commercial street near the Thames.

214. *Metropole:* hotel in Brighton, a seacoast resort city fifty miles south of London.

218. [Eliot] "Tiresias, although a mere spectator and not indeed a 'character,' is yet the most important personage in the poem, uniting all the rest. Just as the one-eyed merchant, seller of currants, melts into the Phoenician Sailor, and the latter is not wholly distinct from Ferdinand Prince of Naples, so all the women are one woman, and the two sexes meet in Tiresias. What Tiresias *sees*, in fact, is the substance of the poem. The whole passage from Ovid is of great anthropological interest. . . ." Eliot then quotes nineteen lines in Latin from Ovid's *Metamorphoses* iii. 320–338, which may be translated as follows: "He [Jupiter] jested with Juno and said: 'Certainly your [women's] pleasure is greater than men's [in love].' She denies it. They decided to ask the opinion of the learned Tiresias: both kinds of love had been known to him [as a man and as a woman]. For he had struck with his staff the bodies of two great serpents mating in a green wood; from a man he was changed, marvelous to say, and spent seven autumns as a woman. In the eighth year he saw the same serpents again and said: 'If there is such potency in striking you that it changes the lot of the striker to the opposite [sex], now I will strike you again!' When he had struck the same snakes, his original form and the shape with which he was born returned. He, then, chosen as arbiter for the playful dispute, confirms the words of Jupiter; it is said that Saturn's daughter [Juno] was more annoyed than she should have been in accordance with the situation and condemned the eyes of her own judge to eternal night. But the almighty father (for it is not permitted to any god to render vain the action of another god), in restitution for his loss of sight, gave [Tiresias] knowledge of the future and so relieved his punishment with dignity."

221. [Eliot] "This may not appear as exact as Sappho's lines, but I had in mind the 'longshore' or 'dory' fisherman, who returns at nightfall." Sappho's "lines" are probably those of a fragment addressed to Hesperus, the Evening Star.

234. *Bradford:* an industrial city in north central England. A Bradford millionaire would be of the "newly rich."

245–246. *I . . . dead:* Tiresias lived and prophesied for several generations in Thebes before he was killed in the destruction of the city. After death he continued to prophesy in Hades, where Ulysses consulted him.

253. [Eliot] "V. Goldsmith, the song in *The Vicar of Wakefield.*"

257. [Eliot] "V. *The Tempest,* as above." See Act I, scene 2, line 391.

258. *Strand:* a street in London.

264. [Eliot] "The interior of St. Magnus Martyr is to my mind one of the first among Wren's interiors. See *The Proposed Demolition of Nineteen City Churches:* (P. S. King & Son, Ltd.)."

266. [Eliot] "The Song of the (three) Thames-daughters begins here. From line 292 to 306 [305] inclusive they speak in turn. V. *Götterdämmerung,* III, i: the Rhine-daughters." The reference is to the opera *Twilight of the Gods,* by the German composer Richard Wagner (1813–1883).

275. *Greenwich reach*: a section of the Thames bordered by Greenwich, a borough of southeastern London on the south side of the river.

276. *Isle of Dogs:* a peninsula in the Thames opposite Greenwich.

277–278. *Weialala . . . leialala:* the refrain in the song of the Rhine-daughters in Wagner's opera.

279. [Eliot] "V. Froude, *Elizabeth,* Vol. I, ch. iv, letter of De Quadra to Philip of Spain: 'In the afternoon we were in a barge, watching the games on the river. (The queen) was alone with Lord Robert and myself on the poop, when they began to talk nonsense, and went so far that Lord Robert at last said, as I was on the spot there was no reason why they should not be married if the queen pleased.'"

293. [Eliot] "Cf. *Purgatorio,* V. 133:

> 'Ricorditi di me, che son la Pia;
> 'Siena mi fe', disfecemi Maremma.'"

(Italian) "Remember me, who am La Pia; Siena made me, Maremma unmade me." La Pia, a woman of Siena, was killed by her husband in the Sienese Maremma. Her soul here addresses Dante in purgatory. Cf. Pound's *Hugh Selwyn Mauberley,* the poem entitled "Siena Mi Fe'; Disfecemi Maremma" (pp. 769 and 1184). *Highbury . . . Kew:* districts in London. *Highbury:* a section of London at the northern edge of the city. *Richmond and Kew:* suburbs just southwest of London on the south bank of the Thames. Both are sites of extensive parks.

296. *Moorgate:* a slum area in London.

300. *Margate Sands:* a seaside resort on the Thames estuary.

307. [Eliot] "V. St. Augustine's *Confessions:* 'to Carthage then I came, where a cauldron of unholy loves sang all about mine ears.'"

308. [Eliot] "The complete text of the Buddha's Fire Sermon (which corresponds in importance to the Sermon on the Mount) from which these words

are taken, will be found translated in the late Henry Clarke Warren's *Buddhism in Translation* (Harvard Oriental Series). Mr. Warren was one of the great pioneers of Buddhist studies in the Occident."

309. [Eliot] "From St. Augustine's *Confessions* again. The collocation of these two representatives of eastern and western asceticism, as the culmination of this part of the poem, is not an accident."

V. What the Thunder Said

[Eliot] "In the first part of Part V three themes are employed: the journey to Emmaus, the approach to the Chapel Perilous (see Miss Weston's book) and the present decay of eastern Europe."

357. [Eliot] "This is *Turdus aonalaschkae pallasii*, the hermit-thrush which I have heard in Quebec Province. Chapman says (*Handbook of Birds of Eastern North America*) 'it is most at home in secluded woodland and thickety retreats. . . . Its notes are not remarkable for variety or volume, but in purity and sweetness of tone and exquisite modulation they are unequalled.' Its 'water-dripping song' is justly celebrated."

360. [Eliot] "The following lines were stimulated by the account of one of the Antarctic expeditions (I forget which, but I think one of Shackleton's): it was related that the party of explorers, at the extremity of their strength, had the constant delusion that there was *one more member* than could actually be counted." Cf. also Luke 24 : 13–34.

367–377. [Eliot] "Cf. Hermann Hesse, *Blick ins Chaos*. . . ." Eliot quotes a passage from Hesse's *A Glimpse into Chaos*, the translation of which from the German reads as follows: "Already half of Europe, at least half of Eastern Europe, is on the way to chaos, travels drunken in sacred madness along the edge of the abyss and the while sings, sings drunken and ecstatic as Dmitri Karamazov sang [see Dostoevski's *The Brothers Karamazov*.] Shocked by these songs the bourgeois laughs; the saint and the prophet listen to them with tears."

388. *chapel:* the Chapel Perilous of the Grail legends, where the knight must meet terrifying and supernatural adventures in order to be granted the sight of the Grail.

396. *Ganga:* Sanscrit name for the Ganges River.

398. *Himavant:* the Himalaya Mountains.

401. *DA:* sound representing the thunder linked by onomatapoeia with the three commands in Sanskrit.

402. [Eliot] "'Datta, dayadhvam, damyata' (Give, sympathize, control). The fable of the meaning of the Thunder is found in the *Brihadaranyaka–Upanishad*, 5, 1. A translation is found in Deussen's *Sechzig Upanishads des Veda*, p. 489." In the *Upanishad*, Prajapati, the Supreme Lord of Creation, speaks the syllable DA in the thunder three times and is interpreted as speaking the three commands.

408. [Eliot] "Cf. Webster, *The White Devil*, V, vi:

> '. . . they'll remarry
> Ere the worm pierce your winding-sheet, ere the spider
> Make a thin curtain for your epitaphs.'"

412. [Eliot] "Cf. *Inferno*, XXXIII, 46:

> 'ed io sentii chiavar l'uscio di sotto
> all'orribile torre.'"

[(Italian) "and below I heard being locked the door of the horrible tower."]

"Also F. H. Bradley, *Appearance and Reality*, p. 346. 'My external sensations are no less private to myself than are my thoughts or my feelings. In either case my experience falls within my own circle, a circle closed on the outside; and, with all its elements alike, every sphere is opaque to the others which surround it. . . . In brief, regarded as an existence which appears in a soul, the whole world for each is peculiar and private to that soul.'"

417. *Coriolanus*: Gaius Marcius Coriolanus, Roman general of the fifth century B.C. See Shakespeare's *Coriolanus*.

425. [Eliot] "V. Weston: *From Ritual to Romance*; chapter on the Fisher King."

426. *Shall . . . order?*: cf. Isaiah 38 : 1.

428. [Eliot] "V. *Purgatorio*, XXVI, 148.

> "'Ara vos prec per aquella valor
> "que vos guida al som de l'escalina,
> "sovegna vos a temps de ma dolor."
> Poi s'ascose nel foco che gli affina.'"

The three lines in Provençal and the fourth in Italian may be translated as follows: "'Now I pray you, by the Goodness that guides you to the summit of this stairway, be mindful in due season of my pain.' Then he hid himself in the fire that refines them." The first three lines are spoken to Dante by Arnaut Daniel (see note to the dedication of *The Waste Land*). In the following Canto, Dante and Virgil leave the seventh circle of Purgatory, pass through a wall of fire, and ascend a stairway that leads to the Earthly Paradise, where Virgil leaves Dante and Beatrice appears to guide the poet to the Heavenly Paradise. For another use of the "stairway" figure by Eliot see Part III of *Ash-Wednesday*.

429. [Eliot] "V. *Pervigilium Veneris*. Cf. Philomela in Parts II and III." The Latin poem "Pervigilium Veneris" ("The Eve of St. Venus") has been dated variously as belonging to the second through fourth centuries A.D. This phrase from near the end of the poem means: "When shall I be as the swallow?"

430. [Eliot] "V. Gerard de Nerval, Sonnet *El Desdichado*." This line from the sonnet "The Unfortunate One," by the French man of letters Gérard de Nerval (1808–1855) means "The Prince of Aquitaine at the ruined tower."

432. [Eliot] "V. Kyd's *Spanish Tragedy*." The subtitle of this play by Thomas Kyd (1557?–1595?) is "Hieronymo Is Mad Againe." The first part of l. 432 is from Act IV, scene 1, l. 69, and is spoken by Hieronymo, who is feigning madness in order to avenge his son's death at the hands of Lorenzo. He tells the unsuspecting Lorenzo that his own plans will fit (agree with) Lorenzo's, Heironymo having planned an entertainment in the course of which he will kill the murderer of his son.

434. [Eliot] "Shantih. Repeated as here, a formal ending to an Upanishad. 'The Peace which passeth understanding' is our equivalent to this word."

The Hollow Men

George Williamson suggests that the title may come from Shakespeare's *Julius Caesar*, Act IV, scene 2, ll. 20–27.

Mistah Kurtz—he dead: in this way is announced the death of the "lost" and "violent" Kurtz, central figure in Joseph Conrad's long short story, *Heart of Darkness*.

A penny . . . Guy: on Guy Fawkes Day (November 5) English children exhibit stuffed effigies of Fawkes and use this phrase to beg pennies for fireworks (see the ending of the poem). Fawkes (1570–1606) was one of the main figures in the Gunpowder Plot, a conspiracy to blow up King James I of England and Parliament on November 5, 1605. The plot was discovered and the leaders executed.

52–67. *The eyes . . . empty men:* for some details see Dante's *Inferno*, III, and *Paradiso*, XXXI–XXXII.

88–89. *Between . . . descent:* cf. Dante's *Purgatorio*, XXXI, 107.

Ash-Wednesday

Ash Wednesday is the first day of Lent and the seventh Wednesday before Easter. On this day in the Roman Catholic and Anglican Churches the priest places ashes on the foreheads of the members of the congregation to remind them of death and the need for penitence for their sins.

4. *Desiring . . . scope:* except for the change of "art" to "gift" this is line 7 in Shakespeare's Sonnet XXIX.

6. *agèd eagle:* cf. Psalm 103 : 5 and Isaiah 40 : 31.

40. *Pray . . . death:* from the prayer "Hail Mary."

42. *Lady:* an idealized woman who may lead the penitent to God, as Beatrice did Dante. *three white leopards:* cf. the leopard, the lion, and the she-wolf in Dante's *Inferno*, I, symbolizing worldly pleasure, ambition, and avarice. *juniper-tree:* see 1 Kings 19 : 4.

43. *cool of the day:* see Genesis 3 : 8.

46. *Shall . . . live?:* see Ezekiel 37 : 1–14.

65. *burden of the grasshopper:* see Ecclesiastes 12 : 5. "Burden" is also to be taken in its musical sense as an accompaniment or a refrain.

69. *Rose:* often a symbol for the Virgin Mary. Cf. the Mystic Rose of Dante's *Paradiso*, XXXI–XXXII.

93–94. *This . . . lot:* see Ezekiel 45 : 1.

96. *stair:* Part III was published separately in 1929 under the title "Som de l'Escalina" ("The Summit of the Stairway"). See the note to line 428 of *The Waste Land* (p. 1111).

117–119. *Lord . . . only:* see Matthew 8 : 8.

123. *Mary:* the Virgin Mary.

130. *Sovegna vos:* (Provençal) "be mindful." See the note to line 428 of *The Waste Land*.

137–138. *Redeem the time:* see Ephesians 5 : 14–16.

142. *yews:* the yew tree is a symbol of immortality.

148. *And . . . exile:* from the prayer "Salve Regina," which reads in part: "And after this our exile, show unto us the blessed fruit of thy womb Jesus."

149–157. *If the . . . Word:* cf. John 1 : 1–5.

158. *O my people . . . thee:* see Micah 6 : 3.

191. *Bless me father:* the beginning of the Catholic Confession.

202. *ivory gates:* see the note to line 8 of "Sweeney Among the Nightingales" (p. 1104).

214. *Our peace in His will:* Dante's lesson. See *Paradiso,* III, 85.

RALPH WALDO EMERSON
1803–1882

Bibliography

Booth, R. A. and Stromberg, Roland. "A Bibliography of Ralph Waldo Emerson, 1908–1920," *Bulletin of Bibliography,* XIX (1948), 180–183.

Bryer, J. R. and Rees, R. A. *A Checklist of Emerson Criticism 1951–1961, with a Detailed Index.* Hartford, Conn.: Transcendental Books, 1964.

Carpenter, F. I. *Emerson Handbook.* New York: Hendricks House, 1953.

Cooke, G. W. *A Bibliography of Ralph Waldo Emerson.* Boston: Houghton Mifflin and Co., 1908.

Stovall, Floyd (ed.). "Emerson," pp. 47–99 in *Eight American Authors: A Review of Research and Criticism.* New York: The Modern Language Association of America, 1956. Mathews, J. C., "Emerson," pp. 424–428 of "Bibliographical Supplement" in paperback reissue by W. W. Norton Co. (New York, 1963).

Concordance

Hubbell, G. S. *A Concordance to the Poems of Ralph Waldo Emerson.* New York: The H. W. Wilson Co., 1932.

Major Writings

Nature (1836)
Essays (1841)
Essays, Second Series (1844)
Poems (1847)
Representative Men: Seven Lectures (1850)
English Traits (1856)
The Conduct of Life (1860)
May-Day and Other Pieces (1867)
Society and Solitude (1870)
Letters and Social Aims (1876)
Selected Poems (1876)
Lectures and Biographical Sketches (1884)

Journals of Ralph Waldo Emerson (1909–1914, 10 Vols., E. W. Emerson and
     W. E. Forbes, eds.)

The Letters of Ralph Waldo Emerson (1939, 6 Vols., R. L. Rusk, ed.)

The Early Lectures of Ralph Waldo Emerson (1959, S. E. Whicher and R. E.
     Spiller, eds.)

The Journals and Miscellaneous Notebooks of Ralph Waldo Emerson (1960–,
     5 Vols. published to date, W. H. Gilman, A. R. Ferguson, G. P. Clark,
     M. R. Davis, M. M. Sealts, Jr., and Harrison Hayford, eds.)

Standard Edition

Emerson, E. W. (ed.). *The Complete Works of Ralph Waldo Emerson*, Centenary
     Edition, 12 Vols. Boston: Houghton Mifflin and Co., 1903–1904. *Poems*,
     Vol. IX, 1904.

Biography

Cabot, J. E. *A Memoir of Ralph Waldo Emerson*, 2 Vols. Boston: Houghton
     Mifflin and Co., 1887.

Rusk, R. L. *The Life of Ralph Waldo Emerson*. New York: Charles Scribner's
     Sons, 1949.

Woodberry, G. E. *Ralph Waldo Emerson*. New York: The Macmillan Co.,
     1907.

Criticism

Blair, Walter, and Faust, Clarence. "Emerson's Literary Method," *Mod. Phil.*,
     XLII (1944), 79–95.

Carpenter, F. I. "The Poetry" and "Aesthetic and Poetic Theory," pp. 79–102
     in *Emerson Handbook*. New York: Hendricks House, 1953.

Foerster, Norman. "Emerson," pp. 52–110 in *American Criticism: A Study in
     Literary Theory from Poe to the Present*. Boston: Houghton Mifflin and Co.,
     1928.

Foerster, Norman. "Emerson," pp. 37–68 in *Nature in American Literature:
     Studies in the Modern View of Nature*. New York: The Macmillan Co., 1923.

Gorely, Jean. "Emerson's Theory of Poetry," *Poetry Review*, XXII (1931),
     263–273.

Gross, S. L. "Emerson and Poetry," *So. Atl. Quart.*, LIV (1955), 82–94.

Hopkins, V. C. *Spires of Form: A Study of Emerson's Aesthetic Theory*. Cam-
     bridge, Mass.: Harvard University Press, 1951.

McEuen, K. A. "Emerson's Rhymes," *Am. Lit.*, XX (1948), 31–42.

Matthiessen, F. O. "From Emerson to Thoreau," pp. 3–175 in *American Ren-
     aissance: Art and Expression in the Age of Emerson and Whitman*. New
     York: Oxford University Press, 1941.

Paul, Sherman. *Emerson's Angle of Vision: Man and Nature in American Ex-
     perience*. Cambridge, Mass.: Harvard University Press, 1952.

Strauch, C. F. "The Year of Emerson's Poetic Maturity: 1834," *Phil. Quart.*,
     XXXIV (1955), 353–377.

Sutcliffe, E. G. "Emerson's Theories of Literary Expression," *University of Illinois Studies in Language and Literature*, VIII (1923), 9–142.

Thompson, F. T. "Emerson's Theory and Practice of Poetry," *PMLA*, XLIII (1928), 1170–1184.

Whicher, S. E. *Freedom and Fate: An Inner Life of Ralph Waldo Emerson*. Philadelphia: University of Pennsylvania Press, 1953.

Comments on Poems

The texts for Emerson's poems here printed are those in Volume IX of the standard Centenary Edition, which was based on J. E. Cabot's text of the poems in the Riverside Edition of Emerson's works (1884). Although the *Selected Poems* of 1876 was the last to come under Emerson's own hand, the J. E. Cabot and Edward Emerson text was carefully edited; furthermore, Emerson's intellectual and critical powers had already failed markedly before he prepared this last collection of his poetry. Cabot put the situation tactfully in his Prefatory Note to the *Poems* in the Riverside Edition: ". . . the readings adopted by [Emerson] in the Selected Poems have not always been followed here, but in some cases preference has been given to corrections made by him when he was in fuller strength than at the time of the last revision."

The Sphinx

In his notes on this poem Emerson's editor, Edward Emerson, quoted a passage from the poet's notebook of 1859 (*Works*, IX, p. 412): "I have often been asked the meaning of the ' Sphinx.' It is this,—The perception of identity unites all things and explains one by another, and the most rare and strange is equally facile as the most common. But if the mind live only in particulars, and see only differences (wanting the power to see the whole—all in each), then the world addresses to this mind a question it cannot answer, and each new fact tears it in pieces, and it is vanquished by the distracting variety."

Discussed in Charles Malloy, *Arena*, XXXI (1904), 138–152, 272–283, 370–380, 494–507; Josephine Miles, *The Primary Language of Poetry in the 1740's and 1840's* (University of California Press, 1950), pp. 302–304; E. J. Rose, *New Eng. Quart.*, XXXVI (1963), 249–258; Andrew Schiller, *Papers of of the Michigan Academy of Science, Arts, and Letters*, XL (1955), 317–320; H. D. Thoreau, *Journal*, Vol. I (Houghton Mifflin and Co., 1906), pp. 229–237; T. R. Whitaker. *Am. Lit.*, XXVII (1955), 179–195.

75. *the pit of the Dragon:* the bottomless pit into which Satan is cast in Revelation 20 : 1–3.

76. *the Blest:* the holy city described in Revelation 21.

91–92. *Lurks . . . remorse:* in the *Selected Poems* (1876) edition these lines read:

> And the joy that is sweetest
> Lurks in stings of remorse.

107. *Rue, myrrh and cummin:* curative herbs.

128. *Monadnoc's head:* Mt. Monadnock in southern New Hampshire.

Each and All

For some of the elements of Emerson's thought and experience that went into this poem see his *Journals* for May 16, 1834 (III, p. 298)—the sea shells and the concept of composition; and for November 26, 1834 (III, p. 373)—the red-cloaked clown. (Here, as elsewhere in the notes on Emerson, *Journals* refers to the edition by E. W. Emerson and W. E. Forbes.)

Discussed in Blair and Faust, *Mod. Phil.,* XLII (1944), 89–91; P. A. C. [Charlotte Porter and H. A. Clarke], *Poet-Lore,* VI (1894), 273–276; R. B. Davis, *Exercise Exchange,* VII (1960), 3–5; Gross, *So. Atl. Quart.,* LIV (1955), 89–91; Strauch, *Phil. Quart.,* XXXIV (1955), 369–373.

The Problem

Emerson entered the germ of this poem in the *Journals* for August 28, 1838 (V, pp. 29–30).

Discussed in K. W. Cameron, *Emerson Society Quarterly,* No. 27 (Second Quarter, 1962), 37–46; Charles Malloy, *Arena,* XXXII (1904), 39–48, 145–151.

10. *awful . . . brought:* the statue of Jove at Olympia, created by Phidias, the fifth-century Greek sculptor.

19. *The hand . . . dome:* Michelangelo designed the great dome of St. Peter's in Rome.

51. *Pentecost:* see Acts 2 : 1–36.

55–56. *The word . . . unbroken:* the prophet is Moses. See Exodus 31 : 18; 32 : 15–19.

65. *Chrysostom:* St. John Chrysostom (347?–407), patriarch of Constantinople, called Chrysostom (Greek for "Golden Mouth") because of his eloquence and his homilies. *Augustine:* St. Augustine, who, Emerson thought, wrote "golden words."

68. *Taylor:* Jeremy Taylor (1613–1667), English bishop, famous for his pulpit oratory and his devotional writings.

Uriel

Uriel is the Archangel of the Sun in Milton's *Paradise Lost,* III, ll. 645–653. The poem may be read as a commentary on the reception of Emerson's *Divinity School Address,* given July 15, 1838.

Discussed in W. T. Harris, *The Genius and Character of Emerson* (Houghton Mifflin and Co., 1885), pp. 381–384; Charles Malloy, *Arena* XXXII (1904), 278–283; Andrew Schiller, *Papers of the Michigan Academy of Science, Arts, and Letters,* XL (1955), 315; Whicher, *Freedom and Fate,* pp. 74–76.

8. *Seyd:* Saadi (1184–1291), Persian poet, used by Emerson to represent the ideal poet. See Emerson's poem "Saadi."

Alphonso of Castile

Alfonso X of Leon and Castile (1221–1284) was called "the Wise" because of his wide learning in letters, law, and science.

Mithridates

Mithridates the Great (131?–163 B.C.), King of Pontus, built up immunity to poisons by taking gradually increased doses of them.

7. *cantharids:* cantharides, a powder that acts as an internal or external irritant.

Hamatreya

This poem is based on a passage from Book IV of the Hindu *Vishnu Purana* that Emerson copied into his journals for 1845 (*Journals*, VII, pp. 127–129). Although a "Maitreya" is named in the scriptural source, Emerson may have derived the title, not from a variant of that word, but from two Greek forms that, joined, mean "Earth-Mother." (See Bridgman below.)

Discussed in Richard Bridgman, *Emerson Society Quarterly*, No. 27 (Second Quarter, 1962), 16; F. I. Carpenter, *Emerson and Asia* (Harvard University Press, 1930), pp. 122–127; Arthur Christy, *The Orient in American Transcendentalism* (Columbia University Press, 1932), pp. 170–176.

1. *Bulkeley . . . Flint:* names of some of the first settlers of Concord. Bulkeley was an ancestor of Emerson.

8. *flags:* blue flags, wild irises.

The Rhodora

Discussed in Gross, *So. Atl. Quart.*, LIV (1955), 91–93; Matthiessen, *American Renaissance*, pp. 48–50; Strauch, *Phil. Quart.*, XXXIV (1955), 361–365.

The Snow-Storm

Discussed in Matthiessen, *American Renaissance*, pp. 138–140; Sister Paul Reiten, *Explicator*, XXII (1964), 39; Strauch, *Phil. Quart.*, XXXIV (1955), 373–377.

18. *Parian:* very white, like the marble from the Greek island of Paros.

21. *maugre:* in spite of.

Ode

William Henry Channing (1810–1884), a nephew of William Ellery Channing, was a Unitarian clergyman and a humanitarian.

Discussed in George Arms, *Coll. Eng.*, XXII (1961), 407–409; Andrew Schiller, *Papers of the Michigan Academy of Science, Arts, and Letters*, XL (1955), 315–317; C. F. Strauch, *Personalist*, XXXIII (1952), 52–53.

16–18. *Behold . . . knife!:* a reference to the Mexican War of 1846–1848, which was probably going on at the time of composition of this poem. Emerson opposed the war as a scheme to extend slave territory.

21. *Contoocook:* a New Hampshire river.

22. *Agiochook:* Indian name of the White Mountains in New Hampshire.

86–87. *Knows . . . lion:* see Judges 14 : 8–14.

90–97. *The Cossack . . . at her side:* possibly a political parable based on events in Polish history. In the Partition of Poland in 1795, Russia received a large share of that country's territory. In the Decembrist Rising of 1825, Russian army officers revolted briefly against the Czar. Subsequently Polish Nationalists in Russian Poland carried out the abortive Revolution of 1830–1831, while in 1846 there was an uprising of Polish nobles in Galicia, then part of Austrian Poland.

93. *Her last poet mute:* perhaps a reference to Adam Mickiewicz (1798–1855), Polish Romantic poet, who in his later years turned from poetry to active revolutionary work.

Ode to Beauty

54. *Salvator, of Guercino:* Salvator Rosa (1615–1673) and Giovanni Francesco Barbieri (1591–1666), called "Guercino," were Italian painters.

55. *Piranesi:* Giambattista Piranesi (1720–1778), Italian engraver.

57. *masters of·the shell:* in Greek mythology Apollo used a turtle shell to make the lyre, the instrument of poetry and music. The "masters" are the poets.

Give All to Love

Discussed in M. H. Cowan, *Explicator*, XVIII (1960), 49.

Merlin

Merlin here is not the magician of Arthurian romance but the legendary Welsh bard, typifying the poet of natural inspiration.

Discussed in N. F. Adkins, *PMLA*, LXIII (1948), 662–671; R. H. Pearce, *The Continuity of American Poetry* (Princeton University Press, 1961), pp. 162–164.

49. *Sybarites:* those devoted to sensuous pleasure and luxury.

126. *Sisters:* the three Fates.

Bacchus

As a motto for this poem Emerson wrote in his own copy of *Poems* a quotation from the *Phaedrus:* "The man who is his own master knocks in vain at the door of poetry."

Discussed in Charles Malloy, *Arena*, XXXII (1904), 504–513; B. J. Paris, *Mod. Lang. Quart.*, XXIII (1962), 150–159.

54. *lote:* the lotus, the eating of which produced forgetfulness.

66. *tablets blue:* the sky.

Blight

29. *the SAME:* Edward Emerson's note on this term reads:"The teaching of Xenophanes and the Eleatic School." Xenophanes (*c.* 570–*c.* 480 B.C.) was a pre-Socratic Greek thinker, whose philosophy, according to Plato, "starts from the principle of the unity of all things."

Musketaquid

The title is the Indian name of the Concord River, on which the town of Concord is situated.

28. *sannup:* a married male American Indian.

Threnody

The first part of this poem, ll. 1–175, was written soon after the death, at the age of five, of Waldo, the Emersons' much-loved first child, on January 27, 1842. The remaining lines, with their spirit of reconcilement, were probably written in 1843. For Emerson's first reaction to the death of his son see *Journals*, VI, pp. 150–154.

Discussed in Blair and Faust, *Mod. Phil.*, XLII (1944), 91–95; B. B. Cohen, *Indiana University Folio*, XIV (1948), 13–15.

176. *The deep Heart:* the heart of Nature, the Over-Soul. See Emerson's "The Over-Soul" in *Essays* (First Series).

183. *the man of eld:* possibly Jacob, who dreamed of the ladder reaching from earth to heaven in Genesis 28 : 12.

Concord Hymn

The battle commemorated was, of course, that at Concord on April 19, 1775. The hymn was written to be sung to the tune of "Old Hundred" by the people assembled at the dedication of the monument on July 4, 1837.

Discussed in George Arms, *Explicator*, I (1942), 23; Paul Goodman, *Ken. Rev.*, XX (1958), 548–551.

Brahma

This poem was based on Emerson's reading in various Hindu scriptural writings, particularly the *Katha Upanishad* and the *Bhagavad Gita*. K. R. Chandrasekharan, to whom the following notes are indebted, writes: "The subject of the poem is not Brahma the Creator, but Brahman, the Absolute or the Universal Soul whom Emerson himself terms elsewhere the 'Oversoul.' The correct title of the poem ought to have been *Brahman* and not *Brahma*."

Discussed in F. I. Carpenter, *Emerson and Asia* (Harvard University Press, 1930), pp. 110–122; K. R. Chandrasekharan, *New Eng. Quart.*, XXXIII (1960), 506–512; Arthur Christy, *The Orient in American Transcendentalism* (Columbia University Press, 1932) pp. 164–170; Robert Frost, *New York Times Book Review* (March 21, 1954), p. 1; W. T. Harris, *The Genius and Character of Emerson* (Houghton Mifflin and Co., 1885), pp. 373–380; W. T. Harris, *Poet-Lore*, I (1889), 253–259; W. B. Stein et al., *Explicator*, XX (1961), 29; Mark Van Doren, *Introduction to Poetry* (William Sloane Associates, 1951), pp. 90–93; R. L. White, *Explicator*, XXI (1963), 63; George Williamson, *University of California Chronicle*, XXX (1928), 274–279.

1. *the red slayer:* Siva the Destroyer, who is one of the three aspects of Brahman, the others being Brahma the Creator and Vishnu the Preserver.

13. *the strong gods:* ". . . the 'devas' of Hindu cosmology, an order of celestial beings akin to angels, who are superior to human beings in their nature and powers and are also immortal, but are as much the creatures of Brahman as human beings are. Salvation for the gods also means reunion with Brahman, and for that reason they too pine for Brahma's abode." [Chandrasekharan, p. 508.]

14. *the sacred Seven:* the "seven sages celebrated in Hindu religious literature for their quest of God through austerities and penance. They are said to 'pine in vain' because realization of God does not come as easily through the observance of religious rites and the mortification of the flesh as through spontaneous surrender to the Divine Will." [Chandrasekharan, p. 508.]

15. *meek lover of the good:* the yogi who achieves spontaneous surrender to the Divine Will.

Days

Discussed in George Arms, *Explicator*, IV (1945), 8; F. I. Carpenter, *Emerson and Asia* (Harvard University Press, 1930), pp. 186–188; E. G. Fletcher, *Explicator*, V (1947), 41; Gross, *So. Atl. Quart.*, LIV (1955), 93–94; Joseph Jones, *Explicator*, IV (1946), 47; Charles Malloy, *Arena*, XXXI (1904), 592–602; Matthiessen, *American Renaissance*, pp. 59–64; E. S. Oliver, *New Eng.*

Quart., XIX (1946), 518–524; C. F. Strauch, *Phil. Quart.*, XXIX (1950), 199–208.

Two Rivers
Emerson entered the first version of this poem in prose form in his journal in early summer, 1856. See *Works*, IX, p. 487.
   1. *Musketaquit:* the Indian name for the Concord River.
   18. *Who drink . . . again:* see John 4 : 14.

Waldeinsamkeit
The German title means "forest solitude."

Terminus
In Roman mythology Terminus was the god of boundaries.
Discussed in A. H. Mason, *Explicator*, IV (1946), 37.

Compensation
The first half of this poem (not to be confused with one by the same title in *Poems*) appeared as the "motto" or epigraph for Emerson's essay "Compensation," published in *Essays* (First Series). It was collected with the second half added in *May-Day and Other Pieces*. For a discussion of Emerson's meaning for this term see, in addition to the essay, H. F. Pommer, *PMLA*, LXXVII (1962), 248–253.

PHILIP FRENEAU
1752–1832

Bibliography

Paltsits, V. C. *A Bibliography of the Separate and Collected Works of Philip Freneau.* New York: Dodd, 1903.
Pattee, F. L. (ed.). *The Poems of Philip Freneau: Poet of The American Revolution*, Vol. III, pp. 401–417. Princeton, N.J.: The University Library, 1907.

Major Writings

The Poems of Philip Freneau (1786)
Poems Written and Published During the American Revolutionary War, and Now Republished from the Original Manuscripts; Interspersed with Translations from the Ancients, and Other Pieces Not Heretofore in Print (1809)
A Collection of Poems, on American Affairs, and a Variety of Other Subjects, Chiefly Moral and Political; Written Between the Year 1897 and the Present Time (1815)

Standard Editions

Clark, Harry Hayden (ed.). *Poems of Freneau* [selections]. New York: Harcourt, Brace and Co., 1929.

Pattee, F. L. (ed.). *The Poems of Philip Freneau: Poet of the American Revolution*. Princeton, N.J.: The University Library, Vol. I, 1902; Vol. II, 1903; Vol. III, 1907.

Biography

Austin, Mary S. *Philip Freneau, The Poet of the Revolution: A History of His Life and Times*. Edited by Helen Kearny Vreeland (great-granddaughter of the poet). New York: Wessels, 1901.
Leary, Lewis. *That Rascal Freneau: A Study in Literary Failure*. New Brunswick, N.J.: Rutgers University Press, 1949.

Criticism

Adkins, Nelson F. *Philip Freneau and the Cosmic Enigma*. New York: New York University Press, 1949.
Allen, Gay Wilson. "Freneau," pp. 1–22. in *American Prosody*. New York: American Book Company, 1935.
Brenner, Rica. *Twelve American Poets Before 1900*, pp. 3–23. New York: Harcourt, Brace and Co., 1933.
Calverton, V. F. "Philip Freneau: An Apostle of Freedom," *Modern Monthly*, VII (October, 1933), 533–546.
Clark, H. H. "Literary Influences on Philip Freneau," *Stud. Phil.*, XXII (January, 1925), 1–33.
Clark, H. H. "What Made Freneau the Father of American Poetry?" *Stud. Phil.*, XVVI (January, 1929), 1–22.
Hustvedt, S. B. "Philippic Freneau," *Am. Sp.*, IV (October, 1928), 1–18.
More, Paul Elmer. "Philip Freneau," *Shelburne Essays*, Fifth Series. Boston: Houghton Mifflin and Co., 1908.
Tyler, M. C. *The Literary History of the American Revolution, 1763–1783*, 2 Vols. New York: G. P. Putnam's Sons, 1897.

Comments on Poems

The Power of Fancy

First version, written in 1770, printed in 1772 edition, was longer; in all editions after 1786 Freneau printed only the first twenty and the last fourteen lines of the earlier version and changed the title to "Ode to Fancy." He used the omitted lines, after extensive revision, in a poem called "Fancy's Ramble." Freneau's conception of "fancy" is partly Deistic, partly preromantic. The poem is indebted to Joseph Wharton's "Ode to Fancy" (1746). The versification shows indebtedness to Milton.

33. Milton's *Paradise Lost*, B. II, V. 1052 [Freneau's note].

67. *Orca:* shortened form of Orcades, ancient name of Orkney Islands, off northern coast of Scotland.

79. *Anson:* George (Baron) Anson, a British admiral who won a great victory over Spanish ships in 1744 despite the fact that storms had reduced his fleet to one ship.

126. *Belinda:* favorite name for a heroine in seventeenth- and eighteenth-century English literature. See, for example, Pope's *The Rape of the Lock* (1712) and several Restoration comedies.

Death

"The House of Night" is a long allegorical poem of 136 stanzas on the theme of the death of Death. The Gothic scene is laid at a solitary palace at midnight. A young man attempts to save the life of his enemy Death, but Death dies in agony and despair. This poem was first printed in *The United States Magazine*, August, 1779, and was published complete only in the 1786 edition of Freneau's *Poems*. The stanzas excerpted here are stanzas 8–10, 109–112, and 116 in the 1786 text.

6. *Whip-poor-will:* A Bird peculiar to America, of a solitary nature, who never sings but in the night. Her note resembles the name given her by the country people [Freneau's note].

The Vanity of Existence

Published in the *Freeman's Journal*, October 24, 1781, as "A Moral Thought," reprinted without change except for title in 1786 edition of *Poems*. *Thyrsis:* herdsman in Theocritus and in Virgil's seventh Eclogue; traditional name in English pastoral poetry for shepherd or rustic.

To the Memory of the Brave Americans

Published in the *Freeman's Journal*, November 21, 1781. The battle at Eutaw Springs, about fifty miles from Charleston, South Carolina, consisted of two encounters. At sunrise the Americans broke the British lines, but the British formed a new line and could not be driven from the field, and the engagements were regarded as a British victory. General Greene suffered over 500 casualties.

25. *Parthian:* a warrior of ancient Parthia, near Caspian Sea, who fought on horseback with bow and arrow, turning his horse as if for flight after each shot.

The Hurricane

"The Hurricane" was first published in the *Freeman's Journal*, April 13, 1785, with the title, "Verses, Made at Sea, in a Heavy Gale," and was reprinted in the *Journal* on August 20, 1788, with the note: "In that violent hurricane at Jamaica, on the night of the 30th of July, 1784, in which no more than eight, out of 150 sail of vessels, in the ports of Kingston and Port-Royal, were saved, Capt. Freneau was at sea, and arrived at Kingston next morning, a mere wreck. On that occasion, the following beautiful lines, extracted from the first volume of his writings, were penned." Text from the edition of 1809.

13. Near the east end of Jamaica, July 30, 1784 [Freneau's note].

The Wild Honey Suckle

Pattee's note in *The Poems of Philip Freneau*, Vol. I: "Freneau doubtless wrote this poem in Charleston, S.C., in July, 1786. It appeared first in the *Freeman's Journal*, August 2, 1786, and was republished in the edition of 1788, and in the later editions, almost without change. The poet probably refers to the *Rhododendron Viscosum*, or as some call it the *Azalia viscosum* since it is the only flower popularly known as the wild honey-suckle that is both white and fragrant. According to Chapman's *Southern Flora*, it flowers in the latitude of Charleston in July and August." Text from 1809 edition.

The Indian Burying Ground

Freneau's note: "The North American Indians bury their dead in a sitting posture: decorating the corpse with wampum, the images of birds, quadrupeds, &c: And (if that of a warrior) with bows, arrows, tomahawks, and other military weapons." In the 1788 edition the poem was entitled "Lines Occasioned by a Visit to an old Indian Burying Ground." The text is from the 1790 edition.

To Sir Toby

Text from 1809 edition, with numerous minor emendations from the 1795 text. The poem was first published in the *National Gazette*, July 21, 1792, with the title "The Island Field Hand," and a note: "Written some years ago at a sugar plantation in Jamaica." Freneau had been shocked before the American Revolution by Negro slavery in the West Indies (see Leary, *That Rascal Freneau*, pp. 68–69), but he wrote this poem while commanding a trading ship to the Caribbean. The Shakespeare quotation is from *The Merchant of Venice*, V. i, 79; Freneau changed "dull as night" to "black as night."

6. *Cudjoe:* from "cudge," a contemporary vernacular term for a Negro slave. Freneau's note: "This passage has a reference to the West India [Indies] custom (sanctioned by law) of branding a newly imported slave on the breast, with a red hot iron, as an evidence of the purchaser's property."

21. A small negro kingdom near the river Senegal [Freneau's note].

48. *Virgil's pencil:* Aeneas descended into Hades to seek his father's advice, *Aeneid*, Book VI.

49. Commanders of slave ships compared to Charon, in Greek mythology, who ferried the dead to Hades across the River Styx.

52. *Plutonian:* in Greek and Roman mythology Pluto was god of the lower world, Hades (Greek) or Dis (Roman).

54. *Liguanes:* The mountains northward of Kingston [Freneau's note].

56. *traitors:* Alluding to the *Independent* negros in the blue mountains, who for a stipulated reward, deliver up every fugitive that falls into their hands, to the English Government [Freneau's note].

Ode

Edmond Charles Édouard Genêt, called "Citizen Genêt," came to the United States in December, 1792, as the first ambassador of the first French Republic. Failing to persuade President Washington to join France in war against England, he attempted to rouse the American citizens to his cause over the head of their President. Friends of France gave a number of public dinners to Genêt, one in Philadelphia on June 1, 1793, at which Freneau's "Ode" was sung to the tune of "God Save the King." Freneau printed the poem in his 1795 edition but dropped it in 1809.

Amanda's Complaint

Text from 1809 edition. Published in New York *Daily Advertiser*, September 7, 1790, under the title "Written at Cape Hatteras," with date June, 1789;

reprinted in the *National Gazette*, March 19, 1892, as "Tormentina's Complaint," with date "Castle Island, Bermuda, Jan. 20, 1789." In the *Advertiser* version the last line read "maidens" instead of "damsels."

Amanda: a virtuous and charming heroine in Colley Cibber's comedy, *Love's Last Shift*, and Sir John Vanbrugh's sequel, *The Relapse*: in the latter she has been deserted but regains her husband's affection.

28. *nymphs:* Though Amanda is probably intended as a real Bermudian "nymph" or "damsel," throughout the poem there are suggested comparisons with the spirits in classical mythology who inhabit trees and streams.

On a Honey Bee
    Published in *Time-Piece*, September 6, 1797, as "On a Bee Drinking from a Glass of Water." After two versions the present text was published in the 1809 edition. "Hezekiah Salem" is a pseudonym.

On the Universality and Other Attributes of the God of Nature
    The "attributes" are those of the Deistic philosophy of Jefferson, Franklin, Thomas Paine, and Freneau.
    23. *Jupiter, optimus, maximus.*—Cicero [Freneau's note].

ROBERT FROST
1874–1963

Bibliography

Clymer, W. B. S., and Green, C. R. *Robert Frost: A Bibliography*. Amherst, Mass.: Jones Library, 1937.
Mertins, Louis, and Mertins, Esther. *The Intervals of Robert Frost: A Critical Bibliography*. Berkeley, Calif.: University of California Press, 1947.

Major Writings

A Boy's Will (1913)
North of Boston (1914)
Mountain Interval (1916)
New Hampshire: A Poem (1923)
West-Running Brook (1928)
A Further Range (1936)
A Witness Tree (1942)
A Masque of Reason (1945)
Steeple Bush (1947)
A Masque of Mercy (1947)
In the Clearing (1962)
The Letters of Robert Frost to Louis Untermeyer (1963, Louis Untermeyer, ed.)
Selected Letters of Robert Frost (1964, Lawrance Thompson, ed.)

Standard Edition

Complete Poems of Robert Frost, 1949 (1949)

Biography

Anderson, M. B. *Robert Frost and John Bartlett: The Record of a Friendship.* New York: Holt, Rinehart and Winston, 1963.

Cook, R. L. *The Dimensions of Robert Frost.* New York: Holt, Rinehart and Winston, 1958.

Cox, Sidney. *A Swinger of Birches: A Portrait of Robert Frost.* New York: New York University Press, 1957.

Gould, Jean. *Robert Frost: The Aim Was Song.* New York: Dodd, Mead, 1964.

Sergeant, E. S. *Robert Frost: The Trial by Existence.* New York: Holt, Rinehart and Winston, 1960.

Criticism

Auden, W. H. "Robert Frost," pp. 337–353 in *The Dyer's Hand and Other Essays.* New York: Random House, 1962.

Brower, R. A. *The Poetry of Robert Frost; Constellations of Intention.* New York: Oxford University Press, 1963.

Cox, J. M. (ed.). *Robert Frost: A Collection of Critical Essays.* Englewood Cliffs, N.J.: Prentice-Hall, 1961.

Greenberg, R. A., and Hepburn, J. C. (eds.). *Robert Frost: An Introduction.* New York: Holt, Rinehart and Winston, 1961.

Lynen, J. F. *The Pastoral Art of Robert Frost.* New Haven, Conn.: Yale University Press, 1960.

Nitchie, G. W. *Human Values in the Poetry of Robert Frost.* Durham, N. C.: Duke University Press, 1960.

Simpson, C. M. "Robert Frost and Man's 'royal role.'" pp. 121–147 in R. M. Ludwig (ed.), *Aspects of American Poetry.* Columbus, Ohio: Ohio State University Press, 1962.

Squires, Radcliffe. *The Major Themes of Robert Frost.* Ann Arbor, Mich.: The University of Michigan Press, 1963.

Thompson, Lawrance. *Fire and Ice: The Art and Thought of Robert Frost.* New York: Holt, Rinehart and Winston, 1942.

Warren, R. P. "The Themes of Robert Frost," pp. 118–136 in *Selected Essays.* New York: Random House, 1958.

Comments on Poems

The Tuft of Flowers
    Discussed in Thomas Shalvey, *Renascence*, XI (1959), 187–188.

Mending Wall
    Discussed in J. W. Beach, *Yale Rev.*, XLIII (1953), 210–211; J. C. Broderick, *Explicator*, XIV (1956), 24; Carson Gibb, *Explicator*, XX (1962), 48; Robert

Hunting, *West. Hum. Rev.*, XVII (1963), 88–89; Lynen, *The Pastoral Art of Robert Frost*, pp. 27–31; Marion Montgomery, *So. Atl. Quart.*, LVII (1958), 349–350; Thomas Shalvey, *Renascence*, XI (1959), 187.

Home Burial
    Discussed in Brower, *The Poetry of Robert Frost*, pp. 18–19; Randall Jarrell, pp. 99–132 in D. C. Allen (ed.), *The Moment of Poetry* (The Johns Hopkins Press, 1962); Lynen, *The Pastoral Art of Robert Frost*, p. 114.

After Apple-Picking
    Discussed in Brower, *The Poetry of Robert Frost*, pp. 23–27; Squires, *The Major Themes of Robert Frost*, pp. 57–59; Louis Untermeyer, E. S. Sergeant and Cleanth Brooks, pp. 2–5 in Greenberg and Hepburn (eds.), *Robert Frost*.

The Road Not Taken
    Discussed in Brower, *The Poetry of Robert Frost*, p. 231; B. W. Griffith, *Explicator*, XII (1954), 55; E. M. Sickels and Laurence Perrine, *Explicator*, XIX (1961), 28; Yvor Winters, *The Function of Criticism* (Alan Swallow, 1957), pp. 163–165.

The Oven Bird
    Discussed in Brower, *The Poetry of Robert Frost*, pp. 28–31; C. F. Burgess, *Explicator*, XX (1962), 59; C. R. B. Combellack, *Explicator*, XXII (1963), 17.

The Witch of Coös
    Coös is the northernmost county of New Hampshire, usually spelled "Coos," but pronounced as two syllables.
    Discussed in Brower, *The Poetry of Robert Frost*, pp. 166–169; Lynen, *The Pastoral Art of Robert Frost*, pp. 115–117.
    13. *Ralle the Sioux Control:* in spiritualism, a control is the particular spirit or intelligence which supposedly takes charge of and uses a medium during a trance. Indians are popular as controls.
    42. *Toffile:* perhaps French-Canadian corruption of Théophile.

Stopping by Woods on a Snowy Evening
    Discussed in Brower, *The Poetry of Robert Frost*, pp. 33–36; J. M. Cox, *Va. Quart. Rev.*, XXXV (1959), 82–84; Robert Frost, Lawrance Thompson, René Wellek and Austin Warren, Leonard Unger and William Van O'Connor, and John Ciardi, pp. 11–30 in Greenberg and Hepburn (eds.), *Robert Frost*; Lynen, *The Pastoral Art of Robert Frost*, pp. 3–6; E. H. Rosenberry, *Coll. Eng.*, XXIV (1963), 526–528.

For Once, Then, Something
    Discussed in Brower, *The Poetry of Robert Frost*, pp. 136–139; D. G. Hoffman, *Explicator*, IX (1950), 17.

The Onset
    Discussed in Brower, *The Poetry of Robert Frost*, pp. 96–98; Lynen, *The Pastoral Art of Robert Frost*, pp. 41–45.

To Earthward
    Discussed in Graham Hough, *Image and Experience* (Gerald Duckworth & Co., 1960), pp. 41–42; W. S. Scott, *Explicator*, XVI (1958), 23.

Two Look at Two
  Discussed in Brower, *The Poetry of Robert Frost*, pp. 153–156.

Acquainted with the Night
  Discussed in Brower, *The Poetry of Robert Frost*, pp. 126–129; Malcolm
Brown, *West. Rev.*, XVI (1952), 266; Yvor Winters, *The Function of Criticism*
(Alan Swallow, 1957), p. 182.

West-Running Brook
  Discussed in J. W. Beach, *Yale Rev.*, XLIII (1953), 212; Brower, *The Poetry
of Robert Frost*, pp. 188–195; R. D. Lord, *Renascence*, 20–25, 31; Lynen, *The
Pastoral Art of Robert Frost*, pp. 122–124; H. H. Watts, *Am. Lit.*, XXVII
(1955), 70–74; H. T. Webster, *Explicator*, VIII (1950), 32.

Two Tramps in Mud Time
  Frost's alternate title to this poem runs: "or, A Full-Time Interest."
  Discussed in R. L. Cook, Charles Kaplan, and Lawrance Thompson, pp.
7–11 in Greenberg and Hepburn (eds.), *Robert Frost*; Malcolm Cowley, pp.
41–42 in Cox (ed.), *Robert Frost*; Lynen, *The Pastoral Art of Robert Frost*,
pp. 157–158; G. F. Whicher, *Am. Schol.*, XIV (1945), 412–414.

Desert Places
  Discussed in R. P. Blackmur, *Nation*, CXLII (1936), 818–819; Brower,
The Poetry of Robert Frost, pp. 108–110; W. C. Brown, *U. Kans. City Rev.*, XV
(1948), 62–63.

Neither Out Far nor In Deep
  Discussed in Brower, *The Poetry of Robert Frost*, pp. 149–151; V. C. Hopkins,
West. Hum. Rev., XIV (1960), 247–263; Randall Jarrell, *Poetry and the Age*
Vintage Books, 1955), pp. 38–40; Laurence Perrine, *Explicator*, VII (1949),
46; R. W. Stallman, *Eng. Jour.*, XLVI (1957), 247–248.

Design
  Discussed in Brower, *The Poetry of Robert Frost*, pp. 104–108; Elizabeth
Drew, *Poetry* (W. W. Norton Co., 1959), pp. 186–188; Randall Jarrell, *Poetry
and the Age* (Vintage Books, 1955), pp. 42–45.
  2. *a white heal-all:* popular name of such plants as *Rhodiola rosea* and *Col-
linsonia canadensis*, since their leaves, when applied to recent minor cuts, are
believed to be curative.

The Gift Outright
  Read before the Phi Beta Kappa Society at William and Mary College,
December 5, 1941. First published in *A Witness Tree* (1942) and republished,
slightly revised, in *In the Clearing* (1962). On January 20, 1961, Robert Frost
recited from memory this poem at the inauguration of President John F.
Kennedy. This was the first time in the history of the United States that a poet
had participated in an inauguration.
  Discussed in Brower, *The Poetry of Robert Frost*, p. 202; J. P. Kreuzer,
Elements of Poetry (The Macmillan Co., 1955), pp. 154–155; Harvey Shapiro,
New York Times Magazine (January 15, 1961), 6, 86.

Directive
  Discussed in M. M. Blum, *Mod. Lang. Notes*, LXXVI (1961), 524–525;

Pearlanna Briggs, *Explicator*, XXI (1963), 71; Brower, *The Poetry of Robert Frost*, pp. 232–242; J. M. Cox, *Va. Quart. Rev.*, XXXV (1959), 85–87; Elizabeth Drew, *Poetry* (W. W. Norton Co., 1959), pp. 229–233; S. P. C. Duvall, *Am. Lit.*, XXXI (1960), 482–488; M. E. Hartsock, *Explicator*, XVI (1958), 42; Randall Jarrell, *Poetry and the Age* (Vintage Books, 1955), pp. 46–49; Robert Peters, *Mod. Lang. Notes*, LXXV (1960), 29–32.

40. *harness gall:* sore spot on a horse's hide caused by rubbing of harness.
59. *as Saint Mark says they mustn't:* see Mark 4 : 11–12.

OLIVER WENDELL HOLMES
1809–1894

Bibliography

Currier, T. F. *A Bibliography of Oliver Wendell Holmes*, completed and edited by E. M. Tilton. New York: New York University Press, 1953.
Small, M. R. "Selected Bibliography," pp. 166–172 in *Oliver Wendell Holmes*. New York: Twayne Publishers, 1962.

Major Writings

Poems (1836)
Poems (1849)
The Autocrat of the Breakfast-Table (1858)
The Professor at the Breakfast-Table (1860)
The Poet at the Breakfast-Table (1872)
Songs of Many Seasons, 1862–1874 (1875)
The Iron Gate and Other Poems (1880)
Over the Teacups (1891)
The Writings of Oliver Wendell Holmes (1891, 13 Vols.)
Letters to James Russell Lowell and Others (1917, W. R. Thayer, ed.)

Standard Editions

The Writings of Oliver Wendell Holmes, Riverside Edition, 13 Vols. Boston: Houghton Mifflin and Co., 1891.
Hayakawa, S. I., and Jones, H. M. (eds.). *Oliver Wendell Holmes: Representative Selections*. New York: American Book Company, 1939.
Scudder, H. E. (ed.). *The Complete Poetical Works of Oliver Wendell Holmes*. Boston: Houghton Mifflin and Co., 1895.

Biography

Howe, M. A. de W. *Holmes of the Breakfast-Table*. New York: Oxford University Press, 1939.
Morse, J. T. *Life and Letters of Oliver Wendell Holmes*, 2 Vols. Boston: Houghton Mifflin and Co., 1896.

Small, M. R. *Oliver Wendell Holmes*. New York: Twayne Publishers, 1962.

Stephen, Leslie. "Oliver Wendell Holmes," pp. 160–195 in *Studies of a Biographer*, II. New York: G. P. Putnam's Sons, 1898.

Tilton, E. M. *Amiable Autocrat: A Biography of Dr. Oliver Wendell Holmes*. New York: Henry Schuman, 1947.

Criticism

Allen, Gay Wilson. "Oliver Wendell Holmes," pp. 193–216 in *American Prosody*. New York: American Book Company, 1935.

Arms, George. "Holmes," pp. 97–114 in *The Fields Were Green*. Stanford, Calif.: Stanford University Press, 1953.

Clark, H. H. "Dr. Holmes: A Re-interpretation," *New Eng. Quart.*, XII (1939), 19–34.

Currier, T. F. "Oliver Wendell Holmes, Poet Laureate of Harvard," *Proceedings of the Massachusetts Historical Society*, LXVII (1945), 436–451.

Hayakawa, S. I. "The Boston Poet-Laureate: Oliver Wendell Holmes," University of Texas *Studies in English*, XVI (1936), 572–592.

Jones, H. M. "Oliver Wendell Holmes (1890–1894)," pp. 84–102 in *History and the Contemporary*. Madison, Wis.: University of Wisconsin Press, 1964.

Kern, A. C. "Dr. Oliver Wendell Holmes Today," *U. Kans. City Rev.*, XIV (1948), 191–199.

Knickerbocker, W. S. "His Own Boswell: A Note on the Poetry of Oliver Wendell Holmes," *Sewanee Rev.*, XLI (1933), 454–466.

Wentersdorf, K. P. "The Underground Workshop of Oliver Wendell Holmes," *Am. Lit.*, XXXV (1963), 1–12.

Woolf, Virginia. "Oliver Wendell Holmes," pp. 232–240 in *Granite and Rainbow: Essays*. London: The Hogarth Press, 1958.

Comments on Poems

The Ballad of the Oysterman
    Discussed in Small, *Oliver Wendell Holmes*, pp. 34–35.

Old Ironsides
    "Old Ironsides," the American frigate *Constitution*, was victor over the British *Guerrière* in the War of 1812. Prompted by the announcement in the Boston *Daily Advertiser* that the vessel, then, as now, lying in the Charlestown Navy Yard, was to be demolished, Holmes wrote this poem, which is credited with saving the ship. The occasion for writing the poem is discussed by Morse, *Life*, I, 79–80.
    Discussed in Small, *Oliver Wendell Holmes*, p. 35.

The Last Leaf
    In a prefatory note to this poem which appears in the Riverside Edition Holmes wrote: "This poem was suggested by the appearance in one of our streets of a venerable relic of the Revolution, said to be one of the party who

threw the tea overboard in Boston Harbor. He was a fine monumental specimen in his cocked hat and knee breeches, with his buckled shoes and his
sturdy cane. The smile with which I, as a young man, greeted him, meant no
disrespect to an honoured fellow-citizen whose costume was out of date,
but whose patriotism never changed with years. I do not recall any earlier
example of this form of verse, which was commended by the fastidious Edgar
Allan Poe, who made a copy of the whole poem which I have in his own hand-
writing. Good Abraham Lincoln had a great liking for the poem, and repeated
it from memory to Governor Andrew, as the governor himself told me."
John Albion Andrew (1818–1867) was Governor of Massachusetts from 1861
to 1866.

   1. *him:* Major Thomas Melville, Herman Melville's grandfather.

The Chambered Nautilus

   The chambered nautilus is a cephalopod found in the South Pacific and
Indian Oceans. Holmes described the genesis of this poem in *The Autocrat of
the Breakfast-Table,* Section IV.

   Discussed in N. F. Adkins, *Am. Lit.,* IX (1938), 458–465; Arms, *The Fields
Were Green,* pp. 108–110; C. D. Eby, Jr., *Emerson Society Quarterly,* No. 27
(1962), 48–50.

   26. *Triton blew:* Triton, in Greek mythology, is sea demigod whose charac-
teristic action is blowing a conch shell. Holmes's line echoes line 14 in
Wordsworth's sonnet "The World Is Too Much with Us": "Or hear old
Triton blow his wreathèd horn."

The Deacon's Masterpiece

   Discussed in Arms, *The Fields Were Green,* pp. 104–105.

   10. *Georgius Secundus:* George II, Hanoverian king of England (1727–1760).

   12. *Lisbon-town:* in 1755 Lisbon, Portugal, was shaken by a great earthquake.

   14. *Braddock's Army:* General Edward Braddock, commander-in-chief of
the British forces in America, led an army to defeat by French and Indians in
the Battle of the Wilderness, July 9, 1755. In the battle Braddock was mortally
wounded.

   17. *the Deacon:* Holmes has in mind the whole·Calvinistic system of logic
as propounded by Jonathan Edwards, whose *Freedom of the Will* appeared in
1754 (not 1755, as implied here).

   20. *felloe:* wooden wheel rim. *thill:* shaft.

   22. *thoroughbrace:* a leather strap, attached to the springs, supporting the
body of a carriage.

Contentment

   The epigraph is taken from "A Ballad," line 31, to be found in Oliver
Goldsmith's *The Vicar of Wakefield,* Chapter 8.

   Discussed in H. H. Scudder, *Am. Lit.,* XX (1949), 443–446.

   3. *brown stone:* in the mid-nineteenth century, the town houses of the rich
customarily had brown-stone fronts.

   21. *Plenipo:* Minister Plenipotentiary.

   22. *St. James:* the court of St. James; that is, he wants only the best of all
ambassadorships, that to Britain.

39. *two, forty-five:* a fast horse, one which can trot a mile in two minutes and forty-five seconds.

60. *Meerschaums:* expensive pipes.

64. *buhl:* inlaid furniture decoration in the manner of A. C. Boulle (1642–1732), French cabinetmaker.

The Two Streams

Discussed in George Arms, *New Eng. Quart.,* XIX (1946), 534–537 and *The Fields Were Green,* pp. 97–99.

1. *rocky wall:* the Continental Divide.

7. *Athabasca:* river in the province of Alberta, Canada, which first flows east then north.

11. *evening's ocean:* the Pacific.

12. *Oregon:* The Columbia River.

19. *frozen tide:* The Arctic Ocean.

Manhood

This is a portion of Holmes's longest philosophical poem.

Dorothy Q.

Dorothy Q. was Dorothy Quincy, Holmes's great-grandmother in the maternal line. Mary Jackson, daughter of Edward and Dorothy Quincy Jackson, married Oliver Wendell. The daughter of Oliver and Mary Jackson Wendell, Sarah, was the mother of the poet. See J. T. Morse, *Life and Letters of Oliver Wendell Holmes,* I, 14.

28. *her name:* Quincy is a Norman name, brought to England with the Conquest.

29. *three-hilled rebel town:* Boston.

Two Sonnets: Harvard

Written for presentation before the Harvard Club of New York on February 21, 1878.

Discussed in Arms, *The Fields Were Green,* pp. 113–114.

"*Christo et Ecclesiæ*": (Latin) "To Christ and the Church." A motto appearing around the edge of the Harvard Seal.

4. *Like David's altar:* commanded by God, King David built an altar on Mount Moriah, the rocky hilltop of Jerusalem, where Solomon later built the temple. See 1 Chronicles 21 : 18 and 2 Chronicles 3 : 1.

6. *ram's-horn:* the trumpet used by Joshua's army to topple the walls of Jericho. See Joshua 6 : 4–5.

14. *Araunah's threshing-floor:* the threshing-floor of Araunah, the Jebusite, which David purchased for the site of the sacrificial altar mentioned in line 4. See 2 Samuel 24 : 15–25 and 2 Chronicles 3 : 1.

"*Veritas*": (Latin) "Truth." This word appears at the center of the Harvard Seal.

15. *older legend: Veritas* appeared on the first seal of Harvard College (the Overseer's Seal of 1643). *Christo et Ecclesiæ,* the third seal of the College, was cast in 1693. See S. E. Morison, *Harvard College in the Seventeenth Century* (Harvard University Press, 1936), p. 493.

24. *phylactery:* an amulet containing a Biblical text to ward off evil. Here Holmes means the text itself (*Veritas*).

The Peau de Chagrin of State Street

La Peau de Chagrin (1831), a novel by Honoré de Balzac (1799–1850), is about a magic skin which regrettably shrinks as one makes wishes. State Street is a financial street in Boston.

Discussed in Arms, *The Fields Were Green*, p. 102.

RANDALL JARRELL
b. 1914

Bibliography

Adams, C. M. *Randall Jarrell: A Bibliography*. Chapel Hill, N.C.: University of North Carolina Press, 1958.

Adams, C. M. "A Supplement to *Randall Jarrell: A Bibliography*," *Analects*, I, No. 2 (1961), pp. 49–56.

Major Writings

Blood for a Stranger (1942)
Little Friend, Little Friend (1945)
Losses (1948)
The Seven-League Crutches (1951)
Poetry and the Age (1953, criticism)
Pictures from an Institution: A Comedy (1954, novel)
Selected Poems (1955)
The Woman at the Washington Zoo: Poems and Translations (1960)
A Sad Heart at the Supermarket: Essays & Fables (1962)
The Lost World (1965)

Criticism

Analects (Woman's College of the University of North Carolina), I, No. 2 (1961). Randall Jarrell number.

Graham, W. S. "'It All Comes Back to Me Now,'" *Poetry*, LXXII (1948), 302–307.

Kobler, J. F. "Randall Jarrell Seeks Truth in Fantasy," *Forum* (Houston), III, No. 6 (1961), 17–20.

Maguire, C. E. "Shape of the Lightning: Randall Jarrell," *Renascence*, VII (1955), 115–120 and 181–186, 195.

Quinn, Sister M. B. *The Metamorphic Tradition in Modern Poetry*, pp. 168–206. New Brunswick, N.J.: Rutgers University Press, 1955.

Ray, David. "The Lightning of Randall Jarrell," *Prairie Schooner*, XXXV (1961), 45–52.

Rideout, W. B. "'To Change, To Change!': The Poetry of Randall Jarrell," pp. 156–178 in Edward Hungerford (ed.), *Poets in Progress: Critical Prefaces to Ten Contemporary Americans*. Evanston, Ill.: Northwestern University Press, 1962.

Tyler, Parker. "The Dramatic Lyrism of Randall Jarrell," *Poetry*, LXXIX (1952), 335–346.

Comments on Poems

90 North

20. *Cloud-Cuckoo-Land*: in Aristophanes' *The Birds*, an imaginary city built in the clouds by the cuckoos; hence any fantastic, illusionary world.

Second Air Force

[Jarrell's note from *Selected Poems*] "In 'Second Air Force' the woman visiting her son remembers what she has read on the front page of her newspaper the week before, a conversation between a bomber, in flames over Germany, and one of the fighters protecting it: 'Then I heard the bomber call me in: "Little Friend, Little Friend, I got two engines on fire. Can you see me, Little Friend?" I said, "I'm crossing right over you. Let's go home."'"

50. *wired fur*: electrically heated flying suits.

The Death of the Ball Turret Gunner

[Jarrell's note from *Selected Poems*] "A ball turret was a plexiglass sphere set into the belly of a B-17 or B-24, and inhabited by two .50 caliber machine-guns and one man, a short small man. When this gunner tracked with his machine-guns a fighter attacking his bomber from below, he revolved with the turret; hunched upside-down in his little sphere, he looked like the foetus in the womb. The fighters which attacked him were armed with cannon firing explosive shells. The hose was a steam hose."

Discussed in Richard Fein, *Analects*, I, No. 2 (1961), 18–20; I. C. Hungerland, *Jour. Aesth. & Art Crit.*, XIII (1955), 352–354; Ray, *Prairie Schooner*, XXXV (1961), 45–51; M. L. Rosenthal, *The Modern Poets: A Critical Introduction* (Oxford University Press, 1960), p. 245.

A Camp in the Prussian Forest

[Jarrell's note from *Selected Poems*] "An American soldier is speaking after the capture of one of the great German death camps. The Jews, under the Nazis, were made to wear the badge of a yellow star. The white Star of David is set over Jewish graves just as the cross is set over Christian graves."

Discussed in Graham, *Poetry*, LXXII (1948), 306; Stephen Spender, *Nation*, CLXVI (1948), 476.

The Woman at the Washington Zoo

For a description of the genesis and development of this poem, see Randall Jarrell, "The Woman at the Washington Zoo," pp. 160–173 in *A Sad Heart at the Supermarket* (Atheneum Publishers, 1962).

Discussed in Michel Benamou, *Analects*, I, No. 2 (1961), 2–3; Sister M. B. Quinn, *Analects*, I, No. 2 (1961), 24–25; Rideout, p. 177 in Edward Hungerford (ed.), *Poets in Progress*.

ROBINSON JEFFERS
1887–1962

Bibliography

Alberts, S. S. *A Bibliography of the Works of Robinson Jeffers.* New York:
    Random House, 1933.

Major Writings

Tamar and Other Poems (1924)
Roan Stallion, Tamar and Other Poems (1925)
The Women at Point Sur (1927)
Cawdor and Other Poems (1928)
Dear Judas, and Other Poems (1929)
Descent to the Dead, Poems Written in Ireland and Great Britain (1931)
Thurso's Landing and Other Poems (1932)
Give Your Heart to the Hawks and Other Poems (1933)
Solstice and Other Poems (1935)
Such Counsels You Gave to Me and Other Poems (1937)
The Selected Poetry of Robinson Jeffers (1938)
Be Angry at the Sun (1941)
Medea, Freely Adapted from the Medea of Euripides (1946)
The Double Axe and Other Poems (1948)
Hungerfield and Other Poems (1954)
The Beginning and the End (1963)

Biography

Sterling, George. *Robinson Jeffers, the Man and the Artist.* New York: Boni &
    Liveright, 1926.

Criticism

Carpenter, F. I. "The Values of Robinson Jeffers," *Am. Lit.*, XI (1940), 353–
    366.
Fletcher, John Gould. "The Dilemma of Robinson Jeffers," *Poetry*, XLIII
    (1934), 338–342.
Gierasch, Walter. "Robinson Jeffers," *Eng. Jour.*, XXVIII (1939), 284–295.
Gilbert, Rudolph. *Shine, Perishing Republic: Robinson Jeffers and the Tragic Sense
    in Modern Poetry.* Boston: Bruce Humphries, 1936.
Gregory, Horace. "Poets Without Critics: A Note on Robinson Jeffers,"
    New World Writing, 7th Mentor Selection (1955), 40–52.
Powell, L. C. *Robinson Jeffers: The Man and His Work.* Los Angeles: Primavera
    Press, 1934; rev. ed., Pasadena, Calif.: San Pasqual Press, 1940.

Schwartz, Delmore, and Taylor, Frajam. "The Enigma of Robinson Jeffers,"
    Poetry, LV (1939), 30–46.
Short, R. W. "The Tower beyond Tragedy," *So. Rev.*, VII (1941), 132–144.
Squires, Radcliffe. *The Loyalties of Robinson Jeffers*. Ann Arbor, Mich.: Univer-
    sity of Michigan Press, 1956.
Waggoner, H. H. "Robinson Jeffers: Here Is Reality," pp. 105–132 in *The
    Heel of Elohim: Science and Values in Modern American Poetry*. Norman,
    Okla.: University of Oklahoma Press, 1950.

Comments on Poems

Textual sources: "Night," "Birds," *Roan Stallion, Tamar, and Other Poems*
(1925); "Apology for Bad Dreams," "Promise of Peace," Modern Library
edition of *Roan Stallion, Tamar, and Other Poems* (1935); "The Eye," *The Double
Axe and Other Poems* (1948); "Ocean," *Hungerfield and Other Poems* (1954); "My
Burial Place," "Let Them Alone," and "But I Am Growing Old and Indolent," *The Beginning and the End* (1963).

Birds
11. *Lobos:* a point of land on Carmel Bay.

Apology for Bad Dreams
The first book of poems solely by Jeffers to include this poem was the
Modern Library reprint of *Roan Stallion, Tamar, and Other Poems* (1935), but
"Apology for Bad Dreams" was published, with several other poems by
Jeffers, in Louis Untermeyer (ed.), *A Miscellany of American Poetry* (Harcourt,
Brace and Co., 1927).

20. *said the prophet:* "I form the light, and create darkness: I make peace,
and create evil: I the Lord do all these things."—Isaiah 45 : 7.

24. *Soberanes:* a point of land just south of Carmel Bay.

31. *this little house:* Tor House, Jeffers' home.

50. *Tamar Cauldwell:* the incestuous heroine of *Tamar*, the title poem of the
volume published by Jeffers in 1924.

52. *Point Pinos:* a point of land just north of Monterey. *Sur Rivers:* about
twenty miles south of Carmel along the California coast. The coastal strip
between Point Pinos and the Sur Rivers is the "Jeffers Country."

Promise of Peace
The first book of poems solely by Jeffers to include this poem was the
Modern Library reprint of *Roan Stallion, Tamar, and Other Poems* (1935), but
"Promise of Peace" was published, with several other poems by Jeffers, in
Louis Untermeyer (ed.), *A Miscellany of American Poetry* (Harcourt, Brace and
Co., 1927).

The Eye
6. *brave dwarfs:* the Japanese. This poem was written during World War II.

But I Am Growing Old and Indolent
5–13. Cf. "Apology for Bad Dreams," ll. 30 ff.
12. *Tamar:* tragic story of incest, based in part on the Biblical story of

Tamar and her brother Amnon. *Cawdor:* tragic story of a middle-aged rancher whose young wife falls in love with her stepson.

13. *Thurso's wife:* the wife in *Thurso's Landing* is hated by her mother-in-law, the cause of her brother-in-law's suicide, and torn by pity and hatred for her husband, whom she has betrayed and caused to become an invalid.

SIDNEY LANIER
1842–1881

Bibliography

Graham, Philip, and Thies, F. C. "Bibliography," pp. 379–412 in C. R. Anderson (general ed.), *The Centennial Edition of Sidney Lanier*, Vol. VI. Baltimore, Md.: The John Hopkins Press, 1945.

Concordance

Graham, Philip, and Jones, Joseph, *A Concordance to the Poems of Sidney Lanier*. Austin, Texas: University of Texas Press, 1939.

Major Writings

Poems (1877)
The Science of English Verse (1880)
Poems of Sidney Lanier (1884, Mary Day Lanier, ed.)
Selected Poems (1947, Stark Young, ed.)

Standard Edition

Anderson, C. R. (general ed.). *The Centennial Edition of Sidney Lanier*, 10 Vols. Baltimore, Md.: The Johns Hopkins Press, 1945.

Biography

Mims, Edwin. *Sidney Lanier*. Boston: Houghton Mifflin and Co., 1905.
Starke, A. H. *Sidney Lanier: A Biographical and Critical Study*. Chapel Hill, N.C.: University of North Carolina Press, 1933.

Criticism

Allen, Gay Wilson. "Sidney Lanier," pp. 277–306 in *American Prosody*. New York: American Book Company, 1935.
Anderson, C. R. (ed.). "Introduction," pp. xxi–xc in *Sidney Lanier: Poems and Poem Outlines*, Vol. I of *The Centennial Edition of Sidney Lanier*. Baltimore: The Johns Hopkins Press, 1945.

Beaver, Joseph. "Lanier's Use of Science for Poetic Imagery," *Am. Lit.*,
    XXIV (1953), 520–533.

Fletcher, J. G. "Sidney Lanier," *U. Kans. City Rev.*, XVI (1949), 97–102.

Graham, Philip. "Sidney Lanier and the Pattern of Contrast," *Am. Quart.*,
    XI (1959), 503–508.

Jones, H. M. "Sidney Lanier," pp. 670–675 in P. H. Boynton (ed.), *American
    Poetry*. New York: Charles Scribner's Sons, 1918.

Leary, Lewis, "The Forlorn Hope of Sidney Lanier," *So. Atl. Quart.*, XLVI
    (1947), 263–271.

Malone, Kemp. "Sidney Lanier," *Johns Hopkins Alumni Magazine* XXI (1933),
    244–249.

Ransom, J. C. "Hearts and Heads," *American Review*, II (1934), 554–571.

Tate, Allen. "A Southern Romantic," *New Republic* LXXVI (August 30,
    1933), 67–70.

Warren, R. P. "The Blind Poet: Sidney Lanier," *American Review*, II (1933),
    27–45.

Webb, Richard, and Coulson, E. R. *Sidney Lanier, Poet and Prosodist*. Athens,
    Ga.: University of Georgia Press, 1941.

Williams, S. T. "Sidney Lanier," pp. 327–341 in John Macy (ed.), *American
    Writers on American Literature*. New York: Horace Liveright, 1931.

Comments on Poems

The texts of Lanier's poems are taken from C. R. Anderson (ed.), *The Centennial Edition of Sidney Lanier*, Vol. I.

Thar's More in the Man Than Thar Is in the Land

This was the first of Lanier's dialect poems, originally published in the Macon, Georgia, *Telegraph and Messenger* (February 7, 1871), 22–23.

Discussed in Starke, *Sidney Lanier*, pp. 148–150.

1. *Jones:* Jones County, in central Georgia, the county just north of Bibb County, of which Lanier's native Macon is the county seat.

Corn

Discussed in Starke, *Sidney Lanier*, pp. 188–194.

157. *Dives's mood:* Dives is the name usually given to the rich man in Jesus' parable of the rich man and Lazarus. See Luke 16 : 19–31.

169. *Bulls' or Bears':* a bull market is one in which prices are rising, a bear market one in which prices are falling.

The Symphony

Discussed in E. J. Hogenes, *Explicator*, XVI (1957), 4; Starke, *Sidney Lanier*, pp. 201–211.

1. *Trade:* Lanier refers to modern capitalism.

4. *tale:* (Archaic) count, reckoning.

42. *Man shall not live . . . :* Jesus, when tempted by Satan, said, "It is written, that man shall not live by bread alone, but by every word of God." Luke 4 : 4. Also see Matthew 4 : 4.

168. *"All for love":* echoes "And all for love, and nothing for reward."
Edmund Spenser, *Faerie Queene*, Book II, Canto viii, stanza 2.

178. *Love thy neighbor:* Jesus said that the second great commandment was,
"Thou shalt love thy neighbor as thyself." Matthew 22 : 39. Also see
Matthew 19 : 19.

182. See Luke 10 : 29 ff.

240. *mercery:* goods to be found in a textile shop.

272. *Mammon's Cave:* a reference to Spenser's *Faerie Queene*, Book II, Canto
vii, in which Sir Guyon (Temperance) goes to the care of Mammon (greed
for wealth).

311. *Pembroke:* apparently a reference to Sir Philip Sidney (1554–1586),
brother of the Countess of Pembroke. Sir Philip fell in battle against the
Spanish near the city of Zutphen, Holland.

333–334. *Never shalt thou . . . :* Jesus said, "Whosoever shall not receive the
kingdom of God as a little child, he shall not enter therein." Mark 10 : 15.
Also see Luke 18 : 17.

368. *Music is Love:* Lanier's echo of Mme de Staël's "Music is love's only
interpreter."

Evening Song

1. *dear Love:* Mary Day Lanier, Mrs. Sidney Lanier.

Song of the Chattahoochee

Discussed in Philip Graham, *University of Texas Studies in English*, XVII
(1937), 111; C. W. Kent, *PMLA*, VII (1892), 33–63; Starke, *Sidney Lanier*,
pp. 290–292.

Chattahoochee: a small river in Georgia.

1. *Habersham:* county in northeast Georgia.

2. *Hall:* another Georgia county, southwest of Habersham.

The Revenge of Hamish

This narrative poem is based upon an incident in William Black's *Macleod
of Dare*, Chapter 3, serialized in *Harper's Magazine*, LVI (February, 1878), 412–
413.

Discussed by Yves Bourgeois, *Revue Anglo-Américaine*, VIII (1931), 431–
432; Starke, *Sidney Lanier*, pp. 310–311; Edmund Wilson, *Patriotic Gore:
Studies in the Literature of the American Civil War* (Oxford University Press,
1962), pp. 522–528.

23. *burn:* (Scottish) brook, small stream.

36. *red as a beacon the wind hath upblown:* signal fire, lighted on a high place
to serve as a warning or signal of danger.

41. *kern:* peasant, boor.

60. *gillie:* in Scottish Highlands, a male attendant.

82. *bairn:* (Scottish) "child."

The Marshes of Glynn

The marshes of Glynn are on the Atlantic coast near Brunswick, Georgia.

Discussed in Graham, *Am. Quart.*, XI (1959), 506–507; Starke, *Sidney
Lanier*, pp. 312–316; Tate, *New Republic*, LXXVI (August 30, 1933), 67–70;
Warren, *American Review*, II (1933), 42–45.

A Ballad of Trees and the Master

See Matthew 26 : 36–46 and Luke 22 : 39–46 for accounts of Christ in Gethsemane.

DENISE LEVERTOV
b. 1923

Major Writings

The Double Image (1946)
Here and Now (1957)
Overland to the Islands (1958)
With Eyes at the Back of Our Heads (1960)
The Jacob's Ladder (1961)
O Taste and See (1964)

Criticism

The criticism is to be found mainly in reviews, samples of which are given below.

Comments on Poems

Pleasures and The Goddess

The first book publication of these poems was in *With Eyes at the Back of Our Heads*, about which Eve Triem wrote in *Poetry*, 96 (1960), 316: "She uses devices, original or in new and disturbing ways. Warning: if you are sensitive only to traditional meanings, you will certainly miss the ideas that Denise Levertov fires at you. They will go by so fast you will not even know they were there ... She is concerned with impact, produced by combining the simplest, uncannily chosen materials." Thomas Parkinson wrote in the San Francisco *Chronicle*, February 28, 1960, p. 22: "Denise Levertov has a special tone of indolence and isolation, sensibility returning upon itself when it is being most objective, a caricature of self from which she reaches but never quite destroys. Her poems are dramas of affection, and her relation with the external world is in the best sense flirtatious. She approaches without inviting, and withdraws. Language is often spoken of as a form of dance: in her poetry the comparison is inevitable."

12. *mamey:* tangy flavor of a tropical apple called the *mamey de Santo Domingo* of Cuba.

The Well

15 ff. Anne Bancroft played the role of Miss Annie Sullivan in *The Miracle Worker*, by William Gibson (Alfred A. Knopf, 1957), produced in New York during the 1959–1960 season. Helen Keller, born in 1880 a normal child, lost both sight and hearing at nineteen months. Anne Sullivan Macy (1866–1936) taught her to communicate by spelling words in her palm.

22. *Valentines:* the place arouses sensations of love. *place of origin:* water is a source of life, both in biological evolution and physiologically because the foetus is encased in a bag of water.

33. *Roding:* a small river in England, near the poet's birthplace.

34. *Alpheus:* river god in Greek mythology.

The Novel

First published in *Hud. Rev.,* winter 1963–1964, Vol. XVI, pp. 539–540, and collected in *O Taste and See.* The two themes of the poem are the processes by which the novel evolves in the author's mind and the imagined characters' awareness of the kind of world (threatened by the atomic bomb) in which they symbolically live.

8. *leaves:* both published versions of this poem have "lives," but the author says (letter to GWA) she intended to write "leaves."

14. *year of the roach:* scientists say that the roach could best survive an atomic war; the poet alludes to the danger of the atom bomb.

HENRY WADSWORTH LONGFELLOW
1807–1882

Bibliography

Livingston, L. S. *A Bibliography of the First Editions . . . of Henry Wadsworth Longfellow.* New York: De Vinne Press, 1908.

Shepard, Odell (ed.), "*Selected Bibliography,*" pp. lvii–lxii in *Henry Wadsworth Longfellow: Representative Selections.* New York: American Book Company, 1934.

Major Writings

Voices of the Night (1839)
Ballads and Other Poems (1842)
The Belfry of Bruges and Other Poems (1846)
The Seaside and the Fireside (1850)
The Courtship of Miles Standish and Other Poems (1858)
Tales of a Wayside Inn (1863)
Dante, The Divine Comedy (1865–1867, translation)
Flower-de-Luce (1867)
Aftermath (1873)
The Masque of Pandora and Other Poems (1875)
Kéramos and Other Poems (1878)
Ultima Thule (1880)
In the Harbor (1882)

Standard Editions

Longfellow, Samuel (ed.). *The Works of Henry Wadsworth Longfellow,* 14 Vols. Boston: Houghton Mifflin and Co., 1886–1891.

Scudder, H. E. (ed.). *The Complete Poetical Works of Henry Wadsworth Long-
      fellow*. Boston: Houghton Mifflin and Co., 1893.

Biography

Austin, G. L. *Henry Wadsworth Longfellow*. Boston: Lee and Shepard, 1883.

Gorman, H. S. *A Victorian American: Henry Wadsworth Longfellow*. New York:
      George H. Doran Co., 1926.

Longfellow, Samuel (ed.). *The Life of Henry Wadsworth Longfellow*, 2 Vols.
      Boston: Ticknor and Co., 1886.

Longfellow, Samuel (ed.). *Final Memorials*. Boston: Ticknor and Co., 1887.

Thompson, Lawrance. *Young Longfellow, 1807–1843*. New York: The Mac-
      millan Co., 1938.

Wagenknecht, Edward. *Longfellow: A Full-Length Portrait*. New York: Long-
      mans, Green and Co., 1955.

Criticism

Allen, Gay Wilson. "Henry Wadsworth Longfellow," pp. 154–192 in
      American Prosody. New York: American Book Company, 1935.

Arms, George. "Longfellow," pp. 204–222 in *The Fields Were Green*. Stanford,
      Calif.: Stanford University Press, 1953.

Arvin, Newton. *Longfellow: His Life and Work*. Boston: Little, Brown and
      Co., 1963.

Bewley, Marius. "The Poetry of Longfellow," *Hud. Rev.*, XVI (1963), 297–
      304.

Elliott, G. R. "Gentle Shades of Longfellow," *Southwest Reveiw*, X (1925),
      34–52.

Hirsch, E. L. *Henry Wadsworth Longfellow*. Minneapolis, Minn.: University of
      Minnesota Press, 1964.

Howells, W. D. "The Art of Longfellow," *No. Am. Rev.*, CLXXXIV
      (March 1, 1907), 472–485.

Jones, H. M. "Longfellow," pp. 105–124 in John Macy (ed.), *American
      Writers on American Literature*. New York: Horace Liveright, 1931.

Mathews, J. C. "Echoes of Dante in Longfellow's Poetry," *Italica*, XXVI
      (1949), 242–259.

More, Paul Elmer. "The Centenary of Longfellow," pp. 132–157 in *Shelburne
      Essays*, Fifth Series. Boston: Houghton Mifflin and Co., 1908.

Nemerov, Howard. "On Longfellow," pp. 143–158 in *Poetry and Fiction:
      Essays*. New Brunswick, N.J.: Rutgers University Press, 1963.

O'Neill, J. E. "Poet of the Feeling Heart," pp. 146–175 in H. C. Gardiner
      (ed.), *American Classics Reconsidered*. New York: Charles Scribner's Sons,
      1958.

Pearson, N. H. "Both Longfellows," *U. Kans. City Rev.*, XVI (1950), 245–
      253.

Von Abele, Rudolph. "A Note on Longfellow's Poetic," *Am. Lit.*, XXIV
      (1952), 77–83.

Comments on Poems

Hymn to the Night

The epigraph is taken from Homer, *Iliad* VIII, 488. It means: "Welcome, thrice prayed for."

Discussed in George Arms, *Explicator*, I (1942), 7.

21. *Orestes-like:* in Aeschylus' tragedy *Eumenides*, Orestes prays for an end to the torments of the Furies.

The Skeleton in Armor

The genesis of this poem is discussed in Samuel Longfellow (ed.), *Life*, I, pp. 286 and 366. It was inspired by the discovery at Fall River, Massachusetts, of a skeleton, supposedly that of a Norseman.

19. *Skald:* Old Norse reciter of heroic verse.

20. *Saga:* an epic tale from the early literature of Scandinavia or Iceland, usually recounting the adventures and travels of a legendary hero.

28. *gerfalcon:* Arctic falcon.

30. *Sound:* Öre Sound, between the island of Sjaelland (Denmark) and southern Sweden. It opens on the north into the Kattegat and on the south into the Baltic Sea.

53. *Berserk's tale:* a berserker was a very fierce Norse warrior.

110. *Skaw:* Cape Skagen, most northern point of Jutland, Denmark.

134. *the lofty tower:* a reference to a tower at Newport, Rhode Island, whose origin is uncertain but supposed by some to be of tenth-century Norse construction.

The Arsenal at Springfield

Inspired by a visit to the United States Arsenal at Springfield, Massachusetts.

7. *Miserere:* (Latin) *Miserere mei, Domine* (Have mercy on me, O Lord). Psalms 51 : 1.

14. *Cimbric forest:* Germanic forests from which the Cimbri came to threaten the Roman Empire.

19. *teocallis:* Aztec temples situated upon flat-topped pyramids.

40. *the curse of Cain:* see Genesis 4 : 11.

Seaweed

Discussed in Arms, *The Fields Were Green*, pp. 209–211.

14. *skerries:* (Scottish) rocky islands, reefs.

The Fire of Drift-Wood

Marblehead is a city on the Atlantic coast in Massachusetts, north of Boston.

Discussed in Arms, *The Fields Were Green*, p. 212.

In the Churchyard at Cambridge

The churchyard described adjoins Christ Church, which faces the Cambridge (Massachusetts) Common.

Discussed in Arms, *The Fields Were Green*, pp. 208–209; I. A., Richards, *Practical Criticism* (Harcourt, Brace and Co., 1949), pp. 162–178.

The Jewish Cemetery at Newport

Discussed in Irving Fitzig, *American Heritage*, XIII (1962), 60–63; Ely Stock, *Rhode Island History*, XX (1961), 81–87.

12. *broken by Moses:* see Exodus 32 : 19.

15. *Alvares and Rivera:* Portuguese and Spanish Jewish names.

32. *Ishmaels and Hagars:* see Genesis 16 and 21. Hagar, Abraham's concubine, and Ishmael, their son, were exiled when Abraham's wife, Sarah, bore him a son, Isaac.

40. *marah:* (Hebrew) bitterness.

41. *Anathema maranatha:* Anathema (Greek) and Maranatha (Aramaic), words used by St. Paul to condemn nonbelievers. See 1 Corinthians 16 : 22.

43. *Mordecai:* Jew prominent in the court of Persian monarch, Ahasuerus. See the Book of Esther.

My Lost Youth

The genesis of this poem is given in Longfellow's journals of March 29 and March 30, 1855, published in Longfellow (ed.), *The Works* XIII, 284, and is discussed in J. T. Hatfield, *PMLA*, XLV (1930), 1189.

Also discussed in George Arms, *Mod. Lang. Notes*, LXI (1946), 389–392.

1. *the beautiful town:* Longfellow's birthplace, Portland, Maine.

8–9. *A boy's will . . . long thoughts:* a literal translation from the German rendering by Johann Gottfried Herder of a Lapland song. J. T. Hatfield says, "After some search, my son has discovered, in an obscure corner of Craigie House, Longfellow's copy of Herder's *Stimmen der Völker in Liedern* [Folk-Voices in Songs] with the poet's characteristic check opposite this poem."

13. *Hesperides:* in classical mythology, a distant land to the west.

37. *sea-fight:* Longfellow says he was thinking of the engagement in 1813 between the American brig, *Enterprise*, and the British brig, *Boxer*, off Portland Harbor. Both captains, slain in battle, were buried in the Montjoy cemetery.

47. *Deering's Woods:* small forest near Portland, Maine.

Snow-Flakes

Discussed in Arms, *The Fields Were Green*, pp. 207–208; Arvin, *Longfellow*, pp. 182–183; Pearson, *U. Kans. City Rev.*, XVI (1950), 252–253.

Killed at the Ford

Discussed in Arms, *The Fields Were Green*, pp. 221–222.

Divina Commedia

Longfellow wrote these sonnets in connection with his translation of Dante. Sonnets I and II were placed before *Inferno*, III and IV before *Purgatorio*, V and VI before *Paradiso*.

Sonnet I

Discussed in George Arms, *Explicator*, II (1943), 7; *The Fields Were Green*, p. 211.

12. *time disconsolate:* the period of the Civil War.

Sonnet III

30. *poet saturnine:* Dante.

41–42. *Although your sins . . . as the snow:* see Isaiah 1 : 18.

Sonnet IV

44. *She:* Beatrice.

47. *with stern rebuke:* Beatrice rebukes Dante in *Purgatorio*, Cantos 30 and 31.

54. *Lethe and Eunoë:* in *Purgatorio*, Canto 28 : 130–144, Dante is told by his guide, Matilda, of the two rivers: Lethe, whose waters cause forgetfulness, Eunoë, whose waters bring memory of past good.

Sonnet V

70. *elevation of the Host:* climax of the Mass, when consecrated bread and wine are raised before the altar by the priest.

The Challenge

Discussed in Arvin, *Longfellow*, pp. 198–200.

5. *brave King Sanchez:* after the death of Ferdinand I of Spain in 1065, his son, Sancho, vainly besieged Zamora (now a part of Portugal), a city given before Ferdinand's death to Sancho's sister, Doña Urroca.

Aftermath

Discussed in Arms, *The Fields Were Green*, pp. 213–214; Arvin, *Longfellow*, pp. 203–204.

The Sicilian's Tale

This tale appears in "Tales of a Wayside Inn, Third Day," first published in the collection *Aftermath* (1873). It has its source in *L'Asino Mutato in Frate* (The Cordelier Metamorphosed), an Italian novella attributed to Michele Colombo. Longfellow could have read the story in translation in Thomas Roscoe's *The Italian Novelists* (London: Printed for Septimus Prowett, 1825), IV, 57–80.

36. *wallets:* knapsacks, packs.

103. *Claudian's Old Man of Verona:* see "Of the Old Man of Verona Who Never Left His Farm," pp. 11–12 in the Latin Carmina Minora (Minor Lyrics) XX, in Julius Koch (ed.), *Carmini Claudii Claudiani* (Leipzig: Teubner, 1893), p. 223. Claudius Claudianus (*c.* 370–404 A.D.) was an Egyptian who became a gifted Greek and Latin epigrammatist.

Milton

11. *Mæonides:* Homer.

Keats

1. *Endymion:* Keats is given the name of the hero of his poem *Endymion*— in Greek mythology a shepherd boy loved by Selene, the moon, who gave him eternal sleep.

10. *Here lieth one:* on Keats's tombstone, in the Protestant Cemetery in Rome, appears the epitaph Keats wrote for himself: "Here lies one whose name was writ in water."

13–14. *The smoking flax . . . reed:* this quotation is an adaptation of Isaiah 42 : 3.

The Chamber over the Gate

The title and the subject of the poem are drawn from 2 Samuel, Chapter 18.

4. *That old man:* King David.

48–49. See 2 Samuel 18 : 33.

Jugurtha

Jugurtha, King of Numidia (ancient kingdom in North Africa), was defeated, captured, and executed by the Romans in 104 B.C.

Discussed in R. E. Amacher, *Explicator*, VI (1948), 29; Arms, *The Fields Were Green*, p. 215.

1. *How cold are thy baths:* a variation on a line in Plutarch's life of Caius Marius in which Jugurtha is reported as saying, "O Hercules! how cold your bath is!" This remark was prompted by Jugurtha's being cast naked into a Roman dungeon.

The Cross of Snow

Longfellow wrote this sonnet on July 10, 1879, and put it in his desk. Found after his death, it was first printed in Samuel Longfellow's *Life*. The image of the cross of snow was suggested by a picture, in a book of western scenery, of the Mountain of the Holy Cross in central Colorado.

Discussed in Arvin, *Longfellow*, pp. 305–306; J. M. Cox, *PMLA*, LXXV (1960), 97–100; R. A. Durr, *Explicator*, VIII (1955), 32.

2. *A gentle face:* the face is that of Longfellow's second wife, Frances Appleton, who was severely burned July 9 and died July 10, 1861.

JAMES RUSSELL LOWELL
1819–1891

Bibliography

Campbell, Killis. "Bibliographical Notes on Lowell," *University of Texas Studies in English*, IV (1924), 115–119.

Clark, H. H., and Foerster, Norman (eds.). "Selected Bibliography," pp. cxliii–clxvi in *James Russell Lowell: Representative Selections*. New York: American Book Company, 1947.

Cooke, G. W. *A Bibliography of James Russell Lowell*. Boston: Houghton Mifflin, and Co., 1906.

Livingston, L. S. *A Bibliography of the First Editions in Book Forms of the Writings of James Russell Lowell*. New York: De Vinne Press, 1914.

Major Writings

A Year's Life and Other Poems (1841)
Poems (1848, 2 Vols.)
A Fable for Critics (1848)
The Biglow Papers: First Series (1848)
Ode Recited at the Harvard Commemoration (1865)
The Biglow Papers: Second Series (1867)
Under the Willows (1868)
Heartsease and Rue (1888)
Letters of James Russell Lowell (1894, 2 Vols., 1904, 3 Vols.; C. E. Norton, ed.)

New Letters of James Russell Lowell (1932, M. A. de W. Howe, ed.)
The Uncollected Poetry of James Russell Lowell (1950, T. M. Smith, ed.)

Standard Editions

Clark, H. H., and Foerster, Norman (eds.). *James Russell Lowell: Representa-*
tive Selections. New York: American Book Company, 1947.
Clark, W. S., II (ed.). *Lowell: Essays, Poems and Letters.* New York: Odyssey
Press, 1948.
Norton, C. E. (ed.). *The Complete Writings of James Russell Lowell.* Elmwood
Edition, 16 Vols. Boston: Houghton Hifflin and Co., 1904.
Scudder, H. E. (ed.). *The Complete Poetical Works of James Russell Lowell.*
Boston: Houghton Mifflin and Co., 1897.

Biography

Beatty, R. C. *James Russell Lowell.* Nashville, Tenn.: Vanderbilt University
Press, 1942.
Greenslet, Ferris. *James Russell Lowell: His Life and Work.* Boston: Houghton
Mifflin and Co., 1905.
Howard, Leon. *Victorian Knight-Errant: A Study of the Early Literary Career*
of James Russell Lowell. Berkeley, Calif.: University of California Press,
1952.
Scudder, H. E. *James Russell Lowell: A Biography,* 2 Vols. Boston: Houghton
Mifflin and Co., 1901.

Criticism

Allen, Gay Wilson. "James Russell Lowell," pp. 244–276 in *American*
Prosody. New York: American Book Company, 1935.
Arms, George. "Lowell," pp. 123–141 in *The Fields Were Green.* Stanford,
Calif.: Stanford University Press, 1953.
Blair, Walter. "A Brahmin Dons Homespun," pp. 77–101 in *Horse Sense in*
American Humor. Chicago: University of Chicago Press, 1942.
Brownell, W. C. "Lowell," pp. 271–335 in *American Prose Masters.* New
York: Charles Scribner's Sons, 1909.
Campbell, Killis. "Lowell's Uncollected Poems," *PMLA,* XXXVIII (1923),
933–937.
Kreymborg, Alfred. "The Poet of Too Many Isms," pp. 116–133 in *Our*
Singing Strength, New York: Coward-McCann, 1929.
Mathews, J. C. "James Russell Lowell's Interest in Dante," *Italica,* XXXVI
(1959), 77–100.
Parsons, E. S. "Lowell's Conception of Poetry," *Colorado College Publica-*
tions, Language Series, II (1908), 67–84.
Pritchard, J. P. "Lowell's Debt to Horace's *Ars Poetica,*" *Am. Lit.,* III
(1931), 259–276.
Voss, Arthur. "Backgrounds of Lowell's Satire in 'The Biglow Papers,'"
New Eng. Quart., XXIII (1950), 47–64.

Voss Arthur. "James Russell Lowell," *U. Kans. City Rev.*, XV (1949), 224–
233.

Comments on Poems

To the Dandelion
   Discussed in Arms, *The Fields Were Green*, pp. 132–133.
   26. *Sybaris*: ancient Greek city of southern Italy famous for its luxury.

[Emerson]
   This and the next six poems are excerpts from a long poem entitled *A Fable for Critics*. The enclosing quotation marks indicate that the passages are from speeches of a critic explaining contemporary American men of letters to Phoebus Apollo.
   Discussed in Howard, *Victorian Knight-Errant*, pp. 260–269.
   27. *Plotinus–Montaigne*: Plotinus (205–270), the Neoplatonist philosopher, was born in Egypt. Michel Eyquem de Montaigne (1533–1592) was from Gascony in southwestern France.
   73. *Fuseli*: Johann Heinrich Fuessli (1742–1825), German-Swiss illustrator of Milton's *Paradise Lost*.
   77. *Flaxman*: John Flaxman (1755–1826), English illustrator of Homer and Dante.

[Bryant]
   5. *Griswold*: Rufus W. Griswold (1815–1857), American editor and critic, says this in his *Poets and Poetry of America* (1842).
   14–15. *inter Nos*: (Latin) between ourselves.
   23. *Berkshire's hills*: Bryant grew up in the Berkshire Mountains of western Massachusetts.
   24. *in loco . . . desipis*: (Latin) "You can be a fool in one place." "Loco-foco" was a name for a group of liberal American political thinkers in the 1840's.
   29. *Mr. Quivis*: Mr. "Whoever-he-is" (Latin).
   37. *Thomson*: James Thomson (1700–1748), English poet of *The Seasons* (1730). *Cowper*: William Cowper (1731–1806), English poet of *The Task* (1785), who was periodically unsound of mind.
   60. *Hesiod's staff*: see l. 40 of *Works and Days,* didactic poem by Hesiod, the Greek poet of the eighth century B.C.

[Whittier]
   11. *Pythoness*: the Pythia, priestess of the oracle at Delphi, Greece, who prophesied seated on a tripod over a vaporous chasm.
   24. *old what's-his-name*: Taillefer, minstrel who sang the *Song of Roland* as he led the charge of Norman cavalry at the battle of Hastings, October 14, 1066. Taillefer fell in the battle.
   30–31. *Anne haec . . . filii tui*: (Latin) a reference to Joseph's brothers speaking to their father, Jacob, about the coat of many colors: "Is this thy son's coat, or not?" See Genesis 37:32.
   31. *Fox*: George Fox (1624), English founder of the Society of Friends (Quakers).
   35. *Castaly's spring*: spring on Mount Parnassus, Greece sacred to Apollo.

[Hawthorne]

12. *a John Bunyan Fouqué:* a writer combining attributes of the German Romantic novelist Baron Fouqué (1777–1843) and John Bunyan (1628–1688), English allegorical writer. *Puritan Tieck:* a Puritan imitator of Johann Ludwig Tieck (1773–1853), German Romantic man of letters.

[Cooper]

16. *Natty Bumppo:* hero of Cooper's *The Pioneers* (1823), first of the Leather-stocking novels.

17. *Long Toms:* Long Tom Coffin is a character in Cooper's *The Pilot* (1823).

22. *dernière chemise:* (French slang) "last resort."

40. *Adams the parson:* Adams is a major character in Henry Fielding's *Joseph Andrews* (1742). *Primrose the vicar:* Dr. Primrose is the chief character in Oliver Goldsmith's *The Vicar of Wakefield* (1766).

[Poe and Longfellow]

1. *Barnaby Rudge:* character who gives his name to a novel by Charles Dickens (1841).

7. *Mathews:* Cornelius Mathews (1817–1889), American critic.

26. *Melesigines:* "born in Melos"; Melos is one of the Greek Cyclades and is one of several locations speculated to be Homer's birthplace.

Ode Recited at the Harvard Commemoration

This ode was first read at Harvard July 21, 1865, to honor Harvard men who had fought in the Civil War.

Discussed in Arms, *The Fields Were Green*, pp. 138–140; H. V. Bail, *Papers of the Bibliographical Society of America*, XXXVII (1943), 169–202; Sydney Mendel, *New Eng. Quart.*, XXXV (1962), 102–103.

37. *Veritas:* (Latin) "Truth." The word appears on the seal of Harvard College.

123. *Baäl's stone:* in 1 Kings 18 is described the contest between Elijah and the priests of the deity, Baal.

150. *our Martyr-Chief:* Abraham Lincoln, fatally shot April 14, 1865.

232. *the Promised Land:* see Exodus 13 : 5. The New England Puritans, too, saw themselves as coming to a Promised Land.

253. *grapes of Canaan:* see Numbers 13 : 23–24, which tells how the spies sent by Moses into Canaan cut a cluster of grapes to bring back as evidence of the richness of the land.

332. *Roundhead and Cavalier:* Roundheads were Puritans and members of the Parliamentary Party led by Oliver Cromwell; the Puritans were early settlers of Massachusetts. Many of the early Virginia colonists were Cavaliers, adherents of Charles I.

339. *Plantagenets:* the English royal family from Henry II to Richard III.

340. *Hapsburgs, and Guelphs:* the Hapsburgs were a German royal family, founded about 1100, which produced kings of Austria and Spain and Holy Roman Emperors; the Guelphs were a German princely family from which the English House of Hanover descended.

386. *Katahdin tell Monadnock, Whiteface he:* Katahdin is a mountain in central Maine, the highest in the state; Monadnock, a mountain in southwestern New Hampshire; Whiteface, a mountain in northwestern Vermont.

Sunthin' in the Pastoral Line

This is No. VI in *The Biglow Papers, Second Series*, collected in 1867. A prose introduction by the Reverend Wilbur is omitted. *The Biglow Papers* consist largely of two sets of verses in Yankee dialect attributed to Hosea Biglow. There are also covering letters by his father, Ezekiel, and commentary by the Reverend Homer Wilbur of Jaalam. The First Series, written as an expression of New England idealist opposition to the Mexican War, which Lowell saw as in the interest of slaveholders, was originally published anonymously in the Boston *Courier*. The Second Series, which appeared in the *Atlantic Monthly* during the Civil War, strongly supports the Northern cause.

Discussed in J. C. Broderick, *Am. Lit.*, XXXI (1959), 163–172.

54. *rile a Shaker:* the Shakers were a plain-living, celibate American religious sect which held that the Second Advent of Christ was imminent.

223. *our Civil War:* the English Civil War between the monarchy and Parliament (1642–1649).

279. *"Smite 'em hip and thigh!"* see Judges 15 : 8.

280. *let every man-child die!:* perhaps an allusion to Herod's command after the birth of Jesus. See Matthew 2 : 16.

281. *Crommle:* Oliver Cromwell (1599–1658), Parliamentary general in the English Civil War and Lord Protector of England.

290. *Charles the Second:* on the restoration of the English monarchy in 1660, Charles II (1630–1685) became King.

299. *Charles's neck gut split:* Charles I (1600–1649) was captured by Parliament and beheaded.

308. *bagnets:* colloquial variant of "bayonets."

The Washers of the Shroud

This poem was inspired by Union defeats in the first months of the Civil War. Written in October, 1861, it first appeared in the *Atlantic Monthly* (November, 1861). Lowell combines the Celtic myth of the Washer with those of the classical Fates and of the Norns of Scandinavian mythology. The legend of the Washer, the Celtic war goddess or warning fairy, is recounted by Gertrude Schoeperle, *Journal of English and Germanic Philology*, XVIII (1919), 60–66.

Discussed in J. Q. Anderson, *Am. Lit.*, XXXV (1963), 361–363; Louise Pound, *Am. Lit.*, XII (1940), 348–350.

10. *Odin's hounds:* Odin, supreme god of Norse mythology, was said to have two wolves, called his hounds, who, like ravens, visited battlefields and ate the slain. See J. A. MacCulloch (ed.), *The Mythology of All Races* (Boston: Marshall Jones Company, 1930), II, 65.

29. *the Sea-Queen's isle:* England.

50. *Hesper:* Hesperus, in Greek mythology, was the land of the setting sun, a remote western land; here, America.

107. *dear ones by Potomac's side:* probably a reference to Union soldiers who fell in the First Battle of Bull Run, July 21, 1861.

Auspex

In Roman religion an auspex was an augur, or soothsayer.

Discussed in R. E. Amacher, *Explicator*, IX (1951), 37; Arms, *The Fields Were Green*, pp. 133–134.

The Recall

10. *Ausonian:* Italian, after the ancient people of southern Italy.

On Receiving a Copy of Mr. Austin Dobson's "Old World Idylls"

Austin Dobson (1840–1921), the English poet and biographer, brought out *Old World Idylls* in 1883. It contained a number of poems in fixed French forms. Lowell's poem is a *rondeau*, one of these forms. See J. K. Robinson, *Mod. Lang. Quart.*, XIV (1953), 31–42.

13. *Lesboum barbiton:* (Latin) "Lesbian lyre"; an echo of Horace, *Odes*, Book I, Ode 1 : 34.

20. *Dick Steele:* Sir Richard Steele (1672–1729), English essayist and playwright.

21. *charmille:* (French) hedge of young hornbeams, arbor.

Verses, Intended to Go with a Posset Dish

Lowell sent the gift of a posset dish and an accompanying poem to the infant daughter of Sir Leslie Stephen (1832–1904), eminent English biographer, critic, and editor. The recipient was to become the novelist Virginia Woolf (1882–1941). A posset dish is a two-handled vessel for making or carrying posset, a hot milk drink.

13. *Amalthea's horn:* horn of plenty, cornucopia.

22. *'Twixt Genesis and Protoplasm:* a reference to the controversy raised between science and religion by such works as Charles Darwin's *On the Origin of Species* (1859).

34. *Watts:* George Frederic Watts (1817–1904), English painter and sculptor, much given to allegorical subjects. The Celia referred to may be the character in Spenser's *Faerie Queene*, mother of Faith, Hope and Charity.

36. *Sir Josh:* Sir Joshua Reynolds (1723–1792), great English portrait painter and first President of the Royal Academy of Arts.

39. *Her mother's beauty:* Virginia's mother, née Julia Jackson, Sir Leslie's second wife, was a great beauty.

ROBERT LOWELL
b. 1917

Bibliography

Mazzaro, Jerome. *The Achievement of Robert Lowell, 1939–1959*. Detroit: University of Detroit Press, 1960.

Major Writings

Land of Unlikeness (1944)
Lord Weary's Castle (1946; with text changes, 1947)

Poems: 1938–1949 (1950; London: Faber & Faber)
The Mills of the Kavanaughs (1951)
Life Studies (1959)
Imitations (1961, translations)
Phaedra (1961, translation)
For the Union Dead (1964)

Criticism

Cambon, Glauco. "Robert Lowell," pp. 219–228 in *The Inclusive Flame: Studies in American Poetry*. Bloomington, Ind.: Indiana University Press, 1963.

Jarrell, Randall. *Poetry and the Age*, pp. 188–199, 230–236. New York: Vintage Books, 1955.

Jones, T. H. "The Poetry of Robert Lowell," *Month*, N. S., IX (1953), 133–142.

Jumper, W. C. "Whom Seek Ye? A Note on Robert Lowell's Poetry," *Hud. Rev.*, IX (1956), 117–125.

Lowell, Robert, and Seidel, Frederick. "The Art of Poetry III: Robert Lowell," *Paris Review*, VII, No. 25 (1961), 56–95.

Lutyens, D. B. "Robert Lowell: Poet of Reconciliation," pp. 128–200 in *The Creative Encounter*. London: Secker & Warburg, 1960.

Rosenthal, M. L. *The Modern Poets: A Critical Introduction*, pp. 226–238. New York: Oxford University Press, 1960.

Standerwick, DeSales. "Notes on Robert Lowell," *Renascence*, VIII (1955), 75–83.

Staples, H. B. "Beyond Charles River to the Acheron: An Introduction to the Poetry of Robert Lowell," pp. 24–37 in Edward Hungerford (ed.), *Poets in Progress: Critical Prefaces to Ten Contemporary Americans*. Evanston, Ill.: Northwestern University Press, 1962.

Staples, H. B. *Robert Lowell: The First Twenty Years*. New York: Farrar, Straus and Cudahy, 1962.

Comments on Poems

The texts of the first twelve Lowell poems are taken from the Faber & Faber (London) edition, *Poems: 1938–1949*, which the poet has designated as the definitive text. Certain minor textual problems have been noted below. The texts of the last three poems are from *Life Studies* and *For the Union Dead*.

In Memory of Arthur Winslow
    Arthur Winslow (1861–1938) was the poet's maternal grandfather.
    Discussed in Staples, *Robert Lowell*, pp. 29–31 *et passim*.
    2. *Phillips' House*: part of the Massachusetts General Hospital on the bank of the Charles River in Boston.
    5. *Charon*: in Greek mythology the boatman who ferried the shades of the dead across the Styx or the Acheron, two of the rivers of Hades.
    7. *Boston Basin*: wide part of the Charles River near the hospital.

10. *resurrexit dominus:* (Latin) "the Lord has risen."

11. *swanboats:* foot-propelled excursion boats peculiar to the small lake in the Boston Public Garden, driven by men seated in the stern and half-enclosed by large metal swans.

Dunbarton: town southwest of Concord, New Hampshire, containing the cemetery of Lowell's mother's ancestors, the Starks and Winslows.

50. *Cotton Mather . . . from hell:* probably a reference to Mather's part in the Salem witchcraft episode of 1692. His book *Memorable Providences, Relating to Witchcraft and Possessions* (1689) had described Satan's war against New England, and his *Wonders of the Invisible World* (1693) was a defense of the magistrates who in witchcraft trials had sentenced a number of supposed witches to death.

52. *Edward:* Edward Winslow (1595–1655), a founder of Plymouth Colony and three times its governor.

54. *Revere:* Paul Revere, of the famous ride, was a Boston silversmith.

55. *General Stark:* John Stark (1728–1822), American general in the Revolution and an ancestor of Lowell on his mother's side.

65. *On these . . . estate:* a fashionable residential area in Boston was made from the 1850's on by the filling in of the "Back Bay" tide flats along the south bank of the Charles River.

69. *like Lazarus from the dead:* see John 11, which describes the raising of Lazarus from the dead by Jesus.

70. *Lavabis . . . delabor:* except for the change from "*me*" (me) to "*nos*" (us), this is the Latin of Psalms 50 : 7 in the Vulgate. See the corresponding English of Psalms 51 : 7 of the King James Bible: ". . . wash me, and I shall be whiter than snow."

71–72. *On Copley Square . . . Church:* Trinity Church on Copley Square in Boston is Episcopalian. It contains large stained glass memorial windows.

80. *Lazarus who was poor:* see Luke 16 : 19–31, where Jesus tells the Pharisees the story of Lazarus the beggar and the rich man.

Christmas Eve Under Hooker's Statue

This poem was originally published in *Partisan Review*, X (1943), 314–315 under the title "The Capitalist's Meditation by the Civil War Monument." Revised, it appeared in *Land of Unlikeness* with the title "Christmas Eve in the Time of War." It was revised and retitled again for *Lord Weary's Castle*.

Joseph Hooker (1814–1879), Union general, was born in Hadley, Massachusetts, hence was a state hero in the Civil War.

Discussed in Lutyens, *The Creative Encounter*, pp. 168–170; Staples, *Robert Lowell*, pp. 90–91.

15. *the Common:* the Boston Common, which the State House borders.

24–25. *When Chancellorsville . . . Melville said:* the quotation is from l. 6 of Melville's "The March Into Virginia," which is printed in this anthology, though the battle there referred to is actually First Manassas (First Battle of Bull Run). At Chancellorsville, Virginia, the Army of the Potomac under Hooker was defeated by Lee's Army of Northern Virginia in a bloody three-day battle in early May, 1863.

The Drunken Fisherman
    7–8. *the moth corrupted:* cf. Luke 12 : 33.

Children of Light
    The ironic title is from Luke 16 : 8.
    Discussed in Cambon, *The Inclusive Flame*, pp. 220–221; Lutyens, *The Creative Encounter*, pp. 137–138; Rosenthal, *The Modern Poets*, pp. 227–228; Staples, *Robert Lowell*, pp. 28–29.
    4. *Geneva's night:* Lowell is attacking the Calvinist theology of the Puritans. John Calvin founded a theocratic government in Geneva, Switzerland.

The Exile's Return
    A number of phrases in this poem are adapted by Lowell from the opening pages of Thomas Mann's novella, *Tonio Kröger*.
    Discussed in Staples, *Robert Lowell*, pp. 33–34.
    8. *Holstenwall:* Lowell draws the word from *Tonio Kröger*, where it refers to the park-like promenade along the site of what used to be the old city walls of Lübeck, Germany, the birthplace of both Thomas Mann and his fictional character Tonio Kröger, the artist later exiled by his temperament and talent from the bourgeois society of his upbringing. The context indicates, however, that the actual reference is to the Holsten-Tor, a medieval fortified gateway still standing at the west entrance to the old city.
    21. *Rathaus:* (German) "Town Hall." Cf. the French "Hôtel de Ville" of ll. 2–3.
    24. *Voi ch'entrate:* (Italian) part of the inscription over the Gate of Hell in Dante's *Inferno*, III, 9: *Lasciate ogni speranza, voi ch'entrate:* "Abandon all hope, you who enter."

Colloquy in Black Rock
    Black Rock is a part of Bridgeport, the industrial city in Connecticut on Long Island Sound.
    Discussed in Staples, *Robert Lowell*, pp. 40–44.
    10. *the martyr Stephen:* Christianity's first martyr, who was stoned to death about 36 A.D. in Jerusalem on the charge of blasphemy. He is to be distinguished from the second St. Stephen (977–1038), who was Stephen I, King of Hungary (see l. 23). St. Stephen's, a Roman Catholic Church where many of the Hungarian machinists attended Mass, is named for this second Stephen.
    22. *Kingfisher:* a symbol for Christ.
    24. *Stupor Mundi:* (Latin) "The Amazement of the World." The phrase was applied to Frederick II (1197–1250), King of Sicily and Holy Roman Emperor, because of his wide learning, his skill in government, and his magnificent manner of living. Lowell may indirectly refer to him as one who struggled long and fruitlessly against the power of the Papacy.

The Quaker Graveyard in Nantucket
    Warren Winslow was a cousin of the poet. During World War II the naval vessel on which he served was lost at sea with all hands. In an excellent

analysis of this poem, Hugh Staples has demonstrated its place "in the great tradition of the English elegy."

Let man . . . upon the earth: cf. Genesis 1 : 26. Lowell, a Roman Catholic convert, quotes from the Douay Version of the Bible.

Discussed in Cleanth Brooks and R. P. Warren, *Conversations on the Craft of Poetry* (Holt, Rinehart and Winston, 1961), pp. 37–40; Cambon, *The Inclusive Flame*, pp. 225–226; Paul Engle, *Eng. Jour.*, XXXVIII (1949), 64; Rosenthal, *The Modern Poets*, pp. 229–230; Standerwick, *Renascence*, VIII (1955), 76–78; Staples, *Robert Lowell*, pp. 45–52, 101–104.

1. *Madaket:* a town and a harbor on the west end of the island of Nantucket.

2–12. *The sea . . . sand:* Staples points out that these lines take much of their imagery from a passage in the first chapter of Thoreau's *Cape Cod*, "The Shipwreck."

15. *Ahab:* the monomaniacal captain of the whaler *Pequod* (see l. 31) in Herman Melville's novel *Moby-Dick* (1851). References to the novel, which describes Ahab's vengeful pursuit of Moby Dick, the White Whale, recur throughout this poem. See especially ll. 43–44, 61–64, 69–77, and 94–106. The *Pequod* sailed from Nantucket, which a century ago was the center of the whaling industry.

19. *heel-bent:* the text in *Lord Weary's Castle* (Harcourt, Brace and Co., 1946) reads "hell-bent."

33. *'Sconset:* Siasconset, a town on the east end of the island of Nantucket.

45. *Poseidon:* in Greek mythology the god of the sea and of earthquakes, both being combined in the epithet "earth-shaker" (l. 22).

62. *IS:* Staples argues that this word combines references to both Old and New Testaments: to Jehovah, the inscrutable God of the Hebrews (as in Exodus 3 : 14—"And God said unto Moses, I AM THAT I AM. . . .") and to Christ the Savior (Iesus Salvator). A similar use of the term occurs in "Where the Rainbow Ends," l. 24.

78. *Clamavimus:* (Latin) "We have cried out."

91. *Wood's Hole:* Woods Hole, a town on the southwestern end of Cape Cod.

92. *Martha's Vineyard:* an island south of Cape Cod and west of Nantucket.

94. *ash-pit of Jehoshaphat:* Jehoshaphat here is the valley where, according to chapter three of the Book of Joel, at the end of the world the Lord will sit in judgment on the heathen nations for their oppression of Israel.

105. *Hide:* the text in *Lord Weary's Castle* (Harcourt, Brace and Co., 1946) omits the comma after "Hide."

106. *Jonas Messias:* cf. Matthew 12 : 40. Near the beginning of *Moby-Dick*, Father Mapple preaches a sermon on Jonah (Jonas).

Our Lady of Walsingham: the Chapel of Our Lady in Walsingham Priory, situated a few miles from the sea in Norfolk, England, was one of the great shrines of medieval England. It was much visited until its destruction by Henry VIII in 1538. Since 1921 parts of the Priory have been restored.

In a prefatory note to *Lord Weary's Castle*, Lowell states that the "Our Lady of Walsingham" section of this poem "is an adaptation of several paragraphs from E. I. Watkin's *Catholic Art and Culture*." See E. I. Watkin, *Catholic Art and Culture* (New York: Sheed & Ward, 1944), pp. 213–214.

114. *Shiloah:* Shiloh, a town in ancient Palestine, the first Israelite sanctuary for the Tabernacle and the Ark of the Covenant.

116. *Sion:* Zion, a hill in Jerusalem on which the Temple was built; later a synonym for the whole city of Jerusalem.

122. *Non est . . . decor:* (Latin) "There is no form nor comeliness." Cf. Isaias (Isaiah) 53 : 2.

134. *Sea-monsters . . . fish:* cf. Milton's *Paradise Lost*, Book I, ll. 462–463.

As a Plane Tree by the Water

Staples notes that the title is taken from the Apocrypha, Ecclesiasticus 24 : 14: "I was exalted like a palm-tree in Engaddi, and as a rose-plant in Jericho, as a fair olive-tree in a pleasant field, and grew up as a plane-tree by the water."

Discussed in Lutyens, *The Creative Encounter*, pp. 139–141; Standerwick, *Renascence*, VIII (1955), 80.

22. *Bernadette:* St. Bernadette (1843–1879), to whom the Virgin Mary appeared in the grotto of Massabieille near Lourdes, France.

25–26. *The grave . . . Christ:* cf. 1 Corinthians 15 : 54.

Mr. Edwards and the Spider

Many phrases in this poem are taken from the writings of Jonathan Edwards (1703–1758), the great Calvinist preacher and theologian: his youthful essay "Of Insects" (stanza one) and two sermons, "Sinners in the Hands of an Angry God" and "The Future Punishment of the Wicked Unavoidable and Intolerable," both delivered in 1741.

Discussed in Staples, *Robert Lowell*, p. 35; D. E. Wiebe, *Wisconsin Studies in Contemporary Literature*, III (1962), 21–31.

18. *How will . . . endure:* see Ezekiel 22 : 14, which was the text for Edwards' sermon "The Future Punishment of the Wicked Unavoidable and Intolerable."

28. *Windsor Marsh:* Edwards was born and brought up at East Windsor, Connecticut.

38. *Josiah Hawley:* if this is Joseph Hawley, Edwards' uncle, who committed suicide, then he is presumably also "the gentleman" in l. 4 of "After the Surprising Conversions," the following poem in *Lord Weary's Castle*. See the discussion of these two poems by D. E. Wiebe.

After the Surprising Conversions

The details of this poem are drawn mainly from two paragraphs near the end of the *Narrative of Surprising Conversions*, an expanded form of a letter originally written on May 30, 1735, to the Reverend Dr. Benjamin Colman of Boston by Jonathan Edwards (see notes for "Mr. Edwards and the Spider"). Edwards was at that time minister at Northampton, Massachusetts, which had been undergoing a religious revival. The expanded form of the letter is dated November 6, 1736, and was published in that year. See *The Works of President Edwards*, Vol. III (New York: Robert Carter & Brothers, 1881), pp. 269–270.

Discussed in G. Giovannini et al., *Explicator*, IX (1951), 53; D. E. Wiebe, *Wisconsin Studies in Contemporary Literature*, III (1962), 21–31.

4. *A gentleman:* see note to l. 38 of "Mr. Edwards and the Spider."

Where the Rainbow Ends

For the derivation of a number of details in this poem, see Revelation, particularly chapters 4 through 9.

Discussed in Marius Bewley, *The Complex Fate* (Chatto and Windus, 1952) pp. 159–160; Jarrell, *Poetry and the Age*, pp. 190–191; Lutyens, *The Creative Encounter*, pp. 147–149; Standerwick, *Renascence*, VIII (1955), 80–81; Staples, *Robert Lowell*, p. 107.

8. *Ararat:* the mountainous region in Armenia in Asia Minor where, according to Genesis 8 : 4, Noah's Ark first rested on land after the flood. *Death:* in Revelation 6 : 8, the fourth horseman of the Apocalypse.

10. *The wild . . . the root:* cf. Romans 11 : 17–18.

12. *Pepperpot:* one of the bridges across the Charles River between Boston and Cambridge, so called because of the "pepperpot" shape of its towers.

14. *The Scales, the pans:* the third horseman of the Apocalypse holds "a pair of balances in his hand." See Revelation 6 : 5.

19–20. *The Chapel's . . . serpent-Time:* King's Chapel, an eighteenth-century church at the corner of Tremont and School Streets in Boston. The eagle and serpent appear to be partly Lowell's invention. Although there are two replicas of eagles in the Chapel, one on either side of a memorial doorway, they are full-feathered and hold nothing in their claws.

24. *IS:* see note to "The Quaker Graveyard in Nantucket," l. 62.

29–30. *Stand . . . to eat:* Staples notes that these words are carved on the gravestone of Lowell's father in Dunbarton Cemetery.

Falling Asleep over the Aeneid

Virgil's Latin epic poem the *Aeneid* describes the escape of the Trojan Aeneas from the fall of Troy, his subsequent wanderings in the Mediterranean, his love affair with Queen Dido of Carthage, her suicide after his desertion of her, and his final establishment of the Roman state in Italy.

5. *lictor:* minor Roman official who carried a bundle of rods bound about an ax (the *fasces*) and cleared the way for a magistrate. Sometimes the lictor also served as an executioner.

12. *Pallas:* a native Italian prince, who helps Aeneas conquer the Rutulians under the leadership of Turnus (see l. 59). Turnus kills Pallas and is then himself killed by Aeneas in single combat. See *Aeneid*, Book XI, ll. 22–99 for Virgil's description of the funeral of Pallas.

22. *Aphrodite:* Aeneas' mother, the Greek name for the Latin Venus (see l. 52).

66. *Turms:* cavalry companies.

68–70. *Alps...Forever:* the text in *The Mills of the Kavanaughs* prints a period after "Alps" and after "Forever."

85. *Augustus:* Augustus Caesar (63 B.C.–14 A.D.), first Roman Emperor, whom Virgil glorifies in the *Aeneid*.

Words for Hart Crane

Discussed in Rosenthal, *The Modern Poets*, p. 235.

1. *Pulitzers:* the annual Pulitzer Prizes established by a bequest of the newspaper publisher Joseph Pulitzer (1847–1911). Especially during the 1920's the

trustees of the awards tended to withhold the prize in literature from books strongly critical of the United States or uncircumspect in some other way.

8. *Catullus redivivus:* (Latin) "Catullus living again." Catullus is the first-century B.C. Roman lyricist, noted for his passionate love poems.

9. *the village:* Greenwich Village, New York's Bohemia, where Crane lived for a number of years.

Skunk Hour

Elizabeth Bishop (b. 1911) is an American poet, on whose "The Armadillo," according to Lowell, this poem is modeled.

Discussed in Anthony Ostroff (ed.), *New World Writing 21* (Lippincott, 1962), pp. 131–159; Rosenthal, *The Modern Poets*, pp. 231–232, 236; Staples, *Robert Lowell*, pp. 82–83.

15. *L. L. Bean:* a Maine mail-order sporting goods firm.

18. *Blue Hill:* low mountain and also a town in Maine near Mt. Desert Island. Lowell had a summer home at Castine, a small coastal town some miles to the west on Penobscot Bay.

35. *I myself am hell:* cf. Satan's remark in *Paradise Lost*, Book IV, l. 75.

ARCHIBALD MACLEISH
b. 1892

Bibliography

Mizener, Arthur. *A Catalogue of the First Editions of Archibald MacLeish.* New Haven, Conn.: Yale University Library, 1938.

Thurber, Gerrish. "MacLeish's Published Books," *Library Journal*, LXIV (1939), 864, 866.

Major Writings

The Pot of Earth (1925)
Streets in the Moon (1926)
The Hamlet of A. MacLeish (1928)
New Found Land: Fourteen Poems (1930)
Conquistador (1932)
Frescoes for Mr. Rockefeller's City (1933)
Public Speech (1936)
A Time to Speak: The Selected Prose of Archibald MacLeish (1941)
A Time to Act: Selected Addresses (1943)
Actfive and Other Poems (1948)
Collected Poems, 1917–1902 (1952)
Songs for Eve (1954)
The Collected Poems of Archibald MacLeish (1963)
J. B.: a play in verse (1957)
Poetry and Journalism (1958)

Poetry and Experience (1961)
The Dialogues of Archibald MacLeish and Mark Van Doren (1964; W. V. Bush, ed.)

Criticism

Ciardi, John. "The Poetry of Archibald MacLeish," *Atlantic*, CXCI (May, 1953), 67–68.

Honig, Edwin. "History, Document, and Archibald MacLeish," *Sewanee Rev.*, XLVIII (1940), 385–396.

Jones, Llewellyn. "Archibald MacLeish: A Modern Metaphysical," *Eng. Jour.*, XXIV (1935), 441–451.

Kohler, Dayton. "MacLeish and the Modern Temper," *So. Atl. Quart.*, XXXVIII (1939), 416–426.

Mizener, Arthur. "The Poetry of Archibald MacLeish," *Sewanee Rev.*, XLVI (1938), 501–519.

Nemerov, Howard. "MacLeish and Viereck," pp. 118–124 in *Poetry and Fiction: Essays*. New Brunswick, N.J.: Rutgers University Press, 1963.

Rosenberg, Harold. "The God in the Car," *Poetry*, LII (1938), 334–342.

Van Ghent, Dorothy. "The Poetry of Archibald MacLeish," *Science and Society*, II (1938), 500–511.

Whittemore, Reed. "MacLeish and the Democratic Pastoral," *Sewanee Rev.*, LXI (1953), 700–709.

Zabel, M. D. "The Poet on Capitol Hill," *Part. Rev.*, VIII (1941), 2–19, and VIII (1941), 128–145.

Comments on Poems

Texts are from *The Collected Poems of Archibald MacLeish* (Houghton Mifflin and Co., 1963).

Ars Poetica
The Latin title: "the art of poetry." Horace's famous epistle on poetry bears these words for its title.

Discussed in V. P. Staudt, *Coll. Eng.*, XIX (1957), 28–29; Donald Stauffer, *The Nature of Poetry* (W. W. Norton Co., 1946), pp. 121–125.

The End of the World
1. *Vasserot:* an imaginary personage, like the others named in the poem.

You, Andrew Marvell
Andrew Marvell (1621–1678) was an English lyric poet. MacLeish was thinking specifically of lines 21–24 in Marvell's "To His Coy Mistress":

> But at my back I always hear
> Time's wingèd chariot hurrying near;
> And yonder all before us lie
> Deserts of vast eternity.

Cf. Eliot's use of this passage in *The Waste Land*, lines 185–186 and 196–198 (p. 847).

Discussed in Cleanth Brooks, *Modern Poetry and the Tradition* (University of North Carolina Press, 1939), p. 122; Nemerov, *Poetry and Fiction: Essays*, pp. 119–120.

1. *here:* according to MacLeish, on the Illinois shore of Lake Michigan.

9. *Ecbatan:* Ecbatana (now Hamadan), ancient capital of the Medes in north-western Iran. Note that each succeeding place name lies farther to the west, suggesting the turn of the earth and the approach of night.

"Not Marble nor the Gilded Monuments"

The title is the first line of Shakespeare's Sonnet LV, which in turn recalls Horace, *Odes*, Book III, Ode 30, line 1: "Exegi monumentum aere perennius" (I have finished a memorial more lasting than bronze).

10–11. *as long as breath . . . is spent:* echoes Shakespeare's Sonnet XVIII, line 13: "So long as man can breathe . . ."

Pole Star

7. *the Wain:* Charles' Wain, that is, the Big Dipper.

HERMAN MELVILLE
1819–1891

Bibliography

Stern, M. R. "A Checklist of Melville Studies," pp. 252–291 in *The Fine Hammered Steel of Herman Melville*. Urbana, Ill.: University of Illinois Press, 1957.

Thorp, Willard. "Selected Bibliography," pp. cxxxiii–clxi in *Herman Melville: Representative Selections*. New York: American Book Company, 1938.

Williams, S. T. "Melville," pp. 207–270 in Floyd Stovall (ed.), *Eight American Authors: A Review of Research and Criticism*. New York: The Modern Language Association of America, 1956. Mathews, J. C., "Melville," pp. 438–445 of "Bibliographical Supplement" in paperback reissue by W. W. Norton Co. (New York, 1963).

Major Writings

Typee: A Peep at Polynesian Life (1846)
Omoo: A Narrative of Adventures in the South Seas (1847)
Mardi: and a Voyage Thither (1849)
Redburn: His First Voyage (1849)
White-Jacket: or The World in a Man-of-War (1850)
Moby-Dick: or, The Whale (1851)
Pierre: or The Ambiguities (1852)
Israel Potter: His Fifty Years of Exile (1855)

The Piazza Tales (1856)

The Confidence-Man: His Masquerade (1857)

Battle-Pieces and Aspects of the War (1866)

Clarel: A Poem and Pilgrimage in the Holy Land (1876)

John Marr and Other Sailors (1888)

Timoleon (1891)

Billy Budd, Foretopman (1924, Raymond Weaver, ed.). Definitive text: *Billy Budd, Sailor: An Inside Narrative* (1962, Harrison Hayford and M. M. Sealts, Jr., eds.)

Journal of a Visit to London and the Continent by Herman Melville (1948, E. M. Metcalf, ed.)

Melville's Journal of a Visit to Europe and the Levant, October 11, 1856–May 6, 1857 (1955, H. C. Horsford, ed.)

The Letters of Herman Melville (1960, M. R. Davis and W. H. Gilman, eds.)

Standard Editions

The Works of Herman Melville, Standard Edition, 16 Vols. London: Constable and Co., 1922–1924. *Clarel*, Vols. 14 and 15, 1924; *Poems*, Vol. 16, 1924. Reissued by Russell & Russell (New York, 1963).

Vincent, H. P. (general ed.). *Complete Works of Herman Melville*. Chicago and New York: Hendricks House, 1947–. *Collected Poems*, Vol. XIV, 1947.

Biography

Howard, Leon. *Herman Melville: A Biography*. Berkeley, Calif.: University of California Press, 1951.

Leyda, Jay. *The Melville Log: A Documentary Life of Herman Melville, 1819–1891*, 2 Vols. New York: Harcourt, Brace and Co., 1951.

Criticism

Abel, Darrel. "'Laurel Twined with Thorn': The Theme of Melville's *Timoleon*," *Personalist*, XLI (1960), 330–340.

Arvin, Newton. *Herman Melville*. New York: William Sloane Associates, 1950.

Arvin, Newton. "Melville's Shorter Poems," *Part. Rev.*, XVI (1949), 1034–1046.

Barrett, Laurence. "The Differences in Melville's Poetry," *PMLA*, LXX (1955), 606–623.

Braswell, William. *Melville's Religious Thought: An Essay in Interpretation*. Durham, N.C.: Duke University Press, 1943.

Chase, Richard. *Herman Melville: A Critical Study*. New York: The Macmillan Co., 1949.

Cohen, Hennig (ed.). "Comment on the Poems," pp. 176–259 in *Selected Poems of Herman Melville*. New York: Anchor, 1964.

Fogle, R. H. "Melville and the Civil War," *Tulane Stud. Eng.*, IX (1959), 61–89.

Fogle, R. H. "The Themes of Melville's Later Poetry," *Tulane Stud. Eng.*,
    XI (1961), 65–86.

Matthiessen, F. O. "Melville as Poet," pp. 77–80 in *The Responsibilities of the
    Critic: Essays and Reviews*. New York: Oxford University Press, 1952.

Montague, G. B. "Melville's *Battle-Pieces*," *University of Texas Studies in English*,
    XXXV (1956), 106–115.

Mumford, Lewis. *Herman Melville: A Study of His Life and Vision*, rev. ed.
    New York: Harcourt, Brace and Co., 1962.

Sedgwick, W. E. *Herman Melville: The Tragedy of Mind*. Cambridge, Mass.:
    Harvard University Press, 1944.

Thorp, Willard (ed.). "Melville's Poetry," pp. lxxxiv–xcvi in *Herman Melville:
    Representative Selections*. New York: American Book Company, 1938.

Warren, R. P. "Melville the Poet," *Ken. Rev.*, VIII (1946), pp. 208–223. Re-
    printed in *Selected Essays* (Random House, 1958), pp. 184–198.

Comments on Poems

The texts of Melville's poems here printed are from the first editions of
Battle-Pieces and Aspects of the War, *Clarel: A Poem and Pilgrimage in the Holy
Land*, *John Marr and Other Sailors*, and *Timoleon*. Subsequent to the publication
of *Battle-Pieces*, Melville entered certain penciled revisions in his own copy of
the book, and those pertaining to the poems here included have been entered
in the notes through the courtesy of Sidney Kaplan. For a list of all such
revisions see Sidney Kaplan (ed.), "Melville's Revisions," pp. xxv–xxviii in
Battle-Pieces and Aspects of the War (Gainesville, Fla.: Scholars' Facsimiles &
Reprints, 1960).

The Portent

Here, as in other selections from *Battle-Pieces*, the date in parentheses is
that assigned by Melville in the text.

On the night of October 16, 1859, John Brown led a successful attack on
the United States Arsenal at Harper's Ferry, Virginia (now West Virginia), at
the confluence of the Shenandoah and Potomac Rivers. Captured on October
18, he was tried, convicted of treason, and, on December 2, hanged.

Discussed in Chase, *Herman Melville*, pp. 231–232; Cohen, *Selected Poems of
Herman Melville*, pp. 176–177; Fogle, *Tulane Stud. Eng.*, IX (1959), pp. 63–64;
Warren, *Ken. Rev.*, VIII (1946), 212.

5. *The cut . . . crown:* Brown had received a head wound at the time of his
capture.

12. *the streaming beard is shown:* Brown's beard was visible below the hood
placed over his face by the hangman.

Misgivings

Discussed in Cohen, *Selected Poems of Herman Melville*, p. 177; Fogle, *Tulane
Stud. Eng.*, IX (1959), 64–65.

The Conflict of Convictions

Melville's note in *Battle-Pieces:* "The gloomy lull of the early part of the
winter of 1860–1, seeming big with final disaster to our institutions, affected

some minds that believed them to constitute one of the great hopes of mankind, much as the eclipse which came over the promise of the first French
Revolution affected kindred natures, throwing them for the time into doubts
and misgivings universal."

Discussed in Chase, *Herman Melville*, pp. 232–234; Cohen, *Selected Poems of
Herman Melville*, pp. 177–178; Fogle, *Tulane Stud. Eng.*, IX (1959), 62, 65–70;
H. F. Pommer, *Milton and Melville* (University of Pittsburgh Press, 1950), pp.
77–79; Warren, *Ken. Rev.*, VIII (1946), 213–218.

10. *Raphael:* H. F. Pommer has demonstrated Melville's use of *Paradise
Lost* in this poem. In Books V and VI of *Paradise Lost*, the Archangel Raphael
relates to Adam and Eve the war in Heaven between God's angels and Satan's.
Pommer suggests that Raphael is called "a white enthusiast" because "he was
certainly not one of the greatest warriors in the celestial conflict" (p. 78).

11. *at which:* Melville's revision: "whereat."

12. *Mammon's slaves:* those enslaved by Mammon, the personification of
materialistic wealth.

44. *the Iron Dome:* construction of an iron dome to replace the original
wood and brick one on the Capitol in Washington was begun in 1855 and
finished in 1863.

48. *Michael:* the Archangel, who in Book VI of *Paradise Lost* leads God's
angels against Satan's. He is here envisaged as defending the Northern side in
the Civil War.

52–54. *His forehead ... wight:* Melville's revision:

> *His forehead bears a taper dim;*
> *Darkness so he feebly braves—*
> *Which foldeth him.*

61. *The Ancient of Days:* God. See Daniel 7 : 9.

The March into Virginia

In both First Manassas (First Battle of Bull Run) and Second Manassas
(Second Battle of Bull Run) on July 21, 1861, and August 29–30, 1862, the
Federal forces were defeated.

Discussed in Barrett, *PMLA*, LXX (1955), 619–620; Cohen, *Selected
Poems of Herman Melville*, p. 179; Warren, *Ken. Rev.*, VIII (1946), 211–215,
220.

33. *are:* Melville's revision: "be."

35. *shame:* according to Sidney Kaplan, a penciled revision in Mrs. Melville's hand in her copy of *Battle-Pieces* gives this word as "some."

36. *The throe ... share:* Melville's revision: "Thy after shock, Manassas,
share."

A Utilitarian View of the Monitor's Fight

The Union *Monitor* and the Confederate *Virginia* (formerly the *Merrimac*)
met in their historic Battle of the Ironclads at Hampton Roads, Virginia, on
March 9, 1862.

Discussed in Cohen, *Selected Poems of Herman Melville*, p. 182.

4. *Orient:* brilliant, shining. Melville's revision: "painted."

27. *yet shall be:* Melville's revision: "shall yet be."

Shiloh

The Battle of Shiloh, which involved great slaughter on both sides, was fought at Shiloh Church and Pittsburgh Landing, Tennessee, on April 6–7, 1862.

Discussed in Cohen, *Selected Poems of Herman Melville*, p. 183.

Malvern Hill

The Seven Days' Battle, which culminated in Malvern Hill, was fought near Richmond June 25–July 1, 1862, and ended General George B. McClellan's advance on the Confederate capital.

Discussed in Cohen, *Selected Poems of Herman Melville*, p. 183.

The House-Top

This poem gives Melville's reactions to the New York draft riots of July 11–13, 1863, during which mobs protested the inequities of the Conscription Act by attacks on Negroes, looting, and arson.

Discussed in Chase, *Herman Melville*, pp. 235–236; Cohen, *Selected Poems of Herman Melville*, p. 185; Fogle, *Tulane Stud. Eng.*, IX (1959), 74–75, 87–89.

13. *priestly spells:* many of the rioters were Irish Catholic workers.

16. *And man . . . in nature:* Melville's note: "'I dare not write the horrible and inconceivable atrocities committed,' says Froissart, in alluding to the remarkable sedition in France during his time. The like may be hinted of some proceedings of the draft-rioters."

18. *shakes:* Melville's revision: "jars."

19. *Draco:* Athenian statesman who drew up a harsh code of laws in 621 B.C.

27. *And . . . scourged:* Roman citizens were legally exempt from whipping.

A Dirge for McPherson

Melville's note on this poem: "The late Major General [James B.] McPherson [1828–1864], commanding the Army of the Tennessee, a native of Ohio and a West Pointer, was one of the foremost spirits of the war. Young, though a veteran; hardy, intrepid, sensitive in honor, full of engaging qualities, with manly beauty; possessed of genius, a favorite with the army, and with Grant and Sherman. Both Generals have generously acknowledged their professional obligations to the able engineer and admirable soldier, their subordinate and junior.

"In an informal account written by the Achilles to this Sarpedon, he says:

"'On that day we avenged his death. Near twenty-two hundred of the enemy's dead remained on the ground when night closed upon the scene of action.' [W. T. Sherman, "The Late Major-General J. B. McPherson," *Hours at Home*, II (April, 1866), 485–493, p. 491.]

"It is significant of the scale on which the war was waged, that the engagement thus written of goes solely (so far as can be learned) under the vague designation of one of the battles before Atlanta."

6. *Lost-Mountain . . . Kenesaw:* mountains near Marietta, Georgia, where the Battle of Kenesaw Mountain was fought on June 27, 1864. McPherson's Army of the Tennessee was Sherman's left wing at that battle.

28. *Sarpedon:* in the *Iliad*, Sarpedon was an ally of the Trojans in the Trojan War, who led the Lycians against the Greeks and was killed by Patroclus. His body was returned to Lycia for a hero's burial.

On the Grave of a Young Cavalry Officer Killed in the Valley of Virginia
  Discussed in Cohen, *Selected Poems of Herman Melville*, p. 196.

Commemorative of a Naval Victory
  Discussed in Cohen, *Selected Poems of Herman Melville*, pp. 196–197; Fogle,
Tulane Stud. Eng., IX (1959), 80–81; Mumford, *Herman Melville*, pp. 210–211;
Warren, *Ken. Rev.*, VIII (1946), 217–218.
  7–8. *The hawk . . . for a king:* Hennig Cohen suggests that "Titian's pic-
ture" may be the portrait "The Man with a Falcon."

Epilogue (from *Clarel*)
  Clarel is a poem in two volumes, four parts, 150 cantos, and over 18,000
lines, based on Melville's reading and thinking and a pilgrimage he made to
Palestine in January, 1857. A slight narrative concerns Clarel, a young theological student, who has begun to question his religious faith and has come to
Jerusalem, where he falls in love with Ruth, a Jewish girl. For ten days he
leaves her to travel with a group of pilgrims who visit various holy places,
then returns to Jerusalem on Ash Wednesday and finds that Ruth has died.
He is left with his grief and his doubts. Melville's major interests in the poem
are to examine the conflicting philosophic and religious currents of his time,
particularly the tensions between faith and doubt, and to analyze the varied
personalities of the pilgrims. In the "Epilogue," the poet himself addresses
the unhappy Clarel.
  The most thorough discussion of the whole poem is Walter E. Bezanson's
long introduction in his edition of *Clarel* (Hendricks House, 1960), pp. ix–cix.
See also Arvin, *Herman Melville*, pp. 269–278, 283–287; N. A. Ault, *Research
Studies of the State College of Washington*, XXVII (1959), 72–84; Merlin Bowen,
The Long Encounter: Self and Experience in the Writings of Herman Melville (Uni-
versity of Chicago Press, 1960), pp. 238–240, 253–280; Braswell, *Melville's
Religious Thought*, pp. 109–113 *et passim*; Chase, *Herman Melville*, pp. 242–257;
Cohen, *Selected Poems of Herman Melville*, pp. 198–210; D. M. Finkelstein,
Melville's Orienda (Yale University Press, 1961), pp. 59–91 *et passim*; R. H.
Fogle, *Tulane Stud. Eng.*, X (1960), 101–116; Howard, *Herman Melville*, pp.
297–309; Ronald Mason, *The Spirit Above the Dust: A Study of Herman Melville*
(John Lehmann, 1951), pp. 224–244; Mumford, *Herman Melville*, pp. 213–225;
Sedgwick, *Herman Melville*, pp. 198–230; Thorp, *Herman Melville: Representa-
tive Selections*, pp. lxxxviii–xciii; H. W. Wells, *The American Way of Poetry*
(Columbia University Press, 1943), pp. 78–88.

The Æolian Harp
  Discussed in Cohen, *Selected Poems of Herman Melville*, pp. 216–217; W. B.
Stein, *Literature and Psychology*, VII (1957), 21–22.
  6. *Ariel's rendering:* see Shakespeare's *The Tempest*, I, ii.
  11. *Alicant:* Alicante, city on east coast of Spain.
  15–26. *Dismasted . . . with hemlocks rolled:* see the description of the floating
wreck in Chapter 22 of *Redburn*.
  18. *kraken:* a legendary Scandinavian sea monster.

The Maldive Shark
  The Maldive Islands are in the Indian Ocean southwest of Ceylon. Cf.

Melville's description of the Shovel-nosed Shark in Chapter 18 of *Mardi*.

Discussed in Cohen, *Selected Poems of Herman Melville*, pp. 218–219; W. B. Stein, *Literature and Psychology*, VII (1957), 22; Warren, *Ken. Rev.*, VIII (1946), 217–218, 222.

The Berg

Discussed in Cohen, *Selected Poems of Herman Melville*, pp. 219–220; W. B. Stein, *Literature and Psychology*, VII (1957), 23.

Pebbles

These brief poetic statements about the sea and the wisdom it teaches conclude the *John Marr* volume.

Discussed in Cohen, *Selected Poems of Herman Melville*, pp. 221–223; Fogle, *Tulane Stud. Eng.*, XI (1961), 73–74.

8. *Orm:* this probably refers to the author of *Ormulum*, a Middle English collection of homilies in verse written about 1200 A.D.

31. *Angels Four:* see Revelation 7 : 1–3.

33. *rosmarine:* from Latin *ros marinus*, "sea-dew." The name of the healing herb rosemary is derived from the Latin by relation to "rose" and the Virgin Mary.

After the Pleasure Party

Amor (Latin for "love") is here the equivalent of Cupid, the god of love in Roman mythology.

Discussed in Abel, *Personalist*, XLI (1960), 333–334; Chase, *Herman Melville*, pp. 220–229; Cohen, *Selected Poems of Herman Melville*, pp. 228–230; Fogle, *Tulane Stud. Eng.*, XI (1961), 77–78; Mumford, *Herman Melville*, pp. 189–194; Wallace Sutton, *Phil. Quart.*, XXX (1951), 316–327.

29. *Vesta:* since the altar fire in the temple of Vesta, the Roman goddess of the hearth, was tended by the Vestal Virgins, her name is synonymous with virginity.

30. *No fable . . . leap:* according to legend, Sappho, the Greek woman poet of the sixth century B.C., threw herself to death in the sea because of an unrequited love.

73. *Decameron folk:* the characters in Boccaccio's *Decameron*, who tell the tales that make up the book.

90–100. *For, Nature . . . life's gate:* see Plato's *Symposium* for a telling of the myth that originally human individuals were simultaneously of both sexes until each was divided into male and female halves, since which time each half has sought its lost mate.

111. *Urania:* the poet addresses the woman, the "I" of the poem, by the name of Urania, the muse of astronomy in Greek mythology. See ll. 45–51 for the woman's astronomical interests.

121. *Albani's porch:* the Villa Albani, which Melville visited in 1857, contained a number of statues that he admired.

138. *armed Virgin:* the Greek Athena or Roman Minerva, goddess of learning and wisdom.

The Ravaged Villa

Discussed in Cohen, *Selected Poems of Herman Melville*, pp. 230–231.

Monody

Discussed in Cohen, *Selected Poems of Herman Melville*, pp. 233–234.

1. *him:* probably Nathaniel Hawthorne, Melville's friend, who died May 19, 1864, and was buried in Concord, Massachusetts.

Art

Discussed in Cohen, *Selected Poems of Herman Melville*, pp. 236–237; Leo Hamalian, *Explicator*, VIII (1950), 40.

10–11. *Jacob's . . . angel:* see Genesis 32 : 24–32.

W. S. MERWIN
b. 1927

Bibliography

Quitslund, Jon. "A Checklist of the Writings of William Stanley Merwin," pp. 94–104 in Sherman Hawkins (ed.), *Seven Princeton Poets*, Princeton, N.J.: Princeton University Library, 1963.

Major Writings

A Mask for Janus (1952)
The Dancing Bears (1954)
Green with Beasts (1956)
Poem of the Cid (1959, translation)
The Drunk in the Furnace (1960)
The Satires of Persius (1961, translation)
Some Spanish Ballads (1961, translation)
The Life of Lazarillo de Tormes, His Fortunes and Adversities (1961, translation)
The Song of Roland (1963, translation)
Moving Target (1963)

Criticism

Bennett, Joseph. "The Moving Finger Writes," *Hud. Rev.*, XVI (1963–1964), 624–625.

Benston, A. N. "Myth in the Poetry of W. S. Merwin," pp. 179–204 in Edward Hungerford (ed.), *Poets in Progress*. Evanston, Ill.: Northwestern University Press, 1962.

Dickey, James. "The Death and Keys of the Censor," *Sewanee Rev.*, LXIX (1961), 327–329.

Roche, T. P., Jr. "Green with Poems," pp. 89–94 in Sherman Hawkins (ed.), *Seven Princeton Poets*. Princeton, N.J.: Princeton University Library, 1963.

Comments on Poems

Dictum: For a Masque of Deluge

Deluge: see account of the flood in Genesis 6–8.

Dido: Dido Milroy, Merwin's wife.

27. *a covered basket:* an allusion to the placing of the baby Moses in an ark of bulrushes. See Exodus 2 : 3.

When I Came from Colchis

1. *Colchis:* the ancient country between the Caucasus and the Black Sea, now a part of Georgia, Soviet Union.

6. *Euxine:* Black Sea.

9. *Jason:* leader of the legendary Argonauts, who came to Colchis in quest of the Golden Fleece. See Euripides, *Medea*.

The Annunciation

The Annunciation was the visit of the Angel Gabriel to Mary to foretell that she would become the mother of Christ. It is described in Luke 1 : 26–38.

John Otto

1. *Brunswick:* Braunschweig, city in northern Germany.

3. *Cumberland Valley:* in central Pennsylvania.

7. *Blain, in Perry County:* small town in the Blue Mountain area about thirty miles west of Harrisburg, Pennsylvania.

12. *Carlisle:* city twenty miles southeast of Blain.

WILLIAM VAUGHN MOODY
1869–1910

Bibliography

Henry, D. D. "Bibliography," pp. 263–272 in *William Vaughn Moody: A Study*. Boston: Bruce Humphries, 1934.

Major Writings

The Masque of Judgment (1900)
Poems (1901)
The Fire-Bringer (1904)
The Great Divide: A Play (1909)
The Faith Healer (1909)
Some Letters of William Vaughn Moody (1913, D. G. Mason, ed.)
Letters to Harriet (1935, Percy MacKaye, ed.)

Standard Edition

Manly, J. M. (ed.). *The Poems and Plays of William Vaughn Moody*, 2 Vols. Boston: Houghton Mifflin and Co., 1912.

Biography

Henry, D. D. "The Growth of a Poet," pp. 9–30 in *William Vaughn Moody: A Study*. Boston: Bruce Humphries, 1934.

Lovett, R. M. "Introduction," pp. ix–xcii·in *Selected Poems of William Vaughn Moody*. Boston: Houghton Mifflin and Co., 1931.

Criticism

Adkins, N. F. "The Poetic Philosophy of William Vaughn Moody," *Texas Review*, IX (1924), 97–112.

Blackmur, R. P. "Moody in Retrospect," *Poetry*, XXXVIII (1931), 331–337.

Buckham, J. W. "The Doubt and Faith of William Vaughn Moody," *Homiletic Review*, LXXXV (1918), 349–353.

Cary, Richard. "Robinson on Moody," *Colby Library Quarterly*, Series VI (1962), 176–183.

Henry, D. D. *William Vaughn Moody: A Study*. Boston: Bruce Humphries, 1934.

Jones, H. M. "The Poet," Part V, pp. 57–64 in *The Bright Medusa*. Urbana, Ill.: University of Illinois Press, 1952.

Jones, H. M. "William Vaughn Moody: An American Milton," *The Double Dealer*, IV (1922), 79–86.

Kreymborg, Alfred. *Our Singing Strength: An Outline of American Poetry* (1620–1930), pp. 286–293. New York: Coward-McCann, 1929.

Lewis, C. M. "William Vaughn Moody," *Yale Rev.*, II (1913), 688–703.

Matthiessen, F. O. "William Vaughn Moody," pp. 93–97 in *The Responsibilities of the Critic: Essays and Reviews*. New York: Oxford University Press, 1952.

Riggs, Thomas, Jr. "Prometheus 1900," *Am. Lit.*, XXII (1951), 399–423.

Weirick, Bruce. "William Vaughn Moody, Nationalist and Mystic," pp. 128–142 in *From Whitman to Sandburg in American Poetry: A Critical Survey*. New York: The Macmillan Co., 1924.

Comments on Poems

The texts of the first six selections by Moody are from *Poems*, the contents of which were reproduced in *The Poems and Plays of William Vaughn Moody*. The text of the last poem, "Thammuz," is from *The Poems and Plays*, where it was first collected.

Gloucester Moors

This poem was begun during a vacation Moody spent in the summer of 1900 on Cape Ann, Massachusetts.

An Ode in Time of Hesitation

First published in the *Atlantic Monthly* for May, 1900, the ode protests the use of American troops to put down the Filipino independence movement then being led by Emilio Aguinaldo.

Discussed in Blackmur, *Poetry*, XXXVIII (1931), 334–335; Frederick Eckman, *University of Texas Studies in English*, XXXVI (1957), 80–92; F. J. and Adaline Glasheen, *Coll. Eng.*, V (1943), 121–129; D. M. McKeithan, *Am. Lit.*, IX (1937), 349–351; F. H. Harrington, *New Eng. Quart.*, X (1937), 651–653.

35. *Pictured Rocks:* many-colored and oddly shaped cliffs on the shore of Lake Superior near Munising on the Upper Peninsula of Michigan.

51. *shawms:* woodwind instruments, forerunner of the oboe.

53. *phylacteries:* small leather boxes containing texts from the Pentateuch fastened by thongs one on the left arm and one on the forehead by Orthodox Jews during prayer. The rivers are here likened to the thongs.

54. *Shasta:* Mt. Shasta, high peak in the Sierra Nevada in northern California.

57. *Mariposa:* a town in central California near Yosemite National Park.

172–173. *Are we . . . youth:* in his *Areopagitica,* Milton described England as "an eagle mewing her mighty youth."

194. *the awful hill slope at San Juan:* San Juan Hill near Santiago de Cuba was the scene of an American victory on July 1, 1898, in the Spanish-American War.

203. *chaffer:* bargaining, trade.

On a Soldier Fallen in the Philippines

Published in the *Atlantic Monthly* for February, 1901, a month before Aguinaldo was captured by American troops. His taking of an oath of allegiance to the United States on April 19, 1901, ended most of the armed resistance by the Filipinos to American occupation.

The Menagerie

Discussed in Henry, *William Vaughn Moody,* pp. 57–59; Kreymborg, *Our Singing Strength,* pp. 288–289.

7. *Gabriel's trump:* in Christian tradition the Archangel Gabriel will announce the day of the Last Judgment with a trumpet blast.

35. *flying jenny:* a merry-go-round.

52. *Forepaugh:* Adam Forepaugh (1831–1890) had been a well-known circus and menagerie owner.

80. *jagged:* slang for "drunk."

Thammuz

Tammuz (or Thammuz) was a Babylonian and Assyrian fertility god, corresponding to the Greek Adonis, whose annual ceremonial death in rivers was mourned by women. Cf. Milton's *Paradise Lost,* Book I, ll. 446–457.

Discussed in William Chislett, Jr., *Dial,* LX (1916), 370.

MARIANNE MOORE
b. 1887

Bibliography

Sheehy, E. P. and Lohf, K. A. *The Achievement of Marianne Moore: A Bibliography, 1907–1957.* New York: New York Public Library, 1958.

Major Writings

Poems (1921)
Observations (1924)
Selected Poems (1935)
The Pangolin and Other Verse (1936)
What Are Years (1941)
Nevertheless (1944)
Collected Poems (1951)
The Fables of La Fontaine (1954, translation)
Predilections (1955, essays)
Like a Bulwark (1956)
O To Be a Dragon (1959)
A Marianne Moore Reader (1961)
The Arctic Ox (1964)

Criticism

Auden, W. H. "Marianne Moore," pp. 296–305 in *The Dyer's Hand and Other Essays*. New York: Random House, 1962.

Beloof, Robert. "Prosody and Tone: The 'Mathematics' of Marianne Moore," *Ken. Rev.*, XX (1958), 116–123.

Blackmur, R. P. "The Method of Marianne Moore," pp. 225–252 in *Form and Value in Modern Poetry*. New York: Anchor, 1957.

Bogan, Louise. "Marianne Moore," pp. 252–257 in *Selected Criticism*. New York: The Noonday Press, 1955.

Burke, Kenneth. "Motives and Motifs in the Poetry of Marianne Moore," *Accent*, II (1942), 157–169.

Fowlie, Wallace. "Marianne Moore," *Sewanee Rev.*, LX (1952), 537–547.

Hoffman, F. J. "Marianne Moore: Imaginary Gardens and Real Toads," *Poetry*, LXXXIII (1953), 152–157.

Jarrell, Randall. "Two Essays on Marianne Moore," pp. 162–187 in *Poetry and the Age*. New York: Vintage Books, 1955.

Monroe, Harriet. "Symposium on Marianne Moore," *Poetry*, XIX (1922), 208–216.

Quarterly Review of Literature, IV (1948). Marianne Moore issue.

Wasserstrom, William. "Marianne Moore, *The Dial*, and Kenneth Burke," *West. Hum. Rev.*, XVII (1963), 249–262.

Williams, W. C. "Marianne Moore," *Dial*, LXXVIII (1925), 393–401.

Comments on Poems

Poetry

Discussed in Lloyd Frankenberg, *Pleasure Dome* (Houghton Mifflin and Co., 1949), pp. 137–141.

23–24. *"business documents and school-books"*: quoted, according to Miss Moore, from Leo Tolstoi's *Diary*. See *The Diaries of Leo Tolstoy*, translated from the Russian by C. J. Hogarth and A. Sirnis (E. P. Dutton, 1917), p. 94. "Where the boundary between prose and poetry lies, I shall never be able to understand. The question is raised in manuals of style, yet the answer to it lies beyond me. Poetry is verse: prose is not verse. Or else poetry is everything with the exception of business documents and school books."

In the notes placed at the end of *Observations* and subsequent volumes, Miss Moore herself identifies the source of most of the quotations in her poems and some of the details.

29–30. "*literalists of the imagination*": quoted, according to Miss Moore, from William Butler Yeats, *Ideas of Good and Evil* (A. H. Bullen, 1903), from the essay, "William Blake and the Imagination," p. 182. "The limitation of his view was from the very intensity of his vision; he was a too literal realist of imagination, as others are of nature; and because he believed that the figures seen by the mind's eye, when exalted by inspiration, were 'eternal existences,' symbols of divine essences, he hated every grace of style that might obscure their lineaments."

The Steeple-Jack

This poem appeared first in a twelve-stanza version in *Selected Poems* (1935), then was cut to eight stanzas and, in 1961, expanded to thirteen stanzas, which version is used here.

Discussed in Louise Bogan, *Coll. Eng.*, XIV (1953), 257–258; Charles Tomlinson, *Sewanee Rev.*, LXV (1957), 682–684.

1. *Dürer:* Albrecht Dürer (1471–1528), German painter and engraver.

No Swan So Fine

1–2. "*No water . . . Versailles*": quoted, according to Miss Moore, from an article in the *New York Times Magazine*, May 10, 1931.

9. *candelabrum-tree:* Miss Moore notes that she had in mind an actual pair of candelabra with figures of swans in Dresden china.

The Pangolin

A pangolin is a scaly anteater, originally from Java.

27–29. *Thomas . . . vine:* according to Miss Moore's note, "a fragment of ironwork in Westminster Abbey."

50–52. *Gargallo's . . . matador:* Pablo Gargallo (1881–1934), Spanish abstractionist sculptor, who worked in forged iron. Actually the "matador" was probably one of Gargallo's heads of a picador; for the picador, unlike the matador, wears a hat with a brim.

What Are Years?

Discussed in Lloyd Frankenberg, *Saturday Review*, XXIX (March 23, 1946), 5; W. V. O'Connor, *Sense and Sensibility in Modern Poetry* (University of Chicago Press, 1948), pp. 229–230.

The Mind Is an Enchanting Thing

7. *Gieseking:* Walter Gieseking (1895–1956), German concert pianist. *Scarlatti:* Alessandro Scarlatti (1659–1725), Italian composer.

37. *Herod's oath:* see Matthew 14 : 3–11.

In Distrust of Merits

Discussed in M. E. Allentuck, *Explicator*, X (1952), 42; Wallace Fowlie, *Quarterly Review of Literature*, IV (1948), 176–177.

Armour's Undermining Modesty

12–13. *our mis-set | alphabet:* in her note Miss Moore quotes from Oscar Ogg's *The 26 Letters*, which explains the ideographic origin of the letter *E*, originally drawn lying on its side.

14. *Arise, for it is day:* the motto, Miss Moore notes, of The John Day Company, a New York publishing house.

28–31. Derived, according to Miss Moore, from *The Book of the Ranks and Dignities of British Society*, attributed to Charles Lamb. Before the Norman Conquest, Saxon commanders of armies were called "dukes." After the Conquest the title died out until it was revived by Edward III, who made his son, the Black Prince, Duke of Cornwall, using in the ceremony a wreath and a silver rod.

35. *in:* corrected from "is" by Miss Moore in note to GWA, June 17, 1965.

Tom Fool at Jamaica

Tom Fool was the best two-year-old thoroughbred in 1951, the best horse of the year in 1953.

Discussed in Marie Borroff, *Coll. Eng.*, XVII (1956), 466–469; Elder Olson, *Chicago Review*, XI (1957), 103–104.

Miss Moore's notes on this poem appear on pages 280–282 in *A Marianne Moore Reader*.

1. *Jonah embarking from Joppa:* see Jonah 1.

6. *mule and jockey:* [Moore] "A mule and jockey by 'Giulio Gomez 6 años' from a collection of drawings by Spanish school children. Solicited on behalf of a fund-raising committee for Republican Spain, sold by Lord and Taylor; given to me by Miss Louise Crane."

8–9. *There . . . said:* [Moore] "The Reverend David C. Shipley, July 20, 1952."

9. *Sentir avec ardeur:* title of poem by Madame Boufflers—Marie-Françoise-Catherine de Beauveau, Marquise de Boufflers (1711–1786). Miss Moore quotes Mme. Boufflers' poem in its entirety. *Sentir avec ardeur* translates, "to feel passionately."

10–11. *"makes an effort . . . rest":* Miss Moore's version of a remark made by Ted Atkinson, quoted by Arthur Daley, *New York Times*, March 3, 1952.

13. *Master Atkinson:* Theodore Atkinson (b.1916), a native of Toronto, has been a leading jockey in the United States since 1944. In her note, Miss Moore quotes a column on Ted Atkinson and Tom Fool by Arthur Daley in the *New York Times* for March 3, 1952, and refers to a picture of Tom Fool and Atkinson in *The Times* for April 1, 1952, which inspired her to "pay him a slight tribute."

14–15. *Chance . . . impurity:* [Moore] "The *I Ching* or *Book of Changes*, translated by Richard Wilhelm and Cary Baynes, Bollingen Series XIX (New York: Pantheon Books, 1950)."

18. *Signor Capossela:* Miss Moore is referring to the remarks of Frederic

Capossela, the announcer at Belmont Park, as quoted by Joseph C. Nichols in the *Times* for July 24, 1952.

23. *a handy horse:* this is Miss Moore's summary of Ted Atkinson's praise of Tom Fool, as quoted by Arthur Daley in the *Times* for March 1, 1955.

29. *Fats Waller:* [Moore] "Thomas Waller, 'a protean jazz figure,' died in 1943." Waller composed *Ain't Misbehavin'*.

31. *Ozzie Smith:* [Moore] "Osborne Smith, a Negro chanter and drummer who improvised the music for Ian Hugo's *Ai-Yé*." *Eubie Blake:* [Moore] "The Negro pianist in *Shuffle Along*." Blake (b. 1883) composed *I'm Just Wild About Harry* and *Lovin' You the Way I Do*.

32. *the Lippizan school:* the Spanish Riding School of the Hofburg, Vienna, where the twenty snow-white Lipizzaner stallions constitute the finest performing troupe in the world.

33. *Tiger Skin:* probably a fictitious race horse. No horse by that name is listed in the *American Racing Manual*.

Melchior Vulpius

Melchior Vulpius was a German composer, pre-eminently of songs and hymns.

8–9. *mastery which none | can understand:* [Moore] "'And not only is the great artist mysterious to us but is that to himself. The nature of the power he feels is unknown to him, and yet he has acquired it and succeeds in directing it.' Arsène Alexander, *Malvina Hoffman—Critique and Catalogue* (Paris: J. E. Pouterman, 1930)."

11. *Mouse-skin-bellows'-breath:* [Moore] "'Bird in a Bush . . . The bird flies from stem to stem while he warbles. His lungs, as in all automatons, consist of tiny bellows constructed from mouse-skin.' Daniel Alain, *Réalités*, April 1957, page 58."

EDGAR ALLAN POE
1809–1849

Bibliography

Heartman, C. F., and Canny, J. R. *A Bibliography of First Printings of the Writings of Edgar Allan Poe*. Hattiesburg, Miss.: The Book Farm, 1940; rev. ed., 1943.

Hubbell, J. B. "Poe," pp. 1–46 in Floyd Stovall (ed.), *Eight American Authors: A Review of Research and Criticism*. New York: The Modern Language Association of America, 1956. Mathews, J. C., "Poe," pp. 421–424 of "Bibliographical Supplement" in paperback reissue by W. W. Norton Co. (New York, 1963).

Robertson, J. W. *Bibliography of the Writings of Edgar A. Poe*, 2 Vols. San Francisco: Russian Hill Private Press, Edwin and Robert Grabhorn, 1934.

Concordance

Booth, B. A. and Jones, C. E. *A Concordance of the Poetical Works of Edgar Allan Poe*. Baltimore: Johns Hopkins University Press, 1941.

Major Writings

Tamerlane and Other Poems (1827)
Al Aaraaf, Tamerlane, and Minor Poems (1829)
Poems (1831)
The Raven and Other Poems (1845)
The Letters of Edgar Allan Poe (1948, 2 Vols., J. W. Ostrom, ed.)

Standard Editions

Campbell, Killis (ed.). *The Poems of Edgar Allan Poe*. Boston: Ginn and Company, 1917.

Harrison, J. A. (ed.). *The Complete Works of Edgar Allan Poe*, Virginia Edition, 17 Vols. New York: Crowell, 1902.

Biography

Quinn, A. H. *Edgar Allan Poe: A Critical Biography*. New York: Appleton-Century-Crofts, 1941.

Rein, D. M. *Edgar A. Poe: the Inner Pattern*. New York: Philosophical Library, 1960.

Wagenknecht, Edward. *Edgar Allan Poe: The Man Behind the Legend*. New York: Oxford University Press, 1963.

Woodberry, G. E. *The Life of Edgar Allan Poe*, rev. ed., 2 Vols., Boston: Houghton Mifflin and Co., 1909.

Criticism

Allen, Gay Wilson. "Edgar Allan Poe," pp. 56–90 in *American Prosody*. New York: American Book Company, 1935.

Campbell, Killis. *The Mind of Poe and Other Studies*. Cambridge, Mass.: Harvard University Press, 1932.

Davidson, E. H. *Poe. A Critical Study*. Cambridge, Mass.: The Belknap Press of the Harvard University Press, 1957.

Eliot, T. S. *From Poe to Valéry*. New York: Harcourt, Brace and Co., 1948.

Kelly, George. "Poe's Theory of Beauty," *Am. Lit.*, XXVII (1956), 521–536.

Marks, E. R. "Poe as a Literary Theorist: A Reappraisal," *Am. Lit.*, XXXIII (1961), 296–306.

Quinn, P. F. *The French Face of Edgar Poe*. Carbondale, Ill.: Southern Illinois Press, 1957.

Stovall, Floyd. "The Conscious Art of Edgar Allan Poe," *Coll. Eng.*, XXIV (1963), 417–421.

Tate, Allen. "The Angelic Imagination: Poe as God," "Our Cousin, Mr. Poe," pp. 56–95 in *The Forlorn Demon*. Chicago: Henry Regnery, 1953.

Wilbur, Richard. "The House of Poe," pp. 21–38 in *Anniversary Lectures 1959*. Washington, D.C.: Library of Congress Reference Department, 1959.

Winters, Yvor. "Edgar Allan Poe: A Crisis in the History of American Obscurantism," pp. 93–122 in *Maule's Curse: Seven Studies in the History of American Obscurantism*. Norfolk, Conn.: New Directions, 1938.

Comments on Poems

Of the many notes Poe wrote to his poems only a very few have been included here. For voluminous scholarly annotation of these poems, the reader is referred to Killis Campbell's *The Poems of Edgar Allan Poe*, the textual source of all the poems reprinted here.

Tamerlane

First published in 1827, drastically revised for 1829 and later editions.

Tamerlane (*c.* 1336–1405) was a Mongol conqueror.

Discussed in Davidson, *Poe*, pp. 4–10.

29. *won usurpingly:* Tamerlane took the crown from his brother.

36. *Taglay:* The mountains of Belur Taglay are a branch of the Imaus, in the southern part of Independent Tartary [Poe].

165. *Samarcand:* Tamerlane's capital; now in the Soviet Union north of Afghanistan.

173. *Timour:* a variant spelling of Tamerlane.

180. *Siroc-wither'd:* withered by the sirocco, a hot wind.

229. *Eblis:* Mohammed's name for the devil.

A Dream Within a Dream

First published under title "Imitation," in 1827; radically revised and entitled "To —— ——" in 1829; further altered and appended, untitled, to "Tamerlane" in 1831. It received its present title when published in *Flag of Our Union*, March 31, 1849. As Killis Campbell says, "This poem emerged from its several recastings as an entirely different poem, no single line, no part of a line, of the original being retained in the final draft."

Sonnet—To Science

Appeared in 1829 and 1831 as untitled preface to "Al Aaraaf."

Discussed in P. C. Hoyt, *Bulletin of the New York Public Library*, LXIII (1959), 568–570.

4. *Vulture:* a recollection of the eagle which fed on Prometheus' liver.

9–14. *Hast thou not dragged . . . tree:* these lines derive from James-Henry-Bernardin de Saint-Pierre, *Studies of Nature* (trans. Henry Hunter; London: C. Dilly, 1796): "It is Science which has dragged down the chaste Dian from her nocturnal car; she has banished the Hamadryads from the antique forests, and the gentle Naiads from the fountains."

10. *Hamadryad:* in classical mythology, a tree nymph.

12. *Naiad:* in classical mythology, a water nymph.

13. *Elfin:* in English mythology, an elf.

14. *tamarind:* Asiatic tree.

Al Aaraaf

The title of this poem comes from the Koran, where it is the name for the place between Heaven and Hell. Poe also uses the fact that this name was given the star discovered by the Danish astronomer, Tycho Brahe. It appeared November 11, 1572, near four stars of the constellation Cassiopeia and disappeared the next month.

Discussed in W. B. Cairns, *Mod. Phil.*, XIII (1915), 35–44; Davidson, *Poe*, pp. 13–27; R. C. and M. M. Pettigrew, *Am. Lit.*, VIII (1937), 439–445; A. H. Quinn, *Poe*, pp. 156–161; Floyd Stovall, *University of Texas Studies in English*, IX (1929), 106–133.

16. *Nesace:* Queen of Al Aaraaf and spirit of beauty.

44. *Capo Deucato:* high cape on Leucas or Leucadia, one of the Greek Ionian islands, from which the poet Sappho is said to have leaped into the sea. Scented lilies are said to have grown on Leucadia.

47. *her:* Sappho [Poe].

48. *The Sephalica:* a flower suggested by Thomas Moore's "The Veiled Prophet of Khorassan," a tale in *Lalla Rookh*.

50. *gemmy flower:* apparently the asphodel. *Trebizond:* medieval Greek empire, in what is now northeast Turkey on the Black Sea.

66. *Nyctanthes:* a night flower, also suggested by Moore's "The Veiled Prophet of Khorassan."

68. *Clytia:* Peruvian flower which follows the path of the sun.

74. *Valisnerian lotus:* There is found, in the Rhone, a beautiful lily of the Valisnerian kind [Poe].

76. *Zante:* The Hyacinth [Poe].

77. *Isola d'oro:* (Italian) "golden island." *Fior di Levante:* (Italian) "flower of the East." Poe probably borrowed this, and the previous phrase, from Chateaubriand, *Itinéraire de Paris à Jerusalem* (Paris, n.d.), p. 15.

78–79. *And the Nelumbo bud ... river:* a lotus wreath on which "Cupid was first seen floating ... down the River Ganges [Poe]."

158. *Therasaean:* Therasaea, or Therasea, the island mentioned by Seneca, which, in a moment, arose from the sea to the eyes of astonished mariners [Poe].

171. *Parian marble:* marble from the island of Paros in the Greek Cyclades.

194. *Tadmor:* Biblical name of Palmyra, Syria. *Persepolis:* ancient capital of Persia.

195 *Balbec:* ancient city where Phoenicians built their temple to the sun-god, Baal or Bel. Its ruins, in central Lebanon, are described by Moore in "Paradise and the Peri," ll. 383–387, *Lalla Rookh*.

196. *Gomorrah:* Biblical city on the plain of the Jordan destroyed for its wickedness.

200. *Eyraco:* Chaldea, ancient region on Euphrates River and Persian Gulf.

258. *Ligeia:* the spirit of harmony, about whom Poe later wrote a short story.

323. *Simoom:* a hot, dust-laden wind in the Middle East.

336. *A maiden-angel and her seraph-lover:* the story of Ianthe and Angelo comes from Thomas Moore's "First Angel Story" in *The Loves of the Angels* (1823). See Campbell, *The Poems of Edgar Allan Poe*, pp. xlvi–xlvii.

367. *Persian Saadi in his Gulistan:* Saadi, or Sa'di (1184–1291), Persian poet whose second book, written in 1258, was called *Gūlistān* ("The Rose Garden"). It consisted of practical wisdom couched in anecdotes in prose and verse.

401–402. *Dread star . . . Earth:* according to Stovall, this is a reference to the prophecy of the destruction of the earth in Luke 17 : 26–30.

Romance

Entitled "Preface" in 1829 and "Introduction" in 1831 edition. The version here published, that of 1845, is almost identical with that of 1829.

Discussed in Davidson, *Poe*, pp. 27–30.

To Helen

According to Poe, this poem was inspired by Mrs. Jane Stanard of Richmond, who died when he was fifteen.

Discussed in P. F. Baum, *Mod. Lang. Notes*, LXIV (1949), 289–297; W. C. Brown, *Coll. Eng.*, V (1944), 382–385; Davidson, *Poe*, pp. 32–34; J. W. Gargano, *Mod. Lang. Notes*, LXXV (1960), 652–653; P. C. Hoyt, *Bulletin of the New York Public Library*, LXIII (1959), 568–570; T. O. Mabbott, *Explicator*, I (1943), 60; Earl Tannenbaum, *Notes and Queries*, V (1958), 353–355.

2. *Nicéan:* perhaps derived from the "Nyseian isle" mentioned in *Paradise Lost*, IV, 275. For various glosses of the word, see Edward Snyder, *Classical Journal*, XLVIII (1953), 159–169.

4. *the weary, way-worn wanderer:* perhaps Odysseus.

Israfel

First published in 1831, considerably revised in present (1845) text.

The epigraph, which Poe ascribes to the Koran, has two sources. The first is from George Sale's translation of the Koran, Section IV, probably found by Poe in a footnote of Thomas Moore's *Lalla Rookh* (1817): "The angel Israfel, who has the most melodious voice of all God's creatures. Sale." (See Moore, *Lalla Rookh*, New York: C. S. Francis & Co., 1849, p. 220n.) The second, which Poe translates "Whose heart-strings are a lute," is a line from the poem, "*Le Refus,*" by the French poet, Pierre Jean de Béranger (1780–1857).

Discussed in Davidson, *Poe*, pp. 34–37; T. O. Mabbott, *Explicator*, II (1944), 57; W. L. Werner, *Explicator*, II (1944), 44.

12. *levin:* lightning.

13. *Pleiads:* a group of seven stars; in Greek mythology, the seven daughters of Atlas.

26. *Houri:* a woman in Mohammedan paradise.

The City in the Sea

Called "The Doomed City" in 1831, then "The City of Sin" and "The City in the Sea. A Prophecy" in periodical publications before present title was adopted.

Discussed in R. E. Amacher, *Explicator*, XIX (1961), 60; R. P. Basler, *Sex, Symbolism, and Psychology in Literature* (Rutgers University Press, 1948), pp. 192–195; Davidson, *Poe*, pp. 37–38; T. F. Keefer, *Coll. Eng.*, XXV (1964), 436–439; T. O. Mabbott, *Explicator*, IV (1945), 1; Louise Pound, *Am. Lit.*, VI (1934), 22–27.

The Sleeper
Entitled "Irene" on publication in 1831, later much revised and given present title.

Discussed in Davidson, *Poe*, pp. 38–40; W. B. Hunter, Jr., *Am. Lit.*, XX (1948), 55–57; T. O. Mabbott, *Am. Lit.*, XXI (1949), 339–340.

17. *Irene:* the "sleeper." "Irene" was an earlier title of this poem.

Lenore
Entitled "A Pæan" on publication in 1831, later much revised and given present title.

Discussed in J. C. Broderick, *Am. Lit.*, XXXV (1964), 504–510.

1. *the golden bowl:* an echo of Ecclesiastes 12 : 6.

3. *Guy de Vere:* Lenore's lover.

13. *Peccavimus:* (Latin) "we have sinned" (from the Confession of the Mass).

The Valley of Unrest
Entitled "The Valley Nis" in a markedly longer first version of 1831.

Discussed in R. P. Basler, *Sex, Symbolism, and Psychology in Literature* (Rutgers University Press, 1948), pp. 197–200.

The Coliseum
15. *Chaldee:* Chaldean astrologer and magician.

18. *mimic eagle:* figure borne on standards of Roman legions.

36. *Memnon:* statue at Thebes, Egypt, which was said to make a harplike sound when rays from the sun struck it.

To One in Paradise
First published, untitled, as part of a story, "The Visionary," in *Godey's Lady's Book*, January, 1834. Entitled "To Ianthe in Heaven" on publication in *Burton's Gentleman's Magazine*, July, 1839. Given present title for publication in 1845.

Discussed in R. P. Basler, *Am. Lit.*, IX (1937), 232–236.

The Haunted Palace
Poe wrote Rufus Griswold in 1841 that this poem was about "a mind haunted by phantoms—a disordered brain" [J. W. Ostrom (ed.), *The Letters of Edgar Allan Poe* (Harvard University Press, 1948), p. 61]. First published separately, the poem was later embedded in the story "The Fall of the House of Usher."

Discussed in Davidson, *Poe*, pp. 79–80; Wilbur, *Anniversary Lectures 1959*, pp. 26–28.

22. *Porphyrogene:* Poe's adaptation of *porphyrogenite*, "born in the purple."

Sonnet—Silence
Discussed in Davidson, *Poe*, pp. 80–81.

The Conqueror Worm
Discussed in Davidson, *Poe*, pp. 81–82; D. R. Swanson, *Explicator*, XIX (1961), 52.

Dream-Land
   Discussed in J. O. Bailey, *Stud. Phil.*, XLV (1948), 517-518; Davidson, *Poe*, p. 82.
   3. *Eidolon:* phantom, ghost.
   6. *ultimate dim Thule:* a variation on Latin *ultima Thule*, "most distant or most northern land."

The Raven
   Poe described how he wrote "The Raven" in "The Philosophy of Composition" (1848).
   Discussed in Davidson, *Poe*, pp. 84-92; H. M. Jones, *History and the Comtemporary* (University of Wisconsin Press, 1964), pp. 145-160; Joseph Jones, *Am. Lit.*, XXX (1958), 185-193.
   41. *Pallas:* Pallas Athene, Greek goddess of wisdom.
   82. *nepenthe:* an ancient pain-removing drug.
   89. *balm in Gilead:* see Jeremiah 8 : 22 and 46 : 11.
   93. *Aidenn:* Eden; Mohammedan paradise.

Ulalume—A Ballad
   This and the remaining four poems were first collected in a posthumous volume: R. W. Griswold (ed.), *The Works of the Late Edgar Allan Poe* (New York: J. S. Redfield, 1850), Vol. II.
   Discussed in J. O. Bailey, *Stud. Phil.*, XLV (1948), 518-523; R. P. Basler, *Sex, Symbolism, and Psychology in Literature* (Rutgers University Press, 1948), pp. 184-187; E. W. Carlson, *Explicator*, XI (1953), 56; Davidson, *Poe*, pp. 93-96; P. C. Hoyt, *Bulletin of the New York Public Library*, LXIII (1959), 568-570; J. P. Kirby, *Explicator*, I (1942), 8; Lewis Leary, *Explicator*, VI (1948), 25; T. O. Mabbott, *Explicator*, I (1943), 25; VI (1948), 57; J. E. Miller, Jr., *Phil. Quart.*, XXXIV (1955), 197-205.
   6. *Auber:* Jean François Auber (1782-1871), French composer of ballets, such as "Lac des Fées."
   7. *Weir:* Robert Walter Weir (1803-1889), popular painter of misty landscapes. See Leary, *Explicator*, VI (1948), 25 on Weir and Auber.
   14. *scoriac:* volcanic lava.
   16. *Yaanek:* Mt. Erebus, volcanic mountain in Antarctica.
   37. *Astarte's bediamonded crescent:* the planet Venus, which sometimes looks like a crescent. Astarte is the Phoenician goddess of Love.
   39. *Dian:* Diana, the chaste Roman goddess of the moon.
   43. *where the worm never dies:* see Isaiah 66 : 24.
   44. *the stars of the Lion:* the constellation Leo, which here implies danger.

Eldorado
   Eldorado is the Spanish word for golden or gilded; hence, any place of fabled wealth.
   Discussed in E. W. Carlson, *Mod. Lang. Notes*, LXXVI (1961), 232-234; O. S. Coad, *Mod. Lang. Notes*, LIX (1944), 59-61; T. O. Mabbott, *Mod. Lang. Notes*, LX (1945), 312-314; W. S. Sanderlin, Jr., *Mod. Lang. Notes*, LXXI (1956), 189-192.

For Annie

Annie was Mrs. Annie Richmond of Lowell, Massachusetts.

35. *naphthaline river:* Phlegethon, the fiery river in Hades.

To My Mother

Addressed to Poe's mother-in-law, Mrs. Maria Clemm.

Annabel Lee

This poem is generally assumed to have been inspired by the memory of Poe's cousin, Virginia Clemm, who married Poe at the age of thirteen in 1836 and died in 1847.

Discussed in Bradford Booth, *Coll. Eng.*, VII (1945), 17–19; W. C. Brown, *Coll. Eng.*, V (1944), 380–382; Davidson, *Poe*, pp. 98–99.

EZRA POUND
b. 1885

Bibliography

Edwards, John. *A Preliminary Checklist of the Writings of Ezra Pound, Especially His Contributions to Periodicals.* New Haven, Conn.: Kirgo-Books, 1953.

Gallup, Donald. *A Bibliography of Ezra Pound.* London: Rupert Hart-Davis, 1963.

Major Writings

A Lume Spento (1908)
Personae of Ezra Pound (1909)
Exultations of Ezra Pound (1909)
Ripostes of Ezra Pound (1912)
Cathay: Translations by Ezra Pound (1915)
Lustra of Ezra Pound (1916)
Quia Pauper Amavi (1919)
Hugh Selwyn Mauberley (1920)
A Draft of XVI Cantos (1925)
Personæ: The Collected Poems of Ezra Pound (1926)
Selected Poems (1928, 1949)
A Draft of XXX Cantos (1930)
Eleven New Cantos: XXXI–XLI (1934)
The Fifth Decad of Cantos (1937)
Cantos LII–LXXI (1940)
The Pisan Cantos (1948)
The Cantos of Ezra Pound (1948)
The Letters of Ezra Pound, 1907–1941 (1950, D. D. Paige, ed.)
The Translations of Ezra Pound (1953)
The Literary Essays of Ezra Pound (1954, T. S. Eliot, ed.)

Section: Rock-Drill: 85–95 de los Cantares (1955)
Thrones: 96–109 de los Cantares (1959)

Biography

Norman, Charles. *Ezra Pound.* New York: The Macmillan Co., 1960.

Criticism

Dekker, George. *The Cantos of Ezra Pound: A Critical Study.* New York: Barnes and Noble, 1963.

Dembo, L. S. *The Confucian Odes of Ezra Pound: A Critical Appraisal.* Berkeley, Calif.: University of California Press, 1963.

Deutsch, Babette. *Poetry in Our Time*, pp. 119–145. New York: Holt, Rinehart and Winston, 1952.

Emery, Clark. *Ideas into Action: A Study of Pound's Cantos.* Coral Gables, Fla.: University of Miami Press, 1958.

Espey, J. J. *Ezra Pound's "Mauberley": A Study in Composition.* Berkeley, Calif.: University of California Press, 1955.

Fraser, G. S. *Ezra Pound.* New York: Grove Press, 1961.

Kenner, Hugh. *The Poetry of Ezra Pound.* London: Faber & Faber, 1951.

Leary, Lewis (ed.). *Motive and Method in the Cantos of Ezra Pound.* New York: Columbia University Press, 1954.

Nagy, N. C. de. *The Poetry of Ezra Pound: The Pre-Imagist Stage.* Bern, Switzerland: Francke Verlag, 1960.

Rosenthal, M. L. *A Primer of Ezra Pound.* New York: The Macmillan Co., 1960.

Russell, Peter (ed.). *An Examination of Ezra Pound: A Collection of Essays.* Norfolk, Conn.: New Directions, 1950.

Watts, H. H. *Ezra Pound and the Cantos.* London: Routledge & Kegan Paul, 1951.

Comments on Poems

Except for the two Cantos, the texts of Pound's poems are taken from *Personæ: The Collected Poems of Ezra Pound* (New Directions edition). John J. Espey's text of *Hugh Selwyn Mauberley*, printed pp. 117–133 in his *Ezra Pound's "Mauberley*," contains several corrections in the text of that poem in *Personæ*; these have been listed in the footnotes. The texts for Canto I and Canto II are from *The Cantos of Ezra Pound.*

Portrait d'une Femme
    Discussed in R. J. Giannone, *Twentieth Century Literature*, V (1959), 131–134.

The Seafarer
    This version of the Old English poem of the same name is one of Pound's best known and most successful "translations."

Discussed in J. B. Bessinger, *Quarterly Journal of Speech*, XLVII (1961), 173–177.

49. *Bosque:* grove, thicket.

The Return

Discussed in Deutsch, *Poetry in Our Time*, pp. 124–125; "Experiment in Verse," *Times Lit. Sup.* (Special Number, August 17, 1956), p. iii; René Taupin, *L'influence du symbolisme français sur la poésie américaine (de 1910 à 1920)* (Champion, 1929), pp. 142–144.

Lament of the Frontier Guard

Like the other poems in *Cathay*, this is a translation from a Japanese version of a Chinese original made on the basis of the manuscripts of the American scholar of the Orient, Ernest Fenollosa (1853–1908), for whom Pound had become unofficial literary executor.

Discussed in Deutsch, *Poetry in our Time*, pp. 131–232.

15. *middle kingdom:* that part of China including the central and lower part of the Yangtze valley.

23. *Rihoku:* Pound's variant for "Rihaku" (the "signature" at the end of the poem), the Japanese form of the name of Li Po (701–762), one of China's greatest poets. Li Po lived during the years when the T'ang Dynasty, under which China had become through military conquest the largest empire on earth, reached its climax of power and began a disastrous decline marked by rebellions and invasions.

Liu Ch'e

Liu Ch'e (156–87 B.C.), sixth emperor of the Han Dynasty of China, was a patron of the arts and himself a poet. Pound's poem is based on one that Liu Ch'e wrote upon the death of a favorite concubine.

For a discussion of Pound's technique of "super-position," which he derived from the Japanese haiku and used in this poem "in the Chinese manner," see Earl Miner, "Pound, *Haiku*, and the Image," *Hud. Rev.*, IX (1957), 570–584.

Hugh Selwyn Mauberley

The editors are glad to acknowledge their indebtedness to John J. Espey's *Ezra Pound's "Mauberley": A Study in Composition* as a source of information for many of the following notes. Espey's book is the most detailed examination of this sequence of poems yet published and is indispensable for anyone who wishes to study it thoroughly. *Hugh Selwyn Mauberley* is also discussed in R. P. Blackmur, *Form and Value in Modern Poetry* (Anchor, 1957), pp. 81–85; T. E. Connolly, *Accent*, XVI (1956), 59–67; Donald Davie, pp. 315–329 in Boris Ford (ed.), *The Modern Age* (Penguin, 1961); Deutsch, *Poetry in Our Time*, 129–131; Fraser, *Ezra Pound*, pp. 52–63; F. J. Hoffman, *The Twenties* (Viking Press, 1955), pp. 36–46; Kenner, *The Poetry of Ezra Pound*, pp. 164–182; F. R. Leavis, *New Bearings in English Poetry* (Chatto and Windus, 1932), pp. 138–151; Rosenthal, *A Primer of Ezra Pound*, pp. 29–41.

At the bottom of the title page of *Personæ: The Collected Poems of Ezra Pound* (1926) appears the following note by Pound: "The sequence is so distinctly a farewell to London that the reader who chooses to regard this as an exclusively American edition may as well omit it and turn at once to page 205" (that is, to the next group of poems in the book, *Homage to Sextus Propertius*).

Vocat æstus in umbram: (Latin) "the heat calls us into the shade." The quotation is from the *Fourth Eclogue* of Nemesianus, a Roman poet who flourished in the late third century A.D.

E. P. Ode pour L'Election de Son Sepulchre
The French title: "E[zra]. P[ound]. Ode for the Choice of His Tomb." Adapted from the poem "*De l'élection de son sepulchre*" in the *Odes* of Pierre de Ronsard (1524–1585), French poet.

8. *Capaneus:* one of the Seven who marched against the city of Thebes. Because he defied Zeus, the god killed him with a thunderbolt.

9. *Ἴδμεν ... Τροίη:* (Greek) "for we know all the things that are in Troy." This is substantially what is sung by the Sirens in the *Odyssey* xii, 189. In order to sail past the Sirens without being drawn to disaster by their song, Odysseus plugs his sailors' ears with wax and has himself, with "unstopped ear," bound to the mast. Note that Penelope (line 13) and Circe (line 15) are also characters in the *Odyssey*.

18–19. *l'an ... eage:* (French) "the thirtieth year of his life." Except for the change of "my" to "his" and a rearrangement of word order, this is the opening line of the *Grand Testament* of François Villon (1431–1463 ?), French poet.

II

31. *kinema:* (Greek) "motion" (whence "cinema").

III

34. *mousseline of Cos:* muslin from the Greek island of Cos.

35. *pianola:* a player (mechanical) piano.

36. *barbitos:* a Greek lyre.

42. *Heracleitus:* Heraclitus, a Greek philosopher (535 ?–475 ? B.C.).

46. *Samothrace:* Pound takes the statue called "The Winged Victory of Samothrace," erected in 306 B.C. on the Greek island of Samothrace and now in the Louvre in Paris, as a symbol of classical beauty and asserts that Christian art represents a falling off from this ideal.

47. *τὸ καλὸν:* (Greek) "the Beautiful."

54. *Pisistratus:* an Athenian Tyrant (d. 527 B.C.), who fostered literature and art.

58. *τίν' ... θεὸν:* (Greek) "what man, what hero, what god," Adapted from Pindar's *Second Olympian Ode*, line 2, where the word order reads, "what god, what hero, what man." To catch Pound's bilingual pun, note that the Greek *τίν'* is pronounced like the English word "tin" (see line 60).

IV

63. *pro domo:* (Latin) "for home."

71–72. *pro patria ... decor:* the whole Latin line adapted here is, "Dulce et decorum est pro patria mori" ("It is sweet and fitting to die for one's country") from Horace, *Odes* iii, 2, 13. Pound adds the Latin "non," meaning "not."

Yeux Glauques

The French title: "sea-green eyes." Espey points out that the words come from the poem "Cærulei Oculi" ("Sea-Green Eyes") in *Émaux et Camées* (*Enamels and Cameos*) (1852) by Théophile Gautier (1811–1872), the French writer. *Hugh Selwyn Mauberley* contains a number of other echoes of Gautier's volume.

In this section of *Hugh Selwyn Mauberley*, Pound reviews the literary and artistic situation in England in the third quarter of the nineteenth century, the Pre-Raphaelite period, to show how it helped shape what the present "age demanded."

98. *"King's Treasuries":* "Of Kings' Treasuries" is the correct title of the first lecture in John Ruskin's *Sesame and Lilies* (1865). Delivered at Manchester, England, in 1864, this lecture attacked the English nation as "a money-making mob" that "cannot with impunity . . . go on despising literature, despising science, despising art, despising nature, despising compassion, and concentrating its soul on Pence."

100. *Buchanan:* Robert Buchanan (1841–1901), English man of letters who in 1871 attacked the "Pre-Raphaelites"—Dante Gabriel Rossetti and others —in an article entitled "The Fleshly School of Poetry."

101. *hers:* Elizabeth Siddal, a model for the Pre-Raphaelite painters and later wife of Dante Gabriel Rossetti (1828–1882), English painter and poet.

104–107. *Burne-Jones . . . rhapsodize:* Sir Edward Coley Burne-Jones (1833–1898), Pre-Raphaelite painter, whose painting, "King Cophetua and the Beggar Maid," hangs in the Tate Gallery in London. Cophetua was a legendary African king who fell in love with and married a beautiful beggar girl.

110. *English Rubaiyat:* Edward Fitzgerald published his translation of *The Rubáiyát of Omar Khayyám* in 1859, but it was at first disregarded by the public.

115. *Jenny:* one of the poems attacked by Buchanan was Rossetti's "Jenny," which concerns a London prostitute.

118. *maquero: maquereau* (French), a pimp.

"Siena Mi Fe'; Disfecemi Maremma"

The Italian title: "Siena made me; Maremma unmade me." See note to Eliot's *The Waste Land*, ll. 293–294 (p. 1109). In his survey of past literary and artistic developments in England, Pound now refers to figures in the "Decadent Movement" of the 1890's.

123. *Verog:* Pound's name for Victor Gustave Plarr (1863–1929), author of a book of poems, *In the Dorian Mood* (see l. 135), and of a book on Ernest Dowson (see l. 125), and librarian of the Royal College of Surgeons. Plarr was born in Strasbourg in Alsace, but his family and he settled in England after the Franco-Prussian War. His move to another country echoes the title of this section of the poem.

124. *Galliffet:* presumably Gaston Alexandre August, Marquis de Galliffet (1830–1909), French general who led a cavalry charge at Sedan in the Franco-Prussian War. Espey corrects "Gallifet" to read "Galliffet."

125. *Dowson:* Ernest Dowson (1867–1900), British poet. *Rhymers' Club:* a literary group founded in 1891 by a number of English "Decadent" poets, including Dowson and Lionel Johnson (see l. 126).

131. *Newman:* John Henry Cardinal Newman (1801–1890), who like John-son had been coverted to Roman Catholicism.

133. *Headlam:* the Reverend Stewart D. Headlam (1847–1924), a friend of many of the Decadent poets. *Image:* Selwyn Image (1849–1930), an editor of *The Hobby Horse*, a little magazine which published the Decadent poets.

Brennbaum

The title is probably Pound's name for Max Beerbohm (1872–1956), English essayist and caricaturist, who was known as "The Incomparable Max."

144. *Horeb . . . years:* Pound seems to assume, incorrectly, that Beerbohm was Jewish and hence would have Old Testament "memories" of the forty years of wandering of the Israelites in the Wilderness of Sinai between the time of their departure from Egypt and that of their conquest of Canaan.

Mr. Nixon

The title is probably Pound's name for Arnold Bennett (1867–1931), English editor and novelist.

160. *Dr. Dundas:* probably, as Espey suggests, a "type of literary pontiff and editor."

168. *Bloughram:* a reference to Robert Browning's satirical poem, *Bishop Blougram's Apology*. Pound has refused to change the spelling "Bloughram."

X

173. *stylist:* probably Ford Madox Ford (1873–1939), English novelist.

XI

184. *Milésien:* the reference is both to the *Milesian Tales*, a collection of erotic romances by Aristides (150?–100? B.C.) of Miletus, the ancient city of Asia Minor, and to a phrase by the French writer, Remy de Gourmont (1858–1915): "Femmes, conservatrices des traditions milésiennes" ("Women, con-servators of Milesian traditions").

186. *Ealing:* a suburb to the west of London.

XII

192. *Daphne:* while Apollo was pursuing the nymph Daphne, she was transformed into a laurel tree. Here Daphne is extending "laurels" to "me."

214. *Fleet St.:* a London street distinguished in the eighteenth century by much literary activity.

215. *Dr. Johnson:* Samuel Johnson (1709–1784), English lexicographer and man of letters.

219. *Pierian roses:* the phrase echoes a line from a poem by Sappho, the Greek lyricist of the sixth century B.C. Also, poetry was celebrated in Pieria in ancient Greece.

Envoi

This poem is patterned after the lyric "Go, Lovely Rose," by the English poet Edmund Waller (1606–1687), who is named in l. 242.

221. *Lawes:* Henry Lawes (1596–1662), English musician, who set many of Waller's lyrics to music, including "Go, Lovely Rose."

Mauberley

Vacuos exercet aera morsus: (Latin) "He bites emptily at the air."

246–247. *eau-forte | Par Jaquemart:* (French) "etching by Jaquemart." Jules Jacquemart (1837–1880) was a French artist.

249. *Messalina:* Valeria Messalina, the dissolute third wife of the Roman emperor Claudius. In this stanza Pound says that Mauberley abandoned ("Turned from") the etching for the medallion as an artistic medium and began engraving a profile ("strait head") of Messalina as seen on an ancient coin.

259. *Pier Francesca:* Piero della Francesca (1420?–1492), Italian painter.

260. *Pisanello:* the common name for Vittore Pisano (1397–1455), Italian medalist and painter.

261. *Achaia:* the name of ancient Greece. "To forge Achaia" means either to recreate the classical world in powerful works of art or create a new form of art. Mauberley lacked the skill of Pisanello, an artist Pound admires.

II

Qu'est . . . un tonnerre?: (French) "What do they know of love, and what can they understand?

"If they do not understand poetry, if they do not feel music, what can they understand of that passion in comparison with which the rose is gross and the perfume of violets a crash of thunder?"

Caid Ali: a pseudonym for Pound himself.

262. *diabolus in the scale:* the devil in the (musical) scale; a term, according to Espey, for "the augmented fourth, which gave the medieval musicians great difficulty."

264. *ANANGKE:* (Greek) "Fate."

268. *NUKTIS' AGALMA:* (Greek) "Night's ornament." Espey corrects "*NUKTIS*" to read "*NUKTOS.*"

278. *TO AGATHON:* (Greek) "the Good."

284. *manifestations:* Pound has written Espey that he now prefers "manifestation."

288. *irides:* plural of "iris," with reference to its meaning both as part of the eye and as a kind of flower.

289. *botticellian:* pertaining to Sandro Botticelli (1444?–1510), Italian painter, particularly well known for his painting "The Birth of Venus."

290. *diastasis:* here meaning both "dilation" and "wide-spaced."

291. *anæthesis:* anesthesia, loss of feeling or sensation. Pound has written Espey that "anæthesis" was a typographical error for "anæsthesis."

295. *Mouths . . . air:* an echo of the Latin epigraph for "Mauberly 1920." Lines 296–298 amplify this suggestion of Mauberley's artistic and psychological ineffectuality.

"The Age Demanded"

302. *Cytheræan:* Aphrodite, whose chariot was drawn by doves.

337. *apathein:* (Greek) "apathy."

IV

360. *Moluccas:* the Spice Islands, near New Guinea.

Medallion

385. *Luini:* Bernardino Luini (*c.* 1480–1532), Italian painter.

391. *Anadyomene:* Aphrodite, the "foam-born." "Anadyomene" is Greek for "rising out of the sea."

392. *Reinach:* Salomon Reinach (1858–1932), French archaeologist, who published his lectures on art as a book entitled *Apollo* (1904).

Canto I

The present Canto I did not always stand at the beginning of *The Cantos* but was adapted by Pound from what was originally the third of the series. The Canto III of *Poetry*, X (1917), 248–254, is a poem of 175 lines, of which the last 95 have become the 76 of the present text. In its original form as Canto III it was given book publication for the first time in *Quia Pauper Amavi* (1919), but in its revised version as Canto I it, like Canto II, was not published in book form until 1925 in *A Draft of XVI Cantos*. For further discussion see Myles Slatin, "A History of Pound's *Cantos I–XVI*, 1915–1925," *Am. Lit.*, XXXV (1963), 183–195.

For much of the information in the following notes to Cantos I and II the editors gratefully acknowledge their indebtedness to Edgar M. Glenn and to Robert D. Mayo, editor of the Northwestern University *Analyst*, which has been publishing a series of explications of the Cantos. Numbers VIII and XVIII of the *Analyst*, both by Glenn, are particularly useful.

The first two and other Cantos are also discussed in Blackmur, *Form and Value in Modern Poetry* (Anchor, 1957), pp. 92–112; Guy Davenport, *Wisconsin Studies in Contemporary Literature*, III (1962), 50–64; Dekker, *The Cantos of Ezra Pound*; Deutsch, *Poetry in Our Time*, pp. 133–145; Emery, *Ideas into Action*; Fraser, *Ezra Pound*, pp. 67–80; Kenner, *The Poetry of Ezra Pound*, pp. 185–304, 314–333; Leary, *Motive and Method in the Cantos of Ezra Pound*; R. H. Pearce, *The Continuity of American Poetry* (Princeton University Press, 1961), pp. 83–101; Sister M. B. Quinn, *The Metamorphic Tradition in Modern Poetry* (Rutgers University Press, 1955), pp. 14–48; Rosenthal, *A Primer of Ezra Pound*, pp. 42–51; Allen Tate, *On the Limits of Poetry* (Alan Swallow, 1948), pp. 350–357; Watts, *Ezra Pound and the Cantos*. Also useful is J. H. Edwards and William Vasse, Jr., *Annotated Index to "The Cantos of Ezra Pound"* (Berkeley, Calif.: University of California Press, 1957).

1–67. [*Analyst*] "This passage is a free rend[er]ing in English of the opening lines of the eleventh book of the *Odyssey*, called the 'Nekuia,' or 'Book of the Dead,' because it describes Odysseus' visit to the underworld. . . . Actually the poet is not translating directly from the *Odyssey*, but from a Renaissance Latin translation by Andreas Divus, but this fact does not emerge until line 68. . . ." One reason for Pound's introduction of Odysseus at the beginning of the Cantos is that Odysseus appears to represent for him "a union of the inquiring mind and the effective will."

3. *We:* Odysseus, who is speaking, and his companions.

7. *Circe's this craft:* [*Analyst*] "The reference is to Circe's powers of magic which provide the wind so that Odysseus' ship may reach its destination."

12. *Kimmerian:* pertaining to the Cimmerians, an ancient people originally living in the Crimea.

17. *the place:* Hades, which Circe had told Odysseus he must visit in order to learn from Tiresias, the dead prophet of Thebes, how he might return to Ithaca, his home. Cf. Eliot's use of Tiresias in *The Waste Land,* Part III.

19. *Perimedes and Eurylochus:* two of Odysseus' men.

21. *pitkin:* a little pit.

29. *Erebus:* the dark part of the Underworld through which the shades of the dead had to pass to reach Hades.

33. *dreory:* (Anglo-Saxon) "bloody." [*Analyst*] "In rendering Homer into English, as earlier commentators have pointed out, the poet gives his lines a pronounced Old English flavor. This is expressed not only in the diction of lines 1–67 (e.g., *pitkin* and *dreory*), but in the rhythm and metrical structure, the alliteration and assonance, the use of epithets, and so on."

42. *Elpenor:* one of Odysseus' companions, who had died as his spirit describes in lines 50–54.

53. *Avernus:* a small crater lake in Campania, Italy, believed by the ancient Romans to be the entrance to the Underworld. The word is often used to refer to the Underworld itself.

58. *Anticlea:* [*Analyst*] "the mother of Odysseus, whose death has occurred in his absence. Odysseus weeps to behold her, but, as instructed by Circe, will not let her drink the blood until Tiresias has first done so."

68. *Lie quiet Divus:* [*Analyst*] "The command is cryptic. It may mean: 'That's enough of that. Let's change the subject.' Or perhaps: 'Divus, rest in peace,' or 'Don't turn over in your grave!'" *Andreas Divus:* the author of a Latin translation of the *Odyssey,* published in Paris in 1538, which Pound states that he found in a Paris bookstall sometime between 1906 and 1910.

69. *In officina Wecheli:* (Latin) "at the workshop of Wechel." This is part of the imprint of the Divus volume.

72. *Venerandam:* (Latin) "compelling admiration." The term is applied to Aphrodite, line 73.

73–76. [*Analyst*] "Without making an allegory of *Canto I* we may point out that Aphrodite seems to present a contrast to Odysseus, whose nature differs from hers as the style of lines 1–67 differs from that of lines 73–75. They represent, so to speak, complementary principles. Odysseus is action and intelligence; Aphrodite is feminine beauty, passion, and perhaps creative force."

73. *the Cretan:* Georgius Dartona Cretensis, whose *Hymni Deorum* (*Hymns of the Gods*), Latin translations of the *Homeric Hymns,* were included in the Divus volume. The Latin words used by Pound are from the second Homeric hymn to Aphrodite, as translated by Dartona.

74. *Cypri . . . est:* "the citadels of Cyprus were her appointed realm." *oricalchi:* Pound's spelling of "orichalchi": (Latin) "of copper." The reference is to a votive gift of copper and gold described in the hymn to Aphrodite as being placed on the goddess.

76. *Argicida:* (Latin) either "slayer of Argus" or "slayer of Greeks." The first would refer to Hermes, herald of the gods, who killed the hundred-eyed Argus at Zeus's command. The second would refer to Aphrodite, who supported the Trojans against the Greeks in the Trojan War. *So that:* [*Analyst*] "possibly from an *ut* in the Latin of Divus or Georgius Dartona. But it can also be construed as a phrase which can only be completed by the cantos

which follow. John Drummond believes that it is an allusion to Browning's *Sordello* (*v.* line 2 of *Canto II*). The words 'So that Sordello . . . ' occur in *Sordello, I, 567*."

Canto II

1. *Robert Browning:* the English poet (1812–1889), whose long poem *Sordello* (1840) is often obscure in meaning.

2–3. *Sordello:* [*Analyst*] "*Sordello* here is used to refer to at least four different things, and each use involves a separate definition: (1) Browning's poem ("*Sordello*," line 2), (2) the actual, historical man, (3) Browning's fabrication (the title character in Browning's poem), and (4) Pound's own conception of Sordello, the man and the poet. Thus the poet systematically inspects the various ways in which Sordello may exist and may be known." The historical Sordello was a thirteenth-century Italian troubadour, who wrote in Provençal.

4. *Lo . . . Mantovana:* (Provençal) "Sordello was from the region around Mantua."

5. *So-shu:* possibly the Japanese version of the name of Chuang Tzǔ, a Chinese Taoist philosopher. See Pound's poem "Ancient Wisdom, Rather Cosmic," which deals with So-Shu. *churned in the sea:* [*Analyst*] "Since *churned* seems to be a metaphor for wrong-headed and ineffectual action, perhaps *sea* is metaphorical, too. Professor [Hugh] Kenner suggests that *sea* stands for the welter (change and multiplicity) of phenomena and of experience. . . .

"Line 5, therefore, may be paraphrased thus: So-shu (Taoist Chuang Tzǔ) dealt ineffectually with life (the welter of phenomena and experience). Interpreted thus, line 5 continues the suggestion in lines 2–4 that phenomena are difficult to deal with because of their fluidity and multiplicity and because of the subjective element that tends to color one's knowledge of them, as indicated by Sordello's various identities."

"Ancient Wisdom, Rather Cosmic" is, however, a "translation" of a poem by Li Po (701–762), the Chinese poet, who is said to have died when he leaned drunkenly out of a boat one night in order to kiss the reflection of the moon in the water, fell in, and drowned. In his article "Fenollosa and Pound" (*Harvard Journal of Asiatic Studies*, XX [1957], 213–238), Achilles Fang suggests (p. 230) that Pound "perhaps confused the poetic philosopher of antiquity with the philosophic poet of T'ang times."

7. *Lir:* a form of the Celtic word for "ocean." In Irish mythology the son of Lir, likewise called Lir, was a god or hero.

11. "*Eleanor . . . ἑλέπτολις!*": [*Analyst*] "Eleanor of Aquitaine, associated here (as elsewhere in the *Cantos*) with Helen of Troy. Both were queens of beauty and the subjects of memorable poetry. . . . The two queens were also sources of discord between great powers. In line 11 only the last parallel is established: the Greek words *elenaus* ('ship-destroying') and *eleptolis* ('city-destroying') are puns used by Aeschylus to describe Helen of Troy in the *Agamemnon*. . . . Pound, however, modifies Aeschylus' series of puns by dropping the Greek *elandros* ('man-destroying') and substituting for it the proper name *Eleanor*, which is similar enough to the Greek *ele* ('destroying') and *aner* ('man') to supply the third pun."

14–22. "*Let her . . . voices*": cf. *Iliad* iii. 139–160. The old men of Troy speak thus of Helen as they watch the combat between Paris and Menelaus.

19. *Schoeney's daughters:* the beautiful Atalanta, daughter of Schoeneus, caused the death of a number of her suitors.

23. *Tyro:* a mortal woman with whom Poseidon (the "sea-god" of line 24) lay, meanwhile making a wave arch over and hide them.

34. *Scios:* [*Analyst*] "Ancient Chios (famous for its wine), modern Scio; an Ionic Greek island off the coast of Asia Minor, about 70 miles north and slightly east of Naxos."

35. *Naxos:* Greek island in the Aegean, known for its wine and for the worship of Dionysus, with whom Bacchus is identified.

36. *Naviform:* shiplike.

40–118. *The ship . . . amid sea:* [*Analyst*] "The story of the attempted rape of Bacchus (Dionysus) is told in the second Homeric hymn to Dionysus and, very briefly, in *The Library* of Apollodorus, but Pound seems to be relying here on the version given in Ovid's *Metamorphoses*, III, 511–733, which may be summarized as follows.

"Tiresias [see l. 115], the blind Theban soothsayer . . . , warned King Pentheus [see l. 59] that the new god Bacchus would come to Thebes, and unless he was worshipped as was his due, Pentheus would be torn to pieces by his mother and sisters. The king scoffed at this prophecy.

"When the new rites were introduced into Thebes, Pentheus obstinately opposed them, denounced Bacchus as an imposter, and ordered his slaves to bring the so-called god before him. They returned from this mission unsuccessful, but produced instead a votary of the god, Accœtes [see l. 62]. Pentheus questioned Accœtes, who told the story of his conversion, as a warning to the king. It is this story which Pound retells in lines 40–118."

42. *young boy:* Bacchus. [*Analyst*] "The plants commonly associated with Bacchus are the ivy and the grape vine; his attendant animals are the lynx, panther, tiger, leopard, and dolphin."

47. *ex-convict:* Lycabas, the Lycabs of line 104.

83. *æther:* (Latin) "air."

95. *Lyæus:* an epithet for Bacchus-Dionysus, meaning "the deliverer from care."

100. *Olibanum:* frankincense.

113. *Medon:* like Lycabas, one of Accœtes' shipmates. *dory:* the sea fish.

115. *Tiresias:* see Canto I, note to l. 17. *Cadmus:* grandfather of Pentheus and founder of Thebes. Both Tiresias and Cadmus had warned Pentheus against suppressing the cult of Dionysus.

124. *Ileuthyeria:* perhaps a name invented by Pound for some nymph or woman turned into coral. *Dafne:* Daphne, the nymph who, pursued by Apollo, was transformed into a laurel tree.

144. *Hesperus:* the Greek name for Venus, the evening star.

153. *Proteus:* in Greek mythology a sea god who could change his shape at will. If he could be caught and held, however, he could be made to foretell future events.

JOHN CROWE RANSOM
b. 1888

Bibliography

Bradbury, J. M. "Selected Bibliography: II. John Crowe Ransom," pp. 277–
279 in *The Fugitives: A Critical Account*. Chapel Hill, N.C.: University of
North Carolina Press, 1958.

Cowan, Louise. "Appendix: Contents of *The Fugitive*," pp. 258–267 in *The
Fugitive Group: A Literary History*. Baton Rouge, La.: Louisiana State
University Press, 1959.

Stallman, R. W. "John Crowe Ransom: A Checklist," *Sewanee Rev.*, LVI
(1948), 442–476.

Major Writings

Poems About God (1919)
Chills and Fever: Poems (1924)
Two Gentlemen in Bonds (1927)
The World's Body (1938, criticism)
The New Criticism (1941)
Selected Poems (1945)
Poems and Essays (1955)
Selected Poems (1963)

Criticism

Beatty, R. C. "John Crowe Ransom as Poet," *Sewanee Rev.*, LII (1944), 344–
366.

Blum, Morgan. "The Fugitive Particular: John Crowe Ransom, Critic,"
West. Rev., XIV (1950), 85–102.

Bradbury, J. M. *The Fugitives: A Critical Account*. Chapel Hill, N.C.: University
of North Carolina Press, 1958.

Cowan, Louise. *The Fugitive Group: A Literary History*. Baton Rouge, La.:
Louisiana State University Press, 1959.

Jarrell, Randall. "John Ransom's Poetry," pp. 87–100 in *Poetry and the Age*.
New York: Vintage Books, 1955.

Koch, Vivienne. "The Poetry of John Crowe Ransom," pp. 33–65 in B.
Rajan (ed.), *Modern American Poetry*, New York: Roy Publishers, 1952.

Long, D. D., and Burr, M. R. (eds.). *John Crowe Ransom: A Tribute from the
Community of Letters*. Gambier, Ohio: The Kenyon Collegian, 1964.

MacCaffrey, I. G. "Ceremonies of Bravery: John Crowe Ransom," pp. 210–
220 in L. D. Rubin and R. D. Jacobs (eds.), *South: Modern Southern
Literature in Its Cultural Setting*. New York: Dolphin, 1961.

Schwartz, Delmore. "Instructed of Much Morality," *Sewanee Rev.*, LIV (1946), 439–448.

Sewanee Review, LVI (1948). "Homage to John Crowe Ransom."

Shenandoah, XIV (1963). "A Tribute to John Crowe Ransom."

Stewart, J. L. *John Crowe Ransom.* Minneapolis, Minn.: University of Minnesota Press, 1963.

Comments on Poems

Winter Remembered
    Discussed in Laura Riding and Robert Graves, *A Survey of Modernist Poetry* (Doubleday, 1928), pp. 229–230.

Bells for John Whiteside's Daughter
    Discussed in R. B. Heilman, *Pacific Spectator*, V (1951), 458–460; Koch, pp. 43–44 in Rajan (ed.), *Modern American Poetry*; D. A. Stauffer, *Sewanee Rev.*, LVI (1948), 430; R. P. Warren, *Selected Essays* (Random House, 1958), pp. 12–16.

Captain Carpenter
    Discussed in Cleanth Brooks, *Modern Poetry and the Tradition* (University of North Carolina Press, 1939), pp. 35–37; Laura Riding and Robert Graves, *A Survey of Modernist Poetry* (Doubleday, 1928) pp. 103–109; Stewart, *John Crowe Ransom*, p. 27.

Antique Harvesters
    Discussed in Koch, pp. 58–61 in Rajan (ed.), *Modern American Poetry*; F. O. Matthiessen, *Sewanee Rev.*, LVI (1948), 394–395; L. D. Rubin, Jr., *Am. Quart.*, IX (1957), 69–70.
    26. *Lady:* a symbol for the South. Here the word has overtones of earthly love and religious veneration as found in chivalric romance.

The Equilibrists
    Discussed in Beatty, *Sewanee Rev.*, LII (1944), 359–360; Bernard Bergonzi, *Critical Quarterly*, IV (1962), 127–137; Cowan, *The Fugitive Group*, pp. 213–215; Elizabeth Drew and J. L. Sweeney, *Directions in Modern Poetry* (W. W. Norton Co., 1940), pp. 208–211; Howard Nemerov, *Sewanee Rev.*, LVI (1948), 419–420; Stewart, *John Crowe Ransom*, pp. 24–25; G. P. Wasserman, *U. Kans. City Rev.*, XXIII (1956), 153, 158–159.
    38. *saeculum:* (Latin) period, age.
    47. *Stuprate:* obsolete word meaning "sexually violated."

Painted Head
    Discussed in Beatty, *Sewanee Rev.*, LII (1944), 365–366; Bradbury, *The Fugitives*, pp. 42–44; Cleanth Brooks, *Modern Poetry and the Tradition* (University of North Carolina Press, 1939), pp. 94–95; Koch, pp. 62–64 in Rajan (ed.), *Modern American Poetry*; Charles Moorman, *Explicator*, X (1951), 15; Virginia Wallach, *Explicator*, XIV (1956), 45.

Master's in the Garden Again

This drastically recast poem in its earliest form was called "Conrad in Twilight" and published in *The Fugitive*, II, No. 5 (March, 1923).

Discussed by W. D. Snodgrass, Leonie Adams, Muriel Rukeyser and John Crowe Ransom, pp. 114–140 in Anthony Ostroff (ed.), *The Contemporary Poet as Artist and Critic: Eight Symposia* (Little, Brown and Company, 1964).

Prelude to an Evening

This poem, first published in *Selected Poems* (1945), Ransom calls "the soliloquy of a man returning home to his wife." It appears revised and explicated in *Selected Poems* (1963). Ransom's commentary appears on pages 101–111 in this edition.

Discussed in Bradbury, *The Fugitives*, pp. 45–46; Cleanth Brooks, *Sewanee Rev.*, LVI (1948), 412–414; Vivienne Koch, pp. 62–64 in Rajan (ed.), *Modern American Poetry*; V. L. Peck, *Explicator*, XX (1962), 41.

EDWIN ARLINGTON ROBINSON
1869–1935

Bibliography

Beebe, Lucius, and Bulkley, Robert J., Jr. *A Bibliography of the Writings of Edwin Arlington Robinson*. Cambridge, Mass.: Dunster House Bookshop, 1931.

Hogan, C. B. *A Bibliography of Edwin Arlington Robinson*. New Haven, Conn.: Yale University Press, 1936.

Lippincott, Lillian. *A Bibliography of the Writings and Criticisms of Edwin Arlington Robinson*. Boston: F. W. Faxon Co., 1937.

Untermeyer, Louis. *Edwin Arlington Robinson: A Reappraisal*. Washington, D.C.: Library of Congress, 1963.

Major Writings

The Torrent and the Night Before (1896)
The Children of the Night: A Book of Poems (1897)
The Town Down the River: A Book of Poems (1910)
The Man Against the Sky: A Book of Poems (1916)
Merlin: A Poem (1917)
The Three Taverns: A Book of Poems (1920)
Lancelot: A Poem (1920)
Avon's Harvest (1921)
Roman Bartholow (1923)
Dionysus in Doubt: A Book of Poems (1925)
Tristram (1927)
Collected Poems (1927)
Matthias at the Door (1931)

King Jasper: A Poem (1935)

Selected Letters of Edwin Arlington Robinson (1940, Ridgely Torrence, ed.)

Letters of Edwin Arlington Robinson to Howard George Schmitt (1945, C. J. Weber, ed.)

Untriangulated Stars: Letters of Edwin Arlington Robinson to Harry de Forest Smith, 1890–1905 (1947, Denham Sutcliffe, ed.)

Standard Editions

Collected Poems of Edwin Arlington Robinson. New York: The Macmillan Co., 1937.

Davis, Charles T. (ed.). *Edwin Arlington Robinson: Selected Early Poems and Letters*. New York: Holt, Rinehart and Winston, 1960.

Thompson, Lawrance (ed.). *Tilbury Town: Selected Poems of Edwin Arlington Robinson*. New York: The Macmillan Co., 1953.

Biography

Hagedorn, Hermann. *Edwin Arlington Robinson: A Biography*. New York: The Macmillan Co., 1938.

Neff, Emery. *Edwin Arlington Robinson*. New York: William Sloane Associates, 1948.

Redman, Ben Ray. *Edwin Arlington Robinson*. New York: Robert M. McBride, 1926.

Criticism

Adams, Richard P. "The Failure of Edwin Arlington Robinson," *Tulane Stud. Eng.* XI (1961), 97–151.

Barnard, Ellsworth. *Edwin Arlington Robinson: A Critical Study*. New York: The Macmillan Co., 1952.

Cestre, Charles. *An Introduction to Edwin Arlington Robinson*. New York: The Macmillan Co., 1930.

Fussell, E. S. *Edwin Arlington Robinson: The Literary Background of a Traditional Poet*. Berkeley, Calif.: University of California Press, 1954.

Kaplan, Estelle. *Philosophy in the Poetry of Edwin Arlington Robinson*. New York: Columbia University Press, 1940.

Lowell, Amy. *Tendencies in Modern American Poetry*, pp. 3–75. New York: The Macmillan Co., 1917.

Morris, Lloyd. *The Poetry of Edwin Arlington Robinson: An Essay in Appreciation*. New York: George H. Doran Co., 1923.

Stovall, Floyd. "The Optimism Behind Robinson's Tragedies," *Am. Lit.*, X (1938), 1–23.

Untermeyer, Louis. *Edwin Arlington Robinson: A Reappraisal*. Washington, D.C.: Library of Congress, 1963.

Waggoner, H. H. *The Heel of Elohim: Science and Values of Modern American Poetry*, pp. 18–40, 195–196, 210–211, *passim*. Norman, Okla.: University of Oklahoma Press, 1950.

Winters, Yvor. *Edwin Arlington Robinson*, Norfolk, Conn.: New Directions, 1946.

Comments on Poems

Robinson revised his poems little, usually merely transferring a poem from its first book publication to a "collected" edition; consequently the dates given in this anthology for Robinson's poems are those of first book publication.

George Crabbe
In *The Village* and other poems George Crabbe (1754–1832), the English poet, described the harshness of rural life in England earnestly and frankly.

Luke Havergal
  12. *the dark will end the dark:* Fussell, *Edwin Arlington Robinson*, p. 473: "The dark ('western gate,' crimson vines,' 'western glooms,' 'twilight') is to be taken as the confrontation and stoic acceptance of tragic experiences . . ." But Barnard, *Edwin Arlington Robinson*, pp. 38–39, sees in the symbols of light and dark the paradox of life through death: "Here we have what might be called a metaphor of the second degree: 'the dark' means 'death,' but the first death is that of the body (through suicide), which in the disordered mind of the bereaved lover promises to end his deathlike loneliness."

Credo
  Untermeyer, *Edwin Arlington Robinson*, p. 6, quotes a reviewer of *The Children of the Night* (in which "Credo" was republished) who regretted the poet's "prison-house" philosophy, to which Robinson replied: "The world is not a prison-house but a kind of spiritual kindergarten where millions of bewildered children are trying to spell God with the wrong blocks." For another interpretation of Robinson's optimism, see Stovall, "The Optimism Behind Robinson's Tragedies," *Am. Lit.*, X (1938), 1–23.

How Annandale Went Out
  1. *it:* the man has become so degenerated that he is no longer a man, in the opinion of the speaker, the physician who performed the mercy killing.
  13. *slight kind of engine:* hypodermic needle.

For a Dead Lady
  Winters, *Edwin Arlington Robinson*, p. 36: "'For a Dead Lady' is an elegy unenlightened by any mitigating idea or feeling; it is purely a lament for the dead. Robinson suggests no way of dealing with the experience except that we understand it and endure it."
  14. *Saturn keeps the years:* Saturn, a Roman god of harvests, became confused with the Greek Cronus, god of agriculture, and then Cronus became confused with the Greek god Chronus, time. Robinson's allusion shows the double confusion, making Saturn measure time.

The Gift of God
  Fussell, *Edwin Arlington Robinson*, p. 611, thinks the mother's future can only contain disillusionment, "the more galling for being totally unexpected," but Barnard, *Edwin Arlington Robinson*, p. 295, finds the poem "essentially and tenderly comic."

Hillcrest
This was the name of the home of Edward MacDowell, at Peterborough,

New Hampshire, which Mrs. MacDowell turned into an artists' colony in 1908. From 1911 until the end of his life Robinson spent every summer there.

Eros Turannos

Title: (Greek) "Love, the tyrant."

Neff, *Edwin Arlington Robinson*, p. 181: "A woman . . . holds to her Judas husband out of pride and out of fear of lonely old age." Cestre, *An Introduction to Edwin Arlington Robinson*, p. 14, similarly interprets the story, but Barnard, *Edwin Arlington Robinson*, p. 278, points out that the woman's husband was a Judas when "she found him."

The Man Against the Sky

Discussed in Barnard, *Edwin Arlington Robinson*, pp. 113–115; Cestre, *An Introduction to Edwin Arlington Robinson*, pp. 60–64; Waggoner, *The Heel of Elohim*, pp. 29–36; Winters, *Edwin Arlington Robinson*, pp. 46–48.

42–46. *As on a day . . . a bird:* see Daniel 3 and 4.

136. *Curse God and die:* see Job 2 : 9.

177–178. *Nahum's . . . soon lost:* see Nahum 3 : 17.

229. *Word:* see John 1 : 1.

Demos

"Demos," from the Greek, means "the common people." Some critics have seen in this poem Robinson's antidemocracy, but as Barnard, *Edwin Arlington Robinson*, p. 259, says: "What he dislikes in democracy is simply the tendencies that might make it cease to be democracy . . . And what he asserts is what no responsible believer in democracy has denied—that a free society cannot survive without the leadership provided by 'an aristocracy of virtue and talent.'"

Mr. Flood's Party

8. *Tilbury Town:* the fictitious name assigned by Robinson in a number of poems to Gardiner, Maine, where he spent his youth.

11. *The poet:* Omar Khayyám. See Edward Fitzgerald's translation of *The Rubáiyát*, stanza vii.

20. *Roland's ghost:* Roland, the hero of the medieval French romance *The Song of Roland*, unwillingly blows his horn to summon Charlemagne's army to save his forces from the Saracen attack.

Karma

Karma: the doctrine in Buddhism and Hinduism that a person's every act affects his soul's next reincarnation.

THEODORE ROETHKE
1908–1963

Bibliography

Matheson, J. W. *Theodore Roethke: A Bibliography*. University of Washington, Master of Librarianship Thesis, 1958.

Major Writings

Open House (1941)
The Lost Son and Other Poems (1948)
Praise to the End! (1951)
The Waking: Poems 1933–1953 (1953)
Words for the Wind: The Collected Verse of Theodore Roethke (1958)
I Am! Says the Lamb (1961)
The Far Field (1964)
On the Poet and His Craft: Selected Prose (1965, R. J. Mills, Jr., ed.)

Criticism

Arnett, Carroll. "Minimal to Maximal: Theodore Roethke's Dialectic," *Coll. Eng.*, XVIII (1957), 414–416.

Burke, Kenneth. "The Vegetal Radicalism of Theodore Roethke," *Sewanee Rev.*, LVIII (1950), 68–108.

Kramer, Hilton. "The Poetry of Theodore Roethke," *West Rev.*, XVIII (1954), 131–146.

Kunitz, Stanley. "News of the Root," *Poetry*, LXXIII (1949), 222–225.

Lee, C. I. "The Line as a Rhythmic Unit in the Poetry of Theodore Roethke," *Speech Monographs*, XXX (1963), 15–22.

Mills, R. J., Jr. "Theodore Roethke: The Lyric of the Self," pp. 3–23 in Edward Hungerford (ed.), *Poets in Progress: Critical Prefaces to Ten Contemporary Americans*. Evanston, Ill.: Northwestern University Press, 1962.

Mills, R. J., Jr. *Theodore Roethke.* Minneapolis, Minn.: University of Minnesota Press, 1963.

Rosenthal, M. L. *The Modern Poets: A Critical Introduction*, pp. 240–244. New York: Oxford University Press, 1960.

Schwartz, Delmore. "The Cunning and the Craft of the Unconscious and the Preconscious," *Poetry*, XCIV (1959), 203–205.

Southworth, J. G. "The Poetry of Theodore Roethke," *Coll. Eng.*, XXI (1960), 326–330, 335–338.

Comments on Poems

The texts of all the poems by Roethke are taken from *Words for the Wind: The Collected Verse of Theodore Roethke.*

Open House
Discussed in Arnett, *Coll. Eng.*, XVIII (1957), 414.

Cuttings, *later*
Discussed in Burke, *Sewanee Rev.*, LVIII (1950), 68–69; Mills, pp. 6–7 in Edward Hungerford (ed.), *Poets in Progress.*

The Lost Son
Discussed in Arnett, *Coll. Eng.*, XVIII (1957), 414–415; Burke, *Sewanee Rev.*, LVIII (1950), 86–93; Babette Deutsch, *Poetry in Our Time* (Holt, Rinehart and Winston, 1952), pp. 182–185; Kramer, *West. Rev.*, XVIII (1954), 138–141;

Mills, pp. 12–16 in Edward Hungerford (ed.), *Poets in Progress*; Mills, *Theodore Roethke*, pp. 24–29; Theodore Roethke, pp. 68–69 in John Ciardi (ed.), *Mid-Century American Poets* (Twayne Publishers, 1950); Rosenthal, *The Modern Poets*, pp. 243–244.

    1. *Woodlawn:* the name of a cemetery.

    The Gibber: inarticulate speech. In selecting this section's title Roethke was apparently thinking of the "ranting" passages.

    84. *Hath the rain a father?:* cf. Job 38 : 28.

    142. *Ordnung!:* (German) "Order!"

Elegy for Jane
    Discussed in Cleanth Brooks and R. P. Warren, *Conversations on the Craft of Poetry* (Holt, Rinehart and Winston, 1961), pp. 59–60.

Four for Sir John Davies
    Sir John Davies (1569–1626), an English poet, was the author of *Orchestra*, in which natural phenomena are described in terms of dancing or ordered motion, and *Nosce Teipsum*, a philosophic poem on the nature of man and the soul. The figure of the bears in Part I of Roethke's poem may have come ultimately from stanza 64 of *Orchestra*, where the bears are the two constellations, Ursa Major and Ursa Minor:

> As the two Bears, whom the First Mover flings
> With a short turn about heaven's axletree,
> In a round dance forever wheeling be.

Other echoes of *Orchestra* occur in Roethke's poem, particularly in the conception of love as a form of dancing.

    Discussed in Arnett, *Coll. Eng.*, XVIII (1957), 415–416; Mills, pp. 17–20 in Edward Hungerford (ed.), *Poets in Progress*; Mills, *Theodore Roethke*, pp. 31–35.

    19. *I take . . . Yeats:* although Roethke may have taken his "cadence" from William Butler Yeats, his meter and stanzaic form are also those of Davies' *Orchestra*, except that his stanza contains six lines instead of seven, Davies' fifth line, which rhymes with the second and fourth, being dropped.

Words for the Wind
    Roethke wrote this poem in honor of his new bride.
    Discussed in Mills, *Theodore Roethke*, pp. 35–37.

First Meditation
    This is the first of the "Meditations of an Old Woman," a group of five poems that concludes *Words for the Wind*.
    Discussed in Mills, pp. 20–22 in Edward Hungerford (ed.), *Poets in Progress*; Mills, *Theodore Roethke*, pp. 40–43.

CARL SANDBURG
b. 1878

Major Writings

Chicago Poems (1916)
Cornhuskers (1918)

Smoke and Steel (1920)
Slabs of the Sunburnt West (1922)
Rootabaga Stories (1922)
Abraham Lincoln: The Prairie Years (1926)
The American Songbag (1927)
Good Morning, America (1928)
The People, Yes (1936)
Abraham Lincoln: The War Years (1939)
Complete Poems (1950)

Biography

Detzer, Karl W. *Carl Sandburg: A Study in Personality and Background.* New
    York: Harcourt, Brace and Co., 1941.
Golden, Harry. *Carl Sandburg.* New York: World, 1961.

Criticism

Aiken, Conrad. "Poetic Realism: Carl Sandburg," pp. 143–148 in *Scepticisms.*
    New York: Alfred A. Knopf, 1919.
Allen, Gay Wilson. "Carl Sandburg: Fire and Smoke," *So. Atl. Quart.,* LIX
    (1960), 315–331.
Arvin, Newton. "Carl Sandburg," in Malcolm Cowley (ed.), *After the Genteel
    Tradition.* New York: W. W. Norton Co., 1959.
Cargill, Oscar. "Carl Sandburg: Crusader and Mystic," *Coll. Eng.,* I (1940),
    649–657.
West, Rebecca. "Introduction" in *Selected Poems of Carl Sandburg.* New York:
    Harcourt, Brace and Co., 1926.
Williams, William Carlos. "Carl Sandburg's Complete Poems," in *Selected
    Essays.* New York: Random House, 1954.

Comments on Poems

The dates of the poems indicate the textual sources for the poems: 1916,
Chicago Poems; 1918, *Cornhuskers;* 1920, *Smoke and Steel;* 1950, *Complete Poems.*

Fog
    This poem has often been called "imagistic," but Sandburg was not active
in the Imagist movement of Ezra Pound and Amy Lowell.

Pool
    A riddle poem: after cremation the gold fillings in the dead man's teeth
melt and form a little pool.

Cool Tombs
    1. *copperheads:* Northern sympathizers (sometimes saboteurs) with the Con-
federacy during the Civil War.
    2. *con men:* "confidential" men, i.e., swindlers; the Grant Administration
became notorious for corruption in both government and business.

When Death Came April Twelve 1945
    This poem was published in the *Woman's Home Companion,* June, 1945, and
first collected in *Complete Poems* (1950).

President Franklin Delano Roosevelt died shortly before the end of World War II.

11–12. *to the music ... ashes:* cf. *Book of Common Prayer*, First Anthem:

> We therefore commit his body to the ground; earth to earth,
> ashes to ashes, dust to dust; in sure and certain hope
> of the Resurrection to eternal life.

KARL SHAPIRO
b. 1913

Bibliography

Quesnel, Louise, and Webster, W. G. "A Bibliography of the Work of Karl Jay Shapiro, 1935–1949." Mimeographed. Baltimore: Enoch Pratt Free Library, 1950.

Major Writings

Person Place and Thing (1942)
V-Letter and Other Poems (1944)
Essay on Rime (1945)
Trial of a Poet and Other Poems (1947)
Poems, 1940–1953 (1953)
Beyond Criticism (1953, criticism)
Poems of a Jew (1958)
In Defense of Ignorance (1960, criticism)
The Bourgeois Poet (1964)

Criticism

Daiches, David. "The Poetry of Karl Shapiro," *Poetry*, LXVI (1945), 266–273.
Fussell, Edwin. "Karl Shapiro: The Paradox of Prose and Poetry," *West. Rev.*, XVIII (1954), 224–244.
Glicksberg, C.I. "Karl Shapiro and the Personal Accent," *Prairie Schooner*, XXII (1948), 44–52.
Kohler, Dayton. "Karl Shapiro: Poet in Uniform," *Coll. Eng.* VII (1946), 243–249.
O'Connor, W. V. "Shapiro on Rime," *Ken. Rev.*, VIII (1946), 113–122.
Seif, Morton. "Poet's Journey: The Struggle in the Soul of Karl Shapiro," *Menorah Journal*, XXXVII (1949), 51–58.

Comments on Poems

The texts of the poems in this anthology are from *Poems, 1940–1953*.

The Potomac
This poem, with an extra stanza, was included in *Person Place and Thing* under

the title "Alexandria" (that is, the city in Virginia just across the Potomac River from Washington, D.C.).

10. *Thomas:* Thomas Jefferson of Virginia, who died in 1826 at his home, Monticello, which may roughly be called "Georgian" in architecture.

11. *Arlington:* the National Cemetery, in northern Virginia across the Potomac from Washington, D. C. The Tomb of the Unknown Soldier, located in this cemetery, is kept under constant guard by single sentries.

Elegy for a Dead Soldier
    Discussed in Paul Engle, *Eng. Jour.*, XXXVIII (1949), 62–63.

22. *Paul:* the chaplain is reading from one of the epistles of Paul in the New Testament.

81–82. *on mourrait . . . industriels?:* (French) "Would one die for the industrialists?"

V-Letter
    During World War II American military men were permitted to write letters on a special form, a small single sheet stamped "V-Letter," which could be folded and sent without postage by air mail. "V" stood for victory.

The Sickness of Adam
    While Adam slept God removed one of his ribs and created Eve out of it. See Genesis 2 : 21–23.

W. D. SNODGRASS
b. 1926

Major Writings

Heart's Needle (1959)

Criticism

Farrelly, David. "Heart's Fling; the Poetry of W. D. Snodgrass," *Perspective*, XIII (1964), 185–199.
Hoffman, D. G. "Arrivals and Rebirths," *Sewanee Rev.*, LXVIII (1960), 122–123.
Lyttle, David. "Snodgrass Walking," *Approach*, 41 (1961), 13–16.
Monteiro, George. "Snodgrass Peoples His Universe," *Publications of the Bibliographical Society of America*, LVI (1962), 494–495.
Torchiana, D. T. "Heart's Needle: Snodgrass Strides Through the Universe," pp. 92–115 in Edward Hungerford (ed.), *Poets in Progress*. Evanston, Ill.: Northwestern University Press, 1962.

Comments on Poems

Returned to Frisco, 1946
    The title refers to the return of American servicemen from the Pacific after

World War II.

13. *Bay Bridge:* bridge across San Francisco Bay between San Francisco and Oakland.

26. *Alcatraz:* island in the Bay until recently used as a federal penitentiary.

April Inventory

32. *Whitehead:* Alfred North Whitehead (1861–1947), English mathematician and philosopher.

33. *Mahler:* Gustav Mahler (1860–1911), conductor and last great composer of the Romantic School of Vienna.

A Flat One

This poem has not been collected in a volume by Snodgrass. It first appeared in *The Quarterly Review of Literature*, 10 (1960), 145–148.

"Flat one" is medical slang for a corpse.

Discussed by W. D. Snodgrass in Paul Engle and Joseph Langland (eds.), *Poet's Choice* (Dial Press, 1962), pp. 247–248.

WALLACE STEVENS
1879–1955

Bibliography

Bryer, J. R., and Riddel, J. N. "A Checklist of Stevens Criticism," *Twentieth Century Literature*, VIII (1962–1963), 124–142.

Mitchell, R. S. "Wallace Stevens: A Checklist of Criticism," *Bulletin of Bibliography*, XXIII (1962), 208–211; XXIII (1963), 232–233.

Morse, S. F. *Wallace Stevens: A Preliminary Checklist of His Published Writings, 1898–1954.* New Haven, Conn.: Yale University Library, 1954.

Concordance

Walsh, T. F. (ed.), *Concordance to the Poetry of Wallace Stevens.* University Park, Pa.: Pennsylvania State University Press, 1963.

Major Writings

Harmonium (1923, enlarged ed., 1931)
Ideas of Order (1935)
Owl's Clover (1936)
The Man with the Blue Guitar and Other Poems (1937)
Parts of a World (1942)
Transport to Summer (1947)
The Auroras of Autumn (1950)
The Necessary Angel: Essays on Reality and the Imagination (1951)
Opus Posthumous (1957, S. F. Morse, ed.)

Standard Edition

The Collected Poems of Wallace Stevens. New York: Knopf, 1954.

Criticism

Benamou, Michel. "Wallace Stevens: Some Relations Between Poetry and Painting," *Comparative Literature*, XI (1959), 47–60.

Blackmur, R. P. *Form and Value in Modern Poetry*, pp. 183–223. New York: Anchor, 1957.

Borroff, Marie (ed.). *Wallace Stevens: A Collection of Critical Essays.* Englewood Cliffs, N.J.: Prentice-Hall, 1963.

Brown, Ashley, and Haller, R. S. (eds.). *The Achievement of Wallace Stevens.* Philadelphia: Lippincott, 1962.

Buttel, Robert. "Wallace Stevens at Harvard: Some Origins of His Theme and Style," *English Literary History*, XXIX (1962), 90–119.

Enck, J. J. *Wallace Stevens: Images and Judgments.* Carbondale, Ill.: Southern Illinois University Press, 1964.

Fuchs, Daniel. *The Comic Spirit of Wallace Stevens.* Durham, N. C.: Duke University Press, 1963.

Harvard Advocate, CXXVII (1940). Wallace Stevens number.

Jarrell, Randall. "Reflections on Wallace Stevens," pp. 121–134 in *Poetry and the Age.* New York: Vintage Books, 1955.

Kermode, Frank. *Wallace Stevens.* Edinburgh: Oliver & Boyd, 1961.

Moore, Marianne. *Predilections*, pp. 32–46. New York: Viking Press, 1955.

Morse, S. F. "Motive for Metaphor," *Origin*, II (1952), complete issue.

O'Connor, W. V. *The Shaping Spirit: A Study of Wallace Stevens.* Chicago: Henry Regnery, 1950.

Pack, Robert. *Wallace Stevens: An Approach to His Poetry and Thought.* New Brunswick, N.J.: Rutgers University Press, 1958.

Perspective, VII (1954). Wallace Stevens issue.

Tindall, W. Y. *Wallace Stevens.* Minneapolis: University of Minnesota Press, 1961.

Winters, Yvor. "Wallace Stevens, or The Hedonist's Progress," pp. 431–459 in *In Defense of Reason.* New York: Alan Swallow, 1947.

Comments on Poems

Domination of Black
    Discussed in Enck, *Wallace Stevens*, pp. 71–72; D. Pettit, *Eng. Jour.*, LI (1962), 346–348; W. J. Rooney, *Jour. Aesth. & Art Crit.*, XIII (1955), 511–514.

The Snow Man
    Discussed in Blackmur, *Form and Value in Modern Poetry*, pp. 200–201; Kermode, *Wallace Stevens*, pp. 34–35; Pack, *Wallace Stevens*, pp. 66–68; Tindall, *Wallace Stevens*, pp. 22–23; C. R. Wagner, *Accent*, XII (1952), 118; Yvor Winters, *In Defense of Reason*, pp. 126–127.

Le Monocle de Mon Oncle

The French title: "My Uncle's Monocle."

Discussed in Blackmur, *Form and Value in Modern Poetry*, pp. 191–192, 203–204; Donald Davie, *Twentieth Century*, CLIII (1953), 457, 462; Richard Ellmann, *Ken. Rev.*, XIX (1957), 97–99; Enck, *Wallace Stevens*, pp. 81–83; W. A. Fahey, *Explicator*, XV (1956), 16; Fuchs, *The Comic Spirit of Wallace Stevens*, pp. 25–26; R. M. Gay, *Explicator*, VI (1948), 27; Kermode, *Wallace Stevens*, pp. 43–45; Pack, *Wallace Stevens*, pp. 7–12; Tindall, *Wallace Stevens*, pp. 13–15.

22. *connaissance:* (French) "acquaintanceship."

27. *Utamaro's:* Kitagawa Utamaro (1753–1806), Japanese master of woodblock prints, particularly famous for his portraits of courtesans with elaborate coiffures.

29. *mountainous coiffures of Bath:* an exceptionally lofty style of hairdressing affected by English beauties of the mid-eighteenth century at Bath, a fashionable watering place. For a discussion of Stanza III, see E. R. Miner, *Explicator*, XIII (1955), 28.

66. *a theme for Hyacinth:* an expression of grief. In Greek mythology a flower is said to have sprung from the blood of the slain youth, Hyacinth, beloved of Apollo, on the petals of which were inscribed the letters AI or AIAI, expressing grief. See Moschus III, 6 and Ovid, *Metamorphoses* X, 211.

93. *Cupido:* Cupid.

A High-Toned Old Christian Woman

Discussed in Fuchs, *The Comic Spirit of Wallace Stevens*, pp. 79–80; W. V. O'Connor, *U. Kans. City Rev.*, XV (1948), 110; Winters, *In Defense of Reason*, pp. 434–435.

2. *nave:* in church architecture, the highest part of the structure, flanked by the aisle.

7. *peristyle:* a system of roof-supporting columns around a building or court.

8. *masque:* A festive dance or revel in which masks are worn.

The Emperor of Ice-Cream

Discussed in Blackmur, *Form and Value in Modern Poetry*, pp. 189–191; Elizabeth Drew and J. L. Sweeney, *Directions in Modern Poetry*. (W. W. Norton Co., 1940), pp. 227–231; Richard Ellmann, *Ken. Rev.*, XIX (1957), 92–95; Enck, *Wallace Stevens*, pp. 199–203; Max Herzberg and Wallace Stevens, *Explicator*, VII (1948), 18; Kenneth Lash and Robert Thackaberry, *Explicator*, VI (1948), 36; Elder Olson, *Coll. Eng.*, XVI (1955), 397–398.

Sunday Morning

Discussed in Blackmur, *Form and Value in Modern Poetry*, pp. 198–200, 202; J. V. Cunningham, *Poetry*, LXXV (1949), 149–165; Richard Ellmann, *Ken. Rev.*, XIX (1957), 95–97; Kermode, *Wallace Stevens*, pp. 41–43; Pack, *Wallace Stevens*, pp. 23–34; R. H. Pearce, pp. 114–115 in Borroff (ed.), *Wallace Stevens*; Tindall, *Wallace Stevens*, pp. 41–42; Winters, *In Defense of Reason*, pp. 431–434, 447–456.

100. *serafin:* serafim, members of an order of celestial beings.

Anecdote of the Jar

Discussed in G. W. Arms et al., *Explicator*, III (1944), 16; Howard Baker, *So. Rev.*, I (1935), 376–377; Tindall, *Wallace Stevens*, pp. 24–25; C. C. Walcutt, *Coll. Eng.*, (1953), 449–451; Winters, *In Defense of Reason*, pp. 435–437.

To the One of Fictive Music

Discussed in R. E. Amacher, *Explicator*, XI (1953), 43; Enck, *Wallace Stevens*, pp. 73–75; Kermode, *Wallace Stevens*, p. 38; J. N. Riddel, pp. 40–41 in Borroff (ed.), *Wallace Stevens*.

Peter Quince at the Clavier

In Shakespeare's *Midsummer Night's Dream*, Peter Quince is the director of the clownish interlude on the "most cruel death of Pyramus and Thisbe."

Discussed in W. S. Johnson, *Jour. Aesth. & Art Crit.*, XIII (1955), 501–503; W. V. O'Connor, *Sense and Sensibility in Modern Poetry* (University of Chicago Press, 1948), pp. 149–150; J. N. Riddel, *Coll. Eng.*, XXIII (1962), 307–309; F. H. Stocking, *Explicator*, V (1947), 47; M. J. Storm, *Explicator*, XIV (1955), 9; Tindall, *Wallace Stevens*, pp. 20–21.

9. *Susanna:* according to the History of Susanna, a book of the Apocrypha, two Hebrew elders attempted to seduce Susanna, the wife of Joachim, after watching her at her bath. When she brought charges against them, they countercharged that she had tried to seduce them. About to be executed, she was proved innocent by the prophet Daniel, and the elders were executed instead.

Thirteen Ways of Looking at a Blackbird

Discussed in Frank Doggett, *Eng. Jour.*, XLVIII (1959), 368; J. V. Hagopian, *American Notes and Queries*, I (1963), 84–85; W. R. Keast, *Chicago Review*, VIII (1954), 48–63; A. W. Levi, *Perspective*, VII (1954), 144–146; P. L. McNamara, *Coll. Eng.*, XXV (1964), 446–448.

25. *Haddam:* a town in Connecticut, southeast of Hartford.

Sea Surface Full of Clouds

Discussed in Blackmur, *Form and Value in Modern Poetry*, pp. 192–194; D. R. Ferry, *Explicator*, VI (1948), 56; A. W. Levi, *Perspective*, VII (1954), 141–142; John Pauker, *Furioso*, V (1950), 34–46; R. H. Pearce, pp. 113–114 in Borroff (ed.), *Wallace Stevens*; J. N. Riddel, *University of Texas Studies in English*, XXXVII (1958), 177–186; Tindall, *Wallace Stevens*, pp. 21–22.

12. *C'était ... âme:* (French) "It was my child, my darling, my soul."

30. *C'était ... or:* (French) "It was my heavenly brother, my life, my gold."

48. *Oh! ... amour:* (French) "Oh! It was my ecstasy and my love."

66. *C'était ... divine:* (French) "It was my faith, divine carelessness."

84. *C'était ... l'ignominie:* (French) "It was my bastard spirit, ignominy."

The Idea of Order at Key West

Discussed in Babette Deutsch, *Poetry in Our Time* (Holt, Rinehart and Winston, 1952), pp. 248–250; Frank Doggett, *Eng. Jour.*, XLVIII (1959), 370–371; Kermode, *Wallace Stevens*, pp. 57–58; L. L. Martz, p. 137 in Borroff (ed.), *Wallace Stevens*.

43. *Ramon Fernandez:* French philosophic literary critic (1894–1944). Wallace Stevens himself has said, "I used two every day names. As I might have expected, they turned out to be an actual name." Quoted in Kimon Friar and John Malcolm Brinnin (eds.), *Modern Poetry* (Appleton-Century-Crofts, 1951), p. 538.

Anglais Mort à Florence
   The French title: "Dead Englishman at Florence."
   Discussed in Kermode, *Wallace Stevens*, pp. 53–54.

A Postcard from the Volcano
   Discussed in Enck, *Wallace Stevens*, pp. 107–108.

Study of Two Pears
   1. *Opusculum paedagogum:* (Latin) "a little work of pedagogy."

The Glass of Water
   Discussed in W. G. French, *Explicator*, XIX (1961), 23; Fuchs, *The Comic Spirit of Wallace Stevens*, pp. 22–23; D. H. Owen, *Perspective*, VII (1954), 181–183; Sister Thérèse, *Explicator*, XXI (1963), 56.
   13. *metaphysica:* (Greek) "aspects after (or beyond) external nature."
   14. *Jocundus:* (Latin) "pleasant (or cheerful) one."

The Sense of the Sleight-of-Hand Man
   Discussed in Fuchs, *The Comic Spirit of Wallace Stevens*, pp. 85–86.

Asides on the Oboe
   Discussed in Kermode, *Wallace Stevens*, pp. 74–75; Pack, *Wallace Stevens*, pp. 150–151; Hi Simons, p. 48 in Borroff (ed.), *Wallace Stevens*.
   5. *the gods that Boucher killed:* perhaps an allusion to *The Loves of the Gods*, a classic of eighteenth-century French tapestry by François Boucher (1703–1770).

Credences of Summer
   Discussed in Enck, *Wallace Stevens*, pp. 175–177; Bernard Heringman, *Perspective*, VII (1954), 171–174; R. J. Mills, Jr., pp. 101–102 in Borroff (ed.), *Wallace Stevens*; Tindall, *Wallace Stevens*, pp. 43–45; H. H. Watts, *Ken. Rev.*, XIV (1952), 122–140.
   47. *Oley:* village in Bucks County, Pennsylvania, near Reading.
   129. *douceurs:* (French) "sweets" or "delights."
   130. *Tristesses:* (French) "sorrows."

To an Old Philosopher in Rome
   The "old philosopher" is George Santayana (1863–1952), Spanish-born philosopher and poet.
   Discussed in Enck, *Wallace Stevens*, pp. 31–32.
   21. *the moving nuns:* Santayana spent the last years of his life at the Convent of the Blue Nuns in Rome.

The Rock
   Discussed in R. J. Mills, Jr., pp. 106–109 in Borroff (ed.), *Wallace Stevens*.

The World as Meditation

The epigraph may be translated from the French: "I have spent too much time working on my violin and travelling. But the essential exercise of the composer—meditation—nothing has ever interrupted this in me ... I live a permanent dream, which stops neither night nor day." Georges Enesco (1881–1955), Rumanian violinist, composer and conductor, teacher of Yehudi Menuhin.

Discussed in L. L. Martz, pp. 133–134 in Borroff (ed.), *Wallace Stevens*.

As You Leave the Room

Discussed in Kermode, *Wallace Stevens*, pp. 18–19.

ALLEN TATE
b. 1899

Bibliography

Bradbury, J. M. "Selected Bibliography: III. Allen Tate," pp. 280–283 in *The Fugitives: A Critical Account*. Chapel Hill, N.C.: University of North Carolina Press, 1958.

Meiners, R. K. "Bibliography," pp. 207–214 in *The Last Alternatives: A Study of the Works of Allen Tate*. Denver: Alan Swallow, 1963.

Tate, Allen. "Bibliographical Note," pp. 112–113 in *Poems: 1920–1945: A Selection*. London: Eyre and Spottiswoode, 1947.

Thorp, Willard. "Allen Tate: A Checklist," *Princeton University Library Chronicle*, III (1942), 85–98.

Major Writings

Mr. Pope and Other Poems (1928)
Poems, 1928–1931 (1932)
The Mediterranean and Other Poems (1936)
Selected Poems (1937)
The Winter Sea (1944)
Poems, 1922–1947 (1948)
Collected Essays (1959)
Poems (1961)

Criticism

Beatty, R. C. "Allen Tate as a Man of Letters," *So. Atl. Quart.*, XLVII (1948), 226–241.

Berland, Alwyn. "Violence in the Poetry of Allen Tate," *Accent*, XI (1951), 161–171.

Bradbury, J. M. "Tate as Poet," pp. 137–174 in *The Fugitives: A Critical Account*. Chapel Hill, N.C.: University of North Carolina Press, 1958.

Feder, Lillian, "Allen Tate's Use of Classical Literature," *Centennial Review of Arts and Science* (Michigan State University), IV (1960) 89–114.

Foster, R. J. "Allen Tate: From the Old South to Catholic Orthodoxy," pp. 107–129 in *The New Romantics*. Bloomington, Ind.: Indiana University Press, 1962.

Hemphill, G. T. *Allen Tate*. Minneapolis, Minn.: University of Minnesota Press, 1964.

Koch, Vivienne. "The Poetry of Allen Tate," *Ken. Rev.*, XI (1949), 355–378.

Meiners, R. K. *The Last Alternatives: A Study of the Works of Allen Tate*. Denver: Alan Swallow, 1963.

Nemerov, Howard. "The Current of the Frozen Streams," pp. 101–111 in *Poetry and Fiction: Essays*. New Brunswick, N.J.: Rutgers University Press, 1963.

Schwartz, Delmore. "The Poetry of Allen Tate," *So. Rev.*, V (1940) 419–438.

Sewanee Review, LXVII (1959), 527–631. "Homage to Allen Tate."

Squires, Radcliffe. "Mr. Tate: Whose Wreath Should Be a Moral," pp. 257–272 in R. M. Ludwig (ed.), *Aspects of American Poetry*. Columbus, Ohio: Ohio State University Press, 1962.

Vivas, Eliseo. "Allen Tate as Man of Letters," pp. 267–281 in *Creation and Discovery*. New York: The Noonday Press, 1955.

Comments on Poems

The texts are taken from Allen Tate, *Poems* (Alan Swallow, 1961).

Mr. Pope

Discussed in M. M. Blum, *Mod. Lang. Notes*, LXXIV (1959), 706–708; Bradbury, *The Fugitives*, pp. 62–63; J. E. Tobin, *Explicator*, XV (1957), 35.

4. *Pope's tight back:* Pope had a spinal deformity.

9. *like a snake:* in *An Essay on Criticism*, Part II, lines 356–357, Pope wrote of inferior versifiers: "A needless Alexandrine ends the Song, / That like a wounded Snake, drags its slow Length along."

The Subway

Discussed in Bradbury, *The Fugitives*, p. 61; Babette Deutsch, *Poetry in Our Time* (Holt, Rinehart and Winston, 1952), pp. 198–199; Joe Horrell, *So. Rev.*, VII (1941), 119–122; J. C. Ransom, *The New Criticism* (New Directions, 1941), pp. 222–225; L. D. Rubin, Jr., *Am. Quart.*, IX (1957), 66–67; Yvor Winters, *In Defense of Reason* (Alan Swallow, 1960), pp. 19–20.

Ode to the Confederate Dead

The fullest discussion of this poem is by Tate himself in "Narcissus as Narcissus," pp. 248–262 in *Collected Essays*.

Also discussed in Cleanth Brooks, *Modern Poetry and the Tradition* (University of North Carolina Press, 1939), pp. 95–96; Denis Donoghue, *Stud. Phil.*, XLIV (1955), 449–450; F. J. Hoffman, *The Twenties* (Viking Press, 1955), pp. 151–153; Vivienne Koch, pp. 24–26 in B. Rajan (ed.), *Modern American Poetry* (Roy Publishers, 1952); L. D. Rubin, Jr., *Am. Quart.*, IX (1957), 70–71; Margaret Schlauch, *Modern English and American Poetry* (C. A. Watts & Co., 1956), pp.

97–98; Yvor Winters, *New Republic*, LVI (October 17, 1928), 255–256; M. D. Zabel, *Poetry*, XXXIII (1929), 282.

33. *Zeno and Parmenides:* Greek philosophers of the fifth century B.C.

47. *Stonewall:* nickname of Confederate General Thomas Jonathan Jackson (1824–1863), earned at the First Battle of Bull Run, July 21, 1861. *the sunken fields of hemp:* hemp fields in the Blue Grass region of Kentucky which fell into neglect during the Civil War (according to Allen Tate in conversation with J. K. Robinson, November 5, 1964).

48. *Shiloh:* a battle fought to a draw April 6 and 7, 1862, at Shiloh, Tennessee. *Antietam:* the bloodiest battle of the Civil War, fought near Sharpsburg, Maryland, September 17, 1862. *Malvern Hill:* the last of the Seven Days' battles, fought July 1, 1862, above the James River, was a great triumph for Union artillery.

The Cross

Discussed in Sister Mary Bernetta, *Renascence*, III (1951), 118; Frederick Morgan, *Hud. Rev.*, I (1948), 263–264; C. C. Walcutt, *Explicator*, VI (1948), 41.

Sonnets at Christmas (1934)

Discussed in L. D. Rubin, Jr., pp. 238–239 in L. D. Rubin, Jr., and R. D. Jacobs (eds.), *South* (Doubleday, 1961); Delmore Schwartz, *So. Rev.*, V (1940), 425–427.

The Mediterranean

The epigraph is a variation on *Quem das finem, rex magne, laborum* (Virgil, *Aeneid* I, 241). Venus says to Jupiter, "What limit to their labors do you give, great king?"

Discussed in R. K. Meiners, *U. Kans. City Rev.*, XXVII (1960), 155–159; L. D. Rubin, Jr., *Am. Quart.*, IX (1957), 64–65.

12. *plates Aeneas bore:* an allusion to Virgil, *Aeneid* VII, 116. The eating of plates fulfilled the prophecy that when Aeneas and his fellows ate their tables they would know that they had reached their destination.

32. *the Gates of Hercules:* the Straits of Gibraltar.

Aeneas at Washington

Discussed in L. D. Rubin, Jr., pp. 232–233 in L. D. Rubin, Jr., and R. D. Jacobs (eds.), *South* (Doubleday, 1961).

Aeneas was the legendary Trojan hero who survived the fall of Troy and journeyed to Italy to found a new nation. Aeneas' description of the fall of Troy appears in Virgil, *Aeneid*, Book II.

1–4. *I myself saw ... fires:* these lines are an almost literal translation of Virgil, *Aeneid* II, 499–502.

2. *Neoptolemus:* son of Achilles, brutal slayer of King Priam of Troy after the fall of the city. *the black Atridae:* the sons of Atreus, Agamemnon and Menelaus, Greek chieftains.

3. *Hecuba:* Priam's queen.

12. *The old man my father:* Aeneas' father, Anchises.

32. *the great Dome:* the dome of the Capitol, Washington, D.C.

36. *ninth buried city:* nine cities of Troy were built one above the other. The Troy of the war was the sixth.

Pastoral

16. *"time is love's fool"*: a variation on "Love's not time's fool." Shakespeare, Sonnet 116, l. 9.

Seasons of the Soul

John Peale Bishop: American poet and essayist, often grouped with Tate and Ransom as a poet of the Southern Renaissance.

The epigraph is from Dante, *Inferno*, Canto XIII, 31–33, and is the speech of the suicide, Pier delle Vigne, in the second ring of the seventh circle. The speech runs: "Then I reached forward with my hand a little and broke off a little branch from a big thorn, and the trunk cried, 'Why do you rend me?'"

Discussed in Beatty, *So. Atl. Quart.*, XLVII (1948), 233–234; Berland, *Accent*, XI (1951), 165–171; Bradbury, *The Fugitives*, pp. 162–165; Cleanth Brooks, *Poetry*, LXVI (1945), 324–329; Babette Deutsch, *Poetry in Our Time* (Holt, Rinehart and Winston, 1952), pp. 199–202; Vivienne Koch, pp. 28–30 in B. Rajan (ed.), *Modern American Poetry* (Roy Publishers, 1952); R. K. Meiners, *Sewanee Rev.*, LXX (1962), 34–80; L. D. Rubin, Jr., pp. 239–243 in L. D. Rubin, Jr., and R. D. Jacobs (eds.), *South* (Doubleday, 1961).

22. *at the June solstice:* a reference to the conquest by German mechanized forces of France in June, 1940.

38. *Balaam and his ass:* in Numbers 22 the ass saw the Angel of God before his master, Balaam, did.

51–60. This is close to a literal translation of Dante, *Inferno*, Canto XII, 77–79.

101–110. This stanza recalls the moment in Dante, *Inferno*, Canto XV, 20–21, when the dead stare at Dante as "an aged tailor does at the eye of his needle."

111–120. These lines echo Sir Thomas Wyatt's lyric, "They Flee from Me."

127. *the drying God above:* probably Christ.

130. *The living wound of love:* echoes *aeterno . . . vulnere amoris*, referring to a description of the conquest of Mars by Venus, in Lucretius' Latin poem *De Rerum Natura*, Book I, l. 34.

172–175. *"We are the men . . . suicide":* again, as in the epigraph, an echo of Dante, *Inferno*, Canto XV.

214. *Platonic cave:* see Plato, *Republic*, Book VII, for the Allegory of the Cave, the prison of the senses.

216. *tired Sisyphus:* in Greek mythology, Sisyphus was condemned after death to the eternal punishment of pushing to the top of a hill a large stone which kept rolling back down on him.

225. *At the window:* in Confessions, Book IX, 23, St. Augustine (354–430), Bishop of Hippo, writes that shortly before his mother, St. Monica, died, "she and I stood alone, leaning in a certain window. . . . We were discoursing there together, alone, very sweetly . . ." *The Confessions of St. Augustine*, translated by E. B. Pusey (J. M. Dent, 1907), p. 194.

The Swimmers

Montgomery County is the county just east of Tate's native county, Clark.

Discussed in Bradbury, *The Fugitives*, pp. 169–170; L. D. Rubin, Jr., pp. 243–244 in L. D. Rubin, Jr., and R. D. Jacobs (eds.), *South* (Doubleday, 1961).

6. *Soft as Nausicaä's palm:* in Homer, *Odyssey* VI, Nausicaä, daughter of King Alcinous of the Phaecians, is several times described as "Nausicaä of the white arms."

EDWARD TAYLOR
c. 1642–1729

Bibliography

Hoffman, C. A. "Edward Taylor: A Selected Bibliography," *Bulletin of Bibliography*, XXIII (1961), 85–87.
Stanford, D. E. (ed.). Appendixes 1 and 2, pp. 499–521 in *The Poems of Edward Taylor*. New Haven, Conn.: Yale University Press, 1960.

Major Writings

Preparatory Meditations before my Approach to the Lords Supper. Chiefly upon the Doctrin preached upon the Day of administration (1939, T. H. Johnson, ed.; 1960, D. E. Stanford, ed.). Johnson gives title as *Sacramental Meditations*.
Gods Determinations touching his Elect: and The Elects Combat in their Conversion, and Coming up to God in Christ together with the Comfortable Effects thereof (1939, T. H. Johnson, ed.; 1960, D. E. Stanford, ed.).

Standard Editions

Johnson, T. H. (ed.). *The Poetical Works of Edward Taylor*. New York: Rockland Editions, 1939. Reissued, Princeton University Press, 1943.
Stanford, D. E. (ed.). *The Poems of Edward Taylor*. New Haven, Conn.: Yale University Press, 1960.

Biography

Grabo, N. S. "The Active Life," pp. 17–39 in *Edward Taylor*. New York: Twayne Publishers, 1961.
Stanford, D. E. (ed.). "Biography," pp. xxxix–xlviii in *The Poems of Edward Taylor*. New Haven, Conn.: Yale University Press, 1960.

Criticism

Black, Mindele. "Edward Taylor: Heavens Sugar Cake," *New Eng. Quart.*, XXIX (1956), 159–181.
Blau, Herbert. "Heaven's Sugar Cake: Theology and Imagery in the Poetry of Edward Taylor," *New Eng. Quart.*, XXVI (1953), 337–360.
Brown, W. C. "Edward Taylor: An American 'Metaphysical,'" *Am. Lit.*, XVI (1944), 186–197.
Grabo, N. S. *Edward Taylor*. New York: Twayne Publishers, 1961.

Johnson, T. H. "Edward Taylor: A Puritan 'Sacred Poet,'" *New Eng. Quart.*, X (1937), 290–322.

Lind, S. E. "Edward Taylor: A Revaluation," *New Eng. Quart.*, XXI (1948), 518–530.

Martz, L. L. "Foreword," pp. xiii–xxxvii in D. E. Stanford (ed.), *The Poems of Edward Taylor*. New Haven, Conn.: Yale University Press, 1960.

Murdock, K. B. "'A Little Recreation of Poetry,'" pp. 137–172 in *Literature & Theology in Colonial New England*. Cambridge, Mass.: Harvard University Press, 1949.

Pearce, R. H. "Taylor," pp. 42–54 in *The Continuity of American Poetry*. Princeton, N.J.: Princeton University Press, 1961.

Warren, Austin. "Edward Taylor's Poetry: Colonial Baroque," *Ken. Rev.*, III (1941), 355–371. Reprinted as "Edward Taylor," pp. 1–18 in *Rage for Order: Essays in Criticism*. Chicago: University of Chicago Press, 1948.

Weathers, W. T. "Edward Taylor and the Cambridge Platonists," *Am. Lit.*, XXVI (1954), 1–31.

Weathers, W. T. "Edward Taylor, Hellenistic Puritan," *Am. Lit.*, XVIII (1946), 18–26.

Wright, Nathalia. "The Morality Tradition in the Poetry of Edward Taylor," *Am. Lit.*, XVIII (1946), 1–18.

Comments on Poems

Taylor refrained from publishing any of his poems and handed them down to his heirs with the injunction that they be kept from publication. Thomas H. Johnson was the first scholar to examine the manuscript of Taylor's "Poetical Works," which had lain in the Yale University Library for years after being deposited there by a nineteenth-century descendant of the poet. The Library was not required to enforce the injunction against publication. Johnson published a selection of the poems in the *New England Quarterly* for June, 1937, and brought out a volume of them, *The Poetical Works of Edward Taylor*, in 1939. A more inclusive edition, *The Poems of Edward Taylor*, was prepared by Donald E. Stanford and published in 1960.

With two exceptions the texts of the Taylor poems printed here are those given by Johnson in the June, 1937, *New England Quarterly* and in his *The Poetical Works of Edward Taylor*. The text of "Meditation 40" is from Johnson's "Some Edward Taylor Gleanings," *New Eng. Quart.*, XVI (1943), 280–296, while the text of "Meditation 68A, Second Series" is from Stanford's *The Poems of Edward Taylor*. The Johnson and Stanford texts have been compared for variations. Generally the two texts differ only in that in the former punctuation has been "very sparingly" modernized. The few instances of disagreement between Stanford and Johnson in the transcription of a word from the Yale manuscript have been listed in the notes on individual poems.

Prologue

In the manuscript of Taylor's "Poetical Works" this poem appears between *Gods Determinations* and *Preparatory Meditations*. Johnson prints it immediately following "The Preface" to *Gods Determinations*, while Stanford believes it to be intended as an introduction to the *Meditations*.

The *Preparatory Meditations* (originally called *Sacramental Meditations* by Johnson) were written in two succeeding series over the period from 1682 to 1725 as Taylor's private poetic commentaries on the sermons to be preached on the Sundays when he administered the sacrament of the Lord's Supper. For a general discussion of them see Grabo, *Edward Taylor*, pp. 136–159; Johnson, *The Poetical Works of Edward Taylor*, pp. 24–28; Martz, "Foreword," pp. xiii–xxxvii in Stanford (ed.), *The Poems of Edward Taylor*.

Discussed in Brown, *Am. Lit.*, XVI (1944), 195–196.

1. *of Earth:* Stanford reads "*of Dust.*"

6. *glore:* glory.

Meditation 1

Unlike the other Meditations this one is headed in the manuscript by no Biblical epigraph. Taylor dated the poem July 23, 1682.

Discussed in Brown, *Am. Lit.*, XVI (1944), 194–195.

The Reflexion

This unnumbered Meditation appears in the manuscript after Meditation 4 and draws its inspiration from the same text in The Song of Solomon (Canticles). It is not dated, but Meditation 4 is dated April 22, 1683.

Discussed in Blau, *New Eng. Quart.*, XXVI (1953), 345–346; John Clendenning, *Am. Quart.*, XVI (1964), 203–210; Grabo, *Edward Taylor*, pp. 157–158; Warren, *Ken. Rev.*, III (1941), 368–370 (*Rage for Order*, pp. 16–17).

4. *Trencher:* platter or plate, usually of wood, for holding food.

35. *Sprindge:* sprinkle, scatter.

Meditation 6

This poem, headed in the manuscript "Another Meditation at the same time," follows Meditation 5, which is dated September 2, 1683.

Discussed in N. S. Grabo, *Explicator*, XVIII (1960), 40; A. M. McNamara, *Explicator*, XVII (1958), 3; Pearce, *The Continuity of American Poetry*, pp. 47–48.

5. *Touchstone:* "A very smooth, fine-grained, black or dark-coloured variety of quartz or jasper . . ., used for testing the quality of gold and silver alloys by the colour of the streak produced by rubbing them upon it. . . ." [*New English Dictionary*].

12. *Angell:* a pun on the double meaning of "angel" as a supernatural being and as the English gold coin stamped with the figure of the Archangel Michael slaying the dragon.

13. *Plate:* coin. A "plate" was a sixteenth-century Spanish silver piece.

Meditation 8

Taylor dated this poem June 8, 1684.

Discussed in Pearce, *The Continuity of American Poetry*, pp. 52–53; Warren, *Ken. Rev.*, III (1941), 365–368 (*Rage for Order*, pp. 12–16).

1. *ken[n]ing:* knowing, recognizing.

7. *Bird of Paradise:* the soul. Paradise refers both to the Garden of Eden and to heaven.

8. *tweedle:* sing, warble.

19. *Gods Tender Bowells:* in Taylor's day the bowels were regarded as the seat of compassion.

24. *in:* Stanford reads "on."

Meditation 20

Taylor dated this poem January 9, 1686.

Discussed in Blau, *New Eng. Quart.*, XXVI (1953), 349–350.

11. *Prince o' th' Aire:* Satan.

13–18. *He did not . . . Throne:* Stanford appropriately notes that the image of the ladder in this stanza is inconsistent with that of the chariot in the preceding and following stanzas.

14. *Elias:* Elijah. See 2 Kings 2 : 11.

15. *Jasper:* the precious stone referred to in Revelation 21 : 18–19.

17. *had:* Stanford reads "trod."

29–30. *Lift up . . . Enter in:* see Psalms 24 : 7.

Meditation 29

Taylor dated this poem November 11, 1688. For the basic figure of grafting see Romans 11 : 16–24.

Discussed in Johannes Hedberg, *Moderna Språk*, LIV (1960), 253–266; Martz, "Foreword," pp. xxxii–xxxiv in Stanford (ed.), *The Poems of Edward Taylor.*

2. *Wits . . . Edens Parke:* mind ruminating over the Garden of Eden.

7–10. *Thou! . . . by Vice:* see John 15 : 5–6.

10. *Chat:* twig. *Writh:* wrenched, twisted.

15. *Nymps:* imps. *Dog's sticks:* sticks for beating dogs. *ding:* beat, strike.

16. *its:* Stanford reads "it's."

22. *Doove:* dove; term of endearment used as in The Song of Solomon 6 : 9.

36. *gamut:* the lowest note on the medieval musical scale; or the major scale itself.

Meditation 38

Taylor dated this poem July 6, 1690.

Discussed in Murdock, *Literature & Theology*, p. 166.

2. *Line:* rule, precept.

14. *Colourings:* putting a good appearance on something in actuality bad.

20. *Regesterer:* court recorder, registrar.

21. *sergeants:* sergeants-at-law, formerly a class of British barristers of high rank in the King's courts.

22. *Evidence:* witnesses.

29. *Carry:* uphold, maintain.

34. *Casts:* defeats.

36. *Sub Forma Pauperis:* (Latin) "under the form of a poor man," hence relieved from costs.

39. *Hit:* Stanford reads "hint."

Meditation 40

Taylor dated this poem February, 1691. The refrain "Was ever Heart like mine?" may echo that in "The Sacrifice" by the English Metaphysical poet George Herbert (1593–1633): "Was ever grief like mine?"

6. *Civit-Box:* civet (perfume) container.

12. *At Nine Pins . . . Fox and Geese:* popular games in England.

16. *Consults:* consultations.

18. *Fuddling Schoole:* a school for befuddling the student.

21. *Play Barlybreaks . . . couple in Hell:* Barly-break is "An old country game . . . originally played by six persons (three of each sex) in couples; one couple, being left in a middle den termed 'hell,' had to catch the others, who were allowed to separate or 'break' when hard pressed, and thus to change partners, but had when caught to take their turn as catchers." [*New English Dictionary*].

22. *Cudgells, Kit-Cat:* field games.

22–24. *Cards . . . One-and-thirty:* except for dice, all card games.

31. *serpents head:* head of Satan. *mall:* maul; beat, strike.

37. *sense:* spiritual sense.

39. *steele:* steel; hardness, lack of feeling.

43. *declare:* Stanford places a period after this word.

49. *down:* Stanford reads "dawns."

54. *jetting:* swaggering.

55. *Anakims:* giant inhabitants of Canaan crushed by the Israelites under Joshua's leadership. See Joshua 11 : 21–22.

56. *Bucking-tub:* tub for washing clothes in lye or soapsuds.

Meditation 68A

Taylor dated this poem December 16, 1705. The First Series of Meditations are dated from July 23, 1682 to February 26, 1693. The Second Series are dated from May, 1693 to October, 1725.

19. *Dozde wood:* rotting wood which gives off phosphorescent light at night.

28. *Shew:* show.

33. *linde:* lined.

The Preface

Gods Determinations, possibly written around 1685, is a series of lyrics organized into a structure that combines elements of the medieval morality play and meditative poetry. After "The Preface," which contrasts God's creative power and the Fall of Man, God's Mercy debates with His Justice, and the souls of the Elect are invited to eternal bliss through God's Grace. In the main body of the work Satan attacks the souls with threats and arguments, while Christ defends and encourages them. A Saint, one of the Elect, then refutes Satan's arguments, and in the concluding six poems of the work the Soul, representing all of the Elect, rejoices in church-fellowship and rides to glory in "Christs Coach." The two selections here printed in addition to "The Preface" are the third from final and final lyrics. For discussions of *Gods Determinations* as a whole, see Grabo, *Edward Taylor*, pp. 159–168; Johnson, *The Poetical Works of Edward Taylor*, pp. 19–24; Murdock, *Literature & Theology*, pp. 159–163; Pearce, *The Continuity of American Poetry*, pp. 49–52; Warren, *Ken. Rev.*, III (1941), 362–365 (*Rage for Order*, pp. 8–12); Weathers, *Am. Lit.*, XXVI (1954), 13–24; Wright, *Am. Lit.*, XVIII (1946), 1–17. Taylor's Calvinist theology is discussed in Grabo, *Edward Taylor*, pp. 40–83;

Johnson, *The Poetical Works of Edward Taylor*, pp. 181–187 ("Glossary");
Stanford, *The Poems of Edward Taylor*, pp. xlix-liv.

Discussed in Grabo, *Edward Taylor*, pp. 45–46; W. R. Manierre II, *Coll.
Eng.*, XXIII (1962), 296–298; Murdock, *Literature & Theology*, pp. 170–172.

3. *Lath:* lathe; that is, a potter's lathe or wheel.

4. *riggalld:* grooved.

10. *Smaragdine:* the color emerald.

11. *Selvedge:* the woven edge of cloth that prevents unraveling.

12. *Quilt Ball:* probably a ball covered with variegated cloth.

30. *Squitchen:* Johnson suggests that this may be a dialect form meaning "a switch or stick."

35. *fet:* fetched.

39. *is:* Stanford reads "then."

The Glory of and Grace in the Church Set Out

Discussed in G. Giovannini, *Explicator*, VI (1948), 26.

The Joy of Church Fellowship Rightly Attended

4. *Encoacht:* Johnson reads "Encroacht," but Stanford's reading "Encoacht" would certainly seem to give Taylor's intended meaning.

An Address to the Soul Occasioned by a Rain

Johnson first printed this poem in *The Poetical Works of Edward Taylor*, reconstructing the present title from the partially obliterated title of the manuscript. Stanford reconstructs the title as "[When] Let by rain," "Let" meaning "hindered." Johnson dates this and the following four poems as having been composed in the 1680's.

Discussed in Johnson, *The Poetical Works of Edward Taylor*, p. 194; Weathers, *Am. Lit.*, XVIII (1946), 24–25; *Am. Lit.*, XXVI (1954), 11–12.

1. *Flippering:* perhaps "fluttering" or "swinging." Taylor appears to have invented this word.

2. *Nippers:* Weathers argues that this means a candle snuffer, the "Flippering Soule" being likened to a flickering candle flame. Considering the figure of the blacksmith's shop in the last two stanzas, it seems more likely that the nippers are the blacksmith's pincers. Gripped by these, the soul cannot act, but is instead acted upon by the "Hammer," which shapes it and strikes sparks from it.

11. *surplic'de see:* Stanford reads "surplice, see."

15. *Crabtree Cask:* cask made from wood of the crabapple tree.

16. *Verjuc'te:* sour, like the tart, sour juice of crabapples.

Upon a Spider Catching a Fly

8. *whorle:* whorl, the fly wheel on the spindle of a spinning wheel. *no[t hasp]:* Stanford reads "not clasp."

18. *froppish:* peevish. *aspish:* Stanford reads "waspish."

26–27. *This goes . . . doth call:* the fly ("This") fails because, unlike the wasp, it is not endowed by nature with a means of self-defense.

31. *Frey:* fray, fight.

49. *Yea:* Stanford reads "And."

Huswifery

The basic image, developed consistently throughout the poem, is of the making of cloth.

Discussed in *Times Lit. Sup.* (November 6, 1959), xiv. (Reprinted pp. 24–25 in *The American Imagination* [Atheneum Publishers, 1960].)

2. *Distaff:* that part of a spinning wheel which holds raw flax or wool.

3. *Flyers:* arms of a spinning wheel that twist the yarn.

8. *quills:* spools.

10. *Fulling Mills:* mills for cleaning cloth.

12. *pinkt:* adorned. *Varnish't:* glossy.

Upon Wedlock and Death of Children

This poem was probably occasioned by the death, on August 22, 1682, of Taylor's daughter Abigail. The four children alluded to in the poem were by his first wife, Elizabeth Fitch, who bore him eight children in all before her death in 1689. Since the fifth child (born January 17, 1684) is not mentioned, Stanford dates the writing of this poem as probably late 1682 or 1683.

Discussed in Grabo, *Edward Taylor*, pp. 125–128.

5–6. *Its Weddens Knot . . . divide:* since the Gordian Knot could not be untied, Alexander the Great cut it with his sword.

14. *a manly flower:* Samuel, born 1675.

16. *another Flowre:* Elizabeth, born 1676, died 1677 (see ll. 19–20).

32. *another manly flower:* James, born 1678.

33. *another, sweet:* Abigail, born 1681, died 1682.

The Ebb and Flow

Discussed in R. J. Jordan, *Explicator*, XX (1962), 67.

7. *Censar:* censer, thurible.

14. *Ignis Fatuus:* (Latin) "foolish fire"; will-o'-the-wisp.

HENRY DAVID THOREAU
1817–1862

Bibliography

Allen, F. H. *A Bibliography of Henry David Thoreau.* Boston: Houghton Mifflin and Co., 1908.

Harding, Walter. *A Thoreau Handbook.* New York: New York University Press, 1959.

Leary, Lewis. "Thoreau," pp. 153–206 in Floyd Stovall (ed.), *Eight American Authors: A Review of Research and Criticism.* New York: The Modern Language Association of America, 1956. Mathews, J. C., "Thoreau," pp. 434–438 of "Bibliographical Supplement" in paperback reissue by W. W. Norton Co. (New York, 1963).

Wade, J. S. "A Contribution to a Bibliography from 1909 to 1936 of Henry David Thoreau," *Journal of the New York Entomological Society*, XLVII (1939) 163–203.

White, William. *A Henry David Thoreau Bibliography 1908–1937*. Boston: F. W. Faxon Co., 1939.

Major Writings

A Week on the Concord and Merrimack Rivers (1849)
Walden; or, Life in the Woods (1854)
Excursions (1863, S. E. Thoreau and R. W. Emerson, eds.)
The Maine Woods (1864, S. E. Thoreau and W. E. Channing, eds.)
Cape Cod (1865, S. E. Thoreau and W. E. Channing, eds.)
A Yankee in Canada, with Anti-Slavery and Reform Papers (1866, W. E. Channing and S. E. Thoreau, eds.)
Poems of Nature (1895, H. S. Salt and F. B. Sanborn, eds.)
Journal (1906, Bradford Torrey and F. H. Allen, eds.)
The Correspondence of Henry David Thoreau (1958, Walter Harding and Carl Bode, eds.)

Standard Editions

Bode, Carl (ed.). *Collected Poems of Henry Thoreau*, Enlarged Edition. Baltimore, Md.: The Johns Hopkins Press, 1964.
Scudder, H. E.; Sanborn, F. B. ; Torrey, Bradford; and Allen, F. H. (eds.). *The Writings of Henry David Thoreau*, Manuscript and Walden Editions, 20 Vols. Boston: Houghton Mifflin and Co., 1906. *Poems*, Vol. V, pp. 393–419.

Biography

Canby, H. S. *Thoreau*. Boston: Houghton Mifflin and Co., 1939.
Salt, H. S. *Life of Henry David Thoreau*, rev. ed. London: Walter Scott, 1896.

Criticism

Atkinson, J. B. *Henry Thoreau: The Cosmic Yankee*. New York: Alfred A. Knopf, 1927.
Benton, Joel. "The Poetry of Thoreau," *Lippincott's Monthly Magazine*, XXXVII (1886), 491–500.
Cook, R. L. *Passage to Walden*. Boston: Houghton Mifflin and Co., 1949.
Foerster, Norman. "Thoreau," pp. 69–142 in *Nature in American Literature: Studies in the Modern View of Nature*. New York: The Macmillan Co., 1923.
Foerster, Norman. "Thoreau as Artist," *Sewanee Rev.*, XXIX (1921), 2–13.
Harding, Walter (ed.). *Thoreau: A Century of Criticism*. Dallas, Tex.: Southern Methodist University Press, 1954.
Krutch, J. W. *Henry David Thoreau*. New York: William Sloane Associates, 1948.
Lorch, F. W. "Thoreau and the Organic Principle in Poetry," *PMLA*, LIII (1938), 286–302.

Matthiessen, F. O. "From Emerson to Thoreau," pp. 3–175 in *American Renaissance: Art and Expression in the Age of Emerson and Whitman*. New York: Oxford University Press, 1941.

Metzger, C. R. "Thoreau's Poetics," pp. 19–27 in *Thoreau and Whitman: A Study of Their Esthetics*. Seattle, Wash.: University of Washington Press, 1961.

Paul, Sherman. *The Shores of America: Thoreau's Inward Exploration*. Urbana, Ill.: University of Illinois Press, 1958.

Seybold, Ethel. *Thoreau: The Quest and the Classics*. New Haven, Conn.: Yale University Press, 1951.

Van Doren, Mark. *Henry David Thoreau: A Critical Study*. Boston: Houghton Mifflin and Co., 1916. Republished, New York: Russell & Russell, 1961.

Wells, H. W. "An Evaluation of Thoreau's Poetry," *Am. Lit.*, XVI (1944), 99–109.

Comments on Poems

The text and order of the following poems by Thoreau are those established by Carl Bode in *Collected Poems of Henry Thoreau*.

Within the Circuit of This Plodding Life
First published without title in *The Dial*, III (July, 1842), 19–20.
16. *Johnswort:* Saint-John's-wort, a field weed.
26. *fieldfare:* the American Robin.

Great God, I Ask Thee for No Meaner Pelf
First published without title in *The Dial*, III (July, 1842), 79–80 in an article by Ralph Waldo Emerson entitled "Prayers."

Light-Winged Smoke, Icarian Bird
First published with the title "Smoke" in *The Dial*, III (April, 1843), 505–506, where it and "Haze" ("Woof of the Sun, Ethereal Gauze") are printed under the greater title "Orphics." Reprinted in *Walden*, Chapter XIII, "House-Warming."
Discussed in Matthiessen, *American Renaissance*, pp. 165–166; Delmer Rodabaugh, *Explicator*, XVII (1959), 47.

Though All the Fates Should Prove Unkind
First printed in *A Week on the Concord and Merrimack Rivers*, "Monday" chapter.

Woof of the Sun, Ethereal Gauze
First published with the title "Haze" in *The Dial*, III (April, 1843), 506, where it and "Smoke" ("Light-Winged Smoke, Icarian Bird") are printed under the greater title "Orphics." Reprinted in *A Week on the Concord and Merrimack Rivers*, "Tuesday" chapter.

Lately, Alas, I Knew a Gentle Boy
First published with the title "Sympathy" in *The Dial*, I (July, 1840), 71–72. Reprinted in *A Week on the Concord and Merrimack Rivers*, "Wednesday" chapter.

The boy of the title was Edmund Quincy Sewall (1828–1908), brother of the Ellen Sewall with whom both Henry and his brother John fell in love. Together with his mother Edmund had visited boarders in the Thoreau household for a week during June, 1839, and in the following March he returned to Concord for several weeks to attend John and Henry's school. See Clayton Hoagland, "The Diary of Thoreau's 'Gentle Boy,'" *New Eng. Quart.*, XXVIII (1955), 473–489.

10. *the House of Fame*: title of a poem by Chaucer.

The Inward Morning

First published in *The Dial*, III (October, 1842), 198–199. Reprinted in *A Week on the Concord and Merrimack Rivers*, "Wednesday" chapter.

My Books I'd Fain Cast Off, I Cannot Read

First published with the title "The Summer Rain" in *The Dial*, III (October, 1842), 224–225. Reprinted in *A Week on the Concord and Merrimack Rivers*, "Thursday" chapter.

11–16. *If juster battles . . . against the host*: Cf. Thoreau's description of the battle between the red and the black ants in *Walden*, Chapter XII, "Brute Neighbors."

I Am a Parcel of Vain Strivings Tied

First published with the title "Sic Vita" in *The Dial*, II (July, 1841), 81–82. Reprinted in *A Week on the Concord and Merrimack Rivers*, "Friday" chapter.

A note in *Poems of Nature* states: "This poem was written on a sheet of paper wrapped round a bunch of violets, tied loosely with a straw, and thrown into the window of a friend. It was read at Thoreau's funeral by his friend Bronson Alcott." The friend who received the poem was Mrs. Lucy Jackson Brown, Emerson's sister-in-law, who in the spring of 1837 was boarding at the house where Thoreau lived.

Inspiration

Portions of this poem were first printed in *A Week on the Concord and Merrimack Rivers*, "Monday" and "Friday" chapters.

The Fall of the Leaf

Two sections of this poem were published separately in the Boston *Commonwealth*: ll. 17–52 with the title "The Fall of the Leaf" in the issue for October 9, 1863; ll. 1–16 with the title "The Soul's Season" in that for November 6, 1863.

HENRY TIMROD
1828–1867

Bibliography

Shepherd, H. E. "Henry Timrod: Literary Estimate and Bibliography," *Publications of the Southern Historical Association*, III (1899), 267–280.

Major Writings

Poems (1860)
Katie (1884)
The Essays of Henry Timrod (1942, E. W. Parks, ed.)
The Uncollected Poems of Henry Timrod (1942, Guy A. Cardwell, ed.)

Standard Editions

Hayne, Paul H. (ed.). *The Poems of Henry Timrod.* New York: Hale and Sons, 1873.

Poems of Henry Timrod [Memorial volume, based on the Hayne edition]. Boston: Houghton Mifflin and Co., 1899.

Biography

Hubbell, J. B. *The Last Years of Henry Timrod: 1864–1867.* Durham, N.C.: Duke University Press, 1941.

Thompson, H. T. *Henry Timrod: Laureate of the Confederacy.* Columbia, S.C.: University of South Carolina Press, 1928.

Wauchope, G. A. *Henry Timrod, Man and Poet:* A Critical Study. Columbia, S.C.: University of South Carolina Press, 1915.

Criticism

Fidler, William, "Henry Timrod: Poet of the Confederacy," *Southern Literary Messenger,* II (1940), 527–532.

Hubbell, J. B. *The South in American Literature, 1607–1900,* pp. 466–474. Durham, N.C.: Duke University Press, 1954.

Comments on Poems

Text: 1873 edition.

Charleston

Fort Sumter, in Charleston harbor, was the scene of the first engagement in the Civil War, April 12, 1861, and was not retaken by the Union army until February 17, 1865.

9. *Calpe:* ancient name of Rock of Gibraltar.

11. *Moultrie:* a fort at the entrance to the Charleston harbor, erected during the War of 1812.

Ode

This poem was written to be sung during memorial observances at Magnolia Cemetery in Charleston. The date has often been given as June 16, 1867, but G. P. Voight discovered in a Charleston newspaper that the date should be 1866: "New Light on Timrod's 'Memorial Ode,'" *Am. Lit.,* IV (1933), 395–396. Timrod may have been influenced by William Collins' "Ode": "How sleep the brave, who sink to rest / By their country's wishes blessed!"

FREDERICK GODDARD TUCKERMAN
1821–1873

Bibliography

Golden, Samuel A. "Bibliography," pp. 70–71 in "Frederick Goddard Tucker-
    man: An American Sonneteer," *University of Maine Bulletin*, LIV (1952),
    1–71.

Major Writings

Poems (1860)
Poems (1864)
Poems (1867)
The Cricket (1950)

Standard Editions

Bynner, Witter (ed.). *The Sonnets of Frederick Goddard Tuckerman*. New York:
    Alfred A. Knopf, 1931.
Momaday, N. Scott (ed.). *The Complete Poems of Frederick Goddard Tuckerman*.
    With a Critical Foreword by Yvor Winters. New York: Oxford Univer-
    sity Press, 1965.

Biography

Golden, Samuel A. "Frederick Goddard Tuckerman: An American Son-
    neteer," *University of Maine Bulletin*, LIV (1952), 1–71.

Criticism

Bynner, Witter (ed.). "Introduction," pp. 3–36 in *The Sonnets of Frederick
    Goddard Tuckerman*. New York: Alfred A. Knopf, 1931.
Eaton, Walter Prichard, "A Forgotten American Poet," *Forum*, XLI (1909),
    62–70.
Winters, Yvor. "A Discovery" [review of *The Cricket*], *Hud. Rev.*, III (1950),
    453–458. Reprinted in Momaday (ed.), *Complete Poems*.

Comments on Poems

The textual source for all the poems reprinted here is the 1864 edition,
published by Ticknor and Fields. Witter Bynner attempted to improve the
punctuation, but in so doing changed the meaning of some lines. The 1864
punctuation has been observed throughout.

The Question
    39. *Phengites stone:* translucent stone used in ancient times for windows.
    55. *Hæmonian:* the Roman name for Thessaly in Greece was Hæmonia; to
the Romans it was a land of magic.

67. *ámomum:* a spice plant from India, mentioned in ancient Greek literature, but not definitely identified.

71. *Chrysophoræ:* probably from *Chrysopa,* a genus of lacewing flies, which might suggest fairies.

94. *Medusa:* one of the Gorgons, a beautiful maiden whose hair was transformed into snakes by Athena, whose sanctuary she had violated.

95. *Pelops:* son of Tantalus and grandson of Zeus; "eburnine" (eburnean, "like ivory") seems to be merely descriptive rather than symbolical.

96. *Ismenean:* like Ismene, meek sister of Antigone, in Sophocles' *Antigone;* here meekness seems to equal sweetness.

97. *Heliades:* possibly an allusion to an Old Testament judge Eli (variant of "Heli"; see I Samuel 12), who fell and killed himself on hearing that his sons had died in battle; hence, "Heliades" indicates people in extreme grief.

Sonnets: Part I

XXIV

11. *Manoah:* father of Samson. See Judges 13 : 9–10.

13. *Deborah:* prophetess of Israel. See Judges 4 : 4, though the poet may have inadvertently transferred the courage of Jael to Deborah.

14. *Mandane:* according to Herodotus, the mother of Cyrus, who dreamed that she must have the infant Cyrus put to death. *Actia* and *Arlotte:* unidentified.

Sonnets: Part II

VII

3. *Hamilcars:* Hamilcar Barca (270?–228 B.C.), Carthaginian general and father of Hannibal.

VIII

6. *Whippoorwill-shoe:* a wild flower known as moccasin flower or lady-slipper. *Sidesaddle-flower:* pitcher plant, *Sarracinia pupurea.*

XI

7. *Whately:* a small town near the poet's home in Greenfield, Massachusetts.

XIII

7. *Hæmanthus:* an African plant, known as "bloodflower" or "blood lily."

XXXIV

13. *Esdras:* another name for Ezra, the priest and scribe in the Old Testament book of Ezra, but the tradition of his eating flowers to become inspired does not have a Biblical source.

JONES VERY
1813–1880

Bibliography

Bartlett, William I. *Jones Very: Emerson's "Brave Saint,"* pp. 209–227. Durham, N.C.: Duke University Press, 1942.

Major Writings

Essays and Poems (1839, R. W. Emerson, ed.)

Standard Editions

Andrews, William P. (ed.). *Poems by Jones Very*. Boston: Houghton Mifflin and Co., 1883.

Clarke, James Freeman, and Bartol, C. A. (eds.). *Poems and Essays*, Complete and Revised Edition. Boston and New York: Houghton Mifflin and Co., 1886. (Despite the claim to completeness, many more poems have been printed from manuscripts in Bartlett, *Jones Very*.)

Biography

Bartlett, William I. *Jones Very: Emerson's "Brave Saint."* Durham, N.C.: Duke University Press, 1942.

Criticism

Baker, Carlos. "Emerson and Jones Very," *New Eng. Quart.*, VII (1934), 90–99.

Berthoff, Warner B. "Jones Very: New England Mystic," *Boston Public Library Quarterly*, II (1950), 63–76.

Winters, Yvor. "Jones Very and R. W. Emerson: Aspects of New England Mysticism" pp. 125–165 in *Maule's Curse, Seven Studies in the History of American Obscurantism*. Norfolk, Conn.: New Directions, 1938. Reprinted in *In Defense of Reason*, pp. 262–282. New York: William Morrow and Co. 1947.

Comments on Poems

In 1839 Emerson edited a thin volume of Very's *Essays and Poems*, the only edition of his writings to appear during his lifetime. There is no definitive edition of Very's poems, but the fullest is the 1886. In the selections for this anthology the 1839 text has been used for those poems which were in the 1839 edition; for poems not in that volume, the 1886 text has been used. In most cases the dates of composition are not known. The form which Very used with most skill was the sonnet, with the Shakespearean rhyme scheme, though, unlike Shakespeare, he frequently employed a final alexandrine, as in "To the Canary Bird" and "Thy Beauty Fades."

To the Canary Bird

First printed in the Salem *Observer*, April 15, 1837. Very was fond of birds and wrote several poems about them, but this poem especially expresses his hatred of tyranny, which he learned as a child from hearing of his father's captivity in Nova Scotia in the War of 1812. Included in 1839 edition, the contents of which were selected by Emerson.

Thy Beauty Fades

Discussed in Bartlett, *Jones Very*, p. 99.

Nature

Very wrote this poem in the summer of 1837 and showed it to Elizabeth Peabody, who brought it, and the poet, to the attention of Emerson, who had recently published his long essay *Nature* (1836). See Bartlett, *Jones Very*, pp. 43 ff.

Life

Discussed in Bartlett, *Jones Very*, p. 88.

The Columbine

1839 text.
Discussed in Bartlett, *Jones Very*, p. 84.

The Dead

1839 text.
Discussed in Bartlett, *Jones Very*, p. 93; Berthoff, *Boston Public Library Quarterly*, II (1960), 71.

The Slave

1839 text. Men who choose freedom of will instead of submission to God's will are slaves. Even nature shows the strength of God's love.

Love

1839 text.
Discussed in Bartlett, *Jones Very*, p. 99.

Thy Brother's Blood

1839 text. A dramatic monologue on the Cain-Abel theme; Jones Very had one living brother, and two had died in their early childhood. But the important theme (in sestet) is redemption.

The Hand and Foot

1883 text.
Discussed in Winters, *In Defense of Reason*, p. 264.

The Barberry-Bush

First published in the Salem *Observer*, November 16, 1839, but not included in the 1839 edition, probably because Emerson did not have it in time to send to the printer—said to be one of his favorite poems. See Bartlett, *Jones Very*, pp. 126, 133.

The Broken Bowl

5. *'T is broken at the cistern:* for the Biblical allusion in this line and in the title see Ecclesiastes 12 : 6.

7. *the preacher:* the Preacher from Ecclesiastes.

13. *the Rock:* Moses "smote the rock twice: and the water came out abundantly." Numbers 20 : 11.

Soul-Sickness

The 1886 edition also contained a similar poem, "Health of Body Dependent on the Soul," a poem admired by Christian Scientists.

The Fugitive Slaves

Probably written around 1850–1851, when New England was excited by the return of fugitive slaves by Federal marshals in compliance with the Fugitive Slave Law of 1850.

On Visiting the Graves of Hawthorne and Thoreau

Thoreau died May 6, 1862; Hawthorne, May 19, 1864. Both were buried in Sleepy Hollow Cemetery, Concord, Massachusetts.

WALT WHITMAN
1819–1892

Bibliography

Allen, Evie Allison. "A Check List of Whitman Publications: 1945–1960," pp. [177]–244 in Gay Wilson Allen, *Walt Whitman as Man, Poet, and Legend*. Carbondale, Ill.: Southern Illinois University Press, 1961.

Allen, Gay Wilson. *Walt Whitman Handbook* [selected bibliographies]. Chicago: Packard and Co., 1946. New York: Hendricks House, 1957; 1962.

Wells, Carolyn, and Goldsmith, Alfred F. *A Concise Bibliography of the Works of Walt Whitman*. Boston: Houghton Mifflin and Co., 1922.

Major Writings

Leaves of Grass (1855) [Revised and enlarged in editions published in 1856, 1860, 1867, 1871, 1876, 1881, 1888, 1889, 1891–1892.]
Specimen Days and Collect (1882–1883)
November Boughs (1888)
Complete Prose Works (1892)

Standard Editions

Allen, Gay Wilson, and Bradley, Sculley (general eds.). *The Collected Writings of Walt Whitman*. New York: New York University Press. So far published: Edwin Haviland Miller (ed.), *The Correspondence of Walt Whitman*, Vol. I, *1842–1867* (1961), Vol. II, *1868–1875* (1961), Vol. III, *1876–1885* (1964); Floyd Stovall (ed.), *Prose Works 1892*, Vol. I, *Specimen Days* (1963), Vol. II, *Collect and Other Prose* (1964); Thomas L. Brasher (ed.), *Early Poems and the Fiction* (1963); Harold Blodgett and Sculley Bradley (eds.), *Leaves of Grass: Readers' Edition* [definitive text of the 1891–1892 edition, with critical notes] (1964). In preparation: Sculley Bradley and Harold Blodgett (eds.), *Leaves of Grass: A Variorum Edition*.

Biography

Allen, Gay Wilson. *The Solitary Singer: A Critical Biography of Walt Whitman*. New York: The Macmillan Co., 1955. Reissued in paperback by Grove Press (New York, 1959).

Asselineau, Roger. *L'Évolution de Walt Whitman après la première Édition des Feuilles d'herbe*. Paris: Didier, 1954. Translation by the author: *The Evolution of Walt Whitman: The Creation of a Personality* [first half of *L'Évolution* . . .]. Cambridge, Mass.: Harvard University Press, 1960. *The Evolution of Walt Whitman: The Creation of a Book* [second half of *L'Évolution* . . .]. Cambridge, Mass.: Harvard University Press, 1962.

Criticism

Alegría, Fernando. *Walt Whitman en Hispanoamerica*. Mexico City: Ediciones Studium, 1954.

Allen, Gay Wilson. *Walt Whitman as Man, Poet, and Legend*. Carbondale, Ill.: Southern Illinois University Press, 1961.

Allen, Gay Wilson. *Walt Whitman Handbook*. Chicago: Packard and Co., 1946. New York: Hendricks House, 1957; 1962.

Allen, Gay Wilson (ed.). *Walt Whitman Abroad: Critical Essays from Germany, France, Scandinavia, Russia, Italy, Spain and Latin America, Israel, Japan, and India*. Syracuse, N.Y. Syracuse University Press, 1955.

Allen, Gay Wilson, and Davis, Charles (eds.). *Walt Whitman's Poems: Selections with Critical Aids* [critical introduction and notes on poems]. New York: New York University Press, 1955.

Beaver, Joseph. *Walt Whitman, Poet of Science*. New York: King's Crown Press, 1951.

Bowers, Fredson (ed.). *Whitman's Manuscripts: Leaves of Grass (1860)*. Chicago: University of Chicago Press, 1955.

Chase, Richard. *Walt Whitman Reconsidered*. New York: William Sloane Associates, 1955.

Hindus, Milton (ed.). *Leaves of Grass One Hundred Years After* [essays by William Carlos Williams, Richard Chase, Leslie Fiedler, Kenneth Burke, David Daiches, J. Middleton Murray, and Milton Hindus]. Stanford, Calif.: Stanford University Press, 1955.

Lawrence, D. H. "Whitman," in *Studies in Classic American Literature*. New York: Thomas Seltzer, 1923. Garden City, N.Y.: Doubleday, 1953.

Matthiessen, F. O. "Whitman," in *American Renaissance: Art and Expression in the Age of Emerson and Whitman*. New York: Oxford University Press, 1941.

Miller, James E., Jr. *A Critical Guide to Leaves of Grass*. Chicago: University of Chicago Press, 1957.

Pearce, Roy Harvey (ed.). *Whitman: A Collection of Critical Essays*. Englewood Cliffs, N.J.: Prentice-Hall, 1962.

Schyberg, Frederik. *Walt Whitman*. København: Gyldendalske Boghandel, 1933. Translation by Evie Allison Allen. New York: Columbia University Press, 1951.

Comments on Poems

Song of Myself

Originally without title in 1855; "A Poem of Walt Whitman" in 1856 edition; "Walt Whitman" in 1860; present title in 1881, used here because it is the title that has become famous. The 1855 text, however, is far superior to the revised versions, being more spontaneous, original, and unconventional in language and punctuation. To mark rhythmical (caesural) or rhetorical pauses Whitman used periods instead of commas. He compounded words freely (see verses 14, 16, etc.), often without using hyphens. He drew recklessly upon all levels of diction, from slang to recondite terms. In attempting to revise the poem to shift the subject from *the self* to *myself* (or himself) the poet became more self-conscious and less inventive. In this first, fresh version the personal self is only an illustration of the universal self.

Discussed in Allen, *The Solitary Singer*, pp. 157–164, 287–288; Allen and Davis, *Walt Whitman's Poems*, pp. 127–131; Chase, *Walt Whitman Reconsidered*, pp. 57–98; Malcolm Cowley, "Introduction," in *Leaves of Grass: The First (1855) Edition* (Viking, 1961), pp. x–xxxvii; James E. Miller, Jr., "'Song of Myself' as Inverted Mystical Experience," *PMLA*, LXX (1955), 636–661, and reprinted in *A Critical Guide to Leaves of Grass*, pp. 6–35.

1. "and sing myself," added in 1881.

41. *entretied:* from French *entretenir*, "to support."

75 ff. This famous description of a "mystical experience" is cited by William James as a "classical example" in *The Varieties of Religious Experience* (Collier Books, 1961), p. 311.

89. *wormfence:* a zigzag rail fence.

100. *Kanuck:* Canadian (Whitman frequently affected the spelling "Kanada"). *Tuckahoe:* inhabitant of eastern Virginia. *Cuff:* a Negro.

193. The *twenty-eight* seems esoteric; possibly it stands for the woman's menstrual period, or a month.

240. *pert:* sophisticated.

282. *Wolverine:* native of Michigan.

318. *Chattahoochee . . . Altamahaw:* rivers in Georgia.

334. *Hoosier:* native of Indiana; *Badger:* of Wisconsin; *Buckeye:* of Ohio.

335. *poke-easy:* loafer, saunterer.

346. *fancy-man:* pimp.

408. *carlacue:* probably a typographical error for "curlicue," but never corrected.

468. *foofoos:* contemporary New York slang; term of contempt for persons without significance.

499. *kosmos:* cosmos, complete in himself; the term also suggests the importance of the poet's individual life, and his role as a cosmical poet-leader.

530. *Translucent mould:* semen.

532. *tilth:* tillage, as in deep plowing.

536 ff. Many phallic metaphors in this passage.

634. *red marauder:* bloodthirsty assassin, like the American Indian attacking a white community on the frontier.

645. *curb:* womb.

658. *compend:* compendium.

671. This pre-Darwinian concept of evolution was not original with Whitman, being common in scientific books of the period.

700. *amie:* feminine form of French noun, but line 701 indicates that masculine gender was intended.

712. *ties, ballasts:* cast off to enable the balloon to soar.

751. *bull-dances:* stag dances.

791. Contemporary astronomers estimated the orbit of Saturn as 79,000 miles.

792. For Whitman's interest in comets, see Beaver, *Walt Whitman, Poet of Science,* pp. 59 ff.

793. Phases of the moon.

867. *murder in cold blood:* massacre of Texan troops on order of General Santa Anna of Mexico near Goliad, Texas, on March 27, 1836.

870–889. After tactical blunders by General Fannin, the U.S. troops were forced to surrender, and were murdered while prisoners of war.

890. ff. Under great odds John Paul Jones, in command of the American ship, *Bonhomme Richard,* defeated the British *Serapis,* commanded by Richard Pearson, on September 23, 1779.

937. *prison ships:* during the American Revolution, captured American sailors were held under inhuman conditions in British ships anchored off the American coast, such as in Wallabout Bay, at the inlet of the East River in Brooklyn, New York.

949. *cholera patient:* cholera epidemics were common in New York and Brooklyn during Whitman's childhood.

969. *Eleves:* French, *élèves,* "pupils"; the poet's disciples.

984. *lie over:* in his exuberance the poet tells the sun to make room for him and humorously calls the earth "old topknot" (l. 987).

993. *scarfed chops:* bandaged jaws, for a sick man or a corpse.

998. *infold:* embrace, accept.

1020 ff. The poet plays the role of founder of a new, eclectic religion. See G. L. Sixbey, "'Chanting the Square Deific'—A Study in Whitman's Religion," *Am. Lit.,* IX (1937), 171–195. Cf. ll. 1092 ff.

1024–1027. *Lithographing:* reproducing image of (borrowing best of all religions). *Kronos, Zeus, Hercules:* Greek gods. *Osiris:* Egyptian god of underworld; *Isis:* his wife, goddess of fertility. *Belus:* son of Poseidon and divinity of various early nations of Asia Minor. *Brahma:* creator-god of Hindu sacred triad. *Adonai:* Hebrew name of God, usually translated "Lord." *Manito:* deity of American Indians (as in Longfellow's *Hiawatha*). *Allah:* Supreme Being to Mohammedans. *Odin:* Norse deity. *Mexitli:* (now spelled Metztli) deity of the Aztecs.

1040. *hostler:* many of the horse grooms and drivers of the New York omnibuses ("horse cars") were personal friends of Whitman, but here he is finding exaggerated Christ-like potentiality in a very unprepossessing person.

1043. *the bull and the bug:* the bull was worshipped in ancient Assyria and the scarab (American "tumble-bug") was sacred in Egypt.

1065. *With dimes on the eyes walking:* people who are dead, having had silver coins placed on their eyelids after death to keep the eyes closed. Interpretation: people so materialistic that they are spiritually dead but do not know it—still walking.

1097. *obis:* perhaps a reference to rites of *obeah* in Caribbean witchcraft.

1099. *phallic:* early Greek religion included phallic worship. *Gymnosophists:* ascetic religious sect observed in India by Alexander the Great.

1100. *Drinking mead from the skull-cap:* rite of pagan Scandinavians or Anglo-Saxons. *Shasta:* a member of a tribe of Indians in the Western U.S., known more familiarly as the Comanches; the context suggests that Whitman confused this name with the sacred writings of India. *vedas:* (usually capitalized) a body of sacred books in the Hindu religion.

1101. *teokallis: teocalli,* "God's house," an Aztec temple, usually built on a mound or pyramid, in Mexico and Central America. *gore:* human sacrifices.

1113. ff. *flukes:* flapping of a whale's tail in its death agony, as described in Melville's *Moby-Dick,* which Whitman had read.

1127. *bad disorder:* venereal disease.

1128. *koboo:* probably some African tribe inaccurately reported in pseudo-anthropology.

1129. *sacs:* jellyfish.

1164. *overlay:* medical term for stricture preventing normal birth.

1182. *scuttle:* sliding door on dome of an astronomical observatory.

1283. *accoucheur:* (French) "obstetrician."

1312. *sidle:* literally to "move sideways," and it is the tilted earth revolving toward the sun that brings the evening; the poet is trying to use kinetic imagery.

1327–1328. The "I" of the poem becomes a comet, consuming itself in flight, as believed by some contemporary astronomers.

From "To Think of Time"

No title in 1855 (version used here); "Burial Poem" in 1856; "Burial," 1860; "To Think of Time" in 1871.

Discussed in Allen and Davis, *Walt Whitman's Poems,* p. 150.

12. *When the dull nights are over:* after a long illness the poet's father, Walter Whitman, died on July 11, 1855, a few days after the publication of the first edition of *Leaves of Grass.*

33. *posh:* mushy ice.

35–52. During the 1850 decade Whitman was especially friendly with drivers of the New York omnibuses, visited them when they were ill, and attended their funerals.

Crossing Brooklyn Ferry

First published in 1856; main revisions in 1860 and 1881; final revision (1881) is present text. Unlike "Song of Myself," the revisions improved the poem.

Discussed in Allen and Davis, *Walt Whitman's Poems,* pp. 157–158; Miller, *A Critical Guide to Leaves of Grass,* pp. 80–89.

Out of the Cradle Endlessly Rocking

First published in the New York *Saturday Press,* a literary weekly, on December 24, 1859, and revised for 1860 edition of *Leaves of Grass*; extensively revised in 1867; final version, 1881—present text.

The poem was formerly regarded as an elegy for some unknown friend or lover, but Allen in *The Solitary Singer,* p. 236, says it stands "not as a cenotaph to a private grief but as a great poet's intuition of the victory of the soul over chaos and death."

Discussed in Allen, *The Solitary Singer*, pp. 231–236; Allen and Davis, *Walt Whitman's Poems*, pp. 164–166; Miller, *A Critical Guide to Leaves of Grass*, pp. 104–110; Stephen E. Whicher, Paul Fussell, Jr., and Richard Chase in R. W. B. Lewis (ed.), *The Presence of Walt Whitman: Selected Papers from the English Institute* (Columbia University Press, 1962), pp. 1–71.

23. *paumanok:* Indian name for Long Island, perhaps meaning "fish-shaped."

From "Children of Adam"

In 1860 a group of fifteen poems called *"Enfans d'Adam,"* ostensibly celebrating the theme of sex as creativity, though some of the poems included the "Calamus" themes and sentiments, i.e., friendship between men. The French title was changed to the present English one in 1867, and the poems were revised until 1881, the text used here.

Discussed in Allen, *The Solitary Singer*, pp. 251–253; Allen and Davis, *Walt Whitman's Poems*, pp. 167–177; Asselineau, *The Evolution of Walt Whitman: The Creation of a Book*, Chap. V; Miller, *A Critical Guide to Leaves of Grass*, pp. 36–51.

57. *act divine:* procreation.

From "Calamus"

The title was given to a group of forty-five poems in the 1860 edition; title retained, with some shifting of poems, in later editions; present text 1881. In his notes Whitman wrote, "Theory of a Cluster of Poems the same to the passion of Woman-Love ['Children of Adam'] as the *Calamus-Leaves* are to adhesiveness, manly love." Quoted in Allen and Davis, *Walt Whitman's Poems*, p. 177. "Adhesiveness" was a cant term in the pseudoscience, phrenology, for emotional attachment between men. For biographical implications see Allen, *The Solitary Singer*, p. 222. In a letter to William Rossetti, Whitman explained the meaning of *calamus:* "It is the very large and aromatic grass, or rush, growing about water-ponds in the valleys: spears about 3 feet high, often called sweet flag—grows all over the Northern and Middle States . . . The recherché or ethereal sense of the term, as used in the book, arises probably from the actual calamus presenting the biggest and hardiest kind of spears of grass, and their fresh, aquatic, pungent bouquet." Quoted in Allen and Davis, *Walt Whitman's Poems*, p. 177. For correspondence concerning the possible homosexual meaning of the poems see Allen, *Walt Whitman as Man, Poet, and Legend*, pp. 165 ff.

Discussed in Asselineau, *The Evolution of Walt Whitman: The Creation of a Book*, Chap. V; Miller, *A Critical Guide to Leaves of Grass*, pp. 52–79. For a most valuable study of the textual evolution of the poems in "Calamus" see Fredson Bowers, *Whitman's Manuscripts: Leaves of Grass (1860)*, pp. 67–123, and *Textual and Literary Criticism* (Cambridge University Press, 1959), pp. 35–65.

Scented Herbage of My Breast

The symbol of the poems as "tomb-leaves" may have come from Whit-

man's interest in Egyptology, or more specifically from the ritual burial of
Osiris, the latter first suggested by Esther Shephard, see Allen and Davis,
Walt Whitman's Poems, p. 181.

I Saw in Louisiana a Live-Oak Growing
    Whitman lived in New Orleans for a few weeks in the spring of 1848. Note
the similarity of this poem to a sonnet, a term Whitman himself applied to the
"Calamus" poems.

From "Drum-Taps"
    Throughout the Civil War Whitman worked on the poems which he collec-
ted in the volume called *Drum-Taps* (1865) and annexed to *Leaves of Grass* in
1867. The poems do not so much tell the history of the war as record the poet's
emotional life during the period. When the war broke out he wrote the re-
cruiting poem "Beat! Beat! Drums!"; but after he had seen the effects of war
on the battlefield in Virginia and in the military hospitals, he became "The
Wound-Dresser" and welcomed peace for the soil "leavened" with the blood
of Northern and Southern men.
    Discussed in Allen, *The Solitary Singer*, pp. 260–377; Allen and Davis, *Walt
Whitman's Poems*, pp. 200–233; Miller, *A Critical Guide to Leaves of Grass*, pp.
219–231.

O Captain! My Captain!
    Written soon after Lincoln's death, included in *Drum-Taps*, printed in May,
1865, and finally placed in *Leaves of Grass* under a section devoted to Lincoln.
The jig tune is not wholly appropriate and the imagery is trite. It is one of the
few poems Whitman wrote in conventional rhyme, metre, and stanza after
1855 and is not characteristic of him; but, like Poe's inferior effort, "The
Raven," this is Whitman's most popular poem.

When Lilacs Last in the Dooryard Bloom'd
    This elegy, usually acknowledged to be one of the greatest in the English
language, was composed slowly throughout the summer of 1865 and was first
published in the autumn in a "Sequel" to *Drum-Taps*. In 1881 it was added to
Leaves of Grass in an appendix, and not fully integrated into the book until
1881—the text used here. Much of the imagery came from the spring of 1865,
while the nation was waiting anxiously for peace, and from the national shock
immediately after Lincoln's assassination on April 15. The lilac, however, derived its symbolical meaning both from the time of year, Easter, with its sug-
gestions of death and resurrection, and the poet's associations from childhood
with lilacs, his grandfather's old farmhouse on Long Island, and maternal love.
At the time of Lincoln's death the evening star was Venus. The bird sings the
Lucretian theme of reconciliation to death. Although the versification is Whitman's characteristic form, the elegy is conventional in imagery, symbolism,
and structure (see Richard P. Adams, "Whitman's 'Lilacs' and the Traditional Pastoral Elegy," *PMLA*, LXXII [1957], 479–487).
    Discussed in Allen, *The Solitary Singer*, pp. 553–558 (biographical-historical
background); Allen and Davis, *Walt Whitman's Poems*, pp. 231–233; Miller,
A Critical Guide to Leaves of Grass, pp. 111–119.

4. *trinity:* two of the three major symbols are mentioned (line 5), but the third is not mentioned until section 4: the bird.

7–11. Imagery from Whitman's notes written on the dark, rainy day after the assassination; see Allen, *The Solitary Singer*, p. 332.

12. *palings:* narrow strips of wood spaced several inches apart to form a picket fence.

20–21. *thrush . . . hermit:* this bird is appropriate for its symbolical use in the poem both because of its shy habits, preferring wooded swamps, dense woods, or pine and hemlock forests, and its ethereal bell-like cadences, which begin with low, flute-like notes, rise to higher, varied sequences, sometimes so high as to be almost inaudible, and end with a tremolo effect.

26–45. Lincoln's body was carried by train from Washington, D.C., to Springfield, Illinois, stopping at principal cities, where mourners presented bouquets.

26 ff. In sections 5, 6, and 16, especially, the syntax shapes the order, rhythm, and emotional tone of the passage. The subject and predicate are withheld until the last line and the envelope of parallel statements advances, develops, and clinches the idea. This device also creates space-empathy—sensation of advancing through space.

79–80. *pictures . . . burial-house:* hardly what would be expected in an American poem; perhaps reminiscent of images in tombs of Pharoahs, indicating the importance of this burial of a national leader.

120. *knowledge of death:* understanding, which finally brings reconciliation, symbolized by bird's song.

121. *thought of death:* pathos of the death of Lincoln, symbolized by the star. The lilac (love) mediates between *knowledge* and *thought* and finally resolves the tension in favor of knowledge.

134. *tallied:* matched, equalled.

163. *tally:* literally count or score, but here, as elsewhere in Whitman's poems, it indicates that a physical object has its spiritual counterpart in the mind or soul. Cf. Emerson's theory of "Symbols" in his essay *Nature* (1836).

A Noiseless Patient Spider
Though not published until 1871, this poem was actually written during the war (see Emory Holloway, ed., *Uncollected Poetry and Prose of Walt Whitman* [Doubleday, 1921], II, p. 9). For its relation to the "Calamus" poems see Allen, *The Solitary Singer*, pp. 341–342. Text of early version, Allen and Davis, *Walt Whitman's Poems*, p. 198. The final version is in the mood of Melville, Emily Dickinson, and Stephen Crane in the post-Civil War period. Mark Van Doren says: "Here is solitude with a vengeance, in vacancy so vast that any soul seen at its center, trying to comprehend and inhabit it, looks terribly minute" [Van Doren, *Introduction to Poetry* (William Sloane Associates, 1951), p. 43].

Good-Bye My Fancy!
Written in 1891 to serve as the final poem for the final edition of *Leaves of Grass*. "I" is the body; "Fancy," poetic faculty. They cannot be separated; either both will die, or both will enjoy a spiritual existence together. Whitman's "Fancy" is more like Coleridge's "imagination" than what Coleridge and Poe called "Fancy."

JOHN GREENLEAF WHITTIER
1807–1892

Bibliography

Currier, Thomas Franklin. *A Bibliography of John Greenleaf Whittier*. Cambridge, Mass.: Harvard University Press, 1937.

Major Writings

Legends of New England in Prose and Verse (1831)
Poems Written During the Progress of the Abolition Question (1837)
Lays of My Home and Other Poems (1843)
Voices of Freedom (1846)
Songs of Labor (1850)
The Chapel of the Hermits (1853)
The Panorama and Other Poems (1856)
Home Ballads, Poems and Lyrics (1860)
In War Time and Other Poems (1864)
Snow-Bound (1866)
The Tent on the Beach (1867)
Among the Hills (1869)
Miriam and Other Poems (1871)
Hazel-Blossoms (1875)
The Vision of Echard (1878)
St. Gregory's Guest (1886)
At Sundown (1890)

Standard Editions

The Writings of John Greenleaf Whittier, Riverside Edition, 7 Vols. Boston and New York: Houghton Mifflin and Co., 1888–1889.
The Complete Poetical Works of John Greenleaf Whittier, Cambridge Edition. Edited by H[orace] E. S[cudder]. Boston and New York: Houghton Mifflin and Co., 1894.

Biography

Bennett, Whitman. *Whittier: Bard of Freedom*. Chapel Hill, N.C.: University of North Carolina Press, 1941.
Carpenter, G. R. *Whittier*. American Men of Letters Series. Boston: Houghton Mifflin and Co., 1903.
Pickard, Samuel T. *Life and Letters of John Greenleaf Whittier*, 2 Vols. Boston: Houghton Mifflin and Co., 1894; revised, 1907.
Pollard, John A. *John Greenleaf Whittier: Friend of Man*. Boston: Houghton Mifflin and Co., 1949.

Criticism

Allen, Gay Wilson, "John Greenleaf Whittier," pp. 127–153 in *American Prosody*. New York: American Book Company, 1935.

Arms, George. "Whittier," pp. 33–96 in *The Fields Were Green*. Stanford, Calif.: Stanford University Press, 1953.

Christy, Arthur. "Orientalism in New England: Whittier," *Am. Lit.*, I (1930), 372–392.

Foerster, Norman. *Nature in American Literature*, pp. 20–36. New York: The Macmillan Co., 1923.

Howe, W. D. "Whittier," pp. 125–134 in John Macy (ed.), *American Writers on American Literature*. New York: Horace Liveright, 1931.

Jones, Howard Mumford. "Whittier Reconsidered," pp. 161–176 in *History and the Contemporary*. Madison, Wis.: University of Wisconsin Press, 1964.

McEuen, Kathryn Anderson. "Whittier's Rhymes," *Am. Sp.*, XX (February, 1945), 51–57.

More, Paul Elmer. "Whittier as Poet," *Shelburne Essays*, Third Series. New York: Houghton Mifflin and Co., 1906.

Scott, W. T. "Poetry in America: A New Consideration of Whittier's Verse," *New Eng. Quart.*, VII (1934), 258–275.

Waggoner, Hyatt H. "What I Had I Gave: Another Look at Whittier," *Essex Institute Historical Collections*, XCX (January, 1959), 32–40.

Wells, Henry W. "Cambridge Culture and Folk Poetry," pp. 44–45 in *The American Way of Poetry*. New York: Columbia University Press, 1943.

Comments on Poems

Unlike some poets, who revise their poems from edition to edition, Whittier let his poems stand as he first published them, except for corrections of typographical errors. Consequently, the dates given for Whittier's poems in this anthology are those of the first book publication, as recorded by Currier (see Bibliography). The actual text reproduced is that of the Cambridge Edition, 1894.

Memories

Whittier placed this poem at the beginning of "Poems Subjective and Reminiscent" in his collected *Writings* (Boston and New York: Houghton Mifflin and Co., 1888–1889). To a friend he remarked that it was so personal he "hardly knew whether to publish it" (Pickard, *Life*, Vol. I, p. 276).

57. *Genevan's:* John Calvin (1509–1564), who fled France to Geneva, Switzerland, where he founded his theocratic community, in 1536.

59. *Derby dalesman's:* George Fox (1624–1690), founder of the "Society of Friends" (called "Quakers"), who was arrested at Derby, England, in 1650 for preaching his Quaker doctrines, and spent a year in prison there.

Proem

Written to introduce a collection of Whittier's poems published in 1849.

Ichabod

Ichabod: Hebrew word meaning "inglorious," used in Bible as name for a child whose mother died in childbirth—1 Samuel 4 : 21. Actually, Whittier regarded Webster's speech as worse than "inglorious."

Whittier's note, from *Writings*, Vol. IV, pp. 61–62: "This poem was the outcome of the surprise and grief and forecast of evil consequences which I felt on reading the seventh of March [1850] speech of Daniel Webster in support of the 'compromise,' and the Fugitive Slave Law. No partisan or personal enmity dictated it. On the contrary my admiration of the splendid personality and intellectual power of the great Senator was never stronger than when I laid down his speech, and, in one of the saddest moments of my life, penned my protest. I saw, as I wrote, with painful clearness its sure results,—the Slave Power arrogant and defiant, strengthened and encouraged to carry out its scheme for the extension of its baleful system, or the dissolution of the Union, the guarantees of personal liberty in the free States broken down, and the whole country made the hunting ground of slave-catchers. In the horror of such a vision, so soon fearfully fulfilled, if one spoke at all, he could only speak in tones of stern and sorrowful rebuke.

"But death softens all resentments, and the consciousness of a common inheritance of frailty and weakness modifies the severity of judgment. Years after, in *The Lost Occasion* [1880], I gave utterance to an almost universal regret that the great statesman did not live to see the flag which he loved trampled under the feet of Slavery, and, in view of this desecration, make his last days glorious in defence of 'Liberty and Union, one and inseparable.'"

Skipper Ireson's Ride

Whittier's note, from *Writings*, Vol. I, pp. 174–175: "In the valuable and carefully prepared *History of Marblehead*, published in 1879 by Samuel Roads, Jr., it is stated that the crew of Captain Ireson, rather than himself, were responsible for the abandonment of the disabled vessel. To screen themselves they charged their captain with the crime. In view of this the writer of the ballad addressed the following letter to the historian:—

"Oak Knoll, Danvers, 5 mo. 18, 1880.

"My dear Friend; I heartily thank thee for a copy of thy *History of Marblehead*. I have read it with great interest and think good use has been made of the abundant material. No town in Essex County has a record more honorable than Marblehead; no one has done more to develop the industrial interests of our New England seaboard, and certainly none have given such evidence of sacrificing patriotism. I am glad the story of it has been at last told, and told so well. I have now no doubt that thy version of Skipper Ireson's ride is the correct one. My verse was founded solely on a fragment of rhyme which I heard from one of my early schoolmates, a native of Marblehead.

"I suppose the story to which it referred dated back at least a century. I knew nothing of the participators, and the narrative of the ballad was pure fancy. I am glad for the sake of truth and justice that the real facts are given in thy book. I certainly would not knowingly do injustice to any one, dead or living.

I am very truly thy friend,

John G. Whittier."

3. *Apuleius's Golden Ass: The Golden Ass* is a story by Lucius Apuleius, a Roman satirist of the second century A.D., in which a young man travels while metamorphosed into an ass ("golden" means excellent).

4. *horse of brass:* allusion to a story in *Arabian Nights*, Chapter 24, about the travels of a Persian prince from country to country on a magic horse of ebony (not brass), which an ugly "sage" or magician had made.

6. *Al-Borák:* a legendary white animal with wings that carried Mohammed to the seventh heaven.

30. *Maenads:* Green *mainad*, from *mainesthai*, to be mad, was a woman participant in orgiastic Dionysian rites; hence, wildly emotional women.

35. *Chaleur Bay:* Canadian bay between New Brunswick and the Gaspé Peninsula.

The Old Burying-Ground

In a letter dated January 1, 1858, Whittier wrote that this poem "was written in part while watching at the sick-bed of my dear mother . . . She passed away a few days ago, in the beautiful serenity of a Christian faith . . ." (Pickard, *Life*, Vol. II, p. 412).

Telling the Bees

Whittier's note, from *Writings*, Vol. I, p. 186: "A remarkable custom, brought from the Old Country, formerly prevailed in the rural districts of New England. On the death of a member of the family, the bees were at once informed of the event, and their hives dressed in mourning. This ceremony was supposed to be necessary to prevent the swarms from leaving their hives and seeking a new home."

1. *place:* Whittier's childhood home, near Haverhill, Massachusetts.

20. *Fernside farm:* the poem accurately describes Whittier's own birthplace, though the story, including the name Fernside, is entirely imaginary. The poem was written long after he had moved from Haverhill to Amesbury, Massachusetts, while his sister Mary, whose garden beside the brook is described in the poem, was still living.

My Playmate

The girl is probably the same as in "Memories," evidently a childhood sweetheart. Tennyson admired this poem.

1. *Ramoth hill:* about two miles from Amesbury, Massachusetts, Whittier's home from 1836 until his death.

36. *Follymill:* near poet's home in Amesbury, locally known for its woodland mayflowers and ground laurel. See Pickard, *Life*, Vol. II, p. 427.

Barbara Frietchie

Whittier's note, from "Writings," Vol. III, p. 245. "This poem was written in strict conformity to the account of the incident as I had it from respectable and trustworthy sources. It has since been the subject of a good deal of conflicting testimony, and the story was probably incorrect in some of its details. It is admitted by all that Barbara Frietchie was no myth, but a worthy and highly esteemed gentlewoman, intensely loyal and a hater of the Slavery Rebellion, holding her Union flag sacred and keeping it with her Bible; that when the Confederates halted before her house, and entered her dooryard, she denounced them in vigorous language, shook her cane in their faces, and drove them out; and when General Burnside's troops followed close upon Jackson's, she waved her flag and cheered them. It is stated that May Quantrell, a brave and loyal lady in another part of the city, did wave her flag in sight of the Confederates. It is possible that there has been a blending of the two incidents."

Snow-Bound

In a long note Whittier explained that the family described in the poem consisted of his father, mother, brother, two sisters, and an uncle and an aunt, both unmarried: "In my boyhood, in our lonely farm-house, we had scanty sources of information; few books and only a small weekly newspaper. Our only annual was the Almanac. Under such circumstances story-telling was a necessary resource in the long winter evenings. My father when a young man had traversed the wilderness to Canada, and could tell us of his adventures with Indians and wild beasts, and of his sojourn in the French villages. My uncle was ready with his record of hunting and fishing and, it must be confessed, with stories which he at least half believed, of witchcraft and apparitions. My mother, who was born in the Indian haunted region of Somersworth, New Hampshire, between Dover and Portsmouth, told us of the inroads of the savages, and the narrow escapes of her ancestors. She described strange people who lived on the Piscataqua and Cocheco, among whom was Bantam the sorcerer. I have in my possession the wizard's 'conjuring book,' which he solemnly opened when consulted. It is a copy of Cornelius Agrippa's *Magic*, printed in 1651 . . ."

In the original edition of *Snow-Bound* (1866) Whittier used as epigraphs a quotation from Agrippa and the first nine lines of Emerson's "The Snow-Storm."

63. *sweep:* a long pole used for lowering and raising a bucket in a shallow well.

90. *Amun:* Egyptian god in the form of a ram, whose ritual death and resurrection paralleled the death and rebirth of vegetation.

183. *brother:* Matthew, a younger brother, who lived until 1883.

215. *Gambia:* region of Gambia River in West Africa.

223. From an Abolitionist poem, "The African Chief," by Sarah Wentworth Morton.

224. *father:* while a young man John Whittier, the poet's father, made several trips to Canada, which he recounts to his family.

225. *Memphremagog:* a lake in Quebec province, Canada.

226. *moose and samp:* venison cooked with coarsely broken grains of corn.

229. *St. François':* St. François de Lac, Quebec, Canada.

256. *mother:* Abigail Hussey Whittier (1781–1857)—see "The Old Burying-Ground" and Whittier's note above.

270. *conjuring book:* Agrippa's *Magic*.

274. *Piscataqua:* a river in New Hampshire.

286. *tome:* William Sewel's *History of the Quakers*.

289. *Chalkley:* itinerant Quaker minister whose *Journal* corroborates Mrs. Whittier's accounts.

305. *ram:* see Genesis 23 : 13.

307. *uncle:* Moses Whittier, unmarried, lived with his brother until his death in 1824.

320. *Apollonius:* there were several Apolloniuses; here probably Apollonius of Tyre, a Greek philosopher of first century A.D. reputed to work miracles.

322. *Hermes Trismegistus:* reputed author of works about Egypt.

323. *Nilus:* the Nile.

332. *White:* Gilbert White, of Surrey County, England, who wrote *Natural History of Selborne* (1789).

350. *aunt:* Mercy Evans Hussey (?–1846).

378. *elder sister:* Mary Whittier Caldwell (1806–1860).

396. *youngest:* Elizabeth Hussey Whittier (1815–1864).

438. *wielder:* George Haskell (1790–1876), Dartmouth student.

476. *Pindus-born Arachthus:* river in Greece, rising in Pindus mountains.

510. *Another guest:* Harriet Livermore (1788–1867), daughter of Judge Livermore of New Hampshire. She was a fanatical believer in the Second Advent of Christ and traveled much proclaiming the impending event. She was later to travel in Europe, live with Lady Hester Stanhope on Mt. Lebanon, and wander in Syria with Arab tribes. At the time of the snowstorm on which the poem is based, she was boarding at nearby Rocks Village.

536. *Kate:* Heroine of Shakespeare's *Taming of the Shrew.*

537. *Siena's saint:* St. Catherine of Siena (1347–1380).

555. *crazy Queen of Lebanon:* Lady Hester Stanhope, religious eccentric, described by Alexander Kinglake in *Eothen, or Traces of Travel Brought Home from the East* (1844), Chap. VIII.

568. *sisters:* the three Fates in Greek and Roman religion.

659. *Doctor:* Dr. Elias Weld of nearby Rocks Village.

683. Thomas Ellwood (1639–1713), who wrote *Davideis* (1712).

684. *heathen Nine:* Muses in Greek mythology who inspired poets.

688. *paper:* the historical events mentioned in the next ten lines indicate that the time being remembered is 1819–1820, but all of them could not have been reported in one issue of the paper.

694–695. Gregor McGregor tried in 1819 to establish by force an American colony in Costa Rica.

696–698. General Ypsilanti led a revolt of the Greeks against their Turkish rulers in 1820.

728. *white amaranth:* a fabulous unfading flower.

739. *aloe:* another name for the century plant, superstitiously thought to bloom only once in a century; its blooming could celebrate the abolishment of slavery in the United States.

747. *Flemish pictures:* Flemish painters were famous for their depiction of homely scenes.

Laus Deo!

Title: "Praise be to God," from the Latin Vulgate Bible.

The constitutional amendment abolishing slavery was adopted by Congress on January 31, 1865, and was ratified by the required number of states on December 18, 1865. The poem celebrates the latter date.

24. *gates of brass:* Psalms 107 : 16: "For he hath broken the gates of brass . . ."

27. *Miriam by the sea:* Miriam the prophetess joining in Moses' song after Pharaoh's army was drowned in the Red Sea—Exodus 15 : 21.

30. See Exodus 15 : 1.

Prelude

The narrative poem called "Among the Hills" is a sentimental story of a cultured woman who married a farmer; it was the principal poem in the small volume (100 pages) published in 1869. The "Prelude" is superior to the body of the poem, and the realism of lines 44–98 reveals a side of Whittier that still surprises his readers.

110. *Canning:* British statesman and Prime Minister (1827) George Canning (1770–1827), who wrote "The Friend of Humanity and the Knife-Grinder."

119–121. See the Book of Ruth.

151. Ophir was fabled in the Old Testament for its gold: see for example 1 Kings 22 : 48, 1 Chronicles 29 : 4, Job 22 : 24, Psalms 45 : 9.

RICHARD WILBUR
b. 1921

Major Writings

The Beautiful Changes and Other Poems (1947)
Ceremony and Other Poems (1950)
A Bestiary (1955, a compilation)
The Misanthrope (1955, translation)
Things of This World (1956)
Poems, 1943–1956 (1957)
Candide: A Comic-Opera Based on Voltaire's Satire (1957, contribution of lyrics)
Advice to a Prophet and Other Poems (1961)
The Poems of Richard Wilbur (1963)

Criticism

Cole, Thomas. "Wilbur's Second Volume," *Poetry*, LXXXII (1953) 37–38.

Dickey, James. "The Stillness at the Center of the Target," *Sewanee Rev.*, LXX (1962), 489–491.

Faverty, F. E. "Well-Open Eyes; or, The Poetry of Richard Wilbur," pp. 59–72 in Edward Hungerford (ed.), *Poets in Progress*. Evanston, Ill.: Northwestern University Press, 1962.

Jarrell, Randall. "Three Poets," pp. 227–230 in *Poetry and the Age*. New York: Vintage Books, 1955.

Rosenthal, M. L. "Unfair question," *Reporter*, 26 (February 15, 1962), 48.

Southworth, J. G. "The Poetry of Richard Wilbur," *Coll. Eng.*, XXII (1960), 24–29.

Warlow, F. W. "Richard Wilbur," *Bucknell Review*, VII (1958), 217–233.

Comments on Poems

First Snow in Alsace

Alsace is a province in eastern France which was liberated from German troops in the autumn of 1944.

Bell Speech

7. *bavardage:* (French) "prattle."

11. *Great Paul:* the bell in St. Paul's Cathedral, London.

16. *Mount Desert:* island off the coast of Maine.

Still, Citizen Sparrow

24. *Ararat:* mountain in modern Turkey near Iran where Noah's ark is said to have come to rest. See Genesis 8 : 4.

The Death of a Toad

Discussed in George Abbe, *You and Contemporary Poetry* (North Guilford, Conn.: Author-Audience Publishers, 1957), pp. 73–76.

Lamarck Elaborated

Jean Baptiste Pierre Antoine de Monet, Chevalier de Lamarck (1744–1829), French scientist, was author of *Philosophie Zoölogique* (1809).

"*The environment creates the organ*": this echoes Lamarck's formulation (in Chapter VII: "Of the Influence of the Environment on the Activities and Habits of Animals..."): "the environment affects the shape and organisation of animals." J. B. Lamarck, *Zoological Philosophy*, Hugh Elliott, trans. (The Macmillan Co., 1914), p. 107.

1. *our eyes have rays:* this idea is suggested by several Greek philosophers; for instance, Plato, *Republic* VI, 508; Alcmeon of Croton (see John Burnett, *Early Greek Philosophy*, third ed., 1930, p. 194); and Democritus (see Kathleen Freeman, *Ancilla to the Pre-Socratic Philosophers*, third ed., 1953, p. 312).

Pangloss's Song: A Comic-Opera Lyric

This poem was one of the lyrics contributed by Wilbur to *Candide*, a comic operetta based on Voltaire's satire, which was first staged in 1956; the score was by Leonard Bernstein. Dr. Pangloss was Voltaire's Leibnitzian optimist who insisted that all was for the best in the best of all possible worlds.

1. *Dear boy:* Candide, the naïve hero of Voltaire's work.

3. *what has paled:* Pangloss is afflicted with syphilis.

26. *chocolate to eat:* chocolate originated in the Western Hemisphere and so did tobacco.

40. *Croix de Guerre:* French military decoration for bravery in war.

WILLIAM CARLOS WILLIAMS
1883–1963

Bibliography

Williams, William Carlos (reported and edited by Edith Heal). *I Wanted to Write a Poem: The Autobiography of the Works of a Poet.* Boston: Beacon Press, 1958. [Bibliography with personal comments.]

Major Writings

A Book of Poems: Al Que Quiere! (1917)
Sour Grapes: A Book of Poems (1921)
Spring and All (1923)
In the American Grain (1925, essays)
Collected Poems, 1921–1931 (1934)
An Early Martyr and Other Poems (1935)
White Mule (1937, a novel)
The Complete Collected Poems of William Carlos Williams, 1906–1938 (1938)
The Wedge (1944)
Paterson (Book One, 1946; Book Two, 1948; Book Three, 1949; Book Four, 1951)
The Autobiography of William Carlos Williams (1951)
The Desert Music and Other Poems (1954)
The Selected Letters of William Carlos Williams (1957, J. C. Thirlwall, ed.)

Standard Editions

The Collected Earlier Poems of William Carlos Williams. Norfolk, Conn.: New Directions, 1951.
The Collected Later Poems of William Carlos Williams. Norfolk, Conn.: New Directions, 1950.

Criticism

Bennett, John. "The Lyre and the Sledgehammer," *Hud. Rev.,* V (1952), 295–307.
Burke, Kenneth. "The Method of William Carlos Williams," *Dial,* LXXXII (1927), 94–98.
Deutsch, Babette. *Poetry in Our Time,* pp. 99–111. Holt, Rinehart and Winston, 1952.
Frankenberg, Lloyd. *Pleasure Dome: On Reading Modern Poetry,* pp. 286–296. Boston: Houghton Mifflin and Co., 1949.
Jarrell, Randall. *Poetry and the Age,* pp. 215–226, 236–246. New York: Vintage Books, 1955.
Koch, Vivienne. *William Carlos Williams.* Norfolk, Conn.: New Directions, 1950.
Koch, Vivienne. "William Carlos Williams: The Man and the Poet," *Ken. Rev.* XIV (1952), 502–510.
Lechlitner, Ruth. "The Poetry of William Carlos Williams," *Poetry,* LIV (1939), 326–335.
Quinn, Sister M. Bernetta. "William Carlos Williams: A Testament of Perpetual Changes," *PMLA,* LXX (1955), 292–322. Reprinted in *The Metamorphic Tradition in 'Modern Poetry,* pp. 89–129. Brunswick, N.J.: Rutgers University Press, 1955.
Thompson, Frank. "The Symbolic Structure of *Paterson,*" *West. Rev.,* XIX (1955), 285–293.

Wagner, Linda Welshimer. *The Poems of William Carlos Williams: A Critical Study*. Middletown, Conn.: Wesleyan University Press, 1964.

Comments on Poems

Spring and All
 Discussed in Winters, *In Defense of Reason* (Alan Swallow, 1947), pp. 78–82.

The Yachts
 Discussed in Deutsch, *Poetry in Our Time*, pp. 102–104; Frankenberg, *Pleasure Dome*, pp. 294–295.

Preface to *Paterson*: Book One
 For discussions of the entire poem *Paterson*, see Deutsch, *Poetry in Our Time*, pp. 104–109; Quinn, *PMLA*, LXX (1955), 292–322 (*The Metamorphic Tradition in Modern Poetry*, pp. 89–129); Thompson, *West. Rev.*, XIX (1955), 285–293.
 Paterson attempts to describe the whole culture of Paterson, New Jersey, from Indian times to the present, in order to show, as Williams writes, "that a man in himself is a city, beginning, seeking, achieving and concluding his life in ways which the various aspects of a city may embody—if imaginatively conceived—any city, all the details of which may be made to voice his most intimate convictions."

The Semblables
 Semblables: "resemblances" (archaic: Chaucerian).
 In *The Collected Earlier Poems* (1951), a group of poems in a section called "The Rose," which contained "The Semblables" and "The Injury," was inadvertently omitted by the publisher and was printed in a pamphlet to accompany the edition. This is the text printed here.
 31. Reading in Randall Jarrell (ed.), *William Carlos Williams: Selected Poems* (New Directions, 1963): "empty tendrils swaying lazily in."

SELECTED BIBLIOGRAPHY

Allen, D. C. (ed.). *The Moment of Poetry* [lectures by John Holmes, May Sarton, Richard Eberhart, Richard Wilbur, Randall Jarrell]. Baltimore: The Johns Hopkins Press, 1962.

Allen, Gay Wilson. *American Prosody*. New York: American Book Company, 1935.

Arms, George. *The Fields Were Green: A New View of Bryant, Whittier, Holmes, Lowell, and Longfellow*. Stanford, Calif.: Stanford University Press, 1953.

Beach, J. W. *The Concept of Nature in Nineteenth-Century English Poetry*. New York: The Macmillan Co., 1936.

Bigelow, G. E. *Rhetoric and American Poetry of the Early National Period*. Gainesville, Fla.: University of Florida Press, 1960.

Bogan, Louise. *Achievement in American Poetry: 1900–1950*. Chicago: Henry Regnery, 1951.

Brenner, Rica. *Twelve American Poets Before 1900*. New York: Harcourt, Brace and Co., 1933.

Cambon, Glauco. *The Inclusive Flame: Studies in American Poetry*. Bloomington, Ind.: Indiana University Press, 1963.

Canby, H. S. *Classic Americans: A Study of Eminent American Writers from Irving to Whitman, with an Introductory Survey of the Colonial Background of Our National Literature*. New York: Harcourt, Brace and Co., 1931.

Deutsch, Babette. *Poetry in Our Time*. New York: Holt, Rinehart and Winston, 1952.

Duncan, J. E. *The Revival of Metaphysical Poetry: The History of a Style, 1800 to the Present*. Minneapolis, Minn.: University of Minnesota Press, 1959.

Feidelson, Charles, Jr. *Symbolism and American Literature*. Chicago: University of Chicago Press, 1953.

Foerster, Norman. *Nature in American Literature: Studies in the Modern View of Nature*. New York: The Macmillan Co., 1923.

Frankenberg, Lloyd. *Pleasure Dome: On Reading Modern Poetry*. Boston: Houghton Mifflin and Co., 1949.

Gardiner, H. C. *American Classics Reconsidered: A Christian Appraisal*. New York: Charles Scribner's Sons, 1958.

Gregory, Horace, and Zaturenska, Marya. *A History of American Poetry: 1900–1940*. New York: Harcourt, Brace and Co., 1946.

Gross, Harvey. *Sound and Form in Modern Poetry: A Study in Prosody from Thomas Hardy to Robert Lowell*. Ann Arbor, Mich.: University of Michigan Press, 1964.

Howard, Leon. *The Connecticut Wits*. Chicago: University of Chicago Press, 1943.

Howard, Leon. *Literature and the American Tradition*. New York: Doubleday, 1960.

Hubbell, J. B. *The South in American Literature, 1607–1900*. Durham, N.C.: Duke University Press, 1954.

Jantz, H. S. *The First Century of New England Verse*. Worcester, Mass.: American Antiquarian Society, 1944.

Jarrell, Randall. *Poetry and the Age*. New York: Alfred A. Knopf, 1953.

Kreymborg, Alfred. *Our Singing Strength: An Outline of American Poetry (1620–1930)*. New York: Coward-McCann, 1929.

Lawrence, D. H. *Studies in Classic American Literature*. New York: Thomas Seltzer, 1923.

Lenhart, C. S. *Musical Influence on American Poetry*. Athens, Ga.: University of Georgia Press, 1956.

Ludwig, R. M. (ed.). *Aspects of American Poetry: Essays Presented to Howard Mumford Jones*. Columbus, O.: Ohio State University Press, 1962.

Matthiessen, F. O. *American Renaissance: Art and Expression in the Age of Emerson and Whitman*. New York: Oxford University Press, 1941.

Murdock, K. B. (ed.). *Handkerchiefs from Paul: Being Pious and Consolatory Verses of Puritan Massachusetts*. Cambridge, Mass.: Harvard University Press, 1927.

Murdock, K. B. *Literature & Theology in Colonial New England*. Cambridge, Mass.: Harvard University Press, 1949.

O'Connor, W. V. *Sense and Sensibility in Modern Poetry*. Chicago: University of Chicago Press, 1948.

Otis, W. B. *American Verse, 1625–1807: A History*. New York: Moffat, Yard & Co., 1909.

Parks, E. W. (ed.). *Southern Poets: Representative Selections*. New York: American Book Company, 1936.

Pearce, R. H. *The Continuity of American Poetry*. Princeton, N.J.: Princeton University Press, 1961.

Quinn, Sister M. B. *The Metamorphic Tradition in Modern Poetry*. New Brunswick, N.J.: Rutgers University Press, 1955.

Rosenthal, M. L. *The Modern Poets: A Critical Introduction*. New York: Oxford University Press, 1960.

Spiller, R. E.; Thorp, Willard; Johnson, T. H.; Canby, H. S.; Ludwig, R. M. (eds.). *Literary History of the United States*, 2 Vols., 3rd ed. New York: The Macmillan Co., 1963.

Stedman, E. C. *Poets of America*. Boston: Houghton Mifflin and Co., 1885.

Stovall, Floyd. *American Idealism*. Norman, Okla.: University of Oklahoma Press, 1943.

Thorp, Willard. *American Writing in the Twentieth Century*. Cambridge, Mass.: Harvard University Press, 1960.

Walker, R. H. *The Poet and the Gilded Age: Social Themes in Late Nineteenth-Century American Verse*. Philadelphia: University of Pennsylvania Press, 1963.

Wells, H. W. *The American Way of Poetry*. New York: Columbia University Press, 1943.

Williams, S. T. *The Beginnings of American Poetry (1620–1885)*. Uppsala, Sweden: Almqvist & Wiksells Boktryckeri Ab, 1951.

Wilson, Edmund. *Axel's Castle: A Study in the Imaginative Literature of 1870 to 1930*. New York: Charles Scribner's Sons, 1931.

Winters, Yvor. *In Defense of Reason*. New York: Alan Swallow, 1947.

INDEXES

Index of Poets and Titles

Index of First Lines